# Your All-in-One Resource

On the CD that accompanies this book, you'll find additional resources to extend your learning.

The reference library includes the following fully searchable titles:

- *Microsoft Computer Dictionary*, 5th ed.
- *First Look 2007 Microsoft Office System* by Katherine Murray
- Windows Vista Product Guide

Also provided are a sample chapter and poster from *Look Both Ways: Help Protect Your Family on the Internet* by Linda Criddle.

The CD interface has a new look. You can use the tabs for an assortment of tasks:

- Check for book updates (if you have Internet access)
- Install the book's sample files
- Find links to helpful tools and resources
- Go online for product support or CD support
- Send us feedback

The following screen shot gives you a glimpse of the new interface.

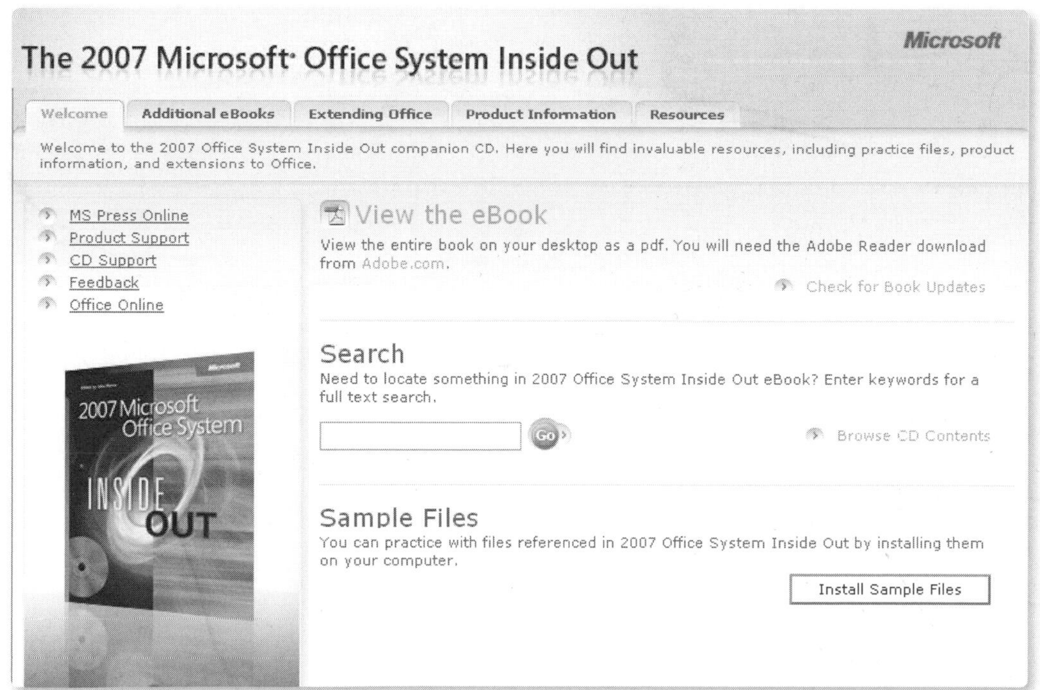

Microsoft®

# Microsoft Office® Access 2007 Inside Out

*John L. Viescas*
*Jeff Conrad*

PUBLISHED BY
Microsoft Press
A Division of Microsoft Corporation
One Microsoft Way
Redmond, Washington 98052-6399



Library of Congress Control Number: 2006940676

Printed and bound in the United States of America.

5 6 7 8 9 10 11 12 13 14 QGT 5 4 3 2 1 0

Distributed in Canada by H.B. Fenn and Company Ltd.

A CIP catalogue record for this book is available from the British Library.

Microsoft Press books are available through booksellers and distributors worldwide. For further information about international editions, contact your local Microsoft Corporation office or contact Microsoft Press International directly at fax (425) 936-7329. Visit our Web site at www.microsoft.com/mspress. Send comments to mspinput@microsoft.com.



**Acquisitions Editor:** Juliana Aldous Atkinson
**Developmental Editor:** Sandra Haynes
**Project Editor:** Melissa von Tschudi-Sutton
**Project Management:** Publishing.com
**Compositor:** Curtis Philips

**Technical Reviewer:** Rozanne Murphy Whalen
**Copy Editors:** Andrea Fox and Kim Wimpsett
**Proofreader:** Andrea Fox
**Indexer:** Rebecca Plunkett

Body Part No. X13-24152

## *Dedication*

*For Suzanne, as always . . .*

– John Viescas

*For the love of my life, Cheryl. Without your love, support, and patience,*
*I would not have been able to complete this project.*
*Thank you for always believing in me.*
*And for Amy, Aaron, and Arica. Thank you*
*for understanding why Daddy could not play*
*very much for a long time.*
*And thank you John for taking a chance*
*and giving an untested, slightly crazy, Access Junkie*
*the opportunity of a lifetime.*

– Jeff Conrad

# Contents at a Glance

## Part 6: After Completing Your Application



***Bonus Content on the Companion CD***

## Part 7: Designing an Access Project



## Part 8: Articles

# Table of Contents

## Part 3: Creating Forms and Reports in a Desktop Application . . . .515

## Part 6: After Completing Your Application . . . . . . . . . . . . . . . . . . . 1281



***See the companion CD for bonus content Parts 7 and 8***

*Bonus Content on the Companion CD*

# Acknowledgments

The folks on the Microsoft Office Access development team provided invaluable technical support as we worked with the beta software and tried to figure out some of the challenging technical details in Microsoft Office Access 2007. Special thanks to Clint Covington, Tim Getsch, Zac Woodall, Suraj Poozhiyil, Neil Black, Viki Selca, and Rob Cooper. You folks make an author's job so much easier. But any errors or omissions in this book are ultimately ours.

A book this large and complex requires a top-notch team to get what we put into Microsoft Office Word documents onto the printed pages you are now holding. We had some of the best in the business at both Microsoft Press and Publishing.com to get the job done. Many thanks to Sandra Haynes and Melissa von Tschudi-Sutton at Microsoft Press. Special thanks to Curt Philips, Rozanne Murphy Whalen, Andrea Fox, Kim Wimpsett, and Publishing.com. We couldn't have done it without you!

And last, but certainly not least, we thank our wives and soul mates. They not only patiently stood by us as we cranked through nearly 3,000 pages of manuscript but also helped behind the scenes reviewing and editing what we did.

*John Viescas* — *Paris, France*

*Jeff Conrad* — *Bend, Oregon*

*February 2007*

# About the CD

The companion CD that ships with this book contains many tools and resources to help you get the most out of your Inside Out book.

**CAUTION!**

If you install the sample files on a Microsoft Windows Vista system, a Windows XP system, or a Windows Server 2003 or later system, you must run the installation program as an Administrator to install the files in the default location. If you do not do that, Microsoft Office Access 2007 opens all the database files as read-only. If you are unable to run the installation program as an Administrator, change the default installation location to a subfolder in My Documents.

## What's on the CD

Your Inside Out CD includes the following:

- **Sample files** Click the Install Sample Files button on the Welcome tab to install the sample files and resources referenced in the book.
- **Additional eBooks** In this section you'll find the following resources:
  - *Microsoft Computer Dictionary*, Fifth Edition
  - *First Look 2007 Microsoft Office System* (Katherine Murray, 2006)
  - Sample chapter and poster from *Look Both Ways: Help Protect Your Family on the Internet* (Linda Criddle, 2007)
  - Windows Vista Product Guide
- **Extending Office** Here you'll find links to Microsoft and other third-party tools that will help you get the most out of your software experience.
- **Resources** In this section, you'll find links to white papers, users assistance articles, product support information, insider blogs, tools, and much more.
- **Bonus content** In the Bonus Content section, you'll find four chapters that will teach you additional skills for creating client/server applications in an Access project. You'll also find six articles that contain important reference materials.

## Sample Applications

Throughout this book, you'll see examples from three sample Office Access 2007 applications included on the companion CD:

- *Wedding List (WeddingMC.accdb and WeddingList.accdb).* This application is an example of a simple database that you might build for your personal use. It has a single main table where you can track the names and addresses of invitees, whether they've said that they will attend, the description of any gift they sent, and whether a thank you note has been sent. Although you might be tempted to store such a simple list in a Microsoft Excel spreadsheet or a Microsoft Word document, this application demonstrates how storing the information in Access makes it easy to search and sort the data and produce reports. The WeddingMC database is automated entirely using macros, and the WeddingList database is the same application automated with Microsoft Visual Basic.
- *Housing Reservations (Housing.accdb).* This application demonstrates how a company housing department might track and manage reservations in company-owned housing facilities for out-of-town employees and guests. This application includes data access pages that could be published on a company intranet for use by employees logging in from remote locations. You'll also find *HousingDataCopy.accdb* and *HousingDataCopy2.accdb* files that contain many of the query, form, and report examples.
- *Conrad Systems Contacts (Contacts.accdb, ContactsData.accdb, Contacts.adp, and ContactsSQL.mdf).* This application is both a contacts management and order entry database—two samples for the price of one! This sample database demonstrates how to build a client/server application using only desktop tools as well as how to "upsize" an application to create an Office Access 2007 project and related Microsoft SQL Server tables, views, stored procedures, and functions. You will need to install Microsoft SQL Server 2005 Express Edition to be able to fully use the project version of this database. You'll also find a *ContactsDataCopy.accdb* file that contains additional query, form, and report examples.

Please note that the person names, company names, e-mail addresses, and Web site addresses in these databases are fictitious. Although we preloaded both databases with sample data, the Housing Reservations and Conrad Systems Contacts databases also include a special form (zfrmLoadData) that has code to load random data into the sample tables based on parameters that you supply.

The examples in this book assume you have installed the 2007 Microsoft Office system, not just Access 2007. Several examples also assume that you have installed all optional features of Access through the 2007 Office release setup program. If you have not installed these additional features, your screen might not match the illustrations in this book or you might not be able to run the samples from the companion CD.

## System Requirements

The following are the minimum system requirements necessary to run the CD:

- Microsoft Windows Vista, Windows XP with Service Pack (SP) 2, Windows Server 2003 with SP1, or newer operating system
- 500 megahertz (MHz) processor or higher
- 2 gigabytes (GB) storage space (a portion of this disk space will be freed after installation if the original download package is removed from the hard drive)
- 256 megabytes (MB) RAM
- CD-ROM or DVD-ROM drive
- 1024×768 or higher resolution monitor
- Microsoft Windows or Windows Vista–compatible sound card and speakers
- Microsoft Internet Explorer 6 or newer
- Microsoft Mouse or compatible pointing device

> **Note**
>
> An Internet connection is necessary to access the hyperlinks on the companion CD. Connect time charges may apply.

## Support Information

Every effort has been made to ensure the accuracy of the contents of the book and of this CD. As corrections or changes are collected, they will be added to a Microsoft Knowledge Base article. Microsoft Press provides support for books and companion CDs at the following Web site: *www.microsoft.com/learning/support/books/.*

If you have comments, questions, or ideas regarding the book or this CD, or questions that are not answered by visiting the site above, please send them via e-mail to *mspinput@microsoft.com.*

You can also click the Feedback or CD Support links on the Welcome page. Please note that Microsoft software product support is not offered through the above addresses.

If your question is about the software, and not about the content of this book, please visit the Microsoft Help and Support page or the Microsoft Knowledge Base at *http://support.microsoft.com.*

In the United States, Microsoft software product support issues not covered by the Microsoft Knowledge Base are addressed by Microsoft Product Support Services. Location-specific software support options are available from *http://support.microsoft.com/gp/selfoverview/*.

Microsoft Press provides corrections for books through the World Wide Web at *www.microsoft.com/mspress/support/*. To connect directly to the Microsoft Press Knowledge Base and enter a query regarding a question or issue that you may have, go to *www.microsoft.com/mspress/support/search.htm*.

**Note**

This companion CD relies on scripting for some interface enhancements. If scripting is disabled or unavailable in your browser, follow these steps to run the CD:

1. From My Computer, double-click the drive that contains this companion CD.
2. Open the Webfiles folder.
3. Double-click Welcome.htm to open the CD in your default browser.

# Conventions and Features Used in This Book

This book uses special text and design conventions to make it easier for you to find the information you need.

## Text Conventions

| Convention | Meaning |
|---|---|
| Abbreviated commands for navigating the Ribbon | For your convenience, this book uses abbreviated commands. For example, "Click Home, Insert, Insert Cells" means that you should click the Home tab on the Ribbon, then click the Insert button, and finally click the Insert Cells command. |
| **Boldface type** | **Boldface** type is used to indicate text that you type. |
| Initial Capital Letters | The first letters of the names of tabs, dialog boxes, dialog box elements, and commands are capitalized. Example: the Save As dialog box. |
| *Italicized type* | *Italicized* type is used to indicate new terms. |
| Plus sign (+) in text | Keyboard shortcuts are indicated by a plus sign (+) separating two key names. For example, Alt+Shift+Tab means that you press the Alt, Shift, and Tab keys at the same time. |

## Design Conventions

INSIDE OUT

**This Statement Illustrates an Example of an "Inside Out" Heading**

These are the book's signature tips. In these tips, you'll get the straight scoop on what's going on with the software—inside information about why a feature works the way it does. You'll also find handy workarounds to deal with software problems.

### Sidebars

Sidebars provide helpful hints, timesaving tricks, or alternative procedures related to the task being discussed.

**TROUBLESHOOTING**

**This statement illustrates an example of a "Troubleshooting" problem statement.**

Look for these sidebars to find solutions to common problems you might encounter. Troubleshooting sidebars appear next to related information in the chapters. You can also use "Index to Troubleshooting Topics" at the back of the book to look up problems by topic.

**Cross-references point you to other locations in the book that offer additional information about the topic being discussed.**

**CAUTION!**

Cautions identify potential problems that you should look out for when you're completing a task or problems that you must address before you can complete a task.

**Note**

Notes offer additional information related to the task being discussed.

When an example has a related file that is included on the companion CD, this icon appears in the margin. You can use these files to follow along with the book's examples.

# Syntax Conventions

The following conventions are used in the syntax descriptions for Visual Basic statements in Chapter 19, "Understanding Visual Basic Fundamentals," Chapter 20, "Automating Your Application with Visual Basic," SQL statements in Article 2, "Understanding SQL," and any other chapter where you find syntax defined. These conventions do not apply to code examples listed within the text; all code examples appear exactly as you'll find them in the sample databases.

You must enter all other symbols, such as parentheses and colons, exactly as they appear in the syntax line. Much of the syntax shown in the Visual Basic chapter has been broken into multiple lines. You can format your code all on one line, or you can write a single line of code on multiple lines using the Visual Basic line continuation character (_).

| Convention | Meaning |
|---|---|
| Bold | Bold type indicates keywords and reserved words that you must enter exactly as shown. Visual Basic understands keywords entered in uppercase, lowercase, and mixed case type. Access stores SQL keywords in queries in all uppercase, but you can enter the keywords in any case. |
| Italic | Italicized words represent variables that you supply. |
| Angle brackets < > | Angle brackets enclose syntactic elements that you must supply. The words inside the angle brackets describe the element but do not show the actual syntax of the element. Do not enter the angle brackets. |
| Brackets [ ] | Brackets enclose optional items. If more than one item is listed, the items are separated by a pipe character (\|). Choose one or none of the elements. Do not enter the brackets or the pipe; they're not part of the element. Note that Visual Basic and SQL in many cases require that you enclose names in brackets. When brackets are required as part of the syntax of variables that you must supply in these examples, the brackets are italicized, as in *[MyTable].[MyField]*. |
| Braces { } | Braces enclose one or more options. If more than one option is listed, the items are separated by a pipe character (\|). Choose one item from the list. Do not enter the braces or the pipe. |
| Ellipsis ... | Ellipses indicate that you can repeat an item one or more times. When a comma is shown with an ellipsis (,...), enter a comma between items. |
| Underscore _ | You can use a blank space followed by an underscore to continue a line of Visual Basic code to the next line for readability. You cannot place an underscore in the middle of a string literal. You do not need an underscore for continued lines in SQL, but you cannot break a literal across lines. |

# Introduction

Microsoft Office Access 2007 is just one part of Microsoft's overall data management product strategy. Like all good relational databases, it allows you to link related information easily—for example, customer and order data that you enter. But Office Access 2007 also complements other database products because it has several powerful connectivity features. As its name implies, Access 2007 can work directly with data from other sources, including many popular personal computer database programs (such as dBASE and Paradox), with many SQL (Structured Query Language) databases on the desktop, on servers, on minicomputers, or on mainframes, and with data stored on Internet or intranet Web servers. Access 2007 also fully supports Microsoft's ActiveX technology, so an Access application can be either a client or a server for all the other 2007 Microsoft Office system applications, including Word, Excel, PowerPoint, Outlook, FrontPage, Publisher, and OneNote.

Access provides a very sophisticated application development system for the Microsoft Windows operating system. This helps you build applications quickly, whatever the data source. In fact, you can build simple applications by defining forms and reports based on your data and linking them with a few macros or Microsoft Visual Basic statements; there's no need to write complex code in the classic programming sense. Because Access uses Visual Basic, you can use the same set of skills with other applications in the Microsoft Office system or with Visual Basic.

For small businesses (and for consultants creating applications for small businesses), the Access desktop development features are all that's required to store and manage the data used to run the business. Access coupled with Microsoft SQL Server—on the desktop or on a server—is an ideal way for many medium-size companies to build new applications for Windows quickly and inexpensively. To enhance workgroup productivity, you can use Access to create an application linked to data on a Microsoft Windows SharePoint Services server. For large corporations with a big investment in mainframe relational database applications as well as a proliferation of desktop applications that rely on personal computer databases, Access provides the tools to easily link mainframe and personal computer data in a single Windows-based application. Access 2007 includes features to allow you to export or import data in XML format (the lingua franca of data stored on the Web).

## Getting Familiar with Access 2007

If you have never used a database program—including Access—you'll find Access 2007 very approachable. Using the results of extensive productivity lab tests, Microsoft has completely revamped the user interface in all the Microsoft Office programs. The new Ribbon technology makes it much easier for novice users to get acquainted with Access and easily discover its most useful features. To get a new user jump-started, Microsoft has provided nearly a dozen local database templates that load onto your hard disk when you install Access. In addition, you'll find many additional database templates available for easy download from the Microsoft Office Web site directly from within

Access. Microsoft plans to continue to add templates after Access 2007 is released to further enhance your productivity.

> **Note**
>
> The Microsoft Office Fluent user interface is the term used to describe the new UI for the 2007 Microsoft Office system. The Ribbon is a component of the Microsoft Office Fluent user interface and the term used throughout this book to refer to the Ribbon component.

But if you have used any prior version of Access, you're in for a big surprise. Menus and toolbars are gone—all replaced by the new Ribbon. The Database window has been replaced by the Navigation Pane. When you first start using Access 2007, you'll probably notice a decrease in productivity—we certainly did—but it won't take you long to get comfortable with the new interface. You'll probably soon discover features that you didn't know were there. Nearly all the old familiar objects are around—tables, queries, forms, reports, macros, and modules, and you'll find that the standard design and data views you've come to know and love are still around. You'll also quickly learn that the new Layout and Report views rapidly increase your productivity.

# About This Book

If you're developing a database application with the tools in Access 2007, this book gives you a thorough understanding of "programming without pain." It provides a solid foundation for designing databases, forms, and reports and getting them all to work together. You'll learn that you can quickly create complex applications by linking design elements with macros or Visual Basic. This book will also show you how to take advantage of some of the more advanced features of Access 2007. You'll learn how to build an Access project that links directly to an SQL Server database. You'll also learn how to use Access tools to link to your Access data from the Web or link your Access application to data stored on the Web.

If you're new to developing applications, particularly database applications, this probably should not be the first book you read about Access. We recommend that you first take a look at *Microsoft Access 2007 Plain and Simple* or *Microsoft Access 2007 Step by Step*.

*Microsoft Office Access 2007 Inside Out* is divided into seven major parts:

- Part 1 provides an overview of Access 2007 and provides you with a detailed look at the new user interface.
    - Chapter 1 explains the major features that a database should provide, explores those features in Access, and discusses some of the main reasons why you should consider using database software.

- Chapter 2 thoroughly explores the new user interface introduced in the 2007 Office release. The chapter also explains content security, working with the Ribbon and the Navigation Pane, and setting options that customize how you work with Access 2007.
- Chapter 3 describes the architecture of Access 2007, gives you an overview of the major objects in an Access database by taking you on a tour through two of the sample databases, and explains the many ways you can use Access to create an application.

- Part 2 shows you how to create your desktop application database and tables and build queries to analyze and update data in your tables.
  - Chapter 4 teaches you how to create databases and tables.
  - Chapter 5 shows you the ins and outs of modifying tables even after you've already begun to load data and build other parts of your application.
  - Chapter 6 explains how to link to or import data from other sources.
  - Chapter 7 shows you how to build simple queries and how to work with data in Datasheet view.
  - Chapter 8 discusses how to design queries to work with data from multiple tables, summarize information, build queries that require you to work in SQL view, and work with the PivotTable and PivotChart views of queries.
  - Chapter 9 focuses on modifying sets of data with queries—updating data, inserting new data, deleting sets of data, or creating a new table from a selection of data from existing tables.
- Part 3 discusses how to build and work with forms and reports in a desktop application.
  - Chapter 10 introduces you to forms—what they look like and how they work.
  - Chapters 11, 12, and 13 teach you all about form design in a desktop application, from simple forms you build with a wizard to complex, advanced forms that use embedded forms or ActiveX controls.
  - Chapter 14 leads you on a guided tour of reports and explains their major features.
  - Chapters 15 and 16 teach you how to design, build, and implement both simple and complex reports in your desktop application.
- Part 4 shows you how to use the programming facilities in Visual Basic to integrate your database objects and make your application "come alive."
  - Chapter 17 discusses the concept of event processing in Access, provides a comprehensive list of events, and explains the sequence in which critical events occur.
  - Chapter 18 covers macro design in depth and explains how to use the new error trapping and embedded macro features.

  - Chapter 19 is a comprehensive reference to the Visual Basic language and object models implemented in Access. The final section of the chapter presents two complex coding examples with a line-by-line discussion of the code.
  - Chapter 20 thoroughly discusses some of the most common tasks that you might want to automate with Visual Basic. Each section describes a problem, shows you specific form or report design techniques you must use to solve the problem, and walks you through the code from one or more of the sample databases that implements the solution.
- Part 5 is all about using Access tools with the Web.
  - Chapter 21 provides an overview of the ways you can publish data on a Web site.
  - Chapter 22 discusses specific ways to publish your Access applications using Windows SharePoint Services (version 3).
  - Chapter 23 covers the features in Access that handle XML, including importing, updating, and publishing data. The chapter also shows you how to use XML to modify table templates and design custom Ribbons.
- Part 6 covers tasks you might want to perform after completing your application.
  - Chapter 24 teaches you how to automate custom Ribbons, how to use the Performance Analyzer tool, how to design a switchboard, and how to set Startup properties.
  - Chapter 25 teaches you tasks for setting up your application so that you can distribute it to others.

- Part 7 expands on what you learned in Parts 2 and 3 by teaching you the additional skills you need to create client/server applications in an Access project.
  - Chapter 26 shows you how to build a new project file and explains how to define SQL Server tables from the project.
  - Chapter 27 teaches you how to design the project equivalent of desktop queries–views, stored procedures, and functions.
  - Chapter 28 builds on what you learned in Chapters 11–13 and shows you how forms work differently in an Access project.
  - Chapter 29 leverages what you learned in Chapters 15–16 and teaches you how to design reports in an Access project.
- The Appendix explains how to install the 2007 Office release, including which options you should choose for Access 2007 to be able to open all the samples in this book. It also discusses how to install Microsoft SQL Server 2005 Express Edition.

The CD also provides six Articles that contain important reference information:

- Article 1 explains a simple technique that you can use to design a good relational database application with little effort. Even if you're already familiar with Access or creating database applications in general, getting the table design right is so important that this article is a "must read" for everyone.
- Article 2 is a complete reference to SQL as implemented in desktop databases. It also contains notes about differences between SQL supported natively by Access and SQL implemented in SQL Server.
- Article 3 discusses how to export data and Access objects to various types of other data formats from your Access application.
- Article 4 lists the functions most commonly used in an Access application categorized by function type.
- Article 5 lists the color names and codes you can use in Access.
- Article 6 lists the macro actions you can use in Access.

PART 1

# Understanding Microsoft Access

CHAPTER 1

# What Is Microsoft Access?



If you're a serious user of a personal computer, you've probably been using word processing or spreadsheet applications to help you solve problems. You might have started a long time ago with character-based products running under MS-DOS but subsequently upgraded to software that runs under the Microsoft Windows operating system. You might also own some database software, either as part of an integrated package such as Microsoft Works or as a separate program.

Database programs have been available for personal computers for a long time. Unfortunately, many of these programs have been either simple data storage managers that aren't suitable for building applications or complex application development systems that are difficult to learn and use. Even many computer-literate people have avoided the more complex database systems unless they have been handed a complete, custom-built database application. The introduction of Microsoft Access more than a decade ago represented a significant turnaround in ease of use. Many people are drawn to it to create both simple databases and sophisticated database applications.

Now that Access is in its eighth release and has become an even more robust product in the sixth edition designed for 32-bit versions of Windows, perhaps it's time to take another look at how you work with your personal computer to get the job done. If you've previously shied away from database software because you felt you needed programming skills or because it would take you too much time to become a proficient user, you'll be pleasantly surprised at how easy it is to work with all the new features rolled into Microsoft Office Access 2007.

Office Access 2007 comes loaded with many existing database templates to solve business and personal needs. These templates are fully functioning applications that can be used as is without having to make any modifications. For users who do want to modify the templates or even start from scratch, this latest version of Access comes with new table templates, new form and report What-You-See-Is-What-You-Get (WYSIWYG) authoring tools, including improved AutoFormats, Quick Create object operations, and a fully revamped user interface (UI) to visually assist the development process.

But how do you decide whether you're ready to move up to a database system such as Access? To help you decide, let's take a look at the advantages of using database application development software.

# What Is a Database?

In the simplest sense, a *database* is a collection of records and files that are organized for a particular purpose. On your computer system, you might keep the names and addresses of all your friends or customers. Perhaps you collect all the letters you write and organize them by recipient. You might have another set of files in which you keep all your financial data—accounts payable and accounts receivable or your checkbook entries and balances. The word processor documents that you organize by topic are, in the broadest sense, one type of database. The spreadsheet files that you organize according to their uses are another type of database. Shortcuts to all your programs on your Windows Start menu are a kind of database. Internet shortcuts organized in your Favorites folder are a database.

If you're very organized, you can probably manage several hundred spreadsheets or shortcuts by using folders and subfolders. When you do this, *you're* the database manager. But what do you do when the problems you're trying to solve get too big? How can you easily collect information about all customers and their orders when the data might be stored in several document and spreadsheet files? How can you maintain links between the files when you enter new information? How do you ensure that data is being entered correctly? What if you need to share your information with many people but don't want two people to try updating the same data at the same time? How do you keep duplicate copies of data from proliferating when people can't share the same data at the same time? Faced with these challenges, you need a *database management system* (DBMS).

## Relational Databases

Nearly all modern database management systems store and handle information using the *relational* database management model. In a relational database management system, sometimes called an *RDBMS,* the system manages all data in *tables*. Tables store information about a single subject (such as customers or products) and have *columns* (or *fields*) that contain the different kinds of information about the subject (for example, customers' addresses or phone numbers) and *rows* (or *records*) that describe all the attributes of a single instance of the subject (for example, data on a specific customer or product). Even when you *query* the database (fetch information from one or more tables), the result is always something that looks like another table.

The term *relational* stems from the fact that each table in the database contains information related to a single subject and only that subject. If you study the relational database management model, you'll find the term *relation* applied to a set of rows (a table) about a single subject. Also, you can manipulate data about two classes of information (such as customers and orders) as a single entity based on related data values. For example, it would be redundant to store customer name and address information with every order that the customer places. In a relational database management system, the information about orders contains a field that stores data, such as a customer number, which can be used to connect each order with the appropriate customer information.

You can also *join* information on related values from multiple tables or queries. For example, you can join company information with contact information to find out the contacts for a particular company. You can join employee information with department information to find out the department in which an employee works.

### Some Relational Database Terminology

**Relation.** Information about a single subject such as customers, orders, employees, products, or companies. A relation is usually stored as a *table* in a relational database management system.

**Attribute.** A specific piece of information about a subject, such as the address for a customer or the dollar amount of an order. An attribute is normally stored as a data *column*, or *field*, in a table.

**Instance.** A particular member of a relation—an individual customer or product. An instance is usually stored in a table as a *record*, or *row*.

**Relationship.** The way information in one relation is related to information in another relation. For example, customers have a *one-to-many* relationship with orders because one customer can place many orders, but any order belongs to only one customer. Companies might have a *many-to-many* relationship with contacts because there might be multiple contacts for a company, and a contact might be associated with more than one company.

**Join.** The process of linking tables or queries on tables via their related data values. For example, customers might be joined to orders by matching customer ID in a customers table and an orders table.

## Database Capabilities

An RDBMS gives you complete control over how you define your data, work with it, and share it with others. The system also provides sophisticated features that make it easy to catalog and manage large amounts of data in many tables. An RDBMS has three main types of capabilities: data definition, data manipulation, and data control.

- **Data definition.** You can define what data is stored in your database, the type of data (for example, numbers or characters), and how the data is related. In some cases, you can also define how the data should be formatted and how it should be validated.
- **Data manipulation.** You can work with the data in many ways. You can select which data fields you want, filter the data, and sort it. You can join data with related information and summarize (total) the data. You can select a set of information and ask the RDBMS to update it, delete it, copy it to another table, or create a new table containing the data.

- **Data control.** You can take advantage of features that help ensure that the right type of data goes into the correct places. In many cases, you can also define how data can be shared and updated by multiple users using the database.

All this functionality is contained in the powerful features of Access. Let's take a look at how Access implements these capabilities and compare them to what you can do with spreadsheet or word processing programs.

## Access as an RDBMS

An Access desktop database is a fully functional RDBMS. It provides all the data definition, data manipulation, and data control features you need to manage large volumes of data.

You can use an Access desktop database (.accdb) either as a stand-alone RDBMS on a single workstation or in a shared client/server mode across a network. A desktop database can also act as the data source for data displayed on Web pages on your company intranet. When you build an application with an Access desktop database, Access is the RDBMS. You can also use Access to build applications in a project file (.adp) connected to Microsoft SQL Server, and you can share the server data with other applications or with users on the Web. When you create an Access project file, SQL Server (or the Microsoft SQL Server Desktop Engine–MSDE) is the RDBMS.

> **Note**
>
> Access 2000, 2002 (XP), and 2003 databases use the .mdb file format, but Office Access 2007 introduces a new file format with an .accdb extension. To maintain maximum backward compatibility, Access 2007 can still open, run, and save .mdb databases created in the Access 2000 or Access 2002-2003 .mdb formats, but in order to take advantage of all the new features in Access 2007, you need to use the new .accdb file format. If you have to create an Access application that will be run by users with previous versions of Access, you should use the Access 2000 or Access 2002-2003 .mdb file formats.

### Data Definition and Storage

As you work with a document or a spreadsheet, you generally have complete freedom to define the contents of the document or each cell in the spreadsheet. Within a given page in a document, you might include paragraphs of text, a table, a chart, or multiple columns of data displayed with multiple fonts. Within a given column on a spreadsheet, you might have text data at the top to define a column header for printing or display, and you might have various numeric formats within the same column, depending on the function of the row. You need this flexibility because your word processing document must be able to convey your message within the context of a printed page, and your spreadsheet must store the data you're analyzing as well as provide for calculation and presentation of the results.

This flexibility is great for solving relatively small, well-defined business problems. But a document becomes unwieldy when it extends beyond a few dozen pages, and a spreadsheet becomes difficult to manage when it contains more than a few hundred rows of information. As the amount of data grows, you might also find that you exceed the data storage limits of your word processing or spreadsheet program or of your computer system. If you design a document or spreadsheet to be used by others, it's difficult (if not impossible) to control how they will use the data or enter new data. For example, on a spreadsheet, even though one cell might need a date and another a currency value to make sense, a user might easily enter character data in error.

Some spreadsheet programs allow you to define a "database" area within a spreadsheet to help you manage the information you need to produce the desired result. However, you are still constrained by the basic storage limitations of the spreadsheet program, and you still don't have much control over what's entered in the rows and columns of the database area. Also, if you need to handle more than number and character data, you might find that your spreadsheet program doesn't understand such data types as pictures or sounds.

An RDBMS allows you to define the kind of data you have and how the data should be stored. You can also usually define rules that the RDBMS can use to ensure the integrity of your data. In its simplest form, a *validation rule* might ensure that the user can't accidentally store alphabetic characters in a field that should contain a number. Other rules might define valid values or ranges of values for your data. In the most sophisticated systems, you can define the relationship between collections of data (usually tables or files) and ask the RDBMS to ensure that your data remains consistent. For example, you can have the system automatically check to ensure that every order entered is for a valid customer.

With an Access desktop database (.accdb), you have complete flexibility to define your data (as text, numbers, dates, times, currency, Internet hyperlinks, pictures, sounds, documents, and spreadsheets), to define how Access stores your data (string length, number precision, and date/time precision), and to define what the data looks like when you display or print it. You can define simple or complex validation rules to ensure that only accurate values exist in your database. You can request that Access check for valid relationships between files or tables in your database. When you connect an Access project (.adp) to an SQL Server database, SQL Server provides all these capabilities.

Because Access is a state-of-the-art application for Windows, you can use all the facilities of ActiveX objects and ActiveX custom controls. ActiveX controls extend the power of Access by allowing you to integrate custom objects created by Microsoft and other software vendors into your database applications. Within your Access forms and reports, for example, you can include ActiveX custom controls to enhance the operation of your application for your users. ActiveX controls provide sophisticated design objects that allow you to present complex data in a simpler, more graphical way. Most ActiveX controls provide a rich set of "actions" (called *methods* in object terminology) that you can call from a procedure and properties you can set to manage how the control looks and behaves. For example, you might want to let your user enter a date by selecting it from a calendar picture. One of the ActiveX controls that you can use in an Access application is the calendar control that provides just such a graphical interface. This control is used in a pop-up form in the Conrad Systems Contacts database that is included with this book. You can see this form in Figure 1-1.

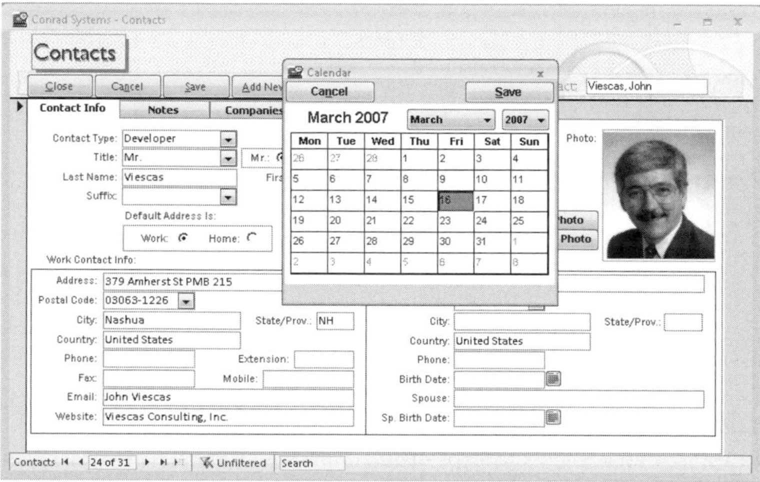


**Figure 1-1** Choose a date using the ActiveX calendar control.

The user can type dates anywhere in the application or click a button next to any date value to open the ActiveX calendar pop-up form.The user can choose a different month or year from the drop-down list boxes on the control, and the control displays the appropriate month. When the user clicks a specific date on the calendar and then clicks Save in the pop-up form, the control passes the date back to the form to update the date field in the record. If you purchase the Office Access 2007 Developer Extensions, you will have several additional ActiveX controls available to use in your applications. Many third-party software vendors have built libraries of ActiveX controls that you can purchase for use with Access.

Office Access 2007 includes a new Attachment data type that can store images and other file types within the record. The Attachment data type can handle multiple attachment files per record via the use of a concept called *Complex Data*. In previous versions of Access, storing images and files through OLE Object data types caused significant bloat of the database file, but in version 2007, Access compresses these files to minimize the size overhead. Examples of files that could be attached to a record using the Attachment data type include a cover letter created in Microsoft Word for each business contact, a bitmap picture of the contact person, or various sales worksheets created in Microsoft Excel. Figure 1-2 shows an example of a form using the Attachment data type to display a contact picture in the Issues template database that comes with Access. (You can find a database created using this template, IssuesSample.accdb, loaded with sample data on the companion CD.)

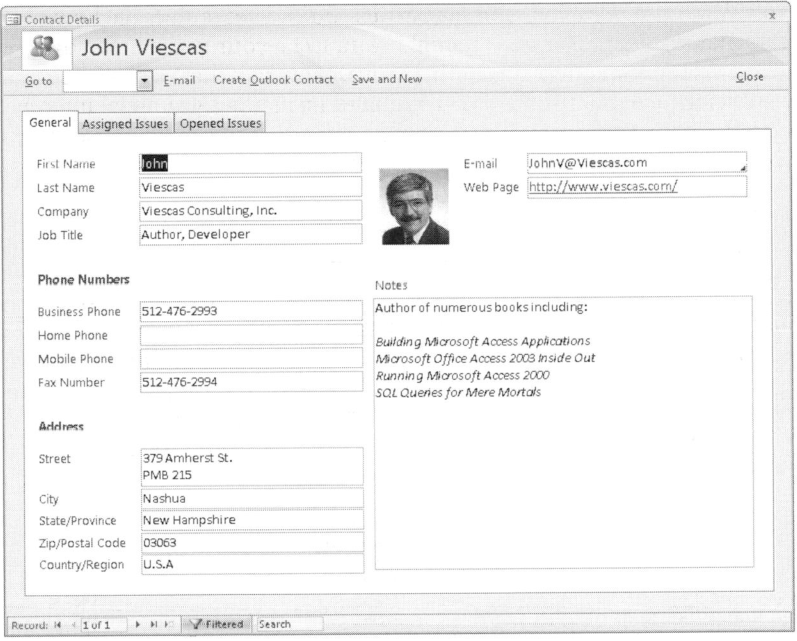


**Figure 1-2** The Attachment data type displays a picture in a form.

Access can also understand and use a wide variety of other data formats, including many other database file structures. You can export data to and import data from word processing files or spreadsheets. You can directly access Paradox, dBASE III, dBASE IV, Microsoft FoxPro, and other database files. You can also import data from these files into an Access table. In addition, Access can work with most popular databases that support the Open Database Connectivity (ODBC) standard, including SQL Server, Oracle, and DB2. Access 2007 has added enhanced functionality to work with Microsoft Windows SharePoint Services (version 3).

## Data Manipulation

Working with data in an RDBMS is very different from working with data in a word processing or spreadsheet program. In a word processing document, you can include tabular data and perform a limited set of functions on the data in the document. You can also search for text strings in the original document and, with ActiveX, include tables, charts, or pictures from other applications. In a spreadsheet, some cells contain functions that determine the result you want, and in other cells you enter the data that provides the source information for the functions. The data in a given spreadsheet serves one particular purpose, and it's cumbersome to use the same data to solve a different problem. You can link to data in another spreadsheet to solve a new problem, or you can use limited search capabilities to copy a selected subset of the data in one spreadsheet to use in problem solving in another spreadsheet.

An RDBMS provides you with many ways to work with your data. You can, for example, search a single table for information or request a complex search across several related tables. You can update a single field or many records with a single command. You can write programs that use RDBMS commands to fetch data you want to display and allow the user to update.

Access uses the powerful SQL database language to process data in your tables. (SQL is an acronym for Structured Query Language.) Using SQL, you can define the set of information that you need to solve a particular problem, including data from perhaps many tables. But Access simplifies data manipulation tasks. You don't even have to understand SQL to get Access to work for you. Access uses the relationship definitions you provide to automatically link the tables you need. You can concentrate on how to solve information problems without having to worry about building a complex navigation system that links all the data structures in your database. Access also has an extremely simple yet powerful graphical query definition facility that you can use to specify the data you need to solve a problem. Using point and click, drag and drop, and a few keystrokes, you can build a complex query in a matter of seconds.

Figure 1-3 shows a complex query used in the desktop database version of the Conrad Systems Contacts application. You can find this query in the Contacts.accdb sample database on the companion CD included with this book. Access displays field lists from selected tables in the upper part of the window; the lines between field lists indicate the automatic links that Access will use to solve the query.

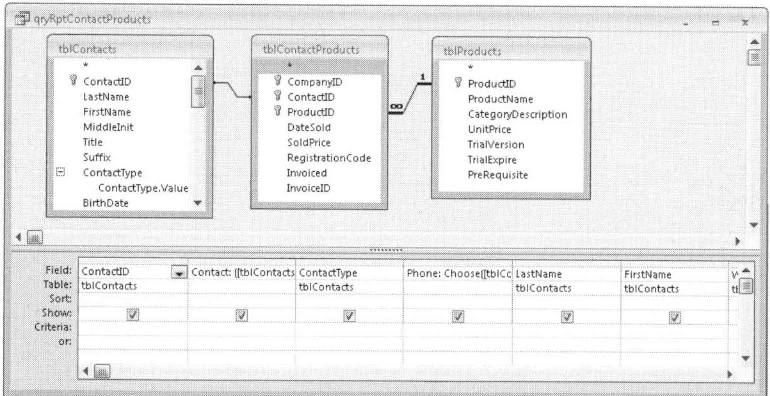


**Figure 1-3** This query will retrieve information about products owned by contacts in the Conrad Systems Contacts sample application.

To create the query, you add the tables containing the data you need to the top of the query design grid, select the fields you want from each table, and drag them to the design grid in the lower part of the window. Choose a few options, type any criteria, and you're ready to have Access select the information you want.

Figure 1-4 shows the same query in the project file version of the Conrad Systems Contacts application, Contacts.adp. You can see that the design interface is similar but also provides an SQL pane so that you can watch Access build the SQL for your query as you

work. You don't need to be an expert to correctly construct the SQL syntax you need to solve your problem, but you can learn a lot about SQL in Chapter 27, "Building Queries in an Access Project," and in Article 2, "Understanding SQL," both found on the companion CD. For certain advanced types of queries, you'll need to learn the basics of SQL.

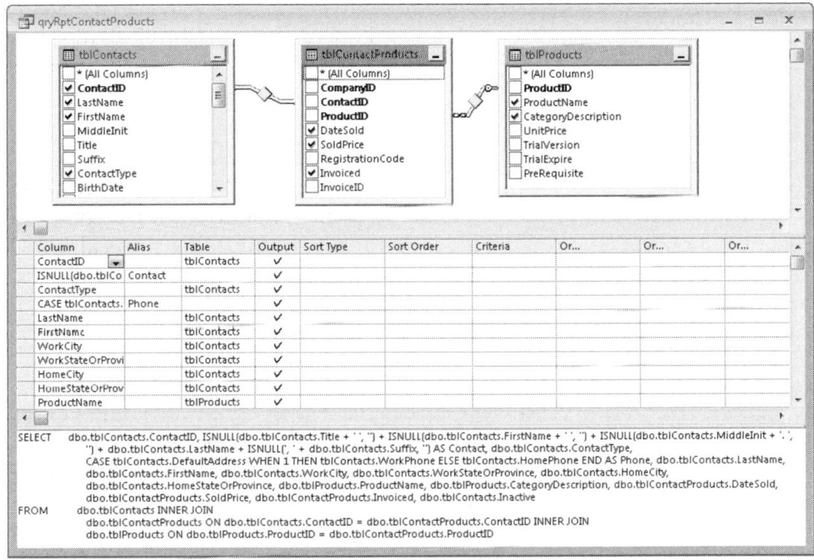


**Figure 1-4** Here is the project file version of a query to retrieve information about products owned by contacts.

Figure 1-5 shows the result of asking the query to return its data.

qryRptContactProducts

| Contact ID | Contact | Contact Type | Phone | Last Name | First Name | Work City | State/Provi | Home Ci |
|---|---|---|---|---|---|---|---|---|
| | Mr. Paul West | Customer | (456) 555-0146 | West | Paul | Kalamazoo | MI | Kalamazc |
| 12 | Mr. Harry Lingg | Customer | (567) 555-0146 | Linggoputro | Harry | Yorktown | VA | Yorktowr |
| 16 | Mr. John Smith | Customer | (789) 555-0137 | Smith | John | Easton | CA | Fresno |
| 23 | Mr. Eugene Zak | Customer | (456) 555-0135 | Zabokritski | Eugene | Riverside | ND | Wahpeto |
| 26 | Dr. Peter Villac | Customer | (234) 555-0138 | Villadsen | Peter | Grandy | NC | Frisco |
| 27 | Mr. Adam Truk | Customer | (567) 555-0113 | Trukawka | Adam | Irrigon | OR | Imnaha |
| 3 | Mr. Tom Micha | Customer | (456) 555-0114 | Michaels | Tom | Youngsville | PA | Kennerd |
| 6 | Mr. Mario Kres | Customer | (234) 555-0140 | Kresnadi | Mario | Grosse Pointe | MI | Grosse Pi |
| 12 | Mr. Harry Lingg | Customer | (567) 555-0146 | Linggoputro | Harry | Yorktown | VA | Yorktowr |
| 15 | Mrs. Shengda Y | Customer | (789) 555-0137 | Yang | Shengda | Easton | CA | Fresno |
| 16 | Mr. John Smith | Customer | (789) 555-0137 | Smith | John | Easton | CA | Fresno |
| 17 | Mr. Douglas Cu | Customer | (789) 555-0137 | Curran | Douglas | Easton | CA | Easton |
| 22 | Mr. Mikael San | Customer | (456) 555-0110 | Sandberg | Mikael | Conway | MA | Colrain |
| 28 | Dr. Mark Hanso | Customer | (567) 555-0113 | Hanson | Mark | Irrigon | OR | Imbler |
| 6 | Mr. Mario Kres | Customer | (234) 555-0140 | Kresnadi | Mario | Grosse Pointe | MI | Grosse Pi |
| 8 | Mr. Joseph Mat | Customer | (234) 555-0140 | Matthews | Joseph | Grosse Pointe | MI | Detroit |
| 12 | Mr. Harry Lingg | Customer | (567) 555-0146 | Linggoputro | Harry | Yorktown | VA | Yorktowr |
| 16 | Mr. John Smith | Customer | (789) 555-0137 | Smith | John | Easton | CA | Fresno |
| 19 | Mr. Dániel Koc | Customer | (678) 555-0137 | Koczka | Dániel | Elias | KY | Sandgap |
| 24 | Dr. Mindy Mart | Customer | (234) 555-0138 | Martin | Mindy | Grandy | NC | Grandy |
| 25 | Mr. Markus Zul | Customer | (234) 555-0138 | Zulechner | Markus | Grandy | NC | Harrellsv |
| 28 | Dr. Mark Hanso | Customer | (567) 555-0113 | Hanson | Mark | Irrigon | OR | Imbler |
| 5 | Mr. Paul West | Customer | (456) 555-0146 | West | Paul | Kalamazoo | MI | Kalamazc |
| 9 | Dr. Jennifer Rie | Customer | (123) 555-0107 | Riegle | Jennifer | Warriors Mark | PA | Wallacet |
| 14 | Ms. Mary E. Gib | Customer | (345) 555-0102 | Gibson | Mary | Matoaka | WV | Kellysvill |

Record: 1 of 92 No Filter Search

**Figure 1-5** The query returns a list of contacts and the products they own.

## Data Control

Spreadsheets and word processing documents are great for solving single-user problems, but they are difficult to use when more than one person needs to share the data. Although spreadsheets are useful for providing templates for simple data entry, they don't do the job well if you need to perform complex data validation. For example, a spreadsheet works well as a template for an invoice for a small business with a single proprietor. But if the business expands and a number of salespeople are entering orders, the company needs a database. Likewise, a spreadsheet can assist employees with expense reports in a large business, but the data eventually must be captured and placed in a database for corporate accounting.

When you need to share your information with others, true relational database management systems give you the flexibility to allow multiple users to read or update your data. An RDBMS that is designed to allow data sharing also provides features to ensure that no two people can change the same data at the same time. The best systems also allow you to group changes (a series of changes is sometimes called a *transaction*) so that either all of the changes or none of the changes appear in your data. For example, while confirming a new order for a customer, you probably want to know that both the inventory for ordered products is updated and the order confirmation is saved or, if you encounter an error, that none of the changes are saved. You probably also want to be sure that no one else can view any part of the order until you have entered all of it.

### Important Changes to User-Level Security

The new .accdb file format in Office Access 2007 no longer supports user-level security through workgroup files for data control. Properly securing an Access database using user-level security was a difficult process for most users to undertake. If any important steps in the process were missed or applied incorrectly, the database would not be properly secured. In some cases it was easy to overlook that a step was missed, which would leave an unknown security hole in the Access database file. Although difficult to set up, user-level security was unfortunately extremely easy to break with tools and utilities available on the Internet. It was simply not possible to fix Access user-level security to comply with Microsoft's current software security standards. For backward compatibility, user-level security defined in databases left in the older .mdb format will continue to be supported. Access 2007 will still allow you to design and modify database object permissions with user-level security if the file is left in the .mdb format. Access 2007 will even continue to honor existing security settings in .mdb and .adp files, but it will not support any of these features in the new .accdb file format. To provide the best security for shared data, Microsoft recommends moving your data to SQL Server or to Microsoft Office SharePoint Server.

Because you can share your Access data with other users, you might need to set some restrictions on what various users are allowed to see or update. Access 2007 has greatly improved the ability to share data with secured Windows SharePoint Services Version 3 lists to ensure data security. With SharePoint-to-Access integration, users can take advantage of improved workflow support, offline SharePoint lists, and a Recycle Bin to undo changes. Access 2007 also has improved data encryption with tougher encryption algorithms. Access automatically provides locking mechanisms to ensure that no two people can update an object at the same time, and Access also understands and honors the locking mechanisms of other database structures (such as Paradox, FoxPro, and SQL databases) that you attach to your database.

## Access as an Application Development System

Being able to define exactly what data you need, how it should be stored, and how you want to access it solves the data management part of the problem. However, you also need a simple way to automate all the common tasks you want to perform. For example, each time you need to enter a new order, you don't want to have to run a query to search the Customers table, execute a command to open the Orders table, and then create a new record before you can enter the data for the order. And after you've entered the data for the new order, you don't want to have to worry about scanning the table that contains all your products to verify the order's sizes, colors, and prices.

Advanced word processing software lets you define templates and macros to automate document creation, but it's not designed to handle complex transaction processing. In a spreadsheet, you enter formulas that define what automatic calculations you want performed. If you're an advanced spreadsheet user, you might also create macros or Visual Basic procedures to help automate entering and validating data. If you're working with a lot of data, you've probably figured out how to use one spreadsheet as a "database" container and use references to selected portions of this data in your calculations.

Although you can build a fairly complex application using spreadsheets, you really don't have the debugging and application management tools you need to easily construct a robust data management application. Even something as simple as a wedding guest invitation and gift list is much easier to handle in a database. (See the Wedding List sample database included with this book.) Database systems are specifically designed for application development. They give you the data management and control tools that you need and also provide facilities to catalog the various parts of your application and manage their interrelationships. You also get a full programming language and debugging tools with a database system.

When you want to build a more complex database application, you need a powerful relational database management system and an application development system to help you automate your tasks. Virtually all database systems include application development facilities to allow programmers or users of the system to define the procedures needed to automate the creation and manipulation of data. Unfortunately, many database application development systems require that you know a programming language, such as C or Xbase, to define procedures. Although these languages are very rich and powerful, you must have experience before you can use them properly. To really take advantage of some database systems, you must learn programming, hire a programmer, or buy a ready-made database application (which might not exactly suit your needs) from a software development company.

Fortunately, Access makes it easy to design and construct database applications without requiring that you know a programming language. Although you begin in Access by defining the relational tables and the fields in those tables that will contain your data, you will quickly branch out to defining actions on the data via forms, reports, macros, and Visual Basic.

You can use forms and reports to define how you want to display the data and what additional calculations you want to perform—very much like spreadsheets. In this case, the format and calculation instructions (in the forms and reports) are separate from the data (in the tables), so you have complete flexibility to use your data in different ways without affecting the data. You simply define another form or report using the same data.

When you want to automate actions in a simple application, Access provides a macro definition facility to make it easy to respond to events (such as clicking a button to open a related report) or to link forms and reports together. Access 2007 makes using macros even easier by letting you embed macro definitions in your forms and reports. When you want to build something a little more complex (like the Housing Reservations database included with this book), you can quickly learn how to create simple Visual Basic event procedures for your forms and reports. If you want to create more sophisticated applications, such as contact tracking, order processing, and reminder systems (see the Conrad Systems Contacts sample database), you can employ more advanced techniques using Visual Basic and module objects.

Access 2007 includes features to make it easy to provide access to your data over your company's local intranet or on the Web. You can share and link to data on a Windows SharePoint Services site. You can also export selected data as a static HTML Web page or link a Microsoft Active Server Page from the Web to your database.

INSIDE OUT

### What Happened to Data Access Pages?

Office Access 2007 no longer supports designing data access pages (DAPs). Usability studies conducted by Microsoft show that DAPs are not a widely used feature within Access, and Microsoft is focusing more of their efforts on Windows SharePoint Services for sharing data in corporate environments. To maintain backward compatibility with previous versions, Access 2007 will continue to support existing .mdb applications that contain DAPs, but you cannot create new data access pages or modify existing pages from within Access 2007.

Access provides advanced database application development facilities to process not only data in its own database structures but also information stored in many other popular database formats. Perhaps Access's greatest strength is its ability to handle data from spreadsheets, text files, dBASE files, Paradox and FoxPro databases, and any SQL database that supports the ODBC standard. This means you can use Access to create a Windows-based application that can process data from a network SQL server or from a mainframe SQL database.

For advanced developers, Access provides the ability to create an Access application in a project file (.adp) that links directly to SQL Server (version 7.0 and later). You store your tables and queries (as views, functions, or stored procedures) directly in SQL Server and create forms for data entry and reports for data output in Access.

## Deciding to Move to Database Software

When you use a word processing document or a spreadsheet to solve a problem, you define both the data and the calculations or functions you need at the same time. For simple problems with a limited set of data, this is an ideal solution. But when you start collecting lots of data, it becomes difficult to manage in many separate document or spreadsheet files. Adding one more transaction (another contact or a new investment in your portfolio) might push you over the limit of manageability. It might even exceed the memory limits of your system or the data storage limits of your software program. Because most spreadsheet programs must be able to load an entire spreadsheet file into memory, running out of memory will probably be the first thing that forces you to consider switching to a database.

If you need to change a formula or the way certain data is formatted, you might find you have to make the same change in many places. When you want to define new calculations on existing data, you might have to copy and modify an existing document or create complex links to the files that contain the data. If you make a copy, how do you keep the data in the two copies synchronized?

Before you can use a database program such as Access to solve problems that require a lot of data or that have complex and changing requirements, you must change the way you think about solving problems with word processing or spreadsheet applications. In Access, you store a single copy of the data in the tables you design. Perhaps one of the hardest concepts to grasp is that you store only your basic data in database tables. For example, in a database, you would store the quantity of items ordered and the price of the items, but you would not usually store the extended cost (a calculated value). You use a query, a form, or a report to define the quantity-times-price calculation.

You can use the query facility to examine and extract the data in many ways. This allows you to keep only one copy of the basic data, yet use it over and over to solve different problems. In a sales database, you might create one form to display vendors and the products they supply. You can create another form to enter orders for these products. You can use a report defined on the same data to graph the sales of products by vendor during specified time periods. You don't need a separate copy of the data to do this, and you can change either the forms or the report independently, without destroying the structure of your database. You can also add new product or sales information easily without having to worry about the impact on any of your forms or reports. You can do this because the data (tables) and the routines you define to operate on the data (queries, forms, reports, macros, or modules) are completely independent of each other. Any change you make to the data via one form is immediately reflected by Access in any other form or query that uses the same data.

### Reasons to Switch to a Database

*Reason 1:* You have too many separate files or too much data in individual files. This makes it difficult to manage the data. Also, the data might exceed the limits of the software or the capacity of the system memory.

*Reason 2:* You have multiple uses for the data—detailing transactions (invoices, for example), and analyzing summaries (such as quarterly sales summaries) and "what if" scenarios. Therefore, you need to be able to look at the data in many different ways, but you find it difficult to create multiple "views" of the data.

*Reason 3:* You need to share data. For example, numerous people are entering and updating data and analyzing it. Only one person at a time can update a word processing document, and although an Excel 2003 and later spreadsheet can be shared among several people, there is no mechanism to prevent two users from updating the same row simultaneously on their local copies of the spreadsheet, requiring the changes to be reconciled later. In contrast, Access locks the row of a table being edited by one person so that no conflicting changes can be made by another user, while still permitting many other users to access or update the remaining rows of the database table. In this way, each person is working from the same data and always sees the latest saved updates made by any other user.

*Reason 4:* You must control the data because different users access the data, because the data is used to run your business, and because the data is related (such as data for customers and orders). This means you must control data values, and you must ensure data consistency.

If you're wondering how you'll make the transition from word processing documents and spreadsheets to Access, you'll be pleased to find features in Access to help you out. You can use the import facilities to copy the data from your existing text or spreadsheet files. You'll find that Access supports most of the same functions you have used in your spreadsheets, so defining calculations in a form or a report will seem very familiar. Within the Help facility, you can find "how do I" topics that walk you through key tasks you need to learn to begin working with a database and "tell me about" and reference topics that enhance your knowledge. In addition, Access provides powerful wizard facilities to give you a jump-start on moving your spreadsheet data to an Access database, such as the Import Spreadsheet Wizard and the Table Analyzer Wizard to help you design database tables to store your old spreadsheet data.

INSIDE OUT

### Design Considerations When Converting from a Spreadsheet to a Database

You can obtain free assistance from us and many other Microsoft MVPs (Most Valuable Professionals) in the Access newsgroups. Some of the most difficult problems arise in databases that have been created by directly copying spreadsheet data into an Access table. The typical advice in this situation is to design the database tables first, then import and split up the spreadsheet data.

You can access the newsgroups using Microsoft Outlook Express or Windows Mail; or you can go to *http://support.microsoft.com/newsgroups/default.aspx*, and in the Community Newsgroups column on the left, expand the Office category and then the Access category to see the available newsgroups. Click one of the links to go to that newsgroup within your Web browser where you can post questions and read answers to questions posted by others.

Take a long look at the kind of work you're doing today. The sidebar, "Reasons to Switch to a Database," summarizes some of the key reasons why you might need to move to Access. Is the number of files starting to overwhelm you? Do you find yourself creating copies of old files when you need to answer new questions? Do others need to share the data and update it? Do you find yourself exceeding the limits of your current software or the memory on your system? If the answer to any of these is *yes*, you should be solving your problems with a relational database management system like Access.

In the next chapter, "Exploring the New Look of Access 2007," you'll learn about all the new user interface changes in Access 2007 including the new Ribbon interface element. You'll also open some of the built-in Access template databases and explore the new Getting Started screen for Access 2007. Finally, you'll learn about the new Navigation Pane to interact with all your various database objects.

CHAPTER 2

# Exploring the New Look of Access 2007



Before you explore the many features of Microsoft Office Access 2007, it's worth spending a little time looking it over and "kicking the tires." Like a new model of a favorite car, this latest version of Access has major changes to the body (user interface) as well as a new engine under the hood (Access Data Engine). In this chapter and the next, we explore the changes to the user interface, show you how to navigate through Microsoft's new replacement for toolbars and menus called the Ribbon, and discuss the various components of an Access database and how they interact.

## Opening Access for the First Time

The first time you open Office Access 2007, you are presented with two preliminary option screens. The first of these, the Privacy Options dialog box seen in Figure 2-1, lists three check boxes, which are selected by default. Note that you must have an active connection to the Internet to use these options. The Get Online Help check box, when selected, allows Access to search Microsoft Office Online's vast resources for content relevant to your search. Access downloads this information to your local computer for faster searching when you search for items in the Help section. Selecting this check box also means you will have the latest Help information at your disposal. The second check box, called Keep Your System Running, is a special tool you can download that interfaces with the 2007 Microsoft Office system. You can use this diagnostic tool to help identify problems with your Office installation. Although not required to run the 2007 Office release or Access 2007, this tool might assist you with locating the cause of any unforeseen system crashes.

The third check box in the Privacy Options dialog box, Make Office Better, allows you to sign up for Microsoft's Customer Experience Improvement Program. This utility tracks various statistics while you use Access 2007 and the 2007 Office release and sends that information to Microsoft. Note that this option does not send any personal information to Microsoft. By tracking how customers are using their products, Microsoft can improve its Office line of products for future releases. Click the Read Our Privacy Statement link in the lower-left corner to read Microsoft's privacy statement. After you make your selections or clear the check boxes you do not want, click the OK button to start using Access 2007.

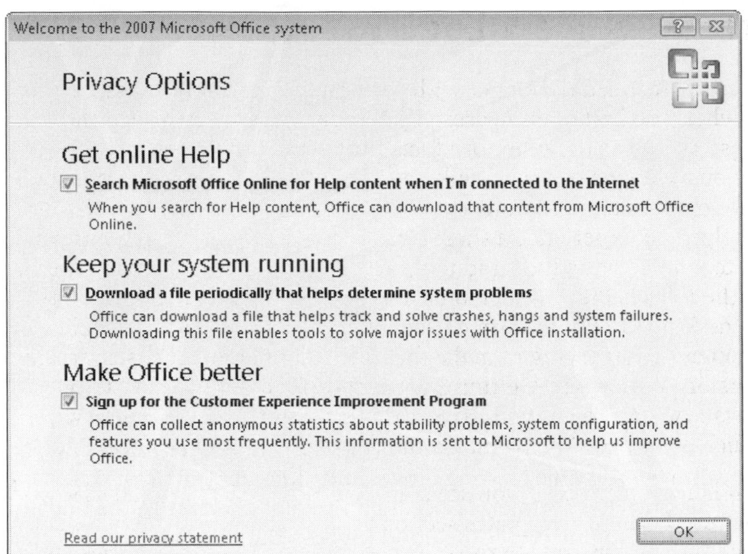


**Figure 2-1** You can choose privacy options when you first launch Access 2007.

Chapter 2

> **Note**
>
> The dialog box shown in Figure 2-1 is what we saw when opening Access 2007 for the first time using Microsoft Windows Vista. You might see a slightly different sequence of prompts if you install the 2007 Office release on Windows XP.

After selecting your options in the Privacy Options dialog box, you can always alter these settings later. For more information on changing these settings, see "Modifying Global Settings via the Access Options Dialog Box" on page 87.

> **CAUTION!**
>
> If you are in a corporate network environment, you should check with your Information Technology department to determine whether your company has established guidelines before making selections in the Privacy Options dialog box.

# Getting Started—A New Look for Access

If you are a seasoned developer with previous versions of Access, be prepared for quite a shock when you first open Access 2007. Microsoft has revamped the entire look and feel of Access as well as the other products in the 2007 Office release. To some degree, users of previous versions of Access will have a challenging task adjusting to all the changes the development team has incorporated into this version. If you are one of these users, you might even experience a short-term decrease in productivity as you become accustomed to where commands and tools are located on the new user interface element called the *Ribbon*. (See "Understanding the New Ribbon Feature" on page 41 for details about the Ribbon.) For first-time users of Access, Microsoft has spent a great deal of development effort trying to make the "Access experience" easier and more intuitive in this version. With a new Getting Started screen, a host of ready-to-use database applications available, and a context-driven, rich graphical Ribbon, users will have an easier and quicker time creating professional-looking database applications.

On first launching Access, you see a new Getting Started screen as shown in Figure 2-2. The Featured Online Templates section in the center of the screen displays database templates created by the Microsoft Access development team. These templates represent some of the more common uses for a database and are therefore presented to you first. On the left side of the screen you can find several different template categories grouped by subject. Click on one of these categories to change the display in the center of the screen to a list of templates in that category. The Local Templates category features database templates available on your local drive that were installed with Access. The From Microsoft Office Online category features database templates that you can download–but you must be connected to the Internet to see and download any templates in each of these categories. Microsoft is continually adding and modifying the selections available in the Microsoft Office Online categories, so the list you see might be different from that shown in Figure 2-2. If you have enabled your privacy options to have Access update these featured links, make sure to check these groups from time to time to see if a new template exists for your specific needs. For more information on Privacy Options, see "Understanding the Trust Center" on page 36.

Just above Featured Online Templates in the middle of the screen is a button labeled Blank Database. You use this button to start the process of creating a new empty database with no objects. See Chapter 4, "Creating Your Database and Tables," for details on how to create a new blank database.

The right task pane on the Getting Started screen displays a list of the Access databases you recently opened. To quickly open any of these databases, click on the file name in the list. Click More to see the Open dialog box where you can search for and open any database not in the list.

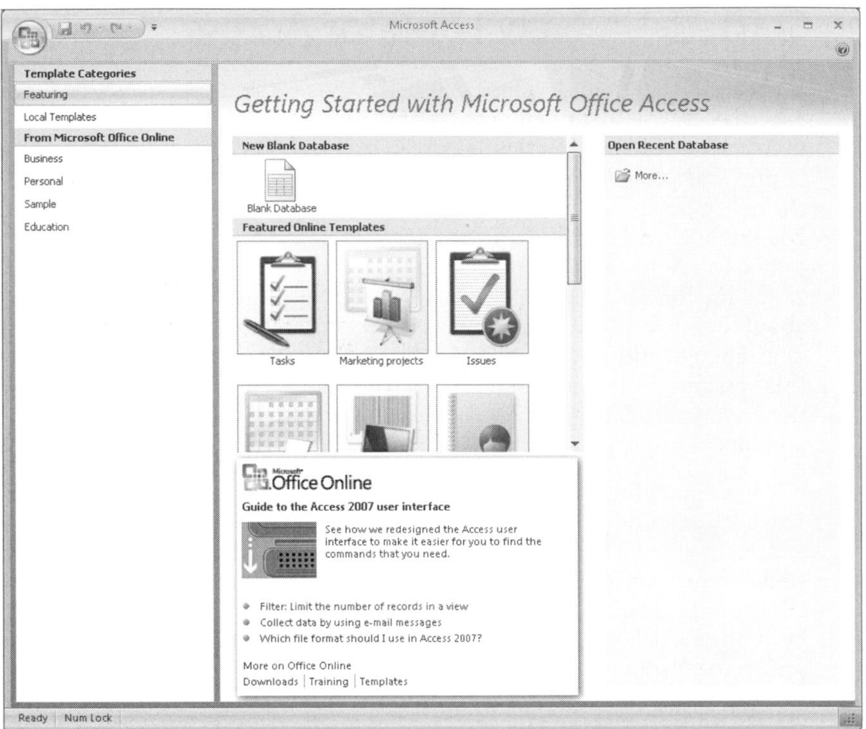


**Figure 2-2** You can create a database from a template, create a new blank database, or search for a database file to open on the Getting Started screen in Access 2007.

At the bottom of the Getting Started screen, you see specific information related to Access 2007 such as articles, additional templates, and downloads available from Microsoft Office Online. The downloads can include tutorials, updates to your Help files, or white papers on advanced topics. Most of this content is aimed at showing you all the new features available in Access 2007 as well as pointing out online training materials that Microsoft has created. If you have enabled your privacy options to have Access update these featured links, this area of the Getting Started screen is automatically updated when new content becomes available. Updating the content occurs only if you have an active Internet connection established.

## Opening an Existing Database

To showcase the new user interface (UI), let's take one of the template databases out for a test drive. Using the IssuesSample.accdb database on the companion CD, based on the Microsoft Issues template, we will highlight some specific areas of Access 2007. First, follow the instructions at the beginning of this book for installing the sample files on your hard drive. If necessary, start Access again to display the Getting Started screen shown in Figure 2-2. Click More under Open Recent Database in the right task pane to see the Open dialog box shown in Figure 2-3.

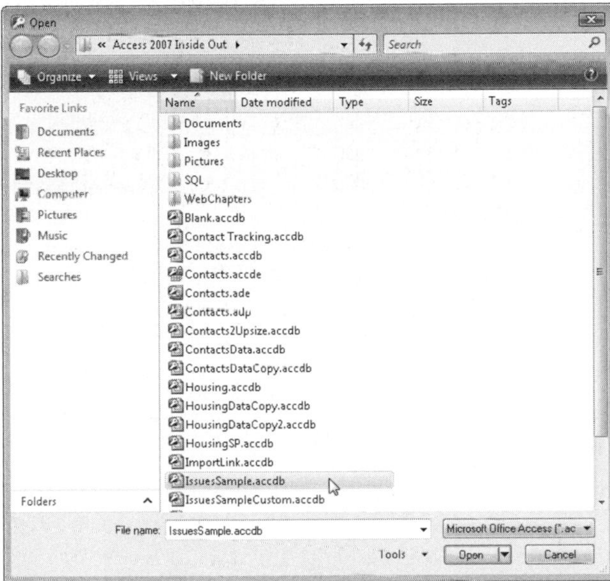


**Figure 2-3** You can use the Open dialog box to find and open any existing database file.

In the Open dialog box, select the IssuesSample.accdb file from the folder in which you installed the sample databases, and then click Open. You can also double-click the file name to open the database. (If you haven't set options in Windows Explorer to show file name extensions for registered applications, you won't see the .accdb extension for your database files.) The Issues sample application will start, and you'll see the startup form for the Issues Sample database along with all the various database objects listed on the left side, as shown in Figure 2-4.

> **Note**
>
> If you installed the sample files for this book in the default location from the companion CD, you can find the files in the Microsoft Press\Access 2007 Inside Out folder on your C drive.

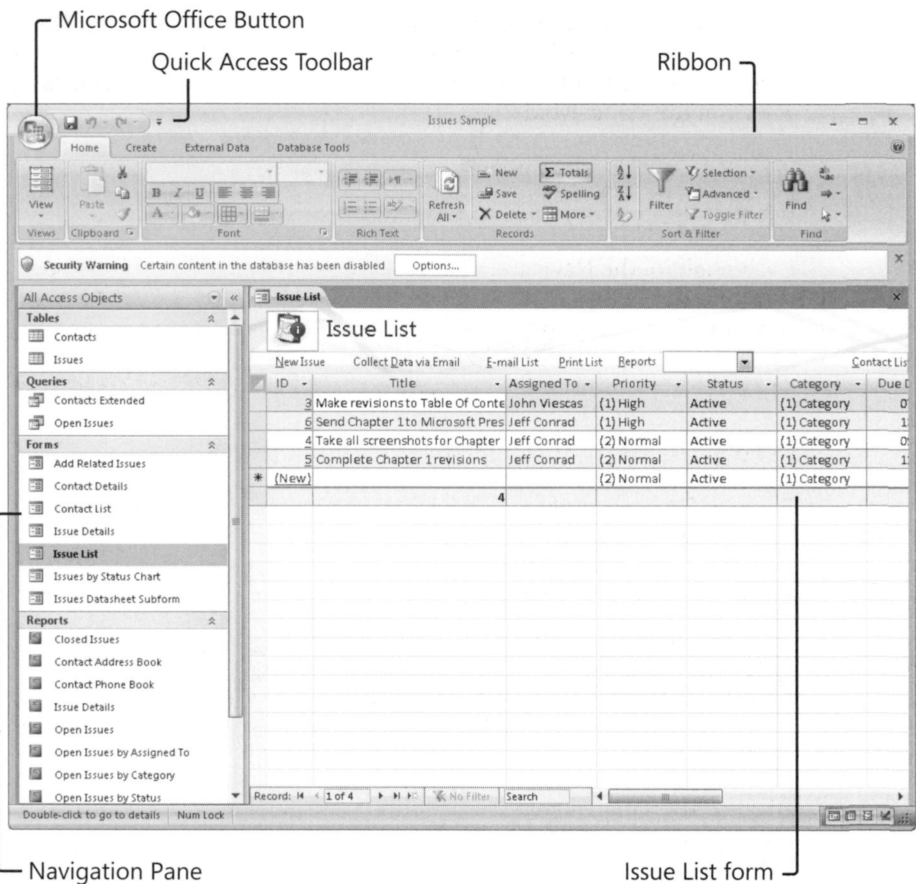


**Figure 2-4** When you open the Issues Sample database, you can see the new user interface for Access 2007.

If you have used previous versions of Access, you immediately notice that Access 2007 has significant changes. We will discuss each of these user interface elements in greater detail in the following sections, but for now, here is a brief overview of the different elements. The upper-left corner of the screen contains a large button with the Microsoft Office logo on it. This button, called the Microsoft Office Button, replaces the File menu from previous editions of Access. Next to this button are a few smaller buttons on what is called the Quick Access Toolbar. This toolbar holds frequently used commands within Access 2007. Beneath the Quick Access Toolbar is a series of four tabs (Home, Create, External Data, and Database Tools) that contain many commands, options, and drop-down list boxes. These tabs are on what Microsoft refers to as the Ribbon and it replaces menu bars and toolbars from previous versions of Access. You will interact heavily with the Ribbon when developing and using Access 2007 databases because most of the commands you need are contained on it.

Beneath the Ribbon is a small message that says *Security Warning*. This Message Bar informs you if Access has disabled potentially harmful content in this database. See "Understanding Content Security" on page 34 to learn what this message means and what you can do to avoid it.

On the left side of the screen is the new Navigation Pane, which replaces the Database window from previous Access versions. In the Navigation Pane, you can find all the various database objects for this database (forms, tables, queries, and so on).

To the right of the Navigation Pane is where your database objects open. In Figure 2-4 you see that the Issue List form is open. All possible views of your database objects appear in this area. Just beneath the Navigation Pane and main object window is the status bar. The status bar displays text descriptions from field controls, various keyboard settings (Caps Lock, Num Lock, and Scroll Lock), and object view buttons.



## Exploring the Microsoft Office Button

Microsoft Office Button

The new Microsoft Office Button in Access 2007, shown in the upper-left corner of Figure 2-5, replaces the File menu from previous versions, and you can display its commands by clicking the Microsoft Office Button from the Getting Started screen or from within any database. Figure 2-5 shows you the available commands.

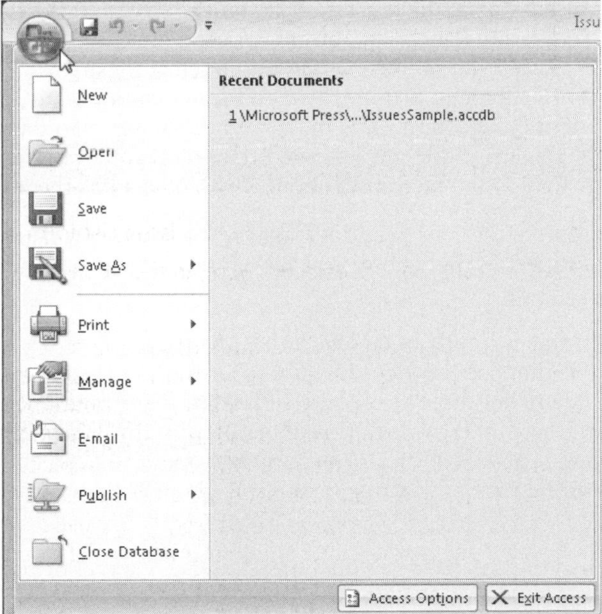


**Figure 2-5** You can view many commands by clicking the Microsoft Office Button.

Using these commands you can do any of the following:

- **New** Create a new database file.
- **Open** Open any existing database file on your computer or network.
- **Save** Save design changes for the database object that is open and has the focus.
- **Save As** Save a copy of the current object, find add-ins to save the object with a different file format, or save a copy of the current database in 2007, 2002/2003, or 2000 Access format. When you click the Save As button, the default is to save a copy of the current open object that has the focus or the object that has the focus in the Navigation Pane. If you rest your mouse pointer on or click the arrow at the right, additional commands appear in a submenu to the right of the arrow. You can choose from these to save a copy of your entire database in any of the formats supported by Access 2007. Note that if you choose to save the entire database, Access closes the database you have open so that it can create the copy.
- **Print** Print the currently open object that has the focus or the object in the Navigation Pane that has the focus using the Print dialog box or the Quick Print feature, or use Print Preview to preview the printed appearance on screen. If you immediately click the Print button, Access opens the Print dialog box to print whatever object currently has the focus. Be careful here because the object that has the focus might not be the one currently on the screen. If the focus is on an object in the Navigation Pane, that object is printed instead of the object currently open. If you rest your mouse pointer on or click the arrow to the right of the Print button, a submenu presents two additional options called Quick Print and Print Preview. Quick Print immediately sends the selected database object to the printer whereas Print Preview lets you preview on your monitor what you are about to print. Here again, be careful about which object has the focus.
- **Manage** Compact and repair your database file, back up your database, or open the Database Properties dialog box to review and change properties specific to this database.
- **E-Mail** Export the currently open object that has the focus or the object in the Navigation Pane that has the focus in various formats and send to another person. Be careful here because the object that has the focus might not be the one currently on the screen. If the focus is on an object in the Navigation Pane, that object is exported instead of the object currently open. You can choose to export and send the object in the following formats: Excel, HTML, Rich Text Format, or as a Text File.
- **Publish** Publish the database to a document manager server or package your database as a CAB file and digitally sign it.
- **Close Database** Close the currently open database and return to the Getting Started screen.

You can also find these two buttons at the bottom of the menu:

- **Access Options** Opens the Access Options dialog box where you can choose and define many different settings and preferences for Access.
- **Exit Access** Closes the currently open database file as well as completely exits Access.

> **Note**
>
> For users of previous versions of Access, the Access Options dialog box is where you'll find many of the settings previously found in the Options dialog box that you opened from the Tools menu. For more information on the options available in this area, see "Modifying Global Settings via the Access Options Dialog Box" on page 87.



## Taking Advantage of the Quick Access Toolbar

Next to the Microsoft Office Button is the Quick Access Toolbar, shown in Figure 2-6. This special toolbar gives you "quick access" to some of the more common commands you will use in Access 2007, and you can customize this toolbar to include additional commands. Here are the default commands available on the Quick Access Toolbar:

- **Save** Saves any changes to the currently selected database object.
- **Undo** Undoes the last change you made to an object or a record.
- **Redo** Cancels the last Undo change you made to an object or a record.

At the right end of the Quick Access Toolbar is a small arrow. Click that arrow, and you'll see the Customize Quick Access Toolbar menu, as shown in Figure 2-6.

The top section of the menu displays common commands that you might want to add to the Quick Access Toolbar. Note that the three default commands–Save, Undo, and Redo–have check marks next to them. You can click any of these to clear the check mark and remove the command from the Quick Access Toolbar. You can click any of the other eight commands (New, Open, E-Mail, Quick Print, Print Preview, Spelling, Mode, and Refresh All) to add them to the right end of the Quick Access Toolbar. Near the bottom of this menu is More Commands, which allows you to fully customize what commands are available and how those commands appear on the Quick Access Toolbar. The Show Below The Ribbon option on the menu allows you to move the Quick Access Toolbar above or below the Ribbon depending on your preference. The last option on this menu, Minimize The Ribbon, causes Access to automatically collapse the Ribbon when it is not being used. When the focus is off the Ribbon, only the Ribbon tabs themselves appear when you click this command. Clicking any of the Ribbon tabs then causes Access to redisplay all the commands on top of any open objects. When you move the focus off any part of the Ribbon, it will again collapse to just the tabs.

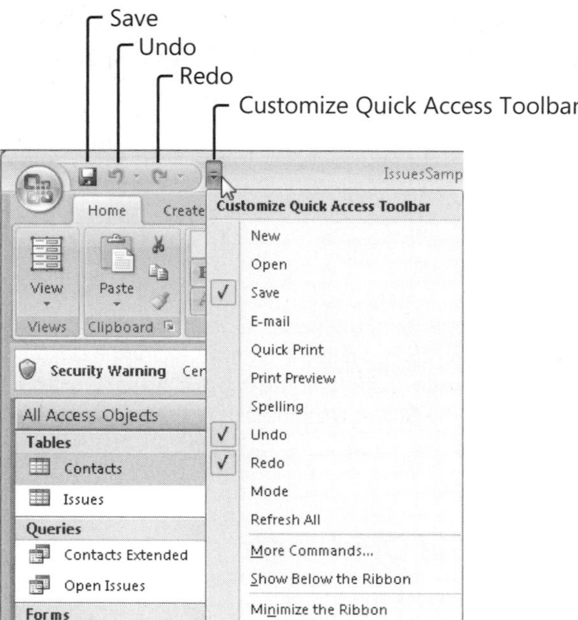


**Figure 2-6** The default Quick Access Toolbar contains the Save, Undo, and Redo commands for the current object, and the command to customize the toolbar.

To customize the Quick Access Toolbar, click the arrow on the right end and click More Commands near the bottom of the menu. The Access Options dialog box with the Customize category selected appears, as shown in Figure 2-7.

On the left you can see a list of built-in Access commands that you can select to add to the Quick Access Toolbar. By default, the list shows commands from the Popular Commands category—commands that are used very frequently. You can change the list of commands by selecting a different category from the Choose Commands From list. The All Commands option displays the entire list of Access commands available in alphabetical order. Just below the list of available commands is a check box that you can select to show the Quick Access Toolbar below the Ribbon. Clear the check box to show the Quick Access Toolbar above the Ribbon.

The list on the right side of the screen by default displays what options are available on every Quick Access Toolbar for all your database files. If you add, remove, or modify the commands shown in the list on the right when you have chosen For All Documents (Default) in the Customize Quick Access Toolbar list, the changes are reflected in every database you open with Access 2007. To customize the Quick Access Toolbar for only the specific database you currently have open, click the arrow in the drop-down list and select the database file path for your current database from the list, as shown in Figure 2-8.

Chapter 2

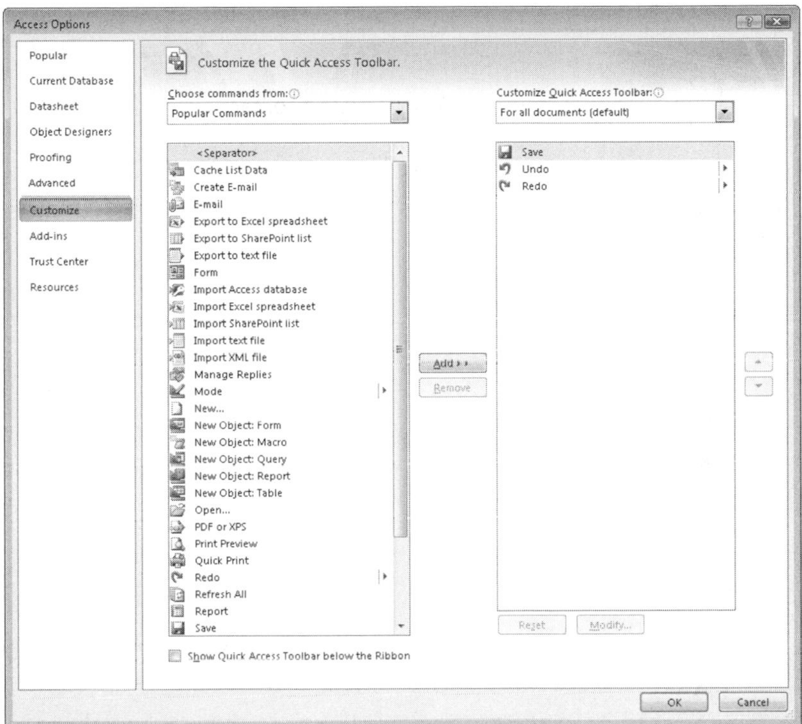


**Figure 2-7** You can add or remove commands on the Quick Access Toolbar and change their sequence using the Customize category in the Access Options dialog box.

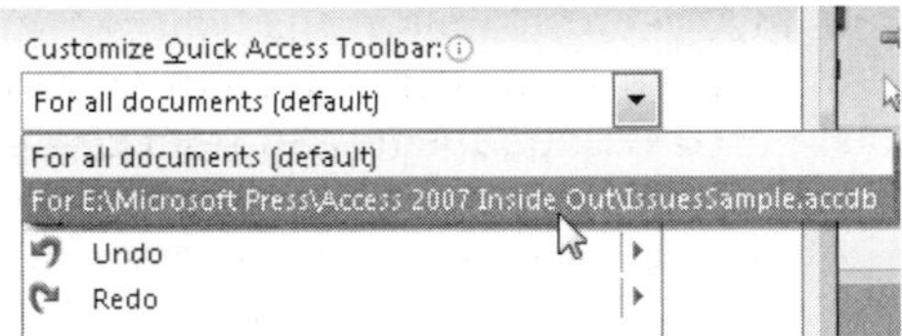


**Figure 2-8** You can add or remove commands on the Quick Access Toolbar for the current database by selecting your database from the Customize Quick Access Toolbar list.

When you select the current database, the command list below it is now empty, awaiting the changes you request. Find a command in the list on the left, and then either double-click it or click the Add button in the middle of the screen to add this command to your custom Quick Access Toolbar, as shown in Figure 2-9. If you make a mistake and select the wrong command, select the command in the list on the right, and click the Remove button to eliminate it from your custom list.

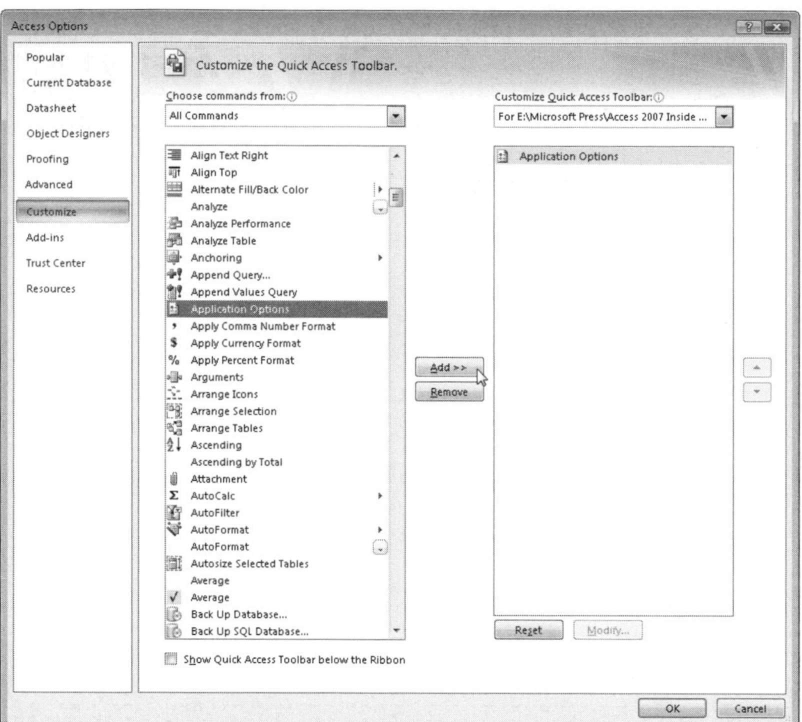


**Figure 2-9** Add a command to the Quick Access Toolbar by selecting it in the list on the left and then clicking the Add button.

In addition to the built-in commands, you can also select any macros you have defined in this current database. To do this, select Macros in the Choose Commands From list on the left. A list of all your saved macro objects appears, and you can add these macros directly to your custom Quick Access Toolbar, as shown in Figure 2-10. We added one macro called mcrSample to this Issues Sample database to illustrate the next steps.

**CAUTION!**

Do not add a macro to your Quick Access Toolbar when you have selected the option to customize the Quick Access Toolbar for all documents. Access displays an error if you try to click your custom macro command in a database that does not contain the macro you selected.

You can also assign custom button images to the macro objects you select. To do so, select one of your macros in the list on the right, and then click the Modify button to open the Modify Button dialog box shown in Figure 2-11. From here you can choose one of the predefined button images available and also change the display name for this option on your custom Quick Access Toolbar.

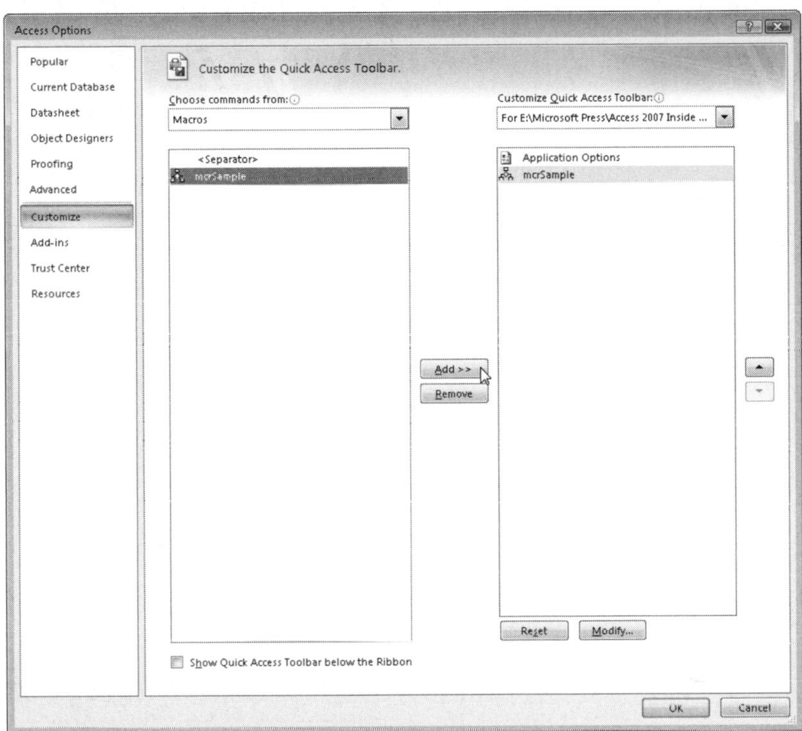


**Figure 2-10** Add a saved macro object to the Quick Access Toolbar by selecting it in the list on the left and then clicking the Add button.

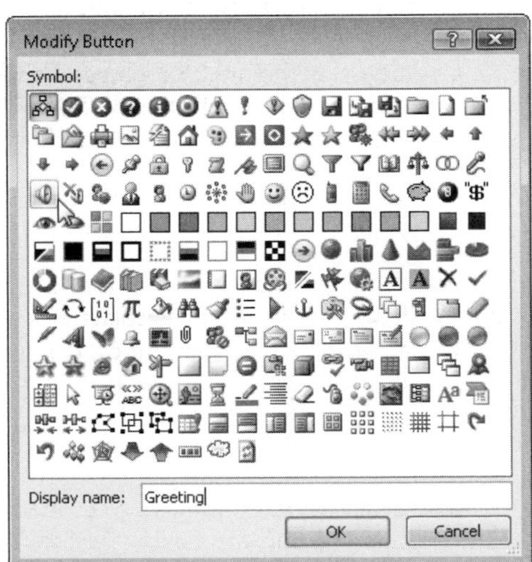


**Figure 2-11** You can change the button face and the display name in the Modify Button dialog box.

After you have all the commands and macros you want on your custom Quick Access Toolbar, you might decide that you do not like the order in which they appear. Access 2007 allows you to easily modify this order using the Move Up and Move Down arrow buttons at the far right of the dialog box. (You can rest your mouse pointer on either button to see the button name.) Select a command you want to move in the list on the right and click the up arrow to move it up in the list as shown in Figure 2-12. Each successive click moves that command up one more place in the custom list. Likewise, the down arrow shifts the selected command down in the list. In Figure 2-12 you can see that we have moved the macro titled Greeting up above the Application Options command.

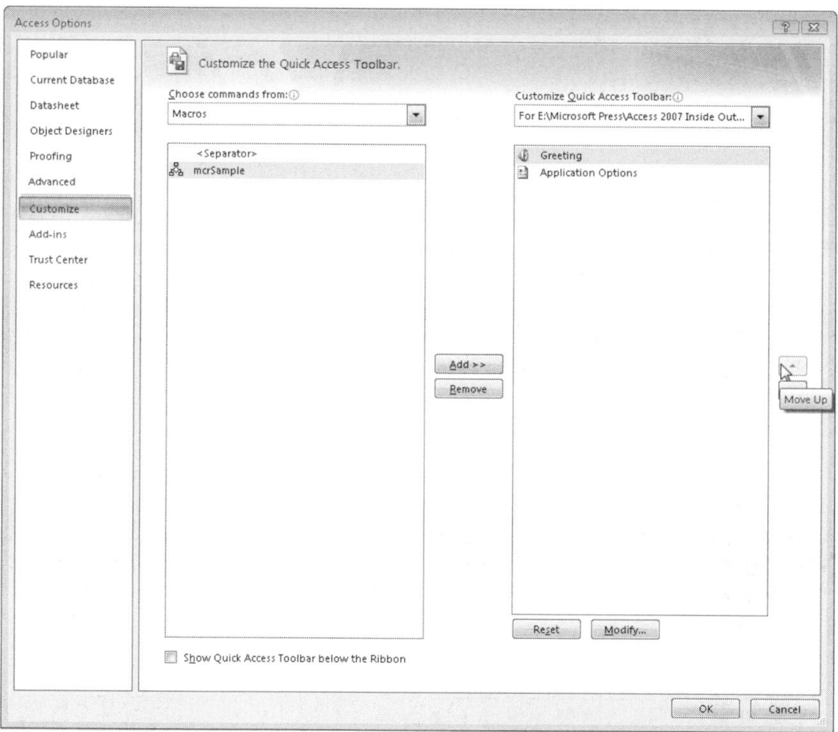


**Figure 2-12** You can change the order of the commands on your Quick Access Toolbar by clicking the Move Up and Move Down arrow buttons.

From top to bottom in the list on the right, the commands appear in left-to-right order on the Quick Access Toolbar after the commands assigned to all databases. When you are completely satisfied with your revisions, click OK to save your changes. Observe that your custom Quick Access Toolbar now appears on the screen above or below the Ribbon depending on the choice you have selected. Figure 2-13 shows our completed changes to the Quick Access Toolbar for this specific database.

**Note**

You might have noticed the <Separator> option in the list on the left. Adding <Separator> to your custom Quick Access Toolbar places a small space below the command currently selected in the list on the right. You can add as many separators as you want to your custom Quick Access Toolbar to visually separate groups of commands.

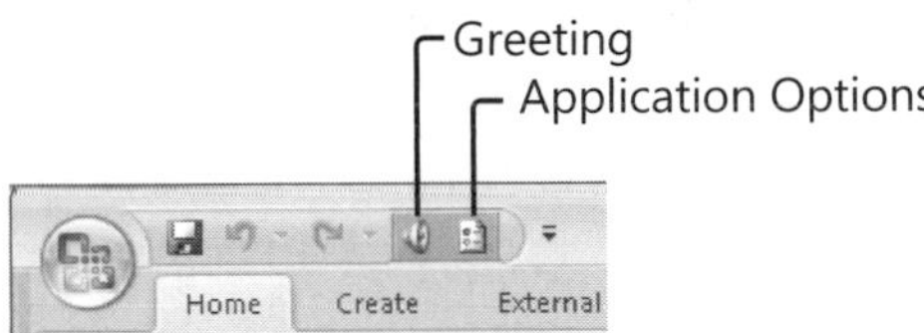


**Figure 2-13** Your two additional commands now appear on the Quick Access Toolbar for this database.

To remove an item from your custom Quick Access Toolbar, reopen the Access Options dialog box with the Customize category selected again by clicking the arrow on the Quick Access Toolbar and then clicking More Commands. To remove an item, select it in the list on the right and click the Remove button, and Access removes it from your list of commands. If you inadvertently remove a command that you wanted to keep, you can click the Cancel button in the lower-right corner to discard all changes. You can also find the command in the list on the left and add it back. Keep in mind that you can remove commands for all databases or for only the current database.

If you wish to restore the Quick Access Toolbar for all databases to the default set of commands, select For All Documents (Default) in the Customize Quick Access Toolbar list, and then click the Reset button. To remove all custom commands for the current database, select the database path in the Customize Quick Access Toolbar list and click Reset. Before removing any commands on the Quick Access Toolbar, Access displays a warning message shown in Figure 2-14. If you click Yes to this Reset Customizations message, Access resets the Quick Access Toolbar for this current database back to the defaults.

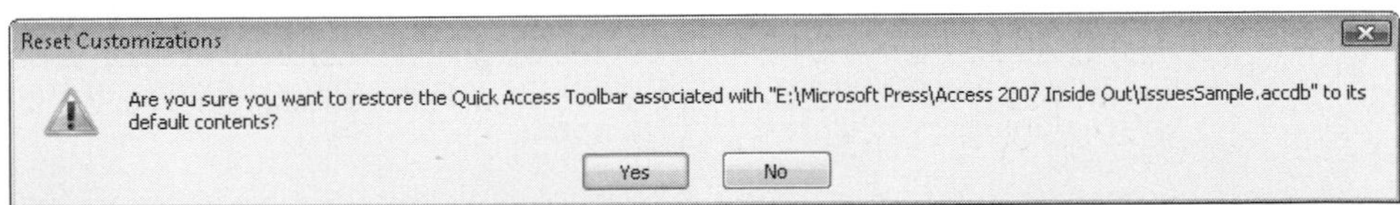


**Figure 2-14** Access asks you to confirm resetting the Quick Access Toolbar back to the default commands.

INSIDE OUT **Adding a Command to the Quick Access Toolbar with Two Mouse Clicks**

If you notice that you are using a command on the Ribbon quite often, Access 2007 provides a very quick and easy way to add this command to the Quick Access Toolbar. To add a command on the Ribbon to the Quick Access Toolbar, right-click the command and click Add To Quick Access Toolbar. This adds the command to the Quick Access Toolbar for all databases. Alternatively, you can quickly remove an item from your custom Quick Access Toolbar by right-clicking on the command and clicking Remove From Quick Access Toolbar.



## Understanding Content Security

In response to growing threats from viruses and worms, Microsoft launched a security initiative in early 2002, called Trustworthy Computing, to focus on making all its products safer to use. In an e-mail sent to employees, Bill Gates summed up the seriousness of the initiative:

"In the past, we've made our software and services more compelling for users by adding new features and functionality, and by making our platform richly extensible. We've done a terrific job at that, but all those great features won't matter unless customers trust our software. So now, when we face a choice between adding features and resolving security issues, we need to choose security. Our products should emphasize security right out of the box, and we must constantly refine and improve that security as threats evolve."

Prior to Microsoft Access 2003, it was quite possible for a malicious person to send you a database file that contained code that could damage your system. As soon as you opened the database, the harmful code would run—perhaps even without your knowledge. Or the programmer could embed dangerous code in a query, form, or report, and your computer would be damaged as soon as you opened that object. In version 11 (Access 2003), you were presented with a series of confusing dialog boxes when you opened an unsigned database file if you had left your macro security level set to medium or high. After wading through the various dialog boxes, you could still be left with a database you were unable to open.

Access 2007 improves upon the security model by adding a new component to the Access interface called the *Trust Center*. This new security interface is far less confusing and intrusive than the Access 2003 macro security feature. With a security level set to high in Access 2003, you would not be able to open any database files because all Access databases could have some type of macros, VBA code, or calls to unsafe functions embedded in their structure. Any database with queries is considered unsafe by Access 2007 because those queries could contain expressions calling unsafe functions. In Access 2007, each database file opens without presenting you with a series of dialog boxes like in Access 2003. Depending on where your file is located on the local computer drive or network share, Access silently disables any malicious macros or VBA code without any intrusive dialog box messages.

> **Note**
>
> The sample databases included on the companion CD are not digitally signed, because they will become unsigned as soon as you change any of the queries or sample code. We designed all the sample applications to open successfully, but each displays a warning dialog box if the database is not trusted. If you have installed the database in an untrusted location, the application displays instructions in the warning dialog box that you can follow to enable the full application. See "Enabling Content by Defining Trusted Locations" on page 39 for information about defining trusted locations.



## Temporarily Enabling a Database That Is Not Trusted

When you open an existing database or template, you might see a Security Warning message displayed in the Message Bar, just below the Quick Access Toolbar and Ribbon as shown in Figure 2-15. This message notifies you that Access has disabled certain features of the application because the file is not digitally signed or is located in a folder that has not been designated as trusted.

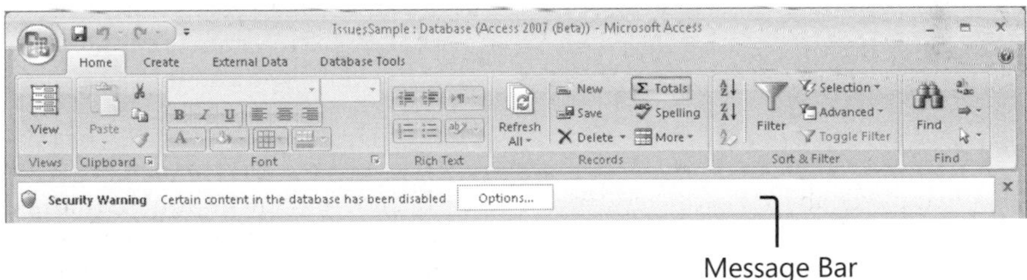


**Figure 2-15** The Message Bar alerts you if Access has disabled certain content.

In order to ensure that any restricted code and macros function in this database, you must manually tell Access to enable this content by clicking the Options button on the Message Bar. This opens a dialog box, called Microsoft Office Security Options, as shown in Figure 2-16. This dialog box warns you that this file's content cannot be verified because a digital certificate was not found.

You can choose to have Access 2007 continue to block any harmful content by leaving the default option set to Help Protect Me From Unknown Content (Recommended). By having Access block any harmful content, you can be assured that no malicious code or macros can execute from this database. However, you also have to realize that because Access blocks all Visual Basic code and any macros containing a potentially harmful command, it is quite possible that this application will not run correctly if you continue to let Access disable potentially harmful functions and code. In order to have Access discontinue blocking potentially harmful content, you must select the Enable This Content option. After you select that option and click OK, Access closes the database and then reopens the file to enable all content. Access does not display the Message Bar after it reopens the file, and all functions, code, and macros are now allowed to run in this specific database.

**Figure 2-16** You can enable blocked content from the Microsoft Office Security Options dialog box.

> **Note**
>
> When you enable content after opening an untrusted database, the database becomes trusted only for the current session. If you close the database and then attempt to reopen it, Access displays the warnings again on the Message Bar.

## Understanding the Trust Center

You might have noticed in the lower-left corner of the Microsoft Office Security Options dialog box a link to the Trust Center. You can also open the Trust Center from the Access Options dialog box, which you can open by clicking the Microsoft Office Button discussed earlier. We will discuss the Access Options dialog box later in this chapter; see "Modifying Global Settings via the Access Options Dialog Box" on page 87.

Click Open The Trust Center in the Microsoft Office Security Options dialog box to view the advanced security settings. If the Message Bar is not currently available, click the Microsoft Office Button in the upper-left corner and then click Access Options. In the Access Options dialog box, click the Trust Center category on the left and then click the Trust Center Settings button. In the Trust Center dialog box, shown in Figure 2-17, you see six categories of security settings.

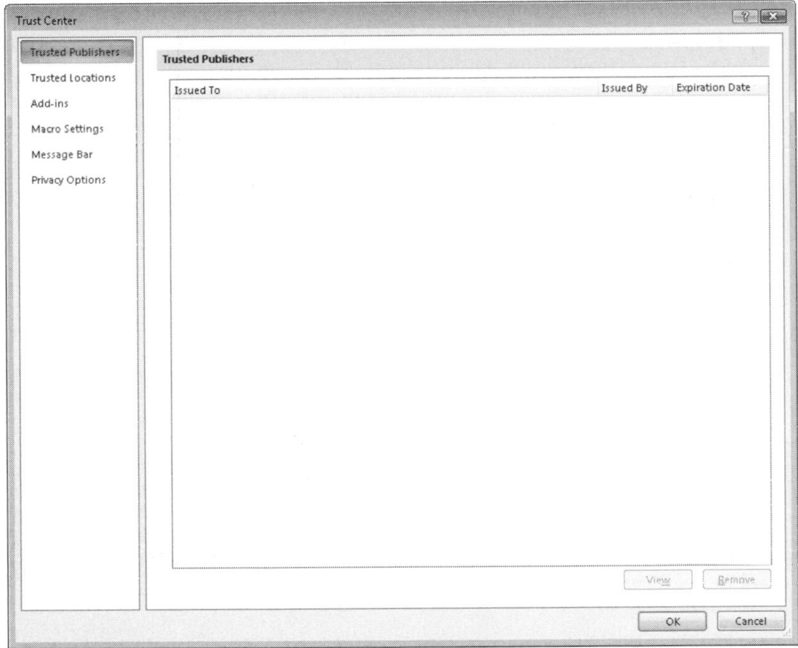


**Figure 2-17** The Trust Center dialog box displays various categories in which you can select trust and privacy options.

Briefly, the categories are as follows:

- **Trusted Publishers.** Use to view and remove publishers you have designated as being trustworthy. When applications are digitally signed by one of these trusted publishers, Access does not disable any content within the database and the Message Bar does not display any warning. By default, digitally signed applications from Microsoft are trusted. You might see one or more additional trusted publishers if you have ever tried to download and run a signed application and have indicated to Windows that you trust the publisher and want to save the publisher's certificate. See Chapter 25, "Distributing Your Application," for information about digitally signing your own applications.
- **Trusted Locations.** Use to designate specific folders and subfolders as trusted locations. Access considers any database files within this folder as trustworthy, and all content in these folders is enabled. In the Trusted Locations category, each

designated trusted folder is listed with the file path, an optional description, and the date the entry was last modified. See "Enabling Content by Defining Trusted Locations" on the next page for details about using the options in this category.

- **Add-Ins.** Use to set specific restrictions on Access add-in files by selecting or clearing the three check boxes in this category. An add-in is a separate program or file that extends the capabilities of Access. You can create these separate files or programs by using Visual Basic for Applications (VBA) or another programming language such as C#. You can require that add-in files be signed by a trusted publisher before Access will load and run them. If you select the option to require that add-ins be signed, you can disable notifications for add-ins that are unsigned. For added security, you can disable all application add-in functionality.

- **Macro Settings.** Use to configure how Access handles macros in databases that are not in a trusted location. Four options are available with this feature, only one of which can be active at any given time. Table 2-1 discusses the purpose of each option.

**Table 2-1 Macro Settings**

| Option | Purpose |
|---|---|
| Disable All Macros Without Notification | Access disables all harmful content, but does not notify you through the Message Bar. |
| Disable All Macros With Notification | Access disables all harmful content but notifies you through the Message Bar that it has disabled the content. This is the default option for new installations of Access. This is equivalent to the Medium macro security level option available in Access 2003. |
| Disable All Macros Except Digitally Signed Macros | Access allows only digitally signed macros (code in digitally signed databases). All other potentially harmful content is disabled. This is equivalent to the High macro security level option available in Access 2003. |
| Enable All Macros (not recommended, potentially dangerous code can run) | Access enables any and all potentially harmful content. In addition, Access does not notify you through the Message Bar. This is equivalent to the Low macro security option available in Access 2003. |

- **Message Bar.** Use to configure Access either to show the Message Bar when content has been disabled or not to display the bar at all.

- **Privacy Options.** Use to enable or disable actions within Access regarding computing privacy, troubleshooting system problems, and scanning suspicious Web site links. The first check box under Privacy Options tells Access to scan Microsoft's online help site when you are connected to the Internet. If you clear this check box, Access scans only your local hard drive when you conduct a search in Help. The second check box, Update Featured Links From Microsoft Office Online, tells Access to display some current Microsoft Office Online featured links on the Getting Started screen. Selecting the third check box instructs Access to download and activate a special file from Microsoft's site that helps you troubleshoot Access and Office program installation and program errors. The fourth check box allows you to sign up for the Customer Experience Improvement Program. Microsoft uses this program to track statistics of the features you use the most frequently and gather information about your Microsoft Office system configuration. These statistics help determine changes in future program releases. The final check box under Privacy Options allows Access to automatically scan Office documents for possible links to and from suspicious Web sites. This last option is turned on by default to help safeguard your computer against documents containing harmful Web links.



## Enabling Content by Defining Trusted Locations

You can permanently enable the content in a database that is not trusted by defining a folder on your hard drive or network that is trusted and then placing the database in that folder. Or, you can define the folder where the database is located as trusted. You define trusted locations in the Trust Center dialog box.

**CAUTION!**

If you are in a corporate network environment, you should check with your Information Technology department to determine whether your company has established guidelines concerning enabling content on Access databases.

To define a trusted location, click the Microsoft Office Button and then click Access Options. In the Access Options dialog box, click the Trust Center category and then click the Trust Center Settings button. Access displays the Trust Center dialog box. Click the Trusted Locations category to see its options, as shown in Figure 2-18.

Click the Add New Location button. Access now displays the Microsoft Office Trusted Location dialog box shown in Figure 2-19.

Click the Browse button and locate the folder you want to designate as trusted. You can optionally designate any subfolders in that directory as trusted without having to designate each individual folder within the hierarchy. Enter an optional description you want for this folder, and click OK to save your changes. The new location you just specified now appears in the list of trusted locations. If you later decide to remove this folder as a trusted location, select that location, as shown in Figure 2-18, and then click the Remove button. Any Access databases in that folder are now treated as unsafe. Figure 2-18 also shows two check boxes at the bottom of the dialog box. The first check box allows you to define network locations as trusted locations. Microsoft recommends you not select this check box because you cannot control what files others might place in a network location. The second check box disables all Trusted Location settings and allows content only from trusted publishers.

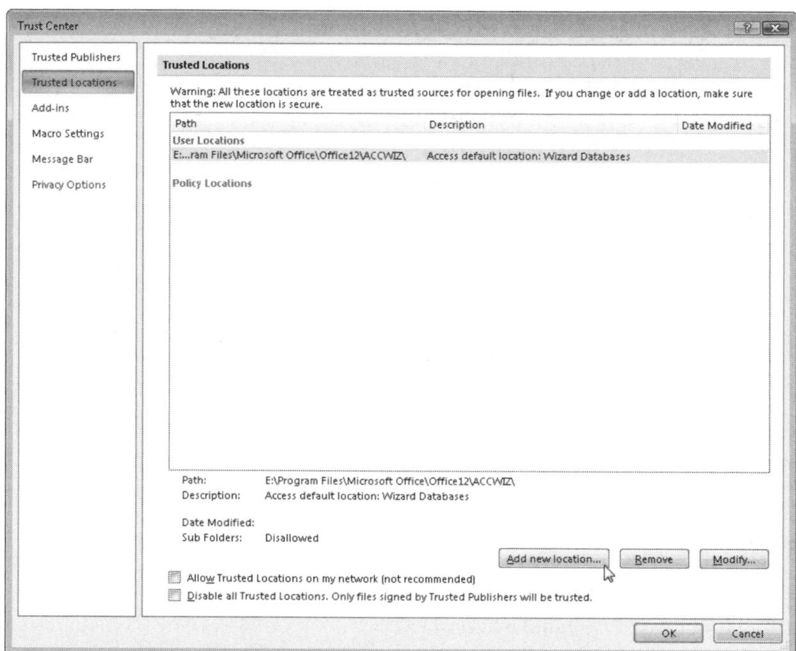


**Figure 2-18** The Trusted Locations category in the Trust Center dialog box shows you locations that are currently trusted.

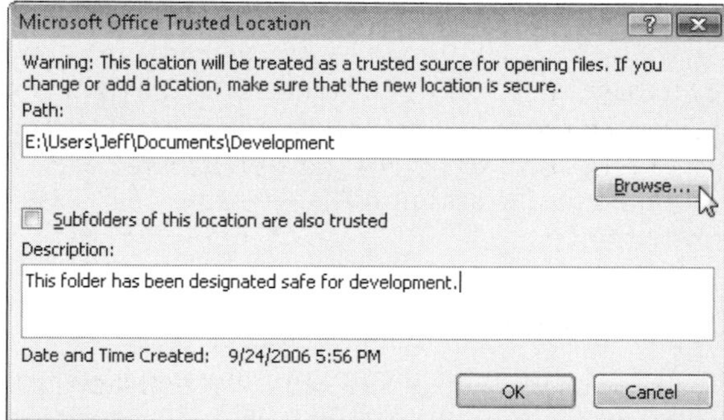


**Figure 2-19** Creating a new trusted location from the Microsoft Office Trusted Location dialog box.

### Note

To ensure that all the sample databases from the companion CD operate correctly, add the folder where you installed the files (the default location is the Microsoft Press\Access 2007 Inside Out folder on your C drive) to your Trusted Locations.

# Understanding the New Ribbon Feature

One of the biggest changes to the new user interface in Access 2007 is the Ribbon, a replacement for the menu bars and toolbars that were in previous versions. The Ribbon, shown in Figure 2-20, is a strip that contains all the functionality of the older menu options (File, Edit, View, and so on) and the various toolbars, condensed into one common area in the application window. Microsoft's usability studies revealed that most users failed to discover many useful features that were previously buried several levels deep in the old menu structure. The Ribbon is a context-rich environment displaying all the program functions and commands, with large icons for key functions and smaller icons for less-used functions. Access displays a host of different controls on the Ribbon to help you build and edit your applications. Lists, command buttons, galleries, and Dialog Box Launchers are all on the Ribbon and offer a new rich user interface for Access 2007 and the other 2007 Microsoft Office system products.

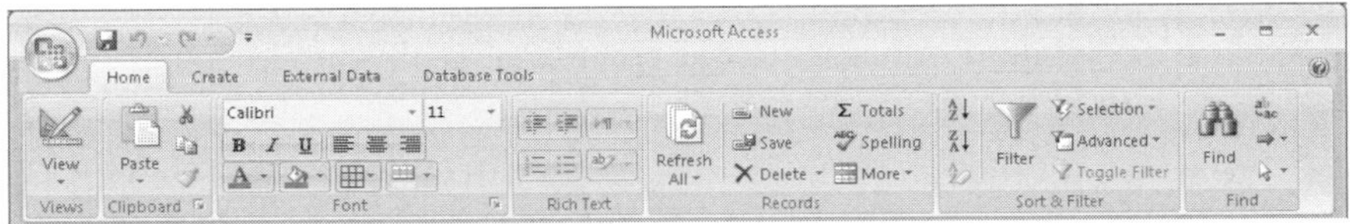


**Figure 2-20** The new Ribbon interface replaces menu bars and toolbars.

The Ribbon in Access 2007 consists of four main tabs—Home, Create, External Data, and Database Tools—that group together common tasks and contain a major subset of the program functions in Access. These main tabs are visible at all times when you are working in Access 2007 because they contain the most common tools you need when working with any database object. Other tabs, called *contextual tabs*, appear and disappear to the right of the Database Tools tab when you are working with specific database objects and in various views. (In the following chapters, we will discuss in detail the various database objects and the contextual tabs that appear when working with each.)

INSIDE OUT

### Scrolling Through the Ribbon Tabs

If you click on one of the Ribbon tabs, you can then scroll through the other tabs using the scroll wheel on your mouse.

Each tab on the Ribbon has commands that are further organized into groups. The name of each group is listed at the bottom, and each group has various commands logically grouped by subject matter. To enhance the user experience and make things easier to find, Microsoft has labeled every command in the various groups. If you rest your mouse pointer on a specific command, Access displays a *ScreenTip* that contains the name of the command and a short description that explains what you can do with the command. Any time a command includes a small arrow, you can click the arrow to display options available for the command.

## Home Tab

Let's first explore the Home tab shown in Figure 2-21.

**Figure 2-21** The Home tab provides common commands for editing, filtering, and sorting data.

The Home tab has the following groups:

- **Views.** Most objects in an Access database have two or more ways to view them. When you have one of these objects open and it has the focus, you can use the View command in this group to easily switch to another view.
- **Clipboard.** You can use the commands in this group to manage data you move to and from the Clipboard.
- **Font.** You can change how Access displays text using the commands in this group.
- **Rich Text.** You can design fields in your database to contain data formatted in Rich Text. (See Chapter 4 for more details about data types.) You can use the commands in this group to format text in a Rich Text field.
- **Records.** Use the commands in this group to work with records, including deleting records and saving changes.
- **Sort & Filter.** You can use these commands to sort and filter your data.
- **Window**. Use the commands in this group to resize windows or select one of several windows you have open. Note that Access displays this group only when you have set your database to display Overlapping Windows rather than Tabbed Documents. For more details, see "Using the Single-Document vs. Multiple-Document Interface" on page 83.
- **Find.** The commands in this group allow you to search and replace data, go to a specific record, or select one or all records.

## Create Tab

The Create tab, shown in Figure 2-22, contains commands that let you create new database objects. Each group on this particular tab arranges its specific functions by database object type.

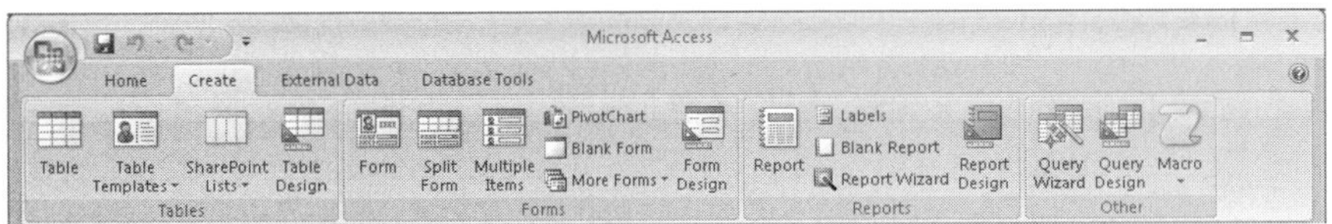


**Figure 2-22** The Create tab provides commands for creating all the various types of database objects.

The Create tab contains the following groups:

- **Tables.** Use the commands in this group to create new tables or link to a Microsoft Windows SharePoint Services list. You can learn more about Windows SharePoint Services in Chapter 22, "Working with Windows SharePoint Services."
- **Forms.** You can create new forms using the commands in this group, including PivotChart and PivotTable forms. For more details about PivotCharts, see Chapter 13, "Advanced Form Design."
- **Reports.** The commands in this group allow you to create new reports using available wizards or to start a new report design from scratch.
- **Other.** Use the commands in this group to create new queries or build macros or modules to automate your application.



## External Data Tab

The External Data tab, shown in Figure 2-23, provides commands to import from or link to data in external sources or export data to external sources, including other Access databases or Windows SharePoint Services lists.

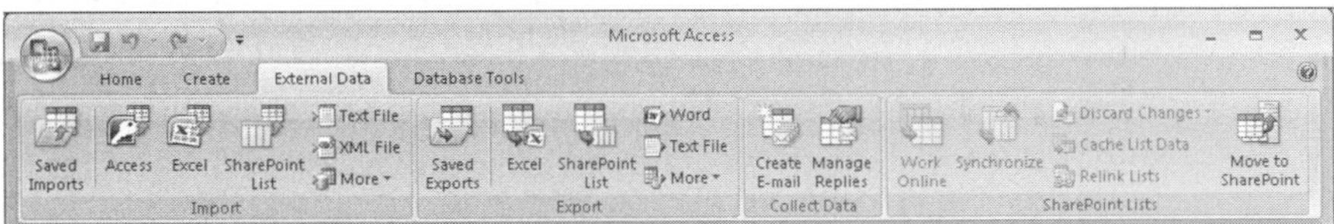


**Figure 2-23** The External Data tab provides commands for working with external data sources.

This tab has the following groups:

- **Import.** The commands in the Import group let you link to data or import data or objects from other sources such as other Access databases, Microsoft Excel spreadsheets, Windows SharePoint Services lists, and many other data sources such as Microsoft SQL Server, dBase, Paradox, and Lotus 1-2-3.
- **Export.** You can use these commands to export objects to another Access database or to export data to Excel, a Windows SharePoint Services site, Microsoft Word, and more.

- **Collect Data.** These two commands allow you to update data in your Access 2007 database from special e-mail options using Microsoft Office Outlook 2007. See Chapter 6, "Importing and Linking Data," for details about using these new features.

- **SharePoint Lists.** Commands in this group allow you to migrate some or all of your data to a Windows SharePoint Services (version 3) site or synchronize offline data with an active Windows SharePoint Services site.



## Database Tools Tab

The last tab that is always available on the Ribbon is the Database Tools tab, shown in Figure 2-24. The top part of Figure 2-24 shows the Database Tools tab when using an Access 2007 database (.accdb) and the bottom part shows the Database Tools tab when using Access 2000, 2002, or 2003 databases (.mdb).

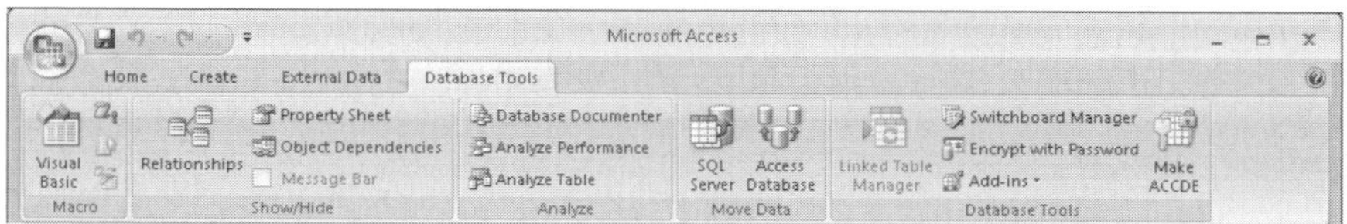


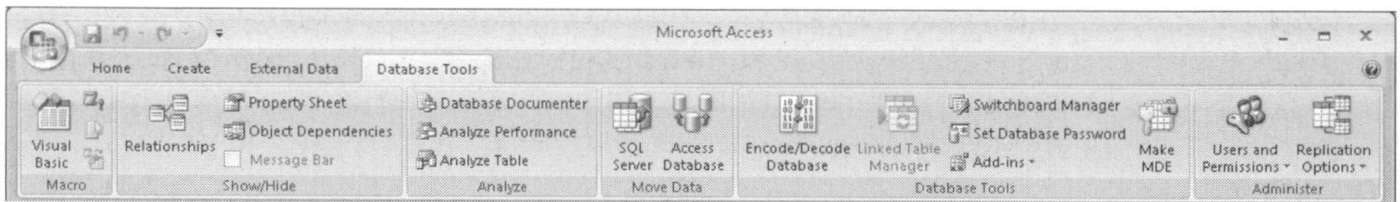


**Figure 2-24** The Database Tools tab gives you access to miscellaneous tools and wizards.

The Database Tools tab on the Ribbon includes the following groups:

- **Macro.** Commands in this group let you open the Visual Basic Editor, run a macro, or covert a macro either to a shortcut menu or to Visual Basic.

- **Show/Hide.** Commands in this group activate useful information windows. Use the Relationships command to view and edit your table relationships. (See Chapter 4 for details.) Click the Property Sheet command to open the Property Sheet dialog box that displays the properties of the object currently selected in the Navigation Pane. Click the Object Dependencies command to see which objects are dependent on the currently selected object. Select the Message Bar check box to reveal the Message Bar that displays any pending security alerts.

- **Analyze.** Use the commands in this group to print a report about your objects or run one of the two analysis wizards.

- **Move Data.** The two wizards available in this group allow you to either move some or all of your tables to SQL Server or move all your tables to a separate Access database and create links to the moved tables in the current database.

- **Database Tools.** You will see a different set of commands in this group depending on whether you have opened an Access 2000, 2002, or 2003 database (.mdb) or an Access 2007 database (.accdb). In both groups, you find commands to run the Linked Table Manager (see Chapter 6), the Switchboard Manager (see Chapter 24, "The Finishing Touches"), make an execute-only version (.mde or .accde) of your database (see Chapter 25), or manage add-ins. In an .mdb file, you can find commands to encode/decode your database (encrypt it) and set a password that a user must know to run your database. In an .accdb file, you can find a command to create an encrypted version with a password (see Chapter 25).
- **Administer.** Access displays this group on the Database Tools tab only when you open an Access database file created in Access 2000, 2002, or 2003 (.mdb). The Users And Permissions command lets you edit and define users and object permissions in the legacy security system no longer supported in Access 2007 format (.accdb) database files. The Replication Options let you manage the legacy replication features no longer supported in Access 2007 format database files. For more information on these features, see *Running Microsoft Access 2000* (Microsoft Press, 1999) or *Microsoft Office Access 2003 Inside Out* (Microsoft Press, 2004).

Chapter 2

INSIDE OUT **Collapsing the Entire Ribbon**

If you need some additional workspace within the Access window, you can collapse the entire Ribbon by double-clicking on any of the tabs. All the groups disappear from the screen, but the tabs are still available. You can also use the keyboard shortcut Ctrl+F1 to collapse the Ribbon. To see the Ribbon again, simply click on any tab to restore the Ribbon to its full height or press Ctrl+F1 again.

## Understanding the New Navigation Pane

As part of the user interface overhaul in Office Access 2007, the development team introduced a new object navigation tool called the Navigation Pane. In previous versions of Access, you navigated among the various database objects through the Database window. Access grouped all database objects together by type and displayed various properties of each object alongside the object name depending on the view you chose.

Office Access 2007 replaces the Database window with the Navigation Pane shown in Figure 2-25. Unlike the Object bar in the old Database window that you could position anywhere in the Access workspace, the new Navigation Pane is a window that is permanently located on the left side of the screen. Any open database objects appear to the right of the Navigation Pane instead of covering it up. This means you still have easy access to the other objects in your database without having to shuffle open objects around the screen or continually minimize and restore object windows. In contrast to the Database window, the new Navigation Pane lets you view objects of different types at the same time. If the list of objects in a particular group is quite extensive, Access provides a scroll bar in each section so that you can access each object.

To follow along in the rest of this section, open the Issues Sample database (IssuesSample.accdb) from the companion CD. Unless you have previously opened this database and changed the Navigation Pane, you should see the Navigation Pane on the left side of the screen, exactly like Figure 2-25.

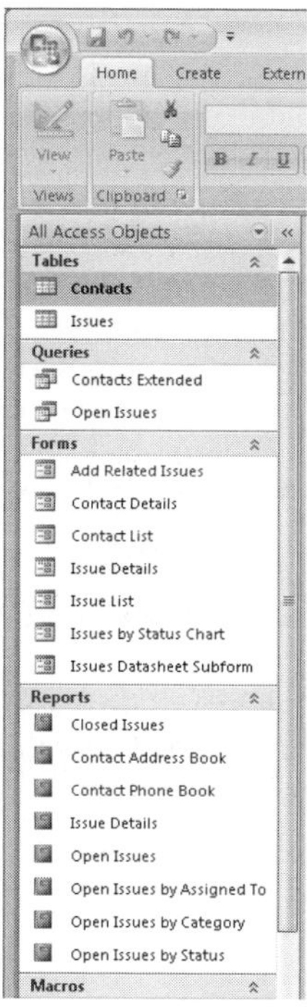


**Figure 2-25** The new Navigation Pane replaces the Database window from previous Access versions.

INSIDE OUT **Quickly Jumping to a Specific Object in the Navigation Pane**

Click an object in one of the groups in the Navigation Pane to select it and then press a letter key to quickly jump to any objects that begin with that letter in that particular group.

Shutter Bar Open/Close Button

You can easily expand or contract the width of the Navigation Pane by positioning your pointer over the right edge of the Navigation Pane and then clicking and dragging the edge in either direction to the width you want. Keep in mind that the farther you expand the width, the less screen area you have available to work with your database objects because all objects open to the right of the Navigation Pane. To maximize the amount of screen area available to work with open objects, you can completely collapse the Navigation Pane to the far left side of the application window by clicking the double-arrow button in the upper-right corner, called the Shutter Bar Open/Close Button. When you do this, the Navigation Pane appears as a thin bar on the left of your screen, as shown in Figure 2-26. After you have "shuttered" the Navigation Pane, the arrows on the button reverse direction and point to the right. Click the button again to reopen the Navigation Pane to its previous width. Access 2007 remembers the last width you set for the Navigation Pane. The next time you open an Access database, the width of the Navigation Pane will be the same as when you last had the database open. Pressing the F11 key alternately toggles the Navigation Pane between its collapsed and expanded view.

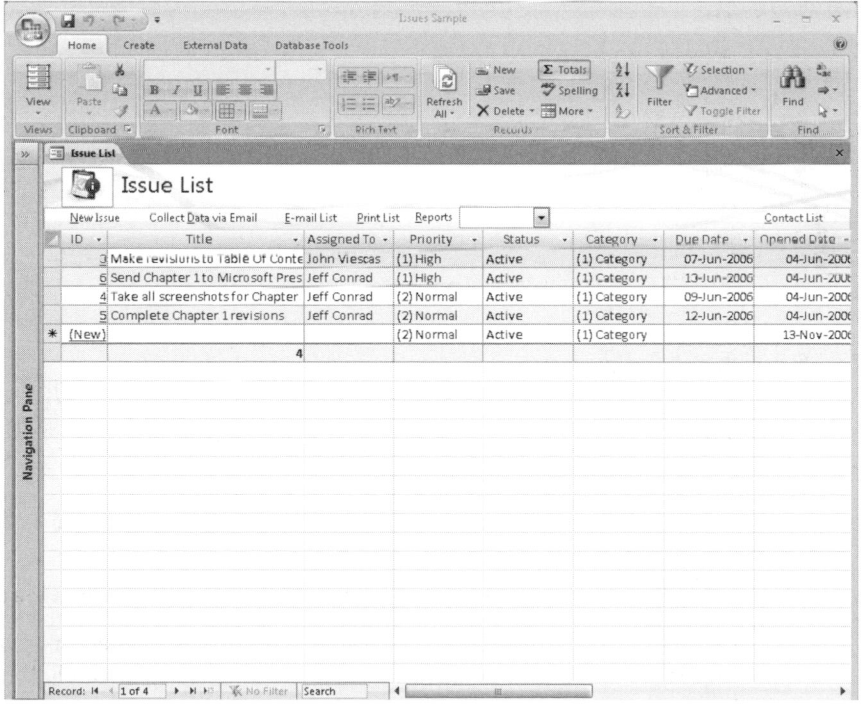


**Figure 2-26** You can collapse the Navigation Pane to give yourself more room to work on open objects.

**We will discuss the various database objects and their purposes within an Access database in Chapter 3, "Microsoft Office Access 2007 Overview."**

## Exploring Navigation Pane Object Views

When you first open the IssuesSample.accdb sample database, the Navigation Pane shows you all the objects defined in the database grouped by object type and sorted by object name. You can verify this view by clicking the menu bar at the top of the Navigation Pane, as shown in Figure 2-27, which opens the Navigation Pane menu. Under Navigate To Category, you should see Object Type selected, and under Filter By Group, you should see All Access Objects selected. This is the view we selected in the database before saving it on the companion CD.

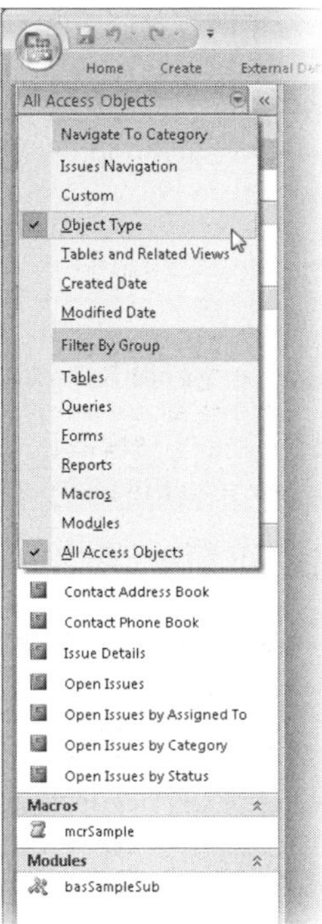


**Figure 2-27** You can change the display in the Navigation Pane by selecting a different category or filter from the Navigation Pane menu.

This view closely matches the Database window in previous versions of Access where you could select tabs to view each object category, and each object type was sorted by object name. The objects in each of the six object types—Tables, Queries, Forms, Reports, Macros, and Modules—are grouped together. When the list of objects is longer than can be displayed within the height of the Navigation Pane, Access provides a scroll bar.

You can customize the Navigation Pane to display the object list in many different ways. Access 2007 provides a set of predefined categories for the Navigation Pane that you can access with a few mouse clicks. You can see these available categories by clicking the top of the Navigation Pane to open the menu, as shown previously in Figure 2-27.

Notice that this Issues Sample database lists six categories under Navigate To Category: Issues Navigation, Custom, Object Type, Tables And Related Views, Created Date, and Modified Date. The first category in the list, Issues Navigation, is a custom category specific to this database. We'll show you how to create and modify custom categories later in this section. Access always provides the other five categories in all databases to allow you to view objects in various predefined ways. We will discuss the Custom and Issues Navigation categories later in "Working with Custom Categories and Groups" on page 53.



INSIDE OUT

### Collapsing an Entire Group in the Navigation Pane

If you click the header of each object type where the double arrow is located, Access collapses that part of the Navigation Pane. For example, if you want to temporarily hide the tables, you can collapse that section by clicking the double arrow next to the word *Tables*. To bring the table list back to full view, simply click the double arrow that is now pointing downward, and the tables section expands to reveal all the table objects.

The Navigation Pane menu also provides commands under Filter By Group to allow you to filter the database object list. The filter commands available change depending on which Navigate To Category command you select. Notice in Figure 2-27 where Navigate To Category is set to Object Type that the Filter By Group section in the lower half of the Navigation Pane menu lists each of the object types that currently exist in your database. When you have the menu categorized by object type, you can further filter the list of objects by selecting one of the object types to see only objects of that type. Click one of the object types, Forms for instance, and Access hides all the other object types as shown in Figure 2-28. This feature is very useful if you want to view and work with only a particular type of database object. Click the All Access Objects filter command to again see all objects by object type.

By default, new blank databases created in the Access 2007 format display the object list in the Navigation Pane in a category called Tables And Related Views. You can switch the Issues Sample database to this category by opening the Navigation Pane menu that contains categories and filters, and then click the Tables And Related Views command as shown in Figure 2-29.

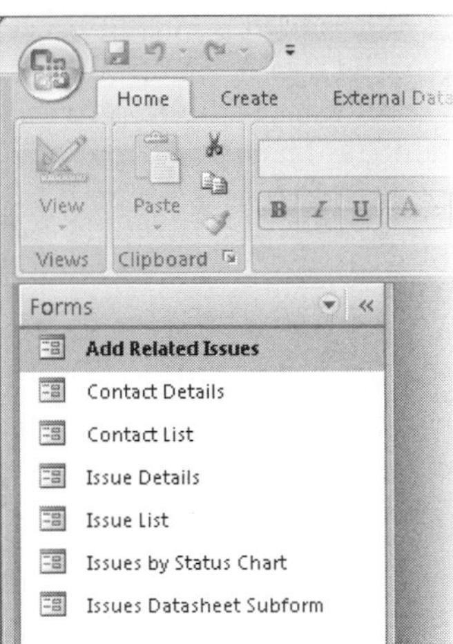


**Figure 2-28** You can display only the Forms group of objects in Object Type view by applying a filter in the Navigation Pane menu.

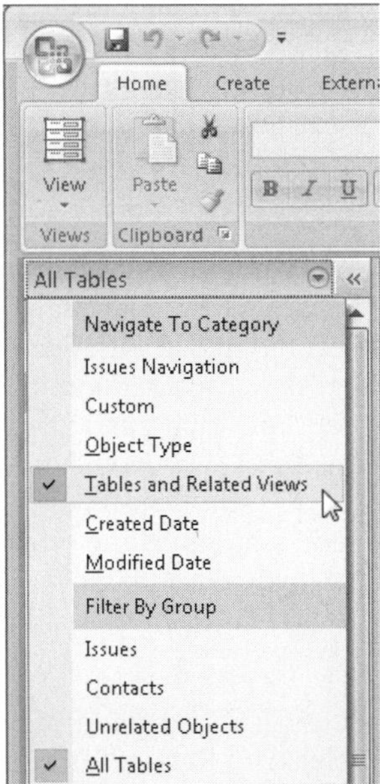


**Figure 2-29** The Tables And Related Views category on the Navigation Pane menu offers a different way to view your database objects.

After you click Tables And Related Views, the Navigation Pane should look similar to Figure 2-30. This particular view category groups the various database objects based on their relation to a common denominator–a table. As you can observe in Figure 2-30, each group of objects is the name of one of the tables. Note that in Figure 2-30 we collapsed the Ribbon in order to show you all the various database objects and groups.

Within each group, you can see the table as the first item in the group followed by all objects that are dependent on the data from the table. So, Access lists all database objects dependent on the Issues data table together in the Issues group, and similarly, it lists all objects dependent on the Contacts table in the Contacts group. At first glance, you might be a bit confused as to the purpose of each object, but notice that the various types of objects each have their own unique icon to help you differentiate them. The Issues table, for example, is listed first with the icon for a table before the name and the word *Table* next to it. The remaining objects in the group are the various objects that are dependent on the Issues table in alphabetical order by name, and each object has an icon before the name that identifies the type of object.



> **Note**
>
> You can find more details about the various object types and related icons in the next chapter.

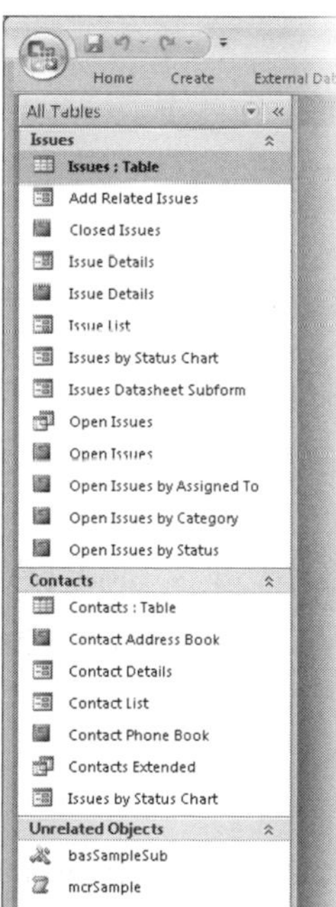


**Figure 2-30** The Tables And Related Views category in the Navigation Pane groups objects under a table.

Some objects appear in a category called Unrelated Objects, such as the macro called mcrSample and the module called basSampleSub in this Issues Sample database. Macros and modules contain code that you can reference from any object in your database. They always appear in the Unrelated Objects category of Tables And Related Views because Access does not search through the macro arguments and module code to see if any table references exist.

INSIDE OUT

### When to Use the Tables And Related Views Category

This particular view category can be quite useful if you are making some changes to a table and want to see what objects might be affected by the change. You can check each query, form, and report that is related to this table one at a time in this view to ensure that no functionality of the database is broken after you make a change to the underlying table.



Now that you have changed to Tables And Related Views, open the Navigation Pane menu again. Notice that the names of both data tables in this database are listed beneath Filter By Group as shown previously in Figure 2-29. Click Issues, and Access reduces the Navigation Pane to show only the objects related to the Issues table as shown in Figure 2-31. By filtering the Navigation Pane to one table, you have reduced the number of objects displayed and can focus your attention on only a small subset of database objects. You can open the Navigation Menu again and click All Tables to restore the complete list.

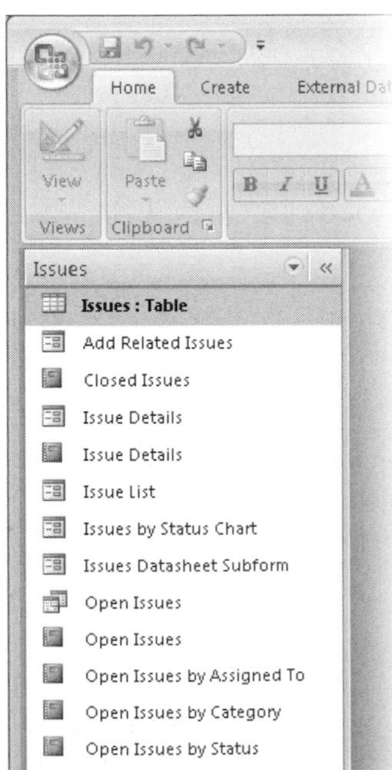


**Figure 2-31** You can filter Tables And Related Views to show only the database objects dependent on one table.

Access provides two related types of object view categories on the Navigation Pane menu called Created Date and Modified Date, as shown in Figure 2-32. These categories list all the objects in descending order based on when you created or last modified the object. These views can be quite useful if you need to locate an object that you created or last modified on a specific date or within a range of dates. When you click either of these commands, Filter By Group on the Navigation Pane menu offers to filter by Today, Yesterday, one of the five days previous to that (listed by day name), Last Week, Two Weeks Ago, Three Weeks Ago, Last Month, Older, or All Dates.

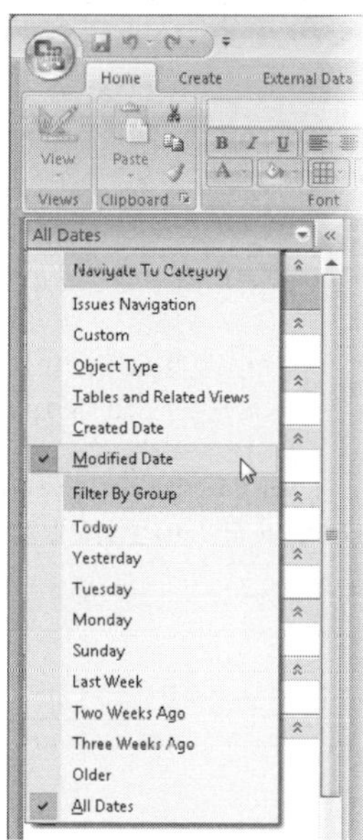


**Figure 2-32** The Created Date and Modified Date categories display objects in the order you created or last modified them.



> **Note**
>
> You will not see the same options listed in Figure 2-32 when you open your copy of Issues Sample because all the Modified dates will be older than three weeks. The only two options you will see are Older and All Dates.

## Working with Custom Categories and Groups

We have not yet discussed the remaining two object categories available on the Navigation Pane menu of the Issues Sample database: Custom and Issues Navigation as shown in Figure 2-33. Whenever you create a new database, Access creates the Custom category that you can modify to suit your needs. Initially, the Custom category contains only one group, Unassigned Objects, containing all the objects defined in your database. As you'll learn later, you can change the name of the Custom category, create one or more custom groups, and assign objects to those groups.

When you create a new database using one of the many templates provided by Microsoft, nearly all these databases contain an additional predefined group designed to make it easier to run the sample application. We created the Issues Sample database using the Issues template, and the Issues Navigation category is predefined in that template. As with any custom category, you can create new groups, modify or delete existing groups, assign additional objects to the groups within the custom category, or delete the category and all its groups altogether.



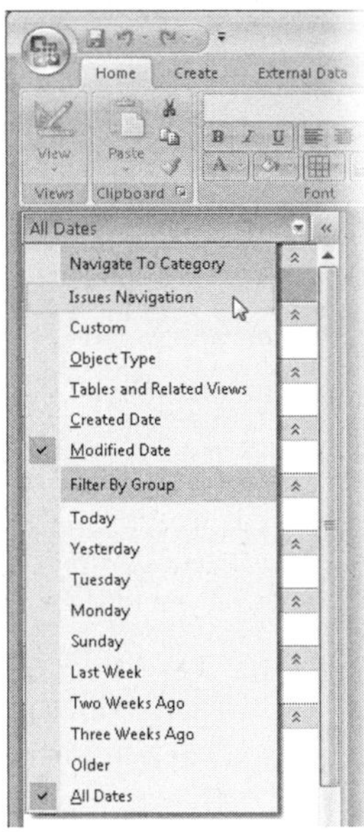


**Figure 2-33** Both Custom and Issues Navigation are custom categories available in the Issues Sample database.

To see an example of a finished custom category in this database, open the Navigation Pane menu and select Issues Navigation. The Navigation Pane changes to display the object list shown in Figure 2-34. This custom category contains three custom groups called Issues, Contacts, and Supporting Objects. There is actually a fourth group called Unassigned Objects, which you cannot see. In the following sections, you'll learn how to hide one or more groups.

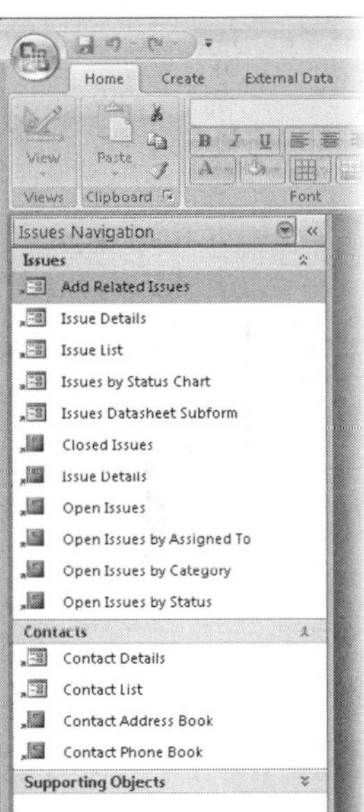


**Figure 2-34** The Issues Navigation category displays a custom view of the various database objects.

In Figure 2-34, notice that each object icon has a small arrow in the lower-left corner. This arrow indicates that you are looking at a shortcut or pointer to the actual object. These shortcuts act similarly to shortcuts in Windows—if you open the shortcut, you're opening the underlying object to which the shortcut points. When you view custom categories and groups in the Navigation Pane, you are always looking at shortcuts to the objects. If you delete one of these shortcuts, you are only deleting the pointer to the object and not the object itself. We'll discuss more about working with these object shortcuts in "Hiding and Renaming Object Shortcuts" on page 69.

## Exploring the Navigation Options Dialog Box

Now that you have seen how a completed custom view category looks in the Navigation Pane, you can create your own new category and groups within that category in this Issues Sample database for the Issues forms and reports and the Contacts forms and reports. If any database objects are currently open, close them so that they do not interfere with the following steps. First, let's create a custom category and then groups within that category to hold our designated database objects. To begin this process, right-click the menu bar at the top of the Navigation Pane and click Navigation Options on the shortcut menu, as shown in Figure 2-35.

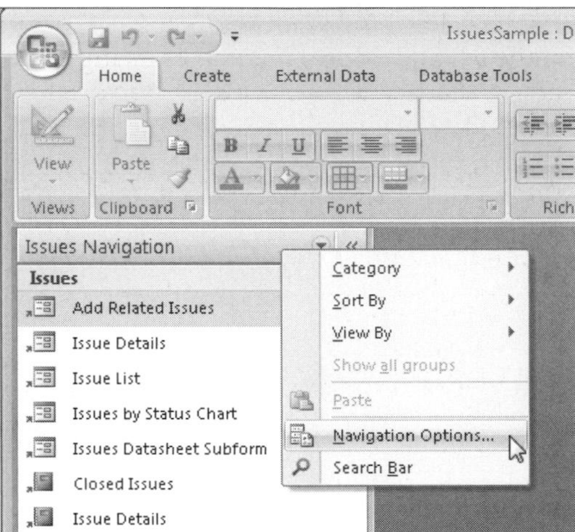


**Figure 2-35** Right-click the top of the Navigation Pane and click Navigation Options to open the Navigation Options dialog box.

Access opens the Navigation Options dialog box as shown in Figure 2-36.

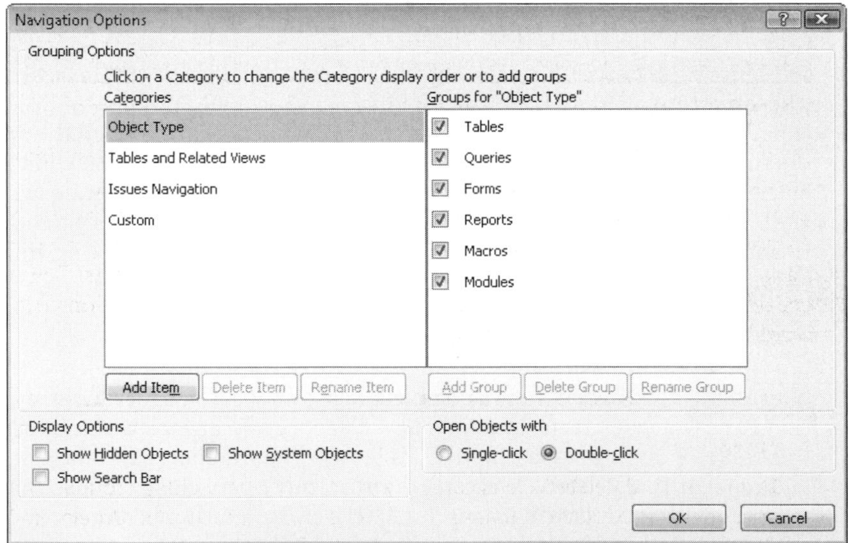


**Figure 2-36** The Navigation Options dialog box lets you create and edit grouping and display options.

The Categories list under Grouping Options lists all the categories that have been defined in this database. In this list, you can see two built-in categories—Object Type and Tables And Related Views—that you cannot delete. The list also shows the Issues Navigation category that was defined in the template and the Custom category that Access defines in all new databases. When you select a different category in the list on the left, the list on the right displays the groups for that category. For example, click the Issues Navigation category on the left and notice that Access changes the list at the right to show the four groups defined in that category–Issues, Contacts, Supporting Objects, and Unassigned Objects, as shown in Figure 2-37.

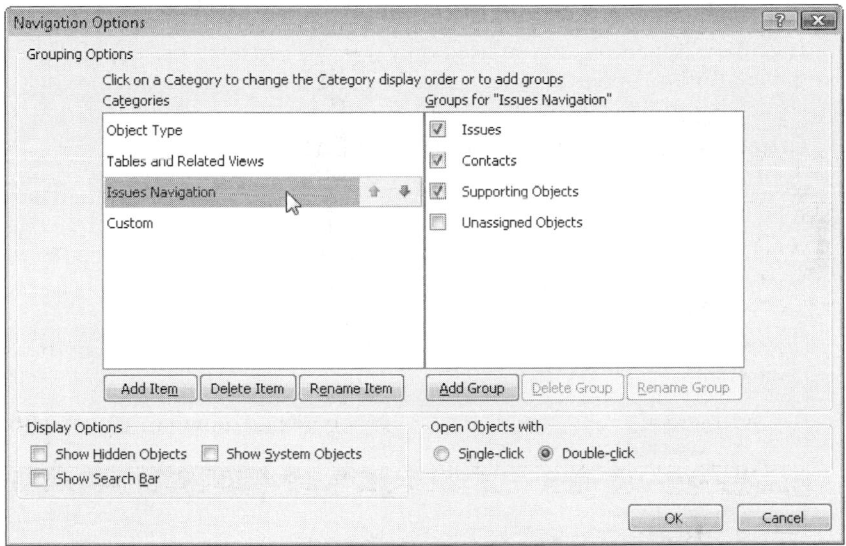


**Figure 2-37** Four groups have been defined in the Issues Navigation category.

Next to each of the four groups for Issues Navigation is a check box. All but the last check box next to Unassigned Objects is selected. When you clear the check box next to any group on the right, Access does not display that group in the Navigation Pane. As you may recall, when you looked at the Issues Navigation category in the Navigation Pane, you could see only Issues, Contacts, and Supporting Objects. Because we cleared the check box next to Unassigned Objects in the Navigation Options dialog box, you are unable to view it in the Navigation Pane.

### Note

The Tables And Related Views category by default includes one group for each table defined in the current database and one additional group called Unrelated Objects. The Object Type category includes one group for each of the six object types—tables, queries, forms, reports, macros, and modules.

In the lower-left corner of this dialog box, the Display Options section contains three check boxes—Show Hidden Objects, Show System Objects, and Show Search Bar. We'll discuss these options in detail in "Hiding and Renaming Object Shortcuts" on page 69 and "Searching for Database Objects" on page 78. The last section in the lower right of the Navigation Options dialog box is a new feature in Access 2007 called Open Objects With. When you select the Single-Click option, each object listed in the Navigation Pane acts like a hyperlink, so you need only one click to open the object. Double-Click, the default option, opens objects in the Navigation Pane with a double-click.



## Creating and Modifying a Custom Category

To create your new navigation category, you could click the Add Item button. Or, because the unused Custom category already exists, you can use it to create your new category. Start by clicking Custom under Categories and then click the Rename Item button, as shown in Figure 2-38.

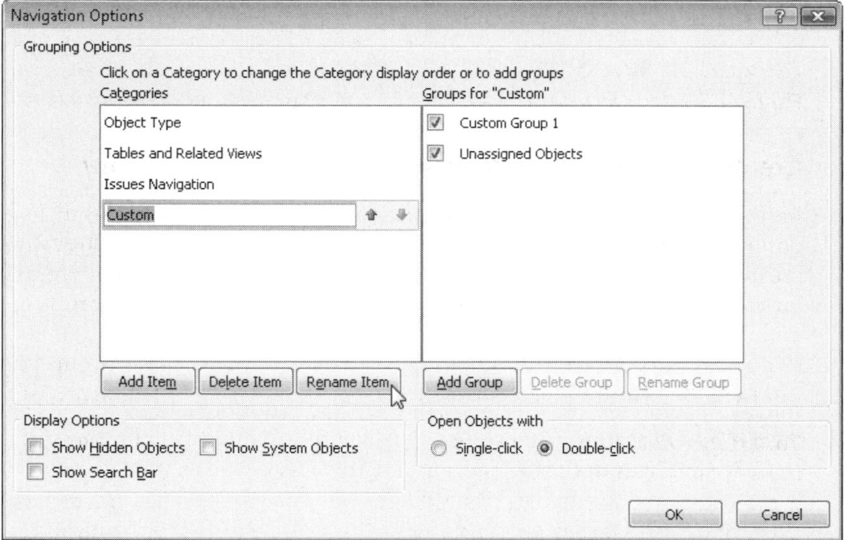


**Figure 2-38** Click the Rename Item button when Custom is selected to rename that category.

After you click the Rename Item button, Access unlocks the Custom field in the Categories list so you can change the name. Delete the word Custom using the Backspace or Delete key and type **Issues Database Objects** for your new name as shown in Figure 2-39.

Under Groups For "Custom" for the Issues Database Objects category, you can see Custom Group 1 and Unassigned Objects, as shown in Figure 2-39. The Custom Group 1 group is an empty placeholder that Access defines in the Custom category in all new Access 2007 database files. By default, no objects are placed in this group for new databases. The Unassigned Objects group is also a built-in Access group for the Custom category. Access places all objects that are not assigned to any other groups in the Unassigned Objects group for display in the Navigation Pane.

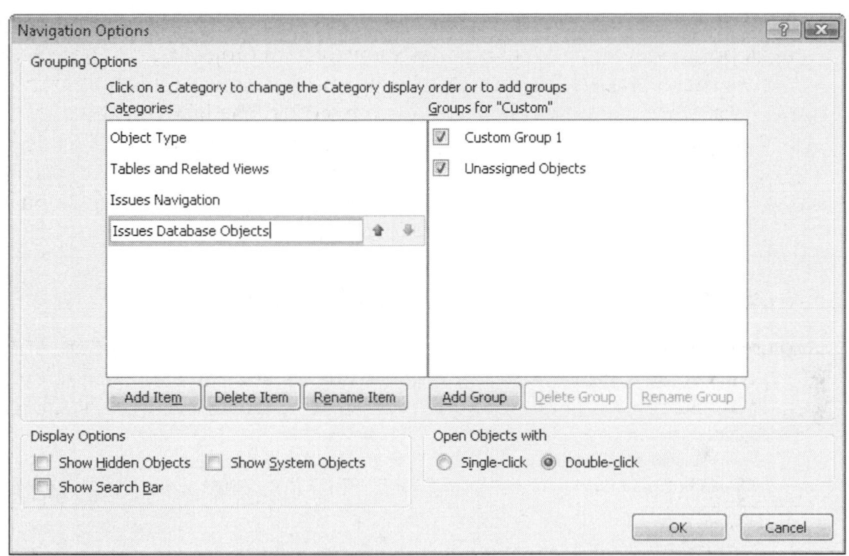


**Figure 2-39** You can rename the Custom group by typing a new name in the field.

## Creating and Modifying Groups in a Custom Category

Beneath the Groups list are three buttons: Add Group, Delete Group, and Rename Group. When you click Custom Group 1 in the list, you can see that all these buttons are available. The Add Group button creates another group under whichever group you have currently selected, the Delete Group button deletes the currently selected group, and the Rename Group button allows you to rename the current group. If you click the Unassigned Objects group, the Delete Group and Rename Group buttons appear dimmed. You cannot delete or rename this built-in group from any custom category.

For the Issues Database Objects category you need to create four groups. You can rename the Custom Group 1 group to a name of your choice, but you also need to create three additional groups. Let's start by renaming Custom Group 1 to Issues Forms. Click Custom Group 1 to select it and then click the Rename Group button. Access unlocks the name of this group so you can change it. Delete the word Custom Group 1 and type **Issues Forms** for your new name as shown in Figure 2-40.

You cannot change the name of the Unassigned Objects group, so you'll need to create additional groups. To create a new group, click the Add Group button. Access creates another group called Custom Group 1 below Issues Forms and unlocks it for you to enter a name as shown in Figure 2-41. Type **Issues Reports** for your new name and press Enter.

Chapter 2

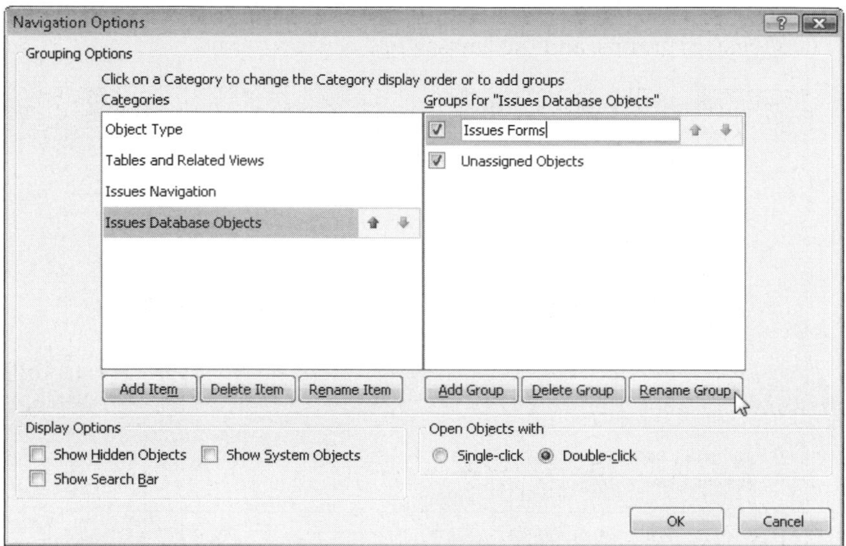


**Figure 2-40** Click the Rename Group button when Custom Group 1 is selected to rename that group.

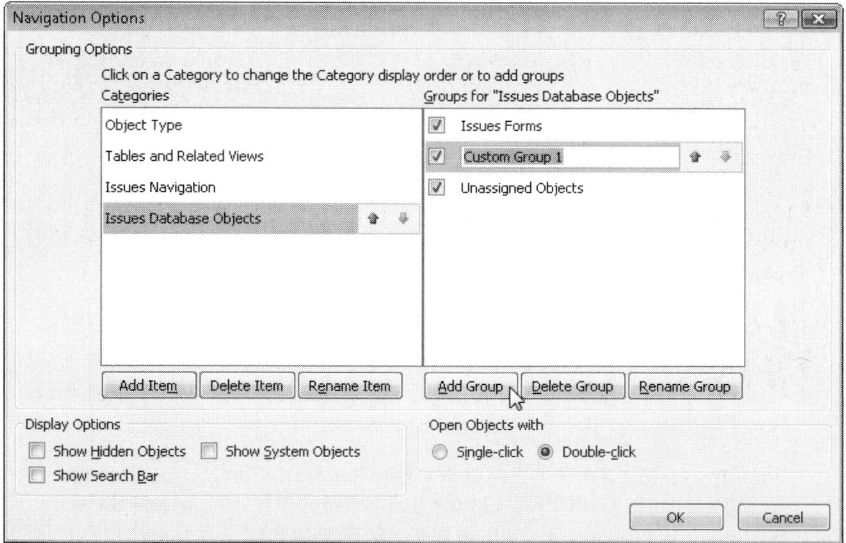


**Figure 2-41** When you click the Add Group button, Access creates another Custom Group 1 group.

Follow the preceding steps to create two additional new groups for the Issues Database Objects category called Contact Forms and Contact Reports. In each case, start by clicking the Add Group button to have Access create another Custom Group 1. Type over that name and enter **Contact Forms** and **Contact Reports** for the two names. Your completed changes should now look like Figure 2-42 with your new custom category, four custom groups, and the Unassigned Objects group.

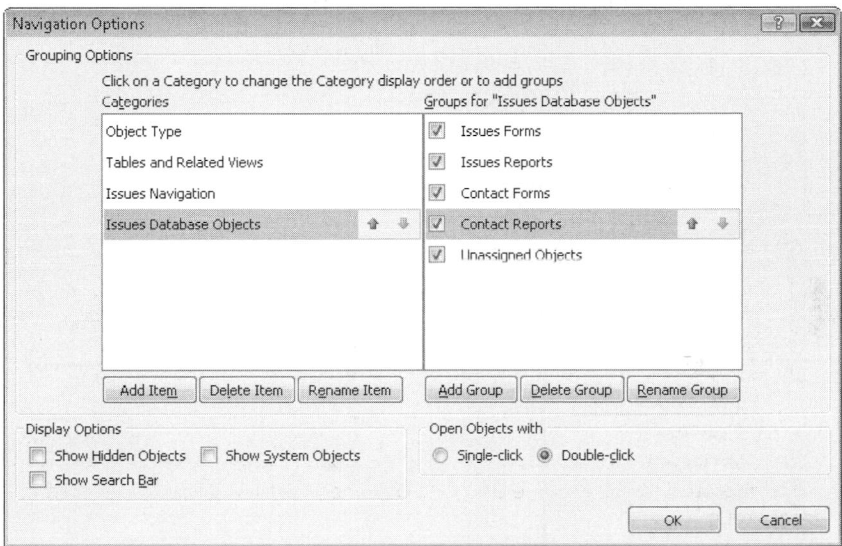


**Figure 2-42** The completed Issues Database Objects category now contains five groups.

Next to whichever custom group is selected on the right are a Move Up arrow and a Move Down arrow that you can click to change the display order of the groups in this category. When you select this category from the Navigation Pane menu, Access displays the groups in the Navigation Pane based on the display order you set in the Navigation Options dialog box. In Figure 2-42, you can see arrow buttons next to the Issues Database Objects category and the Contact Reports group within that category. For now, keep the display order of the custom groups and categories as they are. Click OK to save your current changes.

INSIDE OUT

### Understanding Display Order Rules for Categories and Groups

In the Categories list of the Navigation Options dialog box, you cannot change the display order of the Tables And Related Views and Object Type categories. All custom categories you create must appear below these two built-in categories.

The Unassigned Objects group in all custom groups you create can be displayed only at the bottom of the list of groups. You cannot place any custom groups below this built-in group. Similarly, the Unrelated Objects group within the Tables And Related Views category always appears at the bottom of the list.

To see how your changes appear in the Navigation Pane, click the top of the Navigation Pane to open the menu and select your new Issues Database Objects category, as shown in Figure 2-43.

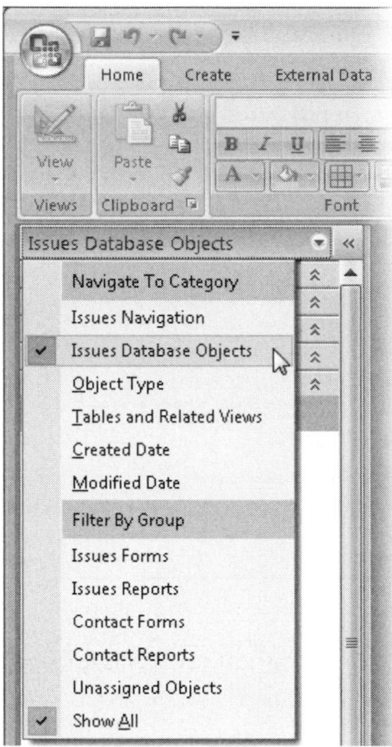


**Figure 2-43** After you select the new Issues Database Objects category, the Navigation Pane displays the custom groups you defined.

The Navigation Pane now displays each of your four custom group names along with the Unassigned Objects category as shown in Figure 2-44. Note that Access placed all your objects into the Unassigned Objects group and listed no database objects in any of the four custom groups. (In Figure 2-44 we collapsed the Ribbon to show you all the objects.)

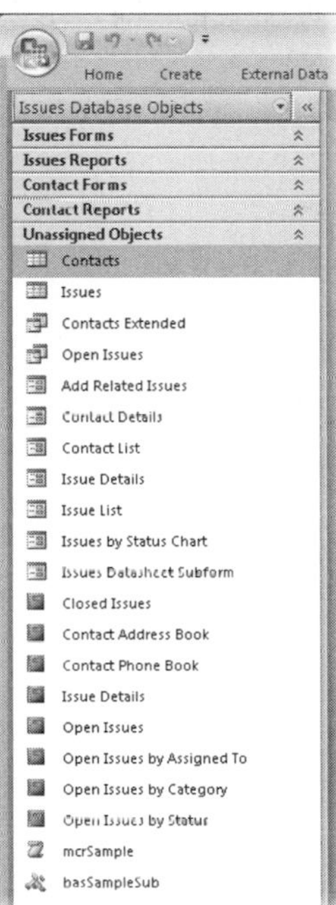


**Figure 2-44** Access initially places all objects into the Unassigned Objects group after you create a custom category.

## Creating Object Shortcuts in Custom Groups

Now that you have finished creating the category and group structure, it's time to move the objects into the groups you set up. You can move the forms that display or edit Issues into the new group called Issues Forms. To accomplish this task, hold down the Ctrl key and single-click each of the five forms that focus on Issues: Add Related Issues, Issue Details, Issue List, Issues by Status Chart, and Issues Datasheet Subform. This action causes Access to select all these objects. If you make a mistake by selecting an incorrect object, continue holding down the Ctrl key and single-click the incorrect object to unselect it. After you have selected all five form objects, right-click one of them and on the shortcut menu that appears click Add To Group and then Issues Forms to move the five selected form objects to that group, as shown in Figure 2-45.

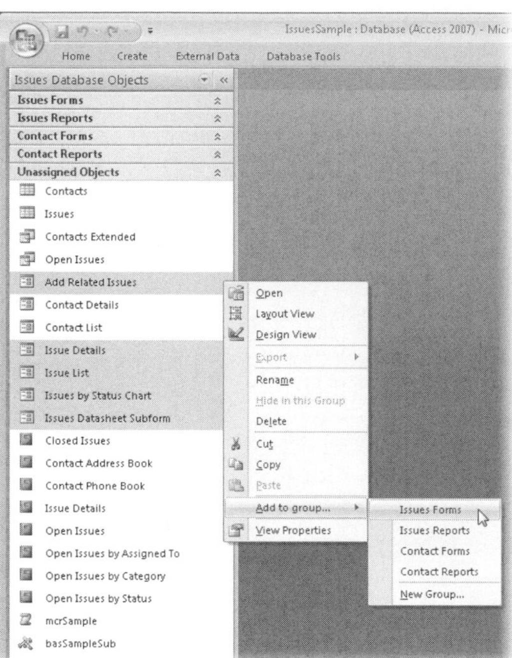


**Figure 2-45** You can move several objects to your custom group at the same time by selecting them and clicking Add To Group from the shortcut menu.

Access creates a shortcut to each of the five objects in the first group, as shown in Figure 2-46. Each of the icons now has a small arrow next to it to indicate that it is actually a shortcut to the respective database object and not the actual object itself, as we discussed earlier. If you delete a shortcut, you are deleting only the shortcut or pointer to the object and not the object itself.

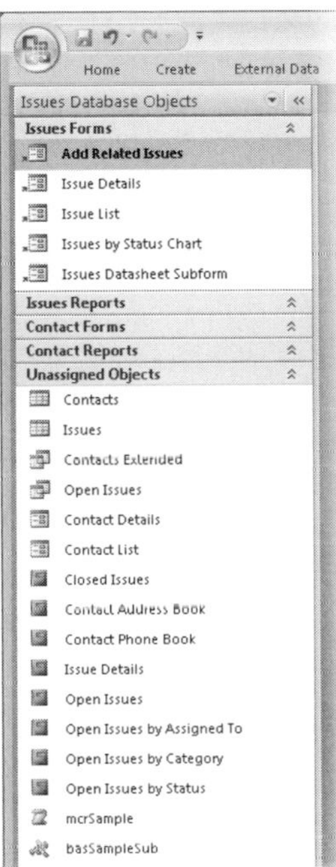


**Figure 2-46** After you move your objects to the first custom group, Access creates a shortcut to each object.

With the first set of objects assigned to a group, let's continue moving the other forms and reports. Hold down the Ctrl key and single-click on each of the following six reports: Closed Issues, Issue Details, Open Issues, Open Issues by Assigned To, Open Issues by Category, and Open Issues by Status. After you have selected these reports, right-click and click Add To Group. Click the group called Issue Reports and again note how Access creates a shortcut to each of these reports in our custom group as shown in Figure 2-47.

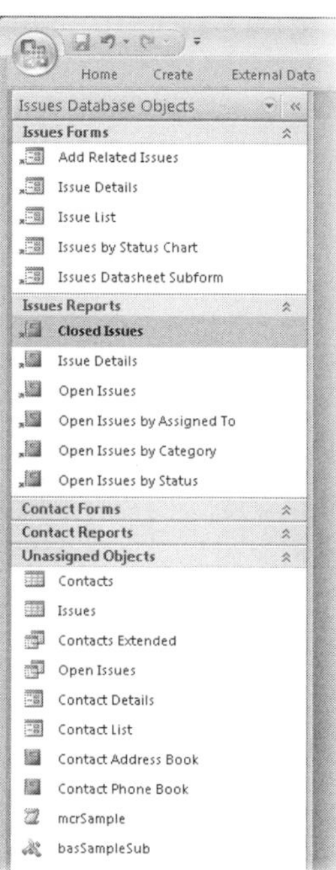


**Figure 2-47** Group all your Issues reports together under Issues Reports by selecting them and clicking Add To Group from the shortcut menu.

## INSIDE OUT Dragging and Dropping Objects into Custom Groups

You can also select objects you want to add to a custom group and drag and drop them into the group with your mouse. If you want a shortcut to appear in more than one group, add it to the first group, select it with your mouse, and while holding down the Ctrl key, drag and drop it into the second group. Holding down the Ctrl key tells Access you want to copy the shortcut, not move it. (Release the mouse button before releasing the Ctrl key to be sure the copy feature works correctly.)

Now repeat this process for the two contact forms called Contact Details and Contact List and move them to the group called Contact Forms. Similarly, move the two contact reports called Contact Address Book and Contact Phone Book to the group called Contact Reports. The Navigation Pane should now look like Figure 2-48.

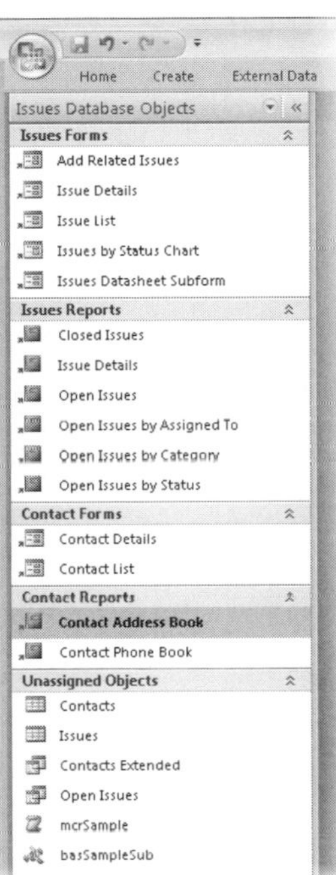


**Figure 2-48** All the form and report objects now have shortcuts in custom groups in the Navigation Pane.

## Hiding Custom Groups in a Category

With the previous steps completed, you should now see only six objects in the Unassigned Objects group—a collection of data tables, queries, one macro, and one module. For now, assume that we do not want to have the users of this database application view these objects. We can hide this entire Unassigned Objects group of objects from the users by going back to the Navigation Options dialog box. Right-click the top of the Navigation Pane, and then click Navigation Options to open the Navigation Options dialog box again. In the Categories list, click the Issues Database Objects category to display our custom groups. Clear the Unassigned Objects check box to tell Access to hide this particular group when showing our custom Issues Database Objects view in the Navigation Pane as shown in Figure 2-49.

Click OK in the Navigation Options dialog box, and Access completely removes this group from view in the Navigation Pane. We are now left with a concise list of form and report objects separated into logical groups as shown in Figure 2-50.

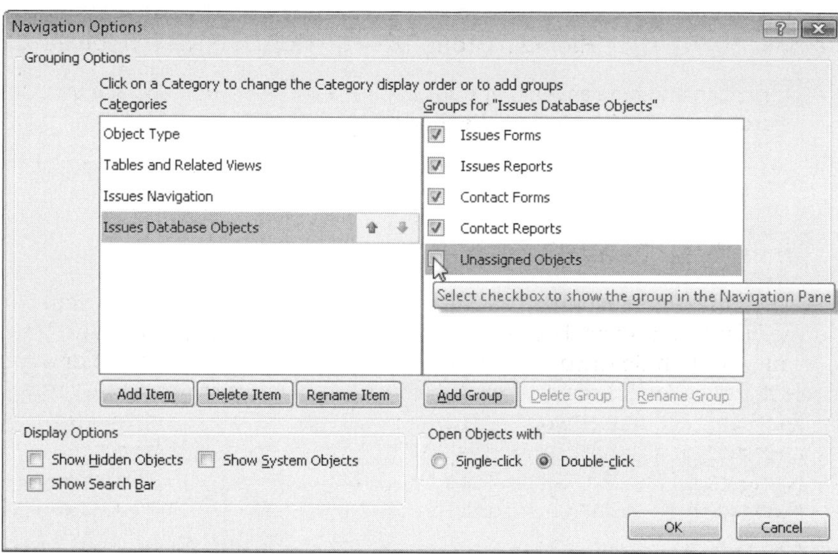


**Figure 2-49** Clear the check box next to Unassigned Objects to hide this group in the Navigation Pane.

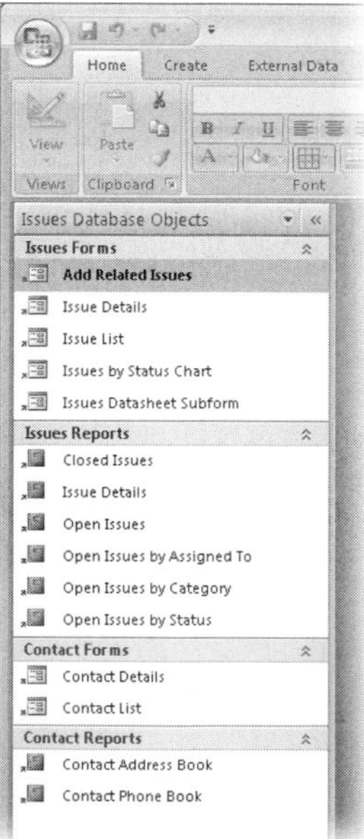


**Figure 2-50** The completed changes to the Navigation Pane now display only form and report object shortcuts in four custom groups.

INSIDE OUT **Hiding a Group Directly from the Navigation Pane**

You can also hide an entire group from view in the Navigation Pane by right-clicking that group and clicking Hide on the shortcut menu that appears.

## Hiding and Renaming Object Shortcuts

We can further customize our list of objects by hiding object shortcuts directly in the Navigation Pane. For example, for illustration purposes right now, assume that you want to hide the data entry form called Issues Datasheet Subform from the current view. (You'll learn in Part 3 that a subform is a form designed to be embedded in another form. A user won't normally need to open subforms directly.) There are two methods for accomplishing this task, both of which you can access directly from the Navigation Pane. For the first method, right-click the Issues Datasheet Subform in the Navigation Pane and click Hide In This Group from the shortcut menu, as shown in Figure 2-51.

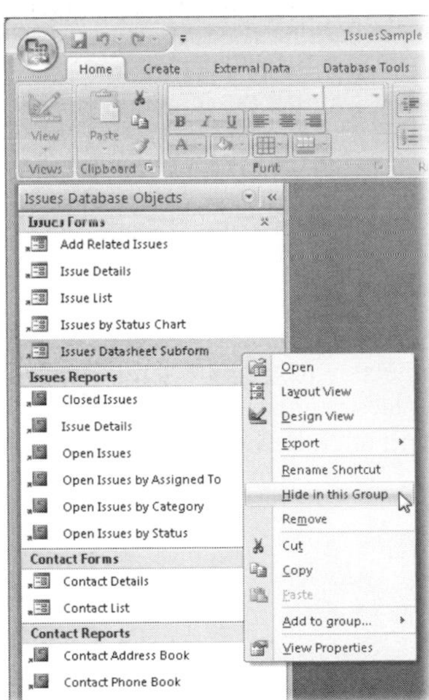


**Figure 2-51** To hide an object in a specific group, right-click it and click Hide In This Group from the shortcut menu.

Access hides this object shortcut from view in the Navigation Pane but does not in any way delete or alter the existing form itself. Alternatively, you can right-click that object in the Navigation Pane and click View Properties from the shortcut menu, shown in Figure 2-51, to open the Properties dialog box for this object, as shown in Figure 2-52.

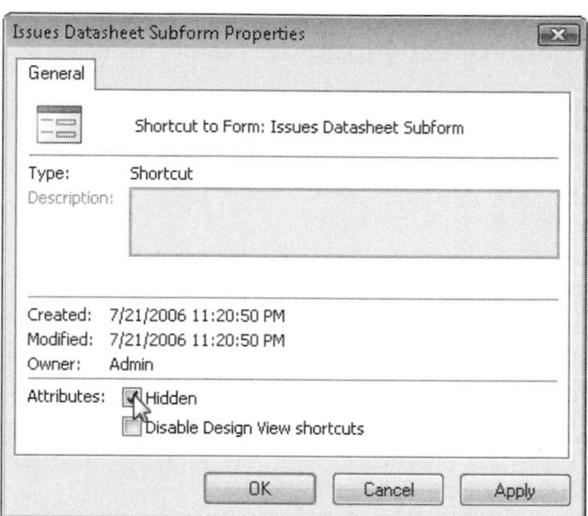


**Figure 2-52** You can hide a database object or an object shortcut from view in the Navigation Pane by selecting the Hidden check box in the Properties dialog box.

The Properties dialog box displays the name of the object and whether this is a shortcut to an object. In the middle of the dialog box you can see any description inherited from the original object (which you can't modify), the date the object was created, the date the object was last modified, and the owner of the object. The Attributes section has two check boxes called Hidden and Disable Design View Shortcuts. We will discuss Disable Design View in Chapter 24. In the Attributes section, select the Hidden check box and then click OK. In the Navigation Pane you will see the Issues Datasheet Subform disappear from view. Remember that you have hidden only the shortcut for this object and have not affected the actual form itself in any way.

You now know how to hide objects or object shortcuts from view in the Navigation Pane, but what if you want to rename the object shortcuts? Access 2007 allows you to easily rename the shortcuts to database objects without affecting the underlying names of the objects. To illustrate this procedure, let's rename one of the report object shortcuts. Right-click the Issue Details report and click Rename Shortcut from the shortcut menu as shown in Figure 2-53.

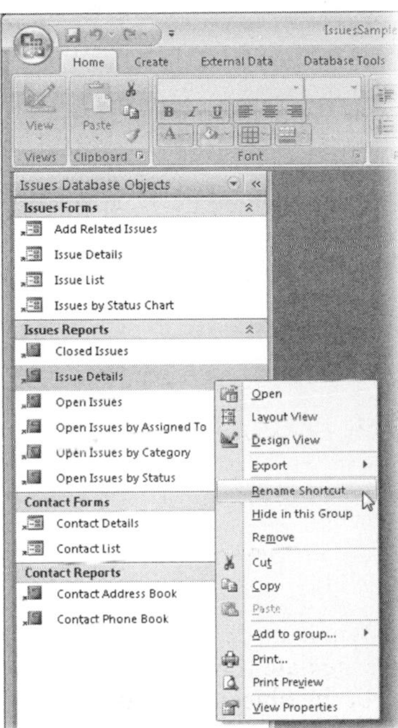


**Figure 2-53** To rename an object shortcut in the Navigation Pane, right-click it and click Rename Shortcut.

Access sets the focus on this report in the Navigation Pane and unlocks the name of the shortcut. Enter a new name for this object, by typing **All Issue Details Report** and then pressing Enter, as shown in Figure 2-54. Access saves the new name of this report shortcut, but does not change the name of the actual report object to which the shortcut points.

The final custom Navigation Pane with all your modifications should now look like Figure 2-55. Behind the scenes, all the database objects are still present and unchanged, but you customized the display view for users of your database. You are now showing only a list of form and report shortcuts while other objects are hidden from view.

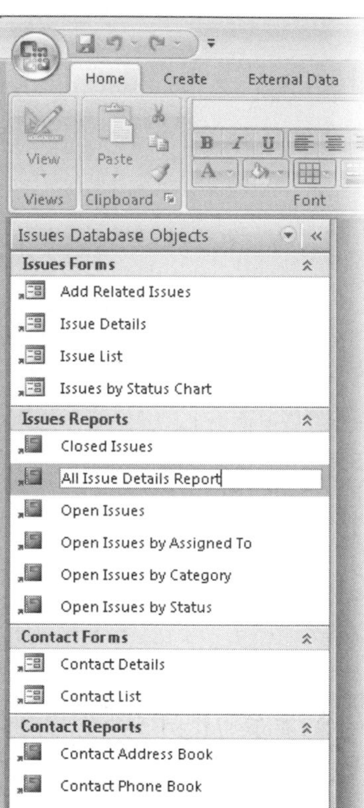


**Figure 2-54** After you click Rename Shortcut, Access unlocks the object shortcut name so that you can change it.

## Revealing Hidden Shortcuts

If you have followed along to this point, remember that you hid the form Issues Datasheet Subform from the current view in the Navigation Pane. To unhide this form, right-click the top of the Navigation Pane and click Navigation Options to open the Navigation Options dialog box. Select the Show Hidden Objects check box, as shown in Figure 2-56. Click OK to save this change and close the Navigation Options dialog box.

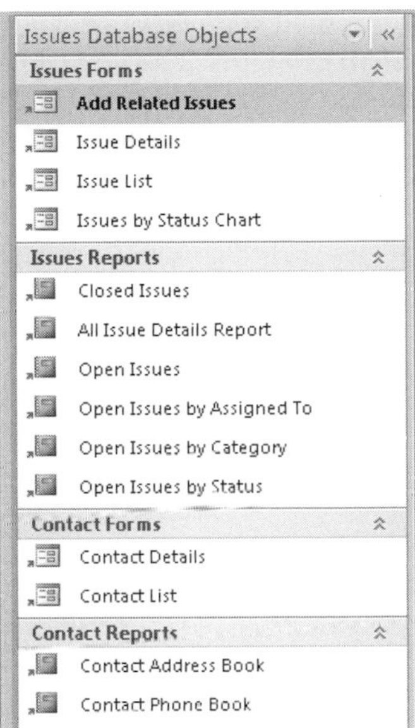


**Figure 2-55** The customized Navigation Pane category and groups now display only form and report shortcuts.

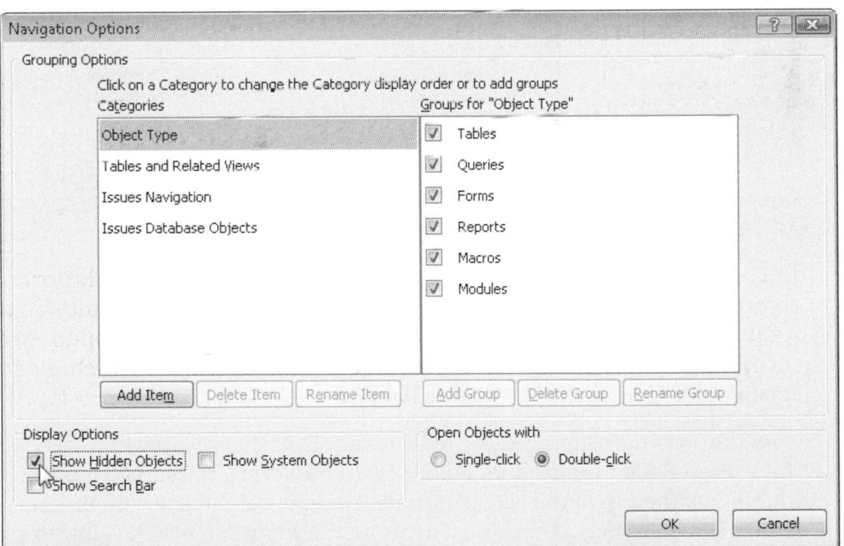


**Figure 2-56** Selecting the Show Hidden Objects check box causes Access to display any hidden object shortcuts in the Navigation Pane.

When you return to the Navigation Pane, Access displays the shortcut to the form Issues Datasheet Subform in the Issues Forms group, as shown in Figure 2-57. If you look closely in Figure 2-57, you can see that Access displays the object dimmed compared to the other object shortcuts. This dimmed state is a visual cue that Access uses to indicate object shortcuts that are hidden. In Figure 2-57 you can also see that Access now shows the hidden group Unassigned Objects and all of the objects contained within it. All the objects in the Unassigned Objects group, along with the group name itself, also appear dimmed in the Navigation Pane.

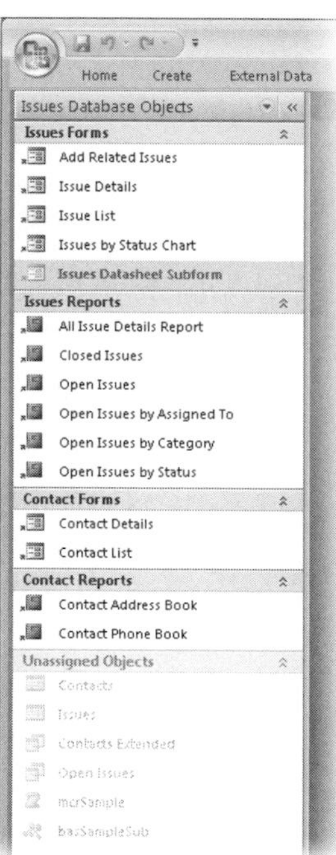


**Figure 2-57** Access displays any hidden shortcuts, objects, or groups in the Navigation Pane when you select the Show Hidden Objects check box.

To change the Hidden property of the form Issues Datasheet Subform, right-click that object in the Navigation Pane and click View Properties to open the Properties dialog box for this object, as shown in Figure 2-58. In the Attributes section, clear the Hidden check box and then click OK. You can see that the Issues Datasheet Subform no longer appears dimmed in the Navigation Pane.

Now that you have changed the form Issues Datasheet Subform to be visible in the Navigation Pane, you need to tell Access to hide the Unassigned Objects group again. Right-click the top of the Navigation Pane and click Navigation Options. Clear the Show Hidden Objects check box, as shown in Figure 2-59. Click OK to save this change and Access once again hides the Unassigned Objects group from view in the Navigation Pane.

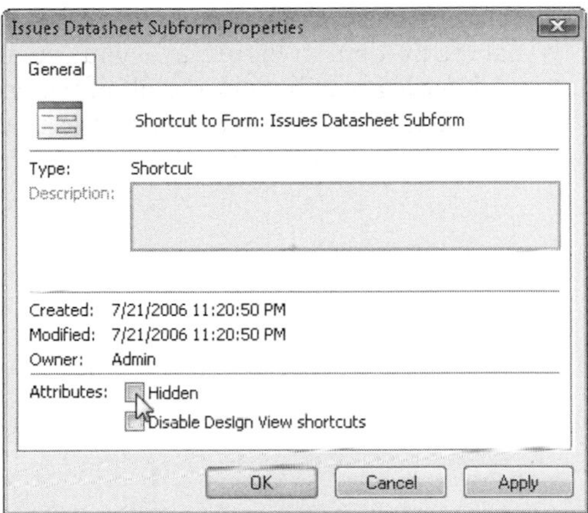


**Figure 2-58** You can unhide a database object or an object shortcut from view in the Navigation Pane by clearing the Hidden check box in the Properties dialog box for the object or shortcut.

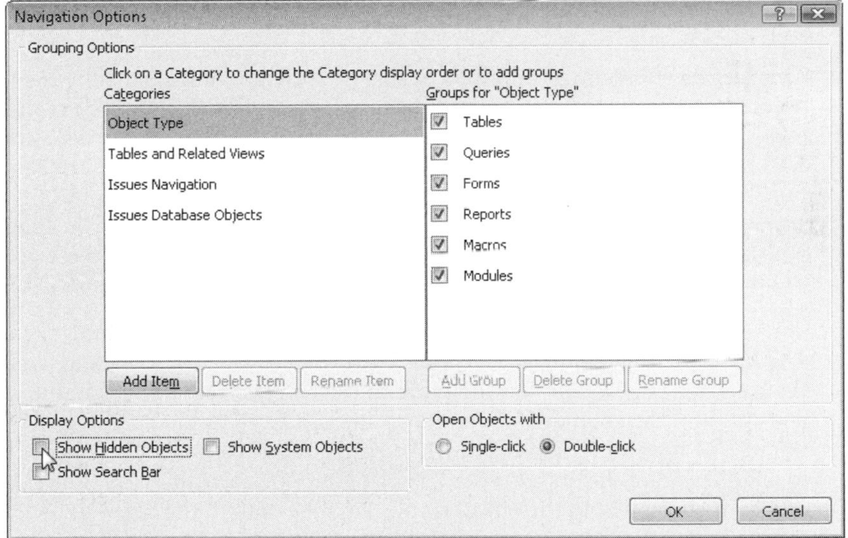


**Figure 2-59** Clear the Show Hidden Objects check box to have Access hide any hidden object shortcuts, objects, or groups in the Navigation Pane.

On the companion CD, you can find a database file called IssueSampleCustom.accdb, which has all the changes from the steps we completed in the preceding sections. If you would like to compare your Issues Database Objects category and groups to our completed sample, open this file from the folder where you installed the sample files.

Chapter 2

## Sorting and Selecting Views in the Navigation Pane

By default, Access sorts the objects in the Navigation Pane by object type in ascending order. The Navigation Pane allows for several other types of object sorting. Right-click the menu at the top of the Navigation Pane and move the mouse pointer over Sort By as shown in Figure 2-60.

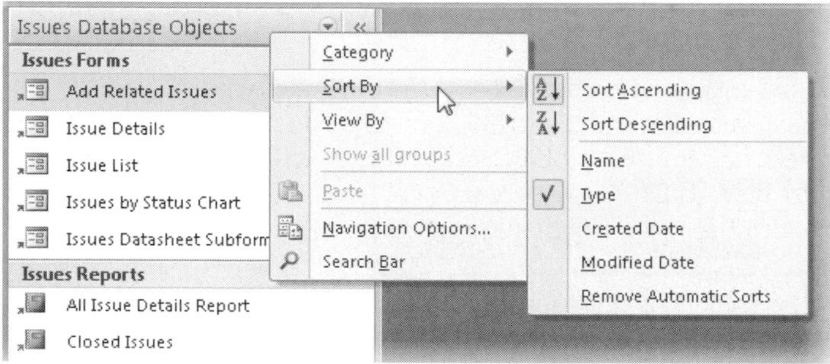


**Figure 2-60** The Sort By submenu on the Navigation Pane menu allows for further Navigation Pane sorting.

The Sort By submenu has options to sort the Navigation Pane list by the name of the object, the object type, the created date, and the modified date. You can change the sort order from ascending to descending for any of these Sort By options by clicking Sort Ascending or Sort Descending at the top of the Sort By submenu. The last option on the Sort By submenu, Remove Automatic Sorts, lets you lay out your object list in any order you want within the Navigation Pane. With this option selected, you can click and drag your objects within their respective groups into any order, and Access will not re-sort them in alphabetical, type, created date, or modified date order after you have repositioned your objects in the list.

The View By submenu has three choices available—Details, Icon, and List—as shown in Figure 2-61. The Details view displays in the Navigation Pane the name of each object, its type, and the creation and modified dates, as well as places a large icon next to the name. The Icon view displays only the name of the object (or the shortcut name) next to a large icon of the object type. The List view similarly displays only the name of the object or shortcut, but the object icon is smaller than in the other two views.

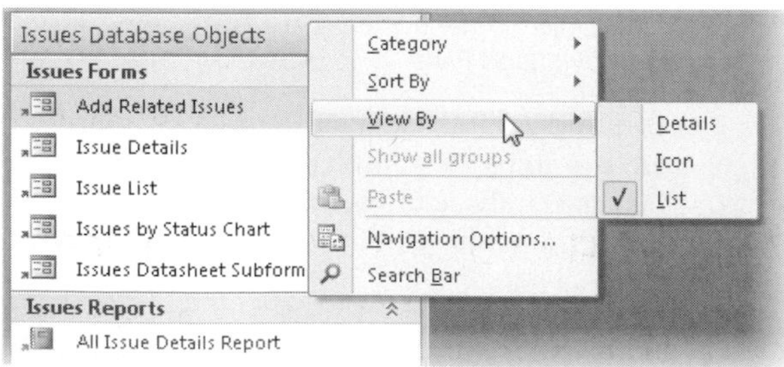


**Figure 2-61** The View By submenu lists commands to view the Navigation Pane objects by Details, Icon, or List.

> **INSIDE OUT** **Viewing Categories from the Navigation Pane Submenus**
>
> You can choose one of the view categories—either a custom category or one of the built-in categories—by right-clicking the Navigation Pane menu and selecting the Category submenu.



In Figure 2-62 you can see what the Navigation Pane looks like with the view set to Details. Notice that more information is displayed about each object, but you see fewer objects. To see the remaining objects you have to use the vertical scroll bar. If you changed your view to Details to test this, go back to the View By submenu and change the view back to List before continuing.

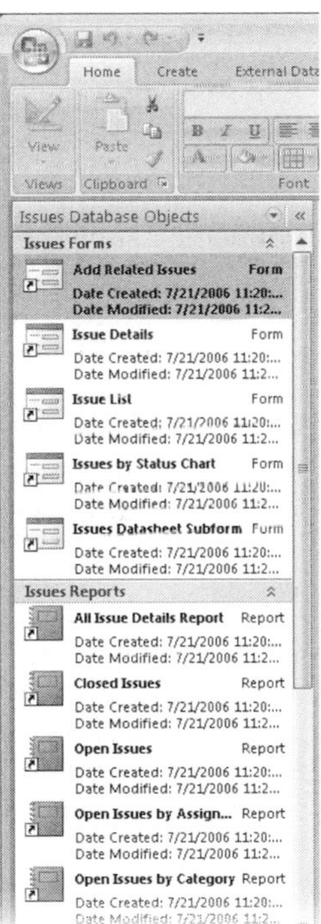


**Figure 2-62** The Details view displays more information about each object in the Navigation Pane than Icon or List view.

## Manually Sorting Objects in the Navigation Pane

So far we have seen how Access can sort the list of objects and object shortcuts in the Navigation Pane automatically for you. Access also allows you to manually sort the object lists so that you can further customize the display order. You must first tell

Access to stop automatically sorting your objects. Right-click the top of the Navigation Pane, click Sort By, and then click Remove Automatic Sorts as shown in Figure 2-63.

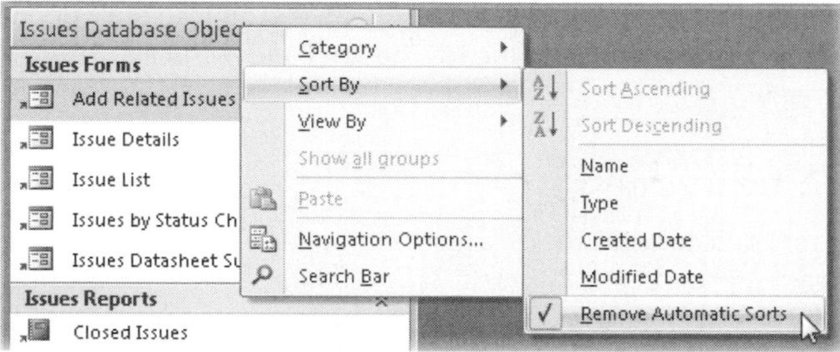


**Figure 2-63** Click the Remove Automatic Sorts command to manually sort your object list in the Navigation Pane.

Now you can click and drag your objects and object shortcuts around into different positions in the Navigation Pane. For example, click and drag the Add Related Issues form shortcut in the Navigation Pane until you have your pointer between the Issue List and Issues by Status Chart forms. An I-beam pointer will appear while you drag to help you position the object, as shown in Figure 2-64. After you release the mouse, Access drops the form shortcut into the new position.

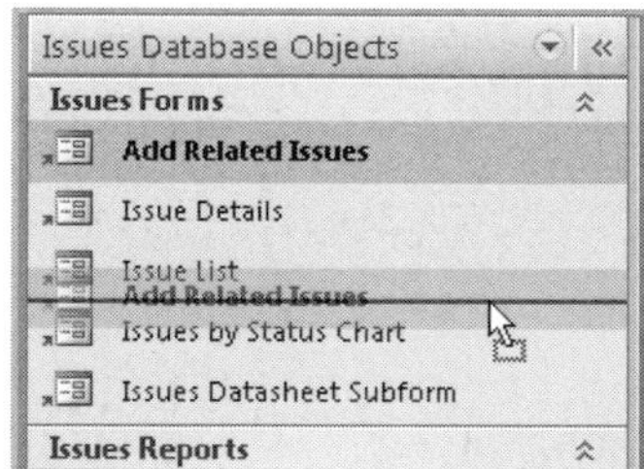


**Figure 2-64** Click and drag your form shortcut into a new position within the Issues Forms category.

To have Access automatically sort the object list again, select any of the four available sort options above Remove Automatic Sorts from the Display Options menu.

## Searching for Database Objects

In databases with a large number of database objects, locating a specific object can be difficult, so Access 2007 includes the Search Bar feature to make this task easier. By default, this feature is turned off, so you must turn it on through the Navigation Pane. You can enable this feature in one of two ways. For the first method, right-click the top of the Navigation Pane and then click Search Bar, as shown in Figure 2-65.

Alternatively, you can right-click the top of the Navigation Pane and then click Navigation Options from the shortcut menu to open the Navigation Options dialog box shown in Figure 2-66.

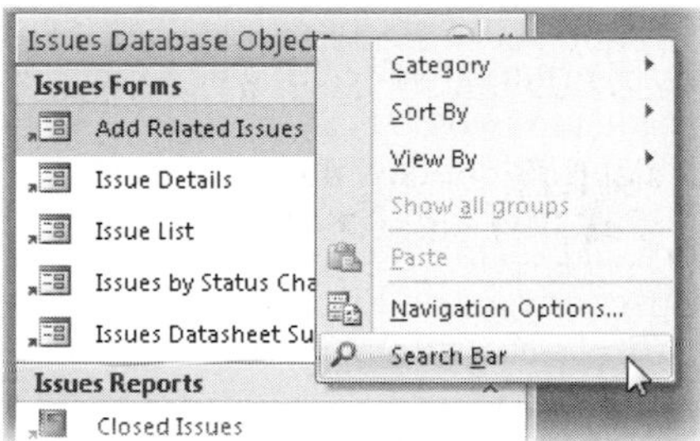


**Figure 2-65** Click the Search Bar command on the Display Options menu to display the Search Bar.

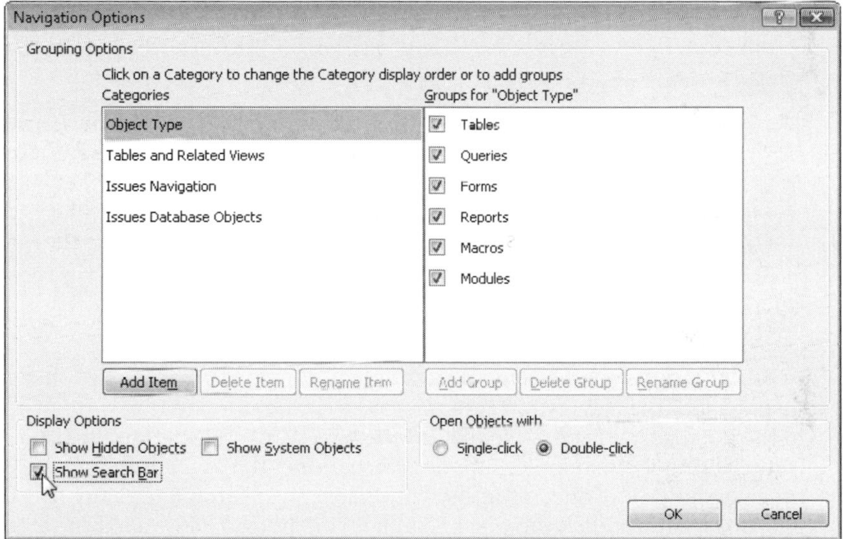


**Figure 2-66** Select the Show Search Bar check box in the Navigation Options dialog box to display the Search Bar.

Select the Show Search Bar check box and then click OK. Access displays a Search Bar near the top of the Navigation Pane, as shown in Figure 2-67.

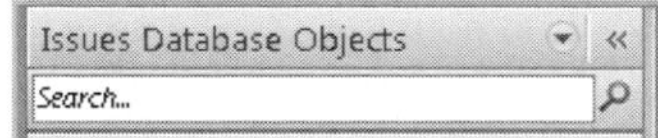


**Figure 2-67** The Search Bar in the Navigation Pane helps you find specific database objects.

We think the Search Bar is misnamed. Rather than "search" for objects that match what you type in the search box, Access filters the list in the Navigation Pane. As you begin to type letters, Access filters the list of objects to those that contain the sequence of characters you enter anywhere in the name. For example, if you want to find an object whose name contains the word Address, type the word **address** in the Search Bar. As you enter each letter in the Search Bar, Access begins filtering the list of objects for any that contain the characters in your entered search string. With each successive letter you type, Access reduces the list of objects shown in the Navigation Pane because there are fewer objects that match your search criteria. Notice that as soon as you have typed the letters *add*, Access has reduced the list to two objects–Add Related Issues and Contact Address Book. The names of both objects contain the letters *add*.

After you finish typing the entire word *address* in the Search Bar, the Navigation Pane should like Figure 2-68. Access collapses any group headers if it does not find any objects (or object shortcuts if you're using a custom category) that meet your search criterion. In this case, Access located one object, Contact Address Book, with the word *address* in its name. To clear your search string if you need to perform another object search, either delete the existing text using the Backspace key or click the Clear Search String button on the right side of the Search Bar. Clearing the search box or clicking the Clear Search String button restores the Navigation Pane to show all displayable objects.

Chapter 2

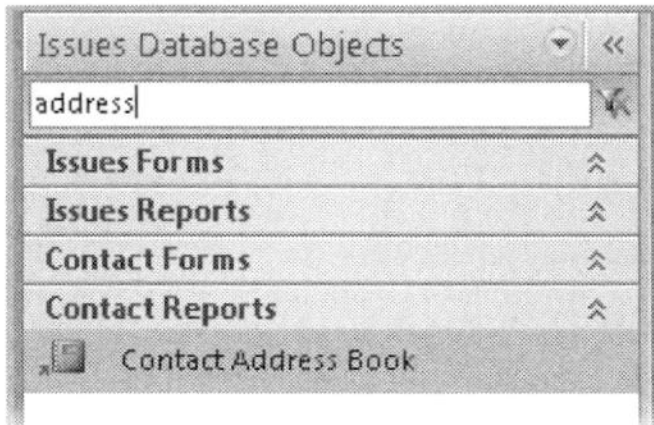


**Figure 2-68** The Search Bar collapses any groups if it does not find any objects in that group that meet your search criterion.

Note that Access searches for objects only in categories and groups that are currently displayed in the Navigation Pane. If Access cannot find an object that you know exists in the database, it is possible that the view you have selected in the Navigation Pane is interfering. For example, suppose you conduct the preceding same search but this time you have only one group showing. Clear the Search Bar of any text by using the Backspace key or click the Clear Search String button. Now click the menu bar at the top of the Navigation Pane and select Issues Forms in the Filter By Group section of the Navigation Pane menu, as shown in Figure 2-69. The only group now displayed in the Navigation Pane is Issues Forms with four object shortcuts.

Enter the word **address** again in the Search Bar and notice that Access cannot locate any objects that meet your criterion. In Figure 2-70 you can see that Access shows an empty Navigation Pane because none of the four form object shortcuts in the Issues Forms groups have the word *address* in their name. This does not mean that no objects in the entire database have the word *address* in their name; it means only that Access could not locate any objects with that search criterion in the *current* view selected in the Navigation Pane.

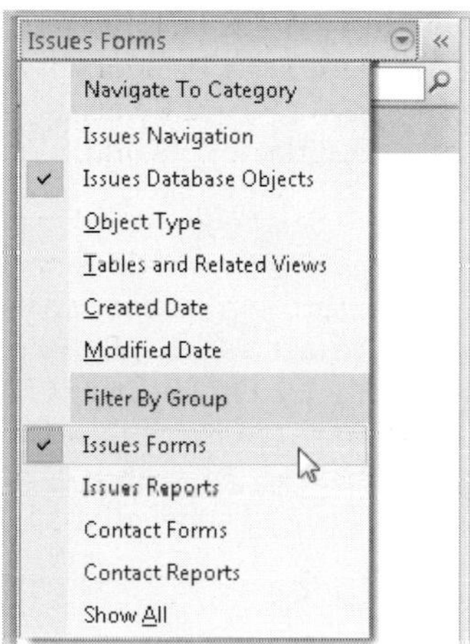


**Figure 2-69** Select Issues Forms from the Navigation Pane menu to show only that group in the Navigation Pane.

**Figure 2-70** Access might not be able to find any objects that meet your criterion if your chosen display view is too restrictive.

If you know exactly the name of the object you want to find and the type of object as well, you can save some additional searching through object types you might not be interested in. For example, suppose you want to find a form that has the word *list* in its name. First open the Navigation Pane menu and click Object Type. Open the menu again and click Forms under Filter By Group to restrict the list of objects to display only forms, as shown in Figure 2-71.



INSIDE OUT **Using the Shortcut Menu to Display Only One Category**

You can also right-click the Forms group header and click Show Only Forms so that only forms show in the Navigation Pane.

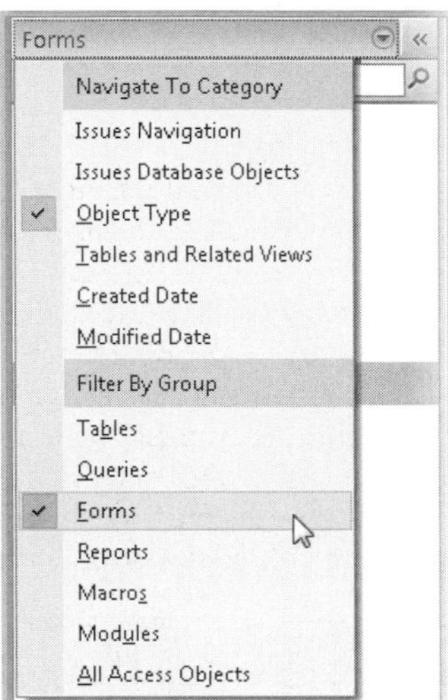


**Figure 2-71** You can limit your search to form objects by selecting the Object Type category and Forms group from the Navigation Pane menu.

Type the word **list** in the Search Bar and Access searches through only data entry forms until it finds a match. In Figure 2-72, Access has found two forms that have the word *list* in their name—Contact List and Issue List.

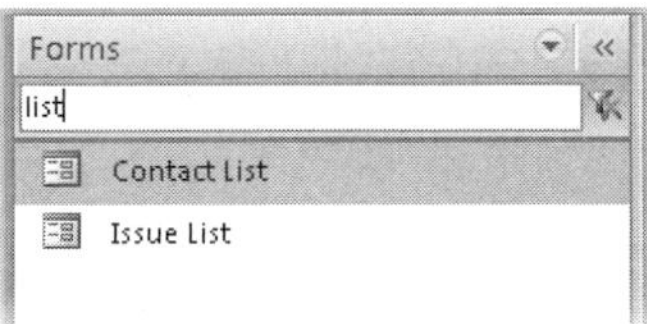


**Figure 2-72** After restricting the Navigation Pane to show only forms, text you enter in the Search Bar searches only in the Forms group.

INSIDE OUT

### Maximizing Your Search to Include All Objects

If you need to search through all your database objects to find a specific named object, we recommend that you set the Navigation Pane menu category to one of the built-in categories such as Object Type or Tables And Related Views. Also check to see that all groups are visible in the Navigation Pane for that category to ensure that Access does not miss any objects when it conducts the search.

# Using the Single-Document vs. Multiple-Document Interface

In previous versions of Access, all objects opened in their own window where you could edit, view, or print them. This type of interface, *multiple-document interface* (MDI for short), was the cornerstone for working with objects in Access. Office Access 2007 introduces a new interface model called *single-document interface* (SDI). In the SDI model, all objects open in a series of tabs along the top of the object window to the right of the Navigation Pane. In the older MDI model, switching between open objects usually meant constantly minimizing, resizing, and maximizing the various objects in order to work with them. In Figure 2-73 you can see two forms, one table, and one report open using MDI format. To switch among these objects you must move the objects around or minimize some of them, as shown near the bottom of the screen.

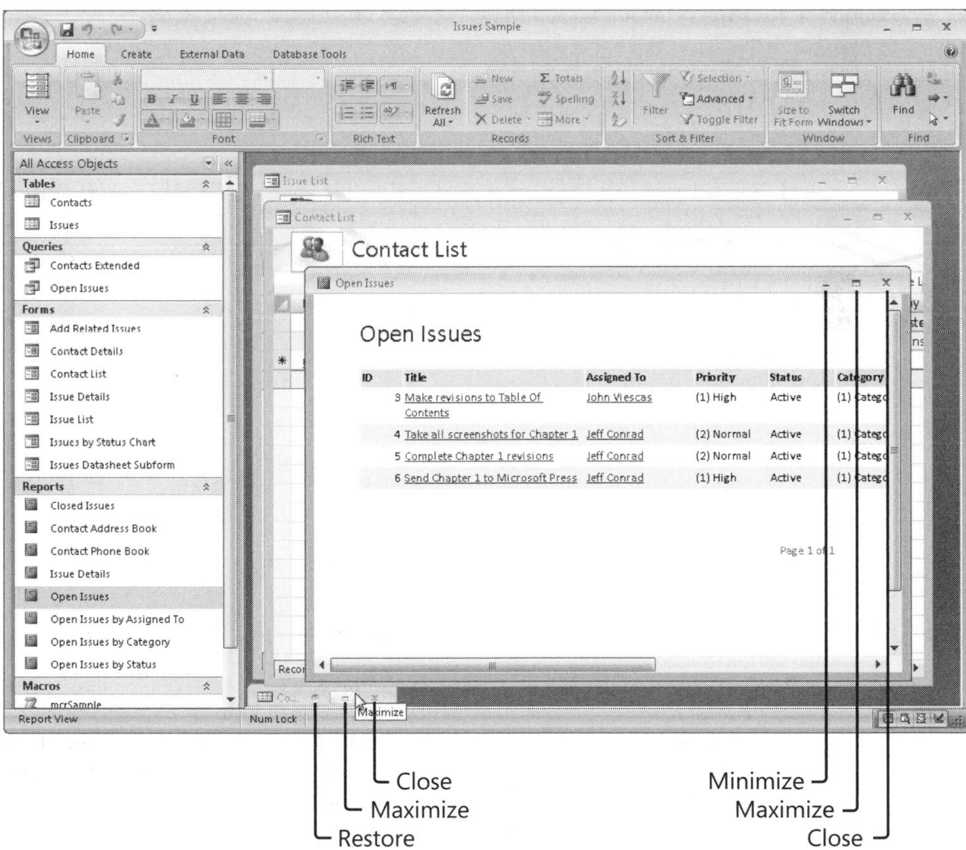


**Figure 2-73** All open objects appear in their own separate window when using the multiple-document interface.

In the new SDI model, each open object appears on a tab to the right of the Navigation Pane. In Figure 2-74 you can see the same four objects open as before, but here each open object has its name listed at the top of a tab next to an icon for that particular type of database object. Switching among open objects is as simple as clicking on a different tab. The end result of this new interface is that you can easily see the names of all open objects and find the ones you need to work with much more quickly.

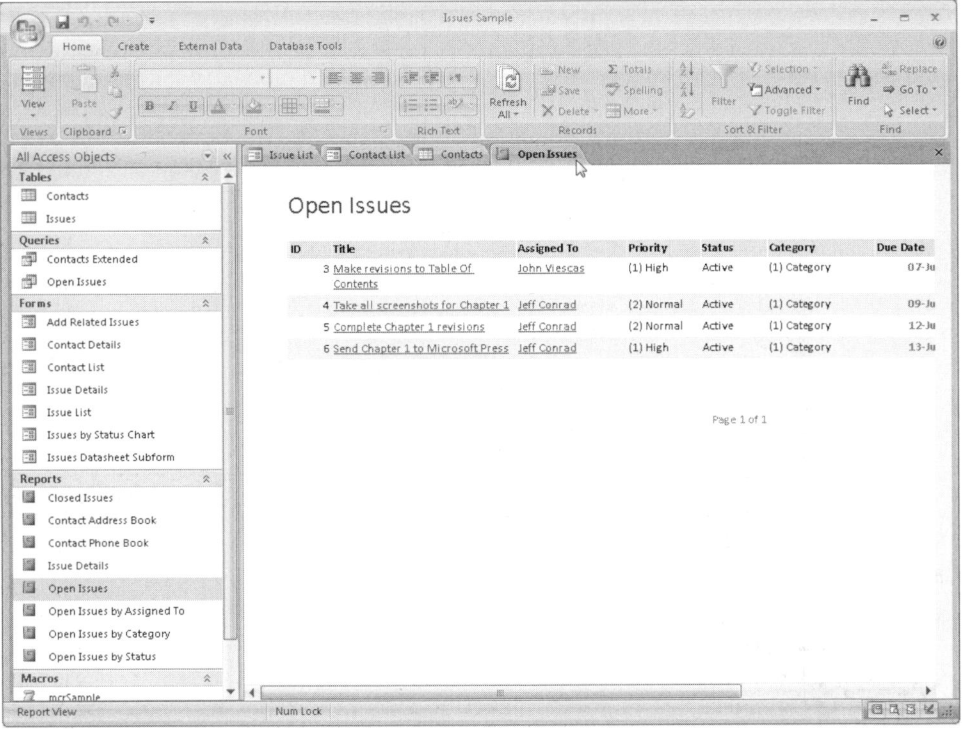


**Figure 2-74** All open objects appear on their own tabs when using the single-document interface.

For new databases created in the Access 2007 format, Access uses the single-document interface by default, but for older databases in the MDB/MDE type format Access 2007 still opens those files in multiple-document interface mode. Access easily allows you to change the interface mode for any database through the Access Options dialog box. Click the Microsoft Office Button, and then click the Access Options button.

The Access Options dialog box opens and displays many options for customizing the look and feel of Access 2007. You can find an explanation of more of the various options in these categories in "Modifying Global Settings via the Access Options Dialog Box" on page 87. Click the Current Database category in the left pane to display a list of settings to tailor this current database. In Figure 2-75, note the section called Document Window Options in the Current Database category of the Access Options dialog box.

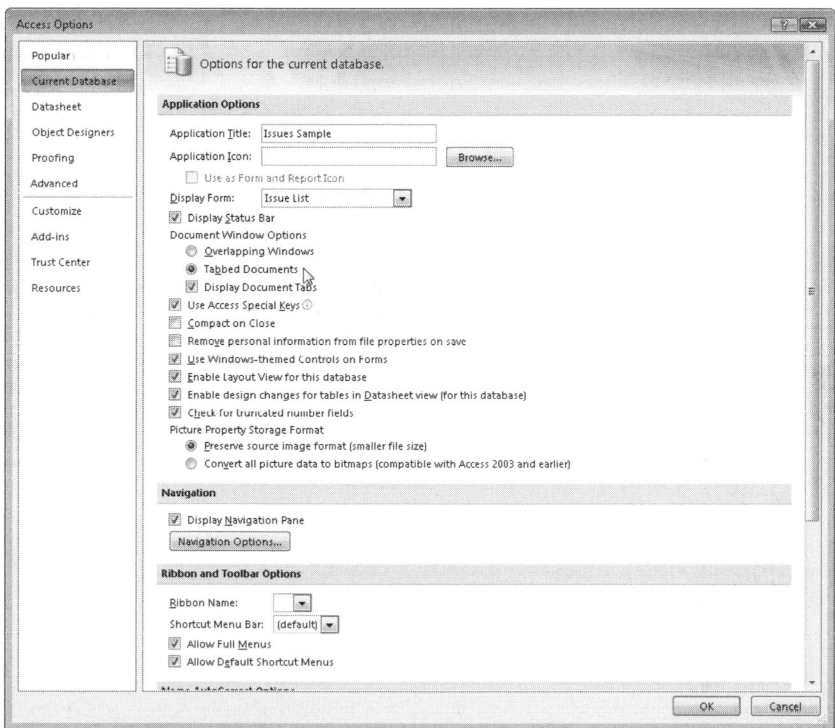


**Figure 2-75** The Document Window Options section in the Current Database category of the Access Options dialog box controls the interface mode.

To work in multiple-document interface mode, select Overlapping Windows. For the single-document interface, with each object on its own tab, select Tabbed Documents. Under these two options is a check box called Display Document Tabs. You can select this check box only in conjunction with the Tabbed Documents option. When you select the Display Document Tabs check box, each object has a tab across the top of the object window with the object's name and an icon for the object type, as was shown in Figure 2-74. If you clear Display Document Tabs, you do not see any tabs for open objects nor do you see any Restore, Minimize, Maximize, or Close buttons for open objects.

In Figure 2-76 we have two forms, one table, and one report open, but you can see only the report because no object tabs are visible. Notice that you do not see any Restore, Minimize, Maximize, or Close buttons along the top of the object window, which means it is more difficult to switch among various open objects. It is possible, but awkward, to switch from one object to another by pressing Ctrl+F6.

After you make your selections in the Access Options dialog box, click OK to save your changes. Access applies these interface settings to this current database the next time you open the file. In order to see the interface change you need to close and reopen the database.

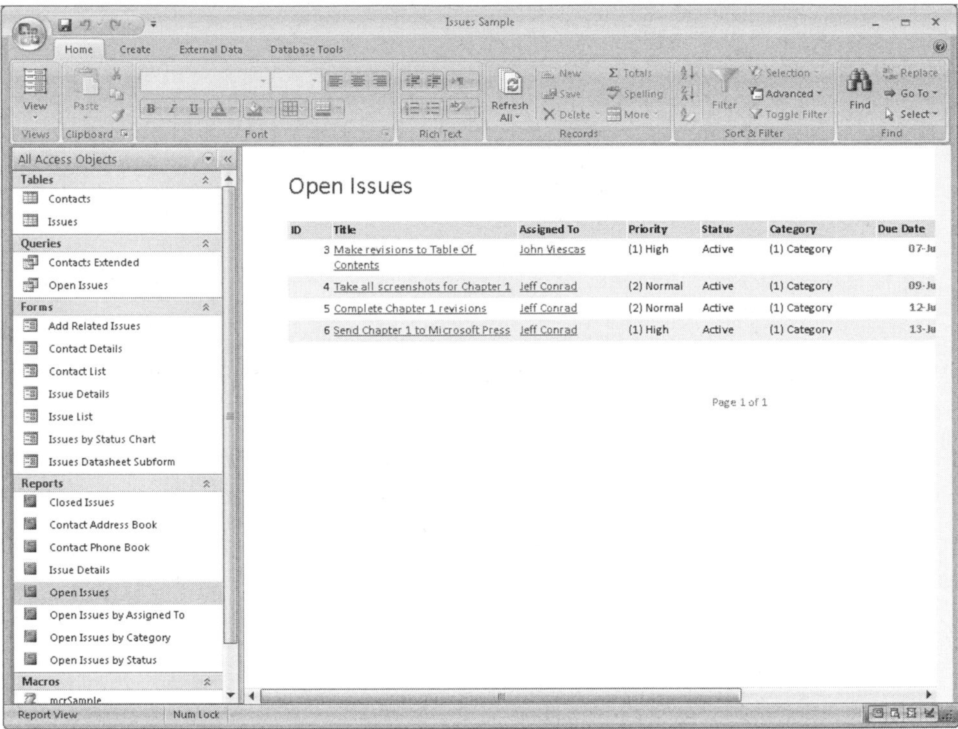


**Figure 2-76** With Tabbed Documents selected and the Display Document Tabs check box cleared, no tabs for open objects appear at the top of the object window.

INSIDE OUT

## Why You Might Want to Use the Tabbed Documents Setting with No Tabs Visible

If you're creating an application for novice users, you might want to set up the application so that the user can work with only one object at a time. Presenting a single object minimizes the choices the user must make. However, you will have to be sure to include a method to allow the user to navigate to other objects, perhaps with command buttons that execute VBA code or macros to open and set the focus to other objects. You must carefully design such an application so the user never gets "trapped" in one object and unable to get to others.

Chapter 2

# Modifying Global Settings via the Access Options Dialog Box

In addition to all the various commands and options available on the Ribbon and in the Navigation Pane, Access 2007 has one central location for setting and modifying global options for all your Access database files or for only the database currently open. This location is the Access Options dialog box. To open the Access Options dialog box, click the Microsoft Office Button and then click Access Options, as shown in Figure 2-77.



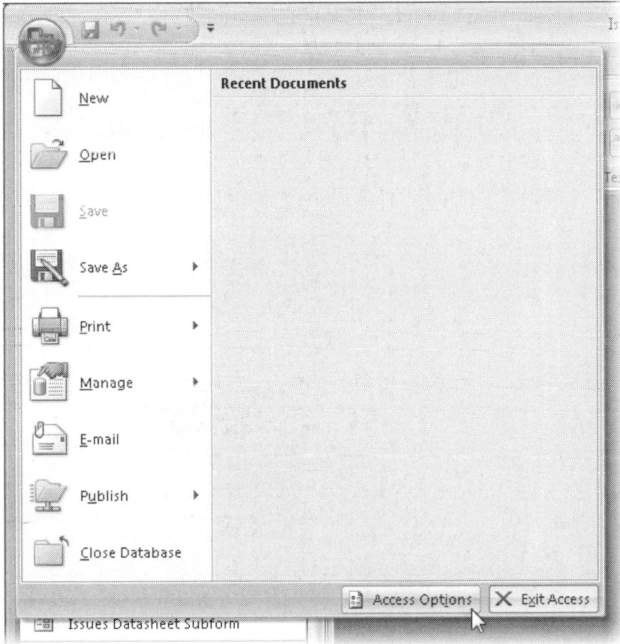


**Figure 2-77** Click the Microsoft Office Button and then click Access Options to open the Access Options dialog box.

The Access Options dialog box contains 10 categories in the left pane to organize the various options and settings. The first category, Popular, has settings that apply not only to Access 2007, but also to any other 2007 Microsoft Office system programs you might have installed. From here you can choose to display ScreenTips, select a color scheme for the application window, and enter a user name for use in all your 2007 Microsoft Office system applications. In the Creating Databases section, you can choose a default file format for new databases you create in Access 2007. By default, the file format is set to create all new databases in Access 2007 format. The Default Database Folder box displays the folder where Access saves all new database files unless you select a different folder when creating the database. Figure 2-78 shows the Popular category of the Access Options dialog box.

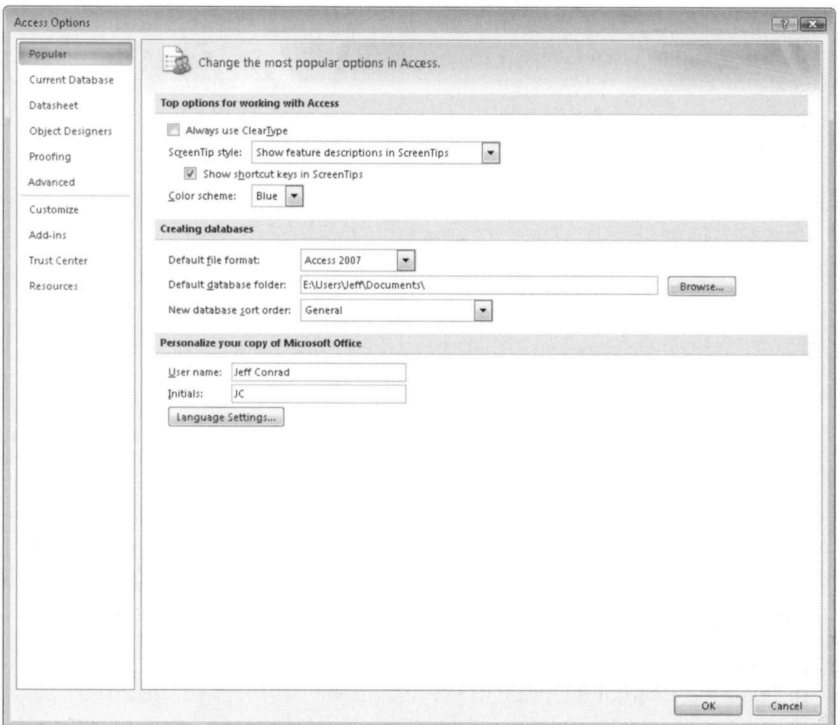


**Figure 2-78** The Popular category has general settings for your Microsoft Office system applications.

The Current Database category, shown in Figure 2-79, has many settings that apply only to the database currently open. This category groups options into these sections: Application Options, Navigation, Ribbon And Toolbar Options, Name AutoCorrect Options, and Filter Lookup Options.

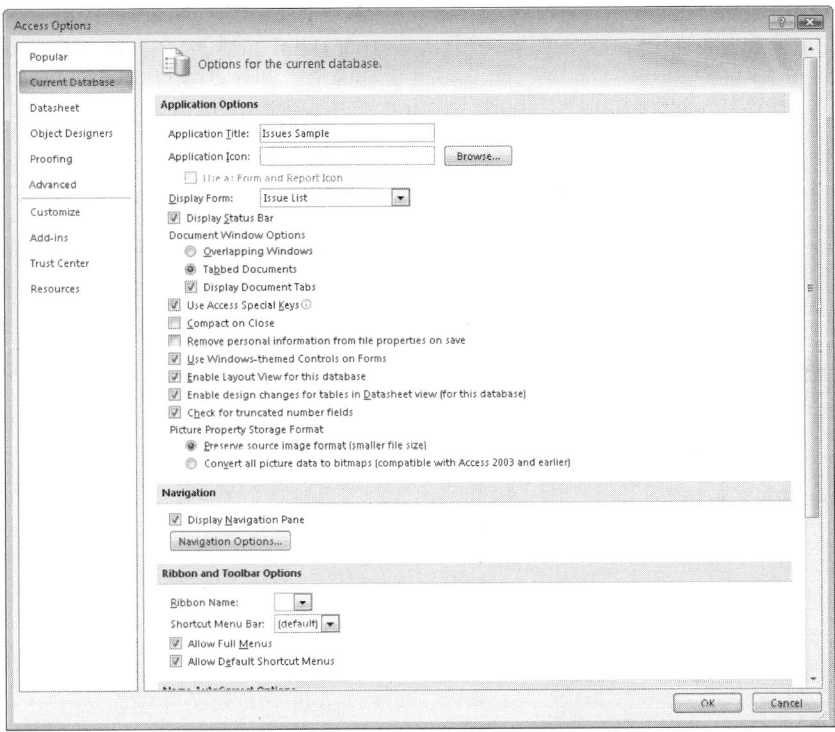


**Figure 2-79** The Current Database category has general settings for the database currently open.

The Document Window Options section in this category was discussed previously in "Using the Single-Document vs. Multiple-Document Interface" on page 83. Use Windows-Themed Controls On Forms will be discussed in Chapter 11, "Building a Form," and Chapter 12, "Customizing a Form." The remaining options in the Current Database category will be discussed in Chapter 24.

The Datasheet category, shown in Figure 2-80, has settings that control the appearance of the datasheet views in your database. This category has options grouped in the following sections—Default Colors, Gridlines And Cell Effects, and Default Font—which allow you to modify the look of your datasheets with different colors, gridlines, and cell effects. You can also select a default font and size under Default Font. You'll learn more about applying these settings to datasheets in "Working in Query Datasheet View" on page 384 and in Chapter 10, "Using Forms," and Chapter 11.

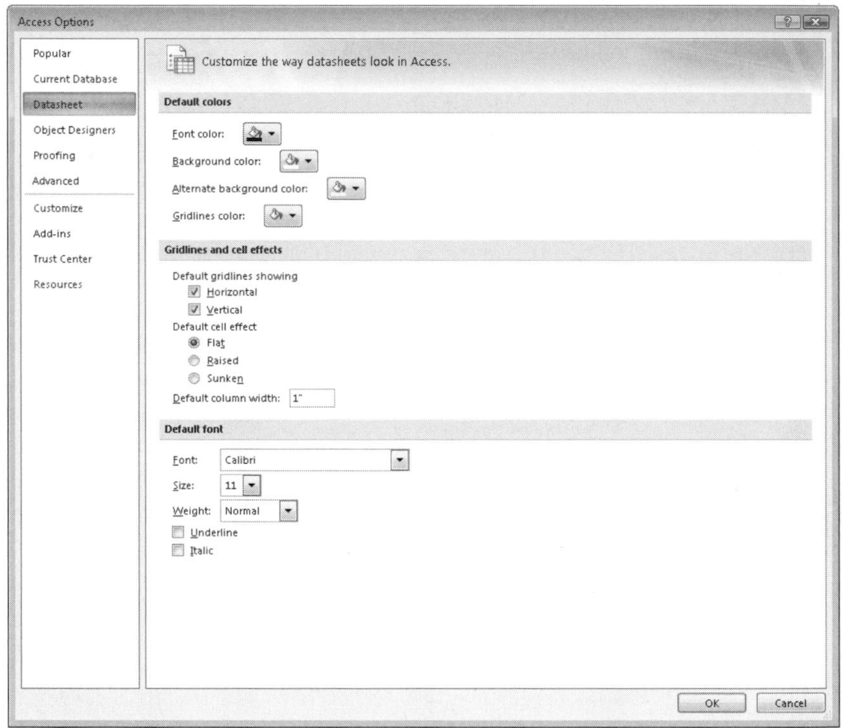


**Figure 2-80** The Datasheet category has general settings to control the look of datasheets.

The Object Designers category, shown in Figure 2-81, includes settings for creating and modifying database objects in all databases. The Object Designers category is divided into four sections: Table Design, Query Design, Forms/Reports, and Error Checking.

The Table Design section has settings for Default Field Type, Default Text Field Size, and Default Number Field Size. You'll learn more about the impact of these settings in Chapter 4. The Query Design section lets you select a default font and size for working in the query design grid. You'll learn more about the impact of these settings in Chapter 8, "Building Complex Queries." The Forms/Reports section has options that allow you to use the existing form and report templates or choose a custom template that you have created. You'll learn more about these settings in Chapter 11. The Error Checking section has several default options that Access looks for when checking for errors in your database file. You'll learn more about these settings in Chapter 19, "Understanding Visual Basic Fundamentals."

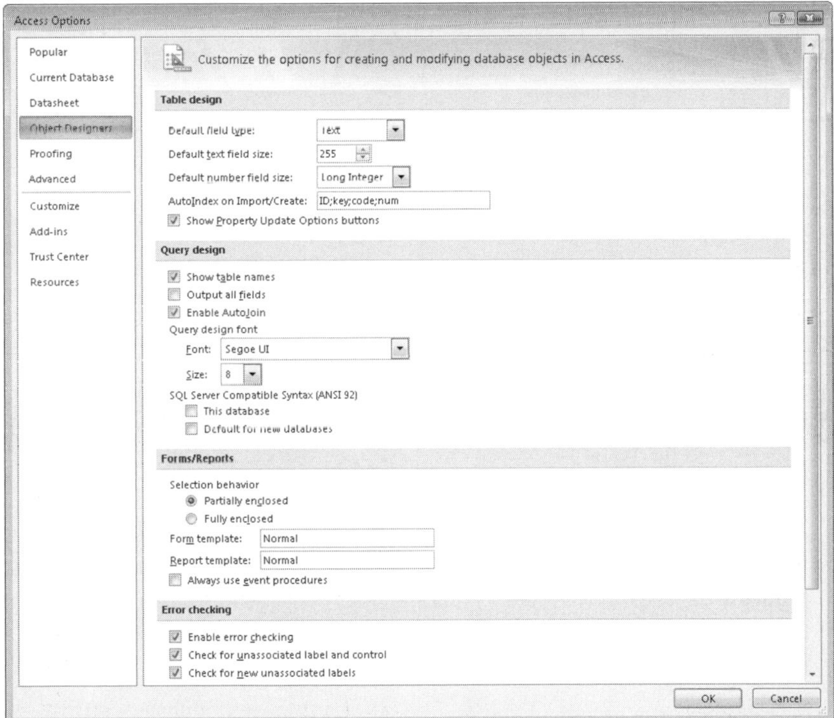


**Figure 2-81** The Object Designers category has settings for working with database objects.

The Proofing category, shown in Figure 2-82, includes options for controlling the spelling and AutoCorrect features. You can click AutoCorrect Options to customize how Access helps you with common typing mistakes. You can also click Custom Dictionaries to select a custom dictionary to use when working with Access 2007 and the other 2007 Office release applications. See Chapter 24 for more information on these options.

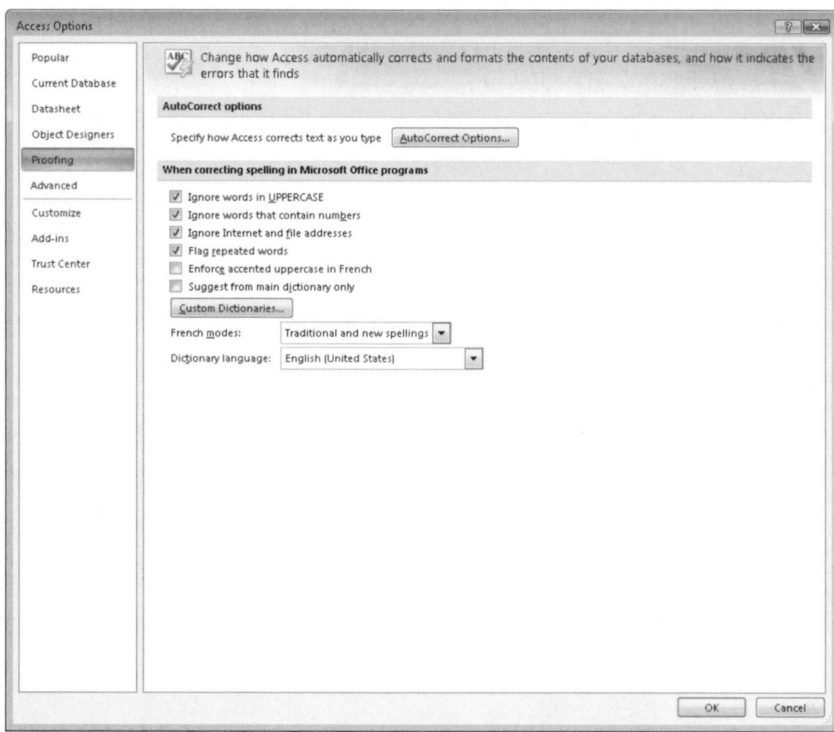


**Figure 2-82** The Proofing category has settings for checking spelling and AutoCorrect.

The Advanced category, shown in Figure 2-83, contains a wide variety of settings for Access 2007. This category has options grouped in the following sections: Editing, Display, Printing, General, and Advanced. Each of the settings in this category applies to all database files you use in Access 2007. Many of these settings are discussed later in various parts of this book. See Chapter 6, Chapter 7, "Creating and Working with Simple Queries," and Chapter 26, "Building Tables in an Access Project," for more information.

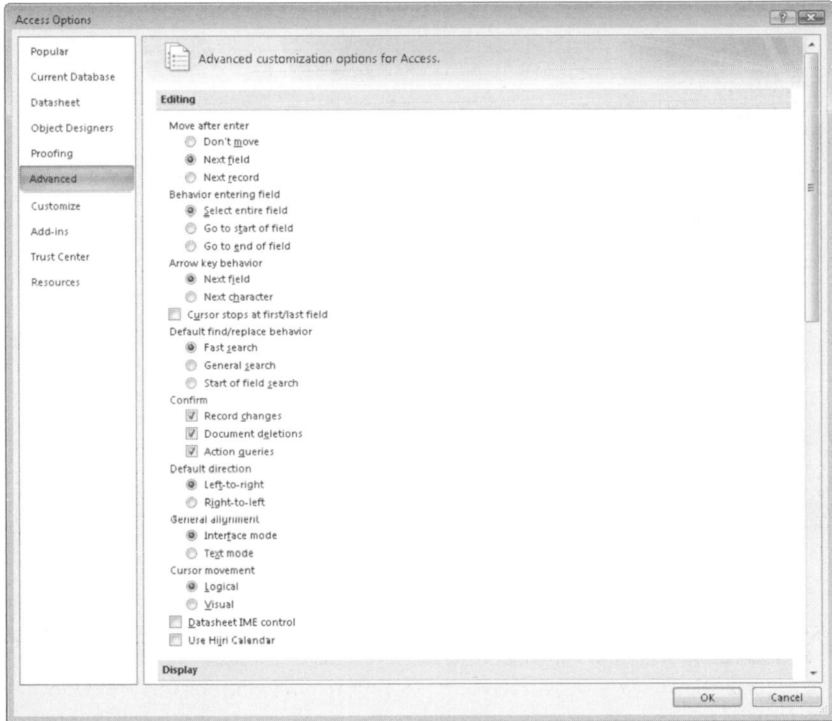


**Figure 2-83** The Advanced category has options for controlling editing, display, and printing.

The Customize category, shown in Figure 2-84, was discussed previously in "Taking Advantage of the Quick Access Toolbar" on page 27. This category is where you customize the Quick Access Toolbar. You can make modifications to the Quick Access Toolbar for this specific database only or to the Quick Access Toolbar for all Access databases.

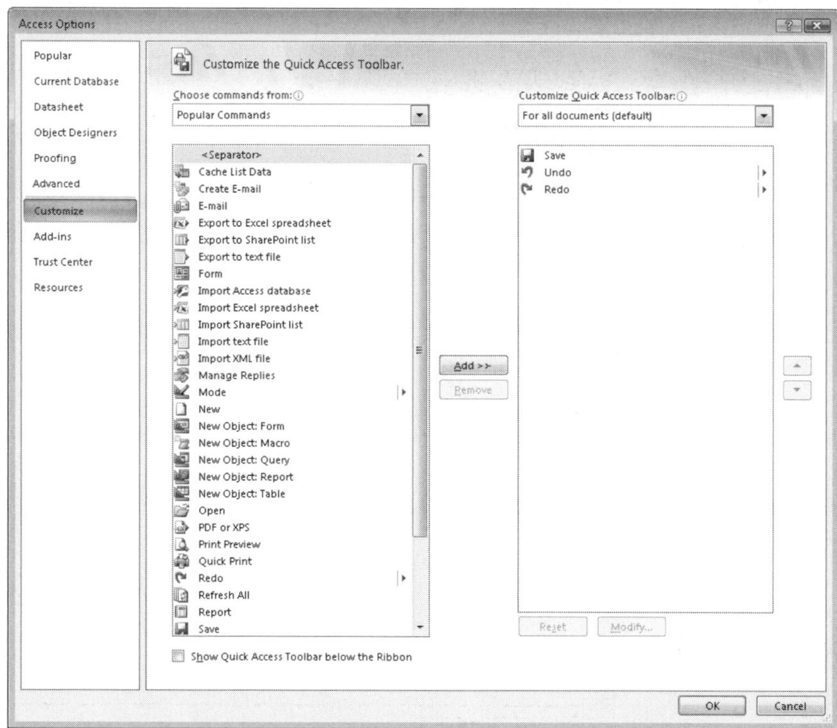


**Figure 2-84** The Customize category allows you to customize the Quick Access Toolbar.

The Add-Ins category, shown in Figure 2-85, lists all the various Access add-ins that might be installed on your computer. You can manage COM add-ins and Access add-ins from this category, and each add-in has its various properties listed. COM add-ins extend the ability of Access and other Microsoft Office system applications with custom commands and specialized features. You can even disable certain add-ins to keep them from loading and functioning.

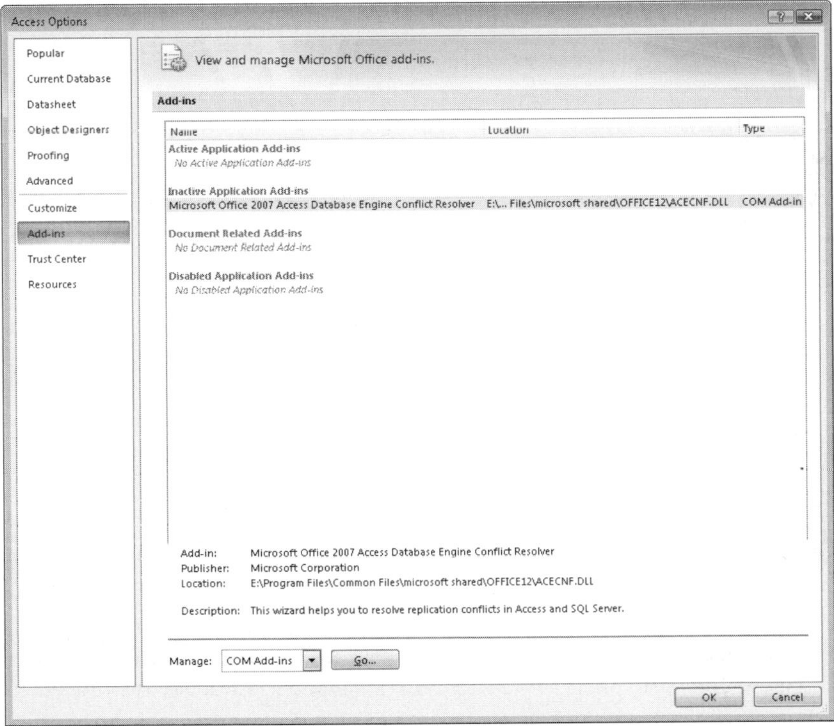


**Figure 2-85** The Add-Ins category lists any installed Access add-ins and COM add-ins.

The Trust Center category, shown in Figure 2-86, is where you access all Trust Center options for handling security. As we discussed earlier in "Understanding Content Security" on page 34, you can open the Trust Center Settings dialog box that controls all aspects of macro security. This category also has links to online privacy and security information.

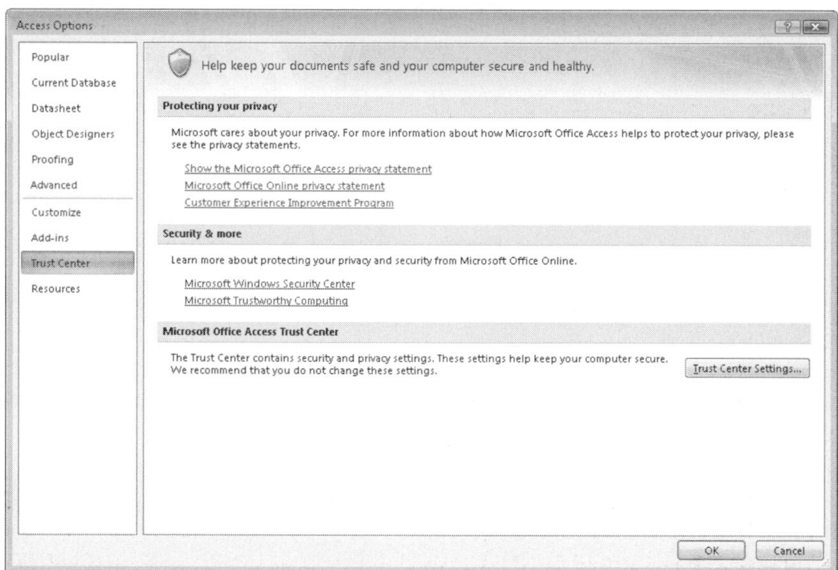


**Figure 2-86** The Trust Center category has links to privacy and security information and the Trust Center Settings button to view more options.

The Resources category, shown in Figure 2-87, is the last category in the Access Options dialog box. This category has options grouped in the following sections: Get Updates, Run Microsoft Office Diagnostics, Contact Us, Activate Microsoft Office, Go To Microsoft Office Online, and About Microsoft Office Access 2007.

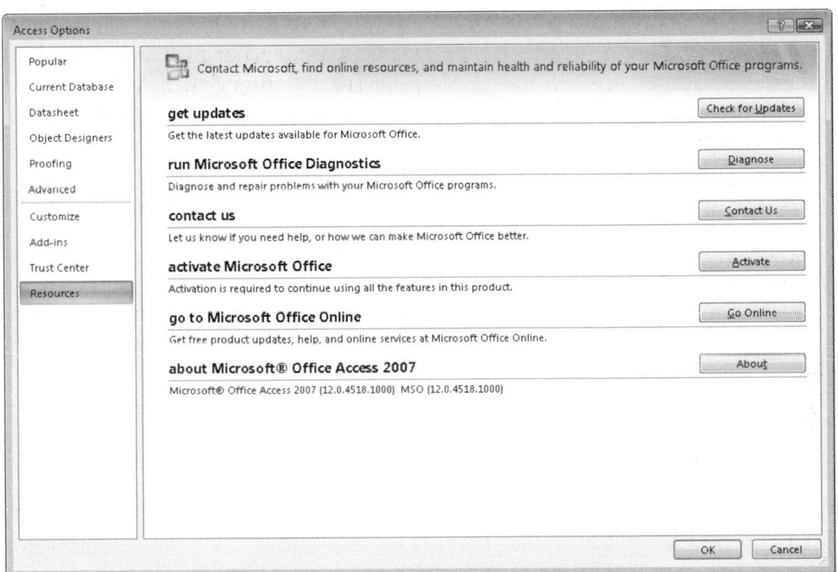


**Figure 2-87** The Resources category has options for contacting Microsoft and utilities to repair problems with your 2007 Microsoft Office system applications.

Click Check For Updates to go to a Web site where you can run a program that verifies that you have the latest updates for your Microsoft Office system. Click Diagnose to run a procedure that verifies your Microsoft Office system installation and fixes most problems. Click Contact Us to go to a Web site where you can find links to support options, go to online support communities, or submit suggestions to improve the product or report a problem. Click Activate to verify that you have a valid installation of the Microsoft Office system and activate all features. Click Go Online to go to Microsoft Office Online to get updates and other services. Click About to open a dialog box that displays your current version and service pack level of Access and provides links to a system analyzer program and online technical support.

In the next chapter, "Microsoft Office Access 2007 Overview," you'll learn about the internal architecture of an Access 2007 application. You'll also open the Housing Reservations and Conrad Systems Contacts sample databases to explore some of the many features and functions of Access. Finally, you'll discover some of the ways that you can use Access as an application solution.

CHAPTER 3

# Microsoft Office Access 2007 Overview



Now that you are more comfortable with the user interface in Microsoft Office Access 2007, it's time to dig deeper into exactly what makes up an Access database. This chapter helps you understand the relationships among the main components in Access and shows you how to move around within the database management system.

## The Architecture of Access

Access calls anything that can have a name an *object*. Within an Access database, the main objects are tables, queries, forms, reports, macros, and modules.

If you have worked with other database systems on desktop computers, you might have seen the term *database* used to refer to only those files in which you store data. In Access, however, a desktop database (.accdb) also includes all the major objects related to the stored data, including objects you define to automate the use of your data. You can also create an Access application using a project file (.adp) that contains the objects that define your application linked to a Microsoft SQL Server database that stores the tables and queries. Here is a summary of the major objects in an Access database:

- **Table.** An object you define and use to store data. Each table contains information about a particular subject, such as customers or orders. Tables contain *fields* (or *columns*) that store different kinds of data, such as a name or an address, and *records* (or *rows*) that collect all the information about a particular instance of the subject, such as all the information about a department named Housing Administration. You can define a *primary key* (one or more fields that have a unique value for each record) and one or more *indexes* on each table to help retrieve your data more quickly.
- **Query.** An object that provides a custom view of data from one or more tables. In Access, you can use the graphical query by example (QBE) facility or you can write SQL statements to create your queries. You can define queries to select, update, insert, or delete data. You can also define queries that create new tables from data in one or more existing tables. When your Access application is a project file connected to an SQL Server database, you can create special types of queries–functions and stored procedures–that can perform complex actions directly on the server.

- **Form.** An object designed primarily for data input or display or for control of application execution. You use forms to customize the presentation of data that your application extracts from queries or tables. You can also print forms. You can design a form to run a macro or a Microsoft Visual Basic procedure in response to any of a number of events—for example, to run a procedure when the value of data changes.
- **Report.** An object designed for formatting, calculating, printing, and summarizing selected data. You can view a report on your screen before you print it.
- **Macro.** An object that is a structured definition of one or more actions that you want Access to perform in response to a defined event. For example, you might design a macro that opens a second form in response to the selection of an item on a main form. You can include simple conditions in macros to specify when one or more actions in the macro should be performed or skipped. You can use macros to open and execute queries, to open tables, or to print or view reports. You can also run other macros or Visual Basic procedures from within a macro.
- **Module.** An object containing custom procedures that you code using Visual Basic. Modules provide a more discrete flow of actions and allow you to trap errors. Modules can be stand-alone objects containing functions that can be called from anywhere in your application, or they can be directly associated with a form or a report to respond to events on the associated form or report.



**For a list of events on forms and reports, see Chapter 17, "Understanding Event Processing."**

INSIDE OUT **What Happened to Data Access Pages?**

Office Access 2007 no longer supports designing *data access pages* (DAPs). Usability studies conducted by Microsoft show that DAPs are not a widely used feature within Access, and Microsoft is focusing more of their efforts on Microsoft Windows SharePoint Services for sharing data in corporate environments. To maintain backward compatibility with previous versions, Office Access 2007 will continue to support existing .mdb applications that contain DAPs, but you cannot create new data access pages or modify existing pages from within Access 2007.

Figure 3-1 shows a conceptual overview of how objects in Access are related. Tables store the data that you can extract with queries and display in reports or that you can display and update in forms. Notice that forms and reports can use data either directly from tables or from a filtered view of the data created by using queries. Queries can use Visual Basic functions to provide customized calculations on data in your database. Access also has many built-in functions that allow you to summarize and format your data in queries.

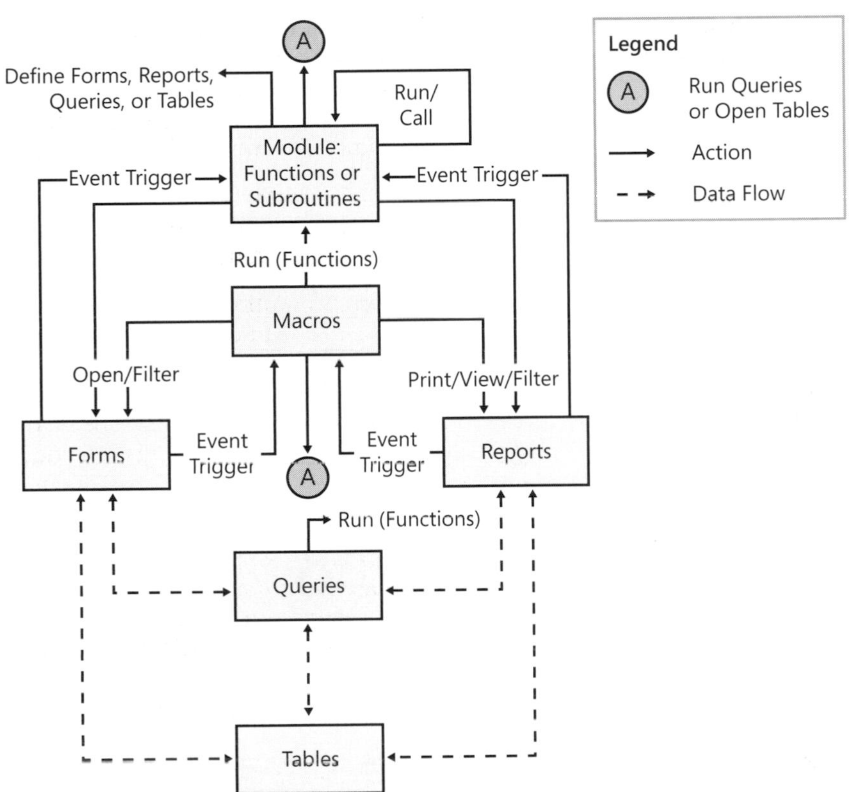


**Figure 3-1.** In an Access application, you can design queries to extract data from or update data in tables; you can build forms or reports on tables or queries, and you can write code in macros or modules to automate your application.

Events on forms and reports can trigger either macros or Visual Basic procedures. An event is any change in the state of an Access object. For example, you can write macros or Visual Basic procedures to respond to opening a form, closing a form, entering a new row on a form, or changing data either in the current record or in an individual control (an object on a form or report that contains data). You can even design a macro or a Visual Basic procedure that responds to the user pressing individual keys on the keyboard when entering data!

**For more information about using Visual Basic within Access, see Chapter 19, "Understanding Visual Basic Fundamentals," and Chapter 20, "Automating Your Application with Visual Basic."**

Using macros and modules, you can change the flow of your application; open, filter, and change data in forms and reports; run queries; and build new tables. Using Visual Basic, you can create, modify, and delete any Access object; manipulate data in your database row by row or column by column; and handle exceptional conditions. Using module code you can even call Windows application programming interface (API) routines to extend your application beyond the built-in capabilities of Access.

# Exploring a Desktop Database—Housing Reservations

Now that you know something about the major objects that make up an Access database, a good next step is to spend some time exploring the Housing Reservations database (Housing.accdb) that comes with this book. First, follow the instructions at the beginning of this book for installing the sample files on your hard drive. When you start Access 2007, it displays the Getting Started window shown in Figure 3-2.

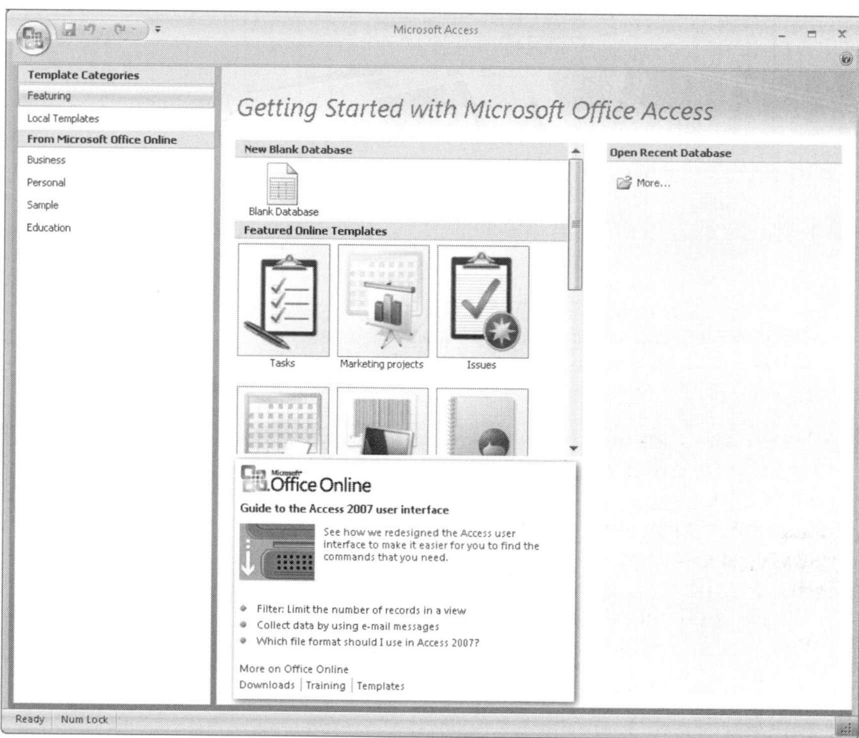


**Figure 3-2** Access 2007 displays the Getting Started window every time you start the program.

Click the More link under Open Recent Database on the right side of the window to see the Open dialog box shown in Figure 3-3. In the Open dialog box, select the file Housing.accdb from the folder in which you installed the sample databases, and then click Open. You can also double-click the file name to open the database. (If you haven't set options in Windows Explorer to show file name extensions for registered applications, you won't see the .accdb extension for your database files.)

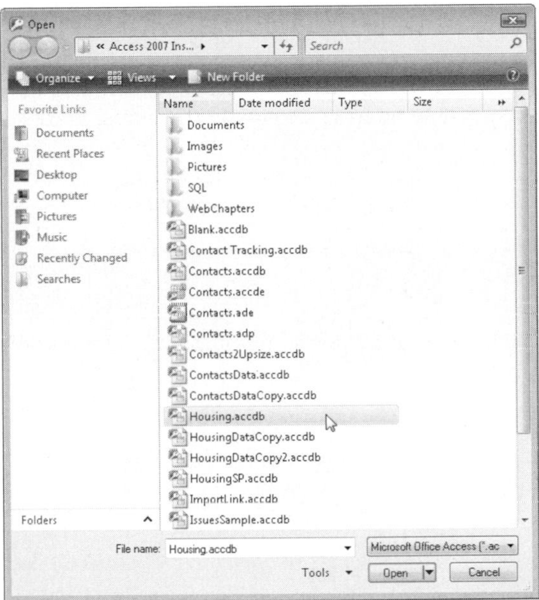


**Figure 3-3** Use the Open dialog box to locate the database that you want to open.

When you open the Housing Reservations application, it displays a Not Trusted dialog box if you have not followed the instructions in the previous chapter to define the location of the sample files as trusted. If this happens, click the Close button to close the dialog box. The application also briefly displays a copyright information notice and then displays a message box instructing you to open the frmSplash form. Click OK to dismiss this message box, and then Access puts the focus on the frmSplash form in the Navigation Pane. (You can open the frmSplash form if you want to run the application.) Your Access window should look similar to Figure 3-4.

For an existing database, the Navigation Pane is always the same width as it was when you last set it. The title bar of the window normally shows the name of the database that you have open. As you'll learn later in this book, you can set options in the database to change the title bar of the main Access window to show the name of your application instead of Microsoft Access—we modified the sample database to display the title Housing Reservations on the title bar.

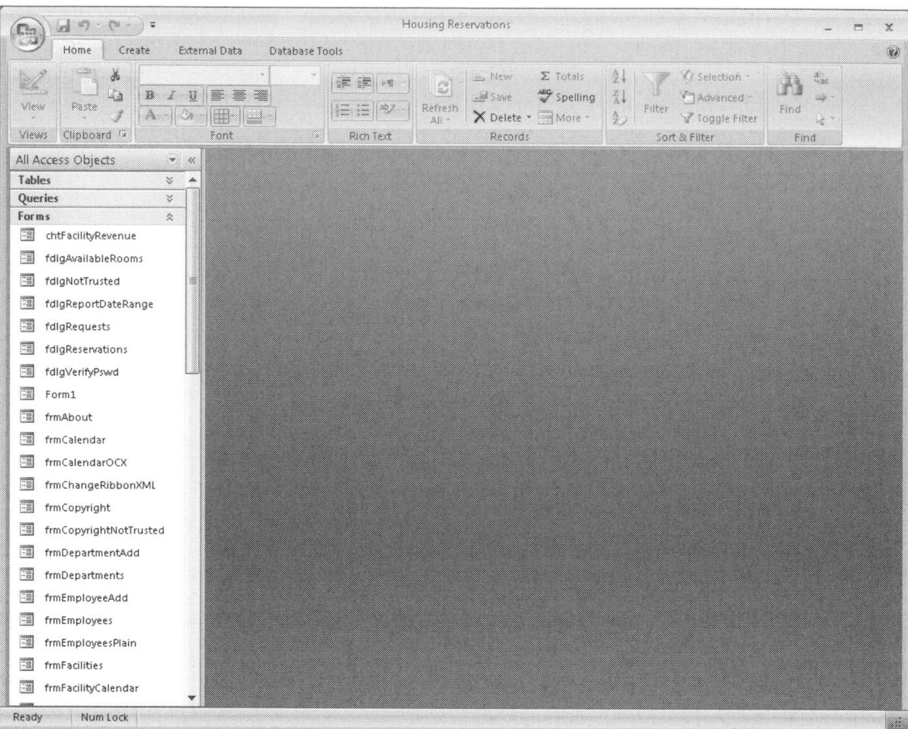


**Figure 3-4** The Navigation Pane displays the objects defined in the Housing Reservations sample database.

As we discussed in the previous chapter, the Ribbon has four main tabs that are displayed at all times. As you explore Access 2007, you'll see that the Ribbon provides several contextual tabs that appear and disappear as you work with specific database objects and areas of the program. These contextual tabs make available commands that are useful only within the context of the object that has the focus and that object's current view. For example, it wouldn't make sense to show you table design commands when you have a table open to display its data (Datasheet view). Likewise, you don't need datasheet commands when you have a query open in Design view. We'll explain the various contextual tabs in more detail as we explore the database objects and other areas of Access in the following chapters.

### Note

You can rest your mouse pointer on any command or option on the various Ribbon tabs for a second (without clicking the button), and Access displays a ScreenTip to help you discover the purpose of the button.

In the previous chapter, you learned that you can change how Access displays the list of objects in the database by using one of the built-in navigation categories (Object Type, Tables And Related Views, Created Date, and Modified Date) or by defining your own custom navigation category. You also learned that you can filter each navigation category to limit what group Access displays within each category so that you don't have to wade through a long list to find what you want.

In this chapter, we'll be exploring each of the types of objects in the Housing Reservations database, so click the Navigation Pane menu at the top of the Navigation Pane and click Object Type under Navigate To Category. Open the menu again and be sure that you have clicked All Access Objects under Filter By Group, as shown in Figure 3-5. Your Navigation Pane should now look similar to Figure 3-4. You can collapse an entire group of objects by clicking on the group's header bar. If you open the Navigation Pane menu, you can see the names of some custom groups we have defined under Navigate To Category to help organize your work. You'll learn how to work with groups later in this chapter.

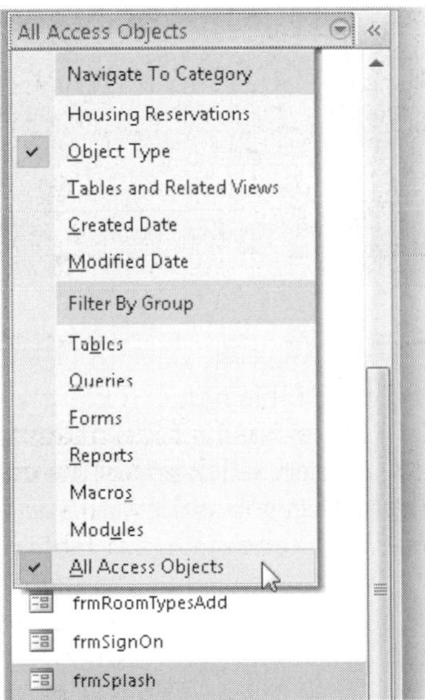


**Figure 3-5** Select Object Type under Navigate To Category and then All Access Objects under Filter By Group to see all objects organized in groups by object type.

## Tables

Click the menu bar at the top of the Navigation Pane and select Object Type under Navigate To Category. Open the menu again and select Tables under Filter By Group to display a list of tables available in the Housing Reservations database, as shown in Figure 3-6.

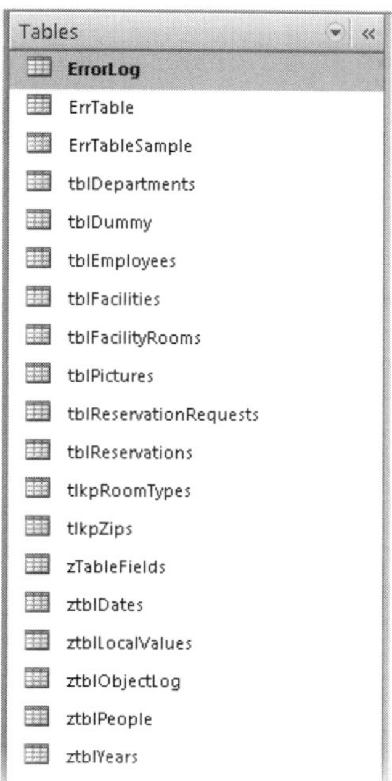


**Figure 3-6** After filtering the Object Type category in the Navigation Pane, you can see only the tables in the Housing Reservations database.



You can open a table in Datasheet view to see the data in the table by double-clicking the table name in the Navigation Pane; or you can open the table in Design view by holding down the Ctrl key and double-clicking the table name. If you right-click a table name, Access displays a shortcut menu, as shown in Figure 3-7, that lets you perform a number of handy operations on the item you selected. Click one of the commands on the shortcut menu, or click anywhere else in the Access window to dismiss the menu.

## INSIDE OUT Turning on Single-Click

If you want to make it easier to open objects from the Navigation Pane, you can right-click the menu bar at the top of the Navigation Pane and select Navigation Options on the shortcut menu. In the lower-right corner of the Navigation Options dialog box, select Single-Click under Open Objects With and click OK. The examples in this chapter assume you are using the default Double-Click setting.

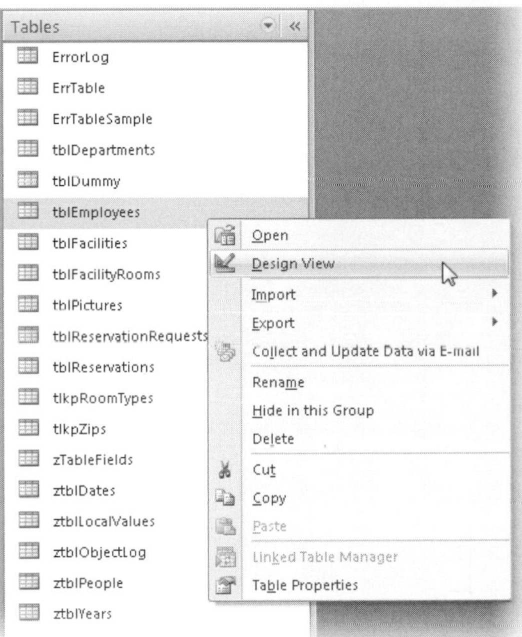


**Figure 3-7** You can access many commands from the shortcut menu for a table in the Navigation Pane.



## Table Window in Design View

When you want to change the definition of a table (the structure or design of a table, as opposed to the data in a table), you must open the Table window in Design view. With the Housing Reservations database open, right-click the tblEmployees table and select Design View from the shortcut menu; this opens the tblEmployees table in Design view, as shown in Figure 3-8. (Collapse the Navigation Pane to be able to see the entire width of the design area.) You'll learn about creating table definitions in Chapter 4, "Creating Your Database and Tables."

In Design view, each row in the top portion of the Table window defines a different field in the table. You can use the mouse to select any field that you want to modify. You can also use the Tab key to move from left to right across the screen, column to column, or Shift+Tab to move from right to left. Use the Up and Down Arrow keys to move from row to row in the field list. As you select a different row in the field list in the top portion of the window, you can see the property settings for the selected field in the bottom portion of the window. Press F6 to move between the field list and the field property settings portions of the Table window in Design view. Unlike previous versions of Access, pressing F6 again does not immediately move the focus back to the field list. If you press F6 repeatedly, the focus goes to the Navigation Pane, to the Ribbon, and then finally back to the field list.

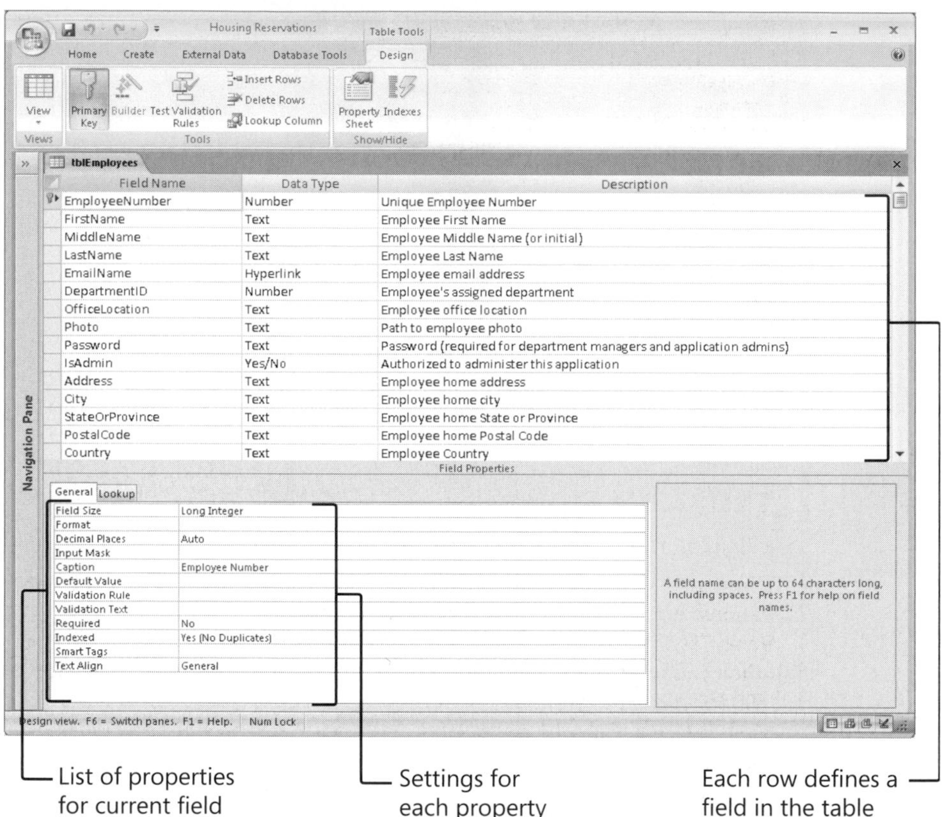


**Figure 3-8** Open a table in Design view to change its structure.

Access has many convenient features. Wherever you can choose from a limited list of valid values, Access provides a list box to assist you in selecting the proper value. For example, when you tab to the Data Type column in the field list, a small arrow appears at the right of the column. Click the arrow or press Alt+Down Arrow to see the list of valid data types, as shown in Figure 3-9.

You can open as many as 254 tables (fewer if you are limited by your computer's memory). If you have selected Overlapping Windows in the Access Options dialog box, you can minimize any of the windows to an icon along the bottom of the Access workspace window by clicking the Minimize button in the upper-right corner of the window. You can also maximize the window to fill the Access workspace to the right of the Navigation Pane by clicking the Maximize/Restore button in that same corner. If you don't see a window you want, you can select it from the list of active windows in the Manage Windows command in the Window group on the Home tab on the Ribbon to bring the window to the front. Click the Close command from the Control Box in the upper-left corner or click the window's Close button in the upper-right corner to close any window.

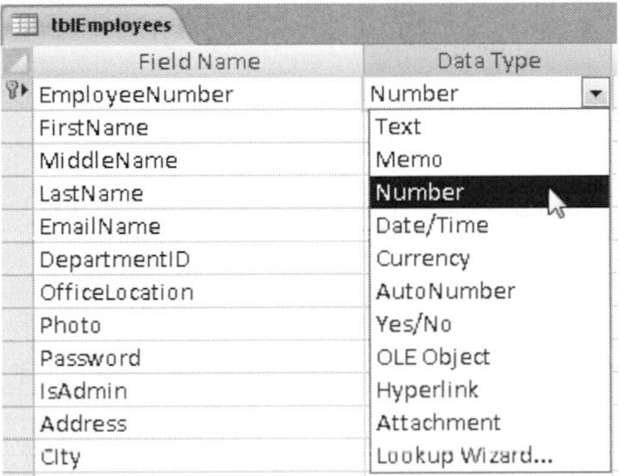


**Figure 3-9** The Data Type list box shows you the available data types.



## TROUBLESHOOTING

### Why can't I see the Maximize/Minimize buttons on my table?

If you are using the tabbed documents interface (the setting used in the Housing Reservations sample database), each open object has its own tab to the right of the Navigation Pane. This option is the default for new databases you create in Access 2007. However, when you open older database files created in earlier versions of Access, the Document Window Options setting in the Access Options dialog box defaults to Overlapping Windows. With the Tabbed Documents setting, there is no need to constantly minimize and maximize object windows to switch views because each open object has an individual tab at the top of the Access workspace (the area below the Ribbon and to the right of the Navigation Pane). Clicking on these object tabs enables you to easily switch among any open objects, so Access 2007 does not provide the Maximize/Minimize buttons. To set your database to Overlapping Windows or Tabbed Documents, see "Using the Single-Document vs. Multiple-Document Interface" on page 83.

## Table Window in Datasheet View

To view, change, insert, or delete data in a table, you can use the table's Datasheet view. A datasheet is a simple way to look at your data in rows and columns without any special formatting. You can open a table's Datasheet view by double-clicking the name of the table you want in the Navigation Pane or by right-clicking on the table name and selecting Open from the shortcut menu. When you open a table in Design view, such as the tblEmployees table shown in Figure 3-8, you can switch to the Datasheet view of this table, shown in Figure 3-10, by clicking the arrow in the Views group on the Ribbon and clicking Datasheet View from the list of available views. Likewise, when you're in Datasheet view, you can return to Design view by clicking the arrow in the Views group and clicking Design View from the available options. You can also switch views for the table by clicking the various view buttons on the status bar located in the lower-right corner of the Access window. You'll read more about working with data in Datasheet view in Chapter 7, "Creating and Working with Simple Queries."

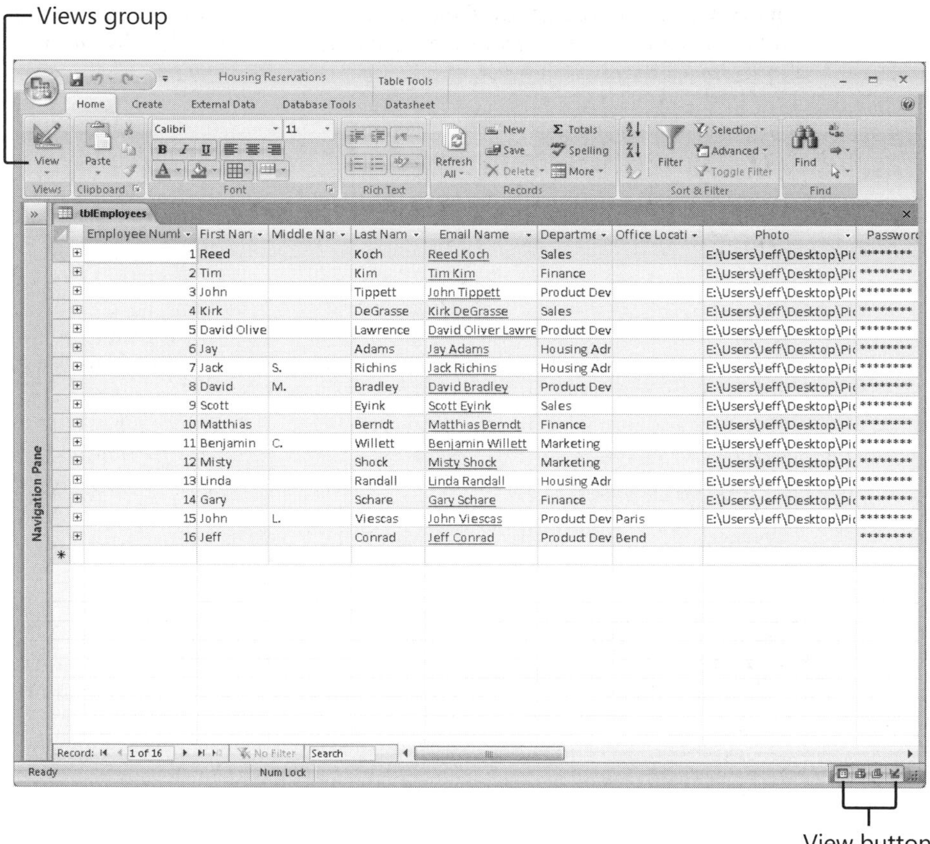


**Figure 3-10** Use the Views button on the Ribbon or the individual view buttons on the status bar to switch from Design to Datasheet view.

As in Design view, you can move from field to field in the Table window in Datasheet view by pressing Tab, and you can move up and down through the records using the arrow keys. You can also use the scroll bars along the bottom and on the right side of the window to move around in the table. To the left of the horizontal scroll bar, Access shows you the current record number and the total number of records in the currently selected set of data. You can select the record number with your mouse (or by pressing F5), type a new number, and then press Enter to go to that record. You can use the arrows on either side of this record number box to move up or down one record or to move to the first or last record in the table. You can start entering data in a new record by clicking the New (Blank) Record button on the right.

## Queries

You probably noticed that the Datasheet view of the tblEmployees table gave you all the fields and all the records in the table. But what if you want to see only the employee names and addresses? Or maybe you would like to see in one view information about employees and all their confirmed room reservations. To fill these needs, you can create a query. Open the Navigation Pane menu, click Object Type under Navigate To Category if it isn't already selected, and then click Queries under Filter By Group to display a list of queries available in the Housing Reservations database, as shown in Figure 3-11.

## TROUBLESHOOTING

### Why does my table have extra rows in the lower half of the sceen like a speadsheet?

You might notice in Figure 3-10 that there are extra rows beneath our existing records, and this grid very much resembles a spreadsheet. This is a departure from previous versions of Access that displayed only one row for each record in that table plus one for a new record. For tables in Datasheet view in Access 2007, the remainder of the space in the application window is filled with dummy rows that you cannot click into. In essence, these extra rows are simply placeholders for possible future records. It might be confusing to think of this grid as a spreadsheet because of its appearance, but you must remember that Access is not a spreadsheet. What you see is only a visual aid and does not denote actual records in the tables.



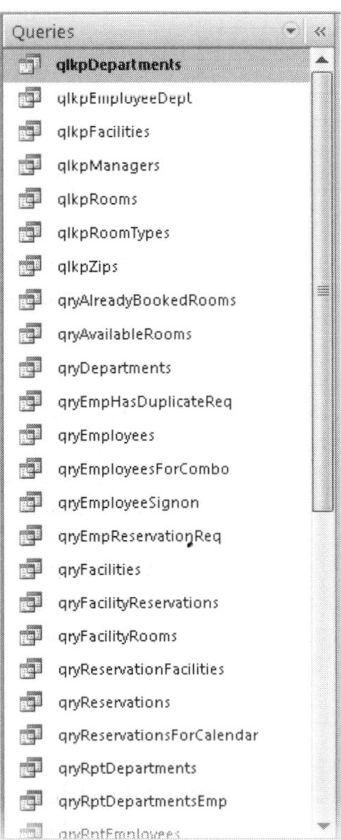


**Figure 3-11** When you filter object types by queries in the Navigation Pane, Access displays a list of only the queries in the Housing Reservations database.

You can open a query in Datasheet view by double-clicking the query name, or you can open it in Design view by clicking on the query to select it, and then pressing Ctrl+Enter. You can also right-click a query and click the Open or Design View command on the shortcut menu.

## Query Window in Design View

When you want to change the definition of a query (the structure or design, as opposed to the data represented in the query), you must open the query in Design view. Take a look at one of the more complex queries in the Housing Reservations query list by scrolling to the query named qryFacilityReservations. Select the query and then press Ctrl+Enter to display the query in Design view, as shown in Figure 3-12. Collapse the Navigation Pane to see more of the width of the query design.

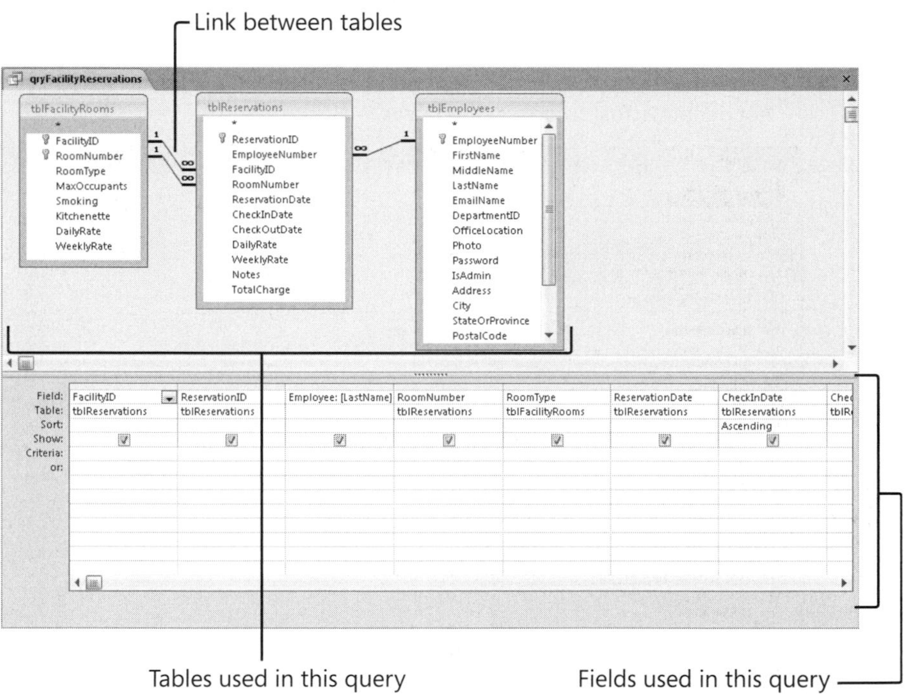


**Figure 3-12** The qryFacilityReservations query in Design view shows data from three tables being linked.

In the upper part of a Query window in Design view, you see the field lists of the tables or other queries that this query uses. The lines connecting the field lists show how Access links the tables to solve your query. If you define relationships between two tables in your database design, Access draws these lines automatically when you include both tables in a query design. See Chapter 4 for details. You can also define relationships when you build the query by dragging a field from one field list and dropping it on another field list.

In the lower part of the Query window, you see the design grid. The design grid shows fields that Access uses in this query, the tables or queries from which the fields come (when you select Table Names in the Show/Hide group on the Ribbon's Design tab), any sorting criteria, whether fields show up in the result, and any selection criteria for the fields. You can use the horizontal scroll bar to bring other fields in this query into view. As in the Design view of tables, you can use F6 to move between the upper and lower portions of the Query window, but the F6 key also cycles through the Query window, the Navigation Pane, and the Ribbon.

You can learn how to build this type of complex multiple-table query in Chapter 8, "Building Complex Queries." You can find this query used in the Housing Reservations database as the source of data for the fsubFacilityReservations form.

## Query Window in Datasheet View

On the Design or Home tab on the Ribbon, click the View button to run the query and see the query results in Datasheet view, as shown in Figure 3-13. You can also right-click the query tab and click Datasheet View on the shortcut menu.

qryFacilityReservations

| Facility | Reservation | Employee | Room | Type | Reservation | Chec |
|---|---|---|---|---|---|---|
| South Campus Housing C | 7 | Koch, Reed | 501 | 2BR Suite - 1 King, 2 Queen, Kitchenette | 2/22/2007 | 2, |
| Main Campus Housing A | 1 | Richins, Jack S. | 810 | Studio - Queen Sofa | 2/6/2007 | |
| North Satellite Housing D | 3 | Lawrence, Davi | 305 | 1BR Suite - 2 Queen Beds | 2/13/2007 | 3, |
| Main Campus Housing B | 2 | Richins, Jack S. | 111 | 2BR Suite - 1 King, 2 Queen, Kitchenette | 2/10/2007 | 3, |
| Main Campus Housing A | 12 | Tippett, John | 207 | Room - King bed | 3/14/2007 | 3, |
| Main Campus Housing B | 11 | Lawrence, Davi | 301 | 1BR Suite - 2 Queen Beds | 3/13/2007 | 3, |
| Main Campus Housing B | 5 | Tippett, John | 214 | Room - 2 Queen beds | 2/15/2007 | 3, |
| Main Campus Housing A | 6 | Berndt, Matthi | 902 | 2BR Suite - 1 King, 2 Queen beds | 2/19/2007 | |
| Main Campus Housing A | 13 | Bradley, David | 111 | 1BR Suite - 1 King Bed, Kitchenette | 3/23/2007 | |
| Main Campus Housing B | 15 | Adams, Jay | 206 | 1BR Suite - 1 King Bed, Kitchenette | 3/27/2007 | |
| Main Campus Housing A | 4 | Tippett, John | 502 | 2BR Suite - 1 King, 2 Queen beds | 2/14/2007 | 4, |
| Main Campus Housing A | 8 | Bradley, David | 509 | Room - 2 Queen beds | 2/25/2007 | 4, |
| Main Campus Housing B | 9 | Kim, Tim | 504 | 1BR Suite - 1 King Bed | 2/25/2007 | 4, |
| Main Campus Housing A | 14 | Richins, Jack S. | 708 | Studio - Queen Sofa, Kitchenette | 3/24/2007 | 4, |
| South Campus Housing C | 17 | DeGrasse, Kirk | 101 | 2BR Suite - 1 King, 2 Queen, Kitchenette | 4/2/2007 | |
| Main Campus Housing A | 10 | Tippett, John | 707 | Room - King bed | 3/8/2007 | |
| South Campus Housing C | 22 | Bradley, David | 103 | 1BR Suite - 1 King Bed | 4/24/2007 | |
| Main Campus Housing A | 20 | Lawrence, Davi | 309 | Room - 2 Queen beds | 4/9/2007 | |
| North Satellite Housing D | 21 | Bradley, David | 402 | 1BR Suite - 1 King Bed, Kitchenette | 4/12/2007 | |
| South Campus Housing C | 16 | Richins, Jack S. | 111 | Studio - Queen Sofa | 3/27/2007 | 5, |
| Main Campus Housing A | 18 | Bradley, David | 702 | 2BR Suite - 1 King, 2 Queen beds | 4/6/2007 | 5, |
| Main Campus Housing B | 19 | Lawrence, Davi | 610 | 2BR Suite - 1 King, 2 Queen, Kitchenette | 4/8/2007 | 5, |
| Main Campus Housing A | 24 | Tippett, John | 207 | Room - King bed | 5/1/2007 | 5, |
| Main Campus Housing B | 28 | Bradley, David | 403 | 2BR Suite - 1 King, 2 Queen beds | 5/7/2007 | 5, |
| Main Campus Housing A | 27 | Willett, Benjar | 505 | Room - King bed | 5/6/2007 | |
| Main Campus Housing B | 30 | Randall, Linda | 103 | 2BR Suite - 1 King, 2 Queen beds | 5/15/2007 | |

Record: 1 of 58 No Filter Search

**Figure 3-13** The Datasheet view of the qryFacilityReservations query shows you fields from three related tables.

The Query window in Datasheet view is similar to a Table window in Datasheet view. Even though the fields in the query datasheet shown in Figure 3-13 are from three different tables, you can work with the fields as if they were in a single table. If you're designing an Access application for other users, you can use queries to hide much of the complexity of the database and make the application simpler to use. Depending on how you designed the query, you might also be able to update some of the data in the underlying tables simply by typing new values in the Query window as you would in a Table window in Datasheet view.

## Forms

Datasheets are useful for viewing and changing data in your database, but they're not particularly attractive or simple to use. If you want to format your data in a special way or automate how your data is used and updated, you need to use a form. Forms provide a number of important capabilities.

- You can control and enhance the way your data looks on the screen. For example, you can add color and shading or add number formats. You can add controls such as list boxes and check boxes. You can display ActiveX objects such as pictures and graphs directly on the form. And you can calculate and display values based on data in a table or a query.
- You can perform extensive editing of data using macros or Visual Basic procedures.
- You can link multiple forms or reports by using macros or Visual Basic procedures that are run from buttons on a form.

Click the menu bar at the top of the Navigation Pane, click Object Type under Navigate To Category, and then click Forms under Filter By Group to display a list of forms available in the Housing Reservations database, as shown in Figure 3-14.

You can open a form in Form view by double-clicking the form name in the Navigation Pane. You can also open the form in Design view by clicking the form to highlight it, and then pressing Ctrl+Enter. Finally, you can right-click a form name and click a command on the shortcut menu. To create a new form, use the commands in the Forms group of the Create tab on the Ribbon.



### Form Window in Design View

When you want to change the definition of a form (the structure or design, as opposed to the data represented in the form), you generally must open the form in Design view. As you'll learn in Chapter 12, "Customizing a Form," you can also set a form property to allow you to make changes in Layout view while you are designing the form. Take a look at the frmEmployeesPlain form in the Housing Reservations database. To open the form, scroll through the list of forms in the Navigation Pane to find the frmEmployeesPlain form, click the form to select it, then press Ctrl+Enter. This form, shown in Figure 3-15, is designed to display all data from the tblEmployees table. Don't worry if what you see on your screen doesn't exactly match Figure 3-15. In this figure, we opened the field list on the right so that you can see some of the main features of the Form window in Design view.

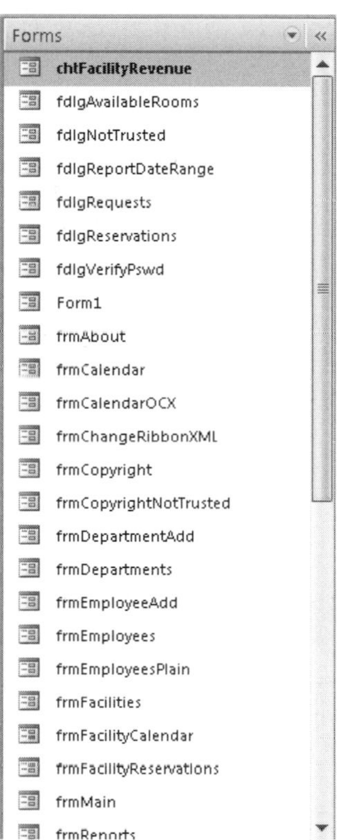


**Figure 3-14** When you filter Object Type by Forms, Access displays a list of only the forms in the Housing Reservations database.

The large window in the center is the form design window where you create the design of the form. When you first open this form in Design view, you should see the Form Design Tools collection of two contextual tabs, Design and Arrange, on the Ribbon just to the right of Database Tools. These tabs are the action centers of form design–you'll use the tools here to add and arrange the design elements of your form.

On the right side of the window shown in Figure 3-15, you can see a field list for this form. This form gets its information from a query called qryEmployees that selects all the fields in the tblEmployees table and then sorts the rows by last name and first name. If you don't see the field list, click the Add Existing Fields command in the Tools group of the Design contextual tab. You can resize this window by clicking on the far left edge of the box and dragging it to a new width toward the left side of the screen. When your mouse pointer is positioned over the title bar, it changes to cross arrows. Click the title bar and drag it to the left and down to undock the window from the right side and position it where you would like. When you undock the Field List window, it becomes a window that floats on top of the design area. When you read about form design in Chapter 11, "Building a Form," you'll see that you can drag a field from the field list to place a control on the form that displays the contents of the field.

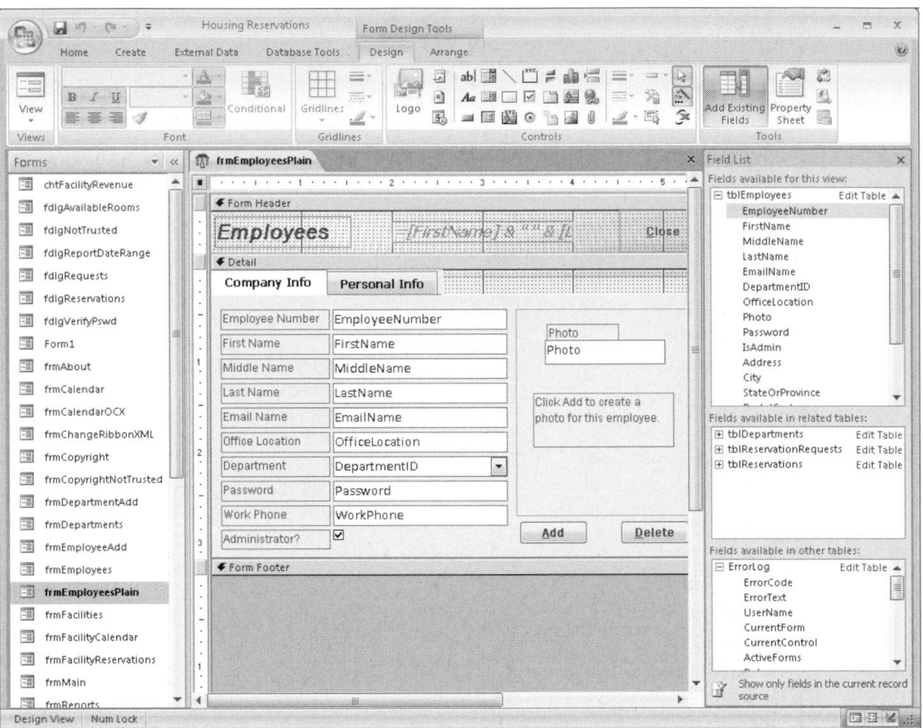


**Figure 3-15** When you open the frmEmployeesPlain form in Design view, you can modify its design.

After you place all the controls on a form, you might want to customize some of them. You do this by opening the property sheet displayed in Figure 3-16. To see the property sheet, click the Property Sheet button in the Tools group of the Design tab. In Figure 3-16 we collapsed the Navigation Pane to show more of the property sheet.

The property sheet always shows the property values for the control selected in the form design. (The property sheet can also display the properties for the form or any section on the form.) Click the tabs at the top of the property sheet to display all properties or to display only properties for formats, data, or events. In the example shown in Figure 3-16, we clicked the text box named EmployeeNumber, near the top of the form, to select it. If you click this text box and then scroll down the list of properties for this text box, you can see the wide range of properties you can set to customize this control. As you learn to build applications using Access, you'll soon discover that you can customize the way your application works by simply setting form and control properties—you don't have to write any code.

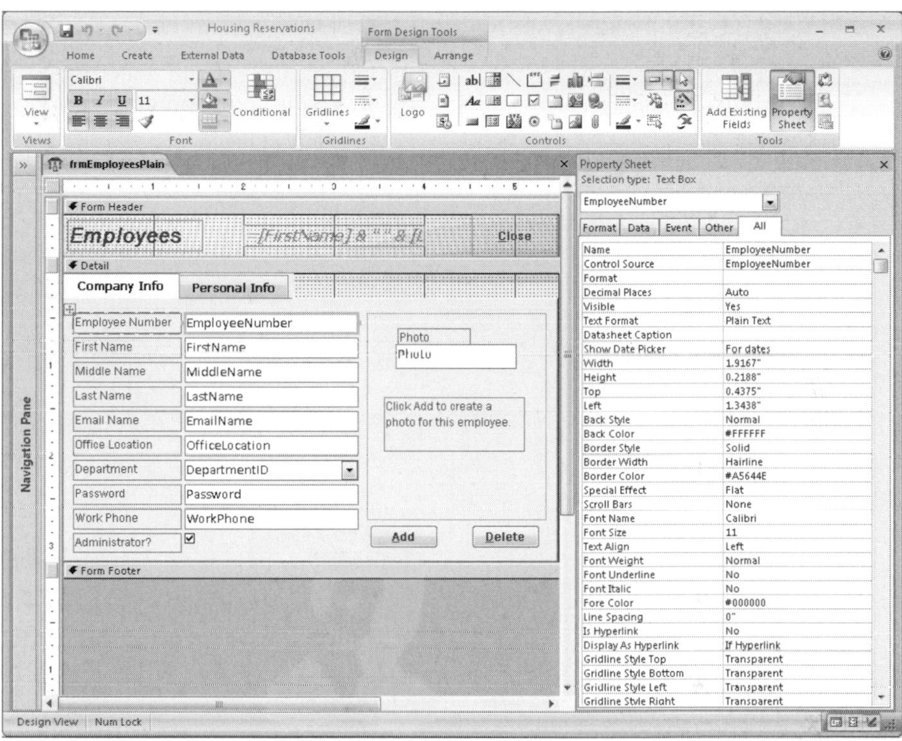


**Figure 3-16** The property sheet lets you set individual properties for a form, form sections, or controls on the form.

If you scroll to the bottom of the property list, or click the Event tab, you'll see a number of properties that you can set to define the macros or Visual Basic procedures that Access runs whenever the associated event occurs on this control. For example, you can use the Before Update event property to define a macro or procedure that performs additional validation before Access saves any changes typed in this control. You can use the On Click or On Dbl Click event properties to perform actions when the user clicks the control. If you need to, you can even look at every individual character the user types in a control with the On Key event properties. As you'll discover later, Access provides a rich set of events that you can detect for the form and for each control on the form.

You might have noticed that Access made available all the commands and options in the Font group of the Design tab when you selected the EmployeeNumber control. When you select a text box on a form in Design view, Access enables the list boxes in this group to make it easy to select a font and font size, and it also enables buttons that let you set the Bold, Italic, and Underline properties. Underneath these buttons are three buttons that let you set text alignment: Align Text Left, Center, and Align Text Right. You can also set the font and fill colors using buttons in this group.

## Form Window in Layout View

Access 2007 introduces a new view for forms called Layout view. If you have the frmEmployeesPlain form open in Design view from the previous section, you can switch to Layout view by right-clicking the frmEmployeesPlain tab and clicking Layout View on the shortcut menu. You should now see the form in Layout view, as shown in Figure 3-17. This unique view for forms gives the developer a fast and easy way to create and modify form designs.

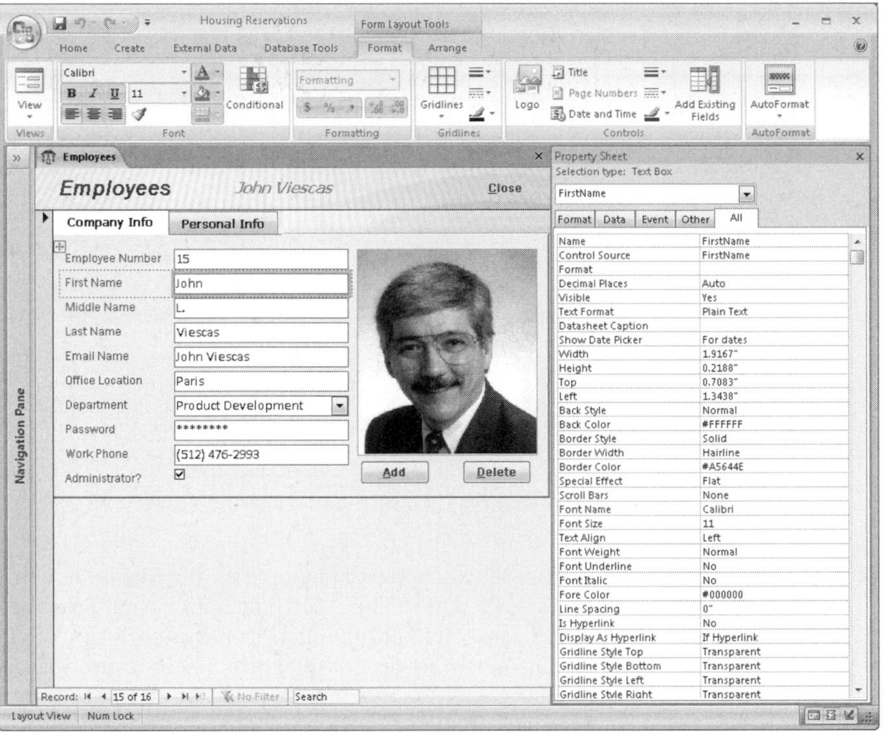


**Figure 3-17** Layout view lets you see your data and also modify the design of the form.

Unlike Design view, Layout view enables you to work with the various control elements and form sections using existing live data. If, for example, you need to resize a text box to fit the available data, you do not have to continually switch back and forth between Form and Design view to see if your size change works effectively–you actually see data in the text box while resizing the control. This new What-You-See-Is-What-You-Get (*WYSIWYG*) form-authoring view provides the best of both worlds by combining the ability to change the structure of the data entry form at the same time you're accessing actual data.

In Layout view, if you have grouped a set of controls you can move them around the form design grid together to maintain their proximity and orientation to one another. In this sample form, we grouped all the controls in the first column in a stacked layout.

In Figure 3-18, you can see that we're dragging the Email Name field down below the Office Location field. A horizontal bar designates where Access will place the control after you release the mouse button. Because these controls are grouped, Access places the Email Name field and its label below the Office Location field and aligns them perfectly.

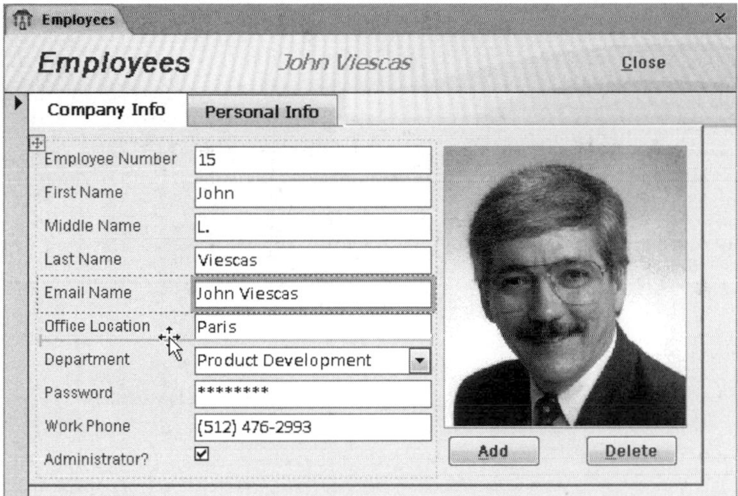


**Figure 3-18** You can move a control within a group in Layout view, and Access keeps them perfectly aligned.

## Form Window in Form View

To view, change, insert, or delete data via a form, you can use Form view. Depending on how you've designed the form, you can work with your data in an attractive and clear context, have the form validate the information you enter, or use the form to trigger other forms or reports based on actions you take while viewing the form. You can open a form in Form view by right-clicking the form's name in the Navigation Pane and clicking Open on the shortcut menu. If you still have the frmEmployeesPlain form open in Layout view from the previous section, you can go directly to Form view by clicking the arrow in the Views group and then clicking Form View.

Figure 3-19 shows a complex form that brings together data from three tables and loads the related employee picture from a file on your hard drive onto a screen that's easy to use and understand. This form includes all the fields from the tblEmployees table. You can tab or use the arrow keys to move through the fields. You can click the Personal Info tab to see additional information about the current employee. You can experiment with filtering by selection to see how easy it is to select only the records you want to see. For example, you can click in the Department field, select the department name, click the Selection button in the Sort & Filter group on the Home tab, and then click Equals "Selected Department" (where "Selected Department" is the department name you selected) to display records only for the current department.

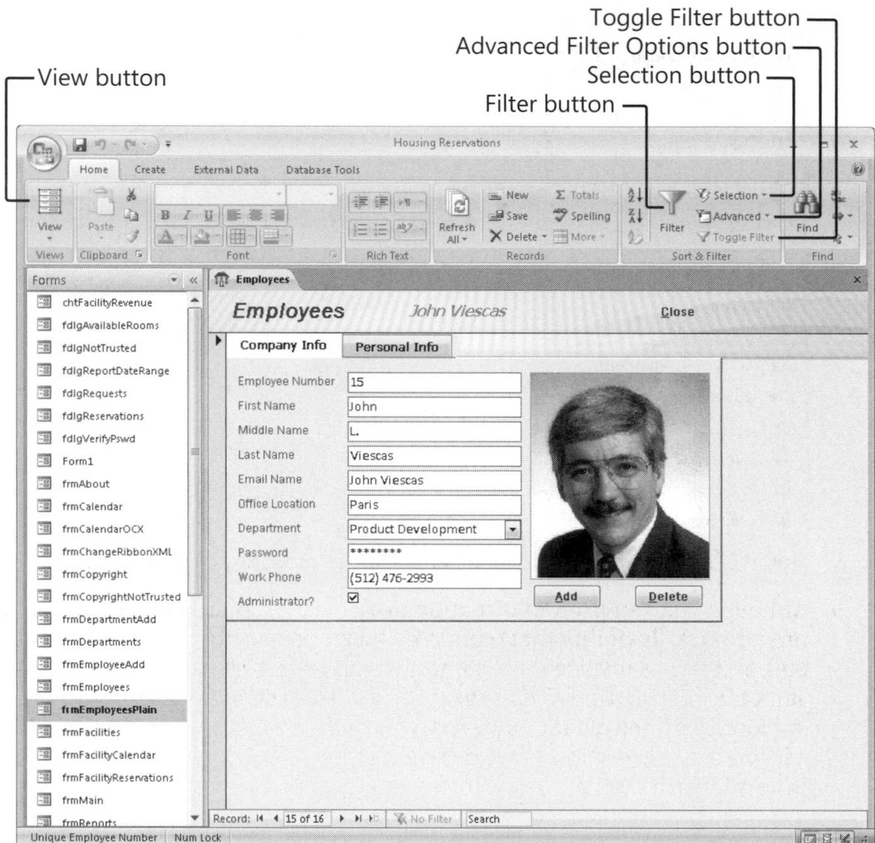


**Figure 3-19** The frmEmployeesPlain form in Form view lets you view and edit employee data.

There are four other ways to look at a form: Datasheet view, PivotTable view, PivotChart view, and Print Preview. You can select the Datasheet view by clicking the arrow in the Views group and clicking Datasheet View to see all the fields in the form arranged in a datasheet—similar to a datasheet for a table or a query. When a form has been designed to display data in a PivotTable (similar to a spreadsheet) or graphed in a PivotChart, you can also select these views with the View button. You can click the Microsoft Office Button, move your mouse pointer to Print, and then click Print Preview on the submenu to see what the form will look like on a printed page. You'll read more about Print Preview in the next section.

## Reports

If your primary need is to print data, you should use a report. Click the menu bar at the top of the Navigation Pane to open the Navigation Pane menu and click Object Type under Navigate To Category. Then open the menu again and click the Reports option under Filter By Group to display a list of reports available in the Housing Reservations database, as shown in Figure 3-20.

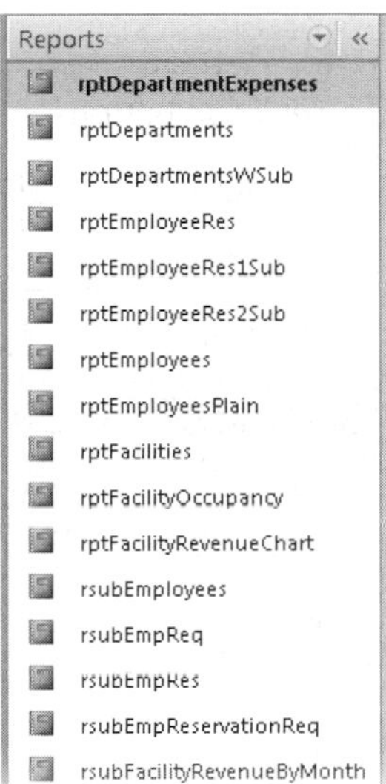


**Figure 3-20** You can filter the Navigation Pane to show only a list of the reports in your database.



Although you can print information in a datasheet or a form, neither of these formats provides the flexibility that reports do when you need to produce complex printed output (such as invoices or summaries) that might include many calculations and subtotals. Formatting in datasheets is limited to sizing the rows and columns, specifying fonts, and setting the colors and gridline effects. You can do a lot of formatting in a form, but because forms are designed primarily for viewing and entering data on the screen, they are not suited for extensive calculations, grouping of data, or multiple totals and subtotals in print.

## Report Window in Design View

When you want to change the definition of a report, you must open the report in Design view. In the report list for Housing Reservations, click on the rptEmployeesPlain report to select it, and then press Ctrl+Enter to see the design for the report, as shown in Figure 3-21. Don't worry if what you see on your screen doesn't exactly match Figure 3-21. We clicked the Add Existing Fields command on the Design tab under Report Design Tools to display the Field List window.

The large window in the center is where you create the design of the report. This report is designed to display all the information about employees by department. Notice that Design view for reports is similar to Design view for forms. (For comparison, see Figure 3-15.) Reports provide additional flexibility, allowing you to group items and to total them (either across or down). You can also define header and footer information for the entire report, for each page, and for each subgroup on the report. When you first open this report in Design view, you should see three new contextual tabs appear on the Ribbon just to the right of Database Tools under Report Design Tools: Design, Arrange, and Page Setup. These contextual tabs are the action centers of report design–you'll use the tools here to add the design elements you want.

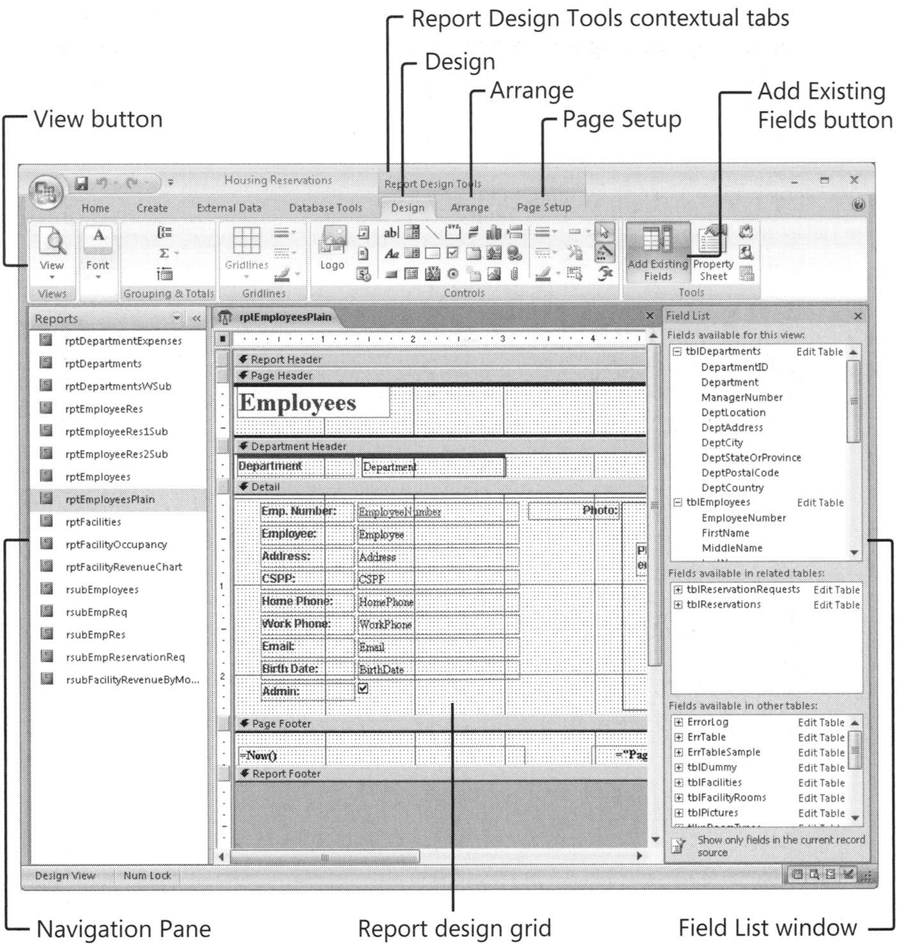


**Figure 3-21** Open the rptEmployeesPlain report in Design view to modify its design.

On the right side of the window shown in Figure 3-21, you can see the field list for this report. This list shows all the fields returned by the record source for the report, qryRptEmployees—all the fields from the tblEmployees table and related fields from the tblDepartments table. If you don't see the field list, click the Add Existing Fields command in the Tools group on the Design contextual tab. You can resize this window by clicking on the far left edge and dragging it to a new width toward the left side of the screen. When your mouse pointer is positioned over the title bar, it changes to cross arrows. Click the title bar and drag it to the left and down to undock the window from the right side and position it where you would like. When you undock the Field List window, it becomes a window that floats on top of the design area. When you read about report design in Chapter 15, "Constructing a Report," you'll see that you can drag a field from the field list to place a control on the report that displays the contents of the field.

After you place all the controls on a report, you might want to customize some of them. Do this by opening the property sheet, which you can see on the right side of the screen in Figure 3-22. To see the property sheet, click the Property Sheet command in the Tools group of the Design tab. In Figure 3-22 we collapsed the Navigation Pane so you can see more of the property sheet.

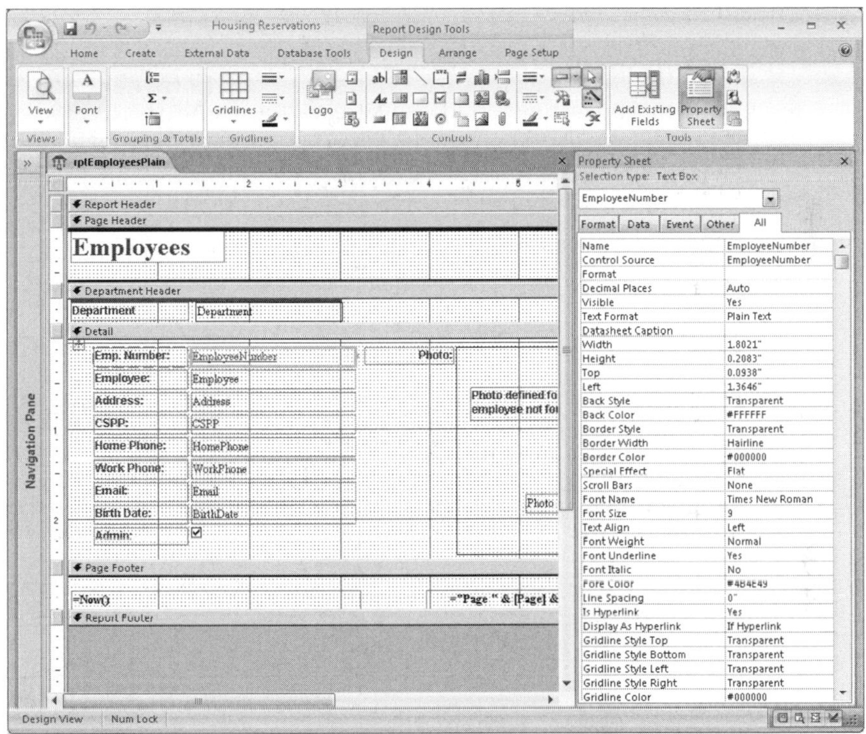


**Figure 3-22** The property sheet lets you set individual properties for a report, report sections, or controls on the report.

The property sheet always shows the property settings for the control selected in the Report window. (The Property Sheet pane can also display the properties for the entire report or any section on the report.) In the example shown in Figure 3-22, we clicked the text box named EmployeeNumber to select it. If you click this text box, you can see that Access displays the EmployeeNumber field from the tblEmployees table as the control source (input data) for this control. You can also specify complex formulas that calculate additional data for report controls.

You might have noticed that Access made available some additional commands and options in the Font group of the Design tab when you selected the EmployeeNumber control. When you select a text box in a report in Design view, Access enables list boxes in the Font group that make it easy to select a font and font size. Access also enables buttons that let you set the Bold, Italic, and Underline properties. Underneath these buttons are three buttons that set text alignment: Align Text Left, Center, and Align Text Right. You can also set font and fill colors using buttons in this group.

Reports can be even more complex than forms, but building a simple report is really quite easy. Access provides report wizards that you can use to automatically generate a number of standard report layouts based on the table or query you choose. You'll find it simple to customize a report to suit your needs after the report wizard has done most of the hard work. You'll learn how to customize a report in Chapter 15 and Chapter 16, "Advanced Report Design."

## Report Window in Print Preview

To see what the finished report looks like, click the arrow in the Views group and then click Print Preview when you're in the Report window in Design view. You can also right-click the report name in the Navigation Pane and then click Print Preview on the shortcut menu. Figure 3-23 shows a report in Print Preview.

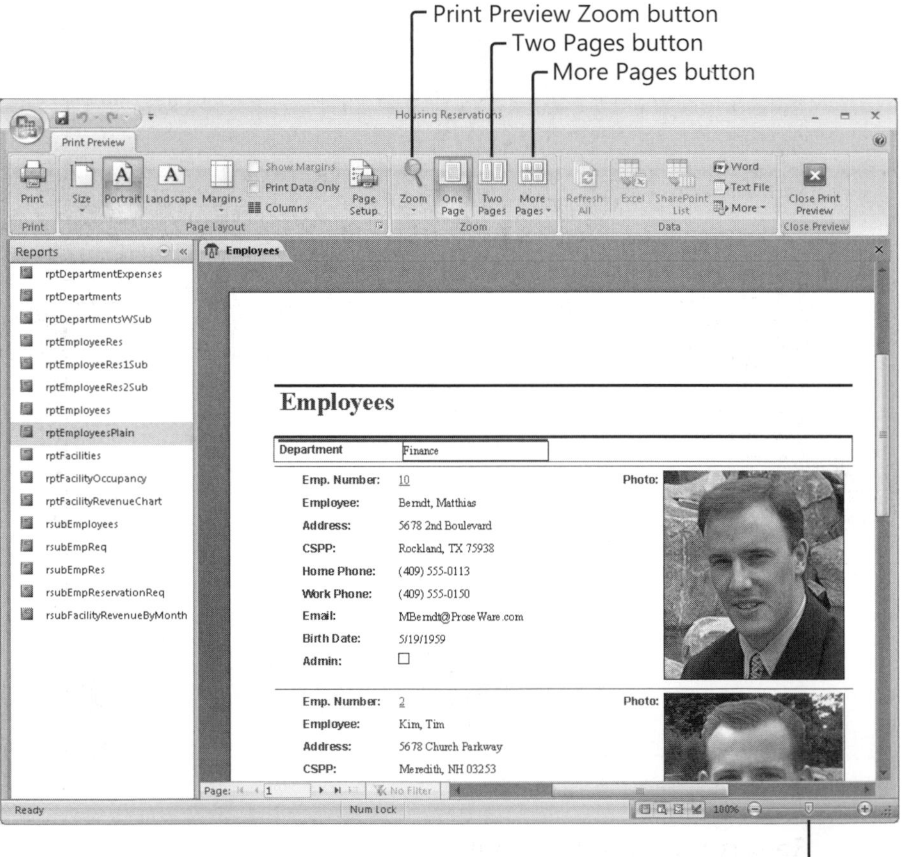


**Figure 3-23** When you open a report in Print Preview, Access shows you how the report will look when you print it.

Access initially shows you the upper-left corner of the report. To see the report centered in full-page view in Print Preview, click the Zoom control in the lower-right corner of the status bar where it says 100%. Clicking that button automatically adjusts the zoom level percent so that you can see a full page of the report. To see two pages side-by-side, click the Two Pages button in the Zoom group of the Print Preview contextual tab. This gives you a reduced picture of two pages, as shown in Figure 3-24, and an overall idea of how Access arranges major areas of data on the report. Unless you have a large monitor, however, you won't be able to read the data. Click the More Pages button and then click an option (Four Pages, Eight Pages, or Twelve Pages) to see more than two pages. When you move the mouse pointer over the window in Print Preview, the pointer changes to a magnifying glass icon. To zoom in, click over an area that you want to see more closely. You can then use the scroll bars to move around in the magnified report. Use the Zoom control on the status bar to magnify or shrink your view. Access also provides several output options such as Word or Excel in the Data group of the Print Preview tab.

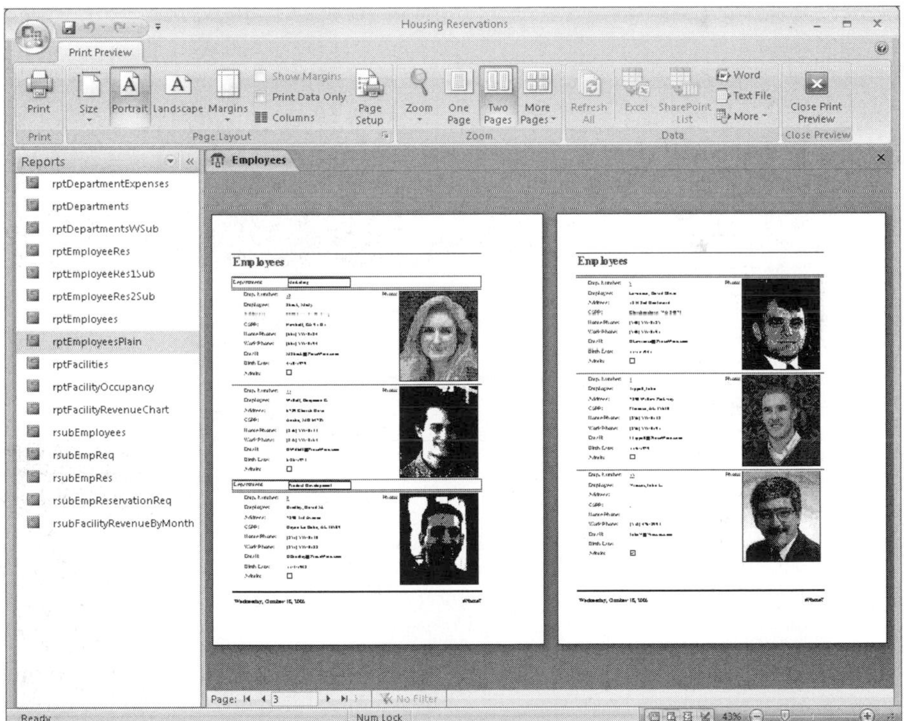


**Figure 3-24** Click the Two Pages button to see two pages side-by-side in Print Preview.

## Report Window in Layout View

Access 2007 introduces a new view for reports called Layout view. This unique view for reports gives the developer a fast and easy way to create and modify report designs.

Unlike Design view, Layout view enables you to work with the various control elements and report sections using existing live data. Similar to Layout view for forms, this new WYSIWYG report-authoring view provides the best of both worlds by combining the ability to change the structure of the report at the same time you're accessing the data.

To open the rptEmployeesPlain in Layout view, find the report in the Navigation Pane, right-click the report name, and click Layout View on the shortcut menu. Figure 3-25 shows the report in Layout view. In Figure 3-25 we collapsed the Navigation Pane so you can see more of the report design grid.

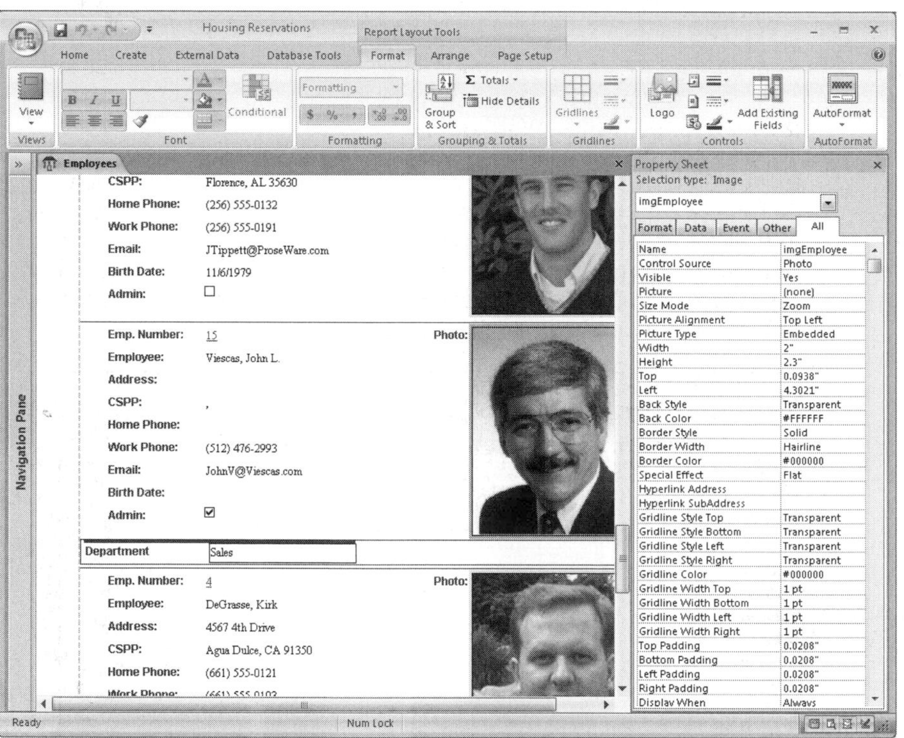


**Figure 3-25** Similar to Layout view for forms, Layout view in reports lets you adjust design elements while looking at the data from your database.

Just like Layout view for forms, if you have grouped a set of controls, you can move them around the report grid together to maintain their proximity and orientation to one another. In Figure 3-26, you can see that we're dragging the Birth Date field above the Email field. A horizontal bar designates where Access will place the control after you release the mouse button. Because these controls are grouped, Access places the Birth Date field and its label above the Email field. The two controls swap places and align perfectly.

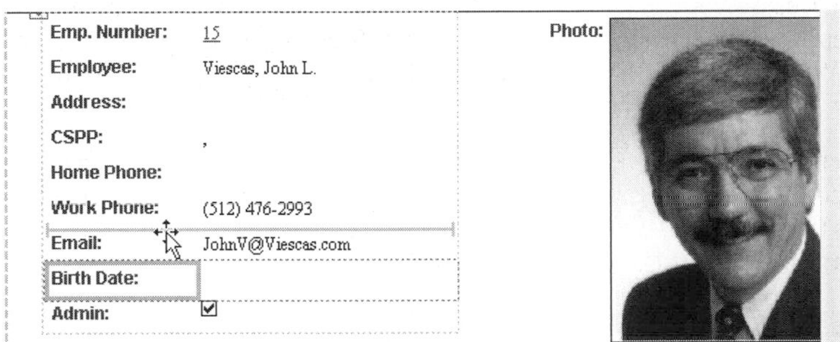


**Figure 3-26** Access makes it easy to move controls around within a group in Layout view.

## Report Window in Report View

In addition to Layout view, Access 2007 includes another new view for reports called Report view, an interactive view for reports that can respond to control events, much like data entry forms. If you have the rptEmployeesPlain report open in Layout view from the previous section, you can switch to Report view by right-clicking the Employees tab and clicking Report View on the shortcut menu. You should now see the report in Report view, as shown in Figure 3-27.

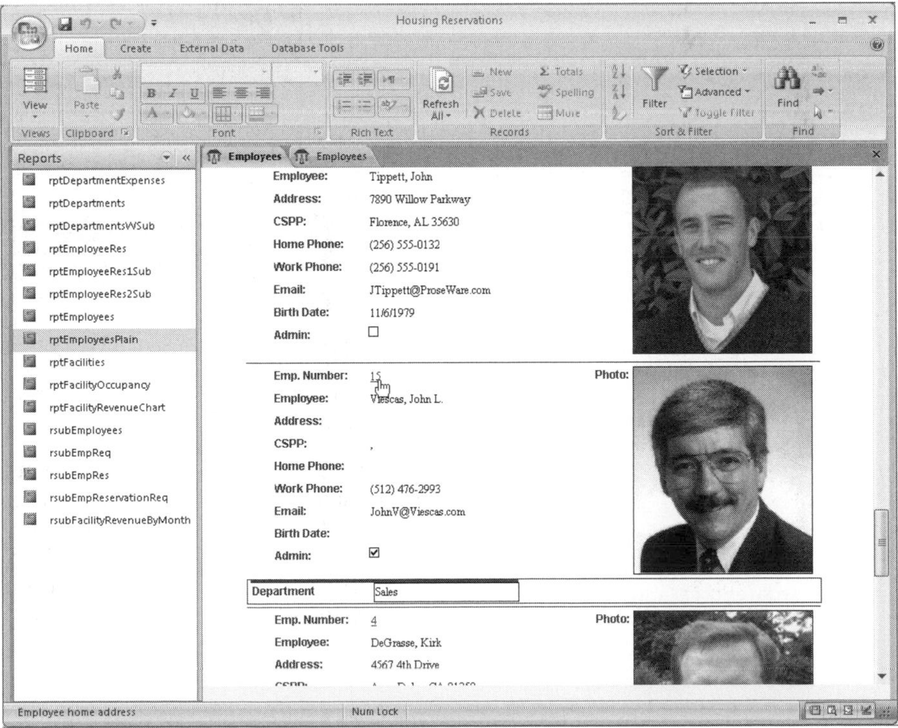


**Figure 3-27** When a report is in Report view, you can program controls to respond to mouse clicks to open a related form.

Chapter 3

Previous versions of Access treat reports on screen as static. After you open a report on the screen, you can only view the report or print it. Report view in Access 2007 gives you the ability to interact with the report through filters to drill down to specific records and then print only this smaller group of records. You can include command buttons on your reports with Access 2007 and program the buttons to respond to a mouse click in Report view. In the new Report view, you can designate controls that respond to events as hyperlinks to provide a visual cue that an event occurs when clicking that control. In Figure 3-27, for example, observe that the Employee Number field looks like a hyperlink with a blue line underneath the data. (In Figure 3-27 we have scrolled down the records to show John's information.) Clicking the Employee Number field opens the frmEmployeesPlain form to display all information for that specific employee so that you can make any necessary changes. After closing the form and returning to the report, click the Refresh All command in the Records group of the Home tab on the Ribbon to see any changes you made to the data using the form reflected in the report. In Figure 3-27 you can see that the frmEmployeesPlain form opens on a new tab because we are using the tabbed interface.

Close the Form window and the Report window to return to the Navigation Pane.



## Macros

You can make working with your data within forms and reports much easier by triggering a macro action. Office Access 2007 provides more than 70 actions that you can include in a macro. They perform tasks such as opening tables and forms, running queries, running other macros, selecting options from menus, and sizing open windows. You can also group multiple actions in a macro and specify conditions that determine when each set of actions will or will not be executed by Access.

Open the Navigation Pane menu and make sure Object Type is selected under Navigate To Category. Then open the menu again and click Macros under Filter By Group to display a list of macros available in the Housing Reservations database, as shown in Figure 3-28. You can run a macro by right-clicking the macro name in the Navigation Pane and clicking Run on the shortcut menu. To open a macro in Design view, right-click the macro name and click Design View on the shortcut menu. To create a brand new macro, click the New Object Macro button in the Other group of the Create tab on the Ribbon.

Macros are a great way to learn about the basics of responding to events and automating actions in an Access database. However, for any application that you intend to distribute to others, you should use Visual Basic to handle events and automate actions. Nearly all the sample databases use Visual Basic exclusively. You can take a look at the design of a macro example in the Housing Reservations database by selecting the SampleMacro macro in the Navigation Pane, and then pressing Ctrl+Enter. Access opens the Macro window in Design view, as shown in Figure 3-29.

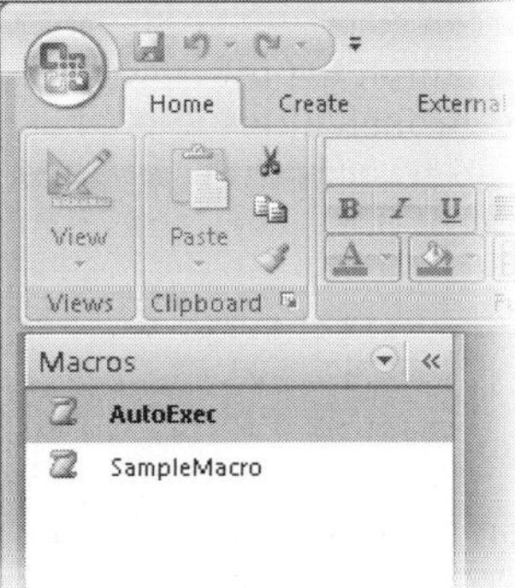


**Figure 3-28** You can filter the Navigation Pane to show the Macros list in the Housing Reservations database.

SampleMacro

| Macro Name | Condition | Action | Comment |
|---|---|---|---|
| Greeting | 4>Hour(Now()) | MsgBox | Test for very late at night |
| | ... | StopMacro | If was true, then done |
| | 6>Hour(Now()) | MsgBox | Test for early in the day |
| | ... | StopMacro | If was true, then done |
| | 12>Hour(Now()) | MsgBox | Display good morning |
| | ... | StopMacro | If was true, then done |
| | 18>Hour(Now()) | MsgBox | Display good afternoon |
| | ... | StopMacro | If was true, then done |
| | 23>Hour(Now()) | MsgBox | Display good night! |

Action Arguments

| | |
|---|---|
| Message | My, You're up VERY LATE! |
| Beep | Yes |
| Type | Warning! |
| Title | Access 2007 Inside Out |

Enter a macro name in this column.

**Figure 3-29** Open the SampleMacro macro object in the Housing Reservations database in Design view to examine and modify its definition.

You can design multiple macro actions within a single macro object and give each one a name in the first column. Any unnamed lines following a line with a name specified all belong to the named macro. In the second column, you can optionally specify a condition test that must be true for the macro command on that line to execute. You can use a continuation indicator (...) on subsequent lines to specify additional commands that should also execute when the condition is true. You select the action you want to run from a list in the Action column and set the arguments required for the action in the Action Arguments section in the lower part of the design window. Some of the limitations of macros include limited ability to branch to other actions and very limited ability to loop through a set of actions.

If you want to see what this macro does, click the Run button in the Tools group of the Design contextual tab to execute it. You should see a greeting message appropriate to the time of day appear on your screen. To learn more about events and the macro design facility, see Chapter 18, "Automating Your Application with Macros." You can find one sample application on the companion CD that is automated entirely using macros–WeddingListMC.accdb.

Close the Macro window now to return to the Navigation Pane.



## Modules

You might find that you keep coding the same complex formula over and over in some of your forms or reports. Although you can build a complete Access application using only forms, reports, and macros, some actions might be difficult or impossible to define in a macro. If that is the case, you can create a Visual Basic procedure that performs a series of calculations and then use that procedure in a form or report.

If your application is so complex that it needs to deal with errors (such as two users trying to update the same record at the same time), you must use Visual Basic. Because Visual Basic is a complete programming language with complex logic and the ability to link to other applications and files, you can solve unusual or difficult programming problems by using Visual Basic procedures.

Version 2 of Access introduced the ability to code Basic routines in special modules attached directly to the forms and reports that they support. You can create these procedures from Design view for forms or reports by requesting the Code Builder in any event property. You can edit this code behind forms and reports by clicking View Code in the Tools group on the Design contextual tab when you have a form or report open in Design view. See Chapters 19 and 20 for details. In fact, after you learn a little bit about Visual Basic, you might find that coding small event procedures for your forms and reports is much more efficient and convenient than trying to keep track of many macro objects. You'll also soon learn that you can't fully respond to some sophisticated events, such as KeyPress, in macros because macros can't access special additional parameters (such as the value of the key pressed) generated by the event. You can fully handle these events only in Visual Basic.

Open the Navigation Pane menu and click Object Type under Navigate To Category. Open the menu again and click Modules under Filter By Group to display a list of modules available in the Housing Reservations database, as shown in Figure 3-30. The Housing Reservations database has several module objects that contain procedures that can be called from any query, form, report, or other procedure in the database. For example, the modMedian module contains a function to calculate the median value of a column in any table or query. The modUtility module contains several functions that you might find useful in your applications.

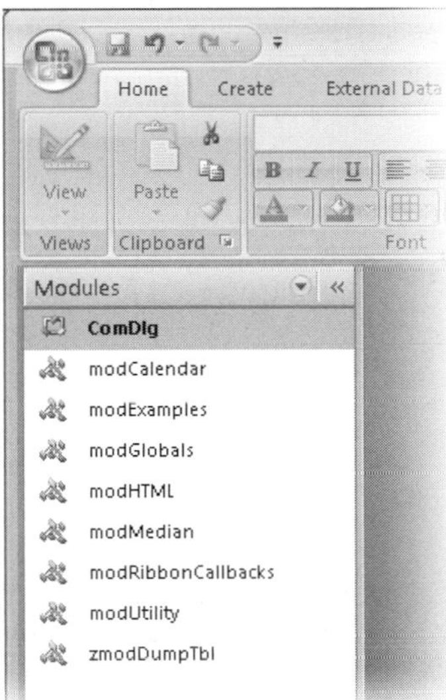


**Figure 3-30** You can filter the Navigation Pane to display only the Visual Basic modules in the Housing Reservations database.

From the Navigation Pane, you can create a new module by clicking the arrow below Macro in the Other group of the Create tab on the Ribbon, or you can open the design of an existing module by double-clicking the name of the module in the Navigation Pane. In addition, you can right-click on the module name in the Navigation Pane and click Design View on the shortcut menu. In a module, you can define procedures that you can call from a macro, a form, or a report. You can also use some procedures (called functions) in expressions in queries and in validation rules that you create for a table or a form. You'll learn how to create procedures in Chapter 19.

Right-click the modUtility module in the Navigation Pane and then click Design View to open the Visual Basic Editor window containing the Visual Basic code in the module. Use the Procedure list box (in the upper right of the Code window) to look at the procedure names available in the sample. One of the functions in this module, IsFormLoaded, checks all forms open in the current Access session to see whether the form name, passed as a parameter, is one of the open forms. This function is useful in macros or in other modules to direct the flow of an application based on which forms the user has open. You can see this function in Figure 3-31.

Note that the Visual Basic Editor runs in an entirely different application window from Access, and it still uses the classic menus and toolbars found in earlier versions of Access. Click the View Microsoft Office Access button on the far left of the toolbar to easily return to the Access window.

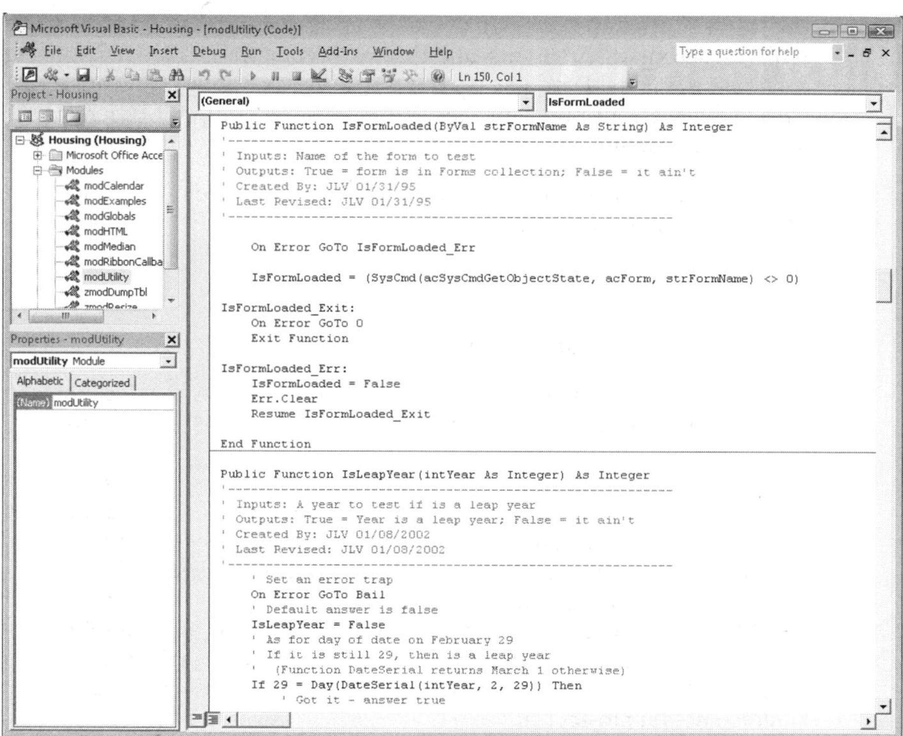

**Figure 3-31** The Visual Basic Editor window displays the IsFormLoaded function in the modUtility module.

This completes the tour of the objects in the Housing Reservations sample database. Close the Visual Basic Editor window if you still have it open, return to the Access window, and close the database.

# Exploring a Project File—Conrad Systems Contacts

Microsoft Access 2000 introduced an advanced facility that allows you to create a project file (with an .adp extension) that contains only your forms, reports, macros, and modules. When you create a new project file, you can specify an SQL Server database to support the project. SQL Server stores the tables and queries you use in the application that you design in the project. You can connect your project file to a Microsoft SQL Server version 6.5 database on a server or to a version 7.0 or later database on a server or on your desktop. Included with the 2007 Microsoft Office release is a special edition of SQL Server 2005, the Microsoft SQL Server Desktop Engine (MSDE), that you can install to run on your desktop computer.

You will see available tables in the server database as table objects in your project. You will also see views, functions, and stored procedures as query objects. Access 2007 includes special table and query editors to allow you to work directly with the objects in SQL Server. Your project file also contains forms, reports, macros, and modules that are virtually identical to those you develop in a desktop database (.accdb).

To see the differences in tables and queries in a project file, start Access and then open the Contacts.adp sample project file.

**INSIDE OUT** **Opening the Sample Project File**

To be able to open the Contacts.adp file successfully, you must first install Microsoft SQL Server 2005 Express Edition or have access to an SQL Server edition that allows you Create authority. You can download SQL Server 2005 Express Edition from *www.microsoft.com/sql/editions/express/default.mspx*. You'll need to attach the sample database files to a computer running a server version of Microsoft Windows, such as Microsoft Windows Server 2003, and possibly modify the connection properties of the sample project so that Access knows where to find the tables and queries required by the project. See the Appendix, "Installing Your Software," for details about how to install and start SQL Server 2005 Express Edition. See Chapter 26, "Building Tables in an Access Project," for details about setting project connection properties. If you are unable to perform these steps at this time, you can still read through this section to gain an understanding of some of the differences in project files.



## Tables

Open the Navigation Pane menu and select Object Type under Navigate To Category. Open the menu again and select Tables under Filter By Group to see all the tables defined in the SQL Server database connected to the project. Figure 3-32 shows you the tables in the ContactsSQL database that is connected to the Conrad Systems Contacts project file.

As you can see, the Navigation Pane in a project file looks very similar to the one in a desktop database. You can see one additional object type listed on the Navigation Pane menu–Database Diagrams. SQL Server allows you to create a diagram of all the tables in your database, and the diagram shows you the relationships that you have defined between the tables.

Select the tblContacts table in the Navigation Pane, and press Ctrl+Enter to see the table in Design view, as shown in Figure 3-33.

**Figure 3-32** The Navigation Pane in a project file shows the tables in the database on SQL Server.

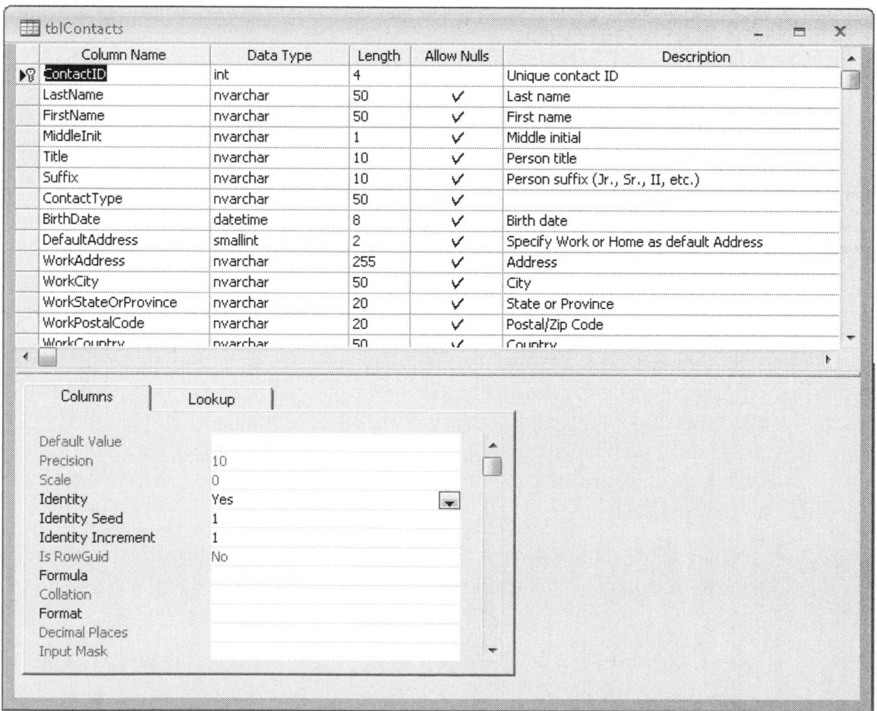


**Figure 3-33** When you open a table in Design view in an Access project, you're editing the table in the database on SQL Server.

As you can see, the table design grid in an Access project is very similar to the one in a desktop database. (See Figure 3-8.) In an SQL Server database, fields are called columns. SQL Server supports a wider variety of data types than does a desktop database. Many of the data types are identical, but they have different names in SQL Server. For example, the int data type in SQL Server is the same as the Long Integer data type in a desktop database. If you want, you can click the Datasheet View option in the Views group to switch to Datasheet view, but you'll find that Datasheet view in an Access project is identical to that in a desktop database. You can learn all the details for creating tables in a project in Chapter 26. Close the table design grid to return to the Navigation Pane.

## Views, Functions, and Stored Procedures

Although all query objects in a desktop database are called simply "queries," you'll find that SQL Server stores three different types of objects—views, functions, and stored procedures—that Access displays when you click Queries under Filter By Group on the Navigation Pane menu, as shown in Figure 3-34.



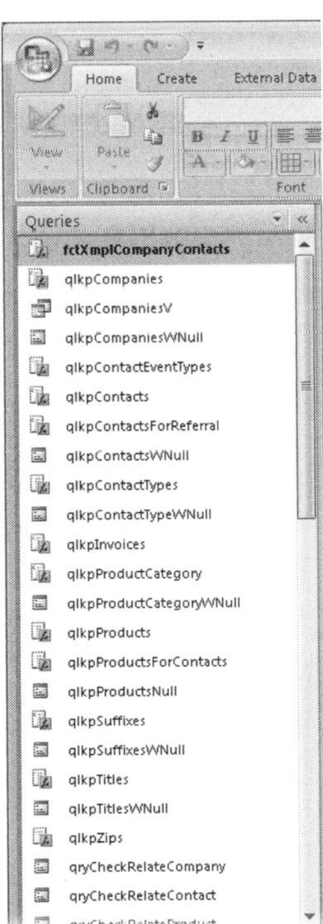


**Figure 3-34** The list of queries in an Access project shows the views, functions, and stored procedures saved in the database on SQL Server.

A *view* returns a filtered view of data from one or more tables. A *function* can return a table, or it can perform a calculation and return a single value, much like a Visual Basic function. The difference is that a function that you see in the queries list in a project file

Navigation Pane executes on SQL Server, and the server returns the result to your project. A *stored procedure* can be as simple as an SQL statement that returns rows from one or more tables, or it can contain a complex program written in Transact-SQL that tests conditions and perhaps updates one or more tables in your database.

In many cases, you can design a view, function, or stored procedure using a query designer that is similar to the designer you use in a desktop database. To see an example of a query in a project file's query designer, scroll down the list of queries in the Conrad Systems Contacts sample project file, select qryContactProductsForInvoice in the Navigation Pane, and then press Ctrl+Enter. Access displays the query in Design view, as shown in Figure 3-35.

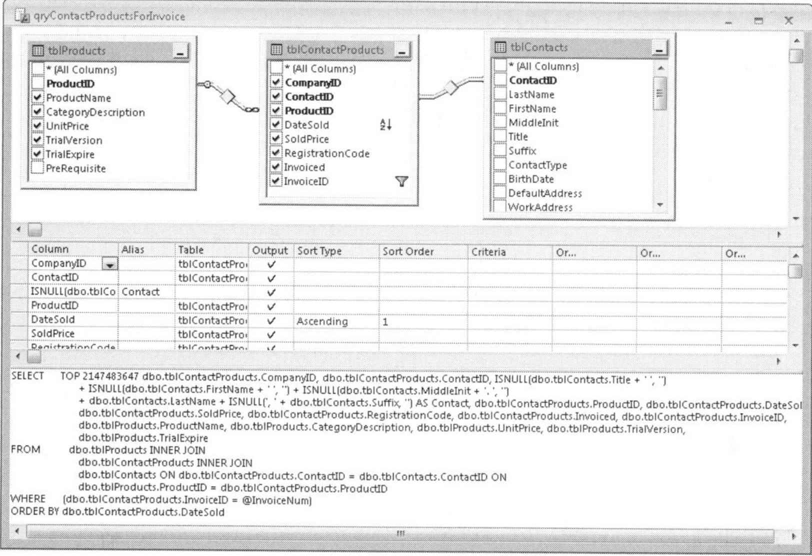


**Figure 3-35** When you open a query in the query designer in an Access project, you're editing the view, function, or stored procedure stored in the server database.

This query is a function that returns columns from three tables. The query designer in an Access project is similar in some ways to the designer in a desktop database (see Figure 3-12). You can see the tables used in the query in the top pane of the designer window. In the center pane are the columns (fields) used in the query, but the columns are listed vertically here instead of horizontally as in the desktop database designer. In the bottom pane, you can see the SQL statement that defines this query on the server. You can close this pane if you like and work exclusively in the designer. Access reflects any change you make on the design grid by modifying the displayed SQL. When you become more expert in SQL, you can also modify the SQL statement, and Access changes the top two panes accordingly.

You can learn about the details of creating a query in an Access project in Chapter 27, "Building Queries in an Access Project," on the companion CD. For details about the SQL database language, see Article 2, "Understanding SQL," also on the companion CD.

Chapter 3

You can close the query design grid now. As noted earlier, the forms, reports, macros, and modules in a project file are virtually identical to those in a desktop database. You can learn about the minor differences for forms and reports in Chapter 28, "Designing Forms in an Access Project," and Chapter 29, "Building Reports in an Access Project," both on the companion CD.

## The Many Faces of Access

Access is not only a powerful, flexible, and easy-to-use database management system, but it is also a complete database application development facility. You can use Access to create and run, under the Windows operating system, an application tailored to your data management needs. Access lets you limit, select, and total your data by using queries. You can create forms for viewing and changing your data. You can also use Access to create simple or complex reports. Forms and reports inherit the properties of the underlying table or query, so in most cases you need to define such properties as formats and validation rules only once. Figure 3-36 gives you an overview of all the ways you can use Access to implement an application.



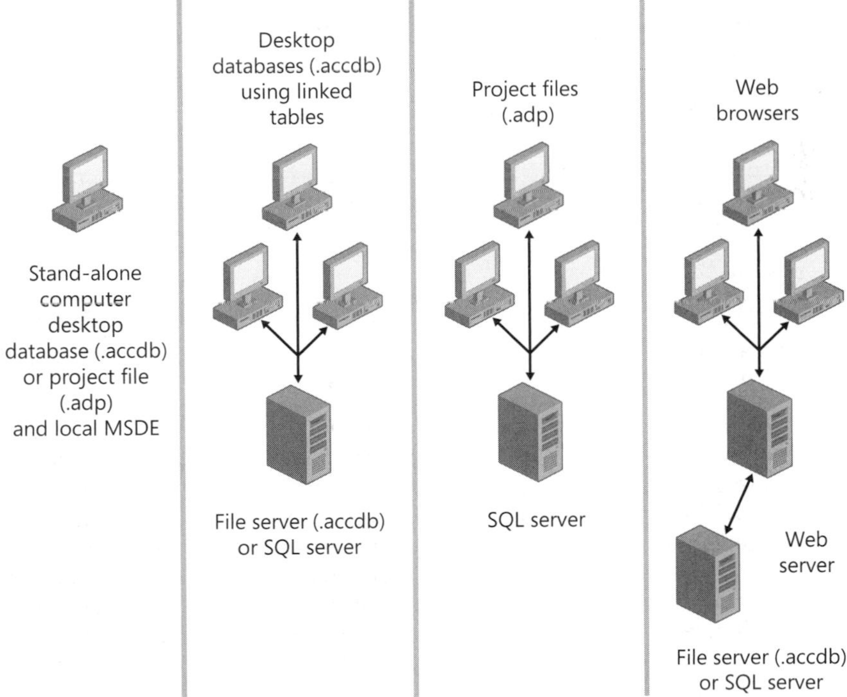


**Figure 3-36** Although Access is primarily a desktop database system, you can use Access to build client/server applications.

The four sections in the figure illustrate ways you can implement an Access application, as follows:

- Using the desktop database facility or an Access project file linked to a local copy of MSDE, you can create a stand-alone application used by a single person.
- You can place a data-only desktop database on a file server or in a database in SQL Server and link the tables over a network to multiple desktop databases so that several users can share the same application.
- You can design your database in SQL Server and connect to the server over a network from multiple Access project files running on different computers.
- Finally, you can create Web pages that connect to data that you designed using Access.

To borrow a cliché, the possibilities are endless . . .

In this chapter, you've had a chance to look at the major objects in the Housing Reservations and Conrad Systems Contacts sample databases. You've also been introduced to the architecture of Access and the wide range of ways that you can use Access. You should be feeling comfortable that you can learn to use Access at the level appropriate to solve your database application needs. In the next chapter you'll learn how to create new databases and the tables you need to store your data."

PART 2

# Building an Access 2007 Desktop Application

CHAPTER 4

# Creating Your Database and Tables



Defining tables in a Microsoft Office Access 2007 desktop database (.accdb file) is incredibly easy. This chapter shows you how it's done. You'll learn how to

- Create a new database application using a database template
- Create a new empty database for your own custom application
- Create a simple table by entering data directly in the table
- Get a jump start on defining custom tables by using table templates
- Define your own tables from scratch by using Design view
- Select the best data type for each field
- Define the primary key for your table
- Set validation rules for your fields and tables
- Tell Access 2007 what relationships to maintain between your tables
- Optimize data retrieval by adding indexes
- Set options that affect how you work in Design view
- Print a table definition

**Note**

All the screen images in this chapter were taken on a Microsoft Windows Vista system using the Blue color scheme.

INSIDE OUT **Take Time to Learn About Table Design**

You could begin building a database in Access 2007 much as you might begin creating a simple single-sheet solution in a spreadsheet application such as Microsoft Excel—by simply organizing your data into rows and columns and then inserting formulas where you need calculations. If you've ever worked extensively with a database or a spreadsheet application, you already know that this unplanned approach works in only the most trivial situations. Solving real problems takes some planning; otherwise, you end up building your application over and over again. One of the beauties of a relational database system such as Access is that it's much easier to make midcourse corrections. However, it's well worth spending time up front designing the tasks you want to perform, the data structures you need to support those tasks, and the flow of tasks within your database application.

To teach you all you might need to know about table design would require another entire book. The good news is Access 2007 provides many examples for good table design in the templates available with the product and online. If you want to learn at least the fundamentals of table and application design, be sure to read Article 1, "Designing Your Database Application," that you can find on the companion CD.

# Creating a New Database



When you first start Office Access 2007, you see the Getting Started screen, as shown in Figure 4-1. We explored the Getting Started screen in detail in Chapter 2, "Exploring the New Look of Access 2007." If you've previously opened other databases, you also see a most recently used list of up to nine database selections under Open Recent Database on the right.

## Using a Database Template to Create a Database

Just for fun, let's explore the built-in database templates first. If you're a beginner, you can use the templates included with Access 2007 to create one of several common applications without needing to know anything about designing database software. You might find that one of these applications meets most of your needs right off the bat. As you learn more about Access 2007, you can build on and customize the basic application design and add new features.

Even if you're an experienced developer, you might find that the application templates save you lots of time in setting up the basic tables, queries, forms, and reports for your application. If the application you need to build is covered by one of the templates, the wizard that builds an application with one of the templates can take care of many of the simpler design tasks.

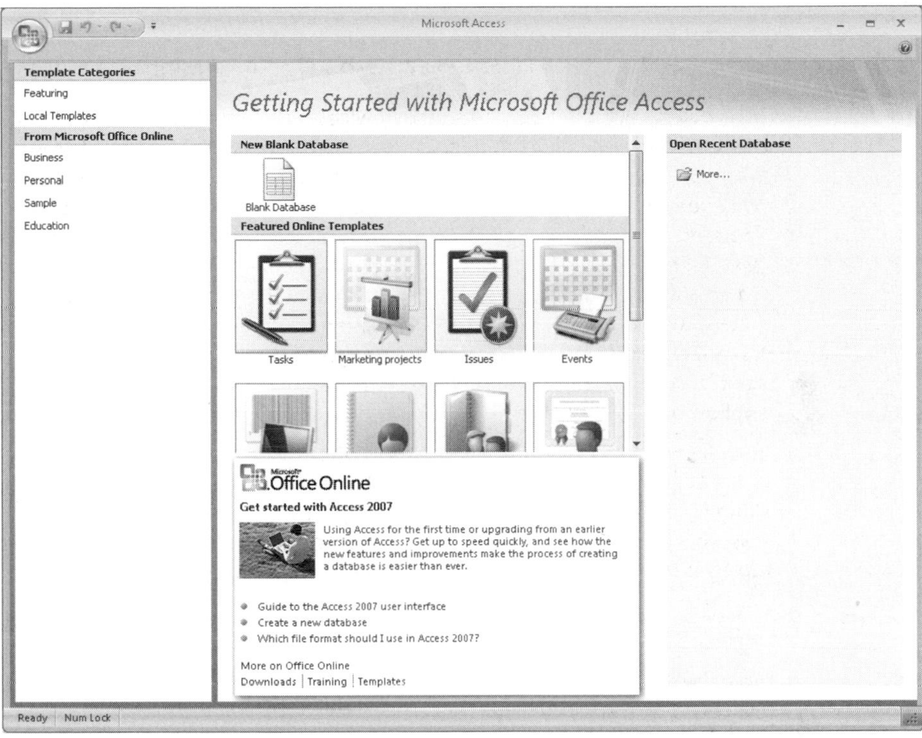


**Figure 4-1** When you first start Access 2007, you see the Getting Started screen.

On the Getting Started screen, you can access the built-in local templates by clicking Local Templates under Template Categories on the left. You can also choose to download a template from Microsoft's Web site by clicking one of the options under From Microsoft Office Online. When you click one of the options under Template Categories or From Microsoft Office Online, the center section of the Getting Started screen changes to show graphics representing of each of the database templates available in that category. Click the Business category under Template Categories to see the list of business template options, as shown in Figure 4-2.

When you click on one of the template graphics in the center of the Getting Started screen, Access 2007 displays additional information about the purpose of the database in the right task pane. Click the Contacts template in the middle of the screen to see detailed information about the local Contacts database template, as shown in Figure 4-3. You can work with all templates from the Getting Started screen in the same way. This example will show you the steps that are needed to build a Contacts database.

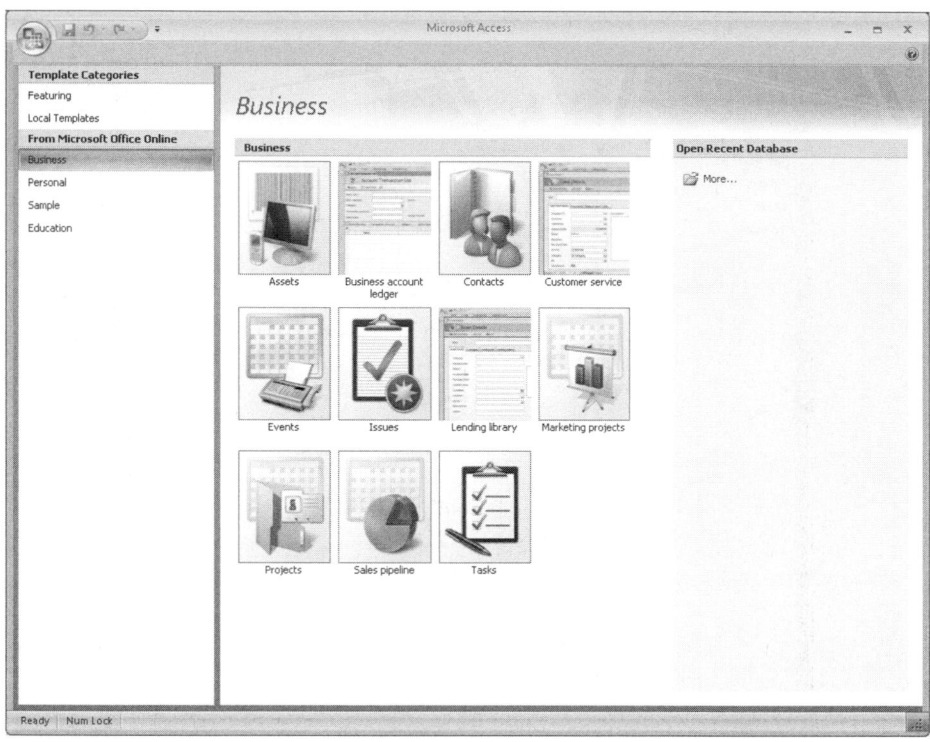


**Figure 4-2** You access templates from Microsoft Office Online by selecting one of the categories to see a list of database templates for that category.

Browse

Access 2007 displays a larger graphic in the right task pane along with a brief description of the template's purpose. When you have selected an online template, Access 2007 also shows you the template size, the approximate download time, and the rating given this template by other users. Access 2007 suggests a name for your new database in the File Name text box and a location to save the file beneath the File Name text box. You can select the optional check box to instruct Access 2007 to link this new database to a Windows SharePoint Services site. For now, do not select this check box. You'll learn more about connecting to a Windows SharePoint Services site in Chapter 22, "Working with Windows SharePoint Services." You can modify the name of this database by typing in the File Name text box. If you want to change the suggested save location, click the Browse button to open the File New Database dialog box, as shown in Figure 4-4.

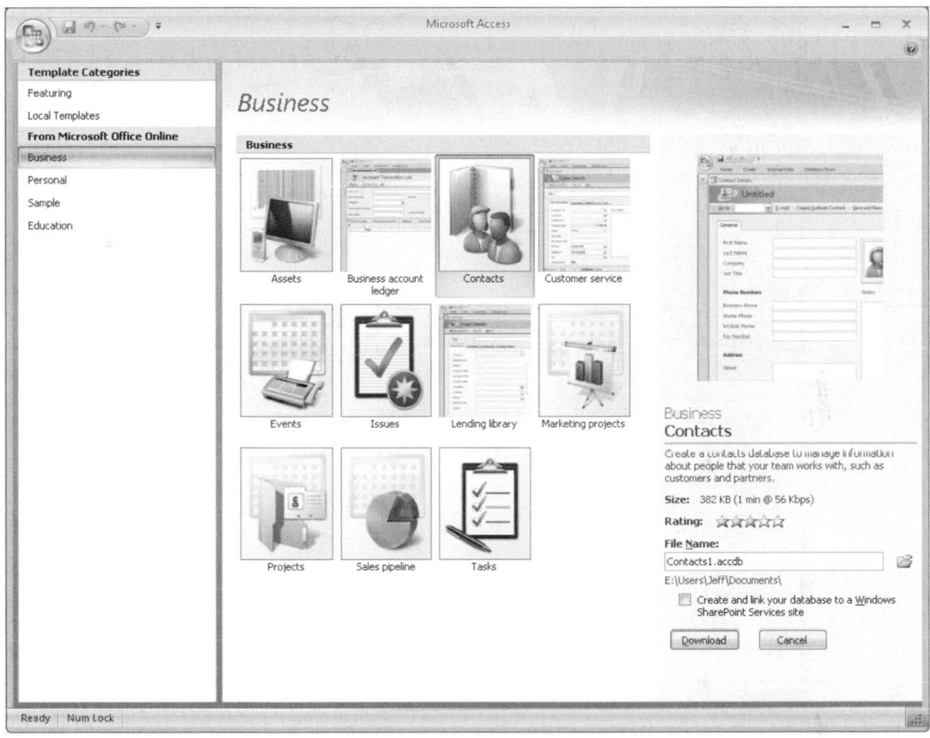


**Figure 4-3** Choosing one of the database templates in the center of the screen shows you more information in the right task pane.

You can select the drive and folder you want by clicking the links on the left and browsing to your destination folder. After you select the specific folder to which you want to save this new database, click OK to return to the Getting Started screen. Your new folder location is shown beneath the File Name text box. If you decide at this point not to create the database, click the Cancel button to stop the process. Click the Download button when working with an online template or the Create button when working with a local template, and Access 2007 begins the process of creating this new database.

The first time you choose to download an online template, Access 2007 displays the Microsoft Office Genuine Advantage confirmation dialog box as shown in Figure 4-5. Each time you download a template, Access 2007 confirms that you have a valid and registered copy of the 2007 Microsoft Office system. If you do not want to see this dialog box again, select the Do Not Show This Message Again check box. Click Continue to proceed with the download and creation of your sample database.

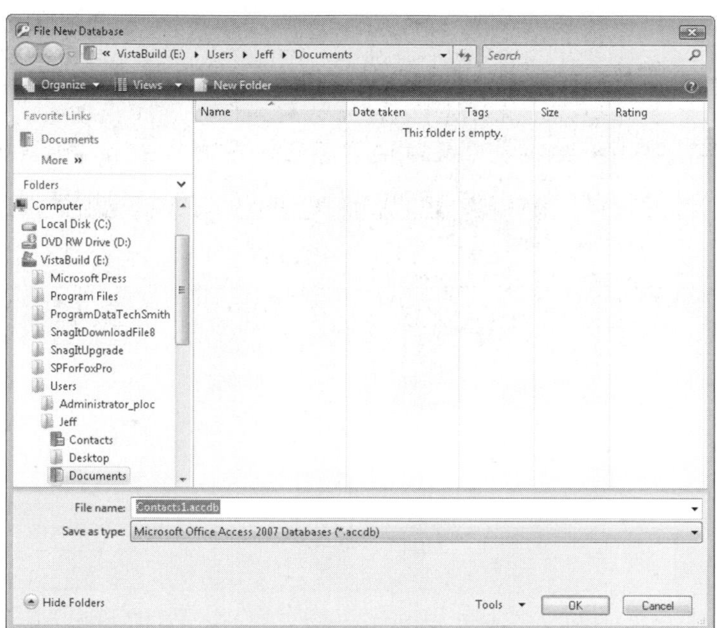


**Figure 4-4** Use the File New Database dialog box to select a folder for saving the new database.

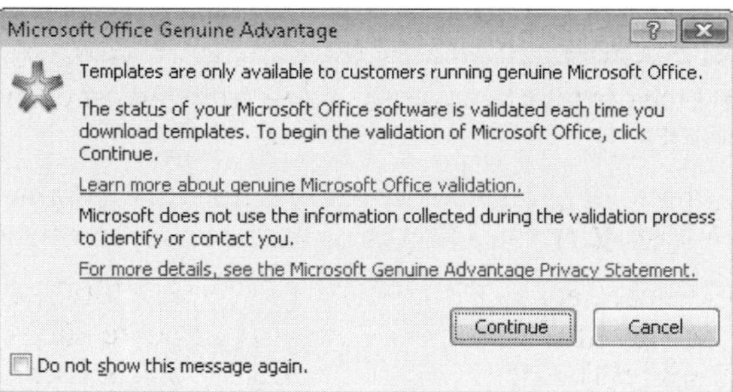


**Figure 4-5** When you ask to download a template, Access verifies that you have a genuine copy of the 2007 Office release.

A progress bar appears on the screen informing you to please wait while Access 2007 creates the database. After a few seconds of preparation, Access opens the new Contacts database and displays the Contact List form, as shown in Figure 4-6. Close this new database for now by clicking the Microsoft Office Button and then clicking Close Database to return to the Getting Started screen.

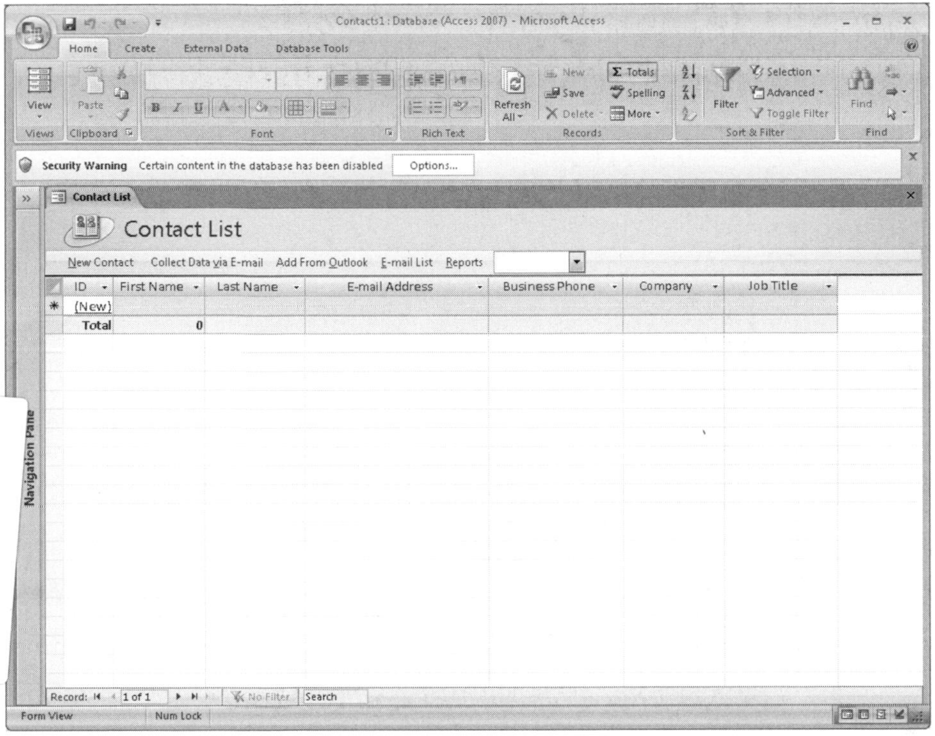

**Figure 4-6** After you create the Contacts database from a template, Access opens the database and displays the Contact List form.



## Creating a New Empty Database

To begin creating a new empty database when you start Access 2007, go to the New Blank Database section in the middle of the Getting Started screen (as shown in Figure 4-1) and click Blank Database. The right side of the Getting Started screen changes to display the Blank Database task pane, as shown in Figure 4-7.

You can click the Browse button to open the File New Database dialog box, shown previously in Figure 4-4, to select the drive and folder you want. In this example, we selected the Documents folder in Windows Vista for the current user. Next, type the name of your new database in the File Name text box–Access 2007 appends an .accdb extension to the file name for you. Access 2007 uses a file with an .accdb extension to store all your database objects, including tables, queries, forms, reports, macros, and modules. For this example, let's create a database with a table containing names and addresses–something you might use to track invitees to a wedding. Type **Kathy's Wedding List** in the File Name box and click the Create button to create your database.

**Figure 4-7** From the Getting Started screen, click Blank Database in the center to open the Blank Database task pane on the right.

Access 2007 takes a few moments to create the system tables in which to store all the information about the tables, queries, forms, reports, macros, and modules that you might create. Access then displays the Navigation Pane for your new database and opens a new blank table in Datasheet view, shown in Figure 4-8.

When you open a database (unless the database includes special startup settings), Access 2007 selects the object you last chose in the Navigation Pane for that database. For example, if the last time you opened this database you worked on a table, Access highlights that object (a table) in the Navigation Pane. Access also remembers the view and filters you applied to the Navigation Pane. For example, if Tables And Related Views was the last selected view applied to the Navigation Pane, Access will remember this the next time you open the database.

Because this is a new database and no objects or special startup settings exist yet, you see a Navigation Pane with only one object defined. For new databases, Access, by default, creates a new table in Datasheet view called Table1 with an ID field already defined. However, Access has not saved this table, so if you do not make any changes to it, Access will not prompt you to save the table if you close it. The following sections show you various methods for creating a new table.

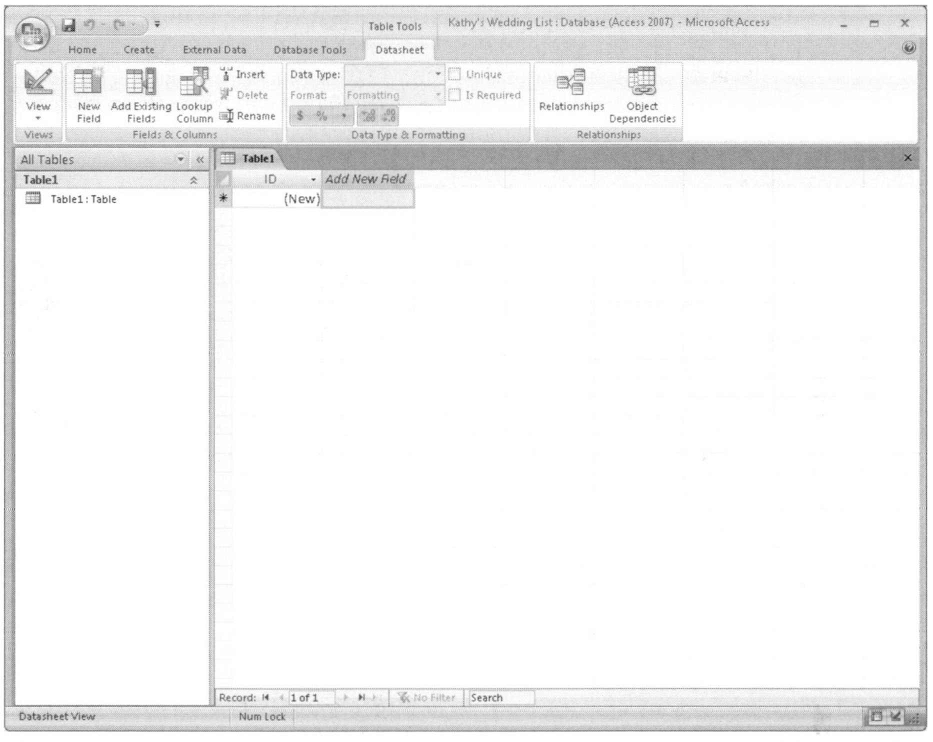


Figure 4-8 When you create a new blank database, Access 2007 opens a new table in Datasheet view for you.



# Creating Your First Simple Table by Entering Data

If you've been following along to this point, you should still have your new Kathy's Wedding List database open with Table1 open in Datasheet view, as shown in Figure 4-8. (You can also follow these steps in any open database.) What you see is an empty datasheet, which looks quite similar to a spreadsheet. Access 2007 automatically created the first field, called ID, in the left column. Leave this field intact for now. In the second column Access has placed another field with the Add New Field heading. You can enter just about any type of data you want in this field—text, dates, numbers, or currency. But unlike a spreadsheet, you can't enter any calculated expressions in a datasheet. As you'll see later in the chapters about queries, you can easily display a calculated result using data from one or more tables by entering an expression in a query.

Because we're starting a list of wedding invitees, we'll need columns containing information such as title, last name, first name, middle initial, street address, city, state, postal code, number of guests invited, number of guests confirmed, gift received, and a gift acknowledged indicator. Be sure to enter the same type of data in a particular column for every row. For example, enter the city name in the seventh column (named Field6 by Access) for every row.

You can see some of the data entered for the wedding invitee list in Figure 4-9. When you start to type in a field in a row, Access 2007 displays a pencil icon on the row selector at the far left to indicate that you're adding or changing data in that row. Press the Tab key to move from column to column. When you move to another row, Access 2007 saves what you typed. If you make a mistake in a particular row or column, you can click the data you want to change and type over it or delete it. Notice that after you enter data in a column, Access 2007 guesses the most appropriate data type and displays it in the Data Type box on the Datasheet tab on the Ribbon.

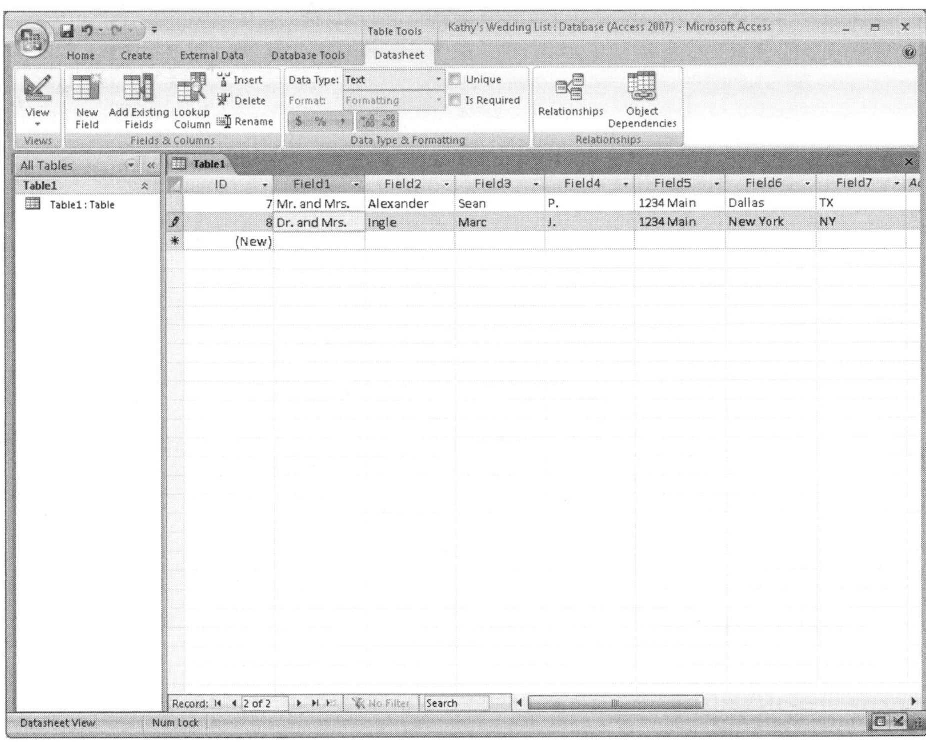


**Figure 4-9** You can create the wedding invitee list table by entering data.

If you create a column of data that you don't want, click anywhere in the column and click Delete in the Fields & Columns group of the Datasheet contextual tab on the Ribbon. Click Yes when Access asks you to confirm the deletion. If you want to insert a blank column between two columns that already contain data, click anywhere in the column to the right of where you want to insert the new column and then click Insert in the Fields & Columns group of the Datasheet tab on the Ribbon. To move a column to a different location, click the field name at the top of the column to select the entire column, and then click again and drag the column to a new location. You can also click an unselected column and drag your mouse pointer through several adjacent columns to select them all. You can then move the columns as a group.

You probably noticed that Access 2007 named your columns Field1, Field2, and so forth—not very informative. You can enter a name for each column by double-clicking the column's field name. You can also click anywhere in the column and then click Rename in the Fields & Columns group on the Datasheet tab. In Figure 4-10, we have already renamed one of the columns and are in the process of renaming the second one.

Table1

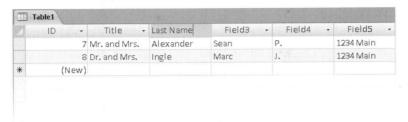

| ID | Title | Last Name | Field3 | Field4 | Field5 |
|---|---|---|---|---|---|
| 7 | Mr. and Mrs. | Alexander | Sean | P. | 1234 Main |
| 8 | Dr. and Mrs. | Ingle | Marc | J. | 1234 Main |
| (New) | | | | | |

**Figure 4-10** Double-click the column heading or click Rename in the Fields & Columns group on the Ribbon to rename a column in Datasheet view.

Save

After you enter several rows of data, it's a good idea to save your table. You can do this by clicking the Save button on the Quick Access Toolbar or by clicking the Microsoft Office Button and then Save. Access 2007 displays a Save As dialog box, as shown in Figure 4-11. Type an appropriate name for your table, and then click OK. If you deleted the ID field by mistake, Access 2007 displays a message box warning you that you have no primary key defined for this table and offers to build one for you. If you accept the offer, Access adds a field called ID and assigns it a special data type named AutoNumber that automatically generates a unique number for each new row you add. See "Understanding Field Data Types" on page 157 for details about AutoNumber. If one or more of the data columns you entered would make a good primary key, click No in the message box. In Chapter 5, "Modifying Your Table Design," you'll learn how to use Design view to define your own primary key(s) or to change the definition of an existing primary key. In this case, Access 2007 should not display a message box, because it already generated the field called ID to serve as the primary key.

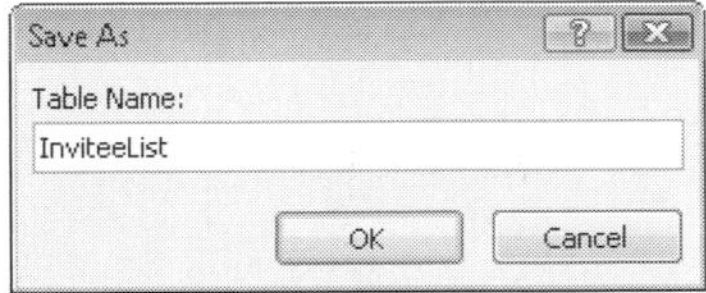


**Figure 4-11** Access 2007 displays the Save As dialog box when you save a new table so that you can specify a table name.

## Creating a Table Using a Table Template

If you look in the Wedding List sample database (WeddingList.accdb) included on the companion CD, you'll find it very simple, with one main table and a few supporting tables for data such as titles, cities, and groups. Most databases are usually quite a bit more complex. For example, the Housing Reservations sample database contains six main tables, and the Conrad Systems Contacts sample database contains more than a dozen tables. If you had to create every table "by hand," it could be quite a tedious process.

Fortunately, Access 2007 comes with table templates to help you build a few common tables. Let's move on to a more complex task–building tables like those you find in Conrad Systems Contacts. Click the Microsoft Office Button and then click New. This returns you to the Getting Started screen, ready to define a new blank database. For this exercise, create a new blank database and give it the name Contact Tracking. We'll use this database to start building tables like some of those you saw in Chapter 3.

To build a table using one of the table templates, close the table that Access 2007 created when you opened the database (Table1), click the Create tab on the Ribbon, and then click the Table Templates button in the Tables group. Access displays a list of five table templates–Contacts, Tasks, Issues, Events, and Assets, as shown in Figure 4-12. Microsoft uses the term *Quick Create* to refer to this one-click table creation feature.

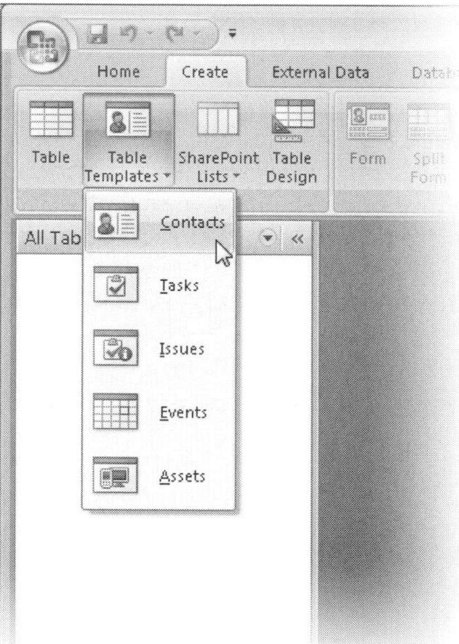


**Figure 4-12** The five types of table templates help you create common types of tables.

The five table templates, which represent some of the more common types of table structures found in databases, are as follows:

- **Contacts** Use this table template when you need to track your personal or business contacts. Key fields in this template include the contact's company, job title, and phone numbers.
- **Tasks** Use this table template for keeping track of various tasks and projects needing completion. Key fields in this template include start and due dates for the task and percentage complete.

- **Issues** Use this table template for recording various personal or business issues. Some key fields in this template include the title of the issue and the issue status.
- **Events** Use this table template as a personal organizer of your appointments. This template includes fields for start and end times of the event, the event date, and even the location.
- **Assets** Use this table template for keeping track of your assets. Key fields in this template include the acquisition date, the original price of the asset, and the current price.

INSIDE OUT

### What Happened to the Table Wizard?

The Table Wizard from previous versions of Access does not exist in Access 2007. Microsoft has replaced the Table Wizard with five table templates so that you can quickly build tables commonly found in most databases.

Click Contacts in the Table Templates list, and Access 2007 builds a complete table structure for a contacts table, as shown in Figure 4-13. Access creates a total of 18 fields to identify the data elements for this contacts table. Use the horizontal scroll bar or press Tab to see the field names to the right. This contacts table template includes fields such as Company, First Name, Last Name, E-mail Address, Job Title, and so on to identify a single subject—a contact. The Table Templates command also automatically defines a data type for each of these fields.

**See Table 4-1 on page 158 for a full discussion of the various data types available within Access 2007.**

INSIDE OUT

### You Can Create and Modify Table Templates

Access 2007 uses special schema files coded in XML to define the properties for the five table templates. These five files have an .accfl extension and are located in the following folder in a default 2007 Office release installation: Program Files\Microsoft Office\Templates\1033\Access. If you choose to modify these template files, we recommend that you back up the original file to a safe location. You can open the .accfl files using Notepad or an XML reader. These XML view files are created using XML Schema Definition (XSD) language to describe the structure of the new table template tables. Access reads these files to determine the structure of the template files and then builds them following the instructions. You can learn how to create and modify these files in Chapter 23, "Using XML."

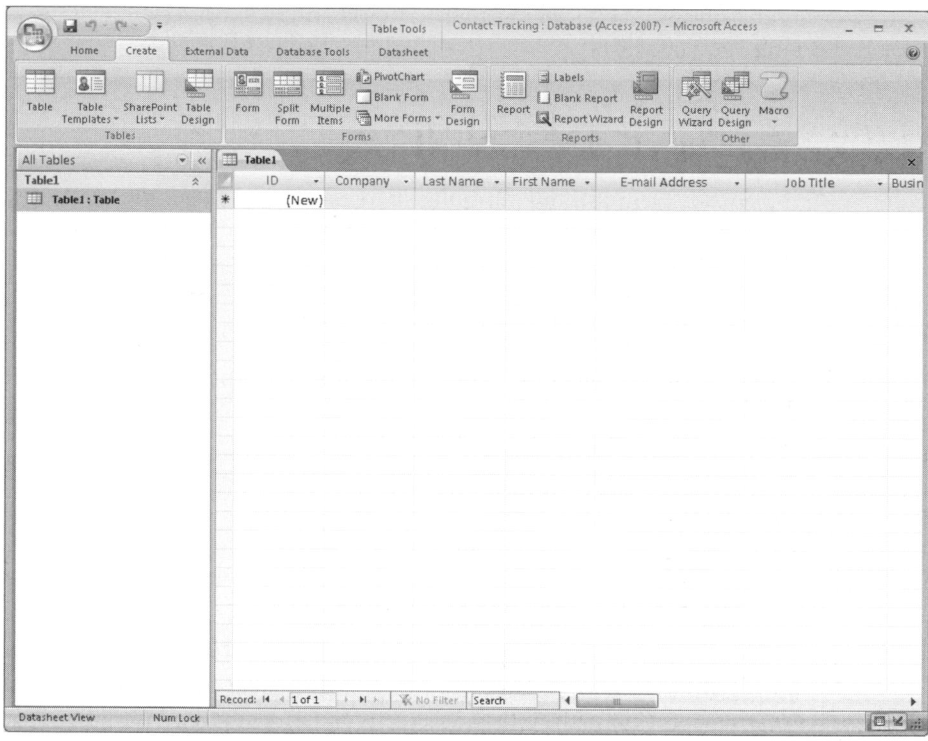


**Figure 4-13** The Table Templates command builds a complete table with appropriate field types.

By default, Access 2007 assigned the name ID to the first field in this Contacts table. This field name is not very descriptive, so we will rename this field ContactID. There are several ways to rename a field using Access 2007, but for now we will focus on one of the easiest methods—renaming the field directly from Datasheet view. Double-click the heading of the ID field and then type **ContactID,** as shown in Figure 4-14. After you press Enter, Access immediately renames the field. Save this table now by clicking the Save button on the Quick Access Toolbar and name the table Contacts.

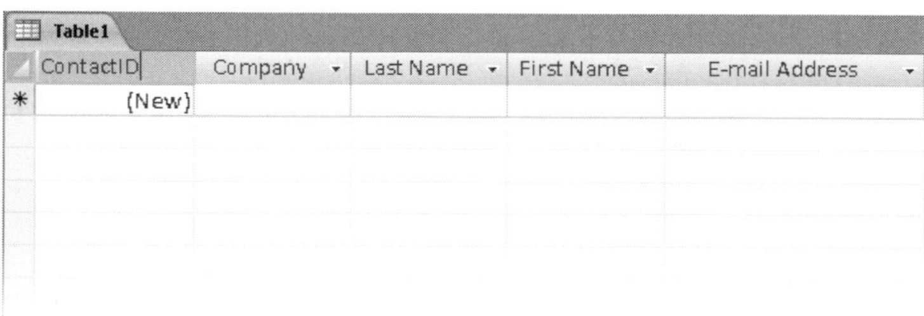


**Figure 4-14** You can double-click a column heading in table Design view to change the name of the field.

You will further change this Contacts table later in this chapter and also in Chapter 5 so that it is more like the final tblContacts table in the Conrad Systems Contacts database. For now, close the Table window so that you can continue building other tables you need.

## Creating a Table in Design View

You could continue to use table templates to build some of the other tables in the Contact Tracking database to mimic those in Conrad Systems Contacts. However, you'll find it very useful to learn the mechanics of building a table from scratch, so now is a good time to explore Design view and learn how to build tables without using table templates. The table templates, unlike the Table Wizard from previous versions of Access, offer only five choices for sample tables, and there is no way to pick and choose which fields to include or exclude. You can modify the template by changing the XML that defines it, and you'll learn how to do that in Chapter 23. By working in Design view, you'll see many additional features that you can use to customize the way your tables (and any queries, forms, or reports built on these tables) work when creating a table from scratch.

To begin creating a new table in Design view, click the Create tab on the Ribbon and then click the Table Design button in the Tables group. Access 2007 displays a blank Table window in Design view, as shown in Figure 4-15.

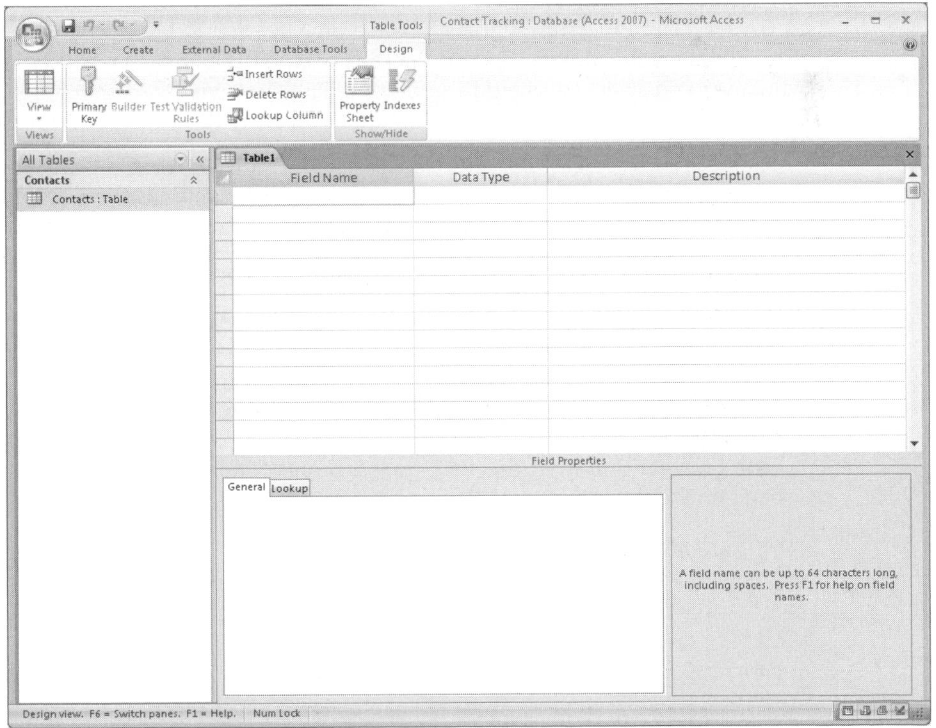


**Figure 4-15** The Table Design command opens a new table in Design view.

In Design view, the upper part of the Table window displays columns in which you can enter the field names, the data type for each field, and a description of each field. After you select a data type for a field, Access 2007 allows you to set field properties in the lower-left section of the Table window. In the lower-right section of the Table window is a box in which Access displays information about fields or properties. The contents of this box change as you move from one location to another within the Table window.

**For details about data type values, see "Understanding Field Data Types" on the next page.**

## Defining Fields

Now you're ready to begin defining the fields for the Companies table that mimics the one you can find in the Conrad Systems Contacts sample database (Contacts.accdb). Be sure the insertion point is in the first row of the Field Name column, and then type the name of the first field, **CompanyID**. Press Tab once to move to the Data Type column. A button with an arrow appears on the right side of the Data Type column. Here and elsewhere in Access 2007, this type of button signifies the presence of a list. Click the arrow or press Alt+Down Arrow to open the list of data type options, shown in Figure 4-16. In the Data Type column, you can either type a valid value or select from the values in the list. Select AutoNumber as the data type for CompanyID.

In the Description column for each field, you can enter a descriptive phrase. Access 2007 displays this description on the status bar (at the bottom of the Access window) whenever you select this field in a query in Datasheet view or in a form in Form view or Datasheet view. For example, enter **Unique Company ID** in the Description column for the CompanyID field.



INSIDE OUT

### Why Setting the Description Property Is Important

Entering a Description property for every field in your table helps document your application. Because Access 2007 also displays the description on the status bar, paying careful attention to what you type in the Description field can later pay big dividends as a kind of mini-help for the users of your database. Also, because this data propagates automatically, you probably don't want to type something nonsensical or silly. Typing **I don't have a clue what this field does** is probably not a good idea—it will show up later on the status bar!

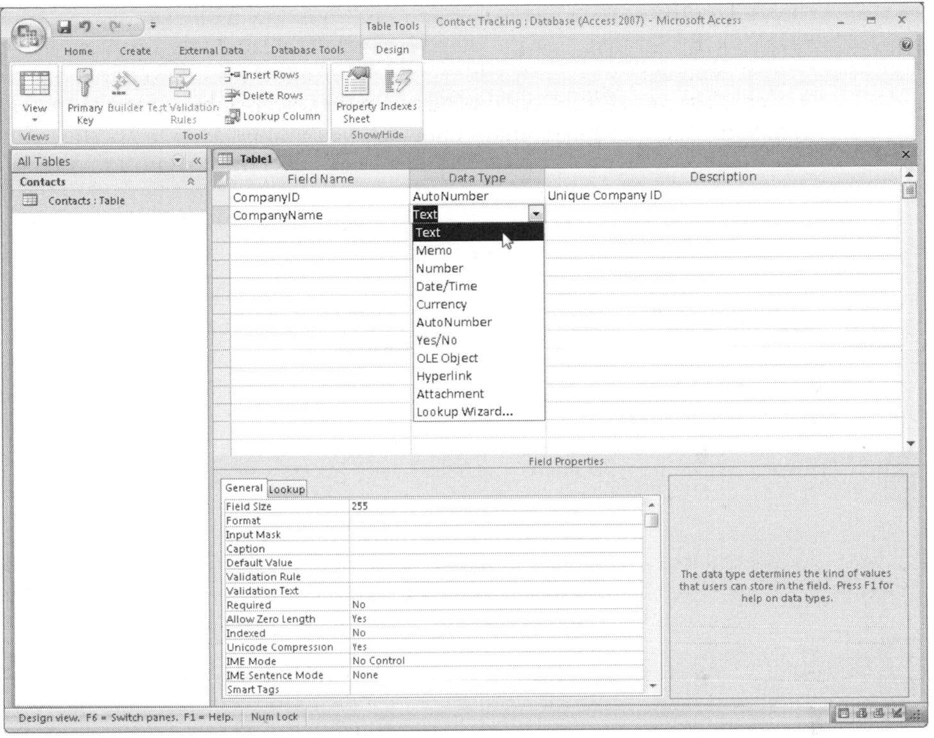


**Figure 4-16** You can choose the data type of a field from a list of data type options.

Tab down to the next line, enter **CompanyName** as a field name, and then choose Text as the data type. After you select a data type, Access 2007 displays some property boxes in the Field Properties section in the lower part of the Table window. These boxes allow you to set *properties*—settings that determine how Access handles the field—and thereby customize a field. The properties Access displays depend on the data type you select; the properties appear with some default values in place, as shown in Figure 4-16.

**For details about the values for each property, see"Setting Field Properties" on page 161.**

## Understanding Field Data Types

Access 2007 supports 10 types of data, each with a specific purpose. You can see the details about each data type in Table 4-1. Access also gives you an eleventh option, Lookup Wizard, to help you define the characteristics of foreign key fields that link to other tables. You'll learn about the Lookup Wizard (and why you shouldn't use it) in the next chapter.

**Table 4-1 Access Data Types**

| Data Type | Usage | Size |
|---|---|---|
| Text | Alphanumeric data | Up to 255 characters |
| Memo | Alphanumeric data—sentences and paragraphs | Up to about 1 gigabyte (but controls to display a memo are limited to the first 64,000 characters) |
| Number | Numeric data | 1, 2, 4, 8 or 16 bytes |
| Date/Time | Dates and times | 8 bytes |
| Currency | Monetary data, stored with 4 decimal places of precision | 8 bytes |
| AutoNumber | Unique value generated by Access for each new record | 4 bytes (16 bytes for ReplicationID) |
| Yes/No | Boolean (true/false) data; Access stores the numeric value zero (0) for false, and minus one (–1) for true | 1 bit |
| OLE Object | Pictures, graphs, or other ActiveX objects from another Windows-based application | Up to about 2 gigabytes |
| Hyperlink | A link "address" to a document or file on the World Wide Web, on an intranet, on a local area network (LAN), or on your local computer | Up to 8,192 characters (each part of a Hyperlink data type can contain up to 2,048 characters) |
| Attachment | You can attach files such as pictures, documents, spreadsheets, or charts; each Attachment field can contain an unlimited number of attachments per record, up to the storage limit of the size of a database file | Up to about 2 gigabytes |
| Lookup Wizard | The Lookup Wizard entry in the Data Type column in Design view is not actually a data type. When you choose this entry, a wizard starts to help you define either a simple or complex lookup field. A simple lookup field uses the contents of another table or a value list to validate the contents of a single value per row. A complex lookup field allows you to store multiple values of the same data type in each row. | Dependent on the data type of the lookup field |

For each field in your table, select the data type that is best suited to how you will use that field's data. For character data, you should normally select the Text data type. You can control the maximum length of a Text field by using a field property, as explained later. Use the Memo data type only for long strings of text that might exceed 255 characters or that might contain formatting characters such as tabs or line endings (carriage returns).

### Choosing Field Names

Office Access 2007 gives you lots of flexibility when it comes to naming your fields. A field name can be up to 64 characters long, can include any combination of letters, numbers, spaces, and special characters except a period (.), an exclamation point (!), an accent grave (`), and brackets ([ ]); however, the name cannot begin with a space and cannot include control characters (ANSI values 0 through 31). In general, you should give your fields meaningful names and should use the same name throughout for a field that occurs in more than one table. You should avoid using field names that might also match any name internal to Access or Visual Basic. For example, all objects have a Name property, so it's a good idea to qualify a field containing a name by calling it CustomerName or CompanyName. You should also avoid names that are the same as built-in functions, such as Date, Time, Now, or Space. See Access Help for a list of all the built-in function names.

Although you can use spaces anywhere within names in Access 2007, you should try to create field names and table names *without* embedded spaces. Many SQL databases to which Access can link (notably Oracle and Ingres) do not support spaces within names. Although SQL Server does allow spaces in names, you must enclose such names in brackets, or use quotes and execute a Set Quoted Identifier On command. If you ever want to move your application to a client/server environment and store your data in an SQL database such as Microsoft SQL Server or Oracle, you'll most likely have to change any names in your database tables that have an embedded space character. As you'll learn later in this book, table field names propagate into the queries, forms, and reports that you design using these tables. So any name you decide to change later in a table must also be changed in all your queries, forms, and reports. See "Setting Table Design Options" on page 191 for details about options to automatically propagate changes.

If you use reserved words or function names for field names, Access 2007 catches most of these and displays a warning message. This message warns you that the field name you chose, such as Name or Date, is a reserved word and you could encounter errors when referring to that field in other areas of the database application. Access still allows you to use this name if you choose, but take note of the problems it could cause. To avoid potential conflicts, we recommend you avoid using reserved words and built-in functions for field names.

When you select the Number data type, you should think carefully about what you enter as the Field Size property because this property choice will affect precision as well as length. (For example, integer numbers do not have decimals.) The Date/Time data type is useful for calendar or clock data and has the added benefit of allowing calculations in seconds, minutes, hours, days, months, or years. For example, you can find out the difference in days between two Date/Time values.

INSIDE OUT

### Understanding What's Inside the Date/Time Data Type

Use the Date/Time data type to store any date, time, or date and time value. It's useful to know that Access 2007 stores the date as the integer portion of the Date/Time data type and the time as the fractional portion—the fraction of a day, measured from midnight, that the time represents, accurate to seconds. For example, 6:00:00 A.M. internally is 0.25. The day number is actually the number of days since December 30, 1899 (there will be a test on that later!) and can be a negative number for dates prior to that date. When two Date/Time fields contain only a date, you can subtract one from the other to find out how many days are between the two dates.

You should generally use the Currency data type for storing money values. Currency has the precision of integers, but with exactly four decimal places. When you need to store a precise fractional number that's not money, use the Number data type and choose Decimal for the Field Size property.

The AutoNumber data type is specifically designed for automatic generation of primary key values. Depending on the settings for the Field Size and New Values properties you choose for an AutoNumber field, you can have Access 2007 create a sequential or random long integer. You can include only one field using the AutoNumber data type in any table. If you define more than one AutoNumber field, Access displays an error message when you try to save the table.

Use the Yes/No data type to hold Boolean (true or false) values. This data type is particularly useful for flagging accounts paid or not paid or orders filled or not filled.

The OLE Object data type allows you to store complex data, such as pictures, graphs, or sounds, which can be edited or displayed through a dynamic link to another Windows-based application. For example, Access 2007 can store and allow you to edit a Microsoft Office Word document, a Microsoft Office Excel spreadsheet, a Microsoft Office PowerPoint presentation slide, a sound file (.wav), a video file (.avi), or pictures created using the Paint or Draw application.

The Hyperlink data type lets you store a simple or complex "link" to an external file or document. (Internally, Hyperlink is a memo data type with a special flag set to indicate that it is a link.) This link can contain a Uniform Resource Locator (URL) that points to a location on the World Wide Web or on a local intranet. It can also contain the Universal Naming Convention (UNC) name of a file on a server on your local area network (LAN) or on your local computer drives. The link can point to a file that is in Hypertext Markup Language (HTML) or in a format that is supported by an ActiveX application on your computer.

The Attachment data type, newly introduced in Access 2007, is very similar to the OLE Object data type in that you can use it to store complex data. However, unlike the OLE Object data type, you can now store *multiple* attachments in a single record. These files are stored in a binary field in a hidden system table. OLE objects usually result in database bloat because the files are not compressed, and Access also stores a bitmap thumbnail of the embedded file that can often be larger than the original file. For the Attachment data type, Access compresses each file, if it isn't already, and uses the original file rather than a generated thumbnail to minimize the amount of database bloat.

**CAUTION!**

You can use the Attachment data type only with databases in the new .accdb file type. If you plan to create a database in the older .mdb format and have users with previous versions of Access use this database, you cannot define any fields as Attachment.

## Setting Field Properties

You can customize the way Access 2007 stores and handles each field by setting specific properties. These properties vary according to the data type you choose. Table 4-2 lists all the possible properties that can appear on a field's General tab in a table's Design view, and the data types that are associated with each property.

**Table 4-2 Field Properties on the General Tab**

| Property | Data Type | Options, Description |
|---|---|---|
| Field Size | Text | Text can be from 0 through 255 characters long, with a default length of 50 characters. |
| | Number | **Byte.** A single-byte integer containing values from 0 through 255. |
| | | **Integer.** A 2-byte integer containing values from –32,768 through +32,767. |
| | | **Long Integer.** A 4-byte integer containing values from –2,147,483,648 through +2,147,483,647. |
| | | **Single.**[1] A 4-byte floating-point number containing values from $-3.4 \times 10^{38}$ through $+3.4 \times 10^{38}$ and up to seven significant digits. |
| | | **Double.**[1] An 8-byte floating-point number containing values from $-1.797 \times 10^{308}$ through $+1.797 \times 10^{308}$ and up to 15 significant digits. |
| | | **Replication ID.**[2] A 16-byte globally unique identifier (GUID). |
| | | **Decimal.** A 12-byte integer with a defined decimal precision that can contain values from approximately $-7.9228 \times 10^{28}$ through $+7.9228 \times 10^{28}$. The default precision (number of decimal places) is 0 and the default scale is 18. |
| New Values | AutoNumber only | **Increment.** Values start at 1 and increment by 1 for each new row. |
| | | **Random.** Access assigns a random long integer value to each new row. |

Chapter 4

| Property | Data Type | Options, Description |
|---|---|---|
| Format | Text, Memo | You can specify a custom format that controls how Access displays the data. For details about custom formats, see "Setting Control Properties" on page 651 or the Access Help topic "Format Property—Text and Memo Data Types." |
| | Number (except Replication ID), Currency, AutoNumber | **General Number (default).** No commas or currency symbols; the number of decimal places shown depends on the precision of the data. |
| | | **Currency.**[3] Currency symbol (from Regional And Language Options in Windows Control Panel) and two decimal places. |
| | | **Euro.** Euro currency symbol (regardless of Control Panel settings) and two decimal places. |
| | | **Fixed.** At least one digit and two decimal places. |
| | | **Standard.** Two decimal places and separator commas. |
| | | **Percent.** Moves displayed decimal point two places to the right and appends a percentage (%) symbol. |
| | | **Scientific.** Scientific notation (for example, 1.05E+06 represents $1.05 \times 10^6$). |
| | | You can specify a custom format that controls how Access displays the data. For details about custom formats, see "Setting Control Properties" on page 651 or the Access Help topic "Format Property—Number and Currency Types." |
| | Date/Time[4] | **General Date (default).** Combines Short Date and Long Time formats (for example, 4/15/2007 5:30:10 PM). |
| | | **Long Date.** Uses Long Date Style from Regional And Language Options in Control Panel (for example, Sunday, April 15, 2007). |
| | | **Medium Date.** 15-Apr-2007. |
| | | **Short Date.**[5] Uses Short Date Style from Regional And Language Options (for example, 4/15/2007). |
| | | **Long Time.** Uses Time Style from Regional And Language Options (for example, 5:30:10 PM). |
| | | **Medium Time.** 5:30 PM. |
| | | **Short Time.** 17:30. |
| | Yes/No | **Yes/No (default).** |
| | | **True/False.** |
| | | **On/Off.** |
| | | You can specify a custom format that controls how Access displays the data. For details about custom formats, see "Setting Control Properties" on page 651 or the Access Help topic "Format Property—Yes/No Data Type." |

| Property | Data Type | Options, Description |
|---|---|---|
| Precision | Number, Decimal | You can specify the maximum number of digits allowed. The default value is 18, and you can specify an integer value between 1 and 28. |
| Scale | Number, Decimal | You can specify the number of digits stored to the right of the decimal point. This value must be less than or equal to the value of the Precision property. |
| Decimal Places | Number (except Replication ID), Currency | You can specify the number of decimal places that Access displays. The default specification is Auto, which causes Access to display two decimal places for the Currency, Fixed, Standard, and Percent formats and the number of decimal places necessary to show the current precision of the numeric value for General Number format. You can also request a fixed display of decimal places ranging from 0 through 15. |
| Input Mask | Text, Number (except Replication ID), Date/Time, Currency | You can specify an editing mask that the user sees while entering data in the field. For example, you can have Access provide the delimiters in a date field such as __/__/__, or you can have Access format a U.S. phone number as (###) 000-0000. See "Defining Input Masks" on page 170 for details. |
| Caption | All | You can enter a more fully descriptive field name that Access displays in form labels and in report headings. (Tip: If you create field names with no embedded spaces, you can use the Caption property to specify a name that includes spaces for Access to use in labels and headers associated with this field in queries, forms, and reports.) |
| Default Value | Text, Memo, Date/Time, Hyperlink, Yes/No | You can specify a default value for the field that Access automatically uses for a new row if no other value is supplied. If you don't specify a Default Value property, the field will be Null if the user fails to supply a value. (See also the Required property.) |
| | Number, Currency | Access sets the property to 0. You can change the setting to a valid numeric value. You can also remove the setting, in which case the field will be Null if the user fails to supply a value. (See also the Required property.) |
| Validation Rule | All (except OLE Object, Replication ID, Attachment, and AutoNumber) | You can supply an expression that must be true whenever you enter or change data in this field. For example, <100 specifies that a number must be less than 100. You can also check for one of a series of values. For example, you can have Access check for a list of valid cities by specifying **"Chicago" Or "New York" Or "San Francisco"**. In addition, you can specify a complex expression that includes any of the built-in functions in Access. See "Defining Simple Field Validation Rules" on page 168 for details. |

| Property | Data Type | Options, Description |
|---|---|---|
| Validation Text | All (except OLE Object, Replication ID, Attachment, and AutoNumber) | You can specify a custom message that Access displays whenever the data entered does not pass your validation rule. |
| Required | All (except AutoNumber) | If you don't want to allow a Null value in this field, set this property to Yes. |
| Allow Zero Length | Text, Memo, Hyperlink | You can set the field equal to a zero-length string ("") if you set this property to Yes. See the sidebar, "Nulls and Zero-Length Strings," on page 166 for more information. |
| Indexed | All except OLE Object and Attachment | You can ask that an index be built to speed access to data values. You can also require that the values in the indexed field always be unique for the entire table. See "Adding Indexes" on page 188, for details. |
| Unicode Compression | Text, Memo, Hyperlink | As of version 2000, Access stores character fields in an .mdb and .accdb file using a double-byte (Unicode) character set to support extended character sets in languages that require them. The Latin character set required by most Western European languages (such as English, Spanish, French, or German) requires only 1 byte per character. When you set Unicode Compression to Yes for character fields, Access stores compressible characters in 1 byte instead of 2, thus saving space in your database file. However, Access will not compress Memo or Hyperlink fields that will not compress to fewer than 4,096 bytes. The default for new tables is Yes in all countries where the standard language character set does not require 2 bytes to store all the characters. |
| IME Mode, IME Sentence Mode | Text, Memo, Hyperlink | On computers with an Asian version of Windows and appropriate Input Method Editor (IME) installed, these properties control conversion of characters in kanji, hiragana, katakana, and hangul character sets. |

| Property | Data Type | Options, Description |
|---|---|---|
| Smart Tags | All data types except Yes/No, OLE Object, Attachment, and Replication ID | Indicates the registered smart tag name and action that you want associated with this field. When the user views this field in a table datasheet, a query datasheet, or a form, Access displays a smart tag available indicator next to the field. The user can click on the indicator and select the smart tag action to perform. For an example using a smart tag, see Chapter 12, "Customizing a Form." |

[1] Single and Double field sizes use an internal storage format called floating point that can handle very large or very small numbers, but which is somewhat imprecise. If the number you need to store contains more than 7 significant digits for a Single or more than 15 significant digits for a Double, the number will be rounded. For example, if you try to save 10,234,567 in a Single, the actual value stored will be 10,234,570. Likewise, Access stores 10.234567 as 10.23457 in a Single. If you want absolute fractional precision, use Decimal field size or Currency data type instead.

[2] In general, you should use the Replication ID field size only in an Access 2003 format and earlier database that is managed by the Replication Manager.

[3] Note that Currency, Euro, Fixed, and Standard formats always display two decimal places regardless of the number of actual decimal places in the underlying data. Access rounds any number to two decimal places for display if the number contains more than two decimal places.

[4] You can also specify a custom format in addition to the built-in ones described here. See Chapter 12 for details.

[5] To help alleviate problems with dates spanning the start of the century, we recommend that you select the Use Four-Digit Year Formatting check box in Access. Click the Microsoft Office Button, click Access Options, and then scroll to the General section in the Advanced category to find this option. You should also be sure that your Short Date Style in the Regional And Language Options dialog box uses a four-digit year. (This is the default in Windows XP and Windows Vista; you can double-check your settings by accessing Regional And Language Options within Control Panel.)



## INSIDE OUT Don't Specify a Validation Rule Without Validation Text

If you specify a validation rule but no validation text, Access 2007 generates an ugly and cryptic message that your users might not understand:

"One or more values are prohibited by the validation rule '<*your expression here*>' set for '<*table name.field name*>'. Enter a value that the expression for this field can accept."

Unless you like getting lots of support calls, we recommend that you always enter a custom validation text message whenever you specify a validation rule.

For details about the properties on the Lookup tab, see "Taking a Look at Lookup Properties," on page 240.

### Nulls and Zero-Length Strings

Relational databases support a special value in fields, called a *Null*, that indicates an unknown value. In contrast, you can set Text or Memo fields to a *zero-length string* to indicate that the value of a field is known but the field is empty.

Why is it important to differentiate Nulls (unknown values) from zero-length strings? Here's an example: Suppose you have a database that stores the results of a survey about automobile preferences. For questionnaires on which there is no response to a color-preference question, it is appropriate to store a Null. You don't want to match responses based on an unknown response, and you don't want to include the row in calculating totals or averages. On the other hand, some people might have responded "I don't care" for a color preference. In this case, you have a known "no preference" answer, and a zero-length string is appropriate. You can match all "I don't care" responses and include the responses in totals and averages.

Another example might be fax numbers in a customer database. If you store a Null, it means you don't know whether the customer has a fax number. If you store a zero-length string, you know the customer has no fax number. Access 2007 gives you the flexibility to deal with both types of "empty" values.

You can join tables on zero-length strings, and two zero-length strings will compare to be equal. However, for Text, Memo, and Hyperlink fields, you must set the Allow Zero Length property to Yes to allow users to enter zero-length strings. (Yes became the default in Microsoft Access 2002.) Otherwise, Access converts a zero-length or all-blank string to a Null before storing the value. If you also set the Required property of the Text field to Yes, Access stores a zero-length string if the user enters either "" (two double quotes with no space) or blanks in the field.

Nulls have special properties. A Null value cannot be equal to any other value, not even to another Null. This means you cannot join (link) two tables on Null values. Also, the question "Is A equal to B?" when A, B, or both A and B contain a Null, can never be answered "yes." The answer, literally, is "I don't know." Likewise, the answer to the question "Is A not equal to B?" is also "I don't know." Finally, Null values do not participate in aggregate calculations involving such functions as Sum or Avg. You can test a value to determine whether it is a Null by comparing it to the special NULL keyword or by using the IsNull built-in function.

## Completing the Fields in the Companies Table

You now know enough about field data types and properties to finish designing the Companies table in this example. (You can also follow this example using the tblCompanies table from the Conrad Systems Contacts sample database.) Use the information listed in Table 4-3 to design the table shown in Figure 4-17.

Table 4-3 **Field Definitions for the Companies Table**

| Field Name | Data Type | Description | Field Size |
|---|---|---|---|
| CompanyID | AutoNumber | Unique Company ID | |
| CompanyName | Text | Company Name | 50 |
| Department | Text | Department | 50 |
| Address | Text | Address | 255 |
| City | Text | City | 50 |
| County | Text | County | 50 |
| StateOrProvince | Text | State or Province | 20 |
| PostalCode | Text | Postal/Zip Code | 10 |
| PhoneNumber | Text | Phone Number | 15 |
| FaxNumber | Text | Fax Number | 15 |
| Website | Hyperlink | Website address | |
| ReferredBy | Number | Contact who referred this company | Long Integer |

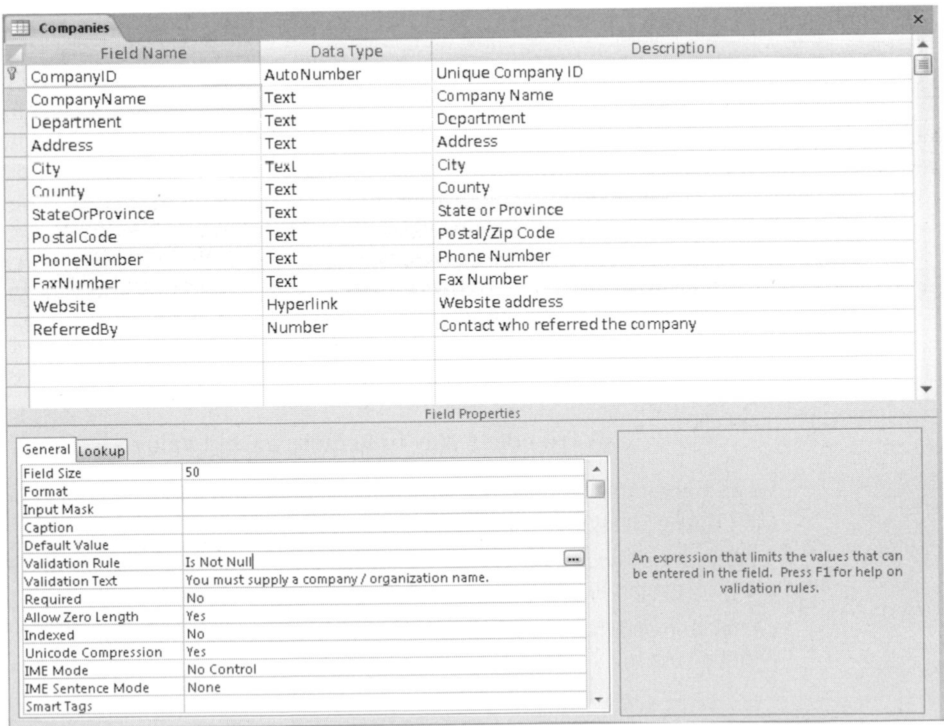


**Figure 4-17** Your fields in the Companies table should look like this. You'll learn how to define validation rules in the next section.

## Defining Simple Field Validation Rules

To define a simple check on the values that you allow in a field, enter an expression in the Validation Rule property box for the field. Access 2007 won't allow you to enter a field value that violates this rule. Access performs this validation for data entered in a Table window in Datasheet view, in an updateable query, or in a form. You can specify a more restrictive validation rule in a form, but you cannot override the rule defined for the field in the table by specifying a completely different rule in the form. For more information on using validation rules in forms, see Chapter 12.

In general, a field validation expression consists of an operator and a comparison value. If you do not include an operator, Access assumes you want an "equals" (=) comparison. You can specify multiple comparisons separated by the Boolean operators OR and AND.

It is good practice to always enclose text string values in quotation marks. If one of your values is a text string containing blanks or special characters, you must enclose the entire string in quotation marks. For example, to limit the valid entries for a City field to the two largest cities in the state of California, enter **"Los Angeles" Or "San Diego"**. If you are comparing date values, you must enclose the date constants in pound sign (#) characters, as in #01/15/2007#.

You can use the comparison symbols to compare the value in the field to a value or values in your validation rule. Comparison symbols are summarized in Table 4-4. For example, you might want to ensure that a numeric value is always less than 1000. To do this, enter **<1000**. You can use one or more pairs of comparisons to ask Access to check that the value falls within certain ranges. For example, if you want to verify that a number is in the range of 50 through 100, enter either **>=50 And <=100** or **Between 50 And 100**. Another way to test for a match in a list of values is to use the IN comparison operator. For example, to test for states surrounding the U.S. capital, enter **In ("Virginia", "Maryland")**. If all you need to do is ensure that the user enters a value, you can use the special comparison phrase **Is Not Null**.



INSIDE OUT **A Friendlier Way to Require a Field Value**

When you set the Required property to Yes and the user fails to enter a value, Access 2007 displays an unfriendly message:

"The field '*<tablename.fieldname>*' cannot contain a Null value because the Required property for this field is set to True. Enter a value in this field."

We recommend that you use the Validation Rule property to require a value in the field and then use the Validation Text property to generate your own specific message.

**Table 4-4 Comparison Symbols Used in Validation Rules**

| Operator | Meaning |
| --- | --- |
| NOT | Use before any comparison operator except IS NOT NULL to perform the converse test. For example, NOT > 5 is equivalent to <=5. |
| < | Less than |
| <= | Less than or equal to |
| > | Greater than |
| >= | Greater than or equal to |
| = | Equal to |
| <> | Not equal to |
| IN | Test for *equal to* any member in a list; comparison value must be a comma-separated list enclosed in parentheses |
| BETWEEN | Test for a range of values; comparison value must be two values (a low and a high value) separated by the AND operator |
| LIKE | Test a Text or Memo field to match a pattern string |
| IS NOT NULL | Requires the user to enter a value in the field |

If you need to validate a Text, Memo, or Hyperlink field against a matching pattern (for example, a postal code or a phone number), you can use the LIKE comparison operator. You provide a text string as a comparison value that defines which characters are valid in which positions. Access understands a number of *wildcard characters*, which you can use to define positions that can contain any single character, zero or more characters, or any single number. These characters are shown in Table 4-5.

**Table 4-5 LIKE Wildcard Characters**

| Character | Meaning |
| --- | --- |
| ? | Any single character |
| * | Zero or more characters; use to define leading, trailing, or embedded strings that don't have to match any specific pattern characters |
| # | Any single digit |

You can also specify that any particular position in the Text or Memo field can contain only characters from a list that you provide. You can specify a range of characters within a list by entering the low value character, a hyphen, and the high value character, as in [A-Z] or [3-7]. If you want to test a position for any characters *except* those in a list, start the list with an exclamation point (!). You must enclose all lists in brackets ([ ]). You can see examples of validation rules using LIKE here.

| Validation Rule | Tests For |
|---|---|
| LIKE "#####" or | A U.S. 5-digit ZIP Code |
| LIKE "#####-####" | A U.S. 9-digit ZIP+ Code |
| LIKE "[A-Z]#[A-Z] #[A-Z]#" | A Canadian postal code |
| LIKE "###-##-####" | A U.S. Social Security Number |
| LIKE "Smith*" | A string that begins with *Smith*[1] |
| LIKE "*smith##*" | A string that contains *smith* followed by two numbers, anywhere in the string |
| LIKE "??00####" | An eight-character string that contains any first two characters followed by exactly two zeros and then any four digits |
| LIKE "[!0-9BMQ]*####" | A string that contains any character other than a number or the letter *B*, *M*, or *Q* in the first position and ends with exactly four digits |

[1] Character string comparisons in Access are case-insensitive. So, smith, SMITH, and Smith are all equal.



## Defining Input Masks

To assist you in entering formatted data, Access 2007 allows you to define an *input mask* for Text, Number (except Replication ID), Date/Time, and Currency data types. You can use an input mask to do something as simple as forcing all letters entered to be uppercase or as complex as adding parentheses and hyphens to phone numbers. You create an input mask by using the special mask definition characters shown in Table 4-6. You can also embed strings of characters that you want to display for formatting or store in the data field.

Table 4-6 **Input Mask Definition Characters**

| Mask Character | Meaning |
|---|---|
| 0 | A single digit must be entered in this position. |
| 9 | A digit or a space can be entered in this position. If the user skips this position by moving the insertion point past the position without entering anything, Access stores nothing in this position. |
| # | A digit, a space, or a plus or minus sign can be entered in this position. If the user skips this position by moving the insertion point past the position without entering anything, Access stores a space. |
| L | A letter must be entered in this position. |

| Mask Character | Meaning |
|---|---|
| ? | A letter can be entered in this position. If the user skips this position by moving the insertion point past the position without entering anything, Access stores nothing. |
| A | A letter or a digit must be entered in this position. |
| a | A letter or a digit can be entered in this position. If the user skips this position by moving the insertion point past the position without entering anything, Access stores nothing. |
| & | A character or a space must be entered in this position. |
| C | Any character or a space can be entered in this position. If the user skips this position by moving the insertion point past the position without entering anything, Access stores nothing. |
| . | Decimal placeholder (depends on the setting in the Regional And Language Options in Control Panel). |
| , | Thousands separator (depends on the setting in the Regional And Language Options in Control Panel). |
| : ; - / | Date and time separators (depend on the settings in the Regional And Language Options in Control Panel). |
| < | Converts to lowercase all characters that follow. |
| > | Converts to uppercase all characters that follow. |
| ! | Causes the mask to fill from right to left when you define optional characters on the left end of the mask. You can place this character anywhere in the mask. |
| \ | Causes the character immediately following to be displayed as a literal character rather than as a mask character. |
| "literal" | You can also enclose any literal string in double quotation marks rather than use the \ character repeatedly. |

An input mask consists of three parts, separated by semicolons. The first part defines the mask string using mask definition characters and embedded literal data. The optional second part indicates whether you want the embedded literal characters stored in the field in the database. Set this second part to **0** to store the characters or to **1** to store only the data entered. The optional third part defines a single character that Access 2007 uses as a placeholder to indicate positions where data can be entered. The default placeholder character is an underscore (_).

Perhaps the best way to learn to use input masks is to take advantage of the Input Mask Wizard. In the Companies table of the Contact Tracking database, the PhoneNumber field could benefit from the use of an input mask. Click the PhoneNumber field in the upper part of the Table window in Design view, and then click in the Input Mask property box in the lower part of the window. You should see a small button with three dots on it (called the *Build* button) to the right of the property box.

Click the Build button to start the Input Mask Wizard. If you haven't already saved the table, the wizard will insist that you do so. Save the table and name it Companies. When Access 2007 warns you that you have not defined a primary key and asks if you want to create a primary key now, click No. We'll define a primary key in the next section. On the first page, the wizard gives you a number of choices for standard input masks that it can generate for you. In this case, click the first one in the list—Phone Number, as shown in Figure 4-18. Note that you can type something in the Try It box below the Input Mask list to try out the mask.

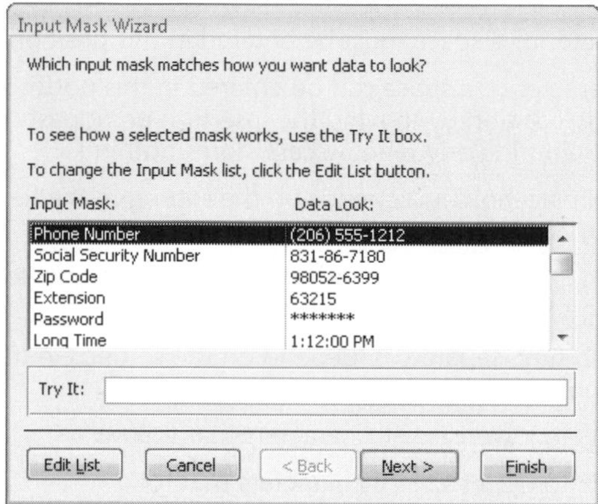


**Figure 4-18** You can choose from several built-in input masks in the Input Mask Wizard.

Click the Next button to go to the next page. On this page, shown in Figure 4-19, you can see the mask name, the proposed mask string, a list from which you select the placeholder character, and another Try It box. The default underscore character (_) works well as a placeholder character for phone numbers.

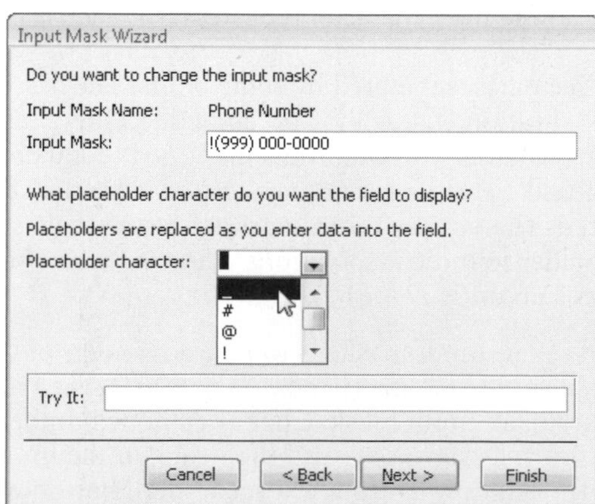


**Figure 4-19** You can choose the placeholder character in the Input Mask Wizard.

Click Next to go to the next page, where you can choose whether you want the data stored without the formatting characters (the default) or stored with the parentheses, spaces, and hyphen separator. In Figure 4-20, we're indicating that we want the data stored with the formatting characters. Click Next to go to the final page, and then click the Finish button on that page to store the mask in the property setting. Figure 4-21 shows the resulting mask in the PhoneNumber field. You'll find this same mask handy for any text field that is meant to contain a U.S. phone number (such as the phone number fields in the Contacts table).

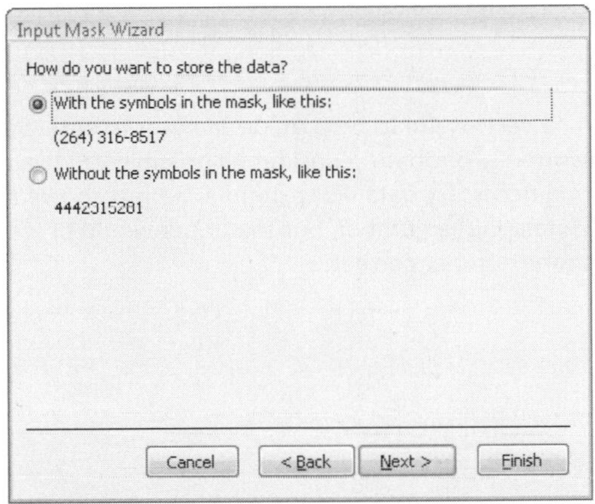


**Figure 4-20** You can choose to store formatting characters.

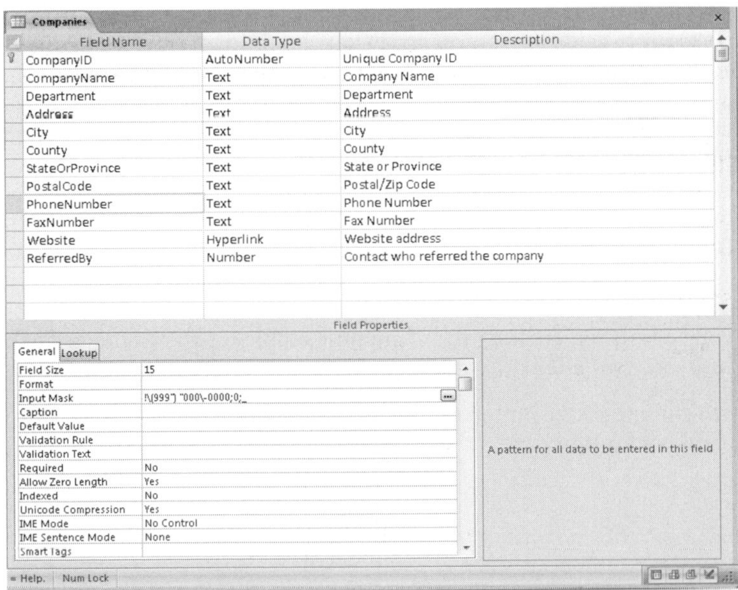


**Figure 4-21** The wizard stores the input mask for PhoneNumber based on the criteria you selected.

**Note**

If you look closely in Figure 4-21, you can see a backslash before the area code and quotation marks around the second parenthesis. When you complete the Input Mask Wizard, Access initially does not display these extra characters. After you click off that field or save the table, Access adds the missing characters. The mask generated by the wizard is incorrect, but the table editor fixes it before saving.

**CAUTION!**

Although an input mask can be very useful to help guide the user to enter valid data, if you define an input mask incorrectly or do not consider all possible valid values, you can prevent the user from entering necessary data. For example, we just showed you how to build an input mask for a U.S. telephone number, but that mask would prevent someone from entering a European phone number correctly.

## Defining a Primary Key

Every table in a relational database should have a primary key. Telling Access 2007 how to define the primary key is quite simple. Open the table in Design view and click the row selector to the left of the field you want to use as the primary key. If you need to select multiple fields for your primary key, hold down the Ctrl key and click the row selector of each additional field you need.

**For details about designing primary keys for your tables, see Article 1, "Designing Your Database Application," on the companion CD.**

After you select all the fields you want for the primary key, click the Primary Key button in the Tools group of the Design contextual tab on the Ribbon. Access 2007 displays a key symbol to the left of the selected field(s) to acknowledge your definition of the primary key. To eliminate all primary key designations, see "Adding Indexes" on page 188. When you've finished creating the Companies table for the Contact Tracking database, the primary key should be the CompanyID field, as shown in Figure 4-22.

Be sure to click the Save button on the Quick Access Toolbar to save this latest change to your table definition.

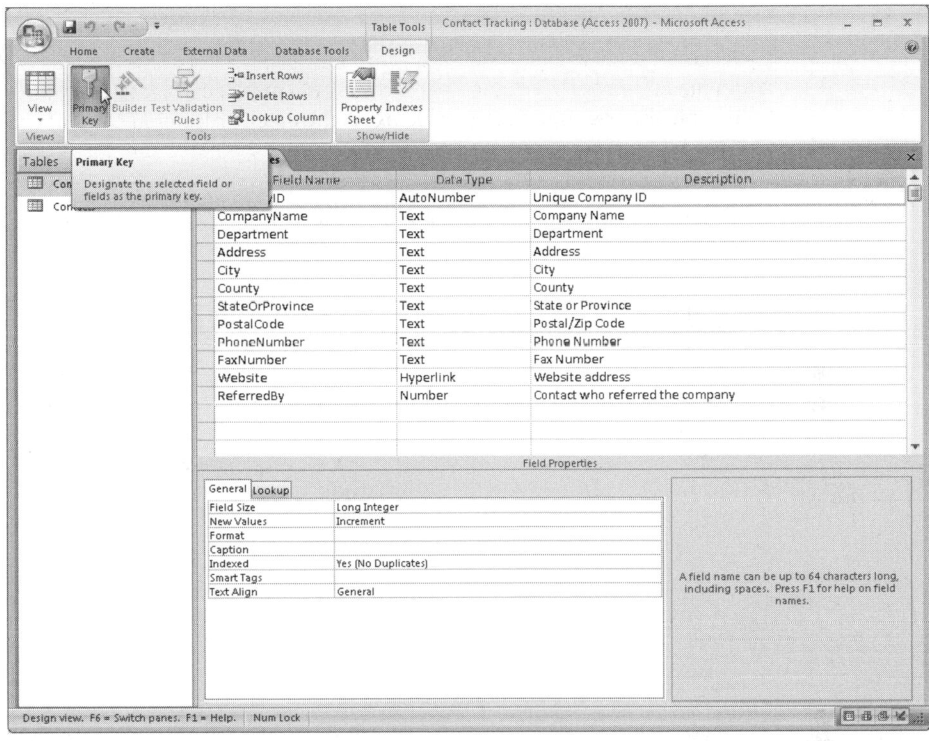


**Figure 4-22** You can easily define the primary key for the Companies table by selecting the field in Design view and clicking the Primary Key button on the Ribbon.



# Defining a Table Validation Rule

The last detail to define is any validation rules that you want Access 2007 to apply to any fields in the table. Although field validation rules get checked as you enter each new value, Access checks a table validation rule only when you save or add a row. Table validation rules are handy when the values in one field are dependent on what's stored in another field. You need to wait until the entire row is about to be saved before checking one field against another.

One of the tables in the Contact Tracking database—Products—needs a table validation rule. Define that table now using the specifications in Table 4-7. Be sure to define ProductID as the primary key and then save the table and name it Products.

**Table 4-7 Field Definitions for the Products Table**

| Field Name | Data Type | Description | Field Size |
|---|---|---|---|
| ProductID | AutoNumber | Unique product identifier | |
| ProductName | Text | Product description | 100 |
| CategoryDescription | Text | Description of the category | 50 |
| UnitPrice | Currency | Price | |
| TrialVersion | Yes/No | Is this a trial version? | |
| TrialExpire | Number | If trial version, number of days before expiration | Long Integer |

To define a table validation rule, be sure that the table is in Design view, and then click the Property Sheet button in the Show/Hide group of the Design contextual tab on the Ribbon, shown in Figure 4-23.

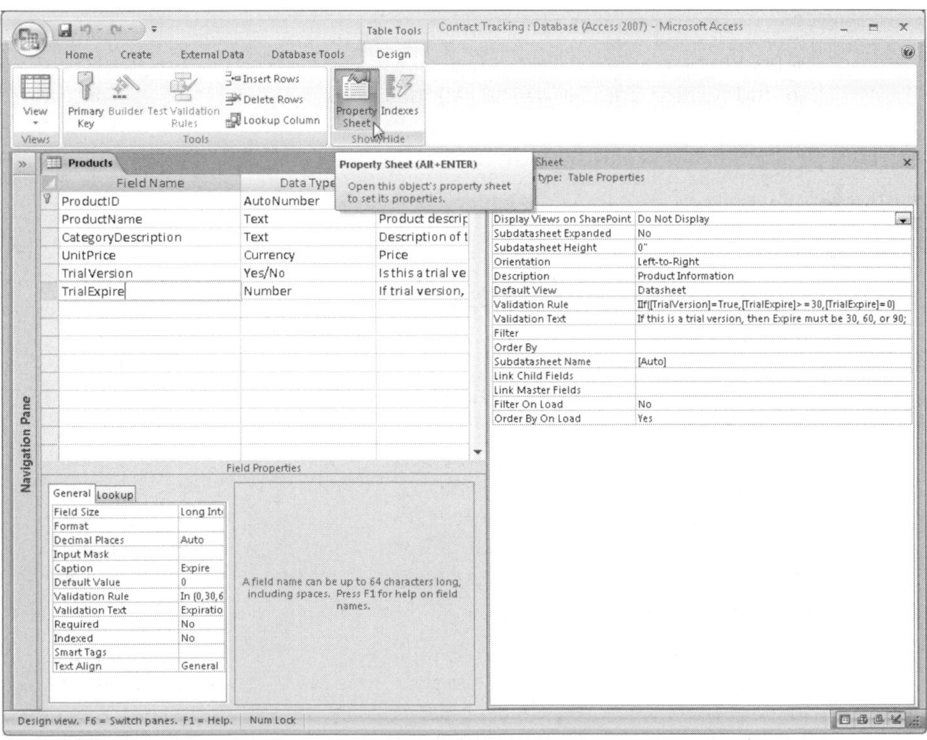

**Figure 4-23** You can define a table validation rule in the property sheet for the table.

**To learn more about expressions, see "Using the Expression Builder" on page 371.**

Chapter 4

On the Validation Rule line in the table's property sheet, you can enter any valid comparison expression, or you can use one of the built-in functions to test your table's field values. In the Products table, we want to be sure that any trial version of the software expires in 30, 60, or 90 days. Zero is also a valid value if this particular product isn't a trial version. As you can see in Figure 4-23, we've already entered a *field* validation rule for TrialExpire on the General tab to make sure the TrialExpire value is always 0, 30, 60, or 90—In (0, 30, 60, 90). But how do we make sure that TrialExpire is zero if TrialVersion is False, or one of the other values if TrialVersion is True? For that, we need to define a *table-level* validation rule in the table's property sheet.

To refer to a field name, enclose the name in brackets ([ ]), as shown in Figure 4-23. You'll use this technique whenever you refer to the name of an object anywhere in an expression. In this case, we're using a special built-in function called *Immediate If* (or *IIF* for short) in the table validation rule to perform the test on the TrialExpire and TrialVersion fields. The IIF function can evaluate a test in the first argument and then return the evaluation of the second argument if the first argument is true or the evaluation of the third argument if the first argument is false. As you will learn in Chapter 19, "Understanding Visual Basic Fundamentals," you must separate the arguments in a function call with commas. Note that we said *evaluation of the argument*—this means we can enter additional tests, even another IIF, in the second and third arguments.

In the Products table, you want to make sure that the TrialVersion and TrialExpire fields are in sync with each other. If this is not a trial version, the TrialExpire field value should be zero (indicating the product never expires), and if it is a trial version, TrialExpire must be set to some value greater than or equal to 30. The expression we used to accomplish this is as follows:

IIf([TrialVersion]=True,[TrialExpire]>=30,[TrialExpire]=0)

So, the first argument uses IIF to evaluate the expression `[TrialVersion] = True`—is the value in the field named TrialVersion True? If this is true (this is a trial version that must have a nonzero number of expiration days), IIF returns the evaluation of the second argument. If this is not a trial version, IIF evaluates the third argument. Now all we need to do is type the appropriate test based on the true or false result on TrialVersion. If this is a trial version, the TrialExpire field must be 30 or greater (we'll let the field validation rule make sure it's exactly 30, 60, or 90), so we need to test for that by entering **[TrialExpire] >= 30** in the second argument. If this is not a trial version, we need to make sure TrialExpire is zero by entering **[TrialExpire] = 0** in the third argument. Got it? If TrialVersion is True, then [TrialExpire] >= 30 must be true or the validation rule will fail. If TrialVersion is False, then [TrialExpire] = 0 must be true. As you might imagine, once you become more familiar with building expressions and with the available built-in functions, you can create very sophisticated table validation rules.

On the Validation Text line of the table's property sheet, enter the text that you want Access to display whenever the table validation rule is violated. You should be careful to word this message so that the user clearly understands what is wrong. If you enter a table validation rule and fail to specify validation text, Access displays the following message when the user enters invalid data: "One or more values are prohibited by the validation rule '< *your validation rule expression here* >' set for '<*table name*>'. Enter a value that the expression for this field can accept."

Not very pretty, is it? And you can imagine what the user will say about your IIF expression!

## Understanding Other Table Properties

As you can see in Figure 4-23, Access 2007 provides several additional table properties that you can set in Design view. You can enter a description of the table in the Description property, and you'll see this description in the Navigation Pane if you ask for the Details view. For Default View, you can choose from Datasheet (the default), PivotTable, or PivotChart. You can read more about PivotTable and PivotChart views in Chapter 13, "Advanced Form Design."

The Filter property lets you predefine criteria to limit the data displayed in the Datasheet view of this table. If you set Filter On Load to Yes, Access applies the filter you defined when you open the datasheet. You can use Order By to define one or more fields that define the default display sequence of rows in this table when in Datasheet view. If you don't define an Order By property, Access displays the rows in primary key sequence. You can set the Order By On Load property to Yes to request that Access always applies any Order By specification when opening the datasheet.



**Note**

If you apply a filter or specify a sorting sequence when you have the table open in Datasheet view, Access 2007 saves the filter in the Filter property and the sorting sequence in the Order By property. If you have Filter On Load or Order By On Load set to Yes, Access reapplies the previous filter or sort sequence criteria the next time you open the datasheet.

You can find five properties—Subdatasheet Name, Link Child Fields, Link Master Fields, Subdatasheet Height, and Subdatasheet Expanded—that are all related. Access 2000 introduced a feature that lets you see information from related tables when you view the datasheet of a table. For example, in the Contact Tracking database you have been building, you can set the Subdatasheet properties in the definition of Contacts to also show you related information from ContactEvents or ContactProducts. In the Housing Reservations sample database, you can see Departments and their Employees, or Employees and their Reservation Requests. Figure 4-24 shows you the Departments table in Housing.accdb open in Datasheet view. For this table, we defined a subdatasheet to show related employee information for each department.

**Figure 4-24** The datasheet for the tblDepartments table in the Housing Reservations sample database shows an expanded subdatasheet.

Notice the small plus and minus signs at the beginning of each department row. Click on a plus sign to expand the subdatasheet to show related employees. Click on the minus sign to shrink the subdatasheet and show only department information. Table 4-8 explains each of the Table Property settings that you can specify to attach a subdatasheet to a table.



## INSIDE OUT Don't Set Subdatasheet Properties in a Table

For a production application, it's a good idea to set Subdatasheet Name in all your tables to [None]. First, when Access 2007 opens your table, it must not only fetch the rows from the table but also fetch the rows defined in the subdatasheet. Adding a subdatasheet to a large table can negatively impact performance.

Also, any production application should not allow the user to see table or query datasheets because you cannot enforce complex business rules. Any data validation in a table or query datasheet depends entirely on the validation and referential integrity rules defined for your tables because you cannot define any Visual Basic code behind tables or queries.

However, you might find the table and query subdatasheets feature useful in your own personal databases. We'll show you how to build a query with a subdatasheet in Chapter 8, "Building Complex Queries," and a form that uses a subdatasheet in Chapter 13.

**Table 4-8 Table Properties for Defining a Subdatasheet**

| Property Name | Setting | Description |
|---|---|---|
| Subdatasheet Name | [Auto] | Creates a subdatasheet using the first table that has a many relationship defined with this table. |
| | [None] | Turns off the subdatasheet feature. |
| | Table.*name* or Query.*name* | Uses the selected table or query as the subdatasheet. |
| Link Child Fields | Name(s) of the foreign key fields(s) in the related table, separated by semicolons | Defines the fields in the subdatasheet table or query that match the primary key fields in this table. When you choose a table or query for the Subdatasheet Name property, Access uses an available relationship definition or matching field names and data types to automatically set this property for you. You can correct this setting if Access has guessed wrong. |
| Link Master Fields | Name(s) of the primary key field(s) in this table, separated by semicolons | Defines the primary key fields that Access uses to link to the subdatasheet table or query. When you choose a table or query for the Subdatasheet Name property, Access uses an available relationship definition or matching field names and data types to automatically set this property for you. You can correct this setting if Access has guessed wrong. |
| Subdatasheet Height | A measurement in inches | If you specify zero (the default), each subdatasheet expands to show all available rows when opened. When you specify a nonzero value, the subdatasheet window opens to the height you specify. If the height is insufficient to display all rows, a scroll bar appears to allow you to look at all the rows. |
| Subdatasheet Expanded | Yes or No | If you specify Yes, all subdatasheets appear expanded when you open the table datasheet. No is the default. |

You can use the Orientation property to specify the reading sequence of the data in Datasheet view. The default in most versions of Access is Left-to-Right. In versions that support a language that is normally read right to left, the default is Right-to-Left. When you use Right-to-Left, field and table captions appear right-justified, the field order is right to left, and the tab sequence proceeds right to left.

The Display Views On SharePoint property by default is set to Follow Database Setting, which means links are created in the views list when this table is upsized to a Windows SharePoint Services site. We'll discuss upsizing a database to a Windows SharePoint Services site in Chapter 22.

## Defining Relationships

After you have defined two or more related tables, you should tell Access 2007 how the tables are related. You do this so that Access 2007 will be able to link all your tables when you need to use them in queries, forms, or reports.

Thus far in this chapter, you have seen how to build the main subject tables of the Contact Tracking database—Companies, Contacts, and Products. Before we define the relationships in this sample database, you need to create a couple of *linking* tables that define the many-to-many relationships between the Companies and Contacts tables and between the Products and Contacts tables. Table 4-9 shows you the fields you need for the Company Contacts table that forms the "glue" between the Companies and Contacts tables.

Table 4-9 **Field Definitions for the Company Contacts Table**

| Field Name | Data Type | Description | Field Size |
|---|---|---|---|
| CompanyID | Number | Company/organization | Long Integer |
| ContactID | Number | Person within company | Long Integer |
| Position | Text | Person's position within the company | 50 |
| DefaultForContact | Yes/No | Is this the default company for this contact? | |

Define the combination of CompanyID and ContactID as the primary key for this table by clicking the selection button next to CompanyID and then holding down the Ctrl key and clicking the button next to ContactID. Click the Primary Key button in the Tools group of the Design tab on the Ribbon to define the key and then save the table as CompanyContacts.

Table 4-10 shows you the fields you need to define the Contact Products table that creates the link between the Contacts and Products tables.

**Table 4-10 Field Definitions for the Contact Products Table**

| Field Name | Data Type | Description | Field Size |
|---|---|---|---|
| CompanyID | Number | Company/organization | Long Integer |
| ContactID | Number | Related contact | Long Integer |
| ProductID | Number | Related product | Long Integer |
| DateSold | Date/Time | Date product sold | |
| SoldPrice | Currency | Price paid | |

The primary key of the Contact Products table is the combination of CompanyID, ContactID, and ProductID. You can click on CompanyID to select it and then hold down the Shift key while you click on ProductID (if you defined the fields in sequence) to select all three fields. Click the Primary Key button in the Tools group of the Design tab on the Ribbon to define the key, and then save the table as ContactProducts.

You need one last table, the Contact Events Table, to define all the major tables you'll need for Contact Tracking. Table 4-11 shows the fields you need. The primary key for this table is the combination of ContactID and ContactDateTime. Note that we took advantage of the fact that a Date/Time data type in Access 2007 can store both a date and a time, so we don't need the two separate date and time fields. Save this last table as ContactEvents.

**Table 4-11 Field Definitions for the Contact Events Table**

| Field Name | Data Type | Description | Field Size |
|---|---|---|---|
| ContactID | Number | Related contact | Long Integer |
| ContactDateTime | Date/Time | Date and time of the contact | |
| ContactNotes | Memo | Description of the contact | |
| ContactFollowUpDate | Date/Time | Follow-up date | |

Now you're ready to start defining relationships. To define relationships, first close any Table windows that are open and then click the Relationships command in the Show/Hide group of the Database Tools tab on the Ribbon to open the Relationships window. If this is the first time you have defined relationships in this database, Access 2007 opens a blank Relationships window and opens the Show Table dialog box, shown in Figure 4-25.

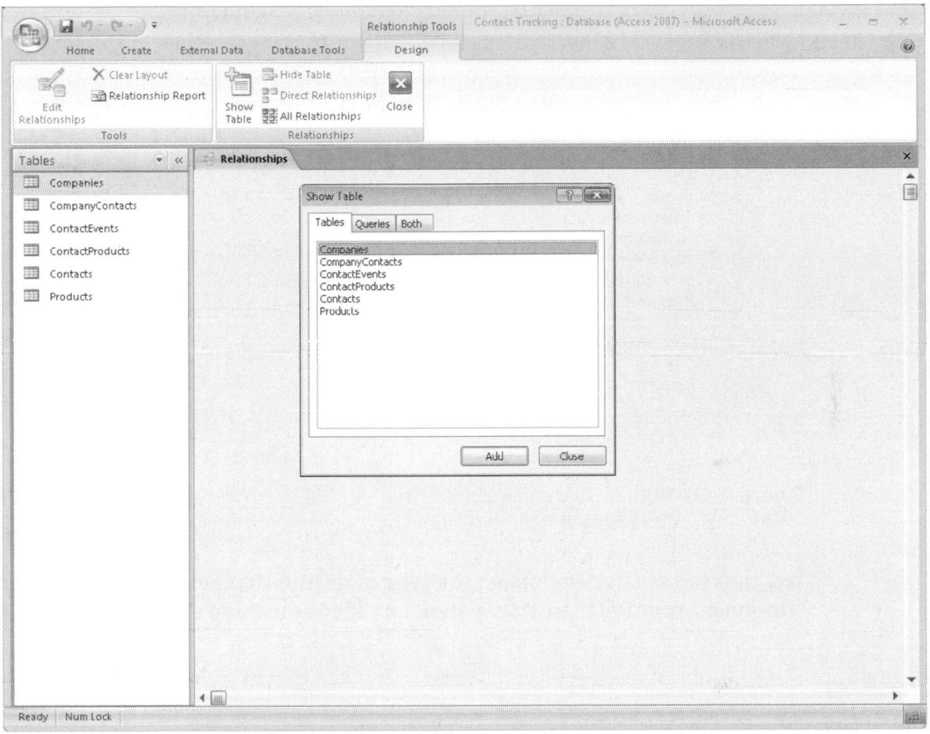


**Figure 4-25** Access displays the Show Table dialog box when you open the Relationships window for the first time.

In the Show Table dialog box, select each table and click the Add button in turn. Click Close to dismiss the Show Table dialog box.



## Defining Your First Relationship

A company can have several contacts, and any contact can belong to several companies or organizations. This means that companies have a many-to-many relationship with contacts. Defining a many-to-many relationship between two tables requires a linking table. Let's link the Companies and Contacts tables by defining the first half of the relationship—the one between Companies and the linking table, CompanyContacts. You can see that for the CompanyID primary key in the Companies table, there is a matching CompanyID foreign key in the CompanyContacts table. To create the relationship you need, click in the CompanyID field in the Companies table and drag it to the CompanyID field in the CompanyContacts table, as shown in Figure 4-26.

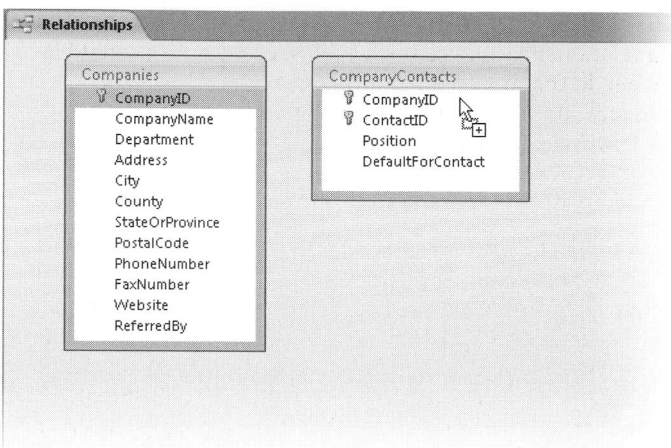


**Figure 4-26** Drag the linking field from the "one" table (Companies) to the "many" table (CompanyContacts) to define the relationship between the tables.

**You can read about determining the type of relationship between two tables in Article 1, "Designing Your Database Application," on the companion CD.**

When you release the mouse button, Access opens the Edit Relationships dialog box, shown in Figure 4-27.

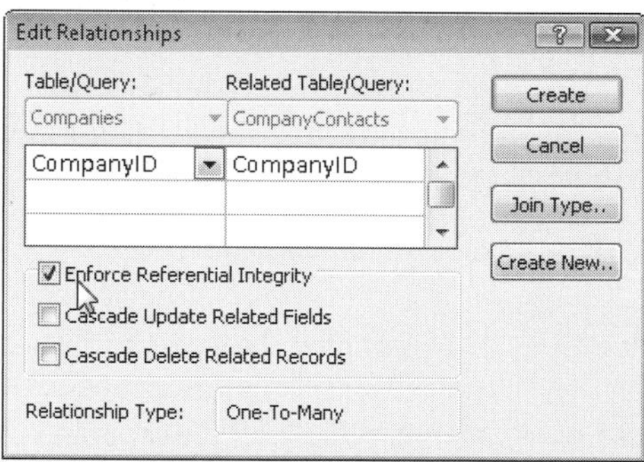


**Figure 4-27** The Edit Relationships dialog box lets you specify the linking fields in two tables.

INSIDE OUT

### Creating Relationships from Scratch

You can also click the Edit Relationships command in the Tools group of the Design contextual tab on the Ribbon to create a new relationship, but you have to fill in the table and field names yourself. Dragging and dropping does some of this work for you.

You'll notice that Access 2007 has filled in the field names for you. If you need to define a multiple-field relationship between two tables, use the additional blank lines to define those fields. (We'll do that in just a second.) Because you probably don't want any rows created in CompanyContacts for a nonexistent company, select the Enforce Referential Integrity check box. When you do this, Access 2007 ensures that you can't add a row in the CompanyContacts table containing an invalid CompanyID. Also, Access won't let you delete any records from the Companies table if they have contacts still defined.

Note that after you select the Enforce Referential Integrity check box, Access 2007 makes two additional check boxes available: Cascade Update Related Fields and Cascade Delete Related Records. If you select the Cascade Delete Related Records check box, Access 2007 deletes child rows (the related rows in the *many* table of a one-to-many relationship) when you delete a parent row (the related row in the *one* table of a one-to-many relationship). For example, if you removed a company from the table Access 2007 would remove the related company contact rows. In this database design, the CompanyID field has the AutoNumber data type, so it cannot be changed once it is set. However, if you build a table with a primary key that is Text or Number (perhaps a ProductID field that could change at some point in the future), it might be a good idea to select the Cascade Update Related Fields check box. This option requests that Access automatically update any foreign key values in the *child* table (the *many* table in a one-to-many relationship) if you change a primary key value in a *parent* table (the *one* table in a one-to-many relationship).

You might have noticed that the Show Table dialog box, shown earlier in Figure 4-25, gives you the option to include queries as well as tables. Sometimes you might want to define relationships between tables and queries or between queries so that Access 2007 knows how to join them properly. You can also define what's known as an *outer join* by clicking the Join Type button in the Edit Relationships dialog box and selecting an option in the Join Properties dialog box. With an outer join, you can find out, for example, which companies have no contacts or which products haven't been sold.

Chapter 4

**For details about outer joins, see "Using Outer Joins" on page 425.**

INSIDE OUT

### Avoid Defining a Relationship with an Outer Join

We recommend that you do not define an outer join relationship between two tables. As you'll learn in Chapter 8, Access 2007 automatically links two tables you include in a query design using the relationships you have defined. In the vast majority of cases, you will want to include only the matching rows from both tables. If you define the relationship as an outer join, you will have to change the link between the two tables every time you include them in a query.

We also do not recommend that you define relationships between queries or between a table and a query. If you have done a good job of naming your fields in your tables, the query designer will recognize the natural links and define the joins for you automatically. Defining extra relationships adds unnecessary overhead in your database application.

Click the Create button to finish your relationship definition. Access draws a line between the two tables to indicate the relationship. Notice that when you ask Access to enforce referential integrity, Access displays a 1 at the end of the relationship line, next to the *one* table, and an infinity symbol next to the *many* table. If you want to delete the relationship, click the line and press the Delete key.

You now know enough to define the additional one-to-many simple relationships that you need. Go ahead and define a relationship on ContactID between the Contacts and CompanyContacts tables to complete the other side of the many-to-many relationship between companies and contacts, a relationship on ContactID between the Contacts and ContactEvents tables, and a relationship on ProductID between the Products and ContactProducts tables. For each relationship, be sure to select the Enforce Referential Integrity check box.

## Creating a Relationship on Multiple Fields

There's one last relationship you need to define in the Contact Tracking database between the CompanyContacts and ContactProducts tables. The relationship between these two tables requires multiple fields from each table. You can start by dragging the CompanyID field from the CompanyContacts table to the ContactProducts table. Access 2007 opens the Edit Relationships dialog box, shown in Figure 4-28.

**Figure 4-28** Select multiple fields in the Edit Relationships dialog box to define a relationship between two tables using more than one field.

When you first see the Edit Relationships dialog box for the relationship you are defining between CompanyContacts and ContactProducts, Access 2007 shows you only the CompanyID field in the two lists. To complete the relationship definition on the combination of CompanyID and ContactID, you must click in the second line under both tables and select ContactID as the second field for both tables, as shown in Figure 4-28. Select the Enforce Referential Integrity check box as shown and click Create to define the compound relationship.

Figure 4-29 shows the Relationships window for all the main tables in your Contact Tracking database. Notice that there are two linking lines that define the relationship between CompanyContacts and ContactProducts.

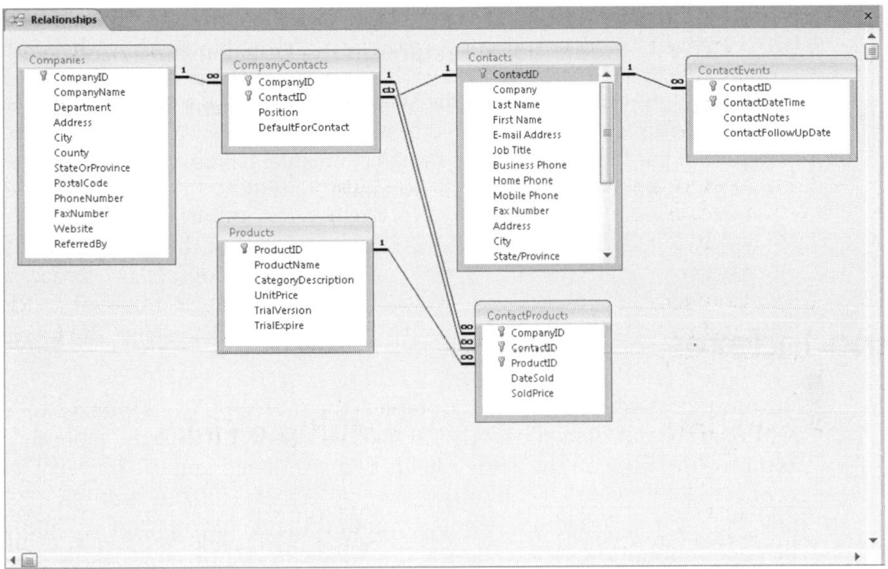


**Figure 4-29** The Relationships window shows a graphical representation of all the main tables in your Contact Tracking database.

If you want to edit or change any relationship, double-click the line to open the Edit Relationships dialog box again. If you want to remove a relationship definition, click on the line linking two tables to select the relationship (the line appears highlighted) and press the Delete key. Access 2007 presents a warning dialog box in case you are asking it to delete a relationship in error.

Note that once you define a relationship, you can delete the table or query field lists from the Relationships window without affecting the relationships. To do this, click the table or query list header and press the Delete key. This can be particularly advantageous in large databases that have dozens of tables. You can also display only those tables that you're working with at the moment. To see the relationships defined for any particular table or query, include it in the Relationships window by using the Show Table dialog box, and then click the Direct Relationships button in the Relationships group of the Design contextual tab on the Ribbon. To redisplay all relationships, click the All Relationships button in the Relationships group.

When you close the Relationships window, Access 2007 asks whether you want to save your layout changes. Click Yes to save the relationships you've defined. That's all there is to it. Later, when you use multiple tables in a query in Chapter 7, "Creating and Working with Simple Queries," you'll see that Access 2007 builds the links between tables based on these relationships.

INSIDE OUT **Additional Features in the Relationships Window**

You can right-click any table in the Relationships window and then choose Table Design from the shortcut menu to open that table in Design view. You can also click Relationship Report in the Tools group of the Design contextual tab on the Ribbon to create a report that prints what you laid out in the window.

# Adding Indexes

The more data you include in your tables, the more you need indexes to help Access 2007 search your data efficiently. An *index* is simply an internal table that contains two columns: the value in the field or fields being indexed and the physical location of each record in your table that contains that value. Access 2007 uses an index similarly to how you use the index in this book—you find the term you want and jump directly to the pages containing that term. You don't have to leaf through all the pages to find the information you want.

Let's assume that you often search your Contacts table by city. Without an index, when you ask Access 2007 to find all the contacts in the city of Chicago, Access has to search every record in your table. This search is fast if your table includes only a few contacts but very slow if the table contains thousands of contact records collected over many years. If you create an index on the City field, Access 2007 can use the index to find more rapidly the records for the contacts in the city you specify.



## Single-Field Indexes

Most of the indexes you'll need to define will probably contain the values from only a single field. Access uses this type of index to help narrow the number of records it has to search whenever you provide search criteria on the field—for example, *City = Chicago* or *PostalCode = 60633*. If you have defined indexes for multiple fields and provided search criteria for more than one of the fields, Access uses the indexes together (using a technology called Rushmore from Microsoft FoxPro) to find the rows you want quickly. For example, if you have created one index on City and another on LastName, and you ask for *City = Bend* and *LastName = Conrad*, Access uses the entries in the City index that equal *Bend* and matches those with the entries in the LastName index that equal *Conrad*. The result is a small set of pointers to the records that match both criteria.

Creating an index on a single field in a table is easy. Open the Contacts table (which you created earlier using a table template) in Design view, and select the field for which you want an index—in this case, City. Click the Indexed property box in the lower part of the Table window, and then click the arrow to open the list of choices, as shown in Figure 4-30.

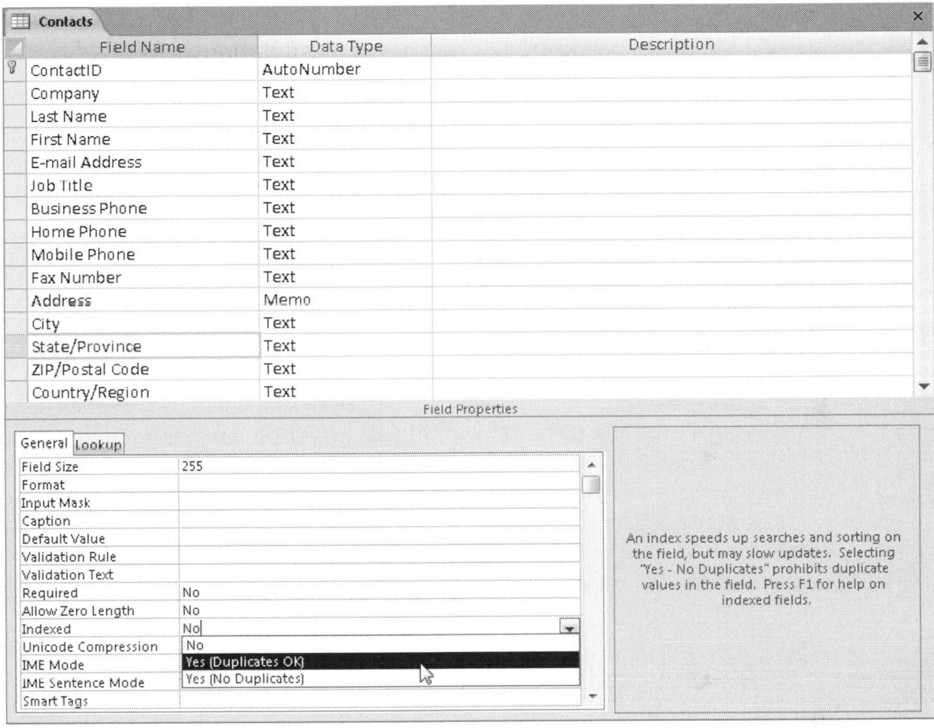


**Figure 4-30** You can use the Indexed property box to set an index on a single field.

When you create a table from scratch (as you did earlier in this chapter for the Companies table), the default Indexed property setting for all fields except the primary key is No. If you use a table template to create a table (as you did for the Contacts table in this chapter), the template indexes fields that might benefit from an index. If you followed along earlier using a table template to build the Contacts table, you will find that the template built an index only for the ContactID and Zip/Postal Code fields. Any tables created using a table template could obviously benefit from some additional indexes.

If you want to set an index for a field, Access 2007 offers two possible Yes choices. In most cases, a given field will have multiple records with the same value—perhaps you have multiple contacts in a particular city or multiple products in the same product category. You should select Yes (Duplicates OK) to create an index for this type of field. By selecting Yes (No Duplicates) you can have Access 2007 enforce unique values in any field by creating an index that doesn't allow duplicates. Access 2007 always defines the primary key index with no duplicates because all primary key values must be unique.

> **Note**
>
> You cannot define an index using an OLE object or attachment field.

## Multiple-Field Indexes

If you often provide multiple criteria in searches against large tables, you might want to consider creating a few multiple-field indexes. This helps Access 2007 narrow the search quickly without having to match values from two separate indexes. For example, suppose you often perform a search for contacts by last name and first name. If you create an index that includes both of these fields, Access can satisfy your query more rapidly.

To create a multiple-field index, you must open the Table window in Design view and open the Indexes window by clicking the Indexes button in the Show/Hide group of the Design contextual tab on the Ribbon. You can see the primary key index and the index that you defined on City in the previous section as well as the index defined by the table template (Zip/Postal Code). Each of these indexes comprises exactly one field.

To create a multiple-field index, move the insertion point to an empty row in the Indexes window and type a unique name. In this example, you want a multiple-field index using the Last Name and First Name fields, so *FullName* might be a reasonable index name. Select the Last Name field in the Field Name column of this row. To add the other field, skip down to the next row and select First Name without typing a new index name. When you're done, your Indexes window should look like the one shown in Figure 4-31.

### INSIDE OUT Inserting New Rows in the Indexes Window

To insert a row in the middle of the list in the Indexes window, right-click in the Index Name column and then choose Insert Rows from the shortcut menu.

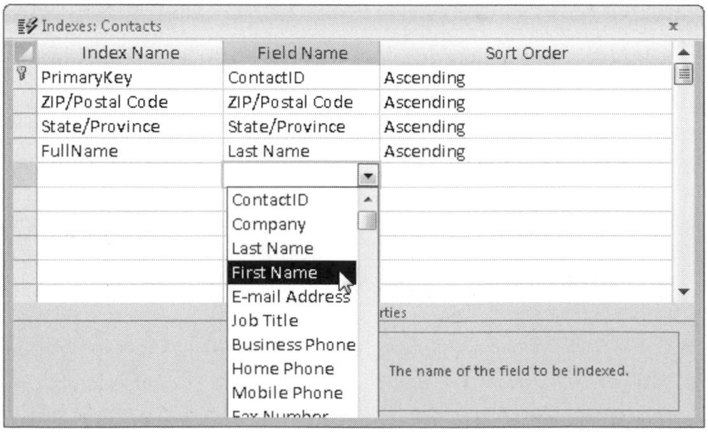

**Figure 4-31** The FullName index includes the Last Name and First Name fields.

You can remove an existing single-field index by changing the Indexed property of a field to No. The only way to remove a multiple-field index is via the Indexes window. To remove a multiple-field index, select the rows (by holding down the Ctrl key as you click each row selector) that define the index and then press Delete. Access 2007 saves any index changes you make when you save the table definition.

Access 2007 can use a multiple-field index in a search even if you don't provide search values for all the fields, as long as you provide search criteria for consecutive fields starting with the first field. Therefore, with the FullName multiple-field index shown in Figure 4-31, you can search for last name or for last name and first name. There's one additional limitation on when Access can use multiple-field indexes: Only the last search criterion you supply can be an inequality, such as >, >=, <, or <=. In other words, Access can use the index shown in Figure 4-31 when you specify searches such as these:

Last Name = "Smith"
Last Name > "Franklin"
Last Name = "Buchanan" And First Name = "Steven"
Last Name = "Viescas" And First Name >= "Bobby"

But Access will not use the FullName index shown in Figure 4-31 if you ask for

Last Name > "Davolio" And First Name > "John"

because only the last field in the search (First Name) can be an inequality. Access also will not use this index if you ask for

First Name = "John"

because the first field of the multiple-field index (Last Name) is missing from the search criterion.

## Setting Table Design Options

Now that you understand the basic mechanics of defining tables in your desktop database, it's useful to take a look at a few options you can set to customize how you work with tables in Design view. Close any open tables so that all you see is the Navigation Pane. Click the Microsoft Office Button and then click Access Options to see all the custom settings offered.

You can find the first options that affect table design in the Advanced category as shown in Figure 4-32. One option that we highly recommend you use is Use Four-Digit Year Formatting, found in the General section. When you enable four-digit year formatting, Access 2007 displays all year values in date/time formats with four digits instead of two. This is important because when you see a value (in two-digit medium date format) such as 15 MAR 12, you won't be able to easily tell whether this is March 15, 1912 or March 15, 2012. Although you can affect the display of some formats in your regional settings in Control Panel, you won't affect them all unless you set four-digit formatting in Access.

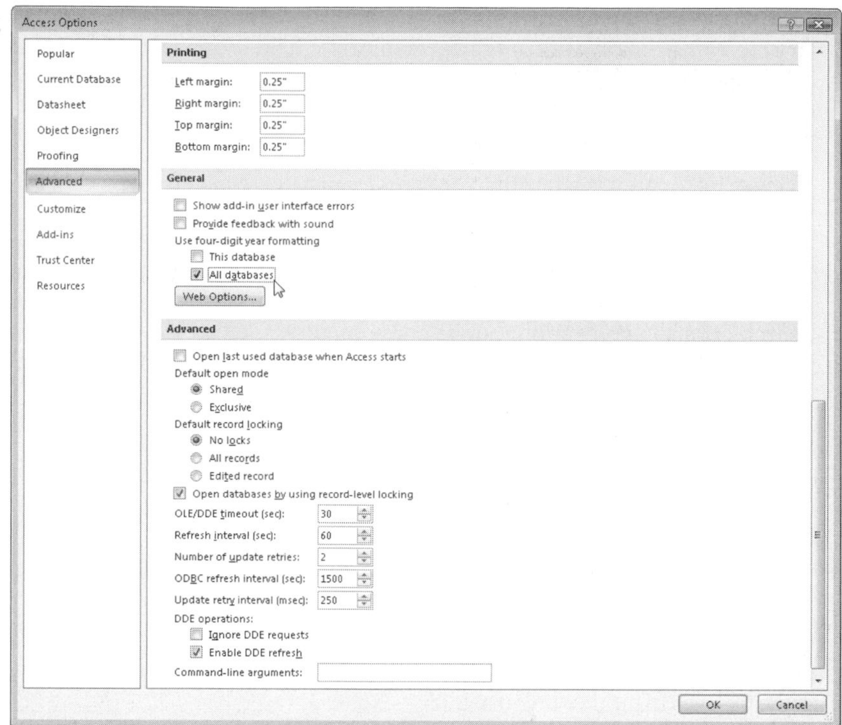


**Figure 4-32** You can find settings that affect table design in the General section in the Advanced category of the Access Options dialog box.

As you can see in Figure 4-32, you have two options under Use Four-Digit Year Formatting in the General section. If you select the This Database check box, the setting creates a property in the database you currently have open and affects only that database. If you select the All Databases check box, the setting creates an entry in your Windows registry that affects all databases that you open on your computer.

In the Current Database category of the Access Options dialog box, you can configure an option that was introduced in Access 2000 called Name AutoCorrect that asks Access to track and correct field name references in queries, forms, and reports. If you select the Track Name AutoCorrect Info check box in the Name AutoCorrrect Options section, Access maintains a unique internal ID number for all field names. This allows you to use the Object Dependencies feature explained in the next chapter. It also allows you to select the next check box, Perform Name AutoCorrect, as shown in Figure 4-33.

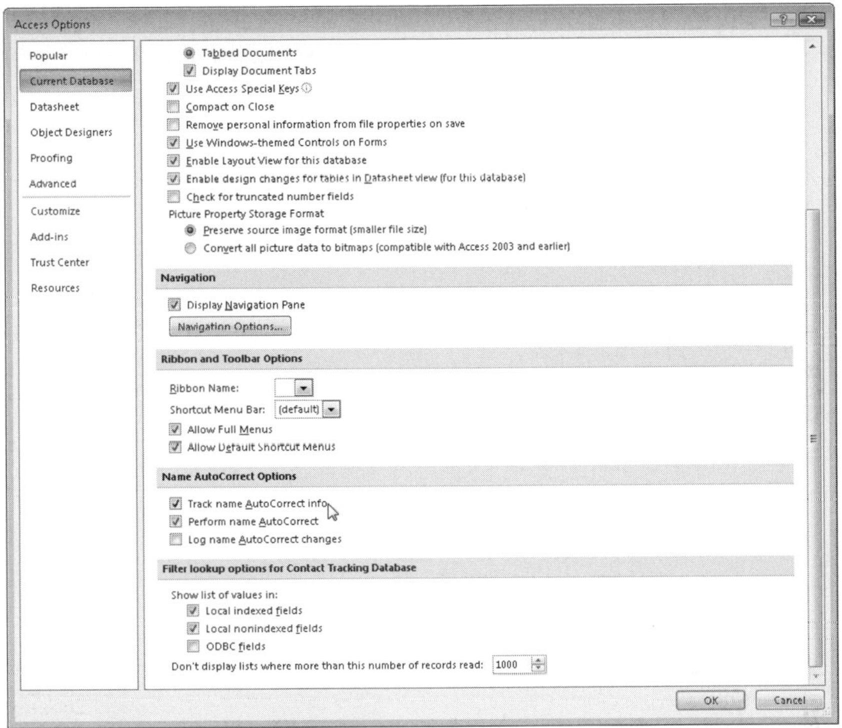


**Figure 4-33** You can set Name AutoCorrect options in the Current Database category of the Access Options dialog box.



If you select the Perform Name AutoCorrect check box, when you change a field name in a table, Access 2007 automatically attempts to propagate the name change to other objects (queries, forms, and reports) that use the field. However, Track Name AutoCorrect Info requires some additional overhead in all your objects, so it's a good idea to carefully choose names as you design your tables so that you won't need to change them later. Finally, if you select the Log Name AutoCorrect Changes check box, Access 2007 logs all changes it makes in a table called AutoCorrect Log. You can open this table to verify the changes made by this feature. (Access doesn't create the table until it makes some changes.)

The next category that contains useful settings that affect table design is Object Designers. Click that category to see the settings shown in Figure 4-34.

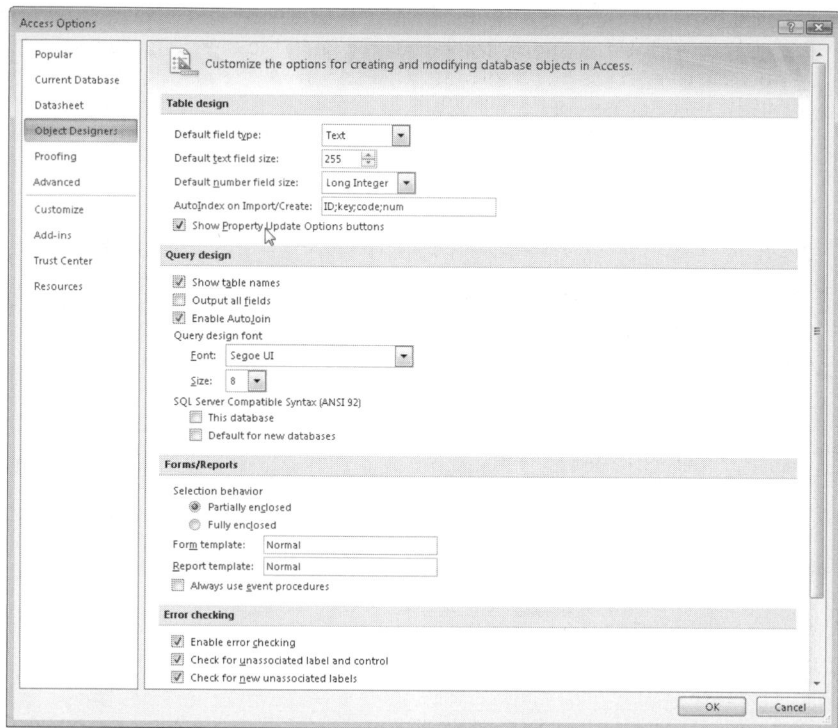


**Figure 4-34** You can find settings that affect table design in the Object Designers category of the Access Options dialog box.

In the Table Design section, you can set the default field type and the default field size for Text and Number fields. The Default Field Type setting allows you to choose the default data type that Access 2007 selects when you type a new field name in table design and then tab to the Data Type column. When you select a data type of Text (either because it is the default data type or you select the Text data type in a new field), Access will automatically set the length you select in the Default Text Field Size box. When you select a data type of Number, Access sets the number size to your choice in the Default Number Field Size box of Byte, Integer, Long Integer, Single, Double, Decimal, or Replication ID. Use the AutoIndex On Import/Create box to define a list of field name prefixes or suffixes for which Access automatically sets the Index property to Yes (Duplicates OK). In the default list, for example, any field that you define with a name that begins or ends with *ID* will automatically have an index.

If you select the Show Property Update Options Buttons check box, a smart tag appears that offers to automatically update related properties in queries, forms, and reports when you change certain field properties in a table design. You can see more details about this option in the next chapter.

You can find the last option that affects how your tables are stored (and, in fact, all objects in your database) in the Popular category, as shown in Figure 4-35. When you create a new database in Access 2007, you actually have a choice of three different file formats. These options also appear in the File New Database dialog box, but this setting in the Access Options dialog box controls which file format appears as the default. You should use the Access 2000 format if others with whom you might share this database are still using Access version 9 (2000), or you should use the 2002-2003 format if others sharing this database are still using Access version 10 (2002) or Access version 11 (2003). Selecting the Access 2007 format ensures maximum compatibility of what you build in Access with future versions of the product.

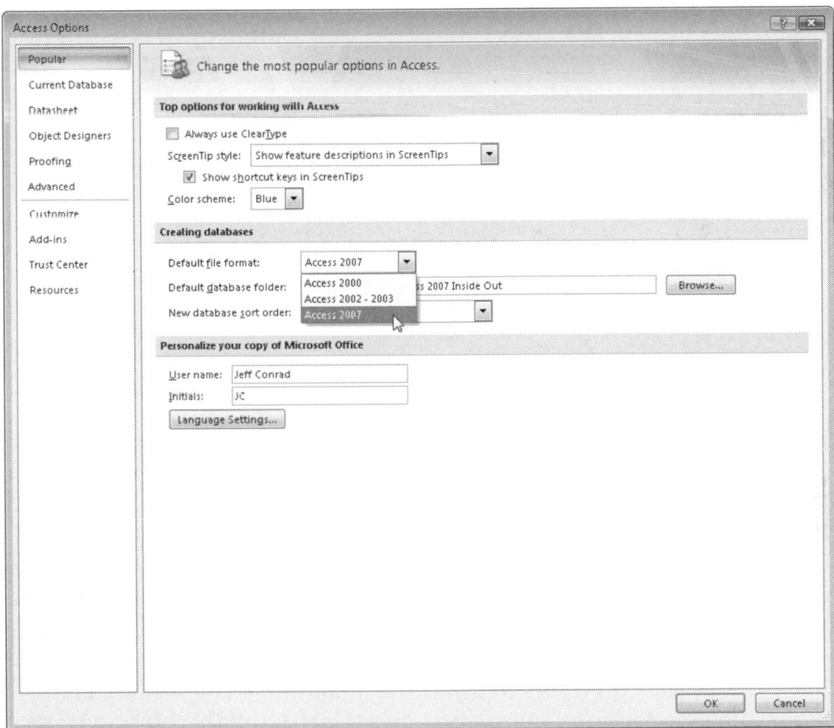


**Figure 4-35** You can select your default database file format in the Creating Databases section of the Popular category in the Access Options dialog box.

# Creating a Default Template for New Databases

Access 2007 introduces a new feature that allows you to create your own default database template for use with all new blank databases. Rather than set options for each new database after you create it, you can set your preferred options only one time and have those settings apply to each new database. To accomplish this, you first need to open a new blank database from the Getting Started screen. Click the Blank Database command on the Getting Started screen to display the Blank Database task pane on the right, as shown in Figure 4-36.

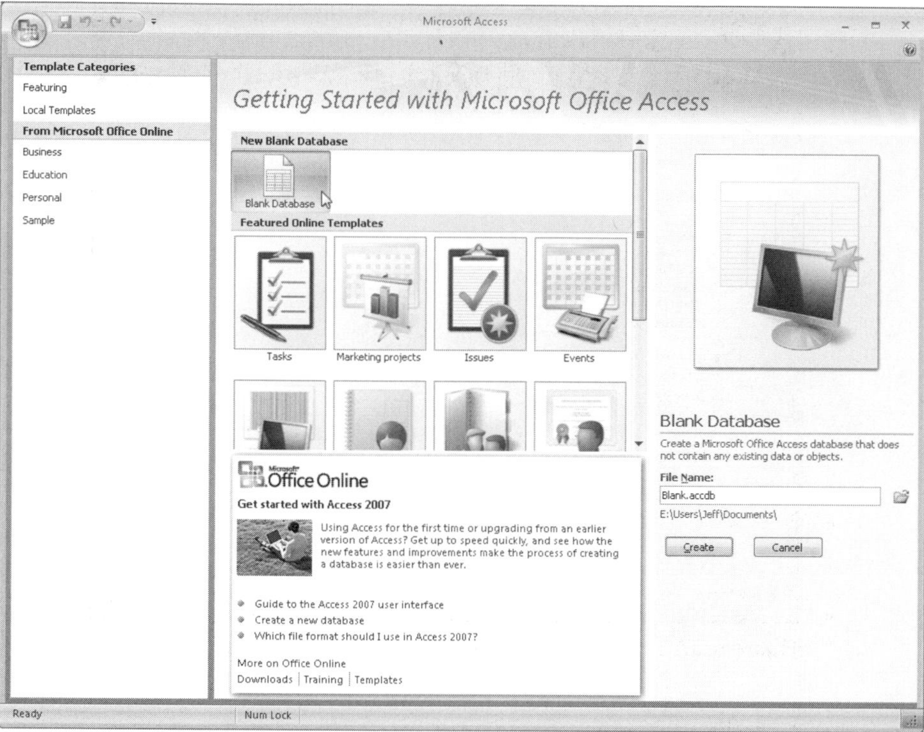


**Figure 4-36** The Blank Database task pane appears on the right when you click the Blank Database command.

You must name this new database Blank in order for this procedure to work. Type **Blank** in the File Name text box, and then click the Browse button to open the File New Database dialog box. So that Access 2007 will use this template file for all new databases, you must place this file in a specific subfolder in the Microsoft Office folder. Navigate to the following folder on your system drive by clicking the folder icons in the left pane of the File New Database dialog box: \Program Files\Microsoft Office\Templates\1033\Access, as shown in Figure 4-37. This file path assumes a default installation of the 2007 Microsoft Office system, so your exact file path might be different if you chose a custom installation and selected a different installation path.

Click OK in the File New Database dialog box to return to the Getting Started screen. If you followed the preceding instructions, the Blank Database task pane on the right should look like Figure 4-38. The File Name text box says Blank.accdb, and the path to the correct template location is displayed above the Create button.

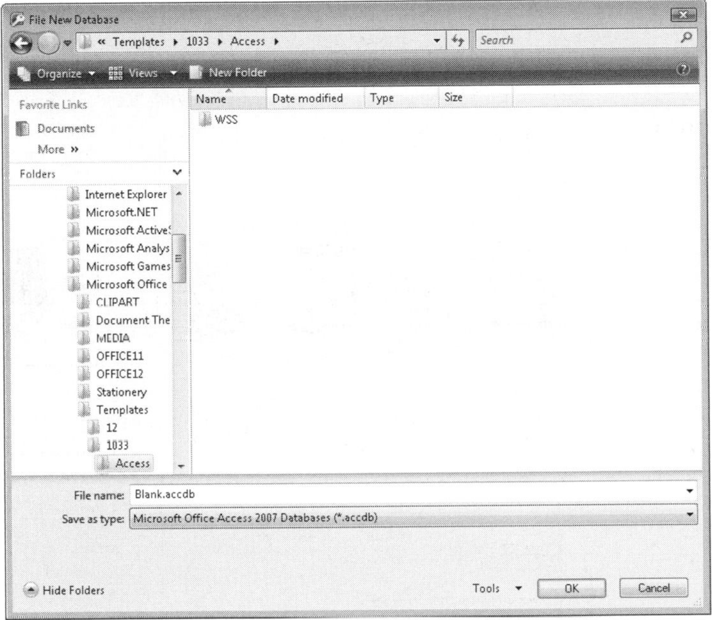


**Figure 4-37** Save the Blank.accdb file in the correct subfolder in the Microsoft Office folder.

**CAUTION!**

If you are using Microsoft Windows Vista, you might not be able to save the Blank.accdb database into the needed template folder. Windows Vista uses User Account Control, which protects critical program folders. If your computer is connected to a domain, you get a prompt dialog box and then you can save to the correct folder. You might need to temporarily turn off User Account Control in order to save the database into the template folder. If you are in a corporate network environment, you should ask your system administrator for assistance with this procedure.

Click the Create button, and Access 2007 creates the new file and saves it in the appropriate template folder. By default, Access opens up a new blank table called Table1. You do not need this table, so close it and do not save it.

Now that you have an empty database with no objects, open the Access Options dialog box by clicking the Microsoft Office Button and then Access Options. Select all the options you want to set for any new databases in the various categories of the Access Options dialog box.

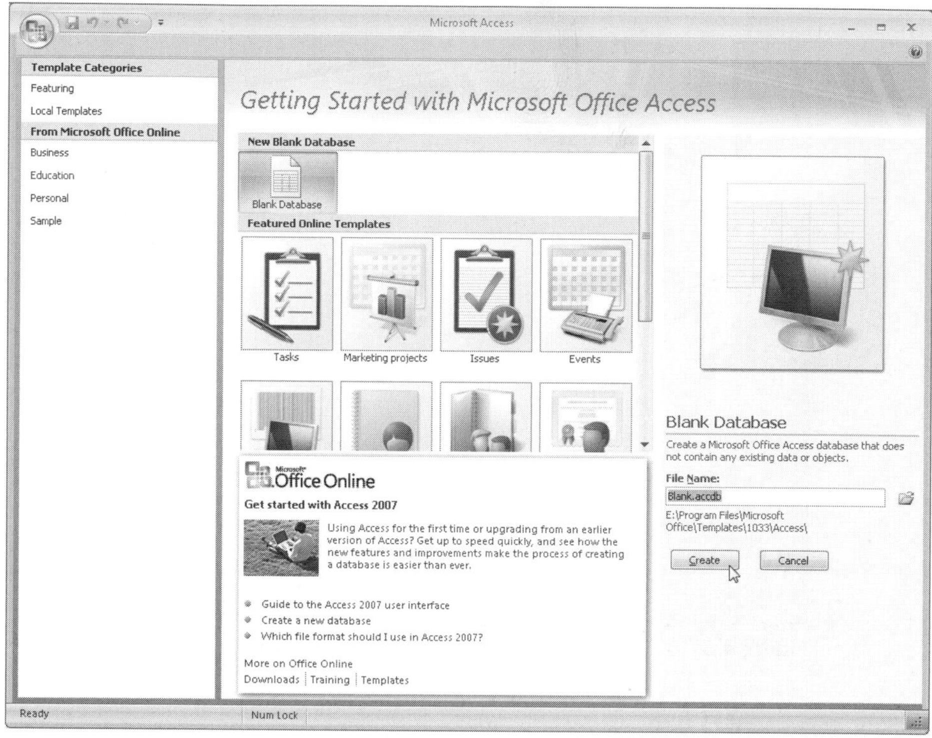


**Figure 4-38** After you enter the correct name and select the correct location, you're ready to create your new database template.

Included on the companion CD is a database called Blank.accdb that has the Access Options settings that we recommend for new databases. In the Current Database category, in the Name AutoCorrect Options section, we cleared the Track Name AutoCorrect Info check box. In the General section of the Advanced category, we selected the Use Four-Digit Year Formatting and This Database check boxes. We left all other options set to the defaults.

> **Note**
>
> You can also open the Visual Basic Editor (VBE) and select Options from the Tools menu to select options that apply to Visual Basic in all new databases. In the Blank.accdb sample database, we selected the Require Variable Declaration check box. We will discuss the VBE Options dialog box in detail in Chapter 19.

After you have defined all the settings you want, close the database and exit Access 2007. Each new blank database you create from the Getting Started screen will now include all the settings you selected for the Blank.accdb file. To make revisions to those settings, open the Blank.accdb file in the template folder and make whatever modifications are necessary. Figure 4-39 shows our Blank.accdb file in the appropriate template folder along with the other local database templates discussed at the beginning of this chapter.

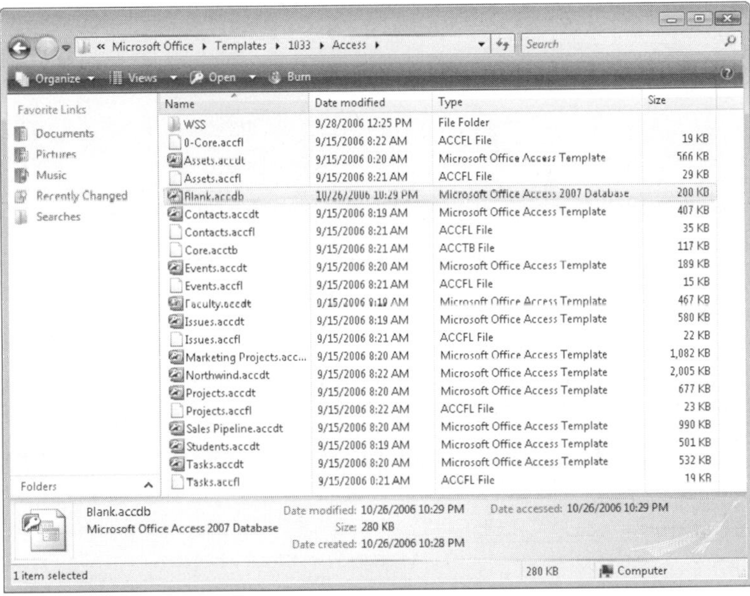


**Figure 4-39** The Blank.accdb file must be located in the same folder as the local database templates.

Creating a custom blank database template saves you time by not having to continually set your personal Access options and VBE options each time you create a new database. In addition to this timesaver, you can also include specific code modules, forms, and any other database objects with new databases. If, for example, you have some common functions and procedures stored in standard code modules that you use in all your database files, you can include them in this Blank.accdb file. Instead of having to manually import these modules into all new databases, Access does all the work for you by including them in new databases. We will discuss creating form templates in Chapter 12. You'll learn about creating public functions in Chapter 19.



# Printing a Table Definition

After you create several tables, you might want to print out their definitions to provide a permanent paper record. You can do this by clicking Database Documenter in the Analyze group of the Database Tools tab on the Ribbon. Access 2007 displays several options in the Documenter dialog box, as shown in Figure 4-40.

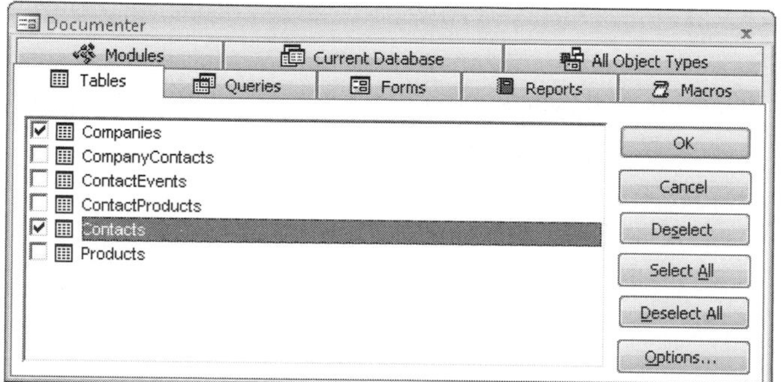


**Figure 4-40** You can select the objects you want to document in the Documenter dialog box.

You can select not only the types of objects you want to document but also which objects you want to document. Click the Options button to select what you want reported. For example, you can ask for the properties, relationships, and permissions for a table; the names, data types, sizes, and properties for fields; and the names, fields, and properties for indexes. Click OK in the Documenter dialog box to produce the report and view it in Print Preview, as shown in Figure 4-41.

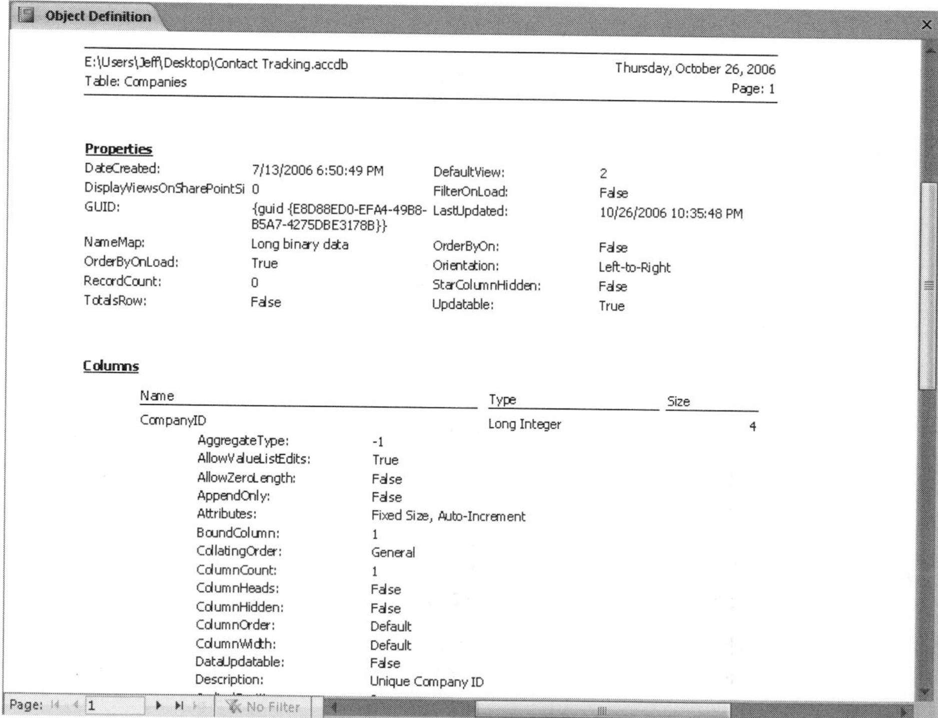


**Figure 4-41** The Database Documenter previews its reports on your screen.

# Database Limitations

As you design your database, you should keep in mind the following limitations:

- A table can have up to 255 fields.
- A table can have up to 32 indexes.

> **Note**
>
> Keep in mind that defining relationships with Referential Integrity turned on creates one additional index in each participating table that counts toward the 32-index limit per table.

- A multiple-field index can have up to 10 fields. The sum of the lengths of the fields cannot exceed 255 bytes.
- A row in a table, excluding memo fields and ActiveX objects, can be no longer than approximately 4 kilobytes.
- A memo field can store up to 1 gigabyte of characters, but you can't display a memo larger than 64 kilobytes in a form or a datasheet.

> **Note**
>
> Clearly, if you try to store a 1-gigabyte memo (which requires 2 gigabytes of storage because of double-byte character set support) or a 2-gigabyte ActiveX object in your database file, your file will be full with the data from one record.

- An ActiveX object can be up to 2 gigabytes in size.
- There is no limit on the number of records in a table, but an Access 2007 database cannot be larger than 2 gigabytes. If you have several large tables, you might need to define each one in a separate Access database and then attach them to the database that contains the forms, reports, macros, and modules for your applications. See Chapter 6, "Importing and Linking Data," for details.

Now that you've started to get comfortable with creating databases and tables, you can read the next chapter to learn how to make modifications to existing tables in a database.

CHAPTER 5

# Modifying Your Table Design



No matter how carefully you design your database, you can be sure that you'll need to change it at some later date. Here are some of the reasons you might need to change your database.

- You no longer need some of the tables.
- You need to perform some new tasks that require not only creating new tables but also inserting some linking fields in existing tables.
- You find that you use some fields in a table much more frequently than others, so it would be easier if those fields appeared first in the table design.
- You no longer need some of the fields.
- You want to add some new fields that are similar to fields that already exist.
- You discover that some of the data you defined would be better stored as a different data type. For example, a field that you originally designed to be all numbers (such as a U.S. ZIP Code) must now contain some letters (as in a Canadian postal code).
- You have a number field that needs to hold larger values or needs a different number of decimal places than you originally planned.
- You can improve your database design by splitting an existing table into two or more tables using the Table Analyzer Wizard.
- You discover that the field you defined as a primary key isn't always unique, so you need to change the definition of your primary key.
- You find that some of your queries take too long to run and might execute more quickly if you add an index to your table.

### Note

The examples in this chapter are based on the tables and data in *Housing.accdb* and *Contacts.accdb* on the companion CD included with this book and the Contact Tracking database you built in Chapter 4, "Creating Your Database and Tables." If you did not create the Contact Tracking database, you can find ContactTracking.accdb in the sample files that you can use to follow along in this chapter. The results you see from the samples you build in this chapter might not exactly match what you see in this book if you have changed the sample data in the files. Also, all the screen images in this chapter were taken on a Microsoft Windows Vista system with the display theme set to Blue, and Use Windows-Themed Controls on Forms has been turned on in the sample databases.

This chapter takes a look at how you can make these changes easily and relatively painlessly with Microsoft Office Access 2007. If you want to follow along with the examples in this chapter, you should first create the Contact Tracking database described in Chapter 4.

### Note

You might have noticed that the Contacts table you defined for the Contact Tracking database in Chapter 4 is quite different from the tblContacts table in the Conrad Systems Contacts database on the companion CD. In this chapter, you'll modify the Contacts table you built in Chapter 4 so that it is more like the one on the companion CD. You'll also learn how to use the Table Analyzer Wizard to help you normalize an existing table that contains data from several subjects.

## Before You Get Started



Office Access 2007 makes it easy for you to change the design of your database, even when you already have data in your tables. You should, however, understand the potential impact of any changes you plan and take steps to ensure that you can recover your previous design if you make a mistake. Here are some things to consider before you make changes.

- Access 2007 does not automatically propagate changes that you make in tables to any queries, forms, reports, macros, or modules. You must make changes to dependent objects yourself, or configure Access to propagate the changes for you. To do so, click the Microsoft Office Button, click Access Options, and then in the Current Database category, select the Perform Name AutoCorrect check box. See "Setting Table Design Options" on page 39 for more details.
- You cannot change the data type of a field that is part of a relationship between tables. You must first delete the relationship and then change the field's data type and redefine the relationship.

- You cannot change the definition of any table that you have open in a query, a form, or a report. You must close any objects that refer to the table you want to change before you open that table in Design view. If you give other users access to your database over a network, you won't be able to change the table definition if someone else has the table (or a query or form based on the table) open.

**INSIDE OUT** **Access Always Prompts You to Save Your Work**

Before saving any changes that permanently alter or delete data in your database, Access 2007 always prompts you for confirmation and gives you a chance to cancel the operation.

## Making a Backup Copy

The safest way to make changes to the design of your database is to make a backup copy of the database before you begin. If you expect to make extensive changes to several tables in your database, you should also make a copy of the .accdb file that contains your database. You could use a utility such as Windows Explorer, but Access 2007 includes a handy feature for making backups easily. When you have the database open that you want to back up, click the Microsoft Office Button, click the Manage command, and then click Back Up Database as shown in Figure 5-1. Access offers to create a copy of your database with the current date appended to the file name.

**Figure 5-1** The Back Up Database command creates a backup of your entire database file.

If you want to change a single table, you can easily make a backup copy of that table right in your database. Use the following procedure to copy any table—the structure and the data together.

1. Open the database containing the table you want to copy. If the database is already open, make sure the list of tables is showing in the Navigation Pane. Click the top of the Navigation Pane to open the Navigation Pane menu and click Object Type beneath Navigate To Category. Click the top of the Navigation Pane again and then click Tables under Filter By Group, as shown in Figure 5-2, to display only the tables contained in your database.

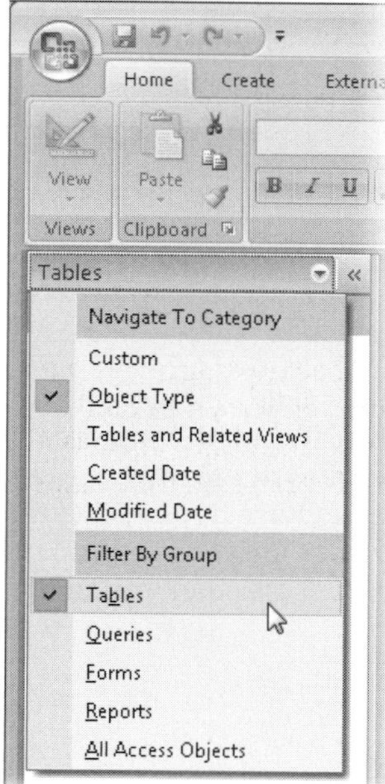


**Figure 5-2** Click Object Type and Tables on the Navigation Pane menu to display only the tables in your database.

2. Select the table you want to copy by clicking the table's name or icon in the Navigation Pane. The table name will be highlighted.

3. Click the Copy command in the Clipboard group on the Home tab of the Ribbon as shown in Figure 5-3. This copies the entire table (structure and data) to the Clipboard.

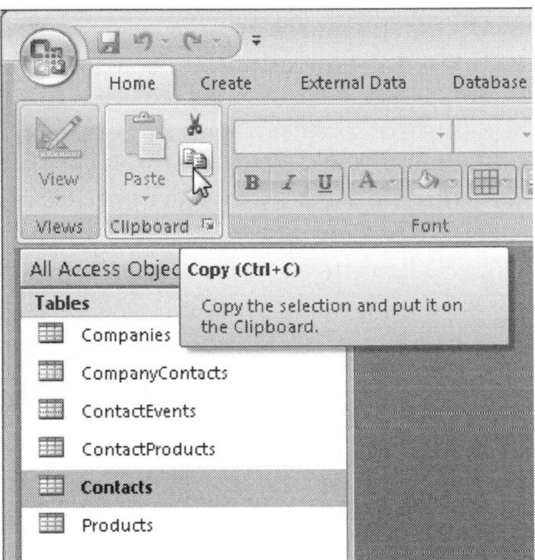


**Figure 5-3** Click the Copy command to copy a table from the Tables list.

4. Click the Paste command in the Clipboard group on the Home tab of the Ribbon. Access opens the Paste Table As dialog box, shown in Figure 5-4. Type a new name for your table. (When naming a backup copy, you might simply add *Backup* and the date to the original table name, as shown in Figure 5-4.) The default option is to copy both the structure and the data. (You also have the option of copying only the table's structure or of appending the data to another table.)

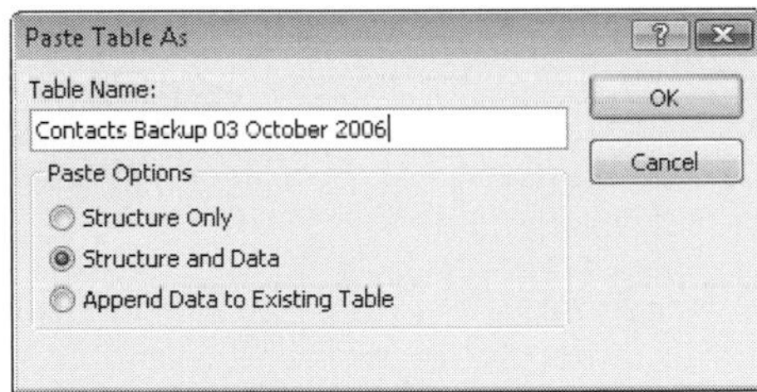


**Figure 5-4** Enter the new name for the copied table in the Paste Table As dialog box.

## Checking Object Dependencies

If you're just starting out and learning Office Access 2007 by reading this book through from the beginning, you probably haven't built anything but tables yet. In Chapter 3 you learned that you can ask Access to show you what queries, forms, and reports are dependent on each table, but the Object Dependencies command in Access won't provide very interesting results in a database with nothing but tables. You'll find this tool invaluable after you have built dozens of objects and then need to make some changes to your tables.

As you learned in the previous chapter, you can select options to track and perform Name AutoCorrect for objects by clicking the Microsoft Office Button, clicking Access Options, and then selecting the check boxes for these features in the Current Database category. Access 2007 uses this AutoCorrect information not only to automatically correct names but also to provide you with detailed information about which objects depend on one another. If you're about to make a change to a field in a table, wouldn't it be good to know which queries, forms, and reports use that table before you make the change? The Perform Name AutoCorrect option will help you out if you have selected it, but it can't always detect and fix field names when you have used them in an expression. You'll learn more about creating expressions in Chapter 7, "Creating and Working with Simple Queries," and in the chapters on using Microsoft Visual Basic later in this book.

If you would like to see object dependencies in action on your computer, open one of your own databases that contains tables, queries, forms, and reports, or open the Conrad Systems Contacts sample database (Contacts.accdb) that you installed from the companion CD. You can find out which other objects depend on a particular object (such as a table) by selecting the object that you're planning to change in the Navigation Pane and then clicking Object Dependencies in the Show/Hide group on the Database Tools tab of the Ribbon. If you haven't selected the Track Name AutoCorrect Info option, Access 2007 shows you the dialog box in Figure 5-5.

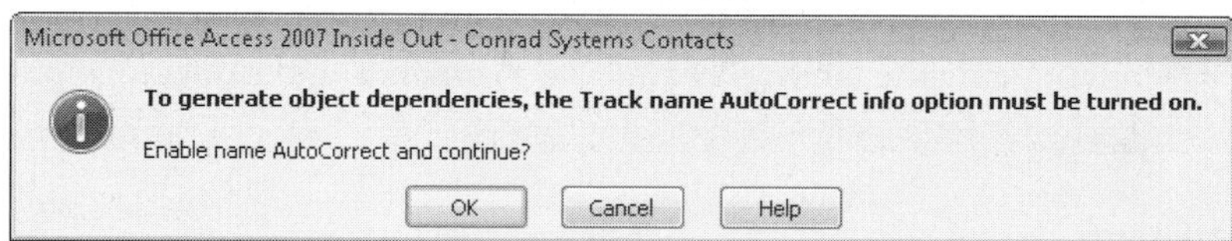


**Figure 5-5** The Object Dependencies feature tells you it needs to turn on Track Name AutoCorrect Info and examine all objects in your database.

Click OK to turn on Track Name AutoCorrect Info—the Object Dependencies command will take a few seconds or minutes to examine all your objects depending on the number of objects you have in your database. Access shows you the result in the Object Dependencies pane as shown in Figure 5-6. At the bottom of the Object Dependencies pane in Figure 5-6, you can see a warning message that some objects were ignored. Access displays this message if there are macros or modules present in your database because macros and modules are not checked for object dependencies.

Notice that in many cases you will have to follow a chain of dependencies to find all the objects that might be affected by the change of a field name in a table. For example, in the Conrad Systems Contacts sample database, we use a query (qryContacts) rather than the table (tblContacts) to provide records to the form that edits contact information (frmContacts). If we were to scroll further down the Object Dependencies pane looking for forms dependent on tblContacts, we would not find the form frmContacts listed.

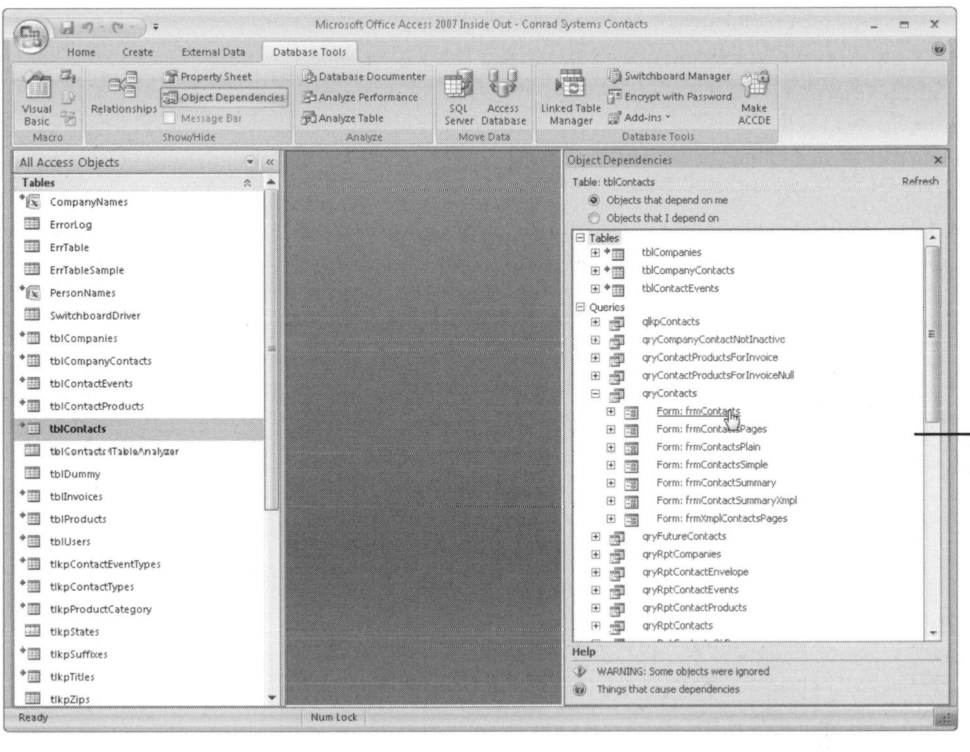


**Figure 5-6** The Object Dependencies pane shows you the list of objects that depend on the object you selected in the Navigation Pane.

You can click the plus sign next to any object name to open an expanded list of dependent objects as we did with qryContacts in Figure 5-6. Notice that we find frmContacts listed there as a dependent object of qryContacts, which is ultimately dependent on the table we're thinking about changing. When you find an object that you want to investigate further, you can click the object name in the Object Dependencies pane to open it in Design view.

As you can imagine, this command can make maintaining your application much easier. Even if you have selected the Perform Name AutoCorrect option, you can use this tool after you have modified your table to verify that the changes you expect were made.



# Deleting Tables

You probably won't need to delete an entire table very often. However, if you set up your application to collect historical information—for example, total product sales by year—you'll eventually want to delete information that you no longer need. You also might want to delete a table if you've made extensive changes that are incorrect and it would be easier to delete your work and restore the table from a backup.

To delete a table, select it in the Navigation Pane and press the Delete key (or click the Delete command in the Records group on the Home tab of the Ribbon). Access 2007 opens the dialog box shown in Figure 5-7, which asks you to confirm or cancel the delete operation.

## INSIDE OUT Access Is Forgiving When You Delete Something by Mistake

Even if you mistakenly confirm the deletion, you can click the Undo command on the Quick Access Toolbar to get your table back. In fact, you can undo up to the last 20 changes that you made in a window—either in the table's Design view or in the Navigation Pane. However, after you save changes to a table design, you will not be able to undo those changes.

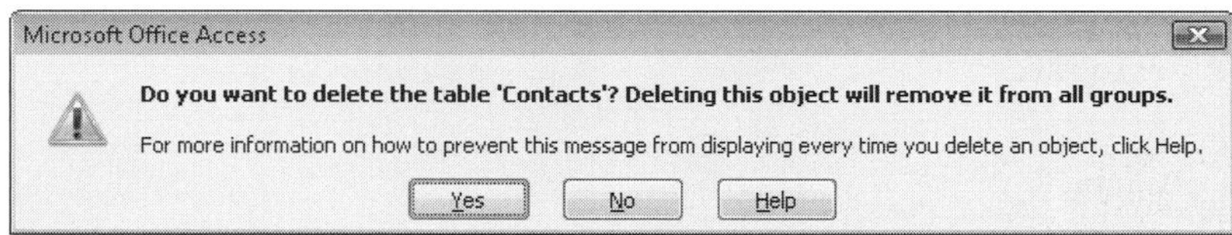


**Figure 5-7** This dialog box gives you the option of canceling the deletion of a table.

## INSIDE OUT Using Cut to Move an Object to the Clipboard

You can use the Cut command in the Clipboard group on the Home tab on the Ribbon to delete a table. This method moves a copy of the table to the Clipboard. After you close the database in which you've been working, you can open another database and paste the table from the Clipboard into it.



If you have defined relationships between the table you want to delete and other tables, Access 2007 displays another dialog box that alerts you and asks whether you want to also delete the relationships. If you click Yes, Access deletes all relationships between any other table and the table you want to delete and then deletes the table. (You can't have a relationship defined to a nonexistent table.) Even at this point, if you find you made a mistake, you can click Undo on the Quick Access Toolbar to restore both the table and all its relationships.

**CAUTION!**

When you undo a table deletion, Access 2007 might not restore all the previously defined relationships between the table and other tables. You should verify the table relationships in the Relationships window.

# Renaming Tables

If you keep transaction data (such as receipts, deposits, or checks written), you might want to save that data at the end of each month in a table with a unique name. One way to save your data is to rename the existing table (perhaps by adding a date to the name). You can then create a new table (perhaps by making a copy of the backup table's structure) to start collecting information for the next month.

To rename a table, right-click on it in the Navigation Pane and click Rename on the shortcut menu. Access 2007 places the name in Edit mode in the Navigation Pane so that you can type a new name, as shown in Figure 5-8. Type the new name, and press Enter to save it.

**Figure 5-8** After clicking Rename on the shortcut menu, you can rename a table in the Navigation Pane.

**INSIDE OUT** **Using the Keyboard to Rename an Object**

You can also edit the name of the object by selecting it in the Navigation Pane and pressing the F2 key. This puts the object name in Edit mode so that you can type a new name.

If you enter the name of a table that already exists, Access 2007 displays a dialog box that asks whether you want to replace the existing table, as shown in Figure 5-9. If you click Yes, Access deletes the old table before performing the renaming operation. Even if you replace an existing table, you can undo the renaming operation by clicking the Undo command on the Quick Access Toolbar.

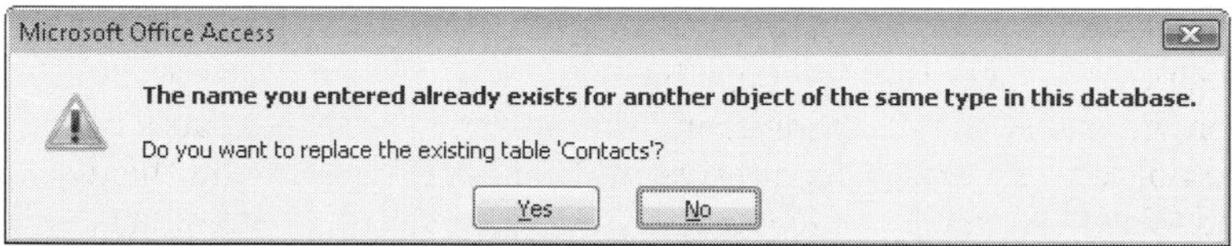


**Figure 5-9** This dialog box asks whether you want to replace an existing table with the same name.

INSIDE OUT **Renaming Other Access Objects**

You can use the techniques you just learned for copying, renaming, and deleting tables to copy, rename, and delete queries, forms, reports, macros, or modules.

## Changing Field Names

Perhaps you misspelled a field name when you first created one of your tables. Or perhaps you've decided that one of the field names isn't descriptive enough. As you learned in Chapter 4, you can change the displayed name for a field by setting its Caption property. But you won't necessarily want the hassle of giving the field a caption every time it appears in a query, a form, or a report. Fortunately, Access 2007 makes it easy to change a field name in a table—even if you already have data in the table.



**Note**

The next several examples in this chapter show you how to change the Contacts table that you created in the previous chapter to more closely match the tblContacts table in the Conrad Systems Contacts sample database.

You created the first draft of the Contacts table by using a table template. Now you need to make a few changes so that it will hold all the data fields that you need for your application. The table template does not give you the option to rename the fields before creating them, but now you decide to rename one of the fields before beginning work on the rest of your application.

Renaming a field is easy. For example, the table template created a field called Address, but you've decided that you want to have two address fields because a contact could have a work address and a home address in this database. It makes sense to change the field name to reflect the actual data you intend to store in the field, so let's change Address to WorkAddress. Open the Contacts table in the Contact Tracking database in Design view, use the mouse to move the insertion point to the beginning of the Address field name, and then type **Work**. You can also click in the field name, use the arrow keys to position the insertion point just before the letter *A*, and type **Work**. As you learned in the previous chapter, we recommend that you not have any spaces in your field names, so do not put a space between the words *Work* and *Address*. Your field should now be called WorkAddress. The table template also chose the Memo data type for this field, which is not necessary. Tab to the Data Type column, click the small arrow in the column (or press Alt+Down Arrow) to open the list, and select **Text** from the list of data types. While you're at it, press F6 to move to the Field Properties section of the window, tab to the Field Size property, and change the field size to **255**. Then, tab down to the Caption property, and change the field caption to **Work Address**. Your result should look like Figure 5-10.

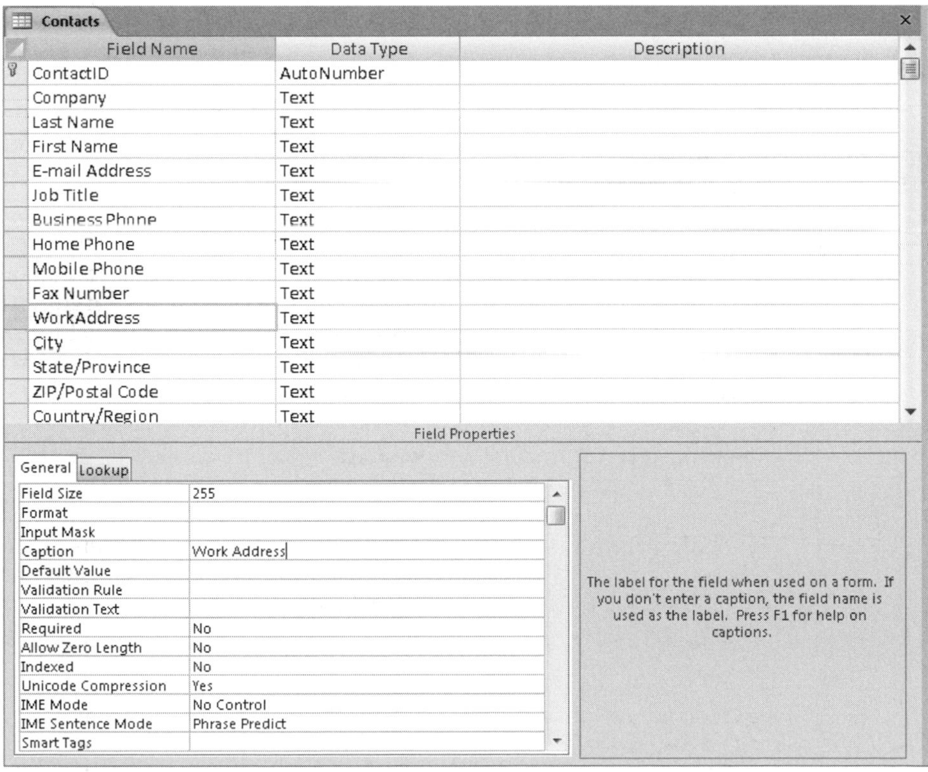


**Figure 5-10** You can change a field name, a field data type, and a field caption in Design view.

## Comparing the Two Contacts Tables

As you follow along with the examples in this chapter, it might be useful to compare the structure of the Contacts table you built in Chapter 4 and the actual tblContacts table in the Conrad Systems Contacts sample database. If you exactly followed the instructions in Chapter 4, your Contacts table in the Contact Tracking database should look like Table 5-1. You can see the actual design of tblContacts in Table 5-2.

Table 5-1 **Contacts**

| Field Name | Type | Length |
|---|---|---|
| ContactID | AutoNumber | |
| Company | Text | 255 |
| Last Name | Text | 255 |
| First Name | Text | 255 |
| E-mail Address | Text | 255 |
| Job Title | Text | 255 |
| Business Phone | Text | 255 |
| Home Phone | Text | 255 |
| Mobile Phone | Text | 255 |
| Fax Number | Text | 255 |
| Address | Text | 255 |
| City | Text | 255 |
| State/Province | Text | 255 |
| Zip/Postal Code | Text | 255 |
| Country/Region | Text | 255 |
| Web Page | Hyperlink | |
| Notes | Memo | |
| Attachments | Attachment | |

Table 5-2 **tblContacts**

| Field Name | Type | Length |
|---|---|---|
| ContactID | Auto Number | |
| LastName | Text | 50 |
| FirstName | Text | 50 |
| MiddleInit | Text | 1 |
| Title | Text | 10 |
| Suffix | Text | 10 |
| ContactType | Text | 50 |
| BirthDate | Date/Time | |
| DefaultAddress | Integer | |
| WorkAddress | Text | 255 |
| WorkCity | Text | 50 |
| WorkStateOrProvince | Text | 20 |
| WorkPostalCode | Text | 20 |
| WorkCountry | Text | 50 |
| WorkPhone | Text | 30 |
| WorkExtension | Text | 20 |
| WorkFaxNumber | Text | 30 |
| HomeAddress | Text | 255 |
| HomeCity | Text | 50 |
| HomeStateOrProvince | Text | 20 |
| HomePostalCode | Text | 20 |
| HomeCountry | Text | 50 |
| HomePhone | Text | 30 |
| MobilePhone | Text | 30 |
| EmailName | Hyperlink | |
| Website | Hyperlink | |
| Photo | Attachment | |
| SpouseName | Text | 75 |
| SpouseBirthDate | Date/Time | |
| Notes | Memo | |
| CommissionPercent | Number | Double |
| Inactive | Yes/No | |

As you can see, we have a lot of work to do to make the two tables identical: rename fields, move fields, insert fields, add new fields, and change data types and lengths.

Before we go any further, you should rename the remaining fields and add captions so that they more closely match the fields in the tblContacts table in the Conrad Systems Contacts sample database. Following the preceding steps for renaming fields and changing the Caption property, go through each of the fields and change them as follows:

| Old Name | New Name | Caption |
|---|---|---|
| Last Name | LastName | Last Name |
| First Name | FirstName | First Name |
| E-mail Address | EmailName | Email Name |
| Job Title | Title | |
| Business Phone | WorkPhone | Work Phone |
| Home Phone | HomePhone | Home Phone |
| Mobile Phone | MobilePhone | Mobile Phone |
| Fax Number | WorkFaxNumber | Fax Number |
| City | WorkCity | Work City |
| State/Province | WorkStateOrProvince | State/Province |
| Zip/Postal Code | WorkPostalCode | Postal Code |
| Country/Region | WorkCountry | Work Country |
| Web Page | Website | |
| Attachments | Photo | |

Your table should now look like Figure 5-11. Click the Save button on the Quick Access Toolbar to save the changes to the table.

INSIDE OUT

### Why the Field Names Have Spaces in the Table Templates

Office Access 2007 provides enhanced capabilities to move not only your data but also your entire application to a Microsoft Windows SharePoint server. You'll learn more about these features in Chapter 22, "Working with Windows SharePoint Services." When you move or copy an Access table to a Windows SharePoint server, Windows SharePoint Services stores the data in an object called a list. One shortcoming of Windows SharePoint Services lists is the fields do not have a Caption property, so a Windows SharePoint Services list always displays the field name for a column of data. Because Microsoft is emphasizing the new Windows SharePoint Services features in Access 2007, all the table templates use spaces in the field names to make them more readable. As you'll learn later in Part 7, "Designing an Access Project," the Conrad Systems Contacts sample database is designed for you to easily migrate to SQL Server, not Windows SharePoint Services. If your application is more likely to upsize to SQL Server, you should consider not using spaces in your field names so that you won't be forced to include bracket or quote delimiters in your references to these field names.

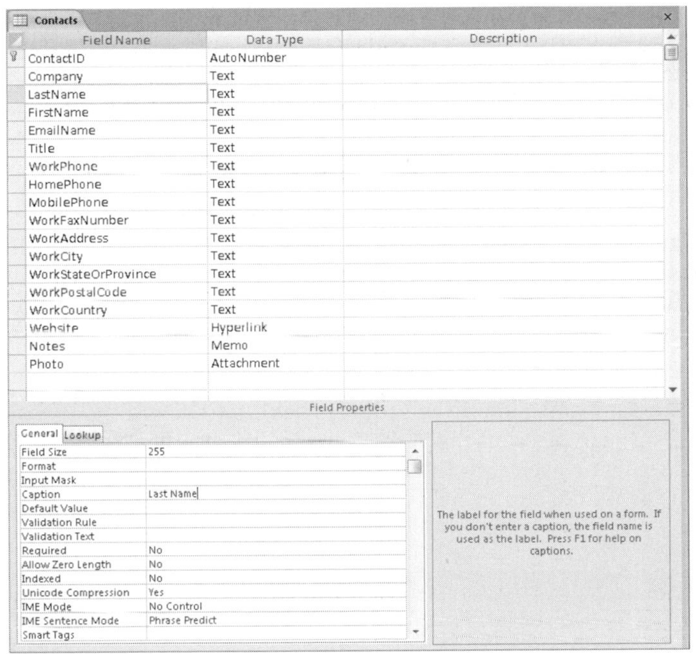


**Figure 5-11** After renaming the fields in the Contacts table created from the template, it is beginning to look more like the table in the Conrad Systems Contacts sample database.

# Moving Fields

You might want to move a field in a table definition for a number of reasons. Perhaps you made an error as you entered or changed the information in a table. Or perhaps you've discovered that you're using some fields you defined at the end of a table quite frequently in forms or reports, in which case it would be easier to find and work with those fields if they were nearer the beginning of your table definition.

INSIDE OUT

### How Important Is the Sequence of Fields in Your Table?

The actual sequence of field definitions in a table is not all that important. In the relational database model, there really is no defined sequence of fields in a row or rows in a table. Access 2007, like most databases that implement the relational model, does allow you to define a field order when you create a table. This order, or sequence of fields, becomes the default order you see in a table datasheet or in a list of field names when you're designing a query, form, or report.

We like to at least group fields together in some reasonable order so that they're easy to find, and we like to place the primary key fields at the top of the list. There's really no hard and fast rule that you must follow for your database to work efficiently.

You can use the mouse to move one or more rows. Simply follow these steps.

1. To select a row you want to move, click its row selector.

   If you want to move multiple contiguous rows, click the row selector for the first row in the group and scroll until you can see the last row in the group. Hold down the Shift key and click the row selector for the last row in the group. The first and last rows and all rows in between will be selected. Release the Shift key.

2. Click and drag the row selector(s) for the selected row(s) to a new location. A small shaded box attaches to the bottom of the mouse pointer while you're dragging, and a highlighted line will appear, indicating the position to which the row(s) will move when you release the mouse button.

In the design for the tblContacts table in the Conrad Systems Contacts database, the EmailName field appears after all the address fields and before the Website field. It certainly makes sense to place all the Web-related fields together. Select the EmailName field by clicking its row selector. Click the row selector again, and drag down until the line between the WorkCountry field and the Website field is highlighted, as shown in Figure 5-12.

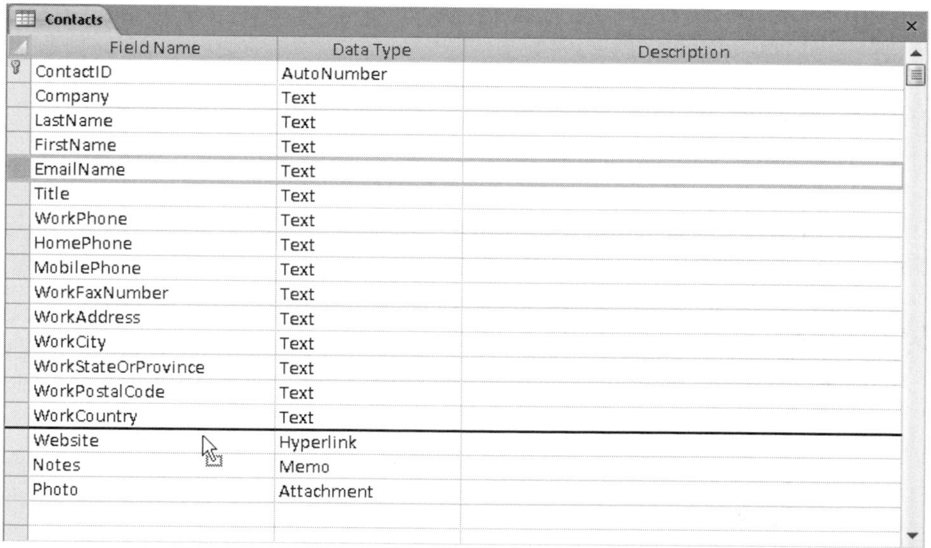

Contacts

| Field Name | Data Type | Description |
|---|---|---|
| ContactID | AutoNumber | |
| Company | Text | |
| LastName | Text | |
| FirstName | Text | |
| EmailName | Text | |
| Title | Text | |
| WorkPhone | Text | |
| HomePhone | Text | |
| MobilePhone | Text | |
| WorkFaxNumber | Text | |
| WorkAddress | Text | |
| WorkCity | Text | |
| WorkStateOrProvince | Text | |
| WorkPostalCode | Text | |
| WorkCountry | Text | |
| Website | Hyperlink | |
| Notes | Memo | |
| Photo | Attachment | |

**Figure 5-12** You can drag the EmailName field to a new position between the WorkCountry and Website fields.

## INSIDE OUT Using the Keyboard Instead of the Mouse in Table Design

When it comes to moving fields, you might find it easier to use a combination of mouse and keyboard methods. Use the mouse to select the row or rows you want to move. Then activate Move mode by pressing Ctrl+Shift+F8, and use the arrow keys to position the row(s). Press Esc to deactivate Move mode. As you experiment with Access 2007, you'll discover more than one way to perform many tasks, and you can choose the techniques that work the best for you.

In Figure 5-13, the fields are positioned correctly.

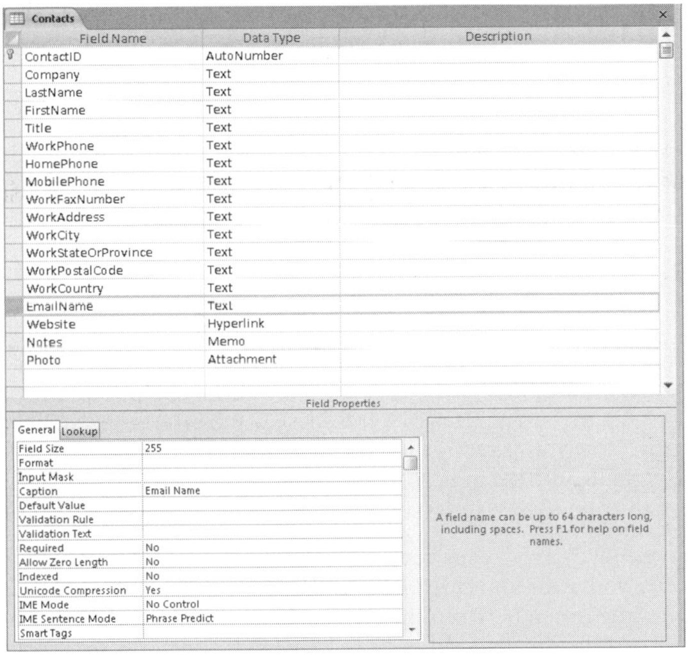

**Figure 5-13** The EmailName field is now correctly placed.

In this exercise, we'll move a couple of additional fields to make the design of Contacts more similar to tblContacts. In the tblContacts table, the HomePhone and MobilePhone fields appear just before the EmailName field. Click the row selector for HomePhone, hold down the Shift key, and click the row selector for MobilePhone to select both fields. Drag and drop the two fields before the EmailName field. Now that you've moved HomePhone and MobilePhone out of the way, you can select both WorkPhone and WorkFaxNumber and drag them to where they belong after the WorkCountry field. Finally, move the Notes field after the Photo field. After you've done this, your table should look like Figure 5-14.

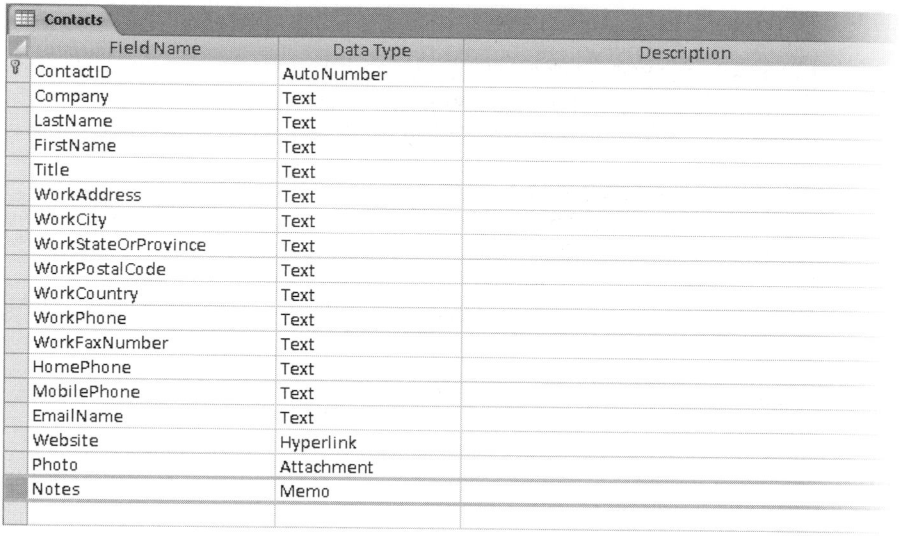

| Field Name | Data Type | Description |
| --- | --- | --- |
| ContactID | AutoNumber | |
| Company | Text | |
| LastName | Text | |
| FirstName | Text | |
| Title | Text | |
| WorkAddress | Text | |
| WorkCity | Text | |
| WorkStateOrProvince | Text | |
| WorkPostalCode | Text | |
| WorkCountry | Text | |
| WorkPhone | Text | |
| WorkFaxNumber | Text | |
| HomePhone | Text | |
| MobilePhone | Text | |
| EmailName | Text | |
| Website | Hyperlink | |
| Photo | Attachment | |
| Notes | Memo | |

**Figure 5-14** After moving several fields, the sequence of fields in your Contacts table is similar to that in tblContacts.

# Inserting Fields

Perhaps one of the most common changes you'll make to your database is to insert a new field in a table. Up until now, we've renamed and moved the available fields to more closely match tblContacts. If you take a look at the comparison of the two tables again (Tables 5-1 and 5-2 on pages 214 and 215), you can see that we need to add several more fields. Now you're ready to insert fields to store the middle initial, suffix, contact type, default address indicator, and more. As you go through adding these new fields, be sure to enter a description for each new field as well as the existing fields.

First, select the row or move your insertion point to the row that defines the field *after* the point where you want to insert the new field. In this case, if you want to insert a field for the middle initial between the FirstName and Title fields, place the insertion point anywhere in the row that defines the Title field. You can also select the entire row by using the arrow keys to move to the row and then pressing Shift+Spacebar or by clicking the row selector. Next, click the Design contextual tab, which is located below Table Tools on the Ribbon. Finally, click the Insert Rows command in the Tools group, as shown in Figure 5-15. (You can also click a field row and press the Insert key to insert a row above your selection.)

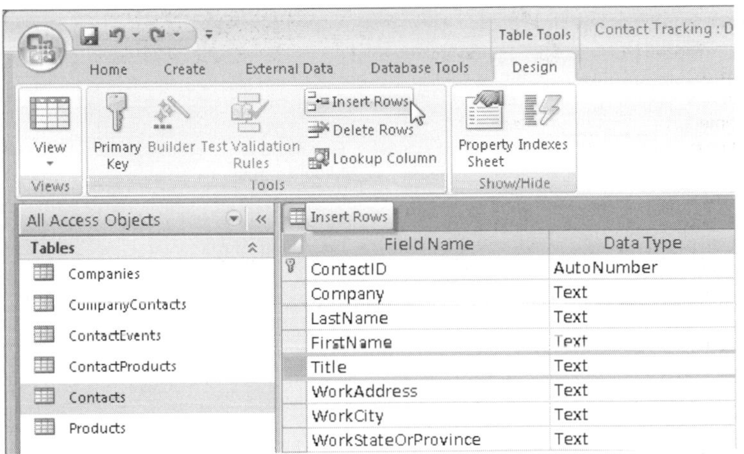


**Figure 5-15** The Insert Rows command inserts a new row above a selected row or above the row in which the insertion point is located.

Access 2007 adds a blank row that you can use to define your new field. Type the definition for the MiddleInit field. Choose the Text data type, and set the Field Size property to **1**. Now move down to the WorkAddress field, and insert another row above it. Enter a Suffix field that has the Text data type with a field size of **10**. Do it one more time and insert a ContactType field between Suffix and WorkAddress, set its data type to Text, and set its length to **50**. Insert a field between ContactType and WorkAddress, name it BirthDate, and set its data type to Date/Time. Insert another field between BirthDate and WorkAddress, name it DefaultAddress, set its data type to Number, and set the field size to Integer. The actual Conrad Systems Contacts application uses this field to indicate whether the work or home address is the default mailing address.

Move down to WorkFaxNumber and insert a field above it. Enter a field name of WorkExtension, set its data type to Text, and set the field size to **20**. Now move down to the bottom of the field list and insert another new field above Notes. Enter a field name of SpouseName, set its data type to Text, and set the field size to **75**. Insert another row between the SpouseName and Notes fields, enter a field name of SpouseBirthDate, and set its data type to Date/Time. Move to the blank row beyond Notes (you can use an existing blank row to add a field at the end), and create a field named CommissionPercent with a data type of Number and a field size of Double. Finally, move down to the empty row below CommissionPercent, create a new field named Inactive, and set its data type to Yes/No.

At this point, your Table window in Design view should look something like the one shown in Figure 5-16. (We entered information in the Description properties of all fields we're going to keep. You can change your descriptions to match the figure.) Don't worry about setting other properties just yet. As you can see, we are getting closer to the exact design specifications of tblContacts in the Conrad Systems Contacts database, but we still have more things to change.

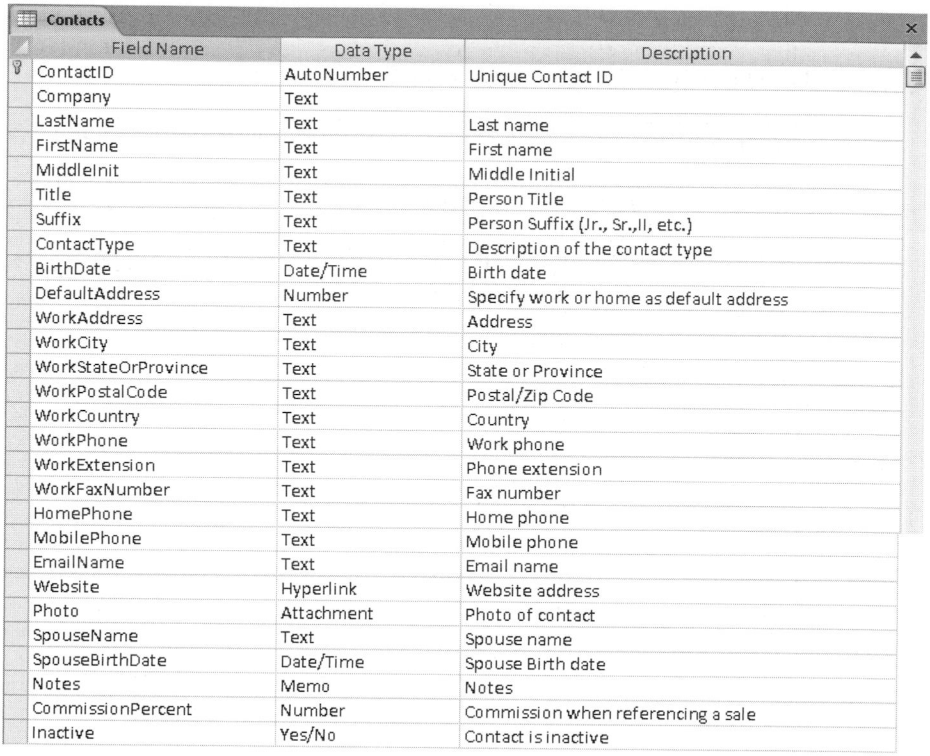

Contacts

| Field Name | Data Type | Description |
|---|---|---|
| ContactID | AutoNumber | Unique Contact ID |
| Company | Text | |
| LastName | Text | Last name |
| FirstName | Text | First name |
| MiddleInit | Text | Middle Initial |
| Title | Text | Person Title |
| Suffix | Text | Person Suffix (Jr., Sr.,II, etc.) |
| ContactType | Text | Description of the contact type |
| BirthDate | Date/Time | Birth date |
| DefaultAddress | Number | Specify work or home as default address |
| WorkAddress | Text | Address |
| WorkCity | Text | City |
| WorkStateOrProvince | Text | State or Province |
| WorkPostalCode | Text | Postal/Zip Code |
| WorkCountry | Text | Country |
| WorkPhone | Text | Work phone |
| WorkExtension | Text | Phone extension |
| WorkFaxNumber | Text | Fax number |
| HomePhone | Text | Home phone |
| MobilePhone | Text | Mobile phone |
| EmailName | Text | Email name |
| Website | Hyperlink | Website address |
| Photo | Attachment | Photo of contact |
| SpouseName | Text | Spouse name |
| SpouseBirthDate | Date/Time | Spouse Birth date |
| Notes | Memo | Notes |
| CommissionPercent | Number | Commission when referencing a sale |
| Inactive | Yes/No | Contact is inactive |

**Figure 5-16** The Contacts table with additional fields inserted and descriptions defined.

INSIDE OUT **Using the Keyboard to Move Between Windows**

You can move the insertion point between the upper part and the lower part of any Table or Query window in Design view by pressing F6.



## Copying Fields

As you create table definitions, you might find that several fields in your table are similar. Rather than enter each of the field definitions separately, you can enter one field definition, copy it, and then paste it as many times as necessary.

To finish defining our Contacts table, we need five additional fields—HomeAddress, HomeCity, HomeStateOrProvince, HomePostalCode, and HomeCountry. You could certainly insert a new row and type all the properties as you just did in the previous section, but why not copy a field that is similar and make minor changes to it?

For this part of the exercise, select the row for the WorkAddress field definition by clicking the row selector at the left of the row. Click the Copy command in the Clipboard group on the Home tab, as shown in Figure 5-17.

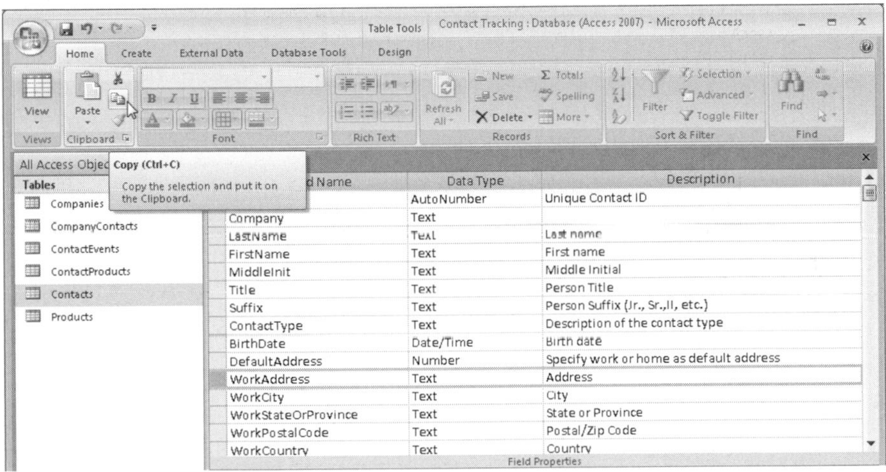


**Figure 5-17** Select the WorkAddress field and click the Copy command on the Home tab of the Ribbon to copy the field to the Clipboard.

Move the insertion point to the row that should follow the row you'll insert. (In this case, move the insertion point to the HomePhone field, which should follow your new field.) Insert a blank row by clicking Insert Rows in the Tools group of the Design contextual tab below Table Tools on the Ribbon. (In this procedure you switch back and forth between the Home tab and the Design contextual tab.) Select the new row by clicking the row selector. Click the Paste command in the Clipboard group on the Home tab of the Ribbon, as shown in Figure 5-18.

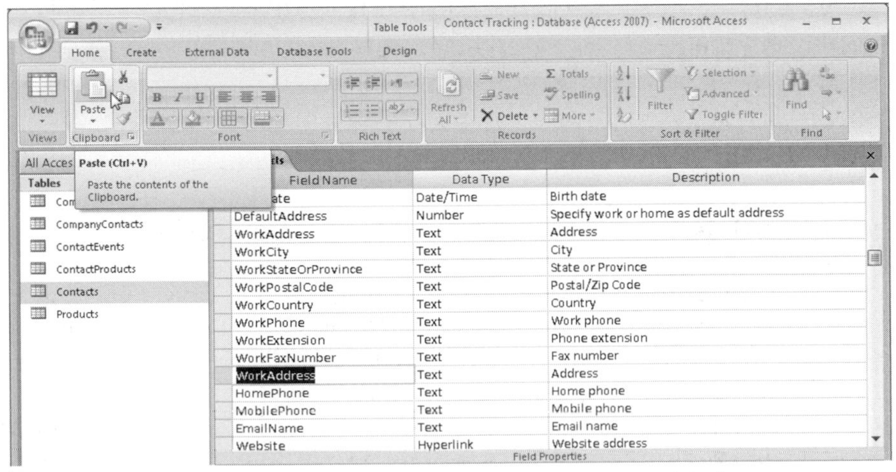


**Figure 5-18** You can paste the copied WorkAddress field into a new blank row.

**CAUTION!**

If you click the Paste command when a row containing data is selected, the copied row will *replace* the selected row. Should you make this replacement in error, click the Undo command on the Quick Access Toolbar to restore the original row.

You can use the Paste command repeatedly to insert a copied row more than once. Remember to change both the name and the description of the resulting field or fields before you save the modified table definition. In this case, it's a simple matter to change the name of the copied row from WorkAddress to HomeAddress and to correct the description and caption accordingly. Note that this procedure also has the benefit of copying any formatting, default value, or validation rule information.

If you're careful, you don't actually have to insert a blank row to paste a field definition from the Clipboard. You can also copy and paste multiple fields at a time. After you fix the HomeAddress field name and description in the upper part of the window and caption in the lower part of the window, select the WorkCity field, hold down the Shift key, and select the WorkCountry field. Click the Copy command to copy all four fields to the Clipboard. Move down to the HomePhone field again and click in the row but *do not select the row*. Click the Paste button in the Clipboard group of the Home tab to insert the four fields just above HomePhone. Change the name of the first one to HomeCity, the second to HomeStateOrProvince, the third to HomePostalCode, and the fourth to HomeCountry and correct the descriptions and captions. You should now have a table that's almost identical to the tblContacts table in the Conrad Systems Contacts sample database as shown in Figure 5-19. Be sure to save your changed table.

Contacts

| Field Name | Data Type | Description |
|---|---|---|
| ContactID | AutoNumber | Unique Contact ID |
| Company | Text | |
| LastName | Text | Last name |
| FirstName | Text | First name |
| MiddleInit | Text | Middle Initial |
| Title | Text | Person Title |
| Suffix | Text | Person Suffix (Jr., Sr.,II, etc.) |
| ContactType | Text | Description of the contact type |
| BirthDate | Date/Time | Birth date |
| DefaultAddress | Number | Specify work or home as default address |
| WorkAddress | Text | Address |
| WorkCity | Text | City |
| WorkStateOrProvince | Text | State or Province |
| WorkPostalCode | Text | Postal/Zip Code |
| WorkCountry | Text | Country |
| WorkPhone | Text | Work phone |
| WorkExtension | Text | Phone extension |
| WorkFaxNumber | Text | Fax number |
| HomeAddress | Text | Address |
| HomeCity | Text | City |
| HomeStateOrProvince | Text | State or Province |
| HomePostalCode | Text | Postal/Zip Code |
| HomeCountry | Text | Country |
| HomePhone | Text | Home phone |
| MobilePhone | Text | Mobile phone |
| EmailName | Text | Email name |
| Website | Hyperlink | Website address |
| Photo | Attachment | Photo of contact |
| SpouseName | Text | Spouse name |
| SpouseBirthDate | Date/Time | Spouse Birth date |
| Notes | Memo | Notes |
| CommissionPercent | Number | Commission when referencing a sale |
| Inactive | Yes/No | Contact is inactive |

**Figure 5-19** The Contacts field list is now almost identical to tblContacts.

# Deleting Fields

Removing unwanted fields is easy. With the Table window open in Design view, select the field that you want to delete by clicking the row selector. You can extend the selection to multiple contiguous fields by holding down the Shift key and pressing the Up and Down Arrow keys to select multiple rows. You can also select multiple contiguous rows by clicking the row selector of the first row and, without releasing the mouse button, dragging up or down to select all the rows you want. After you select the appropriate fields, click Delete Rows in the Tools group of the Design tab below Table Tools on the Ribbon. Or, press the Delete key to delete the selected fields.

We have one extra field in our current Contacts table that we do not need—the Company field that was created by the table template. (Remember that in Chapter 4 you created a Company Contacts table to link contacts to their respective companies.) To delete this field, click the row selector next to the Company field and then click the Delete Rows button in the Tools group of the Design tab on the Ribbon. Your Contacts table now matches the tblContacts table from the Conrad Systems Contacts database in terms of the correct number of fields and field names. Save these latest changes to the Contacts table by clicking the Save button on the Quick Access Toolbar.

If a table contains one or more rows of data, Access displays a warning message when you delete field definitions in Design view, as shown in Figure 5-20. Click No if you think you made a mistake. Click Yes to proceed with the deletion of the fields and the data in those fields. Keep in mind that you can still undo this change up to the point that you save the table.

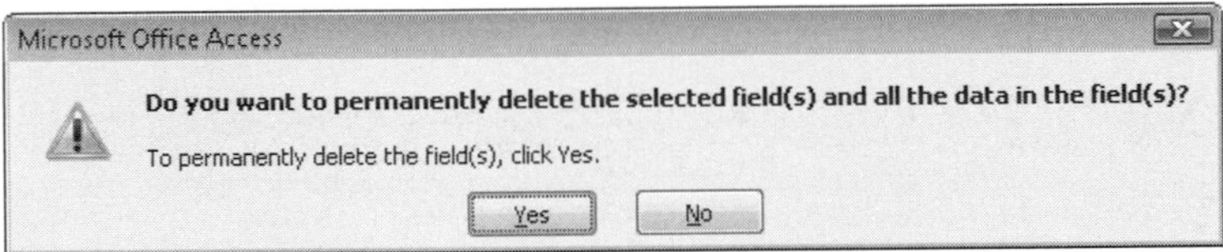


**Figure 5-20** This dialog box asks you to confirm a field deletion.

If you want to test this out in the sample table you have been building, make sure you have saved your latest changes and then switch to Datasheet view by clicking the small arrow below the View button in the Views group on the Home tab and then clicking Datasheet View. Type your name in the Last Name and First Name fields and switch back to Design view by clicking the small arrow below the View button again. Try deleting any field in the design, and Access will warn you that you may be deleting some data as well.

# Changing Data Attributes

As you learned in the previous chapter, Access 2007 provides a number of different data types. These data types help Access work more efficiently with your data and also provide a base level of data validation; for example, you can enter only numbers in a Number or Currency field.

When you initially design your database, you should match the data type and length of each field to its intended use. You might discover, however, that a field you thought would contain only numbers (such as a U.S. ZIP Code) must now contain some letters (perhaps because you've started doing business in Canada). You might find that one or more number fields need to hold larger values or a different number of decimal places. Access allows you to change the data type and length of many fields, even after you've entered data in them.

## Changing Data Types

Changing the data type of a field in a table is simple. Open the table in Design view, click in the Data Type column of the field definition you want to change, click the arrow button at the right to see the available choices, and select a new data type. You cannot convert an OLE Object, an Attachment, or a ReplicationID data type to another data type. With several limitations, Access can successfully convert every other data type to any other data type, even when you have data in the table. Table 5-3 shows you the possible conversions and potential limitations when the table contains data.

**CAUTION!**

When the field contents don't satisfy the limitations noted in Table 5-3, Access 2007 *deletes* the field contents (sets it to Null) when you save the changes.

**Table 5-3 Limitations on Converting One Data Type to Another**

| Convert To | From | Limitations |
|---|---|---|
| Text | Memo | Access truncates text longer than 255 characters. |
| | Hyperlink | Might lose some data if the hyperlink string is longer than 255 characters. |
| | Number, except ReplicationID | No limitations. |
| | AutoNumber | No limitations except ReplicationID. |
| | Currency | No limitations. |
| | Date/Time | No limitations. |
| | Yes/No | Yes (–1) converts to Yes; No (0) converts to No. |
| Memo | Text | No limitations. |
| | Hyperlink | No limitations. |
| | Number, except ReplicationID | No limitations. |
| | AutoNumber | No limitations. |

| Convert To | From | Limitations |
|---|---|---|
| Memo | Currency | No limitations. |
| | Date/Time | No limitations. |
| | Yes/No | Yes (–1) converts to Yes; No (0) converts to No. |
| Hyperlink | Text | If the text contains a valid hyperlink string consisting of a display name, a # delimiter, a valid link address, a # delimiter, and optional bookmark and ScreenTip, Access changes the data type without modifying the text. If the text contains only a valid link address, Access surrounds the address with # delimiters to form the hyperlink field. Access recognizes strings beginning with *http://*, *ftp://*, *mailto:*, *news:*, *servername*, and *d:*\ as link addresses. Access also assumes that a text string in the form *text@text* is an e-mail address, and it adds *mailto:* to the beginning of the string before converting it. If Access does not recognize the text as a link, it converts the text to *[text]#http://[text]#*, where *[text]* is the original contents of the field; the result is probably not a valid link address. |
| | Memo | Same restrictions as converting from Text. |
| | Number, except ReplicationID | Possible, but Access converts the number to a text string in the form *[number]#http://[number]#*, where *[number]* is the text conversion of the original numeric value; the result is probably not a valid link address. |
| | AutoNumber | Possible, but Access converts the AutoNumber to a text string in the form *[number]#http://[number]*, where *[number]* is the text conversion of the original AutoNumber; the result is probably not a valid link address. |
| | Currency | Possible, but Access converts the currency value to a text string in the form *[currency]#http://[currency]*, where *[currency]* is the text conversion of the original currency value; the result is probably not a valid link address. |
| | Date/Time | Possible, but Access converts the date/time to a text string in the form *[date/time]#http://[date/time]#*, where *[date/time]* is the text conversion of the original date or time value; the result is probably not a valid link address. |
| | Yes/No | Possible, but Access converts the yes/no to a text string in the form *[yes/no]#http://[yes/no]*, where *[yes/no]* is the text conversion of the original yes (–1) or no (0) value; the result is probably not a valid link address. |

| Convert To | From | Limitations |
|---|---|---|
| Number | Text | Text must contain only numbers and valid separators. The number value must be within the range for the Field Size property. |
| | Memo | Memo must contain only numbers and valid separators. The number value must be within the range for the Field Size property. |
| | Hyperlink | Not possible. |
| | Number (different field size or precision) | Number must not be larger or smaller than can be contained in the new field size. If you change precision, Access might round the number. |
| | AutoNumber | The number value must be within the range for the Field Size property. |
| | Currency | Number must not be larger or smaller than can be contained in the Field Size property. |
| | Date/Time | If the Field Size is Byte, the date must be between April 18, 1899, and September 11, 1900. If the new Field Size is Integer, the date must be between April 13, 1810, and September 16, 1989. For all other field sizes, there are no limitations. |
| | Yes/No | Yes (–1) converts to –1; No (0) converts to 0. |
| AutoNumber | Text | Not possible if the table contains data. |
| | Memo | Not possible if the table contains data. |
| | Hyperlink | Not possible. |
| | Number | Not possible if the table contains data. |
| | Currency | Not possible if the table contains data. |
| | Date/Time | Not possible if the table contains data. |
| | Yes/No | Not possible if the table contains data. |
| Currency | Text | Text must contain only numbers and valid separators. |
| | Memo | Memo must contain only numbers and valid separators. |
| | Hyperlink | Not possible. |
| | Number, except Replication ID | No limitations. |
| | AutoNumber | No limitations. |
| | Date/Time | No limitations, but value might be rounded. |
| | Yes/No | Yes (–1) converts to $1; No (0) converts to $0. |

| Convert To | From | Limitations |
|---|---|---|
| Date/Time | Text | Text must contain a recognizable date and/or time, such as 11-Nov-08 5:15 PM. |
| | Memo | Memo must contain a recognizable date and/or time, such as 11-Nov-08 5:15 PM. |
| | Hyperlink | Not possible. |
| | Number, except Replication ID | Number must be between –657,434 and 2,958,465.99998843. |
| | AutoNumber | Value must be less than 2,958,466 and greater than –657,433. |
| | Currency | Number must be between –$657,434 and $2,958,465.9999. |
| | Yes/No | Yes (–1) converts to 12/29/1899; No (0) converts to 12:00:00 AM. |
| Yes/No | Text | Text must contain only one of the following values: Yes, True, On, No, False, or Off. |
| | Memo | Text must contain only one of the following values: Yes, True, On, No, False, or Off. |
| | Hyperlink | Not possible. |
| | Number, except Replication ID | Zero or Null converts to No; any other value converts to Yes. |
| | AutoNumber | All values evaluate to Yes. |
| | Currency | Zero or Null converts to No; any other value converts to Yes. |
| | Date/Time | 12:00:00 AM or Null converts to No; any other value converts to Yes. |

If you want to see how this works in the Contacts table you have been building, open the table in Datasheet view and enter any last name and first name in one or two rows. We want to change the EmailName field from the Text data type that the table template provided to Hyperlink. Scroll right and enter an invalid e-mail address in one of the rows in the form: **Proseware email address**. In another row, add the correct URL prefix in the form: **mailto:jeffc@proseware.com**.

Now, switch to Design view and change the data type of the EmailName field from Text to Hyperlink and save the change. Notice that Access 2007 gives you no warning about any conversion problems because it knows it can store any text field that is not larger than 255 characters in a hyperlink, which can be up to 8,192 bytes. Save this change to the table, switch back to Datasheet view, and scroll to the right to find the changed field. You should see a result something like Figure 5-21.

Contacts

| | Mobile Phone | EmailName | Website | Photo |
|---|---|---|---|---|
| | | Proseware email address | | (0) |
| | | mailto:jeffc@proseware.com | | (0) |
| * | | | | (0) |

**Figure 5-21** Access 2007 can convert the Text data type to Hyperlink, but will get it right only if the text contains a recognizable protocol string.

Both entries look fine. However, if you click on the first one, Access 2007 attempts to open your browser because the full text stored in the hyperlink is *Proseware email address#http://Proseware email address#*. Because the link address portion indicates the HTTP protocol, your browser attempts to open instead of your e-mail program. Access displays a message box that says it cannot follow the hyperlink. When you click on the second link, it should open a blank message in your e-mail program with the To: line filled in correctly. Access recognized the mailto: prefix and converted the text correctly.

**You can read more about working with hyperlinks in Chapter 10, "Using Forms." We show you how to make sure that Access correctly recognizes an e-mail name typed into a hyperlink field in Chapter 20, "Automating Your Application with Visual Basic."**

## Changing Data Lengths

For text and number fields, you can define the maximum length of the data that can be stored in the field. Although a text field can be up to 255 characters long, you can restrict the length to as little as 1 character. If you don't specify a length for text, Access 2007 normally assigns the length you specify in the Table Design section in the Object Designers category of the Access Options dialog box. (The default length is 255.) Access won't let you enter text field data longer than the defined length. If you need more space in a text field, you can increase the length at any time; but if you try to redefine the length of a text field so that it's shorter, you will get a warning message (like the one shown in Figure 5-22) stating that Access will truncate any data field that contains data longer than the new length when you try to save the changes to your table. Note also that it warns you that any validation rules you have designed might fail on the changed data.

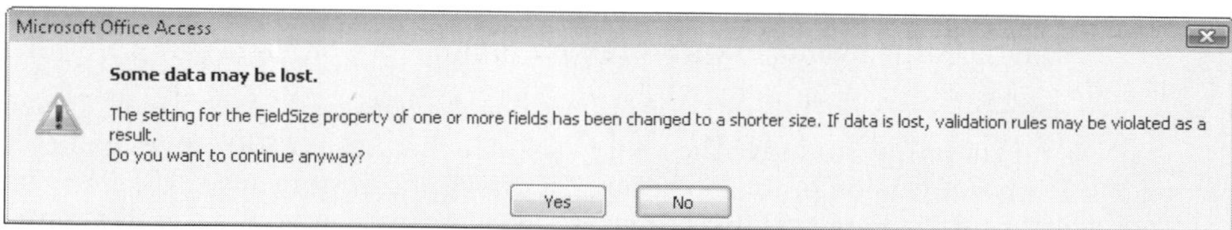


**Figure 5-22** This dialog box informs you of possible data truncation problems.

INSIDE OUT **Setting Field Defaults Through Access Options**

Remember, you can change the default data type for a new field and the default length of new text and number fields by clicking the Microsoft Office Button, clicking Access Options, clicking the Object Designers category of the Access Options dialog box, and then selecting your defaults in the Table Design section.

If you want to try this in your Contacts table, open it in Design view, change the length of the MiddleInit field to **10**, and save the change. Switch to Datasheet view and type more than one character in MiddleInit. Now switch back to Design view and set the length of MiddleInit to **y**. When you try to save the change, you should see the error message in Figure 5-22 (because you're shortening the length of the MiddleInit field). Click Yes to allow the changes and then switch back to Datasheet view. You should find the data you typed truncated to one character in MiddleInit. Review Table 5-2 (page 215) and verify that each field's length in your Contacts table matches tblContacts in the Conrad Systems Contacts database and make any necessary adjustments before proceeding further.

Sizes for numeric data types can vary from a single byte (which can contain a value from 0 through 255) to 2 or 4 bytes (for larger integers), 8 bytes (necessary to hold very large floating-point or currency numbers), or 16 bytes (to hold a unique ReplicationID or decimal number). Except for ReplicationID, you can change the size of a numeric data type at any time, but you might generate errors if you make the size smaller. Access also rounds numbers when converting from floating-point data types (Single or Double) to integer or currency values.

## Dealing with Conversion Errors

When you try to save a modified table definition, Access 2007 always warns you if any changes to the data type or field length will cause conversion errors. For example, if you change the Field Size property of a Number field from Integer to Byte, Access warns you if any of the records contain a number larger than 255. (Access deletes the contents of any field it can't convert at all.) If you examine Table 5-3, you'll see that you should expect some data type changes to always cause problems. For example, if you change a field from Hyperlink to Date/Time, you can expect Access to delete all data. You'll see a dialog box similar to the one shown in Figure 5-23 warning you about fields that Access will set to a Null value if you proceed with your changes. Click Yes to proceed with the changes. You'll have to examine your data to correct any conversion errors.

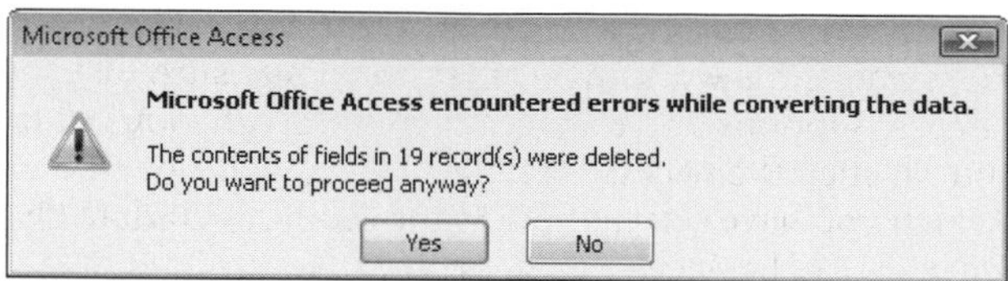


**Figure 5-23** This dialog box informs you of conversion errors.

If you click No, Access 2007 opens the dialog box shown in Figure 5-24. If you deleted any fields or indexes, added any fields, or renamed any fields, Access will save those changes. Otherwise, the database will be unchanged. You can correct any data type or field length changes you made, and then try to save the table definition again.

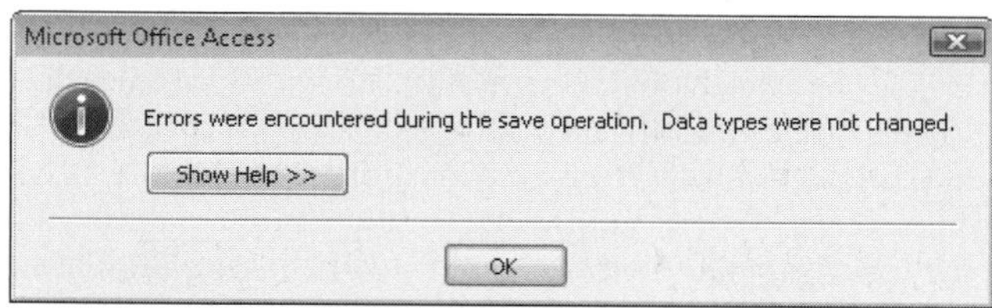


**Figure 5-24** This dialog box appears if you decide not to save a modified table definition.

## Changing Other Field Properties

As you learned in Chapter 4, you can set a number of other properties that define how Access 2007 displays or validates a field that have nothing to do with changing the data type. These properties include Description, Format, Input Mask, Caption, Default Value, Validation Rule, Validation Text, Required, Allow Zero Length, and Indexed.

If you have data in your table, changing some of these properties might elicit a warning from Access. If you change or define a validation rule, or set Required to Yes, Access offers to check the new rule or requirement that a field not be empty against the contents of the table when you try to save the change. If you ask Access to test the data, it checks all the rows in your table and opens a warning dialog box if it finds any rows that fail. However, it doesn't tell you *which* rows failed—we'll show you how to do that in Chapter 7. If you changed the rules for more than one field, you'll see the error dialog box once for each rule that fails.

As you'll learn later, when you define queries, forms, and reports, these objects inherit several of the properties that you define for your table fields. In previous versions of Access, the catch was that once you defined and saved another object that used table fields, any subsequent change that you made to properties in table design didn't change automatically in other dependent objects. You had to go find those properties yourself and fix them, or use a tool such as the Speed Ferret product from Black Moshannon Systems (*www.moshannon.com*). You would get the new property settings in any new objects you created, but the old ones remained unchanged.

The good news is there's a feature in Access 2007 that takes care of this problem for some properties. To see how this works, you must first make sure that you have this option selected in Access Options as we showed you in the previous chapter. Click the Microsoft Office Button, click the Access Options button, click the Object Designers category, and verify that you have selected the Show Property Update Options Buttons check box. Click OK to close the Access Options dialog box.

Next, open the Contacts table in Design view in the Contact Tracking database you have been building. Remember from the previous chapter that Access displays the description on the status bar when the focus is on the Description field in any datasheet or form. Click in the Description column next to the ContactID field and change the description from "Unique contact ID" to just "Contact ID" and then press Tab. As soon as you do this, you'll see an AutoCorrect smart tag that looks like a lightning bolt. If you rest your mouse pointer near the smart tag, it tells you that it offers property update options. Click the arrow next to the tag to see the options you can choose from as shown in Figure 5-25. Access offers you these options whenever you change the Description, Format, or Input Mask properties.

Contacts

| Field Name | Data Type | Description |
|---|---|---|
| ContactID | AutoNumber | Contact Id |
| LastName | Text | ...name |
| FirstName | Text | Update Status Bar Text everywhere ContactID is used |
| MiddleInit | Text | Help on propagating field properties |
| Title | Text | |
| Suffix | Text | Person Suffix (Jr., Sr.,II, etc.) |
| ContactType | Text | Description of the contact type |

**Figure 5-25** When you change a field description, you see a smart tag offering property update options.

You can click Update Status Bar Text Everywhere ContactID Is Used to ask Access to also change this property wherever the ContactID field is used in other objects. Of course, you don't have anything but tables in your sample database right now, so clicking this command won't do anything. You can select Help On Propagating Field Properties to open the Help window to read how this works.



**CAUTION!**

You must click the Update Status Bar Text Everywhere ContactID Is Used command immediately after you make the change in your table definition. If you move to another field or move to another property and make another change, the smart tag disappears. You can make it reappear by returning to the property you changed and changing it again. If you choose to make changes, Access opens an Update Properties dialog box that lists all the objects it plans to change. You can reject all changes or selectively apply the change to only some of the objects.

## Reversing Changes

If you make several changes and then decide you don't want any of them, you can close the Table window without saving it. When you do this, Access opens the dialog box shown in Figure 5-26. Simply click No to reverse all your changes. Click Cancel to return to the Table window in Design view without saving or reversing your changes.

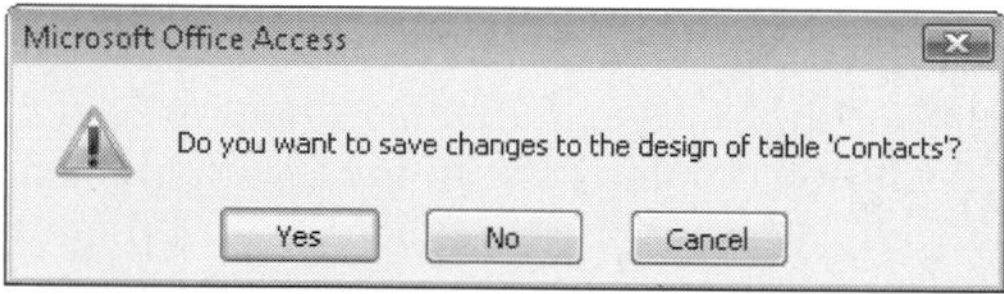


**Figure 5-26** This dialog box gives you the option of reversing unsaved changes to a table.

INSIDE OUT **Reversing Multiple Changes**

You can always reverse up to the last 20 changes you made since you last saved the table design by clicking the Undo button. You can also open the list next to the Undo button to selectively undo a series of changes.

## Using the Table Analyzer Wizard

Even if you use good design techniques (see Article 1, "Designing Your Database Application" on the companion CD) and build a normalized database, you might not arrive at the best design. In fact, you often cannot fully evaluate a database design until you use the database and store data. Access 2007 includes the Table Analyzer Wizard that can examine data in your tables (or data you import from another source) and recommend additional refinements and enhancements to your database design.

One of the key elements of good database design is the elimination of redundant data. The Table Analyzer Wizard is particularly good at scanning data in your tables, identifying data repeated in one or more columns, and recommending alterations to your design that break out the redundant data into separate tables. You can find an example of such redundant data in the Conrad Systems Contacts database (Contacts.accdb). Imagine that a customer sent you a file containing company and contact information. Sounds like a good, easy place to start collecting or adding to your contact data. However, when you open the file, you see that most companies are listed several times because the original data isn't normalized. You'll find just such a table, saved as tblContacts4TableAnalyzer, in the Conrad Systems Contacts sample database.

You can see how the Table Analyzer Wizard works by using it on the tblContacts4TableAnalyzer table. First, open the Conrad Systems Contacts database. Click the Database Tools tab and then click the Analyze Table command in the Analyze group. Access starts the Table Analyzer Wizard and displays the first page, shown in Figure 5-27.

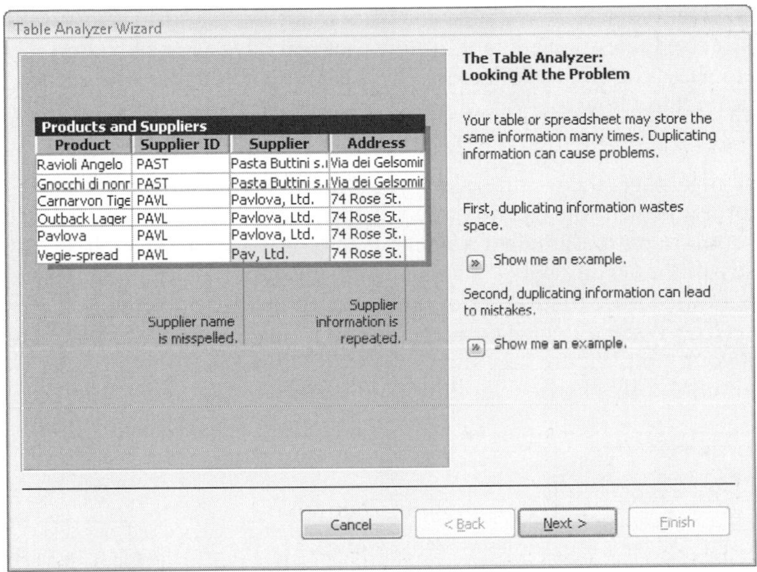


**Figure 5-27** The opening page of the Table Analyzer Wizard informs you about the problems it is designed to correct.

This first page is one of two introductory pages that explain what the wizard can do. Click the Show Me An Example buttons to get a better understanding of the kinds of problems the wizard can solve and to see how the wizard works. Click Next twice to get to the first "action" page in the wizard, shown in Figure 5-28.

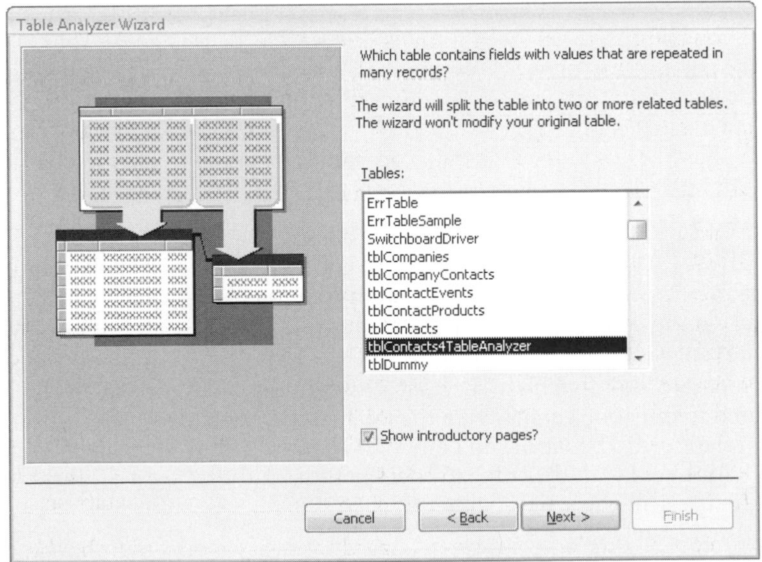


**Figure 5-28** Select the table you want to analyze in the Table Analyzer Wizard.

Chapter 5

On this page, you select the table you want to analyze. For this exercise, select the tblContacts4TableAnalyzer table. (Note that you have a check box on this page to continue to show the two introductory pages each time you start the wizard. If you think you understand how the wizard works, you can clear the check box to skip the introductory pages the next time you start the wizard.) Click Next.

On the next page, the wizard asks if you want to rearrange the fields in the target table or if you want the wizard to decide the arrangement for you. If you know which fields contain redundant data, you can make the decision yourself. Because the wizard handles all the "grunt work" of splitting out lookup data, you might choose the latter option in the future to further normalize tables in your application. For now, select the Yes, Let The Wizard Decide option to see how effective it is. Click Next to start the analysis of your table. Figure 5-29 shows the result of the wizard's analysis. (We've shifted the contents of this figure to fit the result in a single window.)

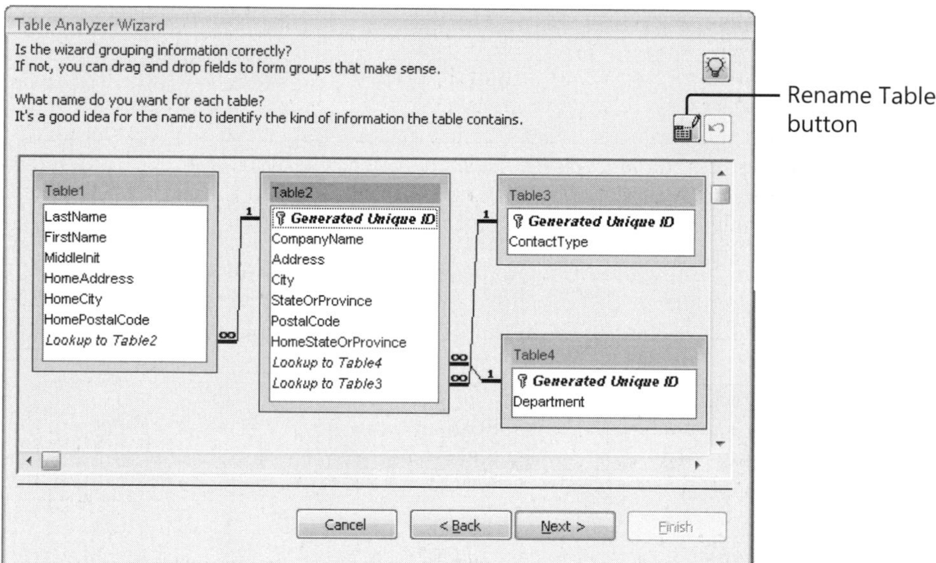


**Figure 5-29** The Table Analyzer Wizard examines the data in your table and makes an initial recommendation.

In this case, the wizard did a pretty good job of identifying the separate company and contact information and splitting the fields into two tables. It also recognized that ContactType and Department have lots of repeating values and perhaps should both be in separate lookup tables. There isn't enough data (only 18 rows–and each contact is related to only one company) in the table for the wizard to have noticed a many-to-many relationship between companies and contacts. It probably kept the HomeStateOrProvince field with the company data because it didn't see a different value across multiple rows for the same company.

We really don't need to do much work to fix this if we're happy with the one-to-many relationships. First, click on HomeStateOrProvince in Table2 and drag and drop it into Table1 between HomeCity and HomePostalCode. Also move the Lookup To Table3 field from Table2 to Table1 to correctly relate the contact type lookup information to contacts instead of companies, and move the Department field from Table4 to Table2 between CompanyName and Address. (The last move should remove Table4 from the design window.)

After you have adjusted the way the wizard split your tables, the next step is to give each of the new tables a new name. To rename a table, first click the table name and then click the Rename Table button in the upper part of the window. (You can also double-click the table's title bar.) The wizard opens a dialog box in which you can enter a new name. You should change Table1 to *Contacts*, Table2 to *Companies*, and Table3 to *ContactTypes*. Click Next when you are finished.

The next page asks you to verify the primary key fields for these tables. You can select new fields for the primary key of each table or add fields to the primary key. The wizard couldn't identify any naturally occurring unique value, so it generated a unique ID (which will be an AutoNumber in the final tables) for two of the tables. You need to select the Contacts table and click the Add Generated Key button to create a primary key for that table. Figure 5-30 shows the result of moving fields, assigning new names to the tables, and adding a primary key. Click Next to accept the settings and go on to an analysis of duplicate values in the lookup tables.

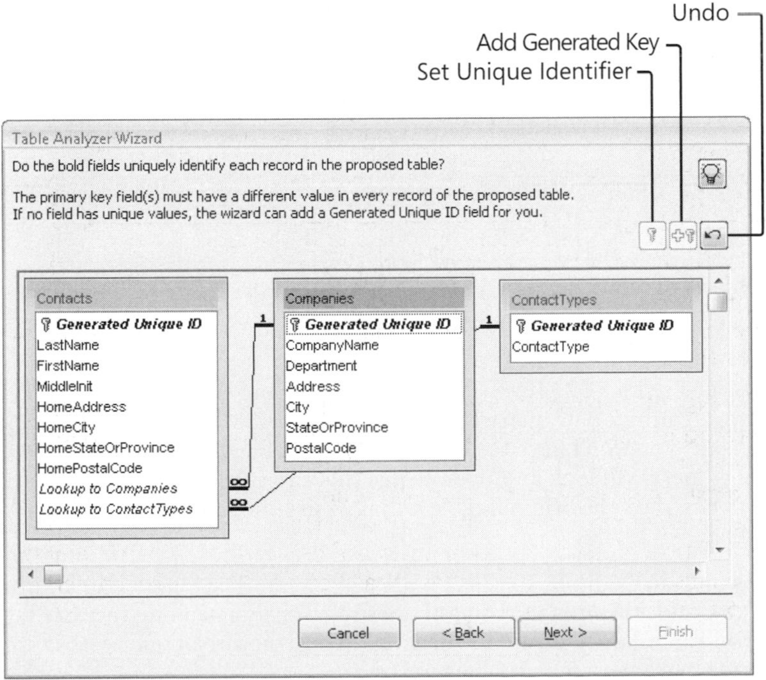


**Figure 5-30** After adjusting what the wizard proposed, you're ready to create the new tables.

The Table Analyzer Wizard looks at values in the new tables to try to eliminate any possible duplicates created by typing errors. Figure 5-31 shows the result of this analysis on the sample table. Because the wizard sees several rows with *Marketing* or *Sales* in them, it suggests that some of these values might, in fact, be the same. You can use this page to tell the wizard any correct values for actual mistyped duplicates. This could be extremely useful if your incoming data had the same company listed several times but with a slightly different spelling or address. The wizard will store only unique values in the final table. You could, if necessary, tell the wizard to substitute one set of similar values for another to eliminate the near duplicates. In this case, you should tell the wizard to use the original value for all the values listed as duplicates by clicking the arrow in the Correction field and selecting the (Leave As Is) option as shown in Figure 5-31. Click Next when you are finished to go on to the next page.

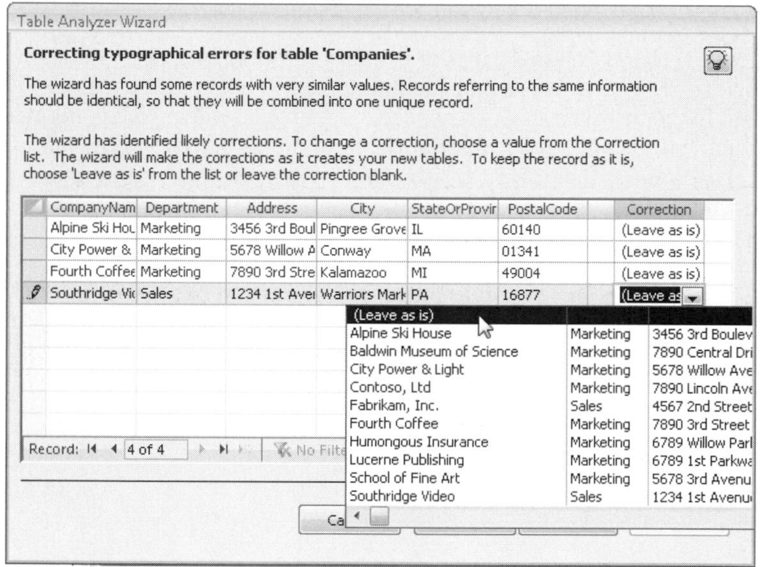


**Figure 5-31** The Table Analyzer Wizard gives you the opportunity to fix potentially duplicate lookup values.

Finally, the wizard offers to create a new query that has the same name as the original table. (See Figure 5-32.) If you've already been using the old table in queries, forms, and reports, creating a new query that integrates the new tables into the original data structure means you won't have to change any other objects in your database. In most cases, the new query will look and operate just like the original table. Old queries, forms, and reports based on the original table will now use the new query and won't know the difference.

This is only an example, so select No, Don't Create The Query. Click Finish to build your new tables. The wizard also creates relationships among the new tables to make sure you can easily re-create the original data structure in queries. Figure 5-33 shows the three new tables built by the wizard.

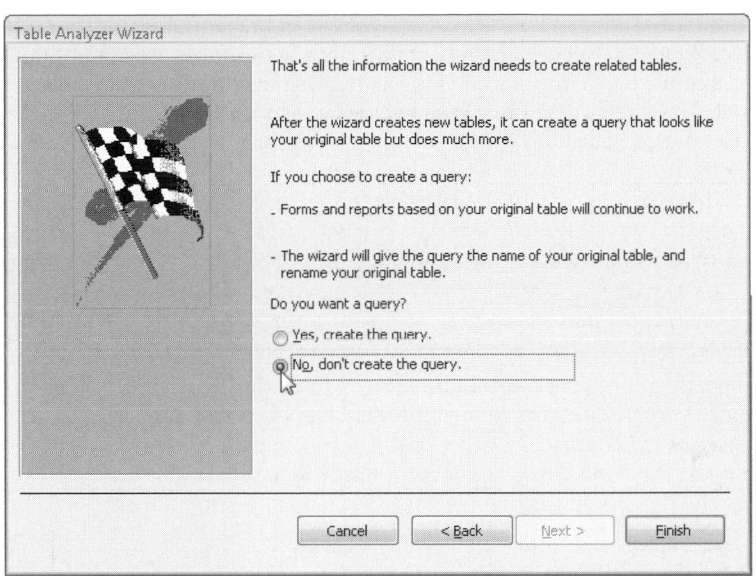


**Figure 5-32** The final page of the Table Analyzer Wizard lets you decide whether you want a query to duplicate the original unnormalized data structure.

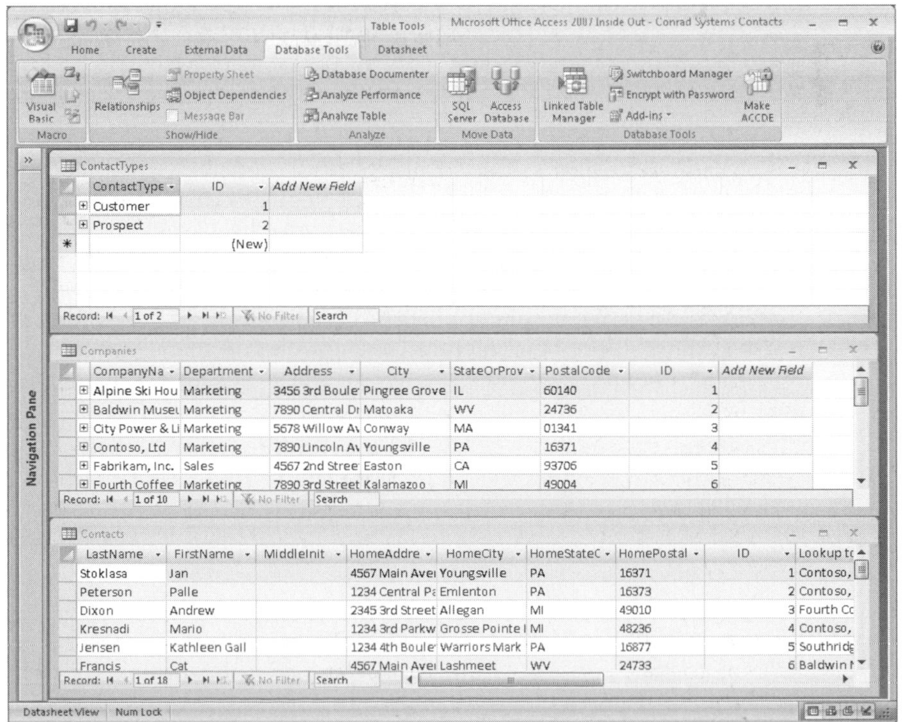


**Figure 5-33** The Table Analyzer Wizard automatically separates your old data into the new table structure.

Notice that the wizard left behind an ID field in the Contacts table as a link to the ContactTypes table. The values in the ContactTypes table are actually unique, so there's no reason not to use the actual value as the primary key instead of an artificial ID. We'll show you how to change the primary key later in this chapter.

## Taking a Look at Lookup Properties

As you have been working with table design, you've probably noticed that there's a Lookup tab available in the lower part of the Table window in Design view. You might have also noticed that Access 2007 offers you a Lookup Wizard entry in the drop-down list of data types and a Lookup Column option in the Tools group on the Design tab. This feature allows you to predefine how you want the field displayed in a datasheet, form, or report. For example, if you have a DepartmentID field in an Employees table that stores the primary key value of the department for which the employee works, you might want to display the department name rather than the number value when you look at the data. If you're displaying a Yes/No field, you might want to provide a drop-down list that shows options for *invoiced* and *not invoiced* instead of *yes* and *no* or *true* and *false*.

In the sample databases, we defined Lookup properties for only a few fields—ones for which we knew that we would later need a combo box with the relevant available choices on one or more forms or reports. (You will also see combo boxes described as drop-down lists.) One such example is in the Housing Reservations sample database (Housing.accdb). Open the database, view the table objects, select tblEmployees, and open it in Design view. Click the DepartmentID field and then click the Lookup tab to see the settings as shown in Figure 5-34.

As you can see, we have set the Display Control property to Combo Box. You see combo boxes in Windows applications all the time. It's a box that you can type in with a button on the right that you can click to drop down a list of values to select. In Access, you tell the combo box what type of list you want (Row Source Type) and specify the source of the list (Row Source). Access is a bit unusual because it lets you define a list that contains more than one column that you can display (Column Count), and it requires you to specify which of the columns (Bound Column) actually supplies the value to be stored when you pick an item from the list. This means that you might see a text value, but the combo box stores a number.

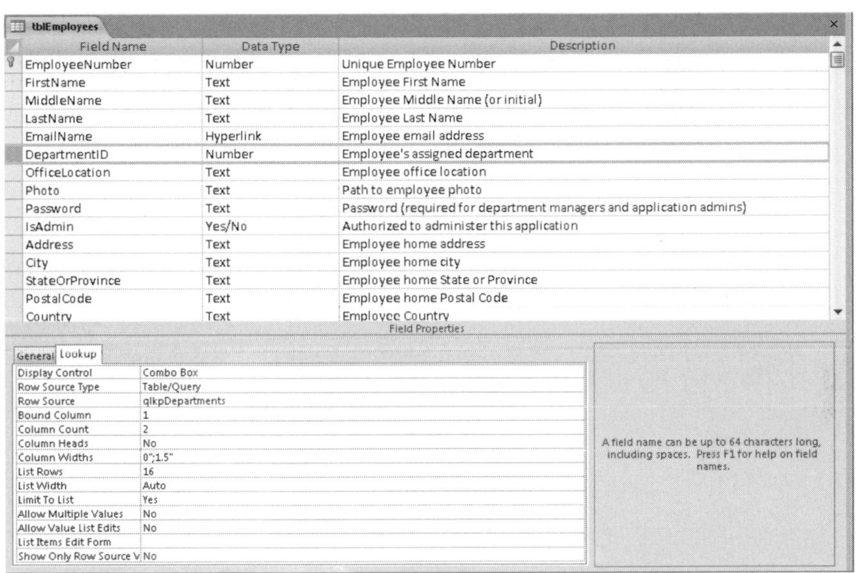


**Figure 5-34** The DepartmentID field in tblEmployees in the Housing Reservations sample database has Lookup properties defined.

You can see this combo box in action by switching to Datasheet view. You can click in the Department field and type a name from the list, or click the arrow on the right and select an item from the list as shown in Figure 5-35. Remember, DepartmentID is actually a number. If you didn't define the special settings on the Lookup tab, you would see a list of numbers in the Department column. For details about these settings, see Table 5-4 on page 243.

tblEmployees

| | Employee Numb | First Nam | Middle Nar | Last Nam | Email Name | Department | Office Locati | Photo |
|---|---|---|---|---|---|---|---|---|
| ⊞ | 1 | Reed | | Koch | Reed Koch | Sales | | E:\Microsoft Pres |
| ⊞ | 2 | Tim | | Kim | Tim Kim | Finance | | E:\Microsoft Pres |
| ⊞ | 3 | John | | Tippett | John Tippett | Housing Administration | | E:\Microsoft Pres |
| ⊞ | 4 | Kirk | | DeGrasse | Kirk DeGrasse | Marketing | | E:\Microsoft Pres |
| ⊞ | 5 | David Olive | | Lawrence | David Oliver Lawre | Product Development | | E:\Microsoft Pres |
| ⊞ | 6 | Jay | | Adams | Jay Adams | Sales | | E:\Microsoft Pres |
| ⊞ | 7 | Jack | S. | Richins | Jack Richins | Housing Administration | | E:\Microsoft Pres |
| ⊞ | 8 | David | M. | Bradley | David Bradley | Product Development | | E:\Microsoft Pres |
| ⊞ | 9 | Scott | | Eyink | Scott Eyink | Sales | | E:\Microsoft Pres |
| ⊞ | 10 | Matthias | | Berndt | Matthias Berndt | Finance | | E:\Microsoft Pres |
| ⊞ | 11 | Benjamin | C. | Willett | Benjamin Willett | Marketing | | E:\Microsoft Pres |
| ⊞ | 12 | Misty | | Shock | Misty Shock | Marketing | | E:\Microsoft Pres |
| ⊞ | 13 | Linda | | Randall | Linda Randall | Housing Administration | | E:\Microsoft Pres |
| ⊞ | 14 | Gary | | Schare | Gary Schare | Finance | | E:\Microsoft Pres |
| ⊞ | 15 | John | L. | Viescas | John Viescas | Product Development | Paris | E:\Microsoft Pres |
| ⊞ | 16 | Jeff | | Conrad | Jeff Conrad | Housing Administration | Bend, OR | E:\Microsoft Pres |
| * | | | | | | | | |

**Figure 5-35** The Lookup tab settings show you a combo box in Datasheet view.

We decided to go ahead and define these properties in this table because we knew we were probably going to use a combo box in one or more forms that we would build later to display related department information while editing an employee record. By setting the values in the table, we can avoid having to define the combo box settings again when we build the forms. If you want to see how this works on a form, you can open frmEmployeesPlain in the Housing Reservations database. (Although you can open the "production" version of frmEmployees from the Navigation Pane, code in that form prevents you from updating any data unless you are signed on to the application.) You can see the result in Figure 5-36.

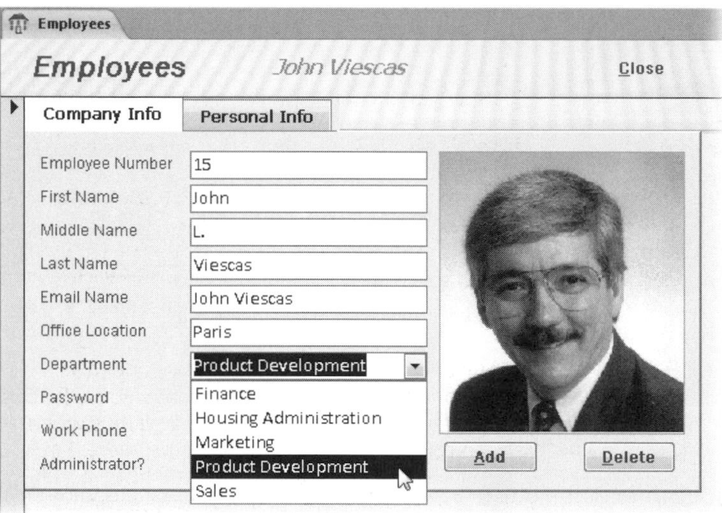


**Figure 5-36** The table Lookup tab properties were inherited by the combo box on frmEmployeesPlain.

## INSIDE OUT Lookup Tab Settings: For Advanced Users Only

We recommend that only experienced users set the Lookup tab properties of a field in a table's Design view. Unless you are fully aware of what the settings do, you can have problems later when you look at the information in a datasheet or try to build a query on the table. For example, if you look at the data in tblEmployees, you could mistakenly decide that "Housing Administration" is a valid value in the DepartmentID field. If you try to build a query and filter the DepartmentID field looking for that department name, your query won't run.



Table 5-4 gives you an overview of what the lookup settings mean. When you study combo box controls later, in Chapter 11, "Building a Form," you'll see how you can also use lookup properties to display lists from related tables in a form. In Chapter 11 we'll also explore the Combo Box Wizard, which makes it easy to correctly define these settings.

Table 5-4 **Lookup Properties**

| Lookup Property | Setting | Meaning |
|---|---|---|
| Display Control | Check Box (Yes/No fields only), Text Box, List Box, or Combo Box | Setting this property to Text Box or Check Box disables lookups. List Box shows a list of values in an open window. Combo Box shows the selected value when closed and shows the available list of values when open. |
| **Properties Available When You Set Display Control to List Box or Combo Box** | | |
| Row Source Type | Table/Query, Value List, or Field List | Table/Query specifies that you want rows from a table or query to fill the list. If you select Value List, you must enter the values you want displayed in the Row Source property, separated by semicolons. The Field List setting shows the names of the fields from the table or query you enter in Row Source—not the data in the rows. |
| Row Source | Table Name, Query Name, or a list of values separated by semicolons | Use a table name, query name, or enter the text of the query (in SQL) that provides the list values when Row Source Type is Table/Query. See Chapters 7 and 8 for details about building queries, and Article 2 on the companion CD for details about SQL. Enter a list of values separated by semicolons when Row Source Type is Value List. Use a table or query name when Row Source Type is Field List. |
| Bound Column | An integer value from 1 to the number of columns in the Row Source | Specify the column in the Row Source that provides the value stored by the list box or combo box. |
| Column Count | An integer value from 1 to 255 | This determines the number of columns available to display. (See Column Widths.) When Row Source Type is Value List, this setting determines how many consecutive values you enter in Row Source make up a logical row. |
| Column Heads | No (default) or Yes | Choose Yes to display the field name at the top of any displayed column when you open the list. |
| Column Widths | One width value per column, separated by semicolons | Specify a zero width if you do not want the combo box or list box to display the column. It is common to not display an AutoNumber ID field, but you might need that field in Row Source as the bound column. |

| Lookup Property | Setting | Meaning |
|---|---|---|
| Allow Multiple Values | No (default) or Yes | Choose Yes to allow the user to select multiple values from Row Source for each record. Caution: If you set this property to Yes and save the table definition, you cannot change the value back to No later. |
| Allow Value List Edits | No (default) or Yes | Choose Yes to allow the user to add and edit items in the underlying Row Source. |
| List Item Edit Form | Form Name | Specify the name of a form that Access will open for the user to add items to the Row Source when the user enters a new value that is not in the list specified in Row Source. |
| **Properties That Apply to Combo Boxes Only** | | |
| List Rows | An integer value between 1 and 255 (default is 8) | Specify how many rows the combo box displays when you open the list. If this setting is less than the number of rows in Row Source, the combo box makes a scroll bar available to move through the list. |
| List Width | Auto or a specific width | Specify the width of the list when you open it. Auto opens the list the width of the field display. |
| Limit To List | No (default) or Yes | Choose No to allow the user to enter a value that's not in the list. When the bound column is not the first displayed column, the combo box acts as though Limit To List is Yes regardless of the setting. |

## INSIDE OUT Allowing Space for the Scroll Bar

When we're designing a combo box that displays multiple columns when dropped down, we always specify a List Width value that's the sum of the Column Width values plus 0.25 inch to allow for the vertical scroll bar.

INSIDE OUT **Why You Should Not Use the Lookup Wizard**

Wait a minute! What about the Lookup Wizard entry under Data Types? We recommend that you *never* use this wizard. It often builds strange SQL for the Row Source property, it always defines a relationship between the table you're editing and the lookup table, and it defines indexes on both fields. If the lookup table contains only a few rows, the index is a waste of time and resources. As you learned in Chapter 4, there's a limit of 32 indexes on a table. We have seen some cases where we haven't been able to build all the indexes we need because the Lookup Wizard built these unnecessary indexes.

## Working with Multi-Value Lookup Fields

In Chapter 1, "What Is Microsoft Access?," we introduced you to the concept of complex data. Access 2007 includes a new feature called Multi-Value Lookup Fields to handle complex data. The purpose of lookup fields, as you just learned, is to *display* one value in a field but actually *store* a different value. For example, a lookup field could store the company ID in a field for an invoice, but display the company name to the user for easier data entry on a form or to show the name on a printed invoice report. Lookup fields in this scenario take the guesswork out of trying to remember a specific company ID number. Multi-Value Lookup Fields take this concept a step further by allowing you to store multiple values in a single lookup field. When you define a field as a Multi-Value Lookup Field, Access provides a special control in the Datasheet view of the table similar to a combo box to display the list of valid values. When you drop down the combo box list, you'll see what looks like a list box that has a check box next to each of the available value choices. Selecting the check box next to one or more of the values stores the selected values in the field.

Figure 5-37 shows an example of a Multi-Value Lookup Field in the Conrad Systems Contacts database. Open the Contacts.accdb database and then open the tblContacts table in Datasheet view. Any specific contact could be one or more contact types. The Contact Type field is designated as a Multi-Value Lookup Field, so the user can select from any of the contact types in the database and mark them as related to the current record. In Figure 5-37 you can see that John Viescas is both a developer and a distributor. By selecting the check boxes next to the available contact types, you tell Access to store multiple values for this single record. Notice that after you tab away from this field, Access separates the values with commas.

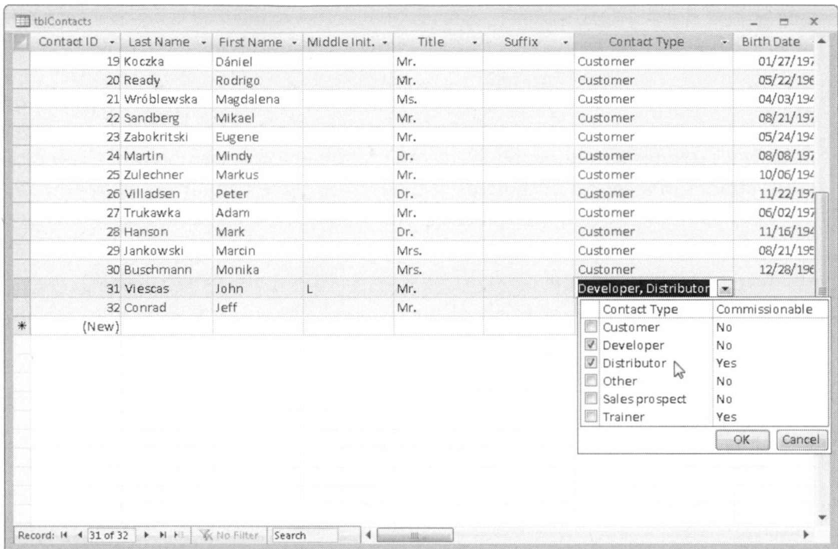


**Figure 5-37** A Multi-Value Lookup Field control allows you to select more than one value for that field.

Access also provides the list box control you see in a table in Datasheet view on a form in Form view. Close the tblContacts table and then open the frmContactsPlain form in Form view. In Figure 5-38 you can see the Contact Type field, which displays an arrow on the right side. Clicking the arrow drops down the list with the available choices of contact types.

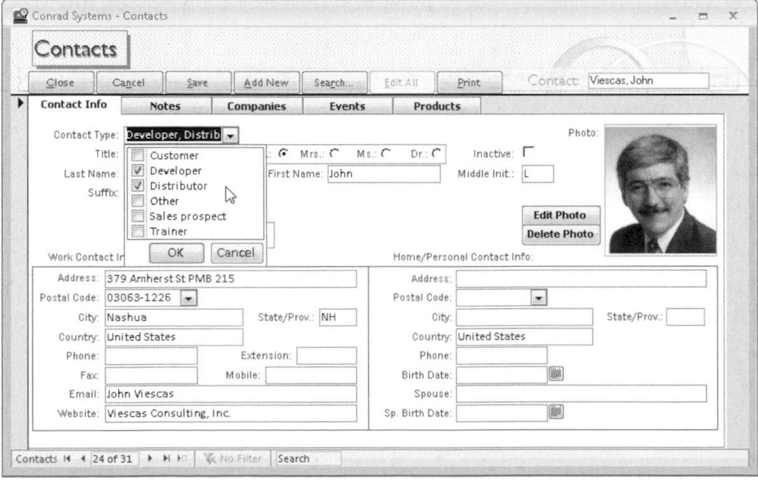


**Figure 5-38** Access also provides a Multi-Value Lookup Field control in the frmContactsPlain form of the Conrad Systems Contacts database.

Chapter 5

To set up a Multi-Value Lookup Field you must set the properties in the table in Design view. Close the frmContactsPlain form and then open the tblContacts table in Design view. (Because this is a linked table, Access will warn you that you cannot modify the design. Click Yes in the warning dialog to open the table design and view the field properties.) Click the ContactType field and then click the Lookup tab under Field Properties to see the settings as shown in Figure 5-39. The Allow Multiple Values property has been set to Yes, which tells Access that it can store multiple values in this field.

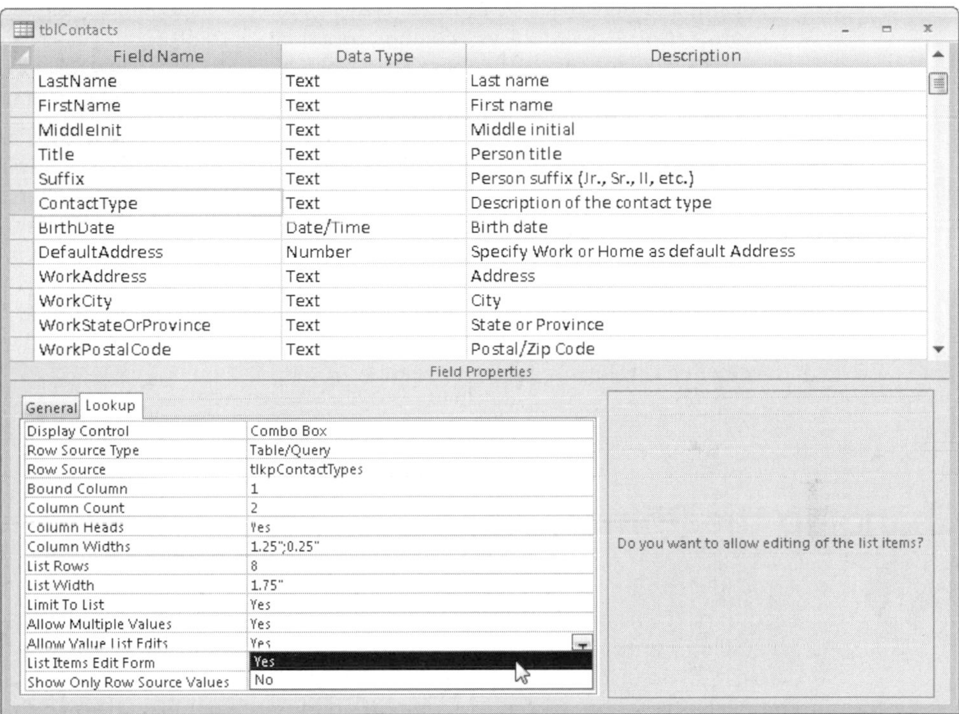


**Figure 5-39** Set the Allow Multiple Values property to Yes to enable this field as a Multi-Value Lookup Field.

### How Do Multi-Value Lookup Fields Maintain Data Normalization Rules?

If you are familiar with data normalization rules, you might be asking yourself how it is possible to store multiple values in a single field and still follow normalization rules. Under the covers and hidden from the standard user interface, Access 2007 actually creates a many-to-many relationship with a hidden join table. All the work of creating this join table and establishing the relationship rules is handled by Access when you set the Allow Multiple Values property to Yes or choose to allow multiple values in the Lookup Wizard. To ensure that only possible related values can be entered in the Multi-Value Lookup Field, Access displays a combo box or list box control containing only the valid related values for data entry. These Multi-Value Lookup Fields allow for better integration with Microsoft Windows SharePoint Services (version 3) complex data structures.

However, you cannot upsize any table that has a Multi-Value Lookup Field to SQL Server. We converted the ContactType field to a standard single-value field to be able to upsize it correctly. Although Multi-Value Lookup Fields can help novice developers create applications that deal with complex many-to-many relationships in a simple way, we recommend that you learn to create such relationships properly when you need them in your database using the appropriate linking table. We wish that Microsoft had made the special multi-value control available for normal many-to-many relationships in Access 2007, but that is not the case. The development team at Microsoft has promised to provide further enhancements in future releases.

## Changing the Primary Key

Article 1, "Designing Your Database Application," on the companion CD discusses the need to have one or more fields that provide a unique value to every row in your table. This field or group of fields with unique values is identified as the *primary key*. If a table doesn't have a primary key, you can't define a relationship between it and other tables, and Access 2007 has to guess how to link tables for you. Even if you define a primary key in your initial design, you might discover later that it doesn't actually contain unique values. In that case, you might have to define a new field or fields to be the primary key.



Let's go back to the three tables we built earlier with the Table Analyzer Wizard. Suppose you discover that users are becoming confused by the fact that ContactTypes_ID is a number instead of the actual text. (See our comments about using the Lookup Wizard on page 245.) You could keep the lookup table to help avoid duplicate values, but there's no reason not to store the actual text value in the Contacts table instead of storing a linking ID.

To fix this, you need to perform the following steps. Be sure to save your work at the end of each step.

1. Open the Contacts table in Design view and insert a new field below ContactTypes_ID named ContactType, data type Text, length 50.

2. Update the new ContactType field with related information from the ContactTypes table. We'll show you how to do this easily with an update query in Chapter 9, "Modifying Data with Action Queries." For now, you can switch to Datasheet view and copy what you see in the Lookup to ContactTypes field to your new ContactType field. (There are only 18 rows, so this shouldn't take you very long.)

3. Open the Relationships window and click the All Relationships button in the Relationships group of the Design tab below Relationship Tools so that you can see the additional relationships that the Table Analyzer Wizard built. Click on the line between Contacts and ContactTypes and press the Delete key to remove the relationship. (You must delete any relationship involving the primary key of a table before you can change the key.) Click Yes to confirm this action.

4. Open the Contacts table in Design view and delete the ContactTypes_ID field.

5. Open the ContactTypes table in Design view and change the primary key from ID to ContactType. (You can also select the ID field and delete it if you like.)

   Access provides several ways for you to accomplish this task. You could open the Indexes window (as you learned in Chapter 4), delete the primary key definition, and build a new one. A simpler way is to select the new field you want as the primary key and then click the Primary Key button in the Tools group of the Design contextual tab below Table Tools, as shown in Figure 5-40.

6. Finally, reopen the Relationships window and define a new relationship between ContactType in the ContactTypes table and your new ContactType field in the Contacts table.

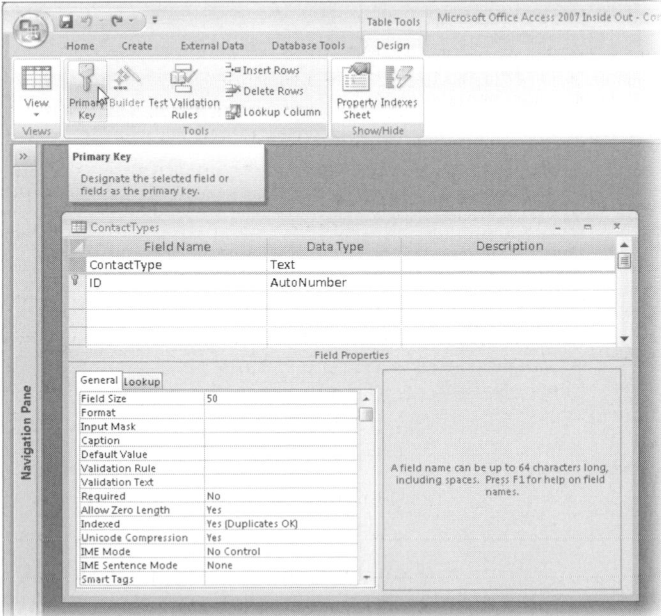


**Figure 5-40** Select the new field that will become the primary key and then click Primary Key on the Design tab to define the key.

Keep in mind that you can directly change the primary key for any table that does not have any relationships defined. Also, when the table contains data, the new fields that you choose for a primary key must have unique values in all the rows.

## Compacting Your Database

As you delete old database objects and add new ones, the space within your .accdb file can become fragmented. The result is that, over time, your database file can grow larger than it needs to be to store all your definitions and data.

To remove unused space, you should compact your database periodically. No other users should be accessing the database you intend to compact. You can compact the database you currently have open by clicking the Microsoft Office Button, clicking the Manage command, and then clicking Compact And Repair Database. If you want to compact another database, you must close your current database and then click the Compact And Repair Database command again. Access 2007 opens the dialog box shown in Figure 5-41.

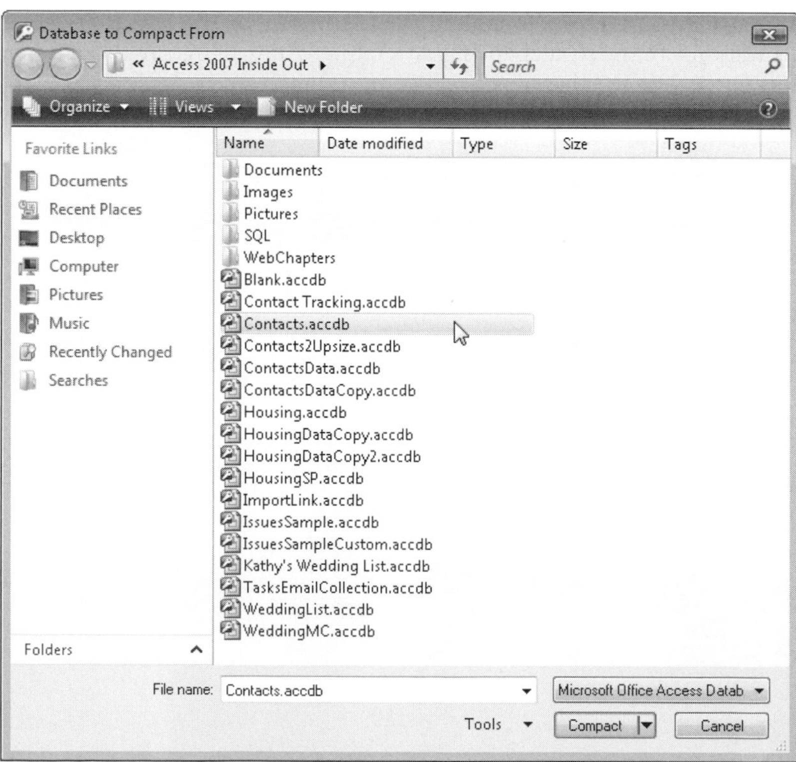


**Figure 5-41** Click the Microsoft Office Button, Manage, and then Compact And Repair Database to open the dialog box for specifying a database to compact.

Select the database you want to compact, and then click Compact. Access asks you for a name for the compacted database. You can enter the same name as the database you are compacting, or you can use a different name. If you use the same name, Access warns you that the original database of the same name will be replaced. If you proceed, Access compacts your database into a temporary file. When compaction is successfully completed, Access deletes your old database and gives its name to the new compacted copy.

INSIDE OUT

### Compacting a Database When You Close It

You can also set an option to compact the database each time you close it. Open your database, click the Microsoft Office Button, and then click the Access Options button. In the Access Options dialog box, select the Current Database category and then select the Compact On Close check box under Application Options. If multiple users are sharing the same database, Access compacts the database when the last user closes it.

You now have all the information you need to modify and maintain your database table definitions. In the next chapter, you'll explore importing data from other sources and linking to data in other files.

CHAPTER 6

# Importing and Linking Data



You can certainly build all your tables, design queries, forms, and reports, and then enter from scratch all the data into your empty tables. However, in many cases you'll have some of the data you need lying around in other files. For example, you might have a customer list in a spreadsheet or a text file. Your list of products might be in another non-Access database file. Microsoft Office Access 2007 provides tools to help you bring the data into your new application.

Although you can use Office Access 2007 as a self-contained database and application system, one of its primary strengths is that it allows you to work with many kinds of data in other databases, in spreadsheets, or in text files. In addition to using data in your local Access 2007 database, you can *import* (copy in) or *link* (connect to) data that's in text files, spreadsheets, other Access databases, dBASE, Paradox, and any other SQL database that supports the Open Database Connectivity (ODBC) software standard (including Microsoft Visual FoxPro). As you'll learn later in Chapter 23, "Using XML," Access also supports files in eXtensible Markup Language (XML), which is the standard format for defining and storing data on the Web.

## A Word About Open Database Connectivity (ODBC)

If you look under the hood of Access, you'll find that it uses a database language called SQL (*Structured Query Language*) to read, insert, update, and delete data. SQL grew out of a relational database research project conducted by IBM in the 1970s. It has been adopted as the official standard for relational databases by organizations such as the American National Standards Institute (ANSI) and the International Organization for Standardization (ISO). When you're viewing a query window in Design view, you can see the SQL statements that Access uses by first clicking the Design tab below Query Tools, clicking the arrow below the View button in the Results group, and then clicking the SQL View command.

**Article 2, "Understanding SQL," on the companion CD provides more details about how Access uses SQL. The Appendix, "Installing Your Software," provides details about installing and managing ODBC connections on your computer.**

In an ideal world, any product that "speaks" SQL should be able to "talk" to any other product that understands SQL. You should be able to build an application that can work with the data in several relational database management systems using the same database language. Although standards exist for SQL, most software companies have implemented variations on or extensions to the language to handle specific features of their products. Also, several products evolved before standards were well established, so the companies producing those products invented their own SQL syntaxes, which differ from the official standard. An SQL statement intended to be executed by Microsoft SQL Server might require modification before it can be executed by other databases that support SQL, such as DB2 or Oracle, and vice versa.

To solve this problem, a group of influential hardware and software companies—more than 30 of them, including Microsoft Corporation—formed the SQL Access Group. The group's goal was to define a common base SQL implementation that its members' products could all use to "talk" to one another. The companies jointly developed the *Common Language Interface* (CLI) for all the major variants of SQL, and they committed themselves to building CLI support into their products. About a dozen of these companies jointly demonstrated this capability in early 1992.

In the meantime, Microsoft formalized the CLI for workstations and announced that Microsoft products—especially those designed for the Microsoft Windows operating system—would use this interface to access SQL databases. Microsoft calls this formalized interface the *Open Database Connectivity (ODBC) standard*. In the spring of 1992, Microsoft announced that more than a dozen database and application software vendors had committed to providing ODBC support in their products by the end of 1992. With Access, Microsoft provides the basic ODBC Driver Manager and the driver to translate ODBC SQL to the SQL understood by Microsoft SQL Server. Microsoft has also worked with several database vendors to develop drivers for other databases. You can see a diagram of the ODBC architecture in Figure 6-1.

Access was one of Microsoft's first ODBC-compliant products, and the ODBC Driver Manager is a standard part of Microsoft's operating systems. Microsoft has further refined this architecture with ActiveX Data Objects (ADO). ADO is a special library of objects that you can use to fetch and modify information about the database structure and fetch and update data from any database, including Access. You can also fetch data from ODBC databases using the standard Data Access Objects (DAO) library used to manipulate native Access tables. After you've added the drivers for the other SQL databases that you want to work with, you can use Access to build an application using data from any of these databases.

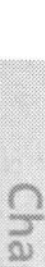

> **Note**
>
> You can use ADO as a "universal interface" to both databases that support ODBC as well as to those that do not. See Chapter 19, "Understanding Visual Basic Fundamentals," for details about working with ADO using Visual Basic.

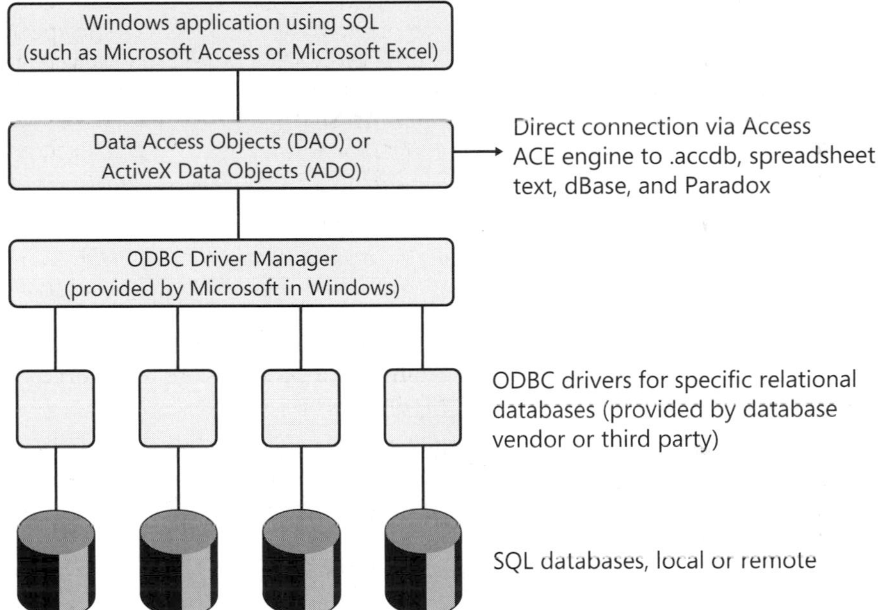


**Figure 6-1** The Microsoft ODBC architecture allows any ODBC-enabled application to link to any SQL database for which you have a driver.

# Creating a Data Source to Link to an ODBC Database

Before you can connect to a database that requires ODBC, you must first create a data source—either a data source name (DSN) file or a data source entry in your Windows registry. A data source is simply a named set of ODBC driver parameters that provide the information the driver needs to dynamically link to the data. To create a new data source name file or registry entry, on the External Data tab, in the Import group, begin importing or linking a file by clicking More and then clicking ODBC Database. Access 2007 opens the Get External Data - ODBC Database dialog box. Select either the Import The Source Data Into A New Table In The Current Database option or the Link To The Data Source By Creating A Linked Table option, and then click OK. Click the New button in the Select Data Source dialog box to begin creating a new data source.

You can also create a new data source directly from the Select Data Source dialog box by clicking the New button on either the File Data Source or Machine Data Source tab. If you create a new file data source, Access 2007 stores a file with a .dsn file name extension in your default folder for data source name files. The resulting text file will contain a list of keyword assignment statements to set the values needed by the driver. (You can find an example of a data source name file at the end of this section.) If you create a new machine data source, Access stores the parameters in the Windows registry.

To create a new machine data source, click the Machine Data Source tab and click the New button. Access displays the Create New Data Source wizard, shown here.

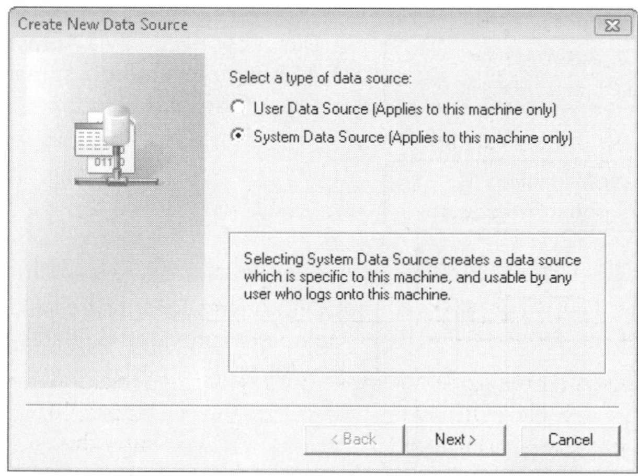


To create a data source that applies to all users on your computer, select System Data Source (Applies To This Machine Only) and click Next. Access displays a list of the available ODBC drivers on your system. To create a data source for SQL Server, select SQL Server at the bottom of the list and click Next. Access confirms that you are ready to create a system data source for the driver you specified. Click Finish, and Access displays the Create A New Data Source To SQL Server wizard, shown here.

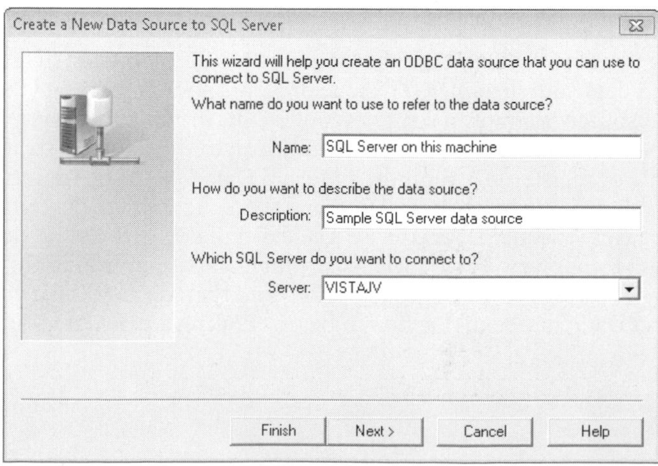

Enter a name and description for your data source. To connect to the server on your computer, enter your computer name in the Server box. If you are authorized to connect to other servers on your network, click the arrow in the Server box. When you do that, Access 2007 searches your network for other SQL servers and places the names of all servers found in the list. Click Next to go to the next page, shown here.

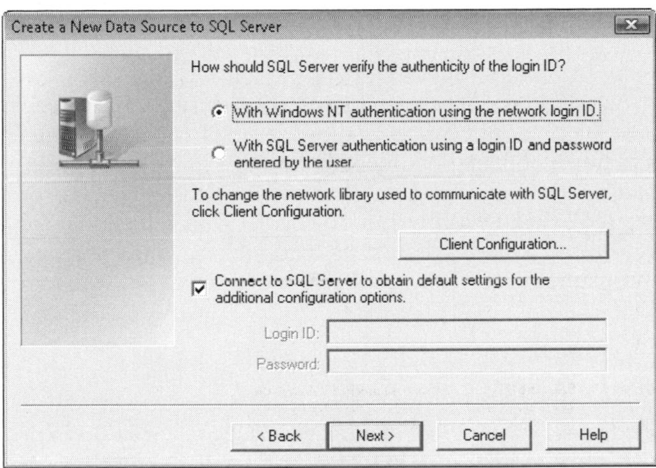


Depending on how SQL Server 2005 is configured, you might need to enter a login ID and password. By default, SQL Server 2005 uses your Windows logon information (your user name and password) to authenticate you. This means that you don't have to enter your user name and password a second time when you access the SQL server. If, however, the server is configured to use SQL authentication, you must select With SQL Server Authentication Using A Login ID And Password Entered By The User, and enter your login ID and password. Click Next to see the page where you can specify the default database for this data source, as shown here.

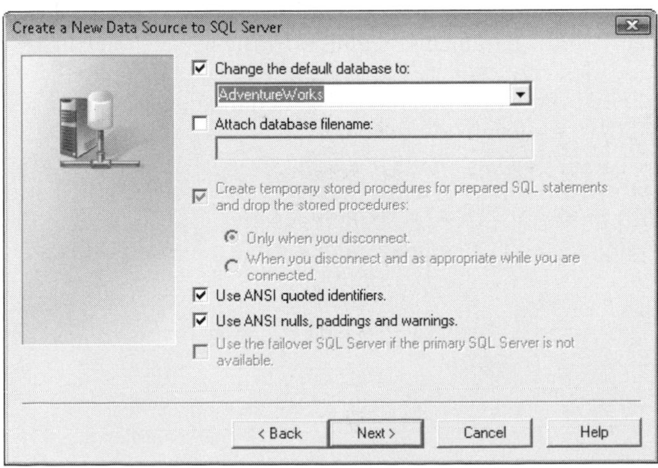

If you are authorized to connect to more than one database on the server and you want to connect to a database other than your default database, select the Change The Default Database To check box. Access logs on to the server and returns a list of available database names. (The preceding figure shows the sample AdventureWorks database that you can install with SQL Server 2005 selected.) If you don't specify a database name and if multiple databases exist on the server, you'll be connected to the default database for your login ID. (You don't need to worry about the other options displayed on this page.) Select the database you want, and click Next.

The last page shows various options, including the ability to change the language of error messages or log data. You can leave these settings as they are and click Finish. Access displays a final confirmation dialog box with a list of the settings you chose. If you need to change anything, click Cancel and then use the Back button in the Create A New Data Source To SQL Server wizard to correct your selections. You can click the Test Data Source button to verify that Access can make a valid connection using your settings. If the test runs successfully, click OK to create your new data source.

## TROUBLESHOOTING

### Why can't I connect to my local instance of SQL Server 2005 Express Edition using Windows authentication on my Windows Vista computer?

When you install SQL Server 2005 Express Edition on a system running Windows Vista, the installation process fails to define your Windows logon ID as an authorized user of the system. To correct this problem, you must install Service Pack 2 for SQL Server 2005 Express Edition. At the end of the installation, you'll be given the chance to define and authorize your logon ID. If you fail to do this, you must uninstall SQL Server 2005 Express Edition, reinstall it with mixed mode authentication, define a system administrator (user ID is "sa") password, and then use that logon to define and authorize your Windows ID.

If you're familiar with the parameters required by the driver, you can create your own data source name file. A data source name file like the one listed here for SQL Server begins with the [ODBC] section delimiter and then includes keyword assignment statements for each piece of information the ODBC service needs to correctly load the driver you want. (You can find this file, named SQLServerLocal.dsn, on the companion CD.) Note that you must supply your Windows user ID (your user name) and computer name for YOURID and YOURCOMPUTER, respectively, to connect to the server running on your computer. You can edit any data source name file using a text editor such as Notepad.

```
[ODBC]
DRIVER=SQL Server
UID=YOURID
DATABASE=AdventureWorks
```

```
WSID=YOURCOMPUTER
APP=Microsoft® Windows® Operating System
Trusted_Connection=Yes
SERVER=YOURCOMPUTER
Description=Sample DSN for SQL Server
```

The first time you create a data source name file, you'll probably want to use the Create New Data Source wizard, but after you understand the structure of a valid data source name file for a particular data source, it's easy to modify an existing file or create a new one.

# Importing vs. Linking Database Files

You have the choice of importing or linking data from other databases, but how do you decide which type of access is best? Here are some guidelines.

You should consider *importing* another database file when any of the following is true.

- The file you need is relatively small and is not changed frequently by users of the other database application.
- You don't need to share the data you create with users of the other database application.
- You're replacing the old database application, and you no longer need the data in the old format.
- You need to load data (such as customers or products as we mentioned earlier) from another source to begin populating your Access tables.
- You need the best performance while working with the data from the other database (because Access performs best with a local copy of the data in Access's native format).

On the other hand, you should consider *linking* another database file when any of the following is true.

- The file is larger than the maximum capacity of a local Access database (2 gigabytes).
- The file is changed frequently by users of the other database application.
- You must share the data on a network with users of the other database application.
- You'll be distributing your application to several individual users, and you will need to make changes to the queries, forms, reports, and modules in the application without disturbing data already entered in the tables.

INSIDE OUT

**Using Linked Tables in a Complex Application Is a Good Idea**

Even when we're building an application that we know will be run by only a single user, we usually create a separate .accdb file that contains all the tables and link those tables back into the .accdb file that contains all our queries, forms, reports, and code. If we've been careful creating our original table design, we rarely have to change it. But users are always thinking up some new feature that they would like to have. We can add a new form or report and send the user an update without having to disturb all the data they've already entered.

If you look closely at the tables in the Conrad Systems Contacts sample database (Contacts.accdb), you can see that most of the tables have a little arrow next to the table icon in the Navigation Pane, like this:

This indicates that these tables are linked from another data source.

**Note**

The samples in this chapter use data you can find in files on the companion CD. You can import the data into or export the data from the Conrad Systems Contacts or Housing Reservations databases. You might want to work from a copy of these databases to follow along with the examples in this chapter. You can find the result of following many of these examples in the ImportLink.accdb sample database, which contains a Companies table that has columns using nearly every available data type in Access.

# Importing Data and Databases

You can copy data from a number of different file formats to create an Access table. In addition to copying data from a number of popular database file formats, Access 2007 can also create a table from data in a spreadsheet or a text file. When you copy data from another database, Access uses information stored by the source database system to convert or name objects in the target Access table. You can import data not only from other Access databases but also from dBASE, Paradox, and—using ODBC—any SQL database that supports the ODBC standard (including Visual FoxPro).

## Importing dBASE Files

To import a dBASE file, do the following:

1. Open the Access database that will receive the dBASE file. If that database is already open, close all open objects so that you see only the Navigation Pane.

2. On the External Data tab, in the Import group, click the More command, and then click dBASE File, as shown here.

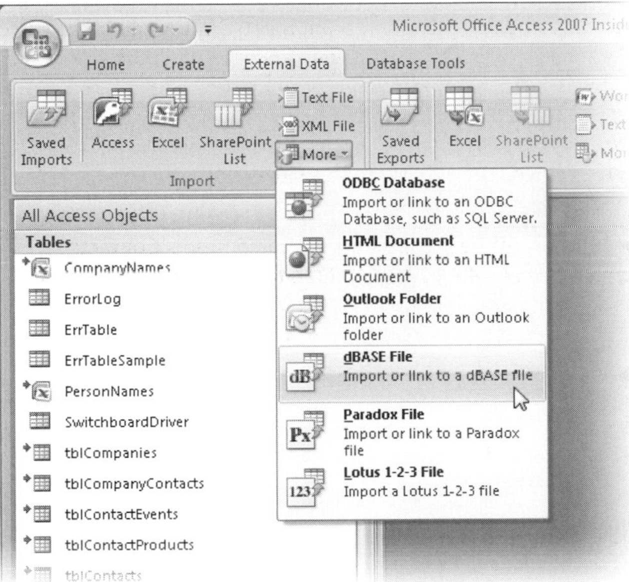


3. Access opens the Get External Data - dBASE File dialog box, shown here. Click the Browse button to browse for the dBASE file you need to import.

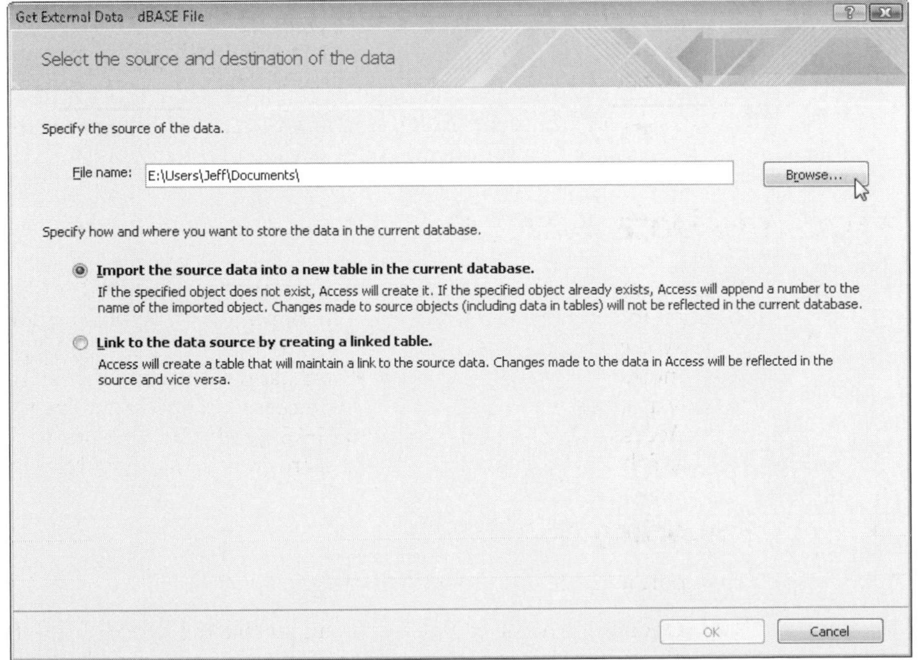

4. Access opens the File Open dialog box, shown next. Select dBASE III, dBASE IV, or dBASE 5, as appropriate, in the list to the right of the File Name box. (In Windows XP, this list is labeled Files Of Type and appears below the File Name box.) Select the source file folder, and then select or type the file name in the File Name box. If you're having difficulty finding the file you want, type a search string in the Search field.

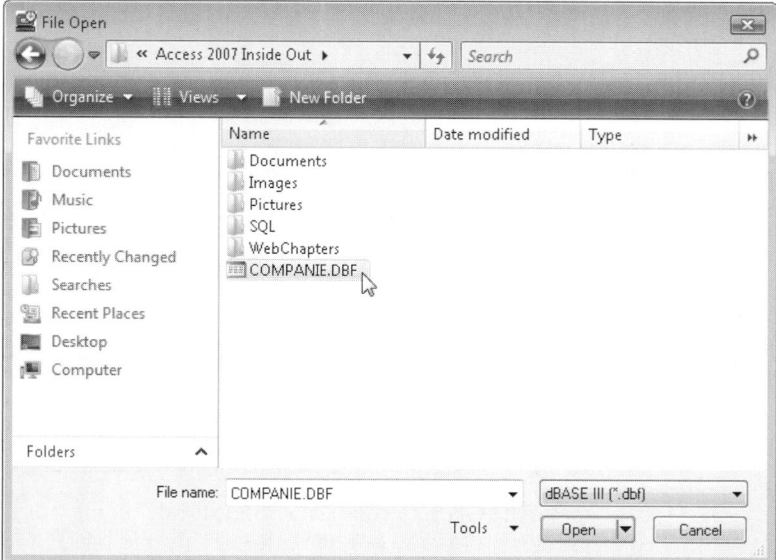


5. Click the Open button to return to the Get External Data - dBASE File dialog box with the file path to the dBASE file you need in the File Name box. Make sure the first option, Import The Source Data Into A New Table In The Current Database, is selected, and then click OK to import the dBASE file you selected. Access displays a message that informs you of the result of the import procedure, as shown next.

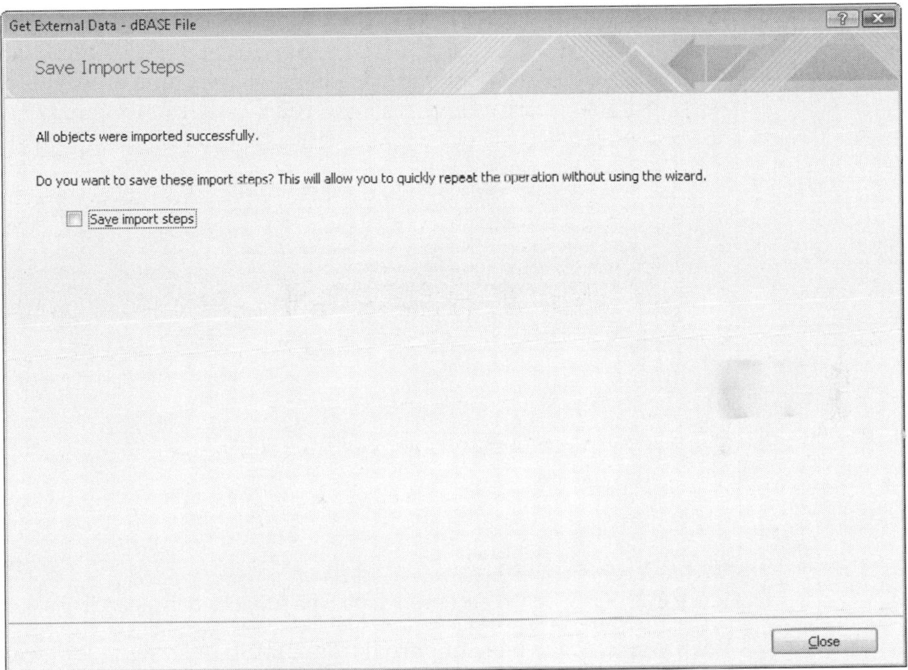


If the import procedure is successful, the new table will have the name of the dBASE file (without the file name extension). If Access finds a duplicate table name, it will generate a new name by adding a unique integer to the end of the name. For example, if you import a file named COMPANY.DBF and you already have tables named Company and Company1, Access creates a table named COMPANY2.

6. Click the Close button to dismiss the message that confirms the import procedure.

You'll find a dBASE 5 file named COMPANIE.DBF on the companion CD. Follow the procedure just described to import this file into the Conrad Systems Contacts sample database or into a new blank database. When you open the table that Access creates from this dBASE format data, you'll see data for the sample companies, as shown in Figure 6-2.

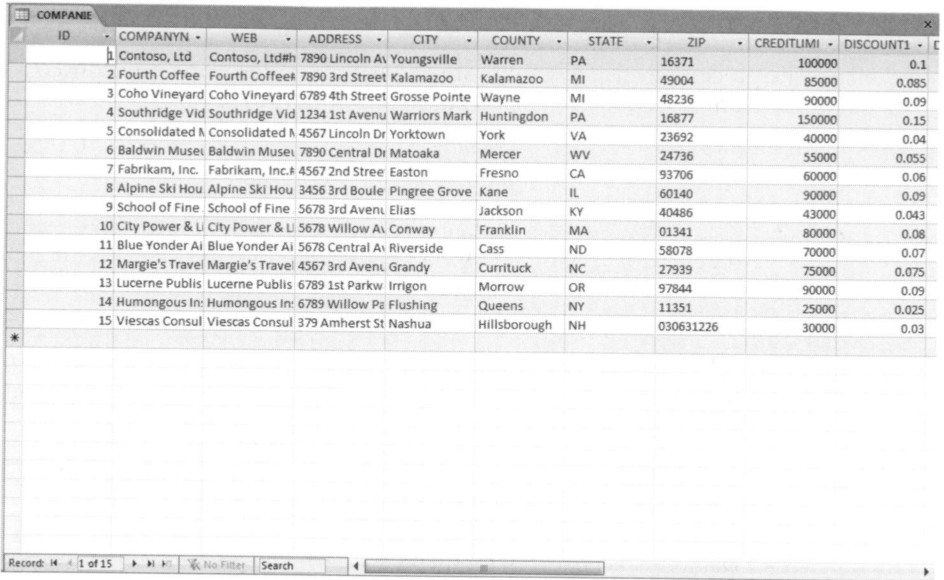

**Figure 6-2** Access can import every data type supported in a dBASE file.

When you look at a table imported from dBASE in Design view, you'll find that Access has converted the data types, as shown in Table 6-1.

**Table 6-1 dBASE-to-Access Data Type Conversions**

| dBASE Data Type | Converts to Access Data Type |
|---|---|
| Character | Text |
| Numeric | Number, Field Size property set to Double |
| Float | Number, Field Size property set to Double |
| Logical | Yes/No |
| Date | Date/Time |
| Memo | Memo |

As we noted earlier, we created the COMPANIE dBASE file from the Companies table you can find in the ImportLink sample database. You can open these two tables side by side to see the differences. First, dBASE doesn't support field names longer than 10 characters. So, CompanyName in the original file is shortened to COMPANYNAM, and LastOrderDate appears as LASTORDERD. Also, dBASE doesn't support Hyperlink, Currency, or Decimal data types, so it stores Hyperlink data types as Memo, and Currency and Decimal data types as Number, Double.

## Importing Paradox Files

The procedure for importing Paradox files is similar to the procedure for importing dBASE files. To import a Paradox file, do the following:

1. Open the Access database that will receive the Paradox file. If that database is already open, close all open objects so that you see only the Navigation Pane.
2. On the External Data tab, in the Import group, click the More command, and then click Paradox File. Access opens the Get External Data - Paradox File dialog box. Click the Browse button to browse for the Paradox file you need to import. Access opens the File Open dialog box, as shown earlier on page 262.
3. Select the source file folder, and then select or type the file name in the File Name box. If you're having difficulty finding the file you want, type a search string in the Search field.
4. Click the Open button to return to the Get External Data - Paradox File dialog box with the file path to the Paradox file you need in the File Name box. Make sure the first option, Import The Source Data Into A New Table In The Current Database, is selected and then click OK to import the Paradox file you selected.
5. If the Paradox file is encrypted, Access opens a dialog box that asks for the password. Type the correct password and click OK to proceed, or click Cancel to start over.

   When you proceed, Access responds with a message that indicates the result of the import procedure. If the import procedure is successful, the new table will have the name of the Paradox file (without the file name extension). If Access finds a duplicate table name, it will generate a new name by adding a unique integer to the end of the name as explained earlier about dBASE files.
6. Click Close to dismiss the message that confirms the import procedure.

You can try this procedure using the Companie.db file that's included on the companion CD.

When you look at a table imported from Paradox in Design view, you'll find that Access has converted the data types, as shown in Table 6-2.

**Table 6-2 Paradox-to-Access Data Type Conversions**

| Paradox Data Type | Converts to Access Data Type |
|---|---|
| Alphanumeric | Text |
| Number | Number, Field Size property set to Double |
| Money | Number, Field Size property set to Double |
| Short Number | Number, Field Size property set to Integer |
| Long Integer | Number, Field Size property set to Long Integer |
| Binary Coded Decimal | Number, Field Size property set to Double |
| Date | Date/Time |
| Time | Date/Time |
| Timestamp | Date/Time |
| Memo | Memo |
| Formatted Memo | Not supported |
| Graphic | Not supported |
| OLE | OLE Object (but Access won't be able to activate the object) |
| Logical | Yes/No |
| AutoIncrement | AutoNumber |
| Binary | Not supported |
| Bytes | Not supported |

## Importing SQL Tables

To import a table from another database system that supports ODBC SQL (such as SQL Server, Visual FoxPro, or Oracle), you must first have the ODBC driver for that database installed on your computer. Your computer must also be linked to the network that connects to the SQL server from which you want to import data, and you must have an account on that server. Check with your system administrator for information about correctly connecting to the SQL server.

If you have SQL Server 2005 installed or have downloaded and installed SQL Server 2005 Express Edition, which you can download from *www.microsoft.com/sql/editions/express/default.mspx*, you already have SQL Server at your disposal. See the Appendix for instructions on how to install SQL Server 2005 Express Edition. One of the best ways to be sure SQL Server is running on your computer is to use the SQL Server Configuration Manager. You can start the Configuration Manager from the Windows Start menu in the Configuration Tools folder under Microsoft SQL Server 2005. You can also start the Configuration Manager by running C:\Windows\System32\SQLServerManager.msc. In the Configuration Manager, select SQL Server 2005 Services and be sure the SQL Server (MSSQLSERVER) service is marked as Running. If it is not running, right-click the service name and click Start on the shortcut menu.

To import data from a SQL table, do the following:

1. Open the Access database that will receive the SQL data. If that database is already open, close all open objects so that you see only the Navigation Pane.
2. On the External Data tab, in the Import group, click the More command, and then click ODBC Database. Access opens the Get External Data - ODBC Database dialog box. Make sure the Import The Source Data Into A New Table In The Current Database option is selected and then click OK.
3. Access opens the Select Data Source dialog box, shown here, from which you can select the data source that maps to the SQL server containing the table you want to import.

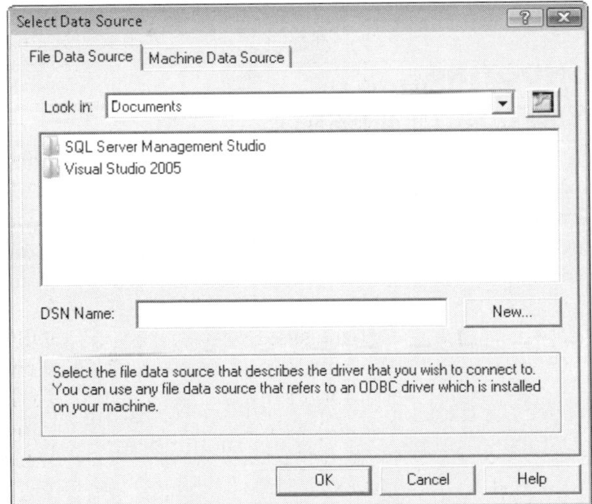


You can select a data source name (.dsn) file that you created previously, or click the Machine Data Source tab, as shown next, to see data sources that are already defined for your computer.

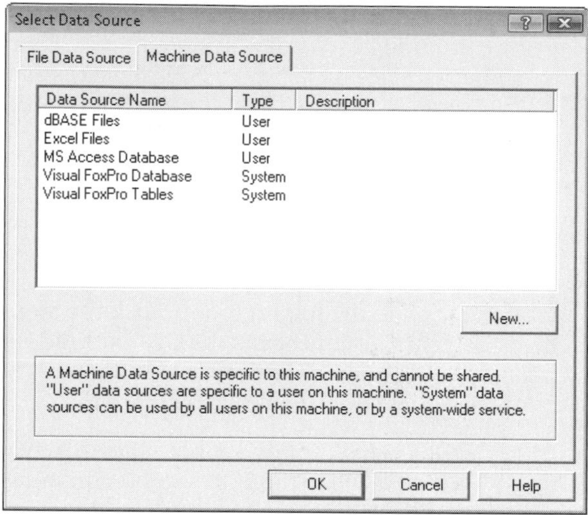


## TROUBLESHOOTING

### Access won't use ODBC for all file types.

Notice that the Machine Data Source tab lists installed sources for dBASE, Microsoft Excel, Access, and Visual FoxPro files. Access will not let you use ODBC for dBASE, Excel, and Access because it uses its own more efficient direct connection via its database engine. Access 2007 uses ODBC to import and link to Visual FoxPro, but you must have Visual FoxPro installed on your computer to be able to work with Visual FoxPro tables from Access.

If you don't see the data source you need, see "Creating a Data Source to Link to an ODBC Database" on page 255 for instructions. After you select a data source, click OK.

4. When Access connects to the server, you'll see the Import Objects dialog box, which lists the available tables on that server, as shown next.

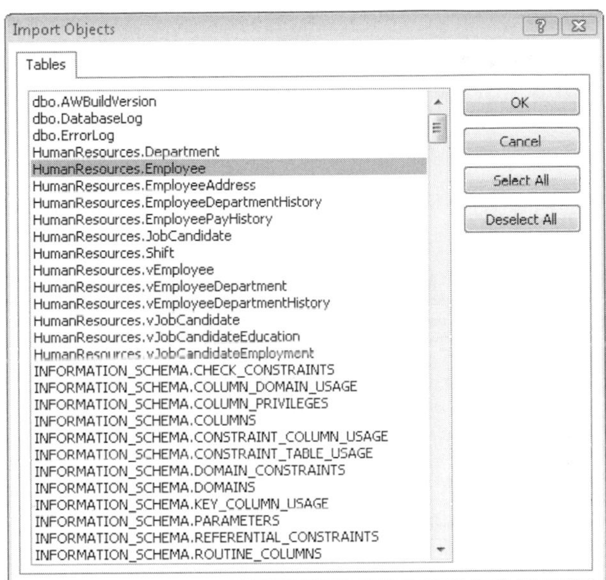


If you want to import a Visual FoxPro table file (.dbf), select the Visual FoxPro Tables driver on the Machine Data Source tab of the Select Data Source dialog box and click OK. Access displays a Configure Connection dialog box. Select Free Table Directory and click the Browse button to locate the folder that contains the file that you want to import. Click OK, and Access displays the Import Objects dialog box similar to the one shown here for SQL Server that lists all the Visual FoxPro tables that exist in the folder you specified.

**Note**

To be able to import or link Visual FoxPro tables, you must download and install the latest Visual FoxPro ODBC driver. You can find the latest driver at *http://msdn.microsoft.com/vfoxpro/downloads/updates/odbc/default.aspx*.

5. From the list of tables or list of files, select the ones you want to import. If you select a table name in error, you can click it again to deselect it or you can click the Deselect All button to start over. Click OK to import the SQL tables you selected.
6. If the import procedure is successful, the new table will have the name of the SQL or Visual FoxPro table. If Access finds a duplicate table name, it will generate a new name by adding a unique integer to the end of the name as explained earlier about dBASE files.

**Note**

You've no doubt noticed by now that the different databases use different style conventions (dbo.newstore, Newstore, NEWSTORE) for table names.

In general, Access converts SQL and Visual FoxPro data types to Access data types, as shown in Tables 6-3 and 6-4.

Table 6-3 **SQL-to-Access Data Type Conversions**

| SQL Data Type | Converts to Access Data Type |
|---|---|
| CHAR[ACTER] | Text, or Memo if more than 255 characters in length |
| VARCHAR | Text, or Memo if more than 255 characters in length |
| TEXT | Memo |
| TINYINT | Number, Field Size property set to Byte |
| SMALLINT | Number, Field Size property set to Integer |
| INT | Number, Field Size property set to Long Integer |
| REAL | Number, Field Size property set to Double |
| FLOAT | Number, Field Size property set to Double |
| DOUBLE | Number, Field Size property set to Double |
| DATE | Date/Time |
| TIME | Date/Time |
| TIMESTAMP | Binary[1] |
| IMAGE | OLE Object |

[1] The ACE database engine supports a Binary data type (raw hexadecimal), but the Access user interface does not. If you link to a table that has a data type that maps to Binary, you will be able to see the data type in the table definition, but you won't be able to successfully edit this data in a datasheet or form. You can manipulate Binary data in Visual Basic.

Table 6-4 **Visual FoxPro-to-Access Data Type Conversions**

| Visual FoxPro Data Type | Converts to Access Data Type |
|---|---|
| Character | Text |
| Numeric | Number, Field Size property set to Integer |
| Float | Number, Field Size property set to Double |
| Date | Date/Time |
| Logical | Yes/No |
| Memo | Memo |
| General | OLE Object |

## Importing Access Objects

If the database from which you want to import data is another Access database, you can import any of the six major types of Access objects: tables, queries, forms, reports, macros, or modules. To achieve the same result, you can also open the source database, select the object you want, click the Copy command in the Clipboard group on the Home tab of the Ribbon, open the target database, and then click the Paste command in the Clipboard group on the Home tab. Using the Import command, however, allows you to copy several objects without having to switch back and forth between the two databases.

To import an object from another Access database, take the following steps:

1. Open the Access database that will receive the object. If that database is already open, close any open objects so that only the Navigation Pane is showing.
2. On the External Data tab, in the Import group, click the Access command. Access opens the Get External Data - Access Database dialog box, shown here.

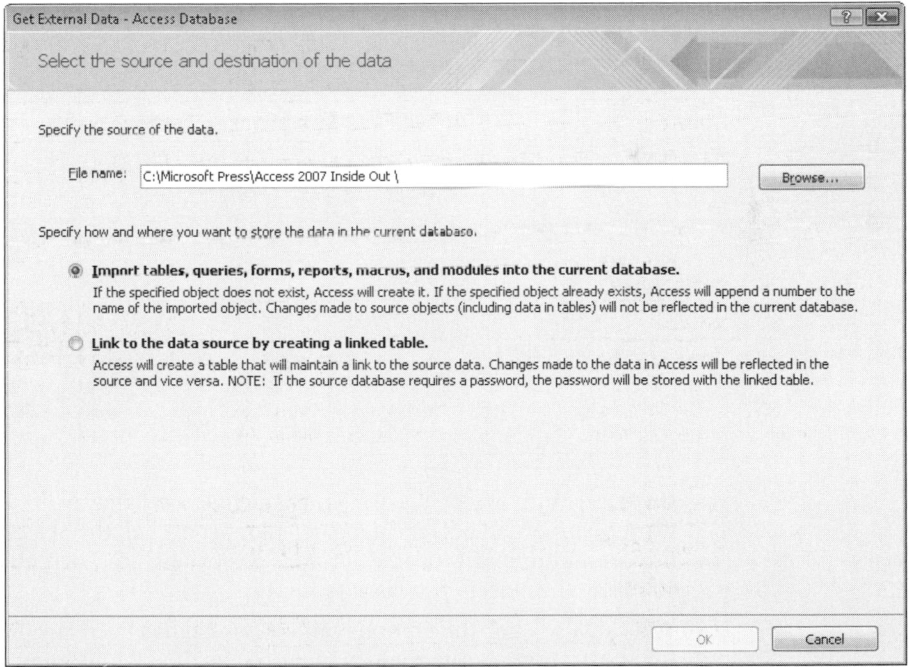


3. Click the Browse button to open the File Open dialog box, previously shown on page 262. Select the folder and the name of the .accdb, .mdb, .adp, .mda, .accda, .mde, .accde, or .ade file containing the object that you want to import, and then click Open.

> **Note**
>
> Microsoft Office Access 2007 provides a database utility to create a compiled version of an .mdb or .accdb desktop application or .adp project file that contains no source code. The compiled versions have .mde, .accde and .ade extensions, respectively. You cannot import forms, reports, or modules from an .mde, .accde or .ade file. For details about creating a compiled version of your application, see Chapter 25, "Distributing Your Application."

4. Click OK. Access opens the Import Objects dialog box, shown here, which provides tabs for each of the object types in the database you selected. First click the tab for the object type, and then select the specific object you want to import.

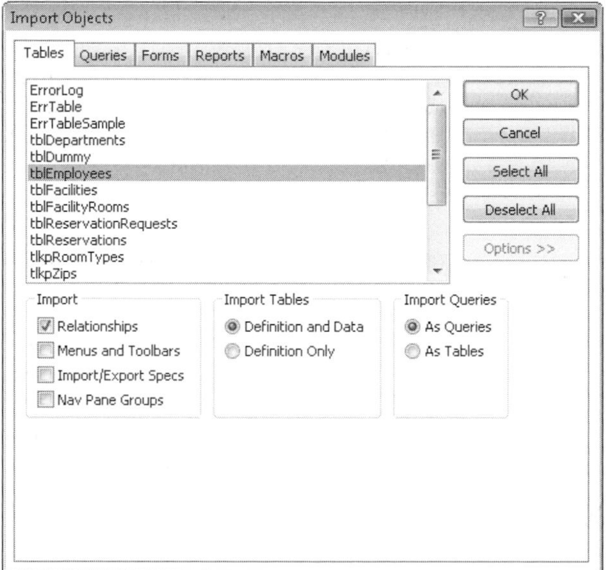


If you select an object in error, you can click the name again to deselect it. If you want to import all objects of a particular type, click the Select All button. You can import multiple objects of different types by clicking each object tab in turn and selecting the objects you want to import.

You can also click the Options button (which has been clicked in the preceding illustration) to select additional options. If you import any tables from the source database, you can select the option to import the table relationships (if any) defined for those tables in the source database. If the object is a table, you can select the option to import the table structure (the table definition) only or to import the structure *and* the stored data. If your source database is an .mdb or

.adp file created in a prior version of Access, you can select the Menus And Toolbars check box to import all the custom menus and toolbars from your source database. Be aware, however, that these items appear on a special Add-Ins tab on the Ribbon, and some of the commands you designed in your custom menus and toolbars might not work in Access 2007. You can also select the Import/Export Specs check box. (See the sidebar, "Defining an Import Specification," on page 291 for details.) If you select the Nav Pane Groups check box, Access imports any custom Navigation Pane groups you have defined in the database. (See Chapter 2, "Exploring the New Look of Access 2007," for details about creating custom groups.) You can also choose to import a query object (the definition of the query) by selecting As Queries under Import Queries; or you can ask Access to run the query and import the data results into a table by selecting As Tables. (See Chapter 7, "Creating and Working with Simple Queries," for details about building and using queries.) Click OK to copy the objects you selected to the current database.

5. If the import procedure is successful, the new object will have the name of the object you selected. If Access finds a duplicate name, it will generate a new name by adding a unique integer to the end of the name as explained previously. Because objects such as queries, forms, reports, macros, and modules might refer to each other or to tables you're importing, you should carefully check name references if Access has to rename an imported object.

> **Note**
>
> If the source Access database is a secured file created in a previous Access version, you must have at least read permission for the database, read data permission for the tables, and read definition permission for all other objects in order to import objects. After you import the objects into your database, you will own the copies of those objects in the target database.

## Importing Spreadsheet Data

Access 2007 also lets you import data from spreadsheet files created by Lotus 1-2-3, Lotus 1-2-3 for Windows, and Microsoft Excel version 3 and later. You can specify a portion of a spreadsheet or the entire spreadsheet file to import into a new table or to append to an existing table. If the first row of cells contains names suitable for field names in the resulting Access table, as shown in the Companies.xlsx spreadsheet in Figure 6-3, you can tell Access to use these names for your fields.

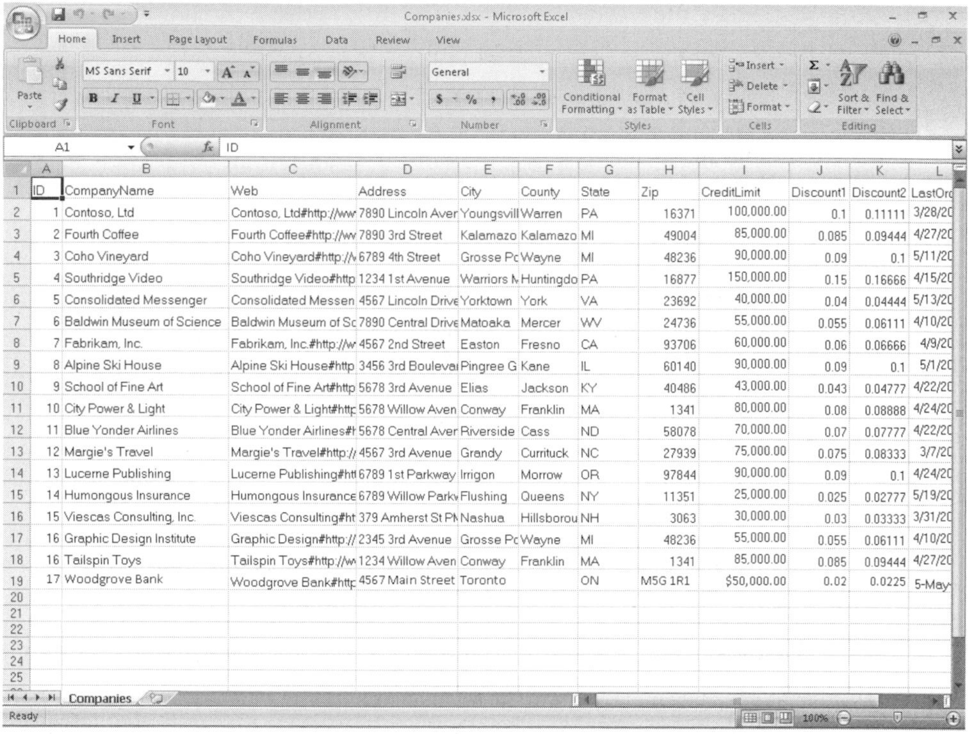

| ID | CompanyName | Web | Address | City | County | State | Zip | CreditLimit | Discount1 | Discount2 | LastOrd |
|---|---|---|---|---|---|---|---|---|---|---|---|
| 1 | Contoso, Ltd | Contoso, Ltd#http://ww | 7890 Lincoln Aver | Youngsvill | Warren | PA | 16371 | 100,000.00 | 0.1 | 0.11111 | 3/28/20 |
| 2 | Fourth Coffee | Fourth Coffee#http://ww | 7890 3rd Street | Kalamazo | Kalamazo | MI | 49004 | 85,000.00 | 0.085 | 0.09444 | 4/27/20 |
| 3 | Coho Vineyard | Coho Vineyard#http://\ | 6789 4th Street | Grosse Pc | Wayne | MI | 48236 | 90,000.00 | 0.09 | 0.1 | 5/11/20 |
| 4 | Southridge Video | Southridge Video#http | 1234 1st Avenue | Warriors M | Huntingdo | PA | 16877 | 150,000.00 | 0.15 | 0.16666 | 4/15/20 |
| 5 | Consolidated Messenger | Consolidated Messen | 4567 Lincoln Drive | Yorktown | York | VA | 23692 | 40,000.00 | 0.04 | 0.04444 | 5/13/20 |
| 6 | Baldwin Museum of Science | Baldwin Museum of Sc | 7890 Central Drive | Matoaka | Mercer | WV | 24736 | 55,000.00 | 0.055 | 0.06111 | 4/10/20 |
| 7 | Fabrikam, Inc. | Fabrikam, Inc.#http://w | 4567 2nd Street | Easton | Fresno | CA | 93706 | 60,000.00 | 0.06 | 0.06666 | 4/9/20 |
| 8 | Alpine Ski House | Alpine Ski House#http | 3456 3rd Boulevai | Pingree G | Kane | IL | 60140 | 90,000.00 | 0.09 | 0.1 | 5/1/20 |
| 9 | School of Fine Art | School of Fine Art#http | 5678 3rd Avenue | Elias | Jackson | KY | 40486 | 43,000.00 | 0.043 | 0.04777 | 4/22/20 |
| 10 | City Power & Light | City Power & Light#http | 5678 Willow Aven | Conway | Franklin | MA | 1341 | 80,000.00 | 0.08 | 0.08888 | 4/24/20 |
| 11 | Blue Yonder Airlines | Blue Yonder Airlines#h | 5678 Central Aver | Riverside | Cass | ND | 58078 | 70,000.00 | 0.07 | 0.07777 | 4/22/20 |
| 12 | Margie's Travel | Margie's Travel#http:// | 4567 3rd Avenue | Grandy | Currituck | NC | 27939 | 75,000.00 | 0.075 | 0.08333 | 3/7/20 |
| 13 | Lucerne Publishing | Lucerne Publishing#htt | 6789 1st Parkway | Irrigon | Morrow | OR | 97844 | 90,000.00 | 0.09 | 0.1 | 4/24/20 |
| 14 | Humongous Insurance | Humongous Insurance | 6789 Willow Parkv | Flushing | Queens | NY | 11351 | 25,000.00 | 0.025 | 0.02777 | 5/19/20 |
| 15 | Viescas Consulting, Inc. | Viescas Consulting#ht | 379 Amherst St PN | Nashua | Hillsborou | NH | 3063 | 30,000.00 | 0.03 | 0.03333 | 3/31/20 |
| 16 | Graphic Design Institute | Graphic Design#http:// | 2345 3rd Avenue | Grosse Pc | Wayne | MI | 48236 | 55,000.00 | 0.055 | 0.06111 | 4/10/20 |
| 16 | Tailspin Toys | Tailspin Toys#http://w | 1234 Willow Aven | Conway | Franklin | MA | 1341 | 85,000.00 | 0.085 | 0.09444 | 4/27/20 |
| 17 | Woodgrove Bank | Woodgrove Bank#http | 4567 Main Street | Toronto | | ON | M5G 1R1 | $50,000.00 | 0.02 | 0.0225 | 5-May |

**Figure 6-3** The data in the first row of this Excel spreadsheet can be used as field names when you import the spreadsheet into a new Access table.

## Preparing a Spreadsheet

Access 2007 determines the data type for the fields in a new table based on the values it finds in the first few rows of data being imported (excluding the first row if that row contains field names). When you import a spreadsheet into a new table, Access stores alphanumeric data as the Text data type with an entry length of 255 characters, numeric data as the Number type with the Field Size property set to Double, numeric data with currency formatting as the Currency type, and any date or time data as the Date/Time type. If Access finds a mixture of data in any column in the first few rows, it imports that column as the Text data type.

## INSIDE OUT Importing to a Temporary Table First

If you want to append all or part of a spreadsheet to a target table, you should import or link the entire spreadsheet as a new table and then use an append query to edit the data and move it to the table you want to update. You can learn about append queries in Chapter 9, "Modifying Data with Action Queries."

If the first several rows are not representative of all the data in your spreadsheet (excluding a potential field names row), you might want to insert a single "dummy" row at the beginning of your spreadsheet with data values that establish the data type you want to use for each column. You can easily delete that row from the table after you import the spreadsheet. For example, if you scroll down in the Companies.xlsx sample spreadsheet shown in Figure 6-3, you'll find that the last entry is a Canadian address, as shown in Figure 6-4.

| | | | | | | | | |
|---|---|---|---|---|---|---|---|---|
| 17 | 16 | Graphic Design Institute | Graphic Design#http:// | 2345 3rd Avenue | Grosse Pc | Wayne | MI | 48236 |
| 18 | 16 | Tailspin Toys | Tailspin Toys#http://w | 1234 Willow Aven | Conway | Franklin | MA | 1341 |
| 19 | 17 | Woodgrove Bank | Woodgrove Bank#http | 4567 Main Street | Toronto | | ON | M5G 1R1 |
| 20 | | | | | | | | |

**Figure 6-4** The Zip field entry contains data that can't be stored in numeric format.

Because Access sees only numbers in the first few rows of the Zip column, it will use a Number data type for the Zip field. However, the entry for the Canadian address has letters and spaces, which requires the field to be defined as text. As you'll see later, if you attempt to import this spreadsheet without fixing this problem, Access generates an error for each row that contains nonnumeric data. Access sets the contents of fields it cannot import to Null. You can solve this by inserting a dummy row at the top with the proper data types in each column, moving the row to the top, or fixing the one bad row after you import the file.

## Importing a Spreadsheet

To import a spreadsheet into an Access database, do the following:

1. Open the Access database that will receive the spreadsheet. If that database is already open, close any open objects so that you see only the Navigation Pane.
2. On the External Data tab, in the Import group, click the Excel command to open the Get External Data - Excel Spreadsheet dialog box shown next. (If you want to import a Lotus 1-2-3 file, on the External Data tab, in the Import group, click More and then click Lotus 1-2-3 File. Because you can only import a Lotus 1-2-3 file, you won't see the options to append or link the data.)

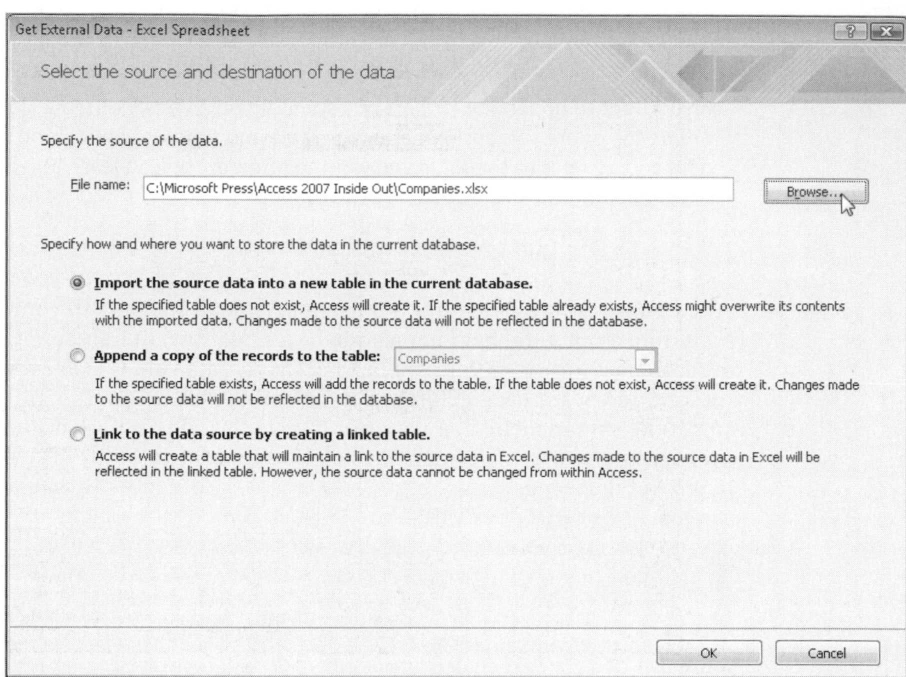


3. Click the Browse button to open the File Open dialog box shown on page 262. Select the folder and the name of the spreadsheet file that you want to import and click Open to return to the Get External Data - Excel Spreadsheet dialog box. If you want to follow along with this example, select the Companies.xlsx file from the companion CD.

4. Make sure the Import The Source Data Into A New Table In The Current Database option is selected and then click OK. If your spreadsheet is from Excel version 5.0 or later, it can contain multiple worksheets. If the spreadsheet contains multiple worksheets or any named ranges, Access shows you the first page of the Import Spreadsheet Wizard, as shown in the following illustration. (If you want to import a range that isn't yet defined, exit the wizard, open your spreadsheet to define a name for the range you want, save the spreadsheet, and then restart the import process in Access.) Select the worksheet or the named range that you want to import, and click Next to continue.

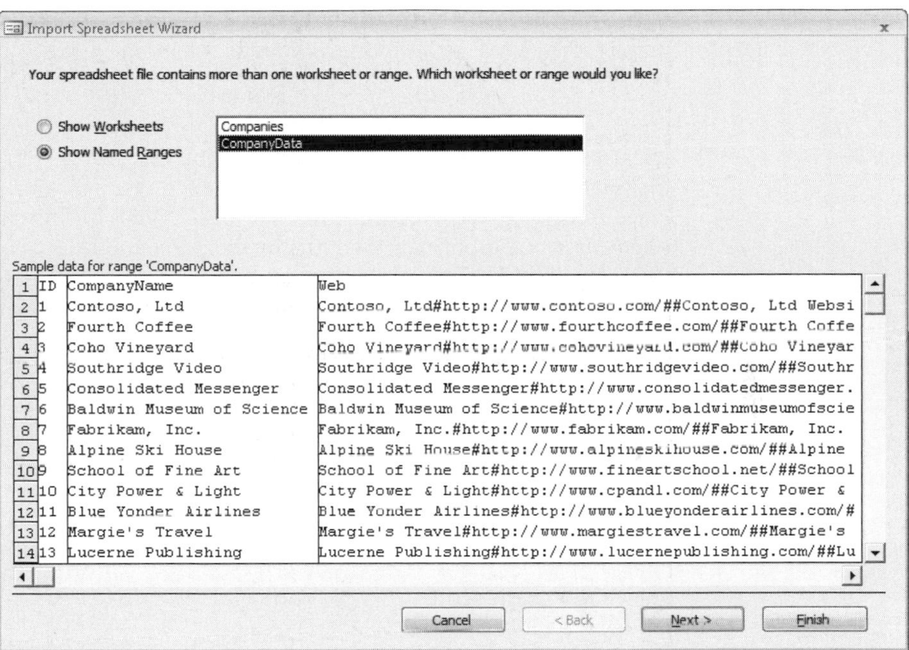


5. After you select a worksheet or a named range, or if your spreadsheet file contains only a single worksheet, the wizard displays the following page.

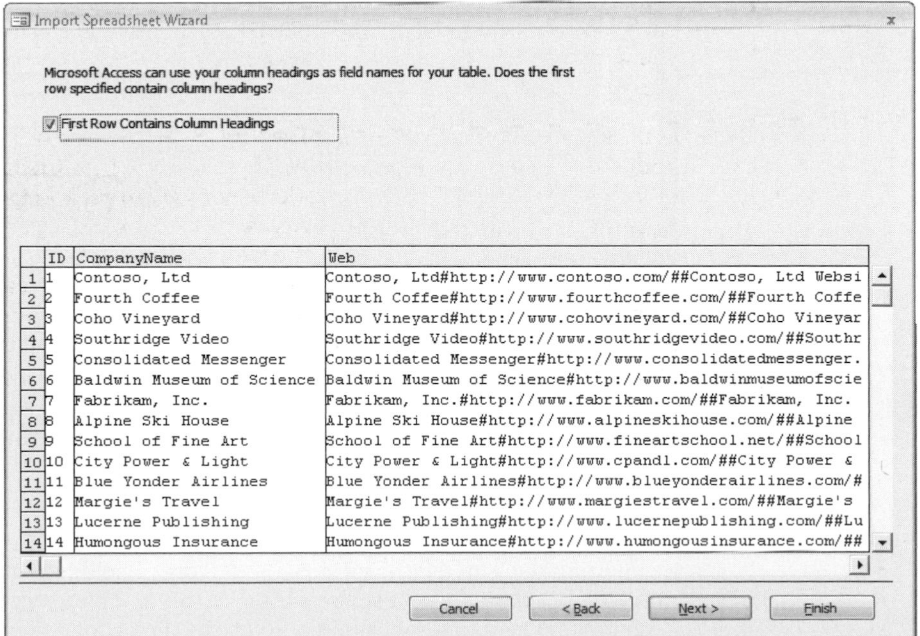

Select the First Row Contains Column Headings check box if you've placed names at the tops of the columns in your spreadsheet. Click Next to go to the next step.

6. On the next page, you can scroll left and right to the various fields and tell the wizard which fields should be indexed in the new table. Your indexing choices are identical to the ones you'll find for the Indexed property of a table field in Design view. You can also correct the data type of the field. In this case, for the ID field, select Yes (No Duplicates) from the Indexed list and select Long Integer from the Data Type list, as shown here, and for the Zip field, select Yes (Duplicates OK).

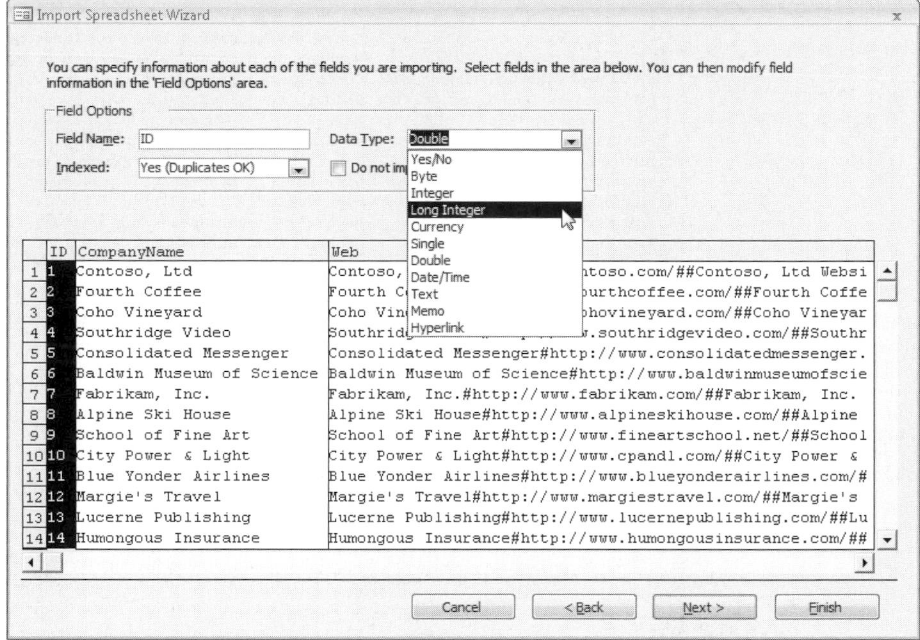


As you move from field to field, the Data Type box displays the data type that the wizard chooses for each field (based on the data it finds in the first few rows). If what you see here is incorrect, click the arrow and select the correct data type from the list. Previous versions of Access would not allow you to change the data type here, but Access 2007 allows you to select the correct data type on this page of the Import Spreadsheet Wizard. You can also choose to eliminate certain columns that you don't want to appear in the final table. For example, it's quite common to have intervening blank columns to control spacing in a spreadsheet that you print. You can eliminate blank columns by scrolling to them and selecting the Do Not Import Field (Skip) check box. Click Next to go to the next step.

7. On the next page, you can designate a field as the primary key of the new table. If you want, you can tell the wizard to build an ID field for you that uses the AutoNumber data type. (It so happens that this sample spreadsheet already has a numeric ID field that we'll attempt to use as the primary key.) If multiple fields

form a unique value for the primary key, you can tell the wizard not to create a primary key. Later, you can open the resulting table in Design view to set the primary key.

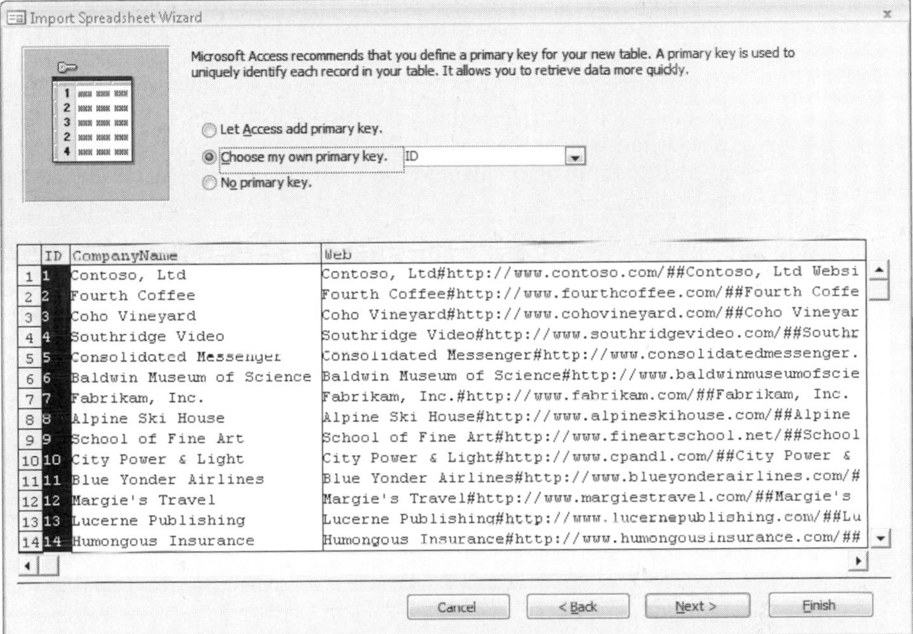


8. Click Next to go to the final page of the wizard, where you can change the name of your new table. (The Import Spreadsheet Wizard uses the name of the spreadsheet or the named range you chose in step 4.) You can also select the option to start the Table Analyzer Wizard to analyze your new table. See Chapter 4, "Creating Your Database and Tables," for details about the Table Analyzer Wizard. If you enter the name of an existing table, Access asks if you want to replace the old table.

9. Click Finish on the last page to import your data. Access opens a dialog box that indicates the result of the import procedure. If the procedure is successful, the new table will have the name you entered in the last step. If you asked to create a new table and Access found errors, you will find a new table that has the name of the import table you specified with a $_ImportErrors suffix. If you asked to append the data to an existing table and Access found errors, you can choose to complete the import with errors or go back to the wizard to attempt to fix the problem (such as incorrectly defined columns). You might need to exit the wizard and correct data in the original spreadsheet file as noted in the following section.

## Fixing Errors

In "Preparing a Spreadsheet" on page 274, you learned that Access 2007 determines data types for the fields in a new table based on the values it finds in the first several rows being imported from a spreadsheet. Figures 6-3 and 6-4 show a spreadsheet whose first few rows would generate a wrong data type for the Zip column in a new Access table. The Number data type that Access would generate for that field, based on the first several entries, would not work for the last row, which contains character data. In addition, one of the rows has a duplicate value in the ID column. If you attempt to use this column as the primary key when you import the spreadsheet, you'll get an additional error.

If you were to import that spreadsheet, Access would first display an error message similar to the one shown in Figure 6-5. This indicates that the wizard found a problem with the column that you designated as the primary key. If you have duplicate values, the wizard will also inform you. When the wizard encounters any problems with the primary key column, it imports your data but does not define a primary key. This gives you a chance to correct the data in the table and then define the primary key yourself.

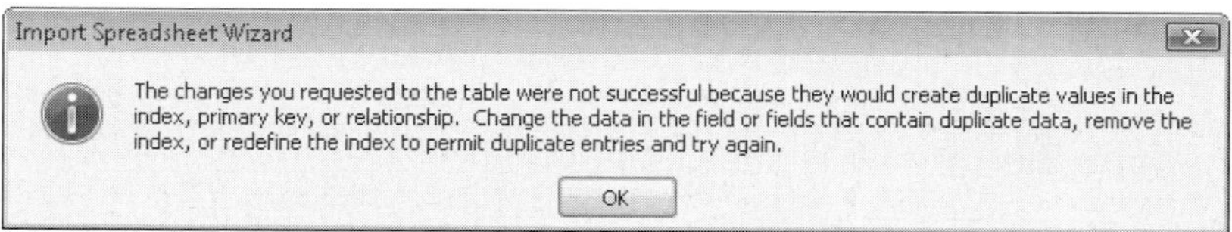


**Figure 6-5** Access displays this error message when it encounters a problem with your primary key values.

In addition, if the wizard has any problems with data conversion, it displays a message similar to the one shown in Figure 6-6.

Note that if your import was successful, you might want to select the Save Import Steps check box before you click Close if you might run the exact same import again in the future. You can find all saved imports by clicking the Saved Imports button in the Import group on the External Data tab.

When the Import Spreadsheet Wizard has problems with data conversion, it creates an import errors table in your database (with the name of the spreadsheet in the title) that contains a record for each error. Figure 6-7 shows the import errors table that Access creates when you import the spreadsheet shown in Figure 6-3. Notice that the table lists not only the type of error but also the field and row in the spreadsheet in which the error occurred. In this case, it lists the one row in the source spreadsheet that contains the Canadian postal code. The row number listed is the relative row number in the source spreadsheet, not the record number in the resulting table.

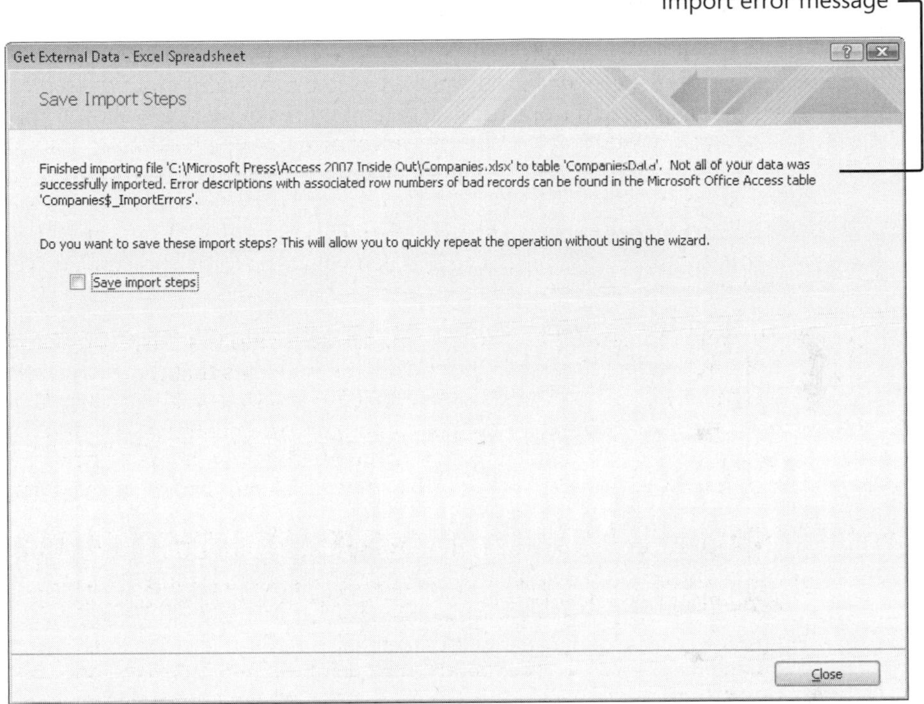


**Figure 6-6** Access displays this message at the top of the Save Import Steps page of the Get External Data - Excel Spreadsheet dialog box if it encounters data conversion errors while importing a spreadsheet.

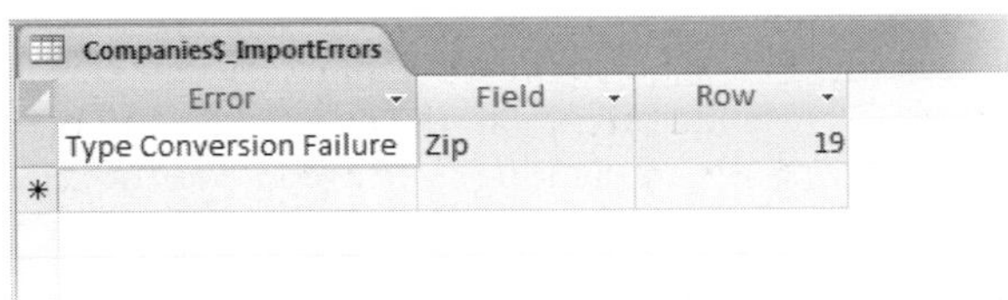
Companies$_ImportErrors

| Error | Field | Row |
|---|---|---|
| Type Conversion Failure | Zip | 19 |
| * | | |

**Figure 6-7** Here is the import errors table that results from importing the spreadsheet shown in Figure 6-3.

Figure 6-8 shows the table that results from importing the spreadsheet shown in Figure 6-3. You can find one row that has no entry in the Zip column. If you switch to Design view, you can see that the Import Spreadsheet Wizard selected the Number data type for the Zip field. If you want to be able to store values that include letters, the Zip field must be a text field. Notice that in Design view there is no primary key defined.

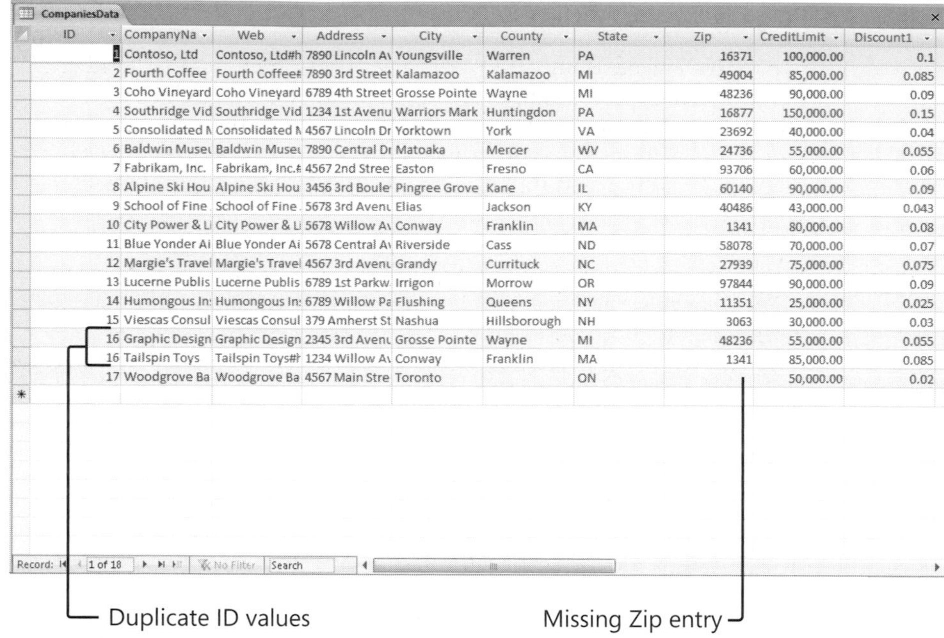

CompaniesData

| ID | CompanyNa | Web | Address | City | County | State | Zip | CreditLimit | Discount1 |
|---|---|---|---|---|---|---|---|---|---|
| 1 | Contoso, Ltd | Contoso, Ltd#h | 7890 Lincoln A | Youngsville | Warren | PA | 16371 | 100,000.00 | 0.1 |
| 2 | Fourth Coffee | Fourth Coffee# | 7890 3rd Street | Kalamazoo | Kalamazoo | MI | 49004 | 85,000.00 | 0.085 |
| 3 | Coho Vineyard | Coho Vineyard | 6789 4th Street | Grosse Pointe | Wayne | MI | 48236 | 90,000.00 | 0.09 |
| 4 | Southridge Vid | Southridge Vid | 1234 1st Avenu | Warriors Mark | Huntingdon | PA | 16877 | 150,000.00 | 0.15 |
| 5 | Consolidated M | Consolidated M | 4567 Lincoln Dr | Yorktown | York | VA | 23692 | 40,000.00 | 0.04 |
| 6 | Baldwin Muset | Baldwin Muset | 7890 Central Dr | Matoaka | Mercer | WV | 24736 | 55,000.00 | 0.055 |
| 7 | Fabrikam, Inc. | Fabrikam, Inc.# | 4567 2nd Stree | Easton | Fresno | CA | 93706 | 60,000.00 | 0.06 |
| 8 | Alpine Ski Hou | Alpine Ski Hou | 3456 3rd Boule | Pingree Grove | Kane | IL | 60140 | 90,000.00 | 0.09 |
| 9 | School of Fine | School of Fine | 5678 3rd Avenu | Elias | Jackson | KY | 40486 | 43,000.00 | 0.043 |
| 10 | City Power & Li | City Power & Li | 5678 Willow Av | Conway | Franklin | MA | 1341 | 80,000.00 | 0.08 |
| 11 | Blue Yonder Ai | Blue Yonder Ai | 5678 Central Av | Riverside | Cass | ND | 58078 | 70,000.00 | 0.07 |
| 12 | Margie's Travel | Margie's Travel | 4567 3rd Avenu | Grandy | Currituck | NC | 27939 | 75,000.00 | 0.075 |
| 13 | Lucerne Publis | Lucerne Publis | 6789 1st Parkw | Irrigon | Morrow | OR | 97844 | 90,000.00 | 0.09 |
| 14 | Humongous In | Humongous In | 6789 Willow Pa | Flushing | Queens | NY | 11351 | 25,000.00 | 0.025 |
| 15 | Viescas Consul | Viescas Consul | 379 Amherst St | Nashua | Hillsborough | NH | 3063 | 30,000.00 | 0.03 |
| 16 | Graphic Design | Graphic Design | 2345 3rd Avenu | Grosse Pointe | Wayne | MI | 48236 | 55,000.00 | 0.055 |
| 16 | Tailspin Toys | Tailspin Toys#h | 1234 Willow Av | Conway | Franklin | MA | 1341 | 85,000.00 | 0.085 |
| 17 | Woodgrove Ba | Woodgrove Ba | 4567 Main Stre | Toronto | | ON | | 50,000.00 | 0.02 |



**Figure 6-8** After importing the spreadsheet shown in Figure 6-3, one row is missing a postal code entry, and there is a duplicate value in the ID column.

You can correct some of the errors in the table in Design view. For example, you can change the data type of the Zip field to Text (and perhaps change the name to PostalCode), save the table, and then enter the missing value. For the row that has a duplicate ID (16), you can switch to Datasheet view and either delete one of the rows or supply a unique value. You can then set ID as the primary key in Design view.

# Importing Text Files

You can import data from a text file into Access 2007 even though, unlike the data in a spreadsheet, the data in a text file isn't arranged in columns and rows in an orderly way. You make the data in a text file understandable to Access either by creating a *delimited text file*, in which special characters delimit the fields in each record, or by creating a *fixed-width text file*, in which each field occupies the same location in each record.

## Preparing a Text File

You might be able to import some text files into Access 2007 without changing them, particularly if a text file was created by a program using standard field delimiters. However, in many cases, you'll have to modify the contents of the file, define the file for Access with an import specification, or do both before you can import it. See the sidebar, "Defining an Import Specification," on page 291 for details.

## Setting Up Delimited Data

Access 2007 needs some way to distinguish where fields start and end in each incoming text string. Access supports four standard separator characters: a comma, a tab, a semicolon, and a space. When you use a comma as the separator (a very common technique), the comma (or the carriage return at the end of the record) indicates the end of each field, and the next field begins with the first nonblank character. The commas are not part of the data. To include a comma within a text string as data, you must enclose all text strings within single or double quotation marks (the text qualifier). If any of your text strings contain double quotation marks, you must enclose the strings within single quotation marks, and vice versa. Access accepts only single or double quotation marks (but not both) as the text qualifier, so all embedded quotes in a file that you want to import into Access must be of the same type. In other words, you can't include a single quotation mark in one field and a double quotation mark in another field within the same file. Figure 6-9 shows a sample comma-separated and double-quote-qualified text file. You can find this file (CompaniesCSV.txt) on the companion CD.

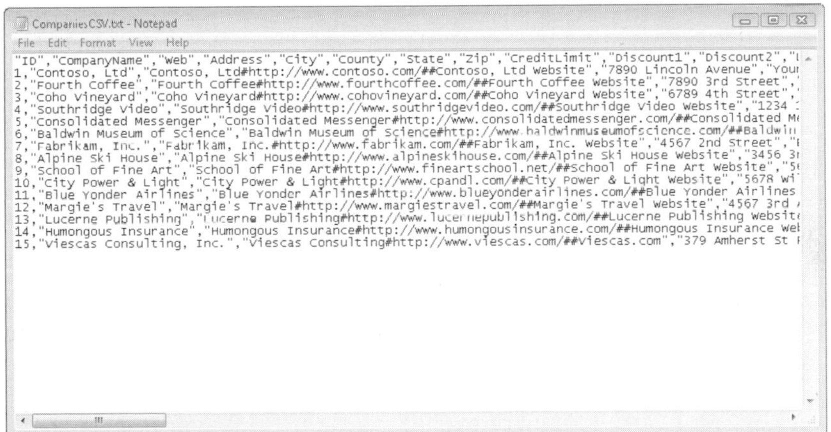


**Figure 6-9** A comma-separated and double-quote-delimited text file uses commas between the field values and surrounds text values in double quotations marks.

Another common way to separate data is to use the tab character between fields. In fact, when you save a spreadsheet file as text in most spreadsheet programs, the program stores the columns with tab characters between them. Figure 6-10 shows one of the worksheets from the CompaniesTABxl.txt Excel spreadsheet saved as text in WordPad. (You can see the tab alignment marks that we placed on the ruler to line up the columns.) Notice that Excel added double quotation marks around several of the text fields—the company names that contain a comma. Because this file is tab delimited, Access accepts the text fields without quotation marks. However, if all or part of your incoming data contains a text qualifier surrounding some of the fields, you should specify that qualifier when you import the data. If you do not do that, Access imports the qualifier characters as well.

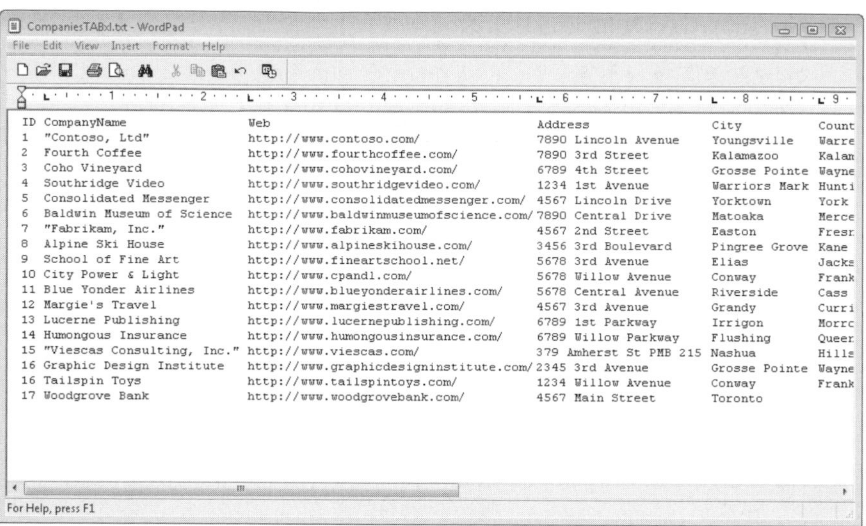


**Figure 6-10** A tab-separated text file uses tab characters to separate the fields.

As with data type analysis, Access examines the first few rows of your file to determine the delimiter and the text qualifier. Notice in Figure 6-10 that tabs are clearly the delimiter, but three of the company name fields are qualified with double quotes. As you'll see later, if you want to import a file that is delimited differently, you can specify different delimiters and separators in the Import Text Wizard. The important thing to remember is that your data should have a consistent data type in all the rows for each column—just as it should in spreadsheet files. If your text file is delimited, the delimiters must be consistent throughout the file.

## Setting Up Fixed-Width Data

Access 2007 can also import text files when the fields appear in fixed locations in each record in the file. You might encounter this type of file if you download a print output file from a host computer. Figure 6-11 shows a sample fixed-width text file. Notice that each field begins in exactly the same location in all the records. (To see this sort of fixed spacing on your screen, you must display the file using a monospaced font such as Courier New.) Unlike delimited files, to prepare this type of file for importing, you must first remove any heading or summary lines from the file. The file must contain only records, with the data you want to import in fixed locations.

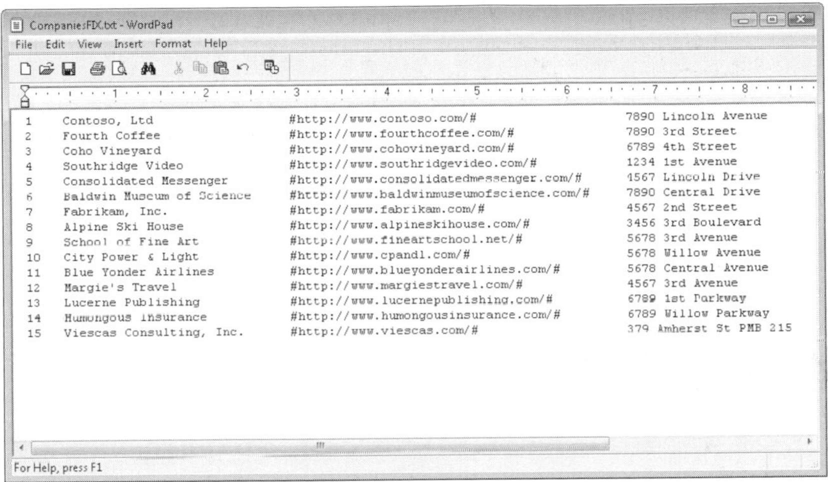


**Figure 6-11** A fixed-width text file contains data in fixed-width columns.

## Importing a Text File

Before you can import a text file, you'll probably need to prepare the data or define the file for Access 2007 with an import specification, or both, as discussed in "Preparing a Text File" on page 282. After you do that, you can import the text file into an Access database by doing the following:

1. Open the Access database that will receive the text data. If that database is already open, close any objects so that only the Navigation Pane is visible.

2. On the External Data tab, in the Import group, click the Text File command, as shown here.

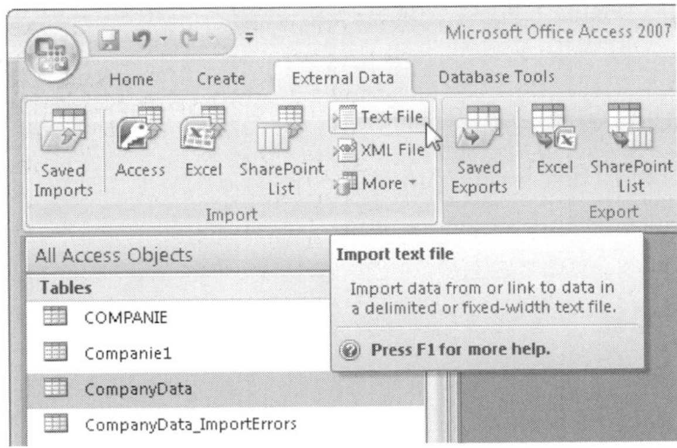


3. Access opens the Get External Data - Text File dialog box shown next. Click the Browse button to open the File Open dialog box shown previously on page 262. Select the folder and the name of the file you want to import. (For these examples,

we used the CompaniesTAB.txt and CompaniesFIX.txt files on the companion CD.) Click the Open button in the File Open dialog box to return to the Get External Data - Text File dialog box.

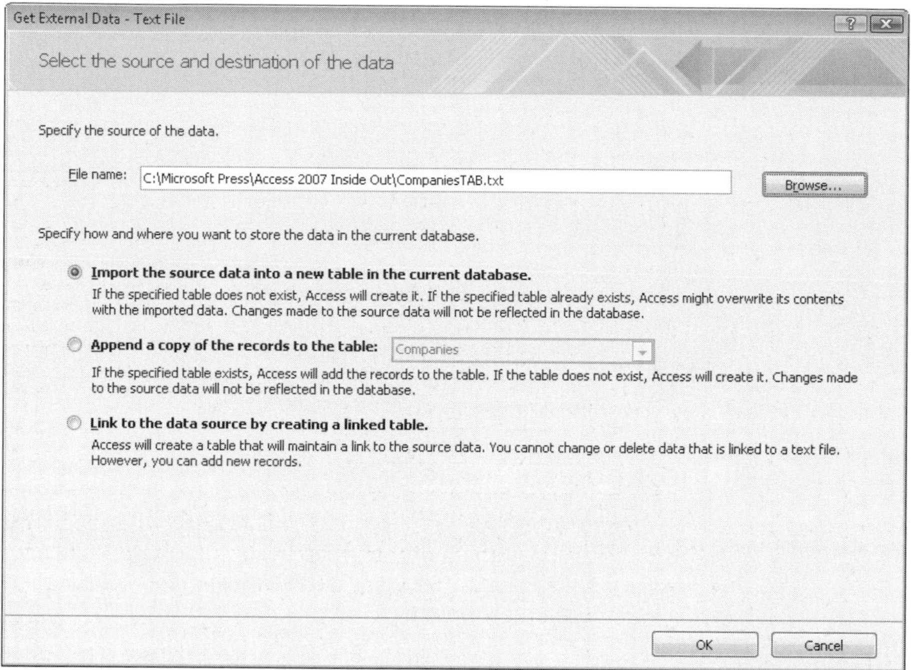


4. Make sure the Import The Source Data Into A New Table In The Current Database option is selected and then click OK. Access starts the Import Text Wizard and displays the first page of the wizard, as shown next. On this page, the wizard makes its best guess about whether the data is delimited or fixed-width. It displays the first several rows of data, which you can examine to confirm the wizard's choice. If the wizard has made the wrong choice, your data is probably formatted incorrectl. You should exit the wizard and fix the source file as suggested in "Preparing a Text File" on page 282. If the wizard has made the correct choice, click Next to go to the next step.

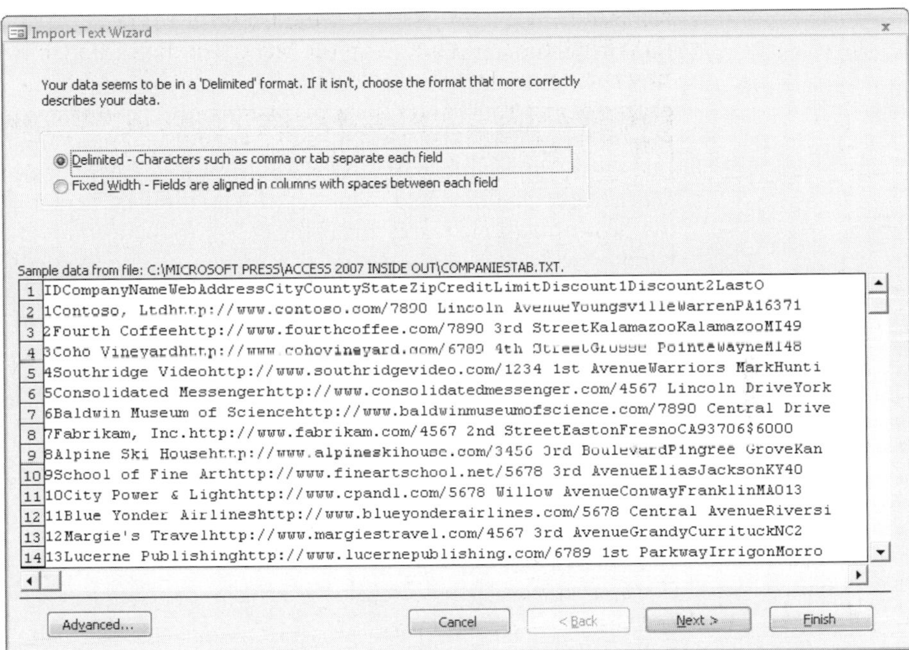

5. If your file is delimited, the Import Text Wizard displays the following page.

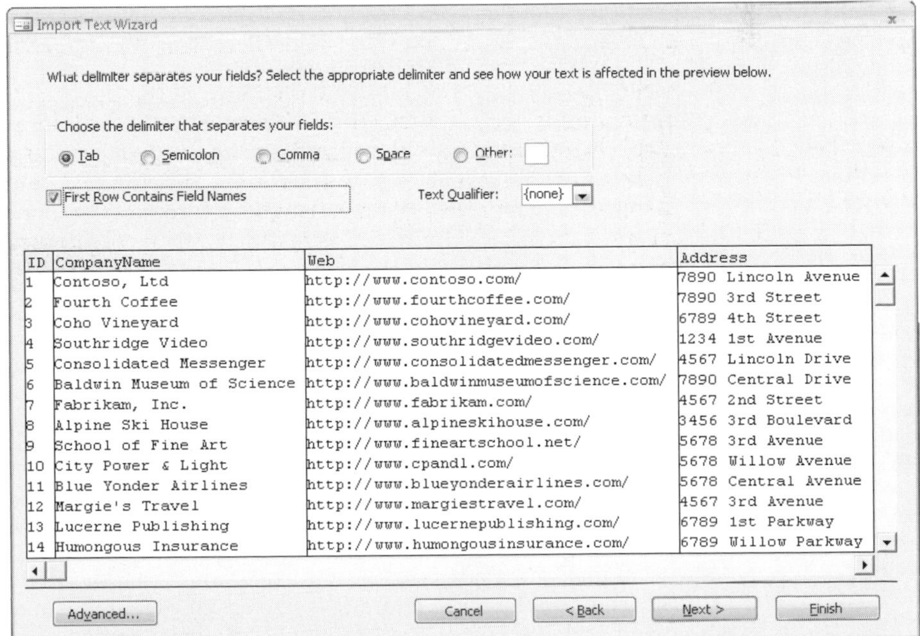

Here you can verify the character that delimits the fields in your text file and the qualifier character that surrounds text strings. Remember that usually when you save a delimited text file from a spreadsheet program, the field delimiter is a tab character and you'll find quotation marks only around strings that contain commas. If the wizard doesn't find a text field with quotation marks in the first few lines, it might assume that no text is surrounded by quotes, and therefore it might set the Text Qualifier field to {none}. You might need to change the Text Qualifier field from {none} to " if this is the case. (You'll need to do this if you use the CompaniesTABxl.txt sample file.) Also be sure to select the First Row Contains Field Names check box if your file has column names in the first row. If you don't do that, the wizard assigns generic field names (Field1, Field2, and so on) and might misidentify the field data types.

If your file is in fixed-width format, the wizard displays this page. (We have scrolled to the right to show one of the problems.)

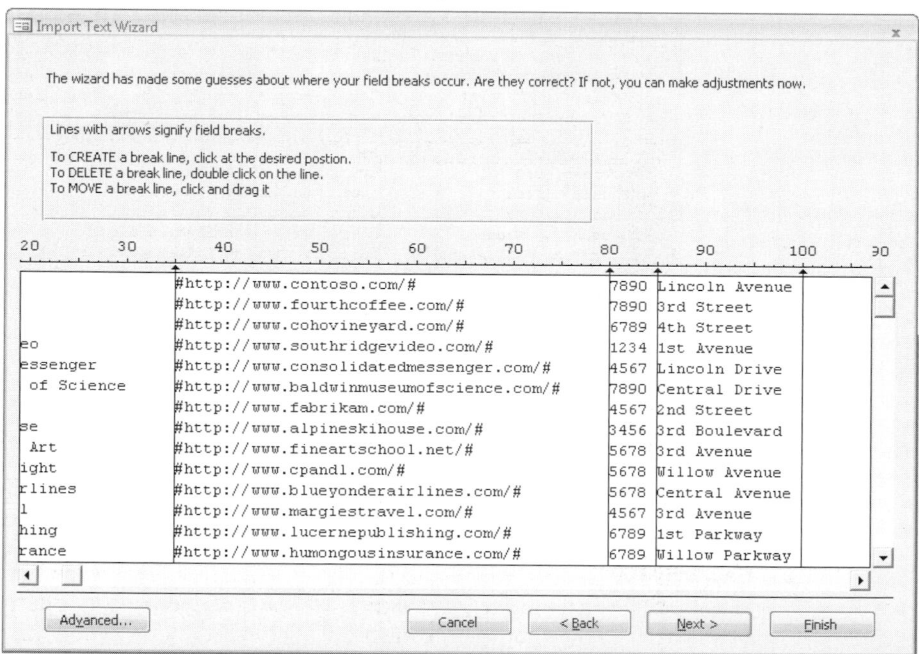


Instead of showing delimiting characters, the wizard offers a graphic representation of where it thinks each field begins. To change the definition of a field, you can drag any line to move it. You can also create an additional field by clicking at the position on the display where fields should be separated. If the wizard creates too many fields, you can double-click any extra delimiting lines to remove them. In the example shown in the preceding illustration (using the CompaniesFIX.txt file on the companion CD), the wizard assumes that the street number is separate from the rest of the address. It also assumes that the State and Zip fields are one field. Because many of the spaces in the sample Comments field line up, it splits this field into several fields. You can double-click the line following the street number to remove it. You can click between the state and zip data to separate those into two fields. Finally, you can double-click all the extra lines the wizard inserted in Comments to turn that into one field. Click Next to go to the next step.

6. If you decided to create a new table in the Get External Data - Text File dialog box, the wizard displays the page shown here. Use this page to specify or confirm field names (you can change field names even if the first row in the text file contains names), select field data types, and set indexed properties. If you're working in a fixed-width text file, you should provide the field names; otherwise, Access names the fields Field1, Field2, and so on.

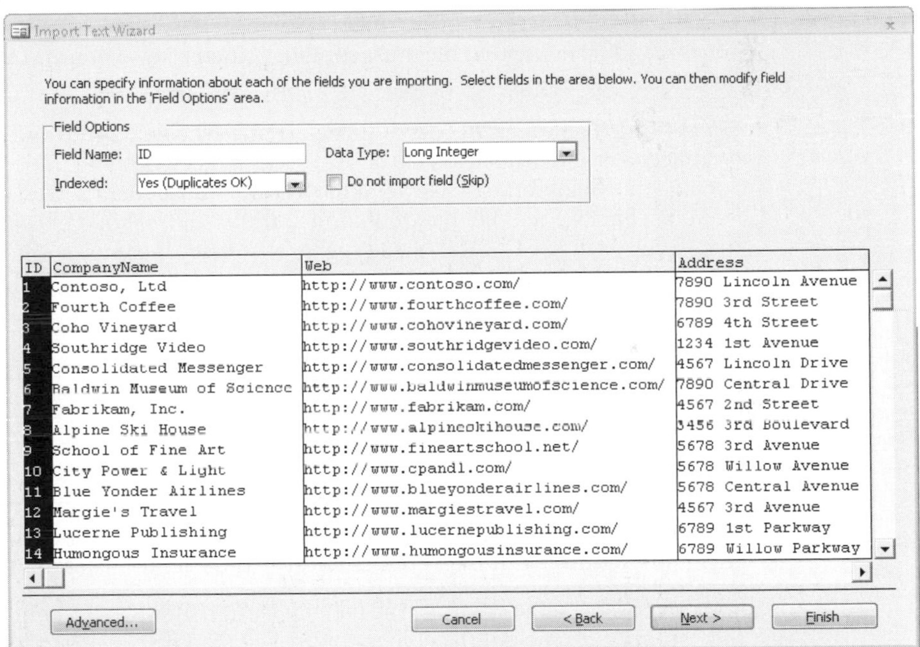


If you decided to append the data to an existing table, either the columns must exactly match both the count and the data type of the columns in the target table (left to right) or the file must be a delimited file with column names in the first row that match column names in the target table.

7. Click Next to go to the next page, where you can select a primary key, much as you did for spreadsheet files. Click Next when you are finished setting a primary key.

8. On the final page of the wizard, you confirm the name of the new table or the target table. You can also select the check box to start the Table Analyzer Wizard to analyze your new table. See Chapter 4 for details about the Table Analyzer Wizard. If you enter the name of an existing table, Access asks if you want to replace the old table. Click Finish to import your data. Access displays a confirmation message at the top of the Get External Data - Text File dialog box

to show you the result of the import procedure. If the wizard encounters an error that prevents any data from being imported, it creates an import errors table in your database (with the name of the text file in the title) that contains a record for each error. The final page of the wizard also includes a check box you can select to save the import steps you just completed.

## Fixing Errors

While importing text files, you might encounter errors that are similar to those described in "Importing Spreadsheet Data" on page 273. For example, when you append a text file to an existing table, some rows might be rejected because of duplicate primary keys. Unless the primary key for your table is an AutoNumber field, the rows you append from the text file must contain primary key fields and the values in those fields must be unique.

For delimited text files, Access 2007 determines the data type (and delimiter and text qualifier) based on the fields in the first several records being imported. If a number appears in a field in the first several records but subsequent records contain text data, you must enclose that field in quotation marks in at least one of the first few rows so that Access will use the Text data type for that field. If a number first appears without decimal places, Access will use the Number data type with the Field Size property set to Long Integer. This setting will generate errors later if the numbers in other records contain decimal places. You can also explicitly tell Access the data type to use by defining a custom import specification. See "Defining an Import Specification" on the next page for details.

Access displays a message if it encounters any errors. As with errors that are generated when you import a spreadsheet, Access creates an import errors table. The table contains a record for each error. The import errors table lists not only the type of error but also the column and row in the text file in which the error occurred. The errors you can encounter with a text file are similar to those described earlier for a spreadsheet file.

You can correct some errors in the table in Design view. For example, you can change the data type of a field if the content of the field can be converted to the new data type. With other errors, you must either add missing data in Datasheet view or delete the imported records and import the table again after correcting the values in the text file that originally caused the errors.

**For details about modifying your table design, see Chapter 5, "Modifying Your Table Design." See Table 5-3 on page 207 for data conversion limitations.**

## Defining an Import Specification

If you are likely to import the same fixed-width file often (for example, a text file you receive from a mainframe once a month) or if you want to be able to use a macro or a Visual Basic procedure to automate importing a text file, you can use the Import Text Wizard to save an import specification for use by your automation procedures. To do so, begin by clicking Text File in the Import group on the External Data tab. Next, select the file you want to import and click OK. Access now opens the Import Text Wizard, which you should use to examine your file, and verify that the wizard identifies the correct fields. At this point, click the Advanced button to see an Import Specification dialog box like the one shown here.

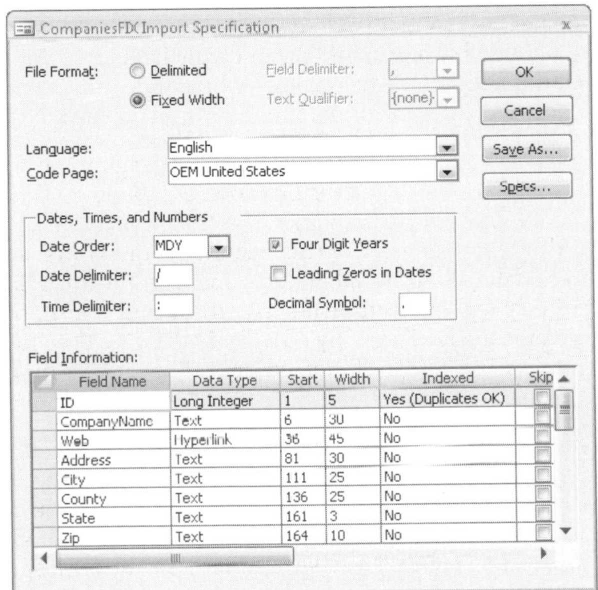


For fixed-width specifications, you can define the field names, data types, start column, width, indexed properties, and whether or not to skip a field. You can identify the language in the Language box and the character set in the Code Page box. You can also specify the way Access recognizes date and time values and numeric fractions. (For example, for a file coming from a non-U.S. computer, the Date Order might be DMY, and the Decimal Symbol might be a comma.) Click the Save As button to save your specification, and give it a name. You can also click the Specs button to load and edit other previously saved specifications. The loaded specification is the one Access uses to import the current file.

## Modifying Imported Tables

When you import data from an external source, Access 2007 often has to use default data types or lengths that can accommodate all the incoming data. You will then need to correct these default settings for your needs. For example, Access assigns a maximum length of 255 characters to text data imported from a spreadsheet or a text file. Even when the source of the data is another database, Access might choose numeric data types that can accept the data but that might not be correct. For example, numeric data in dBASE might be of the Integer type, but Access stores all numeric data from dBASE with a Field Size setting of Double.

Unless you're importing data from an SQL or Paradox database that has a primary key defined, Access does not define a primary key in the new table, so you must do that yourself. Also, if you did not include field names when importing a text or spreadsheet file, you'll probably want to enter meaningful names in the resulting table.

## Linking Files

You can link tables from other Access databases—whether the other databases are local or on a network—and work with the data as if these tables were defined in your current Access database. If you want to work with data stored in another database format supported by Access (dBASE, Paradox, or any SQL database that supports ODBC, including Visual FoxPro), you can link the data instead of importing it.

> **Note**
>
> Although you can *import* queries, forms, reports, macros, and modules from another Access database file, you cannot link these types of objects. Any object that Access needs to run (rather than simply be a container for data) must be in your local database.

In most cases, you can read data, insert new records, delete records, or change data just as if the linked file were an Access table in your database. You can also link text and spreadsheet format data so that you can process it with queries, forms, and reports in your Access database. You can only read the data in linked text and spreadsheet files.

This ability to link data is especially important when you need to access data on a host computer or share data from your application with many other users.

> **Note**
>
> Access 2007 supports linking to dBASE or Paradox versions 5.0 and earlier, and it allows full update if it can find the associated index files. If you need to work with later versions, you must install the Borland Database Engine (BDE).

## Security Considerations

If you attempt to link a file or a table from a database system that is protected, Access 2007 asks you for a password. If the security information you supply is correct and Access successfully links the secured data, Access optionally stores the security information with the linked table entry so that you do not have to enter this information each time you or your application opens the table. Access stores this information in the hidden Connect property of a linked table, so a knowledgeable person might be able to retrieve it by writing code to examine this property. Therefore, if you have linked sensitive information to your Access database and have supplied security information, you should consider encrypting your database. Consult Chapter 25 for information about encrypting your Access database.

If you are linking your database to SQL Server tables and are using Windows domain security, you can set options in SQL Server to accept the Windows domain user ID if the user logs on correctly to the network. Therefore, you won't need to store security information with the link. If your server contains particularly sensitive information, you can disable this option to guard against unauthorized access from logged on but unattended network workstations.

## Performance Considerations

Access 2007 always performs best when working with its own files on your local computer. If you link tables or files from other databases on other computers, you might notice slower performance. In particular, you can expect slower performance if you connect over a network to a table or a file in another database, even if the remote table is an Access table. You won't see any performance difference if you link to Access tables in another .accdb file on your local computer.

When sharing data over a network, you should consider how you and other people can use the data in a way that maximizes performance. For example, instead of working directly with the tables, you should work with queries on the shared data whenever possible to limit the amount of data you need at any one time. When inserting new data in a shared table, you should use an Access form that is set only for data entry so that you don't have to access the entire table to add new data.

You can view and set options for multiple users sharing data by clicking the Microsoft Office Button, clicking Access Options, and then clicking the Advanced category in the Access Options dialog box, as shown in Figure 6-12. The original settings for these options are often appropriate when you share data over a network, so it's a good idea to consult your system administrator before making changes.

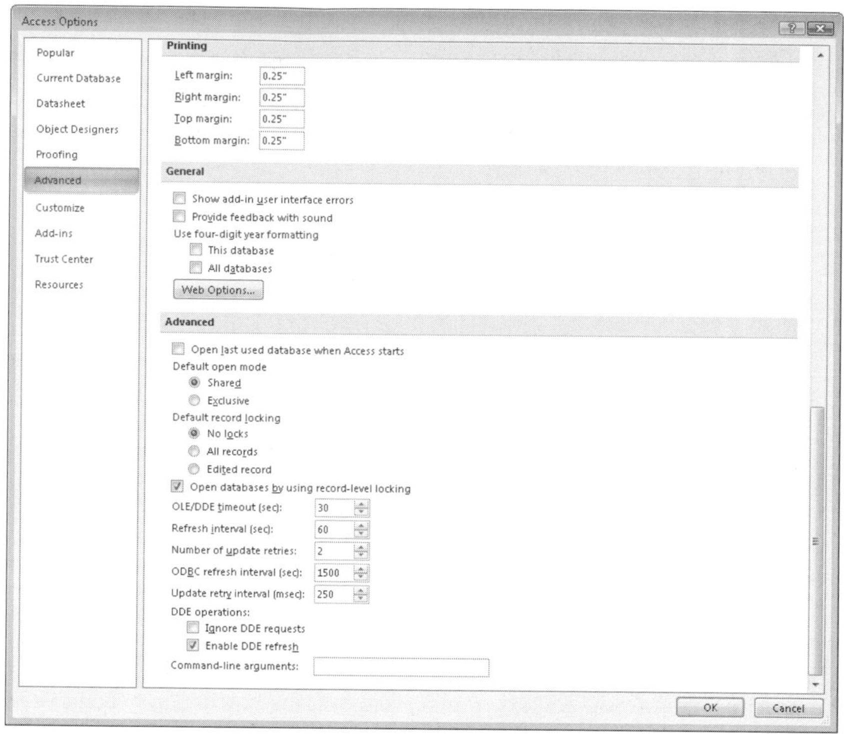


**Figure 6-12** In the Advanced section of the Advanced category in the Access Options dialog box, you can set options that affect the performance of linked tables.

One very important consideration is record locking. When Access 2007 needs to update data in a shared file, it must lock the data to ensure that no other computer is trying to write the same data at the same time. You should set options so that records are not locked if you are simply browsing through data. Even if your application frequently updates and inserts data, you should leave Default Record Locking set to No Locks. With this setting, Access 2007 locks individual records only for the short period of time that it is writing the row, so the chance of receiving an update error while two users are trying to update the same row at the exact same time is very small.

If you want to ensure that no one else can change a record that you have begun to update, you should set Default Record Locking to Edited Record. Note, however, that no other user will be able to edit a record that another has begun to change. If a user begins to type a change in a record and then goes off for lunch, no one else will be able to change that record from another computer until that user either saves the row or clears the edit.

INSIDE OUT **Leave Default Record Locking Alone**

We never set either All Records or Edited Record as the default. Either one can cause extra overhead while updating data and can lock out other users unnecessarily. In the rare case that an update conflict occurs with No Locks, Access gives the second user the opportunity to refresh the data and reenter the blocked update. Also, you can set record locking individually in forms and reports. See Chapter 12, "Customizing a Form," and Chapter 16, "Advanced Report Design," for details.

You can set options to limit the number of times Access 2007 will retry an update to a locked record and how long it will wait between retries. You can also control how often Access reviews updates made by other users to shared data by setting the refresh interval. If this setting is very low, Access will waste time performing this task repeatedly.

Access 97 (version 8) and earlier locked an entire 2-KB page each time you updated, inserted, or deleted rows. This meant that only one user could update any of the rows stored physically within the page. The page size in Access 2000 increased to 4 KB, but Access 2000 (version 9) and later also support record-level locking that eliminates locking collisions when two users attempt to update different rows stored on the same data storage page. Unless you are designing an application that frequently needs to update hundreds of rows at a time (for example, with action queries), you should leave the Open Databases By Using Record-Level Locking check box selected.

## Linking Access Tables

To link a table from another Access database to your database, do the following:

1. Open the Access database to which you want to link the table. If that database is already open, close any objects so that only the Navigation Pane is visible.
2. On the External Data tab, in the Import group, click the Access command, and then select Link To The Data Source By Creating A Linked Table in the Get External Data - Access Database dialog box shown next.

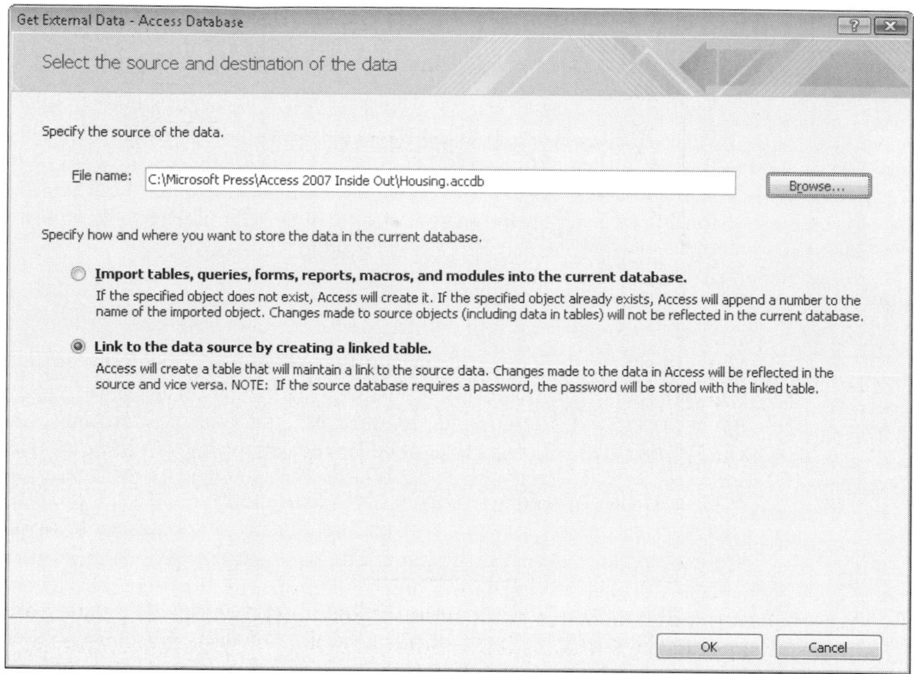


3. Click the Browse button to open the File Open dialog box shown earlier on page 262, which lists the types of databases you can link. Select the folder and the name of the .accdb, .mdb, .mda, .accda, .mde, or .accde file that contains the table to which you want to link. (You cannot link tables from an .adp or .ade file because those are actually tables in SQL Server–use an ODBC link to the server directly as explained in "Linking SQL Tables" on page 301.) If you're connecting over a network, select the logical drive that is assigned to the network server containing the database you want. If you want Access to automatically connect to the network server each time you open the table, type the full network location (also known as the UNC or Universal Naming Convention name) in the File Name box instead of selecting a logical drive. For example, on a Windows network you might enter a network location such as

   ```
   \\dbsvr\access\shared\northwind.accdb
   ```

   After you select the Access database file you want, click the Open button to return to the Get External Data - Access Database dialog box, and then click OK to see the tables in that database.

4. Access opens the Link Tables dialog box, shown next, which lists the tables available in the database you selected. Select one or more tables, and click OK to link the tables to the current database. If the link procedure is successful, the new table will have the name of the table you selected.

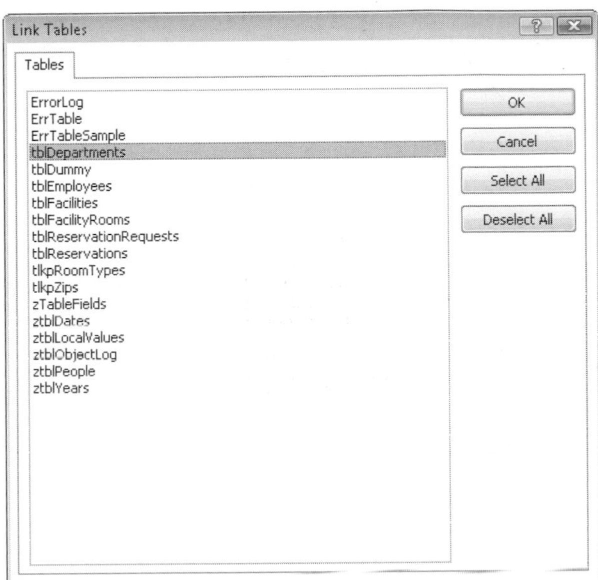


Access marks the icon for linked tables in the Navigation Pane with an arrow, as shown next. If Access finds a duplicate name, it generates a new name by adding a unique integer to the end of the name as described earlier. Because objects such as forms, reports, macros, and modules might refer to the linked table by its original name, you should carefully check name references if Access has to rename a linked table.

## INSIDE OUT Keeping the Connect Property Current

One problem with using linked data in an application that you're going to distribute to someone else is the location of the linked files on your computer might not be exactly the same as it is on your user's computer. For example, the internal Connect property might point to D:\MyDatabases\MyData.accdb, but your user installs the application on the C drive. You might have noticed that a form always opens when you open the Conrad Systems Contacts sample database and that it takes a few seconds before it returns you to the Navigation Pane. We wrote code behind this initial form that verifies the table links and fixes them. You can learn how we built this code in Chapter 25.

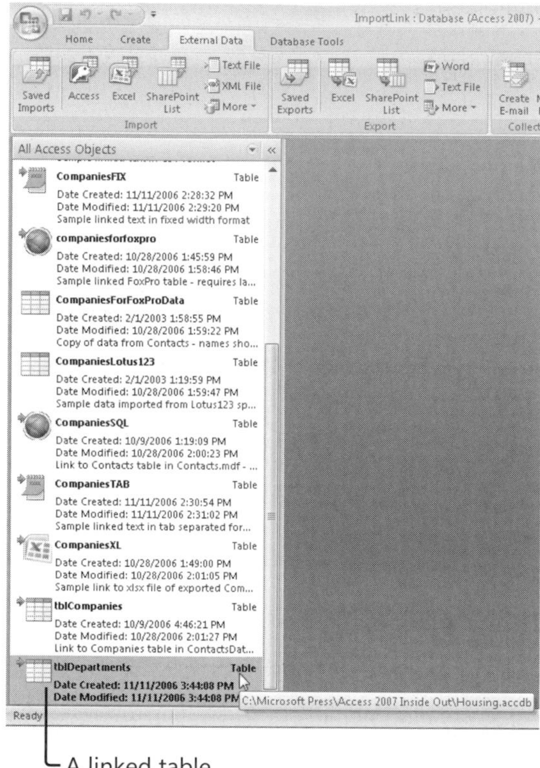


## Linking dBASE and Paradox Files

Linking files from a foreign database is almost as easy as linking an Access table. To link to a file from dBASE or Paradox, do the following:

1. Open the Access database to which you want to link the file. If that database is already open, close any objects so that only the Navigation Pane is visible.
2. On the External Data tab, in the Import group, click the More command, and then click dBASE File or Paradox File, as appropriate. Select Link To The Data Source By Creating A Linked Table in the Get External Data - dBASE File (or Get External Data - Paradox File) dialog box, as shown next.

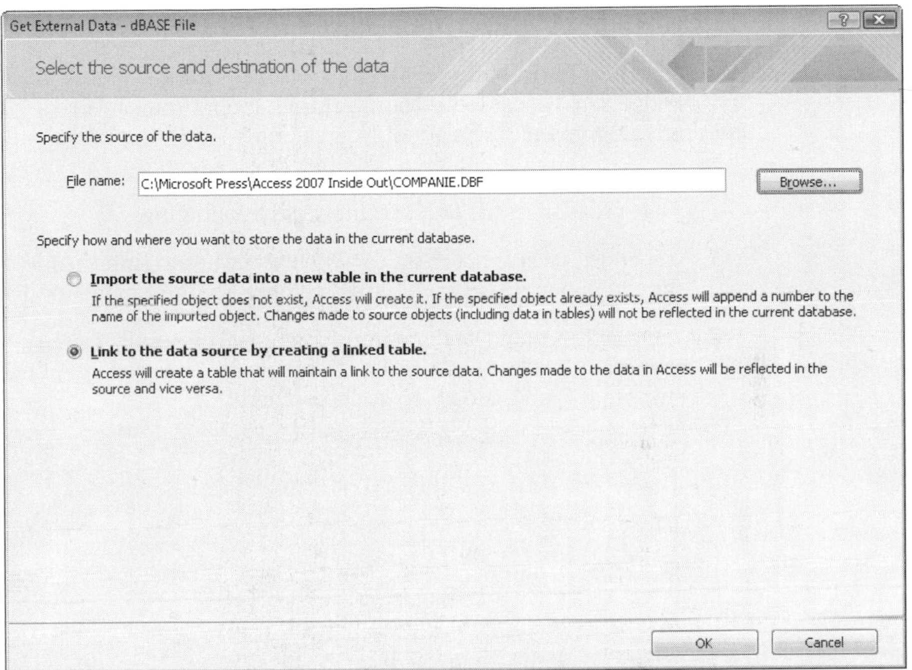


3. Click the Browse button to open the File Open dialog box shown earlier on page 262, which lists the types of dBASE or Paradox files to which you can link. Select dBASE III, dBASE IV, dBASE 5, or Paradox, as appropriate, in the list to the right of the File Name box, and then select the folder and the name of the file to which you want to link. If you're connecting over a network, select the logical drive that is assigned to the network server that contains the database you want. If you want Access to automatically connect to the network server each time you open the linked file, type the full network location in the File Name box instead of selecting a logical drive. For example, on a Windows network you might enter a network location such as

```
\\dbsvr\dbase\shared\newstore.dbf
```

4. Click the Open button to return to the Get External Data - dBASE File dialog box, and then click OK to link to the selected dBASE or Paradox file.

5. If you selected an encrypted Paradox file, Access opens a dialog box that asks you for the correct password. Type the correct password and click OK to proceed, or click Cancel to start over. If the link procedure is successful, the new table will have the name of the file you selected (without the file name extension). If Access finds a duplicate name, it will generate a new name by adding a unique integer to the end of the name.

## Linking Text and Spreadsheet Files

Linking a text file or an Excel spreadsheet file is almost identical to importing these types of files, as discussed earlier in this chapter. (You cannot link Lotus 1-2-3 files; you can only import them.) As noted, you can only read linked text and Excel spreadsheet files.

To link a spreadsheet file or a text file, do the following:

1. Open the Access database to which you want to link the file. If that database is already open, close any objects so that only the Navigation Pane is visible.

2. On the External Data tab, in the Import group, click the Excel or Text File command. Select Link To The Data Source By Creating A Linked Table in the Get External Data dialog box, as shown here.

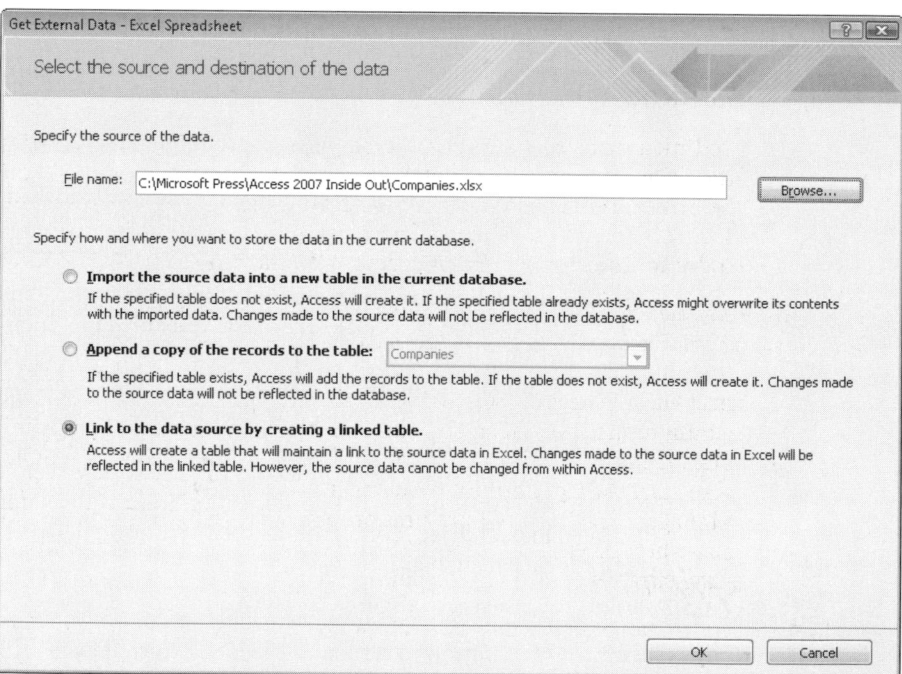


3. Click the Browse button to open the File Open dialog box shown earlier on page 262. Select the folder and the name of the file to which you want to link. If you're connecting over a network, select the logical drive that is assigned to the network server that contains the database you want. If you want Access to automatically connect to the network server each time you open the linked file, type the full network location in the File Name box instead of choosing a logical drive, path, and file name. For example, on a Windows network you might enter a network location such as

```
\\filesvr\excel\shared\companies.xlsx
```

4. Click the Open button to return to the Get External Data dialog box, and then click OK to start the Link Spreadsheet Wizard or the Link Text Wizard.

5. Follow the steps in the wizard, which are identical to the steps for importing a spreadsheet or text file, as described earlier in this chapter.

**CAUTION!**

You can have the same problems with delimiters, text qualifiers, data types, and primary keys noted under importing. You might need to correct or reformat the data in your text or spreadsheet file to be able to successfully link to it. For example, if Access guesses the wrong data type for a column in an Excel file, you will see #Error in fields that have the incorrect data type.

## Linking SQL Tables

To link a table from another database system that supports ODBC SQL, you must have the ODBC driver for that database installed on your computer. Your computer must also be linked to the network that connects to the SQL server from which you want to link a table, and you must have an account on that server. Check with your system administrator for information about correctly connecting to the SQL server.

If you have SQL Server 2005 installed or have downloaded and installed SQL Server 2005 Express Edition, you already have an SQL server at your disposal. See the Appendix for instructions about how to install SQL Server 2005 Express Edition. One of the best ways to be sure SQL Server is running on your computer is to use the SQL Server Configuration Manager. You can start the Configuration Manager from the Windows Start menu in the Configuration Tools folder under Microsoft SQL Server 2005. You can also start the Configuration Manager by running C:\Windows\System32\SQLServerManager.msc. In the Configuration Manager, choose SQL Server 2005 Services and be sure the SQL Server (MSSQLSERVER) service is marked as Running. If it is not running, right-click the service name and click Start on the shortcut menu.

To link an SQL table, do the following:

1. Open the Access database to which you want to link the SQL table. If that database is already open, close all open objects so that you see only the Navigation Pane.

2. On the External Data tab, in the Import group, click the More command, and then click ODBC Database. Access opens the Get External Data - ODBC Database dialog box. Make sure the Link To The Data Source By Creating A Linked Table option is selected and then click OK.

3. Access opens the Select Data Source dialog box, shown earlier on page 267, in which you can select the data source that maps to the SQL server containing the table you want to link. Select a data source, and click OK. If you don't see the data

source you need, see "Creating a Data Source to Link to an ODBC Database" on page 255 for instructions. The ODBC driver displays the SQL Server Login dialog box for the SQL data source that you selected if the server is not set up to accept your Windows login. If you are linking to a Visual FoxPro database or file, the ODBC driver displays the Configure Connection dialog box.

4. When you are required to enter a login ID and password, and if you are authorized to connect to more than one database on the server and you want to connect to a database other than your default database, enter your login ID and password. Then click the Options button to open the lower part of the dialog box. When you click in the Database box, Access logs on to the server and returns a list of available database names. Select the one you want, and click OK. If you don't specify a database name and if multiple databases exist on the server, Access will connect you to the default database for your login ID.

**TROUBLESHOOTING**

**You can't connect to a specific database using trusted authentication because you use more than one data source.**

When you connect to a server using trusted authentication (your Windows user ID), you automatically connect to the database specified in the data source. You might need to create more than one data source if you need to connect to more than one database on that server. See "Creating a Data Source to Link to an ODBC Database" on page 255 for details about defining ODBC data sources.

For Visual FoxPro, specify the database name or FoxPro file folder and click OK.

When Access connects to the server or Visual FoxPro database, you'll see the Link Tables dialog box, similar to the Import Objects dialog box shown earlier on page 269, which lists the available tables on that server.

5. From the list of tables, select the ones you want to link. If you select a table name in error, you can click it again to deselect it, or you can click the Deselect All button to start over. Click OK to link to the tables you selected.

6. If the link procedure is successful, the new table will have the name of the SQL table or Visual FoxPro file (without the file name extension). If Access finds a duplicate name, it will generate a new name by adding a unique integer to the end of the name.

## Modifying Linked Tables

You can make some changes to the definitions of linked tables to customize them for use in your Access 2007 environment. When you attempt to open the table in Design view, Access opens a dialog box to warn you that you cannot modify certain properties of a linked table. You can still click OK to open the linked table in Design view.

You can open a linked table in Design view to change the Format, Decimal Places, Caption, Description, and Input Mask property settings for any field. You can set these properties to customize the way you look at and update data in Access forms and reports. You can also give any linked table a new name for use within your Access database (although the table's original name remains unchanged in the source database) to help you better identify the table or to enable you to use the table with the queries, forms, and reports that you've already designed.

Changing a table's design in Access has no effect on the original table in its source database. However, if the design of the table in the source database changes, you must relink the table to Access. You must also unlink and relink any table if your user ID or your password changes.

## Unlinking Linked Tables

It is easy to unlink tables that are linked to your Access database. In the Navigation Pane, simply select the table you want to unlink and then press the Delete key or click the Delete command in the Records group on the Home tab of the Ribbon. Access displays the confirmation message shown in Figure 6-13. Click Yes to unlink the table. Unlinking the table does not delete the table; it simply removes the link from your table list in the Navigation Pane.

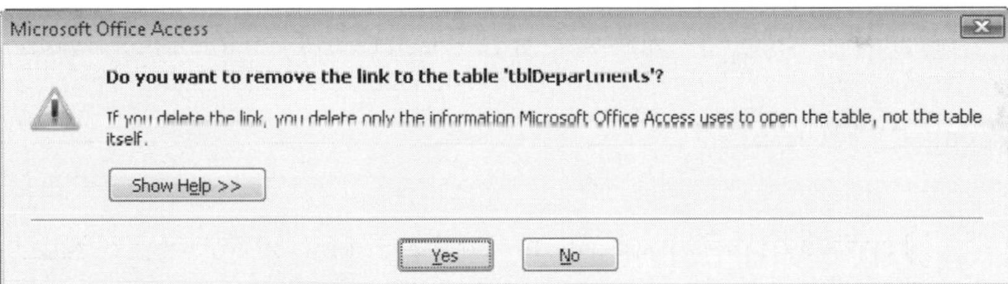


**Figure 6-13** Access displays a message to confirm that you want to unlink a table.

> **Note**
>
> If you click the Cut command in the Clipboard group on the Home tab of the Ribbon to unlink a table, Access does not display the confirmation message shown in Figure 6-13.

## Using the Linked Table Manager

If you move some or all of your linked tables to a different location, you must either delete your linked tables and relink them or update the location information before you can open the tables. You can easily update the location information in the table links by using the Linked Table Manager. To use this handy utility, open the database that contains linked tables that you need to relink, and on the Database Tools tab, in the Database Tools group, click the Linked Table Manager command. The utility opens a dialog box that displays all the linked tables in your database, as shown in Figure 6-14. Simply select the check boxes for the ones that you think need to be verified and updated, and then click OK. If any linked table has been moved to a different location, the Linked Table Manager prompts you with a dialog box so that you can specify the new file location. You can also select the Always Prompt For New Location check box to verify the file location for all linked tables.

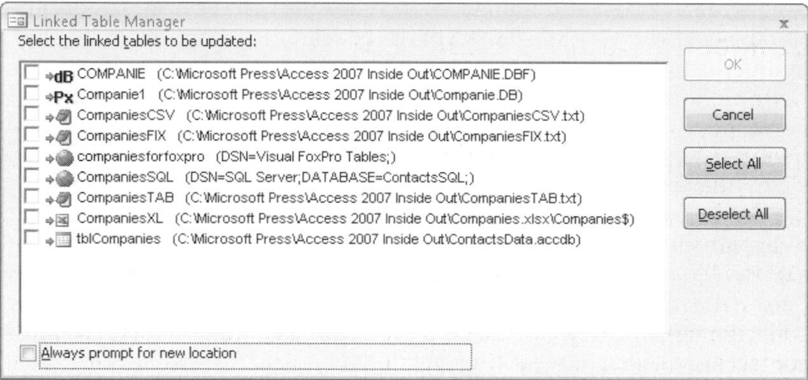


**Figure 6-14** You can use the Linked Table Manager to correct links to files that have moved.

Now you have all the information you need to import and link data using Access 2007. For information on how to export data see Article 3, "Exporting Data," on the companion CD.

## Collecting Data via E-Mail

Access 2007 introduces a new feature that allows you to collect data through e-mail and import it into your database. The data is collected through either HTML forms or rich Microsoft Office InfoPath 2007 forms. Access 2007 allows you to either update existing data in a table or add new records to a table. By integrating Access 2007 with e-mail collection capabilities, you can have users update and add information to your database from different locations. This feature can be used, for example, in a club membership application that periodically needs to update its member records.

To use the e-mail data collection capabilities in Access 2007, you must also have Microsoft Office Outlook 2007 installed to send the data entry forms and to process the data returned. If you are sending the data collection forms in HTML format, your recipients need only have an e-mail client program that accepts HTML. If you want to send Office InfoPath 2007 collection forms, you also need to have InfoPath 2007 installed. The users receiving these forms must also have Office Outlook 2007 and InfoPath 2007 installed to fill out the forms and send them back.

**Note**

To demonstrate the various capabilities of collecting data through e-mail, we use the ContactsDataCopy.accdb and TasksEmailCollection.accdb sample databases on the companion CD. This TasksEmailCollection.accdb sample database is based on the Tasks database template with sample records added to the two tables.

## Collecting Data via HTML Forms

Open ContactsDataCopy.accdb from the folder where you installed your sample files. Click the Navigation Pane menu, click Object Type under Navigate To Category, and then click Tables under Filter By Group to display the list of tables in the database. For the continued success of the Conrad Systems business, its owners need to find new customers who want to purchase their products. One of the best ways to find leads to potential new customers is to ask existing customers. The existing contacts in the Conrad Systems Contacts database could provide names of people through their own personal network of friends who could in turn become new clients. By using the data collection feature in Access 2007, you could send an e-mail form to all the existing contacts in the database, asking whether they know of anyone who might be interested in Conrad Systems' products. To entice existing contacts to provide some names, you could offer an incentive of free support time.

You can update a single table using e-mail data collection, or you can update two or more tables if you use a saved select query as the record source for the data entry form. You'll learn about creating queries using multiple tables in Chapter 8, "Building Complex Queries." For this example, let's create an e-mail form to collect data to add a new record to the tblContacts table. Because we're going to send an e-mail message to the contacts in the tblContacts table, you'll need to add your name and e-mail address if you want to follow along in this section. Open the tblContacts table in Datasheet view, go to the new record at the end, add your name and valid e-mail address, and save the record. Do not add any text to display if you use the Insert Hyperlink dialog box. (We'll explain why later in this section.) Close the table when you're done. Next, right-click the tblContacts table in the Navigation Pane and click Collect And Update Data Via E-Mail on the shortcut menu, as shown in Figure 6-15. Alternatively, you can select the table in the Navigation Pane and click the Create E-Mail button in the Collect Data group on the External Data tab on the Ribbon.

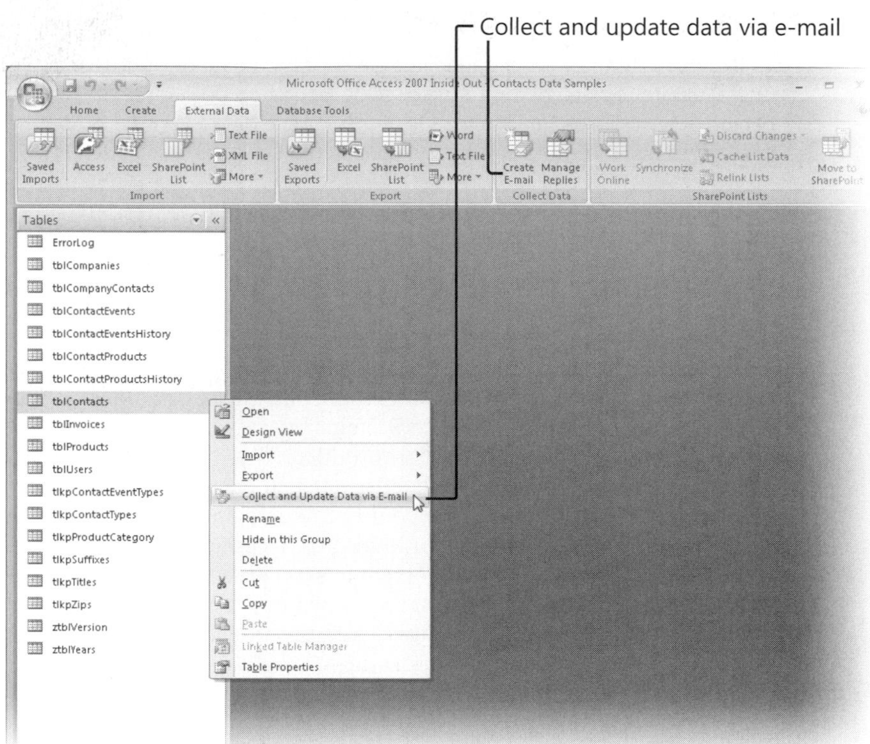


**Figure 6-15** You can begin the process of collecting data via e-mail by using the table's shortcut menu or the Create E-Mail button on the Ribbon.

Access opens the first page of the e-mail collection wizard, as shown in Figure 6-16. This first page is an introductory page, which outlines the steps you take to complete the process. For this example you need to complete six major steps. (If you are adding records to a table with no records, Access displays five steps on this first page.) Click Next to proceed to the second page of the wizard.

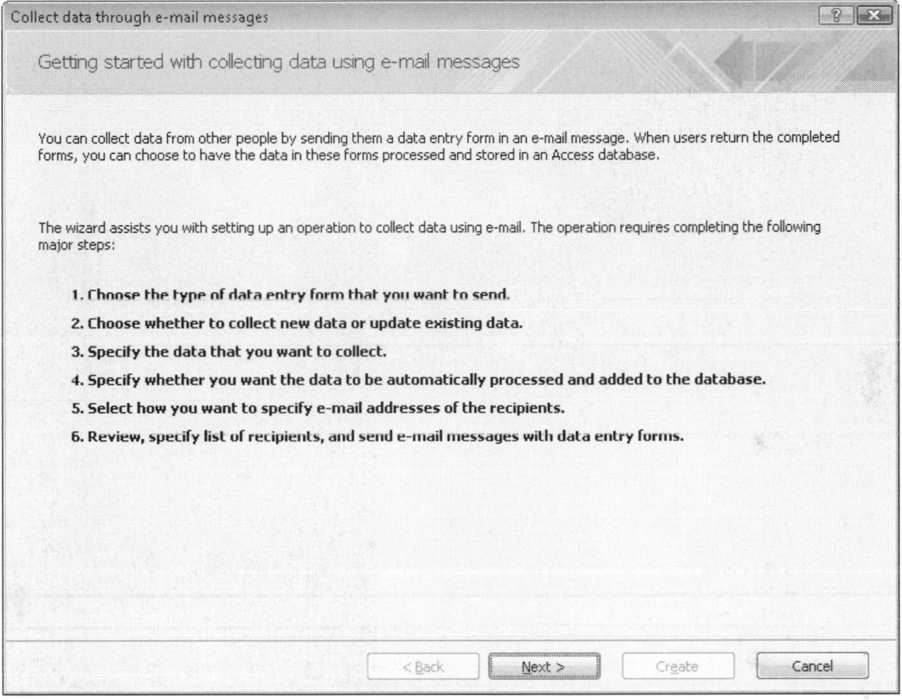


**Figure 6-16** The first page of the e-mail collection wizard is an introductory page.

The second page of the wizard, shown in Figure 6-17, asks you to choose between creating an HTML form or an InfoPath form for data entry. Remember that the people who receive the InfoPath form need to have InfoPath 2007 and Outlook 2007 installed on their computers to be able to read and fill out the data form. When you send an HTML form, the recipient needs only an e-mail client that can handle messages in HTML. For this example, select HTML Form (the default) and click Next.

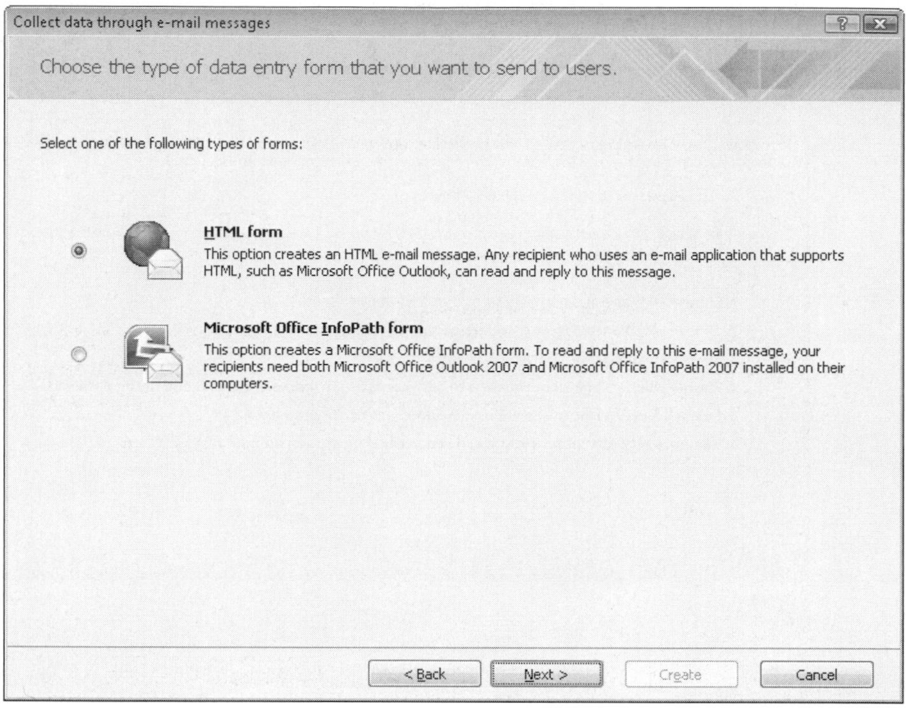


**Figure 6-17** The second page of the wizard asks you to choose a type of form.

The next page of the wizard, shown in Figure 6-18, asks you to choose whether users receive a blank form or a form that includes data from within the database they will update. If you chose a table that has no records, a table that does not have a primary key defined, or a query that combines two or more tables, you will not see this page of the wizard. In those cases, Access assumes you only want to add new records, so it does not display this page. Note also that to send data to update, you must have available within one of your database tables the e-mail address of the recipient.

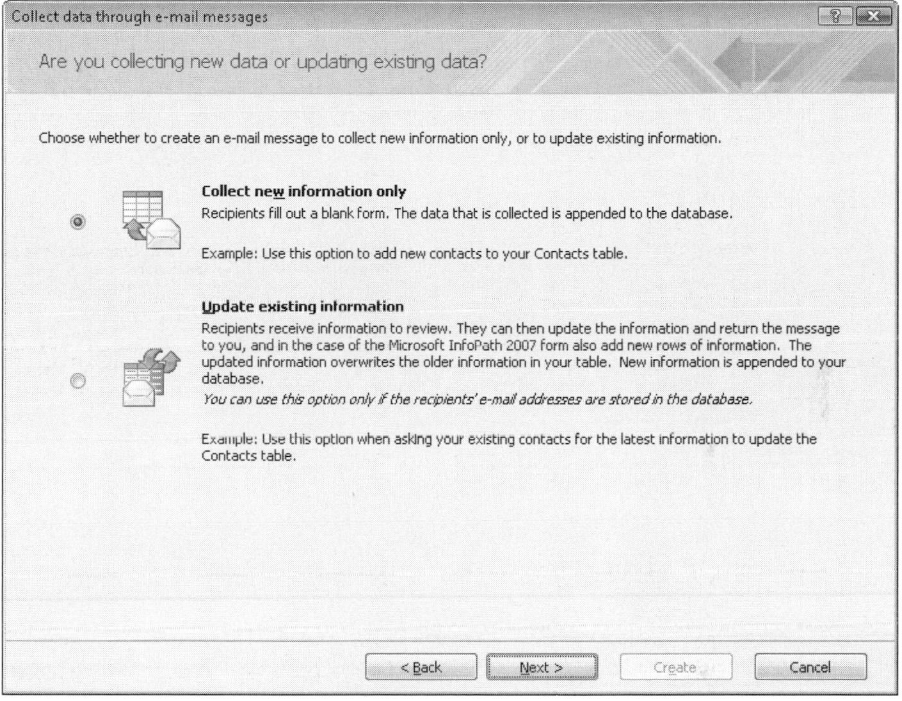


**Figure 6-18** You can choose to collect new information or update existing records on this page of the wizard.

When you select the Collect New Information Only option after choosing to send an HTML message, the recipients can only send back a reply that inserts one record into your table. To insert multiple records, the recipients must send multiple messages. If you select Update Existing Information after choosing to send an HTML message, recipients can view and update all the records you send. The information the recipient returns in a reply will overwrite the existing rows. For this current example, select Collect New Information Only, and then click Next to continue.

On the next page of the wizard, shown in Figure 6-19, you decide which fields from the table or query to include in the e-mail form. By default, Access automatically places any fields whose Required property is set to Yes in the Fields To Include In E-Mail Message list on the right. Access also puts the * symbol next to any required fields.

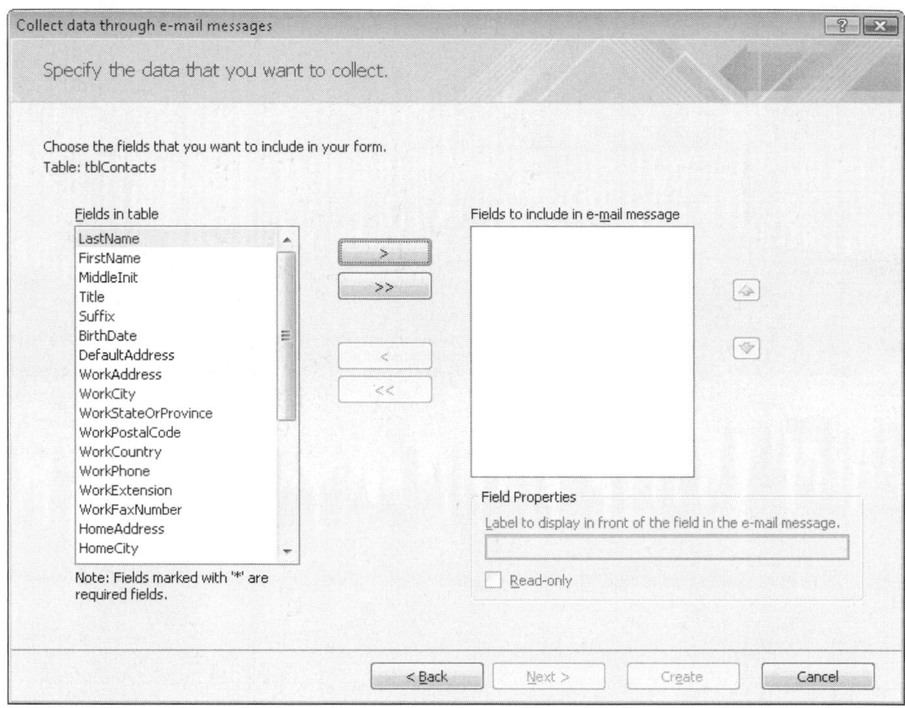


**Figure 6-19** Select which fields to include on the form, in what order to display them, and what labels to display on the form.

You can select any field in the Fields In Table list and click the single right arrow (>) button to copy that field to the Fields To Include In E-Mail Message list. You can also click the double right arrow (>>) button to copy all available fields to the Fields To Include In E-Mail Message list. If you copy a field in error, you can select that field and click the single left arrow (<) button to remove it from the list. You can remove all fields and start over by clicking the double left arrow (<<) button.

## INSIDE OUT Including the Primary Key in the Data Collection Process

Notice that Access did not include the primary key of the tblContacts table (the ContactID field) in the list of available fields. Whenever the primary key is the AutoNumber data type, you cannot include the field regardless of whether you are adding or updating records. If the primary key is not an AutoNumber data type, you should include it only when adding records. When updating records, Access includes the key value in the data it sends in the e-mail form, but the user cannot see nor update it. The only case that requires the primary key field is when the key is not an AutoNumber and the user will be inserting records. When adding records to a table that has a primary key that is not an AutoNumber data type, the user must supply a key value that is unique to be able to add data to the table via e-mail.

For this example, you want to include some of the fields in the tblContacts table, but not all of them. The existing Conrad Systems contacts might not know the information for every field, but they should be able to fill out at least the basic information for new contacts, such as last name, first name, and e-mail address. Select the LastName field and then click the single right arrow (>) to move the field to the Fields To Include In E-Mail Message list. Now repeat this procedure and move the following fields to the Fields To Include In E-Mail Message list: FirstName, MiddleInit, Title, Suffix, WorkPhone, WorkExtension, MobilePhone, EmailName, and Website. These 10 fields should suffice for obtaining information on prospective leads.

After you move fields to the Fields To Include In E-Mail Message list, the up and down arrows to the right of this list become available along with the Field Properties section. You can click the up and down arrows to change the order of the fields you are including in the form. For this example, select the LastName field and click the down arrow twice to move it down two spots in the display order. (You could have moved the FirstName and MiddleInit fields before the LastName field, but we wanted you to see how to change the order of fields within the list.) Access fills in the field's Caption property (or the field name if the field does not have a caption) in the Label To Display In Front Of The Field In The E-Mail Message box under Field Properties. You can customize this label to display different text or leave it as is. (You're limited to using 64 characters for a custom label.) For this example, click the FirstName field and type **Enter the First Name of the new contact here...** as the label for the FirstName field, as shown in Figure 6-20.

If you do not want to allow the recipient to enter any information or change existing data in that field, you could select the Read-Only check box. (This option is more suited for updating data when you want to display data in a field from an existing record, but do not want the user to change it.) For this example, do not select this check box for any of the fields. If you like, you can experiment with entering captions for some of the other fields—we had you change one caption so that you can see the result in the e-mail message. Click Next to continue to the next page.

## TROUBLESHOOTING

### Why can't I see all the fields from my table in the data collection process?

You might have noticed that not only the AutoNumber primary key ContactID field but also the ContactType and Photo fields from the tblContacts table are not shown as available fields. You cannot use AutoNumber, Attachment, OLE Object, or Multi-Value Field Lookup data types in the data collection process. None of these data types are supported for e-mail collection in Access 2007. You will have to add or update these fields manually.

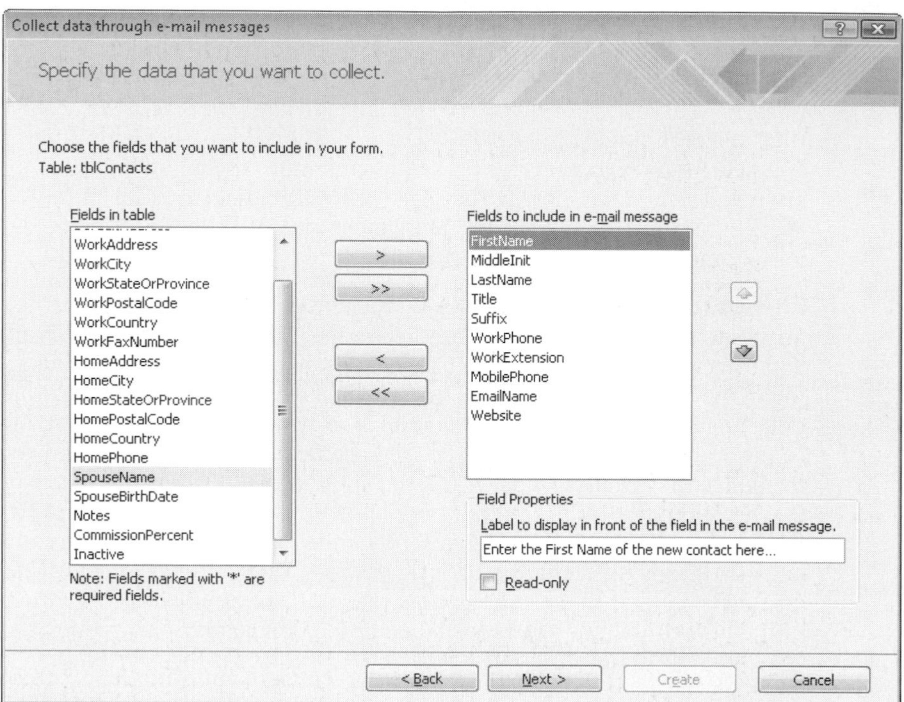


**Figure 6-20** Change the display order by moving the LastName field down two positions and type a more descriptive label for the FirstName field.

The next page of the wizard, shown in Figure 6-21, asks you to specify whether you want to manually process the replies as they arrive (the default) or let Outlook and Access automatically process the replies. By default, all replies are stored in an Outlook folder called Access Data Collection Replies. If you want to change where Outlook saves replies, click the Access Data Collection Replies link on this page. The wizard opens the Select Folder dialog box in Outlook where you can select the Outlook folder you want to use or create a new folder. After you select a different folder, the link on the wizard page changes to the name of this folder.

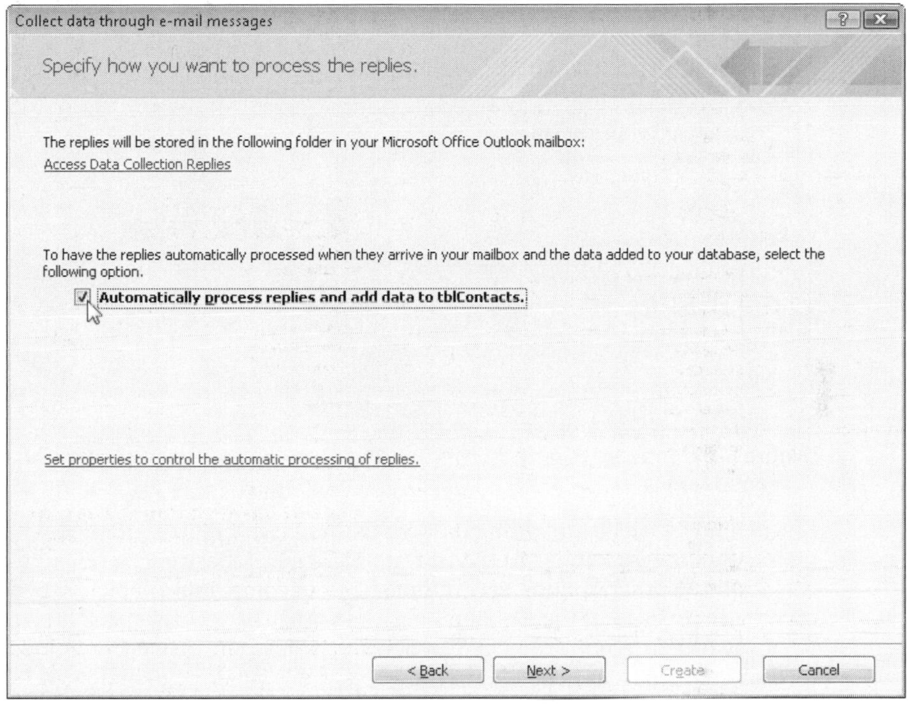


**Figure 6-21** Choose whether to have the replies automatically processed or to manually process them yourself.

To have the replies automatically processed, select the Automatically Process Replies And Add Data To tblContacts check box (the default). For our example, make sure this option is selected. The Set Properties To Control The Automatic Processing Of Replies link allows you to customize various settings for automatic processing. Click this link to open the Collecting Data Using E-Mail Options dialog box, as shown in Figure 6-22.

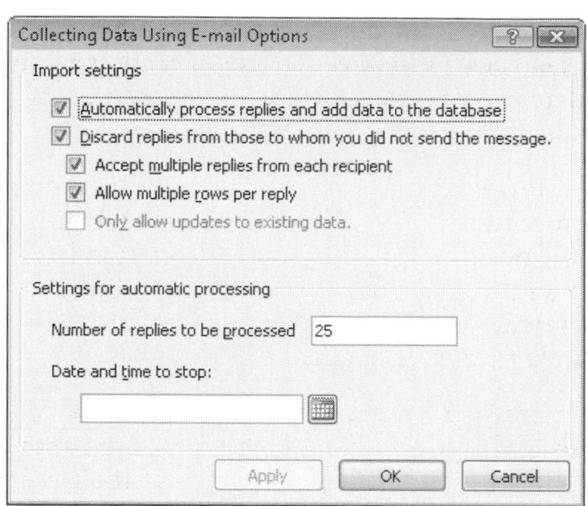


**Figure 6-22** You can set options for processing e-mail forms in the Collecting Data Using E-Mail Options dialog box.

The default settings for adding data are as shown in Figure 6-22. If you clear the Automatically Process Replies And Add Data To The Database check box under Import Settings, all the other options in this dialog box become unavailable, and you will have to manually process all the e-mail replies. Selecting the second check box, Discard Replies From Those To Whom You Did Not Send The Message, instructs Outlook 2007 not to process replies from people to whom you did not send the e-mail form. "Discard" in this case is a bit of a misnomer because the replies will remain in the data collection folder in Outlook—Outlook simply won't process them. You can, however, manually process these replies if you so choose.

Selecting the third check box, Accept Multiple Replies From Each Recipient, allows a recipient to reply to the e-mail form message more than once. Each reply is automatically processed upon arrival. If you clear this check box, only the first reply is processed, but all other replies remain in the Outlook folder. You can then choose to either manually process these additional replies or delete them. In our example, one of your contacts might know the names of several people who could potentially be interested in buying products that Conrad Systems offers. Leaving this check box selected allows the recipient to provide more than one name to you.

> **Note**
>
> The Accept Multiple Replies From Each Recipient check box does not apply to multiple records within an InfoPath form. If a recipient adds more than one record to an InfoPath form, each record is processed because all the records are stored in one e-mail message.



The fourth check box, Allow Multiple Rows Per Reply, applies only to InfoPath forms. If you select this check box, the recipient can insert additional rows in the form to create more records. Each record in the form is then automatically processed. The fifth check box, Only Allow Updates To Existing Data, also applies only to InfoPath forms. Select this check box to prevent a recipient from adding new records in the InfoPath form when updating data. If you clear this check box, the user can add new records in the InfoPath form as well as update existing data. Because we have asked the wizard to collect new information only, this option is unavailable.

Under Settings For Automatic Processing, you can specify the maximum number of replies to be automatically processed. The default for Number Of Replies To Be Processed is 25. You can enter any positive integer between 1 and 10 billion for this setting. If Outlook receives more replies than the number you entered, you can still process the remaining replies manually. If you want all replies to be automatically processed, enter a number larger than the number of replies you expect to receive.

Under Date And Time To Stop, you can define a date and time to have Outlook stop processing any further replies to this message. Any replies received after that time are stored in the Outlook folder, but are not automatically processed. You can, however, choose to manually process replies received after this date. Leave all the settings at their defaults for this example, click Cancel to close the dialog box, and then click Next to go to the next page of the wizard.

INSIDE OUT

### Why Set a Date to Stop Processing Replies?

This setting might be required in time-sensitive situations. For example, you might be conducting a survey that has to be completed before a certain date. To ensure that no records are updated or added after the cutoff date, you can designate a date and time to stop automatic processing in the Collecting Data Using E-Mail Options dialog box.

On the next page of the wizard, shown in Figure 6-23, you can choose whether to enter the e-mail addresses using Outlook 2007 or have Access use e-mail addresses that are stored in the database. If you choose Enter The E-Mail Addresses In Microsoft Office Outlook (the default), you can either type each recipient's address in the Outlook message or you can choose addresses from your Outlook address book. If you select Use The E-Mail Addresses Stored In A Field In The Database, you can use addresses that are stored in the table you are adding or editing. You can also use e-mail addresses stored in a field in a related table. For this example, you'll use the e-mail addresses stored in the tblContacts table, so select Use The E-Mail Addresses Stored In A Field In The Database, and then click Next to continue.

#### Note

This page of the wizard appears only when you are adding new information. If you are updating records, you must have a field containing the e-mail addresses in the table you are updating or in a related table being updated.

**Note**

If you select the Enter The E-Mail Addresses In Microsoft Office Outlook option and click Next, the wizard allows you customize the subject of the message and include an introductory message for your recipients. After Access creates the message, you can click the To button in the Outlook message to open your Outlook address book and select one or more recipients for this message or manually type an e-mail address, and then click Send to send the message.

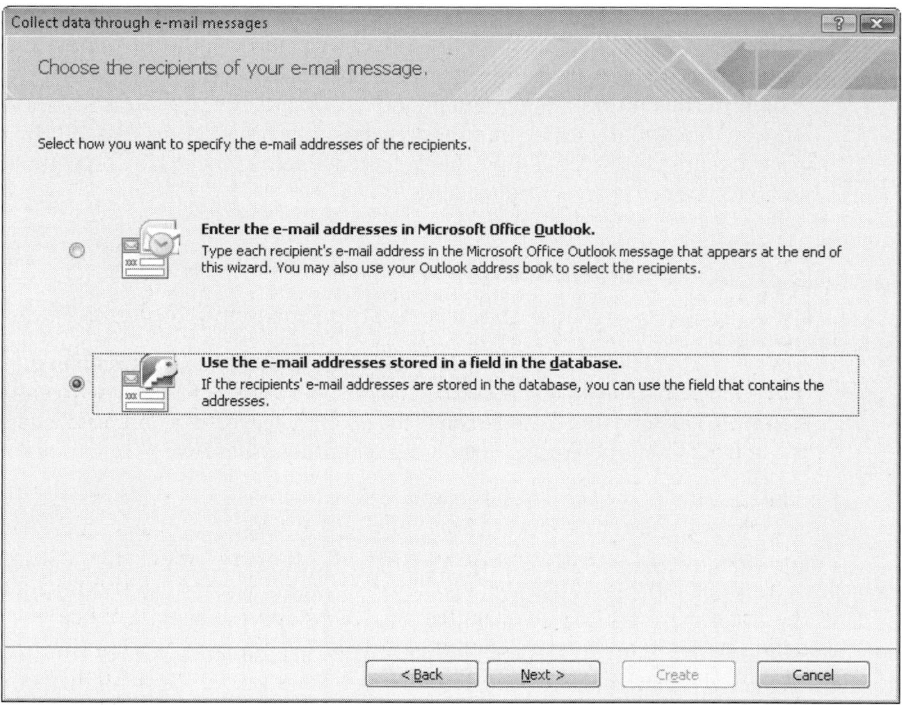


**Figure 6-23** Access asks for the source of the e-mail addresses on this page of the wizard.

On the next page of the wizard, shown in Figure 6-24, you tell Access which field contains the recipients' e-mail addresses. When you first see this page of the wizard, the default option is to select a field within the current table or query. If a field with e-mail addresses exists in the table you are updating, click the arrow in the Select A Field box below The Current Table Or Query and select the field that contains the e-mail addresses. In this example, Access correctly found the EmailName field and selected it for you.

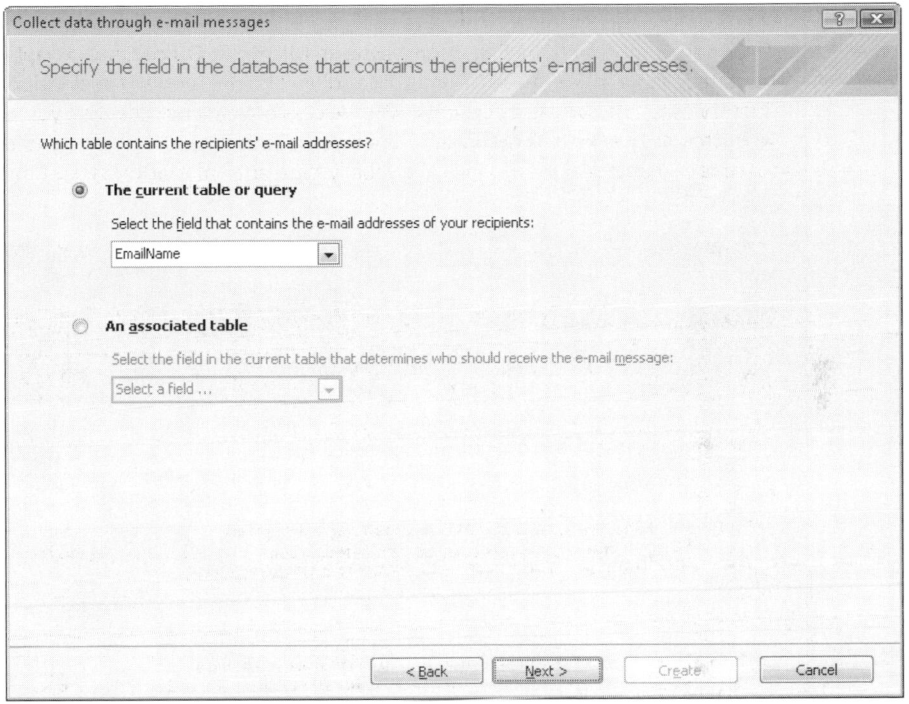


**Figure 6-24** You can choose a field in the current table or query or in an associated table from which to obtain the e-mail addresses.

You can also select the An Associated Table option to find the e-mail addresses in an associated table (one that is defined as related to the target table in the Relationships window). After you select An Associated Table, Access enables the Select A Field box beneath this option. First specify the linking field from the current table or query, and then select the field containing the e-mail addresses in the list of fields from the related table. In this sample database there is a relationship defined between the ContactID field in the tblContacts table and the ContactID field in the tblCompanyContacts, tblContactEvents, and tblCompanies tables. Because ContactID is associated with more than one table, Access displays two lists, as shown in Figure 6-25. The first list displays the names of the associated tables. Choose the table you want, and then select the associated field from the second list, which displays the names of all the fields in the table you select from the first list. Note that if the field you choose under An Associated Table is associated with only one table, Access displays only one list with the names of the fields in the associated table. Because the tblContacts table already contains the e-mail addresses you need, select The Current Table Or Query (if it isn't already), select the EmailName field from the list, and then click Next to continue.

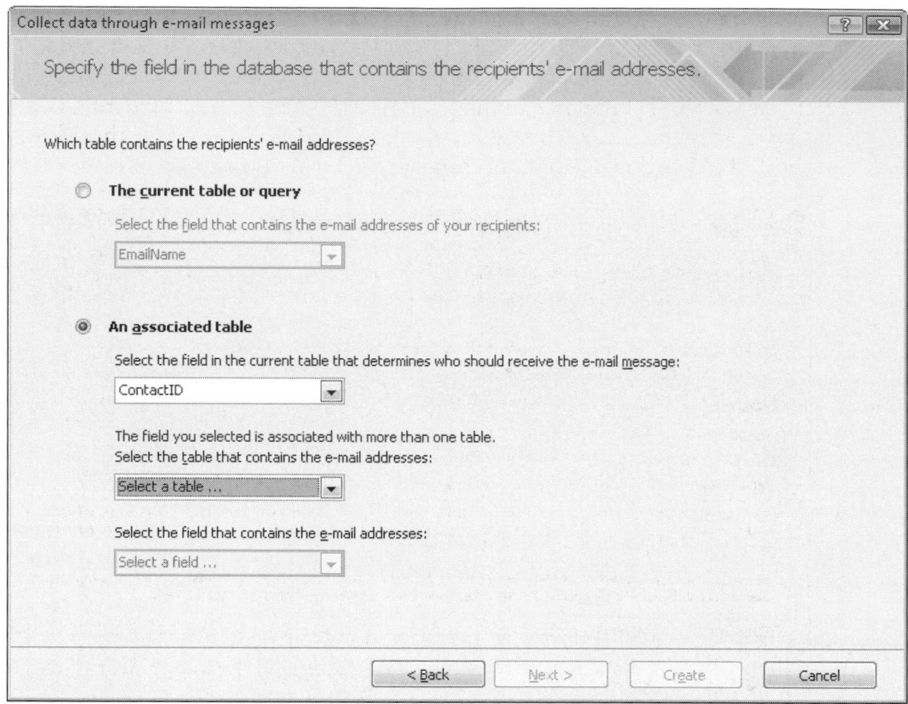


**Figure 6-25** Select the associated table and field that contain the e-mail addresses.

On the next page of the wizard, Customize The E-Mail Message, you can specify the Subject line of the e-mail, write an introductory message, and choose in which Outlook message field the address will appear (To, Cc, or Bcc), as shown in Figure 6-26. We designed our introduction to explain to our customers what the purpose of our message is and to offer them an incentive to provide us with some new contact information. In the Subject box, type

**Special offer for BO$$ customers!**

In the Introduction box, type

**We hope you're enjoying our BO$$ software and find it useful. Send us the contact information for any of your friends whom you think would benefit from our software, and we'll extend your support contract for one month for free for each contact who buys our product. Simply fill in the information below and send it back to us, and we'll do the rest!**

**To start, please make sure to click Reply first to fill out the form. Click Send when you are finished. To send information for more than one contact, click Reply again, fill out another form, and then click Send when you are finished.**

**Thank you for your business!**

**Conrad Systems Development**.

If you were updating existing rows, Outlook must be able to validate the update by matching the e-mail address of the sender with an e-mail field stored in the table being updated or in a related table. You won't be able to specify an e-mail address not already in the database, but you can instruct Access where to put the e-mail address in the message being sent. Leave this set to the default—To Field—to have the address displayed in the To field in the Outlook message. Click Next to continue.

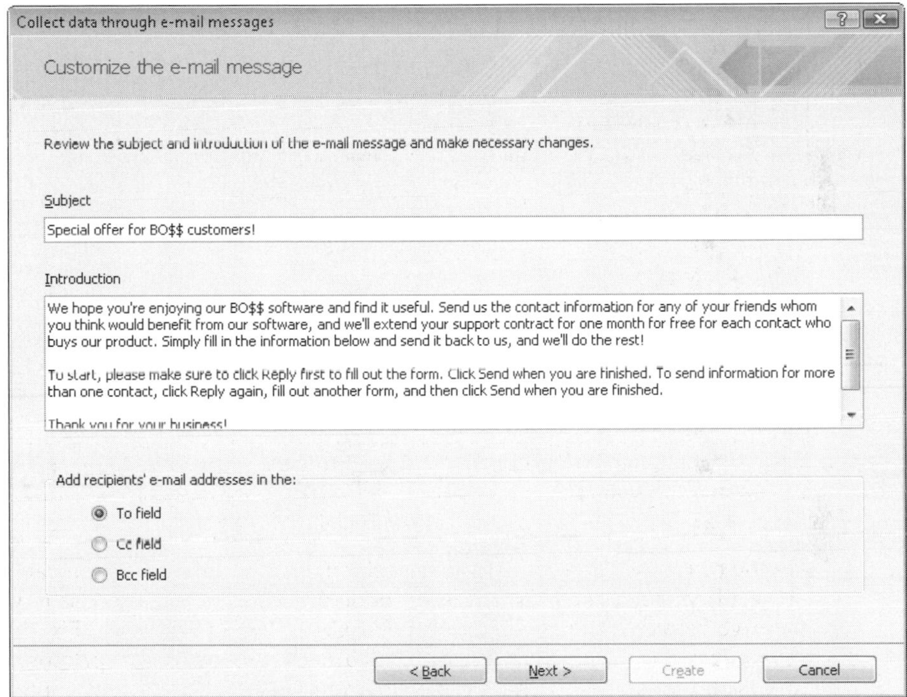


**Figure 6-26** Enter a descriptive subject line and introduction on this page of the wizard and specify where to place the e-mail address in the sent messages.

## INSIDE OUT Instruct the Recipient to Click Reply

We recommend that in your introductory message for HTML forms, you always include text instructing the recipient to click the Reply button before starting. It's not always intuitive from an end user's perspective that they first need to click Reply in order to fill out the form. By including some additional instruction in the introduction, you can avoid potential misunderstandings and support calls.

The next page of the wizard, shown in Figure 6-27, informs you that Access has all the information it needs to create the e-mail form and message. This page also provides information on how to view the status of e-mail messages and how Outlook will process the replies if you chose to have them automatically processed. Click Next to go to the final page of the wizard.

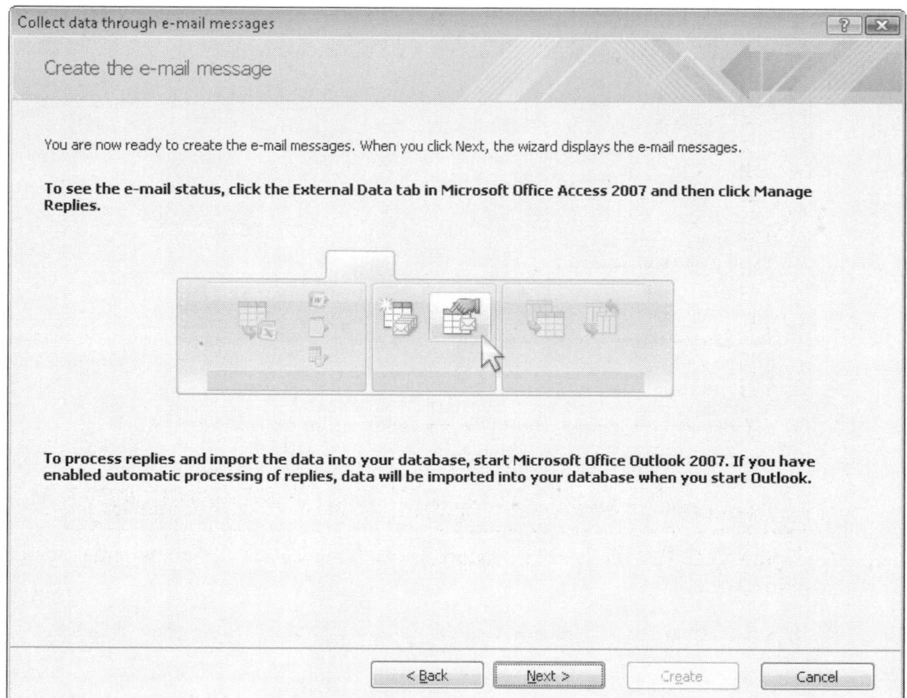


**Figure 6-27** Access is now ready to create your e-mail form.

You can choose which recipients to send the HTML form to on this page of the wizard, as shown in Figure 6-28. Because you asked Access to fetch the e-mail addresses from a field in your table, the wizard shows you the list of addresses that it found. Each e-mail address to which you're about to send the message is shown in the list with a check box at its right. Above the list, on the right, is a Select All check box. If you select this check box, Access selects all the e-mail addresses in the list. You can individually clear any check boxes next to the addresses to have Access not send the e-mail form to that person. If you added your e-mail address in the tblContacts table as instructed at the beginning of this section, select the check box for your e-mail address and clear all the other check boxes. (Much as we like to hear from our readers, we really don't need an e-mail message from you every time you follow this example!) Click Send to have Access create the form message and send it using Outlook. You won't be able to edit the messages further before Access sends them.

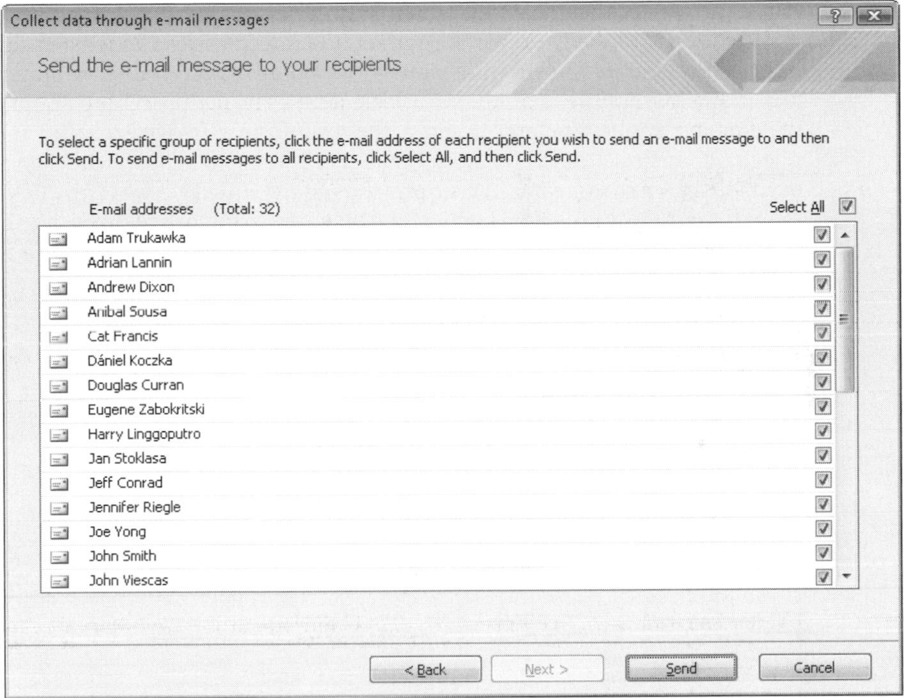


**Figure 6-28** You can select the people to whom you want to send the message on the final page of the wizard.

INSIDE OUT

### Considerations with Hyperlink Fields in Data Collection

In the initial release of Access 2007, there is a bug in the program that might prevent Access from sending the message if the field containing e-mail addresses is a Hyperlink data type and the address is formatted to *display* different text. As you'll learn in Chapter 7, you can add a descriptor in the Text To Display box at the top of the Edit Hyperlink dialog box. All the e-mail addresses in the ContactsDataCopy.accdb sample database display the name of the contact—Jeff Conrad, John Viescas, and so on—as shown in Figure 6-28. If you want to be sure the data collection process works, use e-mail addresses in a plain text field or ensure that the hyperlink includes no display text.

If you chose to enter the e-mail addresses instead of using addresses in the database, Access opens a new Outlook message with the information you provided in the wizard, as shown in Figure 6-29. (The message might not receive immediate focus, so look on your Windows taskbar for the message and maximize the window if necessary.) Figure 6-29 shows what your preview message looks like if you followed the previous instructions but chose to enter the e-mail addresses instead of using addresses in the database.

You can see the subject line you typed in the wizard and the custom introductory message at the top of the body section. Following the introduction, you can see Access has added some important information in a Note section. You can manually adjust the text in this part of the message body or leave it as is. (The warning about not altering the message applies to the recipient.) The rest of the message body has the 10 fields we selected to include in this form. In Figure 6-29, you can also see the custom label we used for the FirstName field. After previewing the message, you can click the To button to open your Outlook address book and select one or more recipients to send this message to or manually type an e-mail address, and then click Send to send the message.

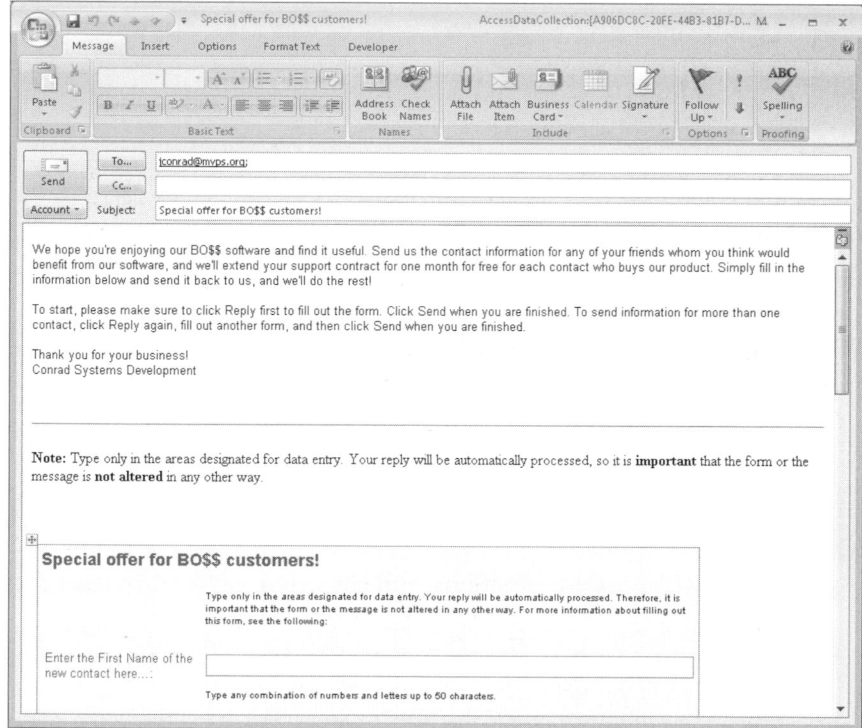


**Figure 6-29** You can preview your message if you choose to manually enter the e-mail addresses.

## Filling Out the HTML Form

When recipients receive the e-mail message form, it appears in their Inbox with the subject line you specified in the wizard, as shown in Figure 6-30. If you sent this message to yourself to see how this process works, open the message now to see what it looks like.

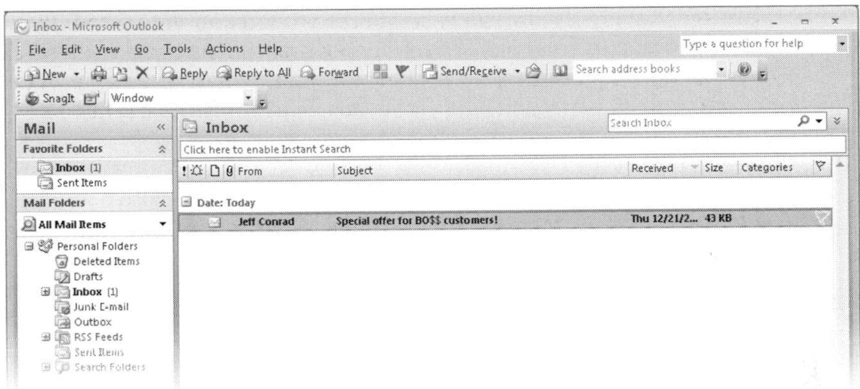


**Figure 6-30** An e-mail data collection form has arrived in the Inbox.

When you open the message as a recipient, you see all the information you previewed in Figure 6-29 if you chose to manually enter the e-mail addresses. (If you chose to use the e-mail addresses found in the table, this is the first time you'll see the completed message.) If you scroll down the message, you can see the form fields you need to fill in, but Outlook locks the fields and prevents you from filling them in. To be able to fill in the form fields, you need to click Reply first, as we discussed previously. Click Reply now and begin filling in the 10 fields, as shown in Figure 6-31. (We entered the information for a fictitious employee found in the Housing Reservations sample database.)

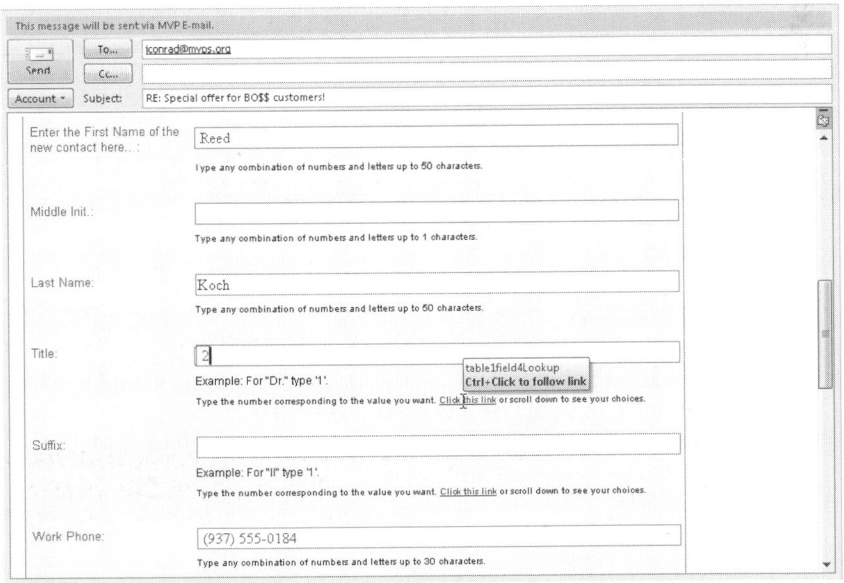

**Figure 6-31** After clicking Reply, you can fill in the fields on the form.

In Figure 6-31, you'll notice additional instructions beneath each form field. The HTML form recognizes the data type and size of each table field and displays some helpful text

Chapter 6

for the user. The FirstName field's Field Size property is set to 50, so the HTML form instructs the user to enter any text up to 50 characters. For fields defined as a Hyperlink data type—such as the EmailName and Website fields—the HTML form instructs the user to enter a hyperlink address in this field. For fields defined as the Number data type, the user is prompted to enter a numeric value. If you look at Figure 6-31, you'll also see that the HTML form includes a link under both the Title and Suffix form fields. These fields are designed to require a specific set of values with a lookup combo box or list box. When Access builds your e-mail message using HTML, it includes the lookup values at the bottom of the HTML form. Press and hold down the Ctrl key and click the link labeled Click This Link (a bookmark actually) beneath the Title field. Outlook moves you to the bottom of the HTML form, as shown in Figure 6-32. You can see the four title values and their numeric equivalents defined in the tlkpTitles table (Dr., Mr. Mrs., and Ms.) and the four suffix values defined in the tlkpSuffixes table (II, Jr., PhD, and Sr.). Find the values you need to enter for the two fields and then either scroll back up in the form or click the Title or Suffix link on the left to move back up in the form. At the bottom of the message, Outlook places a sentence instructing the user to click Send to submit the information. After you finish filling in the form, click Send to send the message back to yourself.

## INSIDE OUT Formatting Rich Text Fields

You might see HTML tags in an HTML or InfoPath update data collection form for fields defined in your table as Memo data types with the Text Format property set to Rich Text. If you highlight all the text and HTML tags in the HTML form field, you'll see a *mini-bar* appear over the field with a group of controls to format the text. (You won't see this mini-bar on an InfoPath form.) These controls are similar to the controls in the Rich Text group on the Home tab in Access 2007. If you change or remove any rich text formatting on the data collection form, Outlook exports the new formats into the Access field.

**CAUTION!**

Be careful when using fields defined as lookup values in a data collection form because Access needs to load all of these values into the HTML or InfoPath form. If your lookup table has hundreds or thousands of records, it will take Access a very long time to load all this information into the data collection form. In this example, we purposely omitted the WorkPostalCode and HomePostalCode fields because the related lookup table (tlkpZips) has more than 50,000 rows!

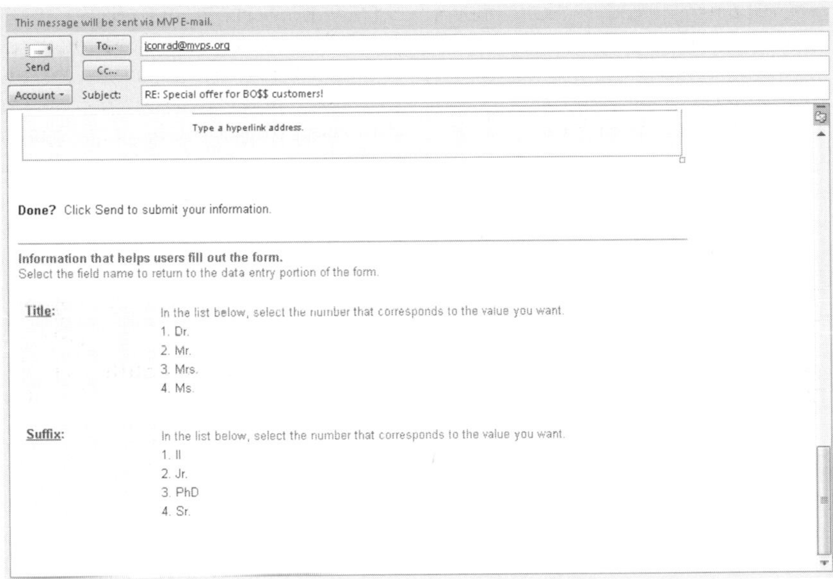


**Figure 6-32** Access includes the lookup values at the bottom of the HTML form to help you enter the correct values in the form fields.

## Having Outlook Automatically Process the Replies

After the message returns to you, Outlook places it in the folder you designated in the wizard. In our example, we left the designated folder set to the default–Access Data Collection Replies. In Figure 6-33, you can see that the message has arrived in the appropriate folder. You chose to have this message automatically processed, so Outlook immediately exported the new record to the tblContacts table. Notice, under the Data Collection Status column, that Outlook successfully exported the record to Access. You can open the message to see how the recipient filled in the form fields, but it's not necessary to open the reply in order to have Outlook export the data.

**CAUTION!**

If you're using an HTTP-based e-mail system such as MSN or Hotmail, your new messages arrive in the inbox for your e-mail account, not the primary Inbox in Outlook. You'll have to move the messages to your Outlook Inbox and process them manually by opening each message and clicking the Export To Access button on the message Ribbon.

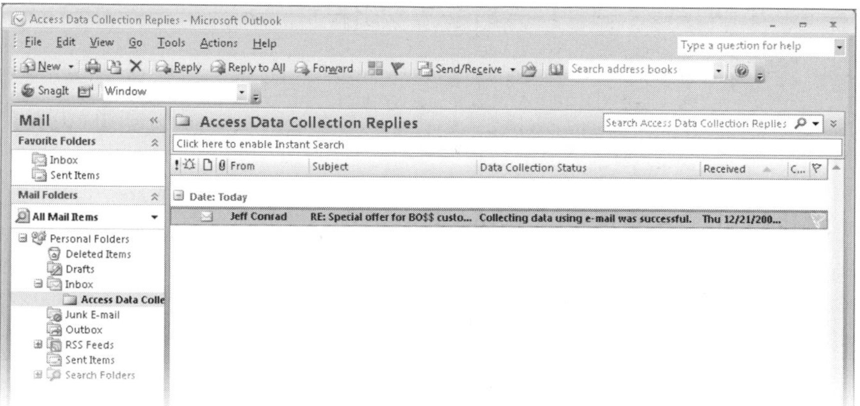


**Figure 6-33** Access automatically processes the message when you receive it.

Minimize your Outlook program and then maximize the ContactsDataCopy.accdb database again (or open the database if you closed it) to see if the record has been added. Select the tblContacts table in the Navigation Pane and then open it in Datasheet view. As you can see in Figure 6-34, a new record has been added to the table with the contact information you provided on the HTML form. Our client has helped add new information to the database without ever opening Access; in fact, the recipients do not even need to have Access installed for this process.

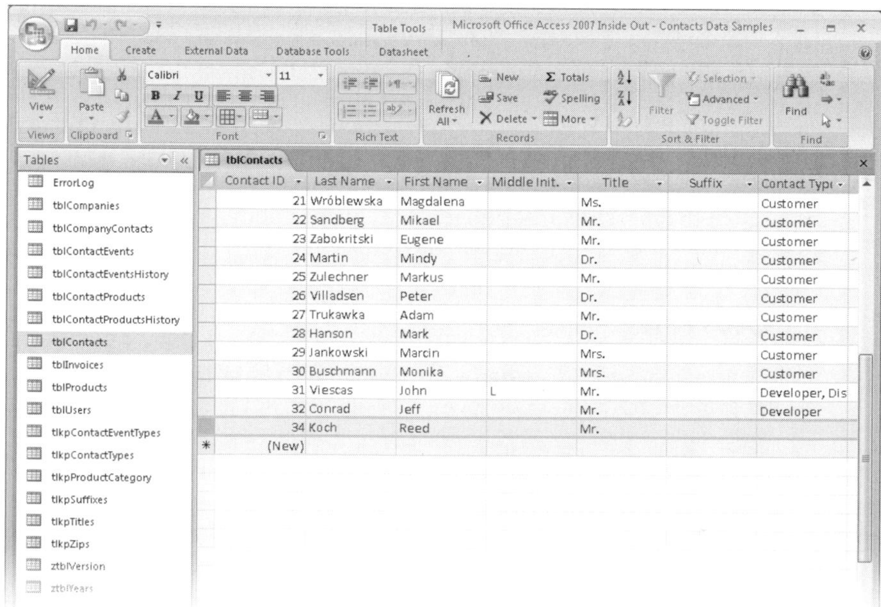


**Figure 6-34** Our new contact information has now been added to the tblContacts table.

Chapter 6

## Collecting Data Using InfoPath Forms

Access 2007 also allows you to send InfoPath forms to e-mail recipients to collect data. Unlike HTML forms, InfoPath forms provide richer tools, such as the ability to display drop-down lists. To be able to reply to messages sent with InfoPath forms, your recipients need to have Outlook 2007 and InfoPath 2007 installed on their computers. In addition to demonstrating collecting data through InfoPath forms, we'll choose different options in the wizard so that you can understand some of the other features available with using InfoPath.

Open TasksEmailCollection.accdb from the folder where you installed your sample files. For this example, we'll update an existing record in the Tasks table and add a new record to the Tasks table. However, because updating data via e-mail requires an e-mail address in the database to validate your authority to perform the update, you'll need to add yourself and your e-mail address if you want to follow along in this section. You'll also need to add a task assigned to you that you can update. Open the Contacts table in Datasheet view, go to the new record at the end, add your name and valid e-mail address, and save the record. Open the Tasks table in Datasheet view, and add a new sample task assigned to yourself. Close both tables when you're done.

Close any open database objects, select the Tasks table in the Navigation Pane, and on the External Data tab, in the Collect Data group, click the Create E-Mail button. Alternatively, you can right-click the table in the Navigation Pane and click Collect And Update Data Via E-Mail on the shortcut menu. Access opens the first page of the e-mail collection wizard, as shown in Figure 6-35. This first page is an introductory page, which outlines the steps you take to complete the process. For this example, you need to complete six major steps. Click Next to proceed to the second page of the wizard.

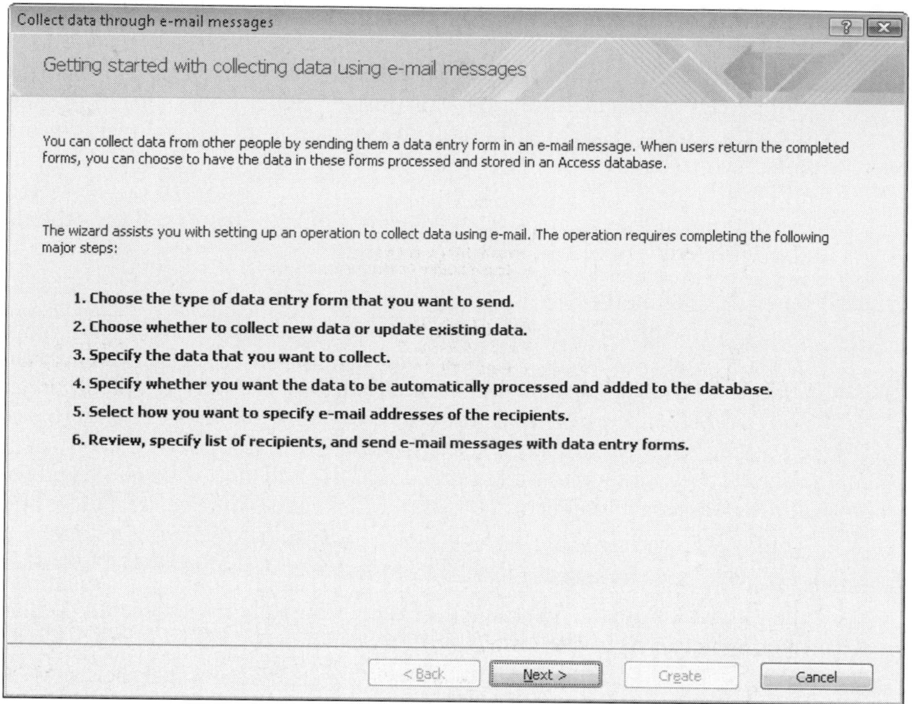


**Figure 6-35** The first page of the wizard outlines the steps you take to collect data through e-mail.

The second page of the wizard, shown in Figure 6-36, asks you to choose between creating an HTML form or an InfoPath form for data entry. Remember that the people who receive the InfoPath form need to have InfoPath 2007 and Outlook 2007 installed on their computers to be able to read and fill out the data form. For this example, select Microsoft Office InfoPath Form and click Next.

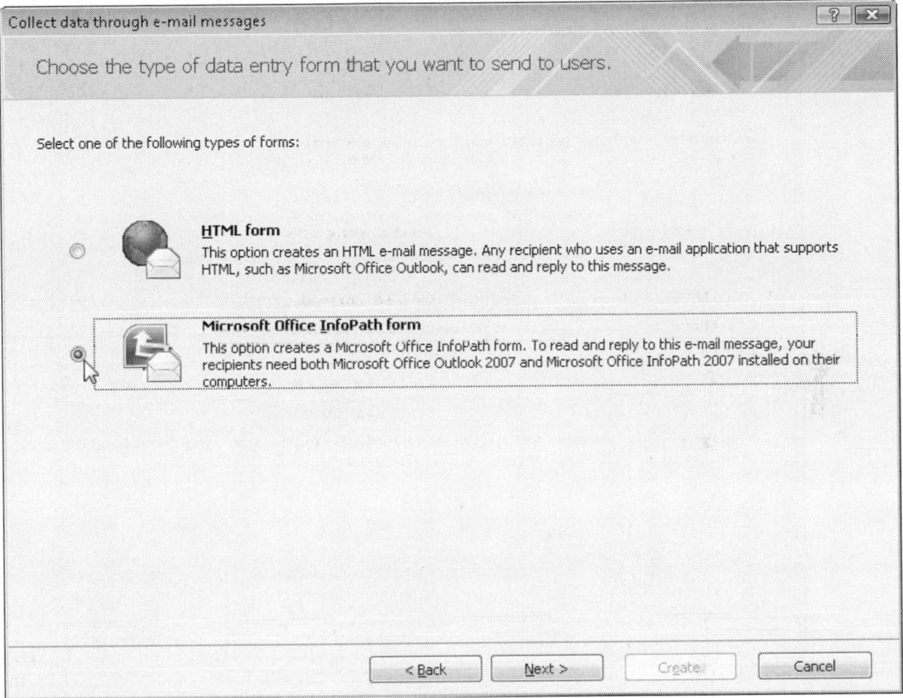


**Figure 6-36** Select the second option to create an InfoPath form.

The next page of the wizard, shown in Figure 6-37, asks you to choose whether users should receive a blank form or a form that includes data from within the database they will update. If you chose a table that has no records, a table that does not have a primary key defined, or a query that combines two or more tables, you will not see this page of the wizard. (You'll learn more about creating queries using two or more tables in Chapter 8.) If you select the first option after having chosen the InfoPath form on the previous page, a recipient of your e-mail can add one or more records with each reply. The recipients can add additional records by clicking the Insert A Row command on the InfoPath form.

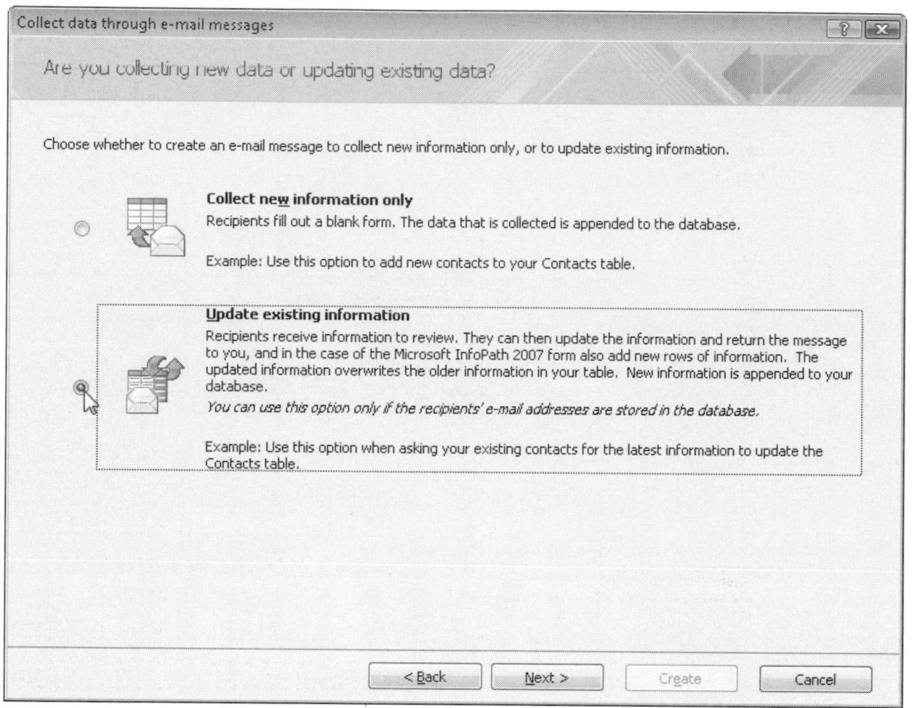


**Figure 6-37** You can choose to collect new information or update existing records on this page of the wizard.

You can use the second option, Update Existing Information, only if e-mail addresses are stored in a field in the table or a related table. With this option, e-mail recipients can view or update one or more records with each reply, depending on how many records are associated with their e-mail address. Recipients can also add additional records by clicking the Insert A Row command on the InfoPath form unless you disable this capability in an option presented later in the wizard. In this example, you will update the existing record in the Tasks table and create a new record, so select Update Existing Information and then click Next to proceed.

On the next page of the wizard, shown in Figure 6-38, you decide which fields from the table or query to include in the e-mail form. By default, Access automatically places any fields whose Required property is set to Yes in the Fields To Include In E-Mail Message list on the right. Notice that Access places the Title and Status fields in the Fields To Include In E-Mail Message list because they are required fields. For this example, we want to use all the fields in the Tasks table, so click the double right arrow (>>) button to move the remaining six fields to the list on the right, as shown in Figure 6-38. If you don't want to include all fields and you move a field in error, you can select that field and move it back by clicking the left arrow (<) button. If you decide you want to start over, you can remove all fields (except the required fields) by clicking the double left arrow (<<) button.

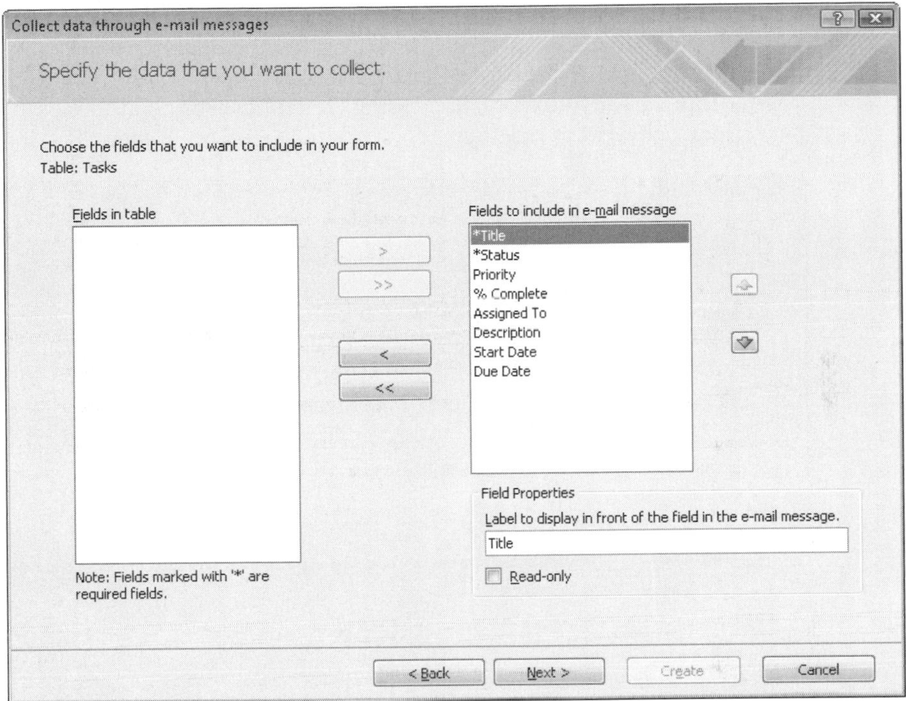


**Figure 6-38** Move all the fields in the Tasks table to the Fields To Include In E-Mail Message list.

Notice that Access fills in the field's Caption property (or the field name if the field does not have a caption) in the Label To Display In Front Of The Field In The E-Mail Message box under Field Properties. You can customize this label to display different text or leave it as is. For this example, leave each of the label captions set to their defaults. The recipients will see the fields in the order that they appear in the list on the right. You can select any field in this list and move it up or down in the sequence by clicking the up and down arrows to the right of the list. The default sequence is fine for this example, so you don't need to move any fields. Also, leave the Read-Only check box cleared for all of the fields, and then click Next to continue to the next page.

The next page of the wizard, shown in Figure 6-39, asks you to specify how you want to manage the replies. By default, all replies are stored in an Outlook folder called Access Data Collection Replies. If you want to change where Outlook saves replies, click the Access Data Collection Replies link. The wizard opens the Select Folder dialog box in Outlook where you can select the Outlook folder you want to use or create a new folder. In this case, leave the default Access Data Collection Replies folder as the destination folder. In the HTML example earlier, you chose to have Outlook automatically process the replies. In this example, leave the Automatically Process Replies And Add Data To Tasks check box cleared so that you can see how to manually process the replies. The Only Allow Updates To Existing Data check box is available only when you are updating data and you have chosen to automatically process the replies. If you choose to automatically process the replies and then select this option, Access does not allow new records to be added to the table. This option appears dimmed in our example because we are going to manually process the replies. Remember also from the HTML example that when you ask Outlook to automatically process replies, you can click Set Properties To Control The Automatic Processing Of Replies. For details, refer to Figure 6-22 on page 314. Click Next to continue.

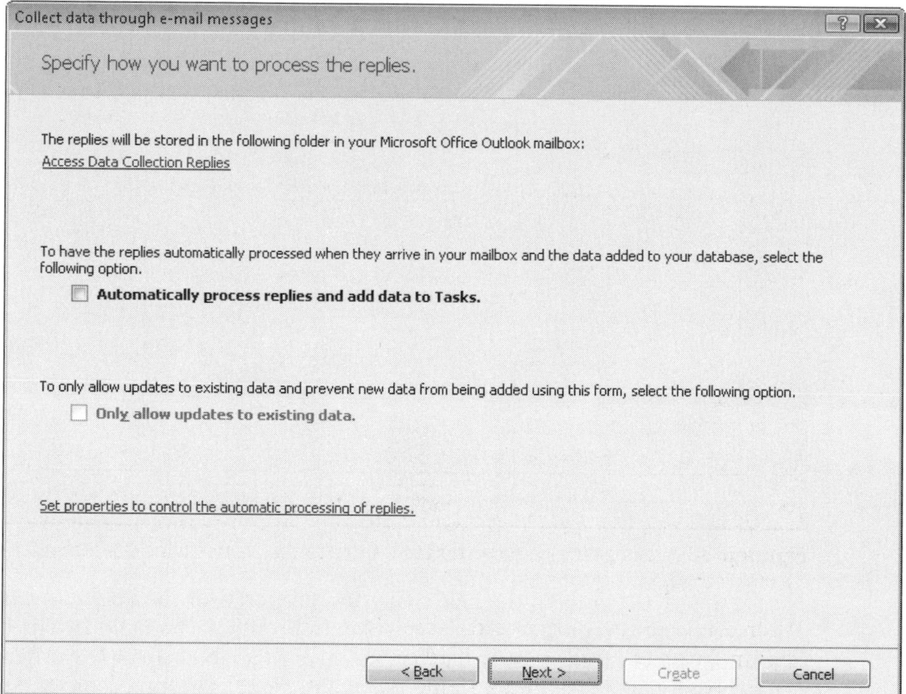


**Figure 6-39** Leave these check boxes cleared to manually process the replies.

On the next page of the wizard, shown in Figure 6-40, you tell Access which field contains the recipients' e-mail addresses. When you first see this page of the wizard, the default option is to select a field within the current table or query. If an e-mail address exists in the table you are updating, click the arrow in the Select A Field box below The Current Table Or Query and select the field that contains the e-mail addresses. However, in this case, no e-mail addresses are stored in the Tasks table in this database; rather, they are stored in the E-mail Address field in the Contacts table, so select the An Associated Table option.

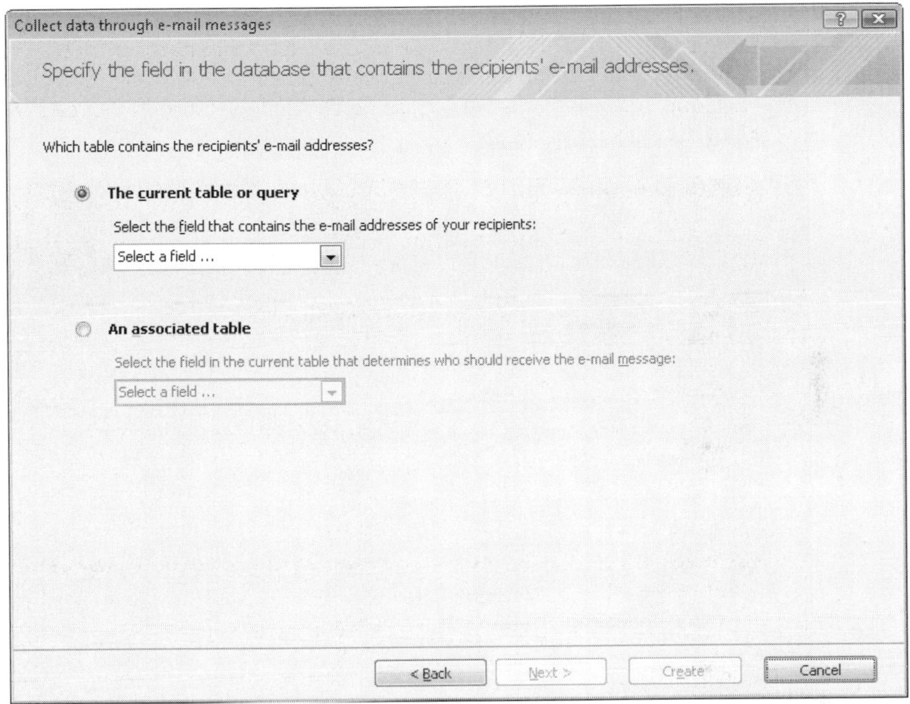


**Figure 6-40** You can choose a field in the current table or query or in an associated table from which to obtain the e-mail addresses.

After you select An Associated Table, Access enables the Select A Field box beneath this option. You need to select the field in the Tasks table that links to a related field in the Contacts table. In this database there is a relationship defined between the Assigned To field in the Tasks table and the ID field in the Contacts table. Select Assigned To in this box, and Access displays one additional option, as shown in Figure 6-41. Access displays all the fields in the Contacts table in the Select A Field box. Select E-mail Address from the list of fields and then click Next to go to the next page of the wizard. Note that if the field you choose under An Associated Table is associated with more than one table, Access displays two lists. The first list displays the names of the associated tables. Choose the table you want, and then select the associated field from the second list, which displays the names of all the fields in the table you select from the first list.

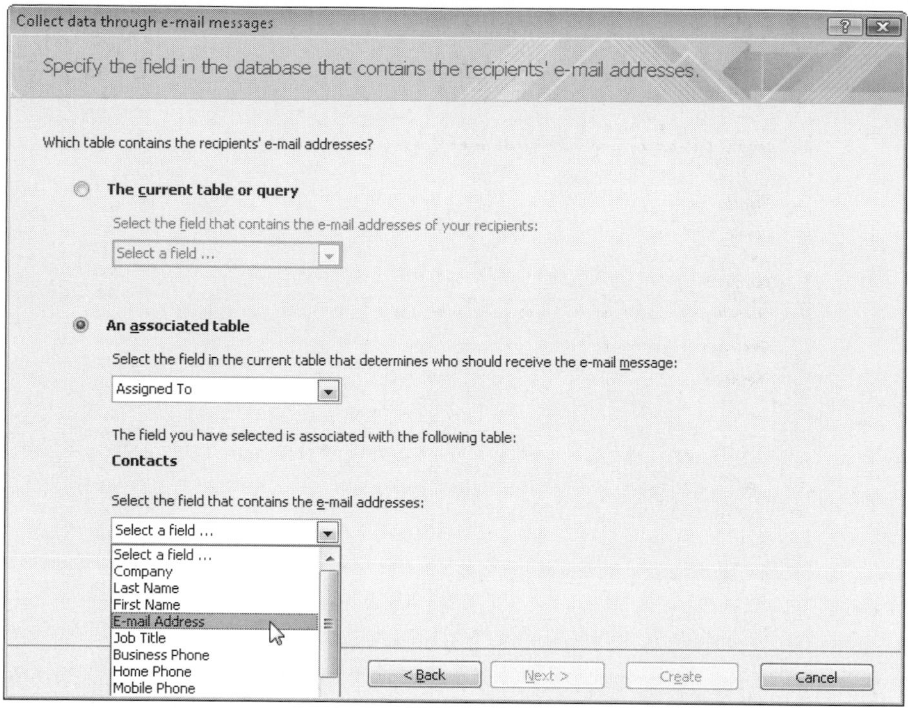


**Figure 6-41** Select E-mail Address from the field list for the Contacts table.

On the next page of the wizard, you can specify the Subject line of the e-mail, write an introductory message, and choose in which Outlook message field the address will appear (To, Cc, or Bcc), as shown in Figure 6-42. In the Subject box, type

**Update Assigned Tasks**

In the Introduction box, type

**Please fill out the form included in this message to update the Task information and send it back to me.**

**Click Submit when you are finished.**

**Thank you.**

Because you chose to update data, three options appear at the bottom of this page, under Add Recipients' E-Mail Addresses In The. To be able to validate the updating of existing rows, Outlook must be able to match the e-mail address of the sender with an e-mail field stored in the table being updated or in a related table. You won't be able to specify an e-mail address not already in the table, but you can tell Access where to put the e-mail address in the message being sent. Leave this set to the default option—To Field—to have the address displayed in the To field in the Outlook message. Click Next to continue.

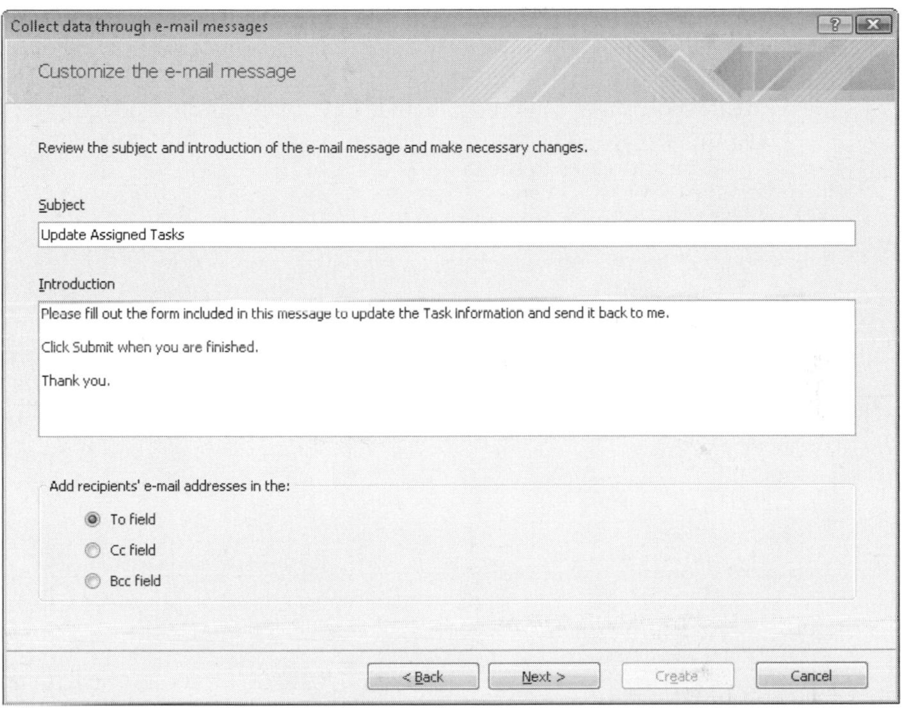


**Figure 6-42** Enter a descriptive subject line and introduction on this page of the wizard and specify where to place the e-mail address in the sent messages.

The last page of the wizard, shown in Figure 6-43, informs you that Access has all the information it needs to create the e-mail form and message. You'll notice in Figure 6-43 that Access displays a warning message at the bottom of this page. You might see any one of three possible messages in this box:

- "Note: These e-mail messages might contain data that is of a confidential or sensitive nature." Access always displays this message when you update existing records because the recipients might see data currently in the table that is of a sensitive nature. You might consider removing from the e-mail any fields with sensitive data if you are concerned that this could be a problem.
- "You currently have an exclusive lock on the database; automatic processing will fail until the lock is released." Outlook cannot process replies if you have the database open in exclusive mode. In order to process the replies, you need to close the database and then reopen it in shared mode. By default, Access should open all databases in shared mode unless you changed the setting in the Advanced category of the Access Options dialog box. You can also open a database in exclusive or shared mode using the Open dialog box if you click the arrow on the Open button and then click the appropriate command (such as Open Exclusive).
- "Some records do not contain a valid address in the specified e-mail address field. No data will be returned for these rows." Before you get to this page of the

wizard, Access runs a quick scan for any Null values in the e-mail address field you designated on the previous page of the wizard. Access displays this warning message if it finds any Null values because it will not be able to send a message for all records that could be updated. You can either proceed with the data collection process with some being left out, or cancel the wizard and then add any missing e-mail addresses to the table.

Click Next to go to the final page of the wizard.

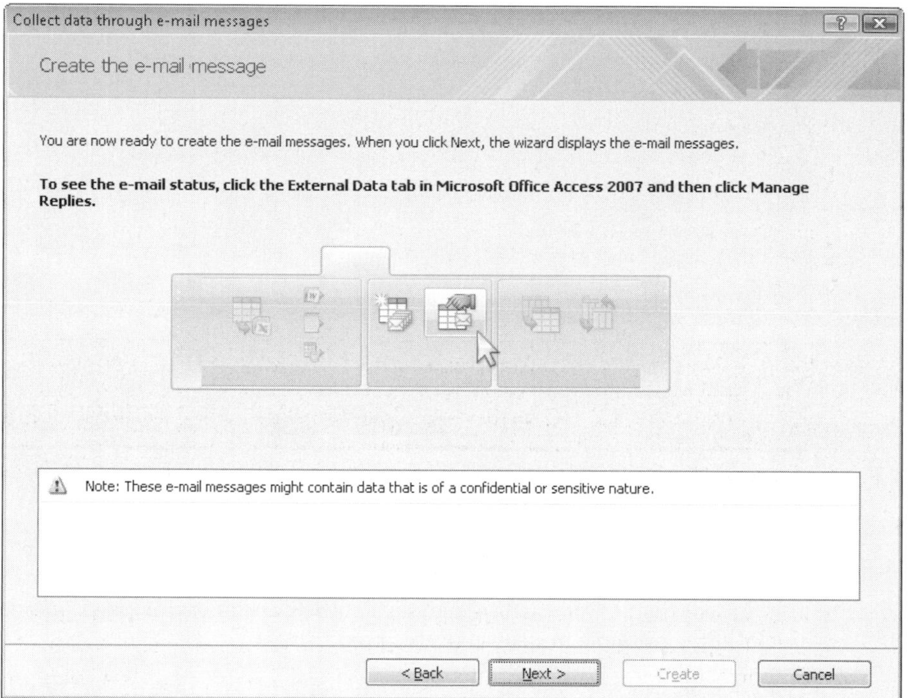


**Figure 6-43** Access displays potential issues that might cause problems with the data collection process.

You can choose which recipients to send the InfoPath form to on the final page of the wizard, as shown in Figure 6-44. Each e-mail address related to a record you're about to send out for update is shown in the list with a check box at its right. Above the list, to the right, is a Select All check box. If you select this check box, Access selects all the e-mail addresses in the list. You can individually clear any check boxes next to the addresses to have Access not send the e-mail form to that person. When we ran our example, there was only one e-mail address related to the one record in the Tasks table. If you added your e-mail address in the Contacts table and a related record in the Tasks table as instructed at the beginning of this section, select your e-mail address and clear the check box next to jconrad@mvps.org. (Much as we like to hear from our readers, we really don't need an e-mail message from you every time you follow this example!) Click Send to have Access create the form message and send it using Outlook 2007.

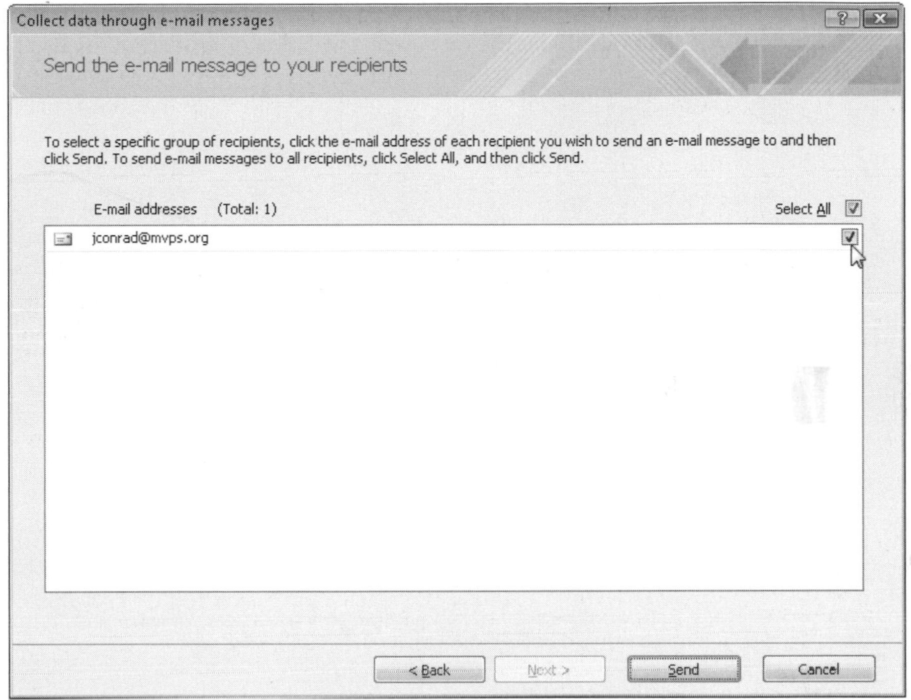


**Figure 6-44** You can select the people to whom you want to send the message on the final page of the wizard.

## Filling Out the InfoPath Form

When recipients receive an e mail form created using InfoPath, the message arrives in their Inboxes with an attachment. After opening the message, a recipient can fill out the form and update the information. Unlike HTML forms, InfoPath allows you to send forms that are easier for the recipients to fill out. In Figure 6-45, you can see that the Status field is displayed as a combo box. The recipient must select from one of the five available Status options because this field is a lookup field in the Tasks table.

With InfoPath forms, you can have more control over the data that comes back in the replies. You achieve this by designing fields in your tables that require a specific set of values with a lookup combo box or list box. When Access builds your e-mail message using InfoPath, it includes the lookup values in the InfoPath form. If you were, for example, to send an HTML form with the same fields in the Tasks table, the recipients can see all the lookup values listed at the bottom of the form. However, they could still type any value into the Status box, including text that is not one of your five choices. Outlook will encounter errors processing the HTML reply if it tries to export that record into the Tasks table in Access because the Limit To List property of the Status field is set to True. In Figure 6-45, you also see a button next to any date field, which opens a calendar for you to select a date, just as you can from within Access. If you use

InfoPath forms, you can reduce the number of problems with inaccurate data, and make it easier for users to fill out the form with the built-in InfoPath form controls.

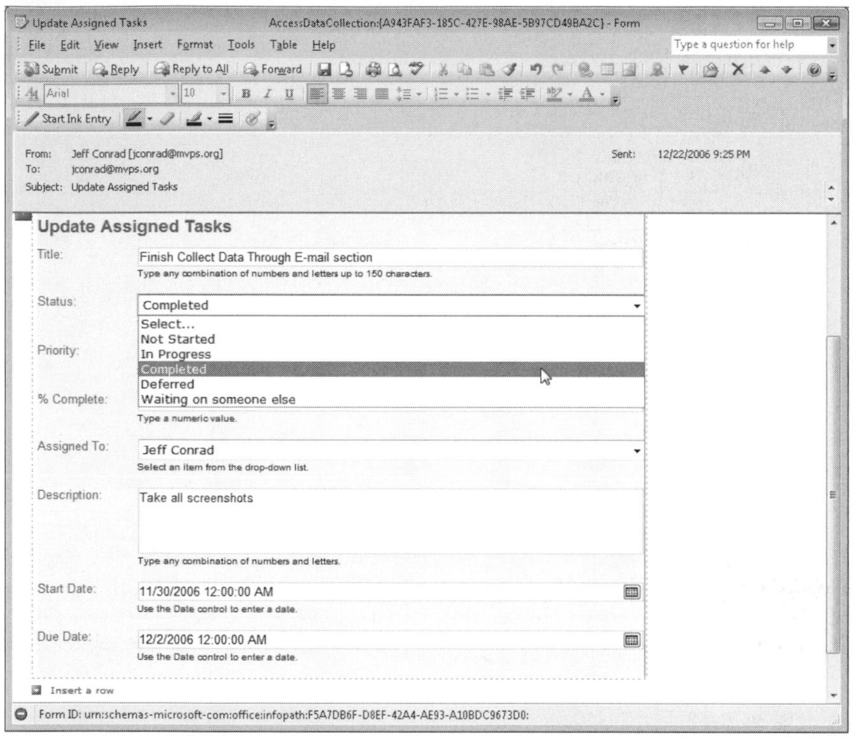


**Figure 6-45** InfoPath forms allow you to use combo box controls for data entry.

For this example, change the status from Not Started to Completed by selecting Completed in the Status box, and change the value in the % Complete field from 0 to 100 to indicate the task is 100 percent complete. You can also create a new record in the InfoPath form by clicking the Insert A Row link in the lower-left corner of the form, as shown in Figure 6-46. For example, you might want to assign a new task to yourself or another contact in the database.

**Figure 6-46** Click Insert A Row on an InfoPath form to add additional records.

After you click the link, a new InfoPath form appears below the existing form with blank fields, as shown in Figure 6-47. You can now fill out the form fields for a new record. You'll notice the two required fields—Title and Status—have a red asterisk on the right to indicate to the recipient that those fields are required. You might also notice the InfoPath form recognizes the data type and size of each table field and displays some helpful text for the user. The Title field's Field Size property is set to 150, so InfoPath instructs the user to enter any text up to 150 characters. The % Complete field is a Number data type in the Tasks table, so InfoPath instructs the user to enter a numeric value in this field.

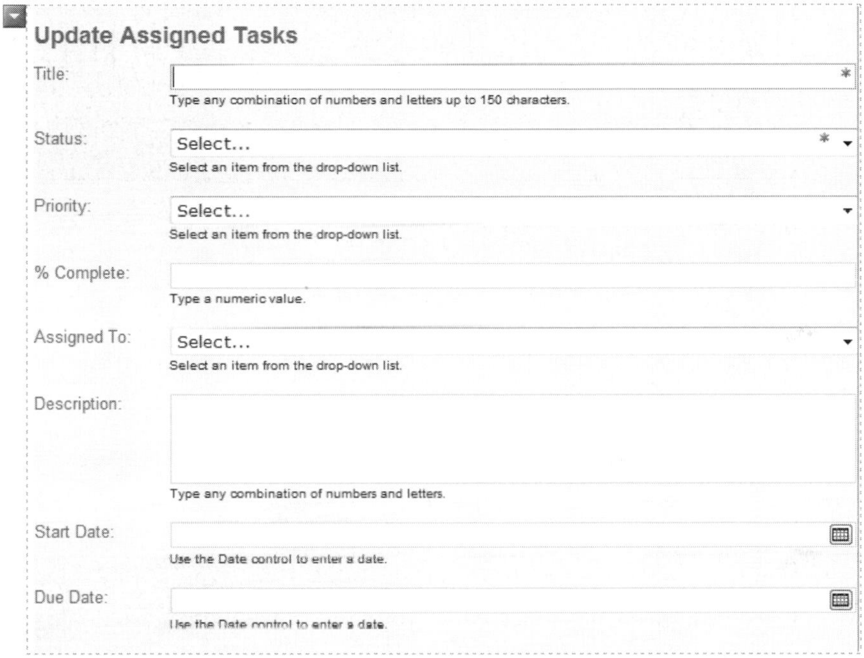

**Figure 6-47** The recipient of the e-mail can add new records in the InfoPath form if you selected this option in the wizard.

If you like, you can create a new record in this blank InfoPath form using the following information:

| | |
|---|---|
| Title | **Review Chapter 6** |
| Status | Not Started |
| Priority | (1) High |
| % Complete | **0** |
| Assigned To | John Viescas |
| Description | **Please review all the changes to Chapter 6** |
| Start Date | Click the calendar control and click the current date |
| Due Date | Click the calendar control and select the date three days after the start date |

Your completed record should be similar to Figure 6-48.

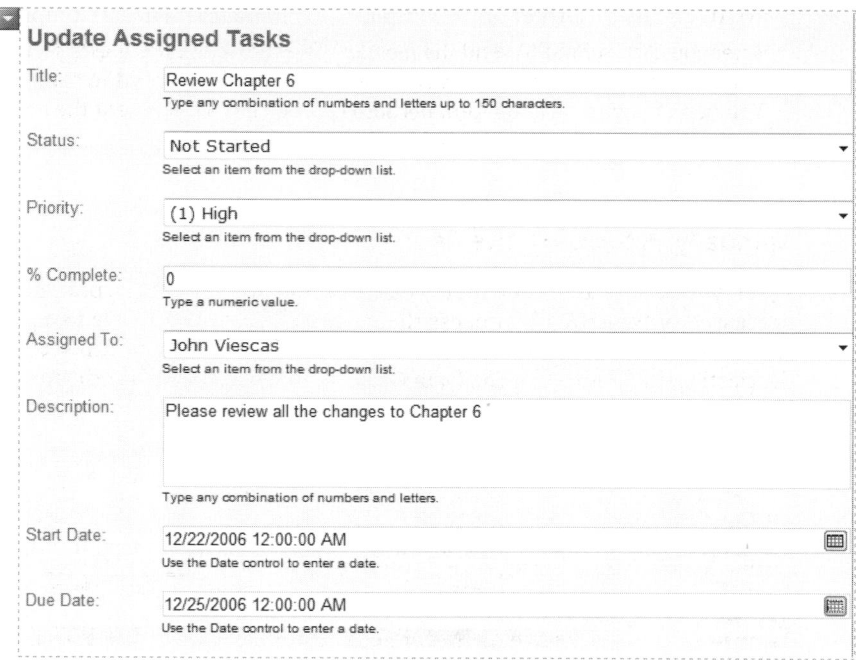


**Figure 6-48** Fill out the blank form to add a new record to the Tasks table.

If you want to create more records, you can scroll down and click the Insert A Row link again to display an additional blank form. If you need to delete a record, click the arrow button in the upper-left corner of the InfoPath form and then click Remove on the menu that appears, as shown in Figure 6-49. You can also insert a new blank record above or below the current record by clicking the Insert Above or Insert Below option.

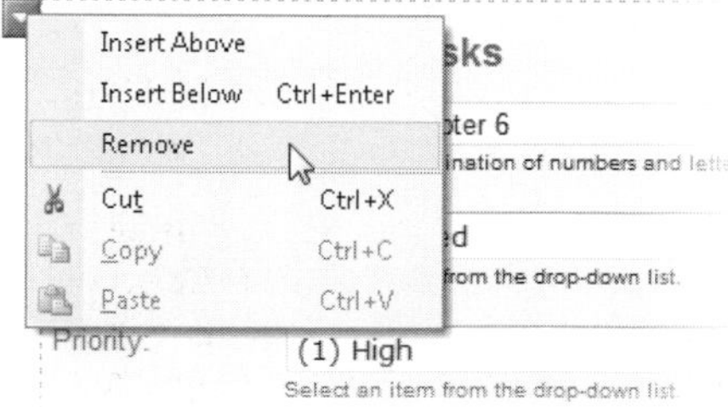


**Figure 6-49** Click Remove to delete a record in the InfoPath form.

After you update the first record and add the new record on this InfoPath form, click Submit on the Outlook Standard toolbar to send this message. Outlook opens a confirmation dialog box where you can modify the To, Cc, or Bcc addresses, change the subject, and enter explanatory text. Click Send in that dialog box to send your updates. Outlook displays a confirmation message box indicating that the form was submitted successfully.

> **Note**
>
> After you click Submit to send the message and then close the message, InfoPath displays a message that the form was changed and asks if you want to save the changes. You don't need to save the form because Outlook has already sent the message.

## Manually Processing the Replies

When you collect data via e-mail, you can choose to have the replies automatically processed or to manually process them yourself. In our example using InfoPath forms, you chose to manually process the replies. In Figure 6-50 you can see the message is in the destination folder, but the Data Collection Status column indicates Message Unprocessed. No data has yet been exported to the Tasks table.

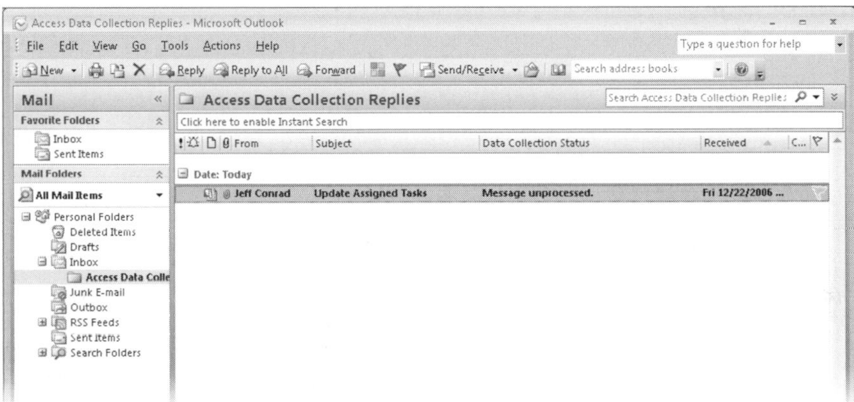


**Figure 6-50** The Data Collection Status column in Outlook indicates that the message has not been processed.

To manually process this reply, right-click the message in Outlook 2007 and click Export Data To Microsoft Office Access on the shortcut menu, as shown in Figure 6-51.

Access opens the Export Data To Microsoft Access dialog box, as shown in Figure 6-52. You can see that the first record is the one with updates, and the second is the new record. You can use the horizontal scroll bar to scroll to the right to see what data will be added or changed in the various fields. If you find something inaccurate, perhaps an invalid Start Date or Due Date value, you can click Cancel to stop the export process. You can then send the message back to the recipient and ask for corrected data. See "Managing and Resending Data Collection Messages from Access" on page 343 for more information. All the data in this example should be fine, so click OK to have Outlook export the data to Access.

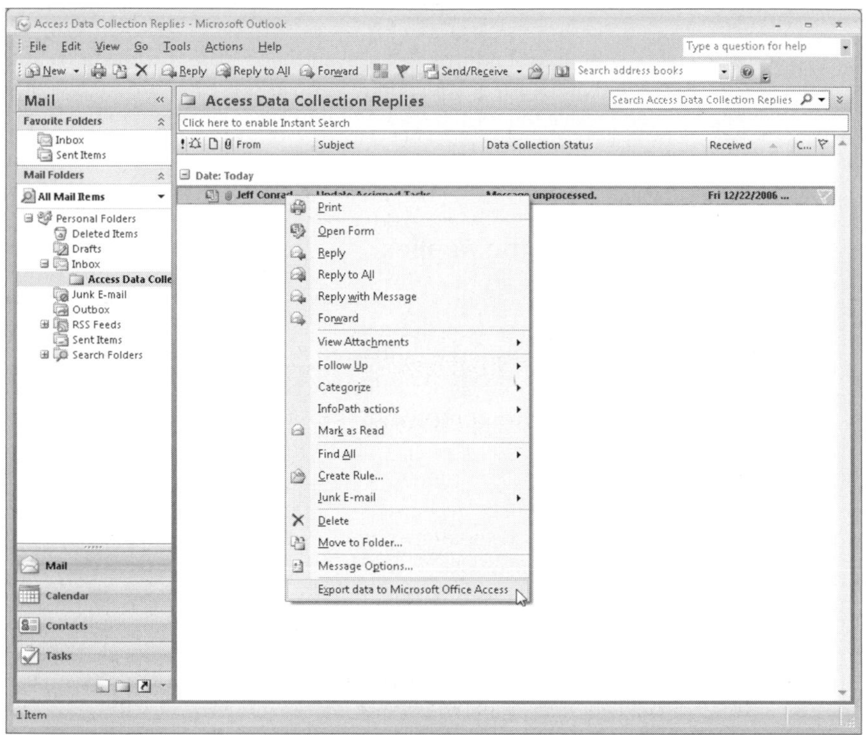


**Figure 6-51** Use the message's context-sensitive menu within Outlook to export the data to Access.

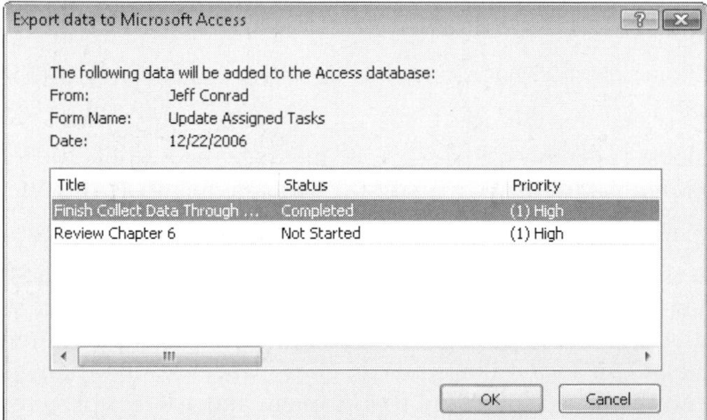


**Figure 6-52** You can review the data to be exported to Access in this dialog box.

If the export process is successful, Outlook displays a confirmation dialog box. Click OK to close the dialog box. If Outlook encounters any errors in the export process, it displays a message indicating that it failed to export all or part of the data. In this case, you should resend the message and ask for corrected data.

Return to the TasksEmailCollection.accdb sample database and open the Tasks table in Datasheet view. In Figure 6-53, you can see the first record is updated with the correct data–the Status field is now changed from Not Started to Completed and the % Complete field is changed from 0 to 100 to indicate the task is 100 percent complete. You can also see that the new record concerning Chapter 6 has been added.

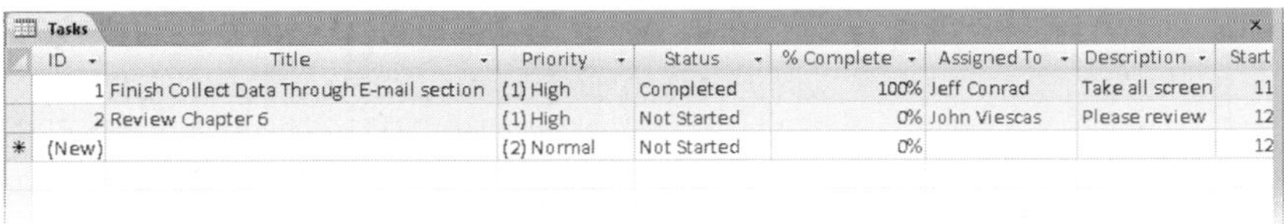


**Figure 6-53** The updated and new data is now added to the Tasks table.

## Managing and Resending Data Collection Messages from Access

You can review the status of sent data collection messages and resend messages by clicking the Manage Replies button in the Collect Data group on the External Data tab on the Ribbon. Access opens the Manage Data Collection Messages dialog box, as shown in Figure 6-54. Under Select A Data Collection Message, you can see the example message we sent, which table or query the message was based on, the message type, and the destination Outlook folder. When you select a message in the list, the Message Details section in the bottom half of the dialog box displays the fields included in the message, the date and time the message was created and last sent, whether the reply was automatically or manually processed, and the date and time to stop automatic processing.

To delete a message from this dialog box, select it and then click the Delete This E-Mail Message button. To review the message options, select the message and click the Message Options button. Access opens the Collecting Data Using E-Mail Options dialog box previously shown in Figure 6 22 on page 314. Here you can review and modify the settings for the message. For example, if you set the original message to automatically process replies, you can turn off automatic processing, change the number of messages to be processed, or change the automatic processing end date. You can also turn on automatic processing if it wasn't enabled in the original message. Note that any changes you make apply to new replies you receive.

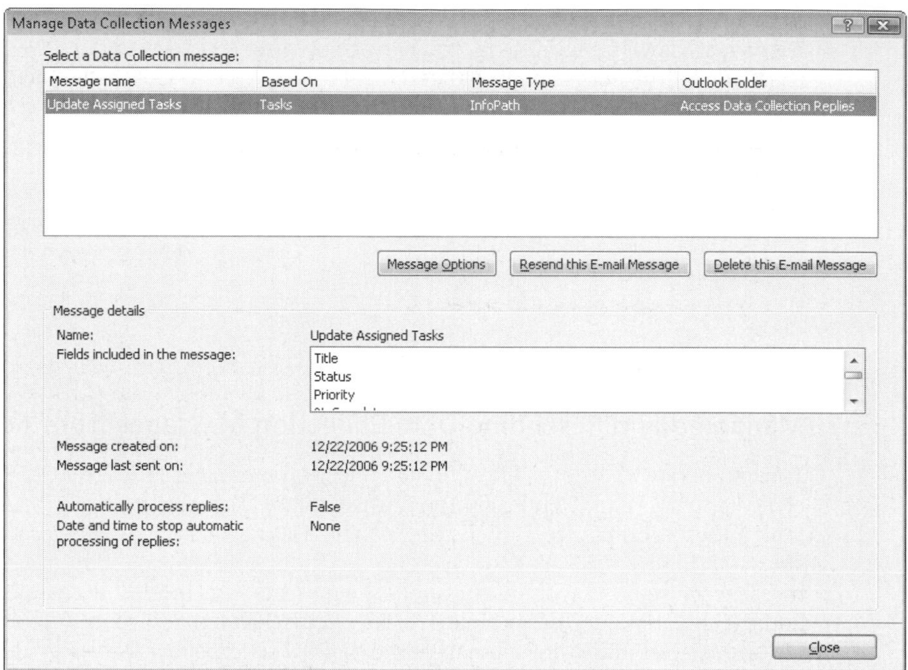


**Figure 6-54** You can review the status of sent messages in the Manage Data Collection Messages dialog box.

If want to send a message again—either because the recipient entered incorrect or incomplete data or you want the recipient to send new data—you can select the message and click the Resend This E-Mail Message button. You might also want to send the same message to additional people or resend it to someone who failed to receive the initial message. Note that you cannot go to Outlook and forward a data collection message; you must use the resend process. When you click the Resend This E-Mail Message button, Access restarts the Collecting Data Through E-Mail Messages wizard beginning with the page that asks you how you want to process replies, as shown in Figure 6-55. (This page is similar to Figure 6-39 page 332.) You can adjust any settings—such as manual or automatic replies or where the e-mail addresses come from—and customize the message details. You can click through the remaining steps of the wizard and then click Create or Send depending on what type of message (HTML or InfoPath) you are sending. Access creates a new message and sends it to the recipients using Outlook 2007.

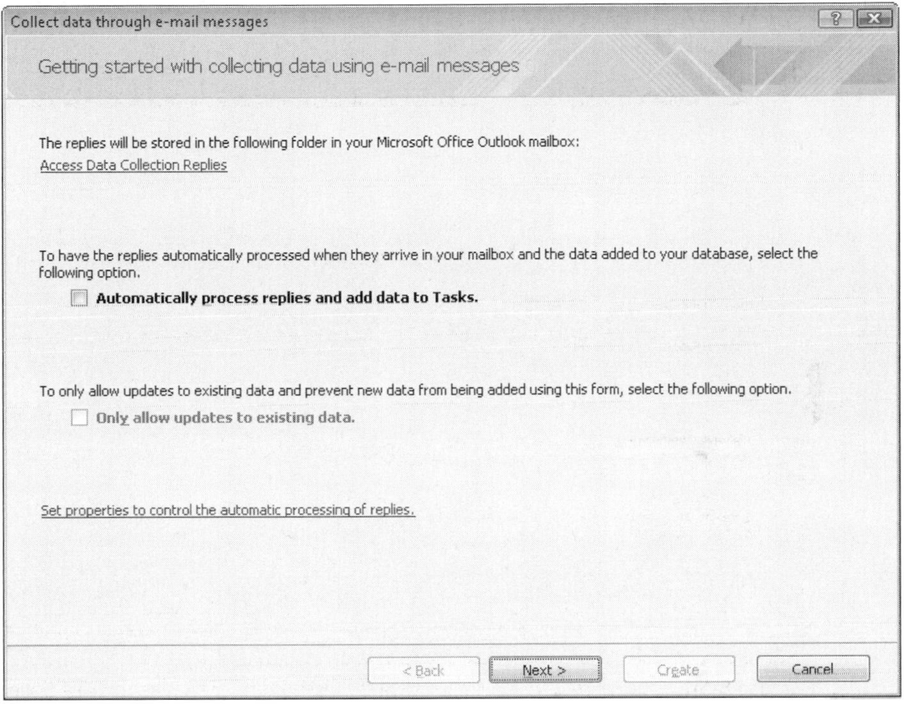


**Figure 6-55** The resend process takes you back to this data collection wizard page.

## INSIDE OUT Starting Over or Resending?

Note that the resend process starts beyond the point in the wizard where you select the format of the message (HTML or InfoPath), choose whether records will be added or updated, and specify the fields in the message. If you do not need to adjust the format of the message, the add or update option, or the fields used in the data collection message, you can simply resend a previous message. If, however, you need to choose different fields or a different table or query to update, you must create a new message.

Now that you know how to build tables, modify them, and import and link them, it's time to move on to more fun stuff—building queries on your tables—in the next chapter.

CHAPTER 7

# Creating and Working with Simple Queries



In the last three chapters, you learned how to create tables, modify them, and link or import tables from other data sources. Although you can certainly build forms and reports that get their data directly from your tables, most of the time you will want to sort or filter your data or display data from more than one table. For these tasks, you need queries.

When you define and run a *select query*, which selects information from the tables and queries in your database, Microsoft Office Access 2007 creates a *recordset* of the selected data. In most cases, you can work with a recordset in the same way that you work with a table: You can browse through it, select information from it, print it, and even update the data in it. But unlike a real table, a recordset doesn't actually exist in your database. Office Access 2007 creates a recordset from the data in the source tables of your query at the time you run the query. *Action queries*—which insert, update, or delete data—will be covered in Chapter 9, "Modifying Data with Action Queries."

As you learn to design forms and reports later in this book, you'll find that queries are the best way to focus on the specific data you need for the task at hand. You'll also find that queries are useful for providing choices for combo and list boxes, which make entering data in your database much easier.

**Note**

The examples in this chapter are based on the tables and data from the Conrad Systems Contacts sample database (Contacts.accdb), a backup copy of the data for the Contacts sample database (ContactsDataCopy.accdb), the Housing Reservations database (Housing.accdb), and the backup copy of the data for the Housing Reservations sample database (HousingDataCopy.accdb) on the companion CD included with this book. The query results you see from the sample queries you build in this chapter might not exactly match what you see in this book if you have reloaded the sample data using zfrmLoadData in either application or have changed any of the data in the tables.

Access 2007 provides two ways to begin creating a new query:

- Click the Query Wizard button in the Other group on the Create tab on the Ribbon. A dialog box appears that lets you select one of the four query wizards. (You'll learn about query wizards in Chapter 8, "Building Complex Queries.")
- Click the Query Design button in the Other group on the Create tab on the Ribbon to begin creating new query using the query designer.

To open an existing query in Design view, make sure you have queries showing in the Navigation Pane. To display all the queries in your database, click the bar at the top of the Navigation Pane and click Object Type under Navigate To Category and then click Queries under Filter By Group. You can open the query you want in Design view by selecting the query in the Navigation Pane and then pressing Ctrl+Enter. You can also right-click a query name in the Navigation Pane and click Design View on the shortcut menu. Figure 7-1 shows the list of queries for the Conrad Systems Contacts database. Please note that the figure shows you only some of the queries in the database. Use the scroll bar in the Navigation Pane to see the complete list of queries available in the Conrad Systems Contacts database.

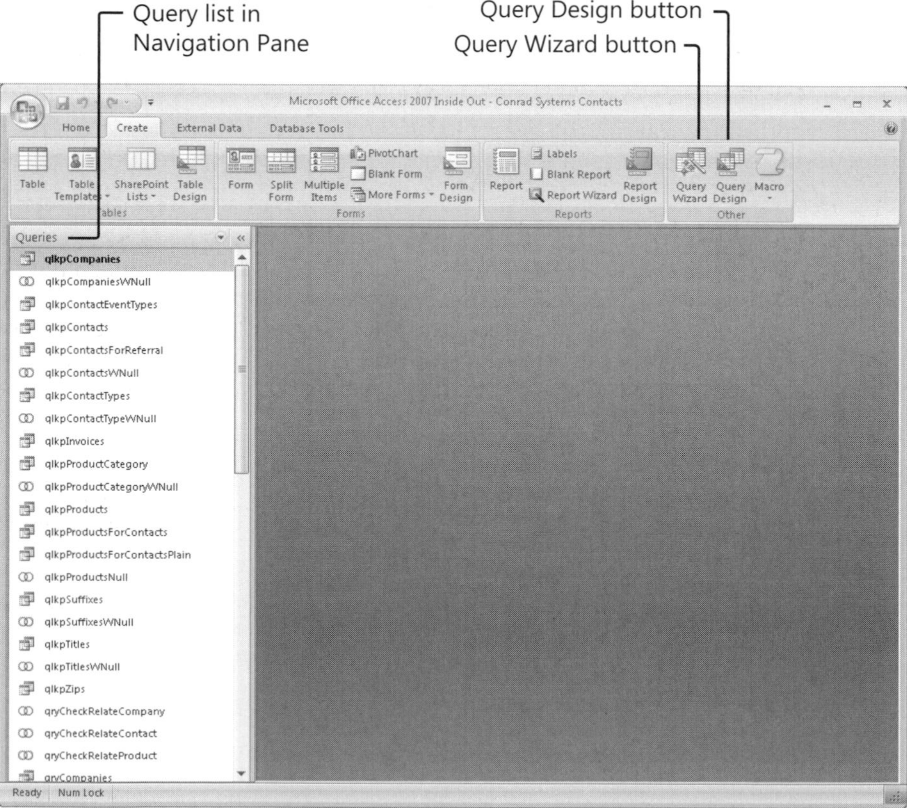


**Figure 7-1** The Navigation Pane has been filtered to show all the queries in the Conrad Systems Contacts database.

Figure 7-2 shows a query that has been opened in Design view. The upper part of the Query window contains field lists, and the lower part contains the design grid.

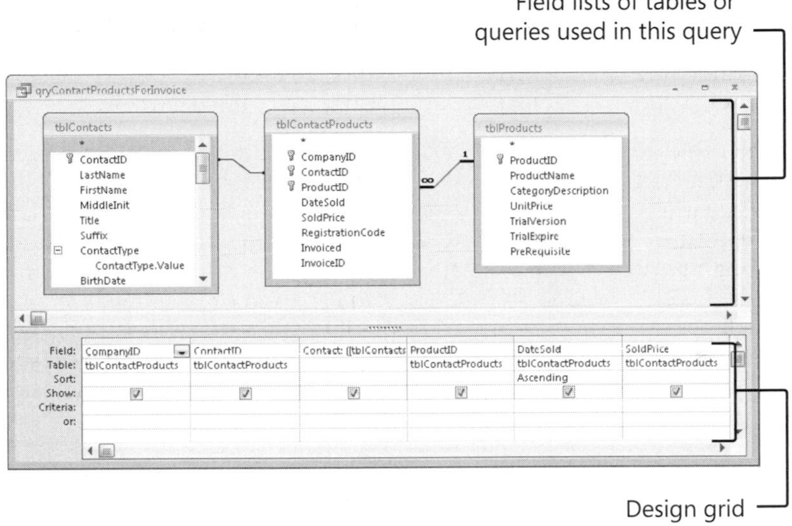


**Figure 7-2** A query open in Design view shows the tables and field lists.

# Selecting Data from a Single Table

One advantage of using queries is that they allow you to find data easily in multiple related tables. Queries are also useful, however, for sifting through the data in a single table. All the techniques you use for working with a single table apply equally to more complex multiple-table queries. This chapter covers the basics about building queries to select data from a single table. The next chapter shows you how to build more complex queries with multiple tables, totals, parameters, and more.

The easiest way to start building a query on a single table is to click the Query Design button in the Other group on the Create tab (see Figure 7-1). Open the Conrad Systems Contacts database and then click the Query Design button. Access 2007 displays the Show Table dialog box on top of the query design grid as shown in Figure 7-3.

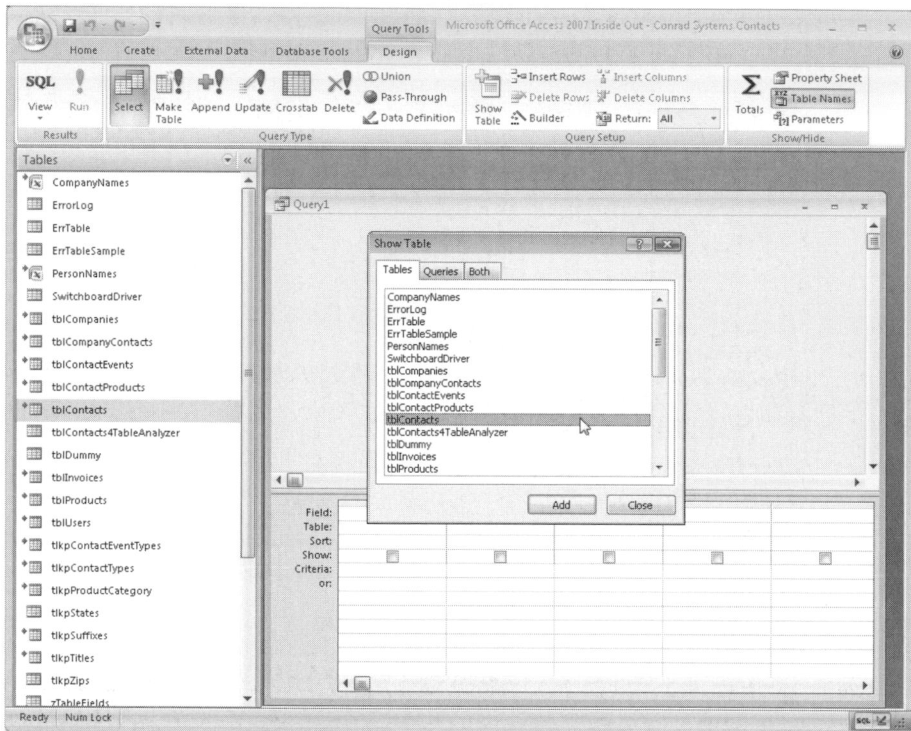


**Figure 7-3** The Show Table dialog box allows you to select one or more tables or queries to build a new query.

Select tblContacts on the Tables tab of the Show Table dialog box and then click Add to place tblContacts in the upper part of the Query window. Click Close in the Show Table dialog box to view the window shown in Figure 7-4.

As mentioned earlier, the Query window in Design view has two main parts. In the upper part you find field lists with the fields for the tables or queries you chose for this query. The lower part of the window is the design grid, in which you do all the design work. Each column in the grid represents one field that you'll work with in this query. As you'll see later, a field can be a simple field from one of the tables or a calculated field based on several fields in the tables.

You use the first row of the design grid to select fields—the fields you want in the resulting recordset, the fields you want to sort by, and the fields you want to test for values. As you'll learn later, you can also generate custom field names (for display in the resulting recordset), and you can use complex expressions or calculations to generate a calculated field.

The second row shows you the name of the table from which you selected a field. If you don't see this row, you can display it by clicking Table Names in the Show/Hide group on the Design tab below Query Tools. This isn't too important when building a query on a single table, but you'll learn later that this row provides valuable information when building a query that fetches data from more than one table or query.

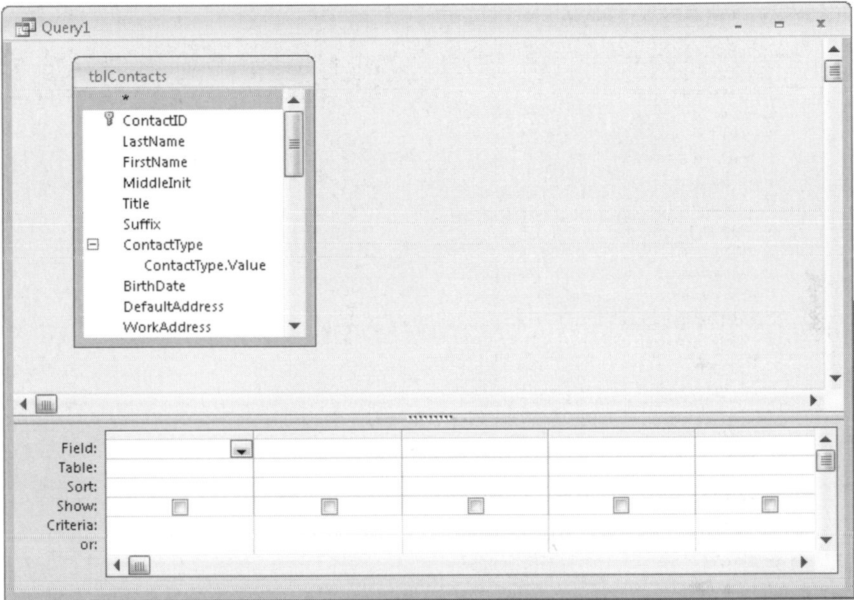


**Figure 7-4** The Query window in Design view for a new query on tblContacts shows the table with its list of fields in the top part of the window.

In the Sort row, you can specify whether Access 2007 should sort the selected or calculated field in ascending or in descending order. In the Show row, you can use the check boxes to indicate the fields that will be included in the recordset. By default, Access 2007 includes all the fields you place in the design grid. Sometimes you'll want to include a field in the query to allow you to select the records you want (such as contacts born in a certain date range), but you won't need that field in the recordset. You can add that field to the design grid so that you can define criteria, but you should clear the Show check box beneath the field to exclude it from the recordset.

Finally, you can use the Criteria row and the row(s) labeled *Or* to enter the criteria you want to use as filters. After you understand how a query is put together, you'll find it easy to specify exactly the fields and records that you want.

## Specifying Fields

The first step in building a query is to select the fields you want in the recordset. You can select the fields in several ways. Using the keyboard, you can tab to a column in the design grid and press Alt+Down Arrow to open the list of available fields. (To move to the design grid, press F6.) Use the Up Arrow and Down Arrow keys to highlight the field you want, and then press Enter to select the field.

Another way to select a field is to drag it from one of the field lists in the upper part of the window to one of the columns in the design grid. In Figure 7-5, the LastName field is being dragged to the design grid. When you drag a field, the mouse pointer turns into a small rectangle.

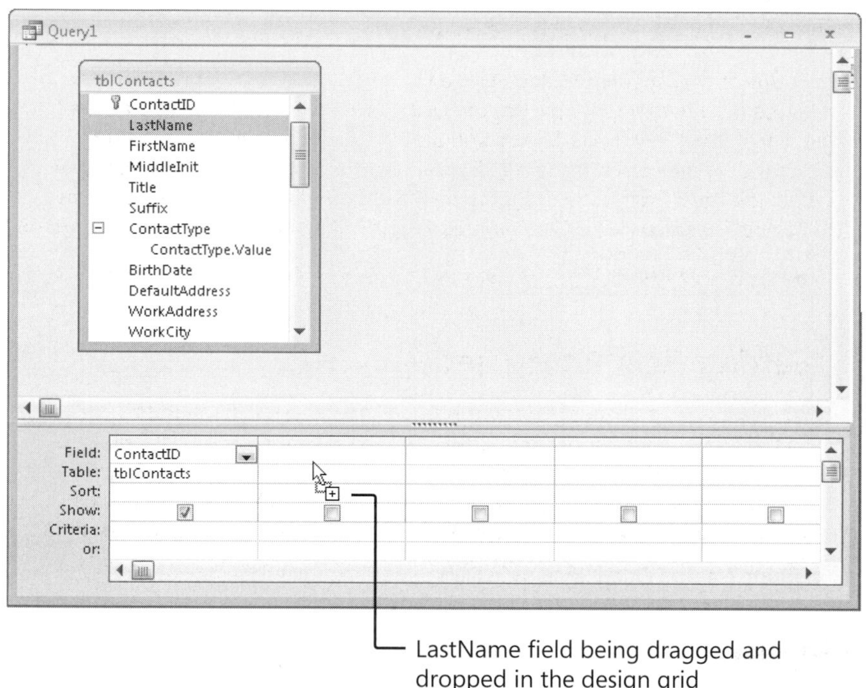


**Figure 7-5** You can drag a field from the table field list to a column in the design grid.

At the top of each field list in the upper part of the Query window (and also next to the first entry in the Field drop-down list in the design grid) is an asterisk (*) symbol. This symbol is shorthand for selecting "all fields in the table or the query" with one entry on the Field line. When you want to include all the fields in a table or a query, you don't have to define each one individually in the design grid unless you also want to define some sorting or selection criteria for specific fields. You can simply add the asterisk to the design grid to include all the fields from a list. Note that you can add individual fields to the grid in addition to the asterisk in order to define criteria for those fields, but you should clear the Show check box for the individual fields so that they don't appear twice in the recordset.

For this exercise, select ContactID, LastName, FirstName, WorkStateOrProvince, and BirthDate from the tblContacts table in the Conrad Systems Contacts database. You can select the fields one at a time by dragging and dropping them in the design grid. You can also double-click each field name, and Access will move it to the design grid into the next available slot. Finally, you can click on one field you want and then hold down the Ctrl key as you click on additional fields or hold down the Shift key to select a group of contiguous fields. Grab the last field you select and drag them all to the design grid. If you switch the Query window to Datasheet view at this point, you'll see all the records, containing only the fields you selected from the underlying table.

**INSIDE OUT** **Another Way to Select All Fields**

Another easy way to select all the fields in a table is to double-click the title bar of the field list in the upper part of the Query window—this highlights all the fields. Then click any of the highlighted fields and drag them as a group to the Field row in the design grid. While you're dragging, the mouse pointer changes to a multiple rectangle icon, indicating that you're dragging multiple fields. When you release the mouse button, you'll see that Access 2007 has copied all the fields to the design grid for you.

## Setting Field Properties

In general, a field that is output by a query inherits the properties defined for that field in the table. You can define a different Description property (the information that is displayed on the status bar when you select that field in a Query window in Datasheet view), Format property (how the data is displayed), Decimal Places property (for numeric data other than integers), Input Mask property, Caption property (the column heading), and Smart Tags property. We'll show you the details of how to use a smart tag in Chapter 12, "Customizing a Form."

**For details about field properties, see Chapter 4, "Creating Your Database and Tables."**

When you learn to define calculated fields later in this chapter, you'll see that it's a good idea to define the properties for these fields. If the field in the query is a foreign key linked to another table, you can also set the Lookup properties as described in Chapter 5, "Modifying Your Table Design." Access propagates Lookup properties that you have defined in your table fields; however, you can use the properties on the Lookup tab in the query's Property Sheet pane to override them.

**Note**

The Access 2007 query designer lets you define Lookup properties for any text or numeric field (other than AutoNumber). The field doesn't have to be a defined foreign key to another table. You might find this useful when you want the user to pick from a restricted value list—such as *M* or *F* for a Gender field.

To set the properties of a field, click any row of that field's column in the design grid, and then click the Property Sheet button in the Show/Hide group of the Design contextual tab to display the property sheet, shown in Figure 7-6. Even though the fields in your query inherit their properties from the underlying table, you won't see those properties displayed here. For example, the BirthDate field in tblContacts has both its Description and Caption set to Birth Date and a Format set to mm/dd/yyyy. If you click in the BirthDate field in your query and open the property sheet, you will see that none of the properties show values. Use the property settings in the property sheet to override any inherited properties and to customize how a field looks when viewed *for this query*. Try entering new property settings for the BirthDate field, as shown in Figure 7-6.

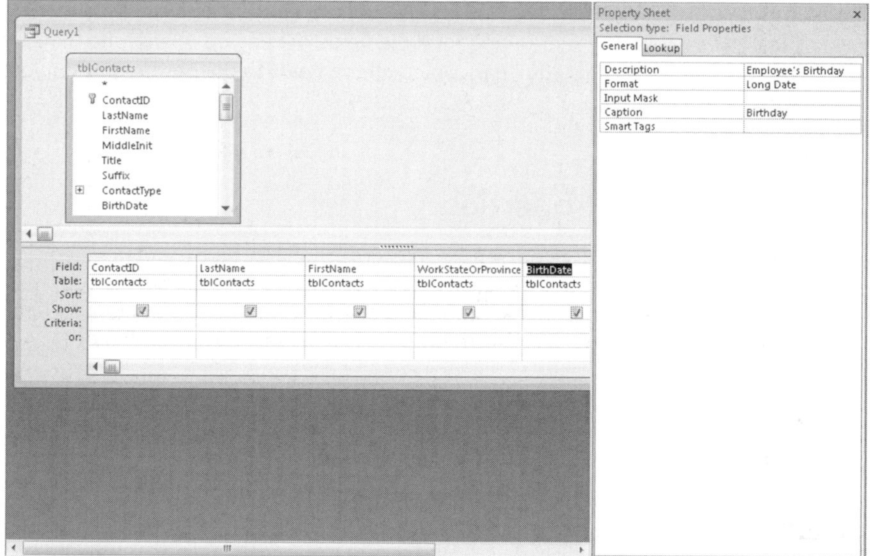


**Figure 7-6** In the property sheet, you can set properties for the BirthDate field.

> **INSIDE OUT** **Switching Views to Check Field Properties**
>
> One of the quickest ways to see if a field in a query has the properties you want is to switch to Datasheet view. If the field isn't displayed the way you want, you can switch back to Design view and override the properties in the query.

If you make these changes and switch to Datasheet view, you'll see that the BirthDate column heading is now *Birthday*; that the date displays day name, month name, day number, and year; and that the text on the status bar matches the new description, as shown in Figure 7-7. (Grab the right edge of the Birthday header with your mouse and drag it right to open the column so that you can see all the date values.)

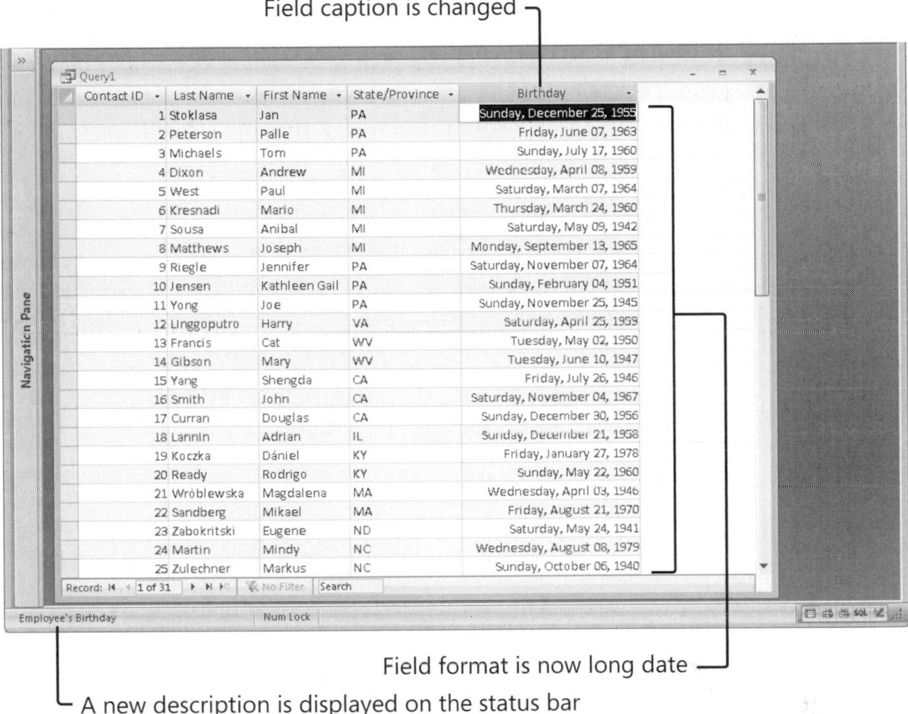


| Contact ID | Last Name | First Name | State/Province | Birthday |
|---|---|---|---|---|
| 1 | Stoklasa | Jan | PA | Sunday, December 25, 1955 |
| 2 | Peterson | Palle | PA | Friday, June 07, 1963 |
| 3 | Michaels | Tom | PA | Sunday, July 17, 1960 |
| 4 | Dixon | Andrew | MI | Wednesday, April 08, 1959 |
| 5 | West | Paul | MI | Saturday, March 07, 1964 |
| 6 | Kresnadi | Mario | MI | Thursday, March 24, 1960 |
| 7 | Sousa | Anibal | MI | Saturday, May 09, 1942 |
| 8 | Matthews | Joseph | MI | Monday, September 13, 1965 |
| 9 | Riegle | Jennifer | PA | Saturday, November 07, 1964 |
| 10 | Jensen | Kathleen Gail | PA | Sunday, February 04, 1951 |
| 11 | Yong | Joe | PA | Sunday, November 25, 1945 |
| 12 | Linggoputro | Harry | VA | Saturday, April 25, 1959 |
| 13 | Francis | Cat | WV | Tuesday, May 02, 1950 |
| 14 | Gibson | Mary | WV | Tuesday, June 10, 1947 |
| 15 | Yang | Shengda | CA | Friday, July 26, 1946 |
| 16 | Smith | John | CA | Saturday, November 04, 1967 |
| 17 | Curran | Douglas | CA | Sunday, December 30, 1956 |
| 18 | Lannin | Adrian | IL | Sunday, December 21, 1958 |
| 19 | Koczka | Dániel | KY | Friday, January 27, 1978 |
| 20 | Ready | Rodrigo | KY | Sunday, May 22, 1960 |
| 21 | Wróblewska | Magdalena | MA | Wednesday, April 03, 1946 |
| 22 | Sandberg | Mikael | MA | Friday, August 21, 1970 |
| 23 | Zabokritski | Eugene | ND | Saturday, May 24, 1941 |
| 24 | Martin | Mindy | NC | Wednesday, August 08, 1979 |
| 25 | Zulechner | Markus | NC | Sunday, October 06, 1940 |

**Figure 7-7** The BirthDate field is now displayed with new property settings.

## Entering Selection Criteria

The next step is to further refine the records you want by specifying criteria on one or more fields. The example shown in Figure 7-8 selects contacts working in the state of California.

Entering selection criteria in a query is similar to entering a validation rule for a field, which you learned about in Chapter 4. To look for a single value, simply type it in the Criteria row for the field you want to test. If the field you're testing is a text field and the value you're looking for has any blank spaces in it, you must enclose the value in quotation marks. Note that Access adds quotation marks for you around single text values. (In Figure 7-8, we typed **CA**, but Access replaced what we typed with "CA" after we pressed Enter.)

If you want to test for any of several values, enter the values in the Criteria row, separated by the word *Or*. For example, specifying *CA Or NC* searches for records for California or North Carolina. You can also test for any of several values by entering each value in a separate Criteria or Or row for the field you want to test. For example, you can enter *CA* in the Criteria row, *NC* in the next row (the first Or row), and so on—but you have to be careful if you're also specifying criteria in other fields, as explained in the section "AND vs. OR" on page 357.

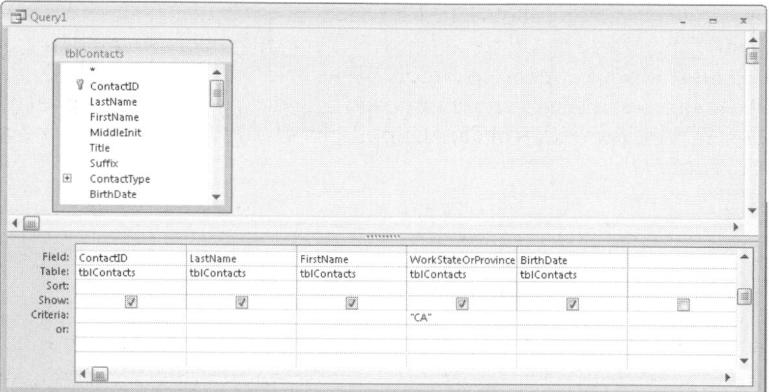


**Figure 7-8** When you specify "CA" as the selection criterion in the design grid, Access returns only records with a WorkStateOrProvince equal to California.

## INSIDE OUT Be Careful When Your Criterion Is Also a Keyword

You should be careful when entering criteria that might also be an Access 2007 keyword. In the examples shown here, we could have chosen to use criteria for the two-character abbreviation for the state of Oregon (OR)—but *or*, as you can see in the examples, is also a keyword. In many cases, Access is smart enough to figure out what you mean from the context. You can enter

```
Or Or Ca
```

in the Criteria row under State, and Access assumes that the first *Or* is criteria (by placing quotation marks around the word for you) and the second *Or* is the Boolean operator keyword. If you want to be sure that Access interprets your criteria correctly, always place double quotation marks around criteria text. If you find that Access guessed wrong, you can always correct the entry before saving the query.

In the section "AND vs. OR," you'll see that you can also include a comparison operator in the Criteria row so that, for example, you can look for values less than (<), greater than or equal to (>=), or not equal to (<>) the value that you specify.

## Working with Dates and Times in Criteria

Access 2007 stores dates and times as 8-byte decimal numbers. The value to the left of the decimal point represents the day (day zero is December 30, 1899), and the fractional part of the number stores the time as a fraction of a day, accurate to seconds. Fortunately, you don't have to worry about converting internal numbers to specify a test for a particular date value because Access 2007 handles date and time entries in several formats.

You must always surround date and time values with pound signs (#) to tell Access that you're entering a date or a time. To test for a specific date, use the date notation that is most comfortable for you. For example, *#April 15, 1962#*, *#4/15/62#*, and *#15-Apr-1962#* are all the same date if you chose English (United States) in the Regional And Language Options in Windows Control Panel. Similarly, *#5:30 PM#* and *#17:30#* both specify 5:30 in the evening.

INSIDE OUT **Understanding Date/Time Criteria**

You must be careful when building criteria to test a range in a date/time field. Let's say you want to look at all records between two dates in the ContactEvents table, which has a date/time field—ContactDateTime—that holds the date *and* time of the contact. For all contact events in the month of January 2007, you might be tempted to put the following on the Criteria line under ContactDateTime.

```
>=#1/1/2007# AND <=#1/31/2007#
```

When you look at the results, you might wonder why no rows show up from January 31, 2007 even when you know that you made and recorded several calls on that day. The reason is simple. Remember, a date/time field contains an integer offset value for the date and a fraction for the time. Let's say you called someone at 9:55 A.M. on January 31, 2007. The internal value is actually 39,113.4132—January 31, 2007 is 39,113 days later than December 30, 1899 (the zero point), and .4132 is the fraction of a day that represents 9:55 A.M. When you say you want rows where ContactDateTime is less than or equal to January 31, 2007, you're comparing to the internal value 39,113—just the day value, which is midnight on that day. You won't find the 9:55 A.M. record because the value is greater than 39,113, or later in the day than midnight. To search successfully, you must enter

```
>=#1/1/2007# AND <#2/1/2007#
```

## AND vs. OR

When you enter criteria for several fields, all the tests in a single Criteria row or Or row must be true for Access 2007 to include a record in the recordset. That is, Access 2007 performs a logical AND operation between multiple criteria in the same row. So if you enter *CA* in the Criteria row for StateOrProvince and *<#1 JAN 1972#* in the Criteria row for BirthDate, the record must be for the state of California *and* must be for someone born before 1972 to be selected. If you enter *CA Or NC* in the Criteria row for StateOrProvince and *>=#01/01/1946# AND <#1 JAN 1972#* in the Criteria row for BirthDate, the record must be for the state of California or North Carolina, *and* the person must have been born between 1946 and 1971.

Figure 7-9 shows the result of applying a logical AND operator between any two tests. As you can see, both tests must be true for the result of the AND to be true and for the record to be selected.

| AND | True | False |
| --- | --- | --- |
| True | True (Selected) | False (Rejected) |
| False | False (Rejected) | False (Rejected) |

**Figure 7-9** When you specify the logical AND operator between two tests, the result is true only if both tests are true.

When you specify multiple criteria for a field and separate the criteria by a logical OR operator, only one of the criteria must be true for Access 2007 to select the record. You can specify several OR criteria for a field, either by entering them all in a single Criteria cell separated by the logical OR operator, as shown earlier, or by entering each subsequent criterion in a separate Or row. When you use multiple Or rows, if the criteria *in any one of the Or rows* is true, Access 2007 selects the record. Figure 7-10 shows the result of applying a logical OR operation between any two tests. As you can see, only one of the tests must be true for the result of the OR to be true and for Access 2007 to select the record.

| OR | True | False |
| --- | --- | --- |
| True | True (Selected) | True (Selected) |
| False | True (Selected) | False (Rejected) |

**Figure 7-10** When you specify the logical OR operator between two tests, the result is true if either or both of the tests is true.

Let's look at a specific example. In Figure 7-11, you specify *CA* in the first Criteria row of the WorkStateOrProvince field and *>=#01/01/1946# AND <#1 JAN 1972#* in that same Criteria row for the BirthDate field. (By the way, when you type #1 JAN 1972# and press Enter, Access changes your entry to #1/1/1972#.) In the next row (the first Or row), you specify *NC* in the WorkStateOrProvince field. When you run this query, you get all the contacts from the state of California who were born between 1946 and 1971. You also get any records for the state of North Carolina regardless of the birth date.

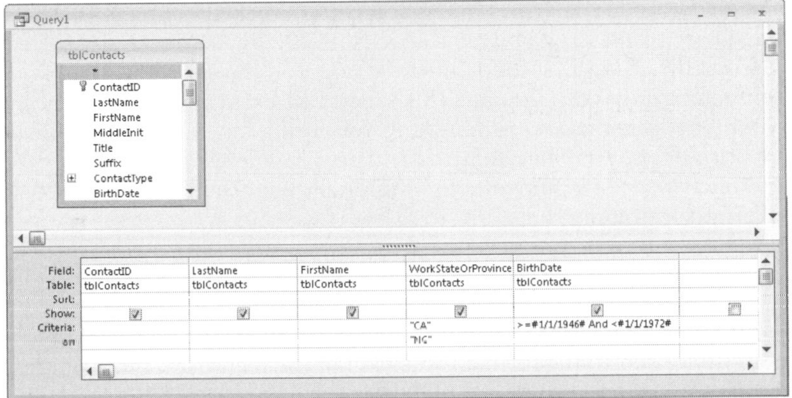


**Figure 7-11** You can specify multiple AND and OR selection criteria in the design grid with additional OR lines.

In Figure 7-12, you can see the recordset (in Datasheet view) that results from running this query:

Query1

| Contact ID | Last Name | First Name | State/Province | Birthday |
|---|---|---|---|---|
| 15 | Yang | Shengda | CA | Friday, July 26, 1946 |
| 16 | Smith | John | CA | Saturday, November 04, 1967 |
| 17 | Curran | Douglas | CA | Sunday, December 30, 1956 |
| 24 | Martin | Mindy | NC | Wednesday, August 08, 1979 |
| 25 | Zulechner | Markus | NC | Sunday, October 06, 1940 |
| 26 | Villadsen | Peter | NC | Saturday, November 22, 1975 |
| (New) | | | | |

Record: 1 of 6 No Filter Search

**Figure 7-12** The recordset of the query shown in Figure 7-11 shows only the records that match your criteria.

## INSIDE OUT Don't Get Confused by And and Or

It's a common mistake to get *Or* and *And* mixed up when typing compound criteria for a single field. You might think to yourself, "I want all the work contacts in the states of Washington *and* California," and then type **WA And CA** in the Criteria row for the WorkStateOrProvince field. When you do this, you're asking Access to find rows where *(WorkStateOrProvince = "WA") And (WorkStateOrProvince = "CA")*. Because a field in a record can't have more than one value at a time (can't contain both the values WA and CA in the same record), there won't be any records in the output. To look for all the rows for these two states, you need to ask Access to search for *(WorkStateOrProvince = "WA") Or (WorkStateOrProvince = "CA")*. In other words, type **WA Or CA** in the Criteria row under the WorkStateOrProvince field.

If you also want to limit rows from contacts in North Carolina to those who were born between 1946 and 1971, you must specify *>=#01/01/1946# AND <#1/1/1972#* again under BirthDate in the second Or row—that is, on the same row that filters for NC under WorkStateOrProvince. Although this seems like extra work, this gives you complete flexibility to filter the data as you want. You could, for example, include people who were born before 1969 in California and people who were born after 1970 in North Carolina by placing a different criterion under BirthDate in the two rows that filter WorkStateOrProvince.

## Between, In, and Like

In addition to comparison operators, Access provides three special operators that are useful for specifying the data you want in the recordset. Table 7-1 describes these operators.

**Table 7-1 Criteria Operators for Queries**

| Predicate | Description |
|---|---|
| Between | Useful for specifying a range of values. The clause *Between 10 And 20* is the same as specifying *>=10 And <=20.* |
| In | Useful for specifying a list of values separated by commas, any one of which can match the field being searched. The clause *In ("CA", "NC", "TN")* is the same as *"CA" Or "NC" Or "TN"*. |
| Like[1] | Useful for searching for patterns in text fields. You can include special characters and ranges of values in the Like comparison string to define the character pattern you want. Use a question mark (?) to indicate any single character in that position. Use an asterisk (*) to indicate zero or more characters in that position. The pound-sign character (#) specifies a single numeric digit in that position. Include a range in brackets ([ ]) to test for a particular range of characters in a position, and use an exclamation point (!) to indicate exceptions. The range *[0-9]* tests for numbers, *[a-z]* tests for letters, and *[!0-9]* tests for any characters except *0* through *9*. For example, the clause *Like"?[a-k]d[0-9]*"* tests for any single character in the first position, any character from *a* through *k* in the second position, the letter *d* in the third position, any character from *0* through *9* in the fourth position, and any number of characters after that. |

[1] As you'll learn in Chapter 27, "Building Queries in an Access Project," and Article 2, "Understanding SQL," the pattern characters supported by SQL Server when you are working in an Access project file are different. The pattern characters discussed here work in desktop applications (.accdb and .accde files) only.

Suppose you want to find all contacts in the state of California or Pennsylvania who were born between 1955 and 1972 and whose first name begins with the letter *J*. Figure 7-13 shows how you would enter these criteria. Figure 7-14 shows the recordset of this query.

## INSIDE OUT Choosing the Correct Date/Time Criteria

If you're really sharp, you're probably looking at Figure 7-13 and wondering why we chose *Between #1/1/1955# And #12/31/1972#* instead of *>= #1/1/1955# And < #1/1/1973#* to cover the case where the BirthDate field might also include a time. In this case we know that the BirthDate field has an input mask that doesn't allow us to enter time values. So we know that using Between and the simple date values will work for this search.

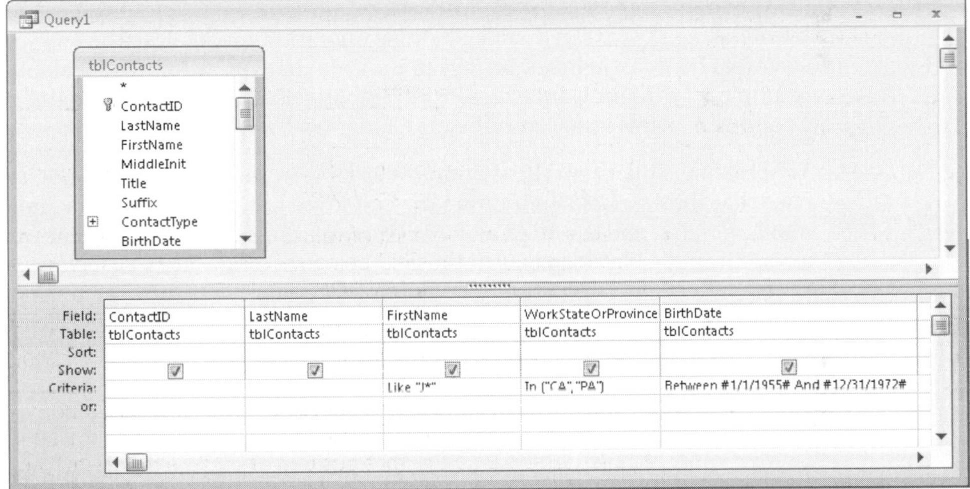


**Figure 7-13** You can also restrict records by using Between, In, and Like all in the same design grid.

Query1

| Contact ID | Last Name | First Name | State/Province | Birthday |
|---|---|---|---|---|
| 1 | Stoklasa | Jan | PA | Sunday, December 25, 1955 |
| 9 | Riegle | Jennifer | PA | Saturday, November 07, 1964 |
| 16 | Smith | John | CA | Saturday, November 04, 1967 |
| (New) | | | | |

Record: 1 of 3 No Filter Search

**Figure 7-14** The recordset of the query shown in Figure 7-13 shows only the records that match your criteria.

**For additional examples that use the Between, In, and Like comparison operators, see "Defining Simple Field Validation Rules" on page 168 and the "Predicate" sections in Article 2, "Understanding SQL," on the companion CD.**

## Using Expressions

You can use an expression to combine fields or to calculate a new value from fields in your table and make that expression a new field in the recordset. You can use any of the many built-in functions that Access 2007 provides as part of your expression. You *concatenate*, or combine, text fields by stringing them end-to-end, or you use arithmetic operators on fields in the underlying table to calculate a value. Let's switch to the HousingDataCopy.accdb database to build some examples.

### Creating Text Expressions

One common use of expressions is to create a new text (string) field by concatenating fields containing text, string constants, or numeric data. You create a string constant by enclosing the text in double or single quotation marks. Use the ampersand character (&) between fields or strings to indicate that you want to concatenate them. For example, you might want to create an output field that concatenates the LastName field, a comma, a blank space, and then the FirstName field.

Try creating a query on the tblEmployees table in the HousingDataCopy.accdb database that shows a field containing the employee last name, a comma and a blank, first name, a blank, and middle name. You can also create a single field containing the city, a comma and a blank space, the state or province followed by one blank space, and the postal code. Your expressions should look like this:

```
LastName & ", " & FirstName & " " & MiddleName
City & ", " & StateOrProvince & " " & PostalCode
```

You can see the Query window in Design view for this example in Figure 7-15. We clicked in the Field row of the second column and then pressed Shift+F2 to open the Zoom window, where it is easier to enter the expression. Note that you can click the Font button to select a larger font that's easier to read. After you choose a font, Access 2007 uses it whenever you open the Zoom window again.

> **Note**
>
> Access 2007 requires that all fields on the Field row in a query have a name. For single fields, Access uses the name of the field. When you enter an expression, Access generates a field name in the form *ExprN:*. See "Specifying Field Names" on page 377 for details about changing the names of fields or expressions. Notice also that Access automatically adds brackets around field names in expressions. It does this so that the field names in the SQL for the query are completely unambiguous. If this table had been designed with blanks in the field names, you would have to type the brackets yourself to ensure that the query designer interprets the names correctly.

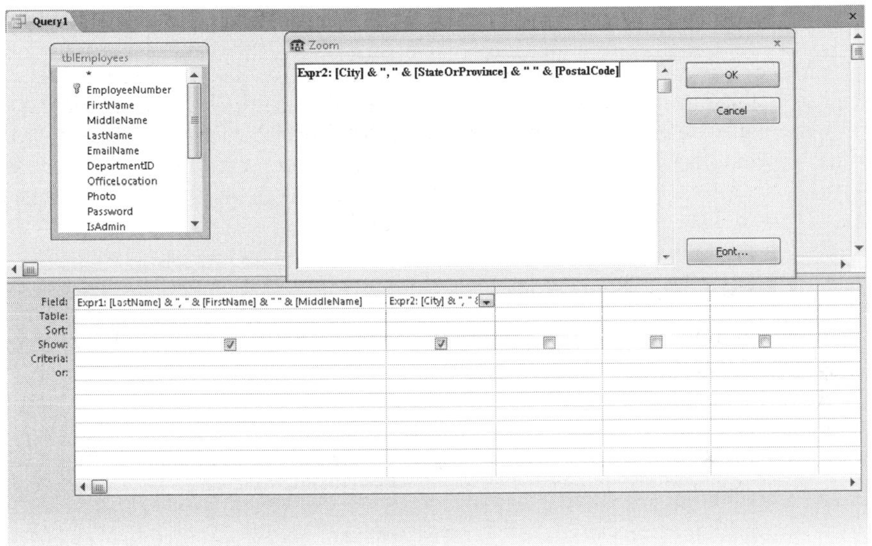


**Figure 7-15** If you use the Zoom window to enter an expression, you can see more of the expression and select a different font.

When you look at the query result in Datasheet view, you should see something like that shown in Figure 7-16.

Query1

| Expr1 | Expr2 |
|---|---|
| Koch, Reed | West Mansfield, OH 43358 |
| Kim, Tim | Meredith, NH 03253 |
| Tippett, John | Florence, AL 35630 |
| DeGrasse, Kirk | Agua Dulce, CA 91350 |
| Lawrence, David Oliver | Christiansburg, VA 24073 |
| Adams, Jay | Ramona, SD 57054 |
| Richins, Jack S. | Saint David, ME 04773 |
| Bradley, David M. | Bayou La Batre, AL 36509 |
| Eyink, Scott | Los Osos, CA 93402 |
| Berndt, Matthias | Rockland, TX 75938 |
| Willett, Benjamin C. | Austin, MO 64725 |
| Shock, Misty | Newhall, CA 91381 |
| Randall, Linda | Trail Creek, IN 46360 |
| Schare, Gary | Rock Springs, AZ 85324 |
| Viescas, John L. | , |
| Conrad, Jeff | , |
| * | |

**Figure 7-16** Here is a query result with concatenated text fields.

Try typing within the Expr1 field in Datasheet view. Because this display is a result of an expression (concatenation of strings), Access 2007 won't let you update the data in this column.

INSIDE OUT

**Eliminating Extra Spaces When Concatenating Null Values**

If you look very closely at Figure 7-16, you can see that we captured the image with the insertion point displayed at the end of the Expr1 field on the first row. Do you notice that there's an extra space after the first name? This happened because that person has no middle name, so what we're seeing is the extra blank we inserted after first name that is supposed to provide spacing between first name and middle name.

This isn't too much of a problem in this particular expression because you're not going to notice the extra blank displayed at the end of the name. But if you create the expression *First (blank) Middle (blank) Last* and if a record has no middle name, the extra blank will be noticeable.

When you use an ampersand, any Null field in the expression doesn't cause the entire expression to be Null. A little secret: You can also use the arithmetic plus sign (+) to concatenate strings. As you'll learn when you create arithmetic expressions, if a field in the expression is Null, the expression evaluates to Null. So, to solve the extra blank problem, you can create an expression to concatenate the parts of a name as follows:

```
FirstName & (" " + MiddleName) & " " & LastName
```

If MiddleName is a Null, the arithmetic expression inside the parentheses evaluates to Null, and the extra blank disappears!

## Defining Arithmetic Expressions

In a reservations record (tblReservations in the Housing Reservations database), code in the form that confirms a reservation automatically calculates the correct TotalCharge value for the reservation before Access 2007 saves a changed row. If you strictly follow the rules for good relational table design (see Article 1, "Designing Your Database Application," on the companion CD), this isn't normally a good idea, but we designed it this way to demonstrate what you have to code to maintain the calculated value in your table. (Access 2007 won't automatically calculate the new value for you.) You can see how this code works in Chapter 20, "Automating Your Application with Visual Basic." This technique also saves time later when calculating a total by month or total by facility in a report.

Table 7-2 shows the operators you can use in arithmetic expressions.

Table 7-2 **Operators Used in Arithmetic Expressions**

| Operator | Description |
|---|---|
| + | Adds two numeric expressions. |
| – | Subtracts the second numeric expression from the first numeric expression. |
| * | Multiplies two numeric expressions. |
| / | Divides the first numeric expression by the second numeric expression. |
| \ | Rounds both numeric expressions to integers and then divides the first integer by the second integer. The result is truncated to an integer. |
| ^ | Raises the first numeric expression to the power indicated by the second numeric expression. |
| Mod | Rounds both numeric expressions to integers, divides the first integer by the second integer, and returns only the remainder. |

The expression to calculate the TotalCharge field is complex because it charges the lower weekly rate for portions of the stay that are full weeks and then adds the daily charge for extra days. Let's say you want to compare the straight daily rate with the discounted rate for longer stays. To begin, you need an expression that calculates the number of days. You can do this in a couple of different ways. First, you can use a handy built-in function called DateDiff to calculate the difference between two Date/Time values in seconds, minutes, hours, days, weeks, months, quarters, or years. In this case, you want the difference between the check-in date and the check-out date in days.

The syntax for calling DateDiff is as follows:

```
DateDiff(<interval>, <date1>, <date2>[, <firstdayofweek>])
```

The function calculates the difference between *<date1>* and *<date2>* using the interval you specify and returns a negative value if *<date1>* is greater than *<date2>*. You can supply a *<firstdayofweek>* value (the default is 1, Sunday) to affect how the function calculates the "ww" interval. Table 7-3 explains the values you can supply for *interval*.

> **Note**
>
> You can also use the settings you find in Table 7-3 for the *interval* argument in the DatePart function (which extracts part of a Date/Time value) and DateAdd function (which adds or subtracts a constant to a Date/Time value).

**Table 7-3 Interval Settings for DateDiff Function**

| Setting | Description |
|---|---|
| "yyyy" | Calculates the difference in years. DateDiff subtracts the year portion of the first date from the year portion of the second date, so *DateDiff*("yyyy", #31 DEC 2006#, #01 JAN 2007#) returns 1. |
| "q" | Calculates the difference in quarters. If the two dates are in the same calendar quarter, the result is 0. |
| "m" | Calculates the difference in months. DateDiff subtracts the month portion of the first date from the month portion of the second date, so *DateDiff*("m", #31 DEC 2006#, #01 JAN 2007#) returns 1. |
| "y" | Calculates the difference in days. DateDiff handles this option the same as "d" below. (For other functions, this extracts the day of the year.) |
| "d" | Calculates the difference in days. |
| "w" | Calculates the difference in weeks based on the day of the week of <*date1*>. If, for example, the day of the week of the first date is a Tuesday, DateDiff counts the number of Tuesdays between the first date and the second date. For example, March 28, 2007 is a Wednesday, and April 2, 2007 is a Monday, so *DateDiff*("w", #28 MAR 2007#, #02 APR 2007#) returns 0. |
| "ww" | Calculates the difference in weeks. When the first day of the week is Sunday (the default), DateDiff counts the number of Sundays greater than the first date and less than or equal to the second date. For example, March 28, 2007 is a Wednesday, and April 7, 2007 is a Monday, so *DateDiff*("ww", #28 MAR 2007#, #02 APR 2007#) returns 1. |
| "h" | Calculates the difference in hours. |
| "n" | Calculates the difference in minutes. |
| "s" | Calculates the difference in seconds. |

The second way to calculate the number of days is to simply subtract one date from the other. Remember that the integer portion of a Date/Time data type is number of days. If you're sure that the fields do not contain any time value, subtract the check-in date from the check-out date to find the number of days. Let's see how this works in the sample database.

Open the HousingDataCopy.accdb database if you have closed it and start a new query on tblReservations. Add EmployeeNumber, FacilityID, RoomNumber, CheckInDate, CheckOutDate, and TotalCharge to the query design grid. You need to enter your expression in a blank column on the Field row. You'll build your final expression in two parts so you can understand the logic involved. Using DateDiff, start the expression by entering

```
DateDiff("d", [CheckInDate], [CheckOutDate])
```

To calculate the number of days by subtracting, the expression is

```
[CheckOutDate] - [CheckInDate]
```

To calculate the amount owed at the daily rate, multiply either of the previous expressions by the DailyRate field. With DateDiff, the final expression is

```
DateDiff("d", [CheckInDate], [CheckOutDate]) * [DailyRate]
```

If you want to use subtraction, you must enter

```
([CheckOutDate] - [CheckInDate]) * [DailyRate]
```

You might be wondering why the second expression includes parentheses. When evaluating an arithmetic expression, Access evaluates certain operations before others, known as *operator precedence*. Table 7-4 shows you operator precedence for arithmetic operations. In an expression with no parentheses, Access performs the operations in the order listed in the table. When operations have the same precedence (for example, multiply and divide), Access performs the operations left to right.

**Table 7-4 Arithmetic Operator Precedence**

| Access Evaluates Operators in the Following Order: | |
|---|---|
| 1 | Exponentiation (^) |
| 2 | Negation—a leading minus sign (-) |
| 3 | Multiplication and division (*, /) |
| 4 | Integer division (\) |
| 5 | Modulus (Mod) |
| 6 | Addition and subtraction (+, -) |

Access evaluates expressions enclosed in parentheses first, starting with the innermost expressions. (You can enclose an expression in parentheses inside another expression in parentheses.) If you do not include the parentheses in the previous example, Access would first multiply CheckInDate times DailyRate (because multiplication and division occur before addition and subtraction) and then subtract that result from CheckOutDate. That not only gives you the wrong answer but also results in an error because you cannot subtract a Double value (the result of multiplying a date/time times a currency) from a date/time value.

After you select the fields from the table and enter the expression to calculate the total based on the daily rate, your query design grid should look something like Figure 7-17.

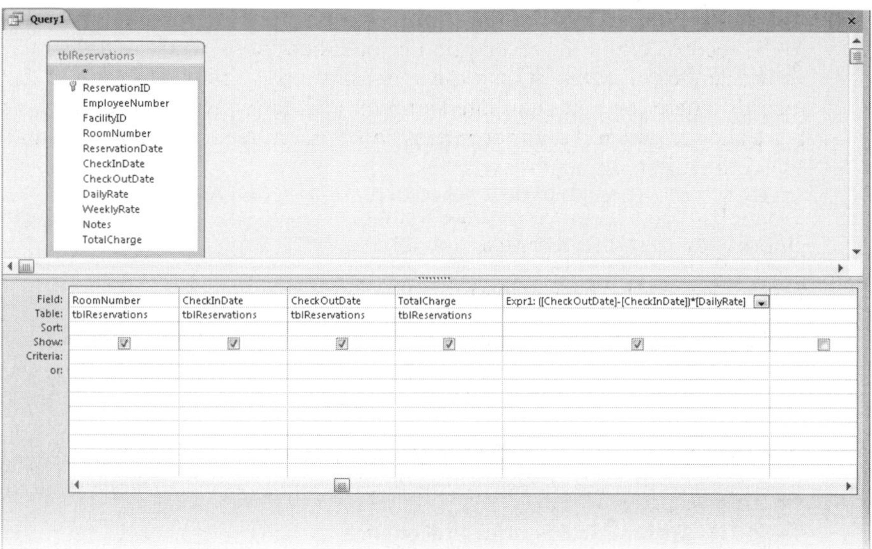


**Figure 7-17** Use an expression to calculate the amount owed based on the daily rate.

When you switch to Datasheet view, you can see the calculated amount from your expression as shown in Figure 7-18.

Query1

| Employee | Facility | Room | Check-In | Check-Out | Charge | Expr1 |
|---|---|---|---|---|---|---|
| 7 | Main Campus Housing A | 810 | 3/6/2007 | 3/18/2007 | $455.00 | 480 |
| 7 | Main Campus Housing B | 111 | 3/24/2007 | 4/4/2007 | $1,040.00 | 1100 |
| 5 | North Satellite Housing D | 305 | 3/20/2007 | 3/23/2007 | $195.00 | 195 |
| 3 | Main Campus Housing A | 502 | 4/14/2007 | 5/1/2007 | $1,420.00 | 1530 |
| 3 | Main Campus Housing B | 214 | 3/26/2007 | 3/28/2007 | $100.00 | 100 |
| 10 | Main Campus Housing A | 902 | 4/1/2007 | 4/20/2007 | $1,600.00 | 1710 |
| 1 | South Campus Housing C | 501 | 2/28/2007 | 3/13/2007 | $1,200.00 | 1300 |
| 8 | Main Campus Housing A | 509 | 4/16/2007 | 4/29/2007 | $620.00 | 650 |
| 2 | Main Campus Housing B | 504 | 4/20/2007 | 4/23/2007 | $210.00 | 210 |
| 3 | Main Campus Housing A | 707 | 5/2/2007 | 5/15/2007 | $680.00 | 715 |
| 5 | Main Campus Housing B | 301 | 3/25/2007 | 4/9/2007 | $895.00 | 975 |
| 3 | Main Campus Housing A | 207 | 3/25/2007 | 4/5/2007 | $570.00 | 605 |
| 8 | Main Campus Housing A | 111 | 4/4/2007 | 4/20/2007 | $1,180.00 | 1280 |
| 7 | Main Campus Housing A | 708 | 4/27/2007 | 5/2/2007 | $250.00 | 225 |
| 6 | Main Campus Housing B | 206 | 4/4/2007 | 4/15/2007 | $830.00 | 880 |
| 7 | South Campus Housing C | 111 | 5/20/2007 | 5/27/2007 | $255.00 | 280 |
| 4 | South Campus Housing C | 101 | 5/1/2007 | 5/22/2007 | $1,920.00 | 2100 |
| 8 | Main Campus Housing A | 702 | 5/23/2007 | 5/28/2007 | $450.00 | 450 |
| 5 | Main Campus Housing B | 610 | 5/23/2007 | 6/6/2007 | $1,280.00 | 1400 |
| 5 | Main Campus Housing A | 309 | 5/5/2007 | 5/22/2007 | $790.00 | 850 |
| 8 | North Satellite Housing D | 402 | 5/9/2007 | 5/20/2007 | $830.00 | 880 |
| 8 | South Campus Housing C | 103 | 5/3/2007 | 5/8/2007 | $350.00 | 350 |
| 12 | Main Campus Housing B | 414 | 6/11/2007 | 6/15/2007 | $195.00 | 200 |
| 3 | Main Campus Housing A | 207 | 5/25/2007 | 5/29/2007 | $220.00 | 220 |
| 5 | South Campus Housing C | 607 | 6/26/2007 | 6/28/2007 | $110.00 | 110 |
| 5 | Main Campus Housing B | 303 | 6/30/2007 | 7/2/2007 | $180.00 | 180 |
| 11 | Main Campus Housing A | 505 | [illegible] | [illegible] | [illegible] | [illegible] |

Record: 1 of 58 No Filter Search

**Figure 7-18** Access displays the results of your calculated expression in Datasheet view.

Note that not all the calculated amounts are larger than the amount already stored in the record. When the reservation is for six days or fewer, the daily rate applies, so your calculation should match the existing charge. You might want to display only the records where the new calculated amount is different than the amount already stored. For that, you can add another expression to calculate the difference and then select the row if the difference is not zero.

Switch back to Design view and enter a new expression to calculate the difference in an empty column. Your expression should look like this:

```
TotalCharge - (([CheckOutDate] - [CheckInDate]) * [DailyRate])
```

In the Criteria line under this new field, enter **<> 0**. Your query design should look like Figure 7-19, and the datasheet for the query now displays only the rows where the calculation result is different, as shown in Figure 7-20.

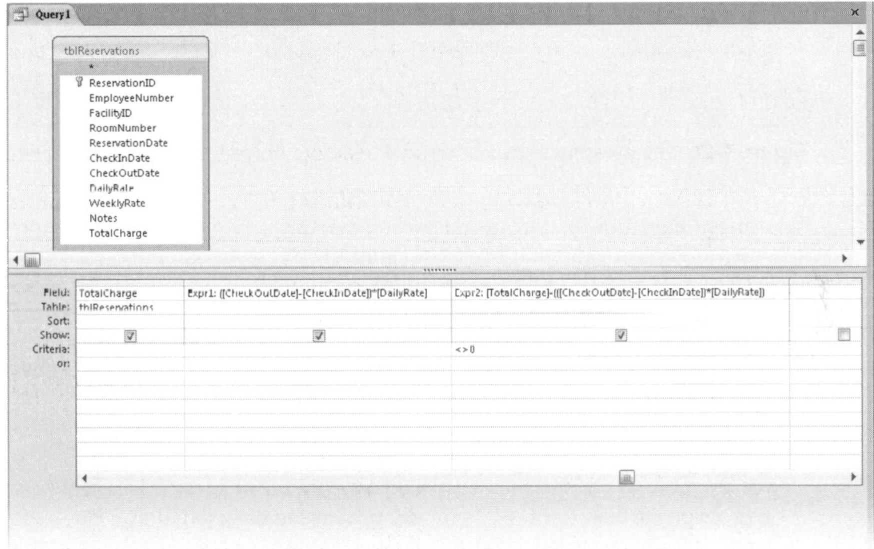


**Figure 7-19** This expression and criterion finds the rows that are different.

Finding the rows that differ in this way has the added benefit of displaying the calculated difference. If you're only interested in finding the rows that differ but don't care about the amount of the difference, you don't need the second expression at all. You can find the rows you want by placing the expression *<>[TotalCharge]* in the Criteria line under the first expression you entered. This asks Access to compare the amount calculated at the straight daily rate with the value in the TotalCharge field stored in the record and display the row only when the two values are not equal.

Query1

| Employee | Facility | Room | Check-In | Check-Out | Charge | Expr1 | Expr2 |
|---|---|---|---|---|---|---|---|
| 7 | Main Campus Housing A | 810 | 3/6/2007 | 3/18/2007 | $455.00 | 480 | ($25.00) |
| 7 | Main Campus Housing B | 111 | 3/24/2007 | 4/4/2007 | $1,040.00 | 1100 | ($60.00) |
| 3 | Main Campus Housing A | 502 | 4/14/2007 | 5/1/2007 | $1,420.00 | 1530 | ($110.00) |
| 10 | Main Campus Housing A | 902 | 4/1/2007 | 4/20/2007 | $1,600.00 | 1710 | ($110.00) |
| 1 | South Campus Housing C | 501 | 2/28/2007 | 3/13/2007 | $1,200.00 | 1300 | ($100.00) |
| 8 | Main Campus Housing A | 509 | 4/16/2007 | 4/29/2007 | $620.00 | 650 | ($30.00) |
| 3 | Main Campus Housing A | 707 | 5/2/2007 | 5/15/2007 | $680.00 | 715 | ($35.00) |
| 5 | Main Campus Housing B | 301 | 3/25/2007 | 4/9/2007 | $895.00 | 975 | ($80.00) |
| 3 | Main Campus Housing A | 207 | 3/25/2007 | 4/5/2007 | $570.00 | 605 | ($35.00) |
| 8 | Main Campus Housing A | 111 | 4/4/2007 | 4/20/2007 | $1,180.00 | 1280 | ($100.00) |
| 7 | Main Campus Housing A | 708 | 4/27/2007 | 5/2/2007 | $250.00 | 225 | $25.00 |
| 6 | Main Campus Housing B | 206 | 4/4/2007 | 4/15/2007 | $830.00 | 880 | ($50.00) |
| 7 | South Campus Housing C | 111 | 5/20/2007 | 5/27/2007 | $255.00 | 280 | ($25.00) |
| 4 | South Campus Housing C | 101 | 5/1/2007 | 5/22/2007 | $1,920.00 | 2100 | ($180.00) |
| 5 | Main Campus Housing B | 610 | 5/23/2007 | 6/6/2007 | $1,280.00 | 1400 | ($120.00) |
| 5 | Main Campus Housing A | 309 | 5/5/2007 | 5/22/2007 | $790.00 | 850 | ($60.00) |
| 8 | North Satellite Housing D | 402 | 5/9/2007 | 5/20/2007 | $830.00 | 880 | ($50.00) |
| 12 | Main Campus Housing B | 414 | 6/11/2007 | 6/15/2007 | $195.00 | 200 | ($5.00) |
| 8 | Main Campus Housing B | 403 | 5/25/2007 | 6/8/2007 | $1,150.00 | 1260 | ($110.00) |
| 13 | Main Campus Housing B | 103 | 6/3/2007 | 6/17/2007 | $1,150.00 | 1260 | ($110.00) |
| 2 | Main Campus Housing A | 410 | 6/8/2007 | 6/27/2007 | $750.00 | 760 | ($10.00) |
| 3 | North Satellite Housing D | 203 | 7/6/2007 | 7/22/2007 | $960.00 | 1040 | ($80.00) |
| 4 | Main Campus Housing B | 402 | 6/26/2007 | 7/14/2007 | $1,180.00 | 1260 | ($80.00) |
| 7 | Main Campus Housing A | 404 | 7/13/2007 | 7/22/2007 | $380.00 | 405 | ($25.00) |
| 5 | Main Campus Housing B | 304 | 7/9/2007 | 7/27/2007 | $1,180.00 | 1260 | ($80.00) |
| 13 | South Campus Housing C | 511 | 7/16/2007 | 7/27/2007 | $415.00 | 440 | ($25.00) |

Record: 1 of 39 No Filter Search

**Figure 7-20** The datasheet now shows only the rows where the calculation is different than the stored value.

You might have inferred from the earlier discussion about entering criteria that you can use only constant values in the Criteria or Or lines. As you can see, you can also compare the value of one field or expression with another field or expression containing a reference to a field.

## INSIDE OUT Adding Parentheses to Expressions for Clarity

You might have noticed that we placed an extra set of parentheses around the original expression we built to calculate the amount at the daily rate before subtracting that amount from the stored value. If you study Table 7-4 carefully, you'll see that we really didn't have to do this because Access would perform the multiplication before doing the final subtract. However, we find it's a good practice to add parentheses to make the sequence of operations crystal clear—we don't always remember the order of precedence rules, and we don't want to have to go looking up the information in Help every time we build an expression. Adding the parentheses makes sure we get the results we want.

So far, you have built fairly simple expressions. When you want to create a more complex expression, sometimes the Expression Builder can be useful, as discussed in the next section.

## Using the Expression Builder

For more complex expressions, Access 2007 provides a utility called the Expression Builder. Let's say you want to double-check the total amount owed for a reservation in the sample database. You have to work with several fields to do this–CheckInDate, CheckOutDate, DailyRate, and WeeklyRate. You need to calculate the number of weeks to charge at the WeeklyRate and then charge the remaining days at the DailyRate. To see how the Expression Builder works, start a new query on the tblReservations table. Click in an empty field in the design grid, and then click the Builder button in the Query Setup group of the Design contextual tab. Access opens the Expression Builder dialog box shown in Figure 7-21.

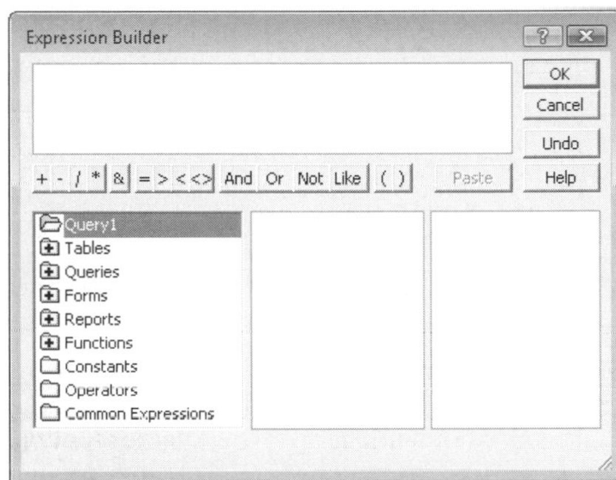


**Figure 7-21** The Expression Builder dialog box helps you build simple and complex expressions.

In the upper part of the dialog box is a blank text box in which you can build an expression. You can type the expression yourself, but it's sometimes more accurate to find field names, operators, and function names in the three panes in the lower part of the dialog box and to use the various expression operator buttons just below the text box.

The expression you need to build, which we'll walk you through in detail in the next few pages, will ultimately look like this:

```
((DateDiff("d", [tblReservations]![CheckInDate], [tblReservations]![CheckOutDate])
\ 7) * [WeeklyRate]) + ((DateDiff("d", [tblReservations]![CheckInDate],
[tblReservations]![CheckOutDate]) Mod 7) * [DailyRate])
```

You can use the Expression Builder to help you correctly construct this expression. Start by double-clicking the Functions category in the left pane, then select Built-In Functions to see the list of function categories in the center pane, and the list of functions within the selected category in the right pane. Select the Date/Time category in the center pane to narrow down the choices. Here you can see the DateDiff function (that you used earlier) as well as several other built-in functions you can use. (You can find a list of the most useful functions and their descriptions in Article 4, "Visual Basic Function Reference," on the companion CD.)

Double-click the DateDiff function in the right pane to add it to the expression text box at the top of the Expression Builder. When you add a function to your expression in this way, the Expression Builder shows you the parameters required by the function. You can click any parameter to highlight it and type a value or select a value from one of the lists in the bottom panes. Click <<interval>> and overtype it with **"d"**. (See Table 7-3 for a list of all the possible interval settings.) You need to insert the CheckInDate field from tblReservations for <<date1>> and the CheckOutDate field for <<date2>>. Click <<date1>> to highlight it and double-click Tables in the left pane to open up the list of table names. Scroll down until you find tblReservations and select it to see the list of field names in the second pane. Double-click CheckInDate. Then click <<date2>>, and double-click CheckOutDate. You don't need the <<firstweekday>> or <<firstweek>> parameters, so click them and press the Delete key to remove them. (You can also remove the extra commas if you like.) The Expression Builder should now look like Figure 7-22.

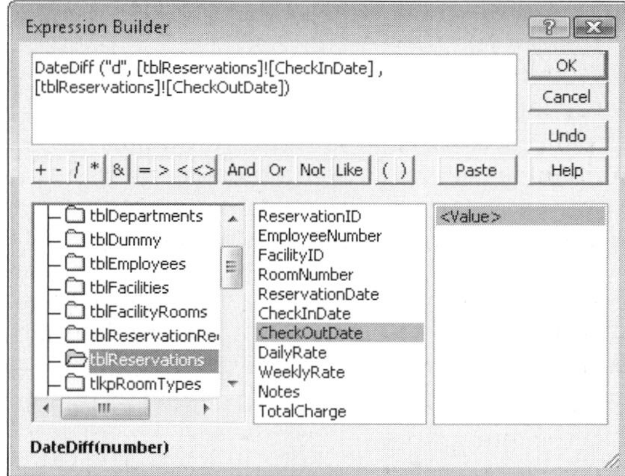


**Figure 7-22** Create a calculation using table field names in the Expression Builder dialog box.

You'll notice that the Expression Builder pastes *[tblReservations]![CheckInDate]* into the expression area, not just *CheckInDate*. There are two good reasons for this. First, the Expression Builder doesn't know whether you might include other tables in this query and whether some of those tables might have field names that are identical to the ones you're selecting now. The way to avoid conflicts is to *fully qualify* the field names by preceding them with the table name. When working in queries, separate the table name from the field name with a period or an exclamation point. Second, you should enclose all names of objects in Access in brackets ([ ]). If you designed the name without any blank spaces, you can leave out the brackets, but it's always good practice to include them.

## INSIDE OUT Understanding Name Separators in SQL

As you'll learn in Chapter 20, in most cases you should separate the name of an object from the name of an object within that object (for example, a field within a table) with an exclamation point. When you build an expression in the Expression Builder, you'll find that the Expression Builder separates names using exclamation points. However, as you'll learn in Article 2, "Understanding SQL," on the companion CD, the standard for the SQL database query language uses a period between the name of a table and the name of a field within the table. To be most compatible with the SQL standard when constructing a query expression, use a period between a table name and a field name. Access accepts either an exclamation point or a period in query design.

Next, you need to divide by 7 to calculate the number of weeks. You're not interested in any fractional part of a week, so you need to use the integer divide operator (\). Note that there is no operator button for integer divide. The operator buttons are arranged horizontally below the expression text box. So, you can either type the operator or scroll down in the leftmost pane, select Operators to open that list, select Arithmetic in the second pane, and then double-click the integer divide operator (\) in the rightmost list to add it to your expression. Make sure the insertion point in the expression box is positioned after the integer divide operator and type the number **7**.

The next operation you need is to multiply the expression you have thus far by the WeeklyRate field from tblReservations. If you like, you can add left and right parentheses around the expression before adding the multiply operator and the field. Remember from Table 7-4 that multiplication and division are of equal precedence, so Access evaluates the division before the multiplication (left to right) even if you don't add the parentheses. But, as we noted earlier, we like to make the precedence of operations crystal clear, so we recommend that you add the parentheses. Press the Home key to go to the beginning of the expression, click the left parenthesis button, press the End key to go to the end, click the right parenthesis button, click the multiply operator (*) button, and finally select the WeeklyRate field from the tblReservations field list.

### Note

WeekyRate and DailyRate are currency fields. DateDiff returns an integer, and the result of an integer divide (\) or a modulus (Mod) operation is an integer. Whenever you ask Access to evaluate an arithmetic expression, it returns a result that has a data type sufficiently complex to contain the result. As you might expect, multiplying an integer (a simple data type) with a currency field (a more complex data type) returns a currency field.

You need to add this entire expression to the calculation for remaining days at the daily rate, so press Ctrl+Home again and add one more left parenthesis, press the Ctrl+End key, and click the right parenthesis button to complete this first part of the expression. Click the addition operator to add it to your expression. Rather than scan back and forth to add parentheses as we build the second part of the expression, click the left parenthesis button twice to start building the calculation for extra days. Add the DateDiff function again, click <<interval>>, and type **"d"**. Click <<date1>>, find CheckInDate in tblReservations again, and double-click it to add it to your expression. Click <<date2>> and double-click the CheckOutDate field. Remove <<firstweekday>> and <<firstweek>> from the function.

Now, you need to know how many days beyond full weeks are in the reservation. You might be tempted to divide by 7 again and try to extract the remainder, but there's a handy operator that returns only the remainder of a division for you–Mod. Scroll down in the left pane and select Operators. In the middle pane, select Arithmetic to see only the arithmetic operators in the right pane. Double-click Mod to add it to your expression after the parentheses.

We're almost done. Type the number **7** and click the right parenthesis button to close the Mod calculation. Click the multiply operator button, and then go back to tblReservations and double-click the DailyRate field. Click the right parenthesis button one last time to finish the expression. Verify that your completed expression exactly matches the one in Figure 7-23.

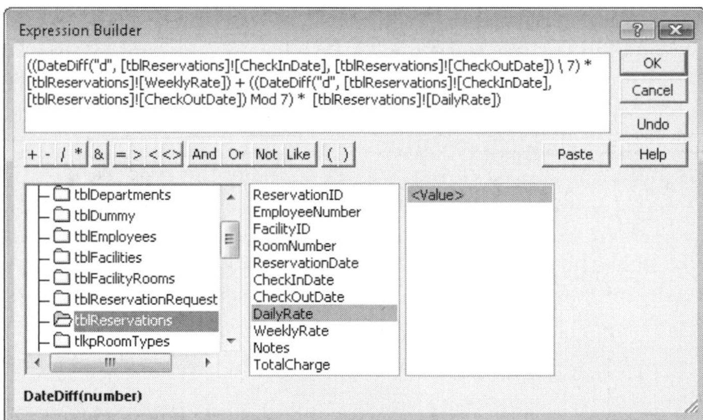


**Figure 7-23** Your completed expression in the Expression Builder dialog box should match this figure.

Click OK to paste your result into the design grid. Go ahead and add ReservationID, FacilityID, RoomNumber, CheckInDate, CheckOutDate, and TotalCharge to your query grid. When you switch to Datasheet view, your result should look like Figure 7-24.

Query1

| Expr1 | Reservation | Facility | Room | Check-In | Check-Out | Charge |
|---|---|---|---|---|---|---|
| $455.00 | 1 | Main Campus Housing A | 810 | 3/6/2007 | 3/18/2007 | $455.00 |
| $1,040.00 | 2 | Main Campus Housing B | 111 | 3/24/2007 | 4/4/2007 | $1,040.00 |
| $195.00 | 3 | North Satellite Housing D | 305 | 3/20/2007 | 3/23/2007 | $195.00 |
| $1,420.00 | 4 | Main Campus Housing A | 502 | 4/14/2007 | 5/1/2007 | $1,420.00 |
| $100.00 | 5 | Main Campus Housing B | 214 | 3/26/2007 | 3/28/2007 | $100.00 |
| $1,600.00 | 6 | Main Campus Housing A | 902 | 4/1/2007 | 4/20/2007 | $1,600.00 |
| $1,240.00 | 7 | South Campus Housing C | 501 | 2/28/2007 | 3/13/2007 | $1,200.00 |
| $620.00 | 8 | Main Campus Housing A | 509 | 4/16/2007 | 4/29/2007 | $620.00 |
| $210.00 | 9 | Main Campus Housing B | 504 | 4/20/2007 | 4/23/2007 | $210.00 |
| $680.00 | 10 | Main Campus Housing A | 707 | 5/2/2007 | 5/15/2007 | $680.00 |
| $895.00 | 11 | Main Campus Housing B | 301 | 3/25/2007 | 4/9/2007 | $895.00 |
| $570.00 | 12 | Main Campus Housing A | 207 | 3/25/2007 | 4/5/2007 | $570.00 |
| $1,180.00 | 13 | Main Campus Housing A | 111 | 4/4/2007 | 4/20/2007 | $1,180.00 |
| $225.00 | 14 | Main Campus Housing A | 708 | 4/27/2007 | 5/2/2007 | $250.00 |
| $830.00 | 15 | Main Campus Housing B | 206 | 4/4/2007 | 4/15/2007 | $830.00 |
| $255.00 | 16 | South Campus Housing C | 111 | 5/20/2007 | 5/27/2007 | $255.00 |
| $1,920.00 | 17 | South Campus Housing C | 101 | 5/1/2007 | 5/22/2007 | $1,920.00 |
| $450.00 | 18 | Main Campus Housing A | 702 | 5/23/2007 | 5/28/2007 | $450.00 |
| $1,280.00 | 19 | Main Campus Housing B | 610 | 5/23/2007 | 6/6/2007 | $1,280.00 |
| $790.00 | 20 | Main Campus Housing A | 309 | 5/5/2007 | 5/22/2007 | $790.00 |
| $830.00 | 21 | North Satellite Housing D | 402 | 5/9/2007 | 5/20/2007 | $830.00 |
| $350.00 | 22 | South Campus Housing C | 103 | 5/3/2007 | 5/8/2007 | $350.00 |
| $200.00 | 23 | Main Campus Housing B | 414 | 6/11/2007 | 6/15/2007 | $195.00 |
| $220.00 | 24 | Main Campus Housing A | 207 | 5/25/2007 | 5/29/2007 | $220.00 |
| $110.00 | 25 | South Campus Housing C | 607 | 6/26/2007 | 6/28/2007 | $110.00 |
| $180.00 | 26 | Main Campus Housing B | 303 | 6/30/2007 | 7/2/2007 | $180.00 |

Record: 7 of 58 No Filter Search

**Figure 7-24** Switch to Datasheet view to see the result of your complex calculation expression.

Do you notice any stored values that don't match what you just calculated? (Hint: Look at the highlighted row.) If you haven't changed the sample data, you'll find several rows that we purposefully updated with invalid TotalCharge values. Here's a challenge: Go back to Design view and enter the criteria you need to display only the rows where your calculated charge doesn't match the TotalCharge stored in the table. You can find the solution saved as qxmplUnmatchedCharges in the HousingDataCopy.accdb sample database.

### INSIDE OUT Is the Builder Useful? You Decide

We personally never use the Expression Builder when we're creating applications in Access 2007. We find it more cumbersome than directly typing the expression we think we need and then trying it out. We included this discussion because some beginning developers might find that the Expression Builder helps them learn how to build correct expression and function call syntax.

We used the DateDiff function to solve this problem, but Access 2007 has several other useful functions to help you deal with date and time values. For example, you might want to see only a part of the date or time value in your query. You might also want to use these functions to help you filter the results in your query. Table 7-5 explains each date and time function and includes filter examples that use the ContactDateTime field in the tblContactEvents table in the Conrad Systems Contacts sample database.

Table 7-5 **Date and Time Functions**

| Function | Description | Example |
|---|---|---|
| Day(*date*) | Returns a value from 1 through 31 for the day of the month. | To select records with contact events that occurred after the 10th of any month, enter **Day([ContactDateTime])** in an empty column on the Field line and enter **>10** as the criterion for that field. |
| Month(*date*) | Returns a value from 1 through 12 for the month of the year. | To find all contact events that occurred in March (of any year), enter **Month([ContactDateTime])** in an empty column on the Field line and enter **3** as the criterion for that field. |
| Year(*date*) | Returns a value from 100 through 9999 for the year. | To find contact events that happened in 2007, enter **Year([ContactDateTime])** in an empty column on the Field line and enter **2007** as the criterion for that field. |
| Weekday(*date*) | As a default, returns a value from 1 (Sunday) through 7 (Saturday) for the day of the week. | To find contact events that occurred between Monday and Friday, enter **Weekday([ContactDateTime])** in an empty column on the Field line and enter **Between 2 And 6** as the criterion for that field. |
| Hour(*date*) | Returns a value from 0 through 23 for the hour of the day. | To find contact events that happened before noon, enter **Hour([ContactDateTime])** in an empty column on the Field line and enter **<12** as the criterion for that field. |
| DateAdd (*interval, amount, date*) | Adds an amount in the interval you specify to a date/time value. | To find contact events that occurred more than six months ago, enter **<DateAdd("m", –6, Date())** as the criterion under ContactDateTime. (See also the Date function below.) |
| DatePart (*interval, date*) | Returns a portion of the date or time, depending on the interval code you supply. Useful interval codes are "q" for quarter of the year (1 through 4) and "ww" for week of the year (1 through 53). | To find contact events in the second quarter, enter **DatePart("q", [ContactDateTime])** in an empty column on the Field line, and enter **2** as the criterion for that field. |
| Date() | Returns the current system date. | To select contact events that happened more than 30 days ago, enter **<(Date() – 30)** as the criterion under ContactDateTime. |

**For additional useful functions, see Article 4, "Visual Basic Function Reference," on the companion CD.**



## Specifying Field Names

Every field must have a name. By default, the name of a simple field in a query is the name of the field from the source table. However, when you create a new field using an expression, the expression doesn't have a name unless you or Access assigns one. You have seen that when you create an expression in the Field row of the design grid, Access adds a prefix such as *Expr1* followed by a colon—that is the name that Access is assigning to your expression. Remember, the column heading for the field is, by default, the field name unless you specify a different caption property setting. As you know, you can assign or change a caption for a field in a query by using the field's property sheet.

### Understanding Field Names and Captions

In the world of tables and queries, every field—even calculated ones—must have a name. When you create a field in a table, you give it a name. When you use a table in a query and include a field from the table in the query output, the name of the field output by the query is the same as the field name in the table. If you create a calculated field in a query, you must assign a name to that field. If you don't, Access assigns an ugly *ExprN* name for you. But you can override this and assign your own field name to expressions. You can also override the default field name for a simple field with another name. When you use a query in another query or a form or report, or you open a query as a recordset in Visual Basic, you use the field name to indicate which field you want to fetch from the query.

You can also define a Caption property for a field. When you do that, what you put in the caption becomes the external label for the field. You'll see the caption in column headings in Datasheet view. Later, when you begin to work with forms and reports, you'll find that the caption becomes the default label for the field. If you don't define a caption, Access shows you the field name instead.

You can change or assign field names that will appear in the recordset of a query. This feature is particularly useful when you've calculated a value in the query that you'll use in a form, a report, or another query. In the queries shown in Figures 7-15, 7-17, and 7-19, you calculated a value and Access assigned a temporary field name. You can replace this name with something more meaningful. For example, in the first query you might want to use something like FullName and CityStateZip. In the second query, RecalculatedCharge might be appropriate. To change a name generated by Access, replace *ExprN* with the name you want in the Field row in the query design grid. To assign a new name to a field, place the insertion point at the beginning of the field specification and insert the new name followed by a colon. Figure 7-25 shows the first query with the field names changed.

Query1

| FullName | CityStateZip |
|---|---|
| Koch, Reed | West Mansfield, OH 43358 |
| Kim, Tim | Meredith, NH 03253 |
| Tippett, John | Florence, AL 35630 |
| DeGrasse, Kirk | Agua Dulce, CA 91350 |
| Lawrence, David Oliver | Christiansburg, VA 24073 |
| Adams, Jay | Ramona, SD 57054 |
| Richins, Jack S. | Saint David, ME 04773 |
| Bradley, David M. | Bayou La Batre, AL 36509 |
| Eyink, Scott | Los Osos, CA 93402 |
| Berndt, Matthias | Rockland, TX 75938 |
| Willett, Benjamin C. | Austin, MO 64725 |
| Shock, Misty | Newhall, CA 91381 |
| Randall, Linda | Trail Creek, IN 46360 |
| Schare, Gary | Rock Springs, AZ 85324 |
| Viescas, John L. | , |
| Conrad, Jeff | , |
| * | |

**Figure 7-25** You can change the *Expr1* and *Expr2* field names shown in Figure 7-16 to display more meaningful field names.

Note that we could have made the column headings you see even more readable by also assigning a caption to these fields via the field's property sheet. We might have chosen something like Person Name for the first field and City-State-Zip for the second field. Keep in mind that setting the caption does not change the actual name of the field when you use the query in a form, a report, or Visual Basic code.

## Sorting Data

Normally, Access 2007 displays the rows in your recordset in the order in which they're retrieved from the database. You can add sorting information to determine the sequence of the data in a query. Click in the Sort row for the field you want to sort on, click the arrow in this row, and then select Ascending or Descending from the list. In the example shown in Figure 7-26, the query results are to be sorted in descending order based on the calculated NewTotalCharge field. (Note that we have given the calculated field a field name.) The recordset will list the most expensive reservations first. The resulting Datasheet view is shown in Figure 7-27. You can find this query saved as qryXmplChargeCalcSorted in the HousingDataCopy.accdb sample database.

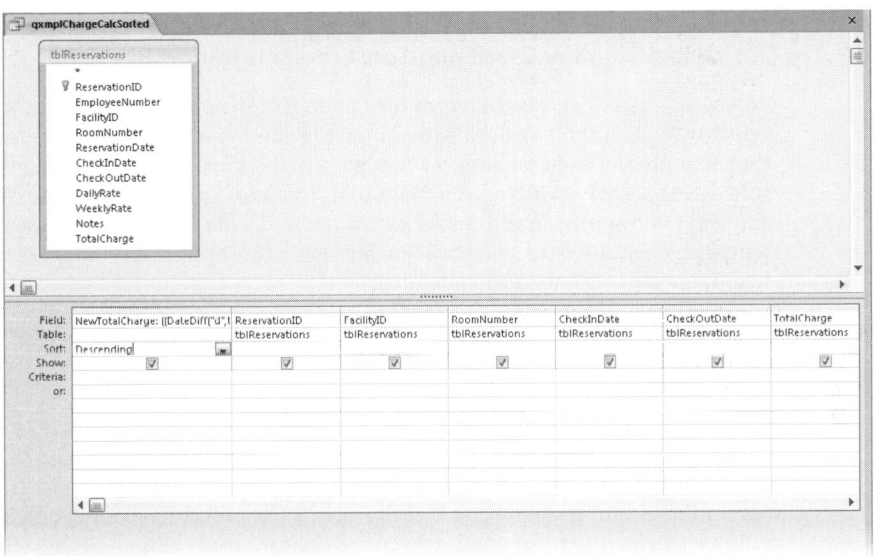


**Figure 7-26** Access sorts the query results on the NewTotalCharge field in descending order.

qxmplChargeCalcSorted

| NewTotalCharge | Reservation | Facility | Room | Check-In | Check-Out | Charge |
|---|---|---|---|---|---|---|
| $1,920.00 | 17 | South Campus Housing C | 101 | 5/1/2007 | 5/22/2007 | $1,920.00 |
| $1,690.00 | 53 | South Campus Housing C | 106 | 8/21/2007 | 9/10/2007 | $1,690.00 |
| $1,600.00 | 6 | Main Campus Housing A | 902 | 4/1/2007 | 4/20/2007 | $1,600.00 |
| $1,420.00 | 4 | Main Campus Housing A | 502 | 4/14/2007 | 5/1/2007 | $1,420.00 |
| $1,380.00 | 41 | South Campus Housing C | 401 | 6/19/2007 | 7/4/2007 | $1,380.00 |
| $1,280.00 | 56 | South Campus Housing C | 109 | 8/10/2007 | 8/24/2007 | $1,280.00 |
| $1,280.00 | 19 | Main Campus Housing B | 610 | 5/23/2007 | 6/6/2007 | $1,280.00 |
| $1,240.00 | 7 | South Campus Housing C | 501 | 2/28/2007 | 3/13/2007 | $1,200.00 |
| $1,180.00 | 13 | Main Campus Housing A | 111 | 4/4/2007 | 4/20/2007 | $1,180.00 |
| $1,180.00 | 35 | Main Campus Housing B | 402 | 6/26/2007 | 7/14/2007 | $1,180.00 |
| $1,180.00 | 38 | Main Campus Housing B | 304 | 7/9/2007 | 7/27/2007 | $1,180.00 |
| $1,150.00 | 30 | Main Campus Housing B | 103 | 6/3/2007 | 6/17/2007 | $1,150.00 |
| $1,150.00 | 28 | Main Campus Housing B | 403 | 5/25/2007 | 6/8/2007 | $1,150.00 |
| $1,040.00 | 48 | Main Campus Housing B | 402 | 8/11/2007 | 8/27/2007 | $1,040.00 |
| $1,040.00 | 2 | Main Campus Housing B | 111 | 3/24/2007 | 4/4/2007 | $1,040.00 |
| $960.00 | 34 | North Satellite Housing D | 203 | 7/6/2007 | 7/22/2007 | $960.00 |
| $960.00 | 49 | Main Campus Housing B | 114 | 8/17/2007 | 9/7/2007 | $960.00 |
| $910.00 | 42 | Main Campus Housing B | 212 | 7/15/2007 | 7/27/2007 | $910.00 |
| $895.00 | 11 | Main Campus Housing B | 301 | 3/25/2007 | 4/9/2007 | $895.00 |
| $850.00 | 43 | South Campus Housing C | 208 | 8/1/2007 | 8/21/2007 | $850.00 |
| $830.00 | 21 | North Satellite Housing D | 402 | 5/9/2007 | 5/20/2007 | $830.00 |
| $830.00 | 15 | Main Campus Housing B | 206 | 4/4/2007 | 4/15/2007 | $830.00 |
| $790.00 | 20 | Main Campus Housing A | 309 | 5/5/2007 | 5/22/2007 | $790.00 |
| $730.00 | 44 | Main Campus Housing B | 102 | 7/22/2007 | 8/2/2007 | $730.00 |
| $710.00 | 32 | Main Campus Housing A | 410 | 6/8/2007 | 6/27/2007 | $750.00 |
| $680.00 | 10 | Main Campus Housing A | 707 | 5/2/2007 | 5/15/2007 | $680.00 |

Record: 1 of 58 No Filter Search

**Figure 7-27** Datasheet view shows the recordset of the query shown in Figure 7-25 sorted on the NewTotalCharge field.

## INSIDE OUT Why Specifying Sort Criteria Is Important

When Access 2007 solves a query, it tries to do it in the most efficient way. When you first construct and run a query, Access might return the records in the sequence you expect (for example, in primary key sequence of the table). However, if you want to be sure Access always returns rows in this order, you must specify sort criteria. As you later add and remove rows in your table, Access might decide that fetching rows in a different sequence might be faster, which, in the absence of sorting criteria, might result in a different row sequence than you intended.

You can also sort on multiple fields. Access honors your sorting criteria from left to right in the design grid. If, for example, you want to sort by FacilityID ascending and then by NewTotalCharge descending, you should include the FacilityID field to the left of the NewTotalCharge field. If the additional field you want to sort is already in the design grid but in the wrong location, click the column selector box (the tinted box above the field row) to select the entire column and then click the selector box again and drag the field to its new location. If you want the field that is out of position to still appear where you originally placed it, add the field to the design grid again in the correct sorting sequence, clear the Show check box (you don't want two copies of the field displayed), and set the Sort specification. Figure 7-28 shows the query shown in Figure 7-26 modified to sort first by FacilityID and then by NewTotalCharge, but leave FacilityID displayed after ReservationID. We saved this query in the HousingDataCopy.accdb sample database as qxmplChargeCalcSortedTwo.

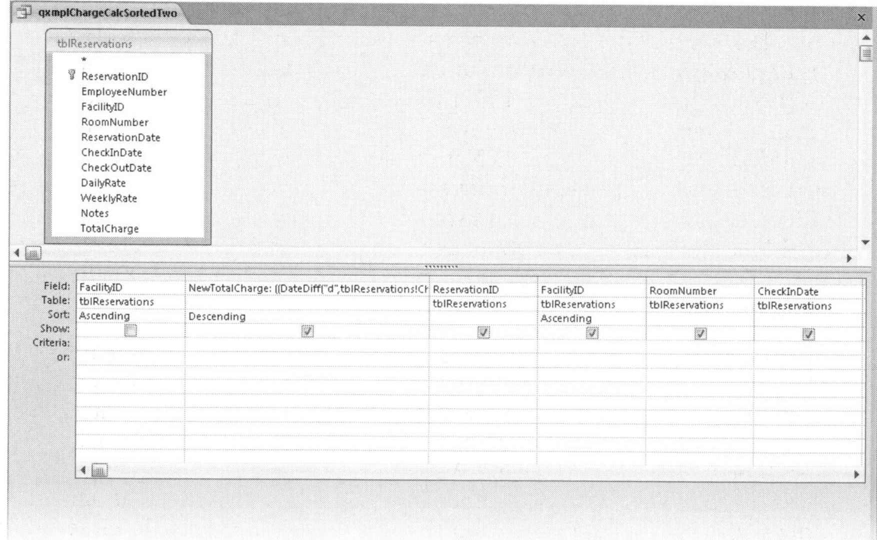


**Figure 7-28** This example sorts on two fields while maintaining the original field sequence in the query output.

INSIDE OUT **A Reminder: Why Lookup Properties Can Be Confusing**

If you open the datasheet of qxmplChargeCalcSortedTwo and scroll down in the recordset, you'll find the Facility column sorted Main Campus Housing A, Main Campus Housing B, South Campus Housing C, and North Satellite Housing D. Why does South appear before North if the values are supposed to be sorted in ascending order? Remember that in Chapter 5 we warned you about Lookup properties confusing the display you see. The information you're seeing in the datasheet comes from the Lookup defined on the FacilityID column in tblReservations—you're seeing the related facility name from tblFacilities. However, the actual value of FacilityID is a number. You can click on the FacilityID column, open the field's property sheet, click the Lookup tab, and set the Display Control property to Text Box to see the actual number value. When you do this and look at the datasheet again, you'll see that the values are sorted correctly.

# Testing Validation Rule Changes

You learned in Chapter 4 how to define both field and table validation rules. You also learned in Chapter 5 that you can change these rules even after you have data in your table. Access 2007 warns you if some of the data in your table doesn't satisfy the new rule, but it doesn't tell you which rows have problems.

## Checking a New Field Validation Rule

The best way to find out if any rows will fail a new field validation rule is to write a query to test your data before you make the change. The trick is you must specify criteria that are the converse of your proposed rule change to find the rows that don't match. For example, if you are planning to set the Required property to Yes or specify a Validation Rule property of Is Not Null on a field (both tests mean the same thing), you want to look for rows containing a field that Is Null. If you want to limit the daily price of a room to <= 90, then you must look for values that are > 90 to find the rows that will fail. Another way to think about asking for the converse of a validation rule is to put the word *Not* in front of the rule. If the new rule is going to be <= 90, then Not <= 90 will find the bad rows.

Let's see what we need to do to test a proposed validation rule change to tblFacilityRooms in the sample database. The daily room rate should not exceed $90.00, so the new rule in the DailyRate field will be <=90. To test for rooms that exceed this new limit, start a new query on tblFacilityRooms. Include the fields FacilityID, RoomNumber, RoomType, DailyRate, and WeeklyRate in the query's design grid. (You need at least FacilityID and RoomNumber–the primary key fields–to be able to identify which rows fail.) Under DailyRate, enter the converse of the new rule: either **>90** or **Not <=90**. Your query should look like Figure 7-29.

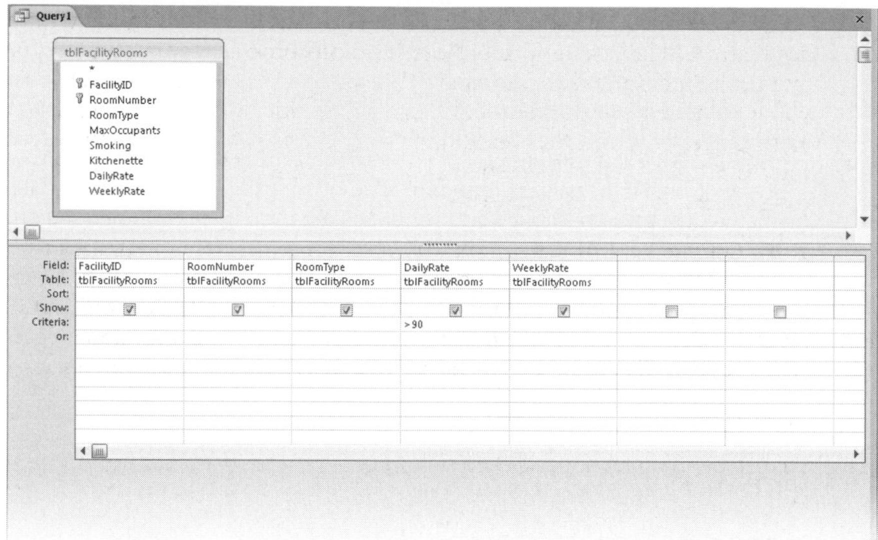


**Figure 7-29** Create a new query to test a proposed new field validation rule.

If you run this query against the original data in the sample database, you'll find 26 rooms that are priced higher than the new proposed rule. As you'll learn in "Working in Query Datasheet View" on page 384, you can update these rows by typing a new value directly in the query datasheet.

Let's try something. Select one of the invalid values you found in the query datasheet and try to type the new maximum value of $90.00. If you try to save the row, you'll get an error message because there's a table validation rule that prevents you from setting a DailyRate value that when multiplied by 7 is more than the WeeklyRate value. It looks like you'll have to fix both values if you want to change your field validation rule.

## Checking a New Table Validation Rule

Checking a proposed new field validation rule is simple. But what about making a change to a table validation rule? Typically, a table validation rule compares one field with another, so to check a new rule, you'll need more complex criteria in your query.

There's already a table validation rule in the tblFacilityRooms table in the HousingDataCopy.accdb sample database. The rule makes sure that the weekly rate is not more than 7 times the daily rate—it wouldn't be much of a discount if it were! Suppose you now want to be sure that the weekly rate reflects a true discount from the daily rate. Your proposed new rule might make sure that the weekly rate is no more than 6 times the daily rate—if an employee stays a full week, the last night is essentially free. Your new rule might look like the following:

```
([DailyRate]*6)>=[WeeklyRate]
```

So, you need to write a query that checks the current values in the WeeklyRate field to see if any will fail the new rule. Note that you could also create an expression to calculate DailyRate times 6 and compare that value with WeeklyRate. When the expression you want to test involves a calculation on one side of the comparison with a simple field value on the other side of the comparison, it's easier to compare the simple field with the expression. Remember, you need to create the converse of the expression to find rows that won't pass the new rule.

You can start with the query you built in the previous section or create a new query. You need at least the primary key fields from the table as well as the fields you need to perform the comparison. In this case, you need to compare the current value of WeeklyRate with the expression on DailyRate. Let's turn the expression around so that it's easier to see what you need to enter in the query grid. The expression looks like this:

```
[WeeklyRate]<=([DailyRate]*6)
```

To test the converse on the WeeklyRate field's Criteria row of your query, you need either

```
>([DailyRate]*6)
```

or

```
Not <=([DailyRate]*6)
```

Your test query should look like Figure 7-30.

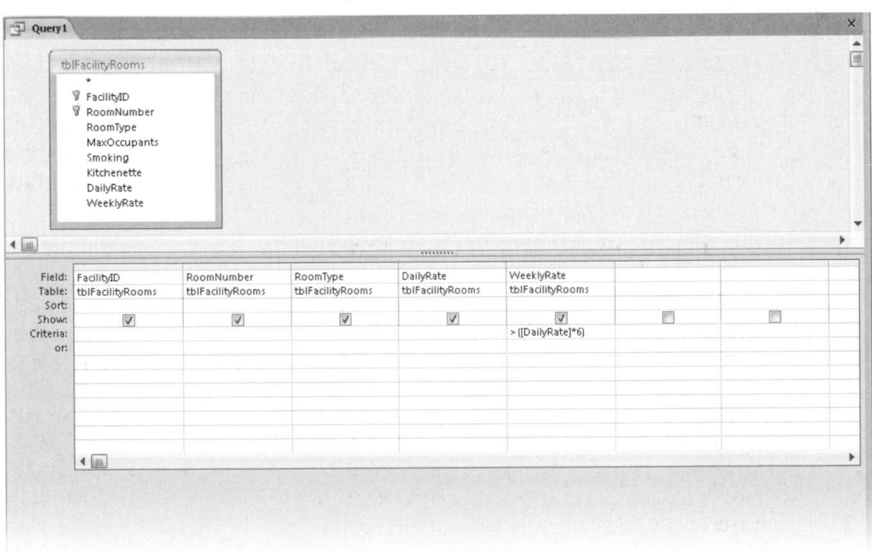


**Figure 7-30** You can create a query to test a new table validation rule.

If you run this query, you'll find that nearly all the rows in the table fail the new test. When we loaded sample data into the table, we created weekly rates that are approximately 6.4 times the daily rate—so none of the rates pass the new test. In Chapter 9, you'll learn how to create an update query to fix both the daily and weekly rates to match the new rules discussed in this section.

# Working in Query Datasheet View

When you're developing an application, you might need to work in table or query Datasheet view to help you load sample data or to solve problems in the queries, forms, and reports you're creating. You might also decide to create certain forms in your application that display information in Datasheet view. Also, the techniques for updating and manipulating data in forms are very similar to doing so in datasheets—so you need to understand how datasheets work to be able to explain to your users how to use your application. If you're using Access 2007 as a personal database to analyze information, you might frequently work with information in Datasheet view. In either case, you should understand how to work with data editing, and the best way to learn how is to understand viewing and editing data in Datasheet view.

Before you get started with the remaining examples in this chapter, open ContactsDataCopy.accdb from your sample files folder. In that database, you'll find a query named qryContactsDatasheet that we'll use in the remainder of this chapter. We defined this query to select key fields from tblContacts and display a subdatasheet from tblContactEvents.

## Moving Around and Using Keyboard Shortcuts

Open the qryContactsDatasheet query in the ContactsDataCopy.accdb database. You should see a result similar to Figure 7-31. Displaying different records or fields is simple. You can use the horizontal scroll bar to scroll through a table's fields, or you can use the vertical scroll bar to scroll through a table's records.

In the lower-left corner of the table in Datasheet view, you can see a set of navigation buttons and the Record Number box, as shown in Figure 7-32. The Record Number box shows the *relative record number* of the current record (meaning the number of the selected record in relation to the current set of records, also called a recordset). You might not see the current record in the window if you've scrolled the display. The number to the right of the new record button shows the total number of records in the current recordset. If you've applied a filter against the table (see "Searching for and Filtering Data" on page 405), this number might be less than the total number of records in the table or query.

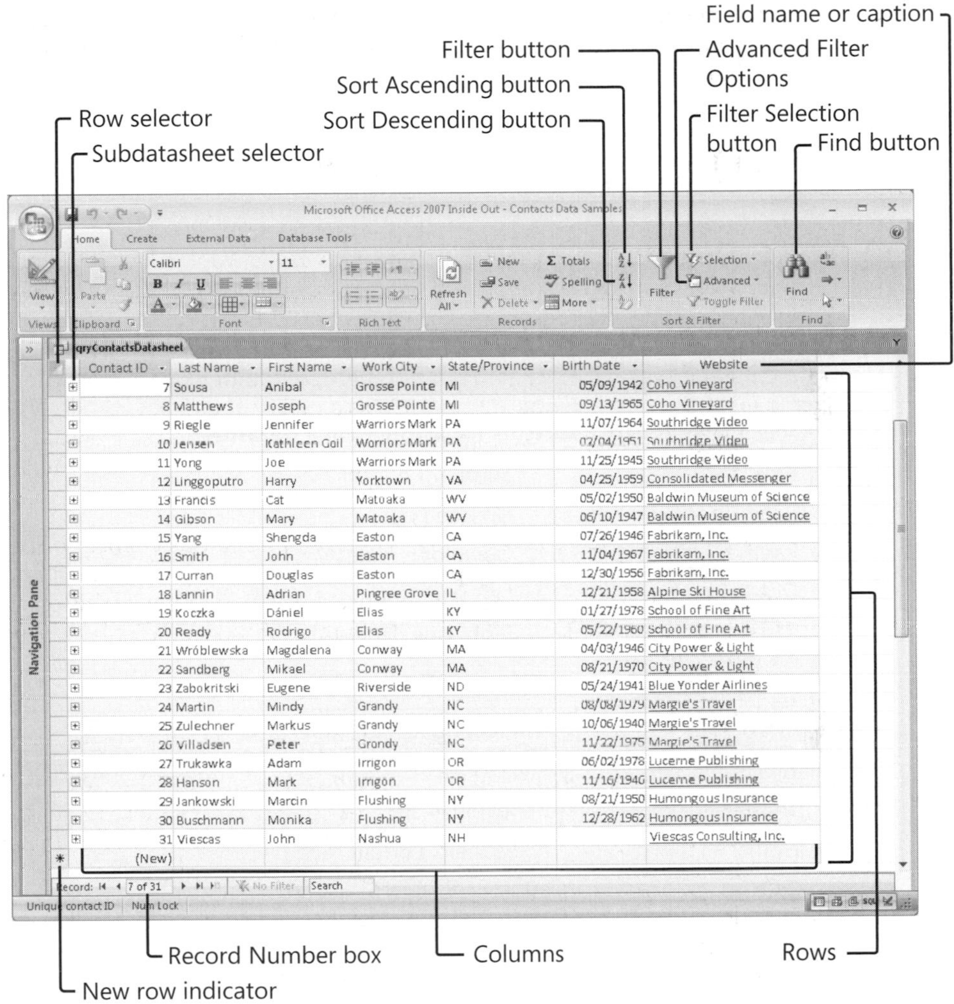


**Figure 7-31** Open the Datasheet view of the qryContactsDatasheet query to begin learning about moving around and editing in a datasheet.

You can quickly move to the record you want by typing a value in the Record Number box and pressing Enter or by using the navigation buttons. You can also click the Go To command in the Find group on the Home tab on the Ribbon to move to the first, last, next, or previous record, or to move to a new, empty record. You can make any record current by clicking anywhere in its row; the number in the Record Number box will change to indicate the row you've selected.

You might find it easier to use the keyboard rather than the mouse to move around in a datasheet, especially if you're typing new data. Table 7-6 lists the keyboard shortcuts for scrolling in a datasheet. Table 7-7 lists the keyboard shortcuts for selecting data in a datasheet.

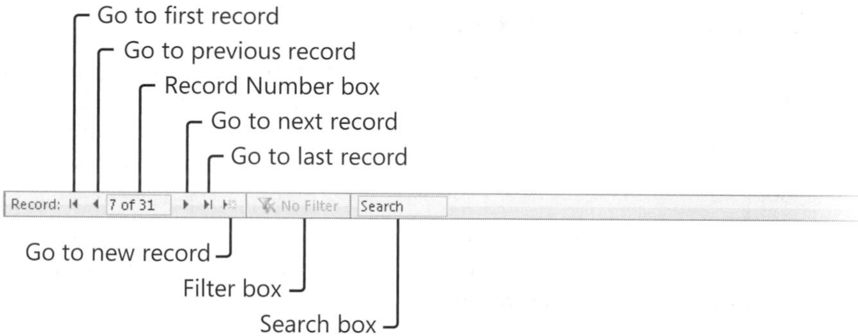


**Figure 7-32** You can navigate through the datasheet records using the navigation buttons and Record Number box.

Table 7-6 **Keyboard Shortcuts for Scrolling in a Datasheet**

| Keys | Scrolling Action |
|---|---|
| Page Up | Up one page |
| Page Down | Down one page |
| Ctrl+Page Up | Left one page |
| Ctrl+Page Down | Right one page |

Table 7-7 **Keyboard Shortcuts for Selecting Data in a Datasheet**

| Keys | Selecting Action |
|---|---|
| Tab | Next field |
| Shift+Tab | Previous field |
| Home | First field, current record |
| End | Last field, current record |
| Up Arrow | Current field, previous record |
| Down Arrow | Current field, next record |
| Ctrl+Up Arrow | Current field, first record |
| Ctrl+Down Arrow | Current field, last record |
| Ctrl+Home | First field, first record |
| Ctrl+End | Last field, last record |
| Alt+F5 | Record Number box |
| Ctrl+Spacebar | The current column |
| Shift+Spacebar | The current record |
| F2 | When in a field, toggles between selecting all data in the field and single-character edit mode |

## Working with Subdatasheets

Microsoft Access 2000 introduced a new feature that lets you display information from multiple related tables in a single datasheet. In the design we developed for the Conrad Systems Contacts sample database, contacts can have multiple contact events and contact products. In some cases, it might be useful to open a query on contacts and be able to see either related events or products in the same datasheet window.

You might have noticed the little plus-sign indicators in the datasheet for qryContacts-Datasheet in Figure 7-31. Click the plus sign next to the second row to open the Contact Events subdatasheet as shown in Figure 7-33.

qryContactsDatasheet

| Contact ID | Last Name | First Name | Work City | State/Province | Birth Date | Website |
|---|---|---|---|---|---|---|
| 1 | Stoklasa | Jan | Youngsville | PA | 12/25/1955 | Contoso, Ltd |
| 2 | Peterson | Palle | Youngsville | PA | 06/07/1963 | Contoso, Ltd |

| Date / Time | Type | Notes | Follow up? | Follow-up D | Add New Field |
|---|---|---|---|---|---|
| 02/24/2007 17:23 | 1 | | ☐ | | |
| 07/03/2007 15:06 | 1 | | ☐ | | |
| * 10/21/2006 9:42 | | | ☐ | | |

| Contact ID | Last Name | First Name | Work City | State/Province | Birth Date | Website |
|---|---|---|---|---|---|---|
| 3 | Michaels | Tom | Youngsville | PA | 07/17/1960 | Contoso, Ltd |
| 4 | Dixon | Andrew | Kalamazoo | MI | 04/08/1959 | Fourth Coffee |
| 5 | West | Paul | Kalamazoo | MI | 03/07/1964 | Fourth Coffee |
| 6 | Kresnadi | Mario | Grosse Pointe | MI | 03/24/1960 | Coho Vineyard |
| 7 | Sousa | Anibal | Grosse Pointe | MI | 05/09/1942 | Coho Vineyard |
| 8 | Matthews | Joseph | Grosse Pointe | MI | 09/13/1965 | Coho Vineyard |
| 9 | [illegible] | Jennifer | Warriors Mark | PA | 11/07/1964 | Southridge Video |
| 10 | Jensen | Kathleen Gail | Warriors Mark | PA | 02/04/1951 | Southridge Video |
| 11 | Yong | Joe | Warriors Mark | PA | 11/25/1945 | Southridge Video |
| 12 | Linggoputro | Harry | Yorktown | VA | 04/25/1959 | Consolidated Messenger |
| 13 | Francis | Cat | Matoaka | WV | 05/02/1950 | Baldwin Museum of Science |
| 14 | Gibson | Mary | Matoaka | WV | 06/10/1947 | Baldwin Museum of Science |
| 15 | Yang | Shengda | Easton | CA | 07/26/1946 | Fabrikam, Inc. |
| 16 | Smith | John | Easton | CA | 11/04/1967 | Fabrikam, Inc. |
| 17 | Curran | Douglas | Easton | CA | 12/30/1956 | Fabrikam, Inc. |
| 18 | Lannin | Adrian | Pingree Grove | IL | 12/21/1958 | Alpine Ski House |
| 19 | Koczka | Dániel | Elias | KY | 01/27/1978 | School of Fine Art |
| 20 | Ready | Rodrigo | Elias | KY | 05/22/1960 | School of Fine Art |
| 21 | Wróblewska | Magdalena | Conway | MA | 04/03/1946 | City Power & Light |
| 22 | Sandberg | Mikael | Conway | MA | 08/21/1970 | City Power & Light |

Record: 1 of 31 No Filter Search

**Figure 7-33** Click the plus sign to view the contact event details for the second contact in a subdatasheet.

A subdatasheet doesn't appear automatically in a query, even if you've defined subdatasheet properties for your table as described in Chapter 4. We had to open the property sheet for the query in Design view and specify the subdatasheet you see. Figure 7-34 shows the properties we set. You can find more details about setting these properties in Chapter 4 and in Chapter 8.

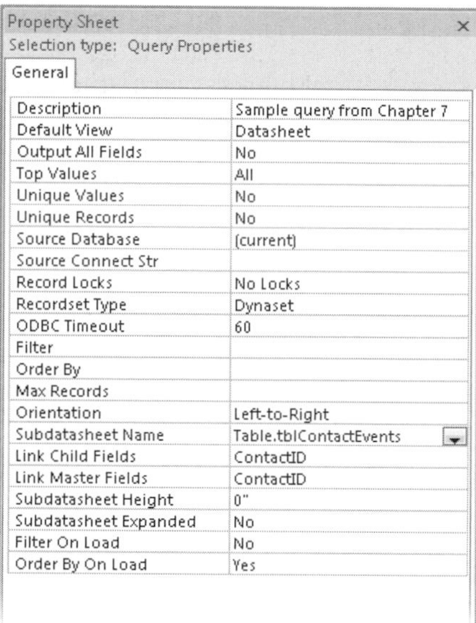


**Figure 7-34** The property sheet for the qryContactsDatasheet query displays the subdatasheet properties.

You can click the plus sign next to each order row to see the contact event detail information for that contact. If you want to expand or collapse all the subdatasheets, click More in the Records group on the Home tab, click Subdatasheet, and then click the option you want as shown in Figure 7-35.

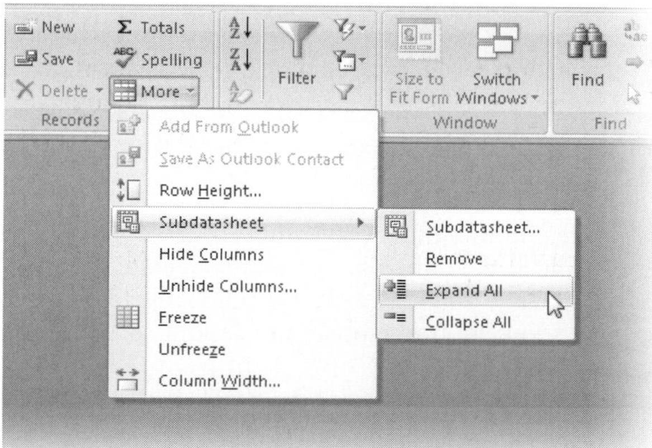


**Figure 7-35** The Subdatasheet menu allows you to easily expand all subdatasheets, collapse all subdatasheets, or remove the currently displayed subdatasheet.

The information from the related tblContactEvents table is interesting, but what if you want to see the products the contact has purchased instead? To do this, while in Datasheet view, click More on the Home tab, click Subdatasheet, and then click Subdatasheet to see the dialog box shown in Figure 7-36.

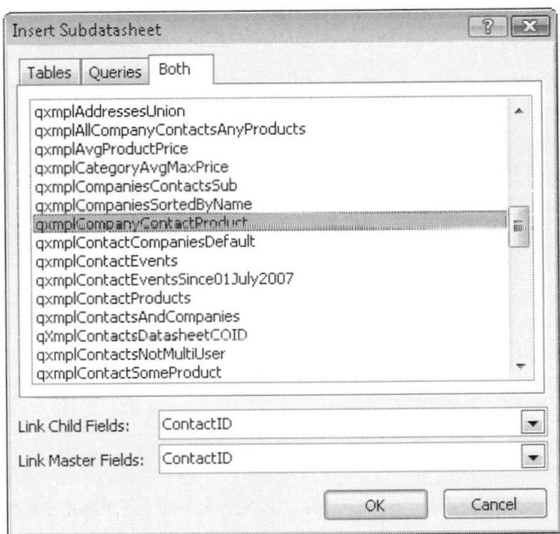


**Figure 7-36** You can choose a different table to display other related information in a subdatasheet from the Insert Subdatasheet dialog box.

We built a query in the sample database that displays the related company and product information for a contact. Click the Queries or Both tab and select qxmplCompanyContactProduct to define the new subdatasheet. Click OK to close the Insert Subdatasheet dialog box.

When you return to the qryContactsDatasheet window, click More on the Home tab, click Subdatasheet, and then click Expand All. You will now see information about each product ordered as shown in Figure 7-37. Note that you can also entirely remove a subdatasheet by clicking Remove on the menu shown in Figure 7-35. Close the query when you are finished.

In the next section, you'll learn more about editing data in Datasheet view. You can use these editing techniques with the main datasheet as well as with any expanded subdatasheet.

**CAUTION!**

When you close qryContactsDatasheet after modifying the subdatasheet as explained in this section, Access will prompt you to ask if you want to save your changes. You should click No to retain the original subdatasheet on tblContactEvents that we defined so that the remaining examples in this chapter make sense.

**Figure 7-37** You can review all product information for a contact from the subdatasheet by expanding it.

## Changing Data

Not only can you view and format data in a datasheet, you can also insert new records, change data, and delete records.

### Understanding Record Indicators

You might have noticed as you moved around in the datasheet that icons occasionally appeared on the row selector at the far left of each row. (See Figure 7-31.) These *record indicators* and their meanings follow. Note also that Access 2007 highlights the current row.

The pencil icon indicates that you are making or have made a change to one or more entries in this row. Access 2007 saves the changes when you move to another row. Before moving to a new row, you can press Esc once to undo the change to the current value, or press Esc twice to undo all changes in the row. If you're updating a database that is shared with other users through a network, Access locks this record when you save the change so that no one else can update it until you're finished. If someone else has the record locked, Access shows you a warning dialog box when you try to save the row. You can wait a few seconds and try to save again.

The asterisk icon indicates a blank row at the end of the table that you can use to create a new record.

## Adding a New Record

As you build your application, you might find it useful to place some data in your tables so that you can test the forms and reports that you design. You might also find it faster sometimes to add data directly to your tables by using Datasheet view rather than by opening a form. If your table is empty when you open the table or a query on the table in Datasheet view, Access 2007 shows a single blank highlighted row with dimmed rows beneath. If you have data in your table, Access shows a blank row beneath the last record as well as dimmed rows below the blank row. You can jump to the blank row to begin adding a new record either by clicking the Go To command on the Home tab and then clicking New Record, by clicking the New button in the Records group on the Home tab, or by pressing Ctrl+Plus Sign. Access places the insertion point in the first column when you start a new record. As soon as you begin typing, Access changes the record indicator to the pencil icon to show that updates are in progress. Press the Tab key to move to the next column.

If the data you enter in a column violates a field validation rule, Access 2007 notifies you as soon as you attempt to leave the column. You must provide a correct value before you can move to another column. Press Esc or click the Undo button on the Quick Access Toolbar to remove your changes in the current field.

Press Shift+Enter at any place in the record or press Tab in the last column in the record to commit your new record to the database. You can also click the Save command in the Records group on the Home tab. If the changes in your record violate the validation rule for the table, Access warns you when you try to save the record. You must correct the problem before you can save your changes. If you want to cancel the record, press Esc twice or click the Undo button on the Quick Access Toolbar until the button appears dimmed. (The first Undo removes the edit from the current field, and clicking Undo again removes any previous edit in other fields until you have removed them all.)

Access 2007 provides several keyboard shortcuts to assist you as you enter new data, as shown in Table 7-8.

**Table 7-8 Keyboard Shortcuts for Entering Data in a Datasheet**

| Keys | Data Action |
|---|---|
| Ctrl+semicolon (;) | Enters the current date |
| Ctrl+colon (:) | Enters the current time |
| Ctrl+Alt+Spacebar | Enters the default value for the field |
| Ctrl+single quotation mark (') or Ctrl+double quotation mark (") | Enters the value from the same field in the previous record |
| Ctrl+Enter | Inserts a carriage return in a memo or text field |
| Ctrl+Plus Sign (+) | Moves to the new record row |
| Ctrl+Minus Sign (–) | Deletes the current record |

## INSIDE OUT Setting Keyboard Options

You can set options that affect how you move around in datasheets and forms. Click the Microsoft Office Button, click Access Options, and click the Advanced category to see the options shown here.

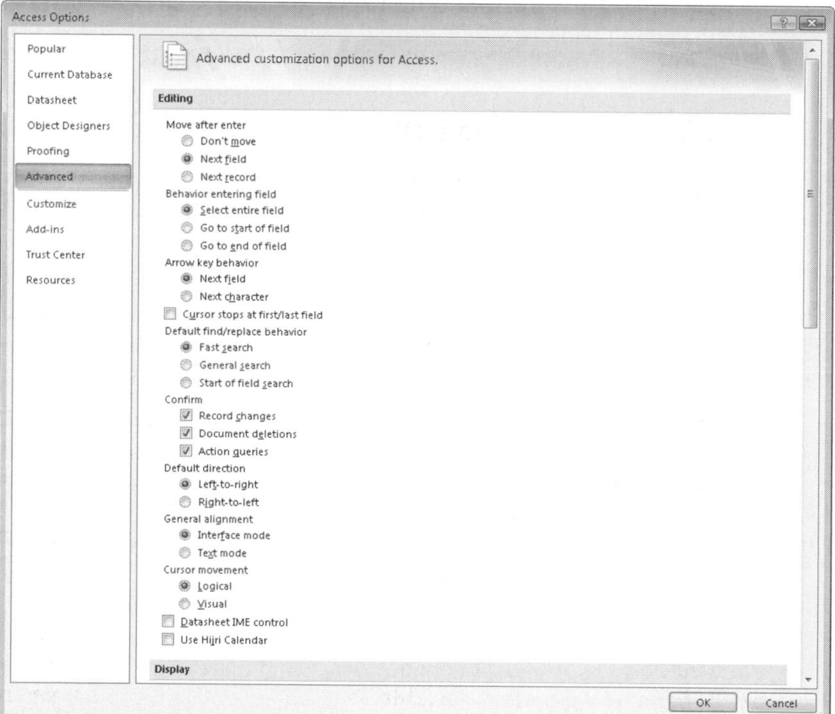


You can change the way the Enter key works by selecting an option under Move After Enter. Select Don't Move to stay in the current field when you press Enter. When you select Next Field (the default), pressing Enter moves you to the next field or the next row if you're on the last field. Select Next Record to save your changes and move to the next row when you press Enter.

You can change which part of the data of the field is selected when you move into a field by selecting an option under Behavior Entering Field. Choose Select Entire Field (the default), to highlight all data in the field. Select Go To Start Of Field to place an insertion point before the first character, and select Go To End Of Field to place the insertion point after the last character.

Under Arrow Key Behavior select Next Field (the default) if you want to move from field to field when you press the Right Arrow or Left Arrow key. Select Next Character to change to the insertion point and move one character at a time when you press the Right Arrow or Left Arrow key. You can select the Cursor Stops At First/Last Field check box if you don't want pressing the arrow keys to move you off the current row.

We personally prefer to set the Move After Enter option to Don't Move and the Arrow Key Behavior option to Next Character. We use the Tab key to move from field to field, and we don't want to accidentally save the record when we press Enter. We leave Behavior Entering Field at the default setting of Select Entire Field so that the entire text is selected, but setting Arrow Key Behavior to Next Character allows us to press the arrow keys to shift to single-character edit mode and move in the field.

## Selecting and Changing Data

When you have data in a table, you can easily change the data by editing it in Datasheet view. You must select data before you can change it, and you can do this in several ways.

- In the cell containing the data you want to change, click just to the left of the first character you want to change (or to the right of the last character), and then drag the insertion point to select all the characters you want to change.
- Double-click any word in a cell to select the entire word.
- Click at the left edge of a cell in the grid (that is, where the mouse pointer turns into a large white cross). Access selects the entire contents of the cell.

Any data you type replaces the old, selected data. In Figure 7-38, we have moved to the left edge of the First Name field, and Access has shown us the white cross mentioned in the last bullet. We can click to select the entire contents of the field. In Figure 7-39, we have changed the value to Mike, but haven't yet saved the row. (You can see the pencil icon indicating that a change is pending.) Access also selects the entire entry if you tab to the cell in the datasheet grid (unless you have changed the keyboard options as noted earlier). If you want to change only part of the data (for example, to correct the spelling of a street name in an address field), you can shift to single-character mode by pressing F2 or by clicking the location at which you want to start your change. Use the Backspace key to erase characters to the left of the insertion point and use the Delete key to remove characters to the right of the insertion point. Hold down the Shift key and press the Right Arrow or Left Arrow key to select multiple characters to replace. You can press F2 again to select the entire cell. A useful keyboard shortcut for changing data is to press Ctrl+Alt+Spacebar to restore the data in the current field to the default value specified in the table definition.

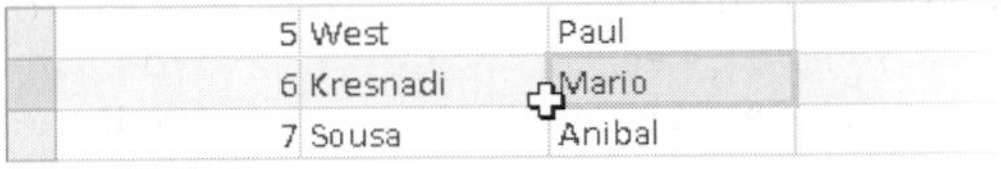

| | | | |
|---|---|---|---|
| | 5 | West | Paul |
| | 6 | Kresnadi | Mario |
| | 7 | Sousa | Anibal |

**Figure 7-38** You can select the old data by clicking the left side of the column.

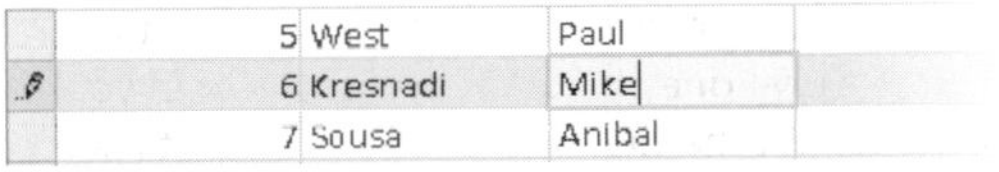

| | | | |
|---|---|---|---|
| | 5 | West | Paul |
| | 6 | Kresnadi | Mike |
| | 7 | Sousa | Anibal |

**Figure 7-39** You can then replace the old data with new data by typing the new information.

## Replacing Data

What if you need to make the same change in more than one record? Access 2007 provides a way to do this quickly and easily. Select any cell in the column whose values you want to change (the first row if you want to start at the beginning of the table), and then click the Replace command in the Find group on the Home tab or press Ctrl+F to see the dialog box shown in Figure 7-40. Suppose, for example, that you suspect that the city name *Easton* is misspelled as *Eaton* in multiple rows. (All the city names are spelled correctly in the sample table.) To fix this using Replace, select the Work City field in any row of qryContactsDatasheet, click the Replace command, type **Eaton** in the Find What text box, and then type **Easton** in the Replace With text box, as shown in Figure 7-40. Click the Find Next button to search for the next occurrence of the text you've typed in the Find What text box. Click the Replace button to change data selectively, or click the Replace All button to change all the entries that match the Find What text. Note that you can select options to look in all fields or only the current field; to select an entry only if the Find What text matches the entire entry in the field; to search All, Up, or Down; to exactly match the case for text searches (because searches in Access are normally case-insensitive); and to search based on the formatted contents (most useful when updating date/time fields).

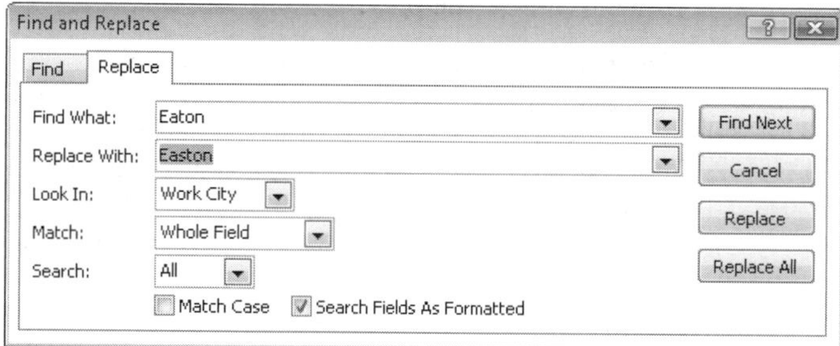


**Figure 7-40** The Find And Replace dialog box allows you to quickly replace data in more than one record.

## Copying and Pasting Data

You can copy or cut any selected data to the Clipboard and paste this data into another field or record. To copy data in a field, tab to the cell or click at the left edge of the cell in the datasheet grid to select the data within it. Click the Copy command in the Clipboard group on the Home tab or press Ctrl+C. To delete (cut) the data you have selected and place a copy on the Clipboard, click the Cut command in the Clipboard group on the Home tab or press Ctrl+X. To paste the data in another location, move the insertion point to the new location, optionally select the data you want to replace, and click the Paste command in the Clipboard group on the Home tab or press Ctrl+V. If the insertion point is at the paste location (you haven't selected any data in the field), Access inserts the Clipboard data.

INSIDE OUT

### Using the Office Clipboard

If you select and copy to the Clipboard several items of text data, Access 2007 shows you the Office Clipboard task pane. Unlike the Windows Clipboard, this facility allows you to copy several separate items, and then select any one of them later to paste into other fields or documents. You might find this feature useful when you want to copy the contents of several fields from one record to another. You can, for example, copy a City field and then copy a State field while in one record and then later individually paste the values into another row. If you don't see the Office Clipboard, you can open it by clicking the Dialog Box Launcher button to the right of the word Clipboard in the Clipboard group of the Home tab. The Office Clipboard task pane will appear just to the left of the Navigation Pane.

To select an entire record to be copied or cut, click the row selector at the far left of the row. You can drag through the row selectors or press Shift+Up Arrow or Shift+Down Arrow to extend the selection to multiple rows. Click the Copy command or press Ctrl+C to copy the contents of multiple rows to the Clipboard. You can also click the Cut command or press Ctrl+X to delete the rows and copy them to the Clipboard.

You can open another table or query and paste the copied rows into that datasheet, or you can click Paste, then Paste Append in the Clipboard group on the Home tab to paste the rows at the end of the same datasheet. When you paste rows into another table, the rows you're adding must satisfy the validation rules of the receiving table, and the primary key values (if any) must be unique. If any validation fails, Access shows you an error message and cancels the paste. You cannot paste copies of entire records into the same table if the table has a primary key other than the AutoNumber data type. (You'll get a duplicate primary key value error if you try to do this.) When the primary key is AutoNumber, Access generates new primary key values for you.

The Cut command is handy for moving those records that you don't want in an active table to a backup table. You can have both tables open (or queries on both tables open) in Datasheet view at the same time. Simply cut the rows you want to move, switch to the backup table window, and paste the cut rows by using the Paste Append command.

When you paste one row, Access inserts the data and leaves your insertion point on the new record but doesn't save it. You can always click Undo on the Quick Access Toolbar to avoid saving the single pasted record. When you paste multiple rows, Access must save them all as a group before allowing you to edit further. Access asks you to confirm the paste operation. (See Figure 7-41.) Click Yes to proceed, or click No if you decide to cancel the operation.

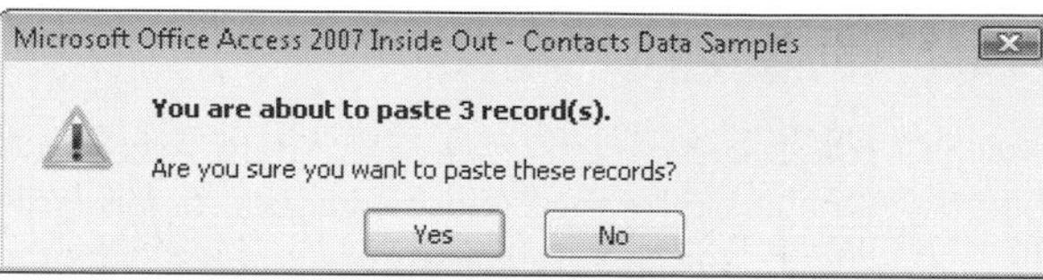


**Figure 7-41** This message box asks whether you want to proceed with a paste operation.

> **Note**
>
> You can't change the physical sequence of rows in a relational database by cutting rows from one location and pasting them in another location. Access always pastes new rows at the end of the current display. If you close the datasheet after pasting in new rows and then open it again, Access displays the rows in sequence by the primary key you defined. If you want to see rows in some other sequence, see "Sorting and Searching for Data" on page 401.

## Deleting Rows

To delete one or more rows, select the rows using the row selectors and then press the Delete key. For details about selecting multiple rows, see the previous discussion on copying and pasting data. You can also use Ctrl+Minus Sign to delete the current or selected row. When you delete rows, Access 2007 gives you a chance to change your mind if you made a mistake. (See Figure 7-42.) Click Yes in the message box to delete the rows, or click No to cancel the deletion. Because this database has referential integrity rules defined between tblContacts and several other tables, you won't be able to delete contact records using qryContactsDatasheet. (Access shows you an error message telling you that related rows exist in other tables.) You would have to remove all related records from tblContactEvents, tblContactProducts, and tblCompanyContacts first.

> **CAUTION!**
>
> After you click Yes in the confirmation message box, you cannot restore the deleted rows. You have to reenter them or copy them from a backup.

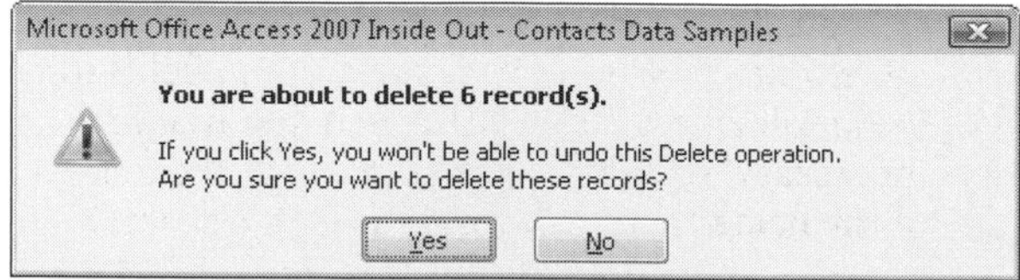


**Figure 7-42** This message box appears when you delete rows.

## Working with Hyperlinks

Microsoft Access 97 (also known as version 8.0) introduced the Hyperlink data type. The Hyperlink data type lets you store a simple or complex link to a file or document outside your database. This link pointer can contain a Uniform Resource Locator (URL) that points to a location on the World Wide Web or on a local intranet. It can also use a Universal Naming Convention (UNC) file name to point to a file on a server on your local area network (LAN) or on your local computer drives. The link might point to a file that is a Web page or in a format that is supported by an ActiveX application on your computer.

A Hyperlink data type is actually a memo field that can contain a virtually unlimited number of characters. The link itself can have up to four parts.

- An optional descriptor that Access displays in the field when you're not editing the link. The descriptor can start with any character other than a pound sign (#) and must have a pound sign as its ending delimiter. If you do not include the descriptor, you must start the link address with a pound sign.
- The link address expressed as either a URL (beginning with a recognized Internet protocol name such as http: or ftp:) or in UNC format (a file location expressed as \\server\share\path\file name). If you do not specify the optional descriptor field, Access displays the link address in the field. Terminate the link address with a pound sign (#).
- An optional subaddress that specifies a named location (such as a cell range in a Microsoft Excel spreadsheet or a bookmark in a Microsoft Word document) within the file. Separate the subaddress from the ScreenTip with a pound sign (#). If you entered no subaddress, you still must enter the pound sign delimiter if you want to define a ScreenTip.
- An optional ScreenTip that appears when you move your mouse pointer over the hyperlink.

For example, a hyperlink containing all four items might look like the following:

```
Viescas Download Page#http://www.viescas.com/Info/links.htm#Downloads
#Click to see the files you can download from Viescas.com
```

A hyperlink that contains a ScreenTip but no bookmark might look like this:

```
Viescas.com Books#http://www.viescas.com/Info/books.htm
##Click to see recommended books on Viescas.com
```

When you have a field defined using the Hyperlink data type, you work with it differently than with a standard text field. We included the Website field from tblContacts in the qryContactsDatasheet sample query (in ContactsDataCopy.accdb). Open the query and scroll to the right, if necessary, so that you can see the Website field, and place your mouse pointer over one of the fields that contains data, as shown in Figure 7-43.

**Figure 7-43** Place your mouse pointer over a hyperlink field in Datasheet view to show the hyperlink or the ScreenTip.

## Activating a Hyperlink

Notice that the text in a hyperlink field is underlined and that the mouse pointer becomes a hand with a pointing finger when you move the pointer over the field. If you leave the pointer floating over the field for a moment, Access displays the ScreenTip. In the tblContacts table, the entries in the Website hyperlink field for some of the contacts contain pointers to Microsoft Web sites. When you click a link field, Access starts the application that supports the link and passes the link address and subaddress to the application. If the link starts with an Internet protocol, Access starts your Web browser. In the case of the links in the tblContacts table, all are links to pages on the Microsoft Web site. If you click one of them, your browser should start and display the related Web page, as shown in Figure 7-44.

## Inserting a New Hyperlink

To insert a hyperlink in an empty hyperlink field, tab to the field or click in it with your mouse. If you're confident about the format of your link, you can type it, following the rules for the four parts noted earlier. If you're not sure, right-click inside the hyperlink field, select Hyperlink from the shortcut menu that appears, and then select Edit Hyperlink from the submenu to see the dialog box shown in Figure 7-45. This dialog box helps you correctly construct the four parts of the hyperlink.

The dialog box opens with Existing File Or Web Page selected in the Link To pane and Current Folder selected in the center pane, as shown in Figure 7-45. What you see in the list in the center pane depends on your current folder, the Web pages you've visited recently, and the files you've opened recently. You'll see a Look In list where you can navigate to any drive or folder on your system. You can also click the Browse The Web button (the button with a globe and a spyglass) to open your Web browser to find a Web site you want, or the Browse For File button (an open folder icon) to open the Link To File dialog box to find the file you want. Click Existing File Or Web Page and click the Recent Files option to see a list of files that you recently opened.

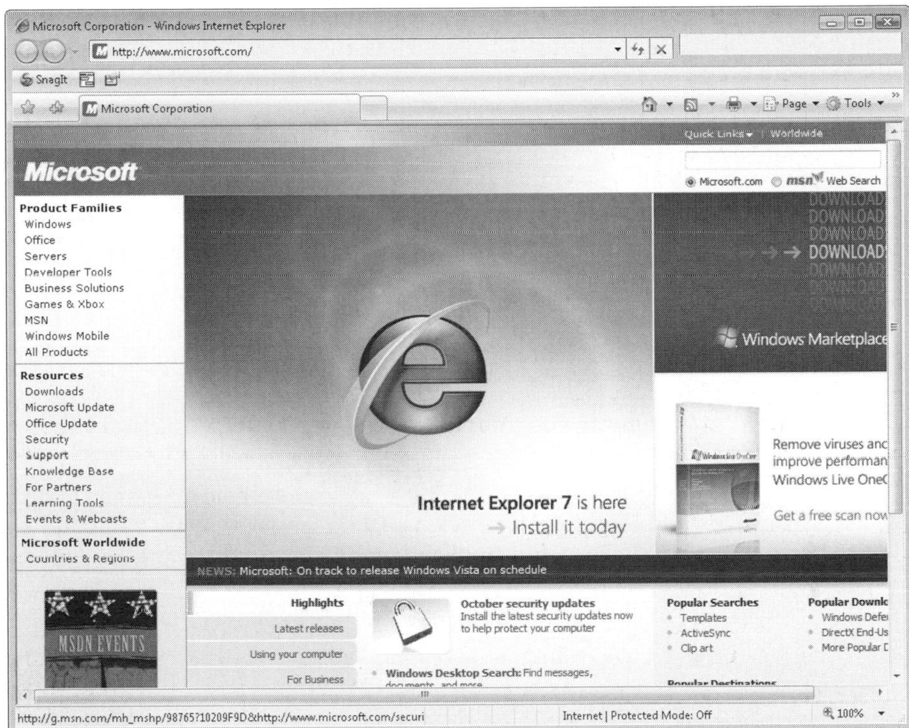


**Figure 7-44** Here is the result of clicking a Web site link in the tblContacts table.

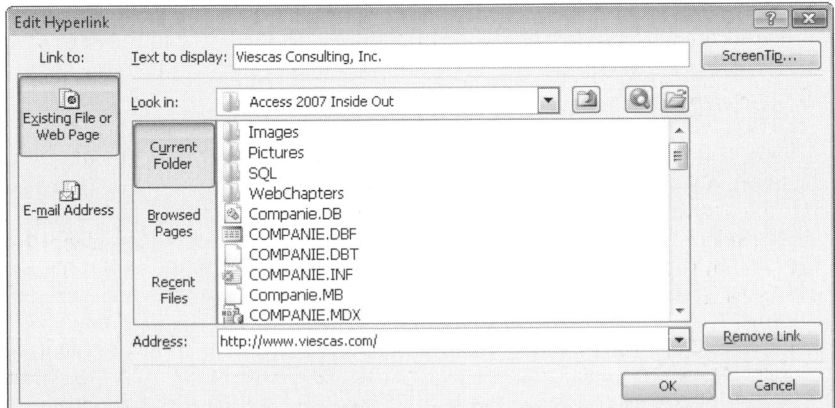


**Figure 7-45** The dialog box used to insert a hyperlink shows you a list of files in the current folder.

We clicked the Browsed Pages option because we knew the hyperlink we wanted was a Web page that we had recently visited. You can enter the descriptor in the Text To Display box at the top. We clicked the ScreenTip button to open the Set Hyperlink ScreenTip dialog box you see in Figure 7-46. You can type the document or Web site address directly into the Address box. (Yes, that's Jeff's real Web site address!)

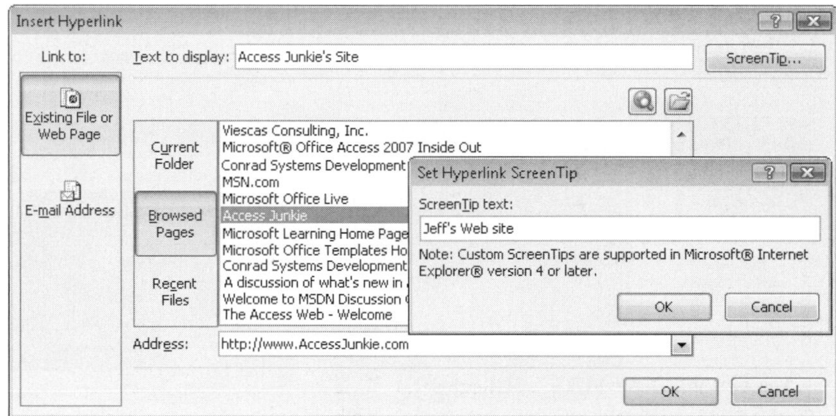


**Figure 7-46** You can choose a Web site address from a list of recently visited Web sites.

The E-Mail Address button in the left pane lets you enter an e-mail address or choose from a list of recently used addresses. This generates a mailto: hyperlink that will invoke your e-mail program and start a new e-mail to the address you enter. You can also optionally specify a subject for the new e-mail by adding a question mark after the e-mail address and entering what you want to appear on the subject line.

Click OK to save your link in the field in the datasheet.

## Editing an Existing Hyperlink

Getting into a hyperlink field to change the value of the link is a bit tricky. You can't simply click in a hyperlink field because that activates the link. What you can do is click in the field before the hyperlink and use the Tab key to move to the link field. Then press F2 to shift to character edit mode to edit the text string that defines the link. Figure 7-47 shows you a hyperlink field after following this procedure. You can use the arrow keys to move around in the text string to change one or more parts. In many cases, you might want to add an optional descriptor at the beginning of the link text, as shown in the figure.

The most comprehensive way to work with a hyperlink field is to right-click a link field to open a shortcut menu. Clicking Hyperlink on this menu displays a submenu with a number of options. You can edit the hyperlink (which opens the dialog box shown in Figure 7-45), open the link document, copy the link to the Clipboard, add the link to your list of favorites, change the text displayed in the field, or remove the hyperlink.

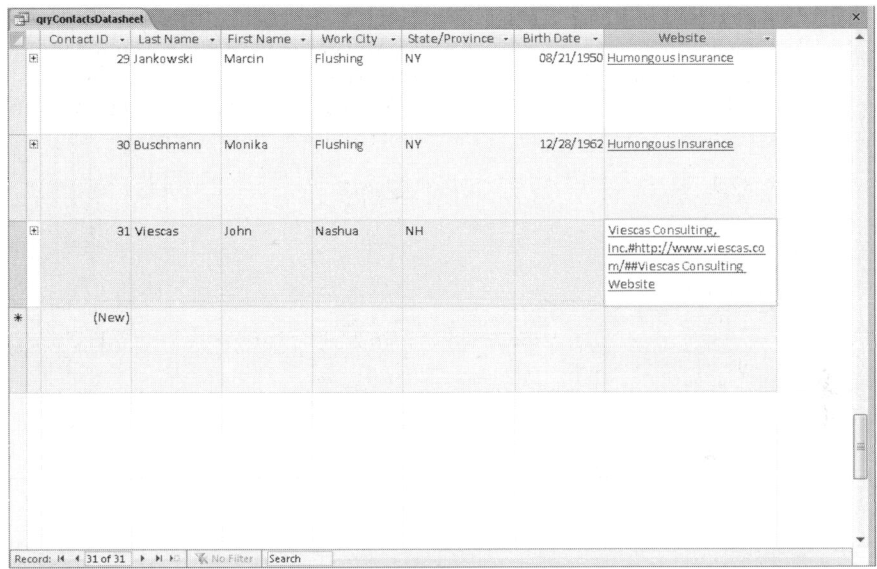

**Figure 7-47** You can edit the text that defines a hyperlink directly in a datasheet.

## Sorting and Searching for Data

When you open a table in Datasheet view, Access 2007 displays the rows sorted in sequence by the primary key you defined for the table. If you didn't define a primary key, you'll see the rows in the sequence in which you entered them in the table. If you want to see the rows in a different sequence or search for specific data, Access provides you with tools to do that. When you open a query in Datasheet view (such as the qryContactsDatasheet sample query we're using in this chapter), you'll see the rows in the order determined by sort specifications in the query. If you haven't specified sorting information, you'll see the data in the same sequence as you would if you opened the table or query in Datasheet view.

### Sorting Data

Access 2007 provides several ways to sort data in Datasheet view. As you might have noticed, two handy Ribbon commands allow you to quickly sort the rows in a query or table datasheet in ascending or descending order. To see how this works, open the qryContactsDatasheet query, click anywhere in the Birth Date column, and click the Descending command in the Sort & Filter group on the Home tab. Access sorts the display to show you the rows ordered alphabetically by Birth Date, as shown in Figure 7-48.

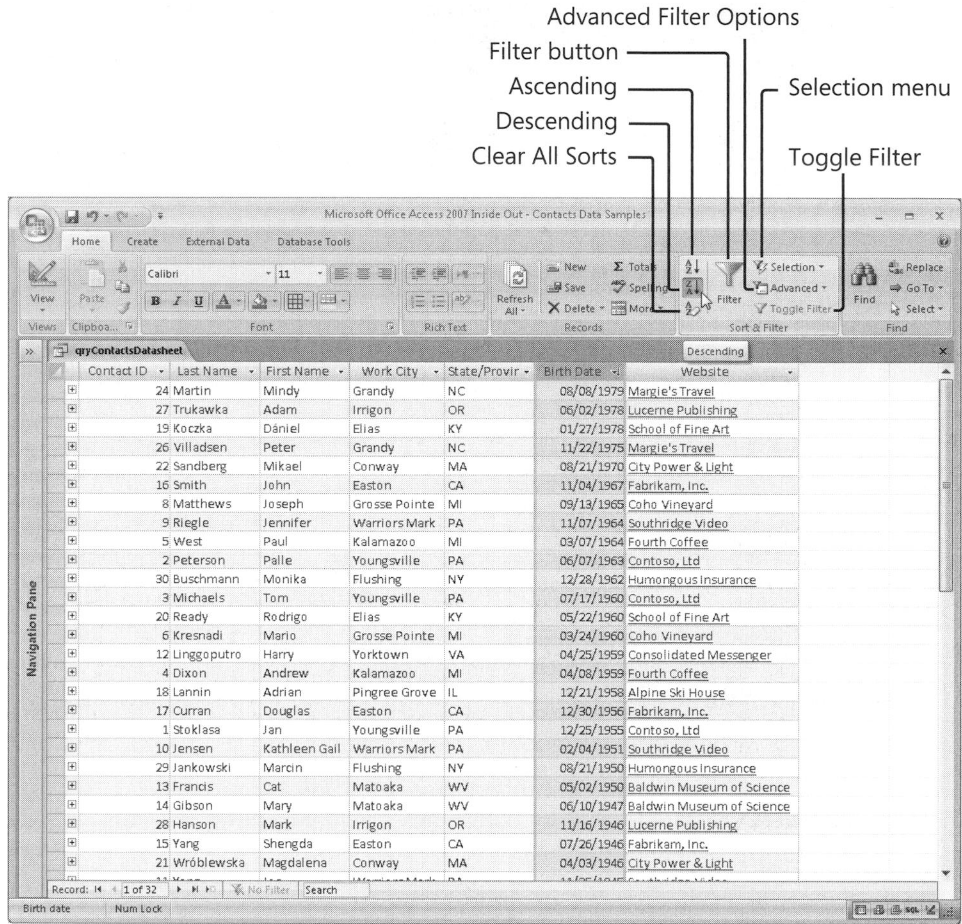


**Figure 7-48** You can sort contacts by birth date by using the sort buttons on the Ribbon.

You can click the Ascending button to sort the rows in ascending order or click the Clear All Sorts button to return to the original data sequence. But before you change the sort or clear the sort, suppose you want to see contacts sorted by state or province ascending and then by birth date descending. You already have the data sorted by birth date, so click anywhere in the State/Province column and click the Ascending button to see the result you want as shown in Figure 7-49.

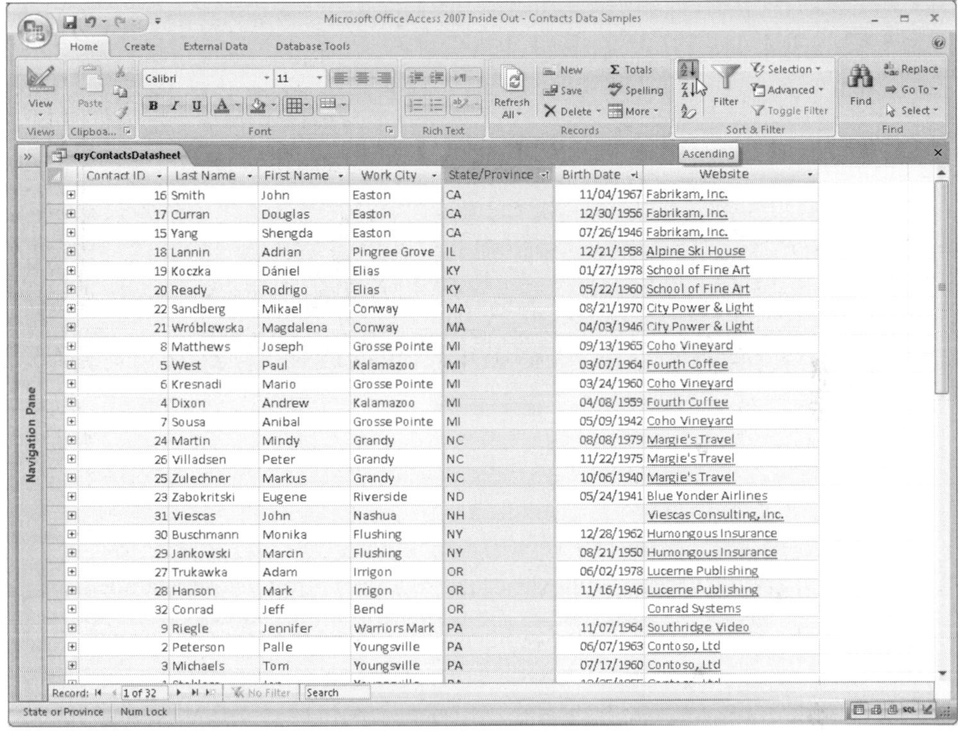

**Figure 7-49** After applying the second sort, the records are now sorted by state or province ascending and then by birth date descending within state or province.

INSIDE OUT

### Applying Multiple Sorts in Reverse Order

Notice that to sort by state or province and then birth date within state or province, you must first sort birth date and then sort state or province. We think that's backwards, but that's the way it works. If you had applied a sort on state or province first and then sorted birth date, you would have seen all the records in date order with any records having the same date subsequently sorted by state or province. If you want to sort on multiple fields, remember to apply the *innermost* sort first and then work your way outward.

Another way to sort more than one field is to use the Advanced Filter/Sort feature. Let's assume that you want to sort by State/Province, then by City within State/Province, and then by Last Name. Here's how to do it:

1. Click the Advanced button in the Sort & Filter group on the Home tab, and then click Advanced Filter/Sort. You'll see the Advanced Filter Design window (shown

in Figure 7-50) with a list of fields in the qryContactsDatasheet query shown in the top part of the window.

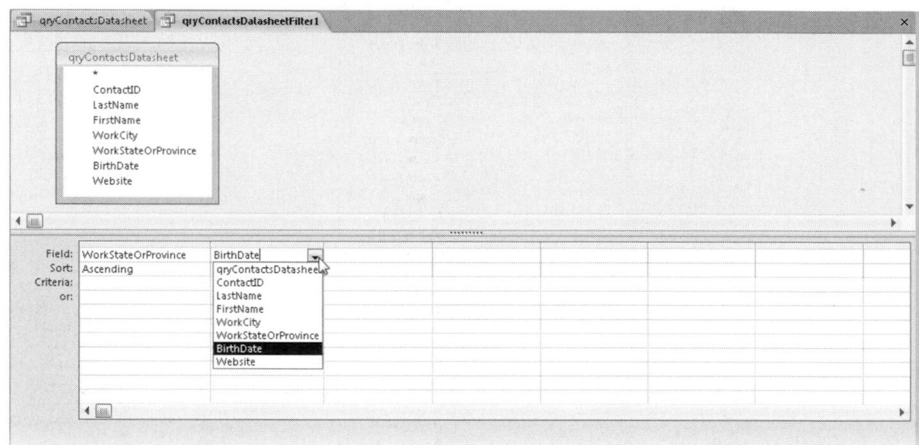


**Figure 7-50** Select the fields you want to sort in the Advanced Filter Design window.

2. If you didn't click the Clear All Sorts button before opening this window, you should see the sorts you previously defined directly in Datasheet view on the WorkStateOrProvince and BirthDate fields. If so, click the bar above the BirthDate field to select it and then press the Delete key to remove the field.

3. Because you recently sorted by State/Province, the Advanced Filter Design window will show this field already added to the filter grid. If you skipped the sort step in Figure 7-48 or closed and reopened the datasheet without saving the sort, open the field list in the first column by clicking the arrow or by pressing Alt+Down Arrow on the keyboard. Select the WorkStateOrProvince field in the list. You can also place the WorkStateOrProvince field in the first column by finding WorkStateOrProvince in the list of fields in the top part of the window and dragging it into the Field row in the first column of the filter grid.

4. Click in the Sort row, immediately below the WorkStateOrProvince field, and select Ascending from the drop-down list.

5. Add the WorkCity and LastName fields to the next two columns, and select Ascending in the Sort row for both.

6. Click the Toggle Filter button in the Sort & Filter group of the Home tab on the Ribbon to see the result shown in Figure 7-51.

qryContactsDatasheet | qryContactsDatasheetFilter1

| Contact ID | Last Name | First Name | Work City | State/Province | Birth Date | Website |
|---|---|---|---|---|---|---|
| 17 | Curran | Douglas | Easton | CA | 12/30/1956 | Fabrikam, Inc. |
| 16 | Smith | John | Easton | CA | 11/04/1967 | Fabrikam, Inc. |
| 15 | Yang | Shengda | Easton | CA | 07/26/1946 | Fabrikam, Inc. |
| 18 | Lannin | Adrian | Pingree Grove | IL | 12/21/1958 | Alpine Ski House |
| 19 | Koczka | Dániel | Elias | KY | 01/27/1978 | School of Fine Art |
| 20 | Ready | Rodrigo | Elias | KY | 05/22/1960 | School of Fine Art |
| 22 | Sandberg | Mikael | Conway | MA | 08/21/1970 | City Power & Light |
| 21 | Wróblewska | Magdalena | Conway | MA | 04/03/1946 | City Power & Light |
| 6 | Kresnadi | Mario | Grosse Pointe | MI | 03/24/1960 | Coho Vineyard |
| 8 | Matthews | Joseph | Grosse Pointe | MI | 09/13/1965 | Coho Vineyard |
| 7 | Sousa | Anibal | Grosse Pointe | MI | 05/09/1942 | Coho Vineyard |
| 4 | Dixon | Andrew | Kalamazoo | MI | 04/08/1959 | Fourth Coffee |
| 5 | West | Paul | Kalamazoo | MI | 03/07/1964 | Fourth Coffee |
| 24 | Martin | Mindy | Grandy | NC | 08/08/1979 | Margie's Travel |
| 26 | Villadsen | Peter | Grandy | NC | 11/22/1975 | Margie's Travel |
| 25 | Zulechner | Markus | Grandy | NC | 10/06/1940 | Margie's Travel |
| 23 | Zabokritski | Eugene | Riverside | ND | 05/24/1941 | Blue Yonder Airlines |
| 31 | Viescas | John | Nashua | NH | | Viescas Consulting, Inc. |
| 30 | Buschmann | Monika | Flushing | NY | 12/28/1962 | Humongous Insurance |
| 29 | Jankowski | Marcin | Flushing | NY | 08/21/1950 | Humongous Insurance |
| 32 | Conrad | Jeff | Bend | OR | | Conrad Systems |
| 28 | Hanson | Mark | Irrigon | OR | 11/16/1946 | Lucerne Publishing |
| 27 | Trukawka | Adam | Irrigon | OR | 06/02/1978 | Lucerne Publishing |
| 10 | Jensen | Kathleen Gail | Warriors Mark | PA | 02/04/1951 | Southridge Video |
| 9 | Riegle | Jennifer | Warriors Mark | PA | 11/07/1964 | Southridge Video |
| 11 | Yong | Joe | Warriors Mark | PA | 11/25/1945 | Southridge Video |

Record: 1 of 32 No Filter Search

**Figure 7-51** After defining your sorts and clicking the Toggle Filter button, you can see the results of your sorting contact records by state or province, city, and then last name.

> **Note**
>
> If you compare Figure 7-49 with Figure 7-51, it looks like the records in Figure 7-49 were already sorted by city name within state. You might be tempted to leave out the sort on city in this exercise, but if you do that, you will not see the city names maintained in the same order. Remember, if you want data presented in a certain sequence, you must ask for it that way!

Close the qryContactsDatasheet window and click No when asked if you want to save design changes. We'll explore using the other options in the Sort & Filter group in the next sections.

## Searching For and Filtering Data

If you want to look for data anywhere in your table, Access 2007 provides several powerful searching and filtering capabilities.

**Using Find** To begin this exercise, open the qryContactsDatasheet query in Datasheet view again. To perform a simple search on a single field, select that field, and then open the Find And Replace dialog box (shown in Figure 7-52) by clicking the Find command in the Find group on the Home tab or by pressing Ctrl+F.

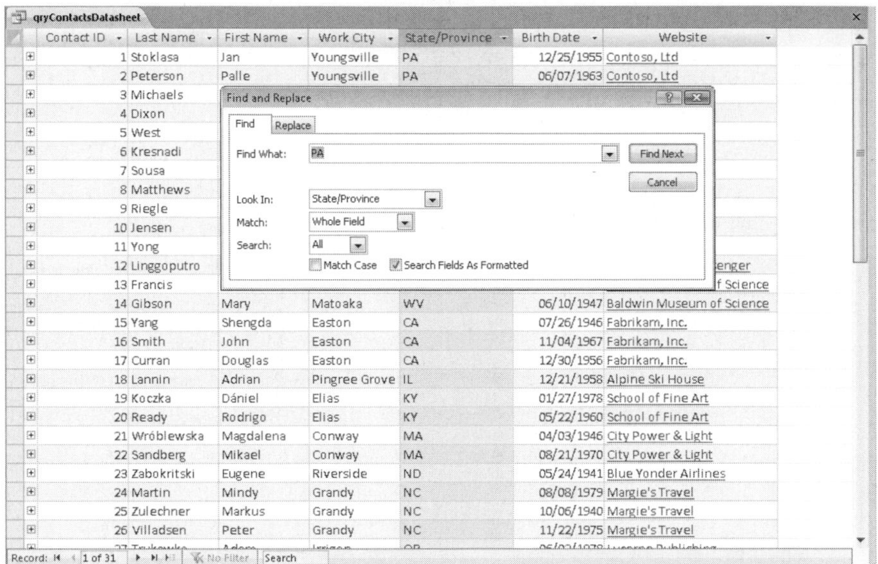


**Figure 7-52** You can use the Find And Replace dialog box to search for data.

In the Find What text box, type the data that you want Access to find. You can include wildcard characters similar to those of the LIKE comparison operator. See "Defining Simple Field Validation Rules" on page 168 to perform a generic search. Use an asterisk (*) to indicate a string of unknown characters of any length (zero or more characters), and use a question mark (?) to indicate exactly one unknown character or a space. For example, *AB??DE* matches *Aberdeen* and *Tab idea* but not *Lab department*.

By default, Access searches the field that your insertion point was in before you opened the Find And Replace dialog box. To search the entire table, select the table or query name from the Look In list. By default, Access searches all records from the top of the recordset unless you change the Search list to search down or up from the current record position. Select the Match Case check box if you want to find text that exactly matches the uppercase and lowercase letters you typed. By default, Access is case-insensitive unless you select this check box.

The Search Fields As Formatted check box appears dimmed unless you select a field that has a format or input mask applied. You can select this check box if you need to search the data as it is displayed rather than as it is stored by Access. Although searching this way is slower, you probably should select this check box if you are searching a date/time field. For example, if you're searching a date field for dates in January, you can specify **-Jan-** if the field is formatted as Medium Date and you select the Search Fields As Formatted check box. You might also want to select this check box when searching a Yes/No field for Yes because any value except 0 is a valid indicator of Yes.

Click Find Next to start searching from the current record. Each time you click Find Next again, Access moves to the next value it finds, and loops to the top of the recordset to continue the search if you started in the middle. After you establish search criteria and you close the Find And Replace dialog box, you can press Shift+F4 to execute the search from the current record without having to open the dialog box again.

**Filtering by Selection** If you want to see all the rows in your table that contain a value that matches one in a row in the datasheet grid, you can use the Selection command in the Sort & Filter group on the Home tab. Select a complete value in a field to see only rows that have data in that column that completely matches. Figure 7-53 shows the value PA selected in the State/Province column and the result after clicking the Selection button in the Sort & Filter group of the Home tab and clicking Equals "PA". If the filtering data you need is in several contiguous columns, click the first column, hold down the Shift key, and click the last column to select all the data; click the Selection button; and then click a filter option to see only rows that match the data in all the columns you selected.

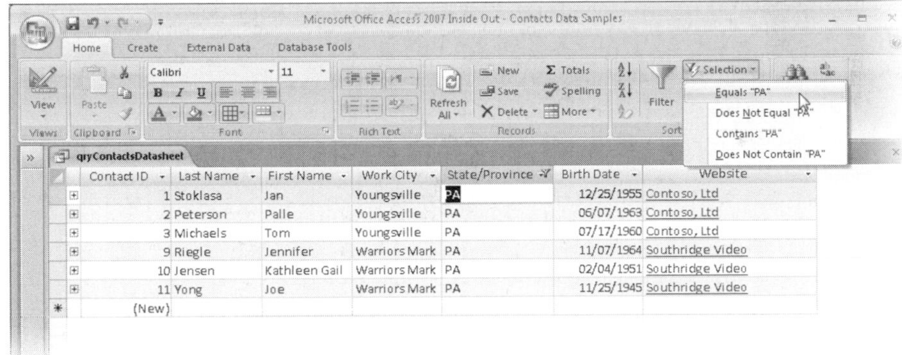

**Figure 7-53** Here is the list of contacts in Pennsylvania, compiled using the Selection filter option.

Alternatively, if you want to see all the rows in your table that contain a part of a value that matches one in a row in the datasheet grid, you can select the characters that you want to match and use Selection. For example, to see all contacts that have the characters *ing* in their work city name, find a contact that has *ing* in the Work City field and select those characters. Click the Selection button in the Sort & Filter group of the Home tab, and then click Contains "ing". When the search is completed you should see only the three contacts who work in the cities named P*ing*ree Grove and Flush*ing*. To remove a filter, click the Toggle Filter button in the Sort & Filter group, or click Advanced in the Sort & Filter group and then click Clear All Filters.

> **Note**
>
> You can open any subdatasheet defined for the query and apply a filter there. If you apply a filter to a subdatasheet, you will filter all the subdatasheets that are open.

You can also add a filter to a filter. For example, if you want to see all contacts who live in Youngsville in Pennsylvania, find the value PA in the State/Province column, select it, click the Selection button in the Sort & Filter group of the Home tab, and then click Equals "PA". In the filtered list, find a row containing the word Youngsville in the Work City field, select the word, click the Selection button again, and click Equals "Youngsville". Access displays a small filter icon that looks like a funnel in the upper-right corner of each column that has a filter applied, as shown in Figure 7-54. If you rest your mouse on one of these column filter icons, Access displays a ScreenTip telling you what filter has been applied to that particular column. To remove all your filters, click the Toggle Filter button or click Advanced in the Sort & Filter group of the Home tab and click Clear All Filters.

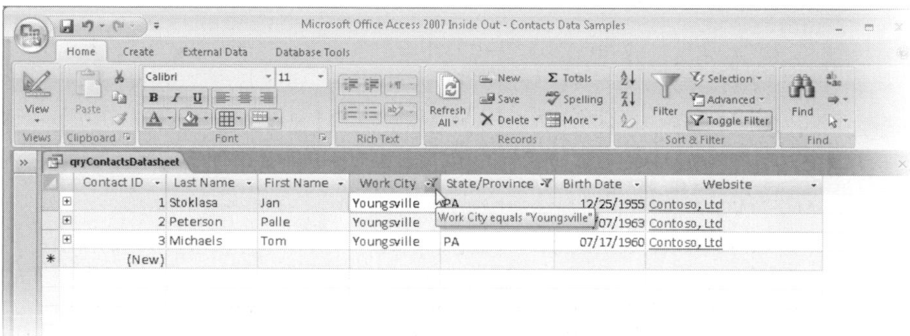


**Figure 7-54** Access displays a ScreenTip on the filter icon in the column header to show you what filter is applied.

**Using the Filter Window** To further assist you with filtering rows, Access 2007 provides a Filter window with predefined filter selections for various data types. Suppose you want to quickly filter the rows for contacts who have birthdays in the month of December. Click inside the Birth Date column in any row and then click the Filter button in the Sort & Filter group of the Home tab, and Access opens the Filter window for this field shown in Figure 7-55.

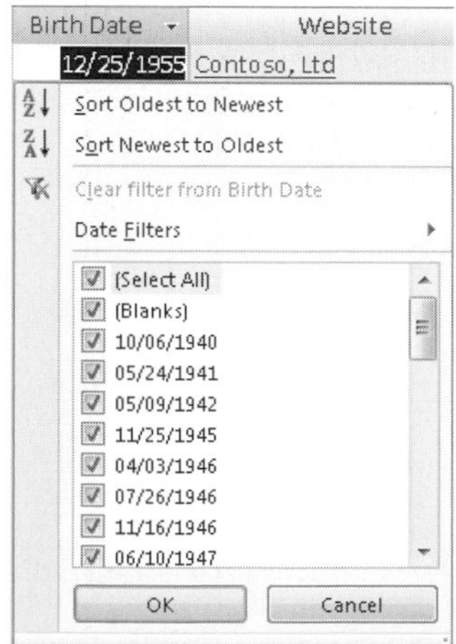


**Figure 7-55** The Filter window for date/time fields displays filter criteria based on the dates entered in the field.

The Ascending and Descending buttons, discussed previously, are the first two options in the Filter window. (For a date/time field, Access shows you Sort Oldest To Newest and Sort Newest To Oldest. For a text field, Access shows you Sort A To Z and Sort Z To A, and for a numeric field, Access shows you Sort Smallest To Largest and Sort Largest to Smallest.) The third option, Clear Filter From Birth Date, removes all filters applied to the Birth Date field. The fourth option is Date Filters, which displays several submenus to the right that allow you to filter for specific date criteria. (For text fields, this option presents a list of text filters. For number fields, Access displays a list of the available numeric values.)

Beneath the Date Filters option is a list. The first two options in this list are the same for all data types. Select All selects all the options presented in the list. Blanks causes Access to search the field for any rows with no value entered—a Null value or an empty string. Beneath Select All and Blanks are every unique value entered into the Birth Date field for the current datasheet. If you select only one of these options, Access filters the rows that exactly match the value you choose.

In our example, to find all contacts who have a birthday in the month of December, click Date Filters, click All Dates In Period, and then you can filter the rows by an individual quarter or by a specific month. Click December and Access filters the rows to display only contacts who have birthdays in December, as shown in Figure 7-56.

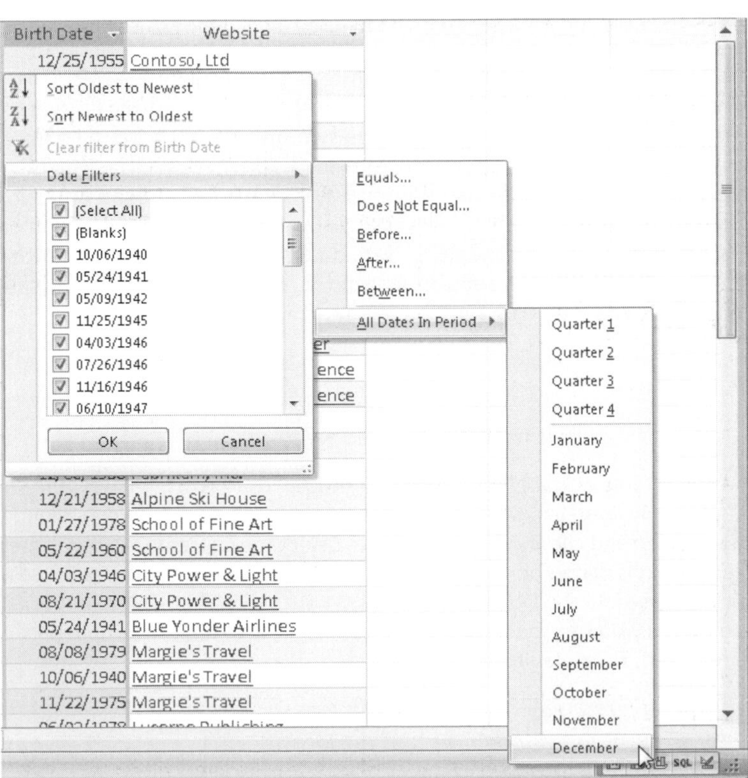


**Figure 7-56** Date Filters presents built-in date filters for periods and months.

The result of this filter should return the four contacts who have birthdays in December as shown in Figure 7-57. Click the Toggle Filter button in the Sort & Filter group of the Home tab to remove the filter.

qryContactsDatasheet

| Contact ID | Last Name | First Name | Work City | State/Province | Birth Date | Website |
|---|---|---|---|---|---|---|
| 1 | Stoklasa | Jan | Youngsville | PA | 12/25/1955 | Contoso, Ltd |
| 17 | Curran | Douglas | Easton | CA | 12/30/1956 | Fabrikam, Inc. |
| 18 | Lannin | Adrian | Pingree Grove | IL | 12/21/1958 | Alpine Ski House |
| 30 | Buschmann | Monika | Flushing | NY | 12/28/1962 | Humongous Insurance |
| (New) | | | | | | |

**Figure 7-57** Four contacts in the table have birthdays in the month of December.

**Using Filter By Form** Applying a filter using Selection is great for searching for rows that match *all* of several criteria (Last Name like "*son*" *and* State/Province equals "OR"), but what if you want to see rows that meet *any* of several criteria (Last Name like "*son" and State/Province equals "OR" or State/Province equals "PA")? You can use Filter By Form to easily build the criteria for this type of search.

When you click the Advanced button in the Sort & Filter group of the Home tab and click Filter By Form, Access 2007 shows you a Filter By Form example that looks like your datasheet but contains no data. If you have no filtering criteria previously defined, Access shows you the Look For tab and one Or tab at the bottom of the window. Move to each column in which you want to define criteria and either select a value from the drop-down list or type search criteria, as shown in Figure 7-58. Notice that each drop-down list shows you all the unique values available for each field, so it's easy to pick values to perform an exact comparison. You can also enter criteria, much the way that you did to create validation rules in Chapter 4. For example, you can enter *Like "*son*"* in the Last Name field to search for the letters *son* anywhere in the name. You can use criteria such as *>#01 JAN 1963#* in the Birth Date date/time field to find rows for contacts born after that date. You can enter multiple criteria on one line, but *all* the criteria you enter on a single line must be true for a particular row to be selected.

INSIDE OUT

### Limiting the Returned Records

When your table or query returns tens of thousands of rows, fetching the values for each list in Filter By Form can take a long time. You can specify a limit by clicking the Microsoft Office Button and clicking Access Options. Select the Current Database category in the Access Options dialog box, and then scroll down to Filter Lookup Options For <name of your database>. In the Don't Display Lists Where More Than This Number Of Records Read option, you can specify a value for display lists to limit the number of discrete values returned. The default value is 1,000.

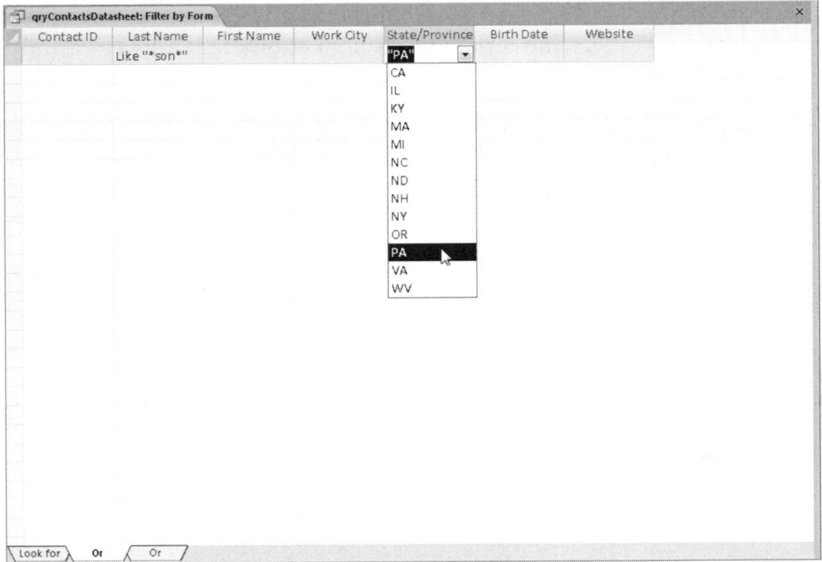


**Figure 7-58** Use Filter By Form to search for one of several states.

If you want to see rows that contain any of several values in a particular column (for example, rows from several states), enter the first value in the appropriate column, and then click the Or tab at the bottom of the window to enter an additional criterion. In this example, "*OR*" was entered in the State/Province column on the Look For tab and "*PA*" on the first Or tab; you can see "PA" being selected for the first Or tab in Figure 7-58.

Each tab also specifies Like "*son*" for the last name. (As you define additional criteria, Access makes additional Or tabs available at the bottom of the window.) Figure 7-59 shows the result of applying these criteria when you click the Toggle Filter button in the Sort & Filter group of the Home tab.

qryContactsDatasheet

| | Contact ID | Last Name | First Name | Work City | State/Province | Birth Date | Website |
|---|---|---|---|---|---|---|---|
| ⊞ | 2 | Peterson | Palle | Youngsville | PA | 06/07/1963 | Contoso, Ltd |
| ⊞ | 28 | Hanson | Mark | Irrigon | OR | 11/16/1946 | Lucerne Publishing |
| * | (New) | | | | | | |

**Figure 7-59** The contacts with names containing *son* in the states of OR and PA.

You can actually define very complex filtering criteria using expressions and the Or tabs in the Filter By Form window. If you look at the Filter By Form window, you can see that Access builds all your criteria in a design grid that looks similar to a Query window in Design view. In fact, filters and sorts use the query capabilities of Access to accomplish the result you want, so in Datasheet view you can use all the same filtering capabilities you'll find for queries.

INSIDE OUT

### Saving and Reusing Your Filters

Access 2007 always remembers the last filtering and sorting criteria you defined for a datasheet. The next time you open the datasheet, click the Advanced button in the Sort & Filter group on the Home tab and click Filter By Form or Advanced to apply the last filter you created (as long as you replied Yes to the prompt to save formatting changes when you last closed the datasheet). If you want to save a particular filter/sort definition, click the Advanced button in the Sort & Filter group on the Home tab, click Save As Query, and give your filter a name. The next time you open the table, return to the Advanced button, and then click Load From Query to find the filter you previously saved.

In the next chapter, we'll explore creating more complex queries—including creating queries from multiple tables or queries, calculating totals, and designing PivotTable and PivotChart views.

# CHAPTER 8
# Building Complex Queries



Creating queries on a single table as you did in the previous chapter is a good way to get acquainted with the basic mechanics of the query designer. It's also useful to work with simple queries to understand how datasheets work.

However, for many tasks you'll need to build a query on multiple tables or queries (yes, you can build a query on a query!), calculate totals, add parameters, customize query properties, or work in SQL view. In fact, there are some types of queries that you can build only in SQL view. This chapter shows you how.

**CAUTION!**

When you build an application, you should *never* allow users to view or edit data directly from table or query datasheets. Although you can protect the integrity of your data somewhat with input masks, validation rules, and relationships, you cannot enforce complex business rules.

For example, in the Housing Reservations application, you need to ensure that a particular room isn't booked more than once for a given time period. In the Conrad Systems Contacts application, your application shouldn't allow a support contract to be sold for a product that the contact hasn't purchased. You can't run such integrity checks from tables or queries. However, you *can* enforce such complex business rules by writing Visual Basic code in the forms you design so that your users can edit data while maintaining data integrity.

The purpose of this chapter is to teach you the concepts you must learn to build the queries you'll need for your forms and reports. In Chapter 20, "Automating Your Application with Visual Basic," you'll learn how to build complex business rule validation into your forms.

# Selecting Data from Multiple Tables

At this point, you've been through all the variations on a single theme—queries on a single table. It's easy to build on this knowledge to retrieve related information from many tables and to place that information in a single view. You'll find this ability to select data from multiple tables very useful in designing forms and reports.

### Note

The examples in this chapter are based on the tables and data in HousingDataCopy.accdb and ContactsDataCopy.accdb on the companion CD included with this book. These databases are copies of the data from the Housing Reservations and Conrad Systems Contacts sample applications, respectively, and they contain the sample queries used in this chapter. The query results you see from the sample queries you build in this chapter might not exactly match what you see in this book if you have changed the sample data in the files. Also, all the screen images in this chapter were taken on a Windows Vista system with the display theme set to Blue. Your results might look different if you are using a different operating system or a different theme.

## Creating Inner Joins

A *join* is the link you need to define between two related tables in a query so that the data you see makes sense. If you don't define the link, you'll see all rows from the first table combined with all rows from the second table (also called the *Cartesian product*). When you use an *inner join* (the default for joins in queries), you won't see rows from either table that don't have a matching row in the other table. This type of query is also called an *equi-join query*, meaning that you'll see rows only where there are *equal* values in *both* tables. For example, in a query that joins departments and employees, you won't see any departments that have no employees or any employees that aren't assigned to a department. To see how to build a query that returns all rows from one of the tables, including rows that have no match in the related table, see "Using Outer Joins" on page 425.

Correctly designing your tables requires you to split out (normalize) your data into separate tables to avoid redundant data and problems updating the data. (For details about designing your tables, see Article 1, "Designing Your Database Application," on the companion CD.) For many tasks, however, you need to work with the data from multiple tables. For example, in the Housing Reservations application, to work with employees and the departments to which they are assigned, you can't get all the information you need from just tblEmployees. Sure, you can see the employee's DepartmentID, but what about the department name and location? If you want to sort or filter employees by department name, you need both tblDepartments and tblEmployees.

In the previous chapter, we built several queries on tblReservations. Because we defined Lookup properties in that table, you can see the facility name in the reservation record, but as you discovered, that's really a numeric field. If you want to sort on the real name value or see other information about the facility, you must create a query that uses both tblFacilities and tblReservations.

Try the following example, in which you combine information about a reservation and about the facility in which the reservation was confirmed. Start by opening the HousingDataCopy.accdb database. Click the Query Design button in the Other group on the Create tab. Microsoft Office Access 2007 immediately opens the Show Table dialog box. In this dialog box, you select the tables and queries that you want in your new query. Select the tblFacilities and tblReservations tables (hold down the Ctrl key as you click each table name), click the Add button, and then close the dialog box.



**TROUBLESHOOTING**

### How can I be sure I'm using the correct table in the query designer?

Whenever your query is based on more than one table, it's a good idea to select the Show Table Names option in the Query Design section of the Object Designers category of the Access Options dialog box. (Click the Microsoft Office Button, click Access Options, and then click the Object Designers category in the left column. Below Query Design, make sure that the Show Table Names check box is selected.) Because you might have the same field name in more than one of the tables, showing table names in the design grid helps to ensure that your query refers to the field you intend it to.

Whenever you have relationships defined, the query designer automatically links (joins) multiple tables on the defined relationships. You might also want to select the Enable AutoJoin check box in the Object Designers category of the Access Options dialog box. When you enable this option and build a query on two tables that aren't directly related, the query designer attempts to link the two tables for you. The query designer looks at the primary key of each table. If it can find a field with the same name and data type in one of the other tables you added to the query designer, the query designer builds the link for you. Some advanced users might prefer to always create these links themselves.

The two tables, tblFacilities and tblReservations, aren't directly related to each other. If you look in the Relationships window (click Relationships on the Database Tools tab), you'll see a relationship defined between tblFacilities and tblFacilityRooms on the FacilityID field. There's also a relationship between tblFacilityRooms and tblReservations on the combination of the FacilityID and the RoomNumber fields. So, tblFacilities is related to tblReservations via the FacilityID field, but indirectly. In other words, the FacilityID field in tblReservations is a *foreign key* that points to the related row in tblFacilities. So, it's perfectly legitimate to build a query that links these two tables on the FacilityID field.

INSIDE OUT

### Query Joins Don't Always Need to Match Relationships

It's a good idea to define relationships between related tables to help ensure the integrity of your data. However, you don't need to define a relationship between the foreign key in a table and the matching primary key in every other related table. For example, if table A is related to table B, and table B is related to table C, you don't necessarily need a relationship defined between table A and table C even though table C might contain a foreign key field that relates it to table A. Even when you haven't explicitly defined a relationship between table A and table C, it is perfectly valid to join table A to table C in a query as long as there's a legitimate matching field in both tables.



The upper part of the Query window in Design view should look like that shown in Figure 8-1. Office Access 2007 first links multiple tables in a query based on the relationships you have defined. If no defined relationship exists, and you have Enable AutoJoin selected in the Object Designers category in the Access Options dialog box (this option is enabled by default), then Access attempts to match the primary key from one table with a field that has the same name and data type in the other table.

Access 2007 shows the links between tables as a line drawn from the primary key in one table to its matching field in the other table. As already noted, no direct relationship exists between these two tables in this example. With Enable AutoJoin selected, however, Access sees that the FacilityID field is the primary key in tblFacilities and finds a matching FacilityID field in tblReservations. So, it should create a join line between the two tables on the FacilityID fields. If you don't see this line, you can click FacilityID in tblFacilities and drag and drop it on FacilityID in tblReservations, just like you learned to do in "Defining Relationships" on page 181.

#### Note

If you haven't defined relationships, when you create a query that uses two tables that are related by more than one field (for example, tblFacilityRooms and tblReservations in this database), the Join Properties dialog box lets you define only one of the links at a time. You must click the New button again to define the second part of the join. If you're using drag and drop, you can do this with only one field at a time even though you can select multiple fields in either table window. We'll discuss the Join Properties dialog box in "Building a Simple Outer Join" on page 425.

In this example, you want to add to the query the FacilityID and FacilityName fields from the tblFacilities table and the ReservationID, EmployeeNumber, FacilityID, RoomNumber, CheckInDate, and CheckOutDate fields from the tblReservations table. (We resized the columns on the query grid in Figure 8-1 so that you can see all the fields.)

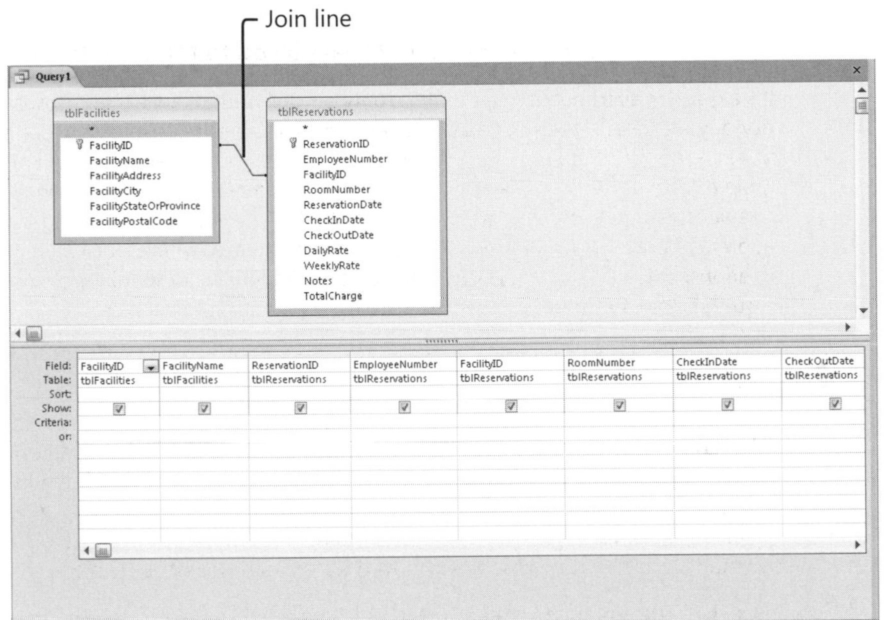


**Figure 8-1** This query selects information from the tblFacilities and tblReservations tables.



When you run the query, you see the recordset shown in Figure 8-2. The fields from the tblFacilities table appear first, left to right. We resized the columns displayed in Figure 8-2 so that you can see all the fields. You might need to scroll right in the datasheet to see them on your computer.

## INSIDE OUT A Query Is Really Defined by Its SQL

The query designer converts everything you build in a query grid into SQL—the lingua franca of database queries. Access 2007 actually stores only the SQL and rebuilds the query grid each time you open a query in Design view. Later in this chapter, we'll examine some of the actual syntax behind your queries, and you can study the full details of SQL in Article 2, "Understanding SQL," on the companion CD.

Notice the facility name in the column for the FacilityID field from the tblReservations table. (The caption for the field is Facility.) If you check the definition of the FacilityID field in the tblReservations table, you'll see a Lookup combo box defined–the query has inherited those properties. Click in a field in the Facility column in this datasheet, and the combo box appears. If you choose a different Facility name from the list, you will change the FacilityID field for that reservation. But the room number already in the row might not exist in the new Facility, so you might get an error if you try to save the row.

This is yet another example of a business rule that you will have to ensure is verified in a form you create for users to edit this data.

Join line — Fields from tblReservations

Query1

| ID | Name | Reservation | Employee | Facility | Room | Check-In | Check-Out |
|---|---|---|---|---|---|---|---|
| 1 | Main Campus Housing A | 1 | 7 | Main Campus Housing A | 810 | 3/6/2007 | 3/18/2007 |
| 1 | Main Campus Housing A | 4 | 3 | Main Campus Housing A | 502 | 4/14/2007 | 5/1/2007 |
| 1 | Main Campus Housing A | 6 | 10 | Main Campus Housing A | 902 | 4/1/2007 | 4/20/2007 |
| 1 | Main Campus Housing A | 8 | 8 | Main Campus Housing A | 509 | 4/16/2007 | 4/29/2007 |
| 1 | Main Campus Housing A | 10 | 3 | Main Campus Housing A | Chicago | 5/2/2007 | 5/15/2007 |
| 1 | Main Campus Housing A | 12 | 3 | Main Campus Housing B | Chicago | /25/2007 | 4/5/2007 |
| 1 | Main Campus Housing A | 13 | 8 | North Satellite Housing D | Chicago | 4/4/2007 | 4/20/2007 |
| 1 | Main Campus Housing A | 14 | 7 | South Campus Housing C | Chicago | /27/2007 | 5/2/2007 |
| 1 | Main Campus Housing A | 18 | 8 | Main Campus Housing A | 702 | 5/23/2007 | 5/28/2007 |
| 1 | Main Campus Housing A | 20 | 5 | Main Campus Housing A | 309 | 5/5/2007 | 5/22/2007 |
| 1 | Main Campus Housing A | 24 | 3 | Main Campus Housing A | 207 | 5/25/2007 | 5/29/2007 |
| 1 | Main Campus Housing A | 27 | 11 | Main Campus Housing A | 505 | 6/2/2007 | 6/3/2007 |
| 1 | Main Campus Housing A | 31 | 5 | Main Campus Housing A | 311 | 7/15/2007 | 7/17/2007 |
| 1 | Main Campus Housing A | 32 | 2 | Main Campus Housing A | 410 | 6/8/2007 | 6/27/2007 |
| 1 | Main Campus Housing A | 36 | 2 | Main Campus Housing A | 507 | 7/8/2007 | 7/14/2007 |
| 1 | Main Campus Housing A | 37 | 7 | Main Campus Housing A | 404 | 7/13/2007 | 7/22/2007 |
| 1 | Main Campus Housing A | 45 | 13 | Main Campus Housing A | 102 | 6/28/2007 | 7/3/2007 |
| 1 | Main Campus Housing A | 46 | 1 | Main Campus Housing A | 501 | 6/21/2007 | 7/1/2007 |
| 1 | Main Campus Housing A | 51 | 9 | Main Campus Housing A | 103 | 8/24/2007 | 9/6/2007 |
| 1 | Main Campus Housing A | 54 | 12 | Main Campus Housing A | 704 | 9/15/2007 | 9/26/2007 |
| 1 | Main Campus Housing A | 57 | 11 | Main Campus Housing A | 104 | 9/14/2007 | 9/22/2007 |
| 1 | Main Campus Housing A | 58 | 10 | Main Campus Housing A | 601 | 8/20/2007 | 8/24/2007 |
| 2 | Main Campus Housing B | 2 | 7 | Main Campus Housing B | 111 | 3/24/2007 | 4/4/2007 |
| 2 | Main Campus Housing B | 5 | 3 | Main Campus Housing B | 214 | 3/26/2007 | 3/28/2007 |
| 2 | Main Campus Housing B | 9 | 2 | Main Campus Housing B | 504 | 4/20/2007 | 4/23/2007 |
| 2 | Main Campus Housing B | 11 | 5 | Main Campus Housing B | 301 | 3/25/2007 | 4/9/2007 |
| 2 | Main Campus Housing B | 15 | 6 | Main Campus Housing B | 206 | 4/4/2007 | 4/15/2007 |

Record: 4 of 58 No Filter Search

**Figure 8-2** Here you can see the recordset of the query shown in Figure 8-1. The facility information in the drop-down list comes from the Lookup properties defined in the tblReservations table.

If you choose a different Facility (the FacilityID field in tblReservations), you can see the ID and Name change on the left side of the datasheet. When you change the value in a foreign key field (in this case, the FacilityID field in tblReservations) in a table on the *many* side of a one-to-many query (there are many reservations for each facility), Access performs an *AutoLookup* to retrieve the related row from the *one* side (tblFacilities) to keep the data synchronized. You'll find this feature handy later when you build a form to display and edit information from a query like this.

Try changing the entry in the Facility column (remember, this is the FacilityID field from tblReservations; you see the name of the facility because we defined Lookup properties on this field.) in the first row from Main Campus Housing A to South Campus Housing C. When you select the new value for the FacilityID field in tblReservations, you should see the ID field from tblFacilities change to 3 and the Name entry (the FacilityName field from tblFacilities) change from Main Campus Housing A to South Campus Housing C. Note that in this case you're changing only the linking FacilityID field in tblReservations, not the name of the facility in tblFacilities. Access is retrieving the row from tblFacilities that matches the changed FacilityID value in tblReservations to show you the correct name.

**Note**

If you change the facility in one of the rows in this query, Access won't let you save the row if the room number in the reservation doesn't exist in the new facility you chose.

One interesting aspect of queries on multiple tables is that in many cases you can update the fields from either table in the query. See "Limitations on Using Select Queries to Update Data" on page 468 for a discussion of when joined queries are not updatable. For example, you can change the facility name in the tblFacilities table by changing the data in the Name column in this query's datasheet.



**CAUTION!**

In most cases, Access lets you edit fields from the table on the *one* side of the join (in this case, tblFacilities). Because the facility name comes from a table on the *one* side of a one-to-many relationship (one facility has many reservations, but each reservation is for only one facility), if you change the name of the facility in any row in this query, you change the name for all reservations for the same facility.

Although the dangers to doing this are apparent, this is actually one of the benefits of designing your tables properly. If the facility is renamed (perhaps it gets renamed in honor of a beloved ex-president of the company), you need to change the name in only one place. You don't have to find all existing reservations for the facility and update them all.

You might use a query like the one in Figure 8-1 as the basis for a report on reservations by facility. However, such a report would probably also need to include the employee name and department to be truly useful. Switch back to Design view, click the Show Table button in the Query Setup group of the Design contextual tab and add tblEmployees and tblDepartments to the query. You can also drag and drop any table or query from the Navigation Pane to your query.

You'll run into a small problem when you add tblDepartments to your query: There are two relationships defined between tblDepartments and tblEmployees. First, each employee must have a valid department assigned, so there's a relationship on DepartmentID. Also, any manager for a department must be an employee of the department, and an employee can manage only one department, so there's a second relationship defined between EmployeeNumber in tblEmployees and ManagerNumber in tblDepartments.

The query designer doesn't know which relationship you want to use as a join in this query, so it includes them *both* in the query grid. If you leave both join lines in your query, you'll see only reservations for managers of departments because the join between EmployeeNumber in tblEmployees and ManagerNumber in tblDepartments forces the query to include only employees who are also managers. Click on the join line between EmployeeNumber in tblEmployees and ManagerNumber in tblDepartments and press the Delete key to remove the join.

If you're going to use this query in a report, you probably don't need EmployeeNumber and FacilityID from tblReservations, so you can delete them. Next click on Room-Number in the design grid and click Insert Columns in the Query Setup group on the Design tab to give you a blank column to work with. You need the employee name for your report, but you most likely don't need the separate FirstName, MiddleName, and LastName fields. Use the blank column to create an expression as follows:



```
EmpName: tblEmployees.FirstName & " " & (tblEmployees.MiddleName + " ") & LastName
```

Note that you're using the little trick you learned in the previous chapter: using an arithmetic operation to eliminate the potential extra blank when an employee has no middle name. Drag and drop the Department field from tblDepartments on top of RoomNumber in the design grid—this should place it between the EmpName field you just defined and RoomNumber. Your query grid should now look like Figure 8-3.

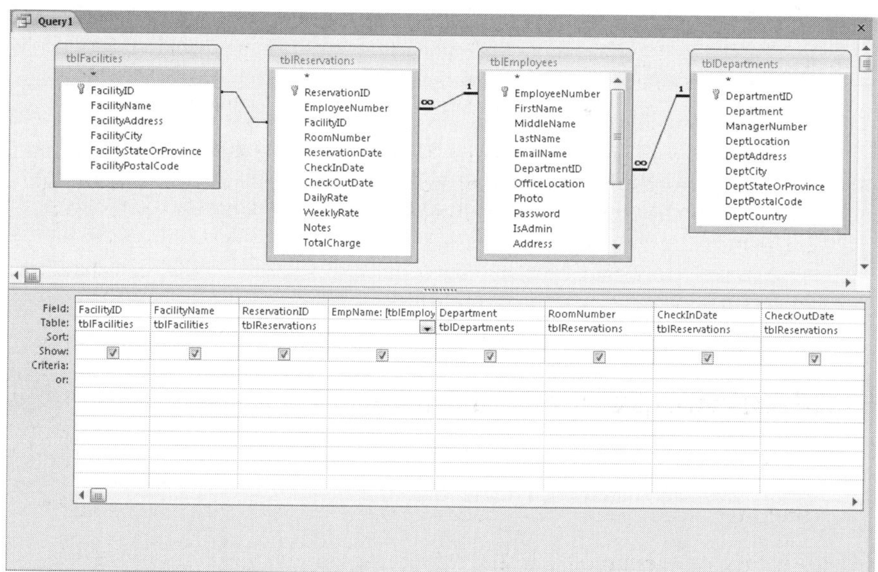


**Figure 8-3** In this example we are creating a complex query using four tables.

You can switch to Datasheet view to see the results of your work as shown in Figure 8-4.

Do you notice anything strange about the sequence of rows? Why aren't the rows sorted by facility name and then perhaps employee name? If you were to put the Employee-Number field back into the query grid and take a look at the data again, you would discover that Access sorted the rows by EmployeeNumber and then by ReservationID. Access looked at all the information you requested and then figured out the quickest way to give you the answer—probably by fetching rows from tblEmployee first (which are sorted on the primary key, EmployeeID) and then fetching the matching rows from tblReservations.

Query1

| ID | Name | Reservation ID | EmpName | Department | Room | Check-In | Check-Out |
|---|---|---|---|---|---|---|---|
| 3 | South Campus Housing C | 7 | Reed Koch | Sales | 501 | 2/28/2007 | 3/13/2007 |
| 1 | Main Campus Housing A | 46 | Reed Koch | Sales | 501 | 6/21/2007 | 7/1/2007 |
| 2 | Main Campus Housing B | 9 | Tim Kim | Finance | 504 | 4/20/2007 | 4/23/2007 |
| 2 | Main Campus Housing B | 29 | Tim Kim | Finance | 206 | 6/20/2007 | 6/25/2007 |
| 1 | Main Campus Housing A | 32 | Tim Kim | Finance | 410 | 6/8/2007 | 6/27/2007 |
| 1 | Main Campus Housing A | 36 | Tim Kim | Finance | 507 | 7/8/2007 | 7/14/2007 |
| 2 | Main Campus Housing B | 44 | Tim Kim | Finance | 102 | 7/22/2007 | 8/2/2007 |
| 1 | Main Campus Housing A | 4 | John Tippett | Product Development | 502 | 4/14/2007 | 5/1/2007 |
| 2 | Main Campus Housing B | 5 | John Tippett | Product Development | 214 | 3/26/2007 | 3/28/2007 |
| 1 | Main Campus Housing A | 10 | John Tippett | Product Development | 707 | 5/2/2007 | 5/15/2007 |
| 1 | Main Campus Housing A | 12 | John Tippett | Product Development | 207 | 3/25/2007 | 4/5/2007 |
| 1 | Main Campus Housing A | 24 | John Tippett | Product Development | 207 | 5/25/2007 | 5/29/2007 |
| 4 | North Satellite Housing D | 34 | John Tippett | Product Development | 203 | 7/6/2007 | 7/22/2007 |
| 3 | South Campus Housing C | 41 | John Tippett | Product Development | 401 | 6/19/2007 | 7/4/2007 |
| 2 | Main Campus Housing B | 55 | John Tippett | Product Development | 212 | 8/6/2007 | 8/12/2007 |
| 3 | South Campus Housing C | 17 | Kirk DeGrasse | Sales | 101 | 5/1/2007 | 5/22/2007 |
| 2 | Main Campus Housing B | 35 | Kirk DeGrasse | Sales | 402 | 6/26/2007 | 7/14/2007 |
| 2 | Main Campus Housing B | 47 | Kirk DeGrasse | Sales | 514 | 7/6/2007 | 7/7/2007 |
| 2 | Main Campus Housing B | 48 | Kirk DeGrasse | Sales | 402 | 8/11/2007 | 8/27/2007 |
| 2 | Main Campus Housing B | 49 | Kirk DeGrasse | Sales | 114 | 8/17/2007 | 9/7/2007 |
| 3 | South Campus Housing C | 53 | Kirk DeGrasse | Sales | 106 | 8/21/2007 | 9/10/2007 |
| 4 | North Satellite Housing D | 3 | David Oliver Lawrence | Product Development | 305 | 3/20/2007 | 3/23/2007 |
| 2 | Main Campus Housing B | 11 | David Oliver Lawrence | Product Development | 301 | 3/25/2007 | 4/9/2007 |
| 2 | Main Campus Housing B | 19 | David Oliver Lawrence | Product Development | 610 | 5/23/2007 | 6/6/2007 |
| 1 | Main Campus Housing A | 20 | David Oliver Lawrence | Product Development | 309 | 5/5/2007 | 5/22/2007 |
| 3 | South Campus Housing C | 25 | David Oliver Lawrence | Product Development | 607 | 6/26/2007 | 6/28/2007 |

Record: 1 of 58 No Filter Search

**Figure 8-4** In Datasheet view you can see the recordset of the query shown in Figure 8-3.

Remember from the previous chapter that the only way you can guarantee the sequence of rows is to specify a sort on the fields you want. In this case, you might want to sort by facility name, employee last name, employee first name, and check-in date. You buried first name and last name in the EmpName expression, so you can't use that field to sort the data by last name. You can find the correct answer saved as qxmplSort-Reservations in the sample database. (Hint: You need to add tblEmployees.LastName and tblEmployees.FirstName to the grid to be able to specify the sort.)

## Building a Query on a Query

When you're building a very complex query, sometimes it's easier to visualize the solution to the problem at hand by breaking it down into smaller pieces. In some cases, building a query on a query might be the only way to correctly solve the problem.

For this set of examples, let's switch to the data in the Conrad Systems Contacts database. Start Access 2007 and open ContactsDataCopy.accdb. Customers who purchase a Single User copy of the BO$$ software marketed by Conrad Systems can later decide to upgrade to the Multi-User edition for a reduced price. Assume you're a consultant hired by Conrad Systems, and the company has asked you to produce a list of all customers and their companies who purchased a Single User copy and then later purchased the upgrade.

To solve this, you might be tempted to start a new query on tblContacts and add the tblCompanies, tblContactProducts, and tblProducts tables. You would include the CompanyID and CompanyName fields from tblCompanies; the ContactID, FirstName, and LastName fields from tblContacts; and the ProductID and ProductName fields from tblProducts. Then you would place a criterion like *"BO$$ Single User" And "Upgrade* *to BO$$ Multi-User*" on the Criteria line under ProductName. However, any one row in your query will show information from only one contact and product, so one row can't contain both "BO$$ Single User" and "Upgrade to BO$$ Multi-User." (See the discussion in "AND vs. OR" on page 357.) Your query will return no rows.

Your next attempt might be to correct the criterion to *"BO$$ Single User" Or "Upgrade to BO$$ Multi-User"*. That will at least return some data, but you'll get an answer similar to Figure 8-5. (You can find this query saved as qxmplTwoProductsWrong in the sample database.)



qxmplTwoProductsWrong

| Compa | Company / Organization | Contact | First Name | Last Name | Product | Product Name |
|---|---|---|---|---|---|---|
| 1 | Contoso, Ltd | 1 | Jan | Stoklasa | 6 | Upgrade to BO$$ Multi-User |
| 2 | Fourth Coffee | 4 | Andrew | Dixon | 6 | Upgrade to BO$$ Multi-User |
| 3 | Coho Vineyard | 6 | Mario | Kresnadi | 3 | BO$$ Single User |
| 3 | Coho Vineyard | 7 | Anibal | Sousa | 6 | Upgrade to BO$$ Multi-User |
| 3 | Coho Vineyard | 8 | Joseph | Matthews | 3 | BO$$ Single User |
| 3 | Coho Vineyard | 8 | Joseph | Matthews | 6 | Upgrade to BO$$ Multi-User |
| 4 | Southridge Video | 10 | Kathleen Gail | Jensen | 6 | Upgrade to BO$$ Multi-User |
| 5 | Consolidated Messenger | 12 | Harry | Linggoputro | 3 | BO$$ Single User |
| 6 | Baldwin Museum of Science | 13 | Cat | Francis | 6 | Upgrade to BO$$ Multi-User |
| 7 | Fabrikam, Inc. | 16 | John | Smith | 3 | BO$$ Single User |
| 7 | Fabrikam, Inc. | 16 | John | Smith | 6 | Upgrade to BO$$ Multi-User |
| 9 | School of Fine Art | 19 | Dániel | Koczka | 3 | BO$$ Single User |
| 9 | School of Fine Art | 19 | Dániel | Koczka | 6 | Upgrade to BO$$ Multi-User |
| 12 | Margie's Travel | 24 | Mindy | Martin | 3 | BO$$ Single User |
| 12 | Margie's Travel | 25 | Markus | Zulechner | 3 | BO$$ Single User |
| 12 | Margie's Travel | 26 | Peter | Villadsen | 6 | Upgrade to BO$$ Multi-User |
| 13 | Lucerne Publishing | 28 | Mark | Hanson | 3 | BO$$ Single User |
| 13 | Lucerne Publishing | 28 | Mark | Hanson | 6 | Upgrade to BO$$ Multi-User |
| 14 | Humongous Insurance | 29 | Marcin | Jankowski | 6 | Upgrade to BO$$ Multi-User |
| * | | | | | (New) | |

Record: 1 of 19 No Filter Search

**Figure 8-5** This query is an attempt to find out which contacts have purchased both BO$$ Single User and the BO$$ Multi-User upgrade.

Because there aren't very many rows in this table, you can scan this 19-row result and see that the correct answer is four contacts—Joseph Matthews, John Smith, Daniel Koczka, and Mark Hanson. But if there were thousands of rows in the database, you wouldn't be able to easily find the contacts who purchased both products. And if you need to display the output in a report, you really need a single row for each contact that meets your criteria.

One way to solve this sort of problem is to build a query that finds everyone who owns BO$$ Single User and save it. Then build another query that finds everyone who purchased the BO$$ Multi-User upgrade and save that. Finally, build a third query that joins the first two results to get your final answer. Remember that a simple join returns only the rows that match in both tables—or queries. So, someone who appears in both queries clearly owns both products! Here's how to build the solution.

1. Build the first query to find customers who own BO$$ Single User.
   a. Start a new query on tblContactProducts and add tblProducts to the query. You should see a join line between tblProducts and tblContactProducts on the ProductID field because there's a relationship defined.
   b. From tblContactProducts, include the CompanyID and the ContactID fields.
   c. Add ProductName from tblProducts, and enter **"BO$$ Single User"** on the Criteria line under this field. Save this query and name it qrySingle.
2. Build the second query to find customers who bought the upgrade.
   a. Start another query on tblContactProducts and add tblProducts to the query.
   b. From tblContactProducts, include the CompanyID and the ContactID fields.
   c. Add ProductName from tblProducts, and enter **"Upgrade to BO$$ Multi-User"** on the Criteria line under this field. Save this query and name it qryMultiUpgrade.
3. Build the final solution query.
   a. Start a new query on tblCompanies. Add your new qrySingle and qryMultiUpgrade queries.
   b. The query designer will link tblCompanies to both queries on CompanyID, but you don't need a link to both. Click on the join line between tblCompanies and qryMultiUpgrade and delete it.
   c. You do need to link qrySingle and qryMultiUpgrade. Drag and drop CompanyID from qrySingle to qryMultiUpgrade. Then, drag and drop ContactID from qrySingle to qryMultiUpgrade. Because you are defining an inner join between the two queries, the query fetches rows only from the two queries where the CompanyID and ContactID match.
   d. Add tblContacts to your query. Because there's a relationship defined between ContactID in tblContacts and ReferredBy in tblCompanies, the query designer adds this join line. You don't need this join (the query would return only contacts who have made referrals), so click on the line and delete it. The query designer does correctly create a join line between tblContacts and qrySingle.
   e. On the query design grid, include CompanyName from tblCompanies, and FirstName and LastName from tblContacts. Your result should look like Figure 8-6.

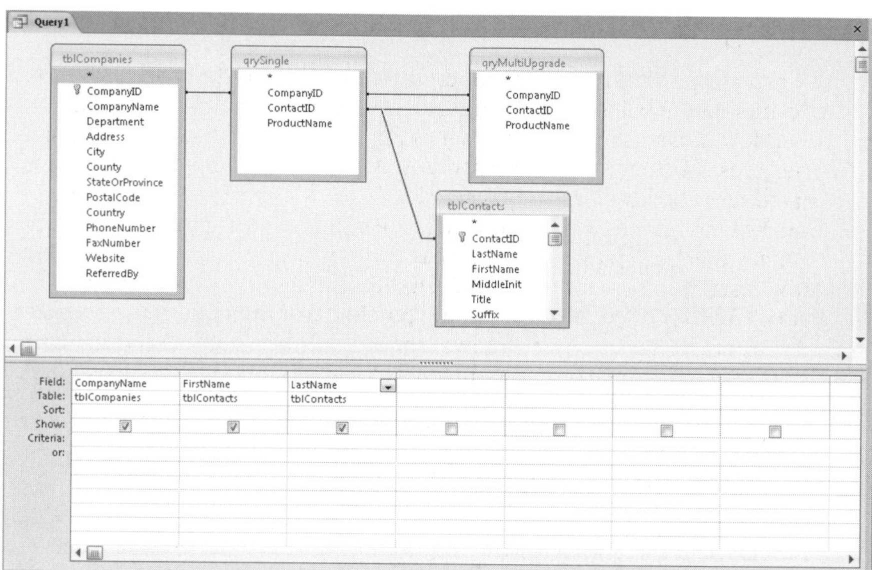


**Figure 8-6** Here you are solving the "contacts who own two products" problem the right way by building a query on queries.

Switch to Datasheet view, and, sure enough, the query gives you the right answer as shown in Figure 8-7.

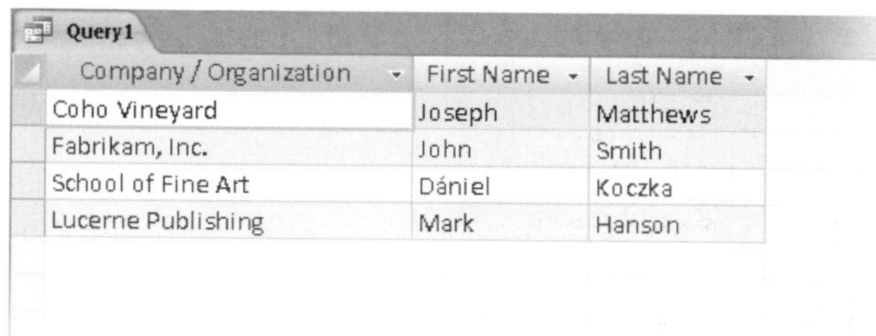
Query1

| Company / Organization | First Name | Last Name |
|---|---|---|
| Coho Vineyard | Joseph | Matthews |
| Fabrikam, Inc. | John | Smith |
| School of Fine Art | Dániel | Koczka |
| Lucerne Publishing | Mark | Hanson |

**Figure 8-7** You can now correctly see the four contacts who purchased a BO$$ Single User edition and later upgraded.

This works because you're using the two queries to filter each other via the join. The qrySingle query finds contacts who own BO$$ Single User. The qryMultiUpgrade query finds contacts who bought the BO$$ Multi-User upgrade. The join lines between these two queries ask the final query to return rows only where the CompanyID and ContactID in the first two queries match, so you won't see rows from qrySingle that don't have a matching combination of CompanyID and ContactID in qryMultiUpgrade, and vice versa.

**For more examples of building queries on queries, see Article 2, "Understanding SQL," on the companion CD.**

## Using Outer Joins

Most queries that you create to request information from multiple tables will show results on the basis of matching data in one or more tables. For example, the Query window in Datasheet view shown in Figure 8-4 contains the names of facilities that have reservations in the tblReservations table—and it does not contain the names of facilities that don't have any reservations booked. As explained earlier, this type of query is called an equi-join query, meaning that you'll see rows only where there are *equal* values in *both* tables. But, what if you want to display facilities that do not have any reservations in the database? Or, how do you find employees who have no reservations? You can get the information you need by creating a query that uses an *outer join*. An outer join lets you see all rows from one of the tables even if there's no matching row in the related table. When no matching row exists, Access returns the special Null value in the columns from the related table.



### Building a Simple Outer Join

To create an outer join, you must modify the join properties. Let's see if we can find any employees who don't have any reservations booked. Start a new query on tblEmployees in the HousingDataCopy database. Add tblReservations to the query. Double-click the join line between the two tables in the upper part of the Query window in Design view to see the Join Properties dialog box, shown in Figure 8-8.

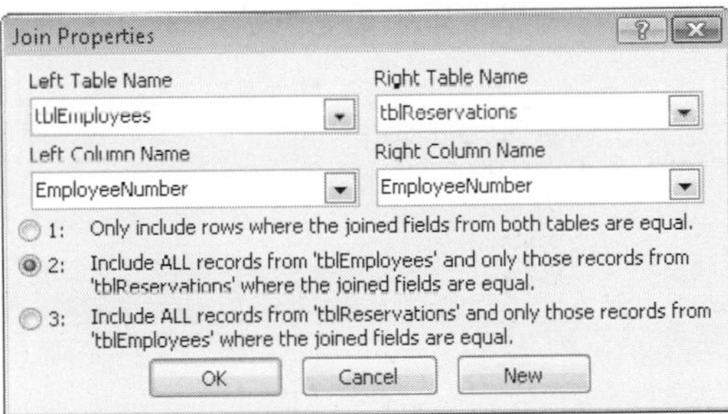


**Figure 8-8** The Join Properties dialog box allows you to change the join properties for the query.

The default setting in the Join Properties dialog box is the first option—where the joined fields from both tables are equal. You can see that you have two additional options for this query: to see all employees and any reservations that match, or to see all reservations and any employees that match. If you entered your underlying data correctly, you shouldn't have reservations for employees who aren't defined in the database. If you asked Access to enforce referential integrity (discussed in Chapter 4, "Creating Your Database and Tables") when you defined the relationship between the tblEmployees table and the tblReservations table, Access won't let you create any reservations for non-existent employees.

Select the second option in the dialog box. (When the link between two tables involves more than one field in each table, you can click the New button to define the additional links.) Click OK. You should now see an arrow on the join line pointing from the tblEmployees field list to the tblReservations field list, indicating that you have asked for an outer join with all records from tblEmployees regardless of match, as shown in Figure 8-9. For employees who have no reservations, Access returns the special Null value in all the columns for tblReservations. So, you can find the employees that aren't planning to stay in any facility by including the Is Null test for any of the columns from tblReservations. When you run this query, you should find exactly two employees who have no reservations, as shown in Figure 8-10. The finished query is saved as qxmplEmployeesNoReservations in the HousingDataCopy.accdb database.



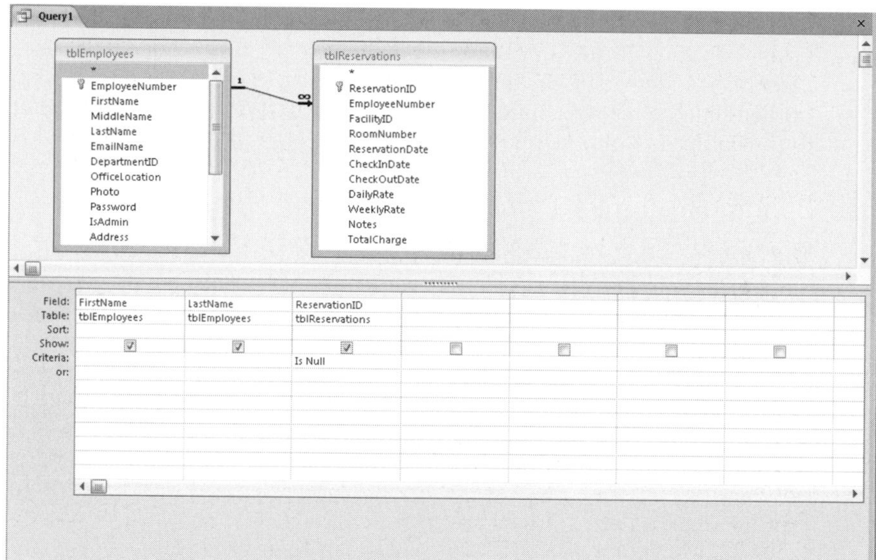


Figure 8-9 This query design finds employees who have no reservations.

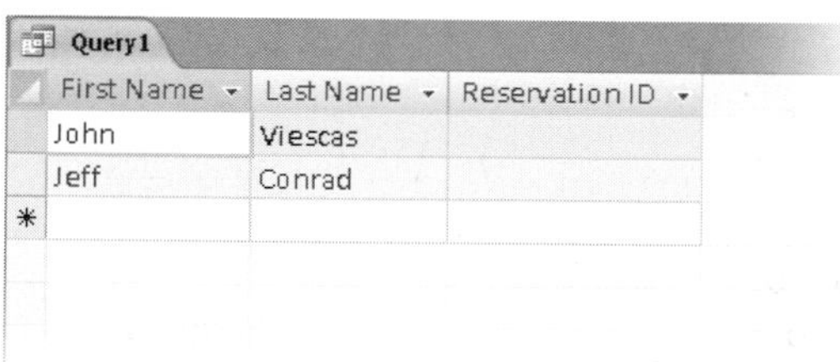

| First Name | Last Name | Reservation ID |
|---|---|---|
| John | Viescas | |
| Jeff | Conrad | |

Figure 8-10 This recordset shows the two employees who have no reservations.

## Solving a Complex "Unmatched" Problem

As discussed earlier in this chapter, you know that to solve certain types of problems you must first build one query to define a subset of data from your tables and then use that query as input to another query to get the final answer. For example, suppose you want to find out which employees have no reservations in a certain time period. You might guess that an outer join from the tblEmployees table to the tblReservations table will do the trick. That would work fine if the tblReservations table contained reservations for only the time period in question. Remember, to find employees who haven't booked a room, you have to look for a special Null value in the columns from tblReservations. But to limit the data in tblReservations to a specific time period–let's say June and July 2007–you have to be able to test real values. In other words, you have a problem because a column from tblReservations can't be both Null and have a date value at the same time. (You can find an example of the wrong way to solve this problem saved as qxmplEmpNotBookedJunJulWRONG in the sample database.)

To solve this problem, you must first create a query that contains only the reservations for the months you want. As you'll see in a bit, you can then use that query with an outer join in another query to find out which employees haven't booked a room in June and July 2007. Figure 8-11 shows the query you need to start with, using tblReservations. This example includes the EmployeeNumber field as well as the FacilityID and RoomNumber fields, so you can use it to search for either employees or facilities or rooms that aren't booked in the target months.



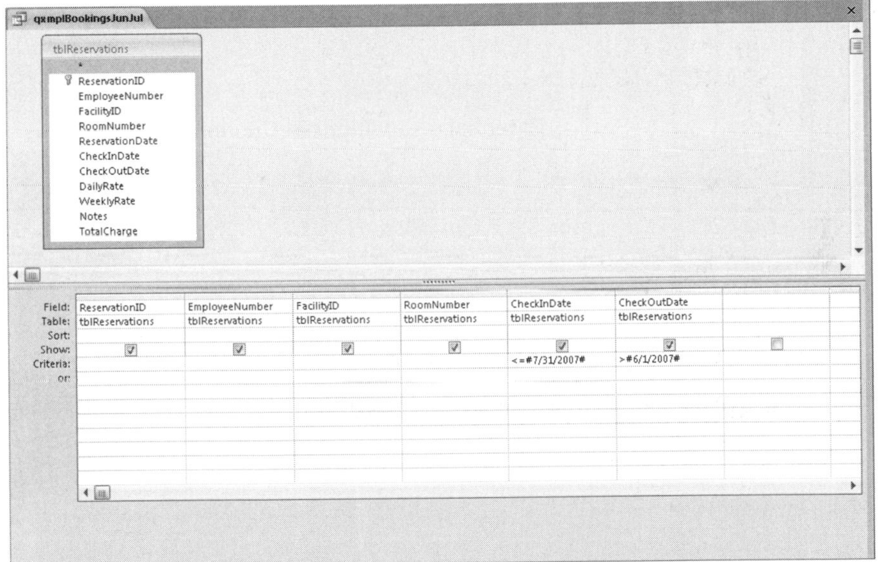


**Figure 8-11** You can add a filter to your query to list reservation data for particular months.

Notice that if you truly want to see all reservations in these two months, you need to specify a criterion on both CheckInDate and CheckOutDate. Anyone who checked in on or before July 31, 2007–provided they didn't check out before June 1, 2007–is someone who stayed in a room between the dates of interest. You don't want anyone who checked out on June 1 (who stayed the night of May 31, but didn't stay over into June), which explains why the second criterion is >#6/1/2007# and not >=#6/1/2007#. This query is saved as qxmplBookingsJunJul in the HousingDataCopy.accdb database.

### Finding Records Across Date Spans

You might be looking at the problem of finding any reservation that crosses into or is contained within a certain date span and scratching your head. You want any reservation that meets one of these criteria:

- The reservation begins before the start of the date span but extends into the date span.
- The reservation is contained wholly within the date span.
- The reservation begins before the end of the date span but extends beyond the date span.
- The reservation starts before the beginning of the date span and ends after the end of the date span.

You can see these four conditions in the following illustration.

**Time frame of interest**

**Potential reservations in the time frame**

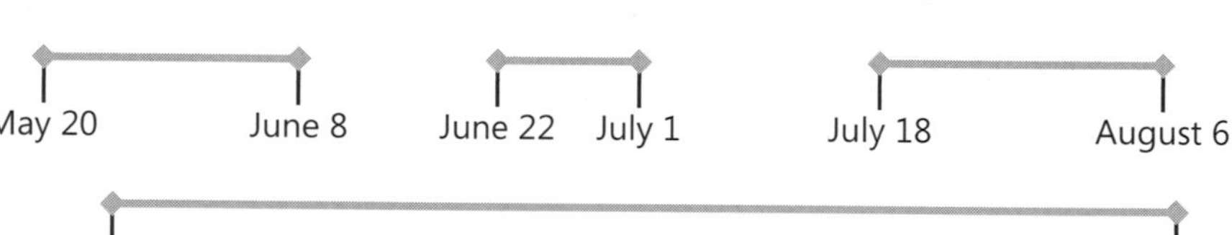


You might be tempted to include four separate criteria in your query, but that's not necessary. As long as a reservation begins before the *end* of the span and ends after the *beginning* of the span, you've got them all! Try out the criteria shown in Figure 8-11 to see if that simple test doesn't find all the previous cases.

After you save the first query, click the Query Design button in the Other group on the Create tab to start a new query. In the Show Table dialog box add tblEmployees to the design grid by double-clicking on tblEmployees. Click the Queries tab in the Show Table dialog box and then double-click on qxmplBookingsJunJul to add it to the query grid. Click Close to close the Show Table dialog box. Access should automatically link tblEmployees to the query on matching EmployeeNumber fields. Double-click the join line to open the Join Properties dialog box, and select option 2 to see all rows from tblEmployees and any matching rows from the query. The join line's arrow should point from tblEmployees to the query, as shown in Figure 8-12.

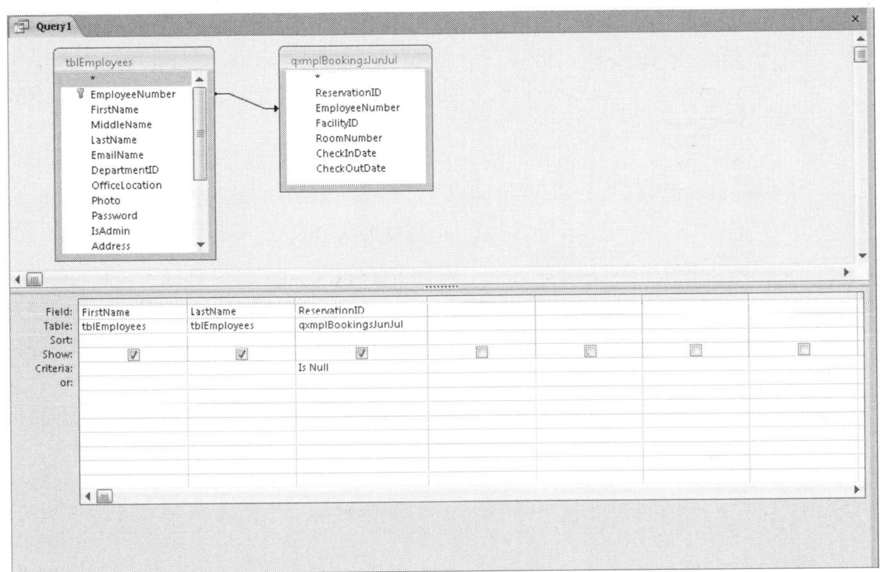


**Figure 8-12** An outer join query searches for employees not booked in June and July 2007.

As you did in the previous outer join example, include some fields from the tblEmployees table and at least one field from the query that contains reservations only from June and July 2007. In the field from the query, add the special Is Null criterion. When you run this query (the results of which are shown in Figure 8-13), you should find six employees who haven't booked a room in June and July 2007—including the two employees that you found earlier who haven't booked any room at all. This query is saved as qxmplEmpNotBookedJunJul in the HousingDataCopy.accdb database.

Query1

| First Nam | Last Nam | Reservation |
|---|---|---|
| Jay | Adams | |
| Scott | Eyink | |
| Matthias | Berndt | |
| Gary | Schare | |
| John | Viescas | |
| Jeff | Conrad | |
| * | | |

**Figure 8-13** These employees have no bookings in June and July 2007.

Let's study another example. When you're looking at reservation requests, and each request indicates the particular type of room desired, it might be useful to know either which facilities have this type of room or which facilities do not. (Not all facilities have all the different types of rooms.) You can find a complete list of the room types in the tlkpRoomTypes table in the Housing Reservations application.

Chapter 8

To find out which room types aren't in a facility, you might try an outer join from tlkpRoomTypes to tblFacilityRooms and look for Null again, but all you'd find is that all room types exist somewhere—you wouldn't know which room type was missing in what facility. In truth, you need to build a query first that limits room types to one facility. Your query should look something like Figure 8-14.

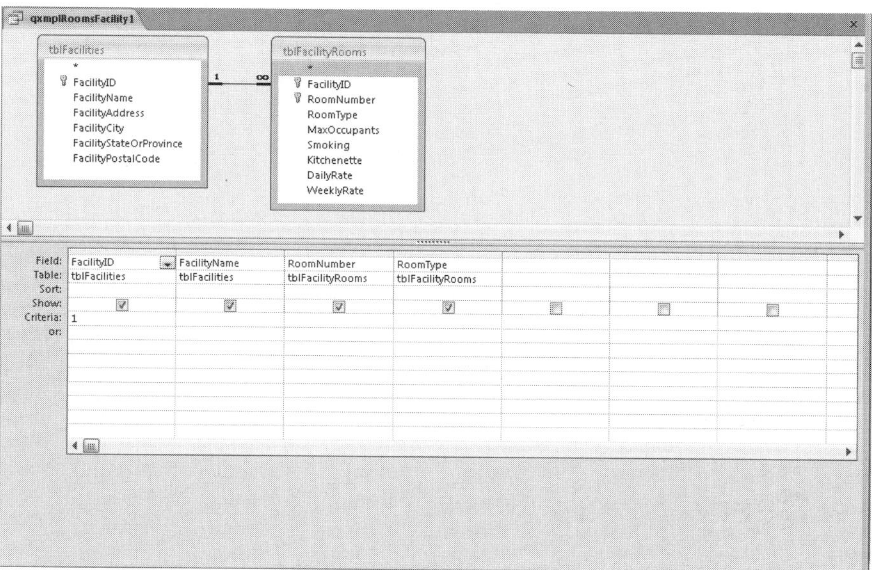


**Figure 8-14** This query lists all the rooms and their room types in Facility 1.

Now you can build your outer join query to find out which room types aren't in the first housing facility. Start a new query by clicking the Query Design button in the Other group on the Create tab. In the Show Table dialog box add tlkpRoomTypes to the design grid by double-clicking tlkpRoomTypes. Click the Queries tab in the Show Table dialog box and then double-click the qxmplRoomsFacility1 query to add it to the query grid. Close the Show Table dialog box. Double-click the join line and ask for all rows from tlkpRoomTypes and any matching rows from the query. Add the RoomType field from tlkpRoomTypes and the FacilityID field from the query to the grid. Under FacilityID, place a criterion of Is Null. Your query should look like Figure 8-15.

If you run this query, you'll find that Facility 1 has no one-bedroom suites with king bed, no one-bedroom suites with two queen beds, and no two-bedroom suites with a king bed, queen bed, and kitchenette. In the sample database, you'll find sample queries that return the room types for the other three facilities, so you can build queries like the one in Figure 8-15 to find out what room types are missing in those facilities.

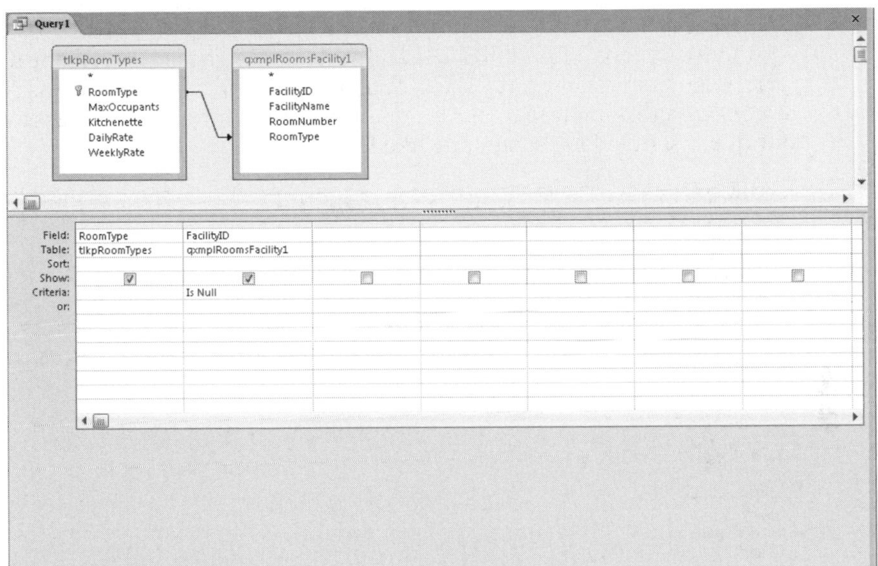


**Figure 8-15** This query determines which room types are not in Facility 1.



# Using a Query Wizard

Every time you have clicked the Query Wizard button in the Other group on the Create tab, you have seen the interesting query wizard entries. You can use query wizards to help you build certain types of "tricky" queries such as crosstab queries (discussed later in this chapter) and queries to find duplicate or unmatched rows. For example, you could have used a query wizard to build the query shown in Figure 8-9 to locate employees who have no room reservations. Let's use a query wizard to build a query to perform a similar search in the ContactsDataCopy.accdb sample file to find contacts who don't own any products.

To try this, click the Query Wizard button in the Other group on the Create tab. Select the Find Unmatched Query Wizard option in the New Query dialog box, as shown in Figure 8-16, and then click OK.

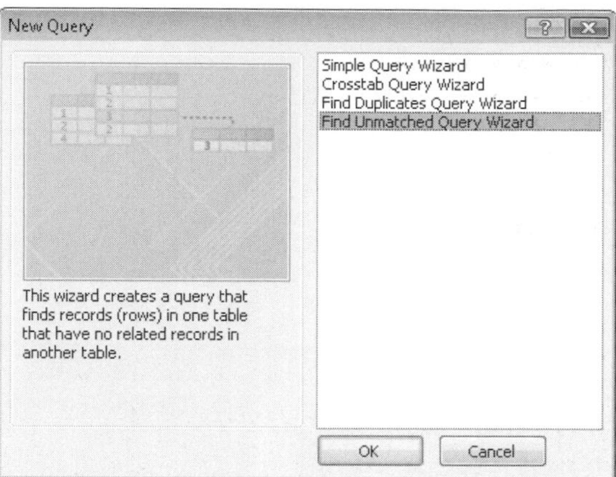


**Figure 8-16** Select a query wizard in the New Query dialog box.

The wizard opens a page with a list of tables from which you can select the initial records, as shown in Figure 8-17. If you want to use an existing query instead of a table, select the Queries option. If you want to look at all queries and tables, select the Both option. In this case, you're looking for contacts who haven't purchased any products, so select the tblContacts table and then click the Next button.

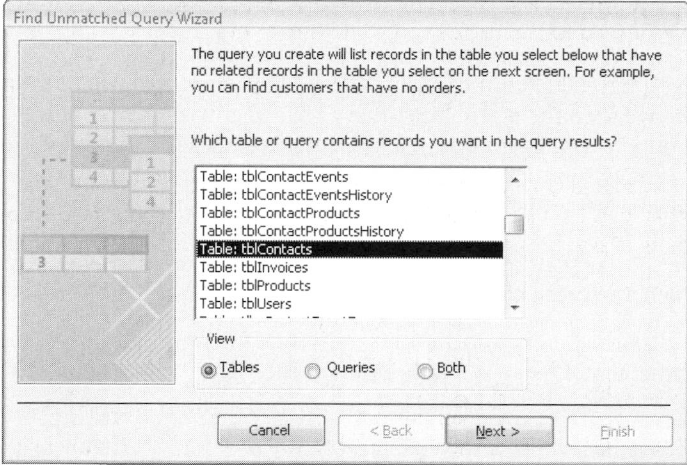


**Figure 8-17** You can select tables or queries on the first page of the Find Unmatched Query Wizard.

On the next page, select the table that contains the related information you expect to be unmatched. You're looking for contacts who have purchased no products, so select the tblContactProducts table and then click the Next button to go to the next page, shown in Figure 8-18.

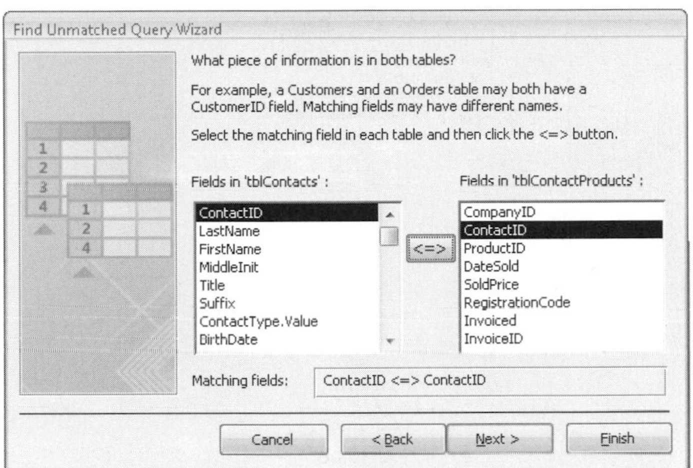


**Figure 8-18** This page is where you define the unmatched link.

Next, the wizard needs to know the linking fields between the two tables. Because no direct relationship is defined between tblContacts and tblContactProducts, the wizard won't automatically choose the matching fields for you. Click on the ContactID field in tblContacts and the ContactID field in tblContactProducts to select those two fields. Click the <=> button between the field lists to add those fields to the Matching Fields box. Click Next to go to the page shown in Figure 8-19.

> **Note**
>
> The Find Unmatched Query Wizard can work with only the tables that have no more than one field that links the two tables. If you need to "find unmatched" records between two tables that require a join on more than one field, you'll have to build the query yourself.

Choose the fields you want to display (see Figure 8-19) by selecting a field in the Available Fields list and then clicking the > button to move the field to the Selected Fields list. The query will display the fields in the order you select them. If you choose a field in error, select it in the list on the right and click the < button to move it back. You can click the >> button to select all fields or the << button to remove all fields. When you're finished selecting fields, click Next. On the final page, you can specify a different name for your query. (The wizard generates a long and ugly name.) You can select an option to either view the results or modify the design. So that you can see the design first, select Modify The Design and then click Finish to open the Query window in Design view. Figure 8-20 shows the finished query to find contacts who have purchased no products.

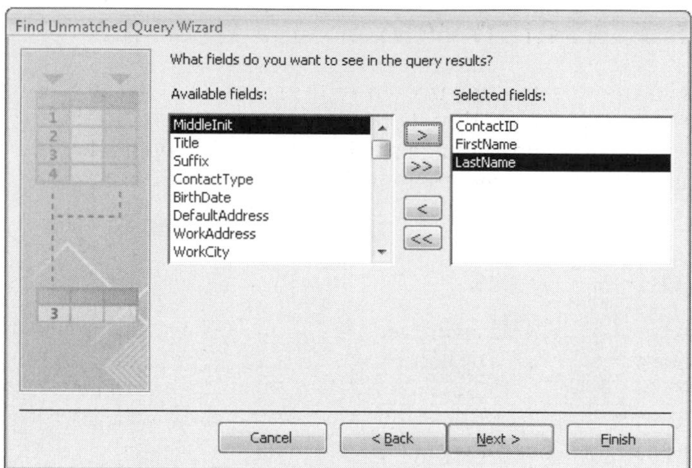


**Figure 8-19** On this page you select the fields to be displayed in a query.

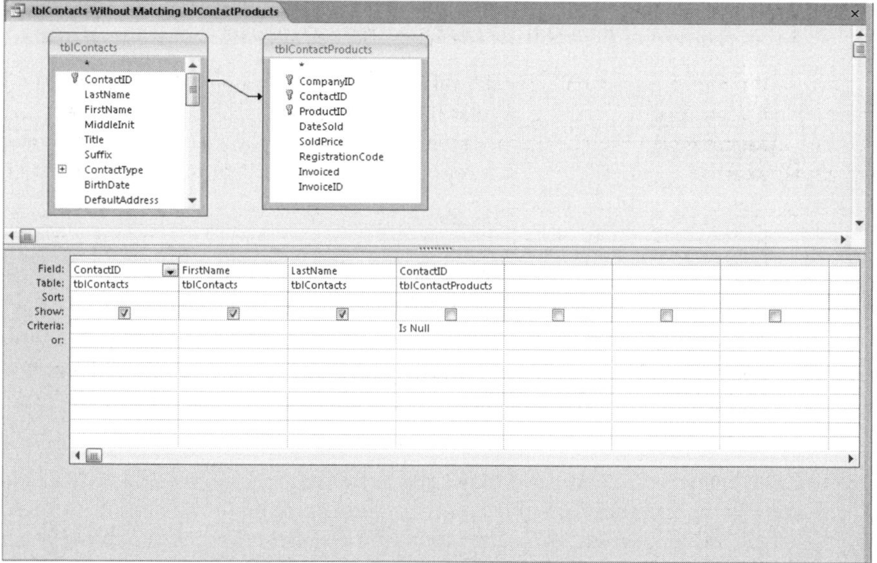


**Figure 8-20** The query wizard has helped you build a query that finds contacts who have purchased no products.

If you run this query, you'll find three contacts who haven't bought anything. Perhaps you should schedule a call to these people to find out why!

# Summarizing Information with Totals Queries

Sometimes you aren't interested in each and every row in your table—you'd rather see calculations across groups of data. For example, you might want the total product purchase amount for all companies in a particular state. Or you might want to know the average of all sales for each month in the last year. To get these answers, you need a *totals query*.

## Totals Within Groups

If you're the housing facilities manager, you might be interested in producing sales and usage numbers by facility or by date range. For this series of exercises, open Housing-DataCopy.accdb and start a new query with tblFacilities and tblReservations in the query design grid. Include in the Field row the FacilityName field from tblFacilities and the CheckInDate and TotalCharge fields from tblReservations.



### INSIDE OUT When Totals Queries Are Useful

We might occasionally build totals queries to display high-level summaries in a report. More often, we create a regular query that fetches all the detail we need and then use the powerful summarization facilities in reports to calculate totals. You'll learn more about summarizing data in a report in Chapter 16, "Advanced Report Design."

A totals query groups the fields you specify, and every output field must either be one of the grouping fields or the result of a calculation using one of the available aggregate functions. (See Table 8-1.) Because all fields are calculated, you cannot update any fields returned by a totals query. So, you're not likely to find totals queries useful in forms.

This does not mean that learning about how to build totals queries is not useful. You need to understand the concepts of grouping and totaling to build reports. You will also find that constructing and opening a totals query in Visual Basic code is useful to perform complex validations.

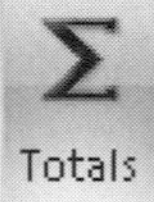


To turn this into a totals query, click the Totals button in the Show/Hide group of the Design contextual tab under Query Tools to open the Total row in the design grid, as shown in Figure 8-21. When you first click the Totals button in the Show/Hide group, Access displays Group By in the Total row for any fields you already have in the design grid. At this point the records in each field are grouped but not totaled. If you were to run the query now, you'd get one row in the recordset for each set of unique values—but no totals. You must replace Group By with an *aggregate function* in the Total row.

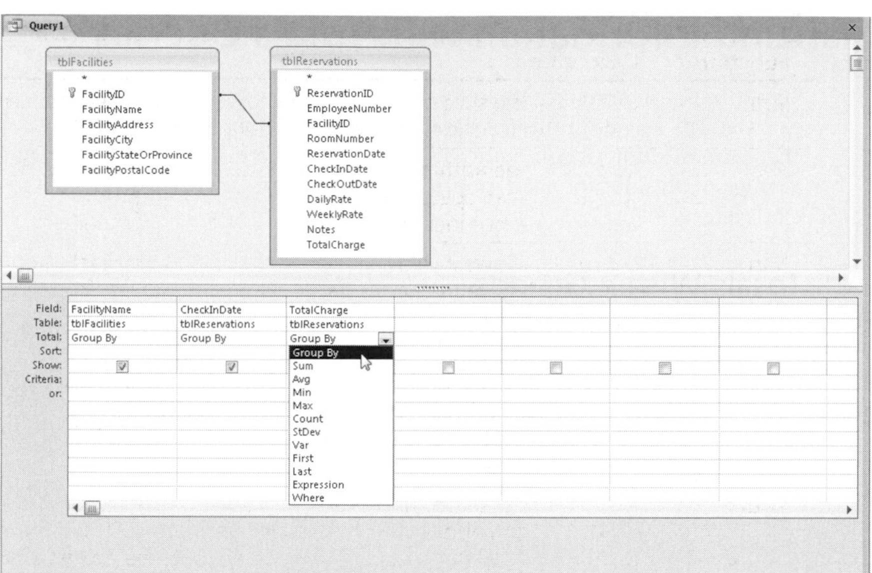


**Figure 8-21** The Total row in the design grid allows you to define aggregate functions.

Access provides nine aggregate functions for your use. You can choose the one you want by typing its name in the Total row in the design grid or by clicking the small arrow and selecting it from the list. You can learn about the available functions in Table 8-1.

Let's experiment with the query you started earlier in this section to understand some of the available functions. First, you probably don't want to see information grouped by individual date. Data summarized over each month would be more informative, so create an expression to replace the CheckInDate field as follows:

```
CheckInMonth: Format([CheckInDate], "yyyy mm")
```

The Format function works similarly to the table field Format property you learned about in Chapter 4. The first parameter is the name of the field or the expression that you want to format, and the second parameter specifies how you want the data formatted. In this case, we're asking Format to return the four-digit year and two-digit month number.

**For more information about Format settings, see "Setting Control Properties" on page 651.**

Change the Total row under TotalCharge to Sum. Add the TotalCharge field from tblReservations three more times, and choose Avg, Min, and Max, respectively, under each. Finally, add the ReservationID field from tblReservations and choose Count in the Total row under that field. Your query design should now look like Figure 8-22.

Table 8-1 **Total Functions**

| Function | Description |
|---|---|
| Sum | Calculates the sum of all the values for this field in each group. You can specify this function only with number or currency fields. |
| Avg | Calculates the arithmetic average of all the values for this field in each group. You can specify this function only with number or currency fields. Access does not include any Null values in the calculation. |
| Min | Returns the lowest value found in this field within each group. For numbers, Min returns the smallest value. For text, Min returns the lowest value in collating sequence ("dictionary"[1] order), without regard to case. Access ignores Null values. |
| Max | Returns the highest value found in this field within each group. For numbers, Max returns the largest value. For text, Max returns the highest value in collating sequence ("dictionary"[1] order), without regard to case. Access ignores Null values. |
| Count | Returns the count of the rows in which the specified field is not a Null value. You can also enter the special expression COUNT(*) in the Field row to count all rows in each group, regardless of the presence of Null values. |
| StDev | Calculates the statistical standard deviation of all the values for this field in each group. You can specify this function only with number or currency fields. If the group does not contain at least two rows, Access returns a Null value. |
| Var | Calculates the statistical variance of all the values for this field in each group. You can specify this function only with number or currency fields. If the group does not contain at least two rows, Access returns a Null value. |
| First | Returns the value for the field from the first row encountered in the group. Note that the first row might not be the one with the lowest value. It also might not be the row you think is "first" within the group. Because First depends on the actual physical sequence of stored data, it essentially returns an unpredictable value from within the group. |
| Last | Returns the value for the field from the last row encountered in the group. Note that the last row might not be the one with the highest value. It also might not be the row you think is "last" within the group. Because Last depends on the actual physical sequence of stored data, it essentially returns an unpredictable value from within the group. |

[1] You can change the sort order for new databases you create by clicking the Microsoft Office Button, clicking Access Options, and then using the New Database Sort Order list in the Popular category. The default value is General, which sorts your data according to the language specified for your operating system.

Switch to Datasheet view to see the results as shown in Figure 8-23. The sample data file has 306 available rooms in four different facilities. From the results of this query, you could conclude that this company has far more housing than it needs! Perhaps the most interesting row is the second row (the row that is highlighted in Figure 8-23). The five reservations for Housing A in April 2007 show how the various functions might help you analyze the data further.

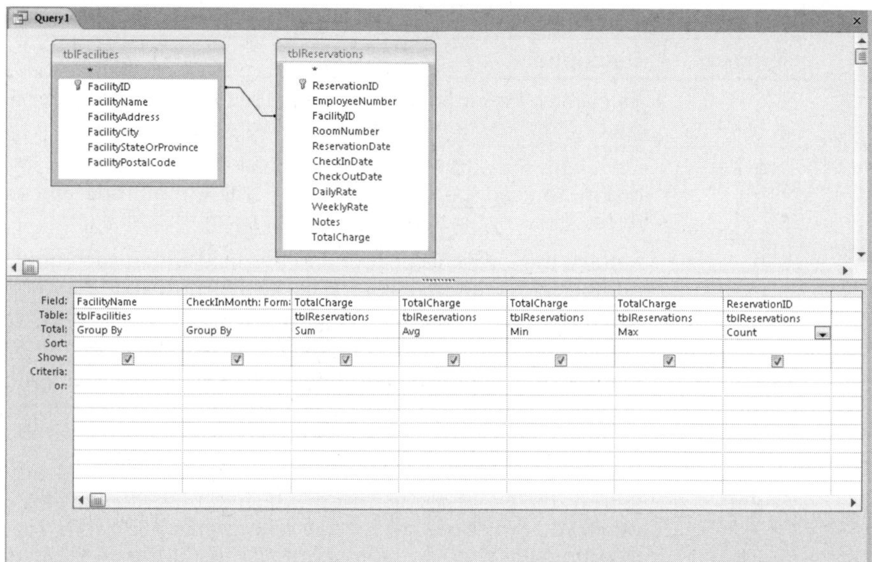


**Figure 8-22** This query design explores many different aggregate functions.

Query1

| Name | CheckInMon | SumOfTotalCharge | AvgOfTotalCharge | MinOfTotalCh | MaxOfTotalCha | CountOfRes |
|---|---|---|---|---|---|---|
| Main Campus Housing A | 2007 03 | $1,025.00 | $512.50 | $455.00 | $570.00 | 2 |
| Main Campus Housing A | 2007 04 | $5,070.00 | $1,014.00 | $250.00 | $1,600.00 | 5 |
| Main Campus Housing A | 2007 05 | $2,140.00 | $535.00 | $220.00 | $790.00 | 4 |
| Main Campus Housing A | 2007 06 | $1,630.00 | $407.50 | $55.00 | $750.00 | 4 |
| Main Campus Housing A | 2007 07 | $870.00 | $290.00 | $160.00 | $380.00 | 3 |
| Main Campus Housing A | 2007 08 | $720.00 | $360.00 | $160.00 | $560.00 | 2 |
| Main Campus Housing A | 2007 09 | $805.00 | $402.50 | $335.00 | $470.00 | 2 |
| Main Campus Housing B | 2007 03 | $2,035.00 | $678.33 | $100.00 | $1,040.00 | 3 |
| Main Campus Housing B | 2007 04 | $1,040.00 | $520.00 | $210.00 | $830.00 | 2 |
| Main Campus Housing B | 2007 05 | $2,430.00 | $1,215.00 | $1,150.00 | $1,280.00 | 2 |
| Main Campus Housing B | 2007 06 | $3,105.00 | $621.00 | $180.00 | $1,180.00 | 5 |
| Main Campus Housing B | 2007 07 | $3,020.00 | $604.00 | $50.00 | $1,180.00 | 5 |
| Main Campus Housing B | 2007 08 | $2,480.00 | $826.67 | $480.00 | $1,040.00 | 3 |
| North Satellite Housing D | 2007 03 | $195.00 | $195.00 | $195.00 | $195.00 | 1 |
| North Satellite Housing D | 2007 05 | $830.00 | $830.00 | $830.00 | $830.00 | 1 |
| North Satellite Housing D | 2007 06 | $280.00 | $280.00 | $280.00 | $280.00 | 1 |
| North Satellite Housing D | 2007 07 | $960.00 | $960.00 | $960.00 | $960.00 | 1 |
| North Satellite Housing D | 2007 08 | $680.00 | $340.00 | $200.00 | $480.00 | 2 |
| South Campus Housing C | 2007 02 | $1,200.00 | $1,200.00 | $1,200.00 | $1,200.00 | 1 |
| South Campus Housing C | 2007 05 | $2,525.00 | $841.67 | $255.00 | $1,920.00 | 3 |
| South Campus Housing C | 2007 06 | $1,490.00 | $745.00 | $110.00 | $1,380.00 | 2 |
| South Campus Housing C | 2007 07 | $415.00 | $415.00 | $415.00 | $415.00 | 1 |
| South Campus Housing C | 2007 08 | $3,820.00 | $1,273.33 | $850.00 | $1,690.00 | 3 |

Record: 2 of 23 No Filter Search

**Figure 8-23** Running the query in Figure 8-22 returns total revenue, average revenue, smallest revenue per reservation, largest revenue per reservation, and count of reservations by facility and month.

## TROUBLESHOOTING

### I didn't specify sorting criteria, so why is my data sorted?

A totals query has to sort your data to be able to group it, so it returns the groups sorted left to right based on the sequence of your Group By fields. If you need to sort the grouping columns in some other way, change the sequence of the Group By fields. Note that you can additionally sort any of the totals fields.



In the list for the Total row in the design grid, you'll also find an Expression setting. Select this when you want to create an expression in the Total row that uses one or more of the aggregate functions listed earlier. For example, you might want to calculate a value that reflects the range of reservation charges in the group, as in the following:

```
Max([TotalCharge]) - Min([TotalCharge])
```

As you can with any field, you can give your expression a custom name. Notice in Figure 8-23 that Access has generated names such as SumOfTotalCharge or AvgOfTotalCharge. You can fix these by clicking in the field in the design grid and prefixing the field or expression with your own name followed by a colon. In Figure 8-24, we removed the separate Min and Max fields, added the expression to calculate the range between the smallest and largest charge, and inserted custom field names. You can see the result in Datasheet view in Figure 8-25.

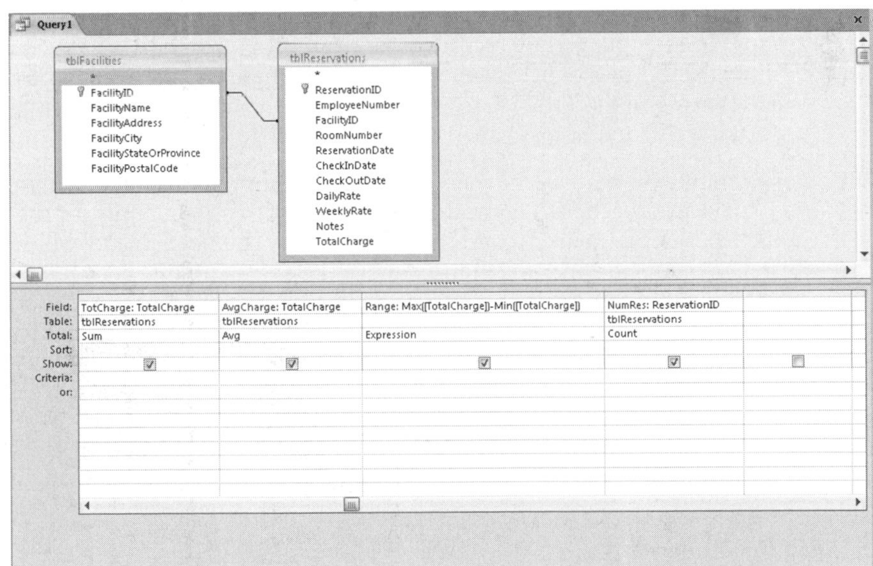


**Figure 8-24** In this figure we are adding an expression and defining custom field names in a totals query.

Query1

| Name | CheckInMonth | TotCharge | AvgCharge | Range | NumRes |
|---|---|---|---|---|---|
| Main Campus Housing A | 2007 03 | $1,025.00 | $512.50 | $115.00 | 2 |
| Main Campus Housing A | 2007 04 | $5,070.00 | $1,014.00 | $1,350.00 | 5 |
| Main Campus Housing A | 2007 05 | $2,140.00 | $535.00 | $570.00 | 4 |
| Main Campus Housing A | 2007 06 | $1,630.00 | $407.50 | $695.00 | 4 |
| Main Campus Housing A | 2007 07 | $870.00 | $290.00 | $220.00 | 3 |
| Main Campus Housing A | 2007 08 | $720.00 | $360.00 | $400.00 | 2 |
| Main Campus Housing A | 2007 09 | $805.00 | $402.50 | $135.00 | 2 |
| Main Campus Housing B | 2007 03 | $2,035.00 | $678.33 | $940.00 | 3 |
| Main Campus Housing B | 2007 04 | $1,040.00 | $520.00 | $620.00 | 2 |
| Main Campus Housing B | 2007 05 | $2,430.00 | $1,215.00 | $130.00 | 2 |
| Main Campus Housing B | 2007 06 | $3,105.00 | $621.00 | $1,000.00 | 5 |
| Main Campus Housing B | 2007 07 | $3,020.00 | $604.00 | $1,130.00 | 5 |
| Main Campus Housing B | 2007 08 | $2,480.00 | $826.67 | $560.00 | 3 |
| North Satellite Housing D | 2007 03 | $195.00 | $195.00 | $0.00 | 1 |
| North Satellite Housing D | 2007 05 | $830.00 | $830.00 | $0.00 | 1 |
| North Satellite Housing D | 2007 06 | $280.00 | $280.00 | $0.00 | 1 |
| North Satellite Housing D | 2007 07 | $960.00 | $960.00 | $0.00 | 1 |
| North Satellite Housing D | 2007 08 | $680.00 | $340.00 | $280.00 | 2 |
| South Campus Housing C | 2007 02 | $1,200.00 | $1,200.00 | $0.00 | 1 |
| South Campus Housing C | 2007 05 | $2,525.00 | $841.67 | $1,665.00 | 3 |
| South Campus Housing C | 2007 06 | $1,490.00 | $745.00 | $1,270.00 | 2 |
| South Campus Housing C | 2007 07 | $415.00 | $415.00 | $0.00 | 1 |
| South Campus Housing C | 2007 08 | $3,820.00 | $1,273.33 | $840.00 | 3 |

Record: 1 of 23 No Filter Search

**Figure 8-25** This is the result in Datasheet view of the query shown in Figure 8-24.

## Selecting Records to Form Groups

You might filter out some records before your totals query gathers the records into groups. To filter out certain records from the tables in your query, you can add to the design grid the field or fields you want to filter. Then, create the filter by selecting the Where setting in the Total row (which will clear the field's Show check box), and entering criteria that tell Access which records to exclude.

For example, the manager of the Sales department might be interested in the statistics you've produced thus far in the query in Figure 8-24, but only for the employees in the Sales department. To find this information, you need to add tblEmployees and tblDepartments to your query (and remove the extra join line between the Employee-Number field in tblEmployees and the ManagerNumber field in tblDepartments). Add the Department field from tblDepartments to your design, change the Total line to Where, and add the criterion **"Sales"** on the Criteria line under this field. Your query should now look like Figure 8-26.

Now, when you run the query, you get totals only for the employees in the Sales department. The result is shown in Figure 8-27.

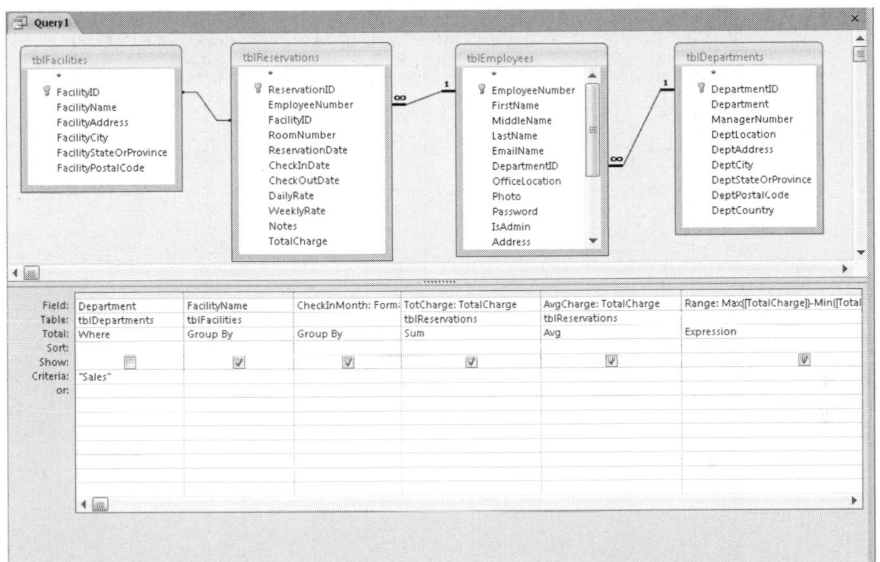


**Figure 8-26** Use the Department field to select the rows that will be included in groups.

| Name | CheckInMonth | TotCharge | AvgCharge | Range | NumRes |
|---|---|---|---|---|---|
| Main Campus Housing A | 2007 06 | $375.00 | $375.00 | $0.00 | 1 |
| Main Campus Housing A | 2007 08 | $560.00 | $560.00 | $0.00 | 1 |
| Main Campus Housing B | 2007 06 | $1,180.00 | $1,180.00 | $0.00 | 1 |
| Main Campus Housing B | 2007 07 | $50.00 | $50.00 | $0.00 | 1 |
| Main Campus Housing B | 2007 08 | $2,000.00 | $1,000.00 | $80.00 | 2 |
| South Campus Housing C | 2007 02 | $1,200.00 | $1,200.00 | $0.00 | 1 |
| South Campus Housing C | 2007 05 | $1,920.00 | $1,920.00 | $0.00 | 1 |
| South Campus Housing C | 2007 08 | $1,690.00 | $1,690.00 | $0.00 | 1 |

**Figure 8-27** This figure displays the recordset of the query shown in Figure 8-26.

## Selecting Specific Groups

You can also filter groups of totals after the query has calculated the groups. To do this, enter criteria for any field that has a Group By setting, one of the aggregate functions, or an expression using the aggregate functions in its Total row. For example, you might want to know which facilities and months have more than $1,000 in total charges. To find that out, use the settings shown in Figure 8-26 and enter a Criteria setting of **>1000** for the TotalCharge field, as shown in Figure 8-28. This query should return five rows in the sample database. You can find this query saved as qxmplSalesHousingGT1000 in the sample database.

Chapter 8

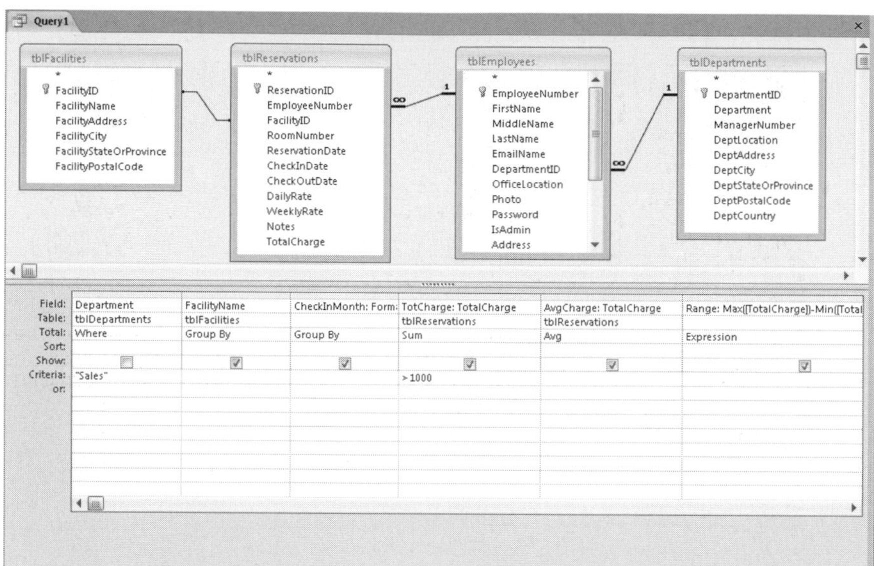

**Figure 8-28** Enter a Criteria setting for the TotCharge field to limit the records to months with more than $1,000 in total charges.

## Building Crosstab Queries

Access 2007 supports a special type of totals query called a *crosstab query* that allows you to see calculated values in a spreadsheet-like format. For example, you can use this type of query to see total revenue by month for each facility in the Housing Reservations application. If you were entering the data in a spreadsheet, the layout of the result you want might look like Figure 8-29.

We have pointed out the key components in the mockup that you'll design into your query.

### Creating a Simple Crosstab Query

Open the HousingDataCopy.accdb database. To see revenue by facility, you'll need tblFacilities and tblReservations. Start a new query on tblFacilities and tblReservations. Add the FacilityName field from tblFacilties to the design grid. Revenue gets collected when the employee checks out, and you want to summarize by month. So, enter **RevMonth: Format(CheckOutDate, "yyyy mmm")** in the next empty field in the design grid. This expression returns the year as four digits and the month as a three-character abbreviation. Finally, add the TotalCharge field from tblReservations.

Click the Design contextual tab below Query Tools on the Ribbon. Then, click the Crosstab command in the Query Type group. Access changes your query to a totals query and adds a Crosstab row to the design grid, as shown in Figure 8-30. Each field in a crosstab query can have one of four crosstab settings: Row Heading, Column Heading, Value (displayed in the crosstab grid), or Not Shown.

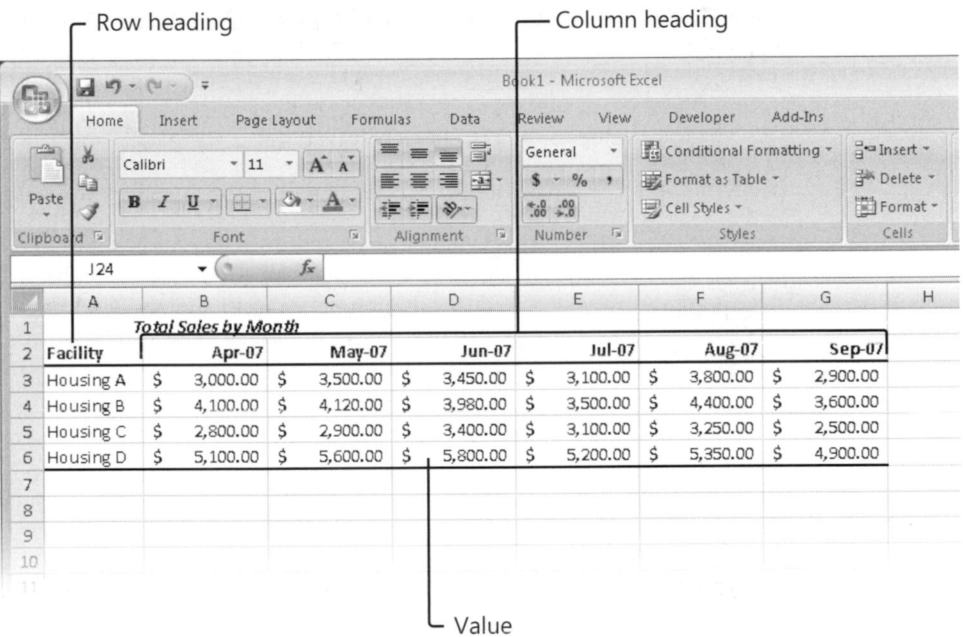


**Figure 8-29** A spreadsheet mockup shows the result you want in your crosstab query.

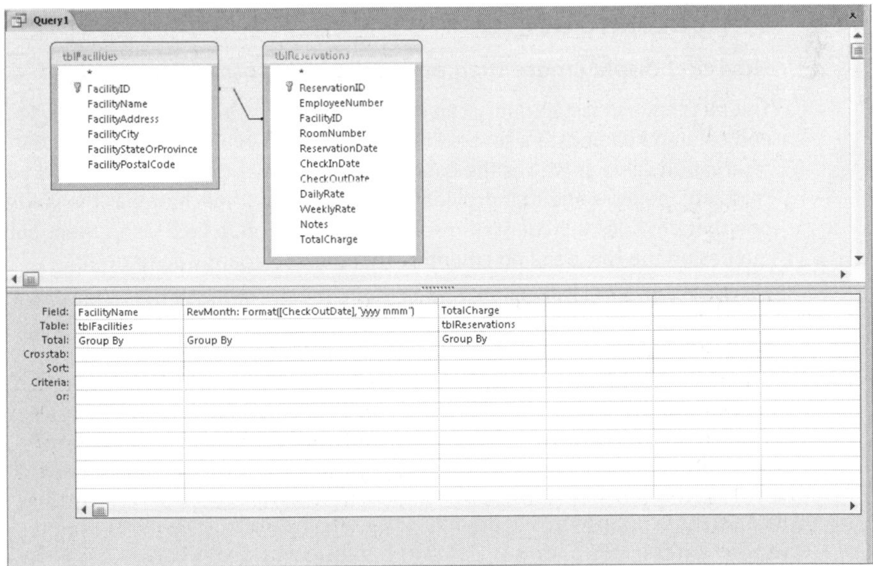


**Figure 8-30** This is a crosstab query in Design view.

You must have at least one row heading in a crosstab query, and you can specify more than one field as a row heading. Each row heading must be a grouped value or expression, and the expression can include one or more of the aggregate functions—Count,

Min, Max, Sum, and so on. The row heading fields form the columns on the left side of the crosstab. Think of the grouped values of the row heading fields as forming the horizontal "labels" of the rows. In this example, we'll be grouping by FacilityName. We'll later modify the basic query we're building here to add a second row heading using Sum—the total value of each facility's reservations.

You must also have one (and only one) field defined as a column heading, and this must also be a grouped or totaled value. These values form the headings of the columns across the crosstab datasheet. Think of a regular totals query where one of the columns "pivots," and the values in the rows become labels for additional columns in the output. These columns appear sorted in value sequence immediately following the columns you define as row headings. Because the values in the data you're selecting determine the column names when you run the query, you cannot always predict in advance the field names that the query will output.

Finally, you need one (and only one) field designated as the value. This field must be a totaled value or an expression that contains one of the aggregate functions. The value appears in the cells that are the intersections of each of the row heading values and each of the column heading values. In the following example, the facility names will appear down the left side, the year and month values will appear as column headings across the top, and the sum of the reservation charge for each group for each month will appear in the intersection.

## TROUBLESHOOTING

### How do I display more than one value in a crosstab?

The fact that a crosstab query can display only one value field in the intersection of row and column headings is a severe limitation. What if you want to display both the total reservation value as well as the count of reservations? One way is to build two separate crosstab queries—one that provides the sum of the total charge as the value field, and one that provides the count of reservations as the value field—and then join the two queries on the row heading columns. That's an inelegant way to do it.

Another solution is to create a simple query that includes all the detail you need and then switch to PivotTable view to build the data display you need. You'll learn about PivotTable and PivotChart views later in this chapter.

As in other types of totals queries, you can include other fields to filter values to obtain the result you want. For these fields, you should select the Where setting in the Total row and the Not Shown setting in the Crosstab row and then enter your criteria. You can also enter criteria for any column headings, and you can sort on any of the fields.

To finish the settings for the crosstab query that you started to build in Figure 8-30, under the FacilityName field in the Crosstab row, click the small arrow and select Row Heading from the list, select Column Heading under the RevMonth expression, and select Value under the TotalCharge field. Also change the Group By setting under the TotalCharge field to Sum.

Switch to Datasheet view to see the result of your query design, as shown in Figure 8-31.

Query1

| Name | 2007 Apr | 2007 Aug | 2007 Jul | 2007 Jun | 2007 Mar | 2007 May | 2007 Sep |
|---|---|---|---|---|---|---|---|
| Main Campus Housing A | $3,970.00 | $160.00 | $1,605.00 | $805.00 | $455.00 | $3,810.00 | $1,365.00 |
| Main Campus Housing B | $2,975.00 | $2,250.00 | $3,650.00 | $4,175.00 | $100.00 | | $960.00 |
| North Satellite Housing D | | $680.00 | $960.00 | $280.00 | $195.00 | $830.00 | |
| South Campus Housing C | | $2,130.00 | $1,795.00 | $110.00 | $1,200.00 | $2,525.00 | $1,690.00 |

**Figure 8-31** This is the recordset of the crosstab query you're building.

Notice that although you didn't specify a sort sequence on the dates, Access sorted the dates left to right in ascending collating order anyway. Notice also that the month names appear in alphabetical order, not in the desired chronological order.

Access provides a solution for this: You can specifically define the order of column headings for any crosstab query by using the query's property sheet. Return to Design view and click in the upper part of the Query window, and then click the Property Sheet button in the Show/Hide group of the Design tab to see the property sheet, as shown in Figure 8-32. (You can verify that you are looking at the property sheet for the query by examining what you see after Selection Type at the top of the property sheet. For queries, you should see "Query Properties.")

Property Sheet
Selection type: Query Properties
General

| | |
|---|---|
| Description | |
| Default View | Datasheet |
| Column Headings | "2007 Jan","2007 Feb","2007 Mar","2007 Apr","2007 May","2007 Jun","2007 Jul","2007 Aug","2007 Sep","2007 Oct","2007 Nov","2007 Dec" |
| Source Database | (current) |
| Source Connect Str | |
| Record Locks | No Locks |
| Recordset Type | Dynaset |
| ODBC Timeout | 60 |
| Orientation | Left-to-Right |
| Subdatasheet Name | |
| Link Child Fields | |
| Link Master Fields | |
| Subdatasheet Height | 0" |
| Subdatasheet Expanded | No |

**Figure 8-32** These entries in the property sheet fix the order of column headings for the query shown in Figure 8-31.

To control the order of columns displayed, enter the headings exactly as they are formatted and in the order you want them in the Column Headings row, separated by commas. In this case, you are entering text values, so you must also enclose each value in double quotes. Be sure to include all the column headings that match the result of the query. (Notice that we specified all the months in 2007 even though the sample data covers only March to September.) If you omit (or misspell) a column heading, Access won't show that column at all. When you run the query with formatted column headings, you see the recordset shown in Figure 8-33.

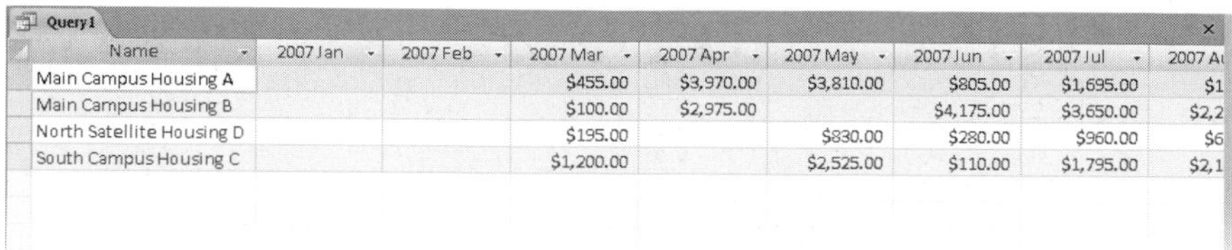

| Name | 2007 Jan | 2007 Feb | 2007 Mar | 2007 Apr | 2007 May | 2007 Jun | 2007 Jul | 2007 A |
|---|---|---|---|---|---|---|---|---|
| Main Campus Housing A | | | $455.00 | $3,970.00 | $3,810.00 | $805.00 | $1,695.00 | $1 |
| Main Campus Housing B | | | $100.00 | $2,975.00 | | $4,175.00 | $3,650.00 | $2,2 |
| North Satellite Housing D | | | $195.00 | | $830.00 | $280.00 | $960.00 | $6 |
| South Campus Housing C | | | $1,200.00 | | $2,525.00 | $110.00 | $1,795.00 | $2,1 |

**Figure 8-33** This crosstab query recordset has custom headings and custom column order, as defined in Figure 8-32.



**CAUTION!**

Specifying correct column headings can be difficult. You must run your query first to determine what headings you'll see. You might be able to define criteria in your query that guarantee the column headings—for example, you could filter the query to return rows only from a specific year. If you misspell a column heading in the query property sheet, the real danger is that Access gives you no warning that your query returns columns that aren't in your column heading specification. You'll see blanks in your misspelled columns, and you could mistakenly assume that no data exists for those columns.

Let's add a grand total for each row (the total per facility regardless of month) and do something about the blank cells. Wouldn't it be nice to see a zero in months when there were no reservations?

Switch back to Design view and add another TotalCharge field to the Field row. Give it a name of GrandTotal, and choose Sum on the Total row and Row Heading on the Crosstab row.

Remember the little trick we used earlier to use a plus sign (+) arithmetic operator in a concatenation to remove extra blanks? In this case, we want to do exactly the reverse—wherever there are no values, the Sum returns a Null that we want to convert to a zero. Also remember that when you concatenate two values with the ampersand (&) operator, that operator ignores Nulls. You can force a Null to a zero by concatenating a leading zero character. If the Sum is not Null, adding a zero in front of the value won't hurt it at all.

In the TotalCharge field you chose as the value field, change Sum to Expression and change the Field line to use this expression:

```
0 & Sum(TotalCharge)
```

Any concatenation returns a string value, so you'll need to convert the value back to a currency number for display. There's a handy "convert to currency" function (CCur) that will perform this conversion for you. Further modify the expression to read:

```
CCur(0 & Sum(TotalCharge))
```

Switch back to Datasheet view, and your query result should now look like Figure 8-34.

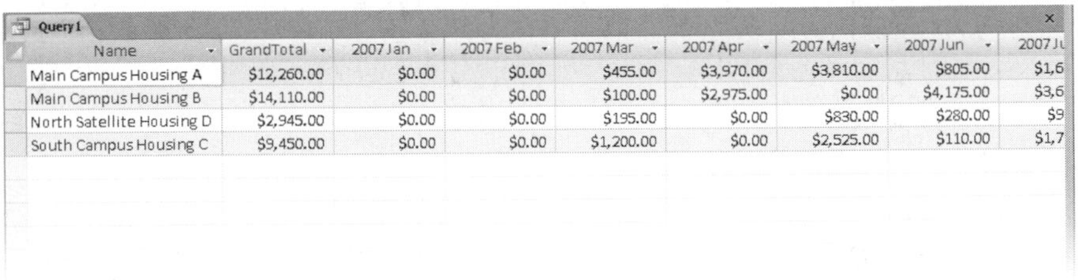

Query1

| Name | GrandTotal | 2007 Jan | 2007 Feb | 2007 Mar | 2007 Apr | 2007 May | 2007 Jun | 2007 Ju |
|---|---|---|---|---|---|---|---|---|
| Main Campus Housing A | $12,260.00 | $0.00 | $0.00 | $455.00 | $3,970.00 | $3,810.00 | $805.00 | $1,6 |
| Main Campus Housing B | $14,110.00 | $0.00 | $0.00 | $100.00 | $2,975.00 | $0.00 | $4,175.00 | $3,6 |
| North Satellite Housing D | $2,945.00 | $0.00 | $0.00 | $195.00 | $0.00 | $830.00 | $280.00 | $9 |
| South Campus Housing C | $9,450.00 | $0.00 | $0.00 | $1,200.00 | $0.00 | $2,525.00 | $110.00 | $1,7 |

**Figure 8-34** Your crosstab query now shows a grand total on each row as an additional row heading, and all empty cells are filled with zero values.

As with most tasks in Access, there's usually more than one way to solve a problem. You can also generate the missing zero values by using the Null-to-zero function (NZ) in your expression instead of using concatenation. Your expression could look like

```
CCur(NZ(Sum(TotalCharge),0))
```

If you're not quite getting the result you expect, you can check what you have built against the qxmplRevenueByFacilityByMonthXtab sample query you'll find in the database.

## Partitioning Data in a Crosstab Query

The total sales by month is interesting, but what can you do if you want to break the data down further? For example, you might want to know the value of sales across a range of room prices. This sort of information might be invaluable to the operator of a commercial hotel. What amount of revenue is the hotel receiving from various room prices?

You'll learn later in Chapter 16 that you can ask the report writer to group data by data ranges. Well, you can also do this in a totals or crosstab query. Let's continue to work in the HousingDataCopy.accdb database to see how this works.

Start a new query with tblFacilities and tblReservations. Add the FacilityName field from tblFacilities, and create a CkOutMonth field by using the Format function to return a four-digit year and month abbreviation as you did earlier. Add the TotalCharge field from tblReservations to the query grid twice. Click the Crosstab button in the Query Type group of the Design tab to convert your query to a crosstab query.

In the Crosstab row, select Row Heading under the FacilityName field, your CkOut-Month expression, and the first TotalCharge field. Change the name of this first TotalCharge field to GrandTotal, and select Sum in the Group By row. For the second TotalCharge field, select Sum in the Group By row and Value in the Crosstab row.

You still don't have a Column Heading field or expression defined, but here's where the fun begins. In this query, your sales manager has asked you for a breakdown of amounts spent per month based on ranges of the DailyRate field. In this database, the lowest daily charge is $40 a day, and the highest is $100 a day. The manager has asked you to display ranges from $40 to $119 in increments of $20 ($40 to $59, $60 to $79, and so on). It turns out there's a handy function called Partition that will split out numbers like this for you. The syntax of the function is as follows:

```
Partition(<number>, <start>, <stop>, <interval>)
```

The *number* argument is the name of a numeric field or expression you want to split up into ranges. *Start* specifies the lowest value you want, *stop* specifies the highest value you want, and *interval* specifies the size of the ranges. The function evaluates each number it sees and returns a string containing the name of the range for that number. You can group on these named ranges to partition your data into groups for this crosstab query. So, the expression you need is as follows:

```
Partition(DailyRate, 40, 119, 20)
```

The function will return values "40: 59", "60: 79", "80: 99", and "100:119". Add that expression to your query grid and select Column Heading in the Crosstab row. Your query should now look like Figure 8-35.



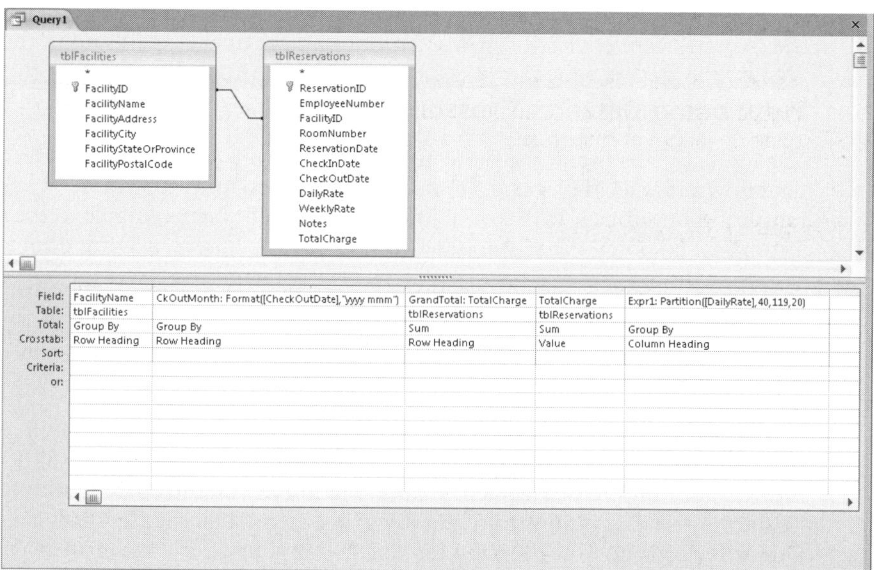


**Figure 8-35** This crosstab query uses partitioned values.

Switch to Datasheet view to see the result that should satisfy your sales manager's request, shown in Figure 8-36. Note that we didn't use the trick discussed earlier to fill blank cells with zeros. In this case, the blank cells seem to visually point out the rate ranges that had no sales. You can find this query saved as qxmplRevenueByFacilityByRateRangeXtab in the sample database.

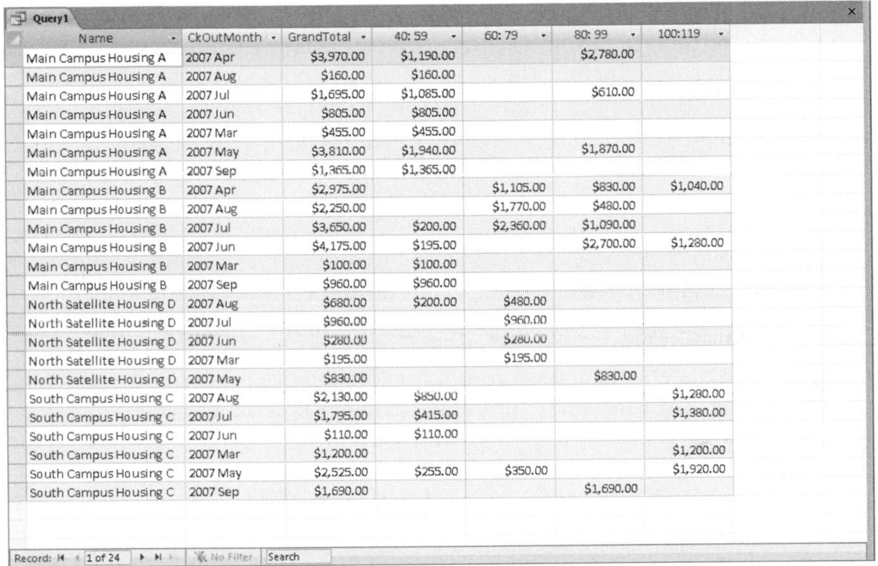

| Name | CkOutMonth | GrandTotal | 40: 59 | 60: 79 | 80: 99 | 100:119 |
|---|---|---|---|---|---|---|
| Main Campus Housing A | 2007 Apr | $3,970.00 | $1,190.00 | | $2,780.00 | |
| Main Campus Housing A | 2007 Aug | $160.00 | $160.00 | | | |
| Main Campus Housing A | 2007 Jul | $1,695.00 | $1,085.00 | | $610.00 | |
| Main Campus Housing A | 2007 Jun | $805.00 | $805.00 | | | |
| Main Campus Housing A | 2007 Mar | $455.00 | $455.00 | | | |
| Main Campus Housing A | 2007 May | $3,810.00 | $1,940.00 | | $1,870.00 | |
| Main Campus Housing A | 2007 Sep | $1,365.00 | $1,365.00 | | | |
| Main Campus Housing B | 2007 Apr | $2,975.00 | | $1,105.00 | $830.00 | $1,040.00 |
| Main Campus Housing B | 2007 Aug | $2,250.00 | | $1,770.00 | $480.00 | |
| Main Campus Housing B | 2007 Jul | $3,650.00 | $200.00 | $2,360.00 | $1,090.00 | |
| Main Campus Housing B | 2007 Jun | $4,175.00 | $195.00 | | $2,700.00 | $1,280.00 |
| Main Campus Housing B | 2007 Mar | $100.00 | $100.00 | | | |
| Main Campus Housing B | 2007 Sep | $960.00 | $960.00 | | | |
| North Satellite Housing D | 2007 Aug | $680.00 | $200.00 | $480.00 | | |
| North Satellite Housing D | 2007 Jul | $960.00 | | $960.00 | | |
| North Satellite Housing D | 2007 Jun | $280.00 | | $280.00 | | |
| North Satellite Housing D | 2007 Mar | $195.00 | | $195.00 | | |
| North Satellite Housing D | 2007 May | $830.00 | | | $830.00 | |
| South Campus Housing C | 2007 Aug | $2,130.00 | $850.00 | | | $1,280.00 |
| South Campus Housing C | 2007 Jul | $1,795.00 | $415.00 | | | $1,380.00 |
| South Campus Housing C | 2007 Jun | $110.00 | $110.00 | | | |
| South Campus Housing C | 2007 Mar | $1,200.00 | | | | $1,200.00 |
| South Campus Housing C | 2007 May | $2,525.00 | $255.00 | $350.00 | | $1,920.00 |
| South Campus Housing C | 2007 Sep | $1,690.00 | | | $1,690.00 | |

**Figure 8-36** Run the crosstab query shown in Figure 8-34 to see the result of partitioning sales totals on ranges of room rates.

# Using Query Parameters

So far you've been entering selection criteria directly in the design grid of the Query window in Design view. However, you don't have to decide at the time you design the query exactly what value you want Access to search for. Instead, you can include a parameter in the query, and Access will prompt you for the criteria each time the query runs.

To include a parameter, you enter a name or a phrase enclosed in brackets ([ ]) in the Criteria row instead of entering a value. What you enclose in brackets becomes the name by which Access knows your parameter. Access displays this name in a dialog box when you run the query, so you should enter a phrase that accurately describes what you want. You can enter several parameters in a single query, so each parameter name must be unique as well as informative. If you want a parameter value to also appear as output in the query, you can enter the parameter name in the Field row of an empty column.

Let's say you're the housing manager, and you want to find out who might be staying in any facility over the next several days or weeks. You don't want to have to build or modify a query each time you want to search the database for upcoming reservations. So, you ask your database developer to provide you with a way to dynamically enter the beginning and ending dates of interest.

Let's build a query to help out the housing manager. Start a new query with tblFacilities in the HousingDataCopy.accdb database. Add tblReservations and tblEmployees. From tblReservations, include the ReservationID, RoomNumber, CheckInDate, CheckOutDate, and TotalCharge fields. Insert the FacilityName field from tblFacilities between ReservationID and RoomNumber. Add an expression to display the employee name in a field inserted between ReservationID and FacilityName. Your expression might look like this:

```
EmpName: tblEmployees.LastName & ", " & tblEmployees.FirstName
```



Now comes the tricky part. You want the query to ask the housing manager for the range of dates of interest. Your query needs to find the reservation rows that show who is in which rooms between a pair of dates. If you remember from the previous example in this chapter where we were looking for employees occupying rooms in June or July, you want any rows where the check-in date is less than or equal to the end date of interest, and the check-out date is greater than the start date of interest. (If they check out on the beginning date of the range, they're not staying in the room that night.) So, you can create two parameters on the Criteria line to accomplish this. Under CheckInDate, enter: **<=[Enter End Date:]**, and under CheckOutDate, enter: **>[Enter Start Date:]**. Your query should look like Figure 8-37.

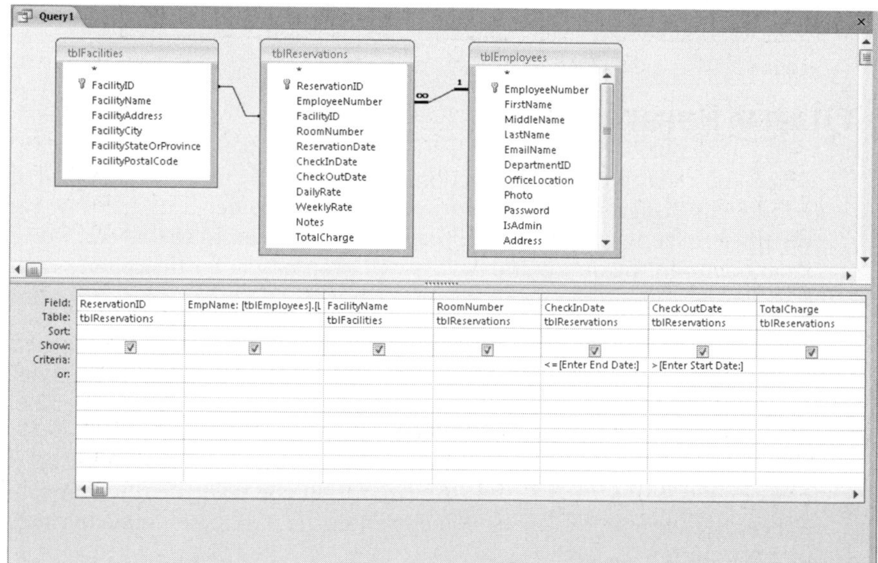


**Figure 8-37** You can use query parameters to accept criteria for a range of reservation dates.

For each parameter in a query, you should tell Access what data type to expect. Access uses this information to validate the value entered. For example, if you define a parameter as a number, Access won't accept alphabetic characters in the parameter value. Likewise, if you define a parameter as a Date/Time data type, Access won't accept anything but a valid date or time value in the parameter prompt. (See Figure 8-39.) By default, Access assigns the Text data type to query parameters. In general, you should always define the data type of your parameters, so click the Parameters command in the Show/Hide group of the Design tab. Access then displays the Query Parameters dialog box, as shown in Figure 8-38.

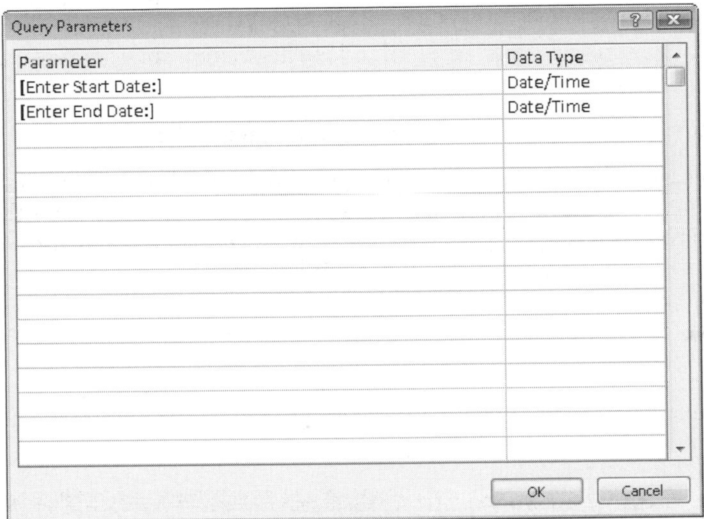


**Figure 8-38** Use the Query Parameters dialog box to assign data types for query parameters.

In the Parameter column, enter each parameter name exactly as you entered it in the design grid. If your parameter name includes no spaces or special characters, you can omit the brackets. (In this case, your parameters include both spaces and the colon character—either of which would require the brackets.) In the Data Type column, select the appropriate data type from the drop-down list. Click OK when you finish defining all your parameters.

When you run the query, Access prompts you for an appropriate value for each parameter, one at a time, with a dialog box like the one shown in Figure 8-39. Because Access displays the "name" of the parameter that you provided in the design grid, you can see why naming the parameter with a useful phrase can help you enter the correct value later. If you enter a value that does not match the data type you specified, Access displays an error message and gives you a chance to try again. You can also click Cancel to abort running the query. If you click OK without typing a value, Access returns a Null value for the parameter to the query.

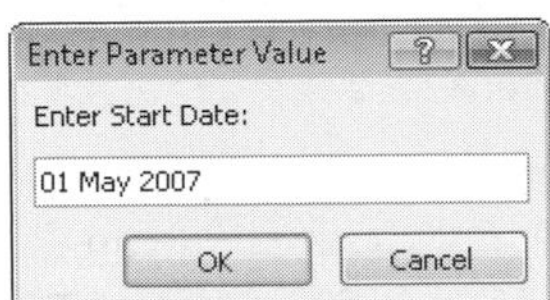


**Figure 8-39** The Enter Parameter Value dialog box asks for the query parameter value.

Notice that Access accepts any value that it can recognize as a date/time, such as a long date or short date format. If you respond to the query parameter prompts with May 1, 2007, for the Start Date and May 12, 2007, for the End Date, you'll see a datasheet like Figure 8-40.

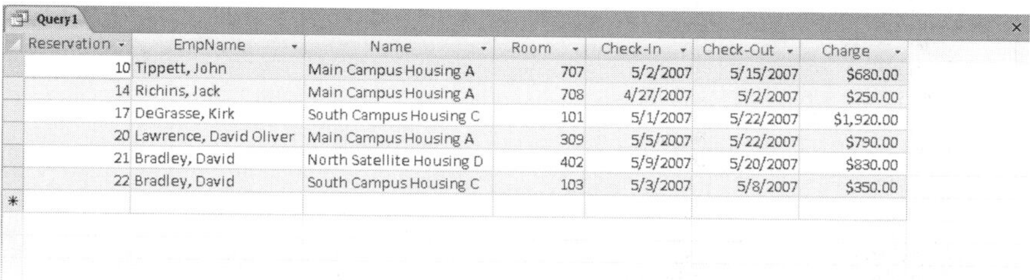
Query1

| Reservation | EmpName | Name | Room | Check-In | Check-Out | Charge |
|---|---|---|---|---|---|---|
| 10 | Tippett, John | Main Campus Housing A | 707 | 5/2/2007 | 5/15/2007 | $680.00 |
| 14 | Richins, Jack | Main Campus Housing A | 708 | 4/27/2007 | 5/2/2007 | $250.00 |
| 17 | DeGrasse, Kirk | South Campus Housing C | 101 | 5/1/2007 | 5/22/2007 | $1,920.00 |
| 20 | Lawrence, David Oliver | Main Campus Housing A | 309 | 5/5/2007 | 5/22/2007 | $790.00 |
| 21 | Bradley, David | North Satellite Housing D | 402 | 5/9/2007 | 5/20/2007 | $830.00 |
| 22 | Bradley, David | South Campus Housing C | 103 | 5/3/2007 | 5/8/2007 | $350.00 |
| * | | | | | | |

**Figure 8-40** This figure displays the recordset of the query shown in Figure 8-37 when you reply with May 1, 2007, and May 12, 2007, to the parameter prompts.

You can find this query saved in the sample database as qxmplReservationLookup-Parameter.



# Customizing Query Properties

Access 2007 provides a number of properties associated with queries that you can use to control how a query runs. To open the property sheet for queries, click in the upper part of a Query window in Design view outside of the field lists and then click the Property Sheet button in the Show/Hide group of the Design contextual tab. Figure 8-41 shows the property sheet Access provides for select queries.

Use the Description property to document what the query does. This description appears next to the query name when you view query objects in Details view in the Navigation Pane. You can also right-click on the query in the Navigation Pane and open the Properties dialog box to enter this property without having to open the query in Design view.

The Default View property determines how the query opens when you open it from the Navigation Pane. Datasheet view is the default, but you might want to change this setting to PivotTable or PivotChart if you have designed either of these views for the query. See "Creating PivotTables and PivotCharts from Queries," page 469, for details.

## Controlling Query Output

You normally select only specific fields that you want returned in the recordset when you run a select query. However, if you're designing the query to be used in a form and you want all fields from all tables used in the query available to the form, set the Output All Fields property to Yes. It's a good idea to keep the default setting of No and change this option only for specific queries.

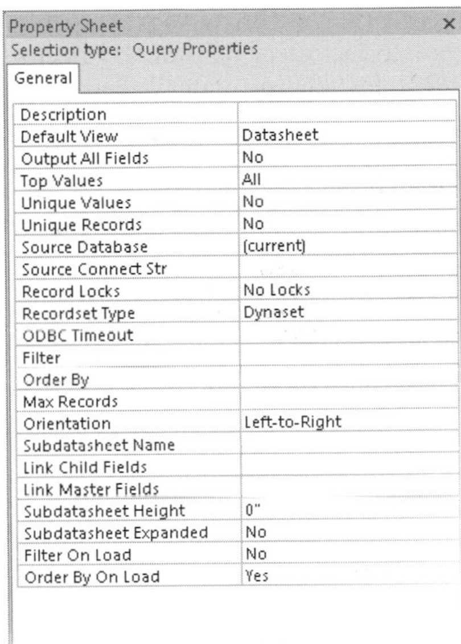


**Figure 8-41** The property sheet for select queries lets you customize the way the query works.



INSIDE OUT

### Don't Change the Default Setting for the Output All Fields Property

You can change the default Output All Fields property for all queries in the Object Designers category of the Access Options dialog box, but we strongly recommend that you do not do this. Queries execute most efficiently when they return only the fields that you need. Also, when your query includes more than one table and a field exists more than once in different tables, an expression you use to reference the field will fail unless you qualify the field name with the table name. You might include the field only once in the design grid, but Output All Fields causes the query to include all copies of the field.

You can use the Top Values property to tell Access that you want to see the first *n* rows or the first *x*% of rows. If you enter an integer value, Access displays the number of rows specified. If you enter a decimal value between 0 and 1 or an integer less than 100 followed by a percent sign (%), Access displays that percentage of rows. For example, you might want to find the top 10 best-selling products or the top 20% of highest paid employees. Note that in most cases you'll need to specify sorting criteria–perhaps by count of products sold descending or salary descending–to place the rows you want at the "top" of the recordset. You can then ask for the top 10 or top 20% to get the answers you want.

When working in a query datasheet, you can define and apply filters and specify sorting just as you can in a table datasheet. Access stores this filtering and sorting criteria in the query's Filter and Order By properties. When you design a query, you can use the Filter and Order By properties to predefine filtering and sorting criteria. When you open the query and click Toggle Filter in the Sort & Filter group on Home tab, Access applies the filter and/or sorts the data using these saved properties. If you change the filter or sorting criteria while in Datasheet view and then save the change, Access updates these properties.



You can also affect whether the fields returned by the query can be updated by changing the Recordset Type property. The default setting, Dynaset, allows you to update any fields on the *many* side of a join. It also lets you change values on the *one* side of a join if you have defined a relationship between the tables and enabled Cascade Update Related Fields in the Edit Relationships dialog box. If you choose Dynaset (Inconsistent Updates), you can update any field that isn't a result of a calculation, but you might update data that you didn't intend to be updatable. If you want the query to be read-only (no fields can be updated), choose the Snapshot setting.

**CAUTION!**

You should rarely, if at all, choose the Dynaset (Inconsistent Updates) setting for Recordset Type. This setting makes fields updatable in queries that might not otherwise allow updating. Although Access still enforces referential integrity rules, you can make changes to tables independently from each other, so you might end up reassigning relationships unintentionally. You can read about the details of when fields are updatable in a query later in this chapter in "Limitations on Using Select Queries to Update Data" on page 468.

## Working with Unique Records and Values

When you run a query, Access often returns what appear to be duplicate rows in the recordset. The default in Access 2007 is to return all records. You can also ask Access to return only unique records. (This was the default for all versions of Access prior to version 8.0, also called Access 97). Unique records mean that the identifier for each row (the primary key of the table in a single-table query or the concatenated primary keys in a multiple-table query) is unique. If you ask for unique records, Access returns only rows with identifiers that are different from each other. If you want to see all possible data (including duplicate rows), set both the Unique Values property and the Unique Records property to No. (You cannot set both Unique Records and Unique Values to Yes. You can set them both to No.)

To understand how the Unique Values and Unique Records settings work, open the ContactsDataCopy.accdb database and create a query that includes both the tblContacts table and the tblContactEvents table. Let's say you want to find out from which cities you've received a contact over a particular period of time. Include the WorkCity and WorkStateOrProvince fields from tblContacts. Include the ContactDateTime field from tblContactEvents, but clear the Show check box. Figure 8-42 shows a sample query with a date criterion that will show contact cities between December 2006 and March 2007. (Remember, ContactDateTime includes a time value, so you need to enter a criterion one day beyond the date range you want.) You can find this query saved as qxmplNoUnique in the sample database.



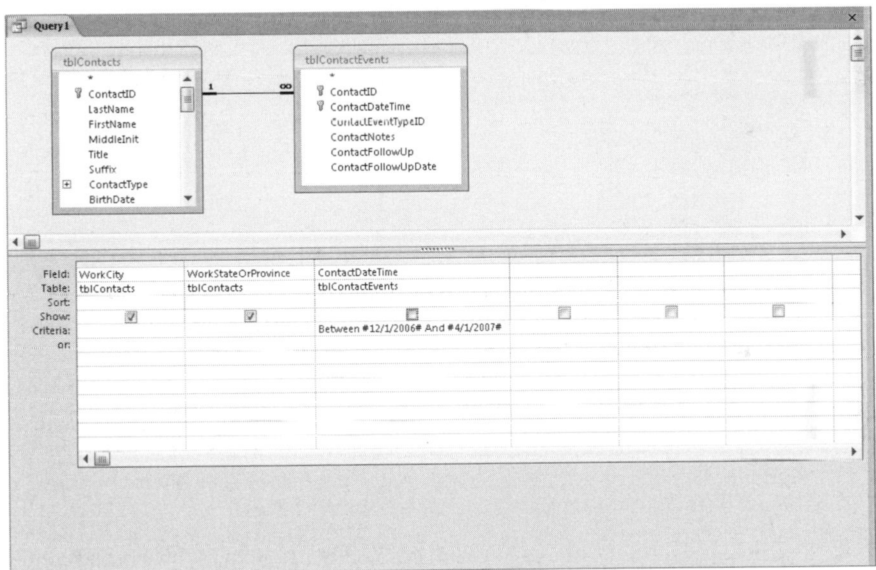


**Figure 8-42** You can build a query that demonstrates setting both Unique Values and Unique Records to No when you're using two tables.

If you switch to Datasheet view, as shown in Figure 8-43, you can see that the query returns 58 rows—each row from tblContacts appears once for each related contact event that has a contact date between the specified days. Some of these rows come from the same person, and some come from different people in the same city. The bottom line is there are 58 rows in tblContactEvents within the specified date range.

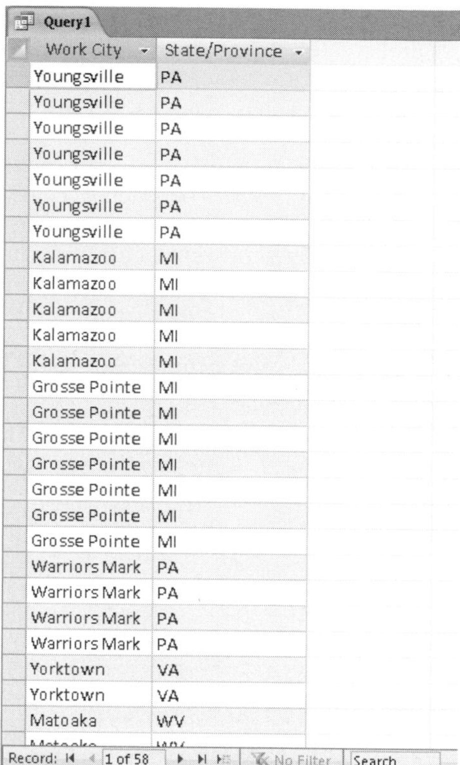


| Work City | State/Province |
|---|---|
| Youngsville | PA |
| Youngsville | PA |
| Youngsville | PA |
| Youngsville | PA |
| Youngsville | PA |
| Youngsville | PA |
| Youngsville | PA |
| Kalamazoo | MI |
| Kalamazoo | MI |
| Kalamazoo | MI |
| Kalamazoo | MI |
| Kalamazoo | MI |
| Grosse Pointe | MI |
| Grosse Pointe | MI |
| Grosse Pointe | MI |
| Grosse Pointe | MI |
| Grosse Pointe | MI |
| Grosse Pointe | MI |
| Grosse Pointe | MI |
| Warriors Mark | PA |
| Warriors Mark | PA |
| Warriors Mark | PA |
| Warriors Mark | PA |
| Yorktown | VA |
| Yorktown | VA |
| Matoaka | WV |

**Figure 8-43** Run your sample query to see the result of retrieving all rows across a join even though the output columns are from only one of the tables.

If you're interested only in one row per contact (per person) from tblContacts, regardless of the number of contact events, you can set the Unique Records property to Yes. The result is shown in Figure 8-44 (saved as qxmplUniqueRecords). This tells us that there were 26 different people who had a contact event within the date range. Again, some of these rows come from different people in the same city, which is why you see the same city listed more than once. The recordset now returns *unique records* from tblContacts (the only table providing output fields in this query).

> **Note**
>
> Setting Unique Records to Yes has no effect unless you include more than one table in your query and you include fields from the table on the *one* side of a one-to-many relationship. You might have this situation when you are interested in data from one table but you want to filter it based on data in a related table without displaying the fields from the related table.

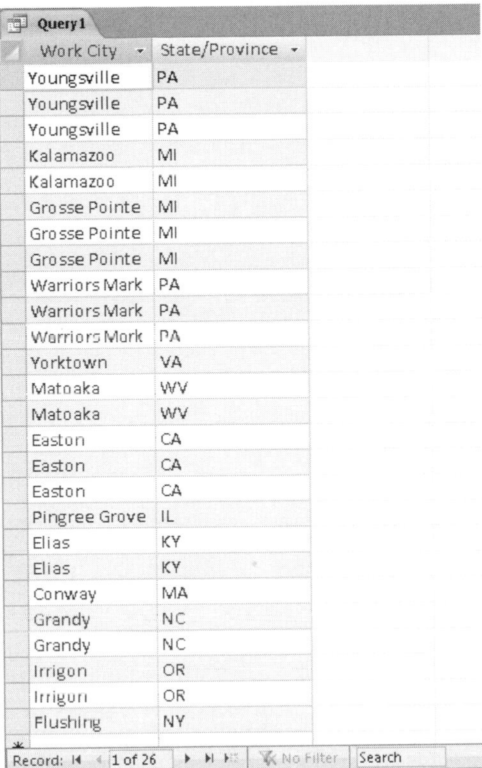


| Work City | State/Province |
|---|---|
| Youngsville | PA |
| Youngsville | PA |
| Youngsville | PA |
| Kalamazoo | MI |
| Kalamazoo | MI |
| Grosse Pointe | MI |
| Grosse Pointe | MI |
| Grosse Pointe | MI |
| Warriors Mark | PA |
| Warriors Mark | PA |
| Warriors Mark | PA |
| Yorktown | VA |
| Matoaka | WV |
| Matoaka | WV |
| Easton | CA |
| Easton | CA |
| Easton | CA |
| Pingree Grove | IL |
| Elias | KY |
| Elias | KY |
| Conway | MA |
| Grandy | NC |
| Grandy | NC |
| Irrigon | OR |
| Irrigon | OR |
| Flushing | NY |



**Figure 8-44** Even though your query uses two tables, when you set the Unique Records property to Yes, your query returns records that are unique in the one table that provides output columns.

Finally, if you're interested in only which distinct cities you received a contact from in the specified date range, and you want to see each city name only once, then set Unique Values to Yes. (Access automatically resets Unique Records to No.) The result is 13 records, as shown in Figure 8-45 (saved as qxmplUniqueValues).

When you ask for unique values, you're asking Access to calculate and remove the duplicate values. As with any calculated value in a query, fields in a unique values query can't be updated.

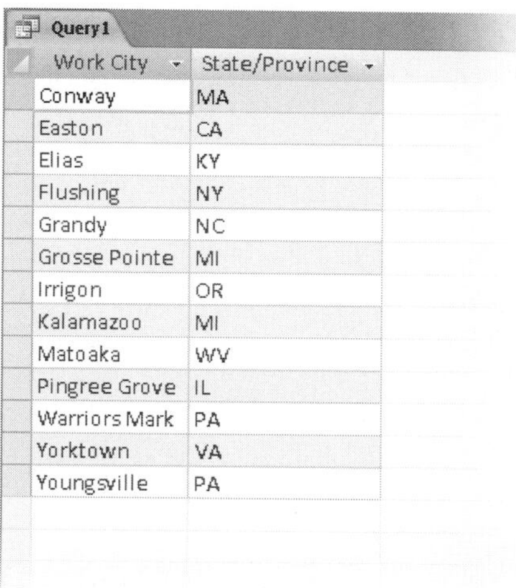

Query1

| Work City | State/Province |
|---|---|
| Conway | MA |
| Easton | CA |
| Elias | KY |
| Flushing | NY |
| Grandy | NC |
| Grosse Pointe | MI |
| Irrigon | OR |
| Kalamazoo | MI |
| Matoaka | WV |
| Pingree Grove | IL |
| Warriors Mark | PA |
| Yorktown | VA |
| Youngsville | PA |

**Figure 8-45** When you set the Unique Values property to Yes, Access removes all the duplicate records.



## Defining a Subdatasheet

In the previous chapter, we showed you how to work with and modify subdatasheets from query Datasheet view. Now, let's take a closer look at the properties you can set in a query to predefine a subdatasheet within the query. Let's say you want to create a query to show company information and make a subdatasheet available that displays information about the primary contact for the company. You can use the qryContacts-Datasheet query that you studied in the previous chapter, but first you'll need to modify that query for this exercise.

In the ContactsDataCopy.accdb database, open qryContactsDatasheet in Design view. To link this query to another that displays company information, you'll need the CompanyID field. Click the Show Table button in the Query Setup group of the Design contextual tab, and add the tblCompanyContacts table to the query. Click Close to close the Show Table dialog box. You should see a join line linking ContactID in the two tables. Add the CompanyID and DefaultForContact fields from tblCompanyContacts to the first two columns in the design grid. It makes sense to list only the default company for each contact, so add a criterion of True on the Criteria line under the Default-ForContact field. You should clear the Show check box because you don't really need to see this field in the output. Your query should now look like Figure 8-46. Click the Microsoft Office Button, click Save As, click Save Object As, and then save the query as qryContactsDatasheetCOID. You can also find this query saved in the sample database as qryXmplContactsDatasheetCOID.

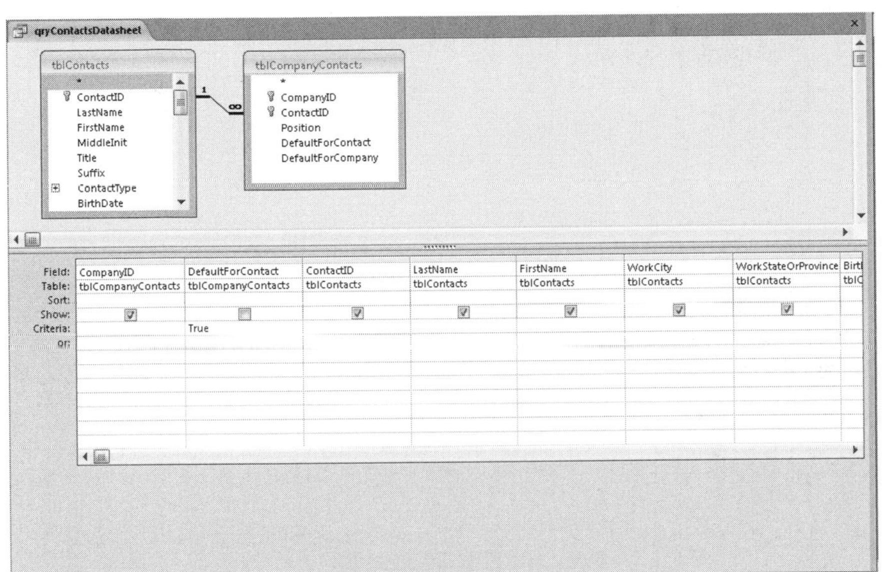


**Figure 8-46** To modify a query to use it as a subdatasheet that displays contacts, include the appropriate linking field.

You need the CompanyID field to provide a link to the outer datasheet that you will build shortly, but you don't necessarily need to see it in your datasheet. Switch to Datasheet view, click in the Company / Org column (this is the CompanyID field), click the More command in the Records group on the Home tab, and select Hide Columns from the list to hide the field. Note that this affects the display only. CompanyID is still a field in the query. (Alternatively, you could clear the Show check box in the design grid.) Close the query and click Yes when Access asks you if you want to save your layout changes.

Now you're ready to build the query in which you'll use the query you just modified as a subdatasheet. Start a new query, add the tblCompanies table to the design grid, and close the Show Tables dialog box. Include the CompanyID, CompanyName, City, and StateOrProvince fields from tblCompanies. Click in the blank space in the top part of the Query window, and click the Property Sheet button in the Show/Hide group on the Design tab to open the property sheet for the query. Click in the Subdatasheet Name property and then click the small arrow to open a list of all tables and queries saved in your database. Scroll down and choose the query that you just saved—qryContacts-DatasheetCOID—and select it as shown in Figure 8-47. (You might have to widen the property sheet in order to see the complete names of queries.)

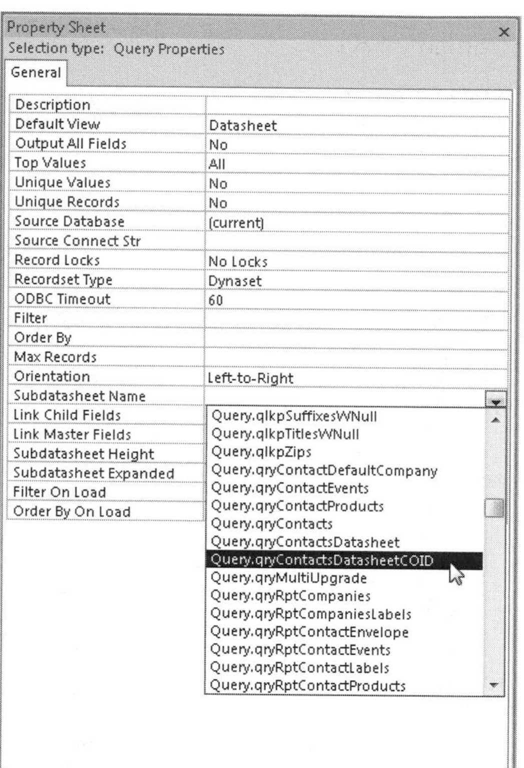


**Figure 8-47** Select the qryContactsDatasheetCOID query to provide the subdatasheet for this query.

You need to tell your query which field links the query you're creating to the query in the subdatasheet. In Link Child Fields, type the name of the field in the subdatasheet query you just selected that matches a field in the query you're designing–in this case, CompanyID. Note that when you're linking to another table or query that requires more than one field to define the relationship, you enter the field names separated by semicolons. In Link Master Fields, enter the name of the field in the query you're creating that should match the value in the field in Link Child Fields—CompanyID again. (You'll see these same properties again when inserting a subform in a form in Chapter 13, "Advanced Form Design.")

Two additional properties apply to subdatasheets—Subdatasheet Height and Subdatasheet Expanded. If you leave Subdatasheet Height at its default setting of 0, the subdatasheet area expands to show all available rows when you open it. You can limit the maximum height by entering a setting in inches (centimeters on a computer with regional settings set to the metric system). If the height you specify isn't large enough to show all rows, you'll see a scroll bar to move through the rows in the subdatasheet. If you set Subdatasheet Expanded to Yes, the subdatasheet for every row opens expanded when you open the query or switch to Datasheet view. Just for fun, change this setting to Yes.

## INSIDE OUT Cycling Through Property Box Values

When a property box has a list of values from which you can select, you can cycle through the values by double-clicking in the property value box instead of clicking the small arrow to the right of the property box.

Switch to Datasheet view, and your result should look like Figure 8-48.

**Figure 8-48** This query shows company information with its contact subdatasheet information expanded.

Do you notice that there are little plus signs on the rows in the subdatasheet? Remember that qryContactsDatasheet, from which you built the new qryContactsDatasheetCOID query, also has a subdatasheet defined. If you click on one of the plus signs in the subdatasheet, you'll see the related contact event subdatasheet information from qryContactsDatasheet as shown in Figure 8-49. You can actually nest subdatasheets like this up to seven levels.

You can find this query saved as qxmplCompaniesContactsSub in the sample database.

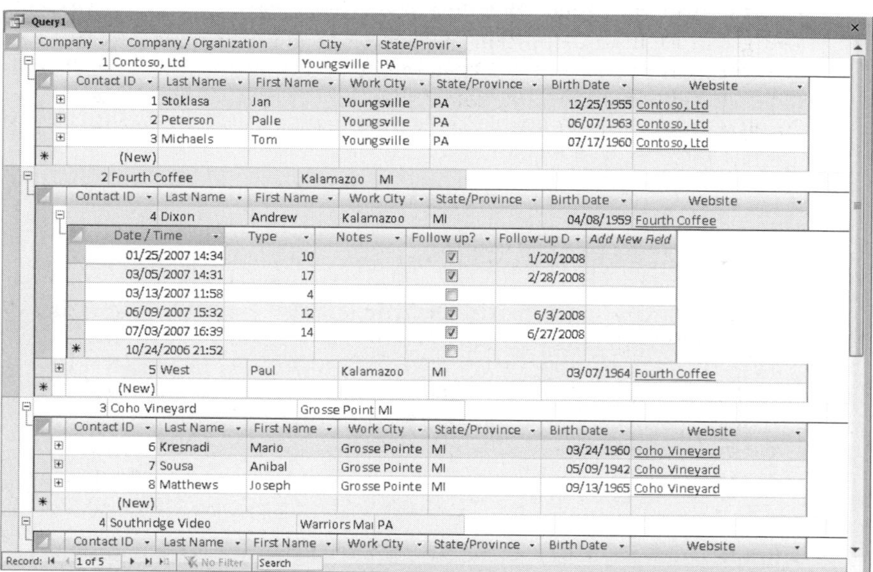

Figure 8-49 You can expand the subdatasheet of the subdatasheet to see contact event information.

## Other Query Properties

Use the Record Locks property to control the level of editing integrity for a query that is designed to access data shared across a network. The default is No Locks—to not lock any records when the user opens the query. With this setting, Access applies a lock temporarily only when it needs to write a row back to the source table. Select the Edited Record setting to lock a row as soon as a user begins entering changes in that row. The most restrictive setting, All Records, locks every record retrieved by the query as long as the user has the query open. Use this setting only when the query must perform multiple updates to a table and other users should not access any data in the table until the query is finished.

Four of the remaining properties—Source Database, Source Connect Str, ODBC Timeout, and Max Records—apply to dynamically linked tables. You can, for example, run a query against tables in another Access database by entering the full path and file name of that database in Source Database. Access dynamically links to the database when you run the query. Use Source Connect Str when you are dynamically linking to an ODBC or non-Access database that requires connection information. ODBC Timeout specifies how long Access will wait (in seconds) for a response from the ODBC database before failing with an error. Use Max Records to limit the number of rows returned to this query from a database server. When you don't specify a number, Access fetches all rows. This might not be desirable when you're fetching data from tables that have hundreds of thousands of rows.

The last property, Orientation, specifies whether you want to see the columns in Left-to-Right or Right-to-Left order. In some languages where reading proceeds right to left, this setting is handy. You can try it out on your system. You'll find that the columns show up right to left, the caption of the query is right-aligned, the selector bar is down the right side of the datasheet, and pressing the Tab key moves through fields from right to left.

## Editing and Creating Queries in SQL View



There are three types of queries that you must create in SQL view: data definition queries, pass-through queries, and union queries.

In a desktop application, Access supports a limited subset of the ANSI-Standard SQL language for data definition. You can execute basic CREATE TABLE and ALTER TABLE commands in a data definition query, but you cannot define any Access-specific properties such as the Input Mask or Validation Rule property. The syntax is so limited that we don't cover it in Article 2, "Understanding SQL," on the companion CD.

When you're using linked tables to a server database system such as Microsoft SQL Server or Oracle, you might need to execute a query on the server that takes advantage of the native SQL supported by the server. You can do most of your work in queries you build in the Access query designer, but the SQL that the query designer builds is only a subset of what your server probably supports. When you need to send a command to your database server in its native syntax, use a pass-through query. If all your data is stored in SQL Server, you should consider building an Access project that links directly to the server data. You can learn about projects in Part 7, "Designing an Access Project."

So, that leaves us with union queries that you might want to build in SQL view. When you create a query that fetches data from multiple tables, you see the related fields side by side in the resulting datasheet. Sometimes it's useful to fetch similar data from several tables and literally stack the rows from different tables on top of one another. Think of pulling the pages containing your favorite recipes out of two different cookbooks and piling them on top of one another to make a new book. For that, you need a union query, and you must build it in SQL view.

Let's say you need to build a mailing list in the Conrad Systems Contacts application. You want to send a brochure to each primary contact for a company at the company's main mailing address. You also want to include any other contacts who are not the primary contact for a company, but send the mailing to their home address. Sounds easy enough to pull the primary contact mailing address from tblCompanies and the address for everyone else from tblContacts. But how do you get all this information in one set of data to make it easy to print your mailing labels in one pass?

## SQL—The Basic Clauses

One way to begin learning SQL (and we strongly recommend that you do) is to take a look at any query you've built in the query designer in SQL view. You can see the SQL view of any query you've built by opening it in Design view and then clicking the small arrow below the View button in the Views group on the Home tab and selecting SQL View. You also find the View button in the Results group on the Design contextual tab below Query Tools. You can learn all the details in Article 2, "Understanding SQL," but a quick overview of the main clauses will help you begin to understand what you see in SQL view.

| SQL Clause | Usage |
|---|---|
| SELECT | This clause lists the fields and expressions that your query returns. It is equivalent to the Field row in the query designer. In a totals query, aggregate functions within the SELECT clause, such as Min or Sum, come from specifications in the Total line. |
| FROM | This clause specifies the tables or queries from which your query fetches data and includes JOIN clauses to define how to link your tables or queries. It is equivalent to the graphical display of table or query field lists and join lines in the top of the query designer. |
| WHERE | This clause specifies how to filter the rows returned by evaluating the FROM clause. It is equivalent to the Criteria and Or lines in the query designer. |
| GROUP BY | This clause lists the grouping field for a totals query. Access builds this clause from the fields indicated with Group By in the Total line of the query designer. |
| HAVING | This clause specifies filtering in a totals query on calculated values. This clause comes from the Criteria and Or lines under fields with one of the aggregate functions specified in the Total line. |

First, build a query to get the information you need for each company's primary contact. In the ContactsDataCopy.accdb database, start a new query with tblCompanies. Add tblCompanyContacts and tblContacts and remove the extra join line between the ContactID field in tblContacts and the ReferredBy field in tblCompanies. In the first column on the Field line, enter:

```
EmpName: (tblContacts.Title + " ") & tblContacts.FirstName & " " &
(tblContacts.MiddleInit + ". ") & tblContacts.LastName & (" " + tblContacts.Suffix)
```

Add the CompanyName and Address fields from tblCompanies. In the fourth column on the Field line, enter:

```
CSZ: tblCompanies.City & ", " & tblCompanies.StateOrProvince & " " &
tblCompanies.PostalCode
```

Chapter 8

Add the DefaultForCompany field from tblCompanyContacts, clear its Show check box, and enter True on the Criteria line. If you switch to Datasheet view, your result should look like Figure 8-50.

Query1

| EmpName | Company / Organization | Billing Address | CSZ |
|---|---|---|---|
| Mrs. Jan Stoklasa | Contoso, Ltd | 7890 Lincoln Avenue | Youngsville, PA 16371 |
| Mr. Andrew Dixon | Fourth Coffee | 7890 3rd Street | Kalamazoo, MI 49004 |
| Mr. Mario Kresnadi | Coho Vineyard | 6789 4th Street | Grosse Pointe, MI 48236 |
| Dr. Jennifer Riegle | Southridge Video | 1234 1st Avenue | Warriors Mark, PA 16877 |
| Mr. Harry Linggoputro | Consolidated Messenger | 4567 Lincoln Drive | Yorktown, VA 23692 |
| Mrs. Cat Francis | Baldwin Museum of Science | 7890 Central Drive | Matoaka, WV 24736 |
| Mrs. Shengda Yang | Fabrikam, Inc. | 4567 2nd Street | Easton, CA 93706 |
| Ms. Adrian Lannin | Alpine Ski House | 3456 3rd Boulevard | Pingree Grove, IL 60140 |
| Mr. Dániel Koczka | School of Fine Art | 5678 3rd Avenue | Elias, KY 40486 |
| Ms. Magdalena Wróblewska | City Power & Light | 5678 Willow Avenue | Conway, MA 01341 |
| Mr. Eugene Zabokritski | Blue Yonder Airlines | 5678 Central Avenue | Riverside, ND 58078 |
| Dr. Mindy Martin | Margie's Travel | 4567 3rd Avenue | Grandy, NC 27939 |
| Mr. Adam Trukawka | Lucerne Publishing | 6789 1st Parkway | Irrigon, OR 97844 |
| Mrs. Marcin Jankowski | Humongous Insurance | 6789 Willow Parkway | Flushing, NY 11351 |

**Figure 8-50** You can switch to Datasheet view to verify that you have correctly built the first part of a union query to display names and addresses.

OK, that's the first part. You do not have to save this query–leave it open in Design view. Start another query with tblContacts and add tblCompanyContacts. Create an EmpName field exactly as you did in the first query. In the second column, enter:

```
CompanyName: ""
```

Say what? Well, one of the requirements to build a union query is that the two recordsets must both have the exact same number of columns and the exact same data types in the relative columns. A mailing label sent to a home address doesn't have a company name, but you need this field to line up with the ones you created in the first query. In Chapter 15, "Constructing a Report," you'll see how the Mailing Label Wizard eliminates the blank row that would otherwise be created by including this field.

Add the HomeAddress field from tblContacts in the third column and create this expression in the fourth column on the Field line:

```
CSZ: tblContacts.HomeCity & ", " & tblContacts.HomeStateOrProvince & " " &
tblContacts.HomePostalCode
```

Finally, include the DefaultForCompany field from tblCompanyContacts, and clear the Show check box but this time set a criterion of False. The Datasheet view of this query should look like Figure 8-51.

Chapter 8

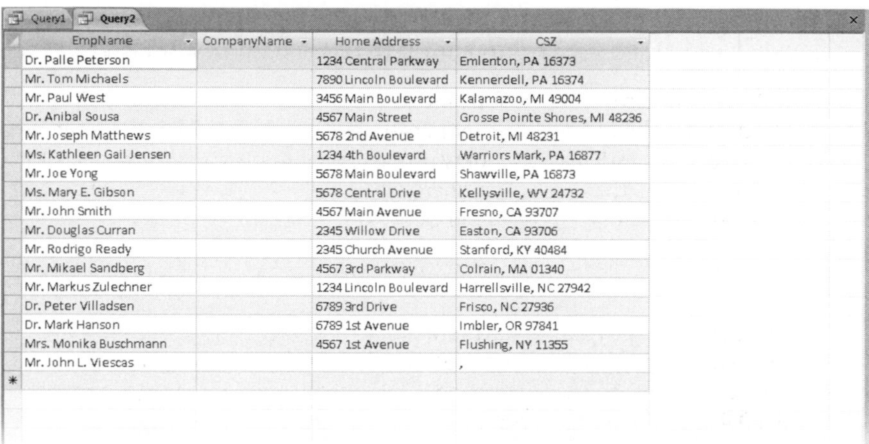

| EmpName | CompanyName | Home Address | CSZ |
|---|---|---|---|
| Dr. Palle Peterson | | 1234 Central Parkway | Emlenton, PA 16373 |
| Mr. Tom Michaels | | 7890 Lincoln Boulevard | Kennerdell, PA 16374 |
| Mr. Paul West | | 3456 Main Boulevard | Kalamazoo, MI 49004 |
| Dr. Anibal Sousa | | 4567 Main Street | Grosse Pointe Shores, MI 48236 |
| Mr. Joseph Matthews | | 5678 2nd Avenue | Detroit, MI 48231 |
| Ms. Kathleen Gail Jensen | | 1234 4th Boulevard | Warriors Mark, PA 16877 |
| Mr. Joe Yong | | 5678 Main Boulevard | Shawville, PA 16873 |
| Ms. Mary E. Gibson | | 5678 Central Drive | Kellysville, WV 24732 |
| Mr. John Smith | | 4567 Main Avenue | Fresno, CA 93707 |
| Mr. Douglas Curran | | 2345 Willow Drive | Easton, CA 93706 |
| Mr. Rodrigo Ready | | 2345 Church Avenue | Stanford, KY 40484 |
| Mr. Mikael Sandberg | | 4567 3rd Parkway | Colrain, MA 01340 |
| Mr. Markus Zulechner | | 1234 Lincoln Boulevard | Harrellsville, NC 27942 |
| Dr. Peter Villadsen | | 6789 3rd Drive | Frisco, NC 27936 |
| Dr. Mark Hanson | | 6789 1st Avenue | Imbler, OR 97841 |
| Mrs. Monika Buschmann | | 4567 1st Avenue | Flushing, NY 11355 |
| Mr. John L. Viescas | | | , |

**Figure 8-51** The second part of a union query to display names and addresses displays the home addresses for persons who are not the primary contact for each company.



Again, you don't have to save this query. Now, you're ready to assemble your union query. Click the Query Design button in the Other group on the Create tab. You'll see a blank third query window with the Show Table dialog box open in front. Click the Close button to dismiss the dialog box. When Access sees that you haven't chosen any tables or queries, it makes SQL the default option on the View button at the left end of the Ribbon. (This means that if you simply click above the View button, which now displays *SQL*, you open the SQL view for the query.) Click the SQL button in the Views group on the Home tab or the Results group of the Design contextual tab to switch to SQL view for this empty query. You should see a blank window with *SELECT;* displayed in the upper-left corner.

Go back to your first query, click the small arrow below the View button on the Home tab, and then click SQL View (or you can follow the same steps using the Results group on the Design contextual tab below Query Tools). You should see a window like Figure 8-52.

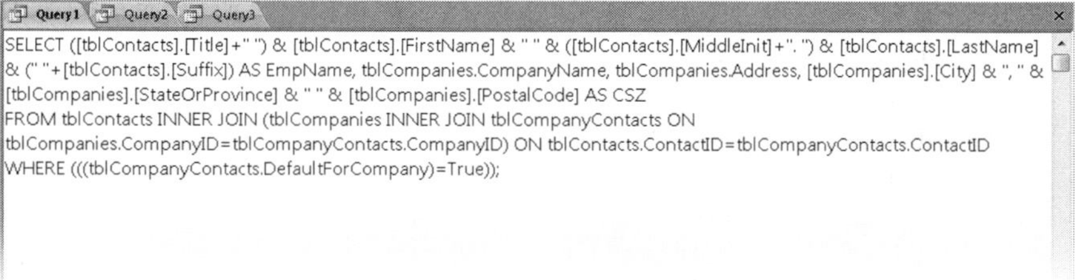

```
SELECT ([tblContacts].[Title]+" ") & [tblContacts].[FirstName] & " " & ([tblContacts].[MiddleInit]+". ") & [tblContacts].[LastName]
& (" "+[tblContacts].[Suffix]) AS EmpName, tblCompanies.CompanyName, tblCompanies.Address, [tblCompanies].[City] & ", " &
[tblCompanies].[StateOrProvince] & " " & [tblCompanies].[PostalCode] AS CSZ
FROM tblContacts INNER JOIN (tblCompanies INNER JOIN tblCompanyContacts ON
tblCompanies.CompanyID=tblCompanyContacts.CompanyID) ON tblContacts.ContactID=tblCompanyContacts.ContactID
WHERE (((tblCompanyContacts.DefaultForCompany)=True));
```

**Figure 8-52** You're going to copy the first part of your union query from the first query's SQL view.

## INSIDE OUT Changing Font Size for the Query Window

By default Access sets the font size for text in the Query window to 8. In order to make Figure 8-52 and Figure 8-53 more readable in the printed book, we temporarily changed our font size to 12 for the Query window. Click the Microsoft Office Button, click Access Options, click the Object Designers category, and then select a font size in the Query Design Font Size text box in the Query Design section. Click OK to save this change.

Select all the text you see in this window and copy it to the Clipboard. Switch to the third empty query, and replace *SELECT;* with the text you copied. Remove the ending semicolon, place the insertion point at the end of the text, press Enter, type the word **UNION**, and press Enter again.

Go to your second query, switch to SQL view, select all the text, and copy it to the Clipboard. Go back to the third query and paste this text at the end. Your new union query should look like Figure 8-53.

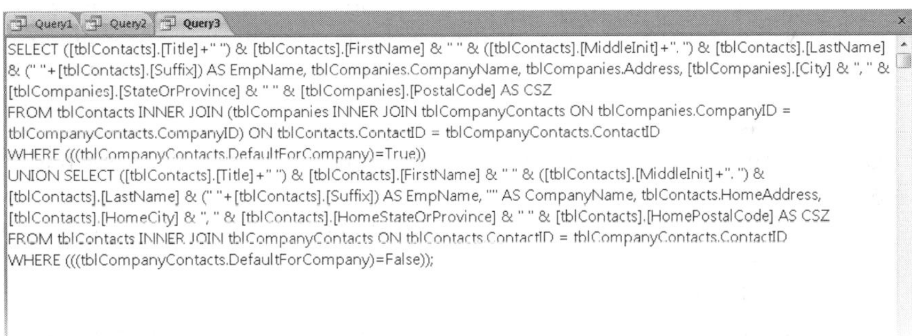
Query1
Query2
Query3
SELECT ([tblContacts].[Title]+" ") & [tblContacts].[FirstName] & " " & ([tblContacts].[MiddleInit]+". ") & [tblContacts].[LastName]
& (" "+[tblContacts].[Suffix]) AS EmpName, tblCompanies.CompanyName, tblCompanies.Address, [tblCompanies].[City] & ", " &
[tblCompanies].[StateOrProvince] & " " & [tblCompanies].[PostalCode] AS CSZ
FROM tblContacts INNER JOIN (tblCompanies INNER JOIN tblCompanyContacts ON tblCompanies.CompanyID =
tblCompanyContacts.CompanyID) ON tblContacts.ContactID = tblCompanyContacts.ContactID
WHERE (((tblCompanyContacts.DefaultForCompany)=True))
UNION SELECT ([tblContacts].[Title]+" ") & [tblContacts].[FirstName] & " " & ([tblContacts].[MiddleInit]+". ") &
[tblContacts].[LastName] & (" "+[tblContacts].[Suffix]) AS EmpName, "" AS CompanyName, tblContacts.HomeAddress,
[tblContacts].[HomeCity] & ", " & [tblContacts].[HomeStateOrProvince] & " " & [tblContacts].[HomePostalCode] AS CSZ
FROM tblContacts INNER JOIN tblCompanyContacts ON tblContacts.ContactID = tblCompanyContacts.ContactID
WHERE (((tblCompanyContacts.DefaultForCompany)=False));

**Figure 8-53** You can assemble a union query by copying and pasting the SQL from two other queries.

Switch to Datasheet view to see the final result as shown in Figure 8-54.

You should save this query, but you can close and not save the first two queries that you used to build this. You can find this query saved as qxmplAddressesUnion in the sample database. If you want to learn more about SQL, see Article 2, "Understanding SQL," on the companion CD.

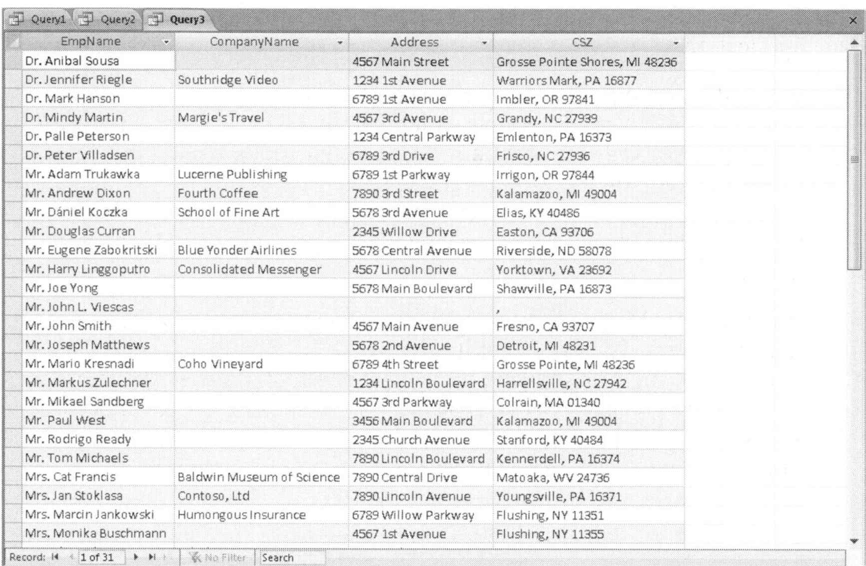

| EmpName | CompanyName | Address | CSZ |
|---|---|---|---|
| Dr. Anibal Sousa | | 4567 Main Street | Grosse Pointe Shores, MI 48236 |
| Dr. Jennifer Riegle | Southridge Video | 1234 1st Avenue | Warriors Mark, PA 16877 |
| Dr. Mark Hanson | | 6789 1st Avenue | Imbler, OR 97841 |
| Dr. Mindy Martin | Margie's Travel | 4567 3rd Avenue | Grandy, NC 27939 |
| Dr. Palle Peterson | | 1234 Central Parkway | Emlenton, PA 16373 |
| Dr. Peter Villadsen | | 6789 3rd Drive | Frisco, NC 27936 |
| Mr. Adam Trukawka | Lucerne Publishing | 6789 1st Parkway | Irrigon, OR 97844 |
| Mr. Andrew Dixon | Fourth Coffee | 7890 3rd Street | Kalamazoo, MI 49004 |
| Mr. Dániel Koczka | School of Fine Art | 5678 3rd Avenue | Elias, KY 40486 |
| Mr. Douglas Curran | | 2345 Willow Drive | Easton, CA 93706 |
| Mr. Eugene Zabokritski | Blue Yonder Airlines | 5678 Central Avenue | Riverside, ND 58078 |
| Mr. Harry Linggoputro | Consolidated Messenger | 4567 Lincoln Drive | Yorktown, VA 23692 |
| Mr. Joe Yong | | 5678 Main Boulevard | Shawville, PA 16873 |
| Mr. John L. Viescas | | | , |
| Mr. John Smith | | 4567 Main Avenue | Fresno, CA 93707 |
| Mr. Joseph Matthews | | 5678 2nd Avenue | Detroit, MI 48231 |
| Mr. Mario Kresnadi | Coho Vineyard | 6789 4th Street | Grosse Pointe, MI 48236 |
| Mr. Markus Zulechner | | 1234 Lincoln Boulevard | Harrellsville, NC 27942 |
| Mr. Mikael Sandberg | | 4567 3rd Parkway | Colrain, MA 01340 |
| Mr. Paul West | | 3456 Main Boulevard | Kalamazoo, MI 49004 |
| Mr. Rodrigo Ready | | 2345 Church Avenue | Stanford, KY 40484 |
| Mr. Tom Michaels | | 7890 Lincoln Boulevard | Kennerdell, PA 16374 |
| Mrs. Cat Francis | Baldwin Museum of Science | 7890 Central Drive | Matoaka, WV 24736 |
| Mrs. Jan Stoklasa | Contoso, Ltd | 7890 Lincoln Avenue | Youngsville, PA 16371 |
| Mrs. Marcin Jankowski | Humongous Insurance | 6789 Willow Parkway | Flushing, NY 11351 |
| Mrs. Monika Buschmann | | 4567 1st Avenue | Flushing, NY 11355 |

Record: 1 of 31 No Filter Search

**Figure 8-54** The union query displays the company address for all primary contacts and the home address for all other contacts.

# Limitations on Using Select Queries to Update Data

The recordset that Access creates when you run a query looks and acts pretty much like a real table containing data. In fact, in most cases you can insert rows, delete rows, and update the information in a recordset, and Access will make the necessary changes to the underlying table or tables for you.

In some cases, however, Access won't be able to figure out what needs to be changed. Consider, for example, a calculated field named Total that is the result of multiplying two fields named Quantity and Price. If you try to increase the amount in a Total field, Access can't know whether you mean to update the Quantity field or the Price field. On the other hand, you can change either the Price field or the Quantity field and then immediately see the change reflected in the calculated Total field.

In addition, Access won't accept any change that might potentially affect many rows in the underlying table. For that reason, you can't change any of the data in a totals query or in a crosstab query. A Group By field is the result of gathering together one or more rows with the same value. Likewise, a Sum is most likely the result of adding values from potentially many rows. A Min or Max value might occur in more than one row.

When working with a recordset that is the result of a join, you can update all fields from the *many* side of a join but only the non-key fields on the *one* side, unless you have specified Cascade Update Related Fields in the relationship. Also, you cannot set or change any field that has the AutoNumber data type. For example, you can't change the

ContactID field values in the tblContacts table in the Conrad Systems Contacts sample application.

The ability to update fields on the *one* side of a query can produce unwanted results if you aren't careful. For example, you could intend to assign a contact to a different company. If you change the company name, you'll change that name for all contacts related to the current CompanyID. What you should do instead is change the CompanyID field in the tblCompanyContacts table, not the company name in the tblCompanies table. You'll learn techniques in Chapter 13 to prevent inadvertent updating of fields in queries.

When you set Unique Values to Yes in the query's property sheet, Access eliminates duplicate rows. The values returned might occur in multiple rows, so Access won't know which one you mean to update. And finally, when Access combines rows from different tables in a union query, the individual rows lose their underlying table identity. Access cannot know which table you mean to update when you try to change a row in a union query, so it disallows all updates.



### Query Fields That Cannot Be Updated

Some types of query fields cannot be updated:

- Any field that is the result of a calculation
- Any field in a totals or crosstab query
- Any field in a query that includes a totals or crosstab query as one of the row sources
- A primary key participating in a relationship unless Cascade Update Related Fields is specified
- AutoNumber fields
- Any field in a unique values query or a unique records query
- Any field in a union query

# Creating PivotTables and PivotCharts from Queries

Microsoft Access 2002 (Office XP) introduced two very useful new features for tables, queries, and forms—PivotTables and PivotCharts. These are additional views of a table, query, or form that you can design to provide analytical views of your data. These views are built into the objects; they're not implemented via a separate ActiveX control as is the old and venerable Microsoft Graph feature.

You learned in this chapter that you can build a crosstab query to *pivot* the values in a column to form dynamic column headings. However, crosstab queries have a major drawback—you can include only one calculated value in the intersection of your row headings and single column heading. PivotTables in Access are very similar to the PivotTable facility in Microsoft Excel. You can categorize rows by several values, just like you can in a crosstab query, but you can also include multiple column categories and multiple raw or calculated values in each intersection of rows and column. As its name implies, you can also pivot the table to swap row headings with column headings.

A PivotChart is a graphical view of the data that you included in your PivotTable. You can build a PivotChart without first defining the PivotTable, and vice versa. When you design a PivotChart, you're also designing or modifying the related PivotTable to provide the data you need for your chart. When you modify a PivotTable, you'll also change (or destroy) the related PivotChart you have already designed.

As you explore the possibilities with PivotTables and PivotCharts, you'll find powerful capabilities to "slice and dice" your data or "drill down" into more detail. Unlike a crosstab query that's built on summarized data, you can begin with a table or query that contains very detailed information. The more detail you have to begin with, the more you can do with your PivotTable and PivotChart.

**CAUTION!**

You might be tempted to design a very detailed query that returns thousands of rows for your user to work with. However, the filtering capabilities inside a PivotTable aren't nearly as efficient as defining a filter in your query to begin with. If you're loading hundreds of thousands of rows over a network, your PivotTable or PivotChart might be very, very slow. You should provide enough detail to get the job done, but no more. You should limit the fields in your query to those focused on the task at hand and include filters in your underlying query to return only the subset of the data that's needed.

## Building a Query for a PivotTable

Although you can build a PivotTable directly on a table in your database, you most likely will need a query to provide the level of detail you want to pivot. Let's build a query in the HousingDataCopy.accdb database that provides some interesting detail.

Start a new query with tblFacilities and add tblReservations, tblEmployees, and tblDepartments. (Be sure to remove the extra relationship between the EmployeeNumber field in tblEmployees and the ManagerNumber field in tblDepartments.) Create an expression to display the employee name in the first field:

```
EmpName: tblEmployees.LastName & ", " & tblEmployees.FirstName &
(" " + tblEmployees.MiddleName)
```

In the query grid, include the Department field from tblDepartments, the ReservationID field from tblReservations (we're going to use this field later to count the number of reservation days), the FacilityName field from tblFacilities, and the RoomNumber field from tblReservations. Add an expression in the next field to calculate the actual charge per day. You could use the DailyRate field from tblReservations, but that's not an accurate reflection of how much the room costs per day when the employee stays a week or more. Your expression should look like this:

```
DailyCharge: CCur(Round(tblReservations.TotalCharge /
(tblReservations.CheckOutDate - tblReservations.CheckInDate), 2))
```

Remember that you can calculate the number of days by subtracting the CheckInDate field from the CheckOutDate field. Divide the TotalCharge field by the number of days to obtain the actual daily rate. This division might result in a value that has more than two decimal places, so asking the Round function to round to two decimal places (the 2 parameter at the end) takes care of that. Finally, the expression uses the CCur (Convert to Currency) function to make sure the query returns a currency value.

Now comes the fun part. Each row in tblReservations represents a stay of one or more days. In this example, we ultimately want to be able to count individual days to find out the length of stay within any month. To do that, we need to "explode" each single row in tblReservations into a row per day for the duration of the reservation. In this sample database, you'll find what we call a "driver" table–ztblDates–full of dates to accomplish this feat. The table contains date values, one per day, for dates from January 1, 1992, to December 31, 2035. We created this table to "drive" the complete list of dates we need (at least, complete enough for our purposes) against the rows in tblReservations in order to provide the explosion.

Include this table in your query and notice that there's no join line to any of the tables. When you add a table with no join defined to another table or set of records, the query returns the Cartesian product of the two sets of records–every row in the first table or set of records is matched with every row in the second table or set of records. For example, if there are 90 rows in one set and 12 rows in the second set, the query returns 1080 rows (90 times 12). In this case, each reservation will now be matched with each of the separate date values in ztblDates.

As we mentioned earlier, you should try to limit the output of a query that you'll use to build a PivotTable to only the rows you need to solve the problem. Let's say the facilities manager is interested in data for June, July, and August of 2007. Add the DateValue field from ztblDates and enter **Between #6/1/2007# And #8/31/2007#** under this field on the Criteria line. You have now limited the explosion of rows to dates in the months of interest.

The final step is to further limit the rows created based on the CheckInDate and CheckOutDate fields in tblReservations. Any reservation that crosses the time span of interest is going to be for a few days or a few weeks. Add the CheckInDate and CheckOutDate fields from tblReservations and clear the Show check box under both. On the Criteria row under CheckInDate, enter **<=ztblDates.DateValue**. Under CheckOutDate, enter **>ztblDates.DateValue**.

This forces the query to keep any rows where the DateValue field from ztblDates is within the time span of each reservation row. Voilà! You now have one row per date for each reservation. Your query should now look like Figure 8-55.

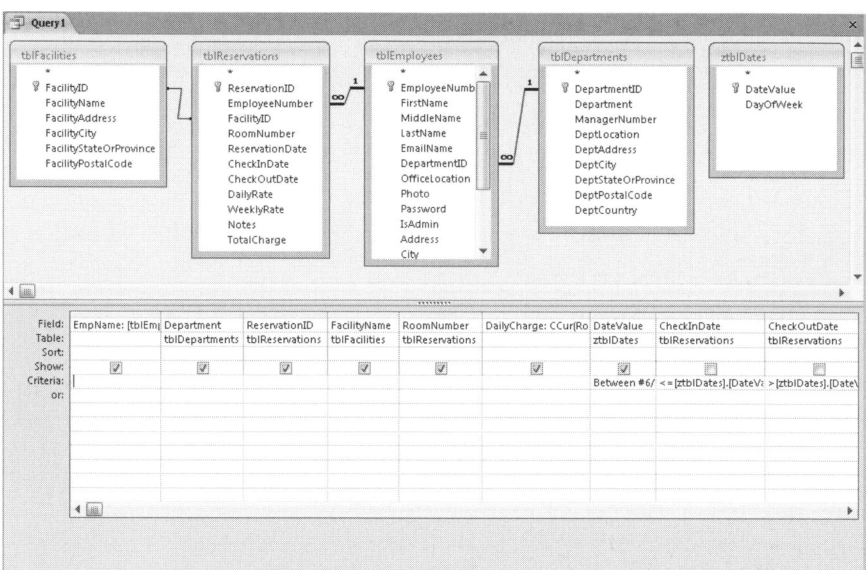

**Figure 8-55** This complex query generates the data you need for a PivotTable.

To better understand how this query expands each reservation into one row per day, take a look at Table 8-2. The table represents expanded rows after applying the final two criteria on CheckInDate and CheckOutDate.

**Table 8-2 How ztblDates Expands Reservation Rows**

| ReservationID | CheckInDate | CheckOutDate | DateValue |
|---|---|---|---|
| 55 | August 6, 2007 | August 12, 2007 | August 6, 2007 |
| 55 | August 6, 2007 | August 12, 2007 | August 7, 2007 |
| 55 | August 6, 2007 | August 12, 2007 | August 8, 2007 |
| 55 | August 6, 2007 | August 12, 2007 | August 9, 2007 |
| 55 | August 6, 2007 | August 12, 2007 | August 10, 2007 |
| 55 | August 6, 2007 | August 12, 2007 | August 11, 2007 |

The end result is that the query selects only the rows from ztblDates that are within the date range of the individual reservation. Because there's one (and only one) row for every date of interest coming from ztblDates, you end up with one row per day that's within the span of days in each reservation. Figure 8-56 shows you the Datasheet view of your query. You can find this query saved as qxmplReservationsByDay in the sample database.

| EmpName | Department | Reservation ID | Name | Room | DailyCharge | DateValue |
|---|---|---|---|---|---|---|
| Lawrence, David Oliver | Product Development | 19 | Main Campus Housing B | 610 | $91.43 | 01-Jun-07 |
| Bradley, David M. | Product Development | 28 | Main Campus Housing B | 403 | $82.14 | 01-Jun-07 |
| Lawrence, David Oliver | Product Development | 19 | Main Campus Housing B | 610 | $91.43 | 02-Jun-07 |
| Bradley, David M. | Product Development | 28 | Main Campus Housing B | 403 | $82.14 | 02-Jun-07 |
| Willett, Benjamin C. | Marketing | 27 | Main Campus Housing A | 505 | $55.00 | 02-Jun-07 |
| Lawrence, David Oliver | Product Development | 19 | Main Campus Housing B | 610 | $91.43 | 03-Jun-07 |
| Bradley, David M. | Product Development | 28 | Main Campus Housing B | 403 | $82.14 | 03-Jun-07 |
| Randall, Linda | Housing Administration | 30 | Main Campus Housing B | 103 | $82.14 | 03-Jun-07 |
| Lawrence, David Oliver | Product Development | 19 | Main Campus Housing B | 610 | $91.43 | 04-Jun-07 |
| Bradley, David M. | Product Development | 28 | Main Campus Housing B | 403 | $82.14 | 04-Jun-07 |
| Randall, Linda | Housing Administration | 30 | Main Campus Housing B | 103 | $82.14 | 04-Jun-07 |
| Lawrence, David Oliver | Product Development | 19 | Main Campus Housing B | 610 | $91.43 | 05-Jun-07 |
| Bradley, David M. | Product Development | 28 | Main Campus Housing B | 403 | $82.14 | 05-Jun-07 |
| Randall, Linda | Housing Administration | 30 | Main Campus Housing B | 103 | $82.14 | 05-Jun-07 |
| Bradley, David M. | Product Development | 28 | Main Campus Housing B | 403 | $82.14 | 06-Jun-07 |
| Randall, Linda | Housing Administration | 30 | Main Campus Housing B | 103 | $82.14 | 06-Jun-07 |
| Bradley, David M. | Product Development | 28 | Main Campus Housing B | 403 | $82.14 | 07-Jun-07 |
| Randall, Linda | Housing Administration | 30 | Main Campus Housing B | 103 | $82.14 | 07-Jun-07 |
| Kim, Tim | Finance | 32 | Main Campus Housing A | 410 | $39.47 | 08-Jun-07 |
| Randall, Linda | Housing Administration | 30 | Main Campus Housing B | 103 | $82.14 | 08-Jun-07 |
| Kim, Tim | Finance | 32 | Main Campus Housing A | 410 | $39.47 | 09-Jun-07 |
| Randall, Linda | Housing Administration | 30 | Main Campus Housing B | 103 | $82.14 | 09-Jun-07 |
| Kim, Tim | Finance | 32 | Main Campus Housing A | 410 | $39.47 | 10-Jun-07 |
| Randall, Linda | Housing Administration | 30 | Main Campus Housing B | 103 | $82.14 | 10-Jun-07 |
| Kim, Tim | Finance | 32 | Main Campus Housing A | 410 | $39.47 | 11-Jun-07 |
| Shock, Misty | Marketing | 23 | Main Campus Housing B | 414 | $48.75 | 11-Jun-07 |

Record: 1 of 307 No Filter Search

**Figure 8-56** The reservations for June, July, and August are expanded into one row per day.

## Designing a PivotTable

Now that you have the data you need, you're ready to start building a PivotTable. From Design or Datasheet view, switch to PivotTable view by clicking the small arrow below the View button and then clicking PivotTable View in the list. (You can find the View button on both the Home tab and the Design contextual tab.) You should see a blank PivotTable design area as shown in Figure 8-57. If you don't see the field list as shown in Figure 8-57, click the Field List command in the Show/Hide group of the Design contextual tab below PivotTable Tools.

In general, you should use as columns those fields that have the fewest values. If you place too many values across your PivotTable, you'll find that you must scroll left a long way to see all the details. In this case, we're interested in statistics by month, and we know there are only three months of data in the underlying recordset. You'll still be able to show the details by day, if you like, because the recordset includes information by date—you can expand any Months field to show all the days in the month. We might want to see the data organized by department and facility. It might also be interesting to provide an easy way to filter on employee name, but we don't need the data from that field displayed in the table.

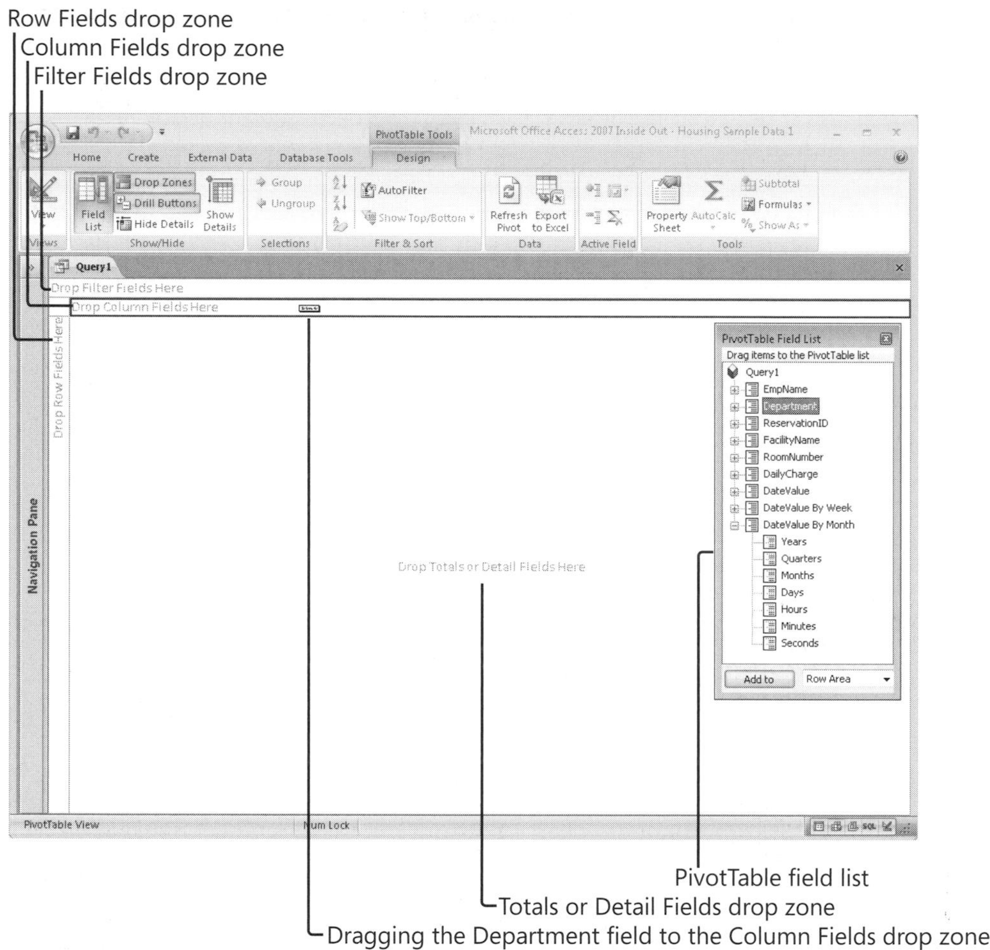


**Figure 8-57** You can design PivotTables using the PivotTable design window.

Expand the DateValue By Month list and drag and drop Months on the Column Fields drop zone. Drag and drop the Department field and the FacilityName field on the Row Fields drop zone. Drag and drop the EmpName field on the Filter Fields drop zone. Finally, drag and drop the ReservationID and DailyCharge fields on the Totals or Detail Fields drop zone. Notice that fields you choose now appear in bold in the PivotTable Field List window. Within the PivotTable, you can click on any plus sign (+) to expand a category or display details, or any minus sign (–) to contract a category or hide details. If you expand Months in the Column Fields drop zone, the PivotTable automatically adds a Days field to the Columns area. You can also expand the categories in the PivotTable Field List window by clicking on the plus sign next to each category. Your PivotTable should look like Figure 8-58.

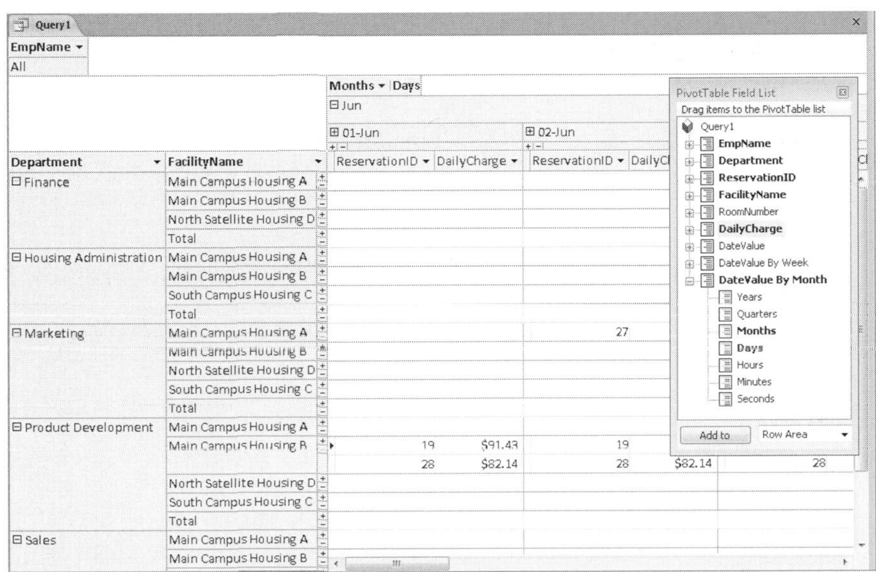


**Figure 8-58** This PivotTable shows fields added to all drop zones.

Now would be a good time to take a quick look at the buttons available on the Design contextual tab below PivotTable Tools, which you saw previously in Figure 8-57. Table 8-3 shows you the details.

**Table 8-3 PivotTable Tools on the Ribbon**

| Button | Usage |
|---|---|
| AutoFilter | When highlighted, indicates automatic filtering is active for the PivotTable. You can click this button to remove all filters. If you define a filter, this button becomes highlighted again. |
| Show Top/Bottom | You can select a column or row field and then click this button to define a filter to display only the first or last number or percentage of rows. This feature works similarly to the Top Values property of a query. |
| AutoCalc | You can select a column, row, or detail/total field and then click this button to insert an aggregate function. The list of available functions includes those you can use in totals queries except for First and Last. (See Table 8-1 on page 437.) The functions available in AutoCalc are appropriate to the field data type and location on the grid. (For example, you can't use a Sum function in a text field.) |
| Subtotal | You can click on a column or row field and then click this button to insert a subtotal based on the values in that field. You must define an AutoCalc field before you add a subtotal. |
| Formulas | You can click this button to insert an expression in the detail/total area that calculates an additional value based on the fields in the recordset. |

| Button | Usage |
| --- | --- |
| Show As | After you insert AutoCalc total fields, you can click in a field and then click this button to convert the value to a percentage of the row, column, or grand totals. |
| Collapse Field | Click on a row or column field and click this button to collapse all subcategories for this field and show summaries only. |
| Expand Field | Performs the opposite of Collapse Field. |
| Hide Details | Hides the details for the selected row or column and shows only totals. |
| Show Details | Performs the opposite of Hide Details. |
| Refresh Pivot | Refetches the underlying data. You might need to do this if others are sharing the data and updating it. |
| Export to Excel | Exports your PivotTable in XML format to an HTML (.htm , .html) file and opens it in Excel. |
| Field List | Opens or closes the PivotTable field list. |
| Property Sheet | Opens or closes the Properties window. |

You're going to need some total calculations for your PivotTable. Click the Reservation ID column heading, click the AutoCalc button to display the list of available functions, and click Count. Click the DailyCharge column heading, click AutoCalc, and click Sum. Click the DailyCharge column heading again, and then click Hide Details to show only totals. Your PivotTable should now look like Figure 8-59. (We closed the PivotTable Field List window to show you more of the PivotTable.)

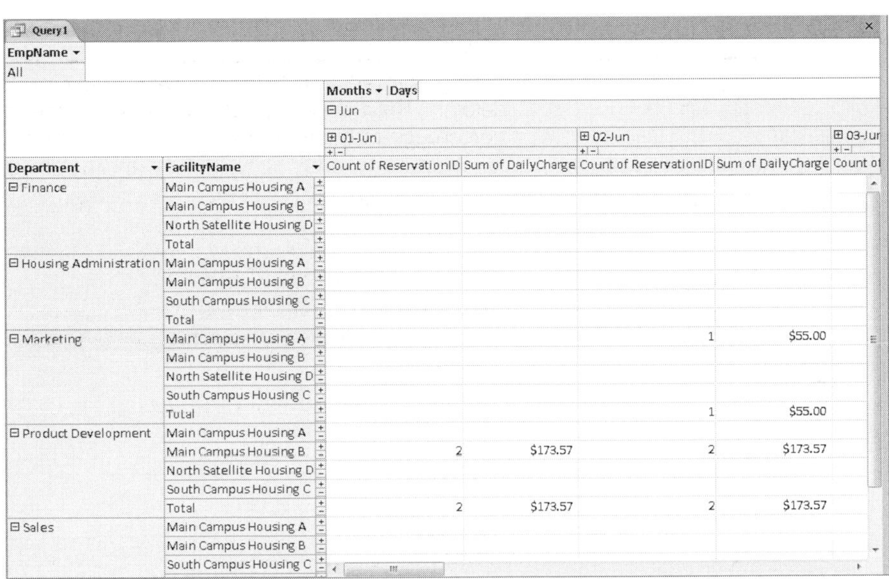


**Figure 8-59** The PivotTable now shows two totals calculations and we are hiding all the details.

There are literally hundreds of properties you can set in a PivotTable. Let's change the captions of the two totals fields to something more meaningful. Click on the Count Of ReservationID field and then click the Property Sheet button in the Tools group of the Design contextual tab below PivotTable Tools to open the Properties window as shown in Figure 8-60.

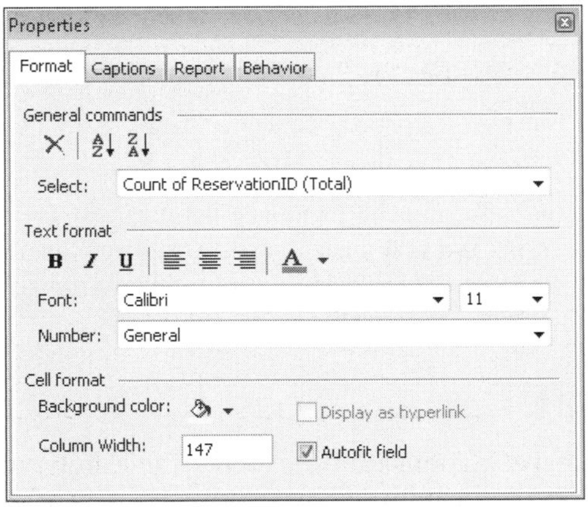

**Figure 8-60** You can change a field's caption in the Properties window for a field in a PivotTable.

As you can see, you can modify the text format on the first tab. You can also click the arrow to the right of Select to choose any other element you have defined thus far. The Properties window changes depending on the type of element you choose. Click the Captions tab and change the caption to Room Days. Go back to the Format tab, select

Sum of Daily Charge (Total) from the Select list, click the Captions tab again, and change the caption to Revenue.

You can spend a couple of days playing around in this PivotTable to see what else you can do. One last thing we might want to do before turning this into a PivotChart is to actually *pivot* the table. You do that by grabbing the fields in the column area and moving them to the row area and vice versa. We decided we'd rather see details about departments first, then facility usage within department, so we placed Department to the left of FacilityName when we moved the fields. You can see the final result in Figure 8-61.

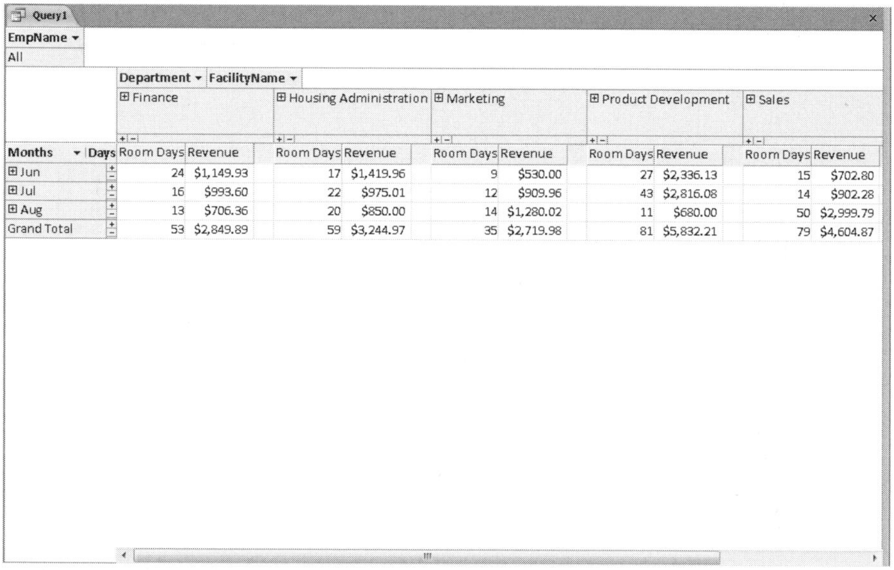

| Months | Days | Finance Room Days | Finance Revenue | Housing Administration Room Days | Housing Administration Revenue | Marketing Room Days | Marketing Revenue | Product Development Room Days | Product Development Revenue | Sales Room Days | Sales Revenue |
|---|---|---|---|---|---|---|---|---|---|---|---|
| Jun | | 24 | $1,149.93 | 17 | $1,419.96 | 9 | $530.00 | 27 | $2,336.13 | 15 | $702.80 |
| Jul | | 16 | $993.60 | 22 | $975.01 | 12 | $909.96 | 43 | $2,816.08 | 14 | $902.28 |
| Aug | | 13 | $706.36 | 20 | $850.00 | 14 | $1,280.02 | 11 | $680.00 | 50 | $2,999.79 |
| Grand Total | | 53 | $2,849.89 | 59 | $3,244.97 | 35 | $2,719.98 | 81 | $5,832.21 | 79 | $4,604.87 |

**Figure 8-61** You can look at the data in a PivotTable another way by "pivoting" the rows and columns and displaying totals only.

If you switch to Design view, you can open the property sheet for the query and set the Default View property to PivotTable. We saved this query as qxmplReservationByDayPT in the sample database. You should save this query under a new name so that you can start fresh building a PivotChart in the next section.

## Designing a PivotChart

Designing a PivotChart is almost as easy as building a PivotTable. You will most likely use PivotCharts in reports (as an embedded subform), but you can also create a PivotChart view of a table, query, or form. As mentioned earlier in the discussion on PivotTables, you most often need to start with a query to pull together the information you need.

To start building a new PivotChart from scratch, open the qxmplReservationsByDay sample query again and switch to PivotChart view. You can see the PivotChart design window in Figure 8-62. (If necessary, click Field List in the Show/Hide group on the Design contextual tab to display the Chart Field List window.)

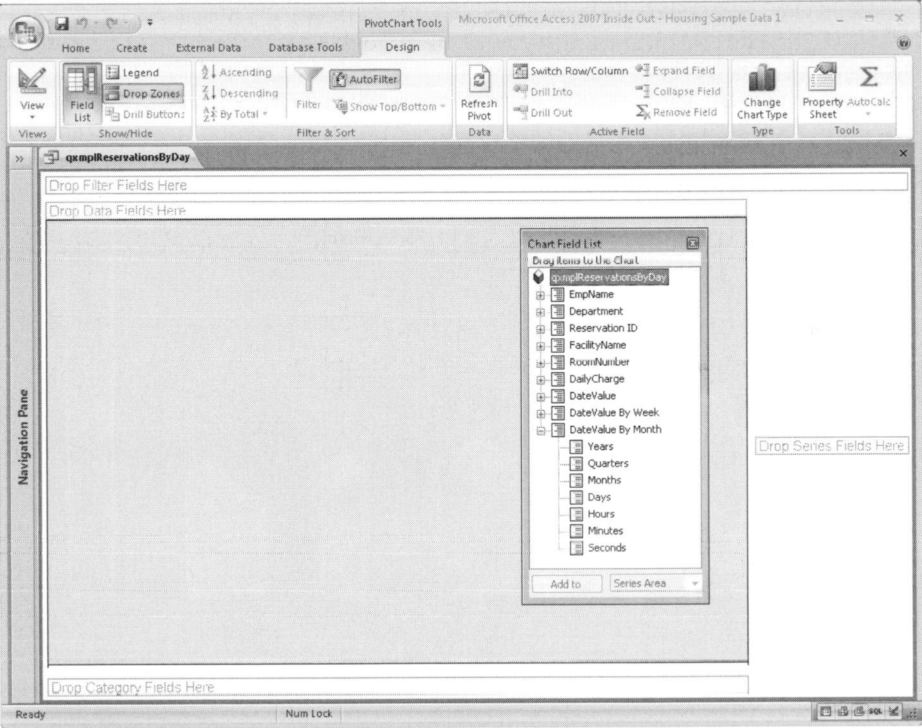


**Figure 8-62** We are beginning to design a PivotChart on a query.

Notice that the filter area is still near the upper-left corner of the window. However, the area for data fields is now along the top of the gray chart drawing area in the center. Drop fields that you want to use for data points along the bottom axis in the bottom-left corner. Drop fields that you want to use for the vertical axis in the right center area. To begin designing your PivotChart, expand DateValue By Month in the field list and drag and drop Months onto the Category Fields drop zone. Next, drag and drop Department onto the Series Fields drop zone on the right.

INSIDE OUT

### Switching into PivotChart View

You can switch directly into PivotChart view from the Design view or Datasheet View of any query. If you haven't previously defined the PivotTable, you can still create your chart by dragging and dropping fields from the field list. Keep in mind that any change you make in PivotChart view also changes what you see in PivotTable view. If you want to keep separate PivotTable and PivotChart views, you should save two versions of your query.

We don't have anything charted yet, so drag the DailyCharge field from the field list to the Data Fields drop zone along the top of the chart. Notice that the chart assumes we want to Sum the field. If you had added the ReservationID field, you would have to click on the Sum of ReservationID field, click the AutoCalc button, and change the calculation to Count. Your PivotChart should now look like Figure 8-63.

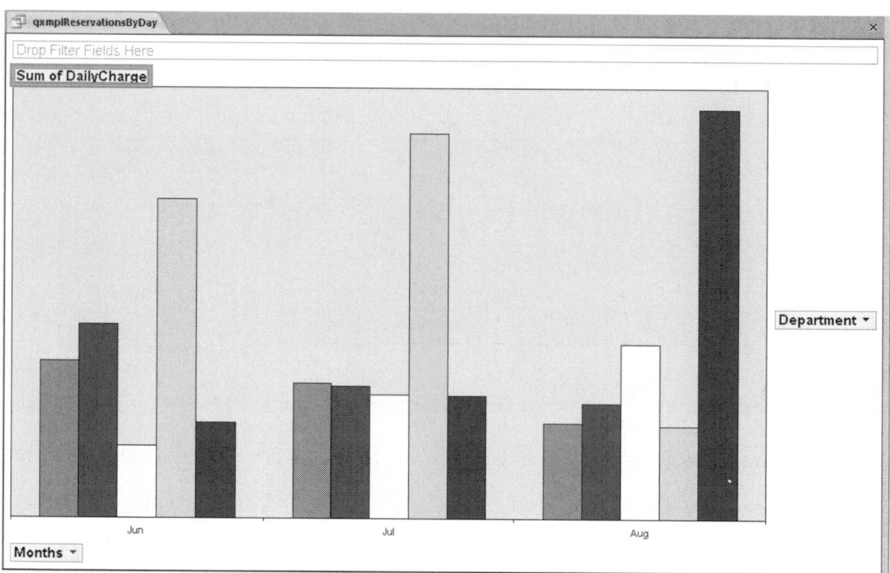


**Figure 8-63** You can create totals and display them using a PivotChart.

This doesn't look all that informative yet, but we're starting to make some progress. It would be nice to add a title, a *legend* (description of each of the colored bars), and a vertical axis with some values. You might also want to display the actual value of each bar at the top of it. Let's get started.

First, open the Properties window (click the Property Sheet button in the Tools group of the Design tab) and select Chart Workspace from the Select list on the General tab as shown in Figure 8-64. (Notice as you go through this exercise that the tabs available in the Properties window change as you select different objects on your PivotChart.)

Click the Title and Legend buttons on the left under Add to create these elements on your PivotChart. Click on the Chart Workspace title you just added (or select Title from the Select list on the General tab), click the Format tab, and change the caption to something like Revenue by Month and Department. Notice that you can also change the font, font size, font color, and position of the title on this tab.

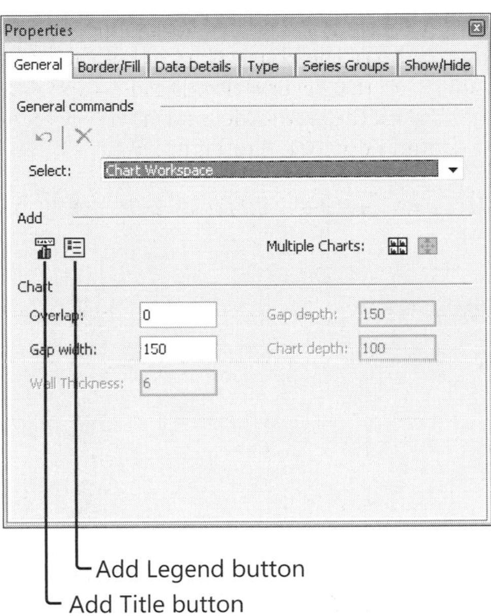


**Figure 8-64** In the Properties window you can add a title and legend to the PivotChart workspace.

Go back to the General tab and select Chart Workspace again. Click the Series Groups tab to see the settings in Figure 8-65. On this tab, you can select one or more items in the Series box and create a separate set of plot bars by placing them in their own group. For each group, you can also add an axis and specify its location. Click on group 1 in the Groups box under Add Axis, select Left in the Axis Position list, and click the Add button to create the axis.

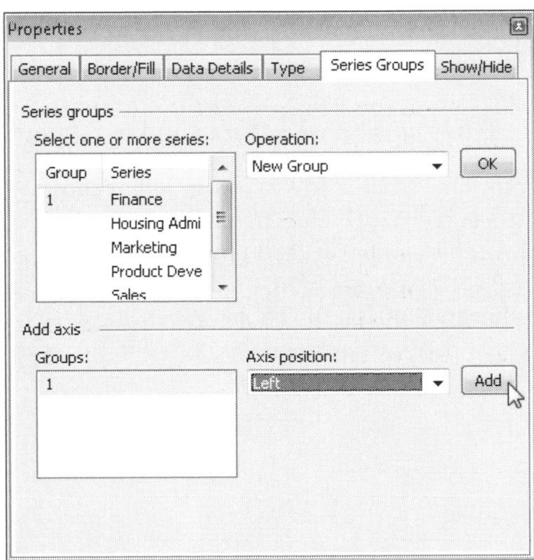


**Figure 8-65** On the Series Groups tab you can add an axis to your PivotChart.

Finally, go back to the General tab and select the five values in the Select list for the Department field one at a time, beginning with Finance. You'll see Add Data Label, Add Trendline, and Add Errorbar buttons as shown in Figure 8-66. Click the Add Data Label button for each department name to add the total value at the top of each column.

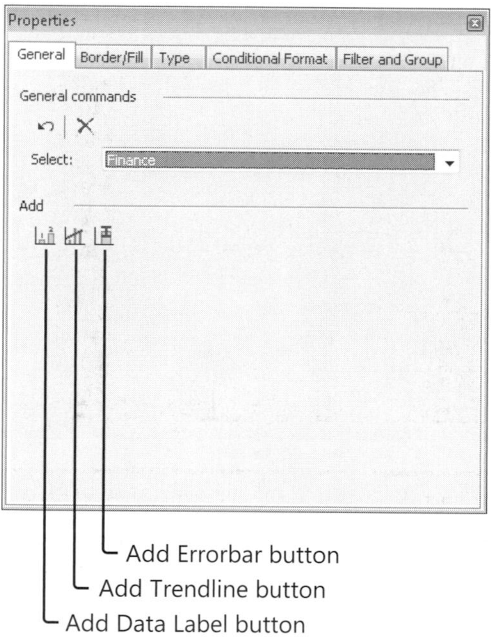


**Figure 8-66** Use the Add Data Label button to display labels on data points on your PivotChart.

Your PivotChart should now like Figure 8-67.



## INSIDE OUT Manipulating the Caption of a Data Field in a PivotChart

If you think about it, you went to some trouble to assign a different caption to Sum of DailyCharge when you built the sample PivotTable. There's actually no way to correct the caption of a data field in PivotChart view. We recommend that you save what you've done so far, and then switch to PivotTable view, hide the details, and change the caption for Sum of DailyCharge to Revenue as you did earlier. When you switch back to PivotChart view, you'll find the new caption displayed. You can find this chart saved as qxmplReservationByDayPC in the sample database.

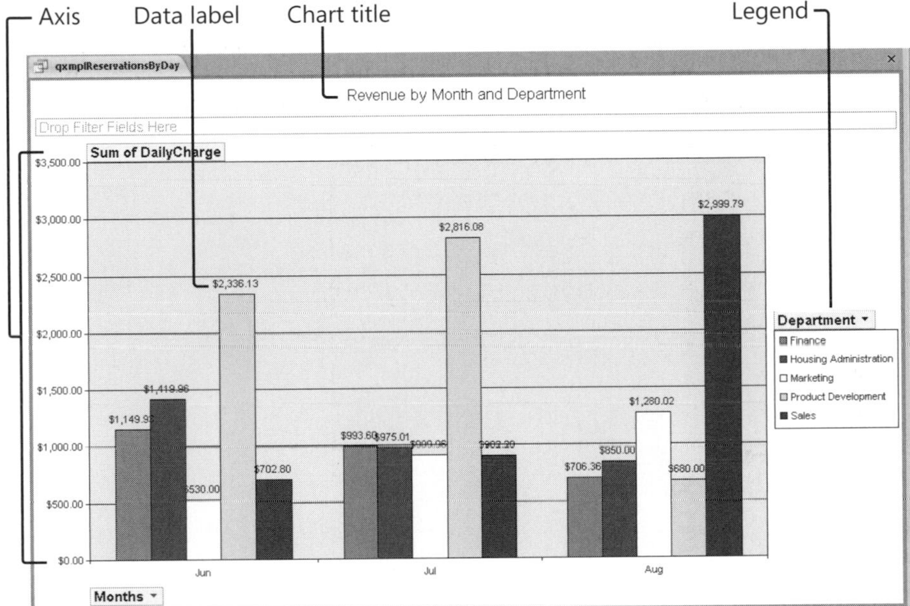


**Figure 8-67** The completed PivotChart shows revenue totals by month and department.

If you want to see what your PivotChart might look like plotted in a different way, you can click the Change Chart Type button in the Type group of the Design contextual tab below PivotChart Tools to open the Properties window with the PivotChart workspace selected and the focus on the Type tab. The chart we've been building thus far is a simple column chart, but you can choose from Bar, Line, Smooth Line, Pie, Scatter, and several other options. Be aware that changing the chart type often throws away some detail settings, so you might have to tweak properties again to get exactly what you want.

Now that you understand the fundamentals of building complex select queries and working with PivotTables and PivotCharts with Access, you're ready to move on to updating sets of data with action queries in the next chapter.

CHAPTER 9

# Modifying Data with Action Queries



In Chapter 7, "Creating and Working with Simple Queries," you learned how to insert, update, and delete single rows of data within a datasheet. In Chapter 8, "Building Complex Queries," you discovered that you can use queries to select the data you want—even from multiple tables. You also learned under what conditions you cannot update a field in a query. Now you can take the concept of queries one step further and use action queries to quickly change, insert, create, or delete sets of data in your database.

The four types of queries you'll study in this chapter are

- **Update query** Allows you to update the fields in one or more rows.
- **Make-table query** Allows you to create a new table by selecting rows from one or more existing tables.
- **Append query** Allows you to copy rows from one or more tables into another table.
- **Delete query** Allows you to remove one or more rows from a table.

Note

The examples in this chapter are based on the tables and data in HousingDataCopy.accdb and ContactsDataCopy.accdb on the companion CD included with this book. These databases are copies of the data from the Housing Reservations and Conrad Systems Contacts sample applications, respectively, and they contain the sample queries used in this chapter. The query results you see from the sample queries you build in this chapter might not exactly match what you see in this book if you have changed the sample data in the files.

# Updating Groups of Rows

It's easy enough to use a table or a query in Datasheet view to find a single record in your database and change one value. But what if you want to make the same change to many records? Changing each record one at a time could be very tedious.

Remember that in Chapter 7 you learned how to construct queries to test proposed new validation rules. In the HousingDataCopy.accdb database, there's a table-level validation rule defined in tblFacilityRooms that doesn't let you enter a WeeklyRate value that is greater than seven times the DailyRate value. If you want to change this rule to ensure that the WeeklyRate value is no more than six times the DailyRate value (thereby ensuring that the weekly rate is a true discount), you must first update the values in the table to comply with the new rule.

You could open tblFacilityRooms in Datasheet view and go through the individual rows one by one to set all the WeeklyRate values by hand. But why not let Microsoft Office Access 2007 do the work for you with a single query?



## Testing with a Select Query

Before you create and run a query to update many records in your database, it's a good idea to first create a select query using criteria that select the records you want to update. You'll see in the next section that it's easy to convert this select query to an update query or other type of action query after you're sure that Office Access 2007 will process the right records.

You could certainly update all the rows in tblFacilityRooms, but what about rows where the WeeklyRate value is already less than or equal to 6 times the DailyRate value? You don't want to update rows that already meet the proposed validation rule change—you might actually increase the WeeklyRate value in those rows. For example, a room might exist that has a DailyRate value of $50 and a WeeklyRate value of $275. If you blanket update all rows to set the WeeklyRate field to six times the DailyRate field, you'll change the WeeklyRate value in this row to $300. So, you should first build a query on tblFacilityRooms to find only those rows that need to be changed.

Open HousingDataCopy.accdb and start a new query on tblFacilityRooms. Include the FacilityID, RoomNumber, DailyRate, and WeeklyRate fields. Enter the criterion **>[DailyRate]*6** under the WeeklyRate field. Your query should look like Figure 9-1.

When you run the query, you'll see 276 records that you want to change, as shown in Figure 9-2. (There are 306 records in the table.)

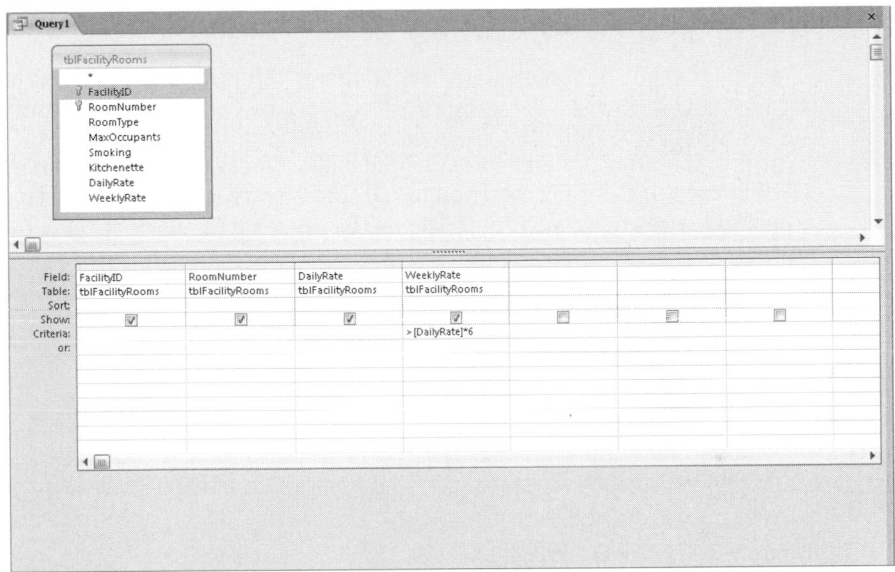


**Figure 9-1** This select query finds weekly rates that will fail the new table validation rule.

Query1

| Facility | Room No. | Daily | Weekly |
|---|---|---|---|
| 1 | 101 | $40.00 | $255.00 |
| 1 | 102 | $90.00 | $575.00 |
| 1 | 103 | $45.00 | $290.00 |
| 1 | 104 | $45.00 | $290.00 |
| 1 | 105 | $55.00 | $350.00 |
| 1 | 106 | $90.00 | $575.00 |
| 1 | 107 | $55.00 | $350.00 |
| 1 | 108 | $45.00 | $290.00 |
| 1 | 109 | $50.00 | $320.00 |
| 1 | 110 | $40.00 | $255.00 |
| 1 | 111 | $80.00 | $510.00 |
| 1 | 201 | $40.00 | $255.00 |
| 1 | 202 | $90.00 | $575.00 |
| 1 | 203 | $45.00 | $290.00 |
| 1 | 204 | $45.00 | $290.00 |
| 1 | 205 | $55.00 | $350.00 |
| 1 | 206 | $90.00 | $575.00 |
| 1 | 207 | $55.00 | $350.00 |
| 1 | 208 | $45.00 | $290.00 |
| 1 | 209 | $50.00 | $320.00 |
| 1 | 210 | $40.00 | $255.00 |
| 1 | 211 | $80.00 | $510.00 |
| 1 | 301 | $40.00 | $255.00 |
| 1 | 302 | $90.00 | $575.00 |
| 1 | 303 | $45.00 | $290.00 |
| 1 | 304 | $45.00 | $290.00 |

Record: 1 of 276 No Filter Search

**Figure 9-2** This is the recordset of the select query shown in Figure 9-1.

## Converting a Select Query to an Update Query

Now you're ready to change the query so that it will update the table. When you first create a query, Access 2007 builds a select query by default. You can find commands for the four types of action queries–make-table, update, append, and delete–in the Query Type group on the Design contextual tab below Query Tools, as shown in Figure 9-3. (Switch back to Design view if you haven't already done so.) Click the Update button to convert the select query to an update query.

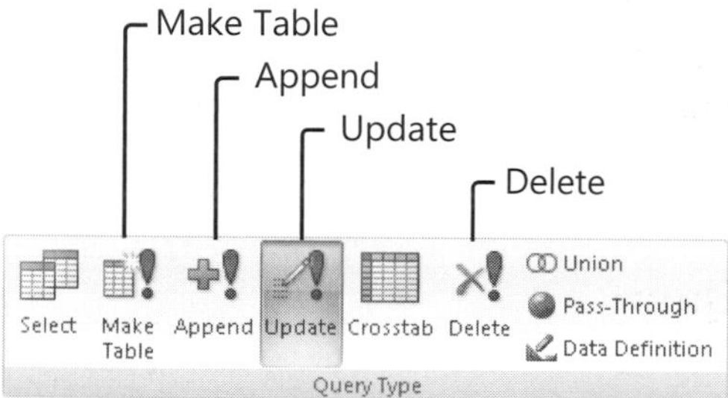


**Figure 9-3** The Query Type group on the Design contextual tab below Query Tools contains commands for the four types of action queries.

When you convert a select query to an update query, Access highlights the Update button in the Query Type group when the query is in Design view and adds a row labeled Update To to the design grid, as shown in Figure 9-4. You use this row to specify how you want your data changed for those rows that meet the query's criteria. In this case, you want to change the WeeklyRate value to **[DailyRate]*6** for all rows where the rate is currently too high.

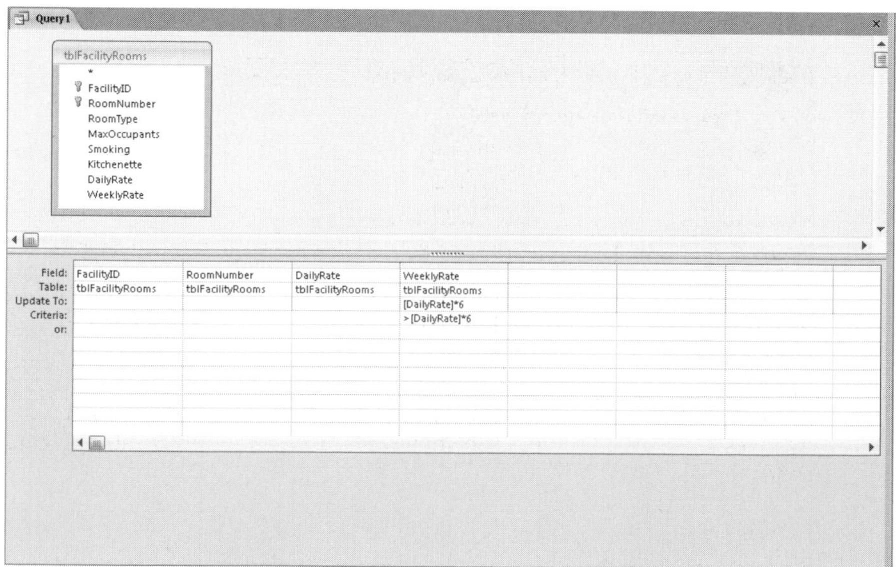


**Figure 9-4** An update query shows an Update To row in the design grid.

INSIDE OUT **What Can I Put in Update To?**

You can enter any valid expression in the Update To row. You can include in the expression one or more of the fields from the source tables in the query. For example, if you want to raise the DailyRate value for a certain type of room by 10 percent, rounded to the nearest dollar (zero decimal places), you can include the DailyRate field in the design grid and enter

```
Round( CCur( [DailyRate] * 1.1 ), 0 )
```

in the Update To row. Note that this formula uses the Round and CCur built-in functions discussed in the previous chapter to round the result to the nearest dollar.

## Running an Update Query

If you want to be completely safe, you should make a backup copy of your table before you run an update query. To do that, go to the Navigation Pane, select the table you're about to update, and click the Copy command in the Clipboard group on the Home tab on the Ribbon. Then click the Paste command in the same Clipboard group, and give the copy of your table a different name when Access prompts you with a dialog box. (Be sure you select the default Structure And Data option.) Now you're ready to run the update query.

To run the query, click the Run command in the Results group on the Design tab below Query Tools. Access first scans your table to determine how many rows will change based on your selection criteria. It then displays a confirmation dialog box like the one shown in Figure 9-5.

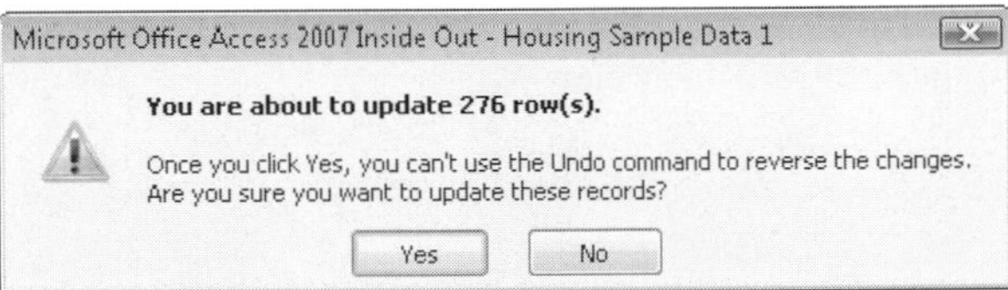


**Figure 9-5** This dialog box reports the number of rows that will be changed by an update query.

You already know that you need to update 276 records, so you can perform the update by clicking Yes in the dialog box. (If the number of rows indicated in the dialog box is not what you expected or if you're not sure that Access will update the right records or fields, click No to stop the query without updating.) After the update query runs, you can look at the table or create a new select query to confirm that Access made the changes you wanted. Figure 9-6 shows the result–no weekly rate is greater than six times the daily rate.

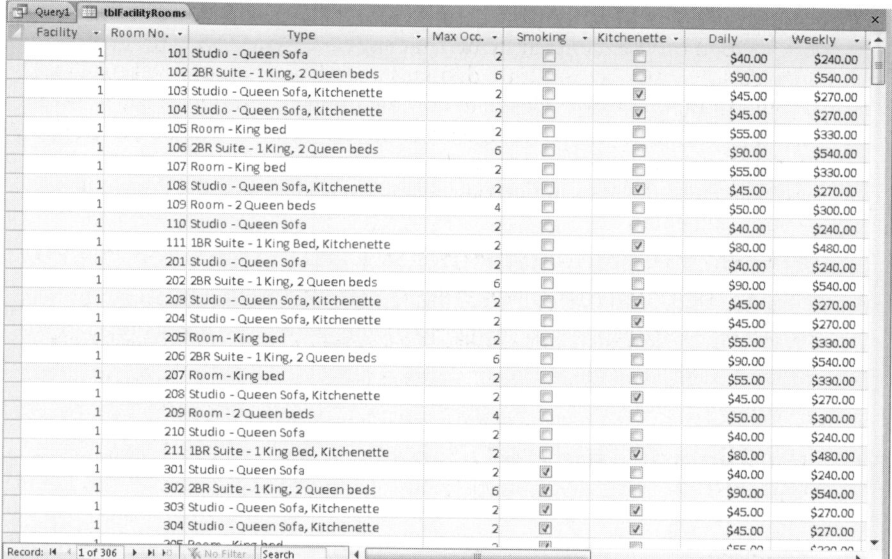


| Facility | Room No. | Type | Max Occ. | Smoking | Kitchenette | Daily | Weekly |
|---|---|---|---|---|---|---|---|
| 1 | 101 | Studio - Queen Sofa | 2 | ☐ | ☐ | $40.00 | $240.00 |
| 1 | 102 | 2BR Suite - 1 King, 2 Queen beds | 6 | ☐ | ☐ | $90.00 | $540.00 |
| 1 | 103 | Studio - Queen Sofa, Kitchenette | 2 | ☐ | ☑ | $45.00 | $270.00 |
| 1 | 104 | Studio - Queen Sofa, Kitchenette | 2 | ☐ | ☑ | $45.00 | $270.00 |
| 1 | 105 | Room - King bed | 2 | ☐ | ☐ | $55.00 | $330.00 |
| 1 | 106 | 2BR Suite - 1 King, 2 Queen beds | 6 | ☐ | ☐ | $90.00 | $540.00 |
| 1 | 107 | Room - King bed | 2 | ☐ | ☐ | $55.00 | $330.00 |
| 1 | 108 | Studio - Queen Sofa, Kitchenette | 2 | ☐ | ☑ | $45.00 | $270.00 |
| 1 | 109 | Room - 2 Queen beds | 4 | ☐ | ☐ | $50.00 | $300.00 |
| 1 | 110 | Studio - Queen Sofa | 2 | ☐ | ☐ | $40.00 | $240.00 |
| 1 | 111 | 1BR Suite - 1 King Bed, Kitchenette | 2 | ☐ | ☑ | $80.00 | $480.00 |
| 1 | 201 | Studio - Queen Sofa | 2 | ☐ | ☐ | $40.00 | $240.00 |
| 1 | 202 | 2BR Suite - 1 King, 2 Queen beds | 6 | ☐ | ☐ | $90.00 | $540.00 |
| 1 | 203 | Studio - Queen Sofa, Kitchenette | 2 | ☐ | ☑ | $45.00 | $270.00 |
| 1 | 204 | Studio - Queen Sofa, Kitchenette | 2 | ☐ | ☑ | $45.00 | $270.00 |
| 1 | 205 | Room - King bed | 2 | ☐ | ☐ | $55.00 | $330.00 |
| 1 | 206 | 2BR Suite - 1 King, 2 Queen beds | 6 | ☐ | ☐ | $90.00 | $540.00 |
| 1 | 207 | Room - King bed | 2 | ☐ | ☐ | $55.00 | $330.00 |
| 1 | 208 | Studio - Queen Sofa, Kitchenette | 2 | ☐ | ☑ | $45.00 | $270.00 |
| 1 | 209 | Room - 2 Queen beds | 4 | ☐ | ☐ | $50.00 | $300.00 |
| 1 | 210 | Studio - Queen Sofa | 2 | ☐ | ☐ | $40.00 | $240.00 |
| 1 | 211 | 1BR Suite - 1 King Bed, Kitchenette | 2 | ☐ | ☑ | $80.00 | $480.00 |
| 1 | 301 | Studio - Queen Sofa | 2 | ☑ | ☐ | $40.00 | $240.00 |
| 1 | 302 | 2BR Suite - 1 King, 2 Queen beds | 6 | ☑ | ☐ | $90.00 | $540.00 |
| 1 | 303 | Studio - Queen Sofa, Kitchenette | 2 | ☑ | ☑ | $45.00 | $270.00 |
| 1 | 304 | Studio - Queen Sofa, Kitchenette | 2 | ☑ | ☑ | $45.00 | $270.00 |

Record: 1 of 306 No Filter Search

**Figure 9-6** You can now see the updated data in the tblFacilityRooms table.

If you think you might want to perform this update again, you can save the query and give it a name. This sample query is saved in the sample database as qxmplUpdateWeekly. In the Navigation Pane, Access distinguishes action queries from select queries by displaying a special icon, followed by an exclamation point, before action query names. For example, Access displays a pencil and an exclamation point next to the new update query that you just created. You'll see later that make-table queries have a small datasheet with a starburst in one corner, append queries have a green cross, and delete queries have a red *X*. Note that if you open an action query from the Navigation Pane, you'll execute it. If you want to see the datasheet of the action query, open it in Design view first, and then switch to Datasheet view.

### Note

It's a good idea to include identifying fields (such as FacilityID and RoomNumber in the preceding example) when you build a test select query that you plan to convert to an action query. However, Access discards any fields for which you have not specified criteria or that you do not want to update when you save your final action query. This is why you won't see anything but the WeeklyRate field in qxmplUpdateWeekly.

To run an action query again, right-click on the query name in the Navigation Pane and click Open on the shortcut menu that appears. When you run an action query from the Navigation Pane, Access 2007 displays a confirmation dialog box similar to the one shown in Figure 9-7. Click Yes to complete the action query. If you want to disable this extra confirmation step (we don't recommend that you do so), click the Microsoft Office Button, click Access Options, and in the Advanced category of the Access Options dialog box, clear the Action Queries check box under Confirm in the Editing section.

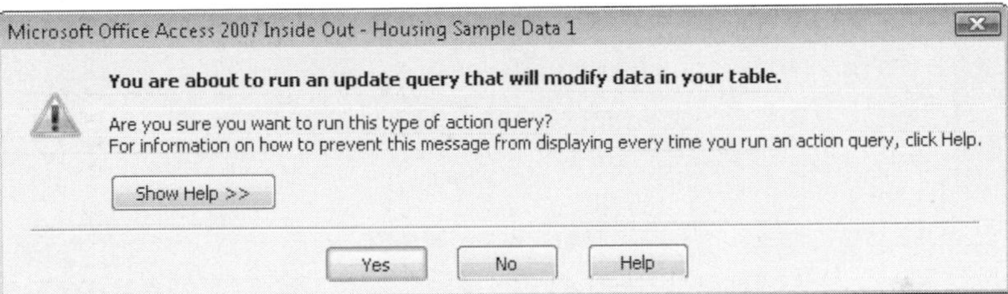


**Figure 9-7** This dialog box asks you to confirm an action query.

## Updating Multiple Fields

When you create an update query, you aren't limited to changing a single field at a time. You can ask Access 2007 to update any or all of the fields in the record by including them in the design grid and then specifying an update formula.

Before Access updates a record in the underlying table or query, it makes a copy of the original record. Access applies the formulas you specify using the values in the original record and places the result in the updated copy. It then updates your database by writing the updated copy to your table. Because updates are made to the copy before updating the table, you can, for example, swap the values in a field named A and a field named B by specifying an Update To setting of [B] for the A field and an Update To setting of [A] for the B field. If Access were making changes directly to the original record, you'd need to use a third field to swap values because the first assignment of B to A would destroy the original value of A.

If you remember from Chapter 7, we also discussed the possibility of reducing the highest daily rate charged for a room to $90. If you do that, you must also update the WeeklyRate value to make sure it doesn't exceed six times the new daily rate. First, build a query to find all rows that have a value in the DailyRate field that exceeds the new maximum. As before, start a query on tblFacilityRooms and include the FacilityID, RoomNumber, DailyRate, and WeeklyRate fields. Place the criterion **>90** under the DailyRate field. Your query should look like Figure 9-8. If you run this query, you'll find 26 rows that meet this criterion in the sample database.

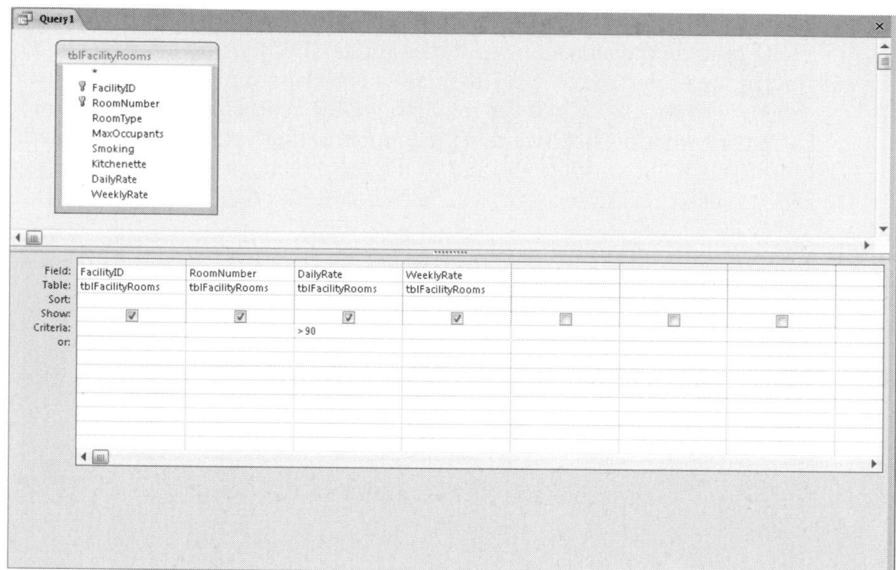


**Figure 9-8** This query finds daily rates greater than $90.

Now comes the tricky part. Change your query to an update query and enter **90** on the Update To row under DailyRate. You might be tempted to set Update To under Weekly-Rate to **[DailyRate]*6** again, but you would be wrong. The reference to [DailyRate] gets you the *original* value of that field in each row—*before* it gets updated to the value 90. You know you're going to set DailyRate in rows that qualify to 90, so enter the constant **540** or the expression **(90 * 6)** in the Update To line under WeeklyRate. Your update query should now look like Figure 9-9.

## INSIDE OUT Performing Multiple Updates with Expressions That Reference Table Fields

If you want to increase (or decrease) DailyRate by some percentage, then you should repeat the calculation for the new DailyRate value and multiply by 6 to calculate the new WeeklyRate value. For example, if you want to increase the rate by 10 percent, your expression in Update To for DailyRate is

```
CCur(Round([DailyRate] * 1.1, 0))
```

Then your expression under WeeklyRate should be

```
CCur(Round([DailyRate] * 1.1), 0)) * 6
```

Remember, DailyRate in any expression references the *old* value in the row before it is updated.

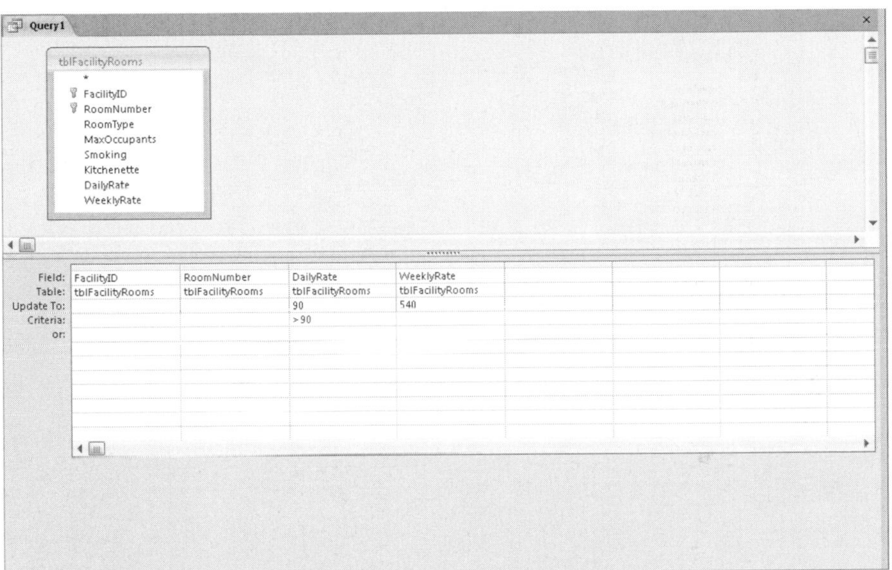


**Figure 9-9** This query finds daily rates greater than $90.

You can find this query saved as qxmplUpdateDailyWeekly in the sample database.



## Creating an Update Query Using Multiple Tables or Queries

The target of an update query should generally be one table, but you might need to update a table based on criteria you apply to a related query or table. Consider the tblContacts table in the Conrad Systems Contacts sample application. The table contains an Inactive field that you can set to Yes to remove that contact from most displays without removing the row from the database. Although you can edit each contact individually and choose to mark them inactive, you occasionally might want to run an update query that automatically sets this flag when the contact hasn't had any activity for a long time.

You studied how to solve a complex unmatched problem in Chapter 8. You need to apply a similar concept to this problem—find the contacts who have activity since a certain date of interest and then use an outer join to identify those who have no activity so that you can mark them inactive.

The sample database contains contact events from January 11, 2007, through July 9, 2007. If you were using this data actively, you would be entering new contact events every day, but this sample data is static. Let's assume that today is January 1, 2008, and you want to flag any contact who hasn't had any event in the last six months.

First, you need to find out who hasn't contacted you since July 1, 2007. Start by opening the ContactsDataCopy.accdb sample database. Start a query with tblContactEvents and include the ContactID and ContactDateTime fields in the query grid. Under ContactDateTime, enter a criterion of **>=#7/1/2007#**. Your query should look like Figure 9-10.

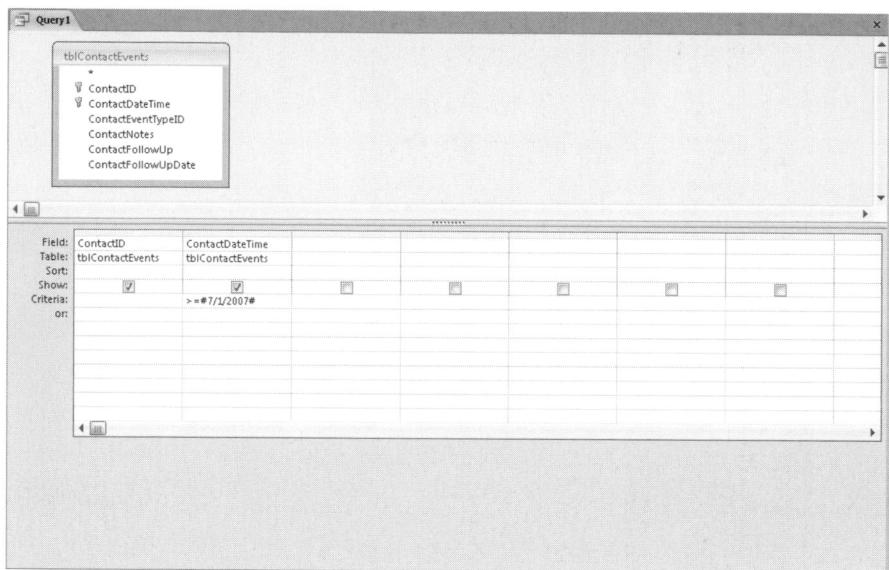


**Figure 9-10** This query finds contact events since July 1, 2007.

If you run this query, you'll find 11 rows for 10 different contacts. Save this query as qryContactsSinceJuly2007. (You can also find the query saved as qxmplContactEvents-Since01July2007 in the sample database.)

Next, you want to find who has not contacted you in this time frame. Start a new query with tblContacts and add the query you just built. You should see a join line linking the ContactID field in tblContacts and the ContactID field in your query. Remember from Chapter 8 that you need an outer join from the table to the query to fetch all rows from tblContacts and any matching rows from the query. Double-click the join line to open the Join Properties dialog box and choose the option to include all rows from tblContacts and any matching rows from qryContactsSinceJuly2007. You should now have an arrow pointing from the table to the query.

Include in the query grid the ContactID, FirstName, LastName, and Inactive fields from tblContacts and the ContactID field from the query. You want contacts who aren't in the list of "recent" contact events, so add the Is Null test on the Criteria line under ContactID from the query. Your query should now look like Figure 9-11.

If you run this query, you'll find out that there are no contact events after the specified date for 22 of the 32 contacts. Remember, this is only an example.

Now you have the contacts you want to set as inactive. In Design view, turn the query into an update query. Under the Inactive field, set Update To to True. You can now run this query to verify that it does mark the 22 contacts as inactive. You can find this query saved as qxmplUpdateInactive in the sample database.

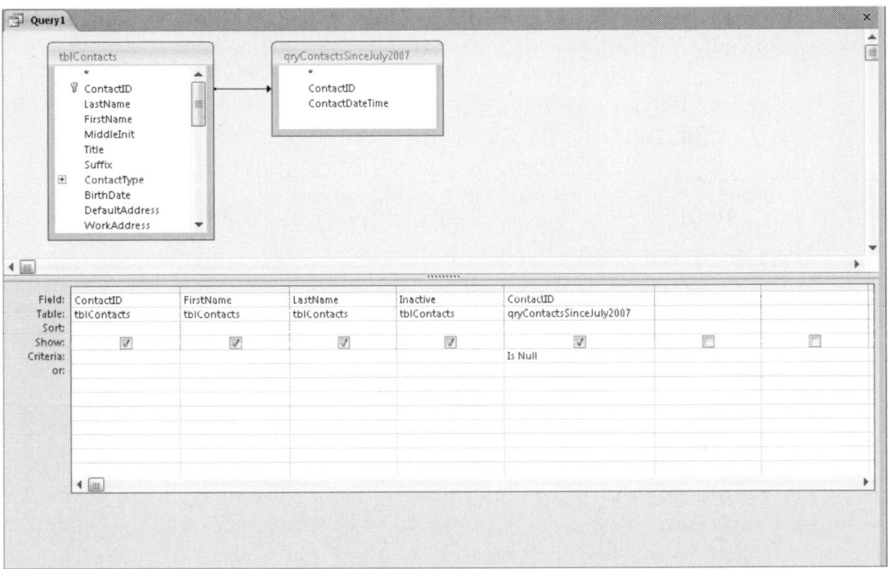


**Figure 9-11** This query finds contacts with no contact events since July 1, 2007.



INSIDE OUT **Making Update Queries Generic with Parameters**

In Chapter 7, you learned how to create a date/time comparison expression using the DateDiff function. In Chapter 8, you learned how to define parameters in your queries. In the example to update inactive status, you entered a specific comparison date in the select query you built. If you really want to save and run a query like this periodically, the select query shouldn't use a static value that you would have to change each time you wanted to perform this update. Using DateDiff, you can define a comparison with an offset relative to the current date. With a parameter, you can create a dynamic prompt for the date you want at the time you run the query.

You might also want to write a converse query that clears the Inactive field for contacts who *do* have recent contact events.

# Creating a New Table with a Make-Table Query

Sometimes you might want to save as a new table the data that you extract with a select query. If you find that you keep executing the same query over and over against data that isn't changing, it can be faster to access the data from a table rather than from the query, particularly if the query must join several tables.

In the last chapter, you created a very complex query using a Cartesian product to drive your PivotTable and PivotChart. At the end of each month or quarter, you might want to use a query like this to create a series of reports. When you have tens of thousands of reservations in your database, this complex query might take a long time to run for each report. You will save a lot of time if you first save the result of the complex query as a temporary table and then run your reports from that table. Also, after reservations are completed for a prior period of time, they're not likely to change, so permanently saving the data selected by a query as a table could be useful for gathering summary information that you intend to keep long after you delete the detailed data on which the query is based.

## Creating a Make-Table Query

In the Housing Reservations application, assume that at the end of each quarter you want to create and save a table that captures reservations detail for the quarter by facility, department, and employee. Open the HousingDataCopy.accdb sample database to follow along with the examples in this section. You might recall from the exercises in building the complex query to provide data for a PivotTable that you need to include tblDepartments, tblFacilities, tblEmployees, and tblReservations. You might also want to include a second copy of tblEmployees to capture the department manager and a copy of tblFacilityRooms to capture the room types. You're essentially unnormalizing the data to create a single archive table that you can also use in reports.



As with most action queries, it's a good idea to start with a select query to verify that you're working with the correct data. Start a new query with tblFacilities, and add tblFacilityRooms, tblReservations, tblEmployees, and tblDepartments. Click the relationship line that the query draws between FacilityID in tblFacilities and FacilityID in tblReservations and press the Delete key to remove this extra join line. Be sure to also remove the extra relationship between the EmployeeNumber field in tblEmployees and the ManagerNumber field in tblDepartments. Add tblEmployees one more time—we plan to use the first instance of tblEmployees to get employees who have reservations, and the second instance to get the managers for the departments. Access names this second table tblEmployees_1 to avoid a duplicate name. Create a join line from EmployeeNumber in tblEmployees_1 to ManagerNumber in tblDepartments.

To avoid confusion with the two copies of tblEmployees, select tblEmployees_1 and click the Property Sheet button on the Design tab below Query Tools to open the property sheet shown in Figure 9-12. You can actually assign an alias name to any field list (table or query) in your query. In this case, change the name of the second copy of tblEmployees to Managers.

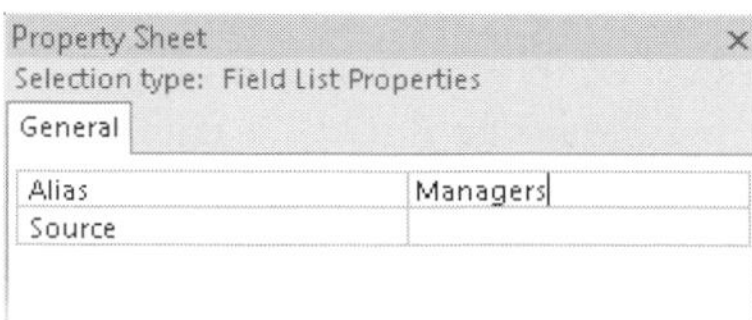


**Figure 9-12** You can use the property sheet to assign an alias name to a field list in a query.

Now you're ready to begin defining fields. Create an expression to display the employee name in the first field:

```
EmpName: tblEmployees.LastName & ", " & tblEmployees.FirstName
& (" " + tblEmployees.MiddleName)
```

In the query grid, include the Department field from tblDepartments, and then add the manager name in the next column with an expression:

```
MgrName: Managers.LastName & ", " & Managers.FirstName
& (" " + Managers.MiddleName)
```

Notice that you're using the new alias name of the second copy of tblEmployees. On the next Field line, add the ReservationID field from tblReservations, the FacilityName field from tblFacilities, the RoomNumber field from tblReservations, and the RoomType field from tblFacilityRooms. Add an expression in the next field to calculate the actual charge per day. Remember, you could use the DailyRate field from tblReservations, but that's not an accurate reflection of how much the room costs per day when the employee stays a week or more. Your expression should look like this:

```
DailyCharge: CCur(Round(tblReservations.TotalCharge /
(tblReservations.CheckOutDate - tblReservations.CheckInDate), 2))
```

Your query design should now look something like Figure 9-13.



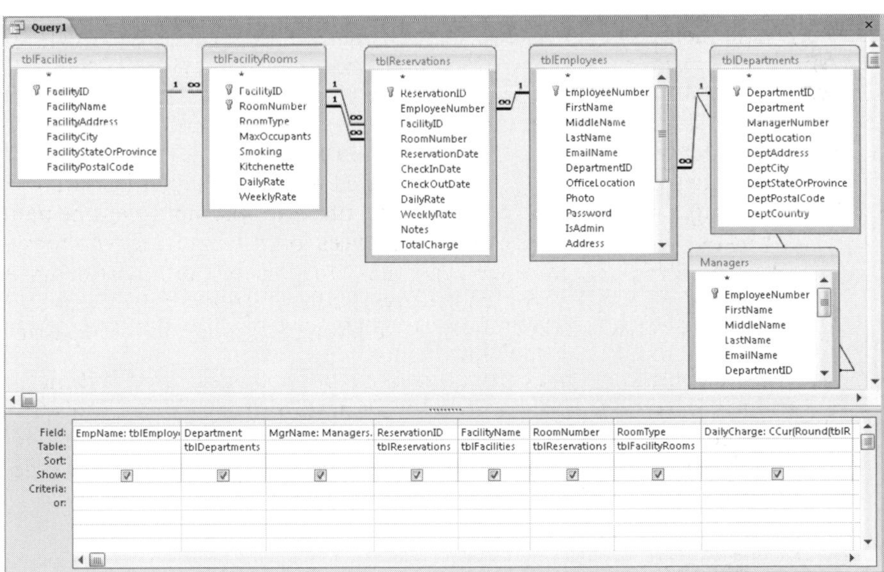


**Figure 9-13** You can design a complex query to gather together many details about reservations.

Each row in tblReservations represents a stay of one or more days, but any report you create later might need to work with detail by individual day. To do that, you need to "explode" each single row in tblReservations into a row per day for the duration of the reservation. Recall from Chapter 8 that you'll find a "driver" table–ztblDates–full of dates to accomplish this task. The table contains date values, one per day, for dates from January 1, 1992, to December 31, 2035.

Include this table in your query and notice that there's no join line from it to any of the tables. When you add a table with no join defined to another table or set of records, the query returns the *Cartesian product* of the two sets of records–every row in the first table or set of records is matched with every row in the second table or set of records. In this case, each reservation will now be matched with each of the separate date values in ztblDates.

When you run this query later to create your working statistics table, you're not going to want to have to open up the query each time in Design view to filter the dates. A couple of parameters would be a good idea here. Add the DateValue field from ztblDates and enter **Between [Start Date] And [End Date]** under this field on the Criteria line. Click the Parameters button in the Show/Hide group of the Design contextual tab, enter both parameters (**[Start Date]** and **[End Date]**), and set the data type to Date/Time. You have now provided a way to limit the "explosion" of rows to the dates of interest.

The final step is to further limit the rows created based on the CheckInDate and CheckOutDate fields in tblReservations. Any reservation that crosses the time span of interest is going to be for a few days or a few weeks. Add the CheckInDate and CheckOutDate fields from tblReservations, and clear the Show check box under both. In the Criteria row under CheckInDate, enter

```
<=ztblDates.DateValue
```

Under CheckOutDate, enter

```
>ztblDates.DateValue
```

This forces the query to keep any rows where DateValue from ztblDates is within the time span of each reservation row. You now have one row per date for each reservation. Your query should now look like Figure 9-14.

Switch to Datasheet view to verify that you'll get the rows you want. The sample data contains reservations from February 28, 2007, through September 15, 2007. To get data for the second quarter of 2007, you can reply to the two parameter prompts with April 1, 2007, and June 30, 2007. Your result should look like Figure 9-15.

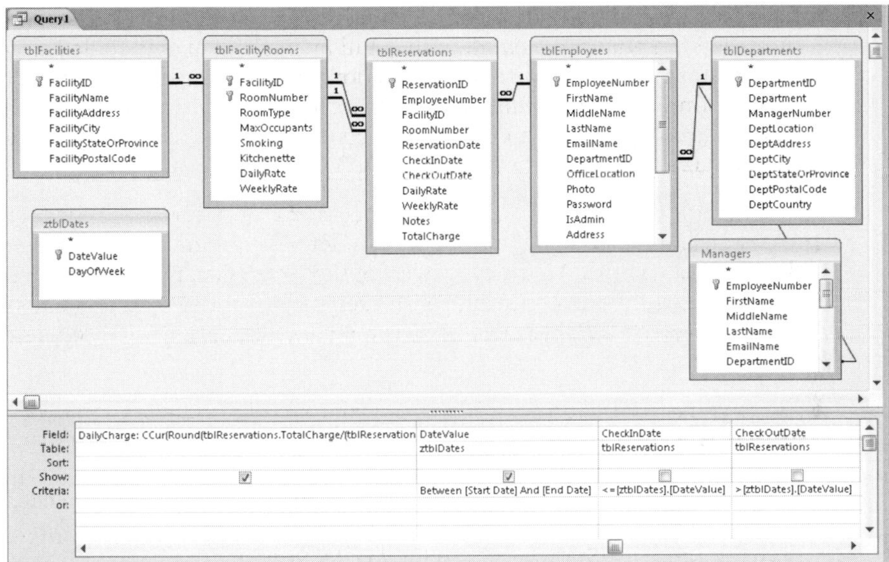


**Figure 9-14** Build a complex parameter query to expand reservation details over a specified time span.

Query1

| EmpName | Department | MgrName | Reservation | Name | Room | Type | DailyCharge | DateValue |
|---|---|---|---|---|---|---|---|---|
| Adams, Jay | Housing Administrat | Richins, Jack S. | 15 | Main Campus | 206 | 1BR Suite - 1 King Be | $75.45 | 04-Apr-2007 |
| Adams, Jay | Housing Administrat | Richins, Jack S. | 15 | Main Campus | 206 | 1BR Suite - 1 King Be | $75.45 | 05-Apr-2007 |
| Adams, Jay | Housing Administrat | Richins, Jack S. | 15 | Main Campus | 206 | 1BR Suite - 1 King Be | $75.45 | 06-Apr-2007 |
| Adams, Jay | Housing Administrat | Richins, Jack S. | 15 | Main Campus | 206 | 1BR Suite - 1 King Be | $75.45 | 07-Apr-2007 |
| Adams, Jay | Housing Administrat | Richins, Jack S. | 15 | Main Campus | 206 | 1BR Suite - 1 King Be | $75.45 | 08-Apr-2007 |
| Adams, Jay | Housing Administrat | Richins, Jack S. | 15 | Main Campus | 206 | 1BR Suite - 1 King Be | $75.45 | 09-Apr-2007 |
| Adams, Jay | Housing Administrat | Richins, Jack S. | 15 | Main Campus | 206 | 1BR Suite - 1 King Be | $75.45 | 10-Apr-2007 |
| Adams, Jay | Housing Administrat | Richins, Jack S. | 15 | Main Campus | 206 | 1BR Suite - 1 King Be | $75.45 | 11-Apr-2007 |
| Adams, Jay | Housing Administrat | Richins, Jack S. | 15 | Main Campus | 206 | 1BR Suite - 1 King Be | $75.45 | 12-Apr-2007 |
| Adams, Jay | Housing Administrat | Richins, Jack S. | 15 | Main Campus | 206 | 1BR Suite - 1 King Be | $75.45 | 13-Apr-2007 |
| Adams, Jay | Housing Administrat | Richins, Jack S. | 15 | Main Campus | 206 | 1BR Suite - 1 King Be | $75.45 | 14-Apr-2007 |
| Richins, Jack S. | Housing Administrat | Richins, Jack S. | 2 | Main Campus | 111 | 2BR Suite - 1 King, 2 | $94.55 | 01-Apr-2007 |
| Richins, Jack S. | Housing Administrat | Richins, Jack S. | 2 | Main Campus | 111 | 2BR Suite - 1 King, 2 | $94.55 | 02-Apr-2007 |
| Richins, Jack S. | Housing Administrat | Richins, Jack S. | 2 | Main Campus | 111 | 2BR Suite - 1 King, 2 | $94.55 | 03-Apr-2007 |
| Richins, Jack S. | Housing Administrat | Richins, Jack S. | 14 | Main Campus | 708 | Studio - Queen Sofa | $50.00 | 27-Apr-2007 |
| Richins, Jack S. | Housing Administrat | Richins, Jack S. | 14 | Main Campus | 708 | Studio - Queen Sofa | $50.00 | 28-Apr-2007 |
| Richins, Jack S. | Housing Administrat | Richins, Jack S. | 14 | Main Campus | 708 | Studio - Queen Sofa | $50.00 | 29-Apr-2007 |
| Richins, Jack S. | Housing Administrat | Richins, Jack S. | 14 | Main Campus | 708 | Studio - Queen Sofa | $50.00 | 30-Apr-2007 |
| Richins, Jack S. | Housing Administrat | Richins, Jack S. | 14 | Main Campus | 708 | Studio - Queen Sofa | $50.00 | 01-May-2007 |
| Richins, Jack S. | Housing Administrat | Richins, Jack S. | 16 | South Campu | 111 | Studio - Queen Sofa | $36.43 | 20-May-2007 |
| Richins, Jack S. | Housing Administrat | Richins, Jack S. | 16 | South Campu | 111 | Studio - Queen Sofa | $36.43 | 21-May-2007 |
| Richins, Jack S. | Housing Administrat | Richins, Jack S. | 16 | South Campu | 111 | Studio - Queen Sofa | $36.43 | 22-May-2007 |
| Richins, Jack S. | Housing Administrat | Richins, Jack S. | 16 | South Campu | 111 | Studio - Queen Sofa | $36.43 | 23-May-2007 |
| Richins, Jack S. | Housing Administrat | Richins, Jack S. | 16 | South Campu | 111 | Studio - Queen Sofa | $36.43 | 24-May-2007 |
| Richins, Jack S. | Housing Administrat | Richins, Jack S. | 16 | South Campu | 111 | Studio - Queen Sofa | $36.43 | 25-May-2007 |
| Richins, Jack S. | Housing Administrat | Richins, Jack S. | 16 | South Campu | 111 | Studio - Queen Sofa | $36.43 | 26-May-2007 |

Record: 1 of 290 No Filter Search

**Figure 9-15** This is the recordset of the select query shown in Figure 9-14, for the second quarter of 2007.

To convert this select query to a make-table query, switch back to Design view and click the Make Table command in the Query Type group of the Design tab below Query Tools. Access displays the Make Table dialog box, shown in Figure 9-16. Type an appropriate name for the summary table you are creating, and click OK to close the dialog box.

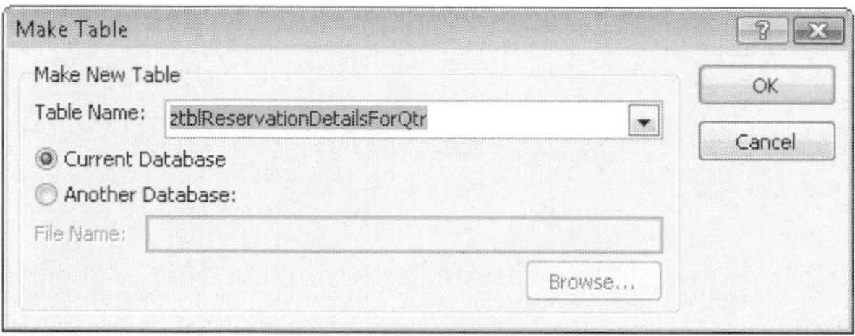


**Figure 9-16** In the Make Table dialog box, type a name for your summary table.



At any time, you can change the name of the table your query creates. Click the Property Sheet button in the Show/Hide group of the Design tab below Query Tools whenever the query is in Design view and change the Destination Table property. In this case, we entered a working table name. (We tend to prefix our working tables with the letter *z* to put them at the bottom of the table list.) After you run this query for a particular quarter, you're probably going to rename the table to indicate the actual quarter's worth of data that the table contains. You can find this make-table query saved in the sample database as qxmplReservationDetailsMakeTable.

## Running a Make-Table Query

After you set up a make-table query, you can run it by clicking the Run command in the Results group on the Design tab below Query Tools. After you respond to the date parameter prompts, Access selects the records that it will place in the new table and displays a confirmation dialog box, as shown in Figure 9-17, that informs you how many rows you'll be inserting into the new table.

Click Yes to create your new table and insert the rows. Click the menu at the top of the Navigation Pane, click Object Type under Navigate To Category, and click Tables under Filter By Group to bring up the table list, which should now include the name of your new table. Open the table in Datasheet view to verify the information, as shown in Figure 9-18.

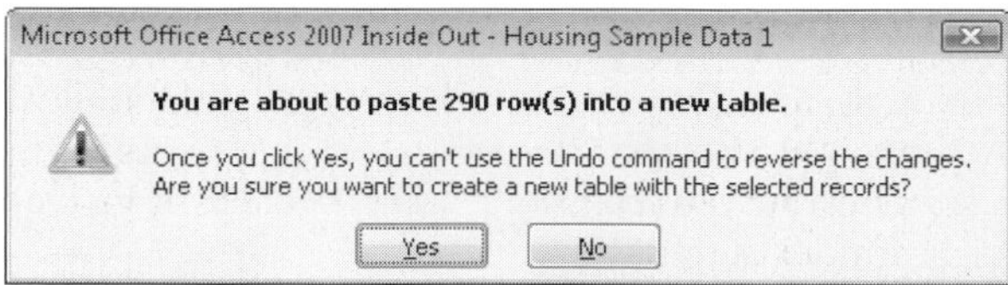


**Figure 9-17** This dialog box asks you to confirm the preliminary results of a make-table query.

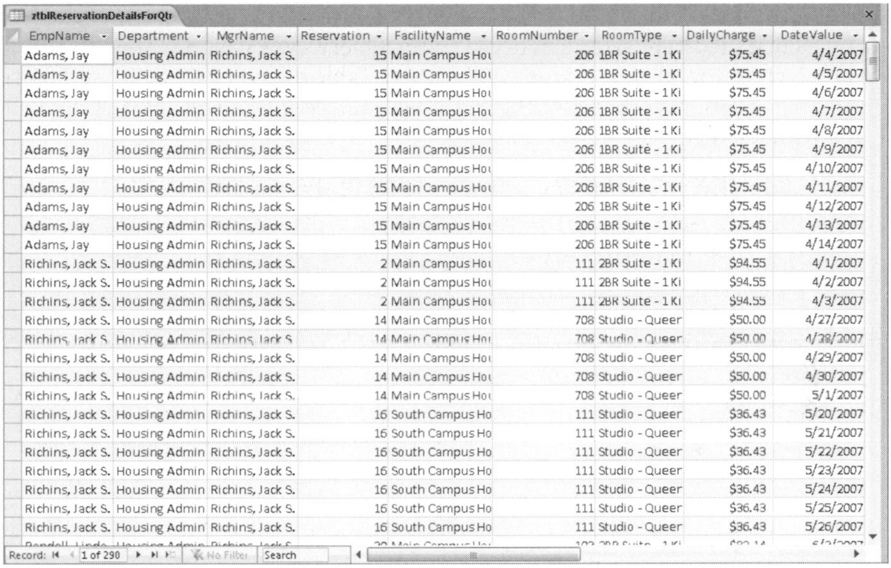
ztblReservationDetailsForQtr

| EmpName | Department | MgrName | Reservation | FacilityName | RoomNumber | RoomType | DailyCharge | DateValue |
|---|---|---|---|---|---|---|---|---|
| Adams, Jay | Housing Admin | Richins, Jack S. | 15 | Main Campus Hot | 206 | 1BR Suite - 1 Ki | $75.45 | 4/4/2007 |
| Adams, Jay | Housing Admin | Richins, Jack S. | 15 | Main Campus Hot | 206 | 1BR Suite - 1 Ki | $75.45 | 4/5/2007 |
| Adams, Jay | Housing Admin | Richins, Jack S. | 15 | Main Campus Hot | 206 | 1BR Suite - 1 Ki | $75.45 | 4/6/2007 |
| Adams, Jay | Housing Admin | Richins, Jack S. | 15 | Main Campus Hot | 206 | 1BR Suite - 1 Ki | $75.45 | 4/7/2007 |
| Adams, Jay | Housing Admin | Richins, Jack S. | 15 | Main Campus Hot | 206 | 1BR Suite - 1 Ki | $75.45 | 4/8/2007 |
| Adams, Jay | Housing Admin | Richins, Jack S. | 15 | Main Campus Hot | 206 | 1BR Suite - 1 Ki | $75.45 | 4/9/2007 |
| Adams, Jay | Housing Admin | Richins, Jack S. | 15 | Main Campus Hot | 206 | 1BR Suite - 1 Ki | $75.45 | 4/10/2007 |
| Adams, Jay | Housing Admin | Richins, Jack S. | 15 | Main Campus Hot | 206 | 1BR Suite - 1 Ki | $75.45 | 4/11/2007 |
| Adams, Jay | Housing Admin | Richins, Jack S. | 15 | Main Campus Hot | 206 | 1BR Suite - 1 Ki | $75.45 | 4/12/2007 |
| Adams, Jay | Housing Admin | Richins, Jack S. | 15 | Main Campus Hot | 206 | 1BR Suite - 1 Ki | $75.45 | 4/13/2007 |
| Adams, Jay | Housing Admin | Richins, Jack S. | 15 | Main Campus Hot | 206 | 1BR Suite - 1 Ki | $75.45 | 4/14/2007 |
| Richins, Jack S. | Housing Admin | Richins, Jack S. | 2 | Main Campus Hot | 111 | 2BR Suite - 1 Ki | $94.55 | 4/1/2007 |
| Richins, Jack S. | Housing Admin | Richins, Jack S. | 2 | Main Campus Hot | 111 | 2BR Suite - 1 Ki | $94.55 | 4/2/2007 |
| Richins, Jack S. | Housing Admin | Richins, Jack S. | 2 | Main Campus Hot | 111 | 2BR Suite - 1 Ki | $94.55 | 4/3/2007 |
| Richins, Jack S. | Housing Admin | Richins, Jack S. | 14 | Main Campus Hot | 708 | Studio - Queer | $50.00 | 4/27/2007 |
| Richins, Jack S. | Housing Admin | Richins, Jack S. | 14 | Main Campus Hot | 708 | Studio - Queer | $50.00 | 4/28/2007 |
| Richins, Jack S. | Housing Admin | Richins, Jack S. | 14 | Main Campus Hot | 708 | Studio - Queer | $50.00 | 4/29/2007 |
| Richins, Jack S. | Housing Admin | Richins, Jack S. | 14 | Main Campus Hot | 708 | Studio - Queer | $50.00 | 4/30/2007 |
| Richins, Jack S. | Housing Admin | Richins, Jack S. | 14 | Main Campus Hot | 708 | Studio - Queer | $50.00 | 5/1/2007 |
| Richins, Jack S. | Housing Admin | Richins, Jack S. | 16 | South Campus Ho | 111 | Studio - Queer | $36.43 | 5/20/2007 |
| Richins, Jack S. | Housing Admin | Richins, Jack S. | 16 | South Campus Ho | 111 | Studio - Queer | $36.43 | 5/21/2007 |
| Richins, Jack S. | Housing Admin | Richins, Jack S. | 16 | South Campus Ho | 111 | Studio - Queer | $36.43 | 5/22/2007 |
| Richins, Jack S. | Housing Admin | Richins, Jack S. | 16 | South Campus Ho | 111 | Studio - Queer | $36.43 | 5/23/2007 |
| Richins, Jack S. | Housing Admin | Richins, Jack S. | 16 | South Campus Ho | 111 | Studio - Queer | $36.43 | 5/24/2007 |
| Richins, Jack S. | Housing Admin | Richins, Jack S. | 16 | South Campus Ho | 111 | Studio - Queer | $36.43 | 5/25/2007 |
| Richins, Jack S. | Housing Admin | Richins, Jack S. | 16 | South Campus Ho | 111 | Studio - Queer | $36.43 | 5/26/2007 |

Record: 1 of 290 No Filter Search

**Figure 9-18** The new table is the result of running the qxmplReservationDetailsMakeTable query.

## INSIDE OUT Make-Table Query Limitations

One of the shortcomings of a make-table query is it propagates only the field name and data type to the resulting table. Running the query does not set other property settings such as Caption or Decimal Places in the target table. This is why you see only field names instead of the original captions in Datasheet view. Notice also that the sequence of rows in the new table (Figure 9-18) does not match the sequence of rows you saw when you looked at the Datasheet view of your make-table query (Figure 9-15). Because the data in a table created with a make-table query has no primary key, Access returns the rows in the order that they're stored physically in the database.

You might want to switch to Design view, as shown in Figure 9-19, to correct field names or to define formatting information. As you can see, Access copies only basic field attributes when creating a new table.

At a minimum, you should define a primary key that contains the DateValue and ReservationID fields. You might also want to define default formats for the date/time fields. If you're planning to create reports on this data that sort or group by department or facility, you should add indexes to those fields.

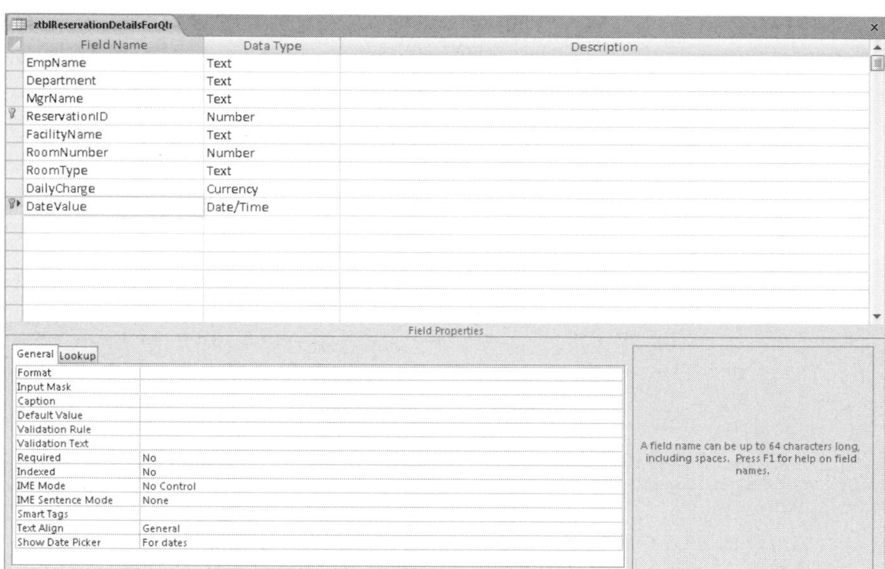


**Figure 9-19** In Design view, you can modify the design of the table created by the qxmplReservationDetailsMakeTable query.



# Inserting Data from Another Table

Using an append query, you can copy a selected set of information from one or more tables and insert it into another table. You can also use an append query to bring data from another source into your database—for example, a list of names and addresses purchased from a mailing list company—and then edit the data and insert it into an existing table. (You learned how to import data from external sources in Chapter 6, "Importing and Linking Data.")

An append query, like a make-table query, provides a way to collect calculated totals or unnormalized rows from several tables. The difference is that a make-table query always creates a new table from the data you select, but an append query copies the data into an existing table that might or might not contain data. You must always modify the design of the table that a make-table query creates (if only to add efficient search indexes) to make it work optimally. Because the target table must already exist for an append query, you can explicitly define needed field properties and indexes (including a primary key) in advance. However, it's easier to run into errors because you're trying to insert data that's already there (based on the primary key you defined), because the data you're adding doesn't match the data type you defined in the table, or because the new data fails one or more validation rules.

**See "Troubleshooting Action Queries" on page 512 for a specific discussion of potential errors.**

## Creating an Append Query

In the previous example, you saw how to take one of the complex queries you learned about in Chapter 8 and turn it into a make-table query. In truth, if you plan to collect such data over several months or years, you should probably design a table to hold the results and use append queries to periodically insert new historical data.

Another good use of append queries is to copy old transaction data to an archive table—either in the current database or another database. For example, after several months or years, the contact events table in the Conrad Systems Contacts application might contain thousands of rows. You might want to keep all events, but copying them to an archive table and deleting them from the main table can improve application performance. (You'll learn about delete queries later in this chapter.)

Let's build an append query to select old contact events and copy them to an archive table. Open the ContactsDataCopy.accdb database to follow along in this exercise. You'll find an empty tblContactEventsHistory table defined in this database.

Start a new query with tblContactEvents. Because the ContactEventTypeID field is a "lookup" to tlkpContactEventTypes, it would be a good idea to preserve the original description of the event rather than the code number. If you kept the original ContactEventTypeID numbers, any changes you made in the future to the related ContactEventTypeDescription information would also change the meaning in the archived records. So, add the tlkpContactEventTypes table so that you can store the current description rather than the ID in the history table. You should see a join line linking the ContactEventTypeID fields in the two tables.

Add the ContactID and ContactDateTime fields from tblContactEvents to the query grid. Include in the grid the ContactEventTypeDescription field from tlkpContactEventTypes. Finally, add to the query design grid the ContactNotes field from tblContactEvents. Because you are saving events in a history table, you don't need the ContactFollowUp and ContactFollowUpDate fields from tblContactEvents.

You want to be able to filter the records on the date and time of the event. Each time you run this query, you probably don't want to archive any recent events, so you need to create a prompt to select events that are a specified number of months old. A couple of handy date/time functions are available for you to do this: DateSerial and DateAdd. DateSerial returns a date value from a year, month, and day input. You can use it to calculate the first date of the current month like this:

```
DateSerial(Year(Date()), Month(Date()), 1)
```

Remember from Table 7-5 on page 376 that the Date function returns today's date, the Year function returns the four-digit year value from a date value, and the Month function returns the month number from a date value. Supplying the value **1** for the day number gets you the date of the first day of the current month.

INSIDE OUT **Using Other Date Expressions**

You can usually think of more than one way to calculate a date value that you want. To calculate the date of the first day of the current month, you could also write the expression

```
(Date() - Day(Date()) + 1)
```

This subtracts the day number of the current date from the current date—resulting in the last day of the previous month—and adds one. For example, August 17, 2007, minus 17 yields July 31, 2007, plus one yields August 1, 2007.

DateAdd adds or subtracts seconds, minutes, hours, days, months, or years from a date value. You specify the interval you want by choosing a value from Table 7-3 on page 366—in this case, you want *m* to indicate that you want to add or subtract months. Finally, you can include a parameter so that you can specify the number of months you want to subtract. So, under the ContactDateTime field, include the criterion

```
<DateAdd("m", -[MonthsAgo], DateSerial(Year(Date()),Month(Date()),1))
```

Click the Parameters button in the Show/Hide group of the Design tab below Query Tools and define the MonthsAgo parameter as Integer. The DateAdd function will return the date that is the number of specified months in the past from the first date of the current month. For example, if today is August 17, 2007, when you respond **6** to MonthsAgo, the expression returns February 1, 2007 (six months prior to August 1). Making sure that the value in ContactDateTime is less than this value ensures that you archive only contacts that are at least six months old. Your query up to this point should look like Figure 9-20.

The sample database contains contact events from January 11, 2007, through July 9, 2007. If you want to experiment with this query, you need to take into account the current date on your computer. For example, if you're running this query in January of 2008, you must specify a MonthsAgo value of no more than 12 to see any records. Likewise, specifying a MonthsAgo value of less than 6 shows you all the records.

Now, it's time to turn this into an append query. Click the Append button in the Query Type group of the Design tab below Query Tools. You'll see the dialog box shown in Figure 9-21, asking you where you want the selected rows inserted (appended).

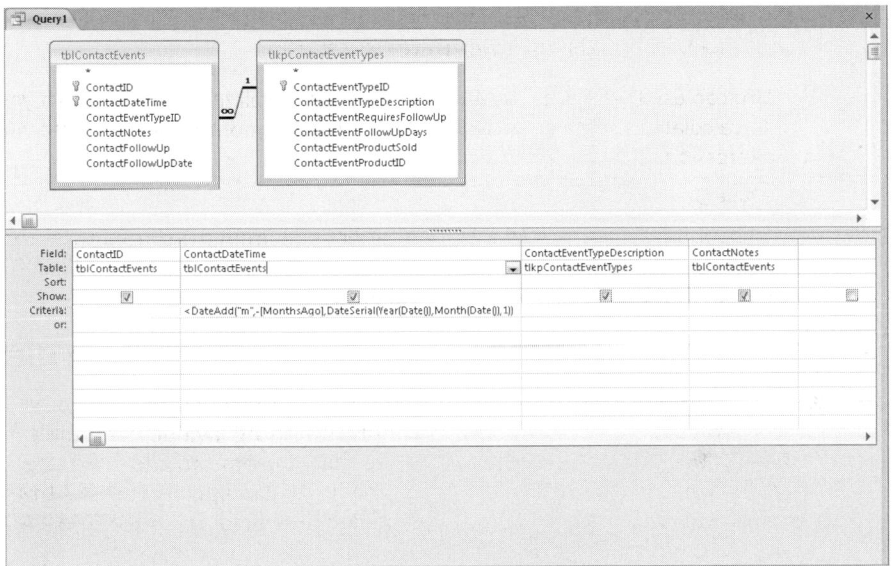


**Figure 9-20** This query finds old contact events to archive.

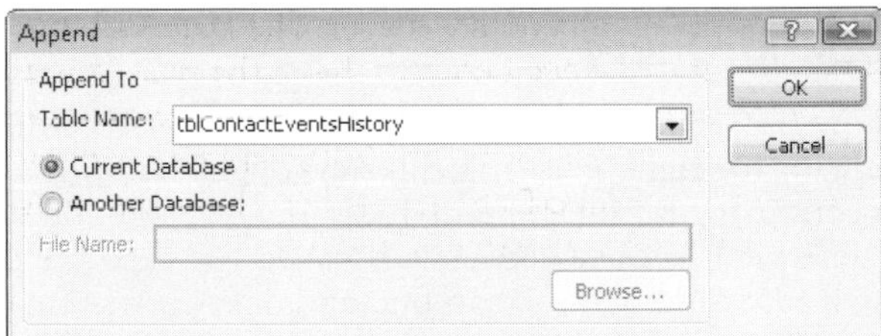


**Figure 9-21** After you click the Append button on the Ribbon, specify the target table of an append query.

Notice that the default is to append the data into a table in the current database. You can select the Another Database option and either type the path and name of the target database or click the Browse button to find the file you want. This feature could be particularly handy if you want to archive the records to another file. In this case, click the arrow to the right of Table Name, select tblContactEventsHistory in the current database, and click OK. Your query design now looks like Figure 9-22.

Notice that Access added an Append To line and automatically filled in the matching field names from the target table. Remember, you want to append the ContactEventTypeDescription field from tlkpContactEventTypes to the ContactEventType field in the history table, so select that field from the list on the Append To line under ContactEventTypeDescription.

You're now ready to run this query in the next section. You can find the query saved as qxmplArchiveContactEvents in the sample database. You'll also find a companion qxmplArchiveContactProducts query.

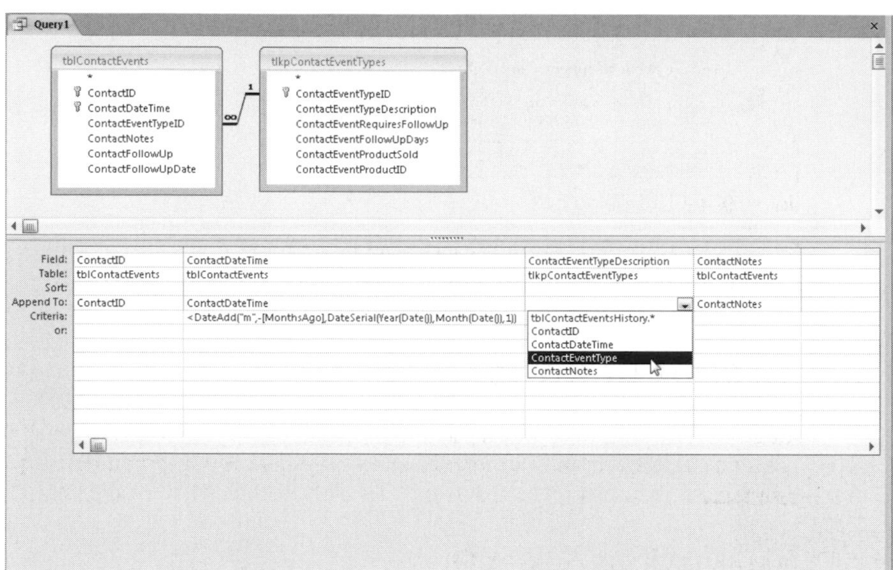


**Figure 9-22** In the Append To row you can specify the target fields in an append query.

## Running an Append Query

As with other action queries, you can run an append query as a select query first to be sure that you'll be copying the right rows. You can start out by building a select query, running it, and then converting it to an append query, or you can build the append query directly and then switch to Datasheet view from Design view to examine the data that the query will add. Although you can find and delete rows that you append in error, you can save time if you make a backup of the target table first.

After you confirm that the query will append the right rows, you can either run it directly from Design view or save it and run it from the Navigation Pane. When you run the qxmplArchiveContactEvents query and respond to the MonthsAgo prompt so that Access archives events earlier than March 1, 2007, Access should tell you that 34 rows will be appended, as shown in Figure 9-23. (For example, if the current date on your computer is any day in May 2007, enter 2 in response to the prompt for the MonthsAgo value.) If you want to append the rows to the tblContactEventsHistory table, click Yes in the confirmation dialog box. Note that after you click Yes, the only way to undo these changes is to go to the target table and either select and delete the rows manually or build a delete query to do it.

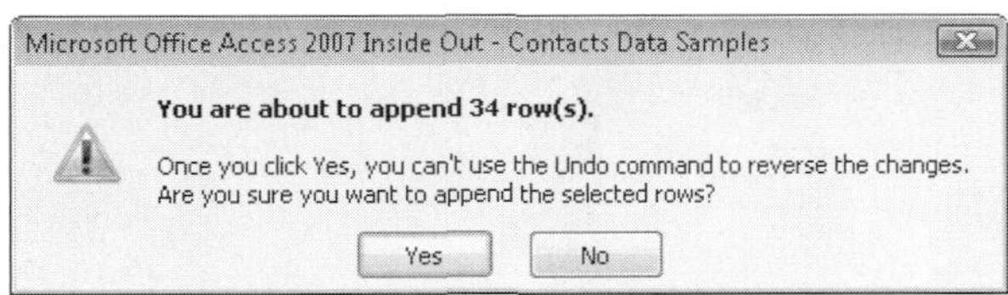


**Figure 9-23** This dialog box asks you to confirm the appending of rows.

Go ahead and append these 34 rows. In "Troubleshooting Action Queries" on page 512, we'll take a look at what happens if you try to run this query again.

# Deleting Groups of Rows

You're not likely to keep all the data in your database forever. You'll probably summarize some of your detailed information as time goes by and then delete the data you no longer need. You can remove sets of records from your database using a delete query.

## Testing with a Select Query

After you have copied all the old contact event and contact product data to the archive tables, you might want to remove this information from the active tables. This is clearly the kind of query that you will want to save so that you can use it again and again. You can design the query to automatically calculate which records to delete based on the current system date and a month parameter as you did in the append queries.

As with an update query, it's a good idea to test which rows will be affected by a delete query by first building a select query to isolate these records. Start a new query with tblContactEvents and include the asterisk (*) field in the query grid. A delete query acts on entire rows, so including the "all fields" indicator will ultimately tell the delete query from which table the rows should be deleted. Add the ContactDateTime field to the design grid, and clear the Show check box. This time, let's use a specific date value to choose rows to delete. In the Criteria line under the ContactDateTime field enter

```
<[Oldest Date to Keep:]
```

Click the Parameters button in the Show/Hide group of the Design tab, and define your parameter as a Date/Time data type. Your query should look like Figure 9-24.

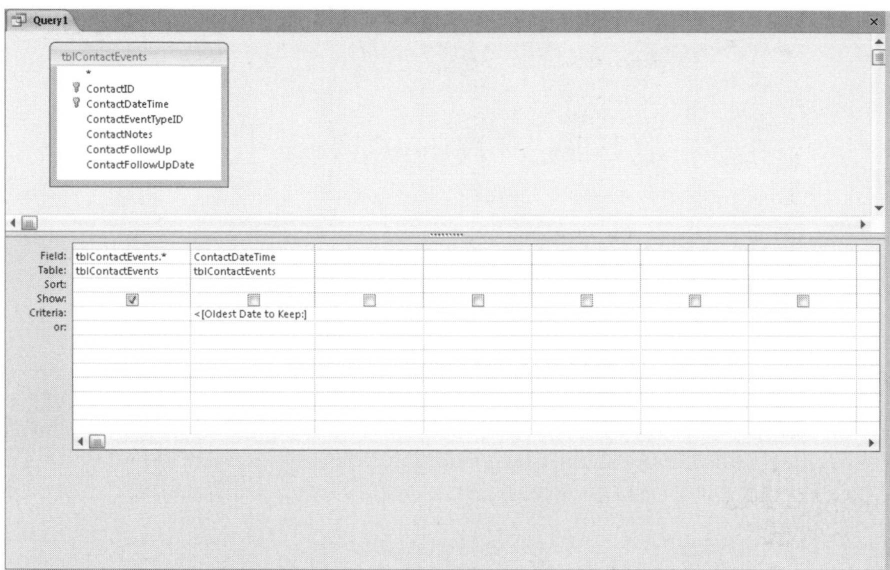

Figure 9-24 This query uses a date parameter to select old contact events.

When you switch to Datasheet view for this query, Access prompts you for a date parameter, as shown in Figure 9-25. In the Enter Parameter Value dialog box, enter **3/1/2007** to see all the old contact events from March 1, 2007 or earlier. The result is shown in Figure 9-26.

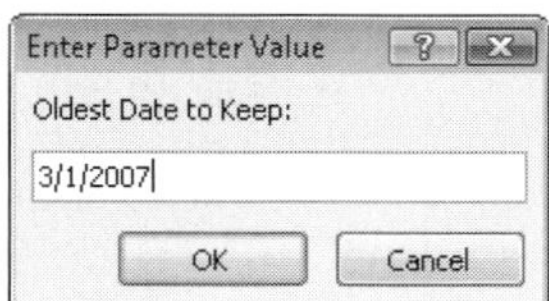

Figure 9-25 Enter the query date parameter when Access prompts you.

INSIDE OUT

### Using Different Date Formats

Access 2007 recognizes several different formats for date parameters. For example, for the first day of March in 2007, you can enter any of the following:

```
3/1/2007      March 1, 2007      1 MAR 2007
```

Query1

| ContactID | Date / Time | Type | Notes | Follow up? | Follow-up Date |
|---|---|---|---|---|---|
| 1 | 02/02/2007 15:57 | 14 | | ☑ | 1/28/2008 |
| 1 | 02/05/2007 14:28 | 12 | | ☑ | 1/31/2008 |
| 2 | 02/24/2007 17:23 | 1 | | ☐ | |
| 3 | 02/13/2007 10:00 | 16 | | ☑ | 3/15/2007 |
| 4 | 01/25/2007 14:34 | 10 | | ☑ | 1/20/2008 |
| 5 | 01/11/2007 11:44 | 17 | | ☑ | 1/6/2008 |
| 5 | 01/23/2007 14:57 | 9 | | ☑ | 1/18/2008 |
| 6 | 01/13/2007 16:24 | 8 | | ☑ | 2/12/2007 |
| 6 | 01/26/2007 10:47 | 5 | | ☐ | |
| 6 | 01/26/2007 13:32 | 1 | | ☐ | |
| 7 | 01/31/2007 11:58 | 5 | | ☐ | |
| 7 | 02/19/2007 16:00 | 13 | | ☑ | 2/14/2008 |
| 8 | 02/22/2007 14:41 | 12 | | ☑ | 2/17/2008 |
| 10 | 02/04/2007 13:03 | 12 | | ☑ | 1/30/2008 |
| 11 | 02/18/2007 13:38 | 10 | | ☑ | 2/13/2008 |
| 13 | 02/14/2007 8:54 | 14 | | ☑ | 2/9/2008 |
| 14 | 02/11/2007 12:50 | 5 | | ☐ | |
| 14 | 02/25/2007 15:27 | 15 | | ☑ | 2/20/2008 |
| 15 | 02/24/2007 15:07 | 4 | | ☐ | |
| 16 | 01/12/2007 8:41 | 12 | | ☑ | 1/7/2008 |
| 16 | 01/16/2007 16:35 | 13 | | ☑ | 1/11/2008 |
| 16 | 02/02/2007 17:06 | 7 | | ☑ | 1/28/2008 |
| 17 | 01/12/2007 12:47 | 5 | | ☐ | |
| 17 | 01/28/2007 8:43 | 4 | | ☐ | |
| 17 | 02/23/2007 9:03 | 8 | | ☑ | 3/25/2007 |
| 18 | 02/06/2007 12:11 | 13 | | ☑ | 2/1/2008 |

Record: 1 of 34 No Filter Search

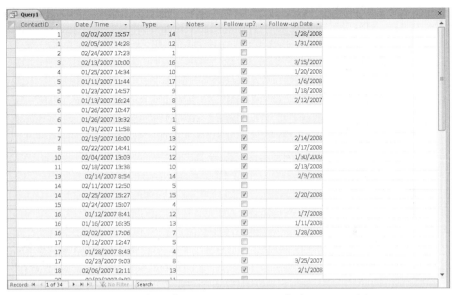

**Figure 9-26** When you run the select query, you can verify the rows to delete.

The append query you saw earlier that copied these rows to an archive table copied 34 rows, which matches what you see here. After you verify that this is what you want, go back to Design view and change the query to a delete query by clicking the Delete command in the Query Type group of the Design tab below Query Tools. Your query should look like Figure 9-27. *Do not run this query!* We'll explain why in the next section.

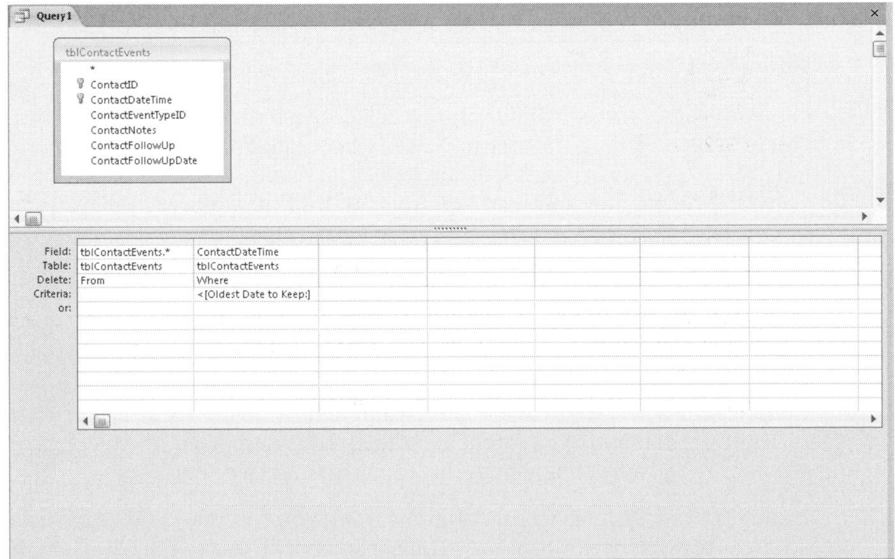


**Figure 9-27** Click the Delete button in the Query Type group on the Ribbon to convert your query to a delete query.

Notice that the query has a new Delete line. In any delete query, you should select From under the "choose all fields" (*) field for the one table from which you want to delete rows. All other fields should indicate Where and have one or more criteria on the Criteria and Or lines.

## Using a Delete Query

Because you won't be able to retrieve any deleted rows, it's a good idea to first make a backup copy of your table, especially if this is the first time that you've run this delete query. Use the procedure described earlier in "Running an Update Query" on page 489 to make a copy of your table.

As you just learned, you can create a delete query from a select query by clicking the Delete command on the Design tab below Query Tools when your query is in Design view. You must be sure that at least one table includes the "choose all fields" indicator (*) and has From specified on the Delete line. Simply click Run in the Results group on the Design tab to delete the rows you specified. Because you included a parameter in this query, you'll need to respond to the Enter Parameter Value dialog box (shown in Figure 9-25) again. Access selects the rows to be deleted and displays the confirmation dialog box shown in Figure 9-28.

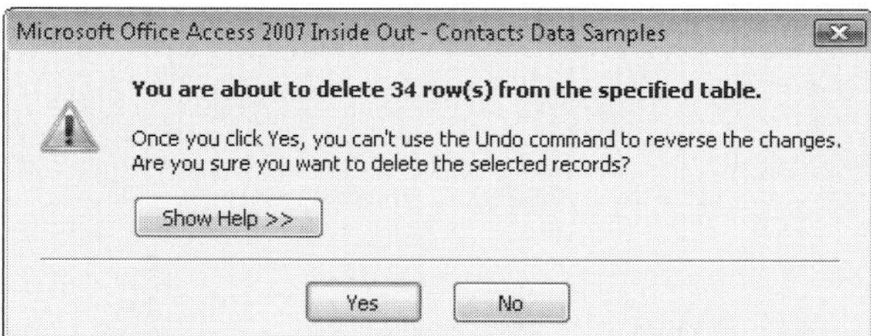


**Figure 9-28** This dialog box asks you to confirm the deletion of rows.

Are you *really, really* sure you want to delete these rows? Are you sure these rows are safely tucked away in the archive table? If so, click Yes to proceed with the deletion. Click No if you're unsure about the rows that Access will delete. (We recommend that you click No for now and read on!) You can find this query saved as qxmplDeleteOldContactEventsUnsafe in the sample database. (Does the query name give you a clue?)

## Deleting Inactive Data

You now know how to copy old contact event and contact product data to an archive table, and how to delete the old contact events from the main table. In some applications, you might want to delete more than just the event records. For example, in an order entry database, you might want to archive and delete the records of old customers who haven't given you any business in more than two years.

In the Conrad Systems Contacts application, you can mark old contacts as inactive so that they disappear from the primary forms you use to edit the data. In "Updating Groups of Rows" on page 486, we showed you how to identify contacts who haven't had any activity in a specified period of time and set the Inactive field so that they don't show up anymore. Because of this feature, archiving and deleting old contacts isn't an issue.

However, you might still want to delete old contact events and contact products that you have archived. We just showed you how to create a delete query to remove rows, but there's a safer way to do it if you have copied the rows elsewhere. Go back to the query you have been building and add tblContactEventsHistory. Create a join line between the ContactID field in tblContactEvents and the ContactID field in tblContactEvents-History. Create another join line between the ContactDateTime field in tblContact-Events and the same field in tblContactEventsHistory. Your query should now look like Figure 9-29.

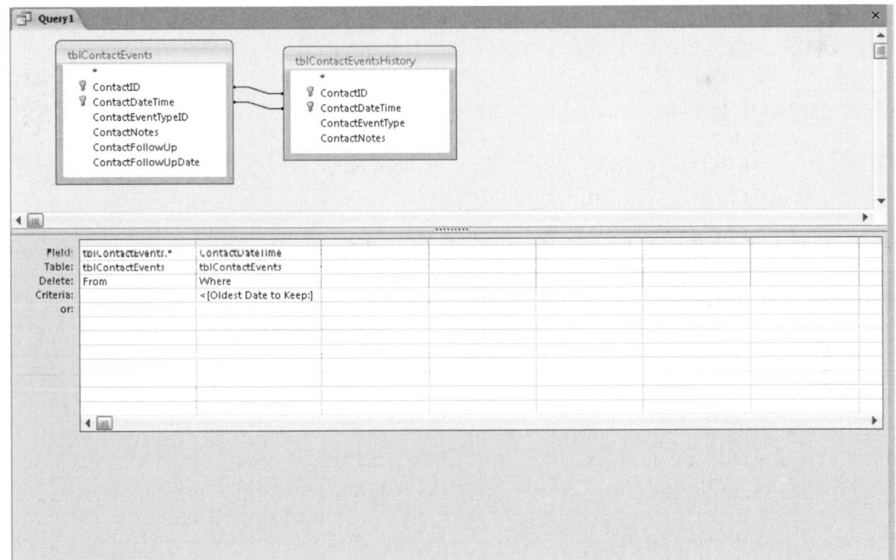


**Figure 9-29** This query allows you to safely delete archived rows.

Remember that the default for a join is to include rows only where the values in both tables match. Now your Delete query won't return any rows from tblContact-Events (where you're performing the delete) unless the row already exists in tblContactEventHistory! Run this query now and reply with any date you like. The query won't delete rows from tblContactEvents unless a copy is safely saved in the archive table. You can find this query saved as qxmplDeleteOldContactEventsSafe in the sample database. There's also a companion query, qxmplDeleteOldContact-ProductsSafe, to deal with contact products.

# Troubleshooting Action Queries

Access 2007 analyzes your action query request and the data you are about to change before it commits changes to your database. When it identifies errors, Access always gives you an opportunity to cancel the operation.

## Solving Common Action Query Errors and Problems

Access identifies (traps) four types of errors during the execution of an action query.

- **Duplicate primary keys** This type of error occurs if you attempt to append a record to a table or update a record in a table, which would result in a duplicate primary key or a duplicate of a unique index key value. Access will not update or append any rows that would create duplicates. For example, if the primary key of a contact event archive table is ContactID and ContactDateTime, Access won't append a record that contains a ContactID and ContactDateTime value already in the table. Before attempting to append such rows, you might have to modify your append query to not select the duplicate rows.
- **Data conversion errors** This type of error occurs if you attempt to append data to an existing table and the data type of the receiving field does not match that of the sending field (and the data in the sending field cannot be converted to the appropriate data type). For example, this error will occur if you attempt to append a text field to an integer field and the text field contains either alphabetic characters or a number string that is too large for the integer field. You might also encounter a conversion error in an update query if you use a formula that attempts a calculation on a field that contains characters. For information on data conversions and potential limitations, see Table 5-3 on page 226.
- **Locked records** This type of error can occur when you run a delete query or an update query on a table that you share with other users on a network. Access cannot update records that are in the process of being updated by some other user. You might want to wait and try again later when no one else is using the affected records to be sure that your update or deletion occurs. Even if you're not sharing the data on a network, you can encounter this error if you have a form or another query open on the data you're updating and have started to change some of the data.
- **Validation rule violations** If any of the rows being inserted or any row being updated violates either a field validation rule or the table validation rule, Access notifies you of an error and does not insert or update any of the rows that fail the validation test. When you have a referential integrity rule defined, you cannot update or delete a row in a way that would violate the rule.

Another problem that can occur, although it isn't an error, is that Access truncates data that is being appended to text or memo fields if the data does not fit. Access does not warn you when this happens. You must be sure (especially with append queries) that you have made the receiving text and memo fields large enough to store the incoming data.

## Looking at an Error Example

Earlier in this chapter, you learned how to create an append query to copy old contact events to an archive table. What do you suppose would happen if you copied rows through December 31, 2006, forgot to delete them from the main table, and then later asked to copy rows through April 30, 2007? If you try this starting with an empty archive table in the ContactsDataCopy.accdb database, run qxmplArchiveContact-Events once, and then run it again with the same or later cut-off month, you'll get an error dialog box similar to the one shown in Figure 9-30.

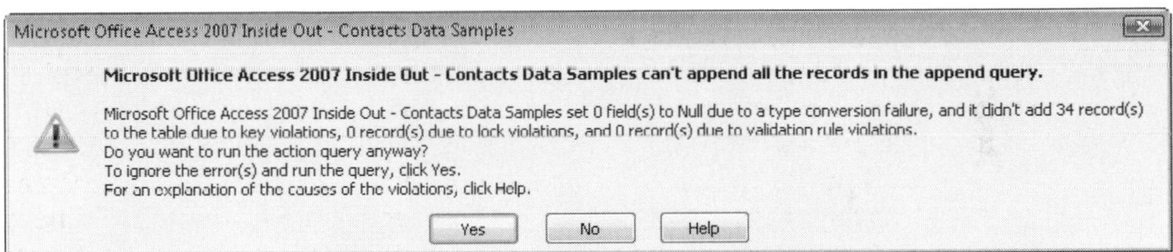


**Figure 9-30** This dialog box alerts you to action query errors.

The dialog box in Figure 9-30 declares that 34 records won't be inserted because of duplicate primary key values. Access didn't find any data conversion errors, locking problems, or validation rule errors. Note that if some fields have data conversion problems, Access might still append the row but leave the field set to Null. When you see this dialog box, you can click Yes to proceed with the changes that Access can make without errors. You might find it difficult later, however, to track down all the records that were not updated successfully. Click No to cancel the append query.

To solve this problem, you can change the "select" part of the query to choose only the rows that haven't already been inserted into the target table. Remember from the previous chapter the technique you used to find "unmatched" rows. You'll apply that same technique to solve this problem.

Open the query you built in the previous section (or qxmplArchiveContactEvents) in Design view. Add tblContactEventsHistory (the target table) to your query. Create join lines from the ContactID field in tblContactEvents to the same field in tblContact-EventsHistory. Do the same with ContactDateTime. Double-click each join line to open the Join Properties dialog box and choose the option to include all rows from tblContactEvents and the matching rows from tblContactEventsHistory. You must do this for each join line so that you end up with both lines pointing to tblContact-EventsHistory. Include the ContactID field from tblContactEventsHistory in the design grid, clear the Append To box underneath it (you don't want to try to insert ContactID twice), and place the criterion Is Null on the Criteria line. Your query should now look like Figure 9-31.

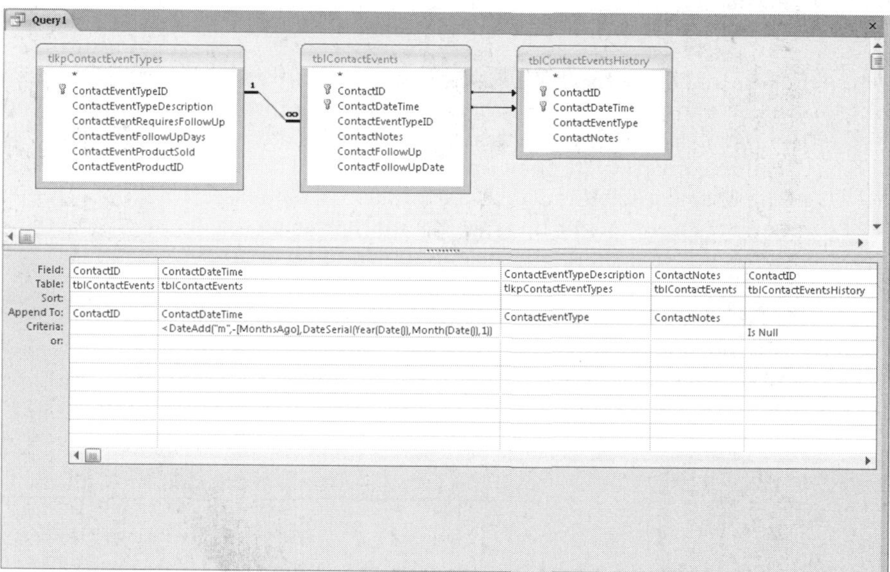


**Figure 9-31** You can design an append query to avoid duplicate row errors.

The end result is that this query will select rows from tblContactEvents only if they don't already exist in the archive table. You can now run this query as many times as you like. If all the rows you choose already exist, the query simply inserts no additional rows. You can find this query saved as qxmplArchiveContactEventsNoDuplicates in the sample database. There's also a companion query, qxmplArchiveContactProducts-NoDuplicates, to handle the archiving of contact product records.

At this point, you should have a reasonable understanding of how action queries can work for you. You can find some more examples of action queries in Article 2, "Understanding SQL," on the companion CD. Now it's time to go on to building the user interface for your application with forms and reports.

PART 3

# Creating Forms and Reports in a Desktop Application

CHAPTER 10

# Using Forms



If you've worked through this book to this point, you should understand all the mechanics of designing and building databases (and connecting to external ones), entering and viewing data in tables, and building queries. An understanding of tables and queries is important before you jump into forms because most of the forms you design will be bound to an underlying table or a query.

This chapter focuses on the external aspects of forms—why forms are useful, what they look like, and how to use them. You'll look at examples of forms from the Conrad Systems Contacts sample database. In Chapters 11, 12 and 13, you'll learn how to design, build, and customize your own forms by learning to build some of the forms you see in the Conrad Systems Contacts and Housing Reservations databases.

## Uses of Forms

Forms are the primary interface between users and your Microsoft Office Access 2007 application. You can design forms for many different purposes.

- **Displaying and editing data** This is the most common use of forms. Forms provide a way to customize the presentation of the data in your database. You can also use forms to change or delete data in your database or add data to it. You can set options in a form to make all or part of your data read-only, to fill in related information from other tables automatically, to calculate the values to be displayed, or to show or hide data on the basis of either the values of other data in the record or the options selected by the user of the form.

- **Controlling application flow** You can design forms that work with macros or with Microsoft Visual Basic procedures to automate the display of certain data or the sequence of certain actions. You can create special controls on your form, called *command buttons*, which run a macro or a Visual Basic procedure when you click them. With macros and Visual Basic procedures, you can open other forms, run queries, restrict the data that is displayed, execute a Ribbon command, set values in records and forms, display customized Ribbons, print reports, and perform a host of other actions. You can also design a form so that macros or Visual Basic procedures run when specific events occur—for example, when someone opens the form, tabs to a specific control, clicks an option on the form, or changes data in the form. See Part 4, "Automating an Access Application," for details about using macros and Visual Basic with forms to automate your application.

- **Accepting input** You can design forms that are used only for entering new data in your database or for providing data values to help automate your application.
- **Displaying messages** Forms can provide information about how to use your application or about upcoming actions. Office Access 2007 also provides a MsgBox macro action and a *MsgBox* Visual Basic function that you can use to display information, warnings, or error messages. See Chapter 20, "Automating Your Application with Visual Basic," for more detail.
- **Printing information** Although you should design and use reports to print most information, you can also print the information displayed in a form. Because you can specify one set of options when Access displays a form and another set of options when Access prints a form, a form can serve a dual role. For example, you might design a form with two sets of display headers and footers, one set for entering an order and another set for printing a customer invoice from the order.

# A Tour of Forms

The Conrad Systems Contacts sample database is full of interesting examples of forms. The rest of this chapter takes you on a tour of some of the major features of those forms and shows you some of the basic techniques for editing data in a form. In the next chapter, you'll learn how to design and build forms for this database.



Begin by opening the Conrad Systems Contacts database (Contacts.accdb) and set the Navigation Pane to display only the forms. To do so, click the Navigation Pane menu, click Object Type under Navigate To Category, and then click Forms under Filter By Group to see the list of available forms. Note that when you open the database, you see a copyright notice followed by a message telling you which form to open to start the application.

## Headers, Detail Sections, and Footers

You'll normally place the information that you want to display from the underlying table or query in the detail section in the center of the Form window. You can add a header at the top of the window or a footer at the bottom of the window to display information or controls that don't need to change as you move through the records.

An interesting form in the Conrad Systems Contacts database that includes both a header and a footer is frmContactSummary. The application uses this form to display the summary results of a contact search whenever the search finds more than five matching contacts. You can also open this form directly from the Navigation Pane—if you do so, it will show you all the contacts in the database. Find the frmContactSummary form in the forms list in the Navigation Pane, right-click the form name, and then click the Open command on the shortcut menu to see a window similar to the one shown in Figure 10-1.

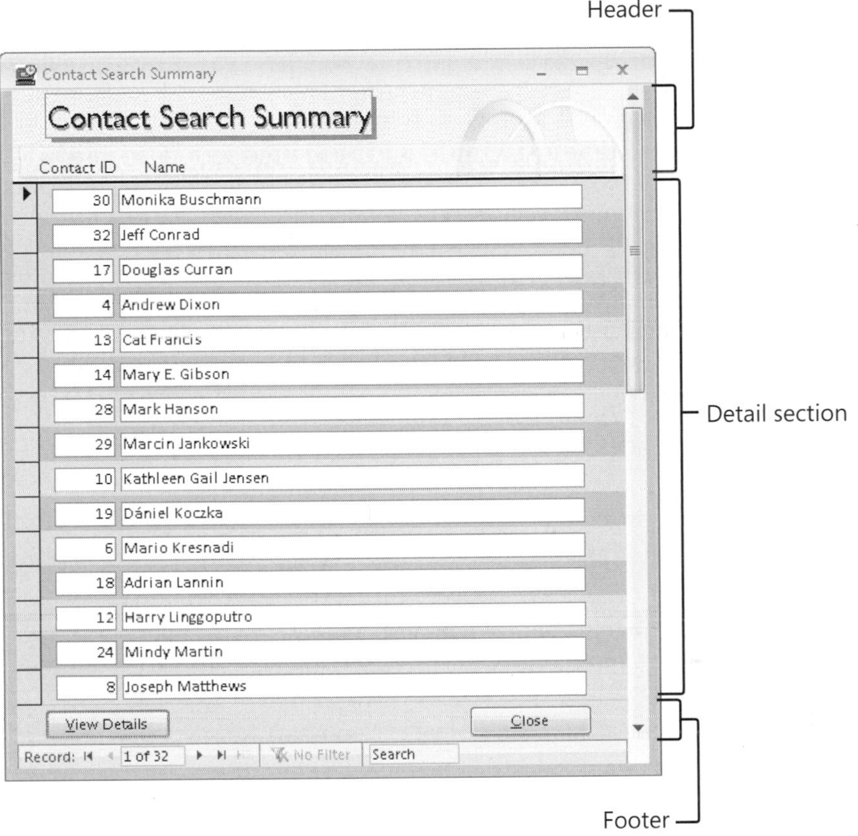


**Figure 10-1** The frmContactSummary form has a header, a detail section, and a footer.

The area at the top of the window containing the title *Contact Search Summary* is the header for the form. The header also includes the column names. The area at the bottom of the window is the footer for the form. You can click the View Details button to see all details for the currently selected contact (the contact with the arrow on the row selector), or you can click Close to close the form. In the lower-left corner of the form is the Record Number box that you saw in tables and queries in Datasheet view. Click the arrow button immediately to the right of the record number to move the row selector arrow to the next contact record in the detail section of the form; notice that the header and footer don't change when you do this. If you move down several records, you can see the records scroll up in the detail section of the form.

If you click the View Details button in the footer, this form closes and the frmContacts form opens, showing details of the contact record that you selected before you clicked the button. The way the form is designed, the View Details button opens the frmContacts form using a filter to show you the currently selected contact. If you decide that you don't want to see details, you can click the Close button in the form footer to dismiss the form.

## Multiple-Page Forms

When you have a lot of information from each record to display in a form, you can design a *multiple-page form*. Open the frmContactsPages form in the Conrad Systems Contacts database to see an example. When you open the form, you'll see the first page of contact data for the first contact. You can use the Record Number box and the buttons in the lower-left corner of the form to move through the records, viewing the first page of information for each contact. Figure 10-2 shows the first page of the second contact record—the records are sorted by last name. (For those of you who want to visit Jeff's Web site, that's his real Web site address in the form!) To see the second page of information for any contact, press the Page Down key. Figure 10-3 shows the second page of Jeff's contact record. (Notice that this form has a header but no footer.) As you view different pages of a multiple-page form, the header at the top of the form (with the form title) doesn't change.

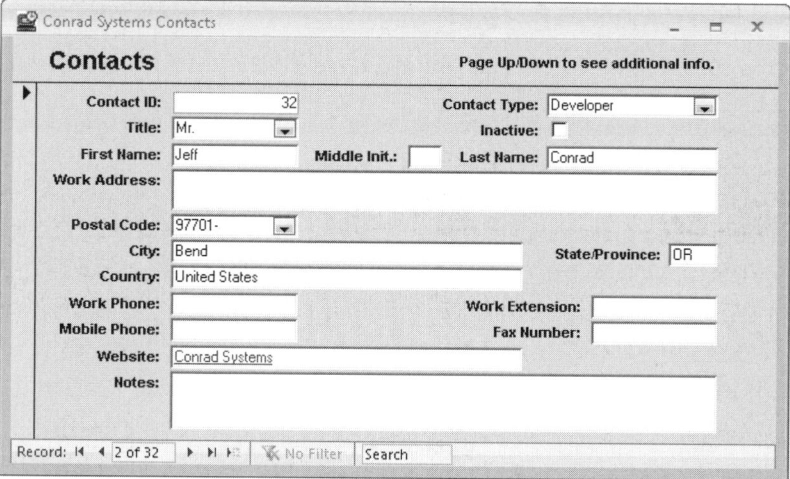


**Figure 10-2** This is the first page of a record in the multiple-page frmContactsPages form.

## Continuous Forms

You can create another type of form that is useful for browsing through and editing a list of records when each record has only a few data fields. This type of form is called a *continuous form*. Rather than showing you only a single record at a time, a continuous form displays formatted records one after the other, in the manner of a datasheet.

The frmContactSummary form shown earlier in Figure 10-1 is a simple continuous form. The frmLkpContactEventTypes form, shown in Figure 10-4, is also a continuous form. You can use the vertical scroll bar to move through the record display, or you can click the buttons in the lower-left corner of the form to move from record to record. Also, you can click the New Record button to move to the blank row below the last record. The application uses this form to let you view and edit the different types of contact events that you might want to log.

Chapter 10

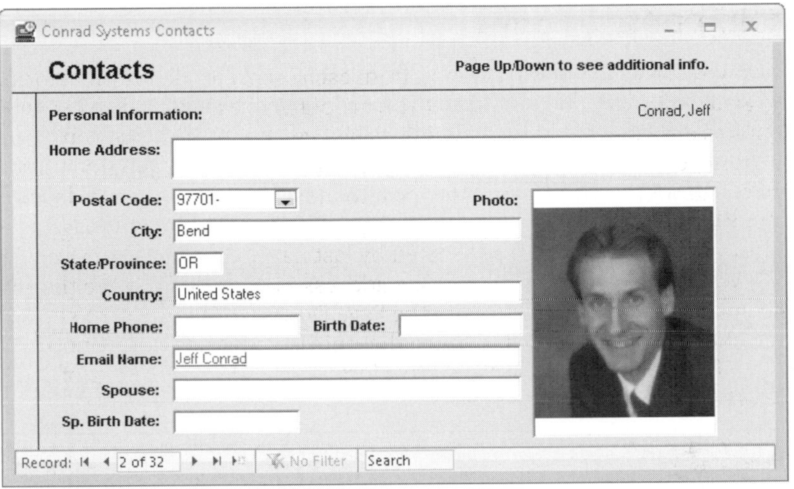


**Figure 10-3** Here is the second page of the same record shown in Figure 10-2.

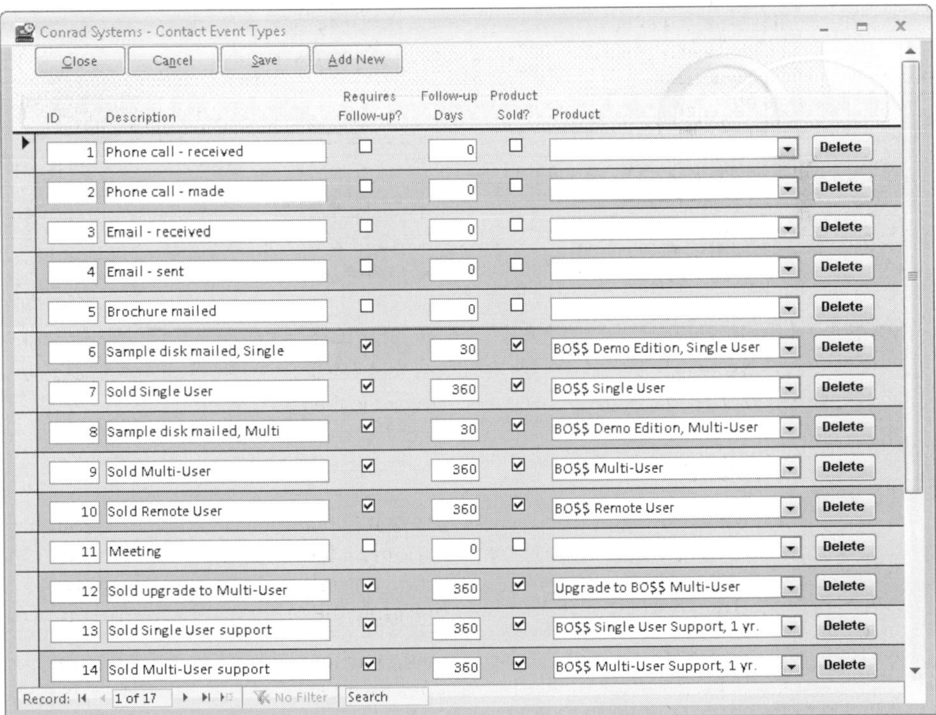


**Figure 10-4** The frmLkpContactEventTypes form in the Conrad Systems Contacts database is a continuous form.

## Split Forms

A new type of form view in Access 2007 called *Split Form* allows you to simultaneously display a record in a regular form view and see a list of records in Datasheet view. Open the frmProducts form in the Conrad Systems Contacts database to see an example, as shown in Figure 10-5. When you open the form, you'll see that the upper half of the form displays the details about one specific product and the lower half of the form displays the complete list of 11 products offered by Conrad Systems.

You can use the Record Number box and the buttons in the lower-left corner of the form to move through the records. Click the Next Record button and notice that the record you are currently viewing in the top half becomes the highlighted record in the bottom half of the form. Depending on the settings in the form's design, you can edit the information about any specific product in either the top or the bottom half of the form.

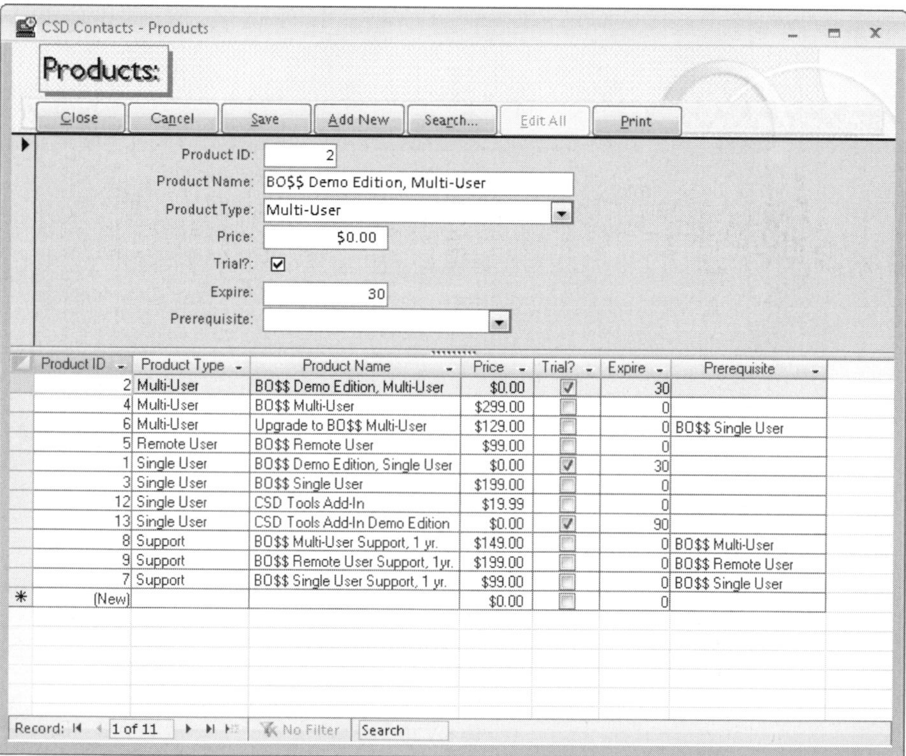


**Figure 10-5** The frmProducts form in the Conrad Systems Contacts database is a split form.

## Subforms

A *subform* is a good way to show related data from the *many* side of a one-to-many relationship. For example, the frmCompanies form, shown in Figure 10-6, has a subform to display the related contacts. Although this form looks much like a single display panel, it has a subform (which looks more like a datasheet than a form) embedded in the main form. The main part of the frmCompanies form displays information from the tblCompanies table, while the subform in the lower part of the window shows information from the tblCompanyContacts table about the contacts related to the current company.

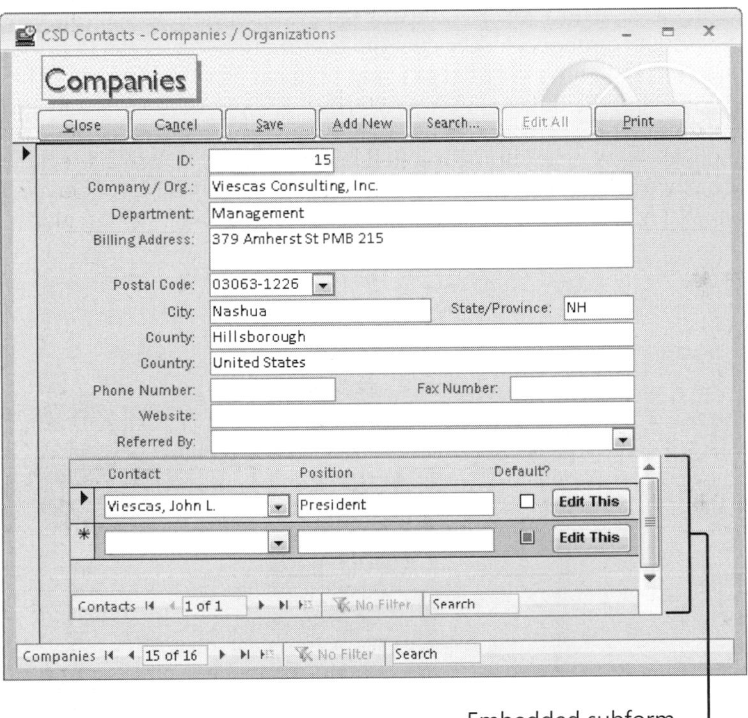


**Figure 10-6** The frmCompanies form has an embedded subform that shows the related contacts.

This form looks quite complicated, but it really isn't difficult to build. Because the Conrad Systems Contacts database is well designed, it doesn't take much effort to build the queries that allow the form to display information from three different tables. Most of the work of creating the form goes into selecting and placing the controls that display the data. To link a subform to a main form, you have to set only two properties that tell Access which linking fields to use. (These are actually the same Link Master Fields and Link Child Fields properties you learned about in Chapter 8, "Building Complex Queries," when you defined a subdatasheet for a query.) In Chapter 13, "Advanced Form Design," you'll build a subform and link it to a form.

## Pop-Up Forms

Sometimes it's useful to provide information in a window that stays on top regardless of where you move the focus in your application. You've probably noticed that the default behavior for windows in Microsoft Windows is for the active window to move to the front and for all other windows to move behind the active one. One exception in Access is the property sheet for any object in Design view. If you grab the property sheet and undock it, it stays floating on top so that you can still access its settings regardless of what you are doing behind it. This sort of floating window is called a *pop-up window*.

You can create forms in Access that open in pop-up windows (called pop-up forms in Access). If you open any form in the Conrad Systems Contacts application and then click the About command on the custom Ribbon, this opens the frmAbout form shown in Figure 10-7, which is designed as a pop-up form. See Chapter 24, "The Finishing Touches," for more details about how to create custom Ribbons for forms. If you still have frmCompanies open, you can click the About command on the Ribbon. Or, you can switch to the Navigation Pane and open the frmAbout form directly to see how it behaves. Notice that if you click in the open form or the window behind it, the frmAbout form stays on top. Click the Close button on the pop-up form to close it.

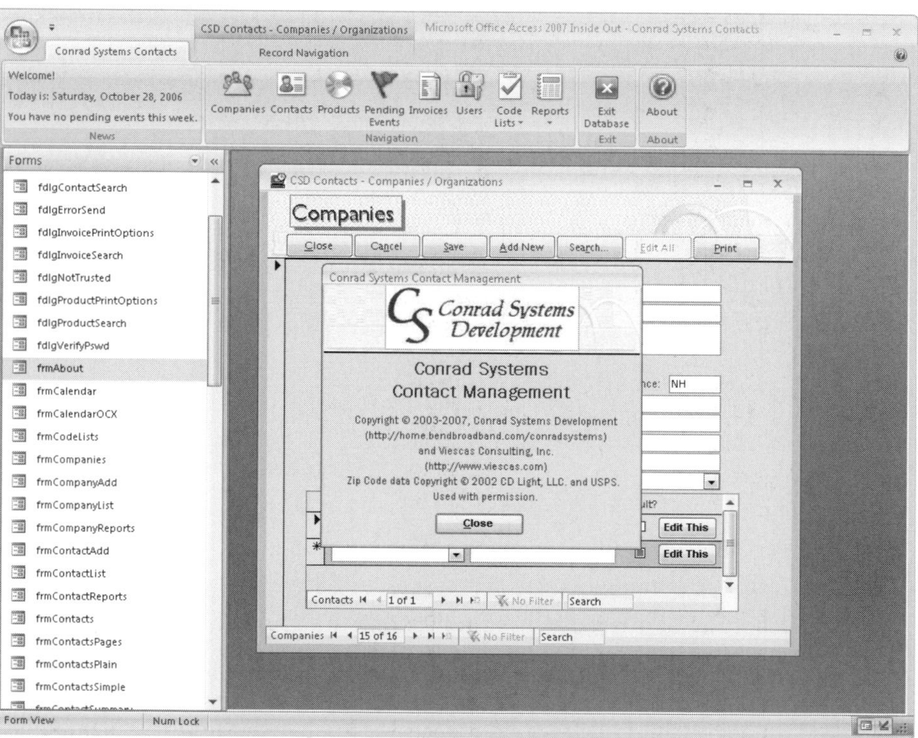


**Figure 10-7** The frmAbout pop-up form "floats" on top of frmCompanies, which has the focus.

## Modal Forms

As you add functionality to your application, you'll encounter situations in which you need to obtain some input from the user or convey some important information to the user before Access can proceed. Access 2007 provides a special type of form, called a *modal form*, which requires a response before the user can continue working in the application. The fdlgContactSearch dialog box in the Conrad Systems Contacts database, shown in Figure 10-8, is a modal form. This dialog box normally opens when you click the Contacts button on the main switchboard form and then click the Search button on the resulting Select Contacts (frmContactList) form. This dialog box also opens if you first open the frmContactsPlain form and then click the Search button. You can open the form on which the dialog box is based directly from the Navigation Pane. You'll notice that as long as this dialog box is open, you can't select any other window or Ribbon command in the application. To proceed, you must either enter some search criteria and click the Search button or click the Cancel button to dismiss the form.

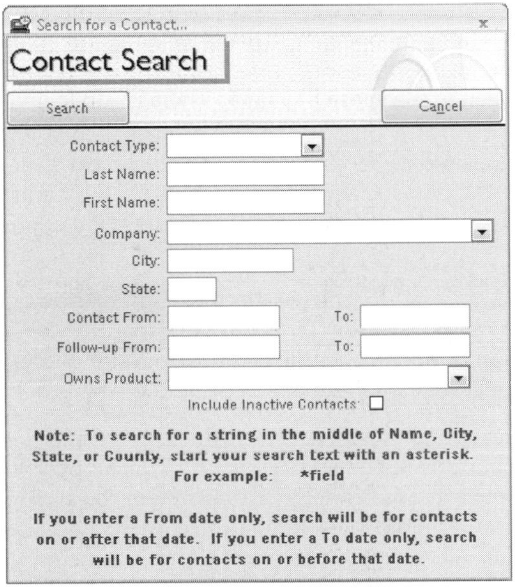

**Figure 10-8** The fdlgContactSearch form in the Conrad Systems Contacts database is a modal form that opens as a Windows dialog box.



## INSIDE OUT Using Name Prefixes to Organize Your Objects

Have you noticed the different prefixes on the form names that we designed in the Conrad Systems Contacts application? We like to create a prefix that helps us know more about the type of form when we look at the form list in the Navigation Pane. For example, we prefix the names of forms that are designed to open in PivotChart view with *cht*. We prefix dialog forms with *fdlg*, normal edit forms with *frm*, forms designed to edit lookup tables with *frmLkp*, and subforms with *fsub*. You may want to adopt a similar naming convention to help you keep your list of forms organized.

## Special Controls

The information in a form is contained in *controls*. The most common control you'll use on a form is a simple text box. A *text box* can display data from an underlying table or query, or it can display the result of an expression calculated in the control. You've probably noticed that many controls allow you to choose from among several values or to see additional content. You can also use controls to trigger a macro or a Visual Basic procedure. These controls are discussed in the next five sections.

### Option Buttons, Check Boxes, Toggle Buttons, and Option Groups

Whenever the data you're displaying can have only two or three valid values, you can use *option buttons*, *check boxes*, or *toggle buttons* to see or set the value you want in the field. For example, when there are two values, as in the case of a simple Yes/No field, you can use a check box to graphically display the value in the field. A check box that's selected means the value is Yes, and a check box that's cleared means the value is No. The Inactive control on the frmContactsPages form (see Figure 10-2) and the Default? control in the subform of frmCompanies (see Figure 10-6) are good examples of the use of a check box.

Stand-alone option buttons and toggle buttons work in the same way as a check box. When the value of an option button is Yes or True, the option button has a black dot in it. When the value of an option button is No or False, the option button appears empty. Likewise a toggle button appears pressed in when True, and not pressed in when False.

To provide a graphical choice among more than two values, you can place option buttons, check boxes, or toggle buttons in an *option group*. When grouped this way, each control in the group should have a unique integer value. When the control appears selected, the value of the option group is the value of the control. Because an option group can have only one value, when you select a control within the group, all other controls in the group appear unselected because their values no longer match the value of the option group.

For example, open frmProducts (this form displays the different products available), and click the Print button to see the fdlgProductPrintOptions form (shown in Figure 10-9) that lists the various contact reporting options. (You cannot open fdlgProduct-PrintOptions directly from the Navigation Pane–it has Visual Basic code that runs when the form opens to verify that the companion frmProducts form is already open. If not, the code tells Access to not allow the form to open.) If you open this form and click the available option buttons, you can see that when you click one button, the previously selected one clears. When you click one of the sales report buttons on this form, the form reveals additional date range options for your sales report.

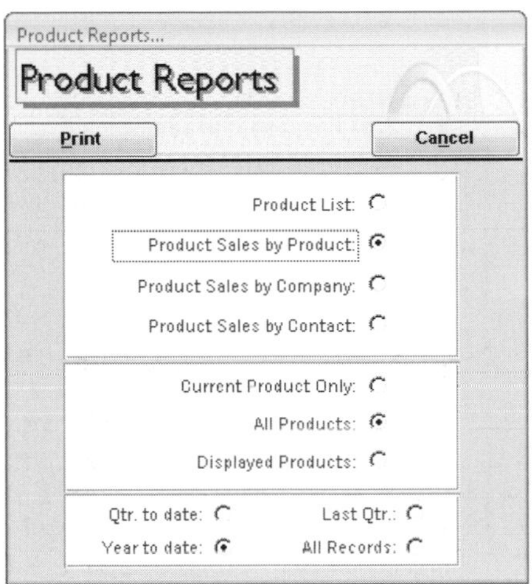


**Figure 10-9** You can see option groups on the fdlgProductPrintOptions form.

## List Boxes and Combo Boxes

When you want to display a list of data values in an open list, a *list box* is a good choice. When you view objects in Windows Explorer, the list of file names and properties in the pane on the right side when you're in Details view is a list box.

A list box can show a list of values you entered when you designed the control, a list of values returned by an SQL statement, the values of one or more fields in a table or in a query, or a list of field names from a table or a query. When you select a value from the list, you set the value of the control. You can use a list box on a form that edits data to display the value of one of the fields. When you choose a new value in the list box, you update the underlying field.

You can also define a list box in which you can select multiple values. When you do this, however, the list box cannot update an underlying field. This type of list box is useful to allow a user to choose multiple items or options that your application code will use to perform some action. As we discussed in "Working with Multi-Value Lookup Fields" on page 245, Multi-Value Field Lookups, when bound to a combo box, do provide a list box that allows you to select and save multiple values back to the table.

In the example shown in Figure 10-10 (the frmContactList form), the list box allows multiple selections and includes the set of names from the tblContacts table. This list box lets you select one or more entries by holding down the Shift key to select a contiguous range or by holding down the Ctrl key to select several noncontiguous entries. When you click the Edit button, a Visual Basic procedure evaluates your choices and opens the frmContacts form (see Figure 10-2) to display the selected contacts.

**Figure 10-10** A list box on the frmContactList form allows you to choose multiple contacts to edit.

A list box like this one can use data from more than one field. In fact, the query behind this list box returns both the ContactID field (the primary key) from tblContacts and the expression that you see containing last name, first name, and middle initial. The list box hides the ContactID, but Visual Basic code behind the form uses that hidden value to quickly find the contacts you want.

Combo boxes are similar to list boxes. The primary difference is that a *combo box* has both a text box *and* a drop-down list. One major advantage of a combo box is that it requires space on the form only for one of the values in the underlying list. However, you can choose only one value in a combo box.

The PostalCode field in the frmCompanies form (see Figure 10-6) is set using a combo box, as shown in Figure 10-11. The combo box uses four fields from the underlying query—the Zipcode, City, State, and County fields from the lookup query qlkpZips. When you select a postal code, the combo box sets the PostalCode field in the underlying record—a very useful feature. Visual Basic code attached to this control also automatically copies the related City, County, and State data from the selected row in the combo box to the fields on the form for you. As long as you know the postal code, you don't have to enter the other related information. You'll find a similar combo box used in the application wherever you need to enter a postal code on a form.



**Note**

In most cases, you will choose settings that disallow choosing a value that's not in the list in your combo boxes that update fields. You can also write Visual Basic code to examine a new value that a user tries to enter and determine whether it should appear in the list. You can learn about how to create code to deal with "not in list" values in Chapter 20.

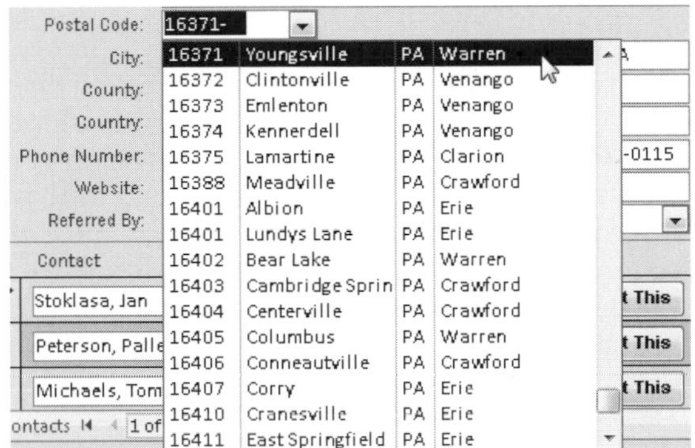


**Figure 10-11** When you click the arrow on a combo box, you can see a list of options.

In Chapter 5, "Modifying Your Table Design," you learned about Multi-Value Lookup Fields. When you define a field as a Multi-Value Lookup Field, Access 2007 provides a special control in the Datasheet view of the table and on a form similar to a combo box to display the valid list of values. When you click the arrow, you'll see a list box with a check box next to each of the available value choices. Selecting the check box next to one or more of the values stores the selected values in the field.

The ContactType field in the frmContactsPlain form is a Multi-Value Lookup Field. Open this form and you can see a Contact Type field with an arrow on its right side. Clicking the arrow opens the list of available choices for Contact Type, as shown in Figure 10-12. You can see that John Viescas is designated as both a Developer and a Distributor. You can have Access store multiple values for this single record by selecting the check box next to an available contact type.

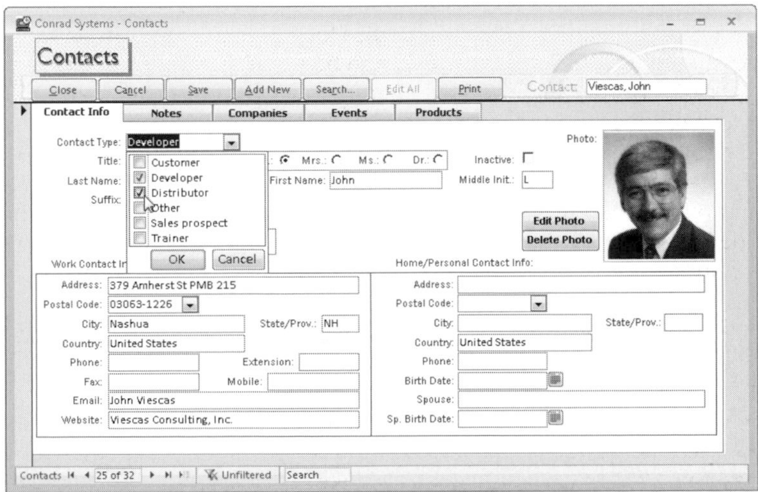


**Figure 10-12** The Contact Type field on the frmContactsPlain form is a Multi-Value Lookup Field control.

Chapter 10

## Tab Controls

Earlier in this chapter, you saw that one way to deal with the need to display lots of information on one form is to use a multiple-page form (frmContactsPages, shown in Figure 10-2 and Figure 10-3). Another way to organize the information on a single form is to use the *tab control* to provide what look like multiple folder tabs that reveal different information depending on the tab chosen—much like the main Ribbon in Access 2007 provides Home, Create, External Data, and Database Tools tabs. In the Conrad Systems Contacts database, a contact has basic contact information and notes, as well as related companies, contact events, and products. Open the frmContactsPlain form to see how the tab control displays only one of these types of information at a time, as shown in Figure 10-13.

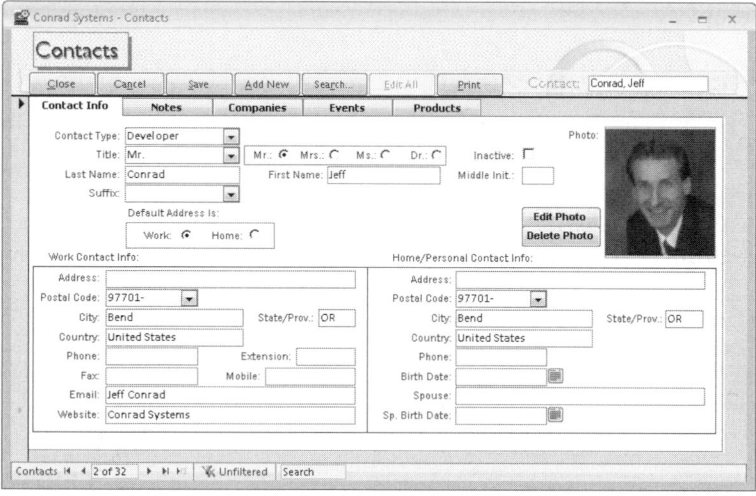


**Figure 10-13** When you first open the frmContactsPlain form, you see information on the Contact Info tab.

You can click the Companies tab (as shown in Figure 10-14) or any of the other tabs to see additional information. Note that there's no programming required to implement tab selection and data display. See Chapter 13 for details about how to use the tab control.

## Attachment Controls

In Chapter 4, "Creating Your Database and Tables," you learned about the new Attachment data type to store complex data. Access 2007 includes a new type of control, called an *attachment control*, to add and delete data from this data type. If you still have the frmContactsPlain form open, click the Contact Info tab to see the contact's picture displayed on the right side of the form. The picture is stored in an attachment field in the contact's record. On the frmContactsPlain form you can use the attachment control to add and delete the contact's picture. When you right-click on the attachment control, Access shows a shortcut menu with Forward, Back, and Manage Attachments commands, as shown in Figure 10-15.

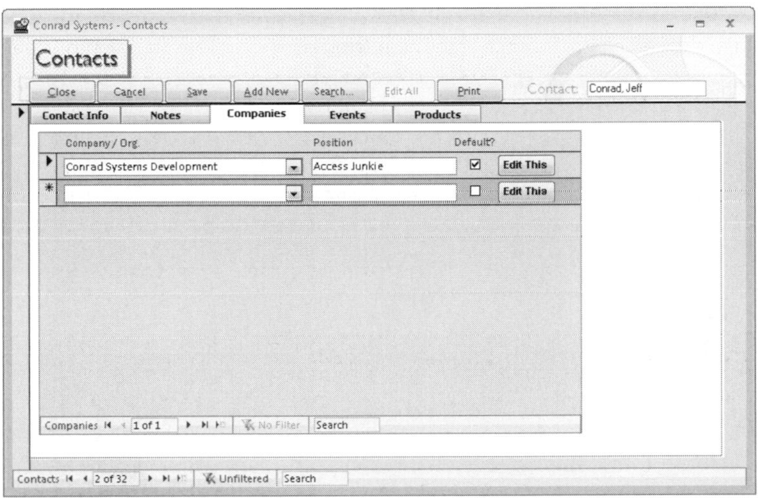


Figure 10-14 When you click another tab in a complex form you can see different data.

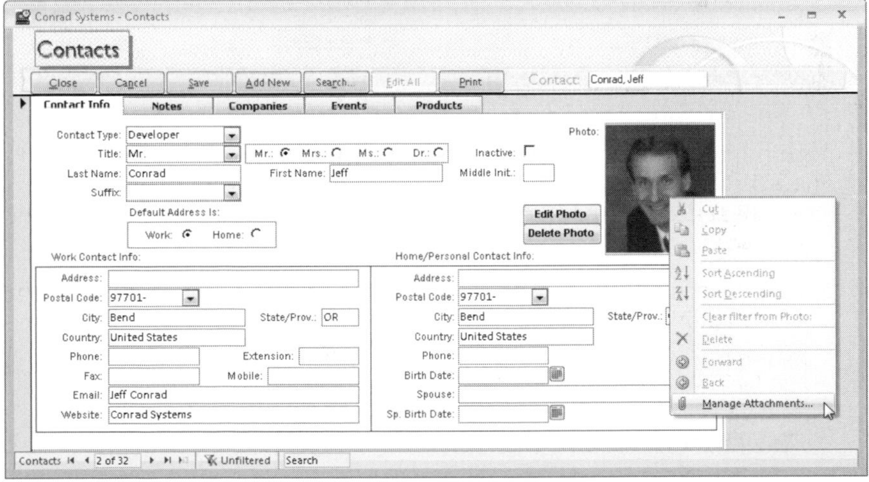


Figure 10-15 Right-click on an attachment control to see a shortcut menu with a Manage Attachments command.



The Forward and Back commands are unavailable because there is only one attachment assigned to the attachment field in this record. Select Manage Attachments and Access displays the Attachments dialog box, as shown in Figure 10-16.

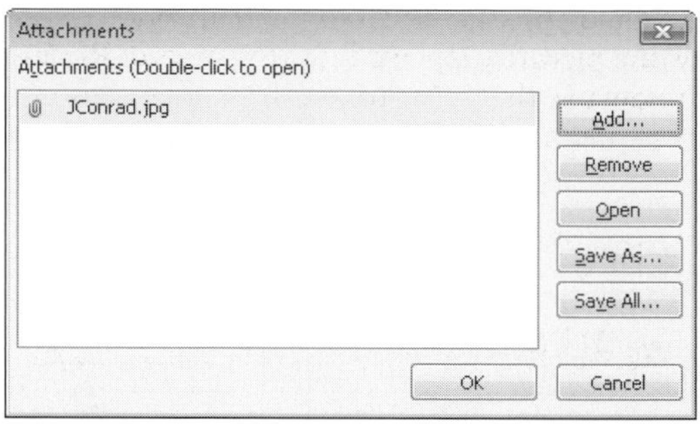


**Figure 10-16** You can add and delete different data files bound to an Attachment data type using the Attachments dialog box.

The left side of the Attachments dialog box lists all the files stored in the attachment field in the current record. The Add button opens the standard Windows Choose File dialog box where you can browse to another file to attach to this field. The Remove button deletes the attachment selected on the left side from the attachment field in the current record.

The Open button opens the selected attachment using the application that's defined in the Windows registry as the default application for this type of data. (On a computer running Windows Vista, the .jpg file opens in the Windows Photo Gallery program unless you have installed another program to view and edit pictures.) The Save As button opens the Save Attachment dialog box where you can save the selected attachment to a folder. The Save All button functions the same as Save As, except that you can save all the attachments (if there are more than one) in this attachment field to a folder in one step.



Use the record navigation buttons to move to Jeff's record, click the Add button to open the Choose File dialog box, browse to the Documents subfolder where you installed the sample files, and select the Microsoft Office Word document for Jeff called JeffConrad.docx. After you select the file, click Open to add the file to the attachment field in the current record. You can see the additional file listed in the Attachments dialog box, as shown in Figure 10-17.

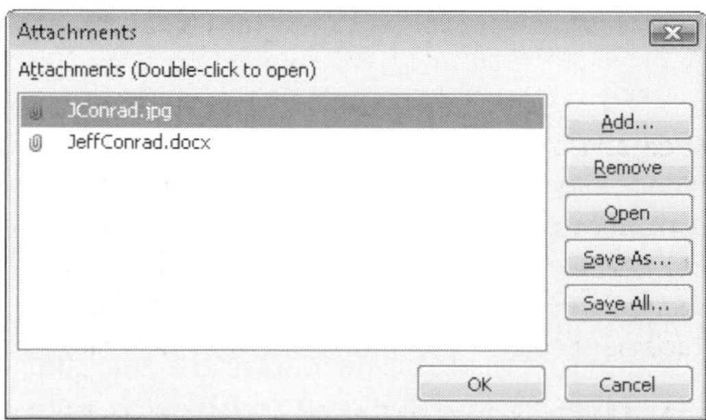


**Figure 10-17** Jeff's document has now been added to the attachment field in the current record.

Click OK in the Attachments dialog box to return to the frmContactsPlain form and notice that you still see only one picture displayed for this record. Right-click the attachment control again. You can now use the Forward and Back commands on the shortcut menu to view the two different files saved in the attachment field in the current record, as shown in Figure 10-18.

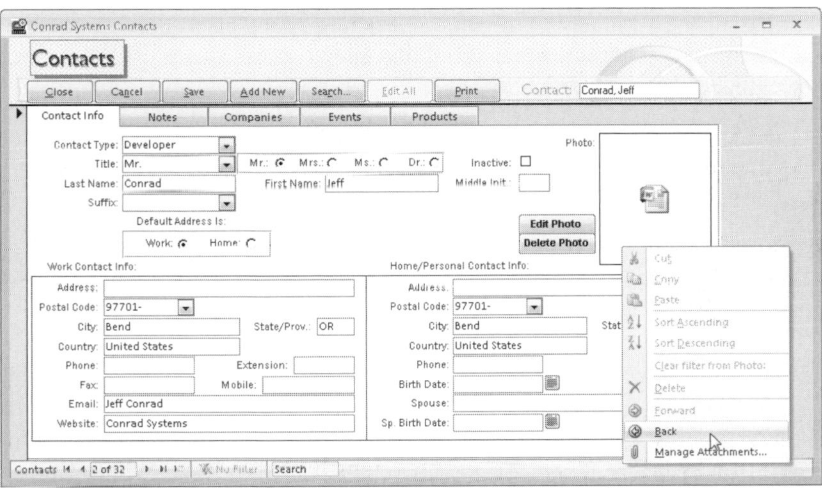


**Figure 10-18** When you store multiple files in an attachment field, you can use the Forward and Back commands on the shortcut menu to view the files.



## ActiveX Objects

To demonstrate an ActiveX object, close the Contacts.accdb database and then open the Contacts2Upsize.accdb database. Open the frmContactsPlain form in this database from the Navigation Pane to see a form that is nearly identical to frmContactsPlain in the Contacts.accdb database. Unlike the contact picture you saw earlier on the frmContactsPlain form in the Contacts.accdb database, this picture is stored in a field in the tblContacts table using Microsoft's ActiveX technology.

> **Note**
>
> The Contacts2Upsize.accdb database is a version of the Conrad Systems Contacts application that has been modified to upsize the data to SQL Server and the application code to an Access project file (.adp). Because SQL Server cannot store the data in attachment fields, we changed the Photo field in the tblContacts table from the Attachment data type to the OLE Object data type. Also, we changed the control on the forms displaying the Photo field from an attachment control to a bound object frame control.

The logo in the top part of the main switchboard form (frmMain) in the Conrad Systems Contacts database, on the other hand, is a picture that Access has stored as part of the form. The control that you use to display a picture or any other ActiveX object is called an *object frame*. A *bound object frame* control is used to display an ActiveX object that is stored in a field in a table—such as the picture on frmContactsPages or frmContactsPlain in this database. When you edit the object in a bound object frame, you're updating a field in the table. Use an *unbound object frame* or an *image* control to display an object that is not stored in a table. Access stores the object with the form definition, and you cannot edit it in Form view.

When you include a bound object frame control on a form and bind the control to an OLE object field in the database, you can edit that object by selecting it and then right-clicking the picture to open the shortcut menu. On the Bitmap Image Object submenu, select Edit, as shown in Figure 10-19.

> **Note**
>
> If you use an unbound object frame or image control on a form, you can edit the contents of the control only when you have the form in Design view.



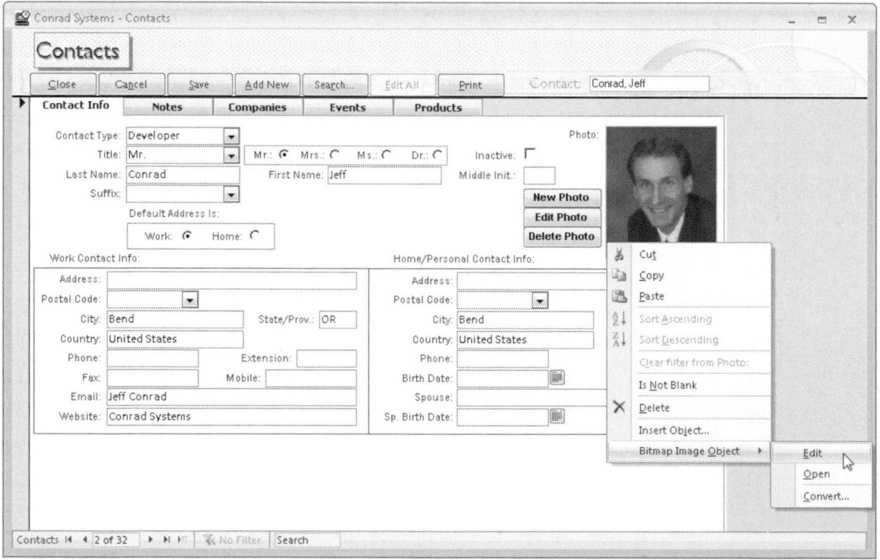


**Figure 10-19** You can select a picture and then edit it by selecting Bitmap Image Object on the shortcut menu and then selecting Edit on the submenu.

**Note**

The Contacts2Upsize application also provides handy New Photo, Edit Photo, and Delete Photo buttons on the frmContactsPlain form. When the form loads, it examines your Windows registry and determines the default program on your computer to edit bitmap (.bmp) or JPEG (.jpg) files. When you click the New Photo or Edit Photo button, Visual Basic code behind the form starts that program for you. You don't have to worry about navigating the complex shortcut menu.

If the object is a picture, a graph, or a spreadsheet, you can see the object in the object frame control and you can activate its application by double-clicking the object. If the object is a sound file, you can hear it by double-clicking the object frame control.

Figure 10-19 shows one of the photographs stored in the tblContacts table that is bound in an object frame control on the frmContactsPlain form. When you double-click the picture—or select the picture, right-click, select Bitmap Image Object from the shortcut menu, and then select Edit from the submenu—Access starts the default application on your computer to edit bitmaps. On most computers, this is the Microsoft Paint application. In Windows, Paint is an ActiveX application that can "activate in place," as shown in Figure 10-20. You can still see a few Access commands listed on the Paint File menu, but Paint has added its own toolbars and menu commands. You can update the picture by using any of the commands on the Paint toolbars and menus. You can paste in a different picture by copying a picture to the Clipboard and clicking the Paste command on Paint's Edit menu. After you make your changes, simply click in another area on the Access form to deactivate Paint and store the result of your edits in the object frame control. If you save the record, Access saves the changed data in your OLE object field.



**Note**

If you have registered an application other than Microsoft Paint to handle bitmap objects, that application will be activated when you select Edit from the submenu.

## Command Buttons

Another useful control is the command button, which you can use to link many forms to create a complete database application. Close the Contacts2Upsize.accdb database and return to the Contacts.accdb database. In the Conrad Systems Contacts database, for example, most of the forms are linked to the main switchboard form (frmMain), shown in Figure 10-21, in which the user can click command buttons to launch various functions in the application. The advantage of using command buttons is simplicity—they offer an easy way to trigger a macro or a Visual Basic procedure. The procedure might do nothing more than open another form, print a report, or run an action query to update many records in your database. As you'll see when you get to the end of this book, you can build a fairly complex application using forms, reports, macros, and some simple Visual Basic procedures.

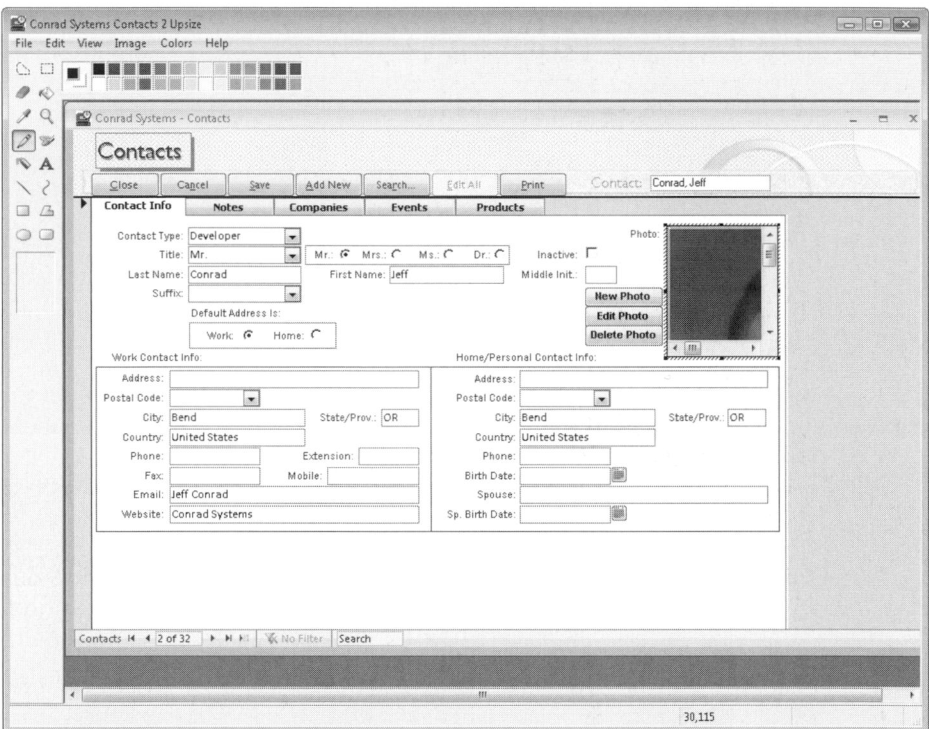


**Figure 10-20** The Photo OLE object field from Figure 10-19 is being edited "in place" with its host application.

## PivotTables and PivotCharts

In Chapter 8, you learned how to create the PivotTable or PivotChart view of a query. You can also build a form that is connected to a table or query and switch to either Pivot-Table or PivotChart view to define a custom view of the underlying data. For example, take a look at the ptContactProducts form shown in Figure 10-22. This form is designed to open only in PivotTable view or Design view. Note that even though the query on which this form is based is updatable, you cannot update any of the field values via the PivotTable.

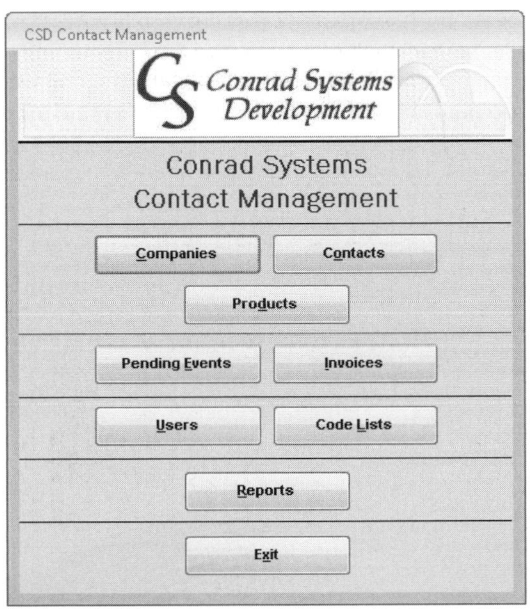


**Figure 10-21** The command buttons on the frmMain switchboard form take the user to various parts of the application.

Contact Products

Drop Filter Fields Here

| | | Months ▾ Days | | | | | | | | |
|---|---|---|---|---|---|---|---|---|---|---|
| | | ⊞ Jan | | ⊞ Feb | | ⊞ Mar | | ⊞ Apr | | ⊞ May |
| Product Type: ▾ | State/Province: ▾ | Number Sold | Revenue | Number Sold | Revenue | Number Sold | Revenue | Number Sold | Revenue | Number Sold |
| | NY | | | | | 1 | $129.00 | | | |
| | OR | | | | | | | | | |
| | PA | | | 2 | $258.00 | | | 2 | $299.00 | |
| | VA | | | | | | | | | |
| | WV | | | | | | | | | |
| | Total | 3 | $428.00 | 4 | $387.00 | 4 | $387.00 | 3 | $598.00 | |
| ⊟ Remote User | CA | | | | | 1 | $99.00 | | | |
| | KY | | | | | | | 1 | $99.00 | |
| | MA | | | | | | | | | |
| | MI | 1 | $99.00 | | | | | | | |
| | NC | | | 1 | $99.00 | | | | | |
| | ND | | | | | | | | | |
| | OR | | | | | | | | | |
| | PA | | | 1 | $99.00 | | | 1 | $99.00 | |
| | Total | 1 | $99.00 | 2 | $198.00 | 1 | $99.00 | 2 | $198.00 | |
| ⊟ Single User | CA | | | 1 | $199.00 | 1 | $0.00 | | | |
| | KY | | | | | | | 1 | $199.00 | |
| | MA | | | | | | | | | |
| | MI | 1 | $19.99 | | | 1 | $19.99 | 1 | $199.00 | |
| | NC | | | | | 2 | $19.99 | | | |
| | ND | | | | | | | 1 | $19.99 | |

**Figure 10-22** The ptContactProducts form is designed to open in PivotTable view.

PivotCharts can be useful in an application to provide a related graphical representation of data displayed on a form. In the Conrad Systems Contacts sample database, you can find the chtProductSales form that charts sales by product and by month. This form is embedded in a report that displays product details (rptProductSalesByProductWChart) and in a sample form that lets you edit product information while viewing the related past sales data as a chart (frmProductsWithSales). You can see frmProductsWithSales in Figure 10-23.

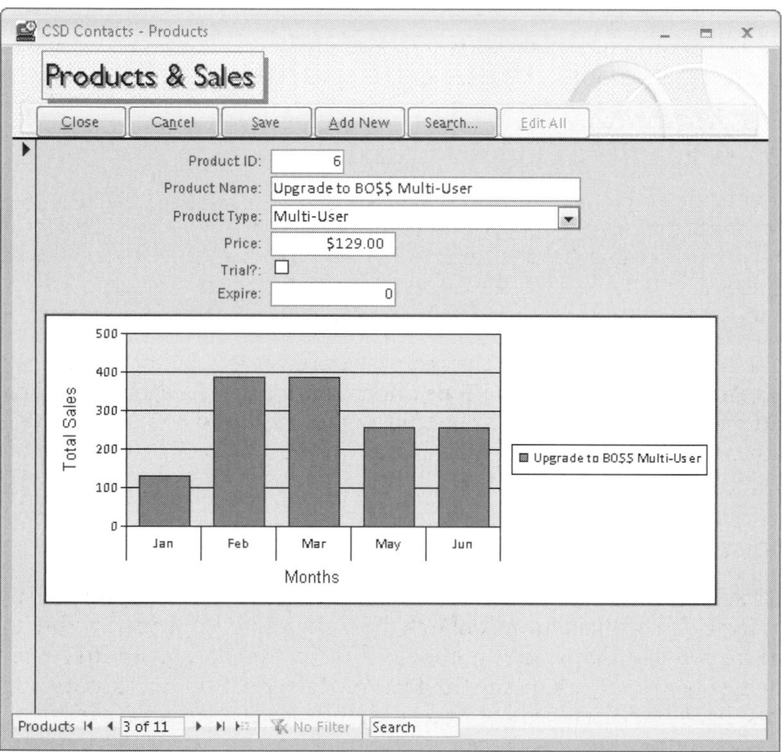


**Figure 10-23** This form to edit product data also has an embedded subform in PivotChart view to show related sales information.

Designing a form as a PivotTable or PivotChart has three distinct advantages over performing these functions in queries.

1. You can restrict the views of the form to display only the PivotTable or the PivotChart or both. You can set a default view for a query, but you cannot prevent the user from switching to Datasheet or Design view.

2. You can embed a form designed as a PivotTable or PivotChart in another form or in a report to display related information. You cannot embed a query in a form or report.

3. You can write Visual Basic code behind the form to dynamically modify the PivotTable or PivotChart. You can also restrict the changes a user can make to the table or chart. You cannot write code behind a query.

You'll learn more about designing forms as PivotTables or PivotCharts in Chapter 13.

# Moving Around on Forms and Working with Data

The rest of this chapter shows you how to move around on and work with data in the various types of forms discussed earlier in the chapter.

## Viewing Data

Moving around on a form is similar to moving around in a datasheet, but there are a few subtle differences between forms and datasheets (usually having to do with how a form was designed) that determine how a form works with data. You can use the frmContactsPlain form in the Conrad Systems Contacts database (which is a copy of frmContacts without custom Ribbons) to explore the ways in which forms work.

First, if necessary, open the Conrad Systems Contacts database. Next, click the Navigation Pane menu, click Object Type under Navigate To Category, and then click Forms under Filter By Group. Select the frmContactsPlain form, right-click on the form name, and click the Open command on the shortcut menu to see the form shown in Figure 10-24.

### Moving Around

The way you move around on a form depends in part on the form's design. For example, the frmContactsPlain form contains three subforms embedded within the tab control–one for contact companies, another for contact events, and a third for contact products. The two boxes you see on the Contact Info tab aren't subforms–they're rectangle controls that we added to enhance the grouping of the main detail fields.

The fsubContactEventsPlain subform on the Events tab is a continuous form. You move around on it similarly to how you move around in a datasheet. On this subform you can use the vertical scroll bar to move the display up or down. You can toggle the subform between two different views–Form view (its current state) and Datasheet view. If you want to see the Datasheet view of the fsubContactEventsPlain subform, right-click in any of the fields on the subform (to ensure that the focus is on the subform), click Subform on the shortcut menu, and then click the Datasheet command. (Notice that the PivotTable and PivotChart options on the shortcut menu appear dimmed–we have disallowed those views in the design of this subform.) The fsubContactEvents subform will now look like Figure 10-25.

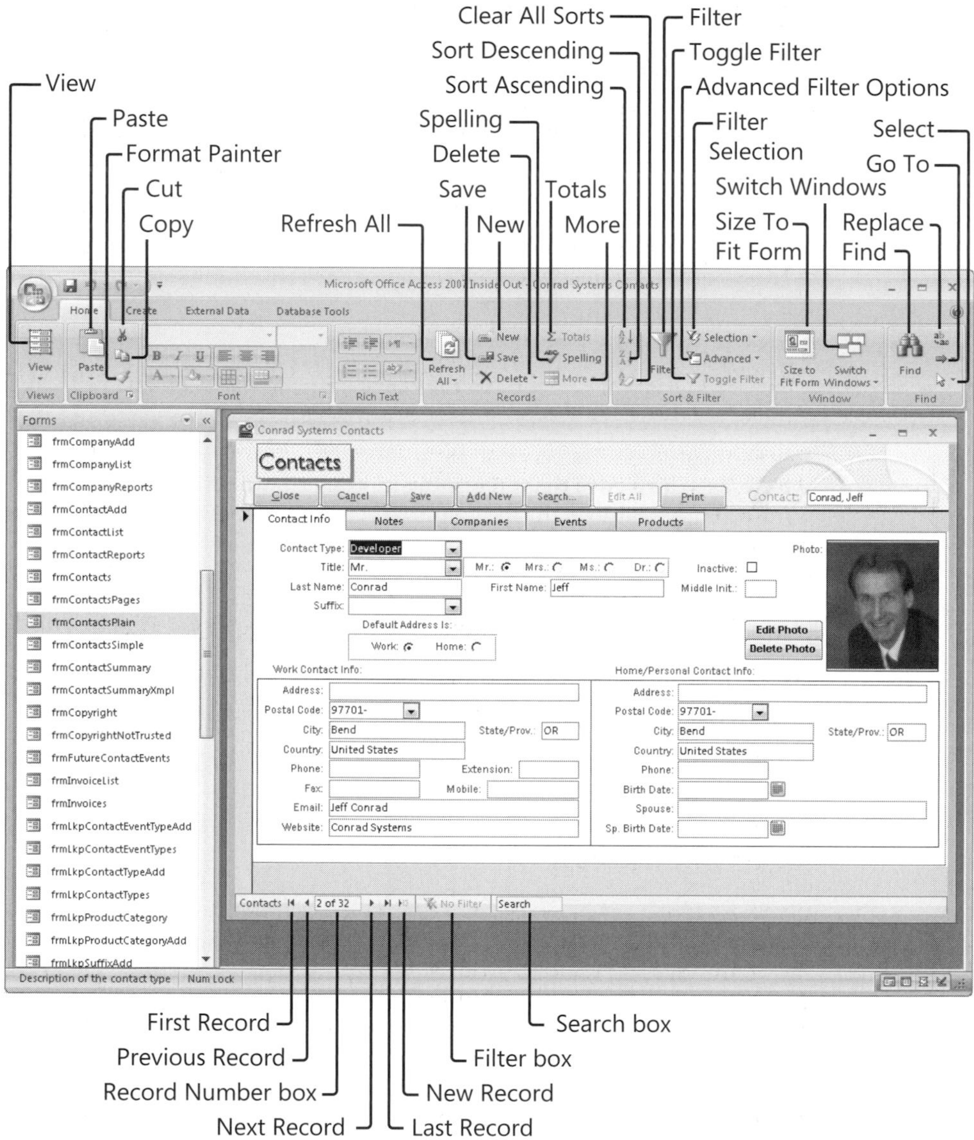


**Figure 10-24** You can use the frmContactsPlain form in the Conrad Systems Contacts database to explore moving around on a form.

Contact Info | Notes | Companies | Events | Products

| | ContactDateTime | ContactEventTypeID | ContactNotes | ContactFollowU | ContactFollowUpDa |
|---|---|---|---|---|---|
| | 04/05/2007 12:36 | Meeting | | ☐ | |
| | 04/05/2007 18:15 | Sold CSD Tools | | ☑ | 3/30/200 |
| | 04/19/2007 13:06 | Phone call - made | | ☐ | |
| | 04/20/2007 12:56 | Sold Remote User support | | ☑ | 4/14/200 |
| | 05/03/2007 12:41 | Phone call - made | | ☐ | |
| | 05/03/2007 14:43 | Brochure mailed | | ☐ | |
| | 05/27/2007 11:34 | Meeting | | ☐ | |
| | 05/31/2007 11:55 | Sample disk mailed, Single | | ☑ | 6/30/200 |
| | 06/06/2007 12:48 | Meeting | | ☐ | |
| | 07/08/2007 9:56 | Sold Remote User | | ☑ | 7/2/200 |
| * | | | | ☐ | |

**Figure 10-25** You can display the fsubContactEventsPlain subform in Datasheet view on the Events tab of frmContactsPlain.

In the frmContactsPlain form, you view different contact records by using the navigation buttons and Record Number box at the bottom of the form. To see the next contact, use the main form's navigation buttons. To see different companies, events, or products for a particular contact, use the vertical scroll bar within the subform or the navigation buttons within the subform window. Note that you can also design a subform without its own Record Number box and navigation buttons. You might want to do this if you think the set of navigation buttons will be confusing to your users.

You can also click the Go To command in the Find group on the Home tab on the Ribbon to move to the first, last, next, or previous record in the main form or in the subform. You can select any field in the form by clicking anywhere in that field. To use the Go To command you must first move to the form or the subform containing those records you want to view.

## Keyboard Shortcuts

If you're typing new data, you might find it easier to use the keyboard rather than the mouse to move around on a form. Some of the keyboard shortcuts you can use with forms are listed in Table 10-1 (for moving around in fields and records) and in Table 10-2 (for actions in a list box or in a combo box). Note that a form that edits data can be in one of two modes: Edit mode or Navigation mode. You're in *Edit mode* on a form when you can see a flashing insertion point in the current field. To enter *Navigation mode*, tab to the next field or press the F2 key to select the current field. As you can see in the following tables, some keyboard shortcuts work differently depending on the mode. Other keyboard shortcuts work in only one mode or the other.

Table 10-1 **Keyboard Shortcuts for Fields and Records**

| Key(s) | Movement in Fields and Records |
|---|---|
| Tab | Moves to the next field. |
| Shift+Tab | Moves to the previous field. |
| Home | In Navigation mode, moves to the first field of the current record. In Edit mode, moves to the beginning of the current field. |
| End | In Navigation mode, moves to the last field of the current record. In Edit mode, moves to the end of the current field. |
| Ctrl+Page Up | Moves to the current field of the previous record. |
| Ctrl+Page Down | Moves to the current field of the next record. |
| Ctrl+Up Arrow | In Navigation mode, moves to the current field of the first record. In Edit mode, moves to the beginning of the current field. |
| Ctrl+Down Arrow | In Navigation mode, moves to the current field of the last record. In Edit mode, moves to the end of the current field. |
| Ctrl+Home | In Navigation mode, moves to the first field of the first record. In Edit mode, moves to the beginning of the current field. |
| Ctrl+End | In Navigation mode, moves to the last field of the last record. In Edit mode, moves to the end of the current field. |
| Ctrl+Tab | If in a subform, moves to the next field in the main form. If the subform is the last field in the tab sequence in the main form, moves to the first field in the next main record.<br>If the focus is on a field on a tab, moves the focus to the first field in the tab order on the next tab. If the focus is on a subform within a tab, moves the focus to the tab. If the subform within the tab is the last control on the form, moves the focus to the tab on the next record.<br>If the focus is on a tab (not a field within the tab), cycles forward through the tabs. |
| Ctrl+Shift+Tab | If in a subform, moves to the previous field in the main form. If the subform is the first field in the tab sequence in the main form, moves to the last field in the next main record.<br>If the focus is on a field on a tab, moves the focus to the first field in the tab order on the previous tab. If the focus is on a subform within a tab, moves the focus to the tab. If the subform within the tab is the first control on the form, moves the focus to the tab on the previous record.<br>If the focus is on a tab (not a field within the tab), cycles backward through the tabs. |
| Ctrl+Shift+Home | In Navigation mode, moves to the first field in the record. When in Navigation mode in a field on a tab, moves the focus to the tab. When the focus is on a tab (not a field within the tab), moves to the first tab on the tab control.<br>In Edit mode, selects all characters from the current insertion point to the beginning of the field. |

| Key(s) | Movement in Fields and Records |
| --- | --- |
| Ctrl+Shift+End | In Navigation mode, moves to the last field in the record. When in Navigation mode in a field on a tab, moves the focus to the tab. When the focus is on a tab (not a field within the tab), moves to the last tab on the tab control.<br>In Edit mode, selects all characters from the current insertion point to the end of the field. |
| Alt+F5 | Moves to the Record Number box. |
| Enter | Depends on your settings for the Move After Enter option in the Editing section of the Advanced category in the Access Options dialog box. |
| Shift+Enter | Saves the current record. |

Table 10-2 **Keyboard Shortcuts for a List Box or a Combo Box**

| Key(s) | Action in a List Box or a Combo Box |
| --- | --- |
| F4 or Alt+Down Arrow | Opens or closes a combo box or a drop-down list box. |
| Down Arrow | Moves down one line in a list box or in a combo box when the list is open. |
| Up Arrow | Moves up one line in a list box or in a combo box when the list is open. |
| Page Down | Moves down to the next group of lines. |
| Page Up | Moves up to the next group of lines. |
| Tab | Exits the box and moves to the next field. |



# Adding Records and Changing Data

You'll probably design most forms so that you can insert new records, change field values, or delete records in Form view or in Datasheet view. The following sections explain procedures for adding new records and changing data.

## Adding a New Record

The procedure for entering a new record varies depending on the design of the form. With a form that's been designed for data entry only, you open the form and enter data in the (usually empty) data fields. Sometimes forms of this type open with default values in the fields or with data entered by a macro or Visual Basic procedure. In the Conrad Systems Contacts application, frmCompanyAdd and frmContactAdd are two examples of forms that open in Data Entry mode. You can see frmContactAdd in Figure 10-26.

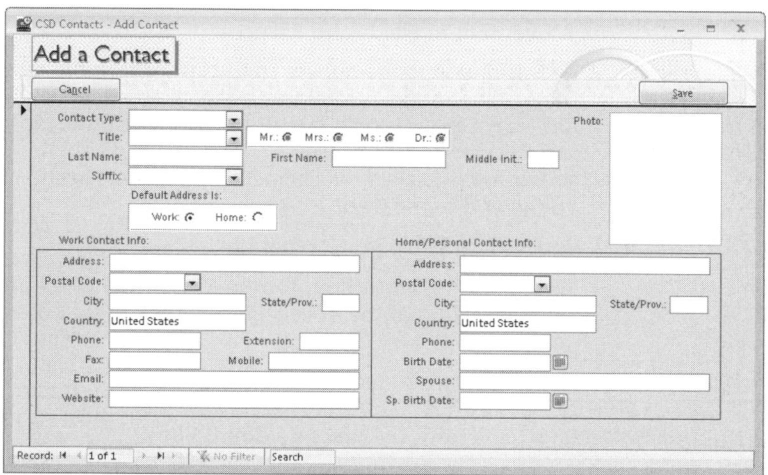


**Figure 10-26** The frmContactAdd form opens in Data Entry mode.

When you're editing company information in frmCompanies and need to enter a new contact that doesn't exist, the application opens this form to allow you to fill in the required information for the new contact. After you save the record, the new contact becomes available to assign to the company displayed in frmCompanies.

You'll normally create a form that allows you to display and edit data and also add new records. The frmContactsPlain form is this type of form. On this form, you can go to a new record in several ways. Open the frmContactsPlain form and try the following:

- Click the Last Record button on the navigation bar at the bottom of the Form window and then click the Next Record button.
- Click the New Record button on the navigation bar at the bottom of the form.
- Click Go To in the Find group on the Home tab and then click New on the submenu.
- Click the New button in the Records group on the Home tab.
- Press Ctrl+Plus Sign.
- Click the Add New command button in the header area of the form. (This last method puts the form into Data Entry mode, something you cannot do from any standard command on the Ribbon.)

The first five methods take you to the empty record at the end of the recordset being edited by this form. This is similar to going to the blank row at the end of a table or query datasheet to begin entering data for a new row. The last method shifts the form into Data Entry mode as shown in Figure 10-27. Notice that there now appears to be only one record—the new record you're about to enter, and that record displays the default value specified for Country even though you haven't started to enter any data yet.

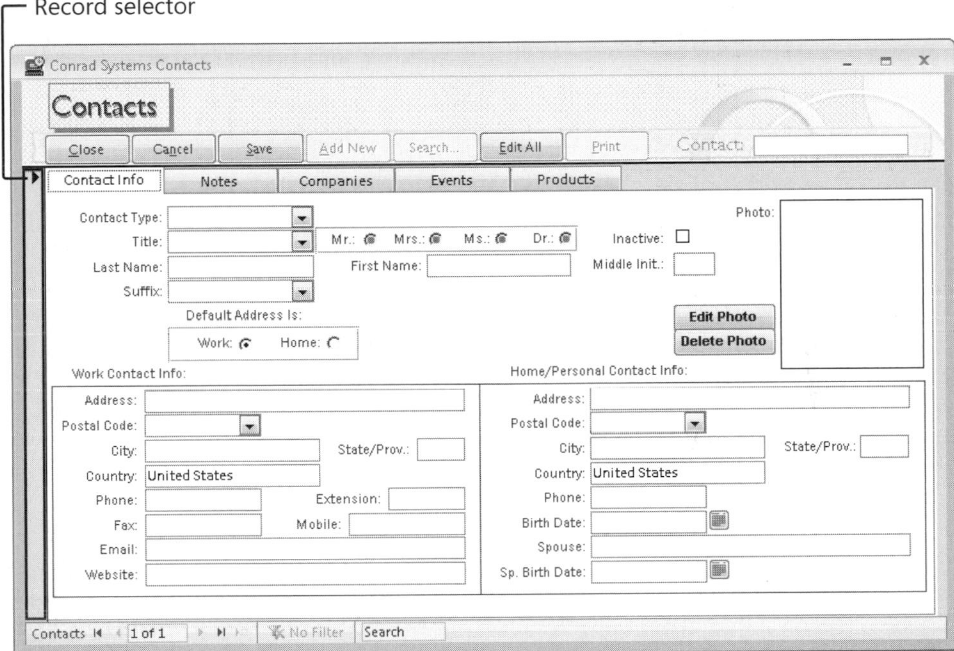


**Figure 10-27** When you click the Add New button in the header of the frmContactsPlain form, Access displays the form in Data Entry mode.

Access places the insertion point in the first field when you start a new record. As soon as you begin typing, Access changes the indicator on the record selector (if your form shows the record selector) to a pencil icon to indicate that updates are in progress. Press Tab to move to the next field.

> **Note**
>
> The frmContactsPlain form provides an Edit All button on the form to return to normal data display if you clicked the Add New button to enter Data Entry mode.

If you violate a field's validation rule, Access notifies you as soon as you attempt to leave the field. You must provide a correct value before you can move to another field. Press Shift+Enter in any field in the record or press Tab in the last field in the record to save your new record in the table. If the data you enter violates a table validation rule, Access displays an error message and does not save the record. If you want to cancel a new record, press Esc twice. (There's also a Cancel button on frmContactsPlain that clears your edits and closes the form.)

If you're adding a new record in a form that has an Attachment or OLE Object data type, you'll encounter a special situation. You'll notice when you tab to the Photo attachment control that you can't type anything in it. This is because the field in the underlying table is an Attachment data type, and this control is an attachment. In fact, when the focus is in this control and you happen to type one of the keyboard navigation letters on one of the command buttons (*C* for Close, *N* for Cancel, and so on), you'll "click" that command button and execute the action programmed in the command button. You'll notice this same problem if you open the frmContactsPlain form in the Contacts2-Upsize.accdb database and tab into the Photo bound object frame control.

To enter data in this type of field in a new record, you must create the object in another application before you can store the data in Access. To insert a file in an attachment field, follow the instructions given earlier to right-click the attachment control and click Manage Attachments on the shortcut menu. Click Add in the Attachments dialog box shown in Figure 10-17 on page 532 to open the Choose File dialog box where you can select the file that you want to store in the attachment field.

If you want to see how to work with an OLE Object field, you'll have to close the Contacts.accdb database and reopen the Contacts2Upsize.accdb database. Open the frmContactsPlain form and go to a new record. To create and store a new file in a bound object frame, right-click on the bound object frame control and click the Insert Object command on the shortcut menu. Access displays the Microsoft Office Access dialog box, shown in Figure 10-28. To create a new object, select the object type you want (in this case, Bitmap Image), and click OK. Access starts the application that's defined in the Windows registry as the default application for this type of data (for bitmaps, usually the Paint application).

Chapter 10

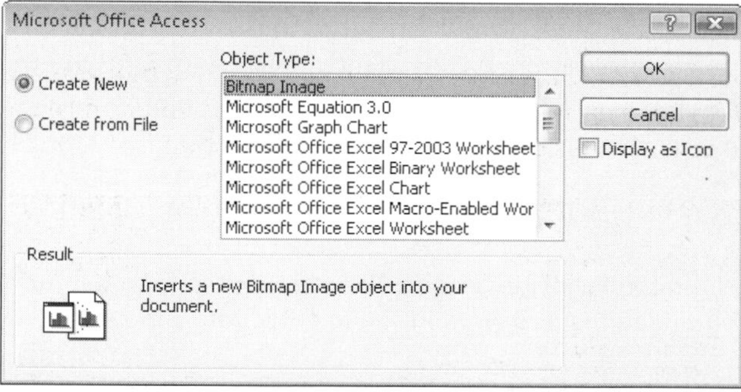


**Figure 10-28** The Microsoft Office Access dialog box allows you to enter data into an OLE object field.

If you have an appropriate file available to copy into the OLE object field in Access, select the Create From File option in the Microsoft Office Access dialog box. Access replaces the Object Type list with a File box where you can enter the path name and file name, as shown in Figure 10-29. You can click the Browse button to open the Browse dialog box, which lets you search for the file you want. After you select a file, you can select the Link check box to create an active link between the copy of the object in Access and the actual file. If you do so, whenever you change the file, the linked object in Access will also change. Select the Display As Icon check box to display the application icon instead of the picture in the bound object frame. Your picture will still be stored or linked in your table even when you choose to display the icon.

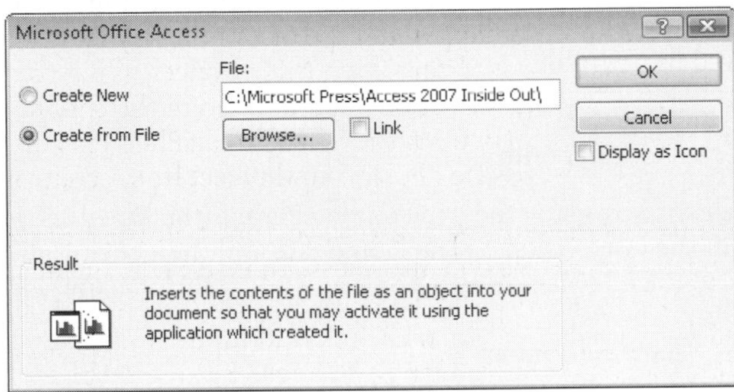


**Figure 10-29** You can insert an object from a file using the Create From File option in the Microsoft Office Access dialog box.

If you opened the Contacts2Upsize.accdb database to experiment with editing in a bound object frame, close it and reopen the Contacts.accdb database.

The frmContactsPlain form also includes two text boxes that let you specify the e-mail address or the Web site address of the contact. To add or edit a hyperlink, you can tab to the hyperlink field (remember that if the link field contains a valid link, clicking in it activates the link!), right click the link field, click Hyperlink on the shortcut menu, and then click Edit Hyperlink on the submenu. Access displays the dialog box shown in Figure 10-30, which lets you edit or define the link.

You can enter the descriptor in the Text To Display box at the top. We clicked the ScreenTip button to open the Set Hyperlink ScreenTip dialog box you see in Figure 10-30. The ScreenTip appears when you rest your mouse pointer on the hyperlink. You can type the document address directly into the Address box.



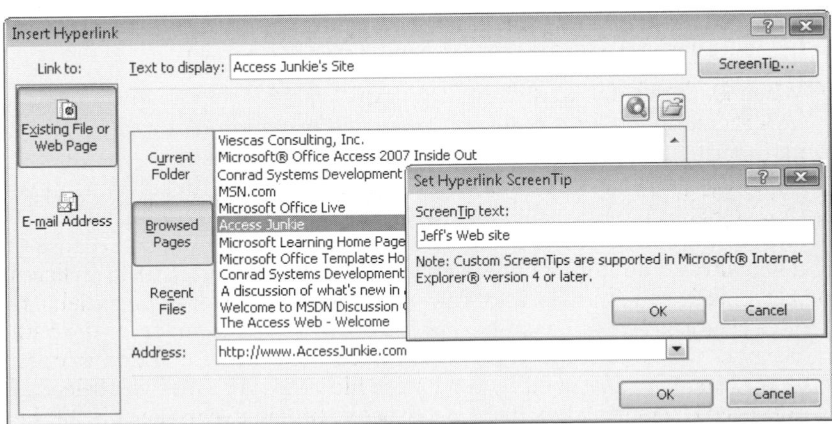


**Figure 10-30** The Insert Hyperlink dialog box shows a link to the AccessJunkie.com Web site.

The second option on the left in the Insert Hyperlink dialog box, E-Mail Address, lets you enter an e-mail address or choose from a list of recently used addresses. This generates a Mailto: hyperlink that will invoke your e-mail program and start a new e-mail message to the address you specify here. You can also optionally enter Subject text for the new e-mail, which adds a question mark after the e-mail address followed by the subject in the stored hyperlink.

Click OK to save your link. See "Working with Hyperlinks" on page 397, for more details and cautions about hyperlinks.

Try adding a new record by using the frmContactsPlain form. Open the form, click the Go To command in the Find group on the Home tab, and then click New. You should see a form similar to the one shown earlier in Figure 10-27. Make any selection you like from the Contact Type drop-down list. Because this field is a Multi-Value Lookup Field, you can select more than one contact type. Click the OK button at the bottom of the list when you have finished selecting one or more contact types. You must enter at least a last name (the only required field in tblContacts). Tab to the Photo field, and follow the procedure discussed previously in "Attachment Controls" on page 530 to add a new picture attachment to this record. You can find several appropriately sized bitmap pictures of contacts on the companion CD in the Pictures subfolder.

To begin adding some events for your new contact, click the Events tab to reveal the appropriate subform. Note that when you click in the subform, Access saves the contact data you entered in the main form. Access does this to ensure that it can create a link between the new record in the main form and any record you might create in the subform. (The new contact ID has to be saved in the main form before you can create related contact category records in a subform.)

Select an event type, as shown in Figure 10-31, or type a new one. As soon as you select an event type, Access automatically fills in the Date/Time field with the current date and time on your computer. You can correct this value or click the small calendar button to open a calendar form to set a new date and time graphically. If you enter an event type that isn't already defined, code behind the form prompts you to ask whether you want to add a new event type. If you click Yes, you'll see a dialog form open to allow you to enter the details for your new event type.

When you press Tab in the last field or press Shift+Enter in any field, Access adds the new event for you. Access also inserts the information required to link the record in the main form and the new record in the subform. Access fetches the ContactID from the record in the outer form and creates the new record in the tblContactEvents table with the related ContactID value. You can't see or edit the ContactID field on either the outer form or the subform. You don't need to see it in the outer form because ContactID in tblContacts is an AutoNumber field. Because Access automatically copies the value for you for new rows in the subform, you don't need to see it there either.

## INSIDE OUT Dealing with AutoNumber Primary Keys and Potentially Duplicate Data

As discussed in Article 1 on the companion CD, "Designing Your Database Application," it's usually preferable to use a combination of data fields that have a unique value in each row to create a primary key. However, choosing a combination of fields in tblContacts that would be guaranteed to be unique in all rows could prove difficult. The combination of first name and last name could easily result in a duplicate when two different people have the same name. Adding postal code might help, but you still might run into two people named *John Smith* who live in the same area.

The simple solution for tables in an Access 2007 desktop database is to use an AutoNumber field as the primary key. In fact, in the Conrad Systems Contacts database, tblCompanies, tblContacts, tblInvoices, and tblProducts all use an AutoNumber field for the primary key. This guarantees that all rows will have a unique primary key, but it doesn't guard against duplicate records—entering the same person twice.

To avoid potential duplicates, you should consider writing Visual Basic code to check a new row just before Access saves it. We included some simple code to perform a Soundex check on the last name in both frmContacts and frmContactsPlain. (Soundex is an algorithm created by the United States National Archive and Records Administration to generate a code from a name to identify names that sound alike.) If you try to add a person in a new row with the last name *Camred*, you'll see a warning about a potential duplicate (*Conrad*, for example) and a list of all similar names. The warning allows you to cancel saving the new row. You can learn how this code works in Chapter 20.

One last point about using AutoNumber: As soon as you begin to enter new data in a table that has an AutoNumber field, Access assigns a new number to that field. If you decide to cancel the new record before saving it, Access won't reuse this AutoNumber value. Access does this to ensure that multiple users sharing a database don't get the same value for a new table row. So, if you want primary key numbers to remain consecutive, you should not use AutoNumber.



**You can define very functional forms using combo boxes, tab controls, and subforms. To really make your application user-friendly, you need to further automate your forms with Visual Basic. For details about how many of the forms in the sample databases are automated with Visual Basic, see Chapter 20.**

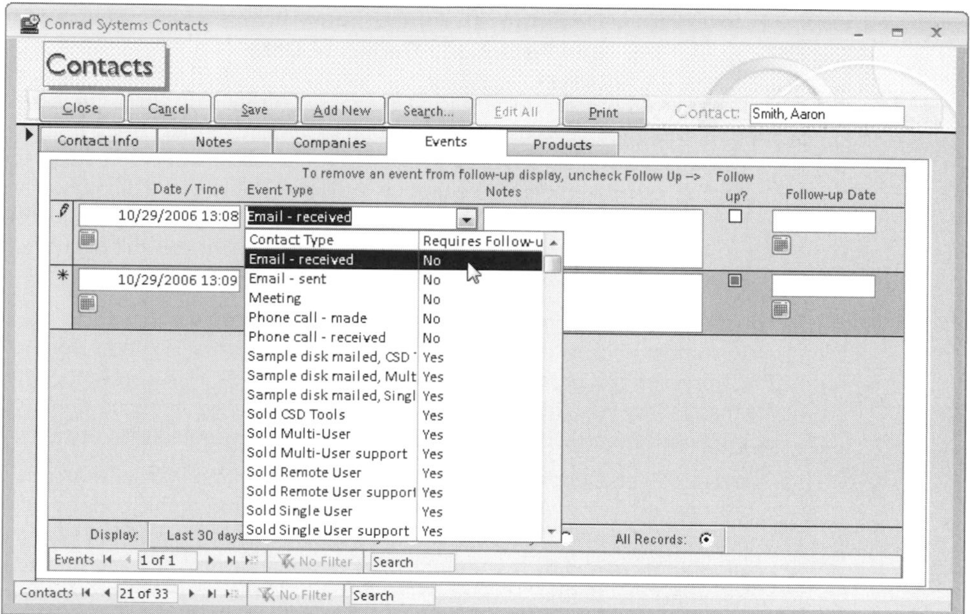


**Figure 10-31** You can add a new contact event record on the Events tab in the frmContactsPlain form.



## Changing and Deleting Data

If your form permits updates, you can easily change or delete existing data in the underlying table or query. If you design the form to be used in Datasheet view, you can use the same techniques you learned in Chapter 7, "Creating and Working with Simple Queries," to work with your data.

In Form view, your data might appear in one of several formats. If you design the form as a single form, you can see the data for only one record at a time. If you design the form as a continuous form, you might be able to see data for more than one record at a time.

As with datasheets, you must select a field in the form in order to change the data in the field. To select a field, either tab to the field or click in the field with the mouse. (Remember, if the field contains a hyperlink, clicking in it will activate the link. To edit a hyperlink, either tab to the field or right-click the field to open the shortcut menu, from which you can click commands to edit the hyperlink.) After you select a field, you can change the data in it by using the same techniques you used for working with data in a datasheet. You can type over individual characters, replace a sequence of characters, or copy and paste data from one field to another.

You might find that you can't tab to or select some fields in a form. When you design a form, you can set the properties of the controls on the form so that a user can't select the control. These properties prevent users from changing fields that you don't want updated, such as calculated values or fields from the *one* side of a query. You can also set the tab order to control the sequence of field selection when you use Tab or Shift+Tab to move around on the form. See Chapter 12, "Customizing a Form," for details.

Deleting a record in a single form or in a continuous form is different from deleting a record in a datasheet. First, you must select the record as you would select a record in a datasheet. If the form is designed with record selectors, simply click the record selector to select the record. If the form does not have record selectors, click the Select command in the Find group on the Home tab, and then click Select on the menu. To delete a selected record, press the Delete key or click the arrow next to the Delete command in the Records group on the Home tab, and then click Delete Record. You can also click the Delete Record command to delete the current record without first having to select it.

When a record you're trying to delete contains related records in other tables, you will see an error message unless the relationship defined between the tables tells Access to cascade delete the related fields and records. See Chapter 4 for details about defining relationships between tables. In frmContacts and frmContactsPlain in the Conrad Systems Contacts application, Visual Basic code behind the forms checks to see if dependent rows exist in other tables. This code issues a custom error message, shown in Figure 10-32, that gives you specific information about the problem. (The standard Access error message is not very user-friendly.) Rather than automatically delete dependent records (you might have asked to delete the contact record in error), the application requires you to specifically go to the tabs that show the related records and delete all these records first. You can see how this code works in Chapter 24.

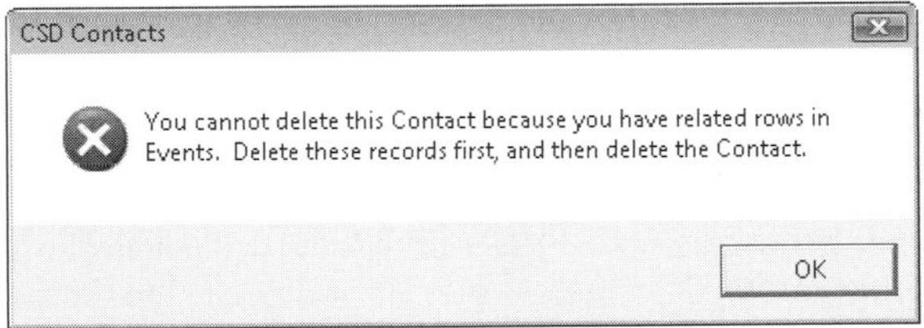


**Figure 10-32** The Conrad Systems Contacts application shows you a custom error message when you attempt to delete a contact that has dependent records in other tables.

## Searching for and Sorting Data

When you use forms to display and edit your data, you can search for data or sort it in a new order in much the same way that you search for and sort data in datasheets. (See Chapter 7.) The following sections show you how to use some of the form filter features to search for data in a form or use the quick sort commands to reorder your data.

## Performing a Simple Search

You can use Access 2007's Find feature in a form exactly as you would in a datasheet. Open the frmContactsPlain form if you closed it, select the field you want to search, and then click the Find command in the Find group on the Home tab to open the Find And Replace dialog box, as shown in Figure 10-33. You can enter search criteria exactly as you would for a datasheet. Note that in a form you can also perform a search on any control that you can select, including controls that display calculated values.

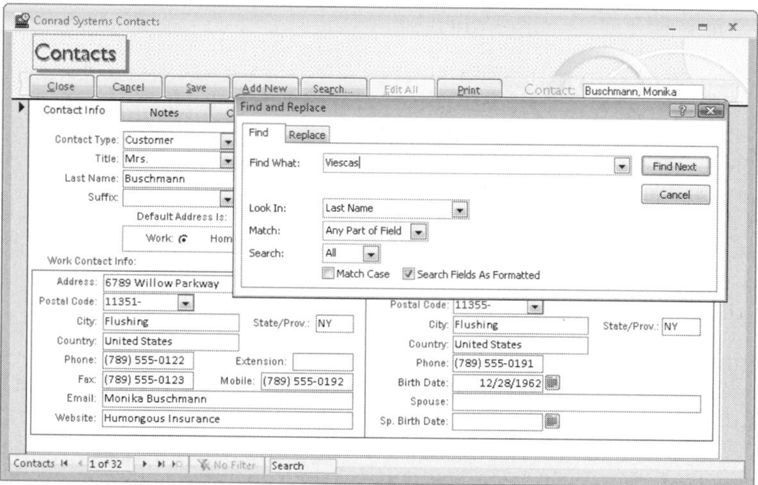


**Figure 10-33** You can use the Find And Replace dialog box to search your records for specific information.

In Figure 10-33 we clicked inside the Last Name field and then opened the Find And Replace dialog box. By default the Look In list in the Find And Replace dialog box remembers what you selected the last time you used Find. If you select Conrad Systems Database from the Look In list, Access will search through all the fields in this form for your criterion. Type the word **Viescas** in the Find What box, and make sure you select Last Name from the Look In list to search through only the Last Name field.

In the Match list, you can ask Access to search Any Part Of Field, Whole Field, or Start Of Field. When you select Any Part Of Field, Access looks for the characters you type in the Find What box anywhere within the field or fields you specified to search. If you select Whole Field, what you type in the Find What box must exactly match the contents of the field. When you select Start Of Field, the characters you type in the Find What box must be at the beginning of the field, but any or no characters can appear in the field after that.

By default, Access searches all records from the beginning of the recordset (the first record displayed in the form) unless you select either Up or Down in the Search list to search up or down from the current record position. Select the Match Case check box if you want to find text that exactly matches the uppercase and lowercase letters you typed. By default, Access is case-insensitive unless you select this check box.

You can select the Search Fields As Formatted check box if you need to search the data as it is displayed rather than as it is stored by Access. Although searching this way is slower, you should select this check box if you are searching a Date/Time field. You should also probably select this check box when searching any field that has a format or input mask applied—such as the Postal Code and phone number fields in this sample form. For example, if you're searching a date field for dates in January, you can specify ***-Jan-*** if the field is formatted as Medium Date and you select the Search Fields As Formatted check box. You might also want to select this check box when searching a Yes/No field for Yes because any value except 0 is a valid indicator of Yes. Clear this check box to improve performance when searching a simple text or numeric field.

After selecting the options you want, click the Find Next button. Access proceeds to search through the last names in the form's recordset for the value Viescas, and it finds John's record. Click Find Next to continue searching from the current record. Each time you click Find Next again, Access moves to the next value it finds. When Access can find no additional records (either by searching up to the first record when you select Up in the Search list or by searching to the last record when you select Down or All), it opens a message box to inform you that it has completed the search. Click OK to dismiss the message box and return to the Find And Replace dialog box. Click Cancel to close the dialog box.

After you have established search criteria in the Find And Replace dialog box, you can press Shift+F4 to execute the search from the current record without having to open the dialog box again.

## Using the Search Box

Access 2007 includes a new Search box on the record navigation bar at the bottom of the Form window, as shown in Figure 10-34. The Search box functions similarly to the Find And Replace dialog box discussed previously. Unlike the Find And Replace dialog box, the Search box does not give you any choices as to what fields to search in, what part of a string to match, or whether to match the string case. When you type something in the Search box, Access immediately begins to search through all fields in the form for the sequence of characters you enter. The characters you type can appear anywhere in the field, and Access performs the match "as formatted." For example, if you type **/196** in the Search box, you're likely to find the first person whose birthday is in the 1960s.

Move to the first record in the frmContactsPlain form and type the letter **c** in the Search box. Notice that Access stays on the first record and highlights the letter *C* of the word Customer in the Contact Type field. Now type the letter **o** after the letter *c* and observe that Access moves the focus to the Last Name field on the second record and highlights the letters *Co* in the name Conrad, as shown previously in Figure 10-34. To clear your search criteria, highlight all the text in the Search box and press Delete or use the Backspace key to remove the text.

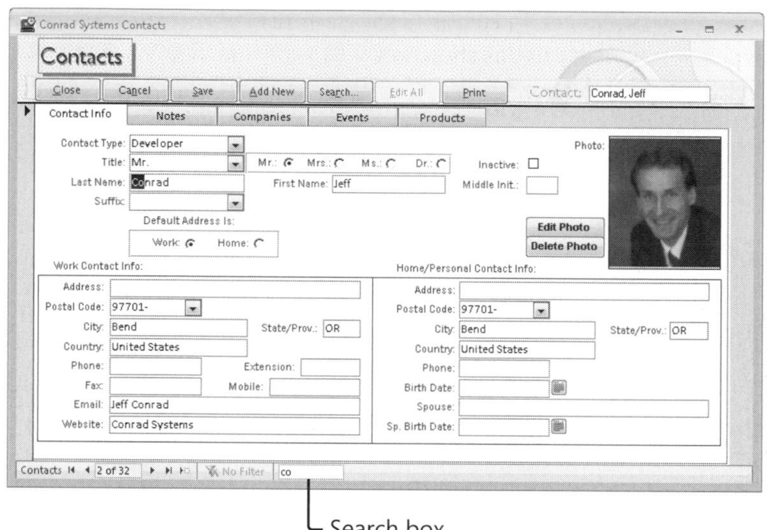


**Figure 10-34** You can also use the Search box to search through your form records.

## Performing a Quick Sort on a Form Field

As you can with a datasheet, you can select just about any control that contains data from the underlying recordset and click the Ascending or Descending button in the Sort & Filter group on the Home tab to reorder the records you see, based on the selected field. If you want to perform a quick sort, open the frmContactsPlain form, click in the Postal Code field in the form under Work Contact Info, and then click the Descending button in the Sort & Filter group on the Home tab. The contact with the highest postal code is displayed first.

## Adding a Filter to a Form

One of Access 2007's most powerful features is its ability to further restrict or sort the information displayed in the form without your having to create a new query. This restriction is accomplished with a filter that you define while you're using the form. When you apply the filter, you see only the data that matches the criteria you entered.

As with datasheets, you can define a filter using Filter By Selection, Filter By Form, or the Advanced Filter definition facility. Open the frmContactsPlain form, click the Advanced button in the Sort & Filter group on the Home tab, and click Filter By Form. Access adds features to the form to let you enter filter criteria, as shown in Figure 10-35. In this example, we're looking for all contacts who are the Developer contact type, whose last name begins with *V*, and who work in the city of Nashua. You'll see that you can click the arrow to the right of each field to display a list that contains all the values for that field currently in the database. If your database contains many thousands of rows, Access might not show the list if the field has more than several hundred unique values—it would take an unacceptably long time to retrieve the entire list. When the list is too long, Access gives you simple Is Null and Is Not Null choices instead. You can also type your own criteria, as shown in the Last Name field in Figure 10-35.

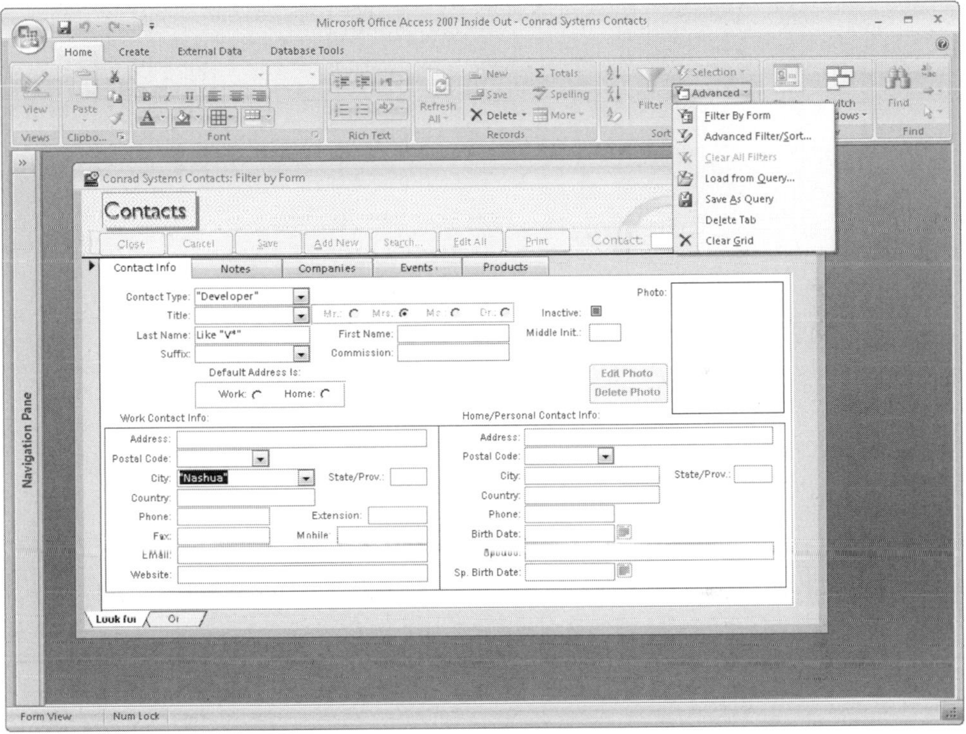


**Figure 10-35** Enter filter criteria for the frmContactsPlain form in the Filter By Form window.

As you can with datasheets, you can enter one set of criteria and then click an Or tab at the bottom of the blank form to enter additional criteria. If you don't like some of the criteria you've entered, click the Advanced button in the Sort & Filter group of the Home tab, and then click Clear Grid to start over. Click the Toggle Filter button in the Sort & Filter group to filter your records. Click the Clear All Filters command to exit the Filter By Form window without applying the new filter. Note that if you specify criteria on a subform, Access applies the filter only for records related to the record currently displayed on the main form. For example, you can't create a filter on the Products tab for contacts who own the BO$$ Multi-User edition and then expect to see all the contacts who own that product—you'll see only products for the current contact that match the value *BO$$ Multi-User*.

To turn off the filter, click the Toggle Filter button in the Sort & Filter group on the Home tab. To see the filter definition, click the Advanced button in the Sort & Filter group and then click Advanced Filter/Sort. After you apply the filter shown in Figure 10-35 and do an ascending quick sort on the WorkPostalCode field, the Advanced Filter/Sort window should look something like that shown in Figure 10-36.

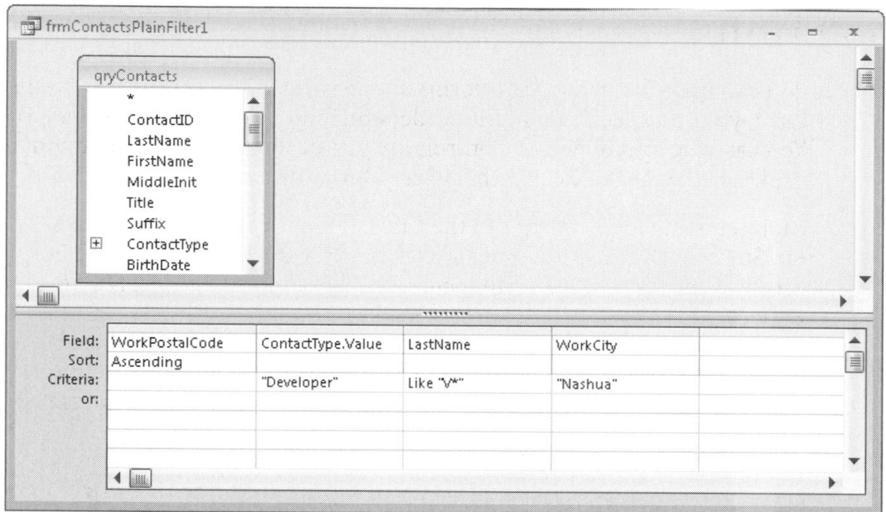


**Figure 10-36** In the Advanced Filter/Sort window for the frmContactsPlain form, you can see criteria previously entered using the Filter By Form command.

> **Note**
>
> If you use one of the Sort (Ascending or Descending) buttons, you'll discover that this "quick sort" uses the form's filter definition to create the sorting criteria. For example, if you do a quick sort to arrange contacts in descending order by last name, you'll find the LastName field in the form filter with the Sort row set to Descending when you click Advanced Filter/Sort under Advanced in the Sort & Filter group on the Home tab.



If you often use the same filter with your form, you can save the filter as a query and give it a name. Open the Advanced Filter/Sort window and create the filter. Click the Advanced command in the Sort & Filter group on the Home tab, click the Save As Query command, and then type a name for the query when Access prompts you.

You can load an existing query definition to use as a filter. Click Advanced in the Sort & Filter group on the Home tab and click Load From Query when you're in the Filter By Form window. Access presents a list of valid select queries (those that are based on the same table or tables as the form you're using).

# Printing Forms

You can use a form to print information from a table or query. When you design the form, you can specify different header and footer information for the printed version. You can also specify which controls are visible. For example, you might define some gridlines that are visible on the printed form but are not displayed on the screen.

An interesting form to print in the Conrad Systems Contacts database is the frmContactSummaryXmpl form. Open the form, click the Microsoft Office Button, click the arrow to the right of the Print command, and then click Print Preview. On the Print Preview tab, click the Zoom button and scroll to the top of the first page. You should see a screen that looks like the one shown in Figure 10-37. Notice that the form footer that you saw earlier in Figure 10-1 (page 519) does not appear in the printed version. In fact, this form has one set of headers and footers designed for printing and another set for viewing the form on the screen.

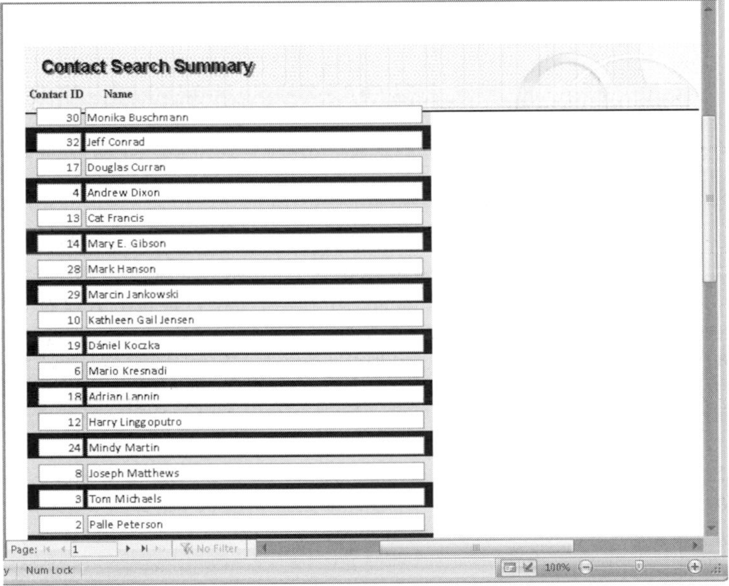


**Figure 10-37** When you view the frmContactSummaryXmpl form in Print Preview, you see a different set of headers and footers.

You can use the scroll bars to move around on the page. Use the Page Number box in the lower-left corner of the Print Preview window in the same way that you use the Record Number box on a form or in a datasheet. Click the Zoom button again to see the entire page on the screen.

Click the Margins command in the Page Layout group on the Print Preview tab to set top, bottom, left, and right margins. Click the Page Setup button in the same Page Layout group to set additional options. Access displays the Page Setup dialog box, in which you can customize the way the form prints. Click the Page tab in the Page Setup dialog box (shown in Figure 10-38) to select Portrait or Landscape orientation, the paper size and source, and the printer. Access will store these specifications with the definition of your form.

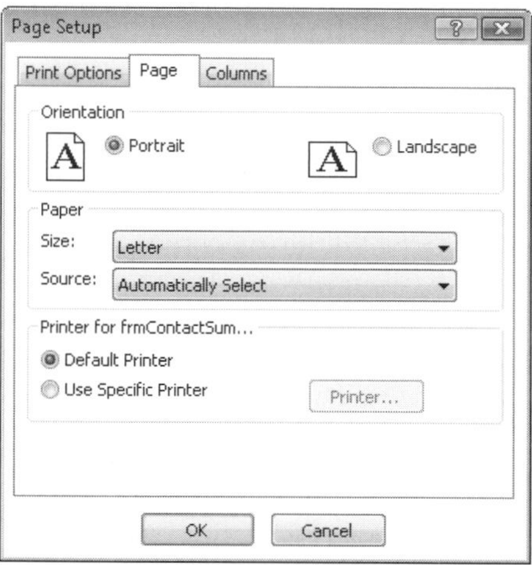


**Figure 10-38** The Page tab of the Page Setup dialog box for forms includes several page options.

Click the Columns tab of the Page Setup dialog box to see additional options, as shown in Figure 10-39. We'll explore the Columns options in detail in Chapter 14, "Using Reports."

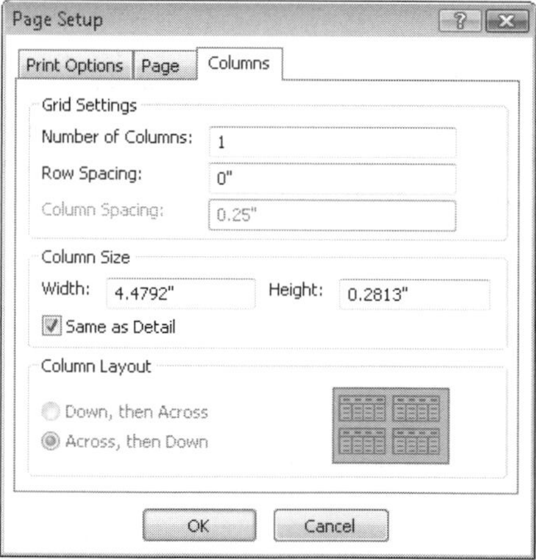


**Figure 10-39** The Columns tab of the Page Setup dialog box for forms lets you define grid and column settings.

You should now have a good understanding of how forms work and of many design elements that you can include when you build forms. Now, on to the fun part—building your first form in the next chapter.

CHAPTER 11

# Building a Form



From the perspective of daily use, forms are the most important objects you'll build in your Microsoft Office Access 2007 application because they're what users see and work with every time they run the application. This chapter shows you how to design and build forms in an Office Access 2007 desktop application. You'll learn how to work with a Form window in Design view to build a basic form based on a single table, and you'll learn how to use the Form Wizard to simplify the form-creation process. The last section of this chapter, "Simplifying Data Input with a Form," shows you how to use some of the special form controls to simplify data entry on your forms.

**Note**

The examples in this chapter are based on the forms, tables, and data in ContactsData-Copy.accdb on the companion CD included with this book. The results you see from the samples in this chapter might not exactly match what you see in this book if you have changed the sample data in the file. Also, all the screen images in this chapter were taken on a Microsoft Windows Vista system with the display theme set to Blue, and Use Windows-Themed Controls On Forms has been turned on in the sample databases. Your results might look different if you are using a different operating system or a different theme. We'll discuss the Use Windows-Themed Controls On Forms option later in this chapter.

## Forms and Object-Oriented Programming

Access was not designed to be a full object-oriented programming environment, yet it has many characteristics found in object-oriented application development systems. Before you dive into building forms, it's useful to examine how Access implements objects and actions, particularly if you come from the world of procedural application development.

In classic procedural application development, the data you need for the application is distinct from the programs you write to work with the data and from the results produced by your programs. Each program works with the data independently and generally has little structural connection with other programs in the system. For example, an order entry program accepts input from a clerk and then writes the order to data files. Later, a billing program processes the orders and prints invoices. Another characteristic of procedural systems is that events must occur in a specific order and cannot be executed out of sequence. A procedural system has difficulty looking up supplier or price information while in the middle of processing an order.

In an object-oriented system, however, an object is defined as a subject that has *properties*, and you can invoke certain actions, or *methods*, to be performed on that subject. Objects can contain other objects. When an object incorporates another object, it inherits the attributes and properties of the other object and expands on the object's definition. In Access, queries define actions on tables, and the queries then become new logical tables known as *recordsets*. That is, a query doesn't actually contain any data, but you can work with the data fetched by the query as though it were a table. You can base a query on another query with the same effect. Queries inherit the integrity and formatting rules defined for the tables. Forms further define actions on tables or queries, and the fields you include in forms initially inherit the underlying properties, such as formatting and validation rules, of the fields in the source tables or queries. You can define different formatting or more restrictive rules, but you cannot override the rules defined for the tables.

Within an Access database, you can interrelate application objects and data. For example, you can set startup properties that prepare your application to run. As part of the application startup, you will usually open a switchboard form. The switchboard form might act on some of the data in the database, or it might offer controls that open other forms, print reports, or close the application.

**For more information about startup properties, see Chapter 24, "The Finishing Touches."**

Figure 11-1 shows the conceptual architecture of an Access form. In addition to operating on tables or queries in a database, forms can contain other forms, called *subforms*. These subforms can, in turn, define actions on other tables, queries, or forms. Events that occur in forms and subforms (such as changing the value of a field or moving to a new record) can trigger macro actions or Microsoft Visual Basic procedures. As you'll learn when you read about advanced form design, macro actions and Visual Basic procedures can be triggered in many ways. The most obvious way to trigger an action is by clicking a command button on a form. But you can also define macros or Visual Basic procedures that execute when an event occurs, such as clicking in a field, changing the data in a field, pressing a key, adding or deleting a row, or simply moving to a new row in the underlying table or query.

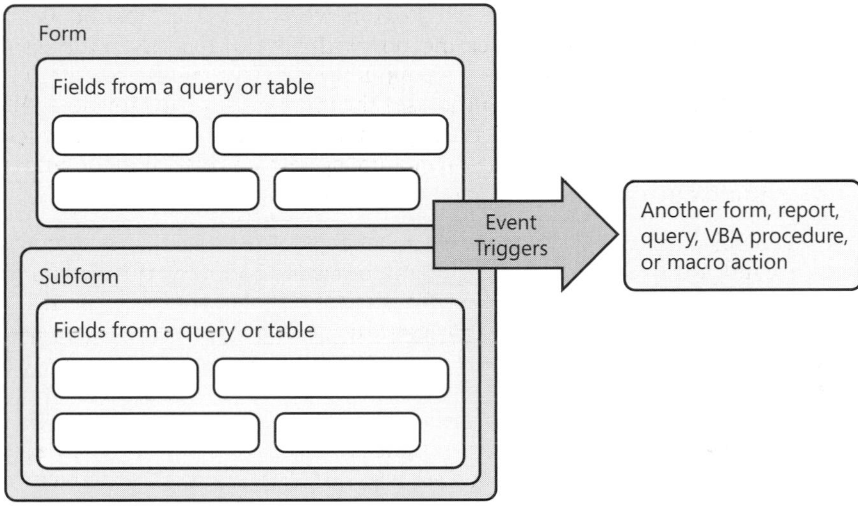


**Figure 11-1** An Access form can contain other objects, including other forms, and you can set some of its properties to define procedures that respond to events.

In Chapter 20, "Automating Your Application with Visual Basic," you'll learn how several of the more complex forms in the Conrad Systems Contacts and Housing Reservations sample databases are automated with Visual Basic. Figure 11-2 shows a few of the automated processes for the frmContacts form in the Conrad Systems Contacts database. For example, printing the contact currently displayed in the form is triggered by using a command button.

In addition to automating print options, code behind the frmContacts form automatically fills in the city and state when you enter a postal code and provides a graphical way to choose a date if you click the button next to a date. On the Events tab, when you enter a sale of a product to the contact, code automatically generates a product record.

Object-oriented systems are not restricted to a specific sequence of events. So a user entering a contact event in Access 2007 can open up a new form object in the Navigation Pane and start a search in a companies or products form window without having to first finalize or cancel work already in progress in frmContacts.

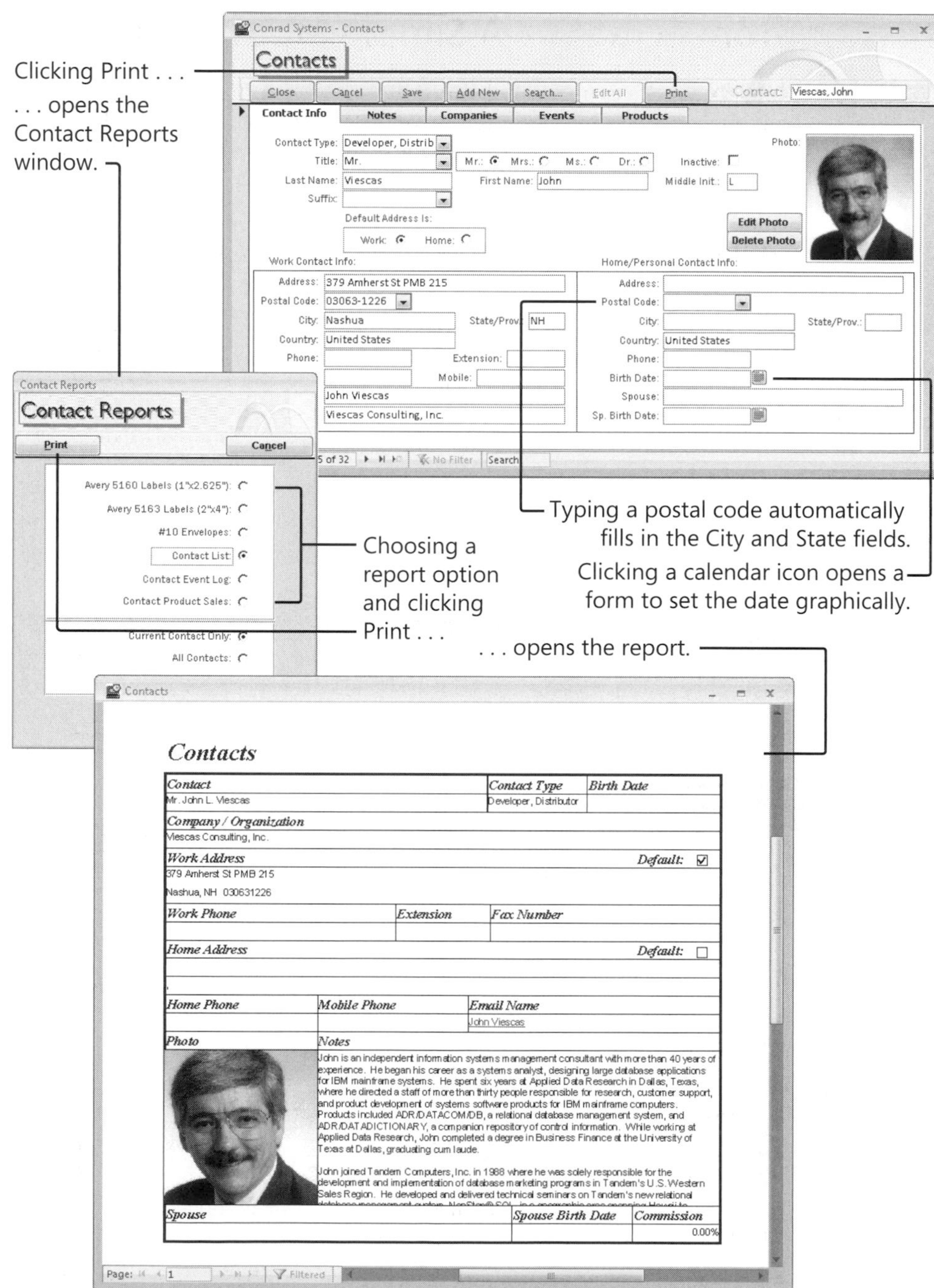


Figure 11-2 Some of the automated processes for the frmContacts form include opening a dialog box to choose a contacts report and automatically filling in the city and state when you enter a postal code.

# Starting from Scratch—A Simple Input Form

To start, you'll create a simple form that accepts and displays data in the tblCompanies table in the Conrad Systems Contacts database. Later, you'll create a form for the tblProducts table in this same database by using the Form Wizard. To follow along in this section, open the ContactsDataCopy.accdb database.

## Building a New Form with Design Tools

To begin building a new form that allows you to display and edit data from a table, you need to start with a blank Form window. You'll build this first form without the aid of the Form Wizard so that you'll understand the variety of components that go into form design. Click the Blank Form command in the Forms group on the Create tab. By default Access opens a blank Form window in Layout view with the field list displayed on the right, as shown in Figure 11-3.

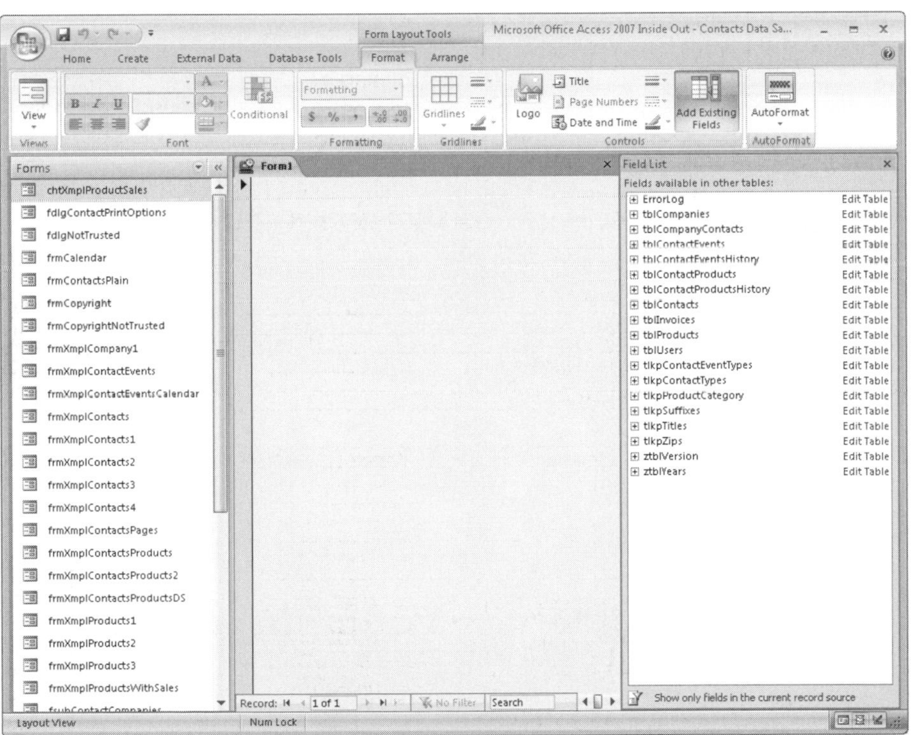


**Figure 11-3** When you click the Blank Form command on the Ribbon, Access opens a new Form window in Layout view.

Access does not know at this point from which tables or queries you want to display and edit data. The field list on the right displays a list of each local or linked table. If you click the plus symbol next to the name of a table, Access expands the list and displays the name of every field in that table. You can click on a field name in the field list and drag and drop it onto your form. If you click the Edit Table hyperlink on the right side of the field list, Access opens that specific table in Design view. We discuss Layout view in more detail in Chapter 12, "Customizing a Form"; for now we will focus on Design view.

When you ask Access to create a new blank form, Access initially displays the form in Layout view. To switch to Design view, click the arrow under the View button in the Views group and click Design View. Access switches the Form window to Design view and provides several design tools on the Design contextual tab under Form Design Tools on the Ribbon, as shown in Figure 11-4.

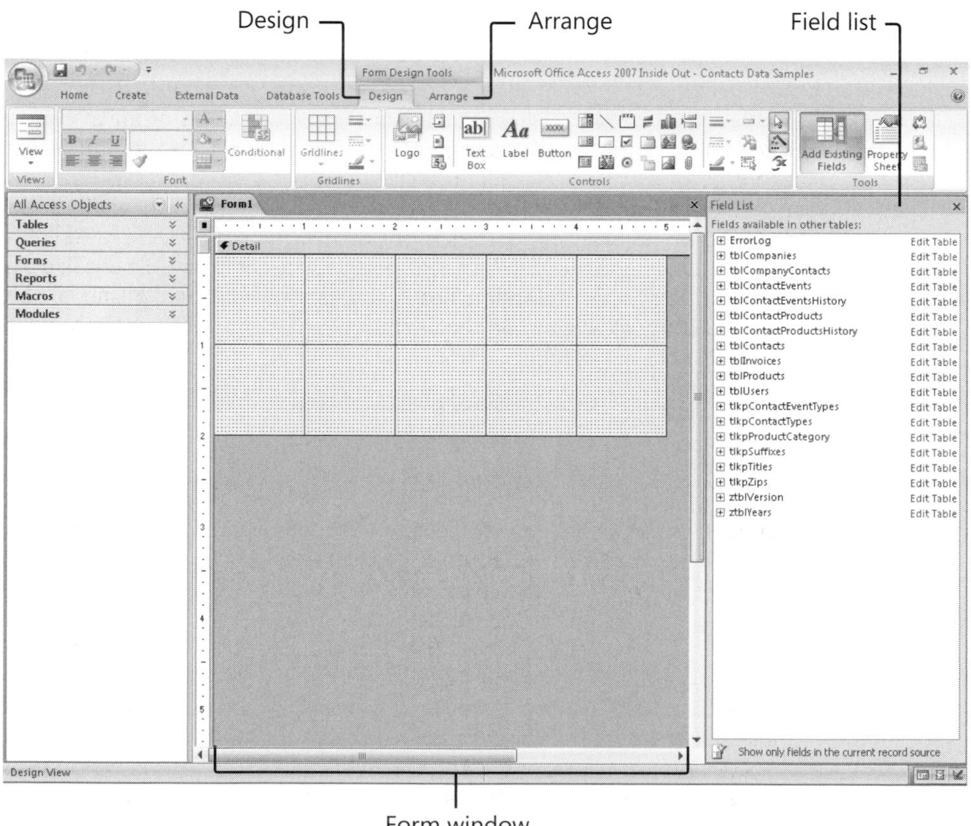


**Figure 11-4** When you open a form in Design view you can use the form grid and tools to create your form elements.

Access starts with a form that has only a *Detail section*. The section has a grid on a background that is the color defined for 3-D objects in the Appearance Settings dialog box—usually a light gray or beige. You can click the edge of the Detail section and then drag the edge to make the section larger or smaller. (To see more of the grid you might also want to collapse the Navigation Pane on the left.) You can remove the grid dots from the Detail section by clicking the Show Grid command in the Show/Hide group on the Arrange tab under Form Design Tools. If you want to add a *Header section* or a *Footer section* to the form, click the Form Header/Footer command in the same Show/Hide group.

**Note**

To set the color for 3-D objects, right-click on the desktop and then click Personalize. Click Windows Color And Appearance. In the Appearance Settings dialog box, click Advanced. In the Item list, click 3D Objects. Use the Color 1 list to set the color you want to use for 3-D objects.

The Detail section starts out at 5 inches (12.7 centimeters) wide by 2 inches (5.08 centimeters) high. The measurement gradations on the rulers are relative to the size and resolution of your screen. By default, Access sets the grid at 24 dots per inch horizontally and 24 dots per inch vertically. You can change the density of the grid dots by altering the Grid X and Grid Y properties in the form's property sheet. To replace the field list with the property sheet, click the Property Sheet command in the Tools group on the Design tab under Form Design Tools. You can find the Grid X and Grid Y properties near the bottom of the list on the Format tab of the property sheet when you have the form selected.

## INSIDE OUT Choosing a Form Width and Height

Although you can design a form that is up to 22 inches (55.87 centimeters) wide, and each form section can also be up to 22 inches high (a total of 66 inches if you include all three sections), you should design your forms to fit on your users' screens. We tend to design all our forms to comfortably fit on the lowest common screen resolution—1024×768. A form to fit this size should be about 9.75 inches (24.8 centimeters) wide, and the sum of the heights of the sections should be about 5.6 inches (14.2 centimeters) to allow space for the Ribbon, status bar, and Windows taskbar. If your user has set a higher screen resolution, and your application is designed using overlapping windows, extra space will be available on the Access desktop to work with multiple form windows at a time. If you are using tabbed documents, extra space appears to the right and bottom of the form when the user opens it on a higher-resolution screen.

You can find a handy form, zsfrm1024x768, in several of the sample databases. When you're working in a higher resolution, you can open this form and overlay it on the form you're designing. If your form fits behind the sample form, your form should be displayed properly at the lowest common resolution.

The Grid X and Grid Y property settings determine the intervals per unit of measurement in the grid. You can enter a number from 1 (coarsest) through 64 (finest). You set the unit of measure (U.S. or metric) by default when you select a country on the Location tab in the Regional And Language Options dialog box. (You open this dialog box by first clicking Clock, Language, And Region in Control Panel and then clicking Regional And Language Options. If your Control Panel is set to Classic View, click Regional And Language Options.)

For example, if your unit of measurement is inches and you specify a Grid X setting of 10, Access divides the grid horizontally into 0.1-inch increments. When your measurement is in inches and you set the Grid X and Grid Y values to 24 or less, Access displays the grid dots on the grid. In centimeters, you can see the grid dots when you specify a setting of 9 or less. If you set a finer grid for either Grid X or Grid Y, Access won't display the grid dots but you can still use the grid to line up controls. Access always displays grid lines at 1-inch intervals (U.S.) or 1-centimeter intervals (metric), even when you set fine Grid X or Grid Y values.

### Some Key Form Design Terms

As you begin to work in form design, you need to understand a few commonly used terms.

A form that displays data from your tables must have a record source. A *record source* can be the name of a table, the name of a query, or an SQL statement.

When a control can display information (text boxes, option groups, toggle buttons, option buttons, check boxes, combo boxes, list boxes, bound object frames, and many ActiveX controls), its *control source* defines the name of the field from the record source or the expression that provides the data to display. A control that has an expression as its control source is not updatable.

When a form has a record source, it is *bound* to the records in that record source—the form displays records from the record source and can potentially update the fields in the records. When a control is on a bound form and its control source is the name of a field in the record source, the control is *bound* to the field—the control displays (and perhaps allows you to edit) the data from the bound field in the current row of the record source. A control cannot be bound unless the form is also bound.

A form that has no record source is *unbound*. A control that has no control source is unbound.



Before proceeding further, you need to specify a record source for your new form. Although you can drag and drop fields from the field list and Access will figure out the appropriate record source for you, you have more control if you select a record source first. Click the All tab in the property sheet, click the arrow to the right of the Record Source property, and select the tblCompanies table from the list as shown in Figure 11-5.

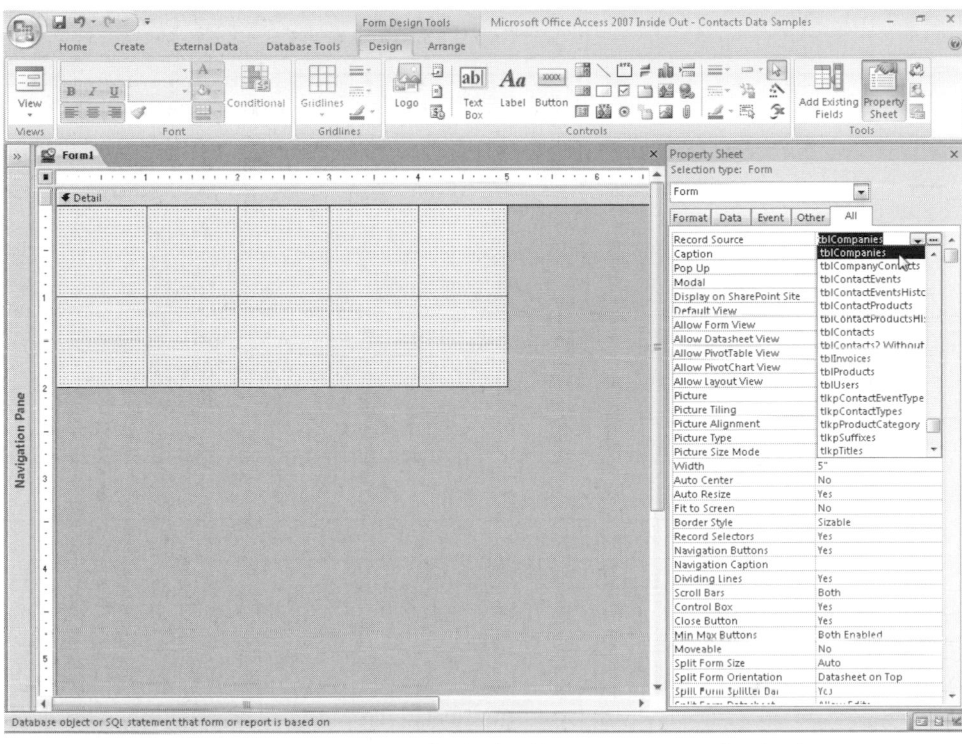


**Figure 11-5** Select a record source to specify which table or query to use for the data on your form.

The following sections describe some of the tools you can use to design a form.

## The Form Design Tools Contextual Ribbon Tabs

As you learned in Chapter 2, "Exploring the New Look of Access 2007," and Chapter 3, "Microsoft Office Access 2007 Overview," the Ribbon provides contextual tabs when Access displays objects in various views. When a form is in Design view, two contextual tabs appear–Design and Arrange under Form Design Tools. These contextual tabs, shown in Figure 11-6, are the "command center" of form design. These tabs provide all the essential tools and commands you need to design and modify your forms.

At the heart of these tabs is the Controls group found on the Design tab. This group contains buttons for all the types of controls you can use when you design a form. It also contains a button (named Insert ActiveX Control) that gives you access to all the ActiveX controls (for example, the calendar control that comes with Access) that you have installed on your system. To select a particular control to place on a form, click the control's button in the group. When you move the mouse pointer over the form, the mouse pointer turns into an icon that represents the control you selected. Position the mouse pointer where you want to place the control, and click the left mouse button to place the control on the form. If you want to size the control as you place it, drag the mouse pointer to make the control the size you want. (You can also size a control after you place it by dragging the sizing handles at its sides or corners.)

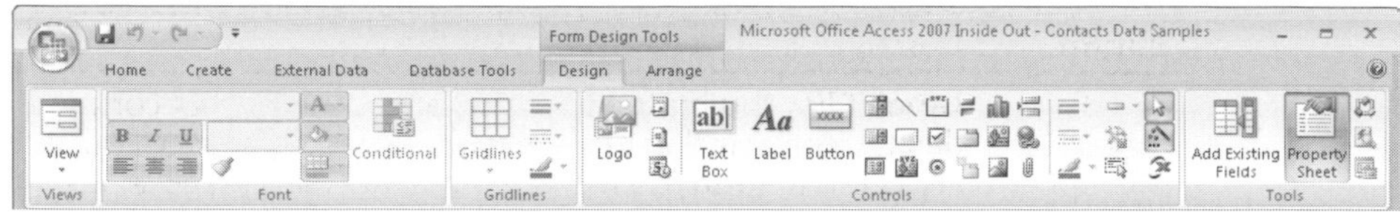


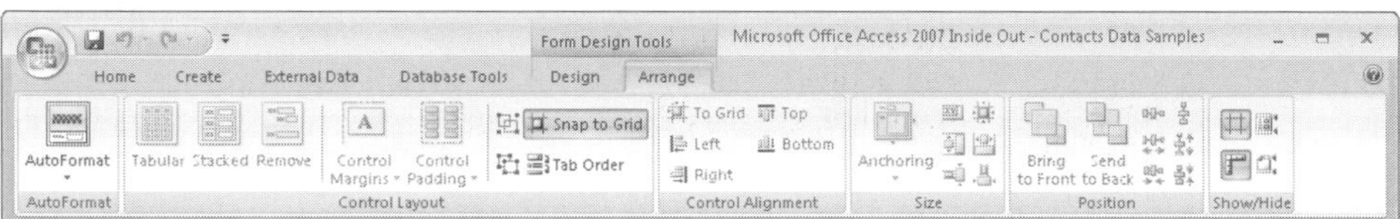


**Figure 11-6** You can use the various commands on the two contextual tabs under Form Design Tools to create and edit your forms.

Top to bottom, left to right, the buttons in the Controls group are described in Table 11-1.

**Table 11-1 Controls Group Buttons**

| Button | Description |
|---|---|
| Logo | **Logo.** Click this button to insert into a form a picture to be used as a logo displayed in an image control. (See the description of the image control later in this table.) When you click Logo, Access opens the Insert Picture dialog box where you can select the graphic or picture that you want to use as a logo. By default, Access places the logo in the form's Header section. If you have not revealed the form header and footer, the command adds those sections to your form before inserting the logo in the Header section. |
| | **Title.** Click this button to insert a new label control in a form's Header section to be used as a title for the form. (See the description of the label control later in this table.) If you have not revealed the form header and footer, the command adds those sections to your form before inserting the label control in the Header section. |
| | **Insert Page Number.** Click this button to open the Page Numbers dialog box where you can choose to insert page numbers in the Page Header or Page Footer section of the form in text box controls. (See the description of the text box control later in this table.) The Page Header and Page Footer sections appear only when you print the form. |
| | **Date & Time.** Click this button to open the Date And Time dialog box where you can choose to insert the date, the time, or both the date and time displayed in text box controls in the form's Header section. (See the description of the text box control later in this table.) You can choose different formats for both the date and time. If you have not revealed the form header and footer, the command adds those sections to your form before inserting the text box controls in the Header section. |
| ab\| Text Box | **Text Box.** Click this button to create text box controls for displaying text, numbers, dates, times, and memo fields. You can bind a text box to one of the fields in an underlying table or query. If you let a text box that is bound to a field be updated, you can change the value in the field in the underlying table or query by entering a new value in the text box. You can also use a text box to display calculated values. |

| Button | Description |
|---|---|
| 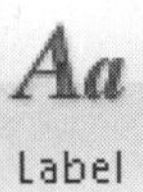 | **Label.** Click this button to create label controls that contain fixed text. By default, controls that can display data have a label control automatically attached. You can use this command to create stand-alone labels for headings and for instructions on your form. |
|  | **Button.** Click this button to create a command button control that can activate a macro or a Visual Basic procedure. You can also specify a hyperlink address that Access opens when a user clicks the button. |
|  | **Combo Box.** Click this button to create a combo box control that contains a list of potential values for the control and an editable text box. To create the list, you can enter values for the Row Source property of the combo box. You can also specify a table or a query as the source of the values in the list. Access displays the currently selected value in the text box. When you click the arrow to the right of the combo box, Access displays the values in the list. Select a new value in the list to reset the value in the control. If you bind the combo box to a field in the underlying table or query, you can change the value in the field by selecting a new value in the list. If you bind the combo box to a multi-value field, Access displays the list with check boxes to allow the user to select multiple values. You can bind multiple columns to the list, and you can hide one or more of the columns in the list by setting a column's width to 0. You can bind the actual value in the control to such a hidden column. When a multiple-column list is closed, Access displays the value in the first column whose width is greater than 0. Access displays all nonzero-width columns when you open the list. |
|  | **List Box.** Click this button to create a list box control that contains a list of potential values for the control. To create the list, you can enter the values in the Row Source property of the list box. You can also specify a table or a query as the source of the values in the list. List boxes are always open, and Access highlights the currently selected value in the list box. You select a new value in the list to reset the value in the control. If you bind the list box to a field in the underlying table or query, you can change the value in the field by selecting a new value in the list. If you bind the list box to a multi-value field, Access displays the list with check boxes to allow the user to select multiple values. You can bind multiple columns to the list, and you can hide one or more of the columns in the list by setting a column's width to 0. You can bind the actual value in the control to such a hidden column. Access displays all nonzero-width columns that fit within the defined width of the control. If the list box control is unbound, you can allow the user to select multiple values in the list (also called a multiple-selection list box). |
|  | **Subform/Subreport.** Click this button to embed another form in the current form. You can use the subform to show data from a table or a query that is related to the data in the main form. Access maintains the link between the two forms for you. |
| 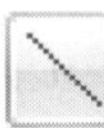 | **Line.** Click this button to add lines to a form to enhance its appearance. |

| Button | Description |
|---|---|
|  | **Rectangle.** Click this button to add filled or empty rectangles to a form to enhance its appearance. |
|  | **Bound Object Frame.** Click this button to display and edit an OLE object field from the underlying data. Access can display most pictures and graphs directly on a form. For other objects, Access displays the icon for the application in which the object was created. For example, if the object is a sound object created in Windows Sound Recorder, you'll see a speaker icon on your form. |
|  | **Option Group.** Click this button to create option group controls that contain one or more toggle buttons, option buttons, or check boxes. (See the descriptions of these controls later in this table.) You can assign a separate numeric value to each button or check box that you include in the group. When you have more than one button or check box in a group, you can select only one button or check box at a time, and the value assigned to that button or check box becomes the value for the option group. If you have incorrectly assigned the same value to more than one button or check box, all buttons or check boxes that have the same value appear highlighted when you click any of them. You can select one of the buttons or check boxes in the group as the default value for the group. If you bind the option group to a field in the underlying query or table, you can set a new value in the field by selecting a button or a check box in the group. |
|  | **Check Box.** Click this button to create a check box control that holds an on/off, a true/false, or a yes/no value. When you select a check box, its value becomes –1 (to represent on, true, or yes), and a check mark appears in the box. Select the check box again, and its value becomes 0 (to represent off, false, or no), and the check mark disappears from the box. You can include a check box in an option group and assign the check box a unique numeric value. If you create a group with multiple controls, selecting a new check box clears any previously selected toggle button, option button, or check box in that group (unless other buttons or check boxes in the group also have the same value). If you bind the check box to a field in the underlying table or query, you can toggle the field's value by clicking the check box. |
|  | **Option Button.** Click this button to create an option button control (sometimes called a radio button control) that holds an on/off, a true/false, or a yes/no value. When you select an option button, its value becomes –1 (to represent on, true, or yes), and a filled circle appears in the center of the button. Select the button again, and its value becomes 0 (to represent off, false, or no), and the filled circle disappears. You can include an option button in an option group and assign the button a unique numeric value. If you create a group with multiple controls, selecting a new option button clears any previously selected toggle button, option button, or check box in that group (unless other buttons or check boxes in the group also have the same value). If you bind the option button to a field in the underlying table or query, you can toggle the field's value by clicking the option button. |

| Button | Description |
|---|---|
|  | **Toggle Button.** Click this button to create a toggle button control that holds an on/off, a true/false, or a yes/no value. When you click a toggle button, its value becomes –1 (to represent on, true, or yes), and the button appears pressed in. Click the button again, and its value becomes 0 (to represent off, false, or no). You can include a toggle button in an option group and assign the button a unique numeric value. If you create a group with multiple controls, selecting a new toggle button clears any previously selected toggle button, option button, or check box in that group (unless other buttons or check boxes in the group also have the same value). If you bind the toggle button to a field in the underlying table or query, you can toggle the field's value by clicking the toggle button. |
|  | **Tab Control.** Click this button to create a series of tab pages on your form. Each page can contain a number of other controls to display information. The tab control works much like many of the option dialog boxes or property sheet windows in Access—when a user clicks a different tab, Access displays the controls contained on that tab. See Chapter 13, "Advanced Form Design," for details about using the Tab Control button. |
|  | **Insert Page.** Click this button to add an additional tab page to your tab control. By default Access creates two pages for a new tab control object. Click on your tab control object on the design grid and then click the Insert Page command to add an additional tab page. |
|  | **Insert Chart.** Click this button to add a chart on your form grid. Clicking this button and then placing the control on your form launches the Chart Wizard to walk you through the steps necessary to create a new chart. |
|  | **Unbound Object Frame.** Click this button to add an object from another application that supports object linking and embedding. The object becomes part of your form, not part of the data from the underlying table or query. You can add pictures, sounds, charts, or slides to enhance your form. When the object is a chart, you can specify a query as the source of data for the chart, and you can link the chart display to the current record in the form by one or more field values. |
|  | **Image.** Click this button to place a static picture on your form. You cannot edit the picture on the form, but Access stores it in a format that is very efficient for application speed and size. If you want to use a picture as the entire background of your form, you can set the form's Picture property. |
|  | **Insert Or Remove Page Break.** Click this button to add a page break between the pages of a multiple-page form. (We think this tool is misnamed. To remove a page break, you must select the page break control and press the Delete key.) |
|  | **Insert Hyperlink.** Click this button to add a hyperlink in a label control to your form design grid. This hyperlink can contain a Uniform Resource Locator (URL) that points to a location on the World Wide Web, on a local intranet, or on a local drive. It can also use a Universal Naming Convention (UNC) file name to point to a file on a server on your local area network (LAN) or on your local computer drives. The link might point to a file that is a Web page or even another object in your current database. Clicking this button opens the Insert Hyperlink dialog box discussed previously in "Working with Hyperlinks" on page 397. |

| Button | Description |
|---|---|
|  | **Attachment.** Click this button to insert an attachment control on the form design grid. You can bind this control to an attachment field in the underlying data. You can use this control, for example, to display a picture or to attach other files. In Form view this control presents the Manage Attachments dialog box where you can attach, delete, and view multiple attachment files stored in the underlying field. |
| 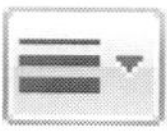 | **Line Thickness menu.** Use this drop-down menu to change the selected line thickness. The available options are Hairline, 1pt, 2pt, 3pt, 4pt, 5pt, and 6pt. |
| 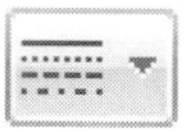 | **Line Type menu.** Use this drop-down menu to change the selected line type. The available options are Transparent, Solid, Dashes, Short Dashes, Dots, Sparse Dots, Dash Dot, and Dash Dot Dot. |
|  | **Line Color menu.** Use this drop-down menu to change the selected line color. You can choose from predefined color schemes or create a custom color from the Color Picker dialog box. |
|  | **Special Effect menu.** Use this drop-down menu to change the look of the control to flat, raised, sunken, etched, shadowed, or chiseled. |
|  | **Set Control Defaults.** Click this button if you want to change the default property settings for all new controls of a particular type. Select a control of that type, set the control's properties to the desired default values, and then click the Set Control Defaults command. The settings of the currently selected control become the default settings for any subsequent definitions of that type of control on your form. |
|  | **Select All.** Click this button to select all the controls on the form design grid. |
|  | **Select.** Click this button to select, size, move, and edit existing controls. This is the default command when you first open a form in Design view. This button becomes selected again after you have used one of the control commands to place a new control on your form. |
|  | **Use Control Wizards.** Click this button to activate a control wizard. Click the button again to deactivate the wizard. When this button appears pressed in, a control wizard helps you enter control properties whenever you create a new option group, combo box, list box, or command button. The Combo Box and List Box Wizards also offer you an option to create Visual Basic code to move to a new record based on a selection the user makes in the combo or list box. The Command Button Wizard offers to generate Visual Basic code that performs various automated actions when the user clicks the button. |
|  | **Insert ActiveX Control.** Click this button to open a dialog box showing all the ActiveX controls you have installed on your system. You can select one of the controls and then click OK to add the control to the form design grid. Not all ActiveX controls work with Access. |

**For more information about using controls on forms, see Chapter 12 and Chapter 13.**

## INSIDE OUT Locking a Control Button

When you click a button that is a form control, your mouse pointer reverts to the Select button after you place the selected control on your form. If you plan to create several controls using the same tool—for example, a series of check boxes in an option group—double-click the button for that control in the Controls group to "lock" it. You can unlock it by clicking any other button (including the Select button).

### The Field List

Use the field list in conjunction with the Controls group to place bound controls (controls linked to fields in a table or a query) on your form. You can open the field list by clicking the Add Existing Fields button in the Tools group on the Design tab. If the form is bound to a table or query, Access displays the name of the underlying table or query along with all the fields available, as shown in Figure 11-7. Any tables that have relationships to the underlying table defined are displayed under Fields Available In Related Tables. The last section of the field list, Fields Available In Other Tables, lists the tables and fields from all other tables in this database. Click the Show Only Fields In The Current Record Source link to remove the bottom two sections of the field list. You can undock the field list by clicking the title bar and dragging it away from the right edge of the Form window. After you undock the field list, you can drag the edges of the window to resize it so that you can see any long field names. You can drag the title bar to move the window out of the way. When the list of available field names is too long to fit in the current size of the window, use the vertical scroll bar to move through the list.

To use the field list to place a bound control on a form, first click the button for the type of control you want in the Controls group. Then drag the field you want from the field list and drop it into position on the form. If you click the button for a control that's inappropriate for the data type of the field, Access selects the default control for the data type. For example, if you click anything but the Attachment button when placing an attachment field on a form, Access creates an attachment control for you anyway. If you try to drag any field after clicking the button for the subform/subreport, unbound object frame, line, rectangle, or page break control, Access creates a text box control or bound object frame control, as appropriate, instead. If you drag a field from the field list without clicking a control, Access uses either the display control you defined for the field in the table definition or a control appropriate for the field data type.

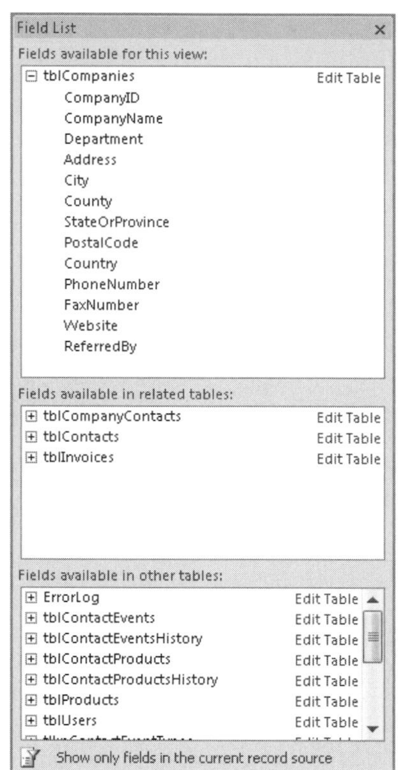


**Figure 11-7** The field list shows the names of the fields in the bound table or query, any related tables, and fields from all other tables in the current database.

## The Property Sheet

The form, each section of the form (header, detail, footer), and each control on the form have a list of properties associated with them, and you set these properties using a property sheet. Each control on a form, each section on a form, and the form itself are all *objects*. The kinds of properties you can specify vary depending on the object. To open the property sheet for an object, select the object and then click the Property Sheet button in the Tools group on the Design tab. Access opens a window similar to the one shown in Figure 11-8 on the right side of the Form window, replacing the field list. (You cannot have both the property sheet and the field list open at the same time.) If you have previously undocked either the field list or property sheet, the property sheet appears in the undocked window. If the property sheet is already open, you can view the properties specific to an object by clicking the object. You can also click the arrow under Selection Type and then select the object name from the list at the top of the property sheet.

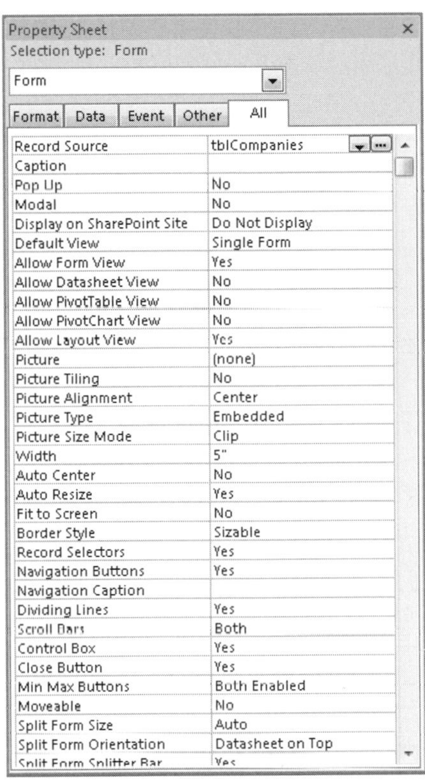


**Figure 11-8** You can view the properties of form controls and sections using the property sheet.

You can drag the title bar to move the property sheet around on your screen. You can also drag the edges of the window to resize it so that you can see more of the property settings. Because a form has more than 100 properties that you can set and because many controls have more than 70 properties, Access provides tabs at the top of the property sheet so that you can choose to display all properties (the default) or to display only format properties, data properties, event properties, or other properties. A form property sheet displaying only the data properties is shown in Figure 11-9.

When you click in a property box that provides a list of valid values, a small arrow appears on the right side of the property box. Click this arrow to see a list of the values for the property. For properties that can have a very long value setting, you can click the property and then press Shift+F2 to open the Zoom dialog box. The Zoom dialog box provides an expanded text box for entering or viewing a value.

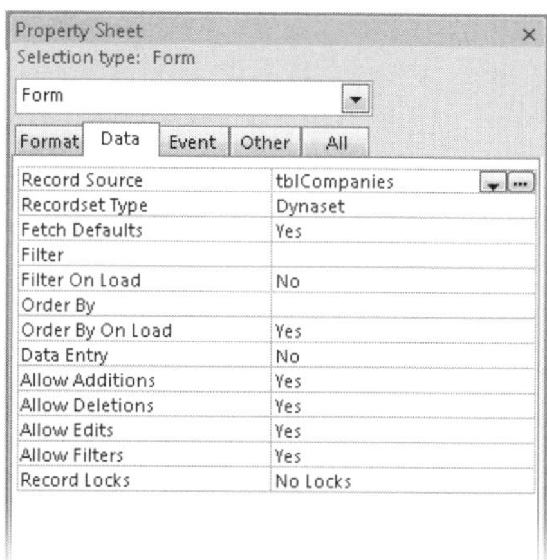


**Figure 11-9** If you click the Data tab on the form property sheet, Access displays only the data properties.

Build

In many cases, a window, dialog box, or wizard is available to help you create property settings for properties that can accept a complex expression, a query definition, or code (a macro or a Visual Basic procedure) to respond to an event. When such help is available for a property setting, Access displays a small button with an ellipsis next to the property box when you select the property; this is the Build button. If you click the Build button, Access responds with the appropriate window, dialog box, or wizard.

For example, suppose that you want to see the companies displayed in this form in ascending order by company name. The easiest way to accomplish this is to create a query that includes the fields from tblCompanies sorted on the CompanyName field, and then specify that query as the *Record Source* property for the form. To start, display the property sheet for the form, click the Data tab to display the form's data properties, click in the Record Source property box, and then click the Build button next to Record Source to start the Query Builder. Access asks whether you want to build a new query based on the table that is currently the source for this form. If you click Yes, Access opens a new Query window in Design view with the tblCompanies field list displayed in the upper part of the window and the property sheet open either in an undocked window or to the right, as shown in Figure 11-10.



### Note

Unlike previous releases, after you open the property sheet in table, query, form, or report Design view, the window will be open for all objects in Design view until you close it. Likewise, if you close the property sheet in Design view, the window will be closed for all other objects in Design view until you reopen it.

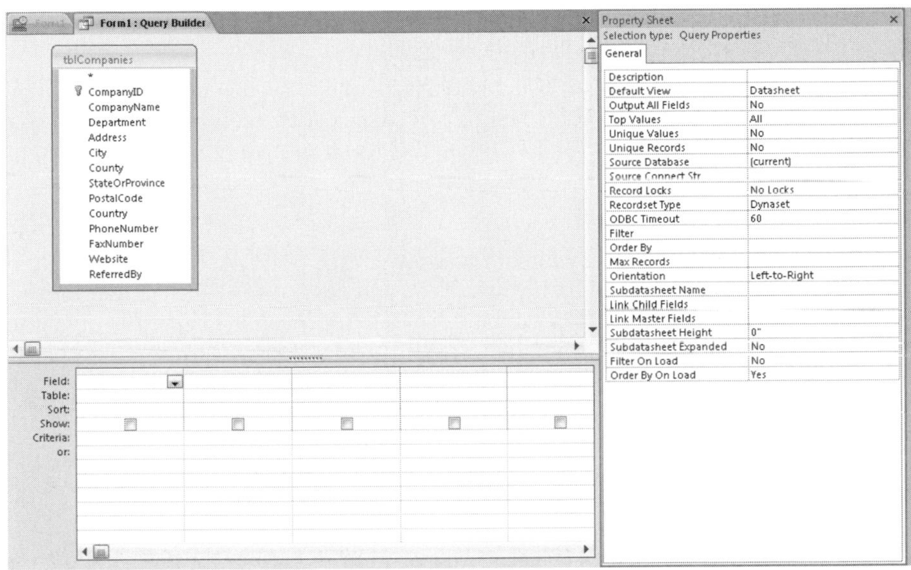


**Figure 11-10** You can use the Query Builder to create a query for the form's Record Source property.

You'll need all the fields in the tblCompanies table for this form, so select them and drag them to the design grid. For the CompanyName field, specify Ascending as the sorting order. Close the property sheet for now by clicking the Close button on its title bar. Your Query Builder window should look like the window shown in Figure 11-11.

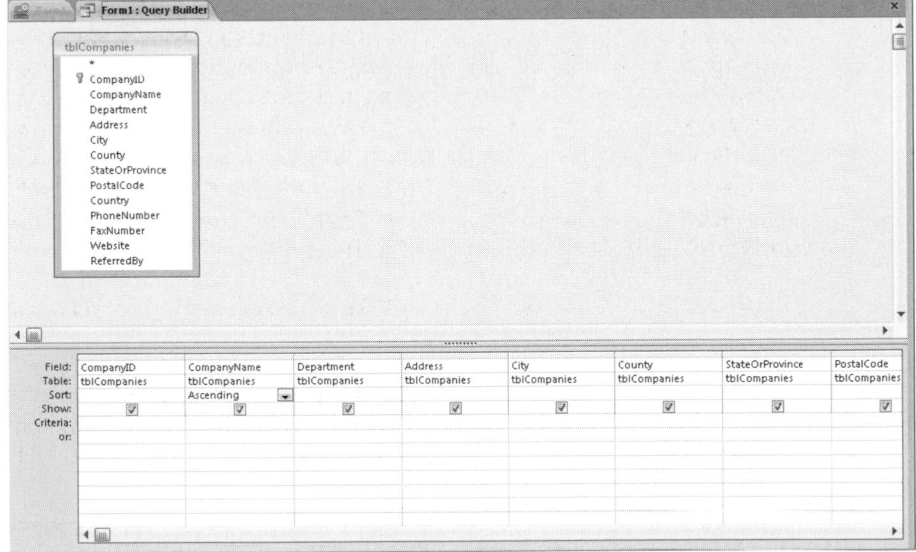


**Figure 11-11** Select all the fields from the table to include them in the query for the Record Source property of the form.

> **INSIDE OUT** **Selecting All the Fields**
>
> To easily select all the fields from a field list displayed in the upper part of the Query window, double-click the title bar of the field list. Access highlights all the fields for you. Then simply click any of them and drag the fields as a group to the design grid.

If you close the Query Builder window at this point, Access asks whether you want to update the property. If you click Yes, Access stores the SQL text for the query in the Record Source property box. A better approach is to save the query and give it a name, such as qryCompaniesSortedByName. Do that now by clicking the Save As command in the Close group on the Design contextual tab under Query Tools, entering **qryCompaniesSortedByName** in the Save As dialog box, and then clicking OK. Now when you close the query, Access asks whether you want to save the query and update the property. Click Yes, and Access places the name of the query (rather than the SQL text) in the property sheet.

## Building a Simple Input Form for the tblCompanies Table

Now let's create a simple input form for the tblCompanies table in the Conrad Systems Contacts database. If you've followed along to this point, you should have a blank form based on the qryCompaniesSortedByName query that you created using the Query Builder. If you haven't followed along, click the Blank Form command in the Forms group on the Create tab.

Click the arrow under View in the Views group on the Design tab and click Design View to switch from Layout view to Design view. You'll see the Form window in Design view and a set of design tools, as shown earlier in Figure 11-4. If necessary, open the property sheet by clicking the Property Sheet command in the Tools group of the Design tab under Form Design Tools. By default this new form is unbound, so click the Record Source property, click the arrow that appears next to the property box, and select tblCompanies from the list. Now the form is bound to the tblCompanies table, but we want to change the record source to a saved query based on the tblCompanies table. Select the Record Source property again, click the Build button, and follow the procedures discussed in the previous sections, whose results are shown in Figures 11-10 and 11-11; this will create the query you need and make it the source for the form.

In the blank form that now has the qryCompaniesSortedByName query as its record source, drag the bottom of the Detail section downward to make some room to work. All the fields in tblCompanies are defined to be displayed with a text box, so you don't need to click a button in the Controls group. If you'd like to practice, though, double-click the Text Box button in the Controls group before dragging fields from the field list. If the field list is not displayed, click the Add Existing Fields button in the Tools group on the Design tab. You can drag fields (for this exercise, all except the ReferredBy field) one at a time to the Detail section of the form, or you can click the first field (CompanyID), hold down the Shift key, and click the last field (Website) to select them all. After you drag and drop the fields, your form should now look something like the one shown in Figure 11-12. If you double-clicked the Text Box button to select it for multiple operations, click the Select button to unlock the selection.

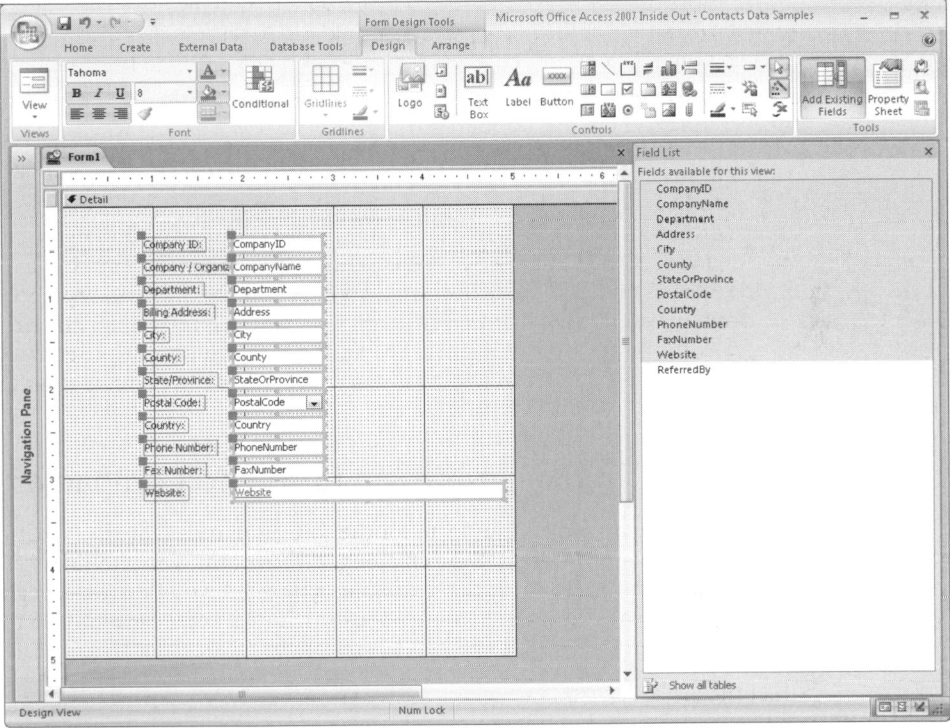


**Figure 11-12** You can drag the fields from the qryCompaniesSortedByName field list to place these text box controls on the form design grid.

## INSIDE OUT Use the Shift or the Ctrl Key to Select Multiple Fields

A quick way to place several successive fields on a form is to click the first field you want in the field list, scroll down until you see the last field you want, and then hold down the Shift key while you click the last field. This procedure selects all the fields between the first and last fields you clicked. Holding down the Ctrl key and clicking several noncontiguous fields works, too. If you include a field in error, hold down the Ctrl key and click the selected field that you don't want. Click any of the selected fields and drag the fields as a group to the Detail section of the form. This has the added benefit of lining up all the controls in a vertical column.



When you position the field icon that you've dragged from the field list, the upper-left corner of the new text box will be at the position of the mouse pointer when you release the mouse button. Note that the default text box control has a label control automatically attached to display the bound field's Caption property (or the field name if the field does not have a caption), positioned 1 inch to the left of the text box. Also, in Design view, the label control displays its Caption property, and the text box control displays its Control Source property (the name of the field to which it is bound).

You should drop each text box about 1.25 inches (3 centimeters) from the left edge of the Detail section to leave room to the left of the text box for Access to place the control labels. If you don't leave room, the text boxes will overlap the labels. Even if you do leave room, if a caption is too long to fit in the 1-inch space between the default label and the default text box (for example, Company / Organization in Figure 11-12), the text box will overlap the label.

If you selected multiple fields in the field list and added them all with one drag-and-drop action, when you click the Property Sheet button immediately after adding the fields, the property sheet indicates that you have selected multiple controls. (In this example, we dragged all the selected fields to the Detail section at one time.) Whenever you select multiple controls on a form in Design view, Access displays the properties that are common to all the controls you selected. If you change a property in the property sheet while you have multiple controls selected, Access makes the change to all the selected controls.

## Moving and Sizing Controls

By default, Access creates text boxes that are 1 inch wide (except for Hyperlink and Memo fields). For some of the fields, 1 inch is larger than necessary to display the field value—especially if you are using the default 8-point font size. For other fields, the text box isn't large enough. You probably also want to adjust the location of some of the controls.

To change a control's size or location, you usually have to select the control first. Be sure that you have clicked the Select button in the Controls group on the Design tab. Click the control you want to resize or move, and moving and sizing handles appear around the control. The handles are small boxes that appear at each corner of the control—except at the upper-left corner, where the larger handle indicates that you cannot use it for sizing. In Figure 11-12, handles appear around all the text boxes because they are all selected. To select just one control, click anywhere in the design area where there is no control; this changes the selection to the Detail section. Then click the control you want. If the control is wide enough or high enough, Access provides additional handles at the midpoints of the edges of the control.



To change the size of a control, you can use the sizing handles on the edges, in either of the lower corners, or in the upper-right corner of the control. When you place the mouse pointer over one of these sizing handles, the pointer turns into a double arrow, as shown in Figure 11-13. With the double-arrow pointer, drag the handle to resize the control. You can practice on the form by shortening the CompanyID text box so that it's 0.5 inch long. You need to stretch the company name, department, and address fields until they are each about 1.75 inches long. You might also want to reduce the state or province field to display two characters and decrease the Web site field to 1.75 inches.

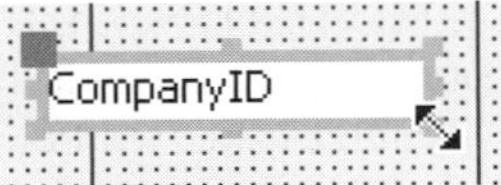


**Figure 11-13** You can drag a corner handle of a selected control to change the control's width or height or both.

To move a control that is not currently selected, click the control and drag it to a new location. After you click a control, you can move it by placing your mouse pointer anywhere between the handles along the edge of the control. When you do this, the mouse pointer turns into a pointer with a four arrow crosshair, as shown in Figure 11-14, and you can then drag the control to a new location. Access displays an outline of the control as you move the control to help you position it correctly. When a control has an attached label, moving either the control or the label in this way moves both of them.

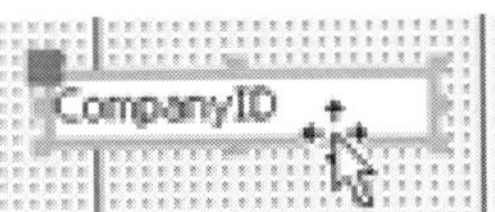


**Figure 11-14** You can drag the edge of a selected control to move the control.

You can position a control and its attached label independently by dragging the larger handle in the upper-left corner of the control or label. When you position the mouse pointer over this handle, the pointer again turns into a pointer with a four arrow crosshair, as shown in Figure 11-15. Drag the control to a new location relative to its label.

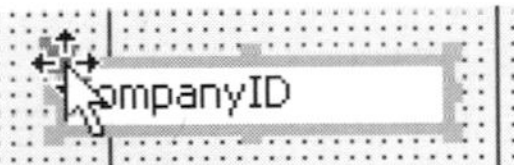

**Figure 11-15** You can drag the large handle of a selected control to move the control independently of its label.

You can delete a label from a control by selecting the label and pressing the Delete key. If you want to create a label that is independent of a control, you can click the Label button. If you inadvertently delete a label from a control and you've made other changes so that you can no longer undo the deletion, you can attach a new label by doing the following:

1. Click the Label button in the Controls group on the Design tab to create a new unattached label.
2. Select the label, and then click the Cut command in the Clipboard group on the Home tab to move the label to the Clipboard.
3. Select the control to which you want to attach the label, and then click the Paste command in the Clipboard group.

## The Font Group

The Font group on the Design tab under Form Design Tools, shown in Figure 11-16, provides a quick and easy way to alter the appearance of a control by allowing you to click buttons rather than set properties. Select the object you want to format and then click the appropriate button in the Font group. The Font group is also handy for setting background colors for sections of the form. Table 11-2 describes each of the buttons in this group.

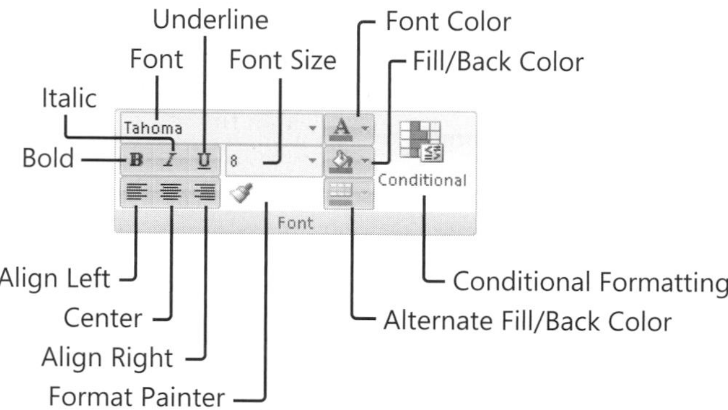


**Figure 11-16** The Font group provides you with tools to change the appearance of form controls.

Table 11-2 **Font Group Buttons**

| Button | Description |
|---|---|
| Font | Use to set the font for labels, text boxes, command buttons, toggle buttons, combo boxes, and list boxes. |
| Bold | Click to set font style to bold. Click again to remove bold. |
| Italic | Click to set font style to italic. Click again to remove italic. |
| Underline | Click to underline text. Click again to remove underline. |
| Font Size | Use to set font size. |
| Align Left | Click to left align text. |
| Center | Click to center text. |
| Align Right | Click to right align text. |
| Format Painter | Use to copy formatting from one control to another control. |
| Font Color | Use to set the font color of the control. |
| Fill/Back Color | Use to set the background color of the control or form area. You can also set the background color to transparent. |
| Alternate Fill/ Back Color | Use to set a background color for alternating rows for forms displayed in Datasheet, Split Form, or Continuous Form view. |
| Conditional Formatting | Use to define dynamic modification of the formatting of text boxes and combo boxes by testing the value in the control, by comparing values in one or more fields, or when the control has the focus. |

**INSIDE OUT** **Using the Alignment Buttons**

You can click only one of the alignment buttons—Align Left, Align Right, or Center—at a time. If you do not click a button, alignment is set to General—text data aligns left and numeric data aligns right. You can also set the Text Align property in the property sheet.

Depending on the object you select, some of the Font group options might not be available. For example, you can't set text color on an attachment or a bound object frame control. If you have the property sheet open and you scroll through it so that you can see the properties the Font group sets, you can watch the settings in the property sheet change as you click different options in the Font group.

## Setting Border Color, Type, Line Thickness, and Special Effect

You can find a special set of commands at the right end of the Controls group on the Design tab below Form Design Tools to further customize the look of the controls on your form, as shown in Figure 11-17. Table 11-3 explains each of these buttons.

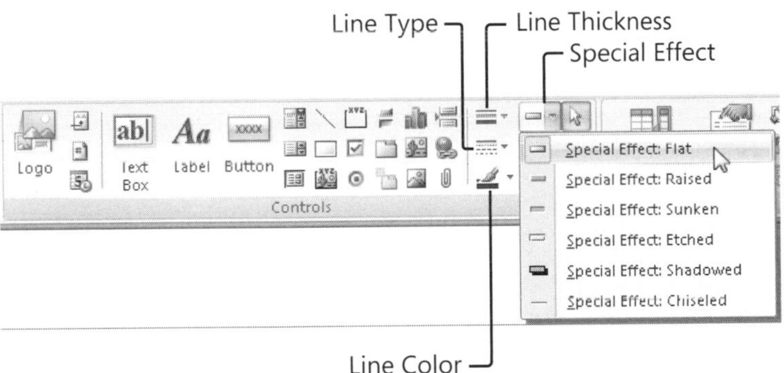


**Figure 11-17** You can use commands in the Controls group on the Design tab to customize the borders of your controls.

Table 11-3 **Border Formatting Commands for Controls**

| Button | Description |
|---|---|
| Line Thickness | When Special Effect is set to Flat (see below), use this command to set the border width from hairline to 6 points wide. |
| Line Type | You can make the border transparent or specify a border that is a solid line, dashes, short dashes, dots, sparse dots, dash dot, or dash dot dot. |
| Line Color | Use this command to set the border color of the control. You can also set the border color to transparent. |
| Special Effect | (Shown with list of options open.) You can set the look of the control to flat, raised, sunken, etched, shadowed, or chiseled. |

Depending on the object you select, some of the Controls group options might not be available. For example, you can't set the border color on a toggle button or command button because the color is always set to gray for this kind of control. If you have the property sheet open and you scroll through it so that you can see the properties these border commands set, you can watch the settings in the property sheet change as you click different options in the group.

## Setting Text Box Properties

The next thing you might want to do is change some of the text box properties. Figure 11-18 shows some of the properties for the CompanyID text box control. Because the CompanyID field in the tblCompanies table is an AutoNumber field, which a user cannot change, you should change the properties of this control to prevent it from being selected on the form. Access provides two properties that you can set to control what the user can do. The *Enabled* property determines whether the control can receive the focus (the user can click in or tab to the control). The *Locked* property determines whether the user can enter data in the control. The defaults are Enabled Yes and Locked No.

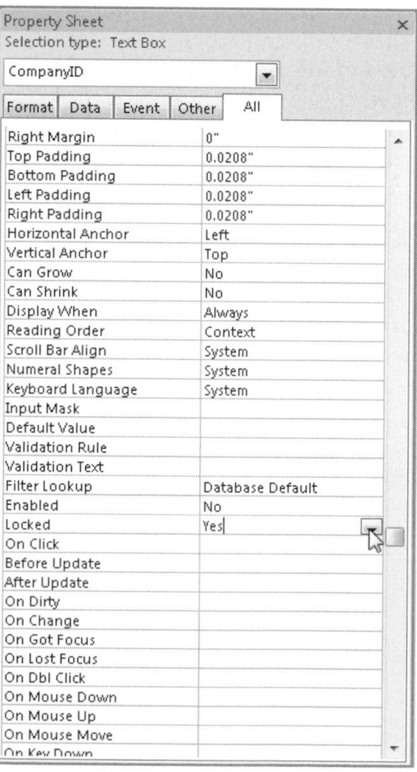


**Figure 11-18** You can set the Enabled and Locked properties of the CompanyID text box control so that users cannot click into that control.

You can set the Enabled property of the control to No so that the user cannot click in or tab to the control. When you do this, Access prohibits access to the field but causes the control and its label to appear dimmed because the control is not locked. (When Access sees that a control is disabled but is still potentially updatable despite being bound to an AutoNumber, it causes the control to appear dimmed.) To display the control and its label normally, just set Locked to Yes.

If you specify a Format, Decimal Places, or Input Mask property setting when you define a field in a table, Access copies these settings to any text box that you bind to the field. Any data you enter using the form must conform to the field validation rule defined in the table; however, you can define a more restrictive rule for this form. Any new row inherits default values from the table unless you provide a different default value in the property sheet. The Status Bar Text property derives its value from the Description property setting you entered for the field in the table. You can learn more about control properties in the next chapter and in Part 4, "Automating an Access Application."

## Setting Label Properties

You can also set separate properties for the labels attached to controls. Click the label for CompanyID to see the property sheet shown in Figure 11-19. Access copies the Caption property from the field in the underlying table to the Caption property in the associated control label. The default settings for the text box control on a form specify that all text boxes have labels and that the caption should have a trailing colon. When you added the CompanyID text box to the form, Access used the caption from the field's definition in the tblCompanies table (Company ID instead of the field name CompanyID), and added the trailing colon. Also, all controls on a form must have a name, so Access generated a name (Label0) that is the control type followed by an integer.

You also can correct the caption from inside a label by selecting the label, moving the mouse pointer inside the label until the pointer changes into an I-beam shape, and then clicking to set the insertion point inside the label text. You can delete unwanted characters, and you can type new characters. When you finish correcting a label caption, Access automatically adjusts the size of the control smaller or larger to adequately display the new name. You can change settings using the property sheet to adjust the size of a label, or you can also select the control and drag the control's handles to override the automatic resizing and manually adjust the size and alignment of the control.

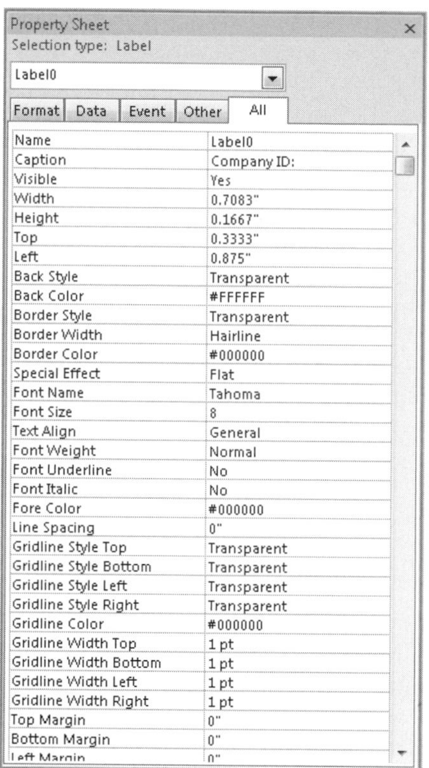


**Figure 11-19** This is the property sheet for the CompanyID label control.

## Setting Form Properties

You can display the form's properties in the property sheet (as shown in Figure 11-20) by clicking anywhere outside the Detail section of the form, by clicking the small square box in the upper-left corner of the Form window, or by selecting Form from the Selection Type combo box on the property sheet. On the Format tab in Figure 11-20, we set the caption to Companies / Organizations. This value will appear on the Form window's title bar in Form view or in Datasheet view.

Toward the bottom of the list of properties on the Format tab are the Grid X and Grid Y properties that control the density of dots on the grid as discussed earlier in this chapter. The defaults are 24 dots per inch across (Grid X) and 24 dots per inch down (Grid Y), if your measurements are in U.S. units. For metric measurements, the defaults are 5 dots per centimeter in both directions. Access also draws a shaded line on the grid every inch or centimeter to help you line up controls. If you decide to turn on the Snap To Grid command in the Control Layout group on the Arrange tab below Form Design Tools to help you line up controls on your form, you might want to change the density of the grid dots to give you greater control over where you place objects on the form.

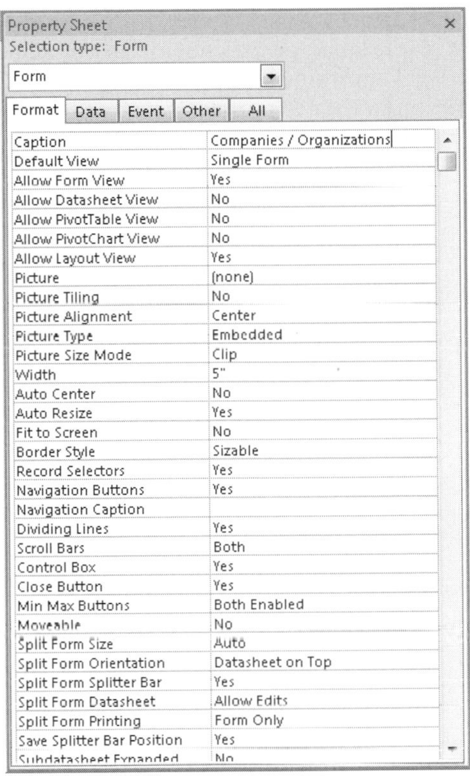

**Figure 11-20** You can use the Caption property on the Format tab of the property sheet for the form to define a title for the form.

> **Note**
>
> You won't see the grid dots if you set either the Grid X or Grid Y property to more than 24 in U.S. measurements or more than 9 in metric measurements.

You can set the properties beginning with On Current on the Event tab of the property sheet to run macros or Visual Basic procedures. The events associated with these properties can trigger macro actions.

## Customizing Colors and Checking Your Design Results

Let's explore some of the interesting effects you can design using colors. To make the fields on the form stand out, you can click in the Detail section and then set the background to dark gray using the Fill/Back Color button in the Font group on the Design tab. To make the labels stand out against this dark background, drag the mouse pointer around all the label controls or click the horizontal ruler directly above all the label controls, and then set the Fill/Back Color to white. If you haven't already moved and resized the labels, you can select all the labels and then widen them all to the left by clicking the left edge sizing handle of any of the labels and dragging left. This pulls the long Company / Organization caption over so that it doesn't overlap the CompanyName field. If you also want to make the Detail section fit snugly around the controls on your form, drag the edges of the Detail section inward.

> **INSIDE OUT**
>
> **Using the Ruler to Select All Controls**
>
> To select all controls in a vertical area, click the horizontal ruler above the area containing the controls you want to select. Likewise, to select all controls in a horizontal area, click the vertical ruler.

When you finish working on this form in Design view, it might look something like the one shown in Figure 11-21.

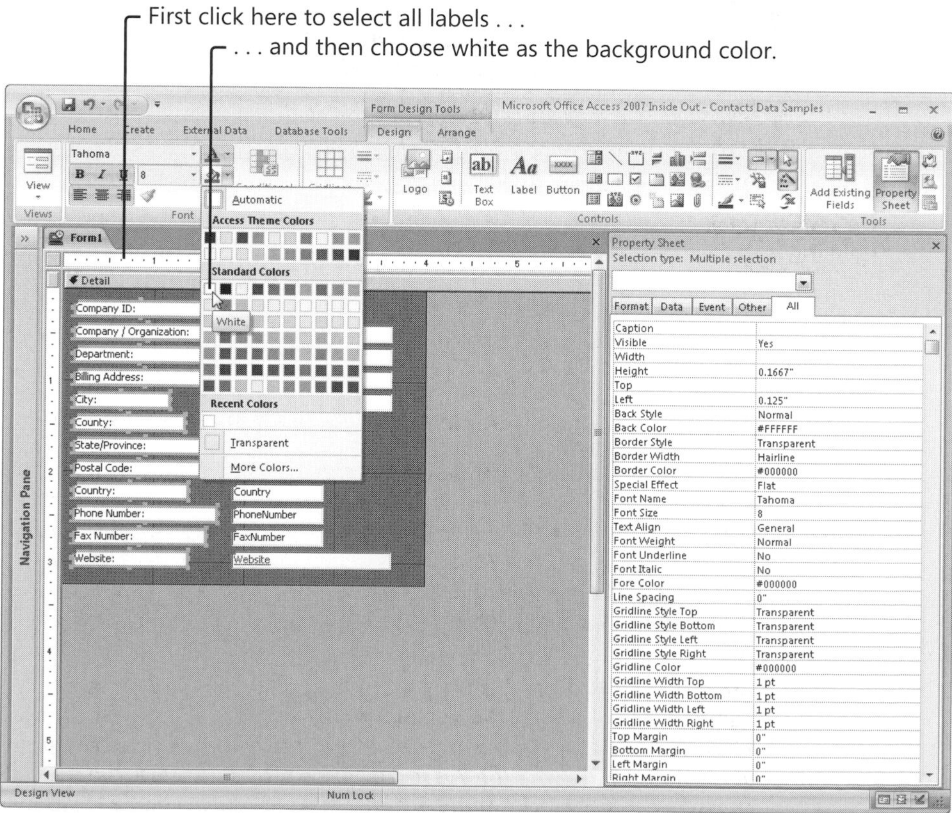


**Figure 11-21** You can add contrast to the Companies / Organizations form by using the Fill/Back Color button.

Click the arrow below the View button in the Views group on the Ribbon and click Form View to see your form. It will look similar to the form shown in Figure 11-22. (You can find this form saved as frmXmplCompany1 in the sample database.) Note that the labels are all different sizes and the contrast might be too distracting. You could further refine the look of this form by making all the labels the same size and perhaps aligning the captions to the right. You could also make the label background transparent or the same color as the Detail section and change the font color to white. You'll learn more about customizing your form design in the next chapter.

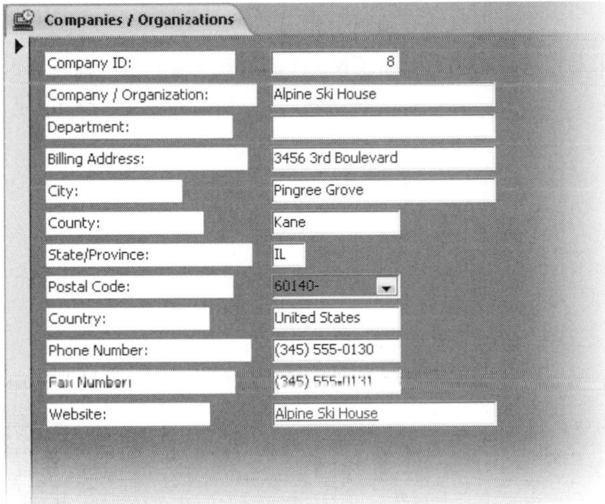


**Figure 11-22** Switch to Form view to see how the Companies / Organizations form looks so far.

Click the Save button on the Quick Access Toolbar or click the Microsoft Office Button and then Save to save your new form design.

INSIDE OUT

### Understanding the Allow Layout View Property

Access 2007 introduces a feature—Allow Layout view—to allow you to further modify the design of your forms even in a finished application. All new forms in Access have the Allow Layout View property set to Yes by default. This lets any user open the form in Layout view to make design changes. You should be sure to set this property to No in all forms before distributing a finished application to users. If you don't do this, users can make design changes to your forms, which is probably not a good idea in a production application.

Note that this property was called Allow Design Changes in Microsoft Access 2003. Setting this property to Yes in Access 2003 allowed the user to open the property sheet while in Form view and make changes to the form design by changing property settings. But Layout view in Access 2007 is much more powerful because the user can not only change properties but also move and add controls. We will discuss Layout view in more detail in the next chapter.

# Working with Quick Create Commands and the Form Wizard

Now that you understand the basic mechanics of form design, you could continue to build all your forms from scratch in Design view. However, even the most experienced developers take advantage of the many wizards built into Access 2007 to get a jump-start on design tasks. This section shows you how to use quick create form commands and the Form Wizard to quickly build a custom form.

## Creating a Form with the Quick Create Commands

Access 2007 introduces new quick create commands so that you can create new forms with one click on a Ribbon command. As you'll learn in this section, you can build forms designed in a variety of different views, so you can pick the style you need for the data-editing task at hand. You just walked through creating a form from scratch, so you should recall how much time it took to place all the fields on the form design grid, resize and move some of the controls, and change some of the form properties. The quick create commands can do a lot of the heavy work in designing a base form, which you can then modify to meet your specific needs.

Suppose you want to create a data entry form for the tblProducts table in the Conrad Systems Contacts database. Begin by opening the ContactsDataCopy.accdb database and click the top of the Navigation Pane to open the Navigation Pane menu. Click Object Type under Navigate To Category and Tables under Filter By Group to display a list of only the tables in this database. Select the tblProducts table in the Navigation Pane and then click the Form command in the Forms group on the Create tab. Access immediately creates a new single form based on the tblProducts table, including a control for every field in that table, and displays it in Layout view as shown in Figure 11-23.

As you can see, Access creates this form very quickly, and it looks professional. Switch to Design view for this form by clicking the arrow below the View button in the Views group on the Home tab and clicking Design View. Notice how Access creates a text box on the form for each field in the tblProducts table and an associated label for each text box with a caption, and aligns all the controls. Access also creates a bitmap picture logo and a label for the form's title in the Header section.

This form could still use some modification, such as entering a different form title and resizing some controls, but overall Access has completed a lot of the hard work of creating the form. Close this form, and do not save it.

Select the tblProducts table again in the Navigation Pane and then click the Split Form command in the Forms group on the Create tab. Access immediately creates a new split form containing every field in the tblProducts table and displays it in Layout view as shown in Figure 11-24.

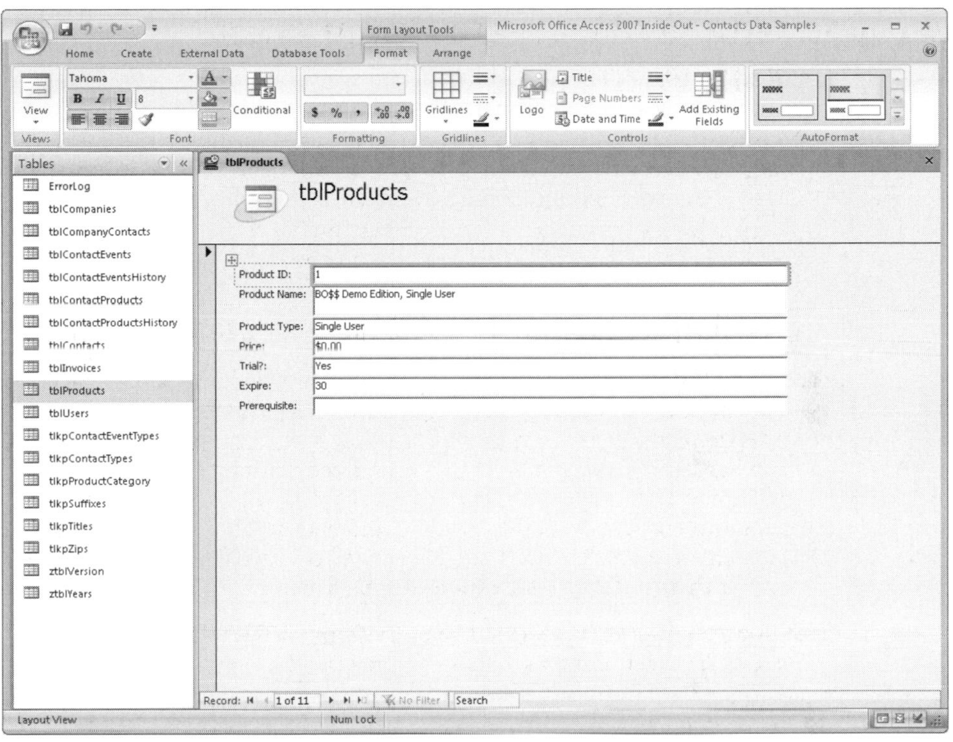


**Figure 11-23** Access can save you time by creating a single form using all the fields in the selected table.

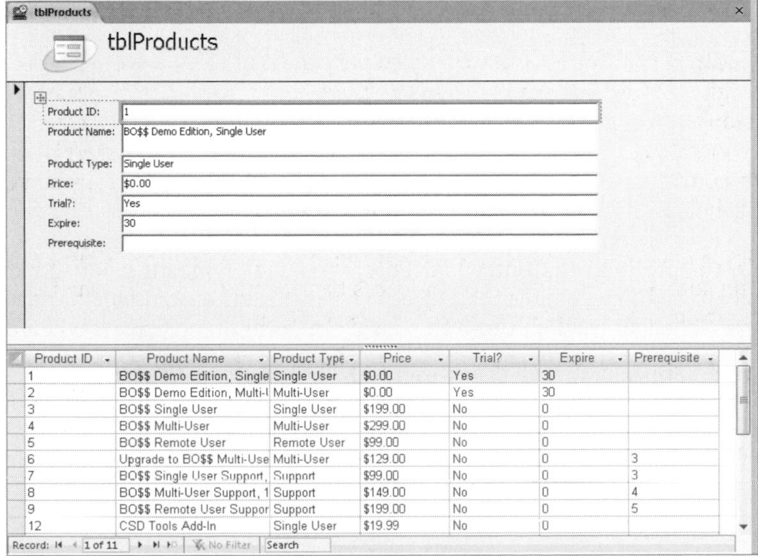


**Figure 11-24** When you click the Split Form command, Access creates a new split form based on your table.

Here again Access creates controls and associated labels for all the fields in the tblProducts table. Switch to Design view by clicking the arrow in the Views group and clicking Design View. The form's Default View property is set to Split Form, and the Split Form Orientation property is set to Datasheet On Bottom. The top of the Form window displays the fields from the tblProducts table in Single Form view, and the bottom of the form displays all the records from the tblProducts table in Datasheet view. Close this form now, and do not save it when prompted.

Select the tblProducts table again in the Navigation Pane and then click the Multiple Items command in the Forms group on the Create tab. Access immediately creates a new continuous form based on all the fields in the tblProducts table and displays it in Layout view as shown in Figure 11-25.

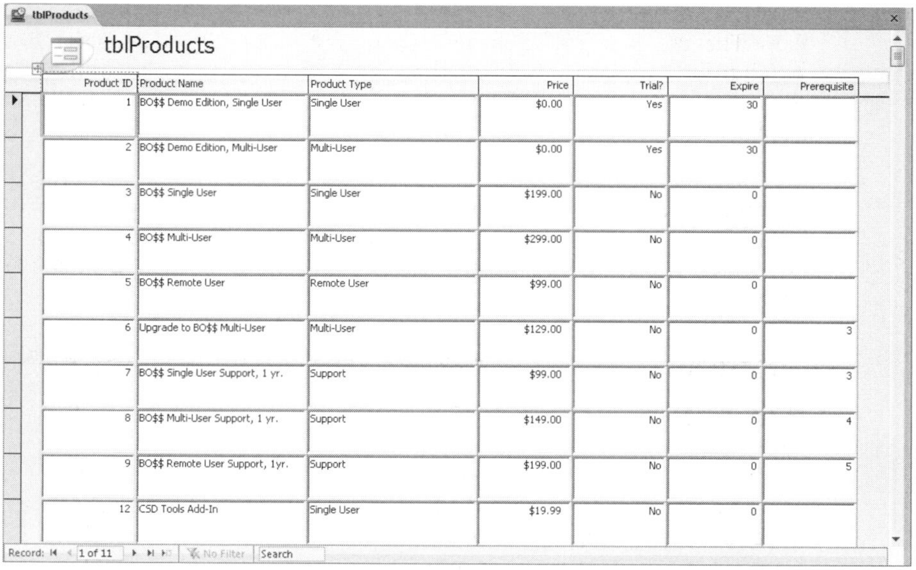

**Figure 11-25** Use the Multiple Items command to create a continuous form.

In this continuous form, Access creates controls for all the fields in the tblProducts table horizontally across the Form window. Switch to Design view by clicking the arrow in the Views group and clicking Design View. The form's properties have been set to display the products in Continuous Form view, which means you can view more than one record at a time. Notice that Access places the associated label for each control in the form's Header section. Close this form now, and do not save it when prompted.

Select the tblProducts table again in the Navigation Pane, click the More Forms command in the Forms group on the Create tab, and then click the Datasheet command. Access immediately creates a new form in Datasheet view using all the fields in the tblProducts table and displays it as shown in Figure 11-26.

tblProducts

| Product ID | Product Name | Product Type | Price | Trial? | Expire | Prerequisite |
|---|---|---|---|---|---|---|
| 1 | BO$$ Demo Edition, Single | Single User | $0.00 | Yes | 30 | |
| 2 | BO$$ Demo Edition, Multi-U | Multi-User | $0.00 | Yes | 30 | |
| 3 | BO$$ Single User | Single User | $199.00 | No | 0 | |
| 4 | BO$$ Multi-User | Multi-User | $299.00 | No | 0 | |
| 5 | BO$$ Remote User | Remote User | $99.00 | No | 0 | |
| 6 | Upgrade to BO$$ Multi-Use | Multi-User | $129.00 | No | 0 | 3 |
| 7 | BO$$ Single User Support, | Support | $99.00 | No | 0 | 3 |
| 8 | BO$$ Multi-User Support, 1 | Support | $149.00 | No | 0 | 4 |
| 9 | BO$$ Remote User Suppor | Support | $199.00 | No | 0 | 5 |
| 12 | CSD Tools Add-In | Single User | $19.99 | No | 0 | |
| 13 | CSD Tools Add-In Demo Ec | Single User | $0.00 | Yes | 90 | |
| * (New) | | | $0.00 | No | 0 | |

**Figure 11-26** This datasheet form was created using the Datasheet command on the More Forms menu.

Switch to Design view by clicking the arrow in the Views group and clicking Design View. The form's properties have been set to display the products in Datasheet view, which means you can view more than one record at a time and all the records are stacked close together like a table datasheet. In datasheet forms, Access places a column header with the name that normally appears for an associated label for each control. Close this form now, and do not save it when prompted.

Access 2007 also has quick create commands for PivotChart and PivotTable views in the Forms group. You can use these commands to get a jump-start on creating PivotChart and PivotTable forms. You'll learn more about creating and using PivotChart forms in Chapter 13.

## Creating the Basic Products Form with the Form Wizard

The quick create form commands are easy to use, but you have no flexibility on how Access initially creates the form. The Form Wizard is another tool you can use to quickly create forms in your database. Begin by opening the ContactsDataCopy.accdb database, and click the top of the Navigation Pane to display the Navigation Pane menu. Select Object Type under Navigate To Category and Tables under Filter By Group to display a list of only the tables in this database. Select the tblProducts table in the Navigation Pane, click the More Forms command in the Forms group on the Create tab, and then click the Form Wizard command. Access opens the first page of the Form Wizard, as shown in Figure 11-27.

You can select any field in the Available Fields list and click the single right arrow (>) button to copy that field to the Selected Fields list. You can also click the double right arrow (>>) button to copy all available fields to the Selected Fields list. If you copy a field in error, you can select the field in the Selected Fields list and click the single left arrow (<) button to remove the field from the list. You can remove all fields and start over by clicking the double left arrow (<<) button. For this example, click the double right arrow button to use all the fields in the tblProducts table in the new form.

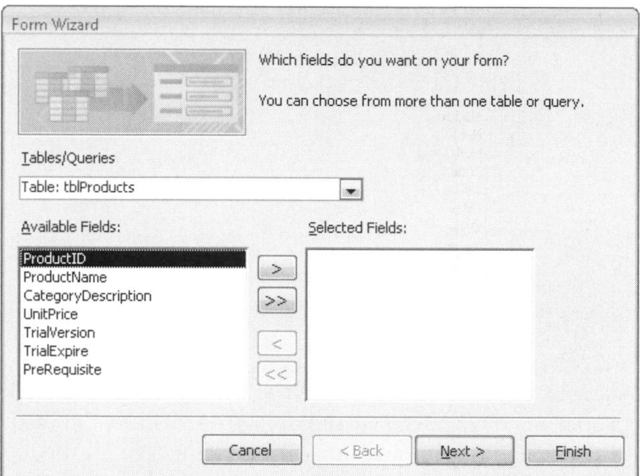


**Figure 11-27** The first page of the Form Wizard displays fields you can select to include in your form.

As you'll learn in Chapter 13, you can select fields from one table or query and then change the data source name in the Tables/Queries combo box to select a different but related table or query. If you have defined the relationships between tables in your database, the Form Wizard can determine how the data from multiple sources is related and can offer to build either a simple form to display all the data or a more complex one that shows some of the data in the main part of the form with related data displayed in an embedded subform. You'll use this technique to build a more complex form in Chapter 13.

At any time, you can click the Finish button to go directly to the last step of the wizard. You can also click the Cancel button at any time to stop creating the form.

After you select all the fields from the tblProducts table, click Next. On the next page, the wizard gives you choices for the layout of your form. You can choose to display the controls on your form in columns, arrange the controls across the form in a tabular format (this creates a continuous form), create a form that opens in Datasheet view, or place the fields in a block "justified" view. For this example, select Columnar, and then click Next.

The wizard next displays a page on which you can select a style for your form, as shown in Figure 11-28. Note that if you choose to display the form in Datasheet view, the style won't apply to the datasheet but will appear if you shift from Datasheet view to Form view. The nice thing about this page is that the wizard shows you a sample of each selection on the left side of the page. You can look at each one and decide which you like best. In this example, the Solstice style is selected. In Chapter 12, you'll learn how to use the AutoFormat facility to create a custom look for your forms.

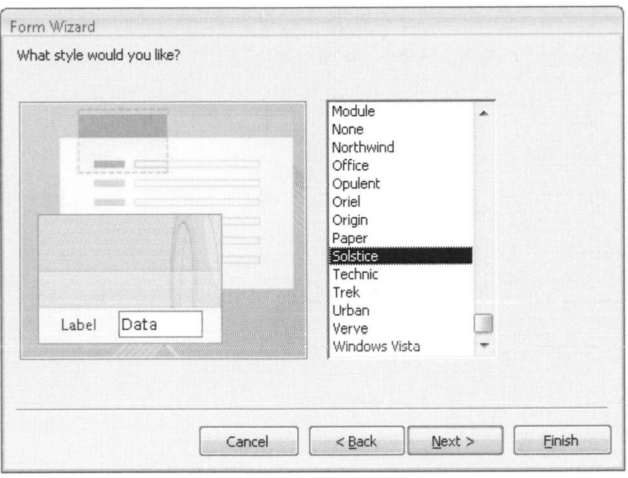


**Figure 11-28** You can select a style for your form on the third page of the Form Wizard.

> **Note**
>
> When you select a style in the Form Wizard, the new style becomes the default for new forms you create using the wizard until you change the style setting again, either in the Form Wizard or with the AutoFormat commands. We'll discuss AutoFormat in the next chapter.

Click Next to display the final page, where the Form Wizard asks for a title for your form. Type an appropriate title, such as **Products**. The wizard places this title in the Caption property of the form and also saves the form with this name. (If you already have a form named Products, Access appends a number to the end of the name to create a unique name.) Select the Open The Form To View Or Enter Information option, and then click the Finish button to go directly to Form view. Or you can select the Modify The Form's Design option, and then click Finish to open the new form in Design view. The finished form is shown in Form view in Figure 11-29.

> **Note**
>
> In the initial release of Access 2007, the Form Wizard failed to apply the background image specified for the style you select when you ask for a Columnar, Datasheet, or Justified form. Microsoft intends to fix this bug in the first service pack. If you do not see the background image, you can reapply the style to your form using AutoFormat. You can read more about AutoFormat in the next chapter. The figures that follow all show the background image applied.

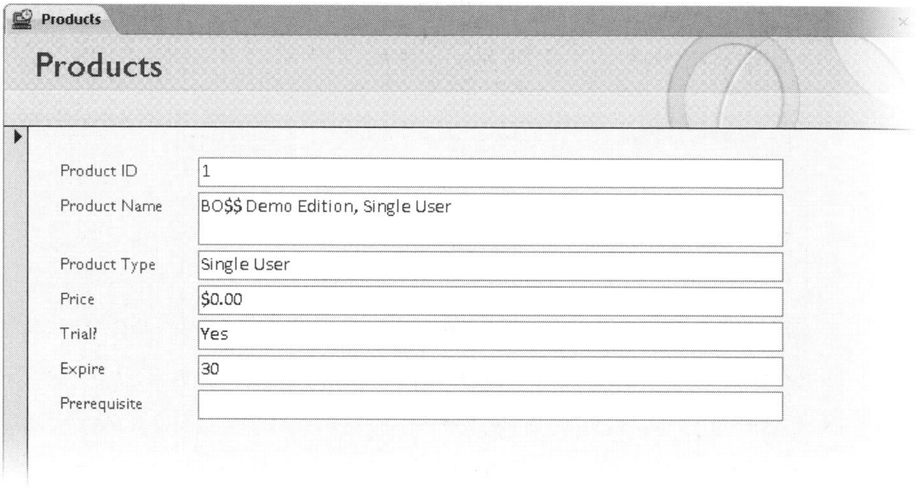

**Figure 11-29** The Form Wizard creates a form in a columnar format using the Solstice style that is very similar to the form produced with the quick create commands.

Notice that the Solstice style uses labels sized alike with no ending colons on the captions. Also notice that all the fields in this style are left-aligned, regardless of data type. You'll learn more about working with styles in the next chapter.

If you're curious to see the tabular format, you can start a new form on the tblProducts table and use the Form Wizard again. Select all the fields on the first page of the Form Wizard, select Tabular for the layout, and set the style to Northwind. For a title, type **Products – Tabular**, and open the new form in Form view. It should look something like the form shown in Figure 11-30. Close this form when you finish looking at it.

> **Note**
>
> We modified the form you see in Figure 11-30 to preserve the default sunken effect for text box controls in the Northwind style. If you create this form on a Windows XP or Windows Vista system, choose Use Windows-Themed Controls On Forms in the Current Database category of the Access Options dialog box, and choose the default Windows XP theme in the Display Properties window in Windows XP, or choose the Windows Vista Basic color scheme in Appearance Settings in Windows Vista, the text boxes appear flat on your form.

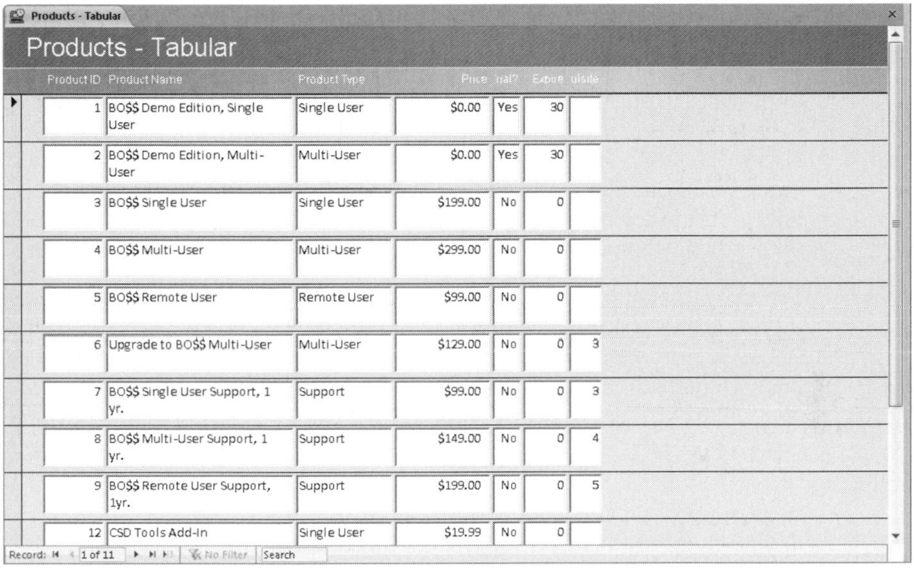

Figure 11-30 This Products form is in a tabular format using the Northwind style.

You can also investigate what a justified form looks like by going through the exercise again and selecting Justified for the layout on the second page in the Form Wizard. If you choose the Office style and name the form **Products – Justified** your result should look something like the one shown in Figure 11-31. Close this form when you finish looking at it.

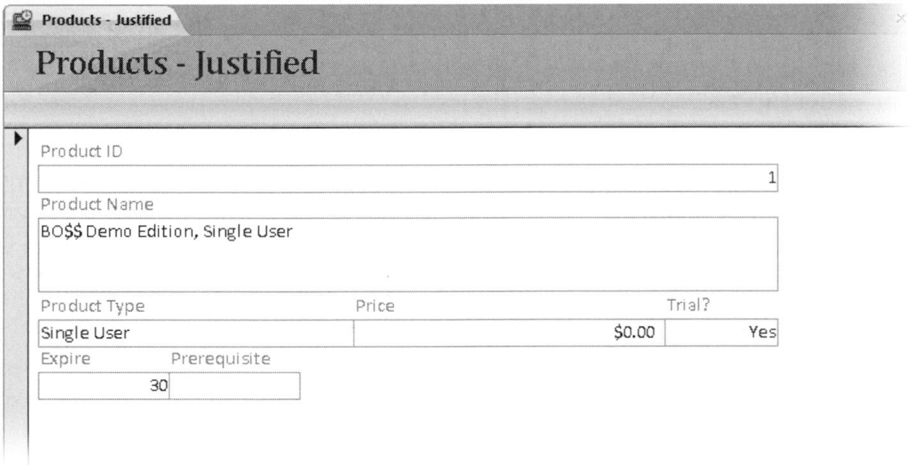

Figure 11-31 This is the Products form in a justified format using the Office style.

## Modifying the Products Form

The Form Wizard took care of some of the work, but there's still a lot you can do to improve the appearance and usability of this form. And even though the Form Wizard adjusted the display control widths, they're still not perfect. Most of the text boxes are larger than they need to be. The Form Wizard created a two-line text box for product name when one should suffice. We personally prefer to see field labels right-aligned and bold so that they're easier to read. Finally, the ProductID field is an AutoNumber data type, so you should probably lock it and disable it so the user cannot type in the field.

You can either start with the columnar format form using the Solstice style (shown in Figure 11-29) or start a new form with the None style. (We decided to modify the Solstice style form from Figure 11-29 for the following examples.) Open the form in Design view. To help align controls, click outside the Detail section so that the form is selected and make sure that the Grid X and Grid Y properties in the form's property sheet are set to 24. (Leave the settings at Grid X = 5 and Grid Y = 5 if you're working in metric measurements.) Be sure the Show Grid command is selected in the Show/Hide group on the Arrange contextual tab.

Begin by selecting the ProductID text box and change the Enabled property to No and the Locked property to Yes as you learned to do earlier. We will leave the Special Effect property of this text box set to Flat to give your users a visual clue that they won't be able to type in the ProductID text box.

The Product ID field does not need to be as wide as it is, so click that control to select it and then click and drag the right edge of the text box control to the left. After the control is about 1 inch wide, release the mouse button and notice that Access resizes all the text box controls to the same width. The Form Wizard has applied a *control layout* so that all the controls will move and resize together. You can tell whether Access has applied a control layout to the controls by the small box with a crosshair inside just to the left of and slightly above the Product ID label, as shown in Figure 11-32. We discuss control layouts in more detail in the next chapter.

To make individual size adjustments to the labels and text box controls, you need to highlight all the controls and turn off this control layout. Start by clicking the horizontal ruler just above the left edge of the label controls, and then drag in the ruler toward the right until the selection indicator touches all the labels and text box controls. (If you can't see the rulers, be sure that you have clicked the Ruler command in the Show/Hide group on the Arrange tab.) Release the mouse button to select all the controls and labels on the form grid, and then click the Remove button in the Control Layout group on the Arrange tab, as shown in Figure 11-32.

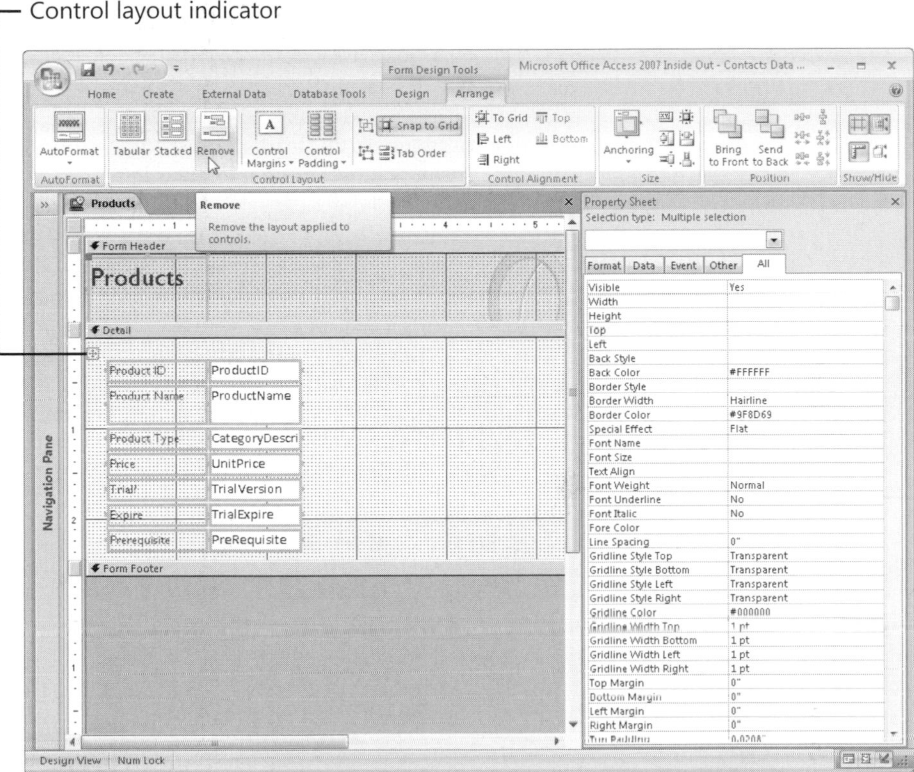


**Figure 11-32** If you or Access has applied a control layout to the form controls, a box with a cross-hair appears next to the controls.

Now that you have removed any control layouts, you can continue making adjustments to the individual controls. The ProductName text box needs to be about 3 inches wide. You can set a specific width by clicking the control, opening the property sheet, clicking the Format tab, and typing **y** in the Width property (the fifth property down the list). The Form Wizard created a text box that is two lines high for ProductName, but it doesn't need to be bigger than one line. Select the control, and then grab the bottom sizing box in the middle of the control and drag it up to make the control smaller. Click the Size To Fit command in the Size group on the Arrange tab to resize the control to display one line. Click the Format tab in the property sheet and change the Scroll Bars property to None—the Form Wizard specified a vertical scroll bar in the two-line control that it designed. It doesn't make sense to show a scroll bar in a one-line control that is already wide enough to display all the data. Select the ProductName label, and then grab the bottom sizing box in the middle of the control and drag it up to make it the same height as the ProductName text box.

Now that you've made the ProductName text box and associated label smaller, you have extra space between it and the CategoryDescription text box. Select the Category-Description, UnitPrice, TrialVersion, TrialExpire, and PreRequisite text boxes and move them up close to the ProductName text box. Unless you turned off Snap To Grid in the Control Layout group on the Arrange tab, it should be easy to line up the controls in their new positions. As you move these four controls, their associated labels will stay aligned with the text boxes.

Next, fix all the labels. Click in the horizontal ruler above the column of labels to select them all. (Access selects the Products label in the form header during this procedure as well, so hold down the Shift key and click the label in the form header to clear it.) Click the Align Right and Bold buttons in the Font group on the Design contextual tab to change the appearance of the labels. Click the Products label in the form header and then click the Italic button in the Font group to add emphasis. Finally, click the Size To Fit command in the Size group on the Arrange tab to make the Product label shrink in size around the text. After you shrink the right margin of your form, move all the controls up closer to the form header and left side of the form grid, and shrink the bottom margin of the form, it should look similar to the one shown in Figure 11-33. Notice that none of the labels attached to the text boxes shows an ending colon. The Solstice style doesn't include them.

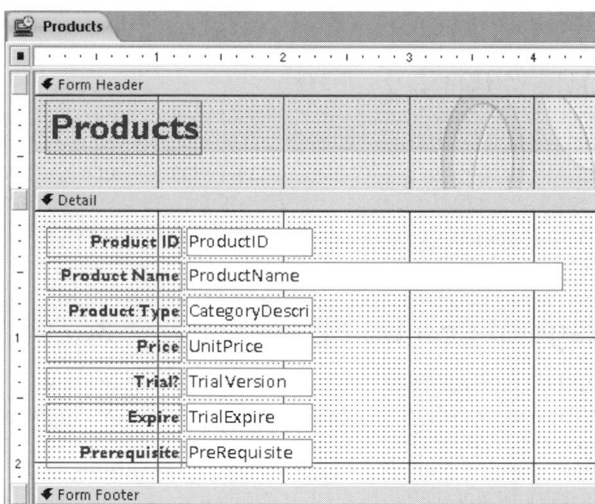


**Figure 11-33** You can now see the modified Products form in Design view with the changes you applied.

Finally, switch to Form view and your form should look something like the one shown in Figure 11-34. The form now looks a bit more customized—and somewhat more like the frmProducts form in the Conrad Systems Contacts application. You can find this form saved as fxmplProducts1 in the sample database.

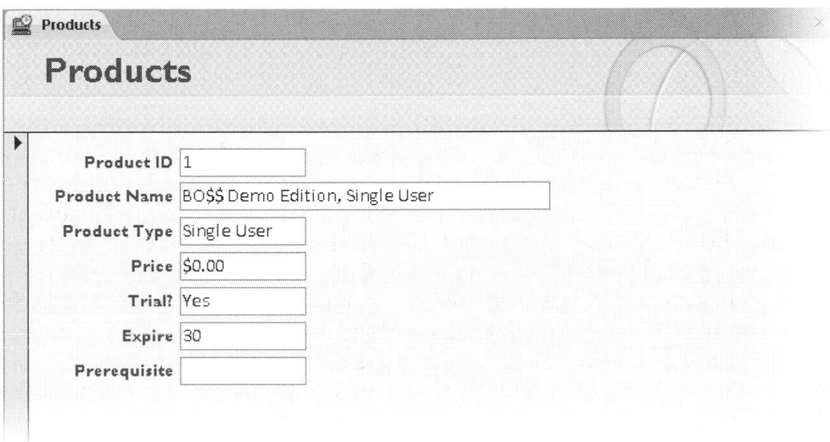


**Figure 11-34** When you switch to Form view, you can see how the modified Products form looks at this point.

# Simplifying Data Input with a Form

One drawback to working with a relational database is that often you have to deal with information stored in multiple tables. That's not a problem if you're using a query to link data, but working with multiple tables can be confusing if you're entering new data. Access 2007 provides some great ways to show information from related tables, thus making data input much simpler.

## Taking Advantage of Combo Boxes and List Boxes

In Chapter 10, "Using Forms," you saw how you can use a combo box or a list box to present a list of potential values for a control. To create the list, you can type the values in the Row Source property box of the control. You can also specify a table or a query as the source of the values in the list. Access 2007 displays the currently selected value in the text box portion of the combo box or as a highlighted selection in the list.

The CategoryDescription field in the tblProducts table is a simple Text data type. To help ensure data consistency, there's a separate lookup table that contains a list of predefined product types. There's also a referential-integrity rule that keeps you from entering anything other than a predefined type in the CategoryDescription field. However, you can type anything you like in the CategoryDescription text box (labeled *Product Type*) that the Form Wizard designed. Go ahead and type any random string of characters in the text box and then try to save the record. You should see an unfriendly technobabble message about "related record is required in 'tlkpProductCategory'."

You can help avoid this problem by providing a combo box to edit and display the CategoryDescription field instead. The combo box can display the list of valid values from the tlkpProductCategory lookup table to make it easy for your user to choose a valid value. The combo box can also limit what the user enters to only values in the list.

In Chapter 20 you'll learn how to write Visual Basic code to detect when a user tries to enter something that's not in the list so that you can provide your own, more user-friendly, message.

To see how a combo box works, you can replace the CategoryDescription text box control with a combo box on the Products form. In Design view, select the CategoryDescription text box control and then press the Delete key to remove the text box control from the form (this also removes the related label control). Be sure the Use Control Wizards button is selected in the Controls group on the Design tab. Display the field list by clicking the Add Existing Fields button in the Tools group on the same Design tab. Next, click the Combo Box button in the Controls group and drag the CategoryDescription field from the field list to the form. The new control appears on the form, and Access starts the Combo Box Wizard, as shown in Figure 11-35, to help you out.

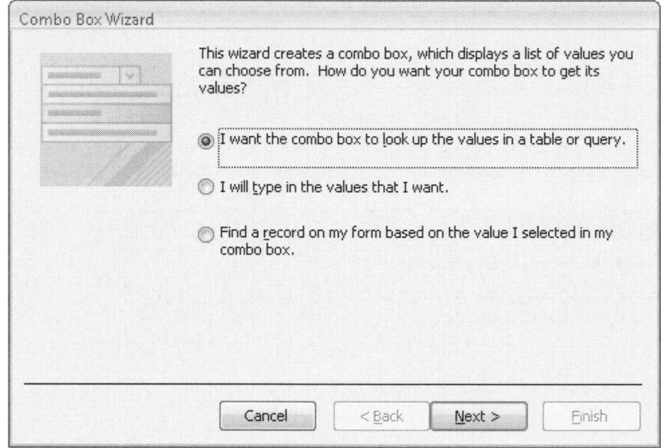


**Figure 11-35** After you drop the CategoryDescription field onto the form grid, Access opens the first page of the Combo Box Wizard.

INSIDE OUT

### Manually Changing a Text Box to a Combo Box

You can change a text box to a combo box by right-clicking on the text box control, clicking Change To on the shortcut menu, and then clicking Combo Box on the submenu. However, after you change a text box to a combo box in this way, you have to set the properties for the display list yourself.



Follow this procedure to build your combo box.

1. You want the combo box to display values from the tlkpProductCategory lookup table, so select the I Want The Combo Box To Look Up The Values In A Table Or Query option, and then click the Next button to go to the next page.

2. On the second page, the wizard displays a list of available tables in the database. Note that the wizard also provides an option to view queries or both tables and queries. Scroll down in the list and click Table: tlkpProductCategory to select that table, and click Next to go to the next page.

3. On the third page, the wizard shows you the single field in the table, CategoryDescription. Select that field and click the right arrow (>) to move it to the Selected Fields list. Click Next to go on.

4. The fourth page allows you to select up to four fields to sort either Ascending or Descending. Click the arrow to the right of the first field and then select the CategoryDescription field. The button next to the first box indicates *Ascending*, and you want to leave it that way. If you click the button, it changes to *Descending*, which is not what you want. (You can click the button again to set it back.) Click Next to go to the next page.

5. The wizard shows you the lookup values that your combo box will display as an embedded datasheet, as shown here. To size a column, click on the dividing line at the right edge of a column at the top, and drag the line. You can adjust the size of the column to be sure it displays all the available descriptions properly. Click Next to go on.

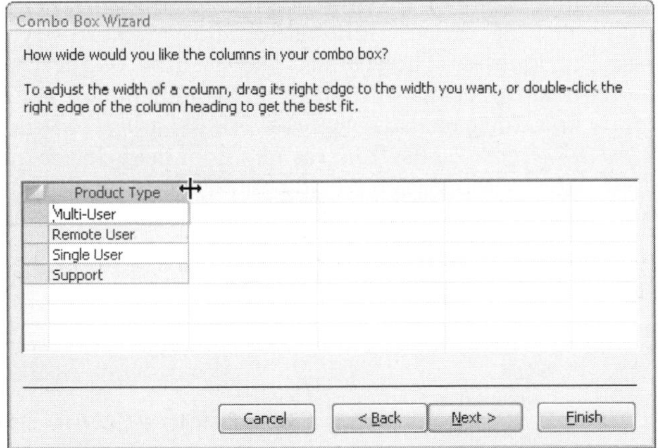


6. On the next page, the wizard asks whether you want to store the value from the combo box in a field from the table or query that you're updating with this form or simply save the value selected in an unbound control "for later use." You'll see in Part 4 of this book that unbound controls are useful for storing calculated values or for providing a way for the user to enter parameter data for use by your macros or Visual Basic procedures. In this case, you want to update the CategoryDescription field, so be sure to select the Store That Value In This Field option and verify that CategoryDescription is selected in the list. Click Next to go to the last page of the wizard.

7. On the final page, shown here, the wizard suggests a caption that you probably want to correct. In this case, enter **Product Type** in the box. Click Finish, and you're all done.

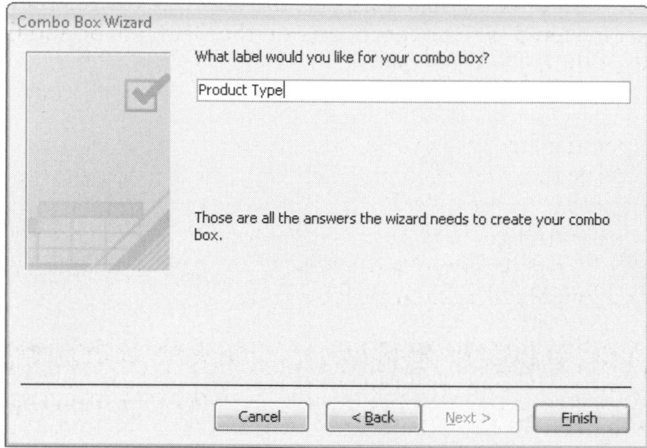


If you have the property sheet open, you can study the properties set by the Combo Box Wizard, as shown in Figure 11-36. The Control Source property shows that the combo box is bound to the CategoryDescription field. The Row Source Type property indicates that the data filling the combo box comes from the table or query entered in the Row Source property box. Notice that the wizard generated an SQL statement in the Row Source property box. You can also specify a value list as the Row Source property, or you can ask Access to create a list from the names of fields in the query or table specified in the Row Source property. Please note in Figure 11-36 that we show both the Data and the Format tabs so that you can see the properties we are discussing.

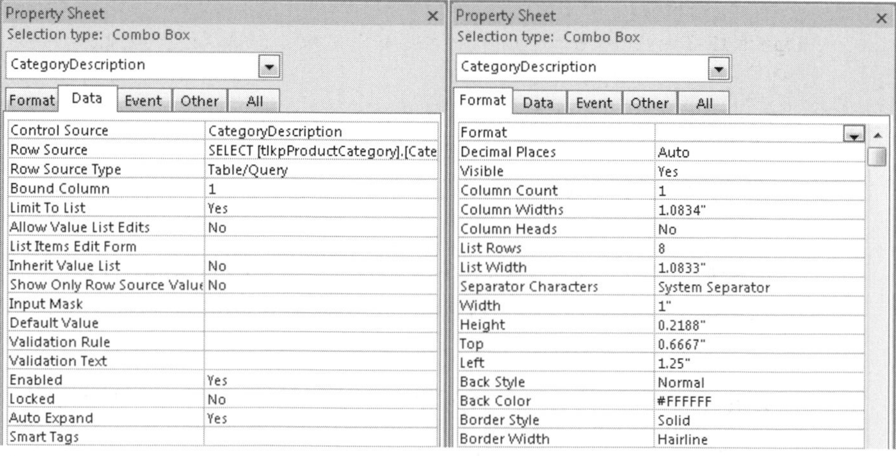


**Figure 11-36** The Combo Box Wizard set these properties for the CategoryDescription field.

The Column Count property is set to 1 to indicate that one column should be created from the list. You have the option of asking Access to display column headings when the combo box is open, but you don't need that for this example, so leave the Column Heads property set to No. The wizard sets the Column Widths property based on the width you set in step 5. The next property on the Data tab, Bound Column, indicates that the first column (the only column in this case) is the one that sets the value of the combo box and, therefore, the value of the bound field in the table.

When you open the form in Form view, it should look like the one shown in Figure 11-37. You can see that the CategoryDescription combo box now shows the list of valid values from the lookup table. Notice also that the label the wizard attached looks more like the labels that the Form Wizard originally created. You can make this label look like the others by changing it to a bold font and right aligning it. (You can find this form saved as fxmplProducts2 in the sample database.)

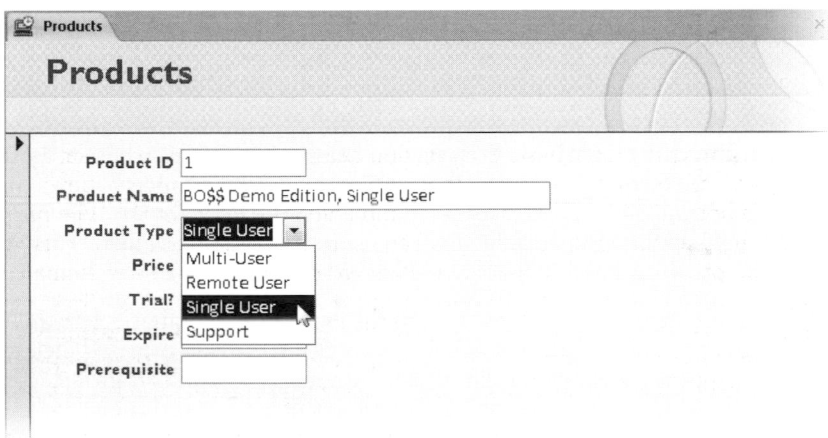


**Figure 11-37** A combo box for the CategoryDescription field makes it much easier for the user to select a correct value.

## INSIDE OUT Having Access Select Closest Matches While Typing

If you want Access to select the closest matching entry when you type a few leading characters in a combo box, set the control's Auto Expand property to Yes.



## Using Toggle Buttons, Check Boxes, and Option Buttons

If your table contains a field that has a yes/no, a true/false, or an on/off value, you can choose from three types of controls that graphically display and set the status of this type of field: toggle buttons, check boxes, and option buttons.

INSIDE OUT **Choosing Toggle Buttons and Check Boxes and Option Buttons—How to Decide?**

Although you can certainly use any of these three controls to display an underlying Yes/No data type, you should try to use these controls in your application similarly to the way Windows uses them. Your users might be confused if you try to use them in a different way.

- Use a *toggle button* to display an option value. A toggle button works best to display an option that is on or off.
- Use a *check box* to display all simple yes/no or true/false values.
- Use an *option button* when the user needs to make a choice from several options. You should not use an option button to display simple yes/no or true/false values.

We personally never use a toggle button or an option button except inside an option group control. You can learn more about working with the option group control in Chapter 13.

The tblProducts table has a TrialVersion field that indicates whether the particular product is a free trial edition that expires in a specific number of days. As you can see in the original text box control created by the Form Wizard (see Figure 11-29), the word Yes or No appears depending on the value in the underlying field. This field might be more appealing and understandable if it were displayed in a check box control.

To change the TrialVersion control on the Products form, first delete the TrialVersion text box control. Display the field list by clicking the Add Existing Fields button in the Tools group. Next, click the Check Box button in the Controls group, and then drag the TrialVersion field from the field list onto the form in the open space you left on the form. Your form in Design view should now look like the one shown in Figure 11-38. Notice that the default check box also includes a label, but the label is positioned to the right of the control and does not include a colon. If you want to move the label, select it, and then use the large handle shown earlier in Figure 11-15 to move the label to the left of the check box. You should also change the font to bold to match the other labels.

After making final adjustments to the TrialVersion label, click the arrow under the Views button and click Form View to see the result. Your form should look like the one shown in Figure 11-39. One of the interesting side effects of using a special control to display data in a form is that the control properties carry over to Datasheet view. Switch to the Datasheet view of this form. The CategoryDescription field is displayed as a drop-down list on the datasheet and the TrialVersion field still looks like a check box. You might decide to design some forms to be used in Datasheet view, but you can customize the look of the datasheet by using controls other than text boxes while in Design view. By the way, this design sample is saved as fxmplProducts3 in the sample database.

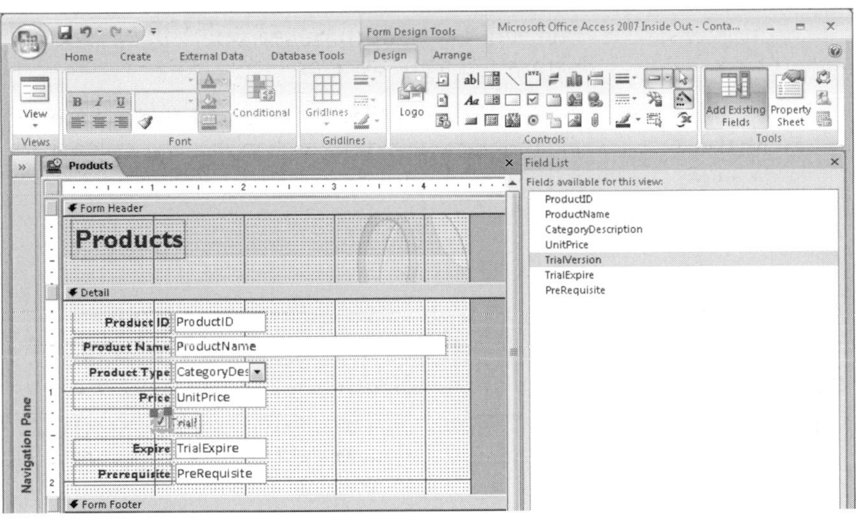


Figure 11-38 The Products form now contains a check box control to display the TrialVersion field.

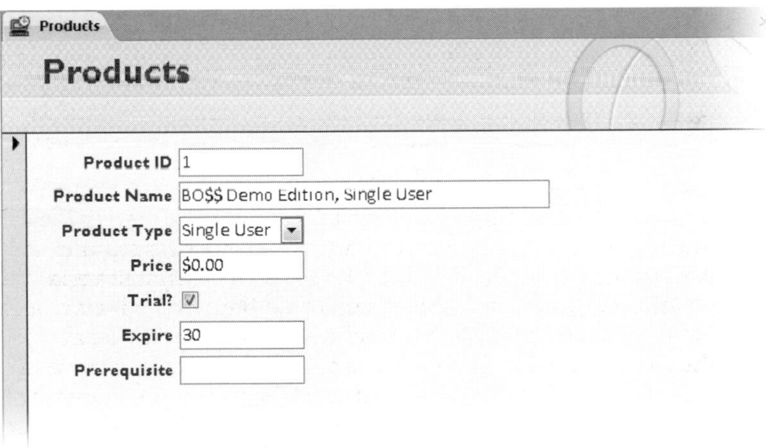


Figure 11-39 Your Products form now has both a combo box control and a check box control to simplify data entry.

By now, you should be getting a feel for the process of building forms. In the next chapter, you'll learn how to customize the appearance of your forms.

CHAPTER 12

# Customizing a Form



In Chapter 11, "Building a Form," you created a form from scratch based on the tblCompanies table in the ContactsDataCopy.accdb sample database. You also had a chance to build a simple form on tblProducts using a wizard and to make some modifications in Design view. These forms are functional, but they're not yet professional grade. In this chapter, you'll learn how to customize your forms in both Design view and the new Layout view to make them more attractive and useful.

**Note**

The examples in this chapter are based on the forms, queries, tables, and data in HousingDataCopy.accdb on the companion CD included with this book. The results you see from the samples in this chapter might not exactly match what you see in this book if you have changed the sample data in the file. Also, all the screen images in this chapter were taken on a Microsoft Windows Vista system with the display theme set to Blue. Your results might look different if you are using a different operating system or a different theme.

## Aligning and Sizing Controls in Design View

To learn how to customize a form, switch to the HousingDataCopy.accdb sample database. You need a form to edit and display employee data, and the easiest way to get started is to create a blank form based on the tblEmployees table. On the Create tab, in the Forms group, click the Blank Form button. A blank form grid appears in Layout view with the field list showing on the right side of the screen. Switch to Design view by clicking the small arrow below the View button in the Views group on either the Home tab or the Format contextual tab under Form Layout Tools. Right now the form is *unbound*—meaning there is no record source—so you need to bind this form to the tblEmployees table. Click the Property Sheet button in the Tools group on the Design tab under Form Design Tools. Find the Record Source property on the All or Data tab of the Property Sheet window for the form, and select tblEmployees from the list of table and query names to bind this form to the tblEmployees table.

Drag down the bottom margin of the Detail section to give yourself some room to work. Click the Arrange contextual tab under Form Design Tools, and make sure Snap To Grid is not selected. (We're asking you to do this on purpose so you can learn ways to line up and evenly space controls.) Open the field list by clicking the Add Existing Fields button in the Tools group on the Design tab. If the field list displays other tables in the bottom half of the field list, click the Show Only Fields In The Current Record Source link at the bottom of the Field List window to show only the fields in the tblEmployees table. Drag and drop each field from the field list into a vertical column on your form about 1.5 inches from the left edge, beginning with the EmployeeNumber field and ending with the BirthDate field. Your starting point should look something like Figure 12-1. (If you don't want to do the work yourself to get to this point, you can find this form saved as frmXmplEmployee1 in the sample database.)

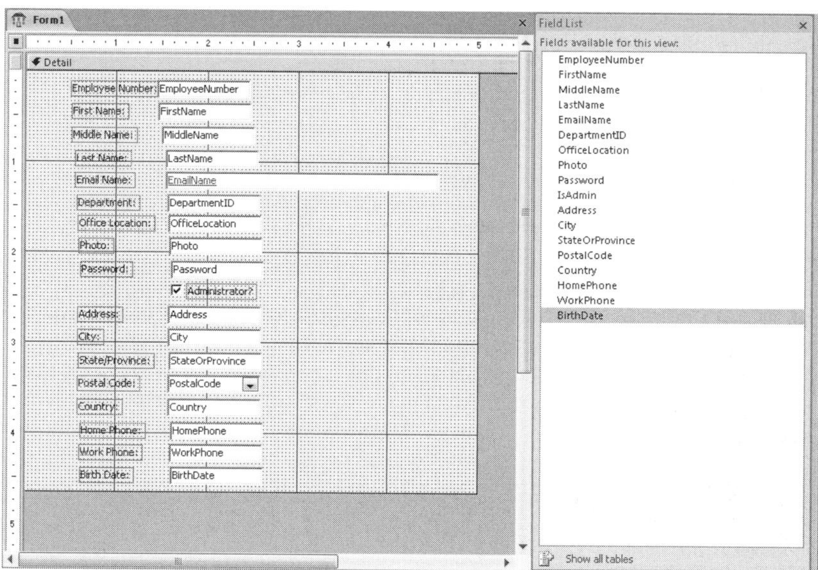


**Figure 12-1** Start to build a form in Design view to display and edit employee data.

> **Note**
>
> The HousingDataCopy.accdb sample database has a special template form called Normal that has its default control properties set to preserve the sunken and etched special effects. This ensures that you'll see the default sunken text boxes when you follow the exercises in this chapter, even when you're running Access on a Windows XP or Windows Vista computer with themed controls enabled. You'll learn more about creating template forms later in this chapter.

If you threw the form together quickly to help you enter some data (as you did in Chapter 11 to create a simple Companies input form in the ContactsDataCopy.accdb database), it probably doesn't matter if the form doesn't look perfect. But all the text boxes except EmailName are the same size, which means some are too large and some are too small to display the data. The long EmailName control looks completely out of place compared to the other controls. Also, the labels are different sizes and not right-aligned. Finally, all the text boxes and labels are out of alignment. If you're designing the form to be used continuously in an application, it's worth the extra effort to fine-tune the design so that it will look professional and be easy to use.

> **Note**
>
> Even if you follow along precisely with the steps described in this chapter, your results might vary slightly. All the alignment commands are sensitive to your current screen resolution. When your screen driver is set to a high resolution (for example, 1280×1024), the distance between grid points is logically smaller than it is when the screen driver is set to a low resolution (such as 800×600). You should design your forms at the same resolution as the computers that will run your application.

To examine the alignment and relative size of controls on your form, you can open the property sheet in Design view and click various controls. For example, Figure 12-2 shows the property sheets for the EmployeeNumber and the FirstName text box controls. You can see by looking at the values for the Left property (the distance from the left edge of the form) that the EmployeeNumber control is a bit closer to the left margin than is the FirstName control.

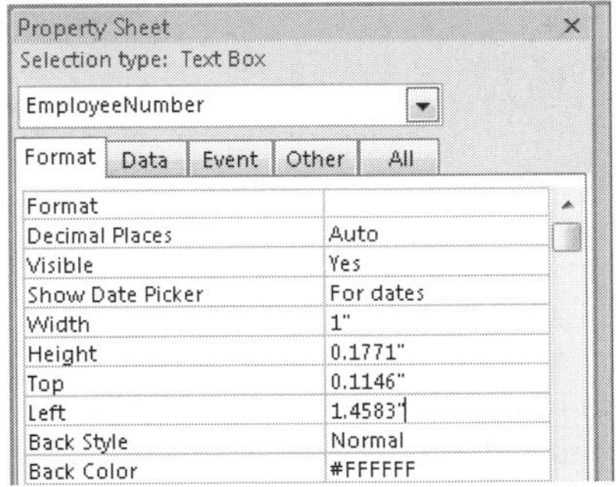


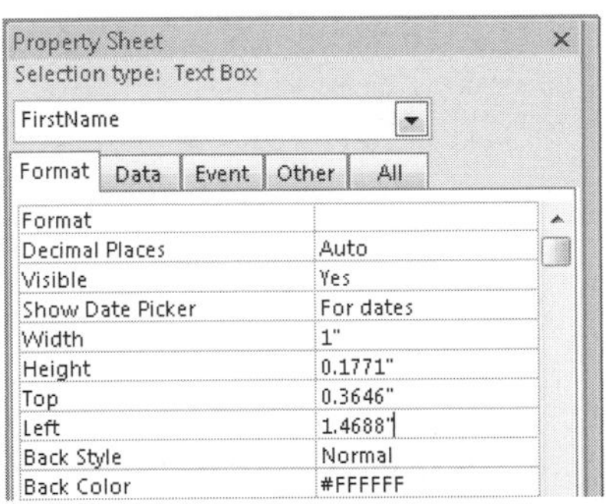


**Figure 12-2** You can see in the Property Sheet windows for the EmployeeNumber and FirstName text box controls that the two controls are not aligned vertically.

You could move around the form and adjust controls so that they fit your data. You could painstakingly enter values for each control's Left property to get all controls in a column to line up exactly and then set the Top property (defining the distance from the top of the Detail section) for controls that you want to appear in a row. You could also adjust the values for the Width and Height properties so that controls and labels are the same width and height where appropriate. Fortunately, there are easier ways to make all these adjustments.

## Sizing Controls to Fit Content

One adjustment you might want to make on this employees form is to bold the font for all the labels. Remember from the previous chapter that you can click the horizontal ruler at the top of the design area to select all controls in a column, so do this to select all the label controls on the left. You can then hold down the Shift key and click the Administrator? label that's not in the column to include it in your selection. Click the Bold button in the Font group on the Design tab to change the font in all selected controls.

INSIDE OUT

### Setting Selection Options

If you think you'll select multiple controls often, you might want to experiment with an option setting that governs how you can select controls with your mouse pointer. Click the Microsoft Office Button, click Access Options, and then click the Object Designers category in the Access Options dialog box. Under Forms/Reports, when you select the Partially Enclosed option, the selection box you draw with your mouse needs to touch only part of a control to select it. If you select the Fully Enclosed option, the selection box must contain the entire control in order for the control to be selected. Fully Enclosed is most useful for complex forms with many controls that are close to each other so that you don't have to worry about inadvertently selecting controls that you touch but don't fully enclose with the selection box.

However, now that you have changed the font, the label controls are no longer large enough to display all the characters, as shown in Figure 12-3. Notice, for example, that the last two letters and the colon in the Employee Number label appear clipped off. Also, although all the text boxes and the combo box appear high enough to adequately display the data in the default Tahoma 8-point font, they're actually too small.

Microsoft Office Access 2007 has a command called Size To Fit that sizes label controls to fit the width of the caption text in the label. This command also ensures that text boxes and combo boxes are tall enough to display your data using the font size you've selected. You can, if you like, select all the controls so that you can resize them all at once. You can click the Select All button in the Controls group on the Design tab to highlight all the controls on your form. To select a specific group of controls, click the first one and then hold down the Shift key as you click each additional control that you want to select. You can also drag the mouse pointer across the form—as long as you don't start dragging while you are on a control—and the mouse pointer will delineate a selection box. (If you start by clicking a control and then attempt to delineate other controls by dragging, you'll only move the control.) Any controls that are inside the selection box when you release the mouse button will be selected. You can also select all controls in a vertical or a horizontal band by making the rulers visible (click the Ruler button in the Show/Hide group on the Arrange tab) and then dragging the mouse along the top or side ruler.

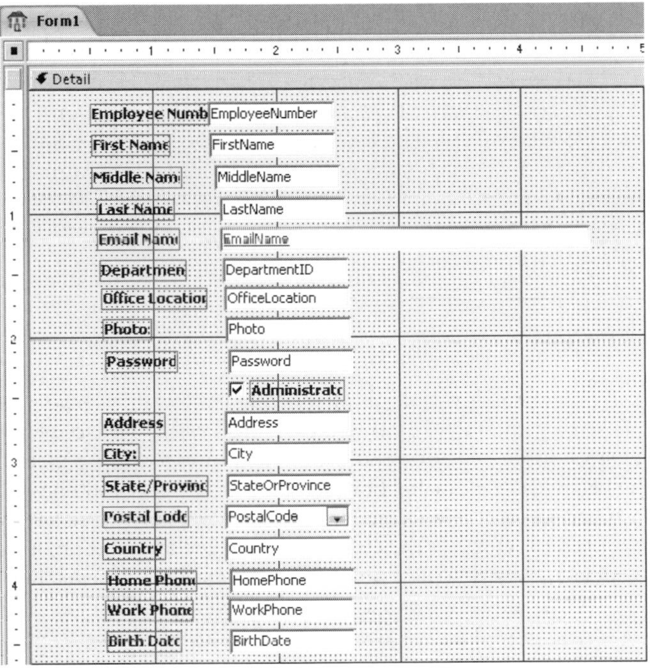


**Figure 12-3** With the bold font, the label controls are no longer large enough to fit the caption text.

> INSIDE OUT **Sizing Individual Controls**
>
> You can "size to fit" any individual control or label by clicking the control to select it and then double-clicking any of its sizing handles.

After you select the controls you want, on the Arrange tab, in the Size group, click the Size To Fit command. The Detail section should now look something like that shown in Figure 12-4. (You cannot see the entire Employee Number label because the right end of it is hidden under the EmployeeNumber text box.)

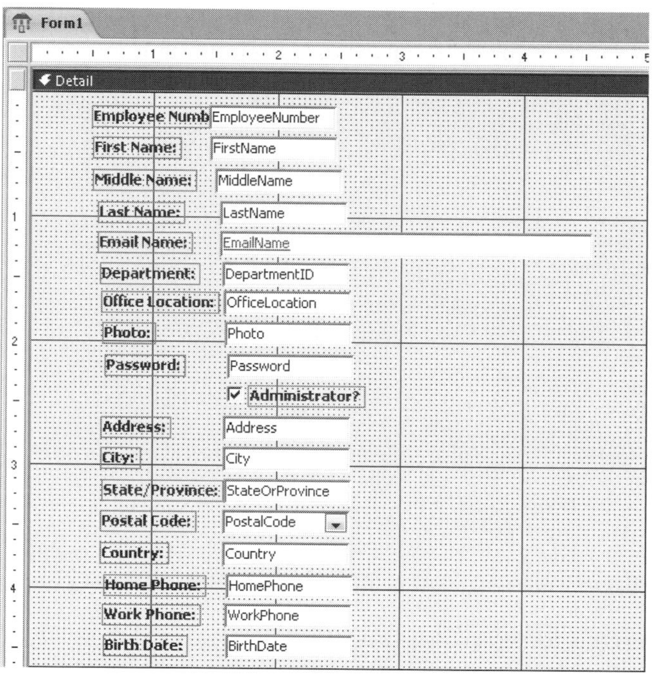


**Figure 12-4** After clicking the Size To Fit command, you can see all the text in the labels.

INSIDE OUT

### Limitations in Use of the Size To Fit Command

The Size To Fit command works very well to set the height of labels, text boxes, and combo boxes based on the font you have chosen. It also does a reasonable job setting the width of labels based not only on the font but also on the characters you have specified in the Caption property. However, it's not perfect, so you should be aware of the following:

- When a label contains a long caption and has a large font that is bold or italic or both, the result of the Size To Fit command is often not wide enough. You will have to adjust the width manually.
- The Size To Fit command does not adjust the width of a text box or combo box because it cannot predict in advance how many characters might need to be displayed from the Control Source property. You must specifically set the width based on the data you expect the control to display.
- The Size To Fit command does not work for list boxes. When you switch to Form view and your list box row source contains enough rows to fill the list box, you might find that you see only part of a row at the bottom. (You'll see only the top part of the characters.) You must switch back and forth between Design view and Form view, adjusting the height of the control manually so that it displays complete rows.

Switch to Form view, and scroll through several of the records to get an idea of which controls aren't wide enough to display the data from the table and which ones could be narrower. You could painstakingly resize each control to exactly fit what you see in the sample data, but this is a bad idea for two reasons:

- The data is a sample of only 16 records, so new data you enter later might be much longer in some fields. You should size the fields that aren't long enough to be 25 percent to 50 percent wider than what you think you need right now.
- A form that has a hodgepodge of a dozen or more different control widths won't make for a very visually pleasing design. You should pick two or three standard widths to use, even if some of the controls end up being wider than necessary.

You can logically group the text box controls and the combo box control in this form into three separate lengths, as follows:

- **Short** EmployeeNumber, DepartmentID, and StateOrProvince
- **Medium** FirstName, MiddleName, LastName, Password, PostalCode, HomePhone, WorkPhone, and BirthDate
- **Long** EmailName, OfficeLocation, Photo, Address, City, and Country

**Note**

The Photo field in tblEmployees is a text field containing the name of the picture file. In Chapter 20, "Automating Your Application with Visual Basic," you'll learn how to load the file into an image control using Visual Basic code to display the picture. Also, although you can resize the check box control, the size of the graphic image inside the control doesn't change.

You can make the necessary adjustments by leaving the medium-length fields as they are and adjusting the fields in the other two groups. Switch back to Design view now so that you can begin resizing the controls. First, select the EmployeeNumber control and then hold down the Shift key while you select the DepartmentID and StateOrProvince controls. Next, click the sizing box in the middle of the right edge of one of the controls, and drag the right edge to the left until all three controls are about half their original sizes. Now, click the EmailName control, and resize this control to about half of its original width. Next, click the OfficeLocation control, and hold down the Shift key while you select the Photo, Address, City, and Country controls. Click the sizing box in the middle of the right edge of one of these controls, and drag the edge right until all three controls are about 50 percent bigger than their original sizes. Your layout should now look something like Figure 12-5.

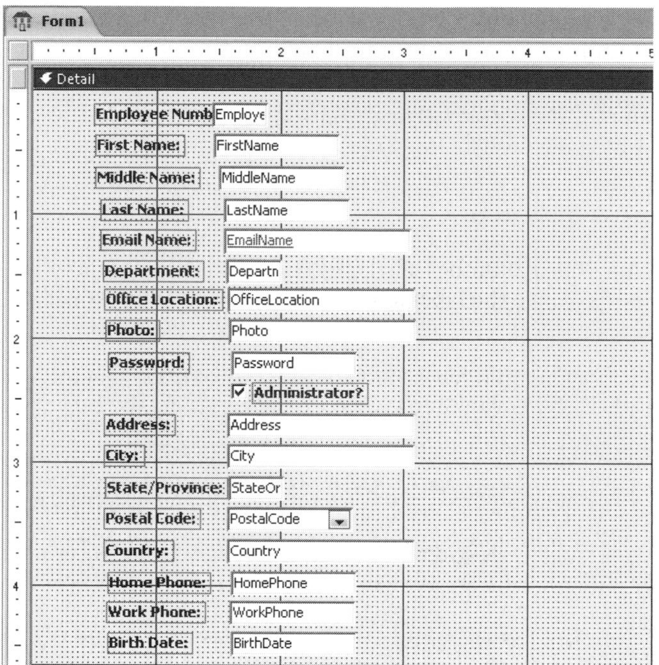


**Figure 12-5** The form for employee data has controls sized to better fit the data.

Before you go on, you might want to save the form and name it frmEmployees. You can find the form at this stage saved as frmXmplEmployee2 in the sample database.

## Adjusting the Layout of Controls

You could have also used the Form Wizard and selected Columnar as the layout to get a jump-start on your employees form. That wizard lays out controls in two columns, without any regard to clusters of fields that might work well lined up side by side. Also, the wizard would put only two controls in the right column, which would make the form look lopsided. Setting up two columns to edit this data is probably a good idea to better use the screen space that is wider than it is tall, but by doing it yourself, you can choose which fields go in which column. For example, you might want to place the work-related fields (EmailName, Department, WorkPhone, OfficeLocation, Password, and IsAdmin) in one column, and place the personal fields (Address, City, StateOrProvince, PostalCode, Country, HomePhone, BirthDate, and Photo) in another.

To adjust your sample employees form in this way, follow these steps:

1. Stretch the Detail section to about 6 inches wide to give yourself some room to work.
2. Select as a group the Address, City, StateOrProvince, PostalCode, Country, and HomePhone controls, and move them into a new column on the right. You're going to end up with two fewer controls in the right column than in the left, so line up the Address control opposite the MiddleName control.

3. Grab the Photo control, and move it under HomePhone opposite Password.
4. Select the WorkPhone control, and move it into the space vacated by Photo.
5. Move the BirthDate control under Photo and across from IsAdmin (the Administrator check box).
6. Grab the lower edge of the Detail section, and shrink the section so that it's now wider than it is high.
7. Select the Employee Number label, grab the positioning handle in the upper-left corner, and move the label to the left out from under the EmployeeNumber text box.

When you're done, you should have a form design that looks something like the one shown in Figure 12-6. Now you're ready to fine-tune your form using alignment and control-size adjustments.

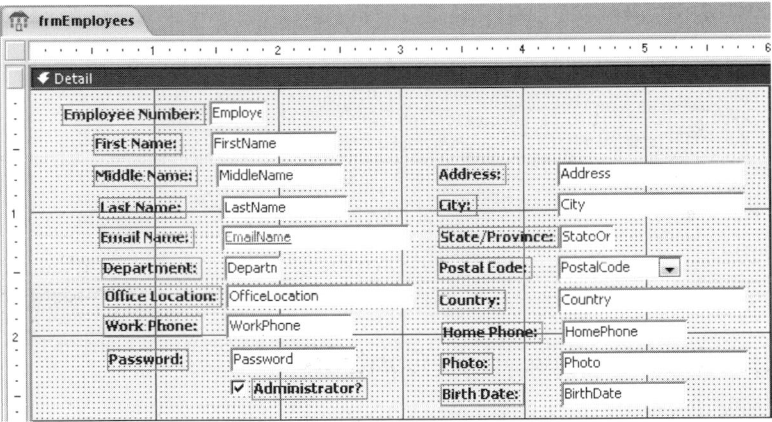


**Figure 12-6** The employees form has the controls arranged into columns that make sense.

## "Snapping" Controls to the Grid

It's a good idea to design your form so that all the controls are spaced evenly down the form and all controls in a column line up. One way that you might find convenient to do this is to take advantage of the grid. If you enable Snap To Grid in the Control Layout group on the Arrange tab, when you move any control, its upper-left corner "snaps" to the nearest grid point. You can use this feature to help you line up controls both horizontally and vertically.

You can adjust the density of the grid by changing the Grid X and Grid Y properties in the property sheet of the form. Be sure that the property sheet is open (Alt+Enter for a shortcut), and then select Form in the Selection Type list near the top of the Property Sheet window. For this example, set the Grid X and Grid Y properties to 16 (0.0625 inch between grid points). This works well for the default 8-point Tahoma font because the "sized to fit" text boxes will be 0.17 inch high. You can place these text boxes every

0.25 inch (four grid points) down the form, which leaves adequate space between the controls. This reduced density also makes it easier to see the grid points so that you can move controls close to the point you want. You could set Grid X and Grid Y to 4, but that reduces flexibility for placing your controls.

The fastest way to snap all controls to the grid is to click Select All in the Controls group on the Design tab and then click the To Grid button in the Control Alignment group on the Arrange tab. The result might look something like that shown in Figure 12-7.

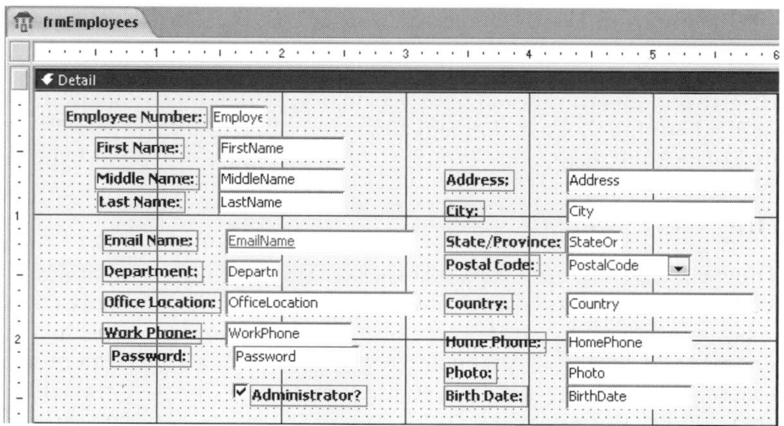


**Figure 12-7** This is how your employees form should look after you "snap" the controls to the grid.

INSIDE OUT

### What's the Difference Between Snap To Grid in Control Layout and To Grid in Control Alignment?

When you enable Snap To Grid, Access aligns the upper-left corner of a control to the grid when you move the control. When you select a control and click To Grid, Access immediately moves that control's upper-left corner to the nearest grid point. The difference is with Snap To Grid, you're moving the control, and with To Grid, Access moves the control for you.

If you want to position each control individually, enable Snap To Grid by making sure it is selected in the Control Layout group on the Arrange tab. (The button appears highlighted and raised when it is active.) Click each text box, combo box, or check box control, and drag it vertically to positions every 0.25 inch (every fourth grid point) down the grid. When you release the mouse button, you'll see the upper-left corner of the control "snap" to the nearest grid point. As you saw in the previous chapter, when you select and move a control that has an attached label, Office Access 2007 moves the control and its label as a unit. If you previously moved a label up or down independent of its attached control by using the positioning handle in the upper-left corner, you might need to select either the control or its label and use the positioning handle again to realign each label and associated control.

> **Note**
>
> For a simple form with a few controls, Snap To Grid works well to help you line up controls. For more complex forms, using the commands in the Control Alignment group produces a better result. Read the next section to learn about these commands.

Snapping to the grid can help you spread the controls apart to make them easier to work with. You'll see in the next few steps that it's easy to line them all up properly.

## Lining Up Controls

You now have your controls spaced down the form, but they might not be equally spaced, and they probably aren't aligned vertically and horizontally. These problems are easy to fix. First, if your form ended up looking like the sample in Figure 12-7 with one or more pairs of controls touching, you need to create some more space by moving down the bottom controls in each column. First, click the IsAdmin check box at the bottom of the first column to select it, and press the Down Arrow once for each pair of touching controls. (We needed to move the control down two rows of dots in our sample.) Do the same, if necessary, to the BirthDate control at the bottom of the second column. Next, select all the text box controls and the check box control in the first column. You can do this by clicking the first text box control (not its associated label) and then holding down the Shift key as you click each of the remaining controls in the column. Or you can click the ruler above the controls. On the Arrange tab, in the Position group, click the Make Vertical Spacing Equal button. Finally, choose all the text box controls and the combo box control in the second column, and click the Make Vertical Spacing Equal button again.

Now you're ready to line up the labels. To get started, select all the labels in the left column except the label for the IsAdmin check box. (You can do this the same way you selected all the data-bound controls in a column.) When you have selected them, your form should look something like the one shown in Figure 12-8. Notice that Access also shows large positioning handles in the upper-left corners of all the related controls but no sizing handles.

The labels will look best if their right edges align. You have two choices at this point. If you turn off the Snap To Grid command, you can have Access align all the labels with the label whose right edge is farthest to the right, even if that edge is between dots on the grid. If you leave Snap To Grid on, you can have Access align the labels with the label farthest to the right and then snap the entire group to the nearest grid point.

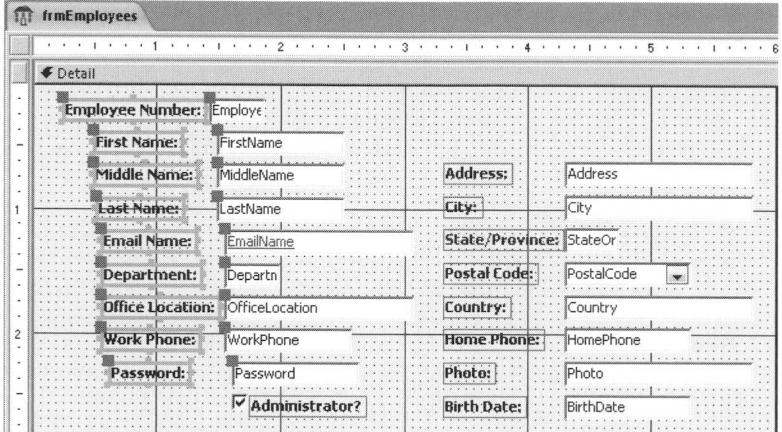


**Figure 12-8** The employees form has a column of labels selected.

> **Note**
>
> For this example, we left Snap To Grid turned on, but you can try it both ways to see which gives you the best result. Try it with Snap To Grid on, and then click the Undo button on the Quick Access Toolbar and try it with Snap To Grid turned off.

When you're ready to align the selected labels on your form, on the Arrange tab, in the Control Alignment group, click the Align Right button. While you're at it, click the Align Text Right button in the Font group on the Design tab to align the captions to the right edges of all the label controls. Click outside the design area to select the form, which will cancel the selection of the labels. Your form should look similar to the one shown in Figure 12-9.

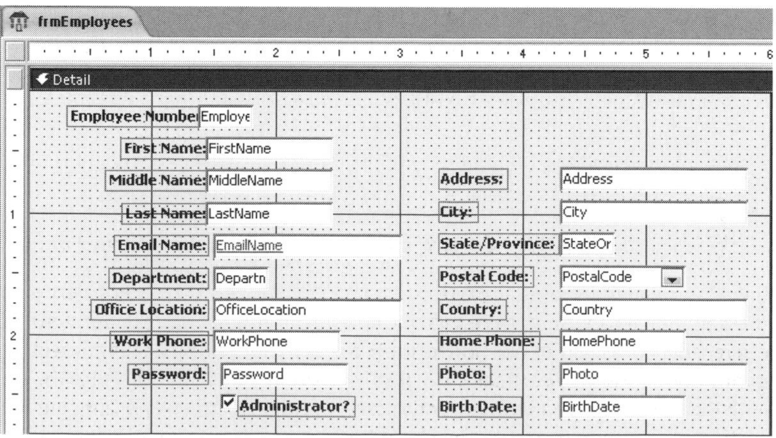


**Figure 12-9** The labels from Figure 12-8 are right-aligned.

To further improve the alignment of the controls on the employees form (assuming your form now looks like Figure 12-9), do the following:

1. The EmployeeNumber text box is a bit too far to the left. Click the control to select it, then click the positioning handle in the upper-left corner, and finally drag the control to the right. If you still have Snap To Grid turned on, it should line up with the FirstName control.
2. Select the EmployeeNumber, FirstName, MiddleName, LastName, EmailName, DepartmentID, OfficeLocation, WorkPhone, Password, and IsAdmin controls. Click the Align Left button in the Control Alignment group on the Arrange tab.
3. Select the labels in the right column and right align them. Also click the Align Text Right button in the Font group on the Design tab to align the captions to the right edge of the label controls.
4. In our sample, the labels in the right column end up a bit too close to the related data controls. Fixing this is a bit tricky. Select the longest label (State/Province), grab its positioning handle in the upper-left corner, and drag it left one row of dots. Grab the sizing handle in the middle of the right edge, and expand the label size until it snaps to one row of dots away from the StateOrProvince text box. Now, select all the labels again, align them left, and then align them right. Note that by first setting the right edge of the longest label and then aligning all the labels first to the left, the longest label is now assured to protrude farthest to the right. Thus, when the labels are all aligned right again, they line up with the new right offset of the longest label.
5. We like all our labels to appear to the left of the related control, so click the Administrator? label to select it, grab its positioning handle in the upper-left corner, and drag it to the left of the IsAdmin check box. If you still have Snap To Grid turned on and you do this carefully, the label should line up vertically with the other labels in the column and horizontally with the check box. While you're at it, click the Align Text Right button in the Font group on the Design tab. If you like, click the Administrator? label, and add a colon to the end of the text.
6. Close up the bottom of the Detail section a bit so that you have the same amount of space below the bottom control as you do above the top control.

After you complete these steps, your form should look something like the one shown in Figure 12-10.

INSIDE OUT

### Moving Controls in a Horizontal or Vertical Plane

If you want to move one or more controls only horizontally or only vertically, hold down the Shift key as you select the control (or the last control in a group) that you want to move, and then drag either horizontally or vertically. When Access detects movement either horizontally or vertically, it "locks" the movement and won't let the objects stray in the other axis. If you inadvertently start to drag horizontally when you mean to move vertically (or vice versa), click the Undo button, and try again. Moving controls in this way is especially useful when you have Snap To Grid turned off.

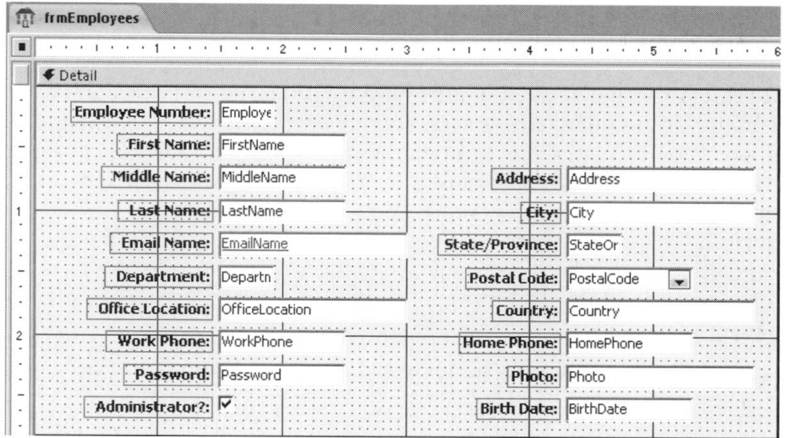


**Figure 12-10** The controls and labels are aligned horizontally and vertically.

If you switch to Form view, you can see the result of your work as shown in Figure 12-11. Click the Save button on the Quick Access Toolbar to save this form. Name the form frmEmployeesDesignView, and then close the form. You can also find this form saved as frmXmplEmployee3 in the sample database.

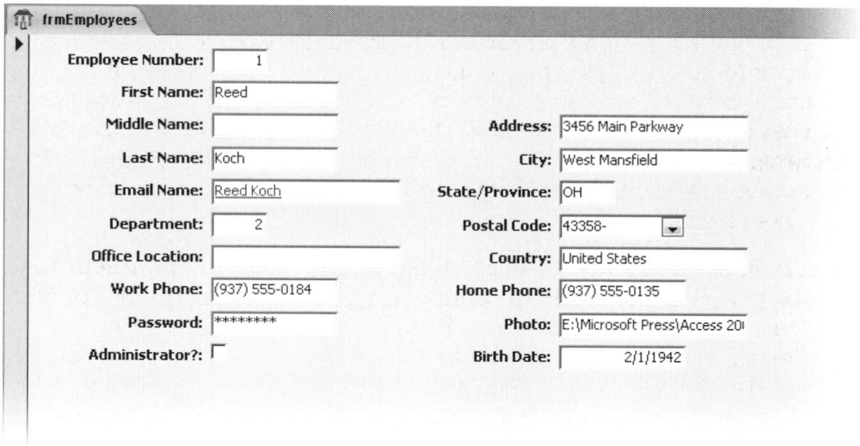

**Figure 12-11** This is your employees form with controls aligned and sized.

## INSIDE OUT Using the Auto Resize Property

Forms have an Auto Resize property. If you set this property to Yes and you are using multiple-document interface mode with overlapping windows, Access sizes the Form window to exactly fit the form. Note that Access won't automatically resize a form in that case if you've switched from Design view to Form view. You can set the Auto Center property to Yes to center the Form window in the current Access workspace if you are using overlapping windows.

# Working in Layout View

Up to this point you've been building a form in Design view to add and edit records in the tblEmployees table. You've seen how to start with a blank form and add fields to the grid, position the controls into a two-column layout, and then align the controls both horizontally and vertically. In this section, you'll follow the same procedure to build an employees form, except this time you'll use the new Layout view in Access 2007. By performing the same steps in Layout view, you will learn how the new Layout view can significantly reduce the amount of time spent aligning and positioning controls. You'll also be able to see live data in the tblEmployees table while working with the controls in Layout view.

Click the Blank Form button in the Forms group on the Create tab. A blank form grid appears in Layout view with the Field List window showing on the right side of the screen. The form does not yet have a record source, so you need to bind this form to the tblEmployees table. Click the Property Sheet button in the Tools group on the Arrange tab under Form Layout Tools. Find the Record Source property on either the All or Data tab in the Property Sheet window for the form, and select tblEmployees from the list of table and query names to bind this form to the tblEmployees table.

## Understanding Control Layouts and Control Anchoring

Now that you have the form bound to the tblEmployees table, you can begin to add the fields to the form grid, as you did previously in Design view, but this time you have left the blank form in Layout view. Open the field list by clicking the Add Existing Fields button in the Controls group on the Format tab. If the field list displays other tables in the bottom half of the field list, click the Show Only Fields In The Current Record Source link at the bottom of the Field List window to show only the fields in the tblEmployees table.

Earlier in the chapter, you were able to drag a control from the field list and drop it on any part of the form grid in Design view. Let's try the same step now in Layout view. Drag and drop the EmployeeNumber field from the field list onto the form grid. (It doesn't matter on what part of the grid you drop the field.) After you release the mouse, you'll notice that Access places the control in the upper-left corner of the form grid, as shown in Figure 12-12. Notice also that you can see actual data from the table in the text box.

Access applied a control layout to the grid and anchored the EmployeeNumber control in the upper-left corner. Access positioned the Employee Number label 0.25 inch from the top of the form and 0.25 inch from the left side of the form. When you anchor a control in a control layout, Access resizes or moves the control if you resize or move the section in which the control resides. In addition to anchoring controls to the default top left, you can choose to anchor controls at the bottom left, top right, and bottom right. You can also choose to stretch the controls across the top, down the left side, across the bottom, down the right side, and down and across the section. On the Arrange tab, in the Position group, click the Anchoring button to see the nine possible anchoring configurations, as shown in Figure 12-13.

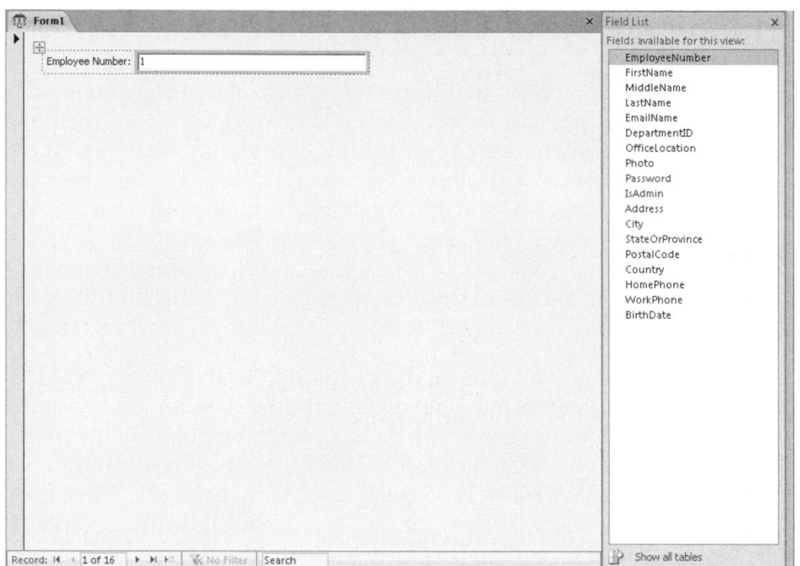


**Figure 12-12** Access positions the EmployeeNumber control in the upper-left corner no matter where you drop it on the form grid.

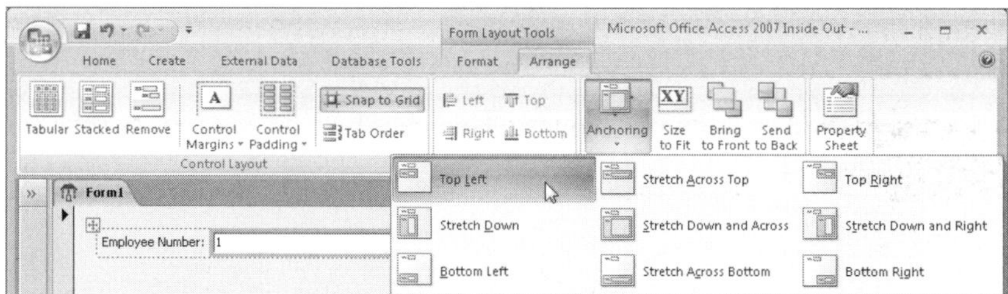


**Figure 12-13** Use the anchoring options to select different anchoring positions for your controls.

To see how another anchoring option appears on the form grid, select the Employee-Number field, if it isn't already selected, and then click Stretch Across Top in the Anchoring gallery. You'll notice that Access increases the width of the EmployeeField so that it extends closer to the right edge of the form. If you close the Field List window, you can see that Access again increases the width of the control. Switch to Form view now by clicking the arrow in the Views group on the Home or Format tab and selecting Form View in the list of available views. Access displays the EmployeeNumber field nearly across the entire top of the form grid, as shown in Figure 12-14. In most cases, a control this wide is not very practical for a simple text field. Return to Layout view, select the EmployeeNumber control, click the Anchoring button in the Position group on the Arrange tab, and change the anchor option back to Top Left.

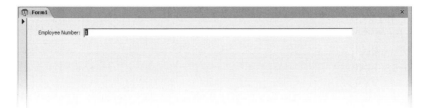

**Figure 12-14** The Stretch Across Top anchoring option produces a very wide control.

If you like, you can try some of the other options, but their names are intuitive. Top Right pins the control in the upper-right corner. Stretch Down expands the control to fill the vertical space on the form. (If you have more than one control stacked in the layout, Access expands them all equally to fill the space.) Stretch Down And Across expands the control to fill the entire space, and so on.

## Lining Up Controls

Now that you have the EmployeeNumber field on the grid, let's add the next field, FirstName, below EmployeeNumber. Click the FirstName field in the field list, drag it onto the form, and drop it just below the EmployeeNumber label and text box, as shown in Figure 12-15. When you have it correctly positioned, Access displays a horizontal I-bar below the EmployeeNumber controls. You'll notice that Access doesn't allow you to drop the FirstName field to the right of the EmployeeNumber control. It displays this I-bar only above or below the EmployeeNumber controls.

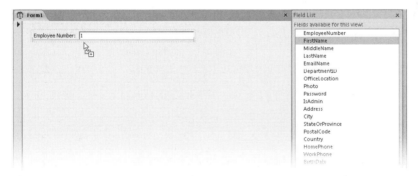

**Figure 12-15** Drag and drop the FirstName field below the EmployeeNumber field.

After you release the mouse, Access places the FirstName field directly below the EmployeeNumber label and text box controls, as shown in Figure 12-16. Now that you have two controls on the grid, you can really begin to see the advantages of using a control layout. Unlike the Design view exercise you performed at the beginning of this chapter, Access creates label and field controls that exactly match the dimensions of the first label and field controls when you use a control layout. Access positions the new controls directly beneath the EmployeeNumber controls and aligns them vertically.

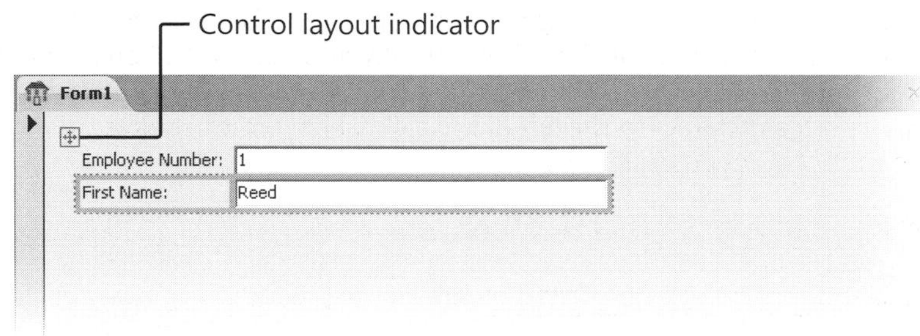


**Figure 12-16** Access sizes all the same types of controls to the same height and width when you use a control layout.

Control layouts help you align and position controls on forms and reports. It might be easier to think of a control layout as being similar to a table in Microsoft Office Word or a spreadsheet in Microsoft Office Excel. When you widen or narrow one control in a column, you change the width of any other controls in that column that are part of that control layout. Likewise, when you increase or decrease the height of a control, you're changing the height of all the controls in that row.

Access 2007 has two kinds of control layouts—*stacked* and *tabular*. In a stacked control layout, Access "stacks" bound controls for different fields in a column and places all the labels down the left side. You can have multiple sets of stacked controls within a section. Any controls (including associated labels) in a stacked layout must all be in one section. In the form you've built thus far, Access has placed the employee number and first name controls in a stacked layout in the Detail section. You can tell these controls are in a control layout by noticing the small box with crosshairs just to the left of and slightly above the Employee Number label, previously shown in Figure 12-16.

In a tabular control layout, Access places bound controls horizontally with labels along the top as column headings—much like rows on a spreadsheet. A tabular control layout can include controls in different sections of a form—for example, the labels can appear in a header section and the data controls in the Detail section of the form.

## Moving Controls Within a Control Layout

Let's add the remaining fields onto the form grid now. Click the MiddleName field in the field list, hold down the Shift key, and then click the BirthDate field to highlight the remaining 16 fields. Drag all the controls as a group onto the form grid and drop them just below the FirstName label and text box. After you drop the fields onto the grid, your form should look like Figure 12-17.

When you work with a control layout in Layout view, you can save time positioning, moving, and resizing controls. As you can see in Figure 12-17, Access sizes all the labels and text box controls to the same dimensions. When you did this same exercise in Design view at the beginning of the chapter, you needed to perform extra steps to make all the labels the same size, change the widths of the labels to accommodate the caption text, and line up the controls both horizontally and vertically. You also had to swap positions for the IsAdmin check box and label. In the new Layout view, though, Access correctly places the label to the left of the check box, which makes this part of the form creation process much easier and faster.

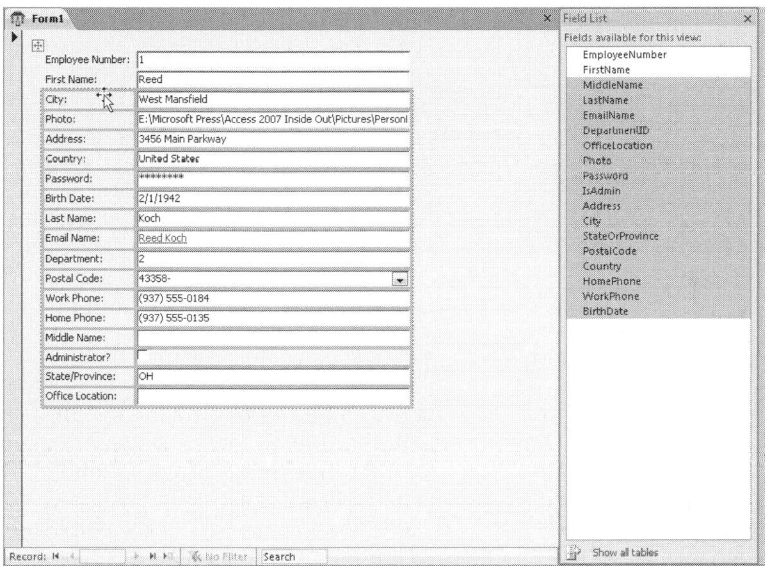


**Figure 12-17** You can quickly move a group of fields from the field list into a control layout in Layout view.

### Note

If you look closely again at Figure 12-17, you'll notice a discrepancy with the order of the fields on the form grid. In the initial release of Access 2007, a bug causes the order of fields to be incorrectly positioned on the form grid when you drag and drop a group of controls from the field list. If you compare your field list on the form grid to the order of fields displayed in the field list, you'll see that the order has been rearranged. To work around this bug, you can drag and drop one field at a time onto the form grid from the field list instead of dragging a group of controls onto the form grid. For now, we'll keep the incorrect order on the grid so that we can show you another advantage to using control layouts.

When you have controls in a control layout and move them around in Layout view, Access automatically snaps them back into proper horizontal and vertical alignment. To see this feature, let's change the order of the controls on the form grid to match the display order shown in the field list. Click the MiddleName text box control or label, drag it up toward the top of the form, and drop it just below the FirstName label and text box. When you have it correctly positioned, Access displays a horizontal I-bar below the FirstName controls, as shown in Figure 12-18.

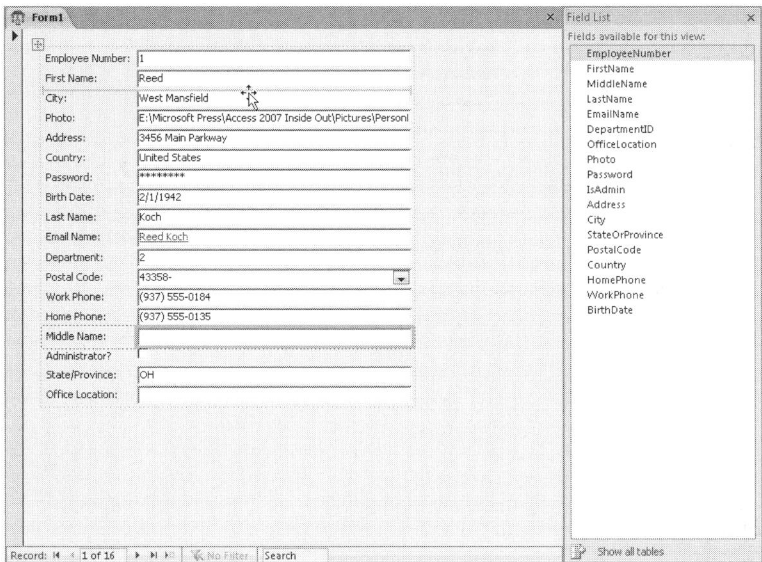


**Figure 12-18** Drag the MiddleName label and text box controls into their correct position.

After you release the mouse, Access moves the MiddleName label and text box controls beneath the FirstName controls and moves all the other controls down to make room, as shown in Figure 12-19. Access also lines up all the controls both horizontally and vertically on the form grid. By using a control layout, you can easily move and swap control positions without having to line up the controls.

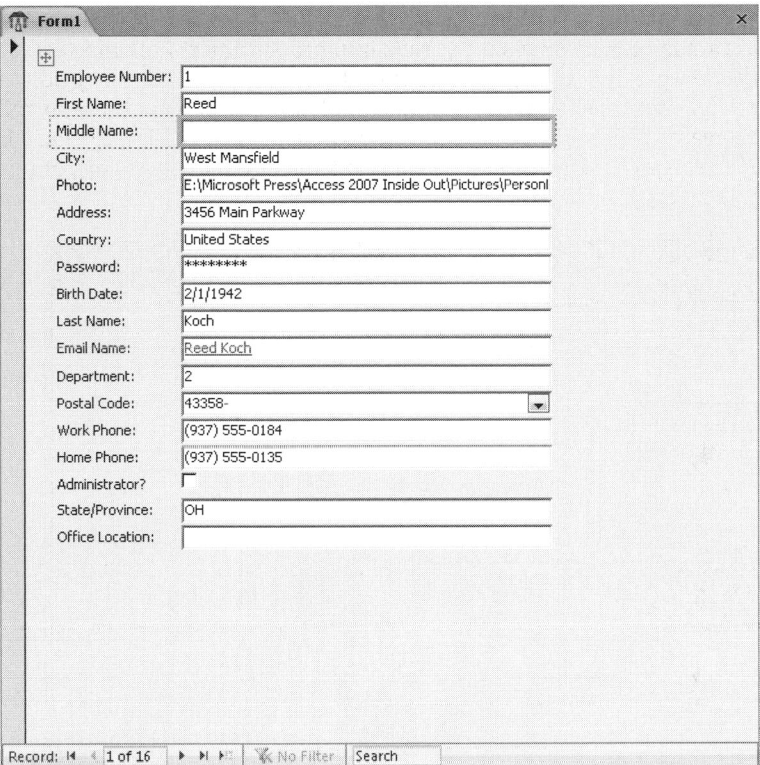


**Figure 12-19** In a control layout, Access repositions controls when you move them around the form grid.

Using the technique you just learned, reposition the remaining fields to match the display order in the field list. Keep the Field List window open during this process so that you can see their correct order.

After you reposition all the controls, your form should look like Figure 12-20. You repositioned and aligned the controls in a matter of seconds, whereas this same procedure in Design view could take much longer.

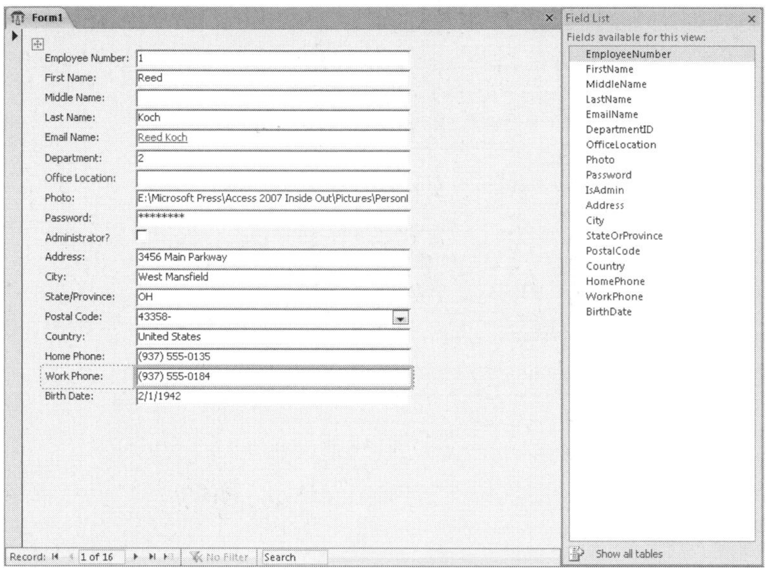


**Figure 12-20** All the controls now match the field list display order.

## Formatting a Column of Controls

As you might recall from earlier in the chapter, we like to right align our labels and bold the font. When you did this procedure in Design view, you clicked the horizontal ruler at the top of the design area to select all controls in a column. In Layout view, however, you cannot display the horizontal ruler. To select all the label controls in a column, select the Employee Number label and then rest your mouse pointer on the top edge of the label until it changes to a down arrow, as shown in Figure 12-21. When you see the down arrow, click once; Access highlights all the labels in that column. Now click the Bold button in the Font group on the Format tab to change the font in all the label controls to bold. Next, click the Align Text Right button in the Font group to right align all the text in the labels.

You'll notice that when you change the font to bold, Access increases the width of all the label controls to make sure all the text still fits within the labels. Access then pushes all the text controls to the right to accommodate the wider labels. Here again, you can see how Layout view saves you time compared to doing the same steps in Design view.

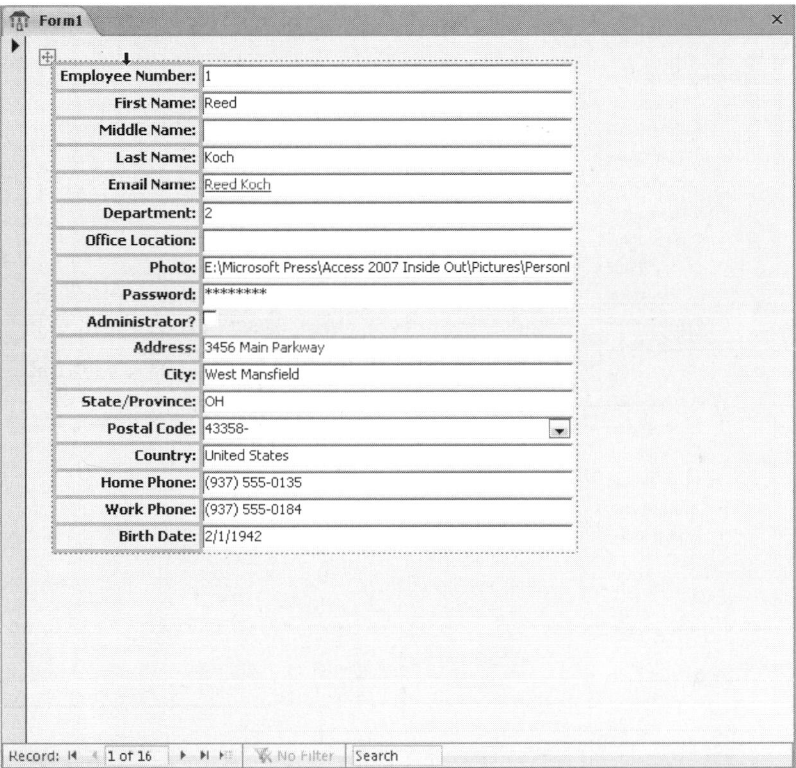


**Figure 12-21** Select all the labels by resting your mouse pointer on the top edge of the Employee Number label.

## Resizing Controls

Now that you have all the labels formatted just the way you want, you should adjust the width of the text box controls. Remember that earlier in the chapter we discussed having three different widths for the various text box controls. Right now, all the text box controls are 3 inches wide, which is much larger than they need to be. Also, we eventually want to have two columns for our fields, so you'll need to make room for the second column of controls. Let's start by resizing all the text box controls to the longest length we want to have, 1.5 inches, and then we'll move the controls into two columns. You'll have an easier time positioning the controls into two columns when you can see the maximum width of the text box controls. Click the sizing box in the middle of the right edge of the EmployeeNumber text box, and drag the right edge to the left until the control is about 1.5 inches wide. As you drag the control to the left, you'll immediately notice that Access resizes every other text box as well, as shown in Figure 12-22.

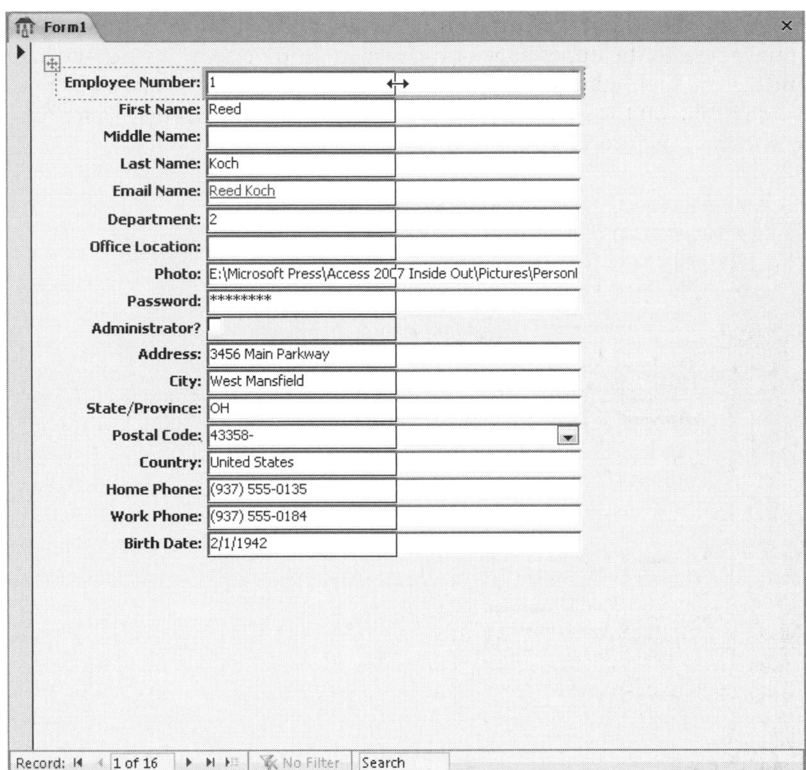


**Figure 12-22** When you resize one control in a control layout, all other controls in the same column are also resized.

Now you can see one of the great advantages *and* disadvantages of using a control layout. If you need to resize all the controls in the same column on a form grid to the same width or height, using a control layout makes this process very simple. However, it is impossible to make *individual* sizing changes to some of the controls inside a control layout. To resize individual controls, you must remove the control layout applied to the controls. But keep in mind that when you remove the control layout, you lose the timesaving features of moving and positioning the controls should you need to insert additional controls.

## Removing a Control Layout

To move eight of your fields into a second column as you did in Design view earlier in this chapter, you need to remove the control layout applied to all the controls on the form grid. Because all the controls are in a stacked layout, Access does not allow you to drag any of the controls into a second column. To remove the control layout, you first need to select all the controls. Click the Employee Number label, and move your pointer to the top edge until it turns into a down arrow. Click, and Access highlights all the labels. Now hold down the Shift key, click the EmployeeNumber text box, and move your mouse to the upper edge of the control until it becomes a down arrow. Click again, and Access highlights all the text box controls as well. Now that all the form controls are selected, on the Arrange tab, in the Control Layout group, click the Remove button, as shown in Figure 12-23.

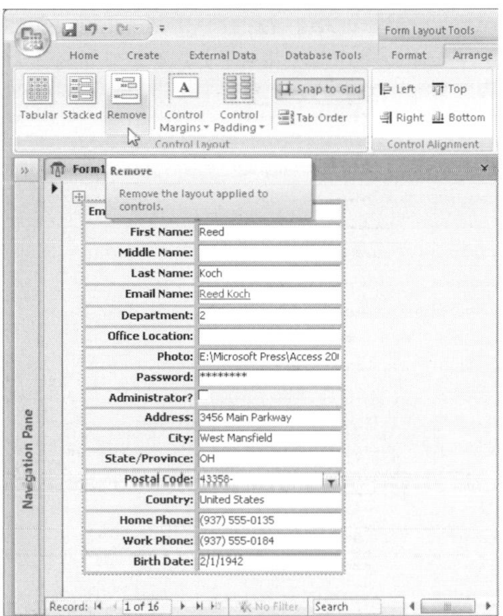


**Figure 12-23** Click the Remove button to remove the control layout applied to the form controls.

INSIDE OUT **Using the Property Sheet to Help Resize Controls**

In Layout view, you cannot display the horizontal ruler across the top of the form grid. When you want to resize a control to a *specific* height or width in this view, it can be difficult trying to guess exactly the right size when you drag the edges of the control. To make this process easier, first display the Property Sheet window by clicking the Property Sheet button in the Tools group on the Arrange tab. Click either the Format or All tab to display the Height and Width property settings, and then type the new height or width directly on the property sheet to resize the control. You can also click a control and then begin dragging the control edges. After you make an adjustment to the control's height or width, release the mouse, and notice that Access adjusts these properties on the property sheet. You'll immediately be able to gauge whether you need to make further adjustments.

Now that you've removed the control layout, you can move and resize any controls independently. You need to move eight fields into a new column to the right of the existing column. To select all of these controls as a group, hold down the Shift key, and then click both the label and the text box for the following fields—Photo, Address, City, StateOrProvince, PostalCode, Country, HomePhone, and BirthDate. After you have all these controls selected, move your mouse onto the middle of one of the controls until it becomes double-sided crosshairs. Now drag the controls as a group to the right and line up the top control even with the MiddleName controls before releasing the mouse, as shown in Figure 12-24. Make sure to leave a little extra room between the two columns. (You don't have to be perfectly precise in this move because you're still going to move things around.)

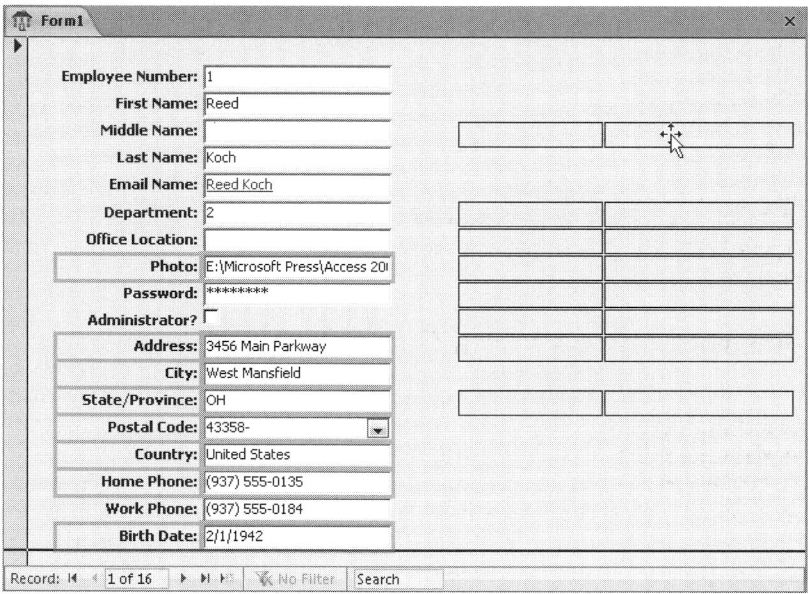


**Figure 12-24** Drag the selected controls into a new column.

After you drop the controls in the second column, your form should look like Figure 12-25. The two columns of controls now have large gaps between the various controls because Access kept the original relative distance between the controls when you moved them as a group. Earlier in this chapter you saw how to fill these missing gaps in Design view by dragging the controls around and then aligning them to existing controls. You could follow the same procedure here in Layout view, but let's use control layouts to save some extra steps.

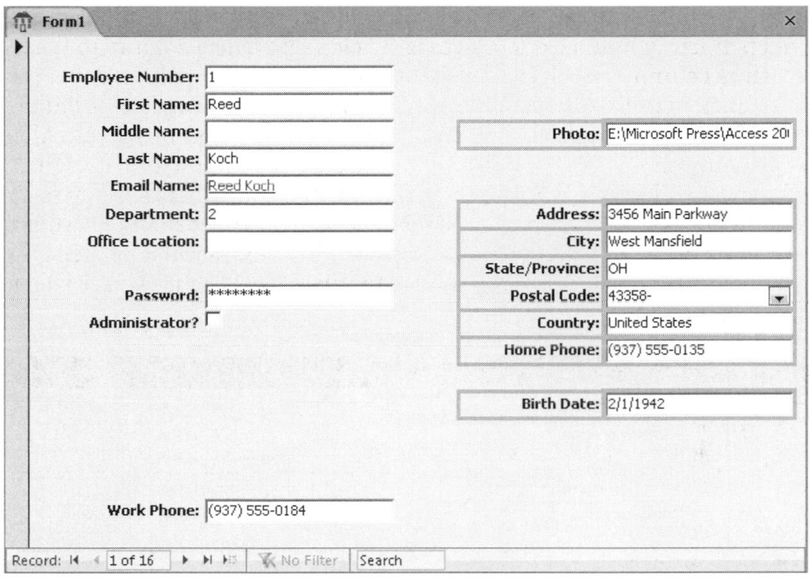


**Figure 12-25** The controls are now separated into two columns, but you still need to move and align them.

## Placing Controls into a Control Layout

If you select all the controls on the form grid and apply them again to a stacked control layout, Access aligns all the controls to the left edge of the form, essentially undoing the work you just did in the preceding step. If, however, you create a new control layout for *each* column of controls, you can still use the features of control layouts. Select all the controls in the left column by holding down the Shift key and then clicking each label and text box (include the IsAdmin check box as well). Next, click the Stacked button in the Control Layout group on the Arrange tab, as shown in Figure 12-26.

After you click the Stacked button, you'll notice that Access snaps the three label and field controls near the bottom of the form grid up next to the other controls. Access aligns them perfectly both horizontally and vertically with one click.

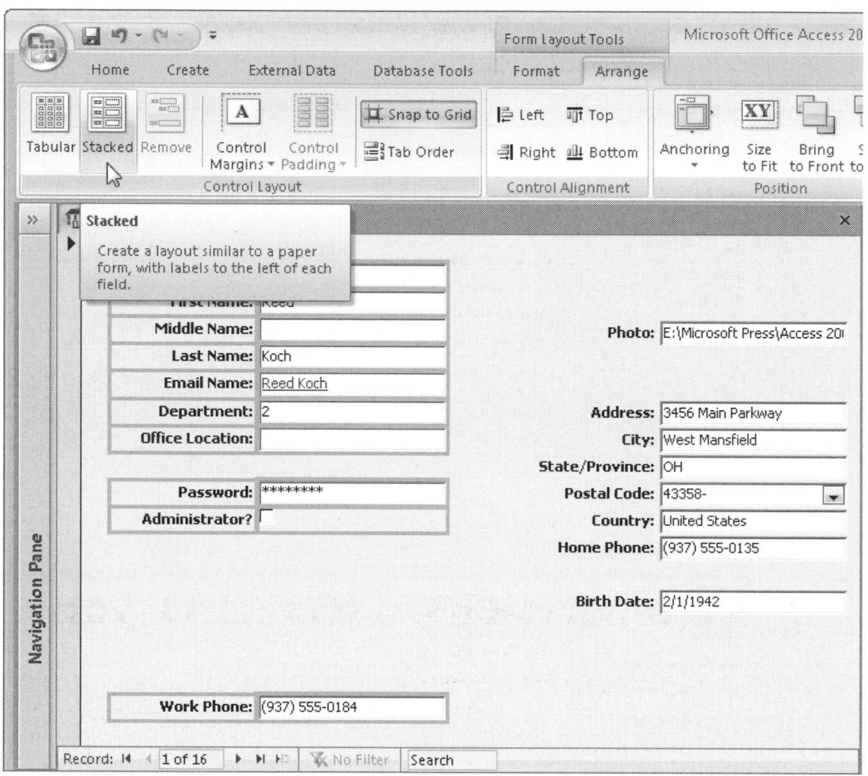


**Figure 12-26** Click the Stacked button to apply a control layout to the controls on the left side of the form grid.

If you look at Figure 12-27, you'll notice that Access 2007 aligned all the label captions back to the left. In a stacked control layout, this is the default, so you'll need to change this to right-aligned. (Notice, however, that placing the controls back into a control layout did not remove the bold font from the labels.) Click the Employee Number label, rest your mouse pointer on the top edge of the label until the cursor changes to a down arrow, and then click to highlight all the label controls. Click the Align Text Right button in the Font group on the Format tab to right align the labels.

Now you need to apply a control layout to the controls on the right side of the form grid. Select each label and text box on the right side of the form, and then click the Stacked button in the Control Layout group on the Arrange tab. Access brings all the label and field controls on the right side up to the Photo controls and aligns them horizontally and vertically. Access again changes all the label captions to be left-aligned, so highlight the labels, and right align them as you did previously. After you make these changes, your form should look like Figure 12-28. You can see how quick and easy it is to align controls when you use control layouts.

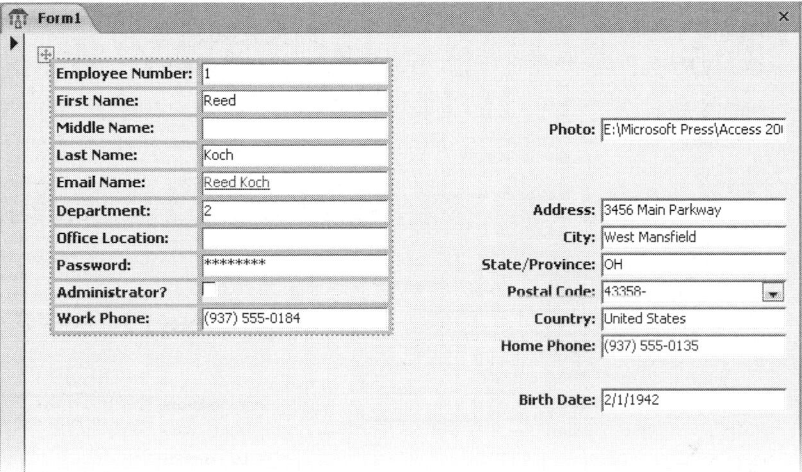


**Figure 12-27** Access aligns all the controls on the left side of the form after you apply a control layout.

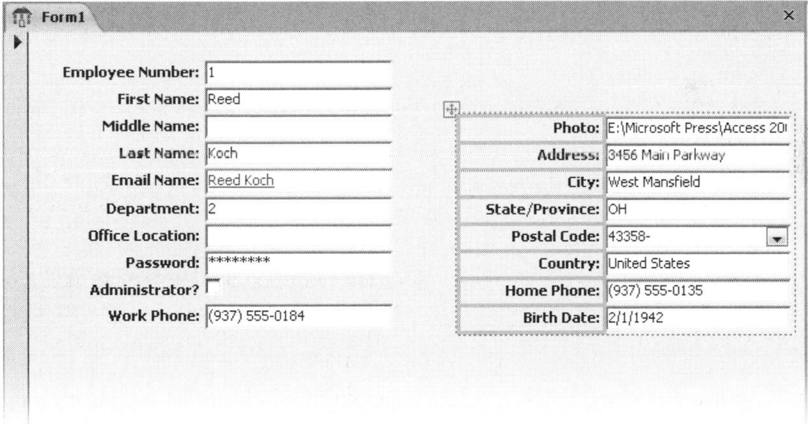


**Figure 12-28** Each column of controls is now within its own stacked control layout.

Now that you have applied a control layout to each column, you should check to make sure that the controls from both columns line up together. Depending upon where you moved the controls to the right side of the form, they could be a little higher or lower than the respective controls on the left side. Because each group of controls is in a control layout, if you move one control, they all move together. To align all the controls vertically, select the MiddleName and Photo controls, and then on the Arrange tab, in the Control Alignment group, click the Top button, as shown in Figure 12-29.

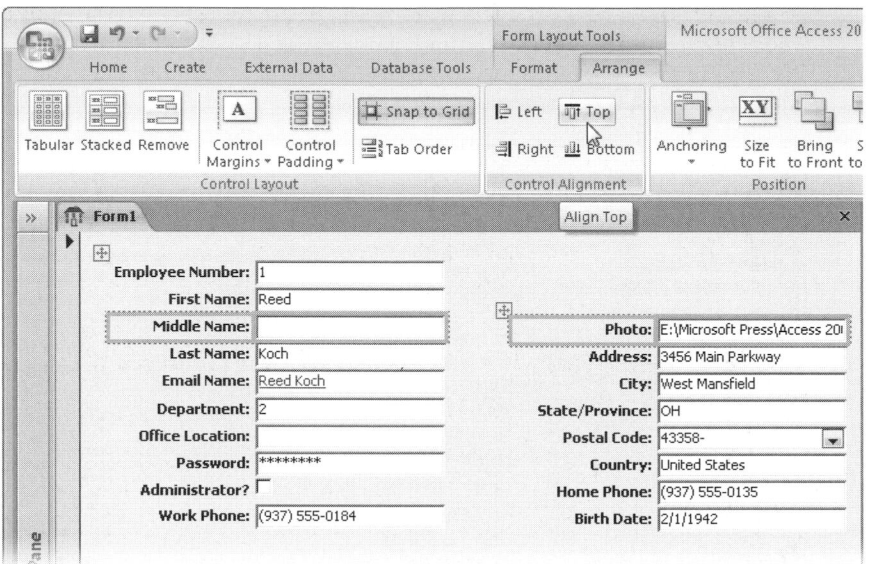


**Figure 12-29** Use the commands in the Control Alignment group to align both control layouts together.

> **Note**
>
> In our test form, we used the Top button to bring the controls up on the right side of the form into alignment with the controls on the left side. If you placed the controls in the right column higher on the form, you might need to select the Birth Date and Work Phone controls and use the Bottom button to bring your controls in the right column down to align them.

## Adding Some Space with Control Padding

All your controls from both sides of the form are now aligned vertically, but they seem to be too close together. Earlier in the chapter, you adjusted the space between the controls by using the grid properties and snapping the controls to the grid. You can also adjust the spacing between the controls by using the *control padding* commands. Control padding adjusts the amount of space between the controls on the form.

Access 2007 has four settings for control padding—None, Narrow (the default), Medium, and Wide. Let's change the control padding around all the controls from Narrow to Medium. Select all the controls on the grid by clicking the Employee Number label, moving the mouse pointer over the top edge until it becomes a down arrow, and then clicking once to highlight all the labels in that column. Hold down the Shift key, and do the same procedure for the EmployeeNumber text box, the Photo label, and the Photo text box. After you have all the controls on the form grid selected, click Control Padding in the Control Layout group on the Arrange tab, and then click Medium, as shown in Figure 12-30.

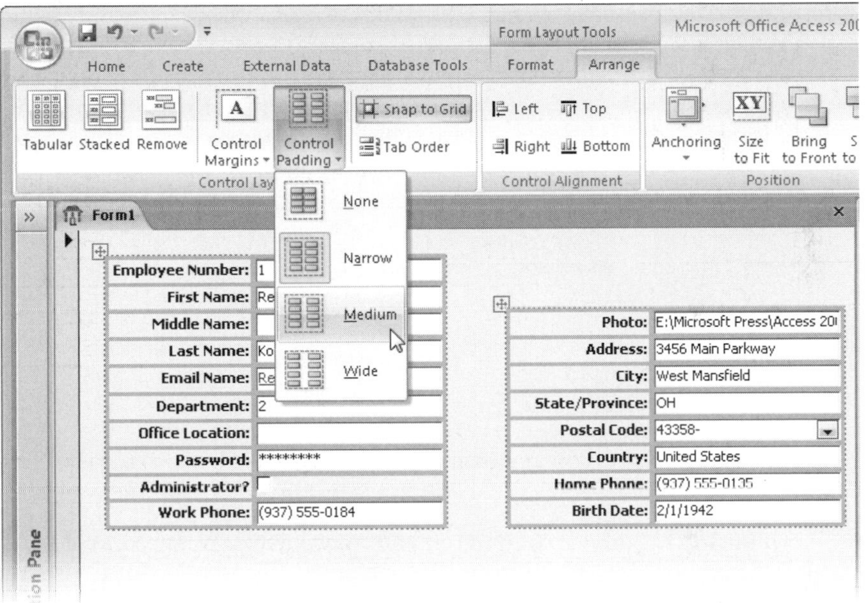

**Figure 12-30** Change the control padding from Narrow to Medium to increase the space between the controls.

## INSIDE OUT Selecting All Controls in a Control Layout

You can quickly select all the controls in a specific control layout by clicking one of the controls and then clicking the small box with crosshairs just to the left of and slightly above the first control in the control layout.

After you click the Medium button, Access increases the padding around all the controls so that they are spaced further apart, as shown in Figure 12-31. You'll notice, however, that the controls from the two separate control layouts don't quite line up. This is easy to fix using the techniques you learned previously–select the MiddleName and Photo controls, and click the Bottom button in the Control Alignment group on the Arrange tab. Access moves down all the controls on the right side of the form to line up with the controls on the left side.

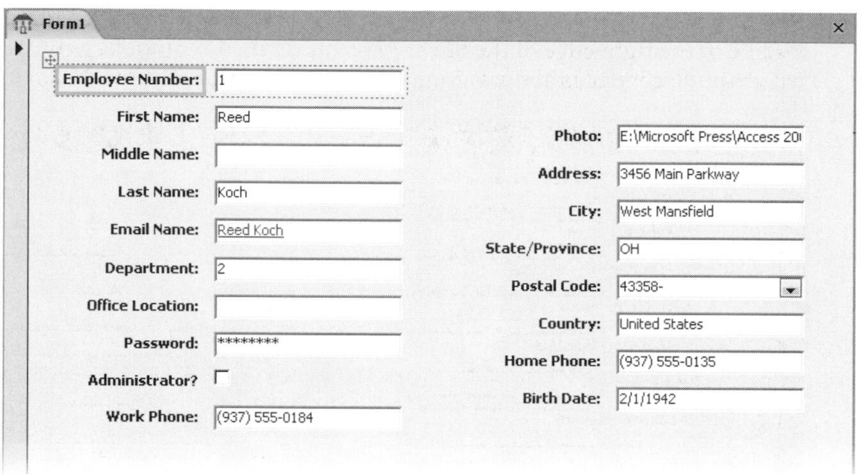


**Figure 12-31** You now have more space between the controls after increasing the control padding.

## Completing the Form

Your form is now looking very similar to the employees form you created in Design view at the beginning of the chapter. The last steps you need to take are to resize the columns to the different widths and move two fields. You need to move the WorkPhone controls above the Password controls and move the Photo controls between the HomePhone and BirthDate controls. Click the WorkPhone label or text box, and drag and drop them just below the OfficeLocation label and text box. Access moves the Password and IsAdmin controls down to allow space for the WorkPhone controls. Similarly, click the Photo label or text box, and drag and drop them just below the HomePhone label and text box. Access moves all the other controls on the right side of the form up to allow space for the Photo controls. All your controls are now positioned correctly and match the layout of the form you previously created in Design view.

In "Resizing Controls," you learned you cannot have different widths and heights for controls contained within a control layout. To individually resize the text boxes, you must remove both control layouts. The control layouts served their purpose in helping you position and align the controls, but they have now reached the limits of their usefulness. To remove the control layout for the controls on the left side of the form, click one of the controls in that group, and then click the small box with crosshairs (just to the left of and slightly above the Employee Number label) to highlight all the controls. Next, click the Remove button in the Control Layout group on the Arrange tab. Remove the control layout for the controls on the right side of the form by following the same steps. You can now resize each label or text box independently.

The text boxes you want to be the longest—EmailName, OfficeLocation, Photo, Address, City, and Country—are already at the correct width, so you need to resize only the remaining text boxes. Let's first resize the text box controls that should be the shortest. Click the EmployeeNumber text box, hold down the Shift key, and then click the

DepartmentID and StateOrProvince text box controls. Next, click the sizing box in the middle of the right edge of the StateOrProvince text box, and drag the right edge to the left until the control is about 0.5 inch wide, as shown in Figure 12-32.

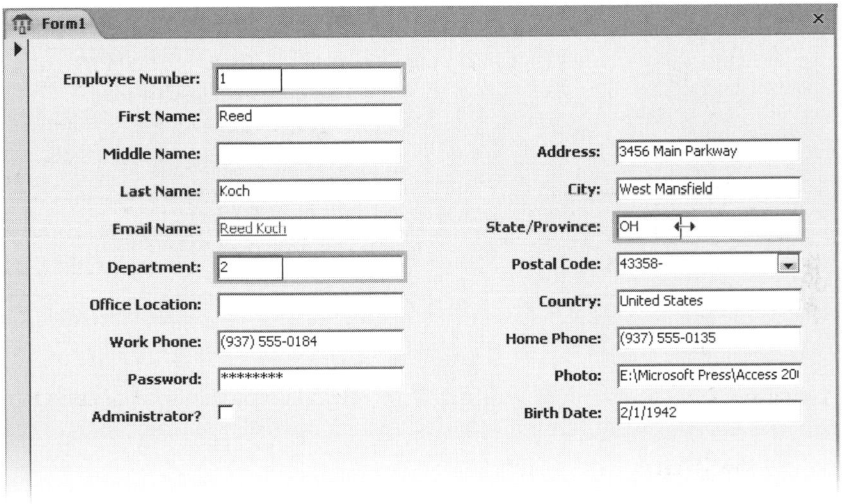

**Figure 12-32** Resize the EmployeeNumber, DepartmentID, and StateOrProvince text boxes to a smaller width.

Now you need to resize the following fields to about 1 inch—FirstName, MiddleName, LastName, Password, PostalCode, HomePhone, WorkPhone, and BirthDate. Select them all by clicking each one while holding down the Shift key, and then drag the right edge of one of the text boxes to the left until the text boxes are about 1 inch wide.

If you switch to Form view, you can see the result of your work, as shown in Figure 12-33. You have now seen how to create the same basic employees form in both Design view and Layout view. Click the Save button on the Quick Access Toolbar to save this form. Name the form frmEmployeesLayoutView, and then close it. You can also find this form saved as frmXmplEmployeeLayout in the sample database.

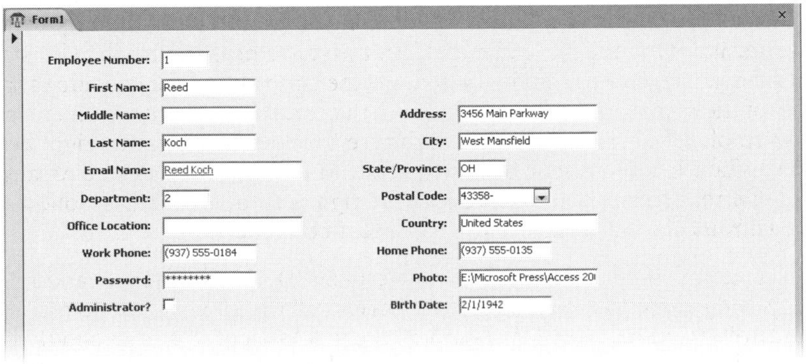

**Figure 12-33** You now have a good, basic employees form created entirely in Layout view.

INSIDE OUT **When to Use Layout View**

Layout view for forms works best for positioning, aligning, and resizing controls. In Layout view, you can see live data in the controls, which makes resizing controls to fit their contents very easy. However, Layout view does have limitations. You cannot, for example, use most of the tools available in the Controls group that you see for a form in Design view. You also cannot see any of the form sections when you display a form in Layout view. This can make it difficult to position controls within specific sections. We've found that using both Design view *and* Layout view increases our productivity.

# Enhancing the Look of a Form

The employees forms you've built thus far in Design view and Layout view look fairly plain. They use default fonts and a background color that's inherited from the color you have defined in Windows for three-dimensional (3-D) objects (sometimes called the Button Face color). In this section, you'll learn about additional enhancements you can make to your form's design. To follow along with the rest of this chapter, you can use either the form you created in Design view, the form you created in Layout view, or one of the example forms saved in the database. We used the form we created using Design view for the remainder of this chapter. Open your form in Design view to continue with the next examples.

## Lines and Rectangles

Access 2007 comes with two drawing tools, the Line tool and the Rectangle tool, that you can use to enhance the appearance of your forms. You can add lines to separate parts of your form visually. Rectangles are useful for surrounding and setting off a group of controls on a form.

On your employees form, it might be helpful to add a line to separate the primary information about the employee in the first column from personal information in the second column. To make sufficient room for the line, you should move the controls in the first column to the left. The easiest way to do this is to switch to Design view, select all the affected controls and labels, and then move them as a group. Start by clicking the top ruler just above the right edge of the controls, and then drag inside the ruler toward the left until the selection indicator touches all the controls in the left column. (If you can't see the rulers, be sure that the Ruler button is selected in the Show/Hide group on the Arrange tab.) Release the mouse button, and all the controls and labels in the left column will be selected. To be sure you move all these controls as a group, click the Group button in the Control Layout group on the Arrange tab. Access shows you that the controls are now grouped by placing a rectangular line around all the controls. Rest the mouse pointer on the square in the upper-left corner of the group so that the pointer changes to a pointer with a crosshairs shape (see Figure 12-34), and slide the entire group left a bit.

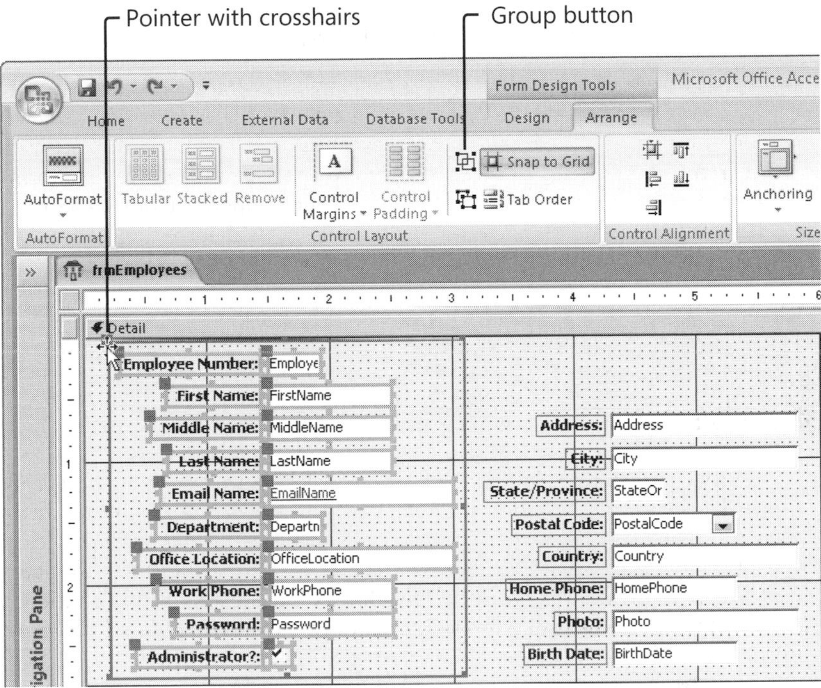


**Figure 12-34** You can group a set of controls and then move them together.

Next, on the Design tab, in the Controls group, click the Line tool. To draw your line, click near the top of the form between the two columns, about two grid rows below the top edge, and drag toward the form's bottom edge. If the line isn't exactly vertical, you can drag the bottom end left or right to adjust it. You can also set its Width property to 0 in the property sheet to make it perfectly vertical. (As you might imagine, setting the Height property to 0 makes the line horizontal.) Use the Line Thickness button in the Controls group on the Design tab to make the line a little thicker if you want. (Or, change the Border Width property in the property sheet.) Click the button, and choose the thickness you want. Your form should now look similar to the one shown in Figure 12-35.

INSIDE OUT **Ensuring Your Lines Are Straight**

When drawing a line on your form, you can make your line exactly horizontal or exactly vertical if you hold down the Shift key as you click and draw the line.

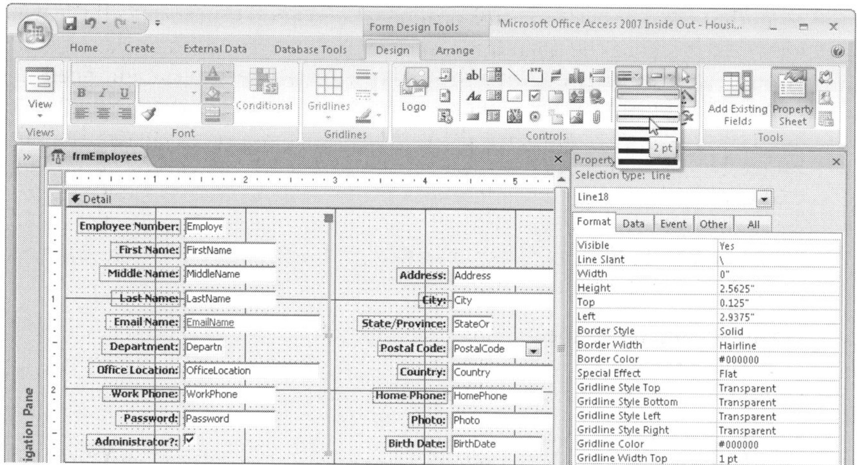


**Figure 12-35** Use the Line tool to draw a line on a form; use the Border Thickness button to adjust the line width.

You can add emphasis to the form by drawing a rectangle around all the controls. To do this, you might first need to move all the controls down and to the right a bit and make the Detail section slightly wider and taller. First, expand your form by about 0.5 inch across and down. Click the Select All button in the Controls group on the Design tab, and then drag all the controls so that you have about 0.25 inch of space around all the edges. (This might seem like too much space, but we'll use the extra space to have some fun later.) Select the Rectangle tool in the Controls group, click where you want to place one corner of the rectangle, and drag to the intended location of the opposite corner. When you draw a rectangle around all the controls, your form will look similar to the one shown in Figure 12-36.

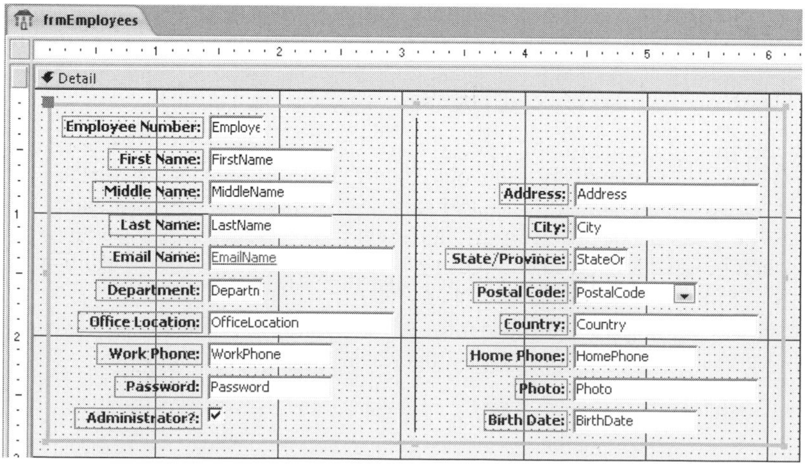

**Figure 12-36** Use the Rectangle tool to place a rectangle with a default etched look on the employees form.

Note that the rectangle control actually covers and is on top of all the other controls. However, because the default rectangle is transparent with an etched special effect, you can see the other controls through the rectangle. (You might need to click the form or another control so that you can see the etched look of the rectangle.) If you prefer a solid rectangle, you can select the rectangle control and then use the Fill/Back Color button in the Font group on the Design tab to select the color you want. (A light gray will work best.) When you add a solid control like this after you've created other controls, the solid control will cover the previous controls. You can select the control and click Send To Back in the Position group on the Arrange tab to reveal the covered controls and keep the solid control in the background.

Go ahead and make the rectangle a solid light gray and send it to the back. Now switch to Form view, and see how your form looks up to this point. Your employees form should look similar to the one shown in Figure 12-37.

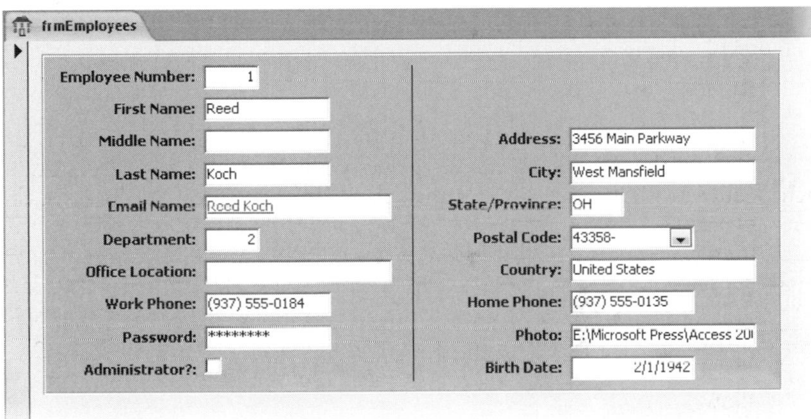


**Figure 12-37** The employees form in Form view has a line and a solid rectangle added.

## Colors and Special Effects

You can also use color and special effects to highlight objects on your form. For example, you can make all the controls appear to "float" on a raised surface on the form. To do so, switch to Design view, and select the rectangle you just created. Click the arrow on the Special Effect button in the Controls group on the Design tab, and then click Special Effect: Raised to change the rectangle from Etched to Raised. Your form in Form view will look similar to the one shown in Figure 12-38.

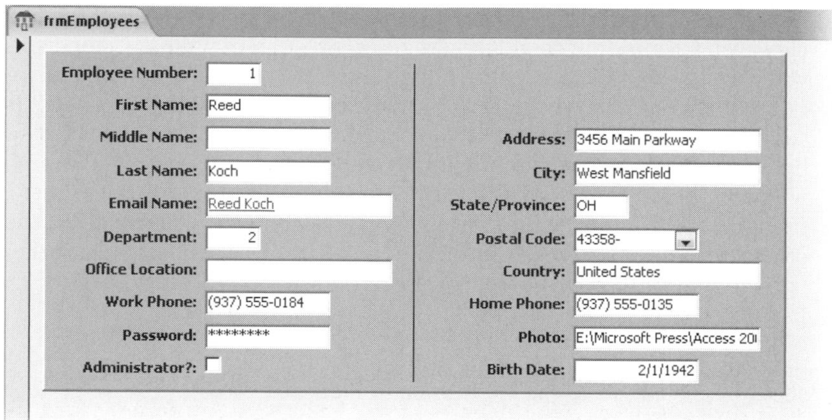


**Figure 12-38** The rectangle behind the controls appears raised above the surface of the form background.

Next, switch to Design view if you changed to Form view, select the Rectangle tool again, and set Back Color to dark gray and Special Effect to Sunken using the buttons in the Font and Controls groups. Draw a second rectangle so that it forms a border about halfway between the edge of the first rectangle and the edge of the grid. Click Send To Back in the Position group on the Arrange tab to send this latest rectangle to the background. Switch to Form view to see the result. The first gray rectangle now appears to float on the form, surrounded by a "moat" of dark gray, as shown in Figure 12-39.

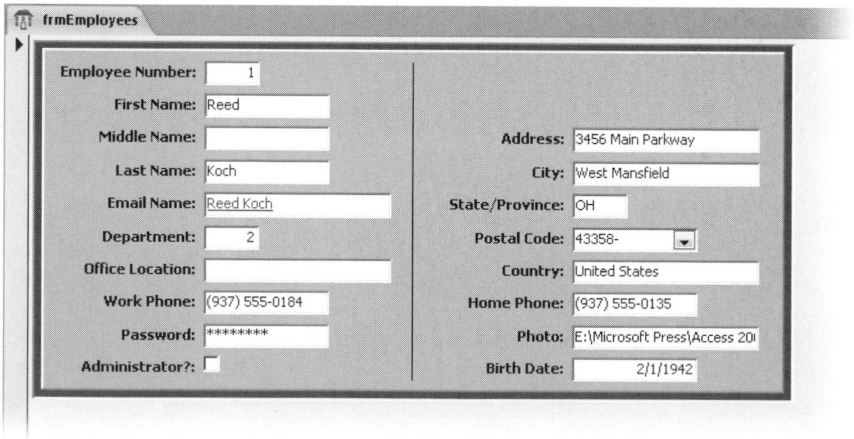

**Figure 12-39** The first light gray rectangle appears to float on the form using special effects.

You can find this form saved as frmXmplEmployee4 in the sample database.

## INSIDE OUT Using System Colors and the Color Palette

Although you can certainly pick from a broad palette of colors for any design object, you might want to design your forms so that they always inherit colors from the options the user has set in the Windows Display dialog box. In fact, if you select the Detail section of the employees form you've been building, open the Property Sheet window, and find the Back Color property, you'll find the property set to System Button Face. This special option tells Access to use the color set in Windows for button faces and other 3-D objects. In any color property, Access lists 31 system color names that you can use to set colors in your forms and controls to match those set in Windows objects. All these color names begin with the word *System*.

You can also see in the Back Color property (or, for that matter, any color property) a list of 20 additional options. These include Alternate Row, Background Form, Background Light Header, Background Dark Header, Borders/Gridlines, Text Black, Text Description, Text Light, Text Dark, Highlight, and Access Theme 1, Access Theme 2, and so on, up to Access Theme 10. These are shades of the color scheme you chose in Access Options—shades of blue for the Blue or Silver theme, and shades of gray and black for the Black theme, and with a shade of orange in all themes for Highlight. If you click the Build button on the Back Color property line or click the arrow next to the Font Color or Fill/Back Color commands in the Font group on the Design tab, Access opens a color palette where you can see the color defined for each of these options, as shown here:

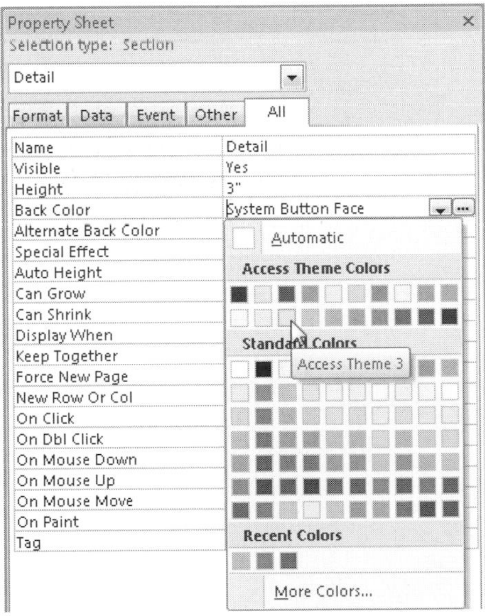

If you select any of the colors under Access Theme Colors, Access enters the name of the theme or color option on the property line. If you click one of the colors under Standard Colors, Access sets a hexadecimal value in the property that represents the red, green, and blue (RGB) color value—#000000 for Black, #FF0000 for Red, #00FF00 for Green, #0000FF for Blue, and #FFFFFF for White, for example. See Article 5, "Color Names and Codes," on the companion CD for a list of common color hexadecimal equivalents.

Under Recent Colors on the color palette, Access displays up to 10 recently used colors. Click one of these to enter the code or name for that color in the color property. If you want to create your own custom color, you can click More Colors to open the Colors dialog box. In the Colors dialog box, you can choose from a wider selection of colors on the Standard tab or define a custom color on the Custom tab by adjusting individual RGB values or selecting the color you want from a color rainbow palette.

## Fonts

Another way you can enhance the appearance of your forms is by varying the fonts and font sizes you use. When you select any control that can display text or data, Access makes font, font size, and font attribute controls available in the Font group on the Design tab so that you can easily change how the text in that control looks. Click the arrow next to the Font Name combo box to open a list of all the available fonts, as shown in Figure 12-40. Select the font you want for the control.

**Figure 12-40** This is a partial list of fonts available to you in the Font Name combo box.

> **Note**
>
> The font list shows all fonts currently installed on your computer. Use the Fonts folder in Windows Control Panel to add or remove fonts. A double-T icon next to the font name in the list indicates a TrueType font that is suitable for both screen display and printing. A printer icon next to the font name indicates a font designed for your printer but that might not look exactly the same when displayed on your screen. A font with no icon indicates a font designed for your screen; a screen font might look different when you print it.

If you want to add some variety, you can use bold or italic type in a few key places. In this case, select all the labels on the form, and select a serif font such as Times New Roman.

You can add a label to the header of the form to display a title such as Employees. You can either do this manually or use a button on the Ribbon designed specifically for this task. If you'd like Access to do most of the work, click the Title button in the Controls group on the Design tab. Access opens the header and footer section, places a new label in the header section, and sets the caption to the name of your form. Double-click the new label to select the existing text, type **Employees** in the label, and press Enter.

To do this same task manually, you need to first open the header and footer of the form by clicking the Form Header/Footer button in the Show/Hide group on the Arrange tab. Grab the bottom edge of the footer, and close it up so that it has zero height. Expand the header to give yourself some room to work. Choose the Label tool in the Controls group on the Design tab, draw a label about 1.5 inches wide and 0.5 inch high, type the word **Employees** in the label, and press Enter.

Set the label in the header to the Tahoma font (a sans serif font), bold, italic, and 18 points in size. Double-click one of the sizing boxes to size the control to fit, and drag the right edge to the right if all the letters don't show in the label. You can see a portion of this work under way in Figure 12-41.

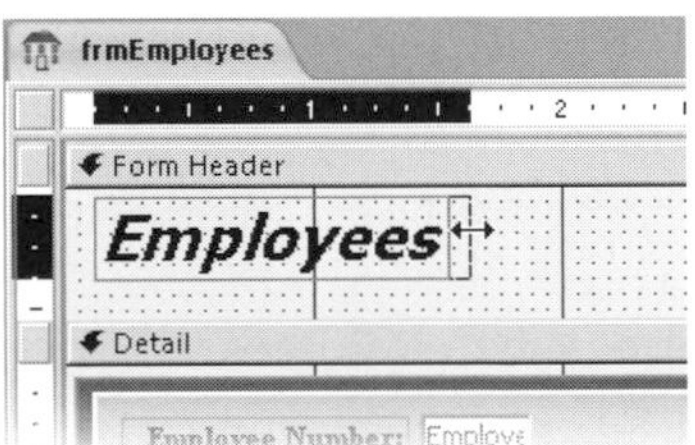


**Figure 12-41** Adjust the size of the label to fit the form header title.

You can create a special "shadowed" effect behind this label in the header by doing the following:

1. Copy the label you just created to the Clipboard, and paste it in the header.
2. Change the font color of the pasted label to white, and then click the Send To Back button in the Position group on the Arrange tab.
3. Turn off the Snap To Grid command if it is on in the Control Layout group on the Arrange tab, and use the arrow keys to move the white label so that it is slightly lower and to the right of the first label.
4. Click the Form Header bar to select that section, and set the background color to light gray to provide some contrast.

When you finish, the form should look similar to the one shown in Figure 12-42. (You can find this form saved in the sample database as frmXmplEmployee5.)

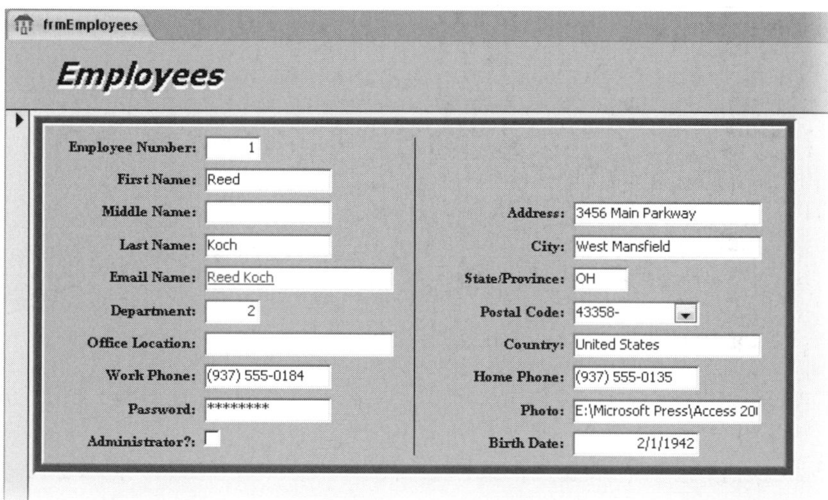


**Figure 12-42** The employees form now has a title and some different fonts for variety.

**INSIDE OUT** **More Is Not Always Better When It Comes to Fonts**

A form with too many fonts or font sizes will look busy and jumbled. In general, you should use only two or three fonts per form. Use one font and font size for most bound data displayed in controls. Make label text bold or colored for emphasis. Select a second font for controls in the headers and perhaps a third (at most) for information in the footers.

# Setting Control Properties

Access 2007 gives you many properties for each control to allow you to customize the way your form works. These properties affect formatting, the presence or absence of scroll bars, the enabling or locking of records, the tab order, and more.

## Formatting Properties

In the property sheet for each text box, combo box, and list box are three properties that you can set to determine how Access displays the data in the form. These properties are Format, Decimal Places, and Input Mask, as shown in Figure 12-43. (The Input Mask property is listed farther down the list on the All tab of the property sheet and isn't shown in Figure 12-43.)

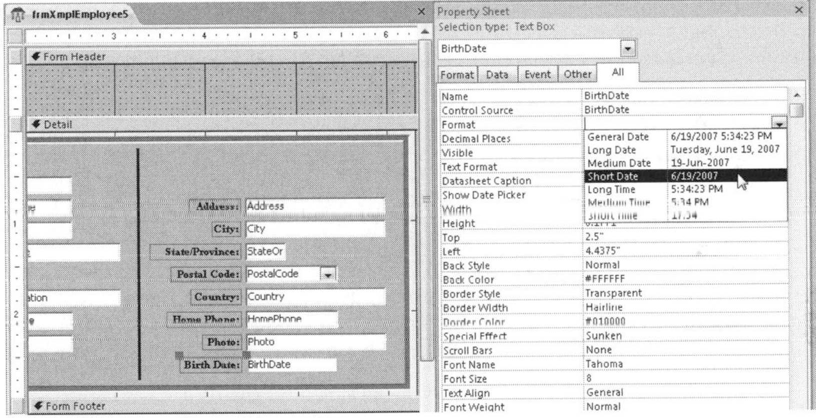


**Figure 12-43** You can select a format from the list of format settings for the BirthDate control, which uses the Date/Time data type.

> **INSIDE OUT** **Always Use Four-Digit Year Values**
>
> We recommended earlier that you change the date display in the Regional And Language Options section of Windows Control Panel to display a four-digit year. Although Access adjusts the century digits automatically when you enter two-digit years, you will avoid confusion about the actual value stored after the year 1999 if you always display the full year. All samples you see in this book using the Short Date format show four-digit years because we changed the settings on our computers. If your computer is set to display a two-digit year, you will see a different result everywhere we used the Short Date format.

**For details on the Input Mask property, see Chapter 4, "Creating Your Database and Tables." For details on dynamically changing format properties (also called *conditional formatting*) based on the value currently displayed, see Chapter 13, "Advanced Form Design."**

Access copies these properties from the definition of the fields in the underlying table. If you haven't specified a Format property in the field definition, Access sets a default Format property for the control, depending on the data type of the field bound to the control. In the control's property sheet, you can customize the appearance of the data on your form by selecting a format setting from the Format property's list or by entering a custom set of formatting characters. The following sections present the format settings and formatting characters available for each data type.

## Specifying a Format for Numbers and Currency

If you don't specify a Format property setting for a control that displays a number or a currency value, Access displays numbers in the General Number format and currency in the Currency format. You can choose from seven Format property settings, as shown in Table 12-1.

**Table 12-1 Format Property Settings for Number and Currency Data Types**

| Format | Description |
|---|---|
| General Number | Displays numbers as entered with up to 11 significant digits. If a number contains more than 11 significant digits or the control you are using to display the value is not wide enough to show all digits, Access first rounds the displayed number and then uses scientific (exponential) notation for very large or very small numbers (more than 10 digits to the right or to the left of the decimal point). |
| Currency | Displays numeric data according to the Currency setting in the Regional And Language Options section of Windows Control Panel. In the U.S. layout, Access uses a leading dollar sign, maintains two decimal places (rounded), and encloses negative numbers in parentheses. |
| Euro | Displays numeric data according to your Currency setting, but always uses a leading euro symbol. |
| Fixed | Displays numbers without thousands separators and with two decimal places. The number displayed is rounded if the underlying value contains more than two decimal places. |
| Standard | Displays numbers with thousands separators and with two decimal places. The number displayed is rounded if the underlying value contains more than two decimal places. |
| Percent | Multiplies the value by 100, displays two decimal places, and adds a trailing percent sign. The number displayed is rounded if the underlying value contains more than four decimal places. |
| Scientific | Displays numbers in scientific (exponential) notation. |

You can also create a custom format. You can specify a different display format for Access to use (depending on whether the numeric value is positive, negative, 0, or Null) by providing up to four format specifications in the Format property. You must separate the specifications by semicolons. When you enter two specifications, Access uses the first for all nonnegative numbers and the second for negative numbers. When you provide three specifications, Access uses the third specification to display numbers with a value of 0. Use the fourth specification to indicate how you want Null values handled.

To create a custom number format, use the formatting characters shown in Table 12-2. Notice that you can include text strings in the format and specify a color to use.

**Table 12-2 Formatting Characters for Number and Currency Data Types**

| Character | Usage |
|---|---|
| Decimal separator | Use to indicate where you want Access to place the decimal point. Use the decimal separator defined in the Regional And Language Options section of Windows Control Panel. In the English (U.S.) layout, the separator is a period (.). |
| Thousands separator | Use to indicate placement of the thousands separator character that is defined in the Regional And Language Options section of Windows Control Panel. In the English (U.S.) layout, the separator is a comma (,). When the position immediately to the left of the separator is # and no digit exists in that position, the thousands separator also is not displayed. |
| 0 | Use this placeholder character to indicate digit display. If no digit exists in the number in this position, Access displays 0. |
| # | Use this placeholder character to indicate digit display. If no digit exists in the number in this position, Access displays a blank space. |
| – + $ ( ) or a blank space | Use these characters anywhere you want in your format string. |
| "text" | Use double quotation marks to embed any text you want displayed. |
| \ | Use to always display the character immediately following (the same as including a single character in double quotation marks). |
| ! | Use to force left alignment. You cannot use any other *digit* placeholder characters (0 or #) when you force left alignment; however, you can use character placeholders as shown in Table 12-3 on page 655. |
| * | Use to designate the immediately following character as the fill character. Access usually displays formatted numeric data right-aligned and filled with blank spaces to the left. You can embed the fill character anywhere in your format string. For example, you can specify a format string for a Currency value as follows: $#,##0*^.00<br>Using the above format, the value $1,234.57 appears as follows:<br>$1,234^^^^^^^^^.57<br>Access generates fill characters so that the displayed text completely fills the display area. |

| Character | Usage |
|---|---|
| % | Place as the last character in your format string to multiply the value by 100 and include a trailing percent sign. |
| E– or e– | Use to generate scientific (exponential) notation and to display a minus sign preceding negative exponents. It must be used with other characters, as in 0.00E–00. |
| E+ or e+ | Use to generate scientific (exponential) notation and to display a minus sign preceding negative exponents and a plus sign preceding positive exponents. It must be used with other characters, as in 0.00E+00. |
| [color] | Use brackets to display the text in the color specified. Valid color names are Black, Blue, Green, Cyan, Red, Magenta, Yellow, and White. A color name must be used with other characters, as in 0.00[Red]. |

INSIDE OUT

### Don't Get Fooled by the Format Property

Keep in mind that what you specify in Format and Decimal Places properties affects only what you see on your screen—these settings do not modify the actual data in the underlying table in any way. For example, if you specify a format that displays two decimal places but the underlying data type contains additional precision (such as a Currency data type that always contains four decimal places), you'll see a rounded value. If you later sum the values, the total might not agree with the sum of the displayed values. Likewise, if you specify a format that displays only the date portion of a Date/Time data type, you won't see any time portion unless you click the control. If we had a penny for every time we've had to explain this concept in the support newsgroups, we would be very wealthy, indeed!

For example, to display a number with two decimal places and comma separators when positive, enclosed in parentheses and shown in red when negative, *Zero* when 0, and *Not Entered* when Null, you would specify the following:

```
#,##0.00;(#,##0.00)[Red];"Zero";"Not Entered"
```

To format a U.S. phone number and area code from a numeric field, you would specify the following:

```
(000) 000-0000
```

## Specifying a Format for Text

If you don't specify a Format property setting for a control that displays a text value, Access left aligns the data in the control. You can specify a custom format with one entry or with two entries separated by semicolons. If you include a second format specification, Access uses that specification to show empty values (a zero-length string). If you want to test for Null, you must use the Immediate If (IIf) and IsNull built-in functions. See "Showing the Null Value in Text Fields" on page 657 for details.

By default, Access fills text placeholder characters (@ and &) using characters from the underlying data from *right to left*. If a text field contains more characters than the number of placeholder characters you provide, Access first uses up the placeholder characters and then displays the remaining characters as though you had specified the @ placeholder character in that position. Table 12-3 lists the formatting characters that are applicable to the Text data type.

**Table 12-3 Formatting Characters for the Text Data Type**

| Character | Usage |
|---|---|
| @ | Use this placeholder character to display any available character in this position. If all available characters in the underlying text have been placed, any extra @ placeholder characters generate blanks. For example, if the text is *abc* and the format is @@@@@, the resulting display is left-aligned and has two blank spaces on the left preceding the characters. |
| & | Use to display any available character in this position. If all available characters in the underlying text have been placed, any extra & placeholder characters display nothing. For example, if the text is *abc* and the format is &&&&&, the resulting display shows only the three characters left-aligned. |
| < | Use to display all characters in lowercase. This character must appear at the beginning of the format string and can be preceded only by the ! specification. |
| > | Use to display all characters in uppercase. This character must appear at the beginning of the format string and can be preceded only by the ! specification. |
| – + $ ( ) or a blank space | Use these characters anywhere you want in your format string. |
| "text" | Use double quotation marks to embed any text you want displayed. |
| \ | Use to always display the character immediately following (the same as including a single character in double quotation marks). |
| ! | Use to force placeholders to fill *left to right* instead of right to left. If you use this specification, it must be the first character in the format string. |

| Character | Usage |
|---|---|
| * | Use to designate the immediately following character as the fill character. Access usually displays formatted text data left-aligned and filled with blank spaces to the right. You can embed the fill character anywhere in your format string. For example, you can specify a format string as follows:<br>>@@*!@@@@@<br>Using the above format, the value *abcdef* appears as follows:<br>A!!!!!!!!!!!!!!!BCDEF<br>(And the above string has a leading blank.)<br>If you force the pattern to be filled from the left by adding a leading exclamation point, the data appears as follows:<br>AB!!!!!!!!!!!!!!CDEF<br>(And the above string has a trailing blank.)<br>Access generates fill characters so that the displayed text completely fills the display area. |
| [color] | Use brackets to display the text in the color specified. Valid color names are Black, Blue, Green, Cyan, Red, Magenta, Yellow, and White. A color name must be used with other characters, as in >[Red].<br>(Keep in mind that in the absence of placeholder characters, Access places the characters as though you had specified @ in all positions.) |

For example, if you want to display a six-character part number with a hyphen between the second character and the third character, filled from the left, specify the following:

```
!@@-@@@@
```

To format a check amount string in the form of *Fourteen Dollars and 59 Cents* so that Access displays an asterisk (*) to fill any available space between the word *and* and the cents amount, specify the following:

```
**@@@@@@@@
```

Using this format in a text box wide enough to display 62 characters, Access displays *Fourteen Dollars and 59 Cents* as

```
Fourteen Dollars and *********************************59 Cents
```

and *One Thousand Two Hundred Dollars and 00 Cents* as

```
One Thousand Two Hundred Dollars and *****************00 Cents
```

## INSIDE OUT Showing the Null Value in Text Fields

As you might have noticed, there is no third optional format specification you can supply for a Null value in a text field as there is with Number, Currency, and Date/Time data types. If the field is Null, Access displays it as though it is empty. If the field can contain an empty string or a Null, you can distinguish it visibly by using the second optional format specification. Assuming your text field is five characters long, your Format specification could look like

```
@@@@@;"<empty string>"
```

If the field has a value, Access displays the value. If the field is an empty string, you will see *<empty string>* in the text box until you click it. If the field is Null, the text box will be blank.

An alternative is to use the IIf and IsNull built-in functions in the Control Source property of the text box. Your control source could look like

```
=IIf(IsNull([FieldToDisplay]), "*Null Value*",[FieldToDisplay])
```

If you do this, however, you won't be able to update the field because the source will be an expression.

## Specifying a Format for Date/Time

If you don't specify a Format property setting for a control that displays a date/time value, Access displays the date/time in the General Date format. You can also select one of the six other Format property settings shown in Table 12-4.

You can also specify a custom format with one entry or with two entries separated by semicolons. If you include a second format specification, Access uses that specification to show Null values. Table 12-5 lists the formatting characters that are applicable to the Date/Time data type.

For example, to display a date as full month name, day, and year (say, *May 29, 2007*) with a color of cyan, you would specify the following:

```
mmmm dd, yyyy[Cyan]
```

Table 12-4 **Format Property Settings for the Date/Time Data Type**

| Format | Description |
| --- | --- |
| General Date | Displays the date as numbers separated by the date separator character. Displays the time as hours, minutes, and seconds separated by the time separator character and followed by an AM/PM indicator. If the value has no time component, Access displays the date only. If the value has no date component, Access displays the time only. Example: 3/17/2007 06:17:55 PM. |
| Long Date | Displays the date according to the Long Date setting in the Regional And Language Options section of Windows Control Panel. Example: Saturday, March 17, 2007. |
| Medium Date | Displays the date as dd-mmm-yyyy. Example: 17-Mar-2007. |
| Short Date | Displays the date according to the Short Date setting in the Regional And Language Options section of Windows Control Panel. Example: 3/17/2007. To avoid confusion for dates in the twenty-first century, we strongly recommend you take advantage of the Use Four-Digit Year formatting options. Click the Microsoft Office Button, click Access Options, click the Advanced category, and then set these options in the General section. |
| Long Time | Displays the time according to the Time setting in the Regional And Language Options section of Windows Control Panel. Example: 6:17:12 PM. |
| Medium Time | Displays the time as hours and minutes separated by the time separator character and followed by an AM/PM indicator. Example: 06:17 PM. |
| Short Time | Displays the time as hours and minutes separated by the time separator character, using a 24-hour clock. Example: 18:17. |

Table 12-5 **Formatting Characters for the Date/Time Data Type**

| Character | Usage |
| --- | --- |
| Time separator | Use to show Access where to separate hours, minutes, and seconds. Use the time separator defined in the Regional And Language Options section of Windows Control Panel. In the English (U.S.) layout, the separator is a colon (:). |
| Date separator | Use to show Access where to separate days, months, and years. Use the date separator defined in the Regional And Language Options section of Windows Control Panel. In the English (U.S.) layout, the separator is a slash (/). |
| c | Use to display the General Date format. |
| d | Use to display the day of the month as one or two digits, as needed. |

| Character | Usage |
|---|---|
| dd | Use to display the day of the month as two digits. |
| ddd | Use to display the day of the week as a three-letter abbreviation. Example: Saturday = Sat. |
| dddd | Use to display the day of the week fully spelled out. |
| ddddd | Use to display the Short Date format. |
| dddddd | Use to display the Long Date format. |
| w | Use to display a number for the day of the week. Example: Sunday = 1. |
| m | Use to display the month as a one-digit or two-digit number, as needed. |
| mm | Use to display the month as a two-digit number. |
| mmm | Use to display the name of the month as a three-letter abbreviation. Example: March = Mar. |
| mmmm | Use to display the name of the month fully spelled out. |
| q | Use to display the calendar quarter number (1–4). |
| y | Use to display the day of the year (1–366). |
| yy | Use to display the last two digits of the year. |
| yyyy | Use to display the full year value (within the range 0100–9999). |
| h | Use to display the hour as one or two digits, as needed. |
| hh | Use to display the hour as two digits. |
| n | Use to display the minutes as one or two digits, as needed. |
| nn | Use to display the minutes as two digits. |
| s | Use to display the seconds as one or two digits, as needed. |
| ss | Use to display the seconds as two digits. |
| ttttt | Use to display the Long Time format. |
| AM/PM | Use to display 12-hour clock values with trailing AM or PM, as appropriate. |
| A/P or a/p | Use to display 12-hour clock values with trailing A or P, or a or p, as appropriate. |
| AMPM | Use to display 12-hour clock values using morning/afternoon indicators as specified in the Regional And Language Options section of Windows Control Panel. |
| – + $ ( ) or a blank space | Use these characters anywhere you want in your format string. |
| "text" | Use double quotation marks to embed any text you want displayed. |
| \ | Use to always display the character immediately following (the same as including a single character in double quotation marks). |

| Character | Usage |
|---|---|
| * | Use to designate the immediately following character as the fill character. Access usually displays formatted date/time data right-aligned and filled with blank spaces to the left. You can embed the fill character anywhere in your format string. For example, you can specify a format string as follows:<br>mm/yyyy ** hh:nn<br>Using the above format, the value March 17, 2007 06:17:55 PM appears as follows:<br>03/2007 ************** 18:17<br>Access generates fill characters so that the displayed text completely fills the display area. |
| [color] | Use brackets to display the text in the color specified. Valid color names are Black, Blue, Green, Cyan, Red, Magenta, Yellow, and White. A color name must be used with other characters, as in ddddd[Red]. |

## Specifying a Format for Yes/No Fields

You can choose from among three standard formats—Yes/No, True/False, or On/Off—to display Yes/No data type values, as shown in Table 12-6. The Yes/No format is the default. As you saw earlier, it's often more useful to display Yes/No values using a check box or a button rather than a text box.

Table 12-6 **Format Property Settings for the Yes/No Data Type**

| Format | Description |
|---|---|
| Yes/No (the default) | Displays 0 as No and any nonzero value as Yes. |
| True/False | Displays 0 as False and any nonzero value as True. |
| On/Off | Displays 0 as Off and any nonzero value as On. |

You can also specify your own custom word or phrase for Yes and No values. Keep in mind that a Yes/No data type is actually a number internally. (–1 is Yes, and 0 is No.) So, you can specify a format string containing three parts separated by semicolons just as you can for a number. Leave the first part empty (a Yes/No value is never a positive number) by starting with a semicolon, specify a string enclosed in double quotation marks (and with an optional color modifier) followed by a semicolon in the second part for the negative Yes values, and specify another string (also with an optional color modifier) in the third part for the zero No values.

To display *Invoice Sent* in red for Yes and *Not Invoiced* in blue for No, you would specify the following:

```
;"Invoice Sent"[Red];"Not Invoiced"[Blue]
```

### How Format and Input Mask Work Together

If you specify both an Input Mask setting (see Chapter 4) and a Format property setting, Access uses the Input Mask setting to display data when you move the focus to the control and uses the Format setting when the control does not have the focus. If you don't include a Format setting but do include an Input Mask setting, Access formats the data using the Input Mask setting. Be careful not to define a Format setting that conflicts with the Input Mask. For example, if you define an Input Mask setting for a phone number that looks like

```
!\(###") "000\-0000;0;_
```

(which stores the parentheses and hyphen with the data) and a Format setting that looks like

```
(&&&) @@@-@@@@
```

your data will be displayed as

```
(206() 5) 55-1212
```

## Adding a Scroll Bar

When you have a field that can contain a long data string (for example, the Notes field in the tblReservationRequests table), it's a good idea to provide a scroll bar in the control to make it easy to scan through all the data. This scroll bar appears whenever you select the control. If you don't add a scroll bar, you must use the arrow keys to move up and down through the data.

To add a scroll bar, first open the form in Design view. Select the control, and open its property sheet. Then set the Scroll Bars property to Vertical. For example, if you open the frmXmplReservationRequests form in Form view and tab to (or click) the Notes text box, the vertical scroll bar appears, as shown in Figure 12-44.

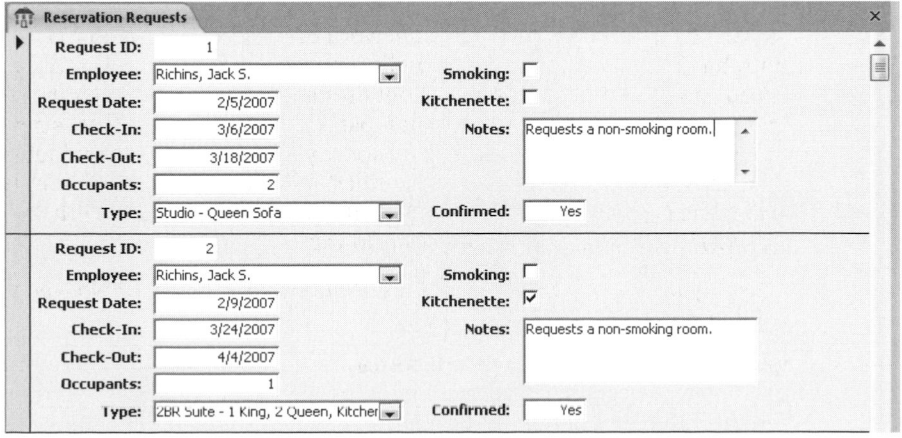


**Figure 12-44** When you click in the Notes text box, Access displays a scroll bar.

Chapter 12

## Enabling and Locking Controls

You might not want users of your form to select or update certain controls. You can set these conditions with the control's Enabled and Locked properties. For example, if you use a control to display an AutoNumber field, you can be certain that Access will provide the field's value. So, it's a good idea to set the control's Enabled property to No (so that the user can't select it) and the control's Locked property to Yes (so that the user can't update it). Table 12-7 shows the effects of the Enabled and Locked property settings. Note, however, that if you want the user to be able to use the Access built-in Find facility to search for a particular AutoNumber value, you should leave Enabled set to Yes to allow the user to select the field and find values in it.

**Table 12-7 Settings for the Enabled and Locked Properties**

| Enabled | Locked | Description |
|---|---|---|
| Yes | Yes | Control can have the focus. Data is displayed normally and can be copied or searched but not changed. |
| No | No | Control cannot have the focus. Control and data appear dimmed. |
| Yes | No | Control can have the focus. Data is displayed normally and can be copied and changed. |
| No | Yes | Control cannot have the focus. Data is displayed normally but can't be copied or changed. |

In some cases, you might want to allow a control to be selected with the mouse but to be skipped over as the user tabs through the controls on the form. You can set the control's Tab Stop property to No while leaving its Enabled property set to Yes. This might be useful for controls for which you also set the Locked property to Yes. Setting the Tab Stop property to No keeps the user from tabbing into the control, but the user can still select the control with the mouse to use the Find command or to copy the data in the control to the Clipboard.

## Setting the Tab Order

As you design a form, Access sets the tab order for the controls in the order in which you place the controls on the form. When you move a control to a new location, Access doesn't automatically change the tab order. Also, when you delete a control and replace it with another, Access places the new control at the end of the tab order. If you want to change the tab order that Access created, you can set a different tab order.

You probably should do this with your sample employees form because you moved controls around after you initially placed them on the form. (If you want to test the existing order, try tabbing through the controls in one record in frmXmplEmployee5—you should see the pointer jump from OfficeLocation in the first column to Photo in the second column and then back to Password in the first column.) Open your form in Design view, select the Detail section (or any control in the Detail section), and then click the Tab Order button in the Control Layout group on the Arrange tab to open the Tab Order dialog box, as shown in Figure 12-45.

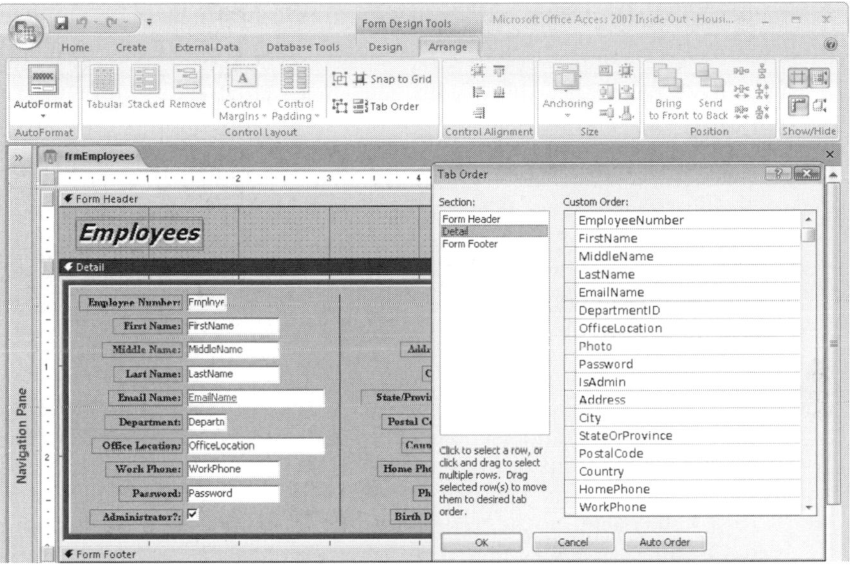


**Figure 12-45** You can change the tab order on the form by using the Tab Order dialog box.

You can click the Auto Order button to reorder the controls so that the tab order corresponds to the arrangement of the controls on the form, from left to right and from top to bottom—but that's probably not what you want in this case. Because this form has two columns, you might want to rearrange the tab order to first move down one column and then the other. You can make custom adjustments to the list by clicking the row selector for a control to highlight it and then clicking the row selector again and dragging the control to its new location in the list. As you can see, the Photo and WorkPhone controls don't appear where they should in the Custom Order list. Click Photo, and drag it down after HomePhone. Click WorkPhone, and drag it up to follow OfficeLocation. Click OK to save your changes to the Custom Order list.

You can also change an individual control's place in the tab order by setting the control's Tab Index property. The Tab Index property of the first control on the form is 0, the second is 1, and so on. If you use this method to assign a new Tab Index setting to a control and some other control already has that Tab Index setting, Access resequences the Tab Index settings for controls appearing in the order after the one you changed. The result is the same as if you had dragged the control to that relative position (as indicated by the new Tab Index setting) in the Tab Order dialog box. (We find it easier to use the Tab Order dialog box.)

## Adding a Smart Tag

Microsoft introduced *smart tags* in Microsoft Office XP. Smart tags are little applications that you can hook into your documents to recognize items such as names, addresses, or stock symbols and provide options, or actions, for recognized fields. For example, you might have an address smart tag in an Office Word document that provides an option to open a map to the location. In an Office Excel spreadsheet, you might define a smart tag for a stock symbol column to go look up the latest price on the Web.

If you have Microsoft Visual Studio, you can actually build your own smart tag applications with Visual Basic. You can download the Smart Tag Software Development Kit (SDK) by going to *www.microsoft.com/downloads/* and performing a search on the keywords *smart tags*. Most Word and Excel smart tag applications have two parts: a recognizer and a set of actions. When a smart tag is active in Word or Excel, the recognizer code runs as you type data and decides whether what you typed is something for which the smart tag has an action. If the smart tag recognizes the text, it passes available actions back to the application, and you see a Smart Tag option available that you can click to invoke one of the actions.

Access 2007 supports smart tags but in a slightly different way than Word or Excel. You can define a smart tag for labels, text boxes, combo boxes, and list boxes. For text boxes, combo boxes, and list boxes, the smart tag uses the current value of the control as specified in the Control Source property. For labels, the smart tag uses the contents of the Caption property. Because data in Access not only has a specific data type but also a specific meaning, the recognizer code in a smart tag does not come into play. Access assumes that you know that the data in the label, text box, combo box, or list box is something the smart tag understands. So, you can use smart tags in Access that have only actions defined.

The 2007 Office release installs a few smart tags that you can use in Access 2007:

- **Date** A smart tag that uses a date/time value to schedule a meeting or show your Microsoft Outlook calendar on that date.
- **Telephone Number** A smart tag that accepts a phone number and opens the matching contact from your contacts list.
- **Financial Symbol** A smart tag that can accept a NYSE or NASDAQ stock symbol and display the latest quote, company report, or news from the MSN Money Central Web site.
- **Person Name** A smart tag that can accept a person name (first name and last name) or e-mail address and send an e-mail, schedule a meeting, open the matching contact from your contacts list, or add the name to your contacts list.

**CAUTION!**

If you assign a smart tag to a control containing data that the smart tag cannot handle, the smart tag won't work, and it might generate an error.



In your employees form, the EmailName is a hyperlink field that opens a new message to the e-mail address when you click it. However, you might also want to use the Person Name smart tag to provide additional options. To add this smart tag, open your form in Design view, click the EmailName text box, open the Property Sheet window, click the

Data tab, and scroll down to the last property in the list–Smart Tags. Click the property, and then click the Build button to open the Smart Tags dialog box, as shown in Figure 12-46.

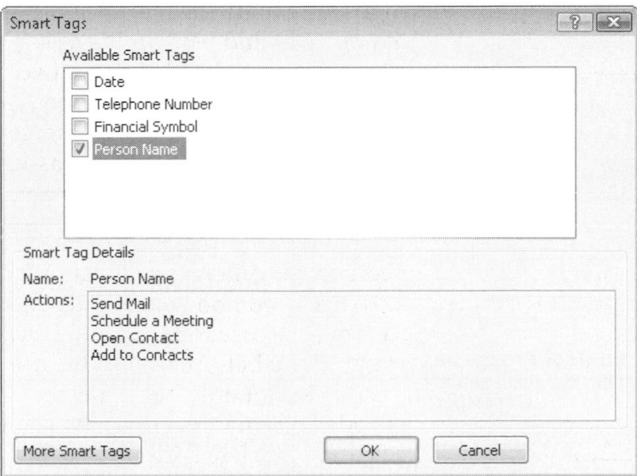


**Figure 12-46** You can define smart tags for your controls using the Smart Tags dialog box.

Select the Person Name check box, and click OK to set the property. Note that you can also click the More Smart Tags button to go to the Microsoft Web site to download and install additional smart tags.

After defining a smart tag, switch to Form view. Controls that have a smart tag defined display a small triangle in the lower-right corner. Rest your mouse pointer on the triangle or tab into the control, and you'll see the smart tag information box appear. Click the down arrow next to the box to see the action choices, as shown in Figure 12-47. Click the action you want to activate that action.

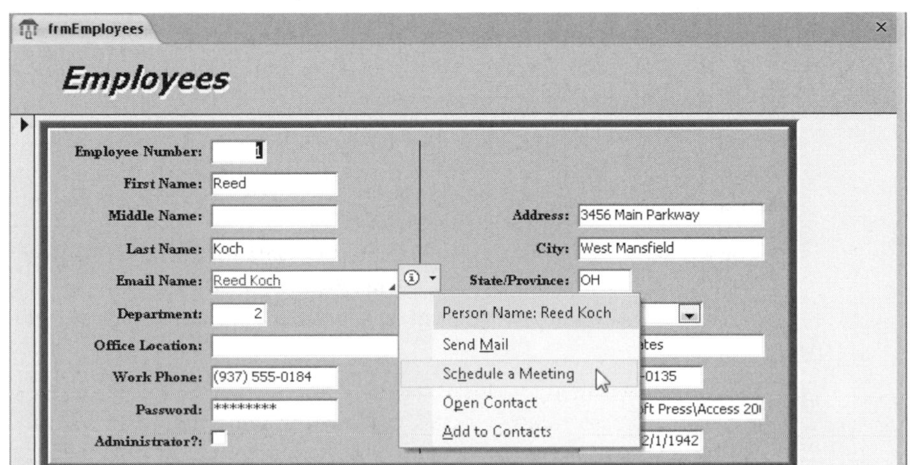


**Figure 12-47** You can select a smart tag action from the menu that appears.

## Understanding Other Control Properties

As you've already discovered, many of the properties for controls that can be bound to fields from your form's record source are exactly the same as those you can set in table Design view on the General or Lookup tab. (See Chapter 4 for more details.) If you do not specify a different setting in the control, the form uses the properties you defined for the field in your table. In some cases, a particular field property setting migrates to a different property in the bound control on your form. For example, the Description property of a field becomes the Status Bar Text property of the bound control. The Caption property of a field moves to the Caption property of a bound control's associated label.

Table 12-8 describes control settings not yet discussed and explains their usage. The table lists the properties in the sequence you will find them on the All tab in the Property Sheet window.

**Table 12-8 Other Control Properties**

| Property | Description |
|---|---|
| Visible | Specify Yes (the default) to make the control visible in Form view. Specify No to hide the control. You will find this property useful when you begin to automate your application and write code to optionally display/hide controls depending on the contents of other fields. See Chapter 20 for details. |
| Text Format | For controls that can display or be bound to text, you can specify whether the data is stored as plain text or rich text. When you set this property to Rich Text, the data can appear with embedded formatting such as *italics* or **bold**. |
| Datasheet Caption | You can assign a caption for this control that will be displayed when the form is in Datasheet view. The caption appears as a column header. |
| Show Date Picker | You can specify For Dates (the default) to instruct Access to display a date picker button to the right of the control when the control is bound to a date/time field. Select Never if you do not want Access to display the date picker control. |
| Width, Height, Top, Left | These properties specify the location and size of the control. Access automatically adjusts these settings when you move a control to a new location or adjust its size. You can enter specific values if you want a control to be placed in a particular location or have a specific size. |
| Back Style | Choose Normal (the default) to be able to specify a color for the background of the control. Choose Transparent to allow the color of any control or section behind the control to show through. |

| Property | Description |
|---|---|
| Back Color, Border Style, Border Width, Border Color, Special Effect, Font Name, Font Size, Font Weight, Font Underline, Font Italic, Fore Color | Access automatically sets these properties when you choose a setting on one of the available buttons in the Font group on the Design contextual tab under Form Tools. You can enter a specific setting in these properties rather than choose an option on the Ribbon. For the color options, you can click the Build button next to the property to select a custom color from the palette of available colors on your computer. |
| Text Align | The default setting is General, which left aligns text and right aligns numbers. You also can choose Left, Center, and Right options (also available in the Font group on the Design tab) to align the text to the left, in the center, or to the right, respectively. The final option, Distribute, spreads the characters evenly across the available display space in the control. |
| Line Spacing | You can specify a different line spacing for the text displayed. The default is 0, which spaces the lines based on the font type and size. |
| Is Hyperlink | Fields that are the Hyperlink data type are always displayed as a hyperlink. You can change this setting to Yes to treat non-Hyperlink data type fields as hyperlinks. The default is No. |
| Display As Hyperlink | Choose If Hyperlink (the default) to instruct Access to display the data as a hyperlink only if the underlying data type is Hyperlink. Choose Always to display the data as a hyperlink even if the data type is not Hyperlink. Choose Screen Only to display the control as a hyperlink only when in Form view. |
| Gridline Style Top, Gridline Style Bottom, Gridline Style Left, Gridline Style Right | These properties control the style of the gridlines around the control. Transparent (the default) specifies that no gridlines appear. You can choose between Solid, Dashes, Short Dashes, Dots, Sparse Dots, Dash Dot, and Dash Dot Dot. You can also use the Style button in the Gridlines group on the Design tab to set these properties. |
| Gridline Color | Specify a color to use if you have set gridlines to a value other than Transparent. You can click the Build button next to the property to select a custom color from the palette of available colors on your computer. The default color is black (#000000). |
| Gridline Width Top, Gridline Width Bottom, Gridline Width Left, Gridline Width Right | These properties control the thickness of the gridlines around controls if you have specified a Control Style setting other than Transparent. You can choose from Hairline, 1 pt (the default), 2 pt, 3 pt, 4 pt, 5 pt, and 6 pt. You can also use the Width button in the Gridlines group on the Design tab to set these properties. |
| Left Margin, Top Margin, Right Margin, Bottom Margin | In a text box control, you can specify alternative margins for the text displayed. The default for all these properties is 0, which provides no additional margin space. You can also use the Control Margins button in the Control Layout group on the Arrange tab to adjust these settings to four options—None, Narrow, Medium, or Wide. |

| Property | Description |
|---|---|
| Top Padding, Bottom Padding, Left Padding, Right Padding | These properties control the amount of space between the control and any gridlines. You can set an amount in inches different from the default of 0.0208 inches. |
| Horizontal Anchor | This specifies how the control is anchored horizontally when it is in a control layout. You can choose Left (the default) to place the control on the left side, Right to place the control on the right side, or Both to stretch the control equally across the control layout. You can also use the Anchoring button in the Size group on the Arrange tab to set this property. |
| Vertical Anchor | This specifies how the control is anchored vertically when it is in a control layout. You can choose Top (the default) to place the control at the top, Bottom to place the control at the bottom, or Both to stretch the control equally across the control layout from top to bottom. You can also use the Anchoring button in the Size group on the Arrange tab to set this property. |
| Can Grow, Can Shrink | These properties apply to controls on a report or in Print Preview. See Chapter 16, "Advanced Report Design," for details. |
| Display When | Choose Always (the default) to display this control in Form view, in Print Preview, and when you print the form. Choose Print Only to display the control only when you view the form in Print Preview or you print the form. Choose Screen Only to display the control only when in Form view. |
| Reading Order | Choose Context (the default) to set the order the characters are displayed based on the first character entered. When the first character is from a character set that is normally read right to left (such as Arabic), the characters appear right to left. Choose Left-To-Right or Right-To-Left to override the reading order. |
| Scroll Bar Align | Choose System (the default) to align scroll bars based on the form's Orientation property setting. See the section "Understanding Other Form Properties" on page 676 for details. Choose Right or Left to override the form setting. |
| Numeral Shapes | On an Arabic or Hindi system, you can choose settings to alter the way numbers are displayed. The default setting is System, which displays numbers based on your system settings. |
| Keyboard Language | System (the default setting) assumes the keyboard being used is the default for your system. You can also choose from any available installed keyboard. |
| Filter Lookup | Choose Database Default (the default setting) to honor the options you set in the Advanced category in the Access Options dialog box. Choose Never to disable the lookup of values in Filter By Form. Choose Always to enable the lookup of values in Filter By Form regardless of your Access Options settings. |
| On Click through On Undo | You can set these properties to run a macro, a function, or an event procedure when the specific event described by the property occurs for this control. See Part 6, "After Completing Your Application," for details. |

| Property | Description |
|---|---|
| Enter Key Behavior | Default (the default setting) specifies that pressing the Enter key in this control performs the action described in the Move After Enter setting in the Advanced category in the Access Options dialog box. The New Line In Field setting specifies that pressing Enter creates a new line in the underlying text. This setting is useful for large text or memo fields, especially when the control is more than one line high and has a vertical scroll bar defined. |
| ControlTip Text | You can enter a custom message that appears as a control tip when you rest your mouse pointer on the control for a few seconds. You might find this especially useful for command buttons to further describe the action that occurs when the user clicks the button. |
| Shortcut Menu Bar | You can design a custom shortcut menu for your forms and reports, and you enter the name of your custom menu in this property. This property exists for backward compatibility with Access 2003 and earlier. |
| Help Context ID | You can create a custom Help file for your application and identify specific topics with a context ID. If you want a particular topic to appear when a user presses F1 when the focus is in this control, enter the ID of the topic in this property. See Chapter 28, "Designing Forms in an Access Project," for details. |
| Auto Tab | Choose Yes to cause an automatic tab to the next field when the user enters a number of characters equal to the field length. The default is No. |
| Vertical | You can design a control that displays text to run vertically down the form (narrow width and tall height). When you do that, you can set Vertical to Yes to turn the text display 90 degrees clockwise. The default is No. |
| Allow AutoCorrect | Specify Yes (the default) to enable autocorrection as you type text, similar to the AutoCorrect feature in Word. You can customize AutoCorrect options by clicking the AutoCorrect Options button in the Proofing category in the Access Options dialog box. Specify No to turn off this feature. |
| IME Hold, IME Mode, IME Sentence Mode | These properties determine how Kanji characters are processed on a Japanese language system. |
| Tag | You can use this property to store additional descriptive information about the control. You can write Visual Basic code to examine and set this property or take a specific action based on the property setting. The user cannot see the contents of the Tag property. |

### Be Careful When Setting Control Validation Rules

Two properties that deserve special mention are Validation Rule and Validation Text. As you know, you can specify these properties for most fields in your table. When you build a form that is bound to data from your table, the validation rules in the table always apply. However, you can also specify a validation rule for many bound controls on your form. You might want to do this if, on this particular form, you want a more restrictive rule to apply.

However, you can get in trouble if you specify a rule that conflicts with the rule in the underlying table. For example, in the HousingDataCopy.accdb sample database, you can find a validation rule on the BirthDate field in the tblEmployees table that disallows entering a birth date for someone who is younger than 18 years old. The validation rule is as follows:

```
<=(Date()-(365*18))
```

What do you suppose happens if you subsequently enter a Validation Rule property for the BirthDate text box control on your form that requires the person to be 18 or younger? You can try it by opening your employees form in Design view, clicking the BirthDate text box, and entering the following in the Validation Rule property in the property sheet:

```
>(Date()-(365*18))
```

So that you can determine which validation rule is preventing you from changing the data, set the Validation Text property to something like "Violating the control validation rule." Now, switch to Form view, and try to type a value that you know violates the table rule, such as 1/1/2007. When you try to tab out of the field, you should see the message from the table: "You cannot enter an employee who is younger than 18 years old." Now, try to enter a date for an older person, such as 1/1/1969, and press Tab to move out of the control. You should see the validation text that you just entered for the control. The bottom line is you have set up the rules so that no value is valid when you try to edit with this form. (You'll have to press Esc to clear your edit to be able to close the form.)

# Setting Form Properties

In addition to the controls on a form, the form itself has a number of properties that you can use to control its appearance and how it works.

## Allowing Different Views

When you build a form from scratch (such as the employees form you've been working on in this chapter), the Default View property of the form is Single Form. This is the view you'll see first when you open the form. With the Single Form setting, you can see only one record at a time, and you have to use the Record Number box, the Previous Record and Next Record arrow buttons to the left and right of the Record Number box, or the Go To command in the Find group on the Home tab to move to another record.

If you set the Default View property of the form to Continuous Forms, you can see multiple records on a short form, and you can use the scroll bar on the right side of the form to scroll through the records. If you set the Default View property of the form to Split Form, you can see your employee records in Datasheet view at the top of the Form window. At the bottom of the Form window, you can see one record at a time displayed in the form controls you've been designing. Because one record's data in the tblEmployees table fills your employees form, the Single Form setting is probably the best choice.

Another set of properties lets you control whether a user can change to Form view, Datasheet view, PivotTable view, PivotChart view, or Layout view. These properties are Allow Form View, Allow Datasheet View, Allow PivotTable View, Allow PivotChart View, and Allow Layout View. The default setting for all these properties is No except Form View and Layout View, meaning that a user cannot use the View button on the Ribbon to switch to Datasheet, PivotTable, or PivotChart view. (Users also cannot switch to these views if they right-click the form tab when their Document Windows Options setting is set to Tabbed Documents). If you're designing a form to be used in an application, you will usually want to eliminate some of the views. For your employees form, set all but the Allow Form View property to No; if you click the arrow in the Views group, the Layout View option should not appear.

INSIDE OUT **Keeping Users Out of Design and Layout Views**

You can make it more difficult to enter Design and Layout views by designing a custom Ribbon for all your forms. See Chapter 24, "The FInishing Touches," for details. You can completely prevent a user from opening a form in Design view or switching to Design view only if you give your users an execute-only copy of your application (see Chapter 25, "Distributing Your Application"). You can prevent users from opening a form in Layout view or switching to Layout view by clearing the Enable Layout View For This Database check box in the Current Database category in the Access Options dialog box. This setting affects all forms *and* reports in your database.

## Setting Navigation Options

Because the employees form you've been designing displays one record at a time, it is not useful to display the row selector on the left side of the form. You've also designed the form to show all the data in a single window, so a scroll bar along the right side of the window isn't necessary. You also don't need a horizontal scroll bar. You probably should keep the Record Number box at the bottom of the form, however. To make these changes, set the form's Record Selectors property on the property sheet to No, the Scroll Bars property to Neither, and the Navigation Buttons property to Yes. Your form should look something like the one shown in Figure 12-48.

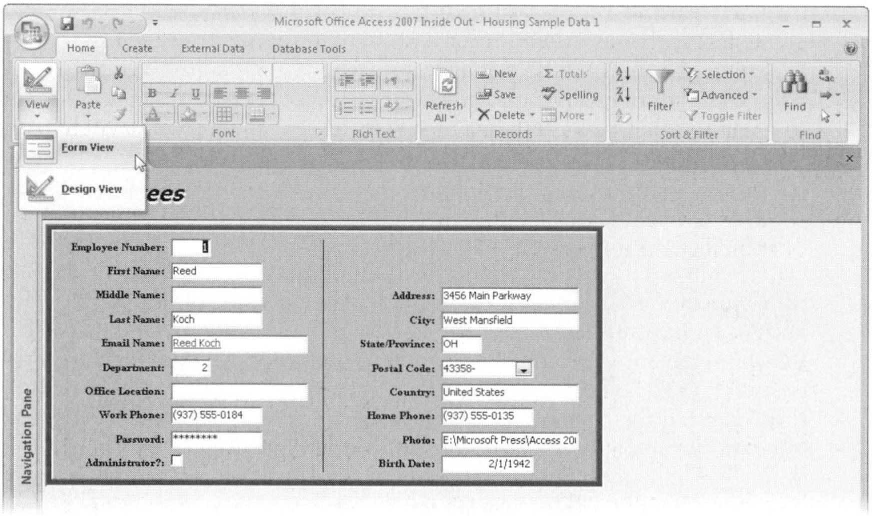

Figure 12-48 The employees form now has views restricted and does not have a record selector or scroll bars.

## Defining a Pop-Up and/or Modal Form

You might occasionally want to design a form that stays on top of all other forms even when it doesn't have the focus. Notice that the undocked property sheet and field list in Design view both have this characteristic. These are called *pop-up forms*. You can make your employees form a pop-up form by setting the form's Pop Up property to Yes. Figure 12-49 shows the employees form as a pop-up form on top of the Navigation Pane, which has the focus. Note that the form can "float" on top of other forms or windows, and it can also be moved on top of the Ribbon. A form that isn't a pop-up form cannot leave the Access workspace below the Ribbon. You might also notice that when you change the employees form's Pop Up property to Yes, the form no longer has the tab across the top. Even though the Document Windows Options setting is still set to Tabbed Documents for this database, this form now looks like we are using the Overlapping Windows setting.

**CAUTION!**

If you play with the frmXmplEmployee5 form to do this, be sure to set the form's Pop Up property back to No or don't save your design changes when you close the form.

As you'll learn in Part 4, "Automating an Access Application," it's sometimes useful to create forms that ask the user for information that's needed in order to perform the next task. Forms have a Modal property that you can set to Yes to "lock" the user into the form when it's open. The user must make a choice in the form or close the form in order to go on to other tasks. When a modal form is open, you can switch to another application, but you can't select any other form or Ribbon button in Access until you dismiss the modal form. You've probably noticed that most dialog boxes, such as the various wizards in Access, are modal forms. Modal isn't a good choice for your employees form, but you'll use the Modal property later to help control application flow.

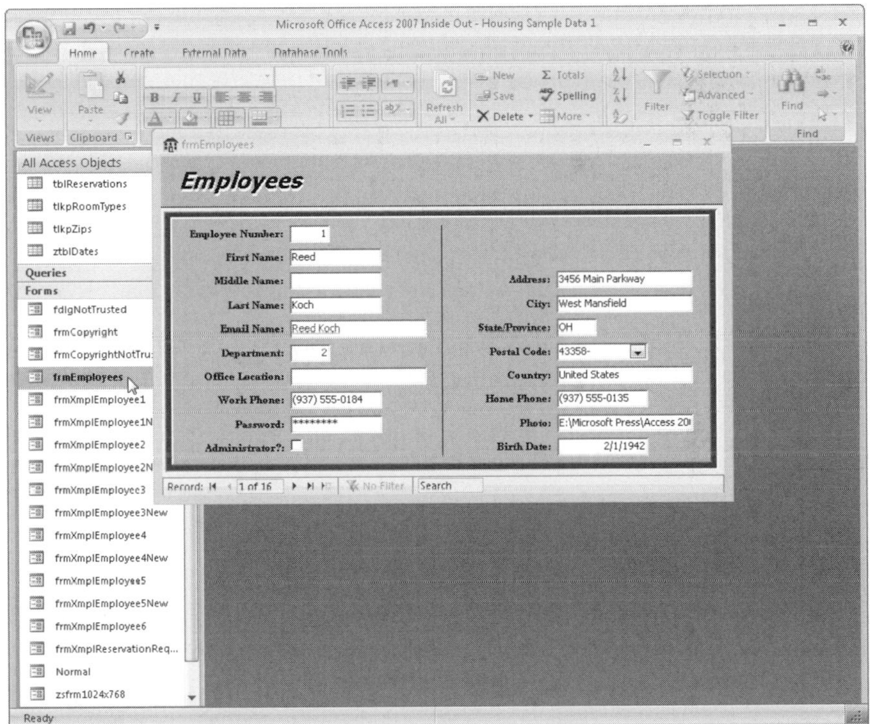


**Figure 12-49** The employees form as a pop-up form floats on top of the Navigation Pane and the Ribbon.

## Controlling Edits, Deletions, Additions, and Filtering

You can set several properties on forms to control whether data in the form can be updated or whether data in the underlying tables can change. You can also prevent or allow user-applied filters on the form. These properties and their settings are shown in Table 12-9.

Table 12-9 **Form Properties for Controlling Editing and Filtering**

| Property | Description |
| --- | --- |
| Filter | Contains the latest criteria applied as a filter on this form. Forms also have a FilterOn property that you can't see in the Form window in Design view. When FilterOn is True, the data displayed in the form is filtered by the criteria string found in the Filter property. On a new form, the Filter property is empty. |
| Filter On Load | You can define criteria in the Filter property and then set Filter On Load to Yes to apply the filter when the form opens. The default setting is No. |
| Order By | Contains the latest sorting criteria applied to this form. Forms also have an OrderByOn property that you can't see in the Form window in Design view. When OrderByOn is True, the data displayed in the form is sorted by the criteria string found in the Order By property. On a new form, the Order By property is empty. |
| Order By On Load | You can define sorting criteria in the Order By property and then set Order By On Load to Yes to apply the sort when the form opens. The default setting is Yes. |
| Data Entry | Determines whether the form opens a blank record in which you can insert new data. Access won't retrieve rows from the form's recordset. The valid settings are Yes and No, and the default setting is No. Setting Data Entry to Yes is effective only when Allow Additions is set to Yes. |
| Allow Additions | Determines whether a user can add records using this form. The valid settings are Yes and No. The default setting is Yes. |
| Allow Deletions | Determines whether a user can delete records in this form. The valid settings are Yes and No. The default setting is Yes. |
| Allow Edits | Determines whether a user can change control values in this form. The valid settings are Yes and No. The default setting is Yes. Note that when you set Allow Edits to No, you cannot change the value of any control on the form, including unbound controls. |
| Allow Filters | Determines whether a user can see selected records by applying filtering and sorting criteria and whether the user can see all records by clicking the Toggle Filter command in the Sort & Filter group. If you set the Data Entry property to Yes and set the Allow Filters property to No, the user can only enter new data and cannot change the form to view other existing records. The valid settings for the Allow Filters property are Yes and No. The default setting is Yes. |

## Defining Window Controls

In some cases, you might want to prevent the user from opening the form's control menu (clicking the control menu button in the upper-left corner of a window displays a shortcut menu containing the Restore, Move, Size, Minimize, Maximize, Close, and Next commands) or from using the Minimize and Maximize buttons. (This applies only if you have your Document Windows Options setting set to Overlapping Windows. If you have Tabbed Documents selected, you see only a Close button on the right side.) If you want to perform special processing before a form closes (such as clearing the application status before your main switchboard closes), you might want to provide a command button to do the processing and then close the form with a Visual Basic command. (See Part 4 for details about writing a command to close a form.) You can set the form's Control Box property to No to remove the control menu button from the form window and the Close button from the upper-right corner. This also removes the Minimize and Maximize buttons.

You can set the form's Close Button property to No to remove the Close button but leave the control menu button (with Close disabled on the control menu). You can set the form's Min Max Buttons property to Both Enabled, None, Min Enabled, or Max Enabled. If you disable a Minimize or Maximize button, the related command on the form's control menu becomes disabled.

**CAUTION!**

If you are using overlapping windows, you can set a form's Control Box property to No to remove all control features from the form's title bar. This means that both the control menu button (which contains the Close command) and the form's Close button (at the right end of the title bar) will not appear. If you also set the form's Modal property to Yes, you should always provide an alternative way to close a modal form, such as a command button that executes a macro or Visual Basic command to close the form. Otherwise, the only way to close the form is to use the Windows Ctrl+F4 key combination. See Part 4 for details about writing a command to close a form.

## Setting the Border Style

In most cases, you'll want to create forms with a regular border–one that allows you to size the window and move it around if you have the Document Windows Options setting set to Overlapping Windows. Forms have a Border Style property that lets you define the look of the border and whether the window can be sized or moved. The Border Style property settings are shown in Table 12-10.

**Table 12-10 Settings for the Border Style Property**

| Setting | Description |
| --- | --- |
| None | The form has no borders, control menu button, title bar, Close button, or Minimize and Maximize buttons. You cannot resize or move the form when it is open. You can select the form and press Ctrl+F4 to close it unless the form's Pop Up property is set to Yes. You should write Visual Basic code to provide an alternative way to close this type of form. |
| Thin | The form has a thin border, signifying that the form cannot be resized. |
| Sizable | This is the default setting. The form can be resized. |
| Dialog | If the Pop Up property is set to Yes, the form's border is a thick line (like that of a true Windows dialog box), signifying that the form cannot be resized. If the Pop Up property is set to No, the Dialog setting is the same as the Thin setting. |

## Understanding Other Form Properties

Table 12-11 describes form settings not yet discussed and explains their usage. The table lists the properties in the sequence you will find them on the All tab in the property sheet.

**Table 12-11 Other Form Properties**

| Property | Description |
| --- | --- |
| Display On SharePoint Site | The default setting, Do Not Display, specifies that if this database is upsized to a Microsoft Windows SharePoint Services (version 3) site, Access will not create a view on the Windows SharePoint Services Version 3 site of this form. The Follow Table Setting option causes Access to honor the setting specified for the underlying table. |
| Picture | Enter the path and file name of a graphic file to use as the background of the form. You can click the Build button next to the property to locate the picture you want. You might find this useful to display an image such as a company logo on the background of your forms. |
| Picture Tiling | The default setting, No, places one copy of the picture on the form. Choose Yes if you want multiple copies "tiled" on the form. When you choose Yes, you must set Picture Alignment to Clip or Zoom, and the picture should be smaller than the form design or form window. Setting Picture Tiling to Yes is useful if your picture is a small pattern bitmap. |
| Picture Alignment | This property applies only when Picture Size Mode is Clip or Zoom. The default setting, Center, centers the picture in the form window area. Form Center centers the picture in the form design area. You can also specify that the picture align in the top left, top right, bottom left, or bottom right of the form. |

| Property | Description |
|---|---|
| Picture Type | Choose Embedded (the default) to store a copy of the picture in your form design. Use Linked to save space in your database, but the form must then always load the picture from the specified picture path when it opens; and if you move the picture to a different location, it might not display. |
| Picture Size Mode | Clip (the default) specifies that the picture appears in its original resolution. If the form is larger than the picture, the picture will not cover the entire form area. If the form is smaller than the picture, you'll see only part of the picture. Use Stretch to stretch the picture to the dimensions of the form, but the picture might appear distorted. Use Zoom to stretch the picture to the dimensions of the form without distorting it; but if the aspect ratio of the picture does not match the display space of the form, the picture won't cover the entire form background. |
| Width | Specifies the width of the form in inches or centimeters. Access automatically updates this property when you drag the right edge of the design area wider or narrower in Design view or Layout view. You cannot set this property to nothing (blank). |
| Auto Center | Choose No (the default) to open the form on the screen wherever it was placed when you last saved its definition from Design view, Layout view, or Form view. Choose Yes to automatically center the form in the Access workspace when you open it. This applies only if you are using a multiple-document interface. |
| Auto Resize | The default Yes setting automatically resizes the form window to its design height and width when you open the form. Choose No if you want to set a specific window size. This applies only if you are using a multiple-document interface. |
| Fit To Screen | The default setting, No, tells Access not to reduce the width of the form if the form window size is reduced. Choose Yes if you want Access to automatically reduce the width of the form to fit within the available screen space. This applies only if you are using a multiple-document interface. |
| Navigation Caption | You can use this property to set descriptive text to be used to the left of the form's navigation buttons. If left blank, Access uses the word Record. |
| Dividing Lines | When you design your form with a Header or a Footer section, Yes (the default) specifies that you will see a horizontal line separating each section. No removes the line(s). |
| Moveable | The default setting, Yes, allows the user to move the form in the Access window if using a multiple-document interface. Set this property to No to lock the form on the screen where you last saved it. |

| Property | Description |
| --- | --- |
| Split Form Size | You can use this setting to adjust the size of the form and datasheet if the form is displayed in Split Form view. If you use a larger setting here, Access displays more of the form and less of the datasheet. The default setting, Auto, tells Access to reset the form and datasheet size. |
| Split Form Orientation | The default setting, Datasheet On Top, displays the datasheet portion of a form in Split Form view at the top of the form window. You can also choose to display the datasheet potion in different positions using the other three options—Datasheet On Bottom, Datasheet On Left, or Datasheet On Right. |
| Split Form Splitter Bar | The default setting, Yes, displays a separator bar between the form and datasheet potions of a form in Split Form view. Choose No to hide the separator bar. When the splitter bar is hidden, the user cannot change the size of the two portions. |
| Split Form Datasheet | The default setting, Allow Edits, allows you to make changes to the data in the datasheet potion of a form in Split Form view. Choose Read Only to disallow any edits of the data in the datasheet portion. |
| Split Form Printing | The default setting, Form Only, specifies that Access prints only the form portion of a form in Split Form view if the user decides to print the form. Choose Datasheet Only to have Access print only the contents of the datasheet portion. |
| Save Splitter Bar Position | The default setting, Yes, specifies that Access attempts to save the splitter bar position when you close a form in Split Form view. You can move the splitter bar to display more or less of either the form or datasheet portion of the form, but you cannot do this when the Split Form Splitter Bar property is set to No. If this property is set to Yes when you close the form, Access prompts you to save the changes to the form. If you choose No, Access does not save the new location. Set this property to No to discard any changes to the splitter bar location upon closing the form. |
| Subdatasheet Expanded and Subdatasheet Height | These properties are identical to those that you can define for tables and queries. Your form must be in Datasheet view and must have a subform that is also in Datasheet view. See Chapter 13 for details. |
| Layout for Print | The default setting, No, indicates that printer fonts installed on your computer will not be available in any font property settings, but screen fonts and TrueType fonts will be available. Choosing Yes disables screen fonts but makes printer fonts and TrueType fonts available. |
| Orientation | The default in most versions of Access 2007 is Left-to-Right. In versions that support a language that is normally read right to left, the default is Right-to-Left. When you use Right-to-Left, captions appear right-justified, the order of characters in controls is right to left, and the tab sequence proceeds right to left. |

| Property | Description |
|---|---|
| Recordset Type | The default setting, Dynaset, specifies that all controls bound to fields in the record source will be updatable as long as the underlying field would also be updatable. If your form is bound to a query, see "Limitations on Using Select Queries to Update Data" on page 468. Dynaset (Inconsistent Updates) specifies that all fields (other than fields resulting from expressions or AutoNumber fields) can be updated, even if the update would break a link between related tables. (We do not recommend this option because it can allow a user to attempt to make a change that would violate integrity rules.) Snapshot specifies that the data is read-only and cannot be updated. |
| Fetch Defaults | Choose Yes (the default) to have the form fetch the default values from the field definitions when you move to a new row. Set this property to No to use only the Default Value settings you have specified for controls. |
| On Current through Before Screen Tip | You can set these properties to run a macro, a function, or an event procedure when the specific event described by the property occurs for this form. See Part 4 for details. |
| Cycle | Use the default setting, All Records, to tab to the next record when you press the Tab key in the last control in the tab order. Choose Current Record to disallow tabbing from one record to another. Choose Current Page on a multipage form to disallow tabbing onto the next or previous page—you must use Page Up or Page Down to move between pages. When you set Current Record or Current Page, you must use the navigation buttons or Ribbon commands to move to other records. |
| Record Locks | No Locks (the default) specifies that Access will not lock any edited row until it needs to write the row back to the table. This is the most efficient choice for most applications. Edited Record specifies that Access apply a lock to the row the instant you begin typing in the record. This can lock out other users in a shared environment. All Records (not recommended) locks every record in the record source as soon as you open the form. |
| Ribbon Name | You can design a custom Ribbon to display for your forms and reports, and you can enter the name of your custom Ribbon in this property. See Chapter 24 for more details. |
| Toolbar, Menu Bar, and Shortcut Menu Bar | Using Access 2000, 2002, or 2003 in an MDB format database, you can design a custom menu bar, toolbar, and shortcut menu for your forms and reports, and you enter the name of your custom menus or toolbars in these properties. These properties are supported in Access 2007 for backward compatibility with earlier versions. |
| Shortcut Menu | The default setting, Yes, indicates shortcut menus will be available for the form and all controls on the form. Choose No to disable shortcut menus. |

| Property | Description |
|---|---|
| Help File | When you create a custom help file for your application, enter the path and file name in this property. See Chapter 24 for details. |
| Help Context ID | You can create a custom help file for your application and identify specific topics with a context ID. If you want a particular topic to appear when a user presses F1 when using this form, enter the ID of the topic in this property. If the focus is in a control that also has a Help Context ID property defined, the topic for that control is displayed. See Chapter 24 for details. |
| Has Module | If you create Visual Basic event procedures for this form, Access automatically sets this property to Yes. If you change this property from Yes to No, Access warns you that doing so will delete all your code and gives you a chance to cancel the change. See Part 4 for details. |
| Fast Laser Printing | The default setting, Yes, specifies that Access will use laser printer line fonts to draw lines and rectangles if you print the form on a printer that supports this option. Choose No to send all lines to your printer as graphics. |
| Tag | You can use this property to store additional descriptive information about the form. You can write Visual Basic code to examine and set this property or take a specific action based on the property setting. The user cannot see the contents of the Tag property. |
| Palette Source | Enter the name of a graphic file or Windows palette file that provides a color palette to display this form. You might need to set this property if you have also set the Picture property so that the colors of the background picture display properly. The default setting, (Default), uses your current Windows palette. |

# Setting Form and Control Defaults

When you're building an application, you should establish a standard design for all your forms and the controls on your forms. Although you can use the AutoFormat templates, you might want to create a standard design that is different.

## Changing Control Defaults

You can use the Set Control Defaults button in the Controls group on the Design tab to change the defaults for the various controls on your form. If you want to change the default property settings for all new controls of a particular type, select a control of that type, set the control's properties to the desired default values, and then click the Set Control Defaults button in the Controls group on the Design tab. The settings of the currently selected control will become the default settings for any subsequent definitions of that type of control on your form.

For example, you might want all new labels to show blue text on a white background. To make this change, place a label on your form, and set the label's Fore Color property to blue and its Back Color property to white using the Font Color and Fill/Back Color buttons in the Font group on the Design tab. Click the Set Control Defaults button in the Controls group on the Design tab while this label is selected. Any new labels you place on the form will have the new default settings.

## Working with AutoFormat

After you define control defaults that give you the "look" you want for your application, you can also set these defaults as an *AutoFormat* that you can use in the Form Wizard. To create an AutoFormat definition, open the form that has the control defaults set the way you want them, click the arrow on the AutoFormat button in the AutoFormat group on the Arrange tab, and then click the AutoFormat Wizard button beneath the gallery of AutoFormats. Click the Customize button in the AutoFormat dialog box to open the Customize AutoFormat dialog box shown in Figure 12-50. Select the Create A New AutoFormat option to save a format that matches the form you currently have open, and then click OK. In the next dialog box, type a name for your new format, and then click OK. Your new format now appears in the list of form AutoFormats. As you saw in Chapter 11, you can select any of the form AutoFormats to dictate the look of a form created by the Form Wizard.

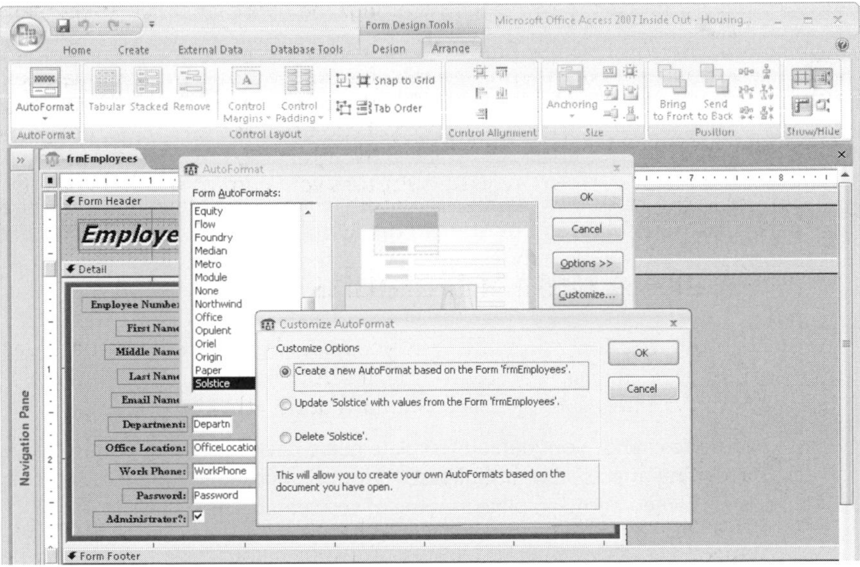


**Figure 12-50** You can create your own custom AutoFormat definitions.

If you have previously defined an AutoFormat, you can update it or delete it using the AutoFormat dialog box. You can also update or delete any of the built-in formats.

## Defining a Template Form

You can also create a special form to define new default properties for all your controls. To do this, open a new blank form and place on it one of each type of control for which you want to define default properties. Modify the properties of the controls to your liking, use these controls to reset the control defaults for the form (by clicking the Set Control Defaults button in the Controls group on the Design tab for each control), and save the form with the name *Normal*. The Normal form becomes the *template form* for the current database. Any new control you place on any new form created after you define your template form (except forms for which you've already changed the default for one or more controls) will use the default property settings you defined for that control type on the Normal form. Note that defining a template form does not affect any existing forms. Also, you can revert to the standard settings by deleting the Normal form from your database.

To define a name other than Normal for your default form and report templates, click the Microsoft Office Button, click Access Options, and then click the Object Designers category. Enter the new name in the Form Template text box in the Forms/Reports section. Then save your template under the new name you specified in the Object Designers category. Note that this new setting becomes the default for all databases on your computer, but if Access doesn't find a form in your database with the name you specified, it uses the standard default settings instead.

If you want to see how this works in the HousingDataCopy.accdb sample database, click the Microsoft Office Button, click Access Options, and then click the Object Designers category. In the Forms/Reports section, enter **zsfrmTemplate** in the Form Template box, and click OK. Next, click the Blank Form button in the Forms group on the Create tab to create a blank form. Your new form should have a header and footer and the Trek background. Try dropping a few controls onto the form. Although we started with the Trek template, we modified the look of labels, text boxes, combo boxes, list boxes, and command buttons in the template form to be different. Figure 12-51 shows you our template in Design view. Note that your new form not only inherits control properties but also inherits the height and width of each of the sections from the template.

**CAUTION!**

Be sure to change your default template name back to Normal before going any further. This setting affects all your databases but won't hurt anything unless you happen to have a form named zsfrmTemplate in some of your databases.

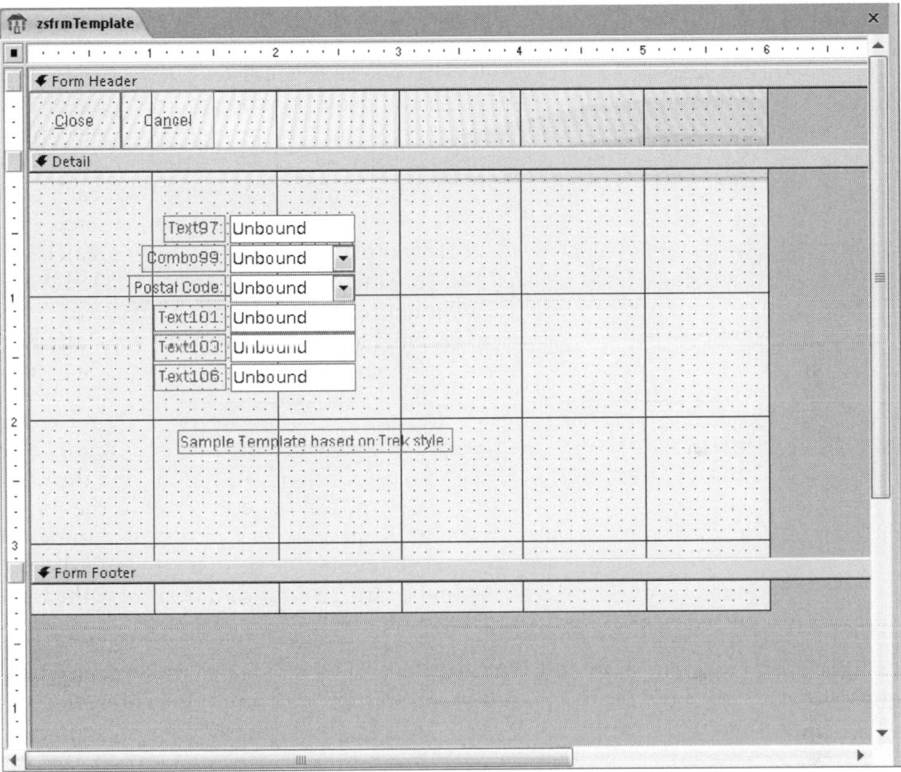


**Figure 12-51** This is the zsfrmTemplate sample template form in the HousingDataCopy.accdb sample database.

Now you should be comfortable with designing forms and adding special touches to make your forms more attractive and usable. In the next chapter, you'll learn advanced form design techniques: using multiple-table queries in forms, building forms within forms, and working with ActiveX controls, PivotTables, and PivotCharts.

CHAPTER 13

# Advanced Form Design



In the previous two chapters, you learned how to design and build a form that works with data from a single table, and you saw how to display data from another table by using a combo box or a list box. You also learned various techniques to enhance the appearance of your forms, and you explored control and form properties you can set to specify how a form looks and works.

In this chapter, you'll learn how to design a form that consolidates information from multiple tables. You'll find out how to

- Create a form based on a query that joins multiple tables
- Embed a subform in a main form so that you can work with related data from two tables or queries at the same time
- Use an option group to display and edit information
- Define conditional formatting of a control based on the data values in the form
- Use the tab control to handle multiple subforms within one area on a form
- Create a form that spreads many data fields across multiple pages
- Use an ActiveX control on your forms
- Design a form in PivotTable or PivotChart view and embed a linked PivotChart form in another form

**Note**

The examples in this chapter are based on the tables and data in HousingDataCopy.accdb and ContactsDataCopy.accdb on the companion CD included with this book. These databases are copies of the data from the Housing Reservations and Conrad Systems Contacts application samples, respectively, and they contain the sample queries and forms used in this chapter. The results you see from the samples you build in this chapter might not exactly match what you see in this book if you have changed the sample data in the files. Also, all the screen images in this chapter were taken on a Microsoft Windows Vista operating system with the display theme set to Blue, and Use Windows-Themed Controls On Forms has been enabled in the Current Database category in the Access Options dialog box for the sample databases.

# Basing a Form on a Multiple-Table Query

When you bring together data from multiple tables using select queries, the result of that query is called a *recordset*. A recordset contains all the information you need, but it's in the unadorned Datasheet view format. Forms enable you to present this data in a more attractive and meaningful way. And in the same way that you can update data with queries, you can also update data using a form that is based on a query.

## Creating a Many-to-One Form

It's easy to design a form that allows you to view and update the data from a single table. Although you can include selected fields from related tables using a list box or a combo box, what if you want to see more information from the related tables? The best way to do this is to design a query based on two (or more) related tables and use that query as the basis of your form.

When you create a query with two or more tables, you're usually working with one-to-many relationships among the tables. As you learned earlier, Microsoft Office Access 2007 lets you update any data in the table that is on the *many* side of the relationship and any nonkey fields on the *one* side of the relationship. This means that when you base a form on a query, you can update all the fields in the form that come from the *many* table and most of the fields from the *one* side. Because the primary purpose of the form is to search and update records on the *many* side of the relationship while reviewing information on the *one* side, this is called a *many-to-one* form.

In Chapter 8, "Building Complex Queries," you learned how to build a multiple-table query that displays information from several tables in the HousingDataCopy.accdb sample database. Later, you explored the fundamentals of form construction by creating simple forms to display company and product data in the ContactsDataCopy.accdb sample database.

In Chapter 12, "Customizing a Form," you built and enhanced a simple form to display employee information from the housing database. (See Figure 12-42 on page 650.)

You could have used a combo box to display a department name instead of a number in your employees form. But what if you want to see the additional details about the department when you view an employee record? To do this, you need to base your employees form on a query that joins multiple tables.

## Designing a Many-to-One Query

To build the query you need, follow these steps:

1. Open the HousingDataCopy.accdb sample database, and on the Create tab, in the Other group, click the Query Design button to open a new Query window in the Design view.
2. Add the tblDepartments table and two copies of the tblEmployees table using the Show Table dialog box. (You need the second copy to fetch the department manager name.) Close the Show Table dialog box after you add the tables to the Query window.
3. Remove the extra relationship line between EmployeeNumber in the first copy of tblEmployees and ManagerNumber in the tblDepartments table.
4. Right-click the second copy of tblEmployees (the title bar of the field list displays *tblEmployees_1*), and click Properties on the shortcut menu, or click the Property Sheet button in the Show/Hide group on the Design tab. In the Property Sheet window, give the field list an alias name of Managers to make the purpose of this field list clear, and then close the Property Sheet window.
5. Click the EmployeeNumber field in the Managers field list, and drag and drop it on ManagerNumber in the tblDepartments field list. This link establishes who the department manager is.
6. Drag the special "all fields" indicator (*) from the tblEmployees field list to the design grid.
7. Create an expression, **Manager: Managers.LastName & ", " & Managers.FirstName**, in the next empty column in the design grid to display the department manager name.
8. From the tblDepartments table, drag DeptLocation, DeptAddress, DeptCity, DeptStateOrProvince, DeptPostalCode, and DeptCountry to the query design grid. Do not include the DepartmentID field from tblDepartments; you want to be able to update the DepartmentID field, but only in the tblEmployees table. If you include the DepartmentID field from the tblDepartments table, it might confuse you later as you design the form. You'll use a combo box on DepartmentID on the form to display the department name. Save your query as qryEmployeesDepartmentManager, and close the query.

You can find a query already built for this purpose (named qryXmplEmployeesDepartmentManager) in the sample database, as shown in Figure 13-1.

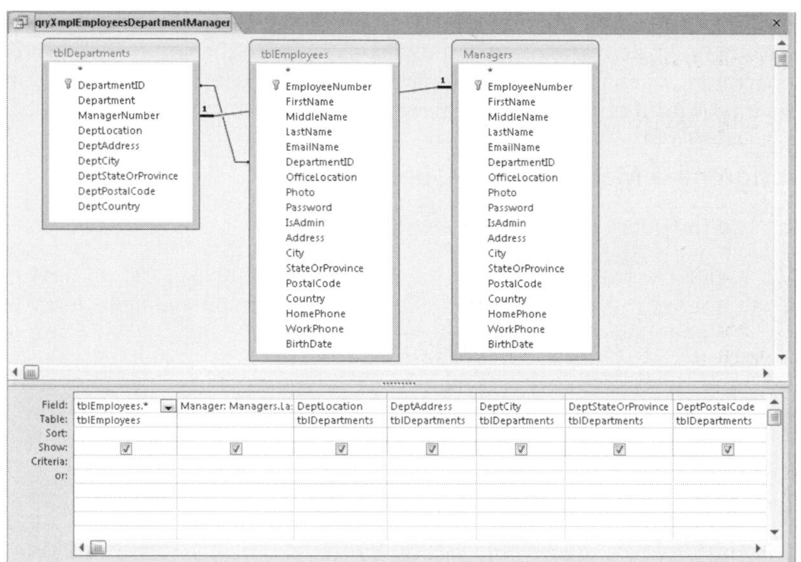


**Figure 13-1** The qryXmplEmployeesDepartmentManager query serves as the record source for your form.

## Designing a Many-to-One Form

Now that you have the query you need, find the query definition in the Navigation Pane, and create a new form based on the query. You can use the Form Wizard to quickly build a starting point for your form. Select the query in the Navigation Pane, click the Create tab, and in the Forms group, click the More Forms button. Click Form Wizard to get started.

You want to include all the fields from the query in this form, so click the double right arrow to move all the fields from the Available Fields list to the Selected Fields list. Click Next to go to the second page of the wizard. Select a columnar layout on the next page, and select the style you want on the page that follows. We started with the Trek style for all forms in the Housing Reservations sample database, as shown in Figure 13-2.

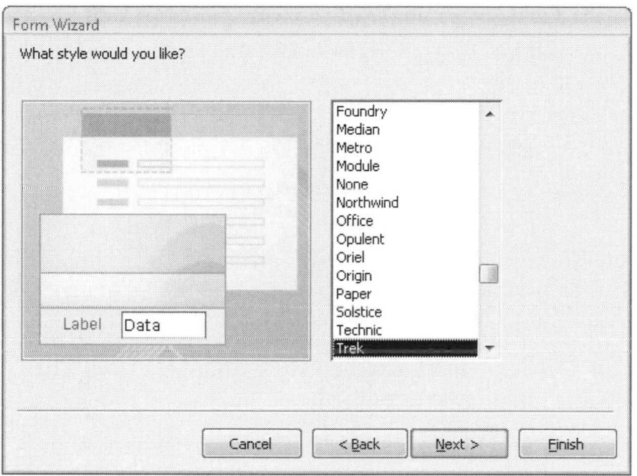


**Figure 13-2** Select a form style on the third page of the Form Wizard.

Give your form a title of Employees on the last page, and click Finish. When the wizard finishes, you should see a form similar to that shown in Figure 13-3.

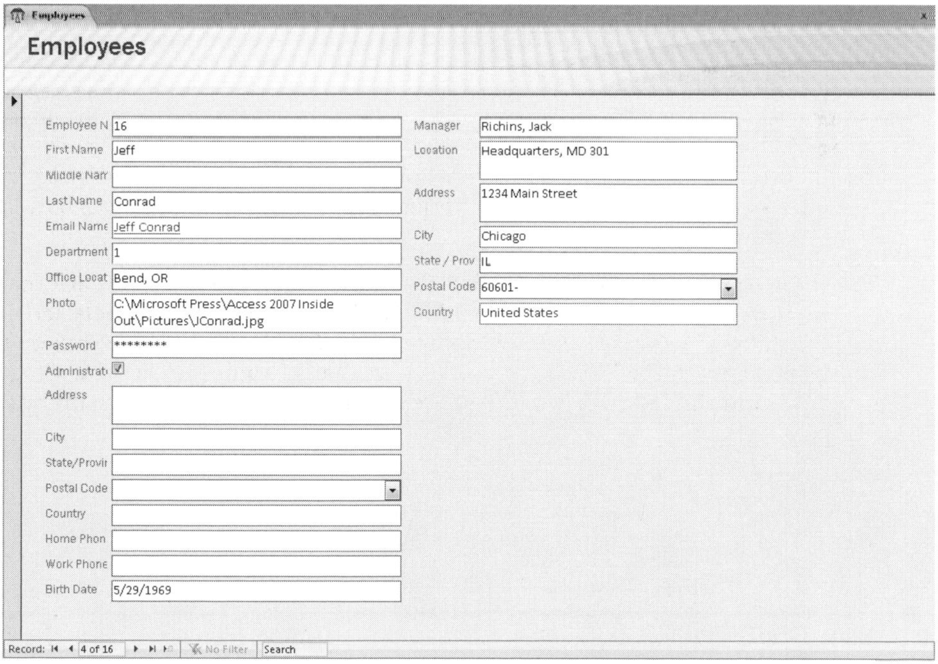

**Figure 13-3** The Employees form is a many-to-one form to display data from multiple tables.

> **Note**
>
> In the initial release of Office Access 2007, the Form Wizard fails to apply the defined background image for the style you select when you create a Columnar, Datasheet, or Justified form. Microsoft is aware of this issue and is looking into it. Figure 13-3 shows the form after we reapplied the Trek style using the AutoFormat command.

This form could use some polishing, but the wizard has placed the fields you chose on the form for you. To be able to see the department name, instead of Department ID, switch to Design view, and perform the following steps:

1. Right-click the DepartmentID text box, click Change To, and then click Combo. This converts the text box to a combo box.
2. Open the property sheet, and set Row Source to tblDepartments, Column Count to 2 (the first two fields of tblDepartments are DepartmentID and Department), and column widths to **0";1.5"** to hide the DepartmentID field and display the department name.

Switch back to Form view, and the result should look like Figure 13-4. You can find this form saved as frmXmplEmployee6 in the sample database.

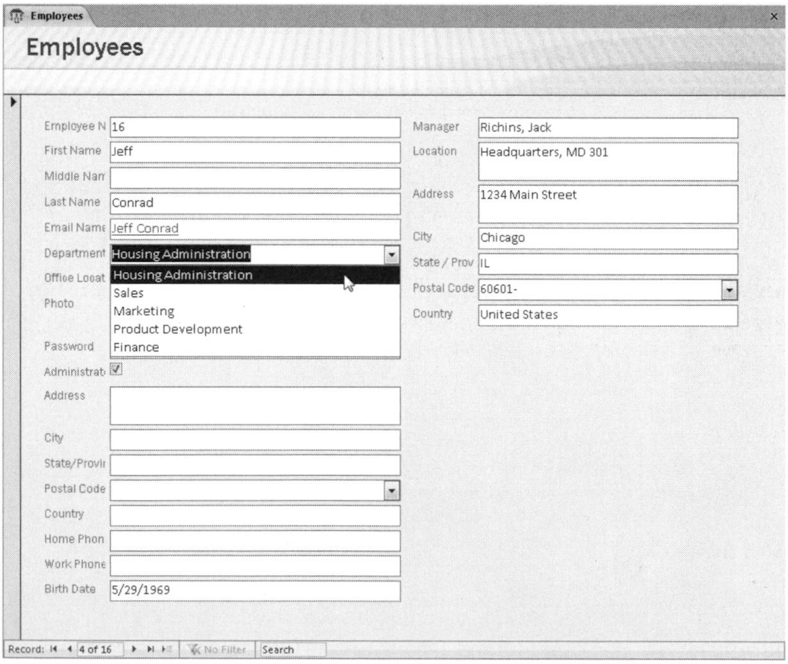

**Figure 13-4** The DepartmentID control displays the related department name after you changed it to a combo box.

Try changing the department in any record to something else, and watch what happens. You should see the corresponding manager name and department location information pop into view, as shown in Figure 13-5. Because you haven't set the Locked property for any of the fields, you can also update the location information for the displayed department. However, if you do this, the new location information appears for all employees assigned to that department.

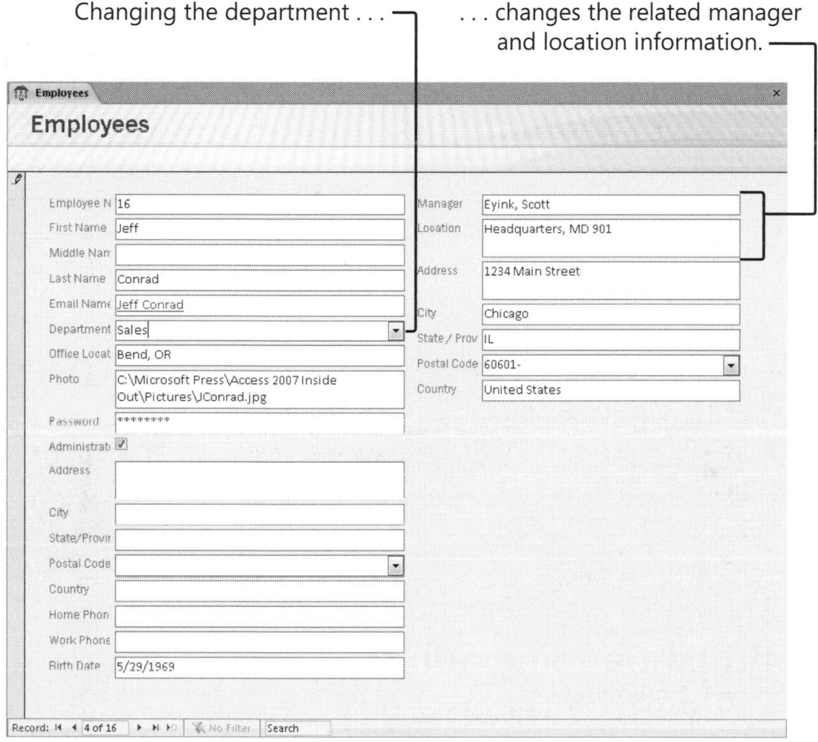


**Figure 13-5** If you change the Department field for the employee, new related information is displayed automatically on this many-to-one form.

INSIDE OUT **Understanding Windows-Themed Controls**

Access 2007 provides an option to help your forms look more consistent with Windows Vista and Windows XP. To enable this feature, click the Microsoft Office Button, click Access Options, and in the Current Database category, select the Use Windows-Themed Controls On Forms check box (displayed under Application Options). You can set this option for each individual database. When you do this, Access uses the Windows Vista or Windows XP theme for your command buttons. It also applies the Windows theme for label, text box, option group, option button, check box, combo box, list box, image, unbound object frame, bound object frame, subform, and rectangle controls. All these controls appear flat when all the following conditions are true:

- Special Effect is Sunken or Etched, or Special Effect is Flat and Border Style is not Transparent.
- Border Style is Solid, or Border Style is Transparent and Special Effect is not Flat.
- Border Color is #000000.
- Border Width is Hairline, 1, or 2.

You can selectively restore the default look for controls by creating a template form in your database. (See the previous chapter for details about creating a template form.) However, the Form Wizard does not honor these settings unless you add your template form as a custom style and instruct the wizard to use that style. The only other solution is to selectively change one of the previously mentioned settings (for example, set Back Color to #010000 instead of #000000) for controls that you do not want themed.

# Creating and Embedding Subforms

If you want to show data from several tables and be able to update the data in more than one of the tables, you probably need to use something more complex than a standard form. In the Conrad Systems Contacts database, the main contact information is in the tblContacts table. Contacts can have multiple contact events and might be associated with more than one company or organization. The information about companies is in the tblCompanies table.

Because any one contact might belong to several companies or organizations and each company probably has many contacts, the tblContacts table is related to the tblCompanies table in a many-to-many relationship. See Chapter 4, "Creating Your Database and Tables," for a review of relationship types. The tblCompanyContacts table provides the link between companies and contacts.

Similarly, a particular contact within a company might own one or more products, and a product should be owned by multiple contacts. Because any one contact might have purchased many different products and any one product might be owned by multiple contacts, the tblCompanyContacts table is related to the tblProducts table in a many-to-many relationship. The tblContactProducts table establishes the necessary link between the contacts and the products owned. Figure 13-6 shows the relationships.

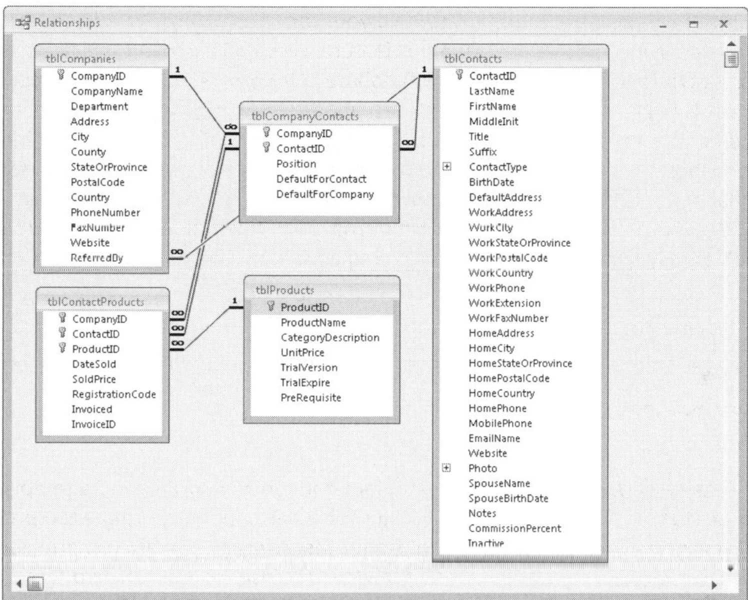


**Figure 13-6** The Relationships window in the Conrad Systems Contacts application shows the relationships between companies, contacts, and products.

When you are viewing information about a particular contact, you also might want to see and edit the related company information and the product detail information. You could create a complex query that brings together the desired information from all five tables and use a single form to display the data, similar to the many-to-one employees form you built in the previous section. However, the focus would be on the contact products (the lowest table in the one-to-many relationship chain), so you would be able to see in a single form row only one product per row. You could design a form that has its Default View property set to Continuous Forms, but you would see the information from tblContacts and tblCompanyContacts repeated over and over.

Subforms can help solve this problem. You can create a main form that displays the contact's information and embed in it a subform that displays all the related rows from tblCompanyContacts. To see the related product information, you could then build a subform within the form that displays the tblCompanyContacts data to show the product information from tblContactProducts.

## Specifying the Subform Source

You can embed up to 10 levels of subforms within another form (a form that has a subform that also has a subform, and so on). It's best to start by designing the innermost form and working outward because you must design and save an inner form before you can embed it in an outer one. In this exercise, you need to build a form on tblContactProducts, embed that in a form that shows data from tblCompanyContacts, and then finally embed that form and subform in a form to display contact information. But first, you must create the record sources for these subforms. Begin by designing the data source for the first subform.

In the example described previously, you want to create or update rows in the tblContactProducts table to create, modify, or delete links between company contact records in the tblCompanyContacts table and products in the tblProducts table. You could certainly base the subform directly on the tblContactProducts table and display the product name via a combo box on the form that looks up the name based on the value in the ProductID field. However, the user might find it useful to have the current list price for the product displayed to be sure the product isn't being sold at the wrong price. To do that, you need a query linking tblContactProducts and tblProducts.

Begin by opening the ContactsDataCopy.accdb sample database, and then start a new query in Design view. In the Show Table dialog box, add the field lists for the tblContactProducts and tblProducts tables to the Query window, and then click Close. You want to be able to update all the fields in the tblContactProducts table, so copy them to the design grid. You can do so by using the all fields indicator (*). Add the ProductName, CategoryDescription, UnitPrice, and TrialVersion fields from the tblProducts table.

Your query should look similar to the one shown in Figure 13-7. (This query is saved as qxmplContactProducts in the sample database.) Notice that the tblProducts table has a one-to-many relationship with the tblContactProducts table. This means that you can update any field in the tblContactProducts table (including all three primary key fields, as long as you don't create a duplicate row) because the tblContactProducts table is on the *many* side of the relationship. Save and close the query so that you can use it as you design the subform. You can save your query as qryContactProductsSub, as shown in Figure 13-7, or use the sample query.

Next, you need a query for the form to display the information from tblCompany-Contacts. You'll embed a subform to display contact products in this form and ultimately embed this form in the outermost form to display contact data. Again, you could use the tblCompanyContacts table as the record source for this form, but you might want to display additional information such as company name and department name from the related tblCompanies table. You also want to restrict the rows displayed to the one row for each contact that defines the default company for the contact.

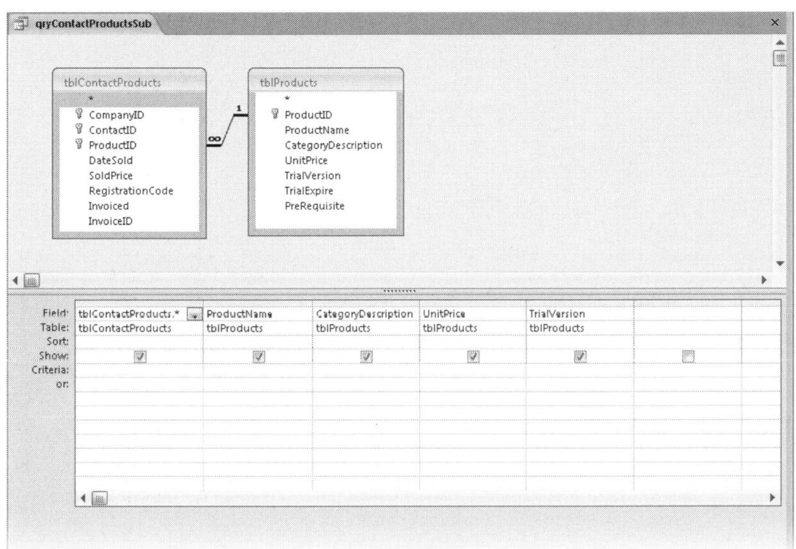


**Figure 13-7** You can use this query to update the tblContactProducts table from a subform while displaying related information from the tblProducts table.

Start a new query on the tblCompanyContacts table. Add the tblCompanies table to the design grid. You should see a link between the two tables on the CompanyID field in each. Close the Show Table dialog box after you add the two tables. In the design grid, include the CompanyID, ContactID, Position, and DefaultForContact fields from tblCompanyContacts. Under the DefaultForContact field, enter a criterion of True to restrict the output to the records that define the default company for each contact. Add the CompanyName and Department fields from the tblCompanies table.

Your query should look like the one shown in Figure 13-8. (This query is saved as qxmplContactCompaniesDefault in the sample database.) Notice that the tblCompanies table has a one-to-many relationship with the tblCompanyContacts table. This means that you can update any field in the tblCompanyContacts table (including the primary key fields, as long as you don't create a duplicate row) because the tblCompanyContacts table is on the *many* side of the relationship. Save the query so that you can use it as you design your form. You can save your query as qryContactCompaniesDefault, as shown in Figure 13-8, or use the sample query.

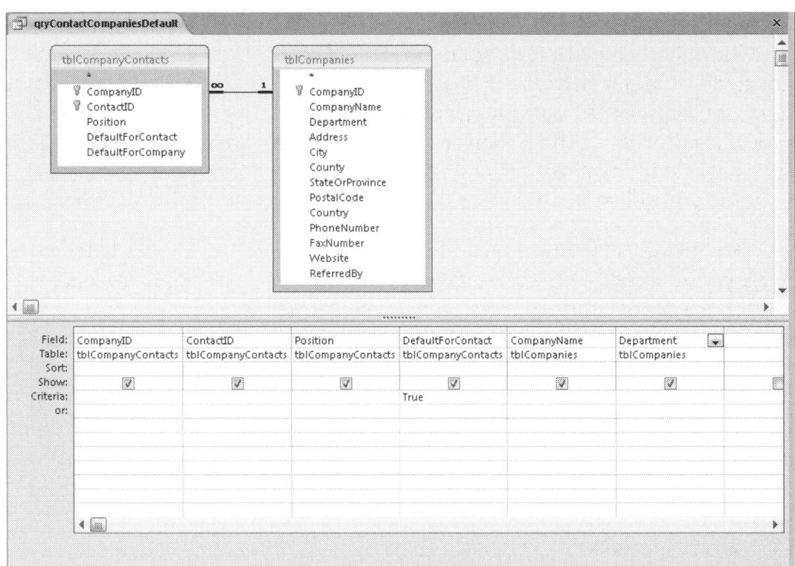

**Figure 13-8** You can use this query to update the tblCompanyContacts table from a subform while displaying related information from the tblCompanies table.

You're now ready to start building the forms and subforms.

## Designing the Innermost Subform

For the innermost subform, you'll end up displaying the single ProductID field bound to a combo box that shows the product name. After you choose a ProductID, you want to show the user the product category, name, and list price—but in controls that can't be updated. (You don't want a user to be able to accidentally change product names and list prices via this form!) Of course, you need the DateSold and SoldPrice fields from tblContactProducts so that you can update these fields.

For this purpose, you could use a form in either Datasheet or Continuous Forms view. It's simple to build a subform designed to be used in Datasheet view because you need to include only the fields you want to display in the Detail section of the form, without any regard to alignment or placement. Access takes care of ordering, sizing, and providing column headers in the datasheet. However, we like to use Continuous Forms view because that view lets you control the size of the columns—in Datasheet view, a user can resize the columns, including shrinking a column so that it's no longer visible. Furthermore, if the subform is in Single Form view or Continuous Forms view, the Size To Fit command will make the subform control on the outer form the right size. If the subform is in Datasheet view, however, the Size To Fit command will size the control to the size of the subform in Form view, not to an even number of datasheet rows wide or high. Also, the user is free to resize the row height and column width in Datasheet view, so how you size the subform control in Design view is only a guess.

It turns out that the Form Wizard does a good job assembling this first subform for you. Click the Navigation Pane menu, click Object Type under Navigate To Category, and then click Queries under Filter By Group. Select either the qryContactProductsSub query you built or the sample qxmplContactProducts query in the Navigation Pane. Click More Forms in the Forms group on the Create tab, and then click Form Wizard to start the wizard. You're going to ask the wizard to create a tabular form, which displays the fields you select in the order you select them in Continuous Forms view.

You don't need the CompanyID and ContactID fields—as you'll learn later, the form in which you'll embed this subform will supply these values via special properties you'll set in the subform control. First, click the ProductID field to select it, and click the single right arrow to move it to the Selected Fields list. Choose the additional fields you need in this order: CategoryDescription, ProductName, UnitPrice, DateSold, and SoldPrice. (If we had planned ahead, we could have placed the fields in this sequence in the query we're using as the record source.) Click Next to go to the next page in the wizard, as shown in Figure 13-9.

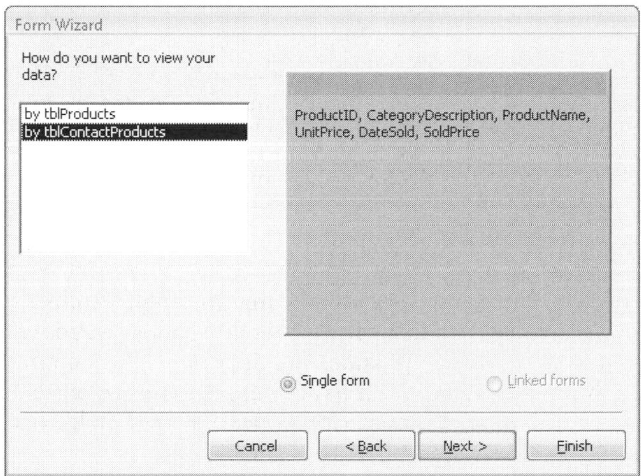


**Figure 13-9** When you use the Form Wizard to build a form on a query using two tables, the wizard offers data layout choices.

Although you won't take advantage of the wizard features shown on this page this time, it's interesting to note the options if you click the By tblProducts option. The wizard offers to build a form on tblProducts and a subform on tblContactProducts or to build two separate forms that are linked with a command button. In this case, you want to build a single continuous form, so click By tblContactProducts, and then click Next to go to the next page. Choose the Tabular layout and the None style on the next two pages. On the final page, give your new form a name such as fsubContactProducts, select the Modify The Form's Design option, and click Finish. Your result should look like Figure 13-10.

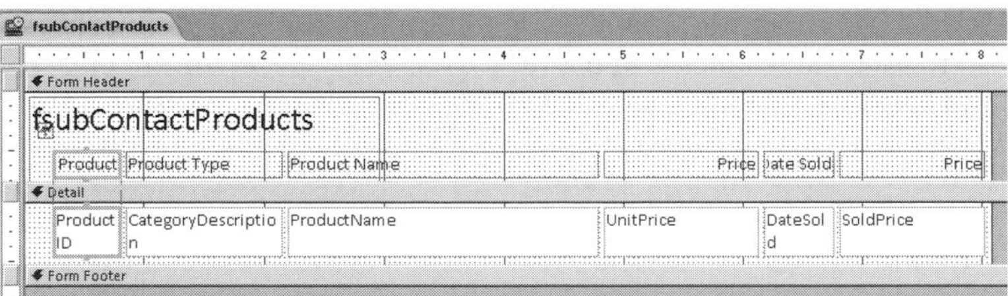

**Figure 13-10** The Form Wizard created a continuous form to edit contact product information.

You could probably use this form as is, but we'll clean it up using the techniques in Design view and Layout view you learned in previous chapters. Perform the following steps to perfect the design:

1. Switch to Layout view, and delete the title label that Access created in the Form Header section.
2. Because you've deleted the title, you can now move all the labels closer to the top of the form. Click the first label, Product; rest your mouse pointer on the middle of the label until it becomes double-sided crosshairs; and then drag the label up near the top of the form. You'll notice that Access moves all the other labels as well because these controls are in a tabular control layout.
3. Select all the labels, and click the Bold button in the Font group on the Format tab to make the captions more readable. You'll notice that Access adjusts the width of all the controls to make room for the larger text.
4. All the controls are set to the Calibri font with a font size of 11. This font and size is too big for our needs, so let's change the font and reduce the size. To select all the labels and text boxes, click the Product label, move your mouse pointer to the top edge until it becomes a down arrow, click the mouse once, hold down the Shift key, and repeat the process with all the labels until all the controls are selected. Next, select the MS Sans Serif font from the Font list, and select 8 from the Font Size list in the Font group on the Format tab.
5. You can move the ProductID label and text box a little closer to the left edge of the form. Click the Product label, and move your mouse pointer to the middle of the left edge of the control until it becomes a double-sided arrow. Next, drag the left edge of the control closer to the left edge of the form. The ProductID controls are now wider than they were, so you can reduce their width by dragging the right edge of the label control to the left. (When you reduce the width, make sure you can still see the caption in the label.) Access moves all the other controls closer to the left side of the form after you reduce the width of the ProductID controls.
6. Now that you've reduced the font size, you could reduce the CategoryDescription controls (the Product Type column) in width. Click the Product Type label, and drag the right edge of the control closer to the left edge of the form. Because you're looking at the form in Layout view, you can easily scroll through the records to make sure you've allowed adequate space in the CategoryDescription.

7. The ProductName text box control does not need to be quite so wide. Click the Product Name label, and drag the right edge of the control closer to the left edge of the form. Make sure you can still see all the data in this control by scrolling through a few of the records. Also, the Form Wizard initially created this text box to be two lines high, but this is unnecessary now. Click the first ProductName text box, move your mouse pointer to the bottom edge of the control until it becomes a double-sided arrow, and then drag the bottom edge up closer until the control is only one line high. Access changes the height of all the text box controls but still leaves a gap below the controls. (We'll fix this in a minute.) To make sure you've sized the text box exactly one line high, you can double-click the edge of the text box or click the Size To Fit command in the Position group on the Arrange tab.

8. The two price text box controls are wider than necessary, so you should reduce the width of these controls as well. Click the UnitPrice label (the first price label), hold down the Shift key and select the SoldPrice label (the second price label), and reduce their width by dragging the right edge of either control closer to the left side of the form. Notice that Access resizes the text box controls for you. Also, because you resized the controls together, they both remain the same width.

9. Now that you've used Layout view to help resize the controls, switch to Design view to make the remaining changes. Click anywhere in the Detail section away from any controls to be sure no controls are selected. Right-click the ProductID text box control, click Change To on the menu, and then click Combo Box to convert the text box to a combo box. Open the Property Sheet window, and set Row Source to tblProducts, Column Count to 2, Column Widths to **0.25"**; **1.5"**, and List Width to **2"**. Access increased the height of the other controls when you changed ProductID to a combo box. To make them all the same height, click the ProductID combo box, hold down the Shift key, and then click the CategoryDescription text box. Next, click the Size To Shortest or the Size To Fit button in the Size group on the Arrange tab.

10. You need to lock the three fields from tblProducts so that they cannot be updated via this form. Click the CategoryDescription text box control, and hold down the Shift key while you click the ProductName text box control and the UnitPrice text box control to add them to the selection. In the Property Sheet window, set Locked to Yes.

11. Because Access originally made the ProductName text box control a two-line control, it will display a vertical scroll bar when you switch to Form view. You sized the control in Layout view to be wide enough to display all product names, so you don't need the scroll bar. Click the ProductName text box, go to the Property Sheet window, and set the Scroll Bars property to None to ensure that this control does not display a scroll bar.

12. Open the form footer by dragging down its bottom edge. Click the Text Box tool in the Controls group on the Design tab, and drop a text box in the Form Footer section under the SoldPrice text box control. Make your new control the same size as the SoldPrice control, and line them up using the Align Left or Align Right

button in the Control Alignment group on the Arrange tab that you learned about in the previous chapter. Click the attached label, set its font to Bold, and in the Property Sheet window type **Total:** in the Caption property. Now move the label closer to the new text box. Click the new text box, and in the Property Sheet window set Control Source to **=Sum([SoldPrice])**, Format to Currency, Enabled to No, and Locked to Yes. Finally, select both the new label and text box controls, and change the font to MS Sans Serif and font size to 8.

All you have left to do is to shrink the bottom of the Detail section to eliminate the extra space below the row of controls, reduce the width of the form, select the form, set the form's Scroll Bars property in the Property Sheet window to Vertical Only (your design should horizontally fit all the fields within the subform control on the main form so that the user won't need to scroll left and right), and set the Navigation Buttons property to No. (You can use the vertical scroll bar to move through the multiple rows.)

Because you didn't choose all the fields from the query, the wizard tried to help you out by creating an SQL statement to fetch only the fields you used on the form. You'll need all the fields for the subform filtering to work correctly. So, delete the SQL statement from the form's Record Source property, and set the property back to the name of your query (qryContactProducts). The result of your work should look something like Figure 13-11.

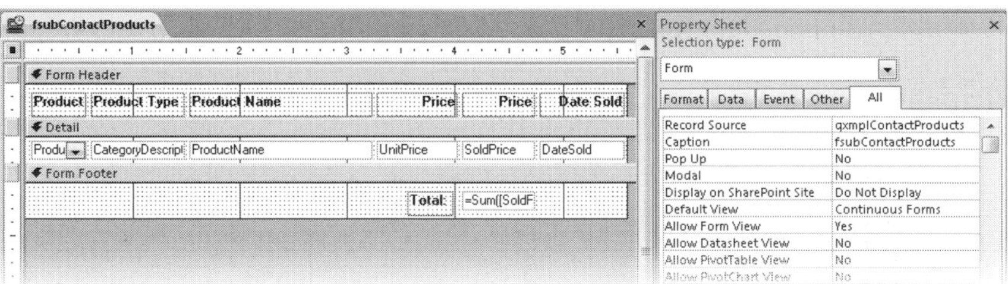


**Figure 13-11** Here is your subform to edit contact products in Design view.

You can switch to the subform's Form view to check your work. You can see the Continuous Forms view in Figure 13-12. Because this form isn't linked as a subform yet (which will limit the display to the current order), the totals displayed in the form footer are the totals for all orders. You can find this form saved as fsubXmplContact-Products in the sample database.

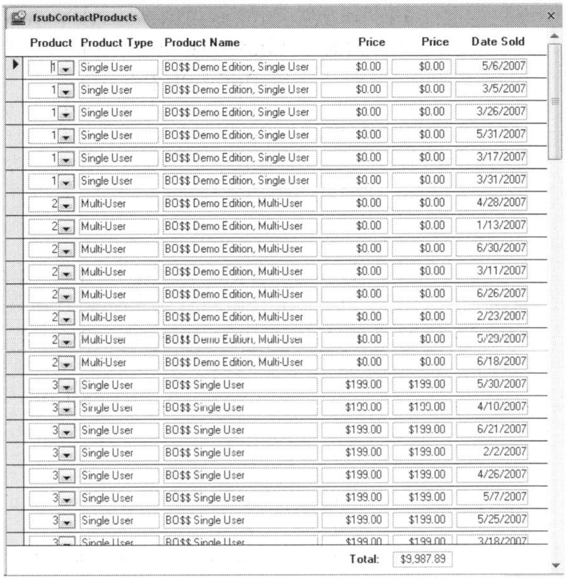

fsubContactProducts

| Product | Product Type | Product Name | Price | Price | Date Sold |
|---|---|---|---|---|---|
| 1 | Single User | BO$$ Demo Edition, Single User | $0.00 | $0.00 | 5/6/2007 |
| 1 | Single User | BO$$ Demo Edition, Single User | $0.00 | $0.00 | 3/5/2007 |
| 1 | Single User | BO$$ Demo Edition, Single User | $0.00 | $0.00 | 3/26/2007 |
| 1 | Single User | BO$$ Demo Edition, Single User | $0.00 | $0.00 | 5/31/2007 |
| 1 | Single User | BO$$ Demo Edition, Single User | $0.00 | $0.00 | 3/17/2007 |
| 1 | Single User | BO$$ Demo Edition, Single User | $0.00 | $0.00 | 3/31/2007 |
| 2 | Multi-User | BO$$ Demo Edition, Multi-User | $0.00 | $0.00 | 4/28/2007 |
| 2 | Multi-User | BO$$ Demo Edition, Multi-User | $0.00 | $0.00 | 1/13/2007 |
| 2 | Multi-User | BO$$ Demo Edition, Multi-User | $0.00 | $0.00 | 6/30/2007 |
| 2 | Multi-User | BO$$ Demo Edition, Multi-User | $0.00 | $0.00 | 3/11/2007 |
| 2 | Multi-User | BO$$ Demo Edition, Multi-User | $0.00 | $0.00 | 6/26/2007 |
| 2 | Multi-User | BO$$ Demo Edition, Multi-User | $0.00 | $0.00 | 2/23/2007 |
| 2 | Multi-User | BO$$ Demo Edition, Multi-User | $0.00 | $0.00 | 5/29/2007 |
| 2 | Multi-User | BO$$ Demo Edition, Multi-User | $0.00 | $0.00 | 6/18/2007 |
| 3 | Single User | BO$$ Single User | $199.00 | $199.00 | 5/30/2007 |
| 3 | Single User | BO$$ Single User | $199.00 | $199.00 | 4/10/2007 |
| 3 | Single User | BO$$ Single User | $199.00 | $199.00 | 6/21/2007 |
| 3 | Single User | BO$$ Single User | $199.00 | $199.00 | 2/2/2007 |
| 3 | Single User | BO$$ Single User | $199.00 | $199.00 | 4/26/2007 |
| 3 | Single User | BO$$ Single User | $199.00 | $199.00 | 5/7/2007 |
| 3 | Single User | BO$$ Single User | $199.00 | $199.00 | 5/25/2007 |
| 3 | Single User | BO$$ Single User | $199.00 | $199.00 | 3/18/2007 |
| | | | Total: | $9,987.89 | |

**Figure 13-12** This is your contact products subform displayed in Continuous Forms view.

INSIDE OUT

### Using a Subform in Datasheet View

If you'll be using a subform in Datasheet view when it's embedded in another form, you have to switch to Datasheet view to adjust how the datasheet looks and then save the subform from Datasheet view to preserve the look you want. You must also use the Datasheet view of the form to make adjustments to fonts and row height. The font in Datasheet view is independent of any font defined for the controls in Form view.

Also, if you build a tabular form such as the one shown in Figure 13-12 and then decide to use it as a subform in Datasheet view, you will see the field names as the column headings rather than the captions. In Datasheet view, columns display the defined caption for the field only when the bound control has an attached label. In a tabular form, the labels are detached from their respective controls and displayed in a separate section of the form design.

## Designing the First Level Subform

You can now move on to the form to display the company contact information and act as a link between contacts and contact products. The purpose of the final form will be to view contacts and edit their contact products, so you don't need to have anything fancy in the middle or allow any updates. To begin, click the Form Design button in the Forms group on the Create tab. Access opens a blank form grid in Design view.

Chapter 13

Open the Property Sheet window, and select in the Record Source property either the query you built earlier (qryContactCompaniesDefault) or the sample query we provided (qxmplContactCompaniesDefault).

To make this form easy to build, set some control defaults first. Click the Label button in the Controls group on the Design tab, and click the Bold button in the Font group on the Design tab to give all your labels a default bold font. Click the Text Box button, and change Special Effect to Flat, Label Align to Right, and Label X (the offset of the label to the right) to **–.05"**.

Open the Field List window by clicking the Add Existing Fields button in the Tools group on the Design tab, and then click the Show Only Fields In The Current Record Source link (if necessary). Click the CompanyID field to select it, and hold down the Ctrl key while you click the CompanyName and Department fields to add them to the selection. Drag and drop these fields together onto your form about 2 inches from the left edge and near the top of the Detail section. Drag and drop the Position field onto the form directly below Department. If you have Snap To Grid turned on, it should be easy to line up the controls. Otherwise, select all the text box controls, and use the Align buttons in the Control Alignment group on the Arrange tab to line them up. Set the Locked property of all text box controls to Yes. Select the label control attached to the CompanyID text box, and change the caption from Company / Org.: to **Company ID:**. At this stage, your design should look like Figure 13-13.

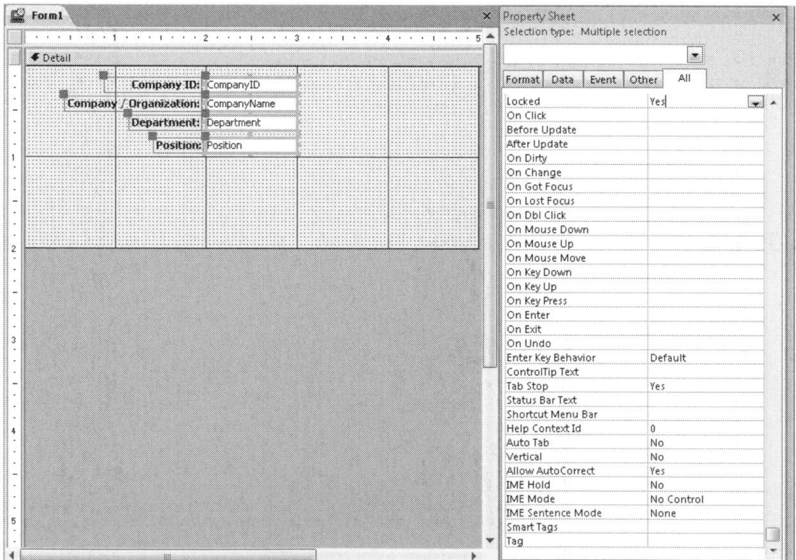


**Figure 13-13** Your form to display company contact information is now beginning to take shape.

## Embedding a Subform

You can use a couple of techniques to embed a subform in your outer form. First, you can cancel the selection of the Use Control Wizards button in the Controls group on the Design tab, select the Subform/Subreport tool in the Controls group, and then click the upper-left corner of the outer form's empty area and drag the mouse pointer to create a subform control. (If you leave the Use Control Wizards button selected, Access starts a wizard to help you build the subform when you place a subform control on your outer form. Because you already built the subform, you don't need the wizard's help.) After you have the subform control in place, set its Source Object property to point to the subform you built (or use the sample fsubXmplContactProducts).

A better way to embed the subform is to expand the Navigation Pane, find the form you want to embed as a subform, and then drag it from the Navigation Pane and drop it onto your form. To do this, expand the Navigation Pane if you collapsed it, open the Navigation Pane menu, click Object Type under Navigate To Category, and then click Forms under Filter By Group to display the list of forms in the database. Click the subform you built in the previous section (or the fsubXmplContactProducts form that we supplied), and drag and drop it onto your form at the left edge below the Position label and text box. Figure 13-14 shows this action in progress.

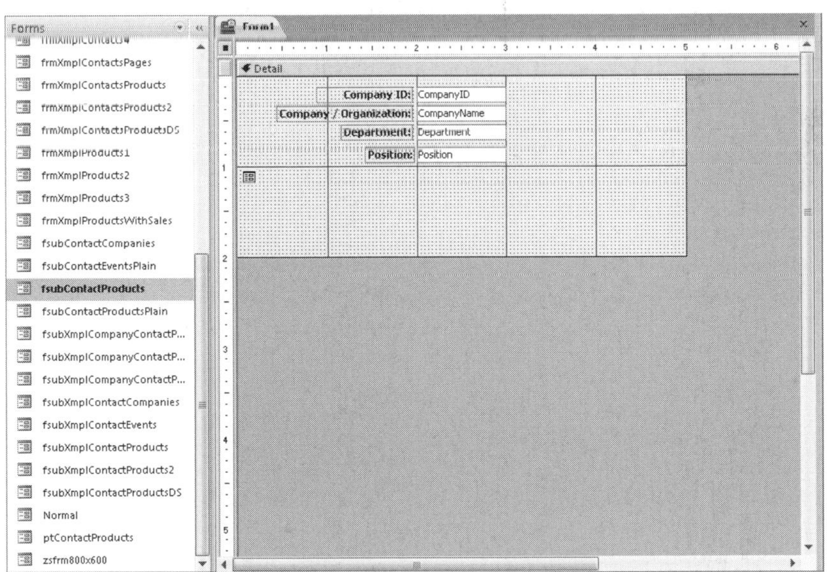


**Figure 13-14** You can drag and drop one form from the Navigation Pane onto the Design view of another form to create a subform.

Adding a subform in this way has the advantages that your new subform control will be sized correctly horizontally, will have a height to display at least one row, and will have some of its other properties automatically set. If the form you are designing has a table as its record source and Access can find related fields of the same name in the record source of the subform you're adding, then Access automatically defines the link properties as well. You'll have to set these properties yourself later in this exercise.

You don't need the label that Access added to your subform control, so you can select it and delete it. Click the subform control to select it (if you click more than once, you'll select an object on the form inside the subform control), drag the sizing handle in the middle of the bottom of the control so that it is about 2 inches high, and then click the Size To Fit button in the Size group on the Arrange tab to correctly size the control to display multiple rows. Move up the bottom of the Detail section of the outer form if necessary so that there's only a small margin below the bottom of the resized subform control. Your form should look something like Figure 13-15.

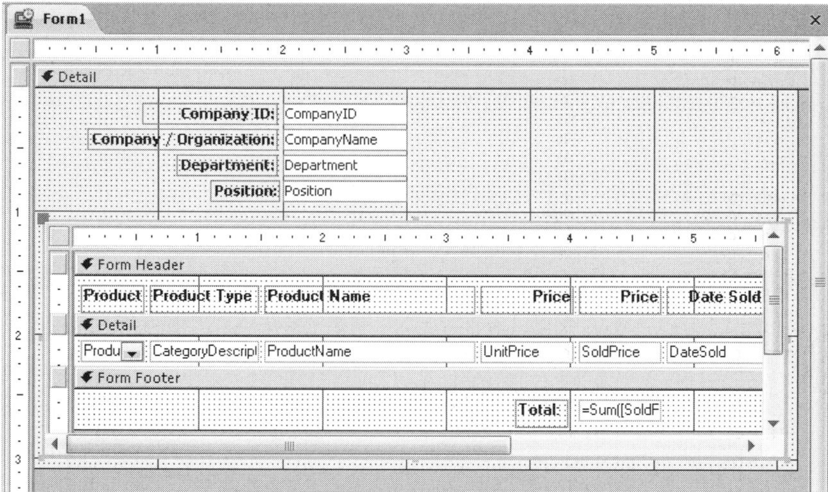


**Figure 13-15** The contact products subform, embedded in your form, displays the products owned by a company contact.

## INSIDE OUT Sizing a Subform Control

Sizing a subform that you display in Form view is quite simple. You might need to do this if you create the subform control directly on the form. Select the subform control, and then click Size To Fit in the Size group on the Arrange tab. In this case, you're using a subform in Continuous Forms view, so Access will size the subform control to the correct width and to the nearest vertical height to fully display rows in the Detail section. Note that if your subform default view is Datasheet view, using the Size To Fit button won't work unless the form's Design view is exactly the same size as the datasheet. You have to switch in and out of Form view and manually adjust the size of the subform control.

You must set a couple of key properties to finish this work. If you remember from Figure 13-6, the tblCompanyContacts table is related to the tblContactProducts table on both the CompanyID and the ContactID fields. When you view records in an outer form and you want Access to filter the rows in the subform to show only related information, you must make sure that Access knows the field(s) that link the two sets of data. With the subform control selected, open the Property Sheet window, and set the Link Child Fields and Link Master Fields properties as shown in Figure 13-16.

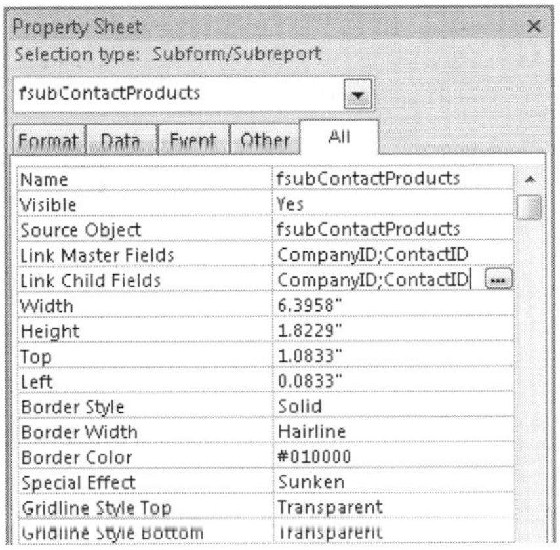

Property Sheet
Selection type: Subform/Subreport

fsubContactProducts

Format | Data | Event | Other | All

| Name | fsubContactProducts |
|---|---|
| Visible | Yes |
| Source Object | fsubContactProducts |
| Link Master Fields | CompanyID;ContactID |
| Link Child Fields | CompanyID;ContactID |
| Width | 6.3958" |
| Height | 1.8229" |
| Top | 1.0833" |
| Left | 0.0833" |
| Border Style | Solid |
| Border Width | Hairline |
| Border Color | #010000 |
| Special Effect | Sunken |
| Gridline Style Top | Transparent |
| Gridline Style Bottom | Transparent |

**Figure 13-16** Set the link field properties of the subform control to tell Access how the data in the outer form is related to the data in the inner form.

The Link Child Fields property refers to the "child" form—the one in the subform. You must enter the names of the fields in the record source of the form inside the subform that should be filtered based on what row you have displayed in the outer form, separated by semicolons. Likewise, the Link Master Fields property should contain the name(s) of the related field(s) on the outer form. In most cases, both properties will contain only one field name, but the names might not be the same. In this case, you know it takes two fields to correctly relate the rows. Switch to Form view, and your form should look like Figure 13-17. As you move from record to record in the outer form, Access uses the values it finds in the field(s) defined in Link Master Fields as a filter against the fields in the subform defined in Link Child Fields.

We don't know yet which contact owns these products because we haven't built the final outer form yet to display contact information. You should return to Design view and make some adjustments to the length of the CompanyName, Department, and Position text boxes. You should also set the form's Scroll Bars property to Neither and the Record Selectors property to No. You really don't want users adding and deleting records in this outer form, so set Allow Additions and Allow Deletions to No. Save your form as fsubCompanyContactProducts. (Note that if you made any changes to the form inside the subform control, Access will also ask you whether you want to save that form, too.) You can also find this form saved as fsubXmplCompanyContactProducts in the sample database.

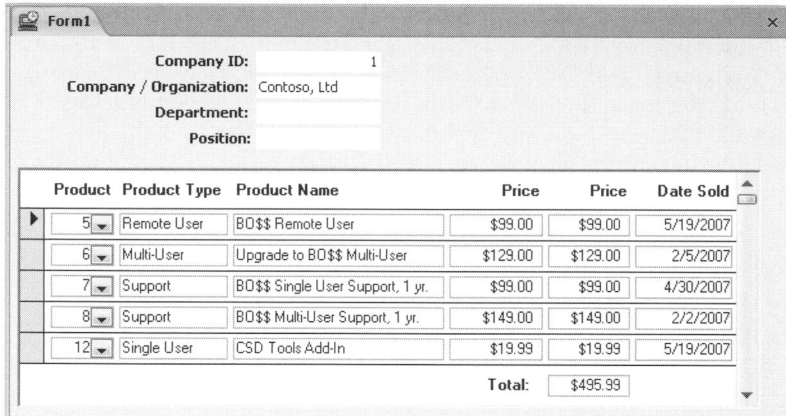


**Figure 13-17** You now have a form to display company contact information with a subform that displays the related products owned.

> INSIDE OUT **Access Might Create the Link for You**
>
> If the record source of the outer form is a single table, Access automatically sets the Link Master Fields and Link Child Fields properties for you when it can find a related field in the table or query that you define as the record source of the form within the subform control. It does this when you either drag the subform to the main form or set the Source Object property of the subform control.

## Specifying the Main Form Source

Now it's time to create the main form. You need a table or a query as the source of the form. You want to be able to view (and perhaps update) the contacts who own the products shown in the form and subform you've built thus far, so your row source should include the tblContacts table. You don't need any other related tables, but you might want to use a query so that you can sort the contacts by name.

Start a new query on the tblContacts table, and include all the fields in the design grid. Add criteria to sort in ascending order under LastName and FirstName. (You'll recall from Chapter 7, "Creating and Working with Simple Queries," that the sequence of fields in the design grid is important for sorting, so be sure that LastName is before FirstName in the query design grid.) Save your query as qryContactsSorted. Your query should look something like that shown in Figure 13-18. You can find this query saved as qxmplContactsSorted in the sample database.

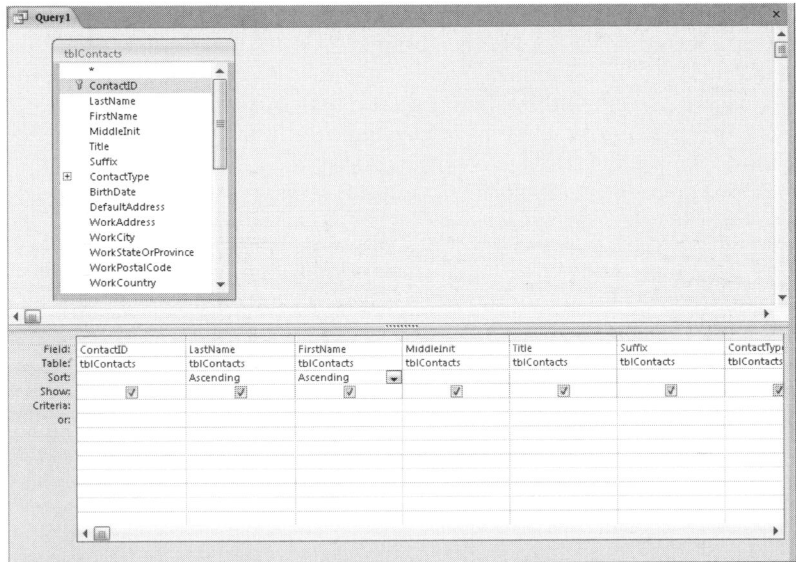

**Figure 13-18** This query sorts the contact records to be used in a form.

## Creating the Main Form

Building the form for the tblContacts table is fairly straightforward. In fact, you can use the Form Wizard to build the basic columnar format form from the query you just created. We recommend that you build this form from scratch as you did to build the form for company contacts because there are only a few fields you need to include, and you want to place them differently than the wizard would. To begin, click the Form Design button in the Forms group on the Create tab. Access opens a blank form grid in Design view. Open the Property Sheet window, and select in the Record Source property either the query you just built (qryContactsSorted) or the sample query we provided (qxmplContactsSorted).

As you did with the company contacts form, set some control defaults first. Click the Label button in the Controls group on the Design tab, and click the Bold button in the Font group to give all your labels a default bold font. Click the Text Box button, and change Label Align to Right and Label X (the offset of the label to the right) to **–0.05"**. If you have Use Windows-Themed Controls On Forms enabled, also make sure that Border Color is set to #010000 and Special Effect is set to Sunken—your new form should have inherited these values from the Normal form we have saved in the database. Click the Combo Box button, and make the same adjustments to the default Label Align, Label X, Border Color, and Special Effect properties.

Disable Use Control Wizards in the Controls group on the Design tab, open the Field List window, click the ContactType field, and with the combo box control still selected, drag and drop the field about 1 inch from the left margin near the top of the design area. One at a time, add the Title, LastName, and Suffix fields in a column under ContactType. In a row aligned with the LastName text box, drag and drop the

FirstName field to about 3 inches out and the MiddleInit field to about 5 inches out. (Access expands the width of the design area when you do this.) You can shrink the MiddleInit text box to about a half-inch wide. Click the ContactType control, and in the Property Sheet window change the Column Widths property to **1.25";0"**. By default Access set this control to display two columns, but you need to display only the first column. Now change the List Width property to **1.5"** to shorten the column display when you open the list in Form view, and change the Column Heads property to No.

The sample design shown in Figure 13-19 has a space at the bottom of the Detail section where you can place the subform to display company contact and product data. You can find this main form saved as frmXmplContacts1 in the sample database.

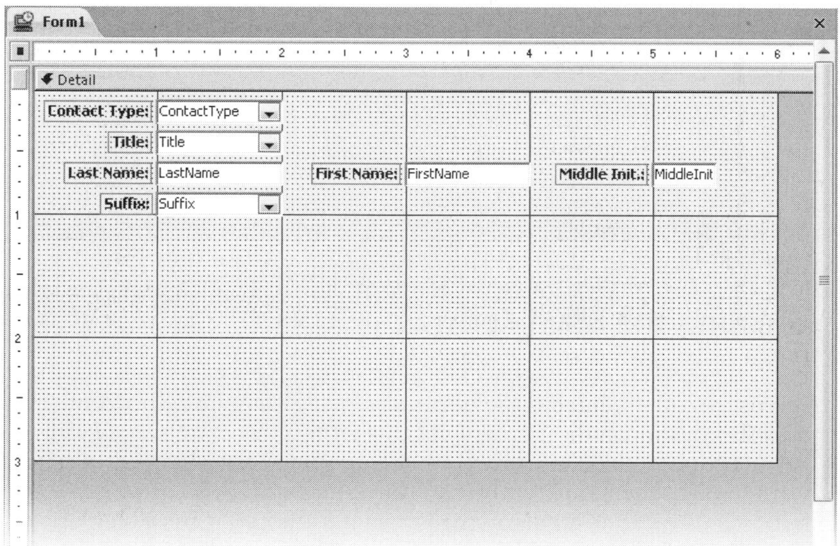


**Figure 13-19** This is the start of your main form with space for a subform.

Now you're ready to add the subform. This time, click the Subform/Subreport button in the Controls group on the Design tab (make sure the Use Control Wizards button is still turned off), and draw the control starting near the left edge under the Suffix combo box and extending to fill the blank area. Select the label control that came with the subform, and delete it. Select the subform control, open the Property Sheet window, and select the fsubCompanyContactProducts form you created earlier (or our sample fsubXmplCompanyContactProducts form) from the list in the Source Object property. Enter **ContactID** in the Link Child Fields and Link Master Fields properties. Finally, double-click one of the subform control sizing handles, or click the Size To Fit button in the Size group on the Arrange tab to properly size the subform control. Your result should look something like Figure 13-20. Save your form as frmContactsProducts. You can find this form saved as frmXmplContactsProducts in the sample database.

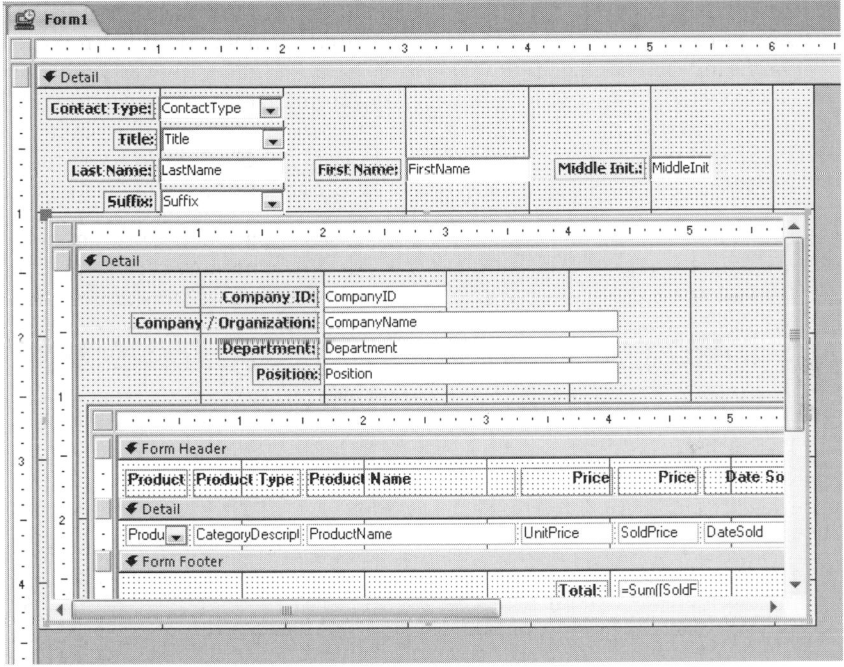


**Figure 13-20** The new subform is embedded in the form to edit contacts.

In this case, the ContactID field from tblContacts on the outer form is the link to the related rows on the subform. If you recall, the combination of CompanyID and ContactID forms the link between the forms on the second and third level.

## INSIDE OUT Editing the Form Inside a Subform Control

Access 2000 introduced a feature that allows you to directly edit your subform after you have defined it as the source for your subform control. As you can see in Figure 13-20, the design of the fsubCompanyContactProducts form is visible in the subform control on the outermost form. Likewise, the design of the fsubContactProducts form is visible inside that. You can click any control in the inner forms and change its size or adjust its properties using the property sheet or the contextual Ribbon tabs under Form Design Tools and Form Layout Tools. You might need to temporarily expand the size of the subform control in order to work with the inner form easily. However, you cannot click the Microsoft Office Button and then click Save As to save your changes to a different form definition. If you want to edit the form inside a subform control in its own window, right-click the subform control, and then click Subform In New Window.

Switch to Form View to see the completed form, as shown in Figure 13-21. Because you properly set the linking field information for the subform controls, you can see the companies for each contact and the products for each company and contact in the subforms as you move from one contact to another. Note that the inner set of navigation buttons is for the first subform. Use the scroll bar in the innermost subform to move through the product detail records. Also, because you locked the controls in the first subform (the company contact information), you cannot edit the controls you see there.

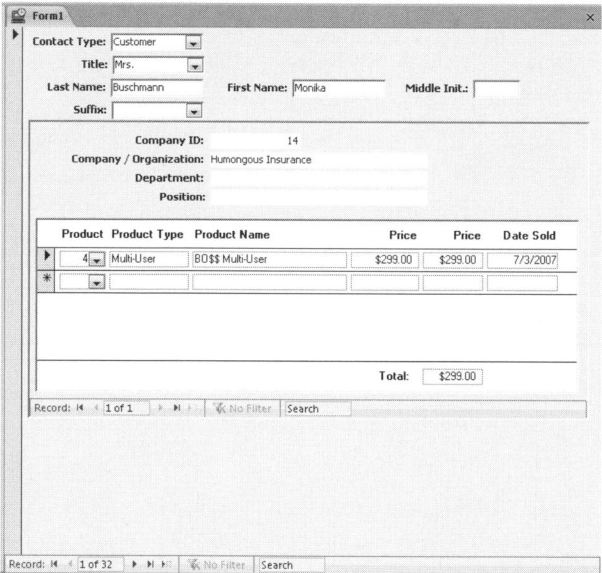


**Figure 13-21** You now have a form to edit contacts in a main form and products owned by the contact in subforms.

> **Note**
>
> If you look at the frmContacts form in the Conrad Systems Contacts application, you'll see a products subform on the Products tab that has no intervening company contacts subform. This form has some Visual Basic procedures that automatically supply the default company ID for the contact and disallow adding a product if the contact doesn't have a default company defined. You can see how this code works in Chapter 20, "Automating Your Application with Visual Basic."

## Creating a Subdatasheet Subform

In Chapter 7, you learned how to define a subdatasheet for a query. You can do the same thing with forms as long as the forms are saved to be displayed in Datasheet view. The best way to see how this works is to create modified versions of the three forms you just built.

Start by opening your fsubContactProducts form (or the sample fsubXmplContact-Products form) in Design view. Change the Default View property of the form to Datasheet, change the Allow Datasheet View property to Yes, and save the form as fsubContactProductsDS. (Click the Microsoft Office Button, click Save As, and then click Save Object As. Type the new object name, and then click OK.) Switch to Datasheet view, and your form now looks like Figure 13-22.

fsubContactProducts

| ProductID | CategoryDescription | ProductName | UnitPrice | DateSold |
|---|---|---|---|---|
| 1 | Single User | BO$$ Demo Edition, Single User | $0.00 | 5/6/ |
| 1 | Single User | BO$$ Demo Edition, Single User | $0.00 | 5/5/ |
| 1 | Single User | BO$$ Demo Edition, Single User | $0.00 | 3/26/ |
| 1 | Single User | BO$$ Demo Edition, Single User | $0.00 | 5/31/ |
| 1 | Single User | BO$$ Demo Edition, Single User | $0.00 | 3/17/ |
| 1 | Single User | BO$$ Demo Edition, Single User | $0.00 | 3/31/ |
| 2 | Multi-User | BO$$ Demo Edition, Multi-User | $0.00 | 4/28/ |
| 2 | Multi-User | BO$$ Demo Edition, Multi-User | $0.00 | 1/13/ |
| 2 | Multi-User | BO$$ Demo Edition, Multi-User | $0.00 | 6/30/ |
| 2 | Multi-User | BO$$ Demo Edition, Multi-User | $0.00 | 3/11/ |
| 2 | Multi-User | BO$$ Demo Edition, Multi-User | $0.00 | 6/26/ |
| 2 | Multi-User | BO$$ Demo Edition, Multi-User | $0.00 | 2/23/ |
| 2 | Multi-User | BO$$ Demo Edition, Multi-User | $0.00 | 5/29/ |
| 2 | Multi-User | BO$$ Demo Edition, Multi-User | $0.00 | 6/18/ |
| 3 | Single User | BO$$ Single User | $199.00 | 5/30/ |
| 3 | Single User | BO$$ Single User | $199.00 | 4/10/ |
| 3 | Single User | BO$$ Single User | $199.00 | 6/21/ |
| 3 | Single User | BO$$ Single User | $199.00 | 2/2/ |
| 3 | Single User | BO$$ Single User | $199.00 | 4/20/ |
| 3 | Single User | BO$$ Single User | $199.00 | 5/7/ |
| 3 | Single User | BO$$ Single User | $199.00 | 5/25/ |
| 3 | Single User | BO$$ Single User | $199.00 | 3/18/ |
| 4 | Multi-User | BO$$ Multi-User | $299.00 | 1/23/ |
| 4 | Multi-User | BO$$ Multi-User | $299.00 | 4/1/ |
| 4 | Multi-User | BO$$ Multi-User | $299.00 | 7/3/ |
| 4 | Multi-User | BO$$ Multi-User | $299.00 | 4/4/ |
| 4 | Multi-User | BO$$ Multi-User | $299.00 | 5/22/ |
| 4 | Multi-User | BO$$ Multi-User | $299.00 | 7/3/ |
| 5 | Remote User | BO$$ Remote User | $99.00 | 5/19/ |
| 5 | Remote User | BO$$ Remote User | $99.00 | 5/18/ |

**Figure 13-22** The contact products subform was changed to be displayed in Datasheet view.

Notice that several of the columns are much wider than they need to be. If you scroll down to the bottom, you don't see the subtotal that's in the form footer anymore. Also, because the labels for these fields are in the form header (see Figure 13-11) and not attached to their respective controls, you see the actual field names instead of the field captions. Let's not worry about the captions for now, but you should adjust the column widths to be more reasonable. You can do that by double-clicking the dividing line to the right of each column heading. This auto-sizes the columns to the widest data (or column caption) displayed. If the data you see isn't representative of the widest data you might store, you need to adjust the width by hand. You must save the form again to preserve this sizing, so click the Save button on the Quick Access Toolbar, and then close the form. You can find this form saved as fsubXmplContactProductsDS in the sample database.

Next, open your fsubCompanyContactProducts form (or the fsubXmplCompany-ContactProducts sample form) in Design view. Change the Default View property of the form to Datasheet. Click the subform control to select it, and change the Source Object property to point to the new datasheet subform you just saved—fsubContactProductsDS. Save the form as fsubCompanyContactProductsDS.

If you like, you can select the form again and change the Subdatasheet Height and Subdatasheet Expanded properties. Because both this form and the embedded subform are set to be displayed in Datasheet view, you can set these properties exactly as you would for a table or query. You can specify a specific height in inches that you want to reserve for the subdatasheet (the subform inside this form). If you leave the default value of 0", the subdatasheet opens to display all available rows when you click the plus sign on any row to expand the subdatasheet for that row. You can also change Subdatasheet Expanded to Yes to always expand all subdatasheets within the subform when you open the form (as though you clicked the plus sign on all displayed rows). For now, leave these properties as they are.

Switch to Datasheet view, and your form should look like Figure 13-23.

fsubCompanyContactProductsDS

| Company ID | Company / Organization | Department | Position |
|---|---|---|---|
| 1 | Contoso, Ltd | | |
| 1 | Contoso, Ltd | | |
| 1 | Contoso, Ltd | | |
| 2 | Fourth Coffee | | |
| 2 | Fourth Coffee | | |
| 3 | Coho Vineyard | | |
| 3 | Coho Vineyard | | |
| 3 | Coho Vineyard | | |
| 4 | Southridge Video | | |

| ProductID | CategoryDescription | ProductName | UnitPrice | DateSold | SoldPrice |
|---|---|---|---|---|---|
| 4 | Multi-User | BO$$ Multi-User | $299.00 | 4/1/2007 | $299.00 |
| 5 | Remote User | BO$$ Remote User | $99.00 | 4/15/2007 | $99.00 |
| 12 | Single User | CSD Tools Add-In | $19.99 | 4/19/2007 | $19.99 |
| 13 | Single User | CSD Tools Add-In Demo Edition | $0.00 | 3/15/2007 | $0.00 |

| Company ID | Company / Organization | Department | Position |
|---|---|---|---|
| 4 | Southridge Video | | |
| 4 | Southridge Video | | |
| 5 | Consolidated Messenger | | |
| 6 | Baldwin Museum of Science | | |
| 6 | Baldwin Museum of Science | | |
| 7 | Fabrikam, Inc. | | |
| 7 | Fabrikam, Inc. | | |
| 7 | Fabrikam, Inc. | | |
| 8 | Alpine Ski House | | |
| 9 | School of Fine Art | | |
| 9 | School of Fine Art | | |
| 10 | City Power & Light | | |
| 10 | City Power & Light | | |
| 11 | Blue Yonder Airlines | | |

Record: 1 of 32 No Filter Search

**Figure 13-23** Your form now displays company contact information in Datasheet view with a subdatasheet to display products.

Because the controls on this form have attached labels (see Figure 13-15), the captions from those labels appear as the column headings. Notice that the subdatasheet form has its columns sized as you saved them when you designed the subform. You can resize the columns in either display and save the form to save the new column width settings. Keep in mind that your user is also free to resize the column widths. However, because these are forms, you have more control over what the user can do than you have in a query. Try to type something in the Company / Organization or Department column. Because the controls in the underlying form are locked, you won't be able to update this information. Close this form now, and save it if you are prompted.

To finish putting this all together, you can now edit your frmContactsProducts form (or the frmXmplContactsProducts sample form) to use these new datasheet subforms. Open your form in Design view, click the subform control to select it, and change its Source Object property to fsubCompanyContactProductsDS. You also need to make the subform control about 7.75 inches wide because the subform in Datasheet view won't fit in the current window. However, you can also shorten the height of the subform control to about 1.5 inches.

Save your modified form as frmContactsProductsDS, and switch to Form view. Your form should now look like Figure 13-24.

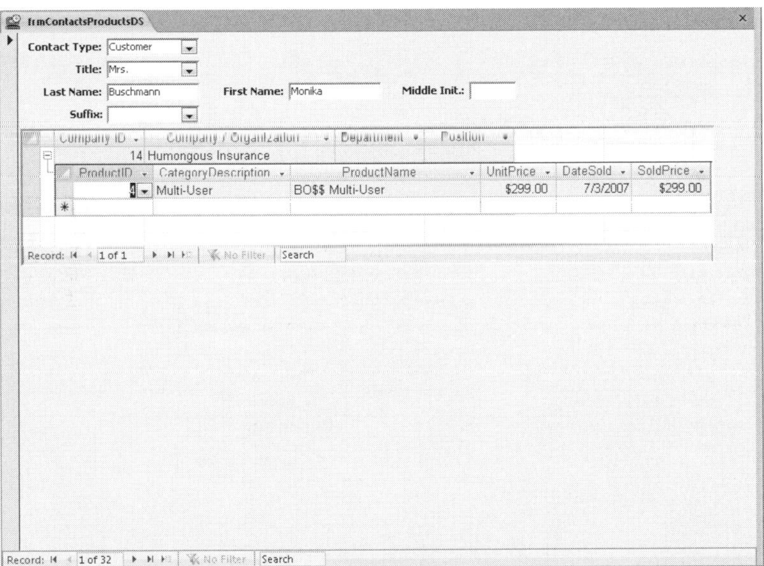


**Figure 13-24** Your modified form now allows you to edit contacts in a main form and products owned by the contact in subforms displayed in Datasheet view.

Remember that one of the shortcomings of designing your form this way is you have to make a "best guess" at the size of the subform window, and your users can modify the width of the columns in both datasheets as they wish. We personally don't like this design very much, but you might find it useful to conserve vertical space in a subform design when displaying complex data levels. You can find this form saved as frmXmplContactsProductsDS in the sample database.

# Displaying Values in an Option Group

Whenever you have a field that contains an integer code value, you need to provide some way for the user to set the value based on what your application knows the code means, not the number. You could certainly use a combo box or a list box to supply a descriptive list. However, when the number of different values is small, an option group might be the ideal solution.

In the Conrad Systems Contacts application, the tblContacts table contains both a home and a work address. The DefaultAddress field contains an integer code value that is used by some reports to generate a mailing address. When DefaultAddress is 1, the application uses the work address; and when DefaultAddress is 2, the home address is the default. However, a user isn't likely to always remember that 1 means work and 2 means home. You should provide a way to make these values obvious.

In the ContactsDataCopy.accdb sample file, you can find a form called frmXmplContacts that has the basic contact information and the two sets of addresses already laid out. Figure 13-25 shows you that form in Form view.

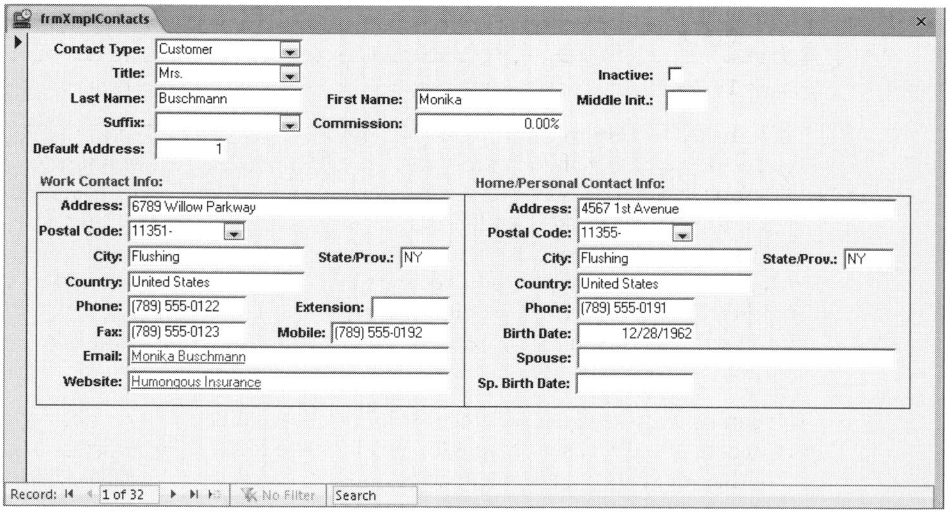

**Figure 13-25** You can use this form to edit contact name and address information.

You can see that the Default Address field could be confusing on this form. To fix this, switch to Design view, and delete the DefaultAddress text box control. Click the Option Group button in the Controls group on the Design tab to select it, and then open the field list and drag the Default Address field onto the form under the Suffix combo box control. (We set the defaults for the option group control on this form so that it should fit nicely under the Suffix control and be wide enough to add some buttons.)

Next, double-click the Option Button command in the Controls group on the Design tab to allow you to define multiple buttons without having to go back to the Controls group to click the button again. When you move your mouse pointer inside the option group control, you'll see the control become highlighted to indicate you're placing the button inside the control. Drag one toward the left end of the control (the label will appear to the right of the button) and a second one to the middle. Figure 13-26 shows what the form looks like as you add the second button.

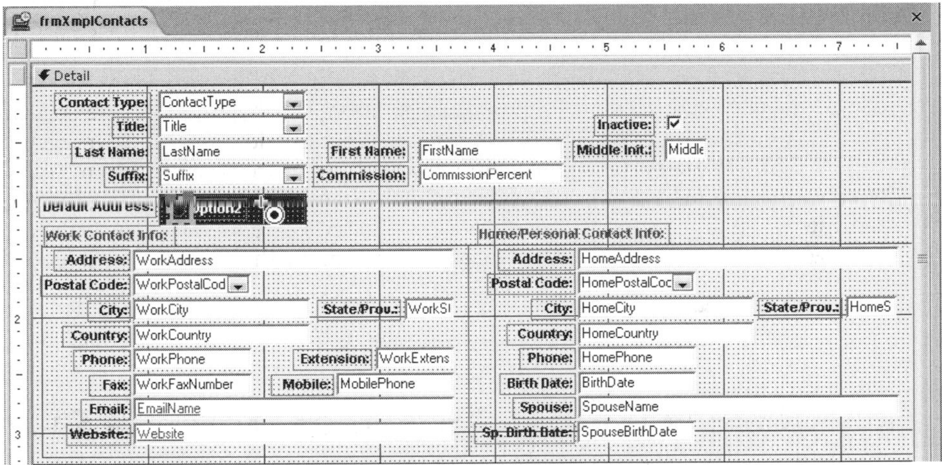


**Figure 13-26** Add two option button controls inside an option group control.

Click the Select button in the Controls group on the Design tab to turn off the Option Button tool. Click the first button, and open the Property Sheet window. Near the top of the list on the All tab, you can see that Access has set the Option Value property of this button to 1. If you click the other button, you'll find that its Option Value property is 2. Because the option group control is bound to the DefaultValue field, the first button will be highlighted when you're on a record that has a value of 1 (work address) in this field, and the second button will be highlighted when the value is 2. If you click a different button when editing a record, Access changes the value of the underlying field to the value of the button.

You can actually assign any integer value you like to each option button in a group, but Access has set these just fine for this field. Note that if you assign the same value to more than one button, they'll all appear selected when you're on a record that has that value.

To make the purpose of these buttons perfectly clear, you need to fix the attached labels. Click the label for the first button, and change the Caption property from Option2 to **Work**. Set the Caption property for the label attached to the second button to **Home**. Switch to Form view to see the results as shown in Figure 13-27. Save this form as frmContacts2. You can also find this form saved as frmXmplContacts2 in the sample database.

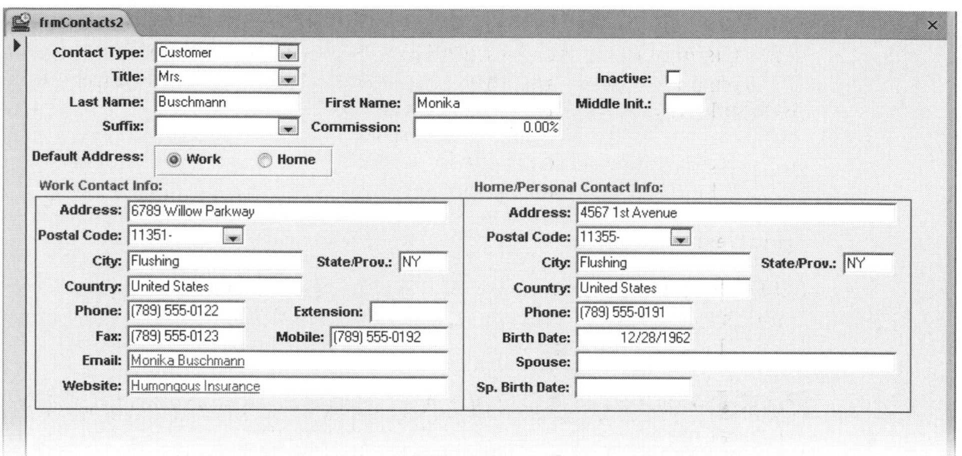


**Figure 13-27** You can use an option group to set the default address for the contacts.

# Using Conditional Formatting

Access 2007 includes a feature that allows you to define dynamic modification of the formatting of text boxes and combo boxes. You can define an expression that tests the value in the text box or combo box or any other field available in the form. If the expression is true, Access will modify the Bold, Italic, Underline, Back Color, Fore Color, and Enabled properties for you based on the custom settings you associate with the expression.

This feature can be particularly useful for controlling field display in a subform in Continuous Forms view. For example, you might want to highlight the ProductName field in the innermost subform shown in Figure 13-21 when the product is a trial version. Or, you might want to change the font of the address fields in the form shown in Figure 13-27 depending on the value of the DefaultAddress field.

For the first example, you can use the fsubCompanyContactProducts subform that you built earlier (or the fsubXmplCompanyContactProducts sample form you'll find in the sample database). To define conditional formatting, first open the form you need to modify in Design view. Click the subform control, and then click the ProductName field within the subform to select it. On the Design tab, in the Font group, click the Conditional button to see the Conditional Formatting dialog box.

In the Default Formatting box, you can see the currently defined format for the control. You can use the Bold, Italic, Underline, Fill/Back Color, Font/Fore Color, and Enabled buttons to modify the default. When you first open this dialog box, Access displays a single blank Condition 1. In the leftmost list, you can choose Field Value Is to test for a value in the field, Expression Is to create a logical expression that can test other fields on the form or compare another field with this one, and Field Has Focus to define settings the control will inherit when the user clicks in the control.

When you choose Field Value Is, the dialog box displays a second list with logical comparison options such as Less Than, Equal To, or Greater Than. Choose the logical comparison you want, and then enter the value or values to compare the field with in the text boxes on the right.

In this case, you want to set the format of ProductName based on the value of the Trial-Version field. So, choose Expression Is, and in the expression box enter the following:

```
[TrialVersion]=True
```

Set the formatting properties you want the control to have if the test is true by using the buttons to the right. In this case, set the Fill/Back Color to a bright yellow as shown in Figure 13-28, and click OK.

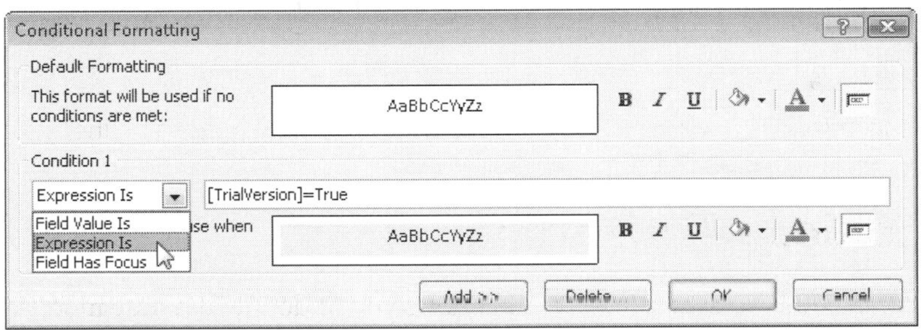


**Figure 13-28** Define conditional formatting for the ProductName field using the Conditional Formatting dialog box.

Switch to Form view to see the result as shown in Figure 13-29, and move to the third company record. You can find the sample saved as fsubXmplCompanyContactProducts2 and the inner subform saved as fsubXmplContactProducts2.

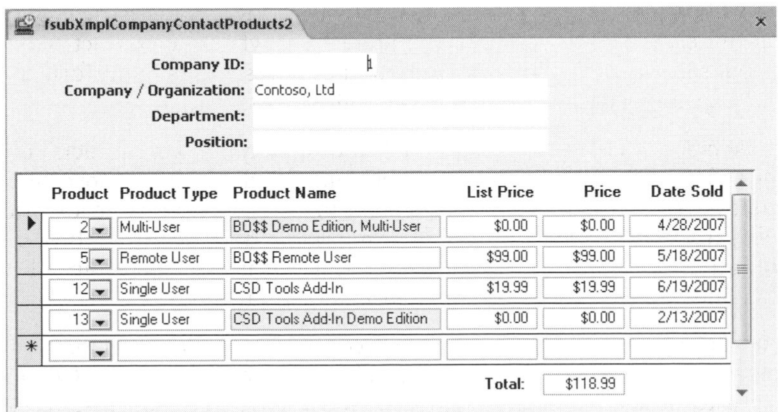


**Figure 13-29** You can now see the effect of defining conditional formatting for the ProductName field.

You can make a similar change to frmContacts2 that you saved earlier, or you can use the sample frmXmplContacts2 form. Open that form in Design view, click the WorkAddress text box control to select it, and hold down the Shift key as you click the WorkPostalCode, WorkCity, and WorkStateOrProvince controls to add them to the selection. (Yes, you can set conditional formatting for multiple controls at one time.) Click the Conditional button in the Font group on the Design tab to see the Conditional Formatting dialog box.

Choose Expression Is in the leftmost list, and enter **[DefaultAddress]=1** in the Condition field to test whether the default is the work address. Underline and highlight the text as shown in Figure 13-30, and click OK to close the dialog box and set the conditional formatting for the controls you selected.

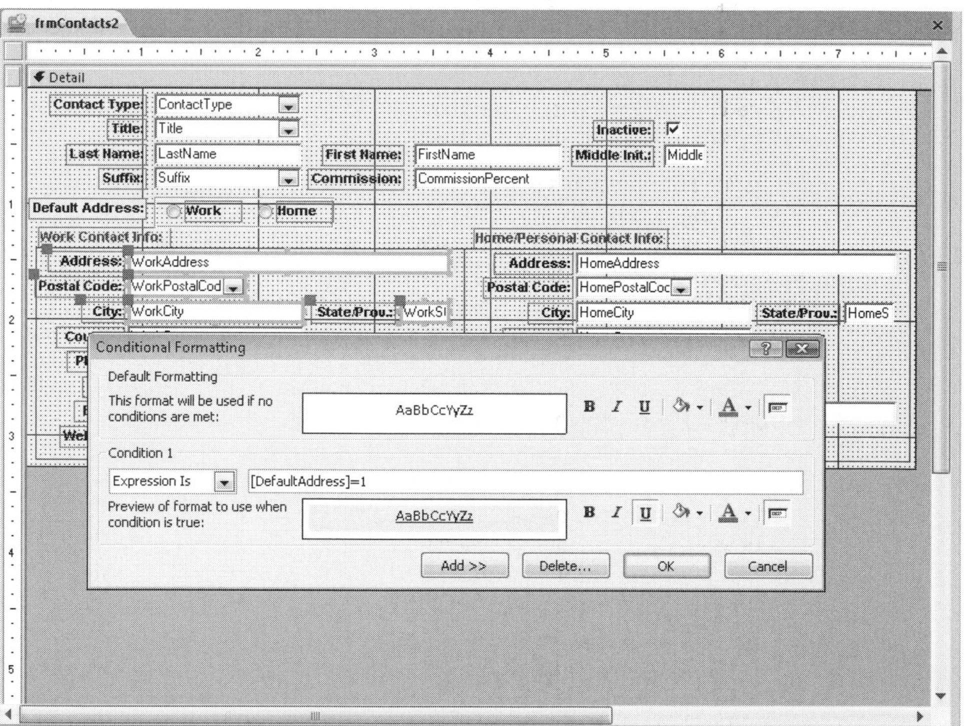


**Figure 13-30** You can also define conditional formatting for a group of controls.

Click the HomeAddress text box, and hold down the Shift key as you click Home-PostalCode, HomeCity, and HomeStateOrProvince to add them to the selection. Click the Conditional button in the Font group again, choose Expression Is in the leftmost list, enter **[DefaultAddress]=2** in the Condition field, and underline and highlight the text. Click OK to save the change, and save your form as frmContacts3. Switch to Form view to see the result as shown in Figure 13-31. All the records in the database have work address as the default, so try changing the Default Address option in one of the records to Home, and you should see the highlight move to the home address fields. You can also find this form saved as frmXmplContacts3 in the sample database.

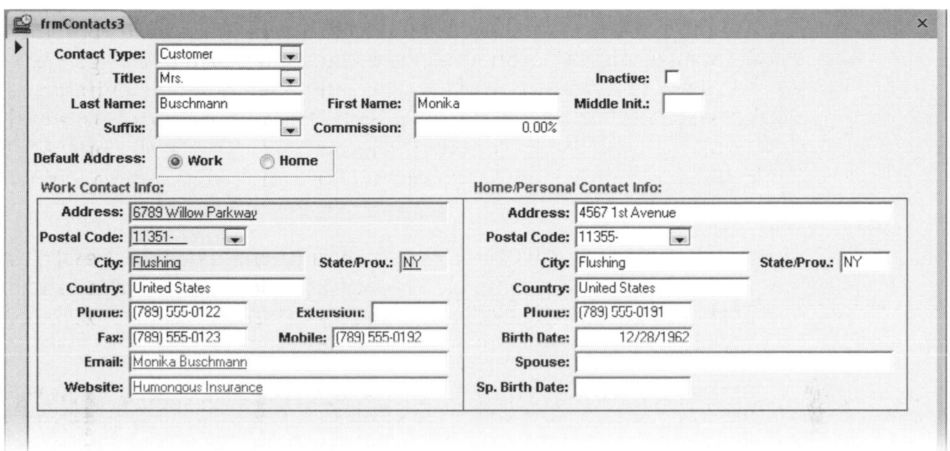


**Figure 13-31** The default address fields are highlighted and underlined in the contacts form based on the value of the DefaultAddress field.

To define additional tests, click the Add button at the bottom of the Conditional Formatting dialog box. Each time you click this button, Access displays an additional Condition definition row. In the second and subsequent rows, you can choose from Field Value Is or Expression Is in the leftmost list. (You can check for focus only in the first test.) For example, you might want to set the background of the product name to one color if it's a trial version and use another color for products priced greater than $200.

# Working with the Tab Control

As you have just seen, a subform is an excellent way to create a form that lets you edit information from the *one* side of a relationship in the main form (contacts) while editing or viewing data from the *many* side of a relationship (contact events or contact products) in the subform window. Building a subform is very simple for a single one-to-many relationship. But what can you do when you have either multiple relationships or lots of data you need to deal with on a form and including all this information makes your form too large to fit on your screen? Access provides a tab control that lets you place multiple controls on individual tabs within a form. The controls on a tab can be as complex as subforms (in the case of the Conrad Systems Contacts database, to display related companies, events, and products) or as simple as text boxes (which can display the potentially lengthy information in the Notes field). You can see the frmContactsPlain form (the simple copy of the form that doesn't have all the bells and whistles of the production form) with the tab that shows contact events selected in Figure 13-32. You can select the other available tabs to see the detail information for the contact—the companies associated with the contact (in a subform on that tab) and the products the contact has purchased (in another subform).

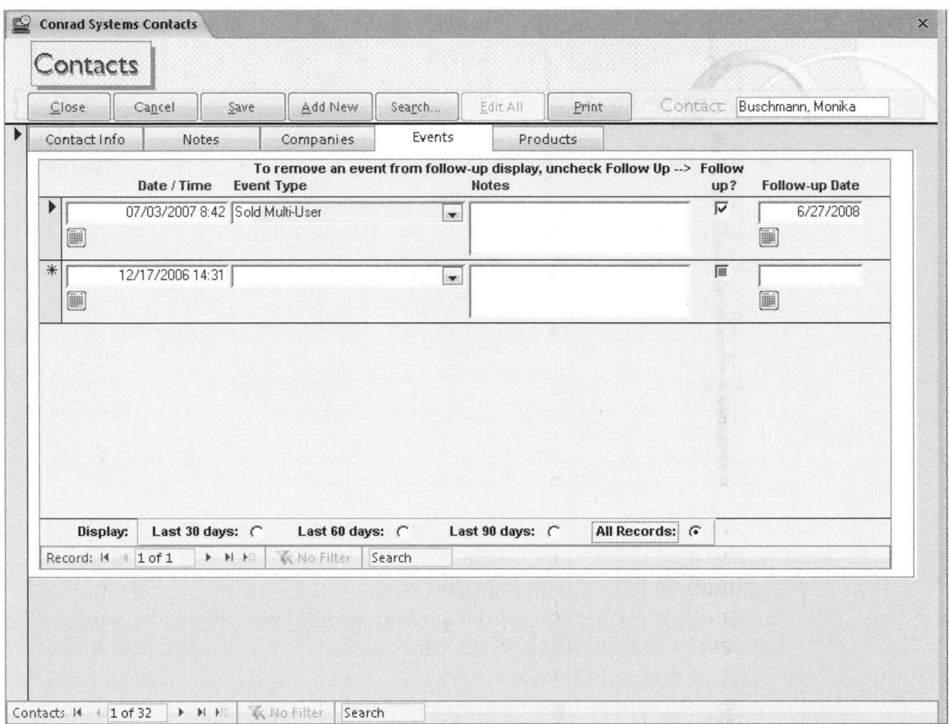


Figure 13-32 The tab control allows you to place multiple subforms and controls on a tab page, such as this tab to edit contact events.

Working with the tab control is quite simple. If you like, you can start with a simple columnar form built by the Form Wizard. Use qxmplContactsSorted as the record source, and include the ContactType, Title, LastName, FirstName, MiddleInit, and Suffix fields. Switch to Design view, and create some space at the bottom of the form to add your tab control. You can also start with frmXmplContacts1, which you can find in the ContactsDataCopy.accdb sample database. To build a control that lets you alternately see company, contact event, or liner notes information for the current contact, perform the following steps:

1. On the Design tab, in the Controls group, click the Tab Control button, and drag an area on the form starting on the left side just under the Suffix combo box control and approximately 6.25 inches wide and 2 inches high. Access shows you a basic tab control with two tabs defined. Open the Property Sheet window, and set the Tab Fixed Width property to **1"** so that all the tabs will be the same size and wide enough to add captions later.

2. While the tab control has the focus, click the Insert Page button in the Controls group on the Design tab, as shown next. Access will add a third tab to the control.

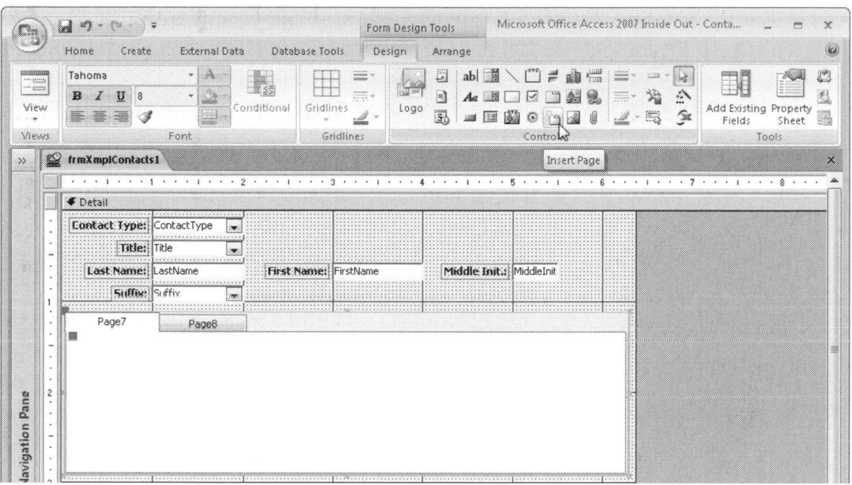


3. Access always inserts new tabs at the end of the tab sequence. If you want to place the new tab in the middle of the tab order, you can select the tab and set its Page Index property. The Page Index of the first tab is 0, the second is 1, and so on. Another way to set the tab sequence is to right-click the control and then click Page Order to see the dialog box shown next. Select a tab, and move it up or down to get the sequence you want.

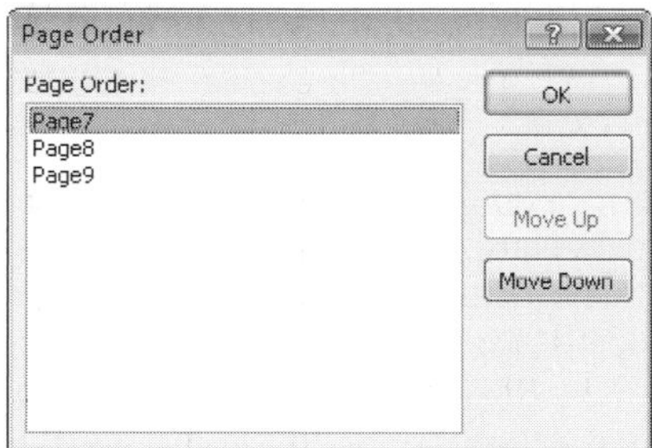


4. Click the first tab, open the Property Sheet window (if it's not already open), and set the Caption property to Companies.

5. Click the second tab, and set the Caption property to Events.

6. Click the third tab, and set the Caption property to Notes.

7. Click the Companies tab to bring it to the front. Click the Subform/Subreport button in the Controls group, and set the Auto Label property in the Property Sheet window to No. Add a subform control to the Companies tab, set its Source Object property to fsubXmplContactCompanies (the sample database contains built-in subforms to make this exercise easy), and set the Link Child Fields and Link Master Fields properties to ContactID. You can also drag the subform from the Navigation Pane and drop it onto the tab if you like.

8. Click the Events tab, and add the fsubXmplContactEvents form to that tab as a subform. Be sure to set the link properties of the subform control to ContactID.

9. Click the Notes tab to bring it to the front. Open the field list, drag the Notes field onto this tab, and remove the attached label. Expand the Notes text box control to almost fill the tab.

10. Adjust the positioning and size of the controls on each tab. Place each control very near the upper-left corner of each tab. The actual Top and Left settings will vary depending on where you placed the tab control. (These settings are relative to the Detail section of the form, not the tab control.) You can place one where you want it and then copy the Top and Left settings to the other two controls so that they exactly line up. It's important to do this so that the controls don't appear to jump around on the tab control as you move from tab to tab. Select each control, and then click the Size To Fit button in the Control Alignment group on the Arrange tab.

Your result should look something like Figure 13-33. You can find this form saved as frmXmplContacts4 in the sample database.

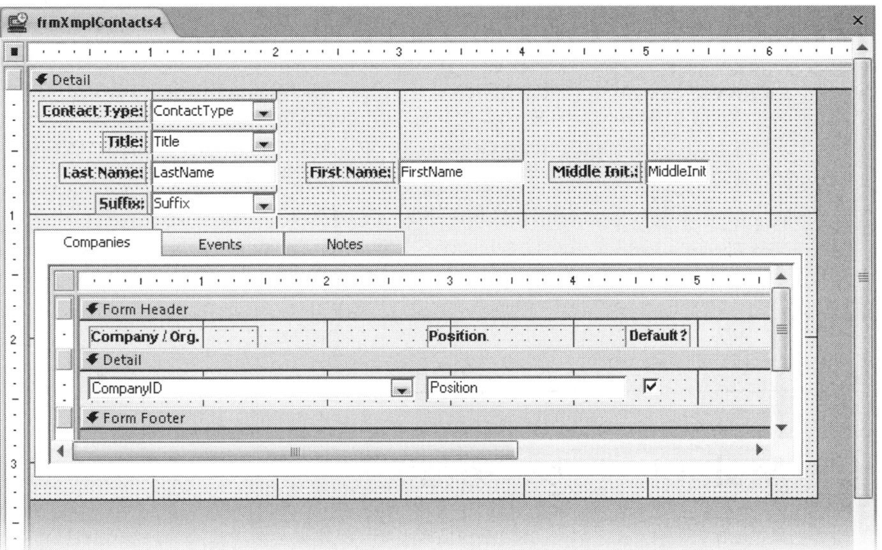


**Figure 13-33** Your completed tab control in Design view shows three tabs with various controls.

Note that clicking each tab in Design view reveals the controls you stored on that tab. Switch to Form view to see the form in action. Table 13-1 lists other useful tab control property settings.

**Table 13-1 Useful Tab Control Formatting Properties**

| Property | Settings | Usage |
|---|---|---|
| Multi Row | No (default) | If the control has more tabs than will fit in a single row, the control displays horizontal scroll arrows in the upper-right corner of the tab control to move through all the tabs. |
| | Yes | If the control has more tabs than will fit in a single row, the control displays multiple rows of tabs. |
| Style | Tabs (default) | The control displays tabs to select the various pages. |
| | Buttons | The control displays buttons (which look like command buttons but work like the buttons in an option group) to select the various pages. |
| | None | The control displays neither tabs nor buttons. Different pages can be displayed from a Visual Basic procedure or a macro by setting relative tab numbers in the tab control's Value property. |
| Tab Fixed Height | 0 (default) | The tab height is based on the font properties of the tab control or the size of the bitmap you define as a picture to be displayed on the tab. |
| | [size in inches] | The tab height is fixed at the value entered. |
| Tab Fixed Width | 0 (default) | The tab width is based on the font properties of the tab control and on the number of characters in the caption or the size of the picture on the tab. |
| | [size in inches] | The tab width is fixed at the value entered. |

# Creating Multiple-Page Forms

As you've seen, Access 2007 makes it easy to display a lot of related information about one subject in a single form, either by using a query as the source of the form or by displaying the related information in a subform. As described in the previous section, if you have too much information to fit in a single, screen-sized form, you can use the tab control. Another way to handle the problem is to split the form into multiple pages.

In Chapter 2, "Exploring the New Look of Access 2007," you learned about the Document Window Options settings in the Access Options dialog box. In previous versions of Access, all objects opened in their own windows where you could edit, view, or print them. This multiple-document interface made multiple-page forms a good method of displaying a lot of information on one form. The ContactsDataCopy.accdb sample database you have been using uses the single-document interface, which shows all open objects in a series of tabs along the top of the object window to the right of the Navigation Pane. Unless you know in advance the height of the Access workspace, it's difficult to design a multiple-page form that works smoothly in the single-document interface. To see how a multiple-page form works in the multiple-document interface, you should close the ContactsDataCopy.accdb database and open the Contacts.accdb database that uses the multiple-document interface.

You can create a form that's up to 22 logical inches high. If you're working on a basic 1024-by-768-pixel screen, you cannot see more than about 5.6 logical inches vertically at one time (if the Ribbon is displayed). If the information you need to make available in the form won't fit in that height, you can split the form into multiple pages by using a page break control. When you view the form, you can use the Page Up and Page Down keys to move easily through the pages.

Creating a smoothly working multiple-page form takes some planning. First, you should plan to make all pages the same height. If the pages aren't all the same size, you'll get choppy movement using the Page Up and Page Down keys. Second, you should design the form so that the page break control is in a horizontal area by itself. If the page break control overlaps other controls, your data might be displayed across the page boundary. You also need to be aware that when you set the form's Auto Resize property to Yes, Access sizes the form to the tallest page.

The frmXmplContactsPagesChap13 form in the Contacts.accdb database is a good example of a multiple-page form. If you open the form in Design view, open the Property Sheet window, and select the Detail section of the form, you can see that the height of this area is exactly 5.8 inches. If you click the page break control, shown at the left edge of the Detail section in Figure 13-34, you'll find that it's set at 2.9 inches from the top of the page. Because this is exactly half the height of the Detail section, the page break control splits the section into two equally sized pages.

When you look at this form in Form view (as shown in Figures 13-35 and 13-36) and use the Page Up and Page Down keys, you'll see that the form moves smoothly from page to page. If you switched from Design view to Form view, you must first click the Size To Fit Form button in the Window group on the Home tab to see the form page up and down correctly. When you open this form from the Navigation Pane, it sizes correctly because the form has its Auto Resize property set to Yes.

If you're in a control on the second page of the form and you press Page Down again, you'll move smoothly to the second page of the next record. Note that certain key information (such as the contact name) is duplicated on the second page so that it's always clear which record you're editing. If you look at the second page of the form in Design view, you'll find a locked text box control at the top of the second page that displays the contact name again.

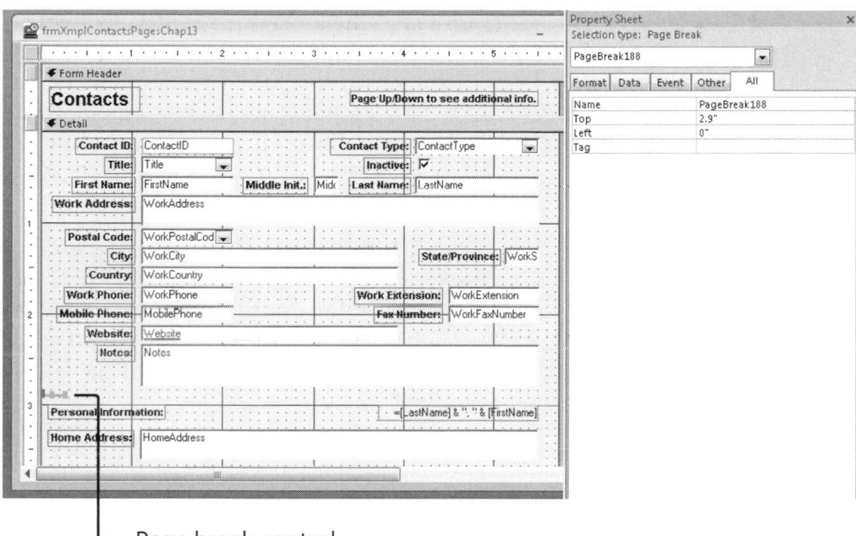


**Figure 13-34** The frmXmplContactsPages form includes a page break control that splits the Detail section exactly in half.

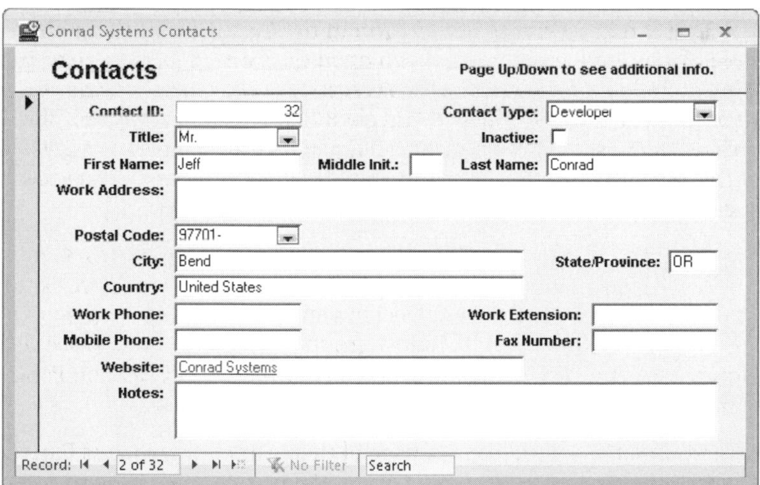


**Figure 13-35** This is the first page of the frmXmplContactsPages form.

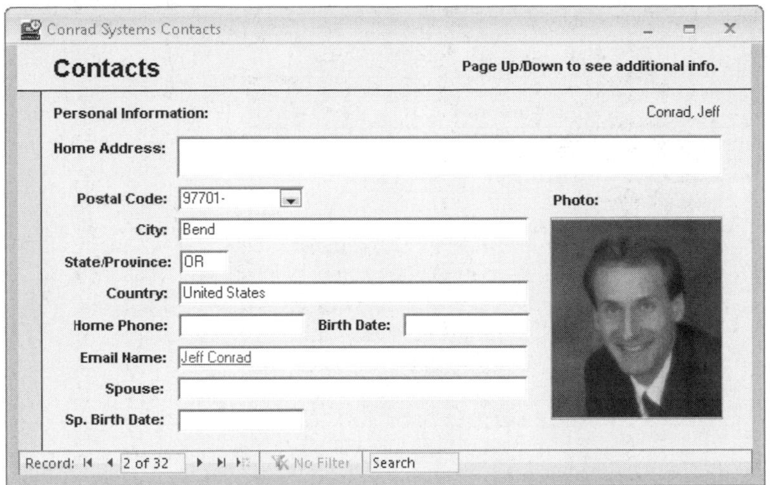


**Figure 13-36** When you press Page Down, you can see the second page of the frmXmplContactsPages form.

A key form property that makes multiple-page forms work is the Cycle property. On this sample form, the Cycle property is set to Current Page. As you learned in Table 12-11 on page 676, other options are All Records (the default) and Current Record. If you don't set the Cycle property to Current Page, you must place the first and last controls on a page that can receive the focus exactly on the page boundary. If you don't do this, you'll find that the form scrolls partially down into the subsequent page as you tab from the last control on one page to the first control on the next page. Because it's not likely that you'll design your form with controls exactly aligned on the page boundary, you must use some special techniques to properly align form pages if you want to allow tabbing between pages or records. See "Controlling Tabbing on a Multiple-Page Form" on page 1080 for details. You can now close the Contacts.accdb database.

# Introducing ActiveX Controls—The Calendar Control

Although Access 2007 certainly provides a useful collection of controls to help you design your forms, for some tasks you might need something more complex. Access supports many ActiveX controls that provide functionality beyond the basic set you can find in the Controls group. An *ActiveX* control is a small program that supports the ActiveX interface to allow Access to see the control's properties and build a window to display the control's user interface.

The 2007 Microsoft Office system installs dozens of ActiveX controls on your computer. It uses many of these in other applications such as Microsoft Office Outlook 2007 or Microsoft Office Excel 2007. Access 2007 makes some of these controls available directly in the Controls group through the Insert ActiveX Control button, such as Office PivotTable, Office Chart, and Office Spreadsheet. These controls are available for forms you design, but they're not intended for that purpose. Controls that you can effectively use in your Access forms include the Calendar control (which presents a calendar to make it easy to select a date value), the ListView control (which allows you to navigate data in a tree structure), the ProgressBar control (which allows you to graphically display progress of a complex task, but you must write code to update the bar), and the Slider control (with which a user can set a value by moving a slider).

The Conrad Systems Contacts application contains many date/time fields, so the Calendar control might be ideal to provide a graphical way to set a date value. In the ContactsDataCopy.accdb sample database, open frmXmplContactEvents as shown in Figure 13-37. This is a simple form to directly edit records from the tblContactEvents table. In this table, the ContactDateTime field includes both a date and a time, but the ContactFollowUpDate field has a date value only. The Calendar ActiveX control, which provides a date value only, might be ideal to use to set this value.

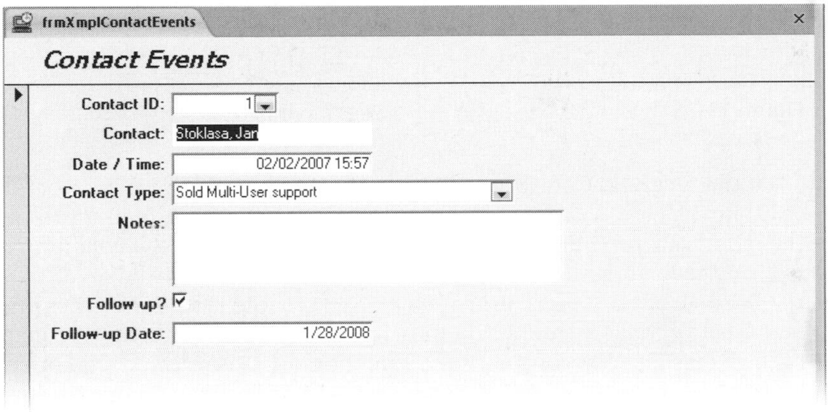

frmXmplContactEvents

Contact Events

Contact ID: 1
Contact: Stoklasa, Jan
Date / Time: 02/02/2007 15:57
Contact Type: Sold Multi-User support
Notes:
Follow up? ☑
Follow-up Date: 1/28/2008

**Figure 13-37** You can use this basic form to edit contact events using standard controls.

> **Note**
>
> Access 2007 provides a new feature called the Date Picker that you can activate for text box controls. If you set the Show Date Picker property of a text box control to For Dates, Access displays a small calendar icon next to the text box when it contains a date/time value and the text box has the focus. You can try it out on the frmXmplContactEvents form by clicking in the Follow-Up Date field and then clicking the icon that appears to the right of the text box.

Switch to the Design view of this form, delete the ContactFollowUpDate text box control, and expand the Detail section downward about 2 inches to give yourself some room to work. Click the ActiveX Controls button in the Controls group on the Design tab to open the Insert ActiveX Control dialog box that lists all the registered ActiveX controls on your computer as shown in Figure 13-38. You can use the scroll bar on the right side to move up or down the list.

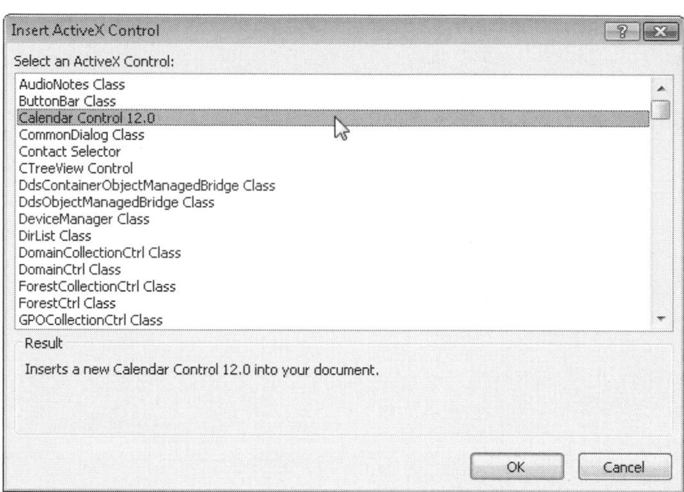


**Figure 13-38** The Insert ActiveX Control dialog box displays all ActiveX controls that are registered on your computer.

Click the Calendar Control 12.0 item in the list to select that control, and then click OK. The dialog box closes, and Access places the new control in the upper-left corner of the Detail section. Click the control and drag it just under the FollowUp check box control, and then align the Calendar control with the other text boxes. (Tip: If you select the FollowUp check box control before inserting the calendar, Access places the calendar below that control.) If you want, resize the Calendar control to match the width of the Notes text box control. Make sure the control is selected, and open the Property Sheet window. Most ActiveX controls have custom properties that Access recognizes and shows in the Property Sheet window. Most controls also display these custom properties in their own dialog boxes. Click the Other tab in the Property Sheet window to see the list of custom properties available for this control. You can click the Custom property and then click the Build button next to the property box to open the Calendar Properties dialog box, as shown in Figure 13-39. (You can't actually type anything in the Custom property box–it's simply a way that Access provides to allow you to easily open the control's Custom Properties dialog box.) Another way to open the Custom Properties dialog box for the Calendar ActiveX control is to right-click the control, click Calendar Object, and click Properties on the submenu.

You're going to set this control bound to the ContactFollowUpDate field, so you don't need to worry about setting the Month, Day, or Year properties of the control. You might set these values if you wanted to use the control to provide a date value for some other purpose. As you can see, you also have options to include the month and year title, include selectors for the month and year, list the days of the week across the top, and show or hide horizontal and vertical grids. Click OK to close the Calendar Properties dialog box.

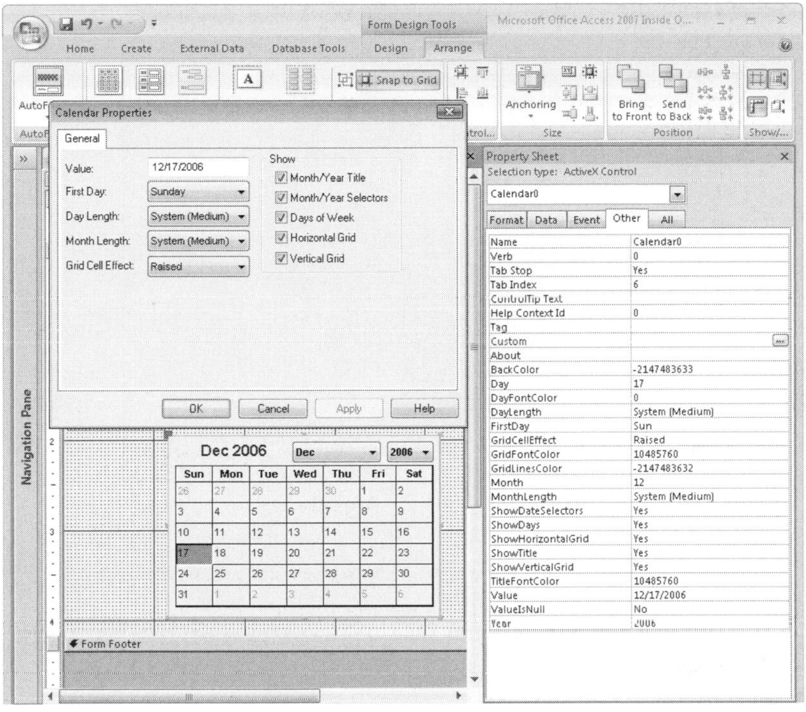

**Figure 13-39** You can set custom properties for the Calendar ActiveX control in the Property Sheet window and in the control's Custom Properties dialog box.

This control might look better with some additional contrast, so click the BackColor property and click the Build button to open the Color Picker to set the color. (If you know the color code you want, you can also enter it directly in the property.) Choose Light Gray 2 under Standard Colors (a value of #C0C0C0 or 12632256 decimal). Click the All tab in the Property Sheet window, and set the Control Source property near the top of the list to the ContactFollowUpDate field. Now add a label to the form grid for the calendar, set its caption to **Follow-Up Date:**, and then align it with the other labels and with the top of the Calendar control. Switch to Form view, and your form should now look like Figure 13-40. Notice that when you move through the records, the calendar changes to display the value stored in the record. You can change the calendar date by clicking one of the date boxes to update the field. You can find this form saved as frmXmplContactEventsCalendar in the sample database.

> **Note**
>
> The initial release of Access 2007 has a bug that prevents the Build button from being displayed on any properties that affect color. As a result, you cannot open the Custom Properties dialog box for these properties, and you can't pick a color from the Color Palette window. To match our example, enter the decimal value **12632256** in the BackColor property.

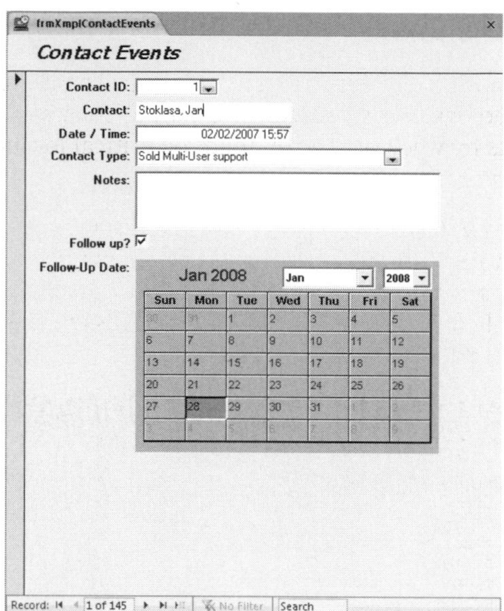


**Figure 13-40** You can see the ActiveX Calendar control in action.

In Chapter 24, "The Finishing Touches," you'll learn how to execute the methods of the ActiveX Calendar control to command it to move to a different year, month, or day.

# Working with PivotChart Forms

Even when the main purpose of your application is to enter, store, and organize data to support an active business function, you probably want to add features that allow management to analyze the business processes. PivotTables and PivotCharts are ideal for this purpose. In Chapter 8, you learned how to create the PivotTable and PivotChart views of a query. Designing the PivotTable or PivotChart view of a form is exactly the same with some interesting twists:

- You can use any query or table as the record source of the form, but only fields bound to controls on the form are available to design the PivotTable or PivotChart.
- You can set form properties to control what users can modify in the PivotTable or PivotChart view, including locking the form so they can't modify what you designed at all.
- Because a form has event properties, you can control what the user can modify by writing a Visual Basic procedure to respond to the event.
- You can embed a form designed in PivotTable or PivotChart view as the subform of another form and set the Link Child Fields and Link Master Fields properties to filter the table or chart to display information relevant to the record on the outer form.

## Building a PivotChart Form

In the Housing Reservations application, you might want to track room revenue by month or quarter. In the Conrad Systems Contacts application, charting product sales or the number of contact events by week or month might be critical for judging how effectively the business is running.

In most cases, you should start by designing a query that fetches the fields you want to display in your PivotTable or PivotChart. In the Conrad Systems Contacts application, you might want to display product sales data by product or by company. The ContactsDataCopy.accdb sample file has a query that gathers this information, qryXmplProductSalesForChart, as shown in Figure 13-41.

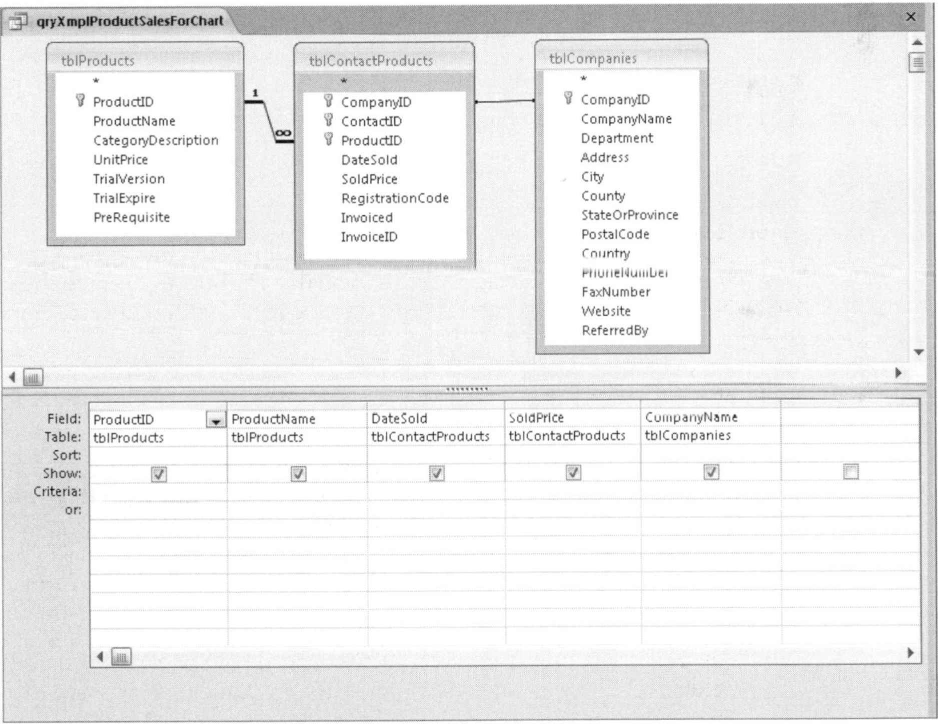


**Figure 13-41** This sample query selects product sales data by product or by company.

Open the ContactsDataCopy.accdb sample database, select the qryXmplProductSalesForChart query in the Navigation Pane, and click the PivotChart button in the Forms group on the Create tab. Now you can begin to design a chart to show sales by product by month in PivotChart view. From the chart's field list (click the Field List button in the Show/Hide group on the Design tab if you don't see this window), drag and drop ProductName onto the Drop Series Fields Here area. Drag and drop SoldPrice onto the Drop Data Fields Here area—the chart automatically calculates a sum for you. Open the Date Sold By Month list, drag and drop Months onto the Drop Category Fields Here area, and then close the field list.

Click the Axis title on the left, and then click the Property Sheet button in the Tools group. Click the Format tab, and enter **Total Sales** in the Caption property box. Click the General tab, and select Category Axis 1 Title in the Select list. Click the Format tab again, and change the Caption property to **Months**. Return to the General tab, and select Chart Workspace in the Select list. Click the Add Legend button in the Add area to create a legend on the right side of the chart. Click the Show/Hide tab, clear all the check boxes in the Let Users View section, and clear the Field Buttons / Drop Zones and Field List check boxes to remove them from the chart. Your chart should now look like Figure 13-42.

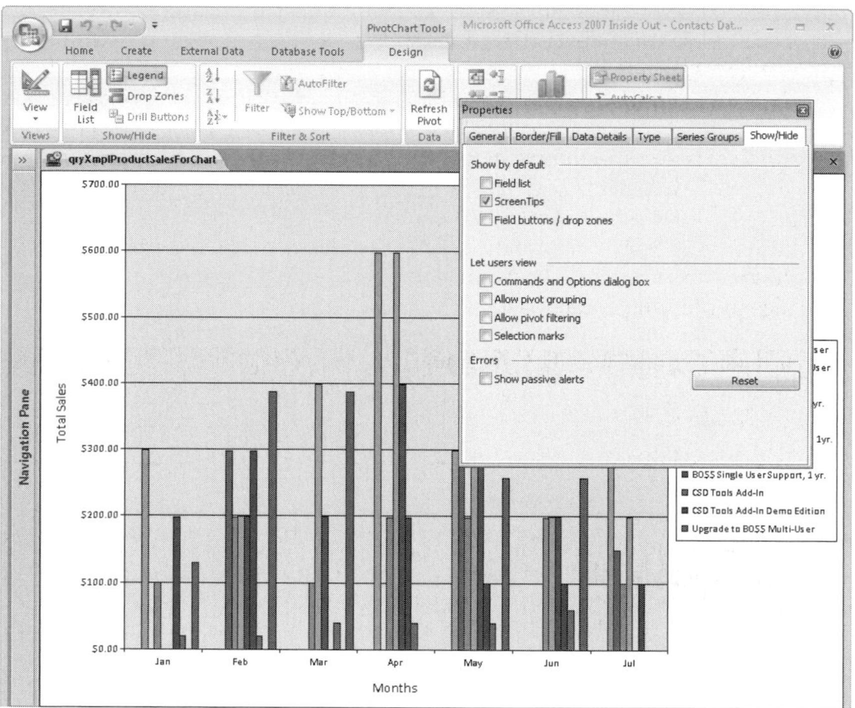


**Figure 13-42** The chart you're building displays product sales by product and month.

Switch to Design view, and set Allow Edits, Allow Deletions, and Allow Additions all to No. Finally, change the Shortcut Menu property to No to keep the user from getting into the chart property settings that way. (You can see how much more control you have over what the user can do in a form.) Save the form as chtProductSalesByProduct. You can also find this form saved as chtXmplProductSales in the sample database.

## Embedding a Linked PivotChart

To demonstrate how you can link the chart you just built into a form that displays product information, you can start with frmXmplProducts3 from Chapter 11, "Building a Form." Open that form in Design view. Widen the design area to about 7.5 inches, and expand the Detail section's height to about 4.25 inches to give you a space to place the chart. Drag and drop the form you just created from the Navigation Pane onto the blank area of the form, and select and delete the attached label.

Notice that Access automatically sizes the subform control to the design height and width of the form, which is probably not big enough to show the chart very well. Access doesn't look at the chart design to determine what height and width might work well to display the PivotChart view of the subform. (Does this remind you of the sizing problems you have with a subform in Datasheet view?) Stretch the width and height of the subform control to fill up the blank space you created. Open the Property Sheet window, and with the subform control selected, set the Locked property to Yes. Verify that the Link Child Fields and Link Master Fields properties are set to ProductID. (Because the outer form is based on a table, dragging and dropping the subform should have set these properties automatically.) Switch to Form view to see the result of your work as shown in Figure 13-43. You can also find this form saved as frmXmplProductsWith-Sales in the sample database.

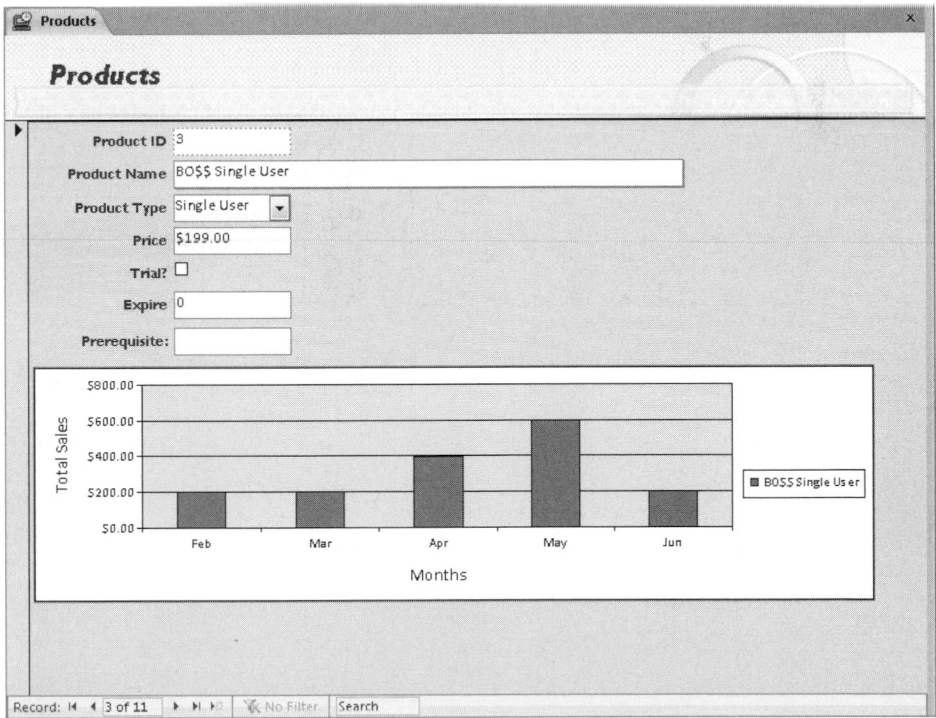


**Figure 13-43** This form displays product information with a sales chart in a subform.

**Note**

You might be wondering why the scale on the left in Figure 13-43 doesn't seem to match what you designed in Figure 13-42. The PivotChart view adjusts its horizontal and vertical scales to match the size of the display window. If you had designed the subform control taller, you might have seen the scale match.

This is the last chapter about designing forms for desktop applications. You'll learn about how form design is different for Access projects in Chapter 28, "Designing Forms in an Access Project," and you'll learn some additional design techniques that you can automate with Visual Basic code in Chapter 20.

CHAPTER 14

# Using Reports



You can certainly format and print tables and queries in Datasheet view, and that technique is useful for producing printed copies of simple lists of information. Although you primarily use forms to view and modify data, you can also use forms to print data—including data from several tables. However, because the primary function of forms is to allow you to view single records or small groups of related records displayed on the screen in an attractive way, forms aren't the best way to print and summarize large sets of data in your database.

This chapter explains why and when you should use a report instead of another method of printing data, and it describes the features that reports offer. The examples in this chapter are based on the Conrad Systems Contacts and Housing Reservations sample databases. After you learn what you can do with reports, you'll look at the process of building reports in the following two chapters.

**Note**

The examples in this chapter are based on the reports, tables, and data in ContactsDataCopy.accdb and Housing.accdb on the companion CD included with this book. You can find similar reports in the Conrad Systems Contacts sample application, but all the reports in that sample file have custom Ribbons defined, so you won't see the main Ribbon tabs when you open those reports. The results you see from the samples in this chapter might not exactly match what you see in this book if you have changed the sample data in the files. Also, all the screen images in this chapter were taken on a Windows Vista system with the display theme set to Blue. Your results might look different if you are using a different operating system or a different theme.

## Uses of Reports

Reports are the best way to create a printed copy of information that is extracted or calculated from data in your database. Reports have two principal advantages over other methods of printing data.

- Reports can compare, summarize, subtotal, and total large sets of data.

- Reports can be created to produce attractive invoices, purchase orders, mailing labels, presentation materials, and other output you might need in order to efficiently conduct business.

Reports are designed to group data, to present each grouping separately, and to perform calculations. They work as follows:

- You can define up to 10 grouping criteria to separate the levels of detail.
- You can define separate headers and footers for each group.
- You can perform complex calculations not only within a group or a set of rows but also across groups.
- In addition to page headers and footers, you can define a header and a footer for the entire report.
- You can have your reports respond to events such as opening forms so that you can view detailed information.
- You can filter the report to drill down to more specific records before printing.

As with forms, you can embed pictures or charts in any section of a report. You can also embed subreports or subforms within report sections.



# A Tour of Reports

You can explore reports in Microsoft Office Access 2007 by examining the features of the sample reports in the ContactsDataCopy.accdb sample database. A good place to start is the rptContactProducts report. Open the database, and go to the Navigation Pane. Click the Navigation Pane menu, click Object Type under Navigate To Category, and then click Reports under Filter By Group to display a list of reports available in the database. Scroll down the list of reports in the Navigation Pane until you see the rptContactProducts report, as shown in Figure 14-1. Double-click the report name (or right-click it and click the Open command on the shortcut menu) to see the report in Print Preview—a view of how the report will look when it's printed.

> **Note**
>
> All the reports in the sample databases are set to print to the system default printer. The default printer on your system is probably not the same printer that we used as a default when we designed the report. Some of the sample reports are designed with margins other than the default of 1 inch on all sides. If your default printer cannot print as close to the edge of the paper as the report is designed, Office Access 2007 will adjust the margins to the minimums for your printer. This means that some reports might not appear exactly as you see them in this book, and some data might appear on different pages.

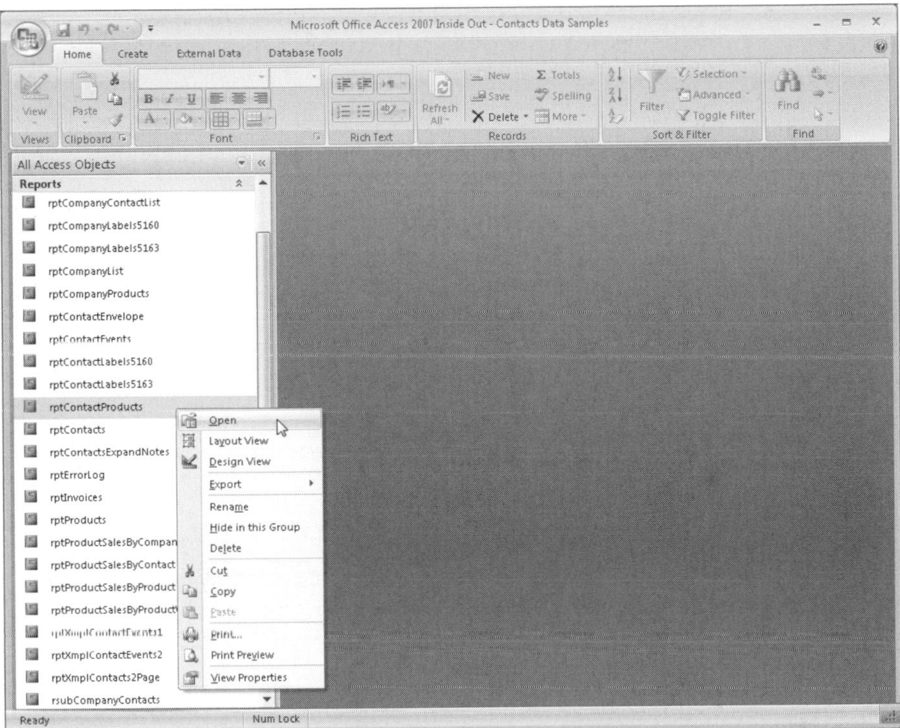


**Figure 14-1** You can use the object shortcut menu to open a report from the Navigation Pane.

## Print Preview—A First Look

The rptContactProducts report is based on the qryRptContactProducts query, which brings together information from the tblContacts, tblProducts, and tblContactProducts tables. When the report opens in Print Preview, you'll see a view of the report in the Contact Products window, as shown in Figure 14-2. When you open the report from the Navigation Pane, the report shows information for all contact product sales.

You can expand the window in Print Preview by collapsing the Navigation Pane to see more of the rptContactProducts report horizontally. Use the vertical and horizontal scroll bars to position the report so that you can see most of the upper half of the first page. If you are using a smaller SVGA screen (800×600 pixels), click the arrow below the Zoom button in the Zoom group on the Ribbon and select 75% to see more of the report. If your screen resolution is 1024×768 or higher, you should be able to easily view the report at 100%. You can also use the Zoom control in the lower-right corner of your window to adjust the zoom level.

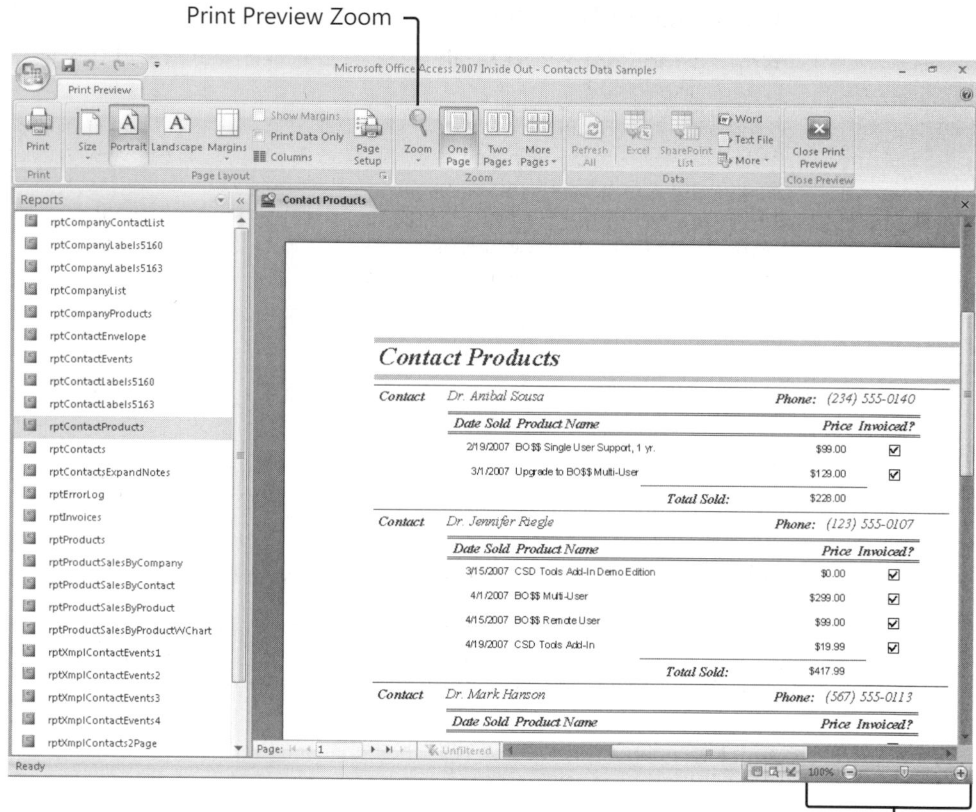


**Figure 14-2** The rptContactProducts report in Print Preview shows sales data gathered from several tables.



## Checking Out Reports in the Sample Application

You can see all the reports described in this chapter in the Conrad Systems Contacts application. Start the application by opening the database (Contacts.accdb), opening frmSplash, and then signing on as either Jeff or John—you don't need a password. To see the final version of the Contact Products report, for example, click the Products button on the main switchboard form, and then click the Print button on the CSD Contacts – Products form to open the Product Reports dialog box. Select Product Sales By Contact. Also select the Current Product Only and All Records options, and then click Print. You'll see the report in Print Preview for the product that was displayed on the Products form. You can also explore the reports by clicking the Reports button on the main switchboard. All reports in the application have custom Ribbons that prevent you from switching to Design view when running the application. When you're finished looking at the reports in Contacts.accdb, be sure to go back to the ContactsDataCopy.accdb file to follow the remaining examples in this chapter.

**TROUBLESHOOTING**

**Why did the Print Preview tab disappear when I collapsed the Navigation Pane?**

If you open a report in Print Preview, Access 2007 displays only the Print Preview contextual Ribbon tab. If you collapse the Navigation Pane while in this view, Access shifts the focus to the Navigation Pane, closes the Print Preview tab, and shows the four main Ribbon tabs. To show the Print Preview tab again, click on the report tab if you are using the Tabbed Documents window option, or click on the report itself to put the focus back on the report and redisplay the Print Preview tab.



To view other pages of the report, use the navigation bar in the lower-left corner of the window, as shown here.

The four buttons, from left to right, are the First Page button, Previous Page button, Next Page button, and Last Page button. The Page Number box is in the middle. To move forward one page at a time, click the Next Page button. You can also click the Page Number box (or press Alt+F5 to select it), change the number, and press Enter to move to the exact page you want. Press Esc to exit the Page Number box. As you might guess, the Previous Page button moves you back one page, and the two outer buttons move you to the first or the last page of the report. You can also move to the top of the page by pressing Ctrl+Up Arrow, move to the bottom of the page by pressing Ctrl+Down Arrow, move to the left edge of the page by pressing Home or Ctrl+Left Arrow, and move to the right edge of the page by pressing End or Ctrl+Right Arrow. Pressing Ctrl+Home moves you to the upper-left corner of the page, and pressing Ctrl+End moves you to the lower-right corner of the page.

## Headers, Detail Sections, Footers, and Groups

Although the rptContactProducts report looks simple at first glance, it actually contains a lot of information. Figure 14-3 shows you the report again with the various sections of the report marked. You can see a page header that appears at the top of every page. As you'll see later when you learn to design reports, you can also define a header for the entire report and choose whether to print this report header on a page by itself or with the first page header.

The data in this report is grouped by contact name, and the detail lines are sorted within contact name by date sold. You can print a heading for each group in your report, and this report has a heading for each contact. This report could easily be modified, for example, to display the product category in a header line (to group the products by category), followed by the related detail lines.

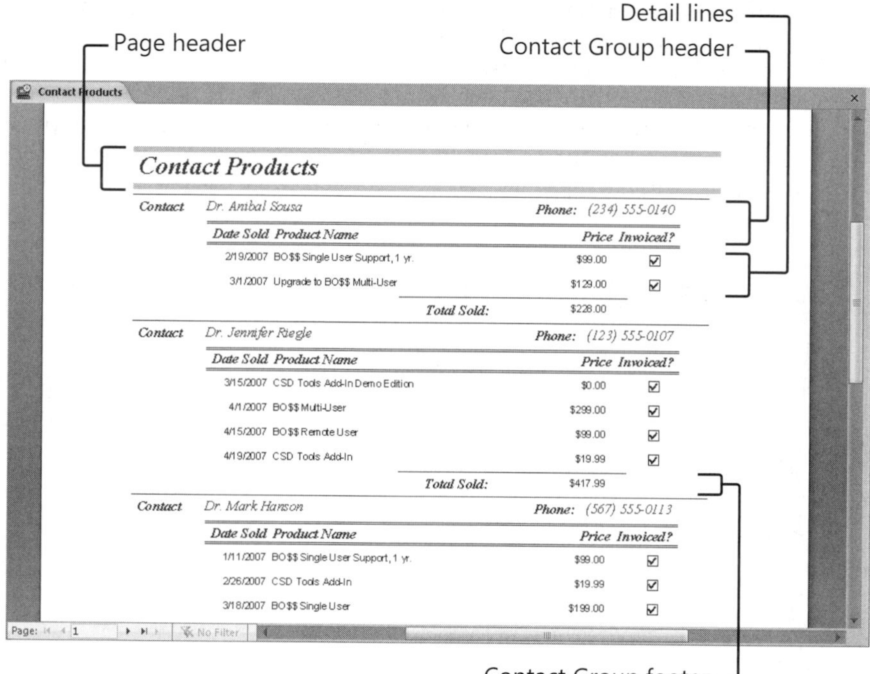


**Figure 14-3** The rptContactProducts report has a subtotal for each contact.

Next Access prints the detail information, one line for each row in the recordset formed by the query. In the Detail section of a report, you can add unbound controls to calculate a result using any of the columns in the record source.

Below the product detail lines for each contact, you can see the group footer for the contact. You could also calculate percentages for a detail record or for a group by including a control that provides a summary in the group footer (total for the group) or report footer (total for the report). To calculate the percentage, you would create an additional control that divides the detail or group value by the total value in an outer group or in the report footer. Access can do this because its report writer can look at the detail data twice—once to calculate any group or grand totals, and a second time to calculate expressions that reference those totals. If you scroll down to the bottom of the page, you'll see a page number, which is in the page footer.

> **Note**
>
> If you're working with a report that has many pages, it might take a long time to move to the first or last page or to move back one page. You can press Esc to cancel your movement request. Access 2007 then closes the report.

A slightly more complex report is rptProductSalesByProduct. Open that report, and go to the last page. At the end of this report, as shown in Figure 14-4, you can see the quantity and sales totals for the last product in the report, for the last category in the report, and for all sales in the database (Grand Total). There are two products in the Single User category, but the first is a demonstration edition that has a zero price, so the total sales amount of the category matches the total sales amount of the second product. The grand total is in the report footer.

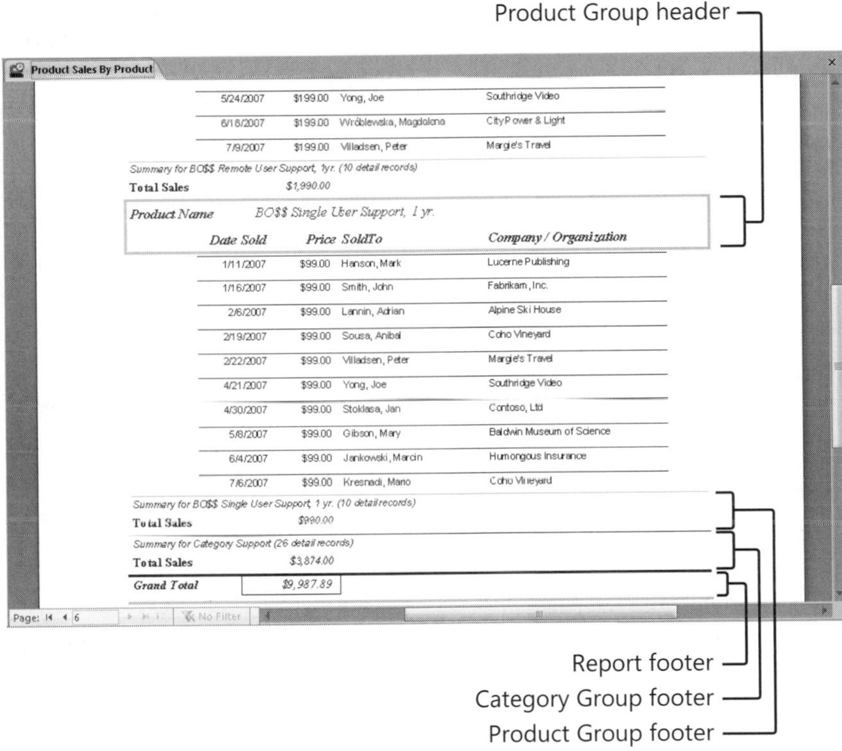


**Figure 14-4** The rptProductSalesByProduct report's grand total calculation is in the report footer.

## Subreports

Just as you can embed subforms within forms, you can embed subreports (or subforms) within reports. Subreports are particularly useful for showing related details or totals for the records that make up the source rows of your report. In the Conrad Systems Contacts database, you can bring together information about contacts and products—either contacts and the products they own or products and the contacts who own them. You can place detailed data about contacts and products in a subreport and then embed that subreport in the Detail section of a report that displays company data—much as you did for the fsubContactProducts form exercise in the previous chapter.

You can see an example of this use of a subreport in the rptCompanyProducts report and in the rsubCompanyProducts subreport in the Conrad Systems Contacts database. In the Navigation Pane, right-click on the rsubCompanyProducts subreport, and then click Design View on the shortcut menu to open the subreport in Design view, as shown in Figure 14-5. The Report window in Design view is shown in Figure 14-6.

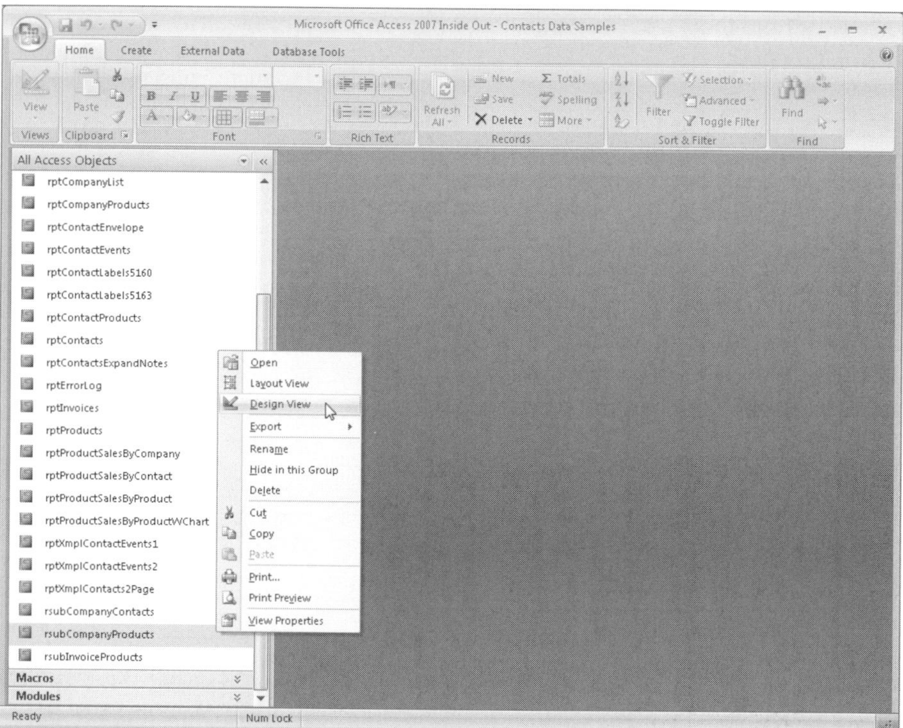


**Figure 14-5** Select Design View from the shortcut menu to open rsubCompanyProducts in Design view.

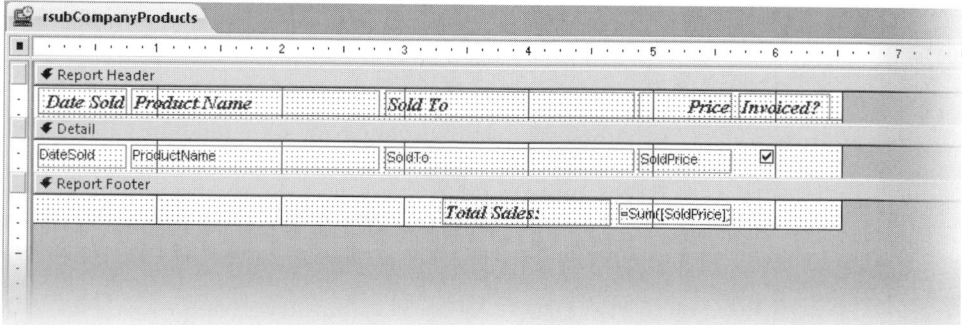


**Figure 14-6** This is the Report window for the rsubCompanyProducts report in Design view.

You can see that this report looks very much like the continuous form you designed earlier to be a subform. If you look at the Record Source property for the subreport, you'll find that it uses the qryRsubCompanyProducts query, which isn't at all simple. The query brings together information from the tblProducts, tblContactProducts, tblContacts, and tblCompanyContacts tables. This subreport doesn't display any company information at all. Switch to Print Preview by clicking the arrow in the Views group on the Ribbon and clicking Print Preview in the list of available views. You'll see a list of various products and the contacts who own them, in date sold order, as shown in Figure 14-7.

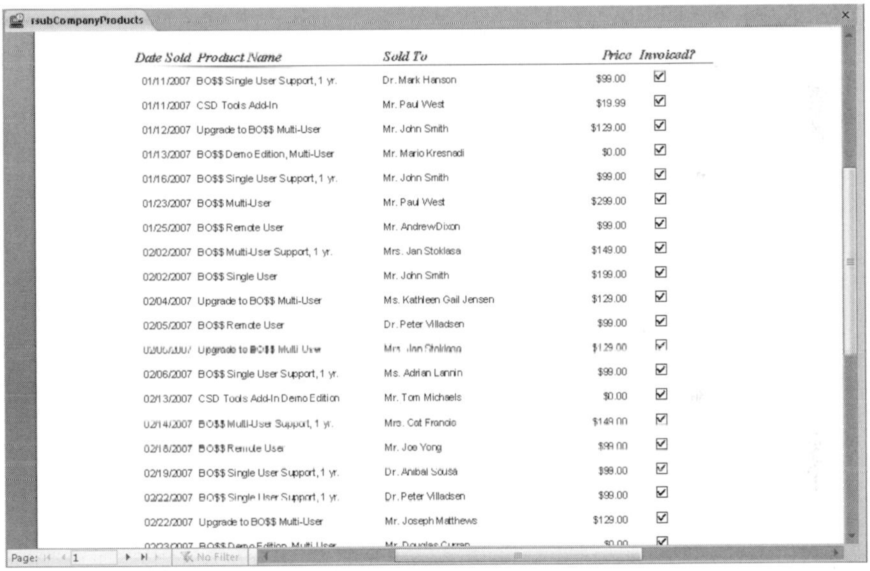

rsubCompanyProducts

| Date Sold | Product Name | Sold To | Price | Invoiced? |
|---|---|---|---|---|
| 01/11/2007 | BO$$ Single User Support, 1 yr. | Dr. Mark Hanson | $99.00 | ☑ |
| 01/11/2007 | CSD Tools Add-In | Mr. Paul West | $19.99 | ☑ |
| 01/12/2007 | Upgrade to BO$$ Multi-User | Mr. John Smith | $129.00 | ☑ |
| 01/13/2007 | BO$$ Demo Edition, Multi-User | Mr. Mario Kresnadi | $0.00 | ☑ |
| 01/16/2007 | BO$$ Single User Support, 1 yr. | Mr. John Smith | $99.00 | ☑ |
| 01/23/2007 | BO$$ Multi-User | Mr. Paul West | $299.00 | ☑ |
| 01/25/2007 | BO$$ Remote User | Mr. Andrew Dixon | $99.00 | ☑ |
| 02/02/2007 | BO$$ Multi-User Support, 1 yr. | Mrs. Jan Stoklasa | $149.00 | ☑ |
| 02/02/2007 | BO$$ Single User | Mr. John Smith | $199.00 | ☑ |
| 02/04/2007 | Upgrade to BO$$ Multi-User | Ms. Kathleen Gail Jensen | $129.00 | ☑ |
| 02/05/2007 | BO$$ Remote User | Dr. Peter Villadsen | $99.00 | ☑ |
| [illegible] | Upgrade to BO$$ Multi-User | Mrs. Jan Stoklasa | $129.00 | ☑ |
| 02/06/2007 | BO$$ Single User Support, 1 yr. | Ms. Adrian Lannin | $99.00 | ☑ |
| 02/13/2007 | CSD Tools Add-In Demo Edition | Mr. Tom Michaels | $0.00 | ☑ |
| 02/14/2007 | BO$$ Multi-User Support, 1 yr. | Mrs. Cat Francis | $149.00 | ☑ |
| 02/18/2007 | BO$$ Remote User | Mr. Joe Yong | $99.00 | ☑ |
| 02/19/2007 | BO$$ Single User Support, 1 yr. | Dr. Aníbal Sousa | $99.00 | ☑ |
| 02/22/2007 | BO$$ Single User Support, 1 yr. | Dr. Peter Villadsen | $99.00 | ☑ |
| 02/22/2007 | Upgrade to BO$$ Multi-User | Mr. Joseph Matthews | $129.00 | ☑ |

Page: 1 No Filter

**Figure 14-7** Switch to Print Preview for the rsubCompanyProducts report to see a complex list of sales history.

Close the subreport and open the rptCompanyProducts report in Print Preview, shown in Figure 14-8. Notice as you move from company to company that the data displayed in the subreport changes to match the company currently displayed. The data from the rsubCompanyProducts report now makes sense within the context of a particular company. Access links the data from each subreport in this example using the Link Master Fields and Link Child Fields properties of the subreport (which are set to the linking CompanyID field)—just as with the subforms you created in Chapter 13, "Advanced Form Design."

As you'll see in the next section, when we examine some features of the rptInvoices report, that report also uses subreports to link information from three related tables to each row displayed from the tblInvoices table.

Chapter 14

Companies and Products Sold

*Companies and Products Sold*

| *Company / Organization* | *Department* | *Billing Address* | *Referred By* |
| --- | --- | --- | --- |
| Alpine Ski House | | 3456 3rd Boulevard<br>Pingree Grove, Kane, IL 60140 | |

| *Date Sold* | *Product Name* | *Sold To* | *Price* | *Invoiced?* |
| --- | --- | --- | --- | --- |
| 02/06/2007 | BO$$ Single User Support, 1 yr. | Ms. Adrian Lannin | $99.00 | ☑ |
| | | *Total Sales:* | $99.00 | |

| *Company / Organization* | *Department* | *Billing Address* | *Referred By* |
| --- | --- | --- | --- |
| Baldwin Museum of Science | | 7890 Central Drive<br>Matoaka, Mercer, WV 24736 | |

| *Date Sold* | *Product Name* | *Sold To* | *Price* | *Invoiced?* |
| --- | --- | --- | --- | --- |
| 02/14/2007 | BO$$ Multi-User Support, 1 yr. | Mrs. Cat Francis | $149.00 | ☑ |
| 02/25/2007 | BO$$ Remote User Support, 1 yr. | Ms. Mary E. Gibson | $199.00 | ☑ |
| 04/02/2007 | BO$$ Remote User Support, 1 yr. | Mrs. Cat Francis | $199.00 | ☑ |
| 05/08/2007 | BO$$ Single User Support, 1 yr. | Ms. Mary E. Gibson | $99.00 | ☑ |
| 05/18/2007 | BO$$ Multi-User Support, 1 yr. | Ms. Mary E. Gibson | $149.00 | ☑ |
| 05/28/2007 | Upgrade to BO$$ Multi-User | Mrs. Cat Francis | $129.00 | ☑ |
| 07/03/2007 | BO$$ Multi-User | Ms. Mary E. Gibson | $299.00 | ☐ |
| | | *Total Sales:* | $1,223.00 | |

| *Company / Organization* | *Department* | *Billing Address* | *Referred By* |
| --- | --- | --- | --- |
| Blue Yonder Airlines | | 5678 Central Avenue | |

Page: 1 No Filter

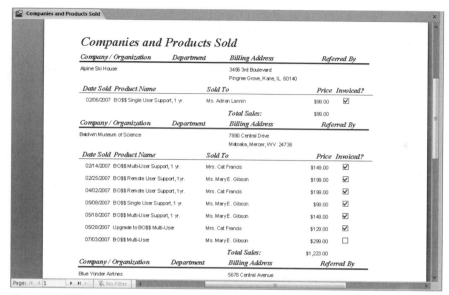

**Figure 14-8** The rptCompanyProducts report has an embedded subreport to display each company's purchase history.

## Objects in Reports

As with forms, you can embed objects in reports. The objects embedded in or linked to reports are usually pictures or charts. You can embed a picture or a chart as an unbound object in the report itself, or you can link a picture or a chart as an object bound to data in your database.

The rptInvoices report in the Conrad Systems Contacts database has an image object. When you open the rptInvoices report in Print Preview, you can see the Conrad Systems logo (a stylized font graphic) embedded in the report title as an unbound bitmap image object, as shown in Figure 14-9. This object is actually a part of the report design.

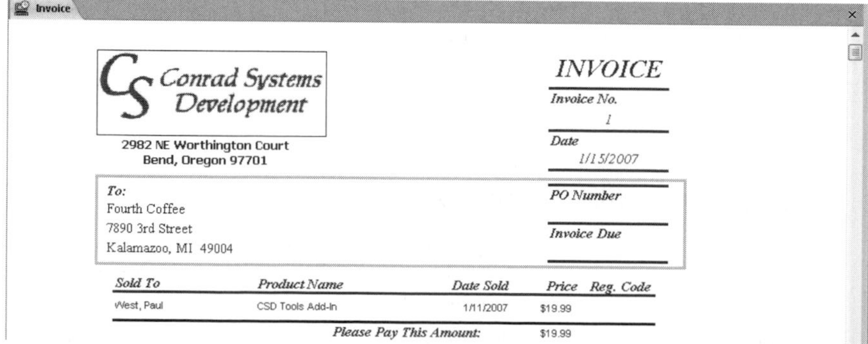

Invoice

Conrad Systems Development
2982 NE Worthington Court
Bend, Oregon 97701

*INVOICE*

*Invoice No.* 1

*Date* 1/15/2007

*To:*
Fourth Coffee
7890 3rd Street
Kalamazoo, MI 49004

*PO Number*

*Invoice Due*

| *Sold To* | *Product Name* | *Date Sold* | *Price* | *Reg. Code* |
| --- | --- | --- | --- | --- |
| West, Paul | CSD Tools Add-In | 1/11/2007 | $19.99 | |
| | | *Please Pay This Amount:* | $19.99 | |

**Figure 14-9** The rptInvoices report has an unbound bitmap image object (the Conrad Systems logo) embedded in the report header.

To see an example of how an object prints when it's stored in a table, open rptContacts, as shown in Figure 14-10. This picture is a bitmap image object stored in an attachment field in the tblContacts table—a picture of the contact.

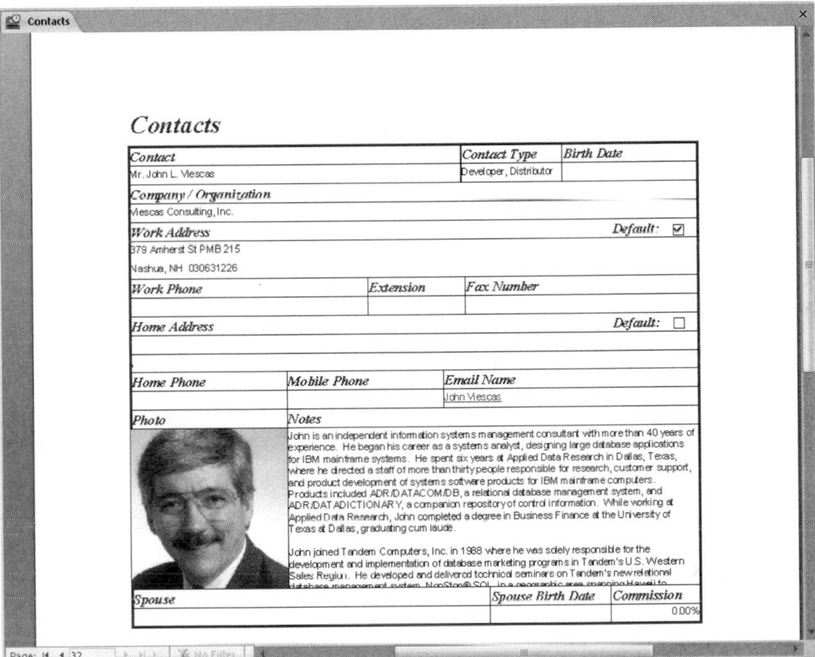


**Figure 14-10** The Photo field in the rptContacts report is a bitmap image object stored in an attachment field.

> **Note**
>
> You might notice that the Notes field in Figure 14-10 doesn't show all the text. There's a special version of this report called rptContactsExpandNotes that fixes this problem with Visual Basic code. See Chapter 20, "Automating Your Application with Visual Basic," for details.

## Report View—A First Look

As you learned in Chapter 3, "Microsoft Office Access 2007 Overview," Access 2007 includes a new view for reports called Report view. Unlike Print Preview, which presents static data, you can use Report view to interact with data in the report. You can explore reports that take advantage of this new view in the Housing.accdb sample database. A good place to start is the rptEmployeesPlain report. Open the database, and go to the Navigation Pane. Click the Navigation Pane menu, and click Object Type under Navigate To Category, and then click Reports under Filter By Group to display a list of reports available in the database. Scroll down the list of reports until you see the rptEmployeesPlain report, as shown in Figure 14-11. Right-click the report, and click Open to see the report in Report view.

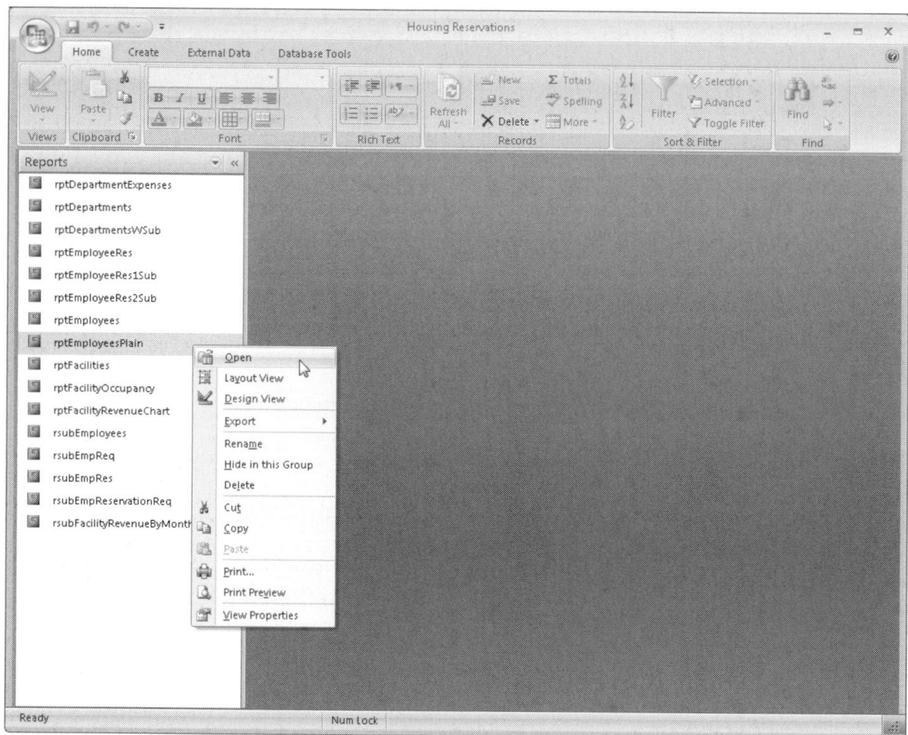


**Figure 14-11** When you click Open on the shortcut menu for the rptEmployeesPlain report, Access opens it in Report view.

INSIDE OUT

### Understanding the Open Command for Reports

You might be wondering why clicking the Open command for the rptEmployeesPlain report opens it in Report view, but the same command opens the rptContactProducts report (discussed earlier) in Print Preview. Access 2007 includes a new report property called Default View. You can define whether a report opens in Report view or Print Preview by using this property. The default setting when you create a new report is Report view. For the rptEmployeesPlain report we left this property set to Report view, so when you double-click on the report in the Navigation Pane or click the Open command on the object shortcut menu, Access opens the report in Report view. We will discuss this new property further in Chapter 16, "Advanced Report Design."

The rptEmployeesPlain report is based on the qryRptEmployees query, which brings together information from the tblEmployees and tblDepartments tables. When the report opens in Report view, you'll see the data from these tables in the Housing Reservations database formatted in the report, as shown in Figure 14-12.

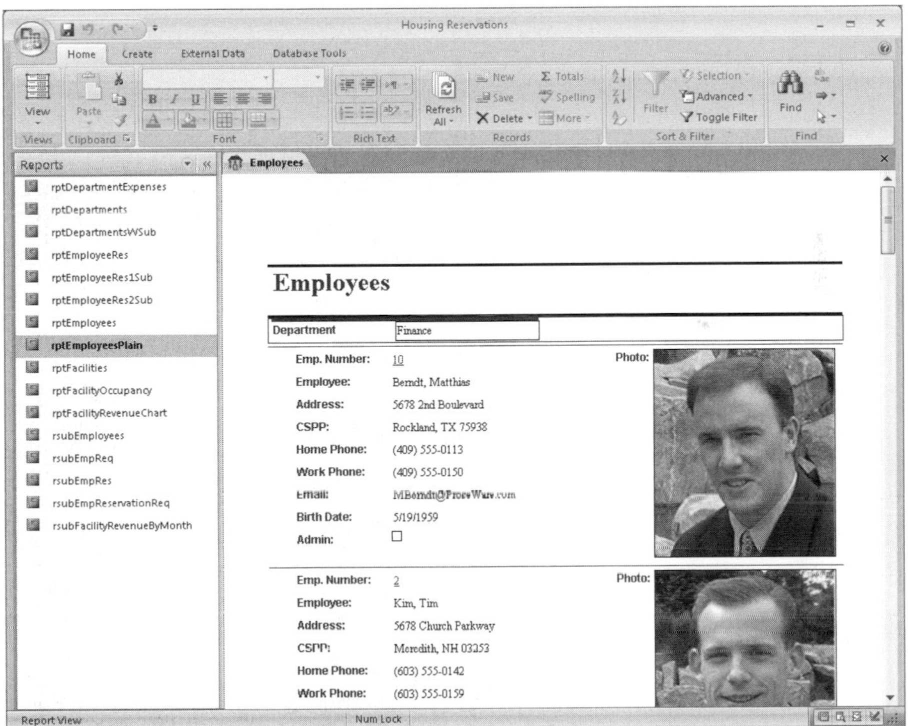


**Figure 14-12** The rptEmployeesPlain report is set to open in the new Report view.

If you look closely at Figure 14-12 you will no doubt notice that there is no Page Number box in the lower-left corner of the window. You can also see that the Print Preview contextual Ribbon tab is not available. Access displays the four main Ribbon tabs in Report view so that you can use filters to interact and drill down to specific records and then print only this smaller group of records. If you were to print this report right now, all 16 employee records would be sent to your printer. Suppose though that you want to print only the records of employees who are in the Finance department. You could create a separate report that would show only the employees in the Finance department, but from within Report view you can ask Access to filter the records to display only the employee records you need. With the rptEmployeesPlain open in Report view, right-click in the Department field for the first record and click Equals "Finance" on the shortcut menu, as shown in Figure 14-13.

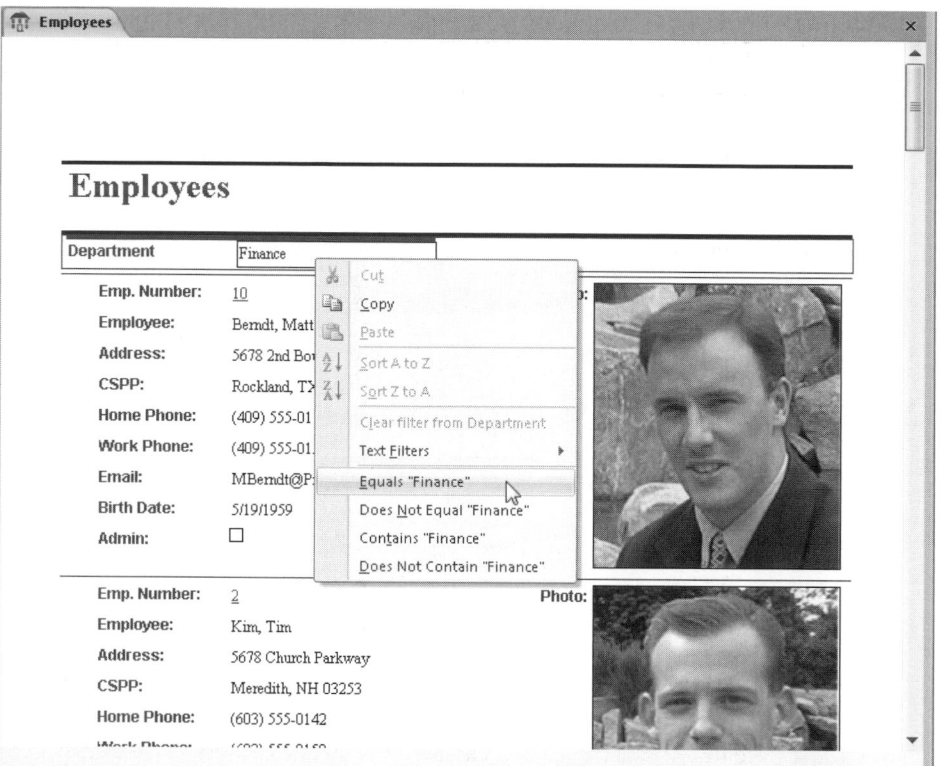


**Figure 14-13** In Report view you can filter the records to show just the ones you want to print.

After you click Equals "Finance," Access filters all the records in the report record source to obtain the three employees in the Finance department, as shown in Figure 14-14. If you print the report at this point, Access prints only a one-page report with the three records.

By using Report view, you can create a single report that returns all records and then use the filtering capabilities of Access to drill down to subsets of the data. To remove the filter applied to this report, click the Toggle Filter button in the Sort & Filter group on the Home tab, and Access again displays all 16 employee records. Report view gives you as many of the filtering and sorting capabilities as you have in forms but in an object that's designed to be printed rather than edit data.

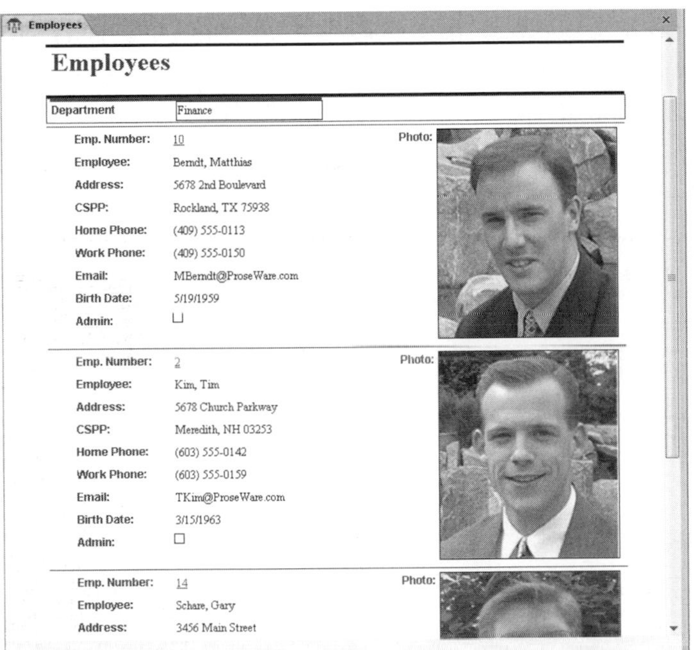


**Figure 14-14** After you apply the filter shown in Figure 4-13, Access shows only the three employees in the Finance department.

In the new Report view, you can also define controls that respond to events, similar to what you can do with forms. We defined a Click event for the employee number text box and styled it as a hyperlink to provide a visual cue to the user. In Figure 4-15, you can see that the Employee Number field looks like a hyperlink with the data in blue and underlined. Clicking the Employee Number field opens the frmEmployeesPlain form as a dialog box displaying all information for that specific employee so that you can make any necessary changes. After closing the form and returning to the report, click the Refresh All command in the Records group on the Home tab to see any changes you made to the data using the form reflected in the report.

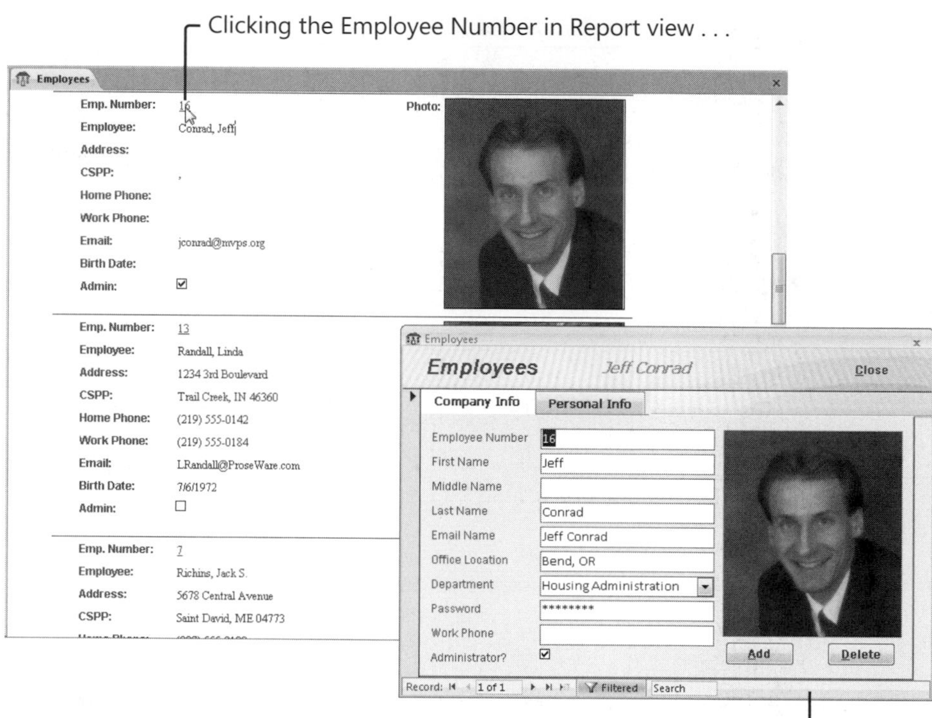


**Figure 14-15** You can use Report view to respond to control events such as opening data entry forms.

# Printing Reports

So far in this chapter you have learned the basics of viewing a report in Print Preview and in Report view. Here are a few more tips and details about setting up reports for printing.

## Print Setup

Before you print a report, you might first want to check its appearance and then change the printer setup. Open the ContactsDataCopy database, right-click the rptContacts report (which you looked at earlier) in the Navigation Pane, and click Print Preview on the shortcut menu to see the report. After Access shows you the report, click the arrow under the Zoom button in the Zoom group on the Print Preview contextual tab, and then size the window to see the full-page view by clicking Fit To Window. Click the Two Pages button in the same group to see two pages side by side, as shown in Figure 14-16.

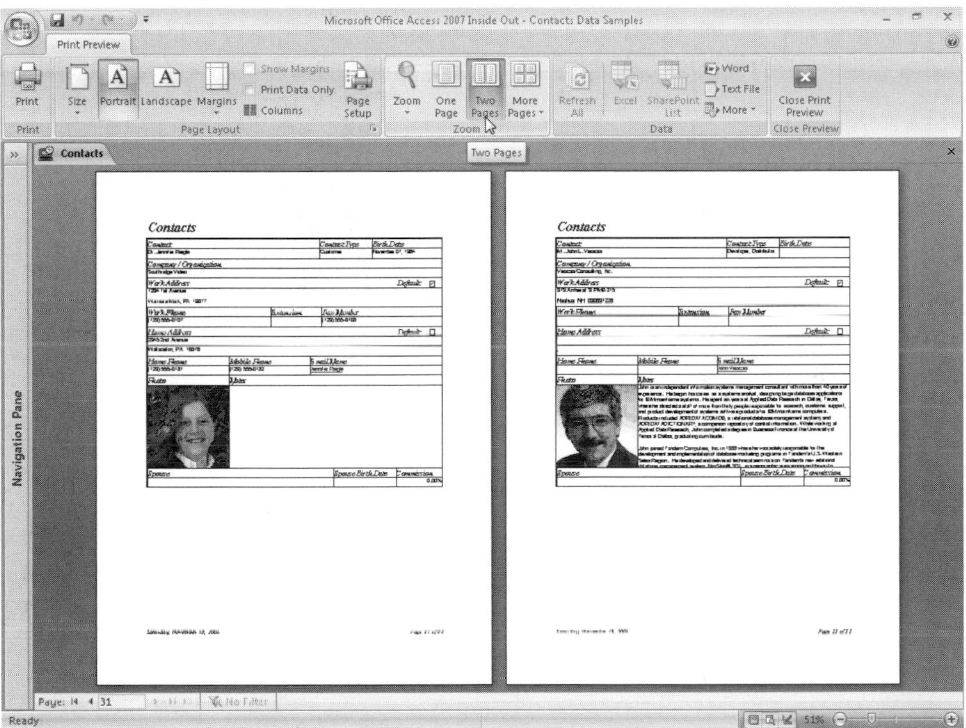


**Figure 14-16** Click the Two Pages button on the Ribbon to display a two-page view of the rptContacts report in Print Preview.

This report is narrow enough to print two contacts side by side in landscape orientation on 14-inch-long paper. To print it that way, you need to modify some parameters in the Page Setup dialog box.

Open the Page Setup dialog box by clicking the Page Setup button in the Page Layout group. Access displays a dialog box similar to the one shown in Figure 14-17.

To print the rptContacts report with two logical pages per physical page, you first need to adjust the margins. You haven't changed the page orientation yet, so the settings that are currently the top and bottom will become the left and right margins, respectively, after you rotate the page. (And left and right margins become top and bottom, respectively.) The pages need to print very close to the edges of the paper, so set the top margin (this becomes the left margin in landscape orientation) to 0.25 inch, set the bottom margin to about 0.5 inch, and set the left and right margins to 0.5 inch. Effectively, the left margin will be the smallest after you change the orientation. Click the Page tab to display the next set of available properties, as shown in Figure 14-18.

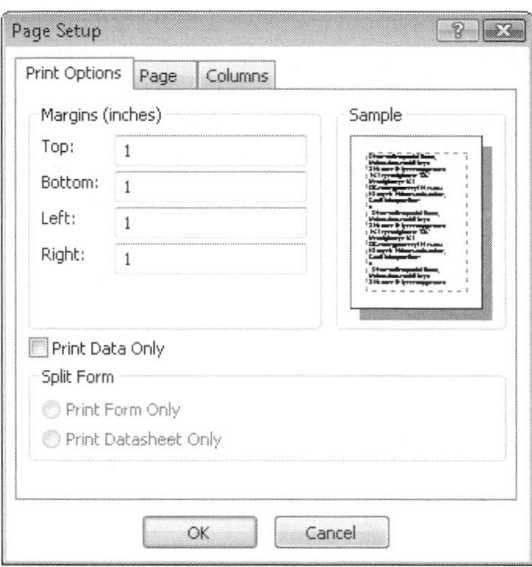


**Figure 14-17** You can adjust the margins in the Page Setup dialog box.

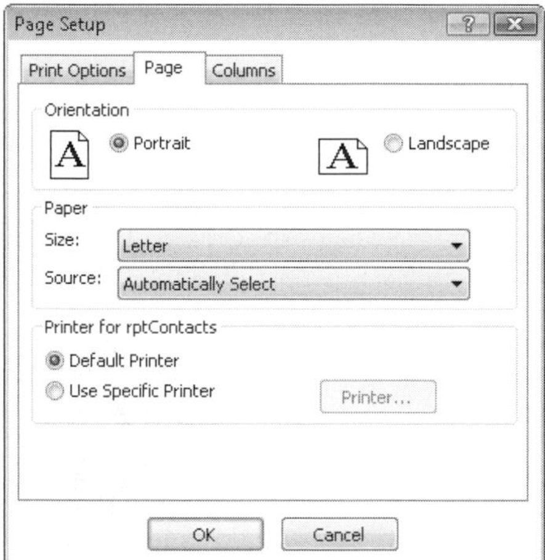


**Figure 14-18** You can set page orientation options on the Page tab of the Page Setup dialog box.

On the Page tab, you can select the orientation of the printed page—Portrait to print vertically down the length of the page, or Landscape to print horizontally across the width of the page. Because we're trying to print two pages across a single sheet of paper, select the Landscape option. The report is also about 6½ inches wide, so you'll need wider paper to fit two logical pages to a printed page. Select Legal (8½-by-14-inch) paper from the Size list under Paper.

In general, it's best to leave the printer set to the default printer that you specified in your Windows settings. If you move your application to a computer that's attached to a different type of printer, you won't have to change the settings. You can print any report you design in Access on any printer supported by Windows with good results.

However, if you've designed your report to print on a specific printer, you can save those settings by using the Page Setup dialog box. To do this, select the Use Specific Printer option on the Page tab and then click the Printer button to open a dialog box in which you can select any printer installed on your system. (The Printer button is available only if you have more than one printer installed on your computer.) Click the Properties button to adjust settings for that printer in its Properties dialog box, shown in Figure 14-19. The Properties dialog box you see might look different, depending on the capabilities of the printer you selected and how Windows supports that printer.



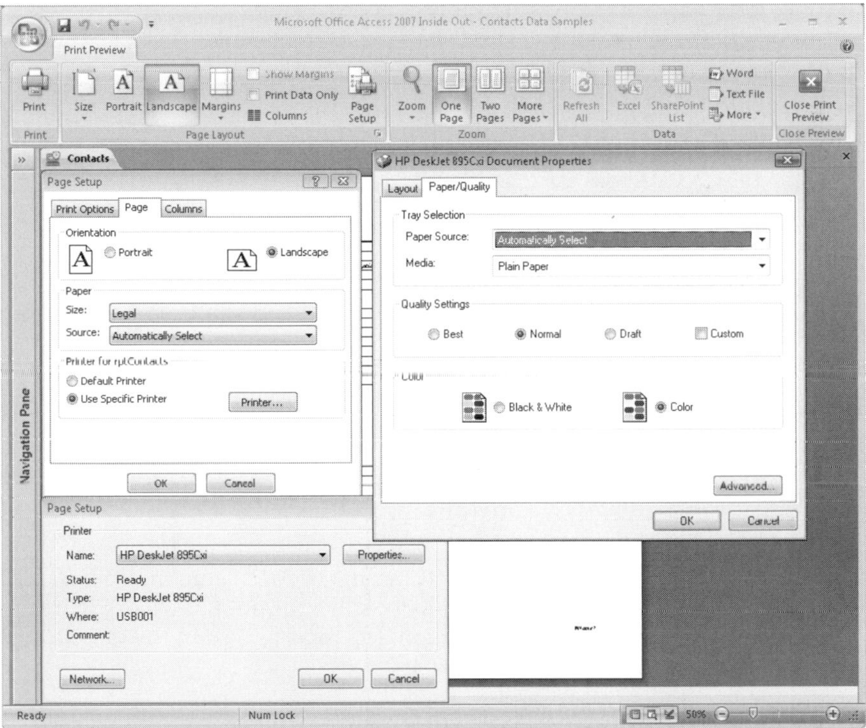


**Figure 14-19** You can define properties for a specific printer to be used with your report.

After you finish selecting options on the Page tab, click the Columns tab, as shown in Figure 14-20, to set up a multiple-column report. In this case, you want to print two "columns" of information. After you set the Number Of Columns property to a value greater than 1 (in this case, 2), you can set spacing between rows and spacing between columns. By default, Access selects the Same As Detail check box and displays the design Width and Height measurements of your report. You can also clear the Same As Detail check box and set a custom width and height that are larger or smaller than the underlying report design size. Note that if you specify a smaller size, Access crops the report. When you have detail data that fits in more than one column or row, you can also tell Access whether you want the detail printed down and then across the page or vice versa.

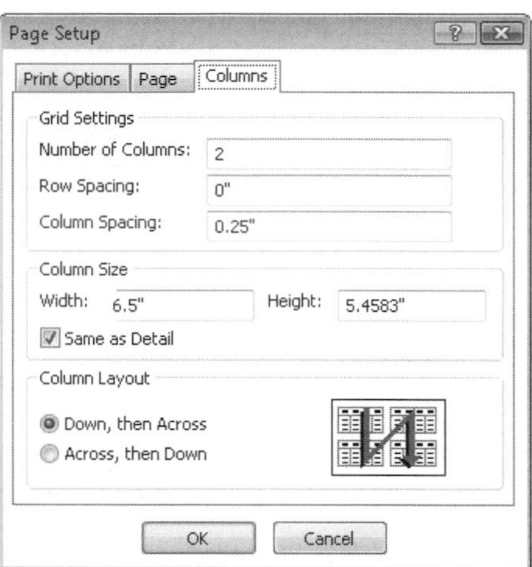


**Figure 14-20** You can set report column properties on the Columns tab of the Page Setup dialog box.

> **Note**
>
> If you created the report or have permission to modify the design of the report, you can change the page layout settings and save them with the report. The next time you print or view the report, Access will use the last page layout settings you specified.

After you enter the appropriate settings in the Page Setup dialog box, click OK, and your report in Print Preview should look like the one shown in Figure 14-21. You can find this modified version of the Contacts report saved in the sample database as rptXmplContacts2Page.

The most common use for setting multiple columns is to print mailing labels. You can find four example reports in the sample database that do this: rptCompanyLabels5160 and rptContactLabels5160 that print company and contact labels two across in Avery 5160 format; and rptCompanyLabels5163 and rptContactLabels5163 that print company and contact labels three across in Avery 5163 format.

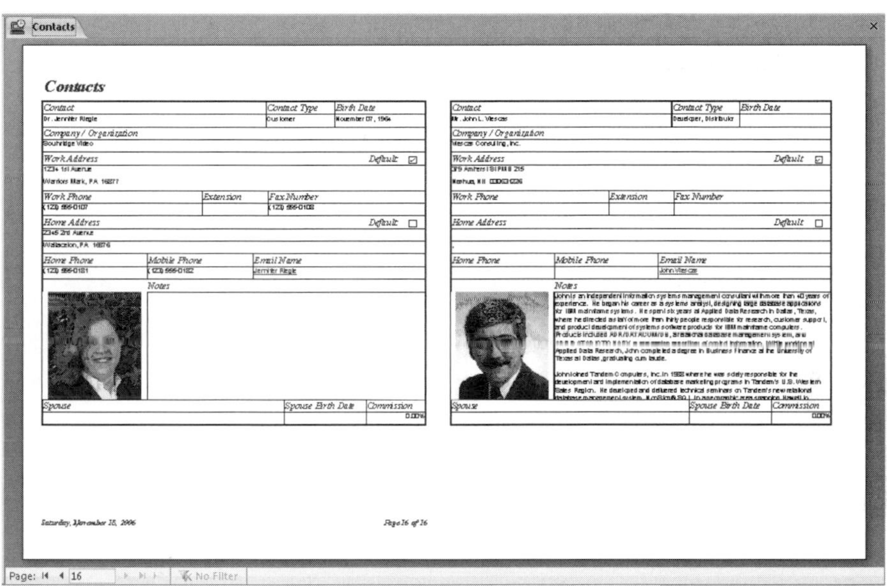


**Figure 14-21** Print Preview now displays the rptContacts report in landscape orientation and in two columns.

That covers the fundamentals of reports and how to view them and set them up for printing. The next two chapters will show you how to design and build reports for your application.

CHAPTER 15

# Constructing a Report



Constructing a report is very similar to building a form. In this chapter, you'll apply many of the techniques that you used in working with forms, and you'll learn about some of the unique features of reports. After a quick tour of the report design facilities, you'll build a simple report for the Conrad Systems Contacts database, and then you'll use the Report Wizard to create the same report. You'll see how to use the new Layout view to modify existing reports and create new ones. Finally, you'll see how to use the quick create Report command to create a report with one mouse click.

**Note**

The examples in this chapter are based on the reports, tables, and data in ContactsDataCopy.accdb on the companion CD included with this book. You can find similar reports in the Conrad Systems Contacts sample application, but all the reports in that sample file have custom Ribbons defined, so you won't see the four main Ribbon tabs when you open those reports. The results you see from the samples in this chapter might not exactly match what you see in this book if you have changed the sample data in the files. Also, all the screen images in this chapter were taken on a Microsoft Windows Vista system with the display theme set to Blue. Your results might look different if you are using a different operating system or a different theme.

## Starting from Scratch—A Simple Report

In a contact tracking application, the user is going to want to take a look at recent events and perhaps work through a list of events that require follow-ups. Although the user could search for events in a form, the application should also provide a report that lists events by contact and shows the phone numbers the user needs. This report can be filtered by the application to print out only recent and upcoming events.

Most reports gather information from several tables, so you'll usually design a query that brings together data from related tables as the basis for the report. In this section, you'll build a relatively simple report to list contact events as you tour the report design facilities. The report you'll build uses the tblContacts, tblContactEvents, and tlkpContactEventTypes tables in the ContactsDataCopy.accdb sample database. The report groups contact event data by contact, prints a single line for each contact event, and calculates the number of contact events and the number of follow-ups for each contact.

## Building the Report Query

To construct the underlying query for the report, you need to start with the tblContactEvents table. Click the Query Design button in the Other group on the Create tab. In the Show Table dialog box, select the tblContactEvents table, click the Add button to add it to the query design grid, and then add the tblContacts and the tlkpContactEventTypes tables as well. Click the Close button in the Show Table dialog box to dismiss it. You should see join lines between tblContacts and tblContactEvents on ContactID, and between tlkpContactEventTypes and tblContactEvents on ContactEventTypeID.

From the tblContacts table, add ContactID to the query design grid. The report needs to show the contact name, but it would be better to show the information concatenated in one field rather than separate title, first name, middle name, last name, and suffix fields. In the next column, enter this expression on the Field line:

```
Contact: ([tblContacts].[Title]+" ") & [tblContacts].[FirstName]
& " " & ([tblContacts].[MiddleInit]+". ") & [tblContacts].[LastName]
& (", "+[tblContacts].[Suffix])
```



Notice that the expression uses the plus sign concatenation operator to eliminate extra blanks when one of the fields contains a Null value—a technique you learned about in Chapter 7, "Creating and Working with Simple Queries."

The query also needs to include the contact's phone number, but the tblContacts table includes both a work and a home phone number. You can create an expression to examine the DefaultAddress field to decide which one to display. Microsoft Office Access 2007 provides a handy function, Choose, which accepts an integer value in its first argument and then uses that value to choose one of the other arguments. For example, if the first argument is 1, the function returns the second argument; if the first argument is 2, the function returns the third argument, and so on. The DefaultAddress field contains a 1 to indicate work address and a 2 to indicate home address. In the third field cell on the query design grid, enter the following:

```
Phone: Choose([tblContacts].[DefaultAddress], [tblContacts].[WorkPhone],
[tblContacts].[HomePhone])
```

To complete your query, include the ContactDateTime field from the tblContactEvents table and the ContactEventTypeDescription field from the tlkpContactEventTypes table. (ContactEventTypeID in tblContactEvents is a meaningless number.) Then include the ContactNotes, ContactFollowUp, and ContactFollowUpDate fields from the tblContactEvents table. Figure 15-1 shows the query you need for this first report. Click the Save button on the Quick Access Toolbar to save your new query. (You can find this query saved as qryRptContactEvents in the sample database.)

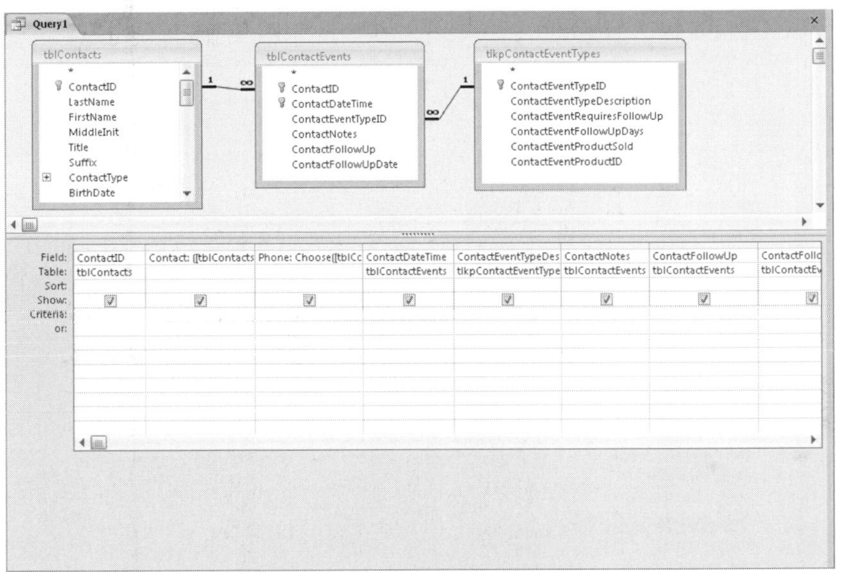


**Figure 15-1** This query selects contact and contact event data for your report.

Note that although you're designing a report that will summarize the data, you are not building a totals query. If you used a totals query as the record source for the report, you would see only the summary in the report. One of the beauties of reports is that you can see the detail information and also ask the report to produce summaries. Also, you don't need to specify any sorting criteria here–you'll do that later in the report's Group, Sort, And Total pane.

## Designing the Report

Now you're ready to start designing the report. Click the Report Design button in the Reports group on the Create tab to tell Office Access 2007 you want to begin creating a report in Design view, as shown in Figure 15-2.

**The field list, the property sheet, and the Font and Controls groups on the Design contextual tab under Report Design Tools are similar to the features you used in building forms. See Chapter 11, "Building a Form," for detailed descriptions of their uses.**

Access 2007 opens a new Report window in Design view, as shown in Figure 15-3. You can see the Report Design Tools collection of Ribbon tabs at the top of the Access window. The Report window is in the middle of the screen, and the property sheet is open to assist you in building your report. (If necessary, you can click the Property Sheet button in the Tools group on the Design tab to open this window.) To begin constructing your report you need to tell Access to use the qryRptContactEvents query as its record source. In the property sheet, select qryRptContactEvents (or the name of the query you just created) in the Record Source property, as shown in Figure 15-3.

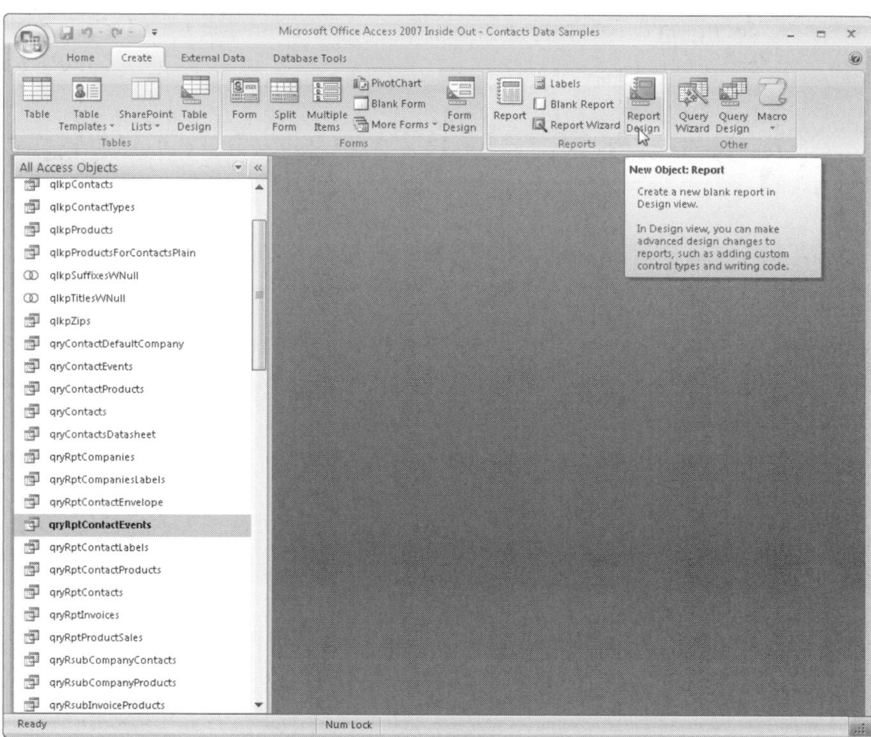


**Figure 15-2** Click the Report Design button to start creating your report.

The blank report has Page Header and Page Footer sections and a Detail section between them, which is 5.25 inches (13.333 cm) high and 6.1694 inches (15.668 cm) wide. The rulers along the top and left edges of the Report window help you plan space on the printed page. If you want standard 1-inch side margins, the body of the report can be up to 6.5 inches wide on an 8.5-by-11-inch page. The available vertical space depends on how you design your headers and footers and how you define the top and bottom margins. As with forms, you can drag the edge of any report section to make the section larger or smaller. Note that the width of all sections is the same, so if you change the width of one section, Access 2007 changes the width of all other sections to match.

Within each section you see a grid that has 24 dots per inch horizontally and 24 dots per inch vertically, with a solid gray line displayed at 1-inch intervals. If you're working in centimeters, Access 2007 divides the grid into 5 dots per centimeter both vertically and horizontally. You can change these settings using the Grid X and Grid Y properties in the report's property sheet. (If the dots are not visible in your Report window, click the Grid command in the Show/Hide group on the Arrange contextual tab; if the Grid command is already selected and you still can't see the dots, try resetting the Grid X and Grid Y properties to lower numbers in the property sheet.)

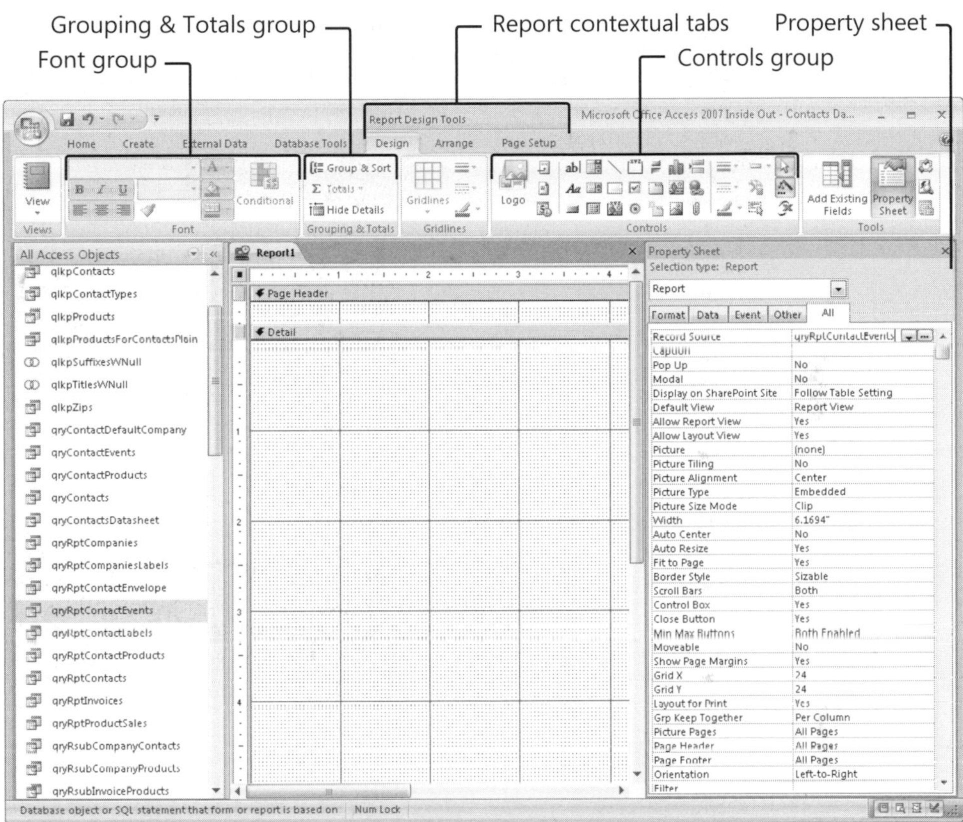


**Figure 15-3** When you open a new Report window in Design view, Access displays all the tools you need to create the report.

The page header and page footer will print in your report at the top and bottom of each page. You can click the Page Header/Footer button in the Show/Hide group on the Arrange tab to add or remove the page header and page footer. You can also add a report header that prints once at the beginning of the report and a report footer that prints once at the end of the report. To add these sections to a report, click the Report Header/Footer button in the same Show/Hide group. You'll learn how to add group headers and group footers in the next section.

## Grouping, Sorting, and Totaling Information

A key way in which reports differ from forms is that on reports you can group information for display using the Group, Sort, And Total pane. Click the Group & Sort button in the Grouping & Totals group on the Design tab (shown in Figure 15-3) to open the Group, Sort, And Total pane beneath the report design grid, as shown in Figure 15-4. (We collapsed the Navigation Pane in Figure 15-4.) In this pane you can define up to 10 fields or expressions that you will use to form groups in the report. The first item in the list determines the main group, and subsequent items define groups within groups.

(You saw the nesting of groups in the previous chapter in the rptProductSalesByProduct report; each product category had a main group, and within that main group was a subgroup for each product.) Because we have not yet defined any grouping or sorting in this report, the Group, Sort, And Total pane opens to a blank pane that allows you to click either Add A Group or Add A Sort.

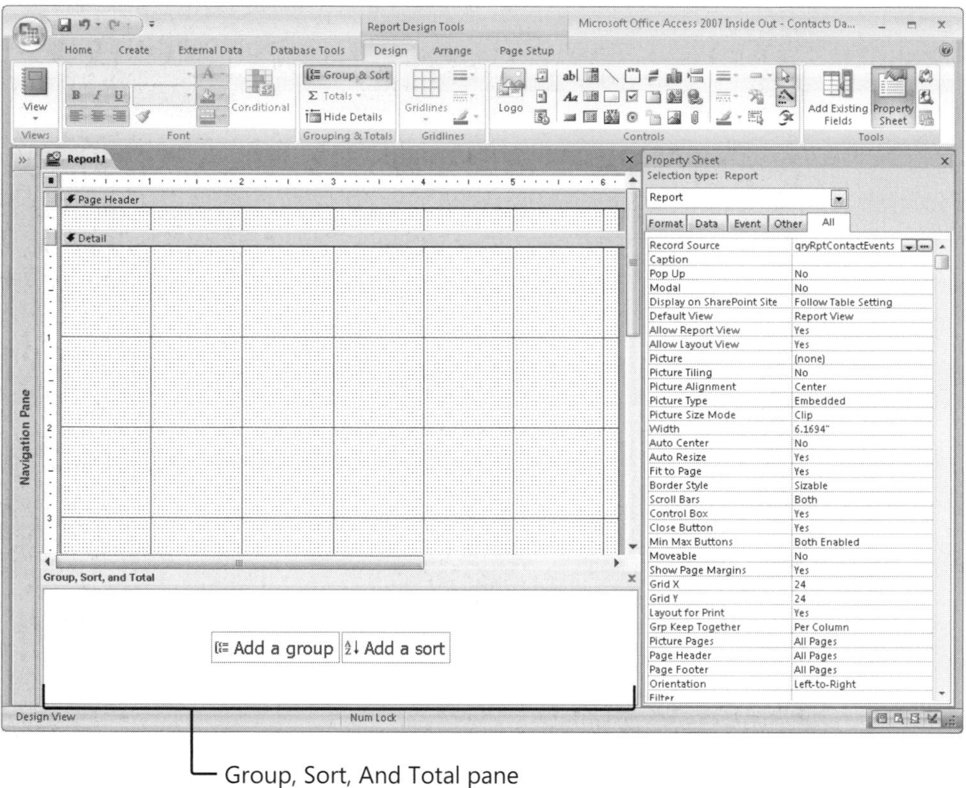


**Figure 15-4** You can create groups and specify their sort order in the Group, Sort, And Total pane.

In the simple report you're creating for contact events, you need to group data by contact ID so that you can total the number of contact events as well as contact events that require follow-up for each contact. Click the Add A Group button in the Group, Sort, And Total pane. Access 2007 creates a new grouping specification and opens a list that contains all fields in the report's record source next to the Group On option, as shown in Figure 15-5. (We collapsed the Navigation Pane and closed the property sheet in Figure 15-5 so that you can see more of the Group, Sort, And Total pane.)

If you click away from the field list before selecting a field to define the group, Access 2007 closes the field list. Click the arrow on the Select Field box (or press Alt+Down Arrow while the focus is on the Select Field box) to open the list of fields from the underlying query or table. Select the ContactID field to place it in the Select Field box. You can also use the Select Field box to enter an expression based on any field in the underlying table or query. Open the field list again and click the Expression option below the list of fields, and Access opens the Expression Builder to help you create the expression. You let Access know you're entering an expression by first typing an equal sign (=) followed by your expression. We discussed the Expression Builder in Chapter 7.

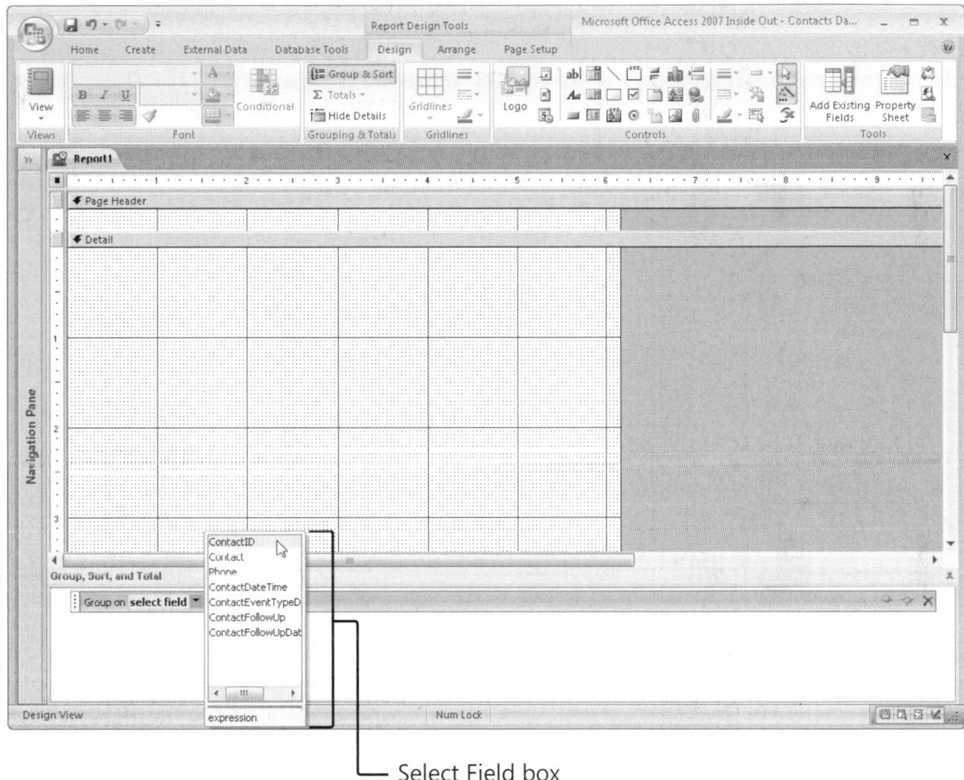


**Figure 15-5** After you click Add A Group in the Group, Sort, And Total Pane, Access creates a new grouping specification and opens a field list to let you select the field that defines the group.

> **Note**
>
> When you define a grouping specification in a report, the report engine actually builds a totals query behind the scenes to perform the grouping. As you learned in Chapter 8, "Building Complex Queries," you cannot use Group By in a totals query on memo, OLE object, hyperlink, or attachment fields. For this reason, you cannot use Memo, OLE Object, Hyperlink, or Attachment data types in the Group, Sort, And Total pane.

After you select ContactID in the Select Field box, Access 2007 adds a new ContactID group header to the report grid beneath the Page Header group level, as shown in Figure 15-6. By default, Access sets the height of this new group level to ¼ inch. Access also displays the Add A Group and Add A Sort buttons beneath the first grouping specification so you can create additional grouping or sorting levels. To the right of Group On ContactID in the Group, Sort, And Total pane, Access now adds two new options–From Smallest To Largest and More.

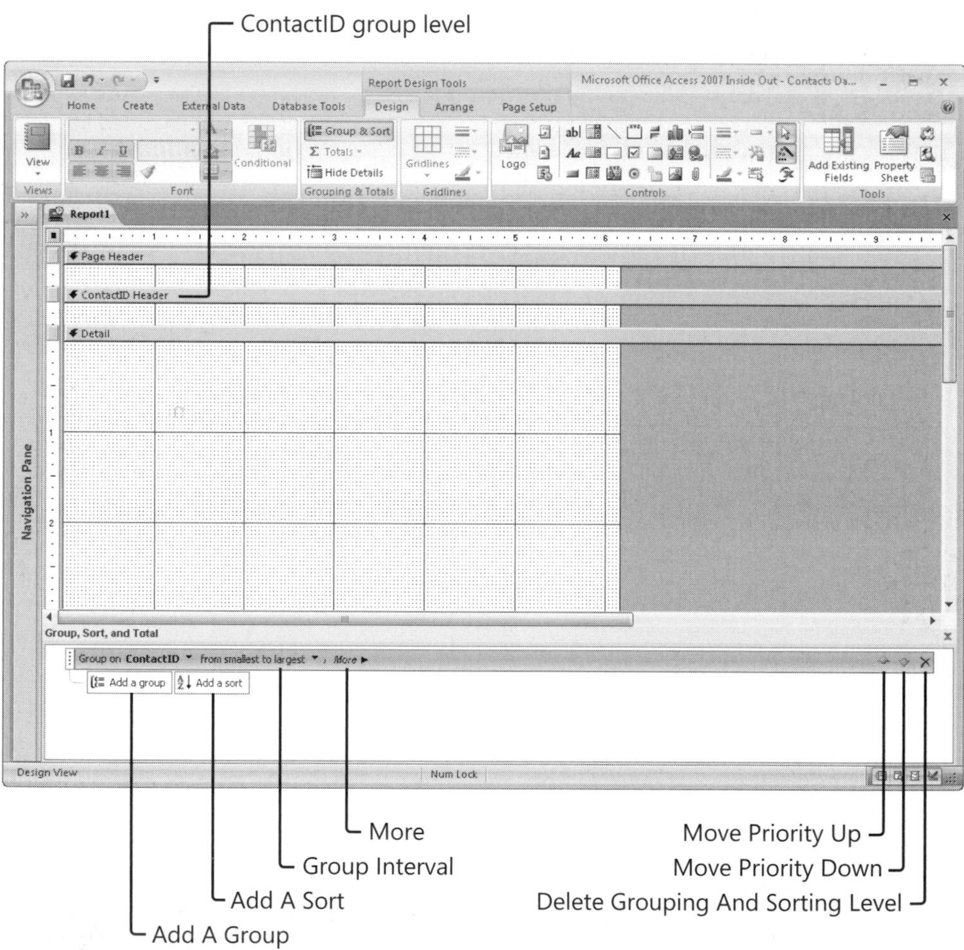


**Figure 15-6** After you add a group in the Group, Sort, And Total pane, Access creates a new group level on the grid.

By default, Access 2007 sorts each field or expression in ascending order. You can change the sort order by selecting From Largest To Smallest from the list that appears when you click the arrow to the right of the second option (From Smallest To Largest in this example). In this case, you want to include the ContactID field so that you can form a group for each contact. Leave the sort order on From Smallest To Largest so that the report will sort the rows in ascending numerical order by the ContactID field. If you wanted to see the contacts in alphabetical order by last name, you would need to include the LastName field in your query (even if you didn't display it on the report), and group and sort on the LastName field. You could use the Contact expression that you included in the query, but then the report would sort the rows by title and first name.

**Note**

Access 2007 changes the choices in the second option in the grouping specification depending on the data type of the field or expression you specified in Group On. When the data type is Text, you'll see With A On Top and With Z On Top options. When the data type is Date/Time, you'll see From Oldest To Newest and From Newest To Oldest. If the data type is Yes/No, you'll see From Selected To Cleared and From Cleared To Selected. As you saw in our example, Access uses From Smallest To Largest and From Largest To Smallest for fields with a Numeric data type.



Click the More option in the ContactID grouping specification to see all the grouping and sorting options, as shown in Figure 15-7. Access now displays a total of eight grouping and sorting options. If you look at Figure 15-7, you can see that Access creates a sentence structure to help you understand how this grouping level will take shape. If you want to collapse the list of options, click Less at the end of the list.

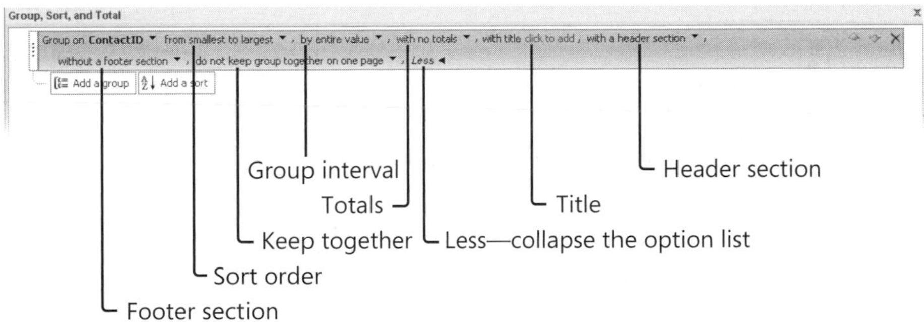


**Figure 15-7** Click More to expand the list of grouping and sorting options.

The third option in the grouping specification (By Entire Value in our example) is called the group interval, which tells Access how to group the records. Click the arrow to the right of this option for a grouping based on the ContactID field, as shown in Figure 15-8. For AutoNumber, Number, and Currency data types, Access displays the following grouping options–By Entire Value, By 5s, By 10s, By 100s, By 1000s, and Custom, which lets you set your own interval. For Text data types, you can set the group interval to By Entire Value, By First Character, By First Two Characters, or Custom, which lets you set your own interval. For Date/Time data types, you can set the group interval to By Entire Value, By Day, By Week, By Month, By Quarter, By Year, or Custom, which lets you set your own interval. Leave the group interval set to By Entire Value for the ContactID group level.

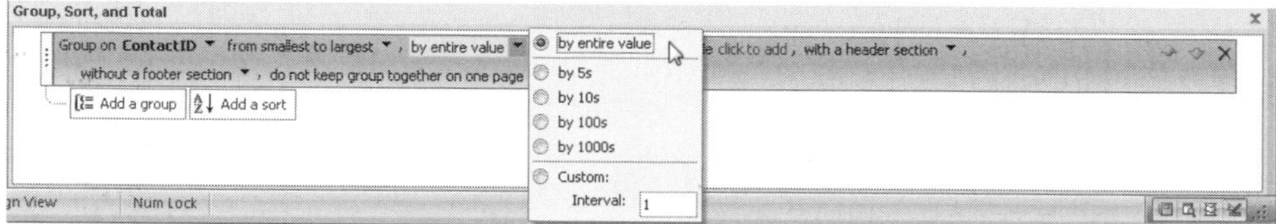


**Figure 15-8** The group interval displays different options based on the field's data type.

You use the fourth option in the grouping specification (which currently displays With No Totals in our example) to configure Access to list totals for a single field or for multiple fields. Click the arrow to the right of this option for a grouping based on the ContactID field, as shown in Figure 15-9. Select the field on which you want Access to calculate and display totals from the Total On list. In the Type box you can choose from several types of calculations based on the data type of the field you chose in the Total On box. Beneath the Type box are four check boxes for additional totaling options. Select the Show Grand Total check box to add a grand total for this field in the report's footer section. Select the Show Group Totals As % Of Grand Total check box if you want Access to calculate the percentage of the grand total for each group and place that percentage in the group header or footer. Select the Show In Group Header check box to place the total and optional percentage in the group's header section and the Show In Group Footer check box to place the total and optional percentage in the group's footer section. Leave the option for the Totals list set at With No Totals for the ContactID group level.

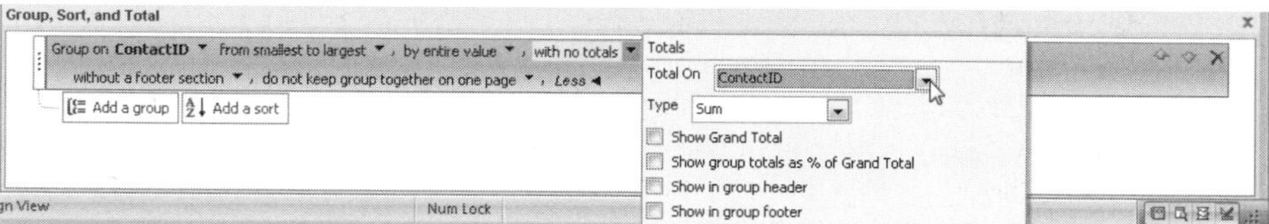


**Figure 15-9** You can ask Access to calculate and display totals in the Totals list.

You use the fifth option in the grouping specification to define a title. You can choose to create a title that appears in a label control in the header section of the group. To create a title, click the blue Click To Add text. Access opens the Zoom dialog box, as shown in Figure 15-10, where you can enter a title. You can click Font to define the font, font style, size, and color of the title letters. After you enter a title, click OK, and Access creates a new label control in the group header section on the report grid. For the grouping based on the ContactID field, click Cancel to not enter a title at this time.

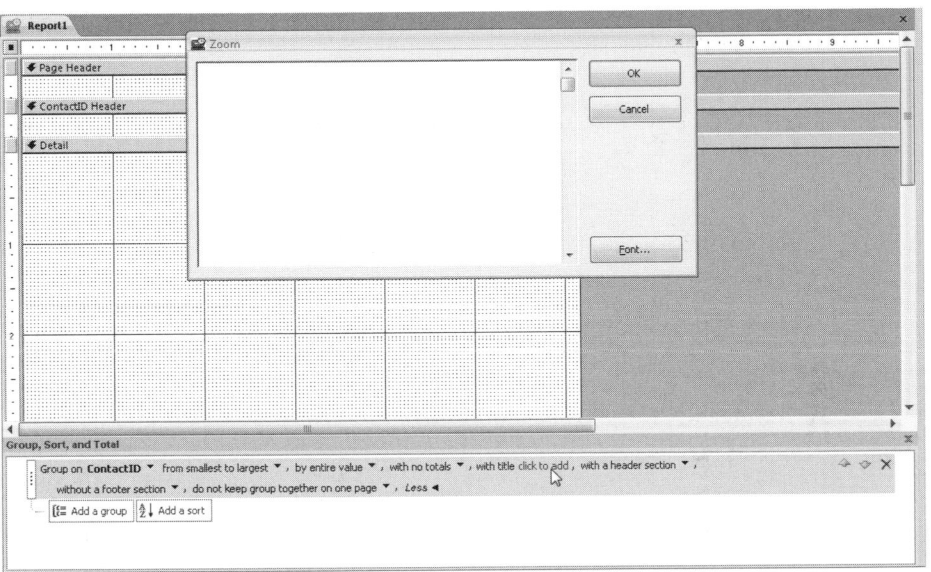


**Figure 15-10** Access displays the Zoom dialog box when you want to add a title to a group header.

You use the sixth option in the grouping specification to display a header section for the specific group. Click the arrow to the right of this option and you can select either With A Header Section (the default selection) or Without A Header Section, as shown in Figure 15-11. When you select the option to include a header, Access creates the header section for the group for you. Conversely, Access removes the group header, and all controls in it, if you select the second option. If you have defined controls in the header section when you choose Without A Header, Access displays a confirmation dialog box explaining that you're deleting both the header and all its controls, and asks you to confirm the deletion. For the ContactID field in our example, leave the option set to the default–With A Header Section.

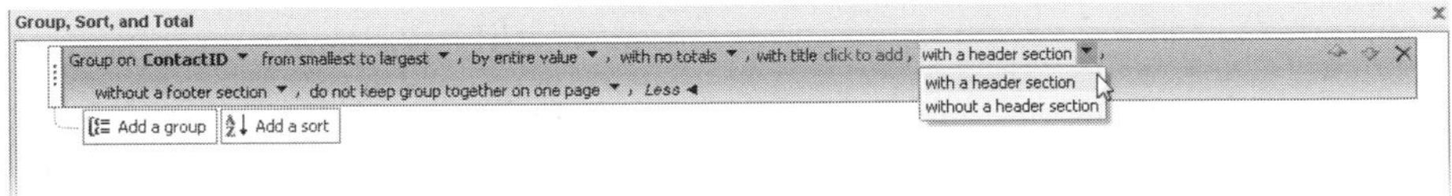


**Figure 15-11** You can choose to have Access create a group header for you.

Similar to the header section option, you can use the seventh option to display a footer section for the grouping specification. Click the arrow to the right of this option and select either With A Footer Section or Without A Footer Section (the default selection), as shown in Figure 15-12. When you select the option to include a footer, Access creates the footer section for you. Conversely, Access removes the group footer, and all controls in it, if you select the second option. If you have defined controls in the footer section when you choose Without A Footer, Access displays a confirmation dialog box explaining that you're deleting both the footer and all its controls, and asks you to confirm the deletion. For the ContactID field you will need a place to put two calculated total fields (the count of contact events and the count of follow-ups). Click the arrow to the right of this option and select With A Footer Section.

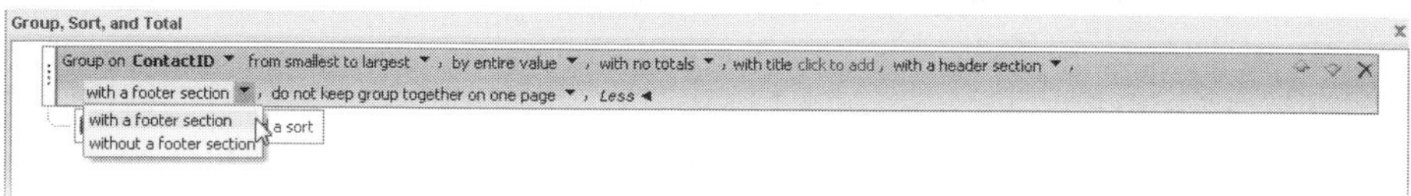


**Figure 15-12** Select the With A Footer Section option to include a footer section for the ContactID group on the report.

You use the last option in the grouping specification, as shown in Figure 15-13, to control how Access will lay out the report when you print it. Click the arrow to the right of this option, and you have three choices—Do Not Keep Group Together On One Page (the default), Keep Whole Group Together On One Page, and Keep Header And First Record Together On One Page.

The Do Not Keep Group Together On One Page option allows a section to flow across page boundaries. The Keep Whole Group Together On One Page option attempts to keep all lines within a section together on a page. If an entire group won't fit on the current page (and the current page isn't blank), Access moves to the top of the next page before starting to print the group, but the group still might overflow the end of the new page.

If you select Keep Header And First Record Together On One Page, Access does not print the header for the group at the bottom of the page if it cannot also print at least one detail record. For the Contact ID field, leave the option set to the default—Do Not Keep Group Together On One Page. You'll learn more about how to use the group on, group interval, and keep together settings in the next chapter.

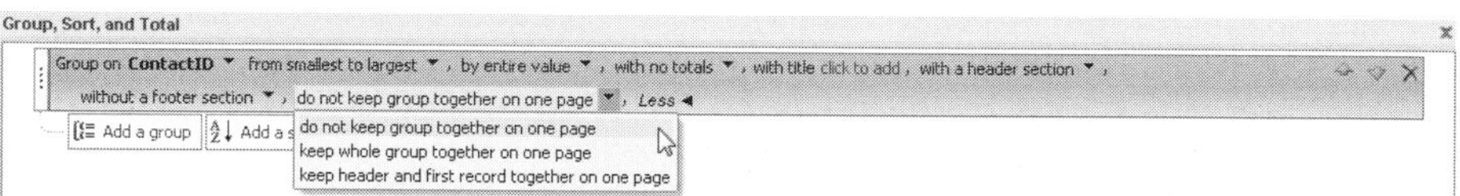


**Figure 15-13** You can choose from among several options to control how the report will look when printed.

It would also be nice to see the contact events in descending date order for each contact (most recent or newest events first). To add the ContactDateTime field below ContactID, click the Add A Sort button and Access creates a new sort specification. Select ContactDateTime in the Select Field box and change the sort order to From Newest To Oldest. Click More to display the rest of the options available to you for the sort specification. Leave the group interval set to By Entire Value, and leave the Totals option set to the default With No Totals. Do not add a title for this field and make sure to not include a group header or group footer. (If you add a header or footer, Access changes your specification from a sorting specification to a grouping specification.) Finally, keep the last option set to Do Not Keep Group Together On One Page. Your completed sorting specification for the ContactDateTime field should look like Figure 15-14.

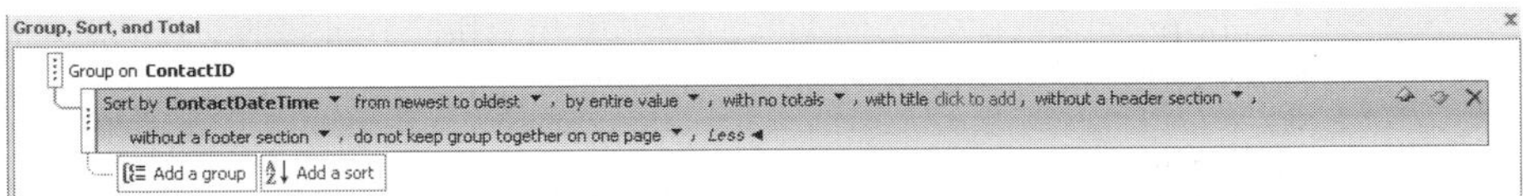


**Figure 15-14** Access will now sort the contact event records for your report in descending order.

You can change the priority of two or more grouping or sorting specifications by using the arrows on the right side of the Group, Sort, And Total pane. If you need to move a group up one level, select that group and then click the up arrow one time. Similarly, if you need to move a group down one level, select that group and then click the down arrow one time. Access repositions any group headers and footers for you during this process. To delete a group level, select it and then click Delete (the *X*) to the right of the up and down arrows. Close the Group, Sort, And Total pane now by clicking the Close button on its title bar or by clicking the Group & Sort button in the Grouping & Totals group on the Design tab.



INSIDE OUT **Understanding Who Controls the Sorting**

You can specify sorting criteria in the query for a report, but after you set any criteria in the Group, Sort, And Total pane, the report overrides any sorting in the query. The best way to ensure that your report data sorts in the order you want is to always specify sorting criteria in the Group, Sort, And Total pane and not in the underlying query.

## Completing the Report

Now you're ready to finish building a report based on the tblContactEvents table. Take the following steps to construct a report similar to the one shown in Figure 15-15. (You can find this report saved as rptXmplContactEvents1 in the sample database.)

1. Click the Title button in the Controls group on the Design tab to place a new label control in the Report Header section. By default, Access enters the name of the report, in this case Report1, in the label. Click inside this label and highlight or delete the existing characters, type **Contact Events**, and press Enter to change the label's caption. With the label control still selected, use the commands in the Font group on the Ribbon to change the font to Arial and the font color to Black. Next, click the Bold and Underline buttons in the Font group, and then click the Size To Fit command in the Size group on the Arrange tab to size the control to accommodate the new font adjustments. Access placed this title in a new section it created–the Report Header. Any control placed in the Report Header section gets printed only on the first page of the report. We want to see this label on every page, so select the label control and drag it down and drop it into the Page Header section. Now remove the Report Header section by clicking the Report Header/Footer button in the Show/Hide group on the Arrange tab.

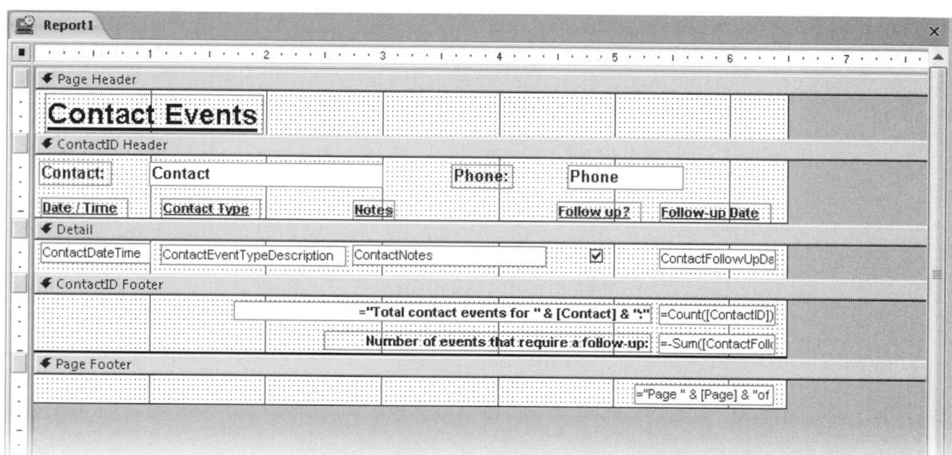


**Figure 15-15** This is the completed Contact Events report that you will create in Design view.

2. Click the Add Existing Fields button in the Tools group on the Design tab to show the field list. If you see Fields Available In Related Tables and Fields Available In Other Tables, click Show Only Fields In The Current Record Source at the bottom of the field list to reduce the number of fields and tables you see. Drag the Contact field from the field list and drop it into the ContactID Header section. Use Arial 10-point bold for the label control and the text box control. Select the text box control and make it about 2 inches wide so that there's room to display all the characters in the contact name. Also drag and drop the Phone field into the header, and set the resulting text box control and the label control to Arial 10-point bold. Size all these controls to fit and line them up near the top of the section.

3. You'll need some column labels in the ContactID Header section. The easiest way to create them is to set up the text box control so that it has an attached label with no colon, set the defaults for the label control to the font you want, drag and drop the fields you need into the Detail section, and then cut the label controls from their respective text box controls and paste them into the header.

   First, widen the design area of the report to about 6.5 inches and increase the height of the ContactID Header section to about 0.5 inch to give yourself some room to work. Next, to set the default properties for the text box and label controls, make sure the property sheet is open (click the Property Sheet button in the Tools group on the Design tab). Click the Text Box button in the Controls group on the Design tab. Select the All tab in the property sheet, scroll down, and check that the Auto Label property is set to Yes and that the Add Colon property is set to No. Also, set the Font Name property to Arial and the Font Size property to 8. Click the Label button in the Controls group, and set its font to Arial 8-point bold and underlined. (You set the font to bold by modifying the Font Weight property.)

Click the Add Existing Fields button in the Tools group to hide the property sheet and open the field list. Now drag the ContactDateTime, ContactEventTypeDescription, ContactNotes, ContactFollowUp, and ContactFollowUpDate fields from the field list and drop them into the Detail section one at a time.

Select the label for ContactDateTime, and then choose the Cut command in the Clipboard group on the Home tab (or press Ctrl+X) to separate the label from the control and move it to the Clipboard. Click the ContactID Header bar, and then click the Paste command in the Clipboard group (or press Ctrl+V) to paste the label in the upper-left corner of the ContactID Header section. Notice that you can now move the label independently in the ContactID Header section. (If you move the label before you separate it from its control, the control moves with it.) Separate the labels from the ContactEventTypeDescription, ContactNotes, ContactFollowUp, and ContactFollowUpDate controls one at a time, and move them to the ContactID Header section of the report.

> **Note**
>
> As you paste each label, you'll see warning smart tags appear that notify you that the labels aren't associated with any control. This is useful to know when you create labels in the Detail section. But in this case, this is what you want, so click the smart tag and select the Ignore Error option to turn off the warning for each label.



4. Line up the column labels in the ContactID Header section, placing the Date / Time label near the left margin, the Contact Type label about 1.1 inches from the left margin, the Notes label about 2.75 inches from the left margin, the Follow Up? label about 4.5 inches from the left margin, and the Follow-Up Date label about 5.4 inches from the left margin. You can set these distances in the Left property of each label's property sheet. Line up the tops of the labels by dragging a selection box around all five labels using the Select button in the Controls group on the Design tab and then clicking the Top command in the Control Alignment group on the Arrange tab.

5. You can enhance the appearance of the report by placing a line control across the bottom of the ContactID Header section. Click the Line button in the Controls group, and place a line in the ContactID Header section. To position this control at the bottom of the section, you need to find out the section's height. Click the ContactID Header bar to select the section, open the property sheet, and find the Height property. Next, select the line control, and set the following properties: Left 0, Width 6.5, and Height 0. Set the Top property equal to the Height of the section. (It's difficult to see this line in Figure 15-15, because it is hidden against the bottom of the section. You'll see it when you switch to Print Preview.)

6. You can make the text box control for ContactDateTime smaller (about 0.9 inch), and you need to make the ContactEventTypeDescription text box control about 1.6 inches wide. Set the Text Align property for the ContactDateTime and ContactFollowUpDate text box controls to Left. Access sized the text box for the ContactNotes field too wide because ContactNotes is a Memo data type. Select the ContactNotes and ContactEventTypeDescription text box controls together, and click the To Narrowest button in the Size group on the Arrange tab to make the ContactNotes text box the same width as the ContactEventTypeDescription text box.
7. Align the text box controls for ContactDateTime, ContactEventTypeDescription, ContactNotes, ContactFollowUp, and ContactFollowUpDate under their respective labels. You can align each one by placing each text box control to the right of the left edge of its label, selecting them both (hold down the Shift key while selecting each one), and then left aligning them by clicking the Left button in the Control Alignment group on the Arrange tab. Align the ContactFollowUp check box control visually under the center of its label. Select all the controls in the Detail section and top align them by clicking the Top button in the same group.
8. The height of the Detail section determines the spacing between lines in the report. You don't need much space between report lines, so make the Detail section smaller, until it's only slightly higher than the row of controls for displaying your data. (About 0.3 inch should suffice.)
9. Expand the height of the ContactID Footer section and then add a text box in this section under the ContactFollowUpDate text box control and delete its attached label. To calculate the number of events, click the text box control, and in the Control Source property in the property sheet, enter

   ```
   =Count([ContactID])
   ```

   It's a good idea to repeat the grouping information in the footer in case the detail lines span a page boundary. One way to do that is to add an expression in a text box. Add a second text box to the left of the first one (also delete its label) and stretch it to about 3.5 inches wide. Click the leftmost text box control to select it, and in the Control Source property in the property sheet, type

   ```
   ="Total contact events for " & [Contact] & ":"
   ```

   Change the text box alignment to Right and change its font to Bold.
10. Add a second text box control in the ContactID Footer section under the first one. In the Control Source property in the property sheet, enter

    ```
    = -Sum([ContactFollowUp])
    ```

    Keep in mind that a True value in a yes/no field is the value –1. So, summing the values and then displaying the negative should give you a count of the contact events that require a follow-up. Click the attached label control and change the Caption property in the property sheet to

```
Number of events that require a follow-up:
```

Change Font Underline to No, right align the label, and size it to fit.

11. Add a line to the bottom of the ContactID Footer section to separate the end of the information about one contact from the next one. You can click the heading bar of the ContactID Footer to select the section and then look in the property sheet to find out the section's height, which should be about 0.5 inch. Select the line again, and in the property sheet set Left to 0, Top to the height of the section, Width to 6.5, Height to 0, and Border Width (the thickness of the line) to 2 pt.

12. Click the Insert Page Number button in the Controls group on the Design tab to open the Page Numbers dialog box shown here.

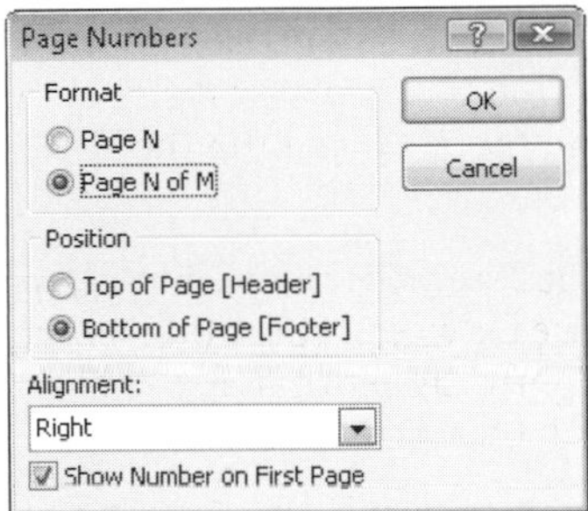


You want to display the current page number and the total number of pages on each page, so select the Page N Of M option under Format. The Page N option displays only the current page number. Next, to display these page numbers at the bottom of the report, select Bottom Of Page [Footer] under Position. The Top Of Page [Header] option places the control in the Page Header section of the report. In the Alignment list, select Right to display the page numbers on the right side of the page. The Left alignment option places the control that displays the page numbers on the left side of the report design grid, and the Center alignment option places the control in the center. The Inside alignment option places one control on the left side and one control on the right side of the report design grid. Access sets the Control Source property of these controls so that page numbers appear in the inside margin of pages in a bound book–odd page numbers appear on the left and even page numbers appear on the right. The Outside alignment option works just the opposite of Inside–even page numbers appear on the left and odd page numbers appear on the right.

Select the Show Number On First Page check box at the bottom of the dialog box to display the page numbers on all pages, including the first page. If you clear this check box, Access creates a control that will not show the page number on the first page. Click OK in the Page Numbers dialog box, and Access creates a new control in the Page Footer section.

13. Click the new text box control that you just created in the page footer, and look at the Control Source property in the property sheet. Access created the expression **="Page " & [Page] & " of " & [Pages]** in the Control Source property of the text box. [Page] is a report property that displays the current page number. [Pages] is a report property that displays the total number of pages in the report. Finally, change the Text Align property to Right for this new control.

After you finish, click the arrow below the View button in the Views group on the Ribbon and click Print Preview to see the result, shown in Figure 15-16. Notice in this figure that the detail lines are sorted in descending order by contact date/time. You'll recall from Figure 15-14 that the grouping and sorting specifications include a request to sort within group on ContactDateTime.



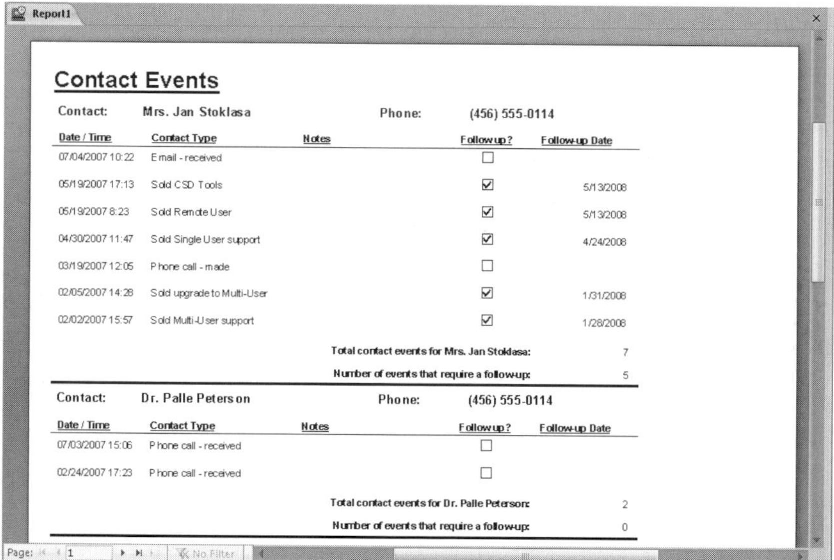


**Figure 15-16** This is how your completed Contact Events report looks in Print Preview.

Now that you've seen how to create a report from scratch, you should have a good understanding of how to work with the individual design elements. In the remaining sections, we'll show you how to get a jump-start on your report design using the quick create Report command, the Report Wizard, and the new Layout view. You'll probably find that using one of these features is a good way to get a report started, and then you can use what you've learned thus far to fully customize your reports.

# Using the Report Command

Access 2007 includes a new quick create Report command that makes it easy for you to quickly create quality reports. Similar to the quick create form commands, the Report command is a one-step process—you're not presented with any options or dialog boxes; Access simply creates a generic report with one click. You can use either a table or query as the base for the report. We'll create two quick reports to illustrate this process using the ContactsDataCopy.accdb sample database.

Open ContactsDataCopy.accdb, click the Navigation Pane menu, click Object Type under Navigate To Category, and then click Queries under Filter By Group to display a list of queries available in this database. The qryContacts query includes all the fields from the tblContacts table and sorts them by last name and then first name. Let's create a nice report of your contacts using this query. Scroll down to this query in the Navigation Pane, select it, and then click the Report command in the Reports group on the Create tab, as shown in Figure 15-17.



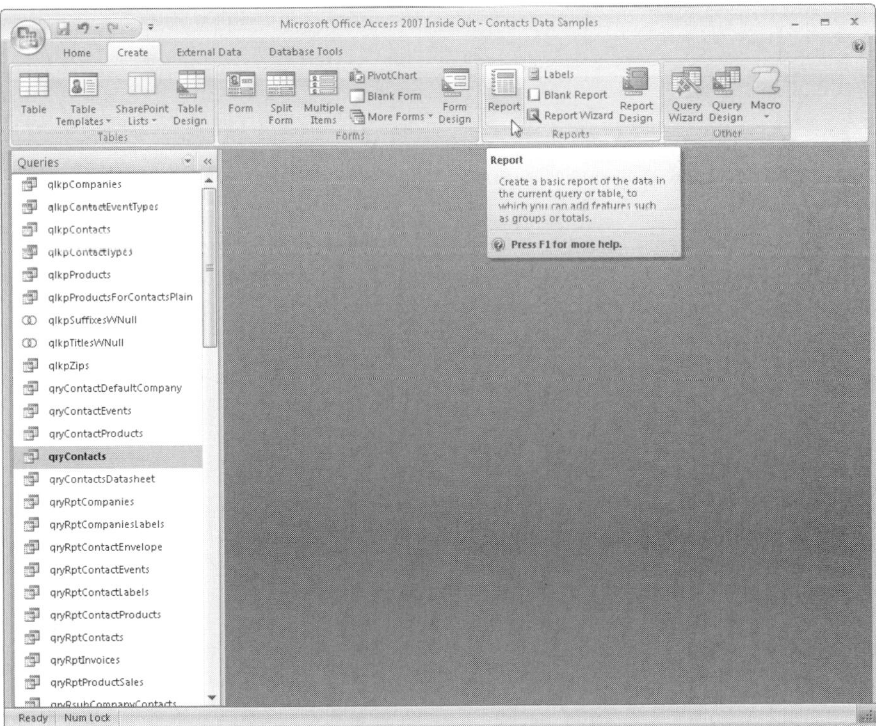


**Figure 15-17** Click the Report command to let Access build a report using the qryContacts query.

After just a second or two, Access 2007 creates an entire report with all the fields in the query, complete with a logo, a title, the current date and time, a colored line beneath the column labels, and even a page count at the bottom of the pages, as shown in Figure 15-18. (You can best see the page count in Print Preview.) Access opens the report in Layout view so that you can begin the process of making modifications.

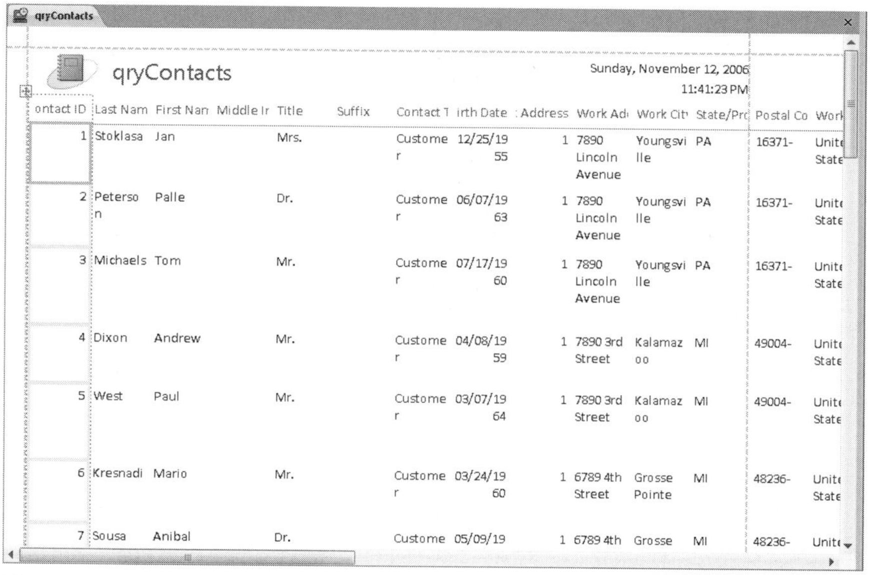

**Figure 15-18** With one click, Access creates an entire formatted report for your convenience.



If you look closely at the report, you'll also see that there are significant problems with this layout. Access spread all the fields out in a tabular control layout. If you switch to Print Preview, you can see that this report would not be easy to read because the data in many columns wraps to multiple lines, and you have to scan across three pages to find all the data for each contact. If the number of contact records were even larger, the report would be extremely hard to follow. Access did much of the hard work for you in creating the report, but you still need to make many modifications in either Layout view or Design view to make the report readable. (We'll discuss Layout view in more detail later in this chapter.) Close this report now, and don't save it when prompted.

The qlkpProducts query includes all the fields from the tblProducts table and sorts them by product name. Select this query in the Navigation Pane and then click the Report command in the Reports group on the Create tab. Access 2007 creates another report very similar to the first one, as shown in Figure 15-19.

This query has only six fields, so Access was able to do a better job of laying out the fields horizontally. However, the Expire field and part of the Price field spill over onto a second page. Using the techniques you learned earlier in this chapter, it would probably take you less than a minute to resize some of the controls to fit everything onto one page and change the title. The rest of the report looks very usable as is. As you can see, the Report command can save you time over starting a report from scratch. Close the report, and don't save it when prompted.

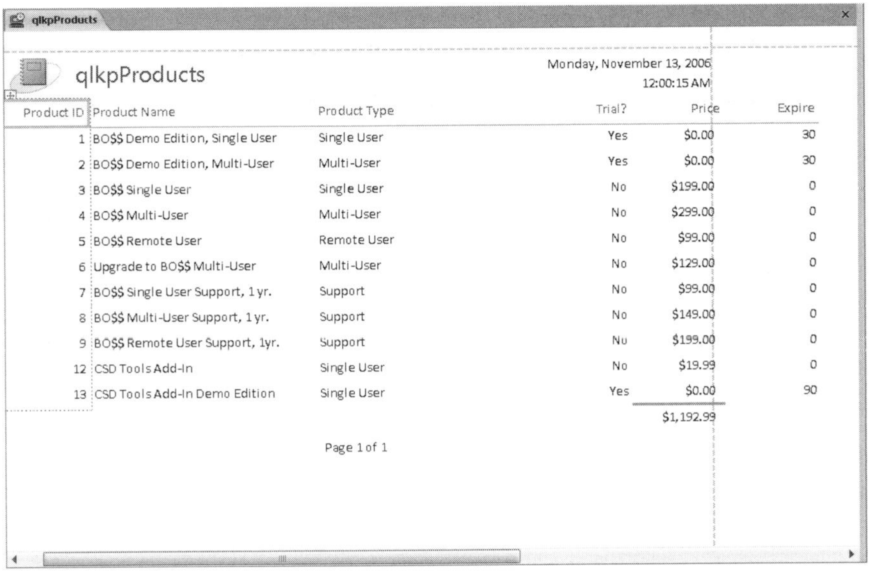

qlkpProducts

qlkpProducts

Monday, November 13, 2006
12:00:15 AM

| Product ID | Product Name | Product Type | Trial? | Price | Expire |
|---|---|---|---|---|---|
| 1 | BO$$ Demo Edition, Single User | Single User | Yes | $0.00 | 30 |
| 2 | BO$$ Demo Edition, Multi-User | Multi-User | Yes | $0.00 | 30 |
| 3 | BO$$ Single User | Single User | No | $199.00 | 0 |
| 4 | BO$$ Multi-User | Multi-User | No | $299.00 | 0 |
| 5 | BO$$ Remote User | Remote User | No | $99.00 | 0 |
| 6 | Upgrade to BO$$ Multi-User | Multi-User | No | $129.00 | 0 |
| 7 | BO$$ Single User Support, 1 yr. | Support | No | $99.00 | 0 |
| 8 | BO$$ Multi-User Support, 1 yr. | Support | No | $149.00 | 0 |
| 9 | BO$$ Remote User Support, 1yr. | Support | No | $199.00 | 0 |
| 12 | CSD Tools Add-In | Single User | No | $19.99 | 0 |
| 13 | CSD Tools Add-In Demo Edition | Single User | Yes | $0.00 | 90 |
| | | | | $1,192.99 | |

Page 1 of 1

**Figure 15-19** This report is easier to understand than the one created on a more complex query.



INSIDE OUT **When to Use the Report Command**

The Report command's strength is speed, not finesse. As the previous two examples demonstrate, this report option is not suited for all occasions. For complex queries or tables with quite a few fields, it might take you longer to clean up a report created with this one-click approach compared to starting from scratch. Although the Report command does create a simple total for the Price field, it does not create any groups or sorts, so you would have to manually add these. We find that the Report command is best suited for simple tables or queries that do not require a lot of complex report analysis.

## Using the Report Wizard

The Report Wizard that Access 2007 provides to assist you in constructing reports is similar to the Form Wizard you used earlier to create forms. To practice using the Report Wizard, we'll build the Contact Events report again. Click the Navigation Pane menu, click Object Type under Navigate To Category, and then click Queries under Filter By Group. Select the qryRptContactEvents query in the Navigation Pane, and then click the Report Wizard button in the Reports group on the Create tab to open the Report Wizard.

## Specifying Report Wizard Options

On the first page of the Report Wizard, shown in Figure 15-20, select the fields you want in your report. (If you have a table or query selected in the Navigation Pane and then click the Report Wizard button, Access automatically uses that object as the record source for the report.) You can select all available fields in the order in which they appear in the underlying query or table by clicking the double right arrow (>>) button. If you want to select only some of the fields or if you want to specify the order in which the fields appear in the report, select one field at a time in the Available Fields list and click the single right arrow (>) button to move the field to the Selected Fields list. If you make a mistake, you can select the field in the Selected Fields list and then click the single left arrow (<) button to move the field to the Available Fields list. Click the double left arrow (<<) button to remove all selected fields from the list on the right and start over.



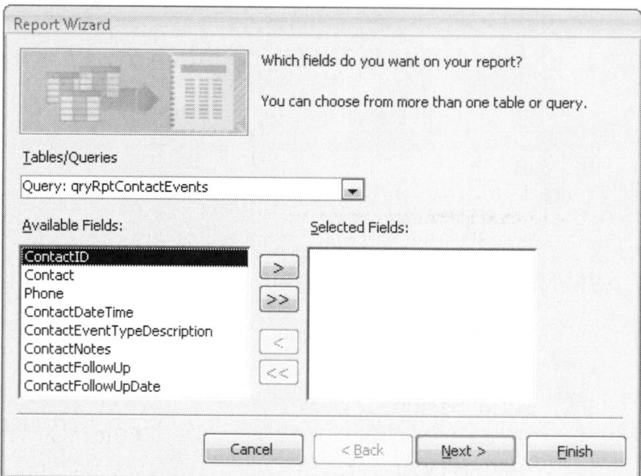


**Figure 15-20** Select fields to include in the report on the first page of the Report Wizard.

To create the Contact Events report, you should select all the fields. Then, click the Next button to go to the next page.

> **INSIDE OUT** **Selecting Fields from More Than One Table and/or Query**
>
> You can also select fields from one table or query and then change the table or query selection in the Tables/Queries list. The Report Wizard uses the relationships you defined in your database to build a new query that correctly links the tables or queries you specify. If the wizard can't determine the links between the data you select, it warns you and won't let you proceed unless you include data only from related tables.

The wizard examines your data and tries to determine whether there are any natural groups in the data. Because this query includes information from the tblContacts table that has a one-to-many relationship to information from the tblContactEvents table, the wizard assumes that you might want to group the information by contacts (the ContactID, Contact, and Phone fields), as shown in Figure 15-21. If you don't want any report groups or you want to set the grouping criteria yourself, select By tblContact-Events. In this case, the Report Wizard has guessed correctly, so click Next to go to the next step.

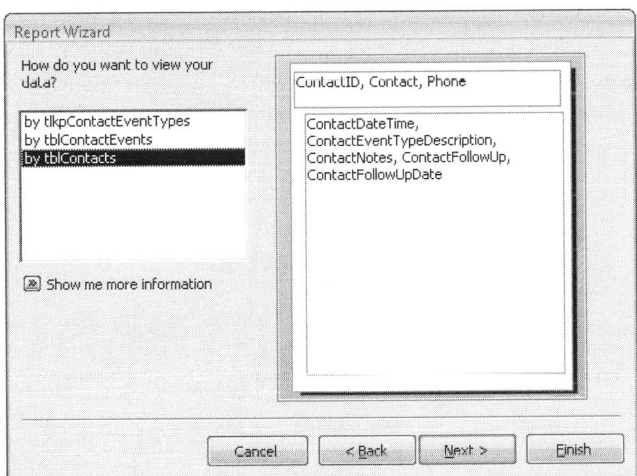


**Figure 15-21** Make sure to verify the primary grouping criteria on the second page of the Report Wizard.

On the next page (shown in the background in Figure 15-22), the Report Wizard shows you the grouping already selected for ContactID and asks whether you want to add any grouping levels below that. (If you chose to set the criteria yourself—by choosing By tblContactEvents on the previous page—you will see a similar window with no first group selected.) You can select up to four grouping levels. The wizard doesn't allow you to enter an expression as a grouping value—something you can do when you build a report from scratch. If you want to use an expression as a grouping value in a report that you create with the Report Wizard, you have to include that expression in the underlying query. For this report, you could also group within each contact by the ContactDateTime field, so select that field and click the single right arrow to temporarily add it as a grouping level.

When you add grouping levels, the Report Wizard makes the Grouping Options button available for those levels. You can select the ContactDateTime By Month grouping level on the right side of this page and then click this button to see the Grouping Intervals dialog box, shown in Figure 15-22. For a text field, you can group by the entire field or by one to five of the leading characters in the field. For a date/time field, you can group by individual values or by year, quarter, month, week, day, hour, or minute. For a numeric field, you can group by individual values or in increments of 10, 50, 100, 500, 1,000, and so on, up to 500,000. As you can see, the Report Wizard has automatically assumed grouping by month when you added the ContactDateTime field as a grouping level. You don't need that grouping level in this sample, so cancel the Grouping Intervals dialog box, select ContactDateTime By Month on the right side of the page, and click the single left arrow to remove it. Then click Next.

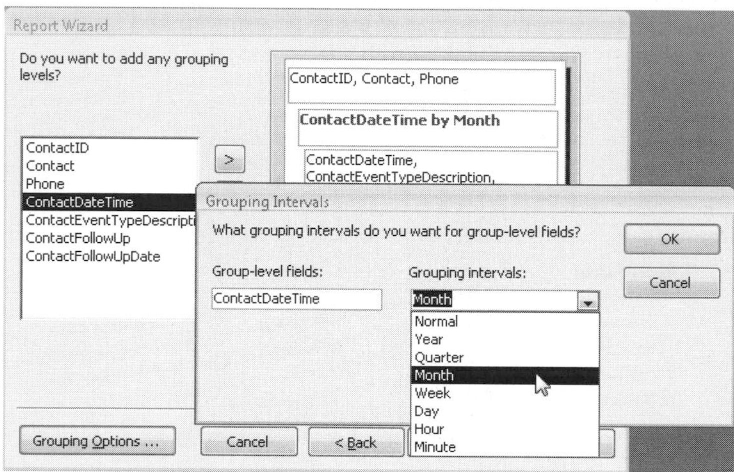


**Figure 15-22** You can set grouping intervals on the grouping fields in the Report Wizard.

On the next page, shown in Figure 15-23, the Report Wizard asks you to specify any additional sorting criteria for the rows in the Detail section. (Access will sort the report at this point by the grouping level fields you specified on the previous page.) You can select up to four fields from your table or query by which to sort the data. By default, the sort order is ascending. Click the button to the right of the field selection list box to switch the order to descending. You can't enter expressions as you can in the Group, Sort, And Total pane. In this report, click the arrow to the right of the first box and select the ContactDateTime field. Click the button to the right once to switch it to Descending, as shown in the figure.

Click the Summary Options button to open the dialog box shown in Figure 15-24. Here you can ask the Report Wizard to display summary values in the group footers for any numeric fields the wizard finds in the Detail section. In this case, the Report Wizard sees that the ContactFollowUp field is the only one in the Detail section that is a number (a Yes/No data type). As you'll see later, the Report Wizard automatically generates a count of the rows, which explains why Count isn't offered as an option.

Select the Sum check box for this field. (You can add the minus sign after the wizard is done to get the correct count.) Note that you also have choices to calculate the average (Avg) of values over the group or to display the smallest (Min) or largest (Max) value. You can select multiple check boxes. You can also indicate that you don't want to see any detail lines by selecting the Summary Only option. (Sometimes you're interested in only the totals for the groups in a report, not all of the detail.) If you select the Calculate Percent Of Total For Sums check box, the Report Wizard will also display, for any field for which you have selected the Sum check box, an additional field that shows what percent of the grand total this sum represents. When you have the settings the way you want them, click OK to close the dialog box. Click Next in the Report Wizard to go on.

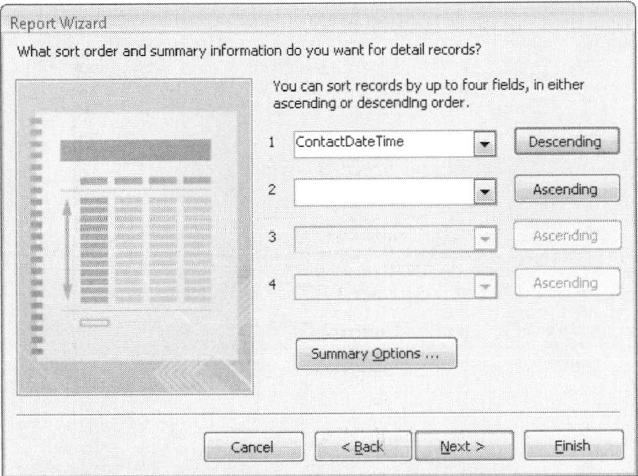


**Figure 15-23** Select ContactDateTime on the fourth page of the Report Wizard to sort on that field.

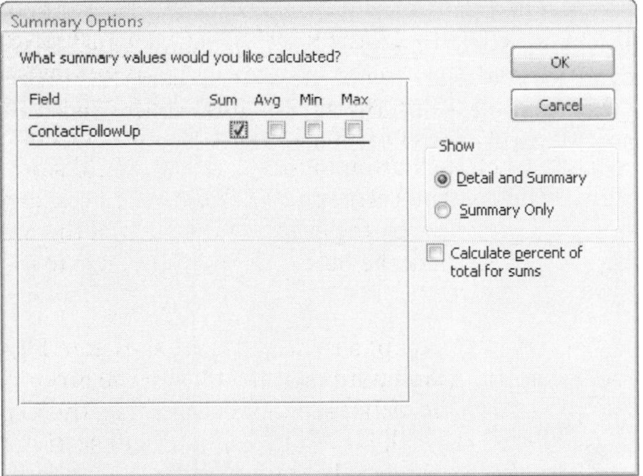


**Figure 15-24** Click the Summary Options button on the fourth page of the Report Wizard to select additional summary options.

On the next page, shown in Figure 15-25, you can select a layout style and a page orientation for your report. When you select a layout option, the Report Wizard displays a preview on the left side of the page. In this case, the Outline layout option in Portrait orientation will come closest to the hand-built report you created earlier in this chapter. You should also select the check box for adjusting the field widths so that all the fields fit on one page.

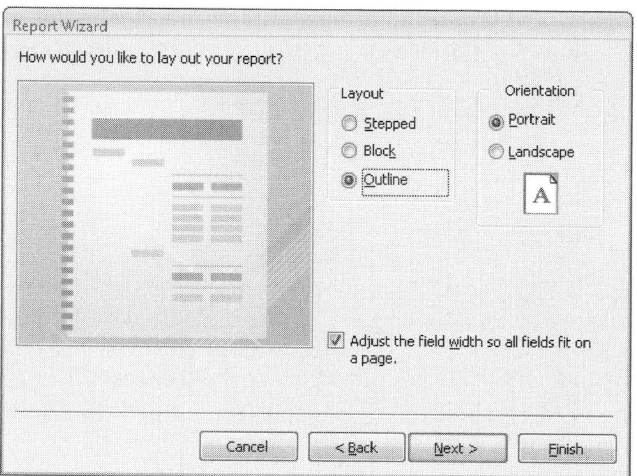


**Figure 15-25** Choose a layout style and page orientation on this page of the Report Wizard.



Click Next to go to the next page of the Report Wizard. On this page you can select from 25 built-in report styles. If you defined your own custom report style using AutoFormat in Design view (similar to the way you defined a format for a form in Chapter 12, "Customizing a Form"), you can also select your custom style. Some of the built-in styles are probably better suited for informal reports in a personal database. Other formats look more professional. Also, some styles include many color elements while others just a few. When you select a style option, the wizard displays a preview on the left side of the page. For this example, select the Access 2007 style. Click Next to go to the final page of the Report Wizard, shown in Figure 15-26.

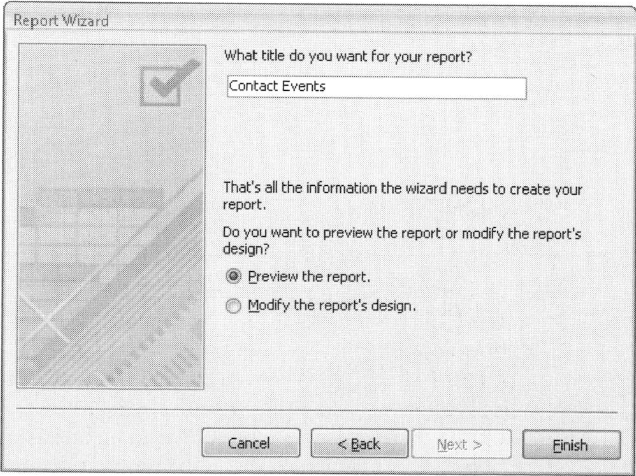


**Figure 15-26** You can specify a report title on the last page of the Report Wizard.

Here, you can type a report title. Note that the wizard uses this title to create the report caption that is displayed in the title bar of the window when you open the report in

Print Preview, the label that serves as the report header, and the report name. It's probably best to enter a title that's appropriate for the caption and label and not worry about the title being a suitable report name. If you're using a naming convention (such as prefixing all reports with *rpt* as we've done in the sample databases), it's easy to switch to the Navigation Pane after the wizard is done to rename your report. In this case, enter **Contact Events** as the title.

## Viewing the Result

Select the Preview The Report option on the final page of the Report Wizard, and then click the Finish button to create the report and display the result in Print Preview, as shown in Figures 15-27. One of the first things you will notice is that Access has created alternating background colors for the detail lines to make it easier to see the data that goes with each record. This feature can be very useful if reports have a lot of information in the detail records and if the lines are packed close together.

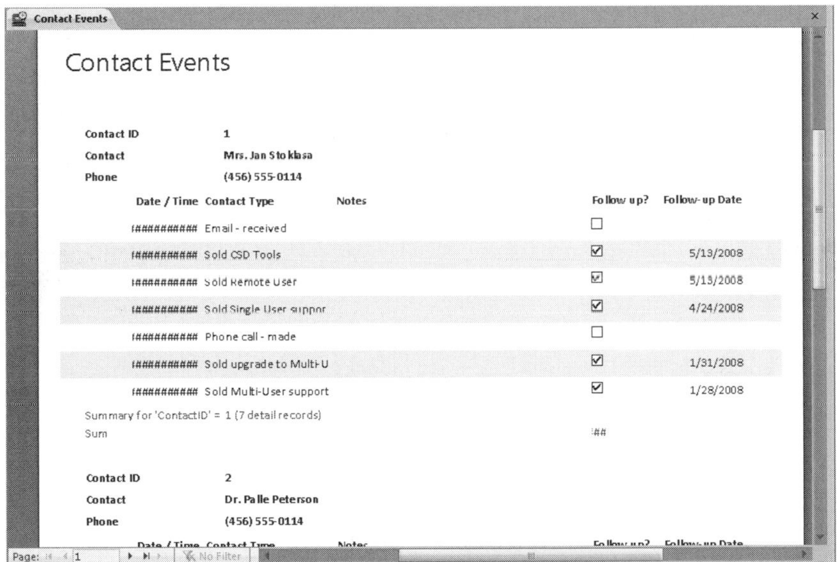


**Figure 15-27** This is the first page of the Contact Events report created using the Report Wizard.

It's easy to use Design view or Layout view to modify minor items (such as adjusting the width and alignment of the ContactDateTime and ContactEventDescription fields and resizing the labels) to obtain a result nearly identical to the report you constructed earlier. You can see in Figure 15-27 that the ContactDateTime field displays # symbols for all the records. Access displays # symbols for date/time and numeric fields when it cannot display all the data in the control, but only when you select the Check For Truncated Number Fields check box under Application Options in the Current Database category of the Access Options dialog box. You also need to fix the expression in the text box that calculates the Sum of the ContactFollowUp field and change the format to display the number. (The Report Wizard set the format to Yes/No.) You should also change the Sum label associated with this calculation. We'll show you how to fix all these problems in the next section. You can find the Report Wizard's report at this point saved as rptXmplContactEvents2 in the sample database. As you might imagine, the Report Wizard can help you to get a head start on more complex report designs.

## Modifying a Wizard-Created Report in Layout View

In the previous section you used the Report Wizard to create a report for contact events. Now you need to clean up this report so that it more closely resembles the Contact Events report you built from scratch earlier in this chapter. Using Layout view makes this process quick and easy. Right-click the Contact Events report in the Navigation Pane (or rptXmplContactEvents2) and click Layout View on the shortcut menu to open this report in Layout view, as shown in Figure 15-28.

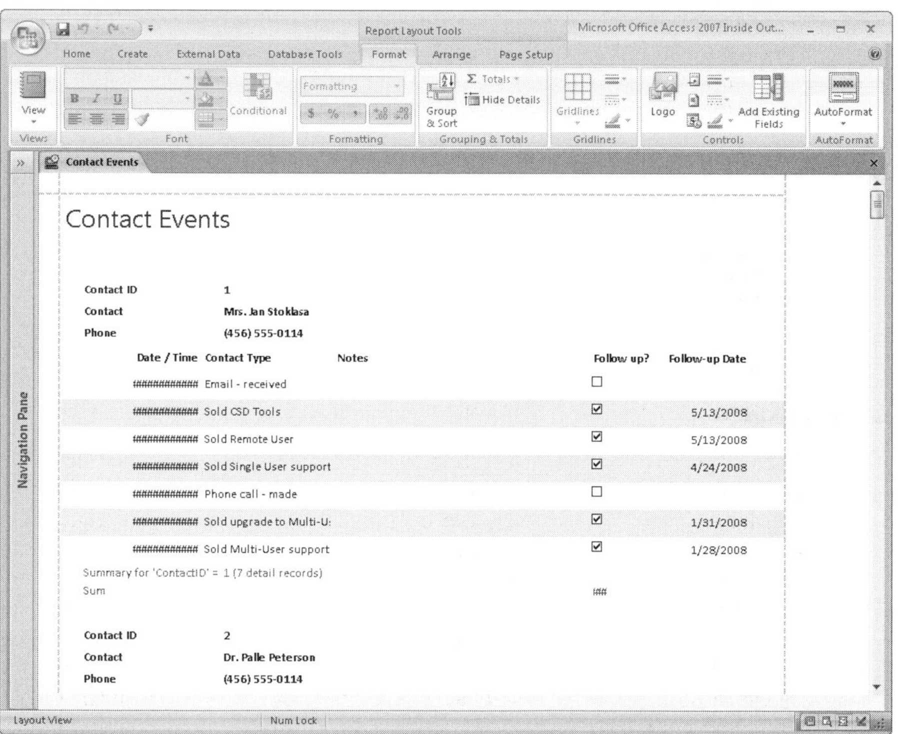


**Figure 15-28** Open the Contact Events report in Layout view to begin making changes.

Access 2007 shows the Report Layout Tools collection of three contextual tabs—Format, Arrange, and Page Setup—on the Ribbon. The report design grid in Layout view looks less like a grid than a sheet of paper. You'll also notice that there are no page breaks in Layout view, and by default Access displays dashed lines along the edges of the report to denote the print margins.

You first need to make the ContactDateTime field wider to accommodate the data. In Layout view you can see live data, so making column adjustments like this is easy.

Click the ContactDateTime label in the first group (the label Date / Time), move your mouse pointer to the left edge of the highlighted control until it becomes a double-sided arrow, and then drag the control to the left until you can see the dates and times in the records, as shown in Figure 15-29. After you adjust the field width for the Date / Time label, click the Center button in the Font group on the Format tab to center the text in the label.

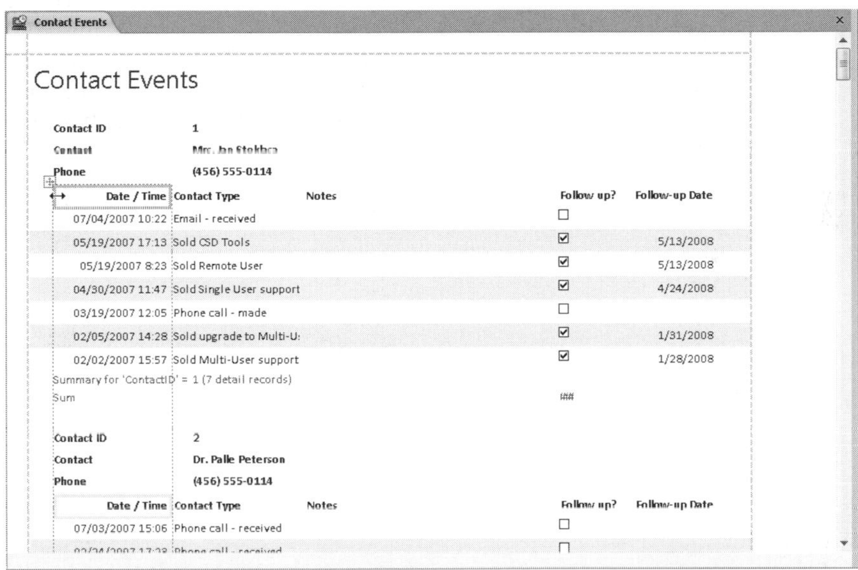


**Figure 15-29** Drag the ContactDateTime label control to the left to resize the entire column.

The ContactEventTypeDescription field also needs to be wider because some of the data is being truncated. Click the ContactEventTypeDescription label in the first group (the label Contact Type), move your mouse pointer to the right edge of the highlighted control until it becomes a double-sided arrow, and then drag the control to the right until you can see all the various contact event descriptions in the records, as shown in Figure 15-30. After you make this adjustment, you can scroll down the records to see whether the increased width accommodates the data in each record. As you make the ContactEventTypeDescription field wider, Access pushes the remaining fields further to the right. If you look closely at Figure 15-30, you can see that the ContactFollowUp-Date field now extends past the print margin. Without even having to switch to Print Preview, you know you have to make further field size adjustments in order to keep the data from spanning across pages.

The Notes field seems to be too wide, so let's shorten this field to make room for the other fields. Click the Notes field label and reduce the width by dragging the right edge to the left until the ContactFollowUpDate field is within the print margin.

The label for the number of events requiring follow-up displays only the word *Sum* at the moment. This label is certainly not very descriptive, so let's change it to something more meaningful. Double-click on the Sum label and type **Number of events that**

**require a follow-up:** directly over the word *Sum*. After you press Enter, Access automatically resizes the control to accommodate the new text, as shown in Figure 15-31.

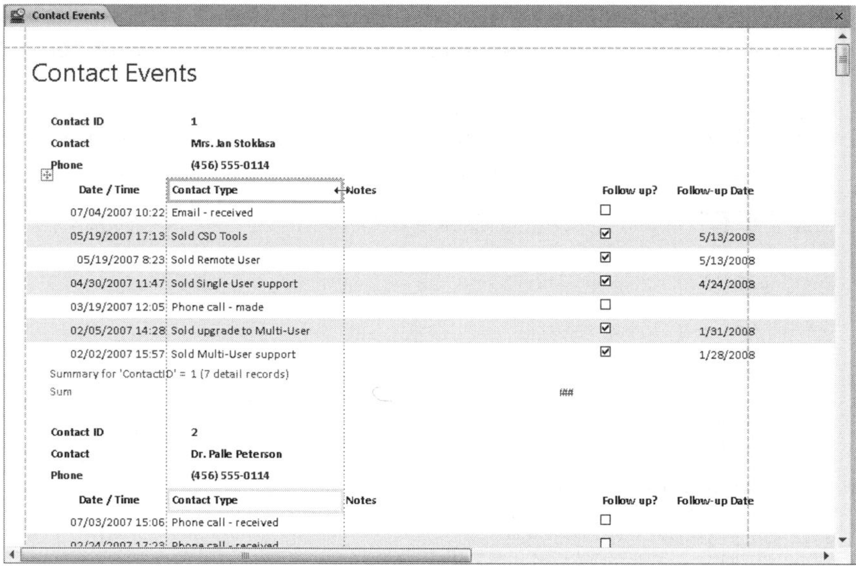


Figure 15-30 When you make the ContactEventTypeDescription field wider, Access moves the other columns to the right.

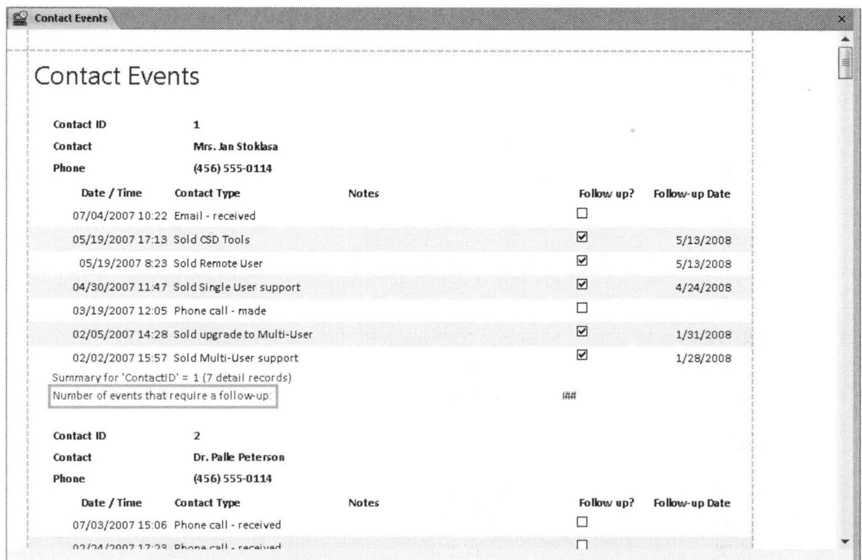


Figure 15-31 Access resizes the control for you in Layout view when you enter a new caption for a label.

You now need to move this label closer to the control that actually lists the sum of the follow-up check boxes. Because there are no controls between the label and the Sum control you have two choices–you can drag the right edge of the label to the Sum control (and right align the text) or you can move the label closer to the Sum control. Let's move this control closer instead of resizing it. Select the label control so that the edges are highlighted with a different color and then drag it closer to the Sum control, as shown in Figure 15-32. As you drag the control, Access displays an outline of the label's size dimensions so that you can easily judge how it will fit in its new position. Release the mouse to drop the label into place next to the Sum control.

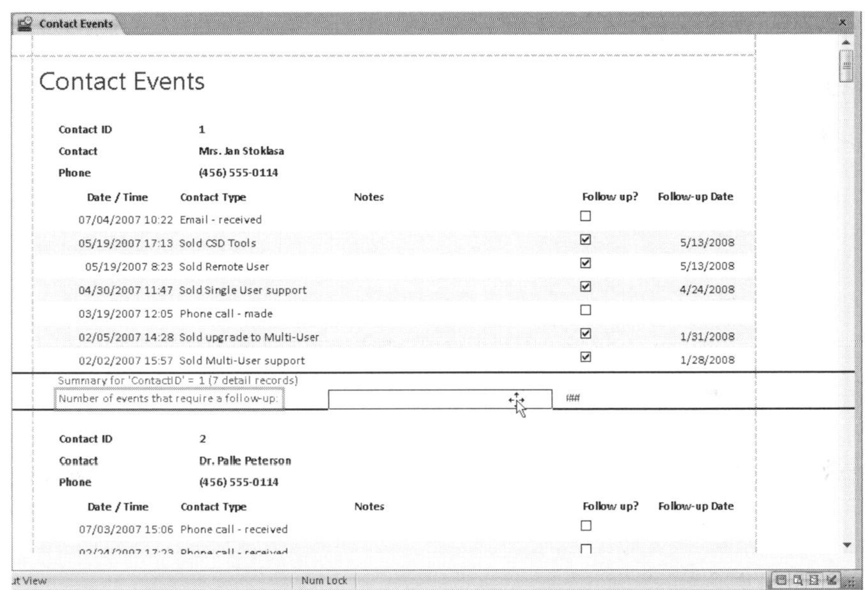


**Figure 15-32** You can easily drag and drop controls into new positions using Layout view.

The Sum control in the Follow Up? column needs to be wider because it is displaying # symbols as was the ContactDateTime field. Resize this control by dragging its right edge. You can now see that Access displays only Yes or No values instead of an actual count. The Report Wizard in this case did not create an expression to correctly calculate the number of follow-ups. Select this control and click the Property Sheet command in the Tools group on the Arrange tab (or press the F4 key) to open the property sheet. Click the All tab on the property sheet and change the Control Source to

```
= -Sum([ContactFollowUp])
```

Move down to the Format property and select Standard from the list of formats to display a number in this control instead of Yes or No. Finally, move down to the Decimal Places property and choose 0 from the list of options to display only whole numbers in the field, as shown in Figure 15-33. Access now displays an integer value representing the number of follow-ups needed. Close the property sheet to see the entire report again.

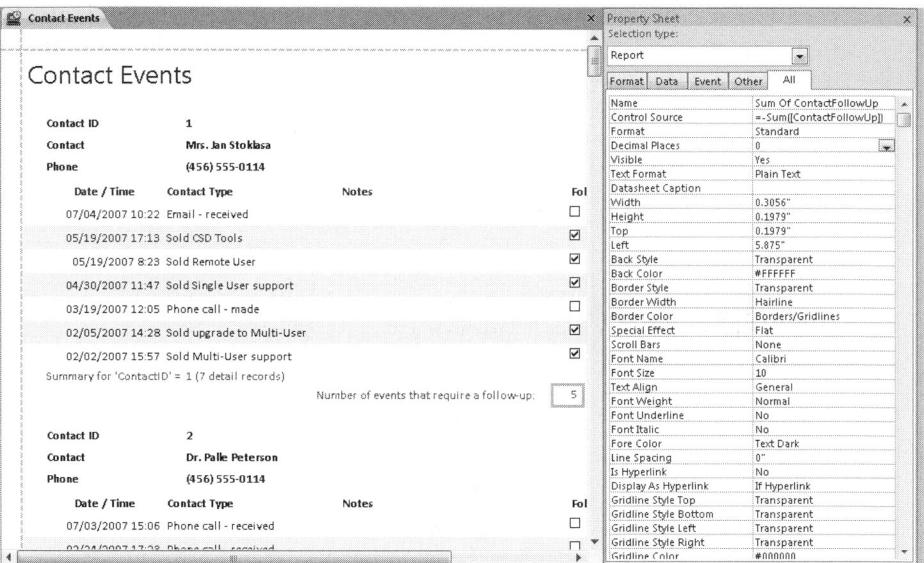


**Figure 15-33** Change the properties of the Sum Of ContactFollowUp control in order to display an integer instead of a Yes or No value.

The Report Wizard created alternating background colors for the detail records in this report. The color is light, so let's change that color to provide more contrast. Click the far left edge of the report next to one of the detail records, and Access highlights all the detail records, as shown in Figure 15-34.

Contact Events

Contact Events

Contact ID 1
Contact Mrs. Jan Stoklasa
Phone (456) 555-0114

| Date / Time | Contact Type | Notes | Follow up? | Follow-up Date |
|---|---|---|---|---|
| 07/04/2007 10:22 | Email - received | | ☐ | |
| 05/19/2007 17:13 | Sold CSD Tools | | ☑ | 5/13/2008 |
| 05/19/2007 8:23 | Sold Remote User | | ☑ | 5/13/2008 |
| 04/30/2007 11:47 | Sold Single User support | | ☑ | 4/24/2008 |
| 03/19/2007 12:05 | Phone call - made | | ☐ | |
| 02/05/2007 14:28 | Sold upgrade to Multi-User | | ☑ | 1/31/2008 |
| 02/02/2007 15:57 | Sold Multi-User support | | ☑ | 1/28/2008 |

Summary for 'ContactID' = 1 (7 detail records)

Number of events that require a follow-up: 5

**Figure 15-34** Click the left side of the report to highlight all the detail records.

Now click the arrow to the right of the Alternate Fill/Back Color button in the Font group on the Format tab to display a color palette. Select Medium Gray 1 to provide more contrast on the report, as shown in Figure 15-35.

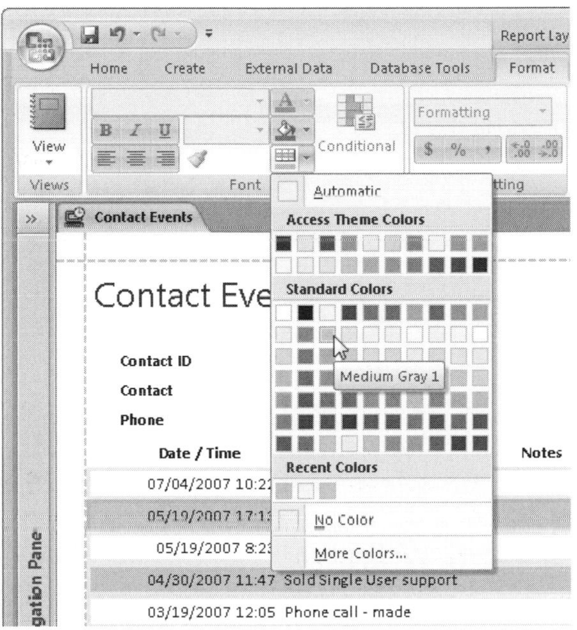


**Figure 15-35** You can select an alternating background color to provide more contrast to your detail records.

Click the Save button on the Quick Access Toolbar to save the changes you made to this report. Switch to Print Preview to see how your completed report looks on paper, as shown in Figure 15-36. This report now looks very close to the Contact Events report you created from scratch earlier in the chapter. You can find this report saved as rptXmplContactEvents3 in the sample database. By using the Report Wizard to do all the heavy lifting and Layout view to make some quick changes, you can create a professional-looking report in a very short time.

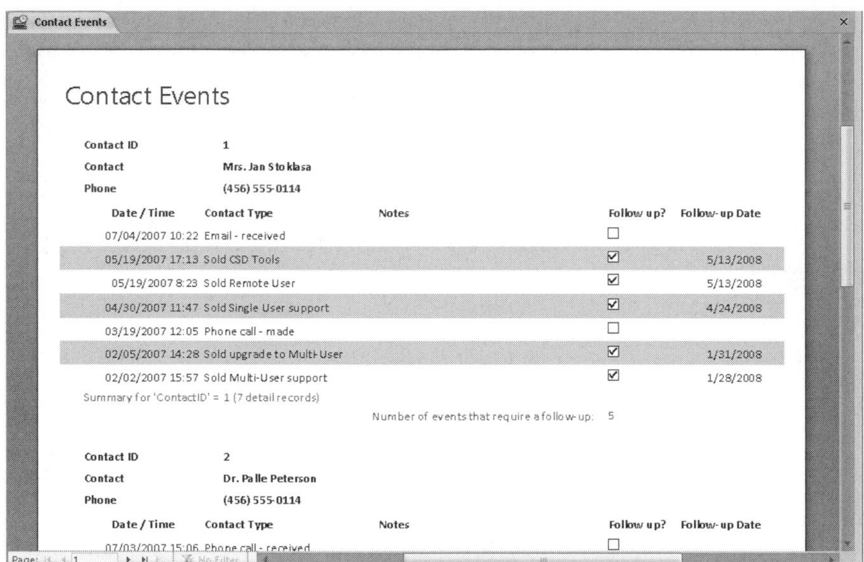


**Figure 15-36** Your completed report now includes all the changes you made in Layout view.



# Building a Report in Layout View

In this chapter you've learned how to create a report from scratch in Design view, to quickly build a simple report using the Report command, to create a report using the Report Wizard to get a jump-start on your work, and to use Layout view to modify an existing report. You've been creating a Contact Events report in the preceding sections, so we'll continue this example now using Layout view.

## Starting with a Blank Report

If you want to follow along in this section, open the ContactsDataCopy.accdb database. Click the Blank Report button in the Reports group on the Create tab. Access 2007 opens a new blank report in Layout view with the field list displayed on the right, as shown in Figure 15-37.

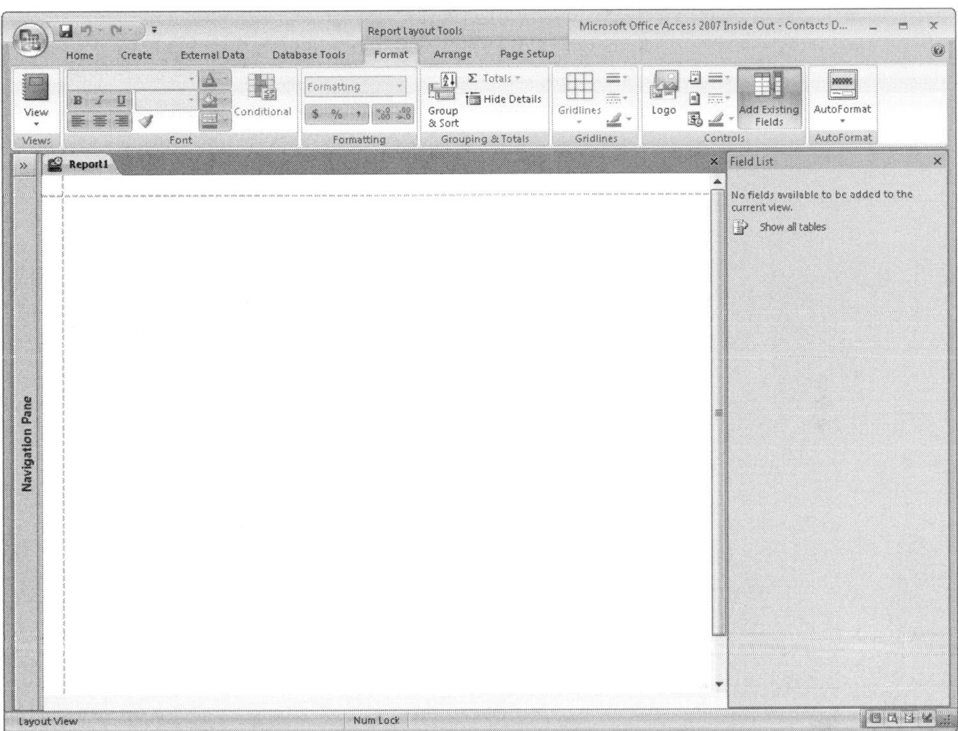


**Figure 15-37** Access always opens in Layout view when you click the Blank Report button.

The report does not yet have a record source, so no fields are displayed in the field list. You can click Show All Tables in the field list to display a list of all tables in this database, but you want to use the saved qryRptContactEvents query that contains all the fields you need from several tables. Click the Property Sheet button in the Tools group on the Arrange tab, click the All tab, and select the qryRptContactEvents query for the Record Source property. Switch back to the field list by clicking the Add Existing Fields button in the Controls group on the Format tab, and then click Show Only Fields In The Current Record Source at the bottom of the field list to show only the eight fields in the query, as shown in Figure 15-38.

You should start this new report by entering a title, so click the Title button in the Controls group on the Format tab. Access places a label control in the upper-left corner of the report and enters the name of the report as Report1. Click inside this label, highlight the existing characters, and change the text to **Contact Events**. As you type the new characters, Access automatically resizes the label to accommodate the length of the new text. Press Enter to save the new title in the control.

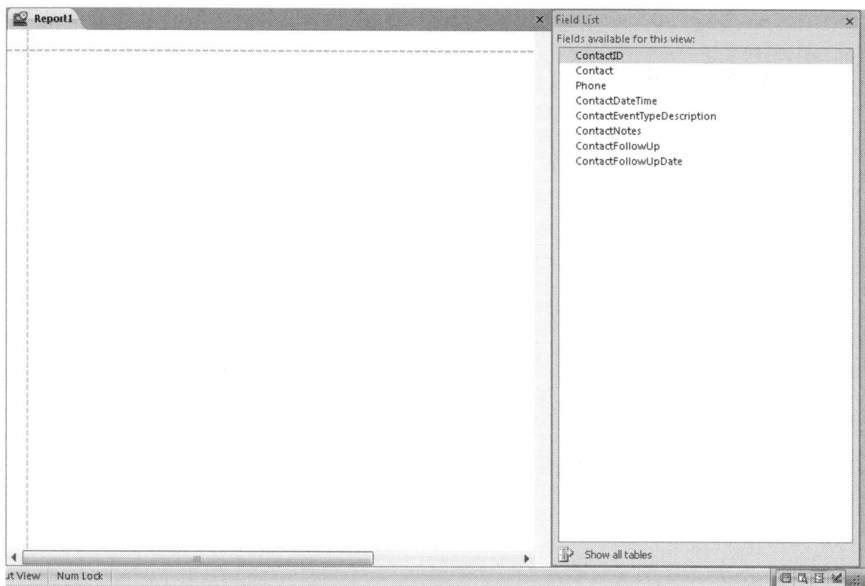


**Figure 15-38** Assign the qryRptContactEvents query as the new report's record source.



## Adding Grouping and Sorting

You need to set up the grouping and sorting options for the ContactID and Contact-DateTime fields as you did earlier in the chapter. Click the Group & Sort button in the Grouping & Totals group on the Format tab to open the Group, Sort, And Total pane. Click the Add A Group button and set the following options for ContactID, as shown in Figure 15-39:

```
Group On ContactID From Smallest To Largest, By Entire Value, With No Totals, With
Title Contact ID, With A Header Section, With A Footer Section, Do Not Keep Group
Together On One Page
```

As soon as you select ContactID in the Select Field box that opens when you click the arrow next to Group On, Access 2007 places a text box bound to ContactID and an associated label on the report. In Layout view, it's hard to see where the different report sections begin and end. When you create the ContactID group level, Access creates a header and footer for this group, but because you see live data in Layout view, the actual design layout can sometimes be hard to visualize. Right now it almost looks like the ContactID field is in the report's Detail section because you see all the records listed one right after another. Switch to Design view for a moment and take a quick look at what Access has created so far. In Figure 15-40, you can see that Access correctly placed the title label in the Report Header section instead of the Page Header section. The ContactID field and label are positioned in the new ContactID group level (as shown in the ContactID Header section). This is what you want, so switch back to Layout view to continue creating your report.

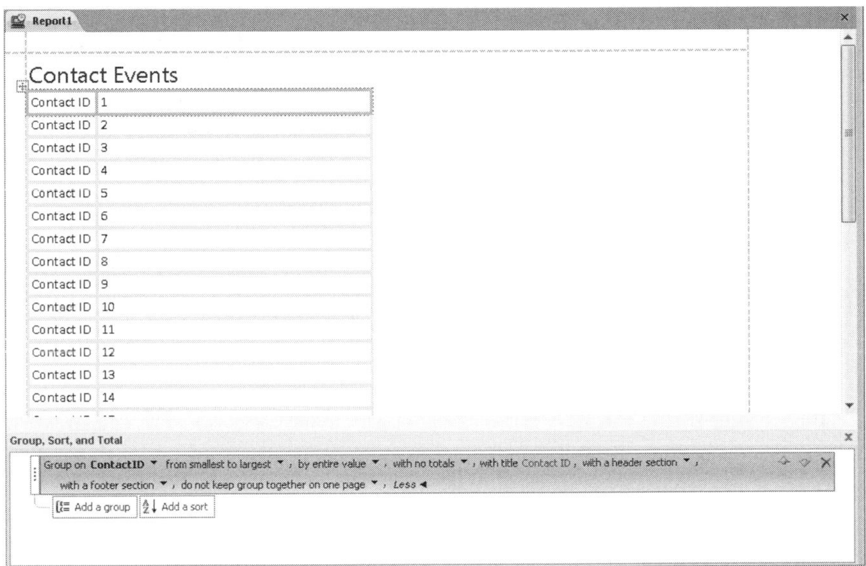


**Figure 15-39** After you add ContactID as a group level, Access adds that field to the report grid.

**Figure 15-40** In Design view, you can see where Access has placed the various controls in the report sections.

You need to add a sort on the ContactDateTime field, so click the Add A Group button in the Group, Sort, And Total pane and set the following options for ContactDateTime:

```
Sort By ContactDateTime From Newest To Oldest, By Entire Value, With No Totals, With
Title Date / Time, Without A Header Section, Without A Footer Section, Do Not Keep
Group Together On One Page
```

Chapter 15

## INSIDE OUT Save a Step by Choosing Add A Group Instead of Add A Sort

You could also click Add A Sort to define the sort on the ContactDateTime field, but Access 2007 won't add the field to the report layout. When you click Add A Group, Access builds a group header section and adds the ContactDateTime field. When you change the grouping specification to Without A Header Section, Access moves the ContactDateTime field into the Detail section for you. This saves having to find the field in the field list and add it yourself.

Just as before, Access places a new control and label on the report for you after you select the ContactDateTime field, as shown in Figure 15-41. In this case, Access places this field in the Detail section of the report when you select Without A Header Section. After you select Without A Header Section, you'll notice that With Title changes from Date / Time to Click To Add. Access moves the label and text box from the new Contact-DateTime Header section into the Detail section. The new label still shows Date / Time, but Access changes the specification to show Click To Add in the With Title column. You can now see the report beginning to take shape with two fields on the grid and the controls displaying live data. Close the Group, Sort, And Total pane now.



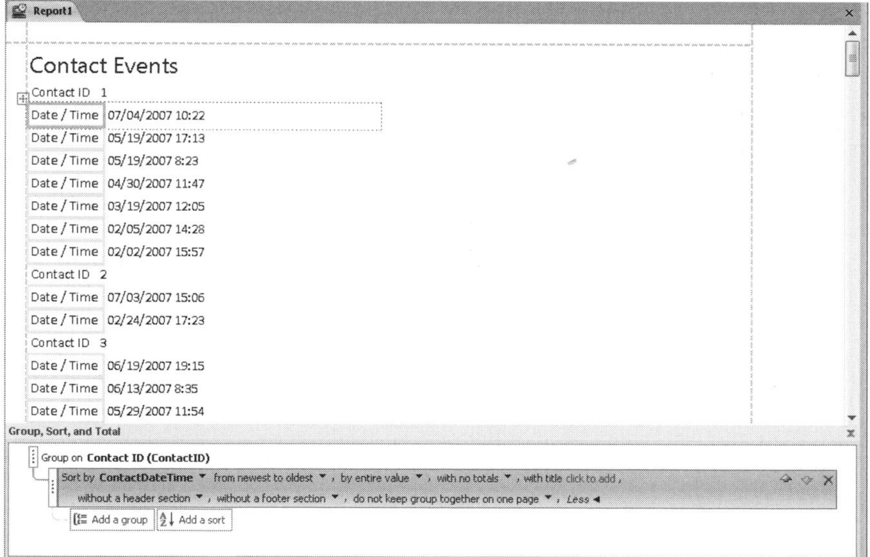


**Figure 15-41** Access adds the ContactDateTime field to the Detail section below the ContactID field.

Now that you have all your grouping and sorting set up, you need to add the additional fields onto the report. If necessary, click the Add Existing Fields button in the Controls group on the Format tab to open the field list again. Click the Contact field in the field list, drag it onto the report, and drop it just below the Contact ID label and text box, as shown in Figure 15-42. When you have it correctly positioned, Access displays a horizontal I-bar below the Contact ID controls.

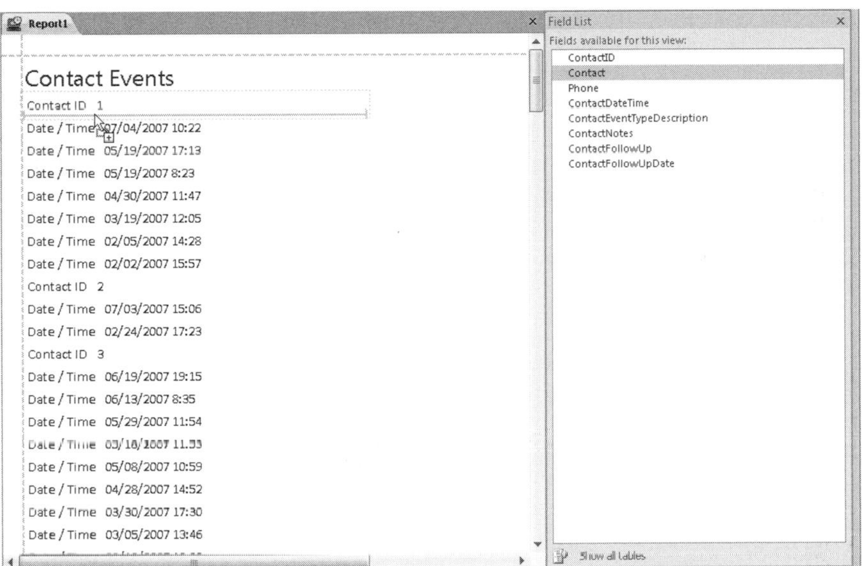


**Figure 15-42** Drag the Contact field and drop it below the ContactID field.

Access places the Contact field right below the Contact ID label and text box controls and appears to push the Date / Time records down the page. Now that you have the Contact field in place, you really don't need the ContactID field at all. Earlier in the chapter when you built this report in Design view, you didn't include the ContactID field because the number itself is probably meaningless to whoever sees this report. The contact's name is more important, so let's delete the ContactID controls now. Click on either the ContactID label or text box and press Delete to remove these two controls from the grid. Alternatively, you can click the Delete button in the Records group on the Home tab. Your report should now look like Figure 15-43.

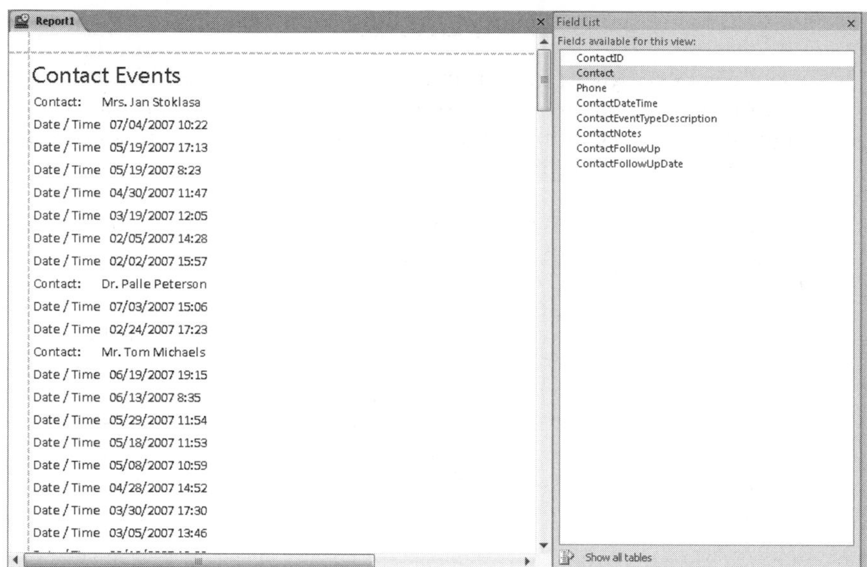


**Figure 15-43** Access moves the other controls up after you delete the ContactID text box and label.

INSIDE OUT **Why Delete the ContactID Controls?**

It's true that you probably could have created the group header directly using the Contact field rather than ContactID to see a similar end result. However, for each contact, only the value in the ContactID field is guaranteed to be unique. (It's the primary key of the tblContacts table.) Although it's highly unlikely to find two contacts with the same name, it could happen, and you would end up with contact event data for multiple unique contact ID values grouped under one heading. Also, creating a group on a numeric value (ContactID) is slightly more efficient than creating a group on a text value (Contact).

Now let's add the Phone field to the report beneath the contact name. Click the Phone field in the field list, drag it onto the report, and drop it just below the label and text box controls for the first contact. As before, make sure the I-bar is right below the contact label and text box controls before releasing the mouse. Access places the Phone field in the ContactID Header section and lines up the control to match the Contact field. (You can switch to Design view if you'd like to see this.)

## Working with Control Layouts

When you're designing a report in Layout view, Access 2007 automatically places any controls that you add to the report inside a *control layout*. Control layouts help you to align and position controls on reports and forms. You can think of a control layout as being similar to a table in Microsoft Word or a spreadsheet in Microsoft Excel. When you widen or narrow one control in a column, you change the width of any other controls in that column that are part of that control layout. Likewise, when you increase or decrease the height of a control, you're changing the height of all the controls on that row.

There are two kinds of control layouts in Access 2007– *stacked* and *tabular*. In a stacked control layout, Access "stacks" bound controls for different fields in a column and places all the labels down the left side. You can have multiple sets of stacked controls within a section. Any controls (including associated labels) in a stacked layout must all be in one section. In the report you've built thus far, Access has placed the contact and phone number controls in a stacked layout in the ContactID Header section. It has also placed the contact date/time controls in a stacked layout in the Detail section.

In a tabular control layout, Access places bound controls horizontally with labels along the top as column headings–much like rows on a spreadsheet. A tabular control layout can include controls in different sections of a report–for example, the labels can appear in a header section and the data controls in the Detail section. You'll learn later in this section how to convert the stacked layout for fields in the Detail section into a tabular layout.



INSIDE OUT

### Is Layout View a Useful Way to Build Reports?

The answer depends on your level of expertise. As experienced developers, we find Layout view somewhat frustrating. It's not always obvious which section contains the controls for a field that we've just added to the report. Notice that we recommend you switch to Design view several times during the design process to verify where Access has placed controls. Also, Access automatically adds any field into a control layout, and you don't have much control over how it does this. Although control layouts can help you align controls in a pleasing way, they severely restrict how you place your controls and how you size them within a layout group. If you're an experienced developer, you might use Layout view to quickly place controls in a new report design, but then you'll probably switch to Design view to selectively remove control layouts so that you can finish customizing your design.

The text box controls for the Phone field and the Contact field are both too wide at this point. You can see this by clicking any of the controls for either field–Access draws a dotted line showing you the boundary of all the controls in the stacked layout group. Start by clicking the Phone field text box, move your mouse to the right edge until it becomes a double-sided arrow, and then click and drag the edge of the field to the left but make sure you don't shorten the field too much. Give yourself more room than you think you might need on the right side because as you resize the Phone field you'll notice that Access resizes the Contact field as well, and you need enough room in that field to display the names on one line. You can see this effect in Figure 15-44. (Note: The longest contact names are near the end of the list.) When you resize the Phone field, you resize the Contact field and vice versa, so if you shorten the Phone field too much, Access has to move some of the data in the Contact field down to a second line.

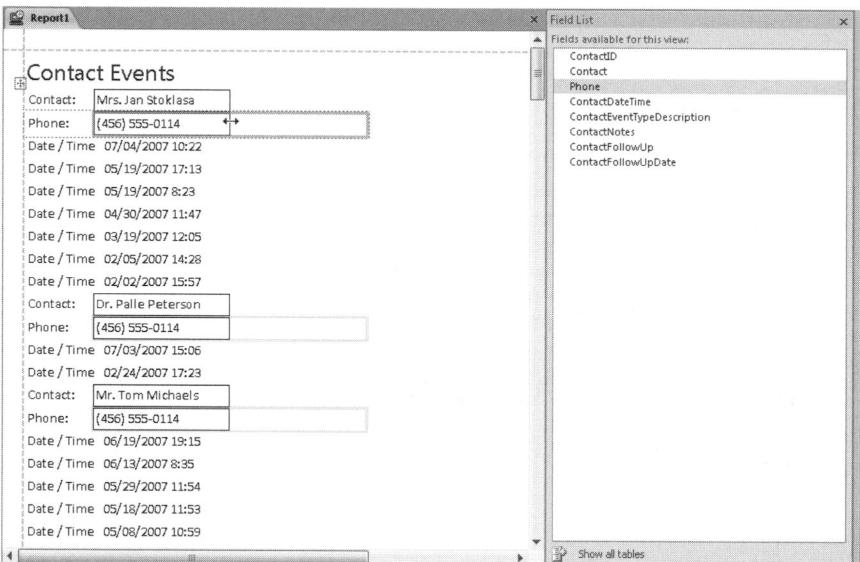


**Figure 15-44** Access resizes the Contact and Phone fields together.

The only control in the Detail section of the report at the moment is the ContactDateTime field. You'll eventually need to convert this stacked control layout to a tabular control layout, and you'll need some additional horizontal space. If you click the ContactDateTime text box, you'll see that it is far wider than it needs to be. Grab the right edge of the control and drag it to the left so that the text box is just wide enough to display all the data.

To see how this affects placing additional controls in the section, click ContactEventTypeDescription in the field list and drag it to the right edge of ContactDateTime. Access lets you place the horizontal I-bar either above or below the ContactDateTime field controls, but not to the right of the field, which is what you want to do. Go ahead and drop it below the first ContactDateTime control, as shown in Figure 15-45.

After you release the mouse, Access places the ContactEventTypeDescription field directly below the ContactDateTime field and sizes it to match the width of the ContactDateTime field, as shown in Figure 15-46. Because the width you chose for the ContactDateTime field won't allow the data in ContactEventTypeDescription to fit on one line for all records, Access expands the height on those records that have more characters.

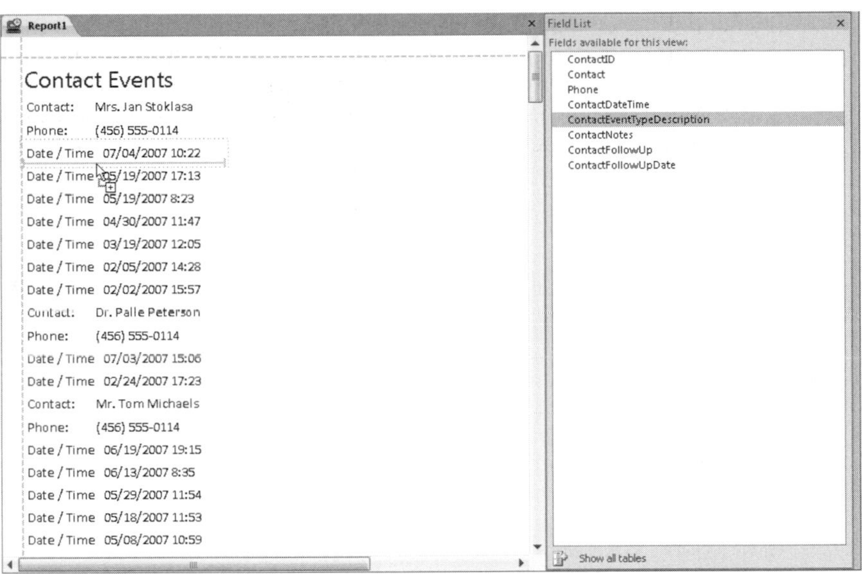


**Figure 15-45** Drop the ContactEventTypeDescription field below the first ContactDateTime field.

**Figure 15-46** Access places the ContactEventTypeDescription field into the stacked control layout with the ContactDateTime field.

If you added the remaining three fields—ContactNotes, ContactFollowUp, and Contact-FollowUpDate—to the report Detail section, Access would also stack these down the left edge on the report. You want to see these fields placed horizontally across the report, so you need to change the control layout in this section from stacked to tabular. Click the Date / Time label or text box, hold down the Shift key, and then click the Contact Type label or text box to select both controls. Click the Remove button in the Control Layout group on the Arrange tab to remove the control layout applied to this section, as shown in Figure 15-47.

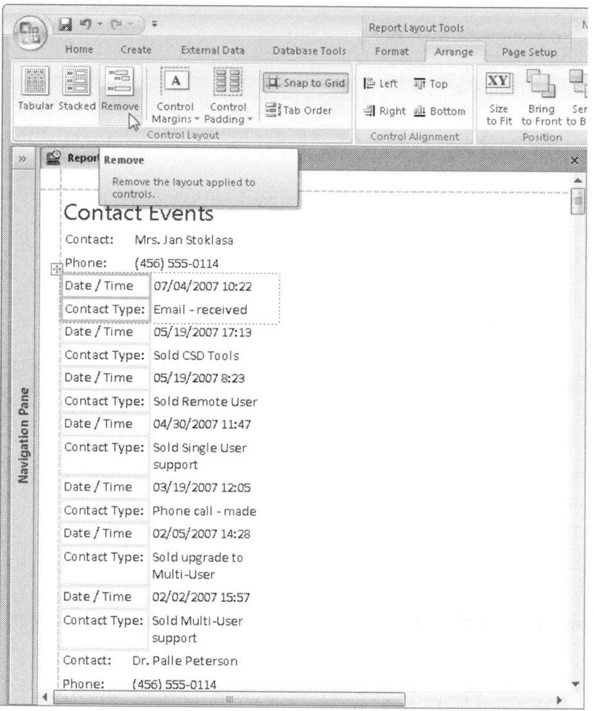


**Figure 15-47** You can remove control layouts by clicking the Remove button on the Arrange tab.

Now that you have removed the control layout for the Detail section, these controls act independently—if you resize one control, the other will not resize. If you add new fields to the Detail section at this point, you might have some extra work in getting everything properly aligned. Because you want to see the other fields displayed horizontally, applying a tabular control layout to the Detail section will make placement and alignment of the new fields much simpler. Select the Date / Time and Contact Type labels or text boxes as you did previously, and then click the Tabular button in the Control Layout group on the Arrange tab, as shown in Figure 15-48.

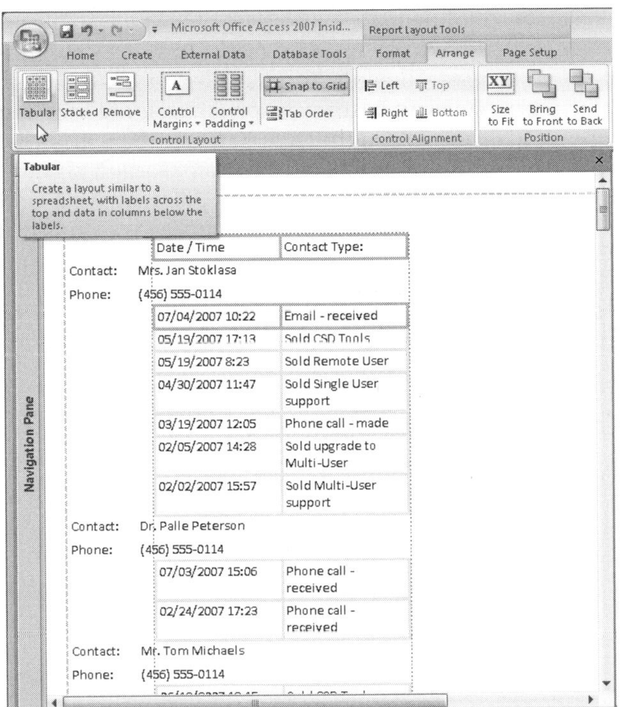

Figure 15-48 The tabular control layout arranges the controls with labels horizontally across the report.



## INSIDE OUT You Don't Have to Remove a Layout Before Converting It

Although we told you to select both controls in the Detail section and then click Remove, you don't actually have to do that. We added that step so that you could see the controls independent of the layout. When you want to convert a layout from stacked to tabular or vice versa, select the controls in the layout and then click the layout you want in order to directly convert it.

Access now places the labels and text box controls for the ContactDateTime and ContactEventTypeDescription fields in a tabular format. The two labels are placed horizontally across the report just below the report title. Access also moves the ContactEventTypeDescription text box to the right of the ContactDateTime text box control. (Access has actually placed the labels in the Page Header section—you can verify this by switching briefly to Design view.) During the switch to tabular format, Access also moves the labels and controls about one inch from the left side of the report. This layout is now closer to the report you built from scratch in Design view earlier in this chapter.

Because these two field controls are now next to each other instead of stacked, you can change the width of one of them without affecting the other. Let's move both the labels and text boxes back to the left margin of the report. Click the Date / Time label and increase the width by dragging its left edge to the print margin dotted line on the left side of the report. The Date / Time label is aligned with the left margin of the report, but now it's too wide, so decrease the width by dragging its right edge toward the left. As you resize the label, Access also resizes the ContactDateTime field control. Release the mouse when you can still see all the data in the ContactDateTime field control. Access moves the Contact Type label and the ContactEventTypeDescription field to the left after you reduce the width of the date/time controls. Now click the Contact Type label and expand the width to the right to allow extra room for the characters in the longest ContactEventTypeDescription field control. After you have expanded the width, Access reduces the height of the ContactEventTypeDescription field control to one line, as shown in Figure 15-49.

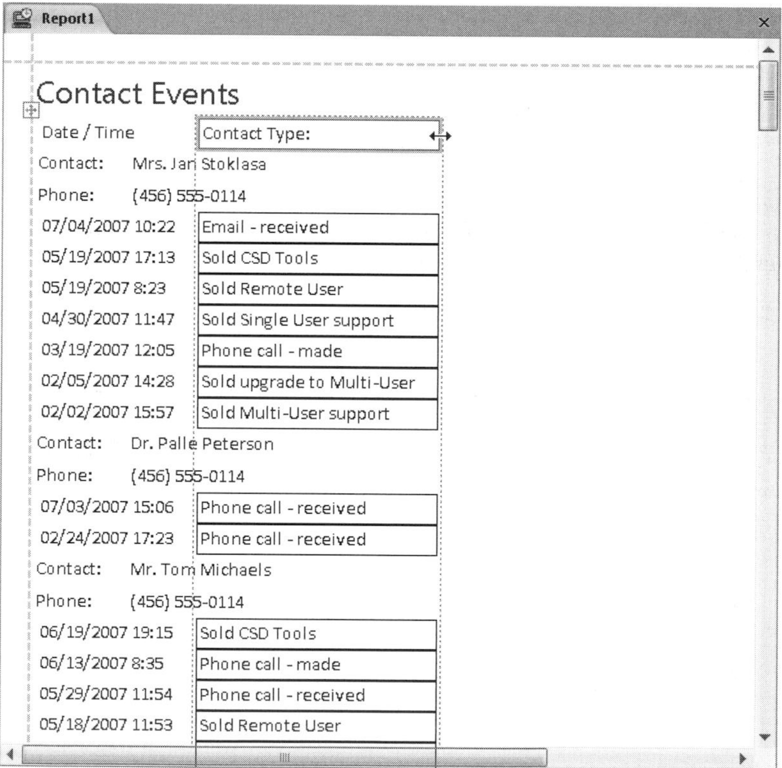


**Figure 15-49** Expand the width of the ContactEventTypeDescription field so that the data fits on one line.

Now you're ready to add the three remaining fields to the report. Click ContactNotes in the field list and drag it to the right edge of the Contact Type label until you see a long vertical I-bar, as shown in Figure 15-50. The vertical I-bar indicates that the field is in the right position, so release the mouse. Access places a Notes label along the same line as the Date / Time and Contact Type labels and a Notes field next to the ContactDate-Time and ContactEventTypeDescription field controls in the Detail section, as shown in Figure 15-51.

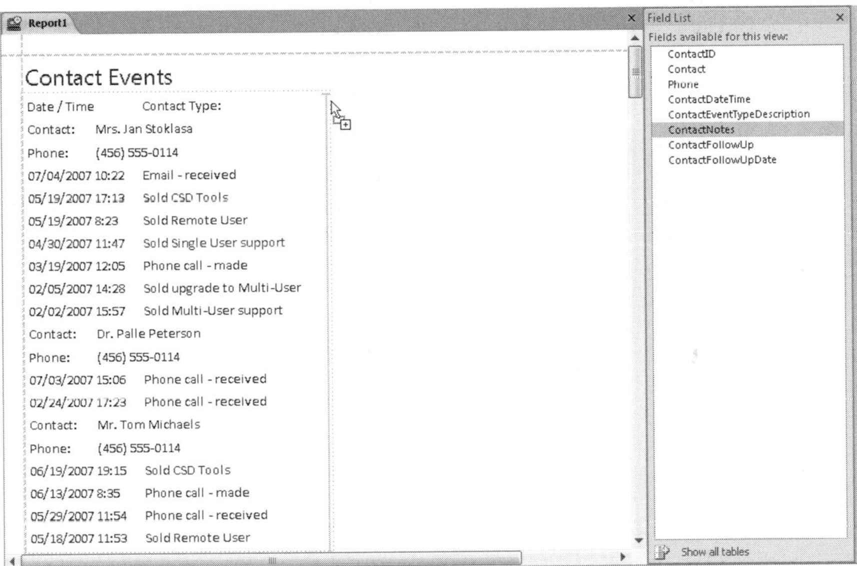

**Figure 15-50** Use the vertical I-bar to help you position the ContactNotes field.

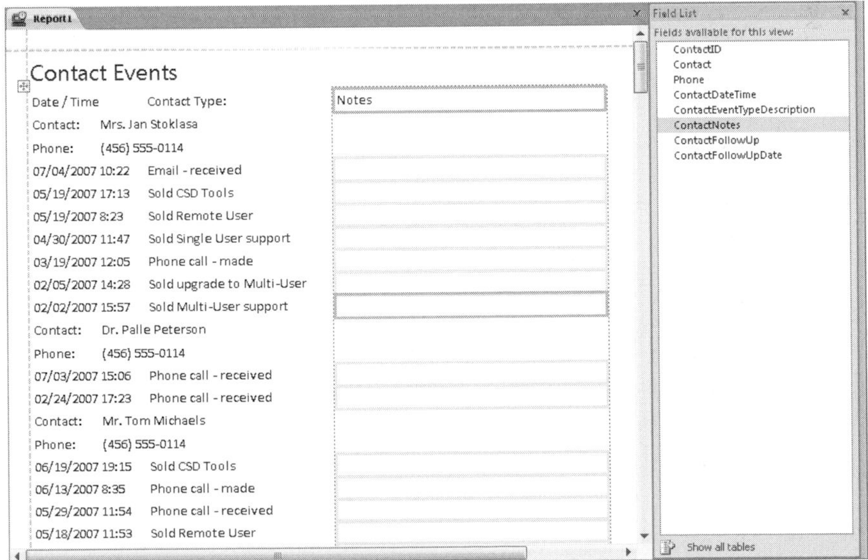

**Figure 15-51** After you drop the ContactNotes field on the report, Access adds a label and text box control to the appropriate report sections.

The ContactNotes field is too wide at this point, so reduce its width by dragging its right edge toward the left side of the report. Now drag the ContactFollowUp field to the right of the Notes label using the same technique. After the ContactFollowUp field is in place, drag the last field, ContactFollowUpDate, into position to the right of the ContactFollowUp field. Close the field list so that you can see the whole report grid and the right print margin. Because these controls are in a tabular control layout, if you resize the width of one of them, the others move to the left or right accordingly. Make any small adjustments you need to the widths of the fields so that you can see all the data, but make sure the ContactFollowUpDate field does not extend past the right print margin. Your report at this point should look like Figure 15-52.

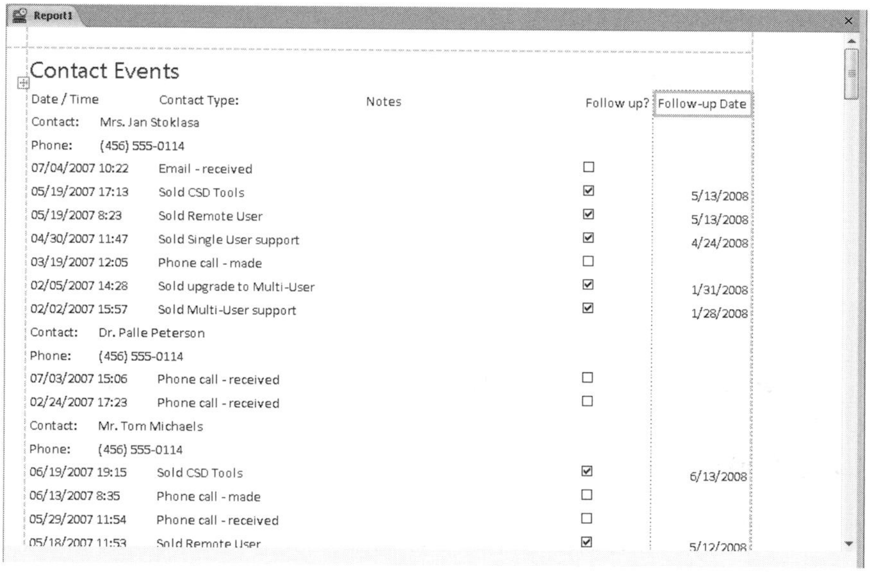

**Figure 15-52** Your report is beginning to take shape with all the fields now in place.



## Adding Totals to Records

All your fields are in place, so now you can add some controls for counting the events and follow-ups. You can add some of these elements to the report while in Layout view, but you'll still have to fine-tune the report using Design view, as you'll soon see. Start with adding a count of the follow-ups by right-clicking on the Follow Up? label and clicking Total Follow Up? and then Count Values, as shown in Figure 15-53.

Access places a new control in the ContactID Footer section in the same column as the ContactFollowUp field, as shown in Figure 15-54. Remember that when you created this report using the Report Wizard, you had to correct the Sum expression for the ContactFollowUp field to display a correct count of the number of contact events requiring a follow-up. (See page 785.) In this case, Access correctly creates an expression to total the number of True values in the ContactFollowUp field. (The Count Records option, shown in Figure 15-53, would ask Access to calculate a simple count of the number of records in that group, which is not we want for this field.) To align the total with the check boxes, click the new control—where you see the number 5—and then click the Align Left button in the Font group on the Format tab.

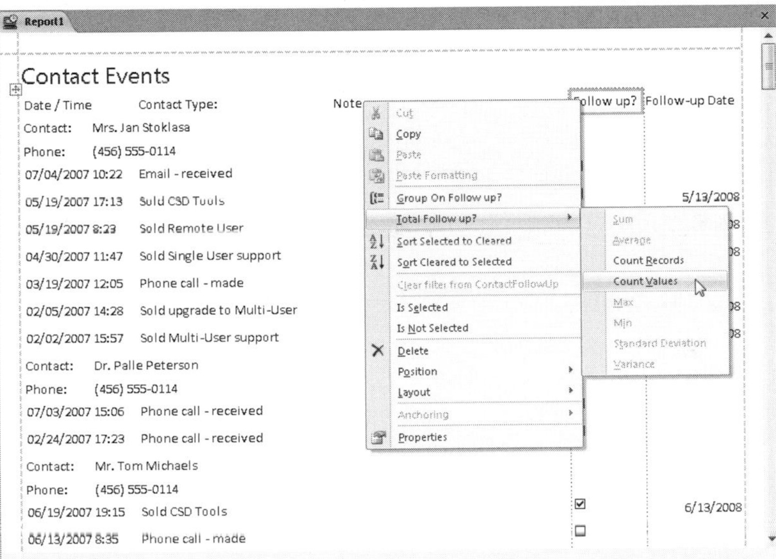


**Figure 15-53** Click the Count Values command to create a control to total the follow-ups for each contact.

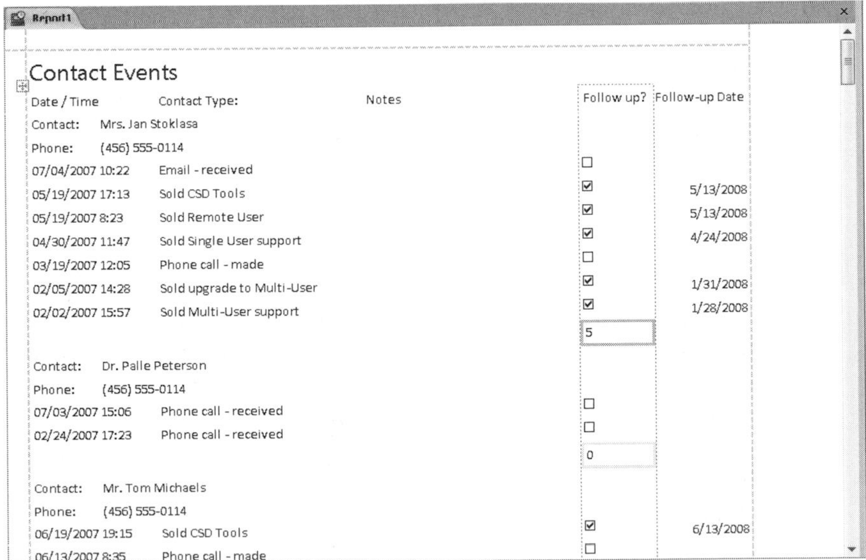


**Figure 15-54** Access creates an expression to count the number of True values for the ContactFollowUp field.

You need to create a similar count of event records for each contact, so right-click the first ContactEventTypeDescription field (under the Phone field), and click Total Contact Type and then Count Values, as shown in Figure 15-55.

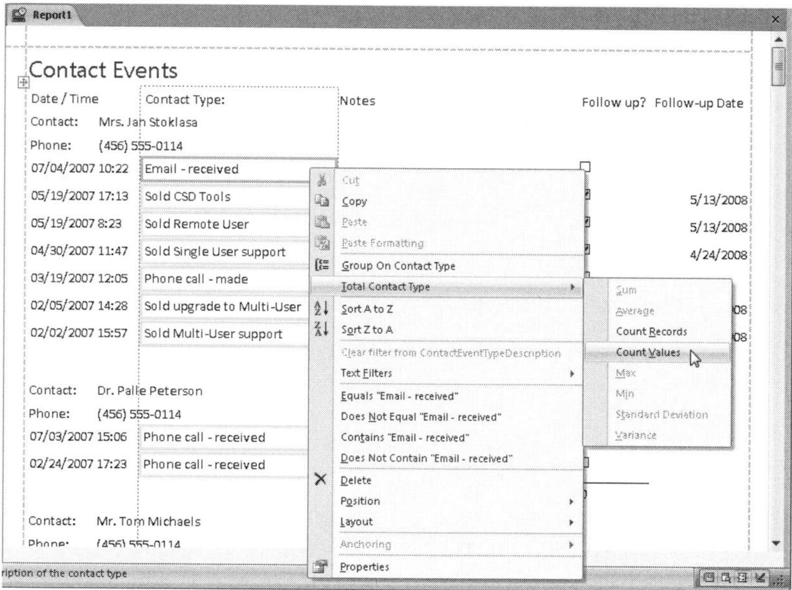


**Figure 15-55** Click the Count Values option to create a control to total the event records.

Access places another new control in the ContactID Footer section in the same column as the ContactEventTypeDescription field, as shown in Figure 15-56. Access now displays a correct count of the number of events.

When the report is printed, it would be nice to have a page number at the bottom of the page. Click the Insert Page Number button in the Controls group on the Format tab to open the Page Numbers dialog box, discussed in "Completing the Report" on page 769. Select the following options in the Page Numbers dialog box: Page N Of M, Bottom Of Page [Footer], Alignment set to Right, and Show Number On First Page. Click OK to close the Page Numbers dialog box.

### Note

You won't immediately see a difference to the report in Layout view after you add a page count. If you scroll to the bottom of this report, you'll see the control says Page 1 Of 1. In Layout view, Access does not count the number of pages because it is not actually formatting the pages for printing. If you switch to Design view, you can see that Access placed the control on the right side of the report in the Page Footer section. If you switch to Print Preview, you can see the correct page numbers displayed on each page.

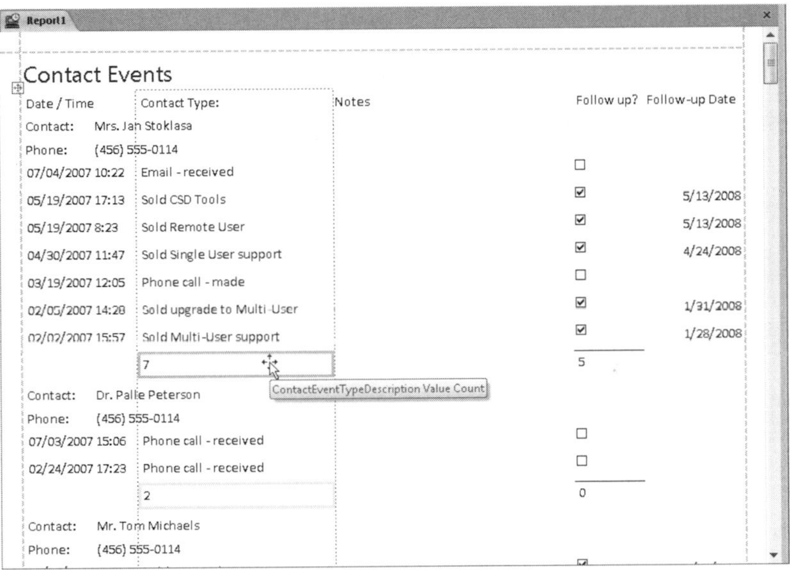


**Figure 15-56** Access now correctly displays a total of events for each contact.



## Applying an AutoFormat

Your report is functional right now, but with a little formatting you can make it look more professional and also easier to read. You could selectively add some color to certain controls to highlight specific areas, but here again you can let Access do most of the work. Access 2007 has 25 built-in AutoFormats to spice up your reports. You can easily click one of the AutoFormats to see what it would look like applied to your report. If you don't like it, click the Undo command on the Quick Access Toolbar and then try another one. To match the report you created previously using the Report Wizard, let's choose the Access 2007 AutoFormat style. Click the arrow under the AutoFormat button in the AutoFormat group on the Format tab to display the gallery of AutoFormats, and then click the Access 2007 style, as shown in Figure 15-57.

You see an instant change to several elements of your report. Access added some background color to all the labels going horizontally across the screen. The font size changed from 11 to 10 in some of the controls, and Access even added some alternating background color to the detail records, as shown in Figure 15-58.

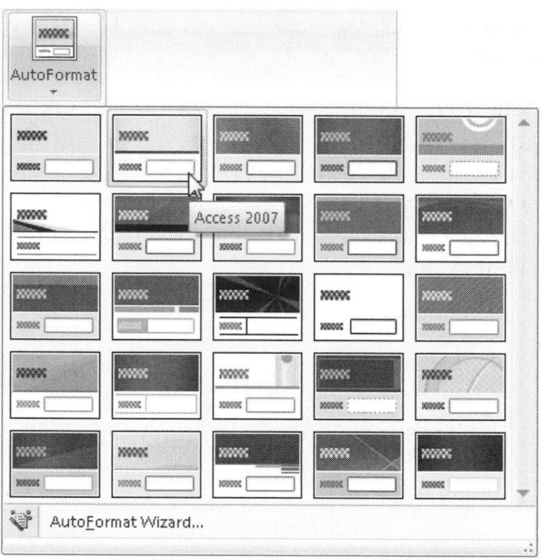


**Figure 15-57** Select one of the AutoFormats to give your report a more professional look.

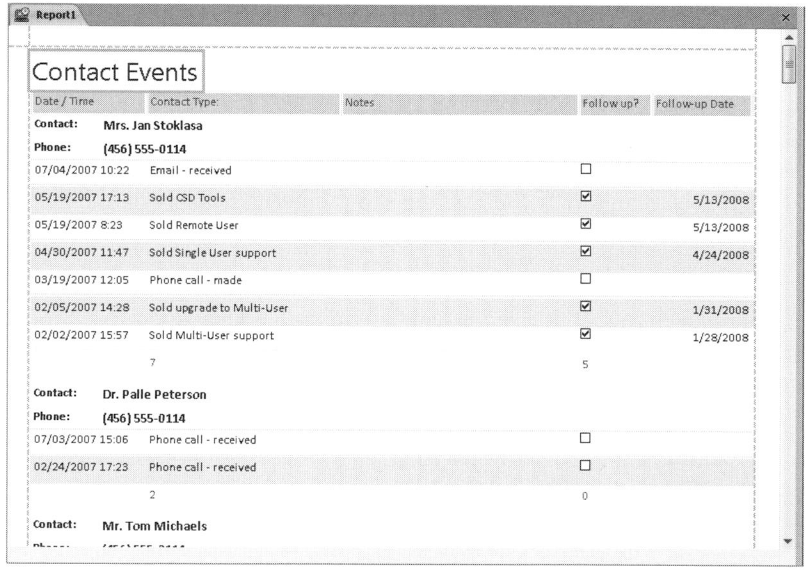


**Figure 15-58** Access makes several visual changes to your report when you select an AutoFormat.

Save your report and then switch to Print Preview to see how your report will print on paper. The report still needs some fine-tuning to exactly match the reports you created earlier in this chapter. You need to add a label and a text box next to the two Sum controls in the ControlID Footer section to list the name of the contact and the descriptive text of follow-up information. You could also move the Title control into the Page Header section so that it appears on every page instead of only the first page. You can find this report (after we made these few changes) saved as rptXmplContactEvents4 in the sample database. As you can see, Layout view allows you to quickly create a professional-looking report in Access 2007.

You should now feel comfortable with constructing reports. In this chapter, you've seen that Access 2007 presents many tools and views to assist you in creating professional and functional reports. In most cases, you'll find that using a combination of these tools—Design view, Layout view, the Report command, and the Report Wizard—is the best way to create reports. In the next chapter, you'll learn how to build more complex reports that contain subreports and calculated values.

CHAPTER 16

# Advanced Report Design



In the previous chapter, you learned how to create a relatively simple report with a single subtotal level. You also saw how the Report Wizard can help you construct a new report. This chapter shows you how to

- Design a report with multiple subtotal groups
- Add complex calculations to a report
- Embed a report within another report
- Create a report with an embedded PivotChart form

To learn how to work with these features, you'll create a Facility Occupancy By Date report for the Housing Reservations database. In a second example, you'll learn how to use the results from two queries in an embedded subreport and an embedded PivotChart to produce a report that summarizes and graphs revenue by facility and month.

**Note**

The examples in this chapter are based on the reports, queries, tables, and data in HousingDataCopy2.accdb on the companion CD included with this book. You can find similar reports in the Housing Reservations sample application, but all the reports in that sample file have custom Ribbons defined, so you won't see the four main Ribbon tabs—Home, Create, External Data, and Database Tools—when you open those reports. The results you see from the samples in this chapter might not exactly match what you see in this book if you have changed the sample data in the files. Also, all the screen images in this chapter were taken on a Microsoft Windows Vista system with the display theme set to Blue. Your results might look different if you are using a different operating system or a different theme.

# Building a Query for a Complex Report

To explore some of the advanced features you can include in a report, let's build a report in the Housing Reservations database that displays room occupancy information by facility, date, room, and employee. As noted in the previous chapter, reports tend to bring together information from many tables, so you are likely to begin constructing a report by designing a query to retrieve the data you need for the report. For this example, you need information from the tblFacilities, tblReservations, and tblEmployees tables in the HousingDataCopy2.accdb database. Open a new Query window in Design view by clicking the Query Design button in the Other group on the Create tab, and add these tables to the Query window.

The tblReservations table contains one row per reservation, and the reservation could span many days. If you want to report on occupancy by day, you must use the special trick you learned in Chapter 8, "Building Complex Queries": Include a table containing all the dates you want, and add special criteria to expand each row in tblReservations into one row per day. The sample database contains a handy table, ztblDates, that has rows containing all the dates from January 1, 1992, to December 31, 2035, so add that table to your query. Close the Show Table dialog box. Next, add the fields listed in Table 16-1 to the design grid. (You can find this query saved as qryXmplRptReservationsByDay in the sample database.)

**Table 16-1 Fields in the qryXmplRptReservationsByDay Query**

| Field/Expression | Source Table | Criterion |
|---|---|---|
| EmpName: tblEmployees.LastName & ", " & tblEmployees.FirstName & (" "+tblEmployees.MiddleName) | | |
| ReservationID | tblReservations | |
| FacilityName | tblFacilities | |
| RoomNumber | tblReservations | |
| DateValue | ztblDates | Between #4/1/2007# And #6/30/2007# |
| CheckInDate | tblReservations | <=[ztblDates].[DateValue] |
| CheckOutDate | tblReservations | >[ztblDates].[DateValue] |
| TotalCharge | tblReservations | |

Your Query window should look similar to the one shown in Figure 16-1.

You might be wondering why the query has a criterion to limit the range of dates returned from the ztblDates table. The sample database contains reservations from February 18, 2007, through October 9, 2007 (340 records). Although you could certainly create a report that includes all reservations, a user is typically going to want to look at records only for a specific date span. (For example, the housekeeping department might be interested in seeing this report only for the next few days or week.) Also, because the ztblDates table contains more than 16,000 rows, this query could take up to a minute to run—or more on a slow computer—unless you filter the rows. In Chapter 20, "Automating Your Application with Visual Basic," you'll learn how to provide the user with a custom date range dialog box to limit the records. For this example, the query includes a filter to limit the rows to the second quarter of 2007.

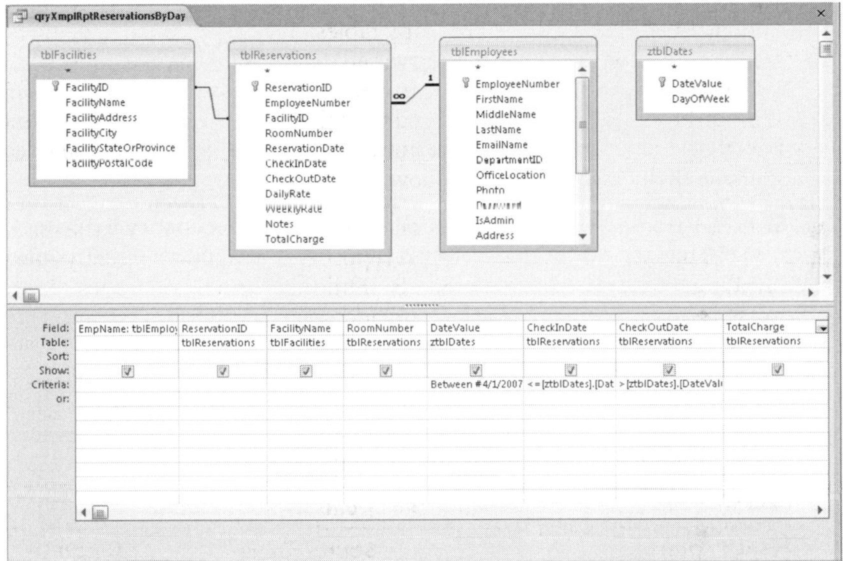

**Figure 16-1** The qryXmplRptReservationsByDay query for the Facility Occupancy By Date report returns one row per day in each reservation.

You can either save your query as qryMyRptReservationsByDay and select it in the Navigation Pane, or select the qryXmplRptReservationsByDay query in the Navigation Pane to follow along in the next section.



# Creating the Basic Facility Occupancy By Date Report

For many reports, building the source query is the most difficult step. Once you have the data you need and understand the grouping options and properties you can set, building the report is easy. We actually like to use the Report Wizard to get a jump-start on laying out our reports. The wizard works especially well when the record source contains 10 or fewer fields.

To start designing the Facility Occupancy By Date report, select the query in the Navigation Pane, and click the Report Wizard button in the Reports group on the Create tab. Build the basic report by taking the following steps:

1. On the first page of the wizard, choose the FacilityName, DateValue, RoomNumber, and EmpName fields, and click Next.
2. On the second page, the wizard suggests grouping the report by the RoomNumber field. However, you need to define custom grouping and sorting later, so click the left arrow to undo that selection, and then click Next.

3. On the next page, the wizard offers to sort the information for you. You can ask the wizard to establish some of the grouping and sorting settings you need by asking for an ascending sort on FacilityName, DateValue, and RoomNumber. Click Next.

4. Because you didn't ask the wizard to create any groups, the wizard suggests a tabular layout, and this is just fine. Be sure that Orientation is set to Portrait and the Adjust The Field Width So All Fields Fit On A Page check box is selected. Click Next.

5. All the reports in this application use the Access 2007 style. Choose that style, and click Next.

6. On the final page of the wizard, enter **Facility Occupancy By Date – 2nd Quarter 2007** as the report title, select the Modify The Report's Design option, and click Finish to create your report.

The report the wizard built should look like that shown in Figure 16-2.

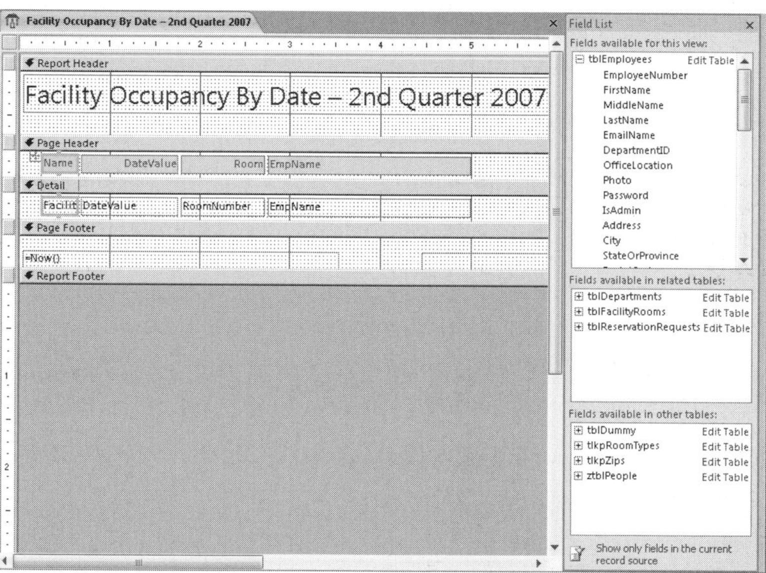


**Figure 16-2** This is the initial Facility Occupancy By Date report created by the Report Wizard.

Close the Field List window to give yourself more room in the object window. The wizard always places the report title label in the Report Header section, but that appears only once on the first page of the report. Especially when the report is likely to contain many pages, we like to see the report title repeated at the top of each page so that the subject of the report is clear throughout. You can move the report title from the Report Header section to the Page Header section. To do this, follow these steps:

1. Expand the bottom of the Page Header section about 0.5 inch.

2. Select any of the label controls in the page header. Move your mouse pointer in the middle of the label until it becomes double-sided crosshairs, and then drag

the label down until it is close to the bottom edge of the Page Header section. You can also use the Down Arrow key to move the controls down to provide some space for the label from the Report Header section. Because the wizard has placed the labels and text boxes into a tabular control layout, you don't have to worry about the labels becoming vertically misaligned from the text box controls in the Detail section. (Caution: If you hold down the Down Arrow key, Microsoft Office Access 2007 moves your selected controls down into the Detail section when they hit the bottom margin of the Page Header section.)

3. Click the label control in the Report Header section, and drag it down into the space you created in the Page Header section. You might want to select a column heading label again and use the Up Arrow key to close any gap below the bottom of the report title label control. Also, move the bottom of the Page Header section up so that there's only a small space between the line and the bottom of the section.

4. Close up the bottom of the Report Header section so that it has zero height.

5. To make sure that all the characters in the report title label fit inside the control, click it and expand it to the right by grabbing the sizing handle in the center of the right edge. (Although the "size to fit" that the wizard performed on the label for you does a pretty good job, we find it safest to always slightly expand labels containing large fonts to make sure all characters show on the printed report.)

While you're refining the look of the report, click the DateValue label control, and change its caption to Date. Also click the EmpName label control, and change its caption to Employee. (You can change captions directly in a label control by selecting the control, clicking inside it with your mouse, and then typing the new caption.) Select all the controls in the Page Footer section, and delete them. You'll learn later how to create controls to display the current date and time and page numbers.

Your report should now look like Figure 16-3. Click the Save button on the Quick Access Toolbar to preserve your work to this point.

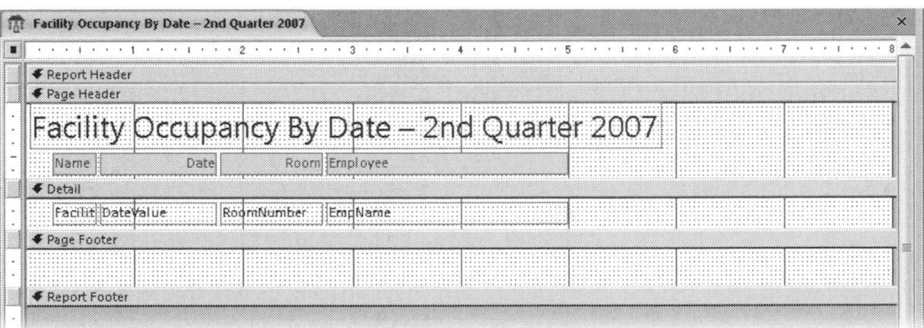


**Figure 16-3** Your Facility Occupancy By Date report should look like this after you adjust what the wizard built.

## Defining the Grouping and Sorting Criteria

The next thing you need to do is define the grouping and sorting criteria for the report. Click the Group & Sort button in the Grouping & Totals group on the Design tab to open the Group, Sort, And Total pane. This report should display the daily reservation data from the query in the Detail section, with summaries of reservations by date, by month, and by facility. Note that in the Group, Sort, And Total pane, you specify grouping values from the outermost to the innermost (like specifying a sorting criteria left to right). So, select the FacilityName sorting specification in the first line of the Group, Sort, And Total pane, click More to expand the options, click the arrow on the Without A Footer box, and then click With A Footer Section. Notice that when you add a group header or group footer for any field or expression in the Group, Sort, And Total pane, Office Access 2007 adds an appropriate section to your report. Access also changes this specification from Sort By to Group On. You want to make sure that a group header doesn't get "orphaned" at the bottom of a page, so click the arrow on the option that says Do Not Keep Group Together On One Page and click Keep Header And First Record Together On One Page. Note that you can also ask Access to attempt to keep all the detail for this level of grouping on one page by clicking the Keep Whole Group Together On One Page option. When you do this, Access will produce a new page if all the detail for the next group won't fit on the current page. As you'll see later, the report sections also have properties that you can set to force a new page with the start of each group.

The DateValue field from the query returns the date each room is occupied across a reservation span. When housing managers review reservations for more than one month, they might want to see subtotals by month. You can create a group on month by clicking the DateValue sorting specification, clicking More to expand the options, clicking the arrow on the group on property box (where it says By Entire Value), and clicking By Month. See the sidebar "Understanding Grouping Options" on page 818 for details about other options you can set. Also click the arrow on the group footer property (where it says Without A Footer Section), and click With A Footer Section to create a space to place monthly totals on your report. (Notice that Access changes this specification from Sort By to Group On.) Click the arrow on the option that says Do Not Keep Group Together On One Page, and click Keep Header And First Record Together On One Page as you did for the FacilityName grouping specification.

You can include the DateValue field in the Group, Sort, And Total pane again, but set the group interval to Each Value to create a subtotal by day. Click the Add A Group button to create a blank specification row for a second DateValue. Click DateValue in the Select Field box, click More to see all the options, click the arrow on the group interval box (where it says By Quarter), and then click By Entire Value. Next, click Without A Header Section in the header section box, and click With A Footer Section in the footer section box. Finally, click Keep Whole Group Together On One Page for the last option so that a set of rows for a particular day doesn't split across a page boundary. You need to move this new grouping specification up one level in the grouping and sorting order, so click the Move Up arrow to move this second DateValue group specification above the RoomNumber sort specification. Remember that there's no sorting specification in the query you built or in the sample qryXmplRptReservationsByDay query. There wouldn't be any point in defining a sort in the query because reports ignore any sorting specification from the query when you define any criteria in the Group, Sort, And Total pane. Your result should look something like that shown in Figure 16-4. (Note that we clicked the first DateValue grouping specification so that you can see the group property settings for that field.)

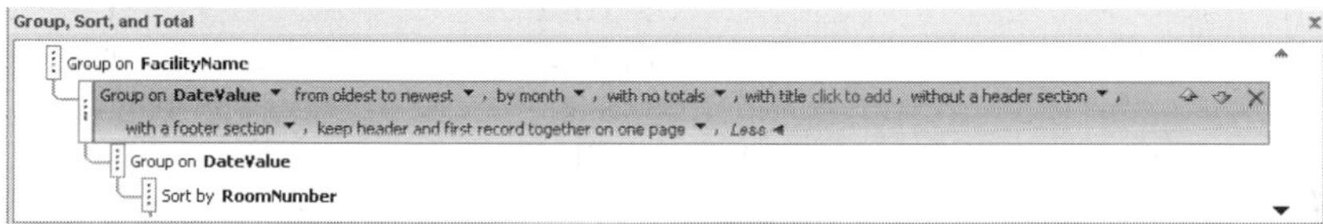


**Figure 16-4** Set your grouping and sorting criteria for the Facility Occupancy By Date report in the Group, Sort, And Total pane.

Your report design should now look like Figure 16-5.

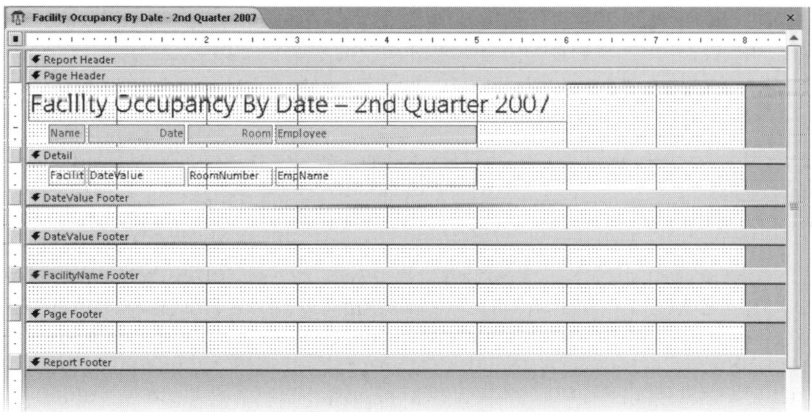


**Figure 16-5** The Facility Occupancy By Date report has new footer sections after you define the grouping and sorting criteria.

Click the Save button again to preserve your work to this point. You can find this stage of the report design saved as rptXmplFacilityDateOccupancyStep1 in the sample database.

### Understanding Grouping Options

For each field or expression in the upper part of the Group, Sort, And Total pane, you can set group on and group interval properties. Normally, you'll want to start a new grouping of data whenever the value of your field or expression changes. You can, however, specify that a new grouping starts whenever a field or an expression changes from one range of values to another. The type of range you can specify varies depending on the data type of the field or the expression.

For text grouping fields, you can tell Access to start a new group based on a change in value of one or more leading characters in the string. For example, you can create a new group based on a change in the first letter of the field (rather than on a change anywhere in the field) to create one group per letter of the alphabet—a group of items beginning with A, a group of items beginning with B, and so on. To group on such a prefix, use the Custom interval, and enter in the Characters box the number of leading characters that differentiates each group.

For numbers, you can enter a setting for the group interval property that clusters multiple values within a range. In the interval list, you can choose from By 5s, By 10s, By 100s, or By 1000s. Access calculates ranges from 0. For example, if you specify By 10s as the interval value, values ranging from –20 to 29 would be grouped from –20 through –11, –10 through –1, 0 through 9, 10 through 19, 20 through 29. You can also specify a Custom interval value.

For date/time fields, you can set the group interval property to calendar or time subdivisions and multiples of those subdivisions, such as By Year, By Quarter, By Month, By Week, or By Day. Use the Custom setting for the group interval property if you want to group on Hours or Minutes or a multiple of the subdivision—for example, select Custom in the group interval property, enter 2 in the By box, and select Years from the interval combo box if you want groupings for every two years.

When you create groupings in which the group interval property is set to something other than Each Value, Access sorts only the grouping value, not the individual values within each group. If you want Access to sort the detail items within the group, you must include a separate sort specification for those items. For example, if you group on the first letter of a LastName field and also want the names within each group sorted, you must select LastName in the field box in the Group, Sort, And Total pane, select With A Header Section (and possibly With A Footer Section), set the sort order to With A On Top, and set the group interval to By First Character. You must then enter LastName again as an additional sorting specification, set the sort order to With A On Top, and set the group interval to By Entire Value.

# Setting Section and Report Properties

You've probably noticed that Access 2007 has a property sheet for each section in the Report window in Design view. You can set section properties not only to control how the section looks but also to control whether Access should attempt to keep a group together or start a new page before or after the group. There's also a property sheet for the report as a whole. You don't need to change any of these properties at this point, but the following sections explain the available property settings.

## Section Properties

When you click in the blank area of any group section or Detail section of a report and then click the Property Sheet button in the Tools group on the Design tab, Access displays a property sheet, such as the one shown in Figure 16-6.

**Figure 16-6** This is a property sheet for a report section.

The available properties and their uses are described in Table 16-2.

Table 16-2 **Properties for a Section**

| Property | Description |
|---|---|
| Name | Access automatically generates a unique section name for you. |
| Visible | Set this property to Yes to make the section visible or to No to make the section invisible. You can set this property from a macro or from a Visual Basic procedure while Access formats and prints your report. You can make sections disappear depending on data values in the report. |
| Height | This property defines the height of the section. You normally change this property by dragging the bottom edge of the section. If you want a specific height, you can enter it here, and Access changes the display to match as long as all controls fit within the defined height. If you attempt to set the height smaller than will accommodate the controls in the section, Access sets the height to the minimum that can contain the controls. |
| Back Color | The default back color of a section is the color value for white, #FFFFFF. You can also choose a custom color by clicking in the property and then clicking the Build (...) button to open the color picker. Click More Colors to open the Colors dialog box. You can also choose colors by clicking the Fill/Back Color button in the Font group on the Design tab. |
| Alternate Back Color | The default alternate back color of a section is No Color. With this setting Access applies the defined back color to all rows of data in that section. If you use the Report Wizard to create your report, Access might set an alternating back color in the Detail section of your report depending upon which style you choose. If you want to display a different back color on alternating rows of data in a section, click the Build (...) button to open the color picker. Click More Colors to open the Colors dialog box. You can also choose alternating colors by clicking the Alternate Fill/Back Color button in the Font group on the Design tab. When you define an Alternate Back Color, Access applies the Back Color to the first, third, and so on rows, and it applies the Alternate Back Color to the second, fourth, and so on, rows. This property is not available in page headers and footers. |
| Special Effect | The default setting is a flat effect. You can also set a raised or sunken effect for a section using the Special Effect button in the Controls group on the Design tab or by clicking this effect from the drop-down list for the property. |
| Auto Height | The default setting, Yes, causes the section's height to adjust automatically when you resize controls resized in Layout view. If you shrink the height of controls in Layout view, for example, Access shrinks the height of the section as well. If no controls exist in a section, Access reduces the section height to 0 inches. Change this property to No to not allow Access to automatically resize the section when controls are resized. |

| Property | Description |
|---|---|
| Can Grow | Setting this property to Yes allows the section to expand to accommodate controls that might expand because they display memo fields or long text strings. You can design a control to display only one line of text, but you should allow the control to expand to display more lines of text as needed. If you set the Can Grow property for any control in the section to Yes, Access automatically sets the Can Grow property of the section to Yes. This property is not available in page headers and footers. |
| Can Shrink | This property is similar to Can Grow. You can set it to Yes to allow the section to become smaller if controls in the section become smaller to enclose less text. Unlike Can Grow, setting the Can Shrink property for any control in the section to Yes does not automatically set Can Shrink for the section to Yes. The default setting is No. This property is not available in page headers and footers. |
| Display When | The default setting, Always, displays this section in Report view, Layout view, Print Preview, and when you print the report. Choose Print Only to display the section only when you view the report in Print Preview or you print the report. Choose Screen Only to display the section only when in Report view and Layout view. |
| Keep Together | Set this property to No to allow a section to flow across page boundaries. The default Yes setting tells Access to attempt to keep all lines within a section together on a page. (You can tell Access to attempt to keep detail lines together with group headers and footers by setting the Keep Together property in a Group, Sort, And Total specification to either Keep Whole Group Together On One Page or to Keep Header And First Record Together On One Page.) This property is not available in page headers and footers. |
| Force New Page | Set this property to Before Section to force the section to print at the top of a new page. Set this property to After Section to force the next section to print at the top of a new page. You can also set this property to Before & After to force the section to print on a page by itself. The default setting is None. This property is not available in page headers and footers. |
| New Row Or Col | When you use the Page Setup dialog box to format your report with more than one column (vertical) or more than one row (horizontal) of sections, you can set this property to Before Section, After Section, or Before & After to produce the section again at the top, bottom, or both top and bottom of a new column or row. This property is useful for forcing headers to print at the top of each column in a multiple-column report. The default setting is None. This property is not available in page headers and footers. |
| On Click | Enter the name of a macro or a Visual Basic procedure that you want Access to execute when a user clicks inside this section in Report view. See Part 4, "Automating an Access Application," for details. |

| Property | Description |
|---|---|
| On Format | Enter the name of a macro or a Visual Basic procedure that you want Access to execute when it begins formatting this section. See Part 4 for details. |
| On Dbl Click | Enter the name of a macro or a Visual Basic procedure that you want Access to execute when a user double-clicks inside this section in Report view. See Part 4 for details. |
| On Mouse Down | Enter the name of a macro or a Visual Basic procedure that you want Access to execute when a user clicks the mouse button while the mouse pointer rests on this section in Report view. See Part 4 for details. |
| On Mouse Up | Enter the name of a macro or a Visual Basic procedure that you want Access to execute when a user releases a mouse button while the mouse pointer rests on this section in Report view. See Part 4 for details. |
| On Mouse Move | Enter the name of a macro or a Visual Basic procedure that you want Access to execute when a user rests their mouse pointer on this section in Report view. See Part 4 for details. |
| On Paint | Enter the name of a macro or a Visual Basic procedure that you want Access to execute when this section is redrawn in Print Preview or Report view. See Part 4 for details. |
| On Print | Enter the name of a macro or a Visual Basic procedure that you want Access to execute when it begins printing this section or when it displays the section in Print Preview. See Part 4 for details. |
| On Retreat | Enter the name of a macro or a Visual Basic procedure that you want Access to execute when it has to "back up" over a section after it finds that the section won't fit on the current page and you've set the Keep Together property to Yes. This event happens after On Format but before On Print, so you can use it to undo settings you might have changed in your On Format routine. Access calls On Format again when it formats the section on a new page. See Part 4 for details. This property is not available in page headers and footers. |
| Tag | Use this property to store additional identifying information about the section. You can use this property in macros and in Visual Basic procedures to temporarily store information that you want to pass to another routine. |

## Report Properties

If you select the Report option from the Selection Type list in the Property Sheet window (or click in the Report window beyond the right edge of the Detail section and then click the Property Sheet button in the Tools group on the Design tab), Access displays the report's properties in the property sheet, as shown in Figure 16-7.

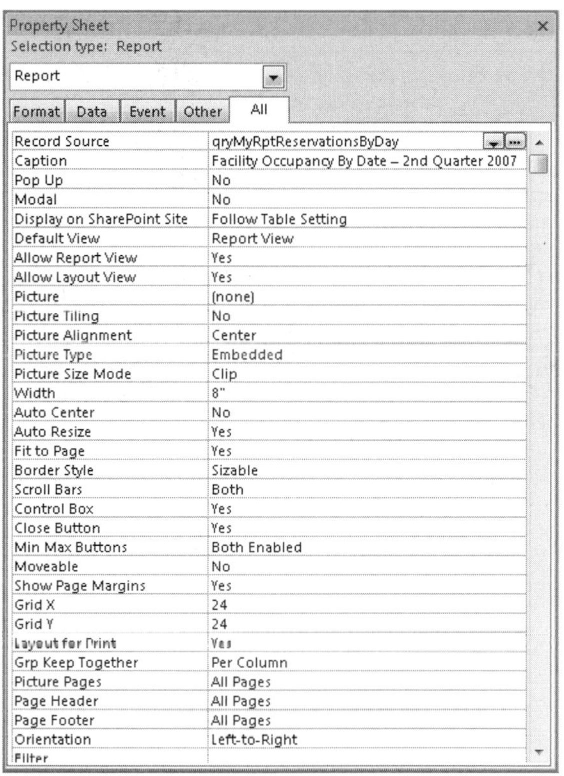


**Figure 16-7** The property sheet for a report displays many properties that you can customize for the report object.

Some of the available properties and their uses are described in Table 16-3.

**Table 16-3 Properties for a Report**

| Property | Description |
|---|---|
| Record Source | This property displays the name of the table or query that provides the data for your report. You can also enter a valid SQL statement for the record source. |
| Caption | Use this property to set the text that appears in the title bar when you open the report in Report view, Layout view, and Print Preview. If you don't specify a caption, Access displays Report: and the name of the report in the window title bar if you are using multiple-document interface or on the report's tab if you are using single-document interface. |
| Pop Up | Set this property to Yes to make the report window in Report view and Print Preview open as a pop-up. A pop-up window stays visible on top of other windows even when another window has the focus. The default setting is No. If you're using a single-document interface, Access does not display a tab for this report but instead shows the report as a pop-up window. |

| Property | Description |
|---|---|
| Modal | Set this property to Yes to disallow clicking any other window or clicking the Ribbon when the Report window is open in Report view or Print Preview. The default setting is No. |
| Display On SharePoint Site | Use this property to tell Access to create a view for this report if the database is migrated to a Microsoft Windows SharePoint Services (version 3) site. The default setting, Follow Table Setting, tells Access to honor the setting specified for the underlying table. Choose Do Not Display to not have Access create a view on the Windows SharePoint Services Version 3 site of this report. |
| Default View | Use this property to tell Access in which view to first open the report. The default setting, Report view, tells Access to open the report in Report view when you double-click the report in the Navigation Pane or click Open on the report's shortcut menu. Select Print Preview to have Access open the report in Print Preview when opened from the Navigation Pane or from the Open command on the report's shortcut menu. If you set the Default View property to Report View and set the Allow Report View property to No, Access removes the Report View option from the Views group and opens the report in Print Preview. |
| Allow Report View | The default setting, Yes, specifies that you can open this report in Report view and you can switch to Report view from other views. If you change the setting to No, Access removes Report View as an option in the Views group on the Ribbon. |
| Allow Layout View | The default setting, Yes, specifies that you can open this report in Layout view and you can switch to Layout view from other views. If you change the setting to No, Access removes Layout View as an option in the Views group on the Ribbon. |
| Picture, Picture Type | To use a bitmap as the background of a report, you enter the full path name and file name in the Picture property. If you set the Picture Type property to Embedded, Access copies the bitmap specified to the Report object. If you set the Picture Type property to Linked, Access uses the path name stored in the Picture property to load the bitmap each time you open the report. The default setting for Picture is (none), and the default setting for Picture Type is Embedded. |
| Picture Tiling | When you set the Picture Size Mode property to Clip or Zoom and your picture is smaller than the page size, you can set the Picture Tiling property to Yes so that Access will place multiple copies of the picture across and/or down the page. The default setting is No. |
| Picture Alignment | When you set the Picture Size Mode property to Clip or Zoom, you can use Picture Alignment to place the picture in the center of the page or in one of the corners. The default setting is Center. |

| Property | Description |
|---|---|
| Picture Size Mode | When your background picture is not the same size as your page, you can set the Picture Size Mode property so that Access adjusts the size. The Clip setting displays the picture in its original size, and if the page is smaller than the picture, Access clips the sides and top and bottom edges of the picture as necessary. The Zoom setting maintains the aspect ratio and shrinks or enlarges the picture to fit the page. If your picture doesn't have the same horizontal-to-vertical dimensions (aspect ratio) as your page, Access centers the image and shows some blank space at the sides or top and bottom of the page. The Stretch setting expands the picture to fit the page size and will distort the image if the aspect ratio of the picture does not match the aspect ratio of the page. The default setting is Clip. |
| Width | Access sets this property when you increase the width of the report in the design grid. If you want a specific width, you can enter it here, and Access changes the display to match as long as all controls fit within the defined width. If you attempt to set the width smaller than will accommodate the controls in any section, Access sets the width to the minimum that can contain the controls. |
| Auto Center | This setting affects the positioning of the Report window when you open the report in Report view or Print Preview using the multiple-document interface. This property has no effect when you are using the single-document interface unless you have also set the Pop Up or Modal property to Yes. The default setting, No, leaves the upper-left corner in the same location as when you last saved the Report window from Design view. When you specify Yes, the Report window opens centered in the Access workspace to the right of the Navigation Pane or opens centered in the Access window if you set either Pop Up or Modal to Yes. If you collapse the Navigation Pane after you open the report, Access moves the report to the left but does not center it again in the object workspace. |
| Auto Resize | This setting affects the size of the Report window when you open the report in Print Preview. The default setting, Yes, asks Access to zoom the report to show the first entire page and size the window to fit within the Access workspace on your screen when you're using a multiple-document interface. When you're using a single-document interface, the report opens in a window sized to approximately 80 percent of the height available in the Access workspace, with a width relative to the layout of the page (portrait or landscape) and the report sized to display the entire first page. Unless you have a very high-resolution monitor, most portrait layout reports will be unreadable with this setting. When you specify No, the report opens at 100 percent resolution. When you're using a single-document interface, Access sizes the window the same as when you last saved the Report window from Design view or Layout view. We recommend you change this setting to No for most reports. |

| Property | Description |
|---|---|
| Fit To Page | Use this property to make Access expand the width of the report to fit a page while you are working in Layout view. The default setting, Yes, tells Access to automatically expand the width of the report to fit within the page margins. When you specify No, Access does not automatically expand the width and honors any width you specify for the report. |
| Border Style | The default setting, Sizable, allows you to resize the Report window in Report view or Print Preview when you use a multiple-document interface or you have set the Pop Up or Modal property to Yes. This property has no effect when you use a single-document interface and both Pop Up and Modal are set to No.<br>When you choose None, the report's Report view and Print Preview windows have no borders, control menu, title bar, Close button, or Minimize and Maximize buttons. You cannot resize or move the report when it is open. You can select the report and press Ctrl+F4 to close it unless the report's Pop Up property is set to Yes. You should write Visual Basic code to provide an alternative way to close this type of report.<br>When you choose Thin, the Report window in Report view or Print Preview has a thin border, signifying that the report cannot be resized.<br>When you choose Dialog and the Pop Up property is set to Yes, the border of the Report window in Report view or Print Preview is a thick line (like that of a true Windows dialog box), signifying that you can resize the report. If the Pop Up property is set to No, the Dialog setting is the same as the Thin setting. |
| Scroll Bars | Use this property to tell Access to display scroll bars for a report displayed in Report view or Layout view. The default setting, Both, causes Access to display both a horizontal and vertical scroll bar if needed to display the entire report. If you choose Neither, Access does not display either scroll bar, even if one is needed. You will not be able to scroll to see the rest of the report. Choose Horizontal Only to display only a horizontal scroll bar, or choose Vertical Only to display only a vertical scroll bar. |
| Control Box | You can set the Control Box property to No to remove the control menu and the Close, Minimize, and Maximize buttons from the Report window in Report view or Print Preview when you're using a multiple-document interface. The default setting is Yes. You must use Ctrl+F4 to close the window when this property is set to No. This property has no effect when you're using the single-document interface. |
| Close Button | You can set the Close Button property to No to remove the Close button from the Report window in Report view or Print Preview. When you're using a multiple-document interface or you have set the Pop Up or Modal property to Yes, the control menu is still available unless you have also set the Control Box property to No, but the Close command is disabled on the menu. The default setting is Yes. |

| Property | Description |
|---|---|
| Min Max Buttons | You can set the Min Max Buttons property to Both Enabled, None, Min Enabled, or Max Enabled when you are using a multiple-document interface or you have set the Pop Up or Modal property to Yes. If you disable a Minimize or Maximize button, the related command on the control menu becomes dimmed when the Report window is in Report view or Print Preview. The default setting is Both Enabled. |
| Moveable | The default setting, Yes, allows you to move the Report window in Report view or Print Preview when you're using a multiple-document interface or the Pop Up or Modal property is set to Yes. Set this property to No to lock the form on the screen where you last saved it. |
| Show Page Margins | The default setting, Yes, displays print margins for your report when you open it in Layout view. The print margins are determined by your printer settings. You can use this setting in Layout view to make sure no controls extend past the print margins. Set this property to No to not display print margins. |
| Grid X, Grid Y | Specify the number of horizontal (X) or vertical (Y) divisions per inch or per centimeter for the dots in the grid. When you use inches (when Measurement is set to U.S. in the Regional And Language Options section of Windows Control Panel), you can see the dots whenever you specify a value of 24 or less for both X and Y. When you use centimeters (when Measurement is set to Metric), you can see the dots when you specify values of 9 or less. The default setting is 24 for inches and 10 for metric. |
| Layout For Print | When you set this property to Yes, you can select from among the TrueType and printer fonts installed on your computer. When you set this property to No, only TrueType and screen fonts are available. The default setting is Yes. |
| Grp Keep Together | Set this property to Per Page if you want Access to honor the Group, Sort, And Total keep together setting by page. Set it to Per Column (the default) for a multiple-column report if you want Access to attempt to keep a group together within a column. This property has no effect in a typical report with a single column. |
| Picture Pages | You can set this property to show the picture on all pages, the first page, or no pages. The default setting is All Pages. |
| Page Header | This property controls whether the page header appears on all pages. You might choose not to print the page header on the first page if the report contains a report header. Valid settings are All Pages (the default), Not With Rpt Hdr, Not With Rpt Ftr, and Not With Rpt Hdr/Ftr. |
| Page Footer | This property controls whether the page footer appears on all pages. You might choose not to print the page footer on the last page if the report contains a report footer. Valid settings are All Pages (the default), Not With Rpt Hdr, Not With Rpt Ftr, and Not With Rpt Hdr/Ftr. |

| Property | Description |
| --- | --- |
| Orientation | The default in most versions of Access 2007 is Left-to-Right. In versions that support a language that is normally read right to left, the default is Right-to-Left. When you use Right-to-Left, captions appear right-justified, and the order of characters in controls is right to left. |
| Filter | This property shows any filter applied by a macro or Visual Basic procedure the last time the report was opened. You can also define a specific Filter setting that you want to save with the report definition. You can define a filter for a report, as you can with a form, using Ribbon commands when the report is in Report view. To activate the Filter in code, set the report's FilterOn property (not displayed in the property sheet) to True. |
| Filter On Load | Set this property to Yes if you want Access to apply the filter defined for the report automatically each time the report opens. Note that you can set the Filter and FilterOn properties from a macro or a Visual Basic procedure. The default setting is No. |
| Order By | This property shows any ordering criteria applied by a macro or a Visual Basic procedure the last time the report was opened. You can also define a specific Order By setting that you want to save with the report definition. You can activate the ordering criteria in code by setting the OrderByOn property (not displayed in the property sheet) to True. |
| Order By On Load | Set this property to Yes if you want the Order By property defined for the report to be applied automatically each time the report opens. Note that you can set the OrderBy and OrderByOn properties from a macro or a Visual Basic procedure. Remember that Order By and Order By On Load have no effect if you have specified any settings in the Group, Sort, And Total pane. The default setting is No. |
| Allow Filters | Use this property to determine whether a user can see selected records in Report view by applying filtering and sorting criteria using the commands in the Sort & Filter group on the Home tab or by applying the shortcut menu filtering options. If you set the Allow Filters property to No, the user cannot change the report to view other existing records, and Access dims all commands in the Sort & Filter group. The valid settings for the Allow Filters property are Yes and No. The default setting is Yes. |
| On Current through On Page | You can set these properties to run a macro, a function, or an event procedure when the specific event described by the property occurs for this report. See Part 4 for details. |
| Date Grouping | Use this property to determine how Access groups date and time values that you've specified in the Group, Sort, And Total pane. You can set this property to US Defaults or Use System Settings (the default). For US Defaults, the first day of the week is Sunday, and the first week of the year starts on January 1. If you specify Use System Settings, the first day of the week and first week of the year are determined by the Regional And Language Options section in Windows Control Panel. |

| Property | Description |
| --- | --- |
| Cycle | Use the default setting, All Records, to tab to the next record when you press the Tab key in the last control in the tab order. This setting applies when you display the report in Layout view or Report view. Choose Current Record to disallow tabbing from one record to another. Choose Current Page to disallow tabbing onto the next or previous record—you must use Page Up or Page Down to move between the records. When you set Current Record or Current Page, you must use the navigation buttons or Ribbon commands to move to other records. |
| Record Locks | Set this property to All Records if the data for your report is on a network shared by others and you want to be sure that no one can update the records in the report until Access creates every page in the report. You should not set this property to All Records for a report that you plan to view in Layout view, Report view, or Print Preview because you'll lock out other users for the entire time that you're viewing the report on your screen. The default setting is No Locks. |
| Ribbon Name | Enter the name of a custom Ribbon. Access displays the Ribbon when you open the report in Report view or Print Preview. See Chapter 24, "The Finishing Touches," for details. |
| Toolbar | Enter the name of a custom toolbar. Access displays the toolbar when you open the report in Report view or Print Preview. You can use this setting only if your database is in the .mdb file format and you defined custom toolbars in the database using a prior version of Access. |
| Menu Bar | Enter the name of a custom menu bar. Access displays the menu bar when you open the report in Report view or Print Preview. You can use this setting only if your database is in the .mdb file format and you defined custom menu bars in the database using a prior version of Access. |
| Shortcut Menu Bar | Enter the name of a custom shortcut menu. Access displays the shortcut menu when you open the report in Report view or Print Preview and right-click in the Report window. You must create custom shortcut menu bars by using Visual Basic code or by using the design facilities in a prior version of Access. |
| Help File, Help Context Id | You can set the Help File property to specify the location of a Help file in any format supported by Windows and the 2007 Microsoft Office system, including the HTML help format. Use the Help Context Id property to point to a specific help topic within the file. |
| Has Module | This property indicates whether the report has associated Visual Basic procedures. Access automatically changes this setting to Yes when you define any Visual Basic event procedures for the report. Caution: If you change this property to No when the report has procedures, Access warns you that this deletes your code. |

| Property | Description |
|---|---|
| Use Default Paper Size | The default setting, No, tells Access to not use the default paper size of your default printer when printing the report. Instead, Access honors the section size properties you defined. Change this setting to Yes to have Access use the default printer settings. |
| Fast Laser Printing | Some laser printers support the drawing of lines (such as the edges of rectangles, the line control, or the edges of text boxes) with rules. If you set the Fast Laser Printing property to Yes, Access sends rule commands instead of graphics to your printer to print rules. Rules print faster than graphics. The default setting is Yes. |
| Tag | Use this property to store additional identifying information about the report. You can use this property in macros and in Visual Basic procedures to temporarily store information that you want to pass to another routine. |
| Palette Source | With this property, if you have a color printer, you can specify a device-independent bitmap (.dib) file, a Microsoft Windows Palette (.pal) file, a Windows icon (.ico) file, or a Windows bitmap (.bmp) file to provide a palette of colors different from those in the Access default palette. You might need to set this property if you have also set the Picture property so that the colors of the background picture display properly. The default setting, (Default), uses your current Windows palette. |
| Key Preview | This property determines whether the report-level keyboard event procedures (KeyUp, KeyDown, and KeyPress) are invoked before a control's keyboard event procedures. The default setting, No, tells Access that only the active control can receive keyboard events when the report is displayed in Layout view or Report view. Choose Yes to have the report receive keyboard events before the active control receives keyboard events when the report is displayed in Layout view or Report view. |



# Using Calculated Values

Much of the power of Access 2007 reports comes from their ability to perform both simple and complex calculations on the data from the underlying tables or queries. Access also provides dozens of built-in functions that you can use to work with your data or to add information to a report. The following sections provide examples of the types of calculations you can perform.

## Adding the Print Date and Page Numbers

One of the pieces of information you might frequently add to a report is the date on which you prepared the report. You'll probably also want to add page numbers. Access provides two built-in functions that you can use to add the current date and time to your report. The Date function returns the current system date as a date/time value with no time component. The Now function returns the current system date and time as a date/time value.

> **Note**
>
> When you create a report using the Report Wizard, it adds a similar control to the Page Footer section, and it uses the Now function that returns the date and the time. However, the wizard sets the Format property to Long Date, which displays only the date portion.

To add the current date to your report, create an unbound text box control (delete the label) in the Page Footer section, and set its Control Source property to **=Date()**. Then, in the Format property box, specify Long Date. You can see an example of using the Date function in Figure 16-8. The result in Print Preview is shown in Figure 16-9.

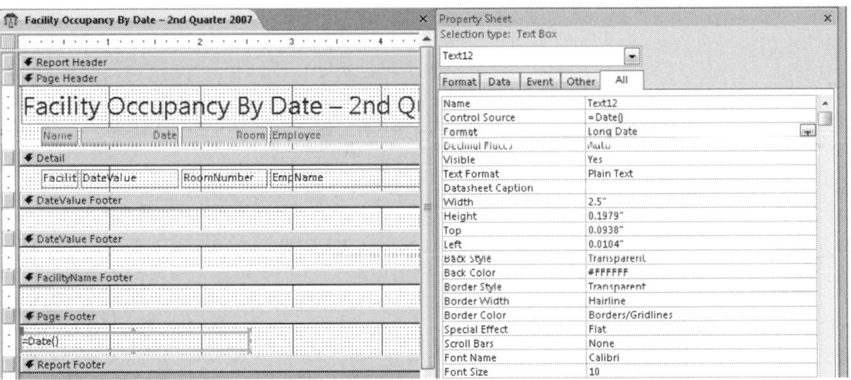


**Figure 16-8** Use the Date function in an unbound control to add the date to a report.

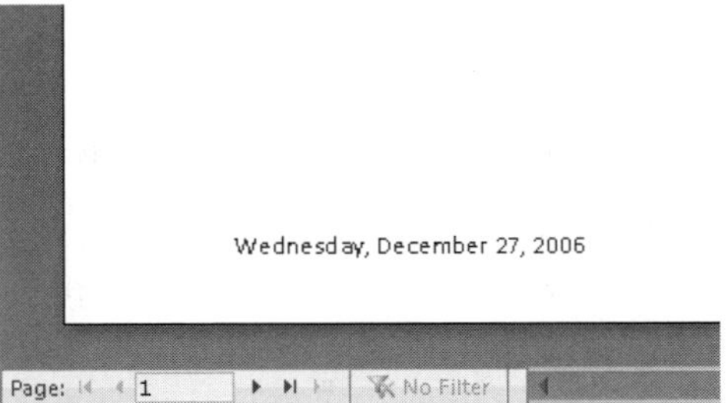


**Figure 16-9** You can now see the current date displayed in the report in Print Preview.

In the Controls group on the Design tab, Access 2007 includes a button that helps you create this type of control on your report. Click the Date & Time button in the Controls group, and Access opens the Date And Time dialog box, shown in Figure 16-10. You can choose to insert the date, the time, or both the date and time displayed in a text box control into the report's Report Header section. You can choose different formats for both. Access displays a sample of what the control will display at the bottom of the dialog box. However, the tool does not offer you any choices of where it will place the control–Access always places this control in the Report Header section on the right side. You could create the control using this feature (selecting only the Include Date check box and the Long Date format), drag and drop it into the Page Footer on the left, set the alignment to left, and shrink the Report Header back to zero height, but we think it's just as easy to create the control yourself. Click Cancel to close the dialog box because you've already added a control to the report to display the date.

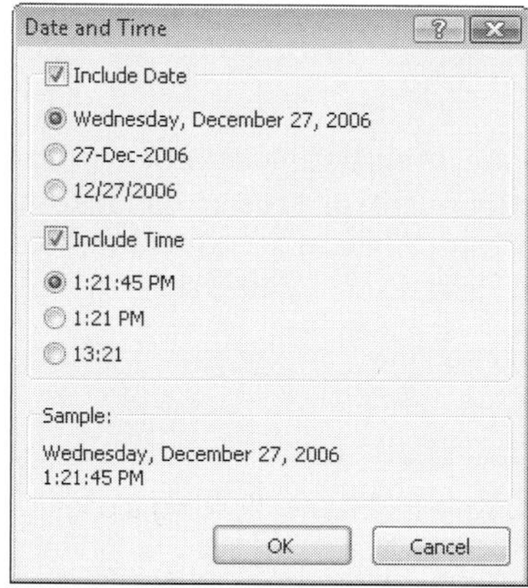


**Figure 16-10** Use the Date And Time dialog box to assist you in building a report date control.



To add a page number, use the Page property for the report. You can't see this property in any of the property sheets because it is maintained by Access. Access also provides the Pages property, which contains a count of the total number of pages in the report. To add the current page number to a report (in this example, in the Page Footer section), create an unbound text box control (delete the label), set its Control Source property to **="Page " & [Page] & " of " & [Pages]** as shown in Figure 16-11, and set the Text Align property to Right.

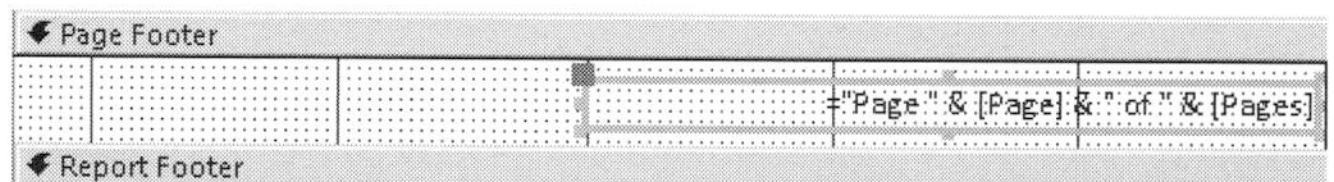


**Figure 16-11** Use the Page and Pages properties to add page numbers to a report.

In the Controls group on the Design tab, Access 2007 includes a button that helps you create this type of control on your report. Click the Insert Page Numbers button in the Controls group, and Access opens the Page Numbers dialog box, shown in Figure 16-12. (Remember, we discussed this command in Chapter 15, "Constructing a Report.") You can choose to insert the page number or the page number and count of pages. Access also offers an option to display the page text box control in the report's Page Header or Page Footer section. In the Alignment drop-down list you can choose where to have Access place the control–Left, Center, Right, Inside, or Outside. Note that Access adds two controls for the Inside and Outside options and includes a logical expression in the control source to display each text box on alternate pages. When you choose Inside, even page numbers appear on the right, and odd page numbers appear on the left. When you choose Outside, even page numbers appear on the left, and odd numbers appear on the right. Select the Show Number On First Page check box at the bottom of the dialog box to display the page numbers on all pages, including the first page. If you clear this check box, Access creates a control that will not show the page number on the first page. You can try this feature using the settings in Figure 16-12 to compare the result with the text box you created previously, or you can click Cancel to close the dialog box.

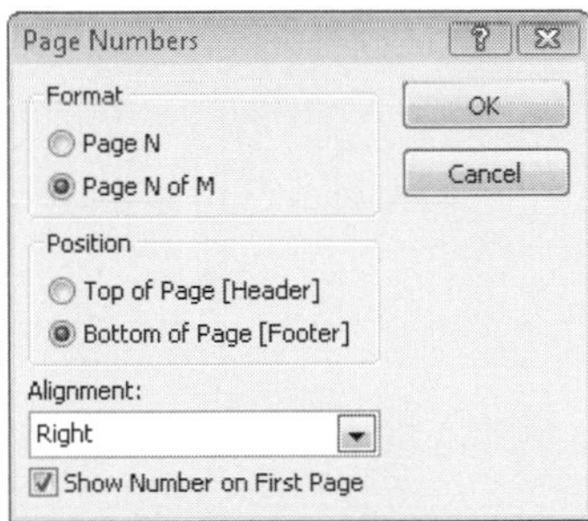


**Figure 16-12** Use the Page Numbers dialog box to assist you in building a page number control.

INSIDE OUT **You Can Change the Value of the Page Property in Code**

You can reset the value of the Page property in a macro or a Visual Basic procedure that you activate from an appropriate report property. For example, if you're printing several multiple-page invoices for different customers in one pass, you might want to reset the page number to 1 when you start to format the page for a different customer. You can include a Group Header section for each customer and then use a macro or a Visual Basic procedure to set the Page property to 1 each time Access formats that section (indicating that you're on the first page of a new customer invoice).



## Performing Calculations

Another task you might perform frequently is calculating extended values from detail values in your tables. If you understand the principles of good table design (see Article 1, "Designing Your Database Application," on the companion CD), you know that it's usually redundant and wasteful of storage space to define a field in your tables that you can calculate from other fields. The only situations in which this is acceptable are when saving the calculated value will greatly improve performance in parts of your application and when you have collected static historical data in a table designed specifically to support reporting.

## Performing a Calculation on a Detail Line

You can use arithmetic operators to create complex calculations in the Control Source property of any control that can display data. You can also use any of the many built-in functions or any of the functions you define yourself in a module. If you want, you can use the Expression Builder that you learned about in Chapter 7, "Creating and Working with Simple Queries," to build the expression for any control. You let Access know that you are using an expression in a Control Source property by starting the expression with an equal sign (=).

> **Note**
>
> To use a field in a calculation, that field must be in the table or query specified in the Record Source property of the report.

One calculated value that housing management might find useful is the daily revenue for each room. You could have calculated that value in the query that is the record source of the report, but you can also calculate it as an expression in a text box in the Detail section of the report. To add the expression you need to the Facility Occupancy By Date report that you have been creating, follow these steps:

1. Before you add your new control to the Detail section, you should first expand the width of the FacilityName control because it is too narrow to display all the facility names. Click the FacilityName control, and drag its left edge toward the left side of the report to make it flush with the left side. Next, drag its right edge toward the right edge of the report to expand the width of the control until it is about 1.6 inches in width. (You can check this in the Property Sheet window if you want.) As you expand the width, Access moves the other controls in the Detail section to the right (along with their labels in the Page Header section). When the Report Wizard created this report, it placed all the controls in the Detail section into a tabular control layout, so when you resize the FacilityName control, Access adjusts the other controls as well. Note that you could make these changes in Layout view in order to see the data while resizing the control. However, Access collapses the height of the two DateValue footer sections and the FacilityName footer section when you switch to Layout view. Go ahead and change the caption for the facility name label as well from Name to Facility by clicking the label and typing **Facility**.
2. Reduce the width of the DateValue controls to 0.9 inch, the RoomNumber controls to 0.8 inch, and the EmpName controls to 1.6 inches.

3. On the Design tab, in the Controls group, click the Text Box button, and place a text box in the Detail section to the right of the EmpName text box. Select the attached label, and delete it.

4. In the Control Source property of the new text box, enter

   ```
   =CCur(Round([TotalCharge]/([CheckOutDate]-[CheckInDate]),2))
   ```

   Because you included the TotalCharge, CheckInDate, and CheckOutDate fields in the query, you can reference them in your expression. This expression calculates the daily revenue by dividing the total charge for the reservation by the number of days. Set the Format property of the text box to Currency, and set the Width property to 0.75 inch. Move this text box close to the EmpName text box, and line up the tops of the two text boxes. Also, make sure the height of both text boxes is the same by selecting them both and then clicking the Size To Tallest button in the Size group on the Arrange tab.

5. Click the Line button in the Controls group on the Design tab, and place a horizontal line in the Page Header section below the labels. Move the line to the left edge of the report, and set its Width property to 5.9 inches so that it stretches over all the controls in the Detail section, including your new text box. Make sure the height of the control is 0 inches. Click the Line Thickness button in the Controls group, and select 2 PT for the thickness.

6. Click the Label tool in the Controls group on the Design tab, and draw a label control next to the Employee label in the page header. Type **Charge** in the label, and press Enter. (If you don't type anything, the label disappears when you click away from it.)

7. The default Label control in the Access 2007 style has no background color, but the other labels have a light blue background. You can click one of the other labels in the page header, click the Format Painter button in the Font group on the Design tab, and then click your new label to transfer the format.

8. Make the new label the same height as the other labels in the page header, and give it the same width as the text box below it (0.75 inch). Align the left edge of the label with the left edge of the text box, and align the top of the label with the top of the other labels in the section.

Your report in Design view should now look like Figure 16-13.

Figure 16-14 shows the result in Print Preview. (Note that the Access 2007 report style has an alternating color defined for the Detail section.) You can see that Access has performed the required calculations for each day of each reservation.

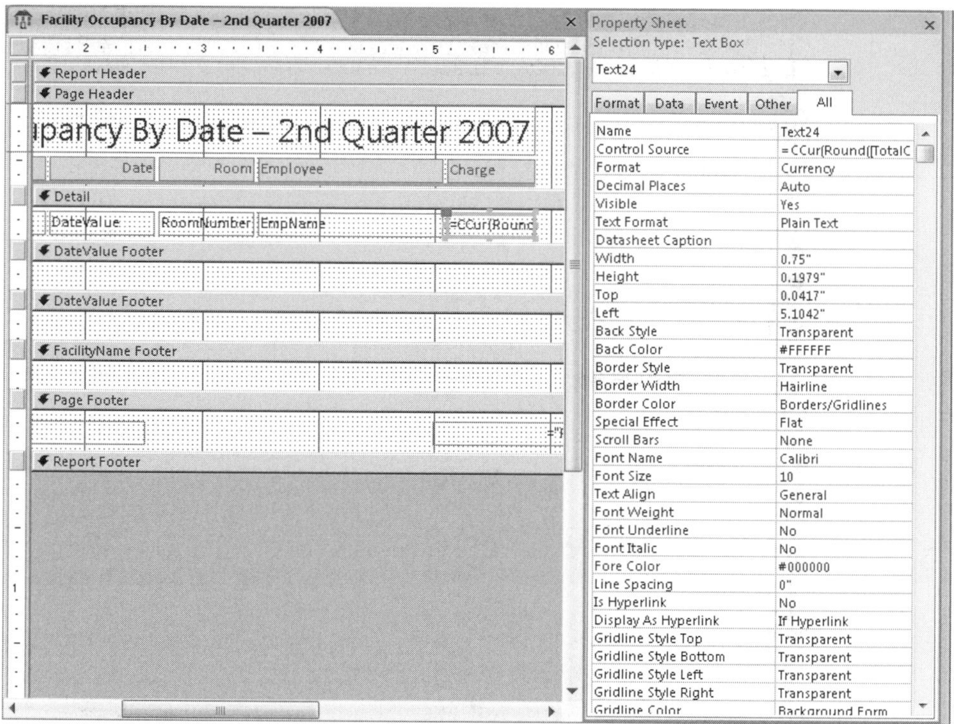

Figure 16-13 Add an expression to the Detail section to calculate daily revenue.



## INSIDE OUT Avoiding #Error in a Calculated Control

Instead of starting with an unbound text box to perform a calculation, you might decide to drag and drop one of the fields that you'll use in the calculation from the field list onto your report. When you do that, Access gives the text box the same name as the field. If you modify the control source to an expression that uses the field, you'll see #Error in the text box when you view or print the report.

When you enter a name in an expression, Access first searches for another control that has that name. If it doesn't find the control, then it looks in the field list. So, if the name of the control is TotalCharge and you include an expression that uses [TotalCharge], the expression is referencing itself! Access can't figure out how to display the value of the TotalCharge text box, so it displays #Error instead. If you decide to drag and drop a field that you'll change to an expression, be sure to change the Name property of the control (for example, txtTotalCharge) before you enter the expression.

Of course, you'll also see #Error if your expression references a function that doesn't exist or provides invalid parameters to a function. However, using the name of the control itself inside the expression that is the control source is one of the most common sources of #Error.

Facility Occupancy By Date – 2nd Quarter 2007

# Facility Occupancy By Date – 2nd Quarter 2007

| Facility | Date | Room | Employee | Charge |
|---|---|---|---|---|
| Main Campus Housing A | 01-Apr-2007 | 201 | Petculescu, Cristian | $37.22 |
| Main Campus Housing A | 01-Apr-2007 | 401 | Meyyappan, Ramesh | $36.88 |
| Main Campus Housing A | 01-Apr-2007 | 410 | Sazanovich, Vadim | $36.43 |
| Main Campus Housing A | 01-Apr-2007 | 507 | Fort, Garth | $50.33 |
| Main Campus Housing A | 01-Apr-2007 | 507 | Cheng, Yao-Qiang | $50.00 |
| Main Campus Housing A | 01-Apr-2007 | 808 | Maxwell, Taylor | $45.00 |
| Main Campus Housing A | 02-Apr-2007 | 401 | Meyyappan, Ramesh | $36.88 |
| Main Campus Housing A | 02-Apr-2007 | 410 | Sazanovich, Vadim | $36.43 |
| Main Campus Housing A | 02-Apr-2007 | 507 | Fort, Garth | $50.33 |
| Main Campus Housing A | 02-Apr-2007 | 507 | Cheng, Yao-Qiang | $50.00 |
| Main Campus Housing A | 02-Apr-2007 | 808 | Maxwell, Taylor | $45.00 |
| Main Campus Housing A | 03-Apr-2007 | 410 | Sazanovich, Vadim | $36.43 |
| Main Campus Housing A | 03-Apr-2007 | 507 | Fort, Garth | $50.33 |

Page: 1 No Filter

**Figure 16-14** The calculated detail line values within a group now appear in Print Preview.

## Adding Values Across a Group

Another task commonly performed in reports is adding values across a group. In the previous chapter, you saw a simple example of this in a report that used the built-in Sum function. In the Facility Occupancy By Date report, you have three levels of grouping: one by facility, another by month, and another by date. When you specified grouping and sorting criteria earlier in this chapter, you asked Access to provide group footers. This gives you sections in your report in which you can add unbound controls that use any of the aggregate functions (Sum, Min, Max, Avg, Count, First, Last, StDev, or Var) in expressions to display a calculated value for all the rows in that group. In this example, you can create unbound controls in the Facility footer and both DateValue footers to hold the totals by facility, by month, and by date, for the daily charge for each room, as shown in Figure 16-15. In the Control Source property of each, enter

```
=Sum(CCur(Round([TotalCharge]/([CheckOutDate]-[CheckInDate]),2)))
```

Set the Format property to Currency for each of the three new controls. Notice that in this case, you must repeat the original expression inside the aggregate function rather than attempt to sum the control you placed in the Detail section. (See "How to Calculate Totals on Expressions" on the next page for an explanation.)

You should also add a line control at the top of each footer section to provide a visual clue that the values that follow are totals. When you place a line control on the grid in any footer section using the Access 2007 report style, Access sets Border Style to Transparent. Change the Border Style property to Solid for each of these lines. In this example, we placed lines approximately 4.85 inches in from the left and made them about 1 inch long, but they're difficult to see in Design view because they're right up against the top of the section. Also move the page number control so the right edge lines up with these new calculated controls, and reduce the width of the design grid to 6.5 inches.

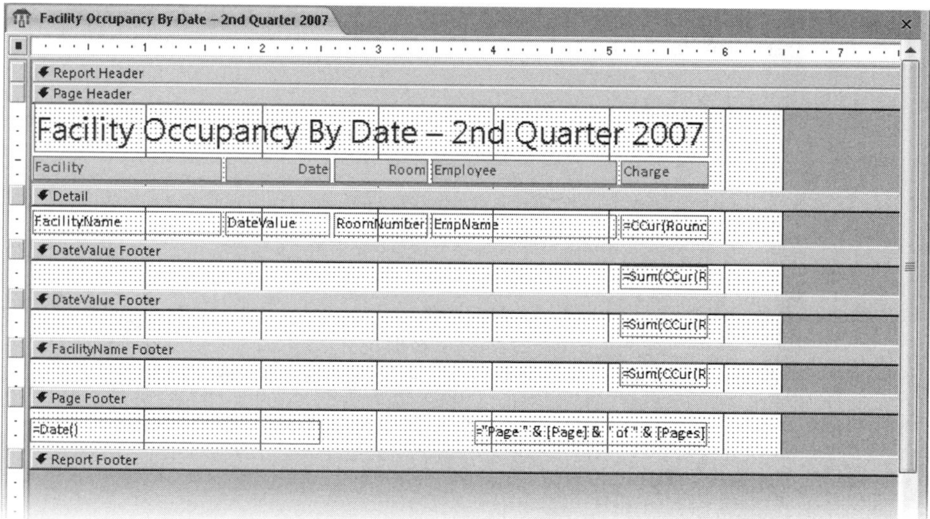


**Figure 16-5** Add summaries by facility, by month, and by date into the three footer sections.



## INSIDE OUT How to Calculate Totals on Expressions

An important point to remember about using an aggregate expression in a group section is that the expression cannot refer to any calculated controls in the Detail section. As you'll learn later, you can reference an outer control from an inner one (for example, a total calculation in a group from inside the Detail section), but not vice versa. So, you cannot create a calculated field in the Detail section, for example, that multiplies two numbers and then reference that control in the summary expression. You can, however, repeat the calculation expression in the summary. If a detail control named Total has an expression such as =[Quantity] * [Price], you must use an expression such as =Sum([Quantity] * [Price]) in your grouping section, not =Sum([Total]).

## Creating a Grand Total

Use the Report Footer section to create grand totals for any values across the entire set of records in a report. You can use any of the aggregate functions in the report footer just as you did in the two grouping section footers. Expand the Report Footer section to about 0.43 inch to give yourself some room. Add a new text box control to the Report Footer section, and set the Control Source property to the same expression used in the three footer controls. Set Format to Currency, and change the width of the text box to 1 inch to allow extra room for a larger number total. Align the right edge of the text box to the other three calculated controls. Click inside the label for this new text box, type **Grand Total:**, and align the text to the right. Finally, bold the text in the label, and move the label so that its right edge is next to the left side of the text box. Figure 16-16 shows you this Sum function used in the new control in the report footer to produce a total for all records in the report.

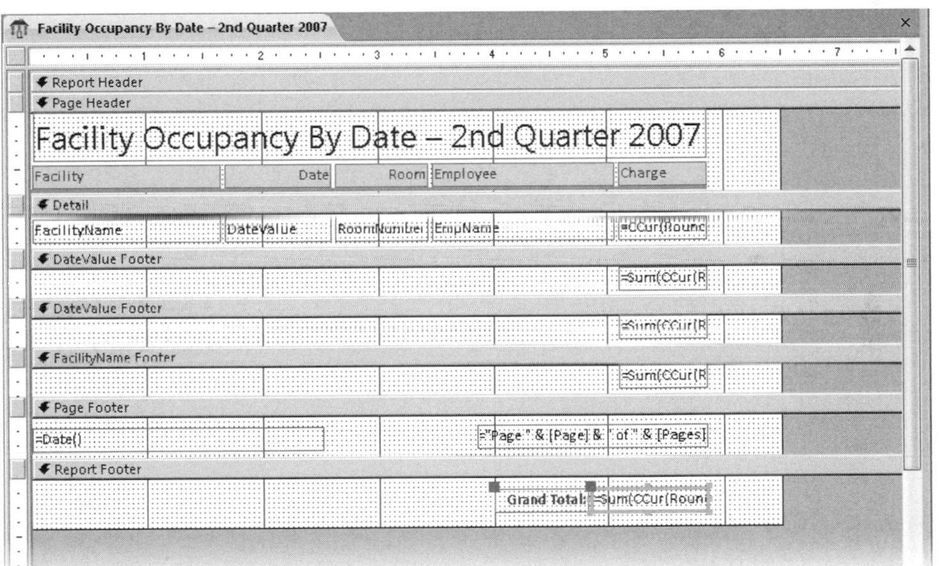


**Figure 16-16** Use the Report Footer section to create a grand total control for all records.

If you switch to Print Preview, go to the last page in the report, and scroll down, you should see a result similar to that shown in Figure 16-17. (You should set the name of this grand total field to txtSumGrand so that you can use it to calculate percentages later.) You can find this stage of the report design saved as rptXmplFacilityDateOccupancyStep2 in the sample database.

| | | | | |
|---|---|---|---|---|
| South Campus Housing C | 30-Jun-2007 | 409 | Beasley, Shaun | $93.68 |
| South Campus Housing C | 30-Jun-2007 | 409 | Shimshoni, Daniel | $93.68 |
| South Campus Housing C | 30-Jun-2007 | 502 | Meisner, Darrell | $37.37 |
| South Campus Housing C | 30-Jun-2007 | 509 | Worden, Joe | $100.00 |
| South Campus Housing C | 30-Jun-2007 | 509 | Shimshoni, Daniel | $94.00 |
| South Campus Housing C | 30-Jun-2007 | 511 | Shimshoni, Daniel | $37.37 |
| South Campus Housing C | 30-Jun-2007 | 601 | Browne, Kevin F. | $91.43 |
| | | | | $792.58 |
| | | | | $17,047.07 |
| | | | | $44,479.28 |
| | | | Grand Total: | $134,987.92 |

**Figure 16-17** You can see the various totals displayed in the report in Print Preview.

> **Note**
>
> If you want to create percentage calculations for any of the groups over the grand total, you must create the control for the grand total in the report footer so that you can reference the total in percentage calculation expressions. See "Calculating Percentages" on page 843. If you don't want the total to print, set the control's Visible property to No.



## Hiding Redundant Values and Concatenating Text Strings

You probably noticed in several of the preceding examples that the FacilityName and DateValue fields print for every detail line. When a particular detail line displays or prints values that match the previous line, the report looks less readable and less professional. You can control this by using the Hide Duplicates text box property (which is available only in reports). Switch to the Design view of this report, and set the Hide Duplicates property to Yes for the FacilityName text box and the DateValue text box in the Detail section. The report will now print the facility name and the date only once per group or page, as shown in Figure 16-18. (The figure shows information from the last page of the report.) When Access moves to a new grouping level or page, it prints the facility name even if it matches the previous value displayed.

Facility Occupancy By Date – 2nd Quarter 2007

| Facility | Date | Room | Employee | Charge |
|---|---|---|---|---|
| South Campus Housing C | 29-Jun-2007 | 201 | Lysaker, Jenny | $93.33 |
| | | 301 | Saddow, Peter | $94.55 |
| | | 302 | Martin, Benjamin | $36.88 |
| | | 309 | Tallman, Tracy | $91.43 |
| | | 409 | Shimshoni, Daniel | $93.68 |
| | | 409 | Beasley, Shaun | $93.68 |
| | | 502 | Meisner, Darrell | $37.37 |
| | | 509 | Shimshoni, Daniel | $94.00 |
| | | 509 | Worden, Joe | $100.00 |
| | | 511 | Shimshoni, Daniel | $37.37 |
| | | 601 | Browne, Kevin F. | $91.43 |
| | | 608 | Browne, Kevin F. | $41.43 |
| | | | | $905.15 |
| South Campus Housing C | 30-Jun-2007 | 110 | Cheng, Yao-Qiang | $60.29 |
| | | 201 | Lysaker, Jenny | $93.33 |
| | | 309 | Tallman, Tracy | $91.43 |
| | | 409 | Beasley, Shaun | $93.68 |
| | | 409 | Shimshoni, Daniel | $93.68 |
| | | 502 | Meisner, Darrell | $37.37 |
| | | 509 | Worden, Joe | $100.00 |
| | | 509 | Shimshoni, Daniel | $94.00 |
| | | 511 | Shimshoni, Daniel | $37.37 |
| | | 601 | Browne, Kevin F. | $91.43 |
| | | | | $792.58 |
| | | | | $17,047.07 |
| | | | | $44,479.28 |
| | | | Grand Total: | $134,987.92 |

**Figure 16-18** Set the Hide Duplicates property to Yes to eliminate redundant values in each group.

Notice that when the report gets to the end of data for a month or a facility, it's not clear what the total lines mean. For example, on the last page of the report as shown in Figure 16-18, $792.58 is clearly the total for the last date, but it's not obvious that $17,047.07 is the total for the month of June for the facility or that $44,479.28 is the total revenue for the facility. You can use string concatenation to display data that looks like a label but that also includes information from the record source. Sometimes it's useful to combine descriptive text with a value from a text field in the underlying query or table or to combine multiple text fields in one control. In Figure 16-19, you can see a descriptive label (created by a single text box control) on one of the subtotal lines. (In Figure 16-19 we dragged the Property Sheet window below the new text box so that you could see the Control Source property.)

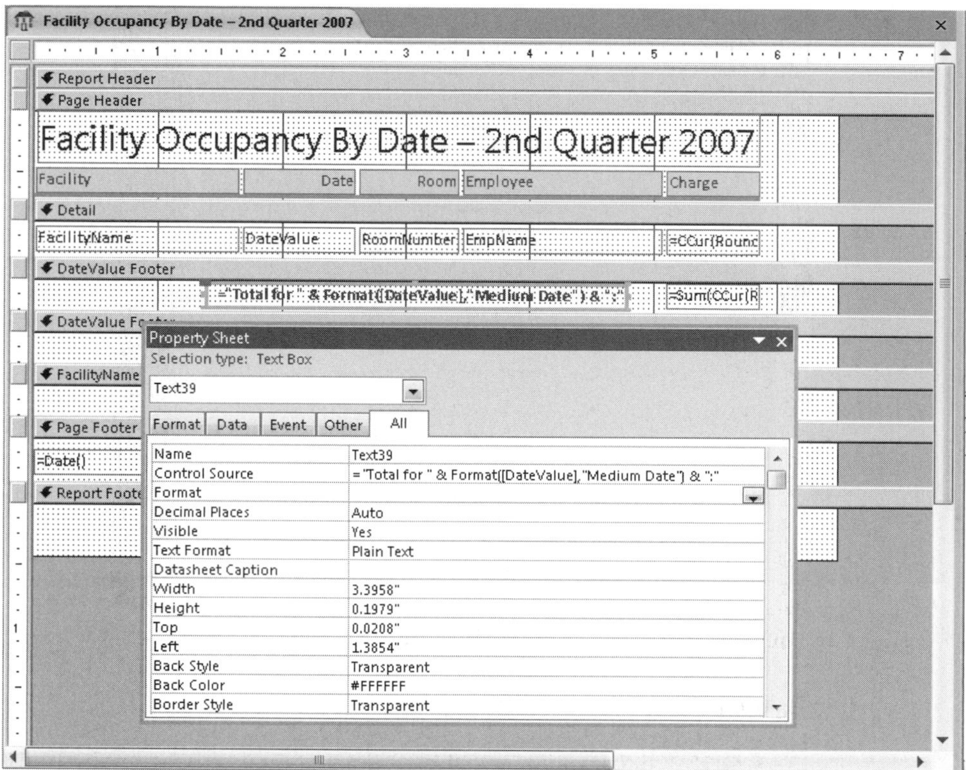


**Figure 16-19** A text constant and a string derived from a field in the record source are concatenated as a "label" in a text box.

This "label" concatenates the words *Total for* with an expression that uses the Format function—applied here to the DateValue field to get the date in medium date format—and an ending string containing a colon. You can use the same technique in the group footer to create a "label" that reads *Total for facility* followed by the facility name and a trailing colon. You could certainly define a label followed by a text box followed by another label to create the same display. The advantage of using a single control is that you don't have to worry about lining up three controls or setting the font characteristics. In fact, because the string in the middle, containing the facility name, could vary significantly in length, you cannot create three separate controls that correctly line up all possible values end-to-end. Set the Text Alignment property of these controls to Right so that they line up correctly next to the summary controls, and match the formatting of the grand total label in the Report Footer section by selecting the grand total label, double-clicking the Format Painter button to lock it, and then clicking the three text boxes. Click the Format Painter button again when you're done to unlock it.

When you look at the report in Print Preview, as shown in Figure 16-20, you can see that the duplicate values for the facility name and for the date have been eliminated. You can also see the nice result from using a concatenated string in a text box to generate labels for the total lines.

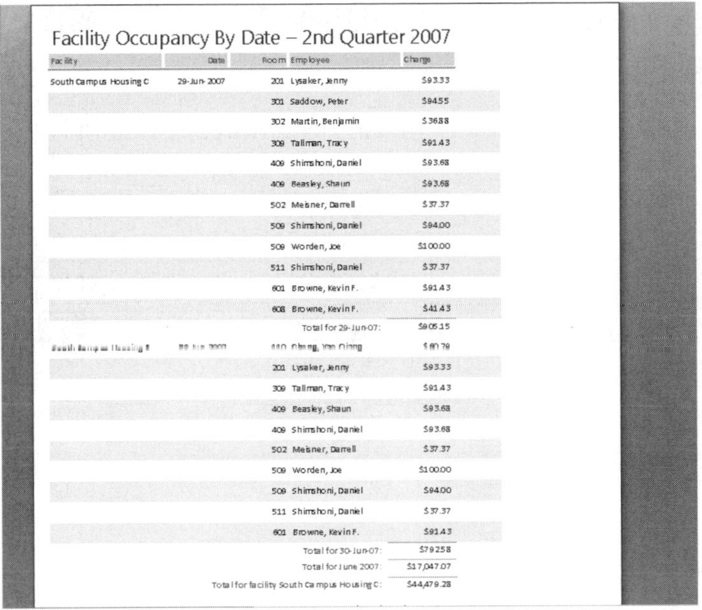

Facility Occupancy By Date – 2nd Quarter 2007

| Facility | Date | Room | Employee | Charge |
|---|---|---|---|---|
| South Campus Housing C | 29-Jun-2007 | 201 | Lysaker, Jenny | $93.33 |
| | | 301 | Saddow, Peter | $94.55 |
| | | 302 | Martin, Benjamin | $36.88 |
| | | 309 | Tallman, Tracy | $91.43 |
| | | 409 | Shimshoni, Daniel | $93.68 |
| | | 409 | Beasley, Shaun | $93.68 |
| | | 502 | Meisner, Darrell | $37.37 |
| | | 509 | Shimshoni, Daniel | $94.00 |
| | | 509 | Worden, Joe | $100.00 |
| | | 511 | Shimshoni, Daniel | $37.37 |
| | | 601 | Browne, Kevin F. | $91.43 |
| | | 608 | Browne, Kevin F. | $41.43 |
| | | | Total for 29-Jun-07: | $905.15 |
| [illegible] | [illegible] | [illegible] | [illegible] | [illegible] |
| | | 201 | Lysaker, Jenny | $93.33 |
| | | 309 | Tallman, Tracy | $91.43 |
| | | 409 | Beasley, Shaun | $93.68 |
| | | 409 | Shimshoni, Daniel | $93.68 |
| | | 502 | Meisner, Darrell | $37.37 |
| | | 509 | Worden, Joe | $100.00 |
| | | 509 | Shimshoni, Daniel | $94.00 |
| | | 511 | Shimshoni, Daniel | $37.37 |
| | | 601 | Browne, Kevin F. | $91.43 |
| | | | Total for 30-Jun-07: | $792.58 |
| | | | Total for June 2007: | $17,047.07 |
| | | | Total for facility South Campus Housing C: | $44,479.28 |

**Figure 16-20** The total lines now have descriptive captions using data from the record source.

## Calculating Percentages

In any report that groups and summarizes data, you might want to determine what percentage of an outer group total or the grand total is represented in a particular sum. You can do this in a report because Access makes two passes through the data. On the first pass, it calculates simple expressions in detail lines, sums across groups, sums across the entire report, and calculates the length of the report. On the second pass, it resolves any expressions that reference totals that were calculated in the first pass. Consequently, you can create an expression in a detail or group summary section that divides by a sum in an outer group or the grand total to calculate percentages.

Figure 16-21 shows an example of a percentage calculation in the FacilityName Footer section. (We dragged the Property Sheet window down below the control so that you could see the Control Source property.) The expression divides the sum of the calculated charge for this facility by the value in a field called txtSumGrand—the name of the grand total control in the report footer. (Remember that when you created the grand total, we instructed you to give it this name.)

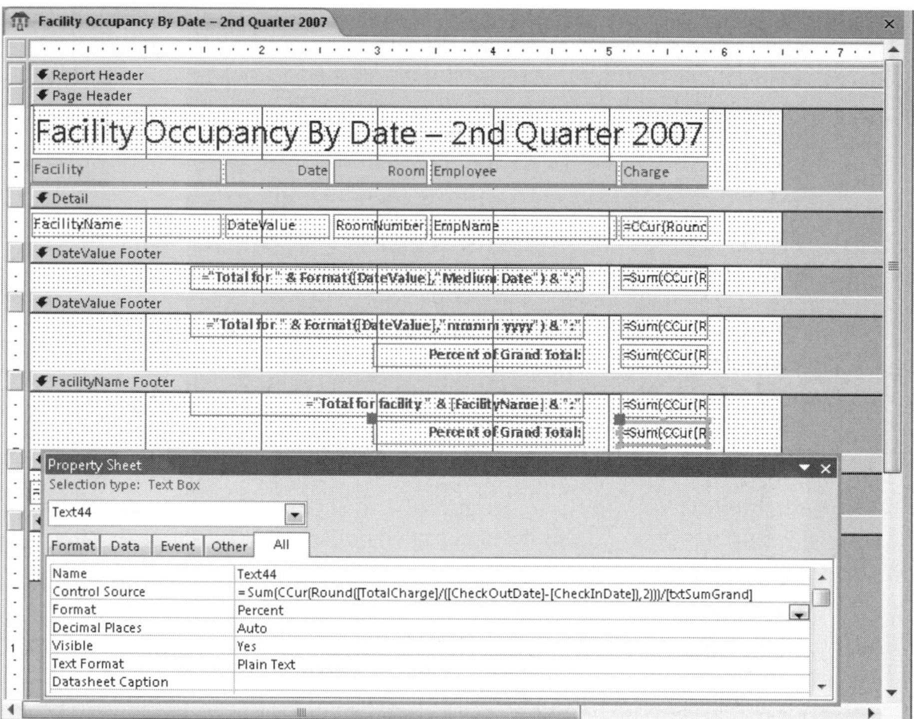


**Figure 16-21** You can add a calculation in the group footer for a percentage of a grand total.

Set the Format property of the text box to Percent, and switch to Print Preview. Scroll down to find a total by month or by facility, and you'll also see the percent of the grand total, as shown in Figure 16-22. You can find this stage of the report design saved as rptXmplFacilityDateOccupancyStep3 in the sample database.

| | | | | |
|---|---|---|---|---|
| Main Campus Housing A | 30-Jun-2007 | 203 | Moseley, Julia | $41.88 |
| | | 210 | Wycoff, Pieter | $37.06 |
| | | 411 | Fort, Garth | $72.86 |
| | | 709 | Glimp, Diane R. | $45.71 |
| | | 802 | Cheng, Yao-Qiang | $84.50 |
| | | 906 | Mohamed, Shammi | $83.89 |
| | | 909 | Schmidt, Steve | $46.84 |
| | | | **Total for 30-Jun-07:** | $412.74 |
| | | | **Total for June 2007:** | $7,040.91 |
| | | | **Percent of Grand Total:** | 5.22% |
| | | | **Total for facility Main Campus Housing A:** | $26,699.89 |
| | | | **Percent of Grand Total:** | 19.78% |

**Figure 16-22** At the end of the report, you can see percentage calculations for two groups in Print Preview.

## Using Running Sum

In addition to producing totals for any group you define, Access lets you create running totals within the Detail section or any group header or footer. For any text box that displays a numeric value, you can set the Running Sum property to produce a total that is reset at the start of each group or that continues totaling through the entire report. Let's further refine rptXmplFacilityDateOccupancyStep3 to see how this works.

Before you can add any controls horizontally, you need to adjust the sizes of some of the controls to provide more horizontal space within the design width of the report. Select the Room label control, and change the width to 0.5 inch in the Property Sheet window. Access moves the EmpName controls to the left so that they remain close to the Room controls. Click the Employee label control, and set the width to 1.3 inches. Select both the Charge label control and the calculated text box control below it, and slide them both to the left about 0.3 inch. (The Left property for these controls should be about 4.8 inches now.) Click the line control in the page header that runs beneath all the labels, and set its width to 6.45 inches. Select all the controls in both DateValue footers, the FacilityName footer, and the report footer, and slide them to the left so that they now line up with the new position of the charge calculation text box in the Detail section.

Now you have some horizontal room to add another label control and companion text box control. Start by selecting the Charge label control, copy it to the Clipboard, and paste it back into the page header. Move it just to the right of the existing Charge label control, and line it up vertically with all the other labels. Now change its caption to **Cum. Charge**, and set its width to 0.85 inch.

> INSIDE OUT
>
> **Select the Section Before Pasting**
>
> If you select the Page Header section before you perform the paste, Access places the control in the upper-left corner of the section and doesn't change the size of the section. If you leave the original control selected when you perform the paste, Access places the new copy below the original and expands the section, which you might not want it to do.

Likewise, select the text box control below the original Charge label control, copy it to the Clipboard, and paste it back into the Detail section. Move it to the left of the existing charge calculation text box, and line it up horizontally with all the other text boxes. Line up the new text box control with the label control above it, and set its width to 0.85 inch to allow room for larger numbers. Finally, select the new text box control, and set its Running Sum property in the Property Sheet window to Over Group. Your report should now look like Figure 16-23.

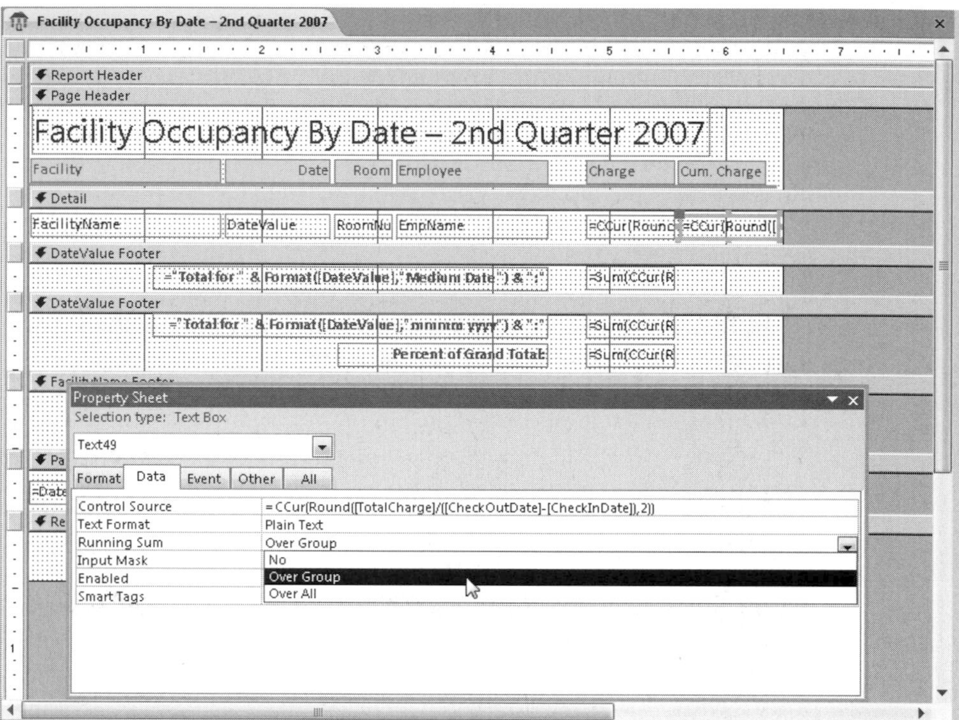

**Figure 16-23** For the Running Sum property of the new calculated text box, select Over Group to add a running sum calculation on the charge.

No, this isn't a second copy of the charge calculation. As you'll see when you look at the report in Print Preview, this produces (as the name of the property implies) a running sum of the charge calculation within the Detail section. As Access encounters each new row in the Detail section, it adds the current value of calculation to the previous accumulation and displays the result. Because you asked for the sum Over Group, Access resets the accumulating total each time it encounters a new group.

Next, let's use a little trick to generate a line number for each line in the Detail section. To make room for this line number, click the Facility label, and drag its right edge to the right side of the report until it moves the Employee label control and EmpName text box control next to the Charge label control. Now drag the left side of the Facility label to the right to reduce its width and create enough space for a small text control. (The Facility label and FacilityName text box controls should be about 1.65 inches in width when you complete these steps.) Insert a small text box in the space you just created in the Detail section. Above this text box, create a label that displays # as its caption. (You can use the Format Painter button again to copy the format from one of the existing label controls to the new one.)

Remember that as Access formats each detail line, it takes the current value of the field (actually, the current value of the text box), adds it to the previous total, and displays the result. If you set the text box equal to any constant numeric value, Access uses that value for each detail line it produces. So, the trick is to set this text box equal to 1 (=1 in the Control Source property) and then set the Running Sum property. If you choose Over All for Running Sum, Access will number the first line 1, add 1 for the second line and display 2, add 1 for the third line and display 3, and so on throughout the report. If you choose Over Group, Access increases the number for each line but resets the number back to 1 when a new group starts. Select Over Group on the Running Sum property for this control to sequentially number all the reservations on the same date, as shown in Figure 16-24. Also set the Format property of the control to **0.** to place a period after each displayed value.

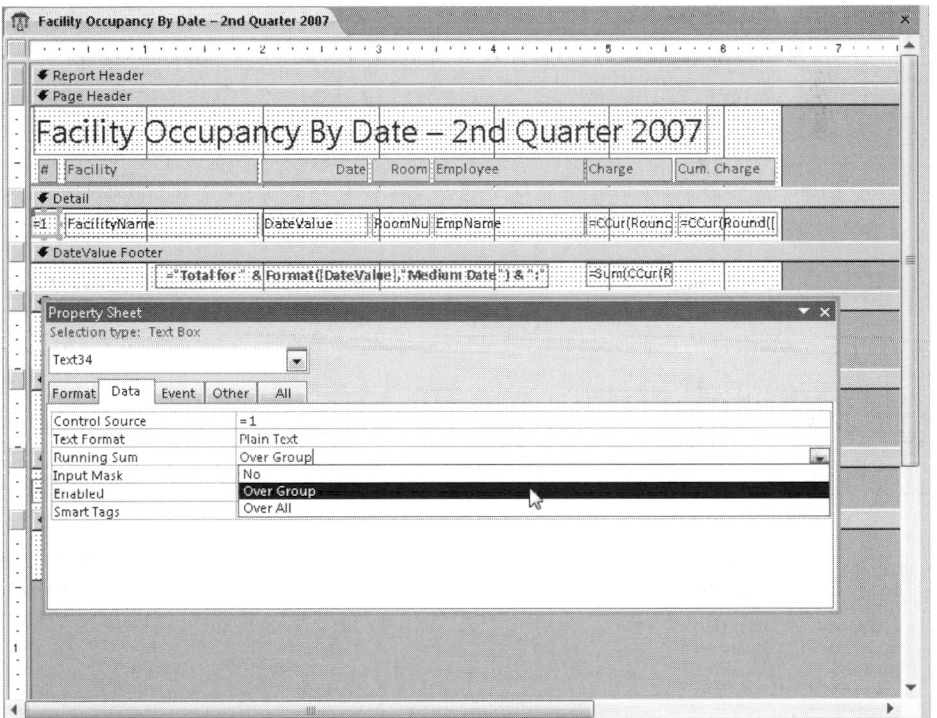


**Figure 16-24** Use the Running Sum property to generate a line number.

If you switch to Print Preview, you can see the result of using Running Sum, as shown in Figure 16-25. The charge accumulates over each group and then resets for the next group. The line numbers start at 1 and also reset for each group. You can find this report saved as rptXmplFacilityDateOccupancyStep4 in the sample database.

Facility Occupancy By Date – 2nd Quarter 2007

| # | Facility | Date | Room | Employee | Charge | Cum. Charge |
|---|---|---|---|---|---|---|
| 1. | Main Campus Housing A | 01-Apr-2007 | 201 | Petculescu, Cristian | $37.22 | $37.22 |
| 2. | | | 401 | Meyyappan, Ramesh | $36.88 | $74.10 |
| 3. | | | 410 | Sazanovich, Vadim | $36.43 | $110.53 |
| 4. | | | 507 | Fort, Garth | $50.33 | $160.86 |
| 5. | | | 507 | Cheng, Yao-Qiang | $50.00 | $210.86 |
| 6. | | | 808 | Maxwell, Taylor | $45.00 | $255.86 |
| | | | | Total for 01-Apr-07: | $255.86 | |
| 1. | Main Campus Housing A | 02-Apr-2007 | 401 | Meyyappan, Ramesh | $36.88 | $36.88 |
| 2. | | | 410 | Sazanovich, Vadim | $36.43 | $73.31 |
| 3. | | | 507 | Fort, Garth | $50.33 | $123.64 |
| 4. | | | 507 | Cheng, Yao-Qiang | $50.00 | $173.64 |
| 5. | | | 808 | Maxwell, Taylor | $45.00 | $218.64 |
| | | | | Total for 02-Apr-07: | $218.64 | |
| 1. | Main Campus Housing A | 03-Apr-2007 | 410 | Sazanovich, Vadim | $36.43 | $36.43 |
| 2. | | | 507 | Fort, Garth | $50.33 | $86.76 |
| 3. | | | 507 | Cheng, Yao-Qiang | $50.00 | $136.76 |

**Figure 16-25** You can see the result of using Running Sum to produce a cumulative total for each group and a line number for each detail line.

## Taking Advantage of Conditional Formatting

In Chapter 13, "Advanced Form Design," you learned how to define conditional formatting for a text box control. Access makes an identical facility available to you for reports. Let's say, for example, that you want to highlight any daily total that is more than $400 or any monthly total that is greater than $10,000. To do this, open the report from the previous example in Design view, select the Sum text box in the first DateValue Footer section that displays the sum of the charge, and click the Conditional button in the Font group on the Design tab. Access displays the Conditional Formatting dialog box, as shown in Figure 16-26.

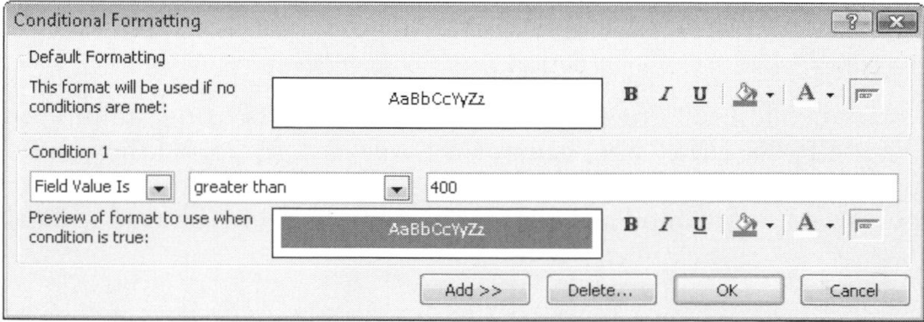


**Figure 16-26** Set conditional formatting for the Sum text box in the first DateValue Footer section.

Chapter 16

Just as you can in a text box control on a form, you can define a test against the current value in the control or enter an expression. In this case, verify that Field Value Is appears in the first list, click Greater Than in the second list, and enter the value **400** in the box. Under Condition 1, set Back Color to some dark color, and set Fore Color to white. Click OK to save the conditional format. You can specify a similar condition for the Sum text box in the second DateValue footer (by month) to test for a monthly total greater than 10,000.

### Note

In the Detail section, you can reference any other field in the current row to create an expression. But, when you create a conditional formatting expression in a grouping section, any field reference you use in an expression uses the value of the current row. In a group footer, for example, the current row is the last row displayed in the previous Detail section.

In order for the new formats to appear in Print Preview, you need to make one quick change to the two Sum controls. Select the Sum control in the first DateValue Footer section, hold down the Shift key, and then select the Sum control in the second DateValue Footer section. Open the Property Sheet window, and change the Back Style property from Transparent to Normal. If you leave these controls set to Transparent, you won't see any text in these controls when the conditions are met.

Before viewing the report one more time, let's change the margins on the report to center the printed area left to right on the page. Assuming a standard U.S. paper width of 8.5 inches and with the report print area designed at 6.5 inches, we need a 1-inch margin on both sides. Click the Page Setup button in the Page Layout group on the Page Setup tab. Access opens the Page Setup dialog box shown in Figure 16-27. On the Print Options tab, change the Top, Bottom, Left, and Right margins from .25 inch to 1 inch. Click OK to save your changes and close the Page Setup dialog box. When you switch to Print Preview, you can see the result, as shown in Figure 16-28. You can find this sample saved as rptXmplFacilityDateOccupancyStep5. (Page 20 in the sample shows both conditional formats in action.)

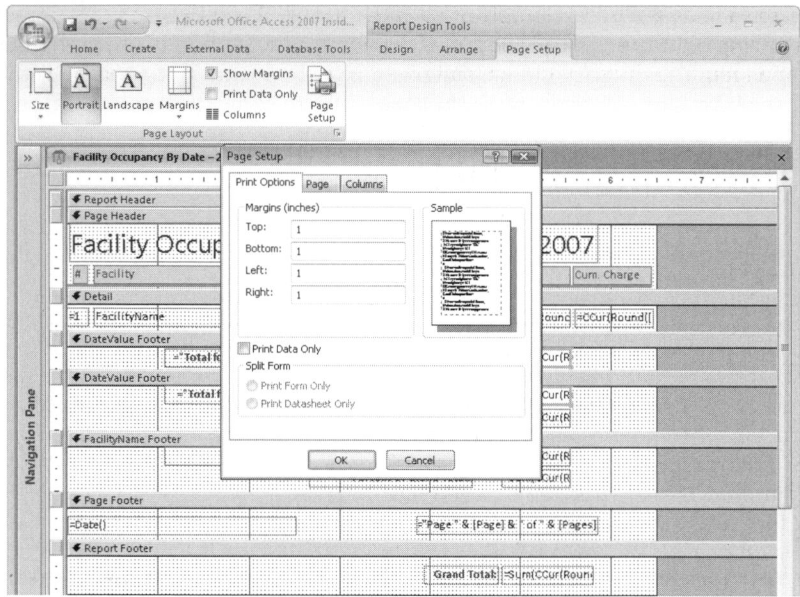


Figure 16-27 Change all the page margins to 1 inch.

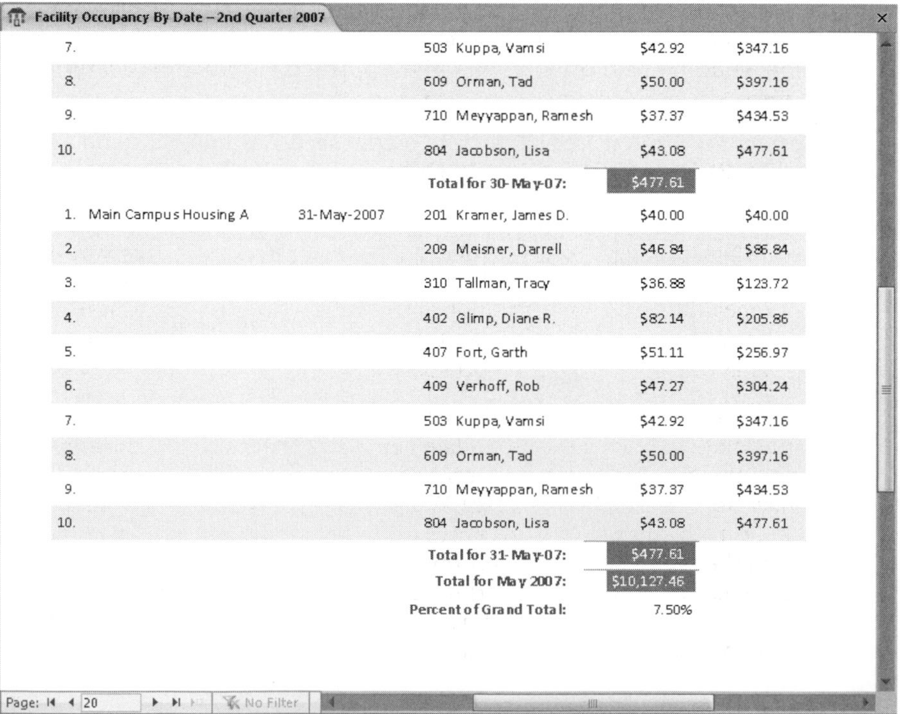


| | | | | | |
|---|---|---|---|---|---|
| 7. | | | 503 Kuppa, Vamsi | $42.92 | $347.16 |
| 8. | | | 609 Orman, Tad | $50.00 | $397.16 |
| 9. | | | 710 Meyyappan, Ramesh | $37.37 | $434.53 |
| 10. | | | 804 Jacobson, Lisa | $43.08 | $477.61 |
| | | | **Total for 30-May-07:** | $477.61 | |
| 1. | Main Campus Housing A | 31-May-2007 | 201 Kramer, James D. | $40.00 | $40.00 |
| 2. | | | 209 Meisner, Darrell | $46.84 | $86.84 |
| 3. | | | 310 Tallman, Tracy | $36.88 | $123.72 |
| 4. | | | 402 Glimp, Diane R. | $82.14 | $205.86 |
| 5. | | | 407 Fort, Garth | $51.11 | $256.97 |
| 6. | | | 409 Verhoff, Rob | $47.27 | $304.24 |
| 7. | | | 503 Kuppa, Vamsi | $42.92 | $347.16 |
| 8. | | | 609 Orman, Tad | $50.00 | $397.16 |
| 9. | | | 710 Meyyappan, Ramesh | $37.37 | $434.53 |
| 10. | | | 804 Jacobson, Lisa | $43.08 | $477.61 |
| | | | **Total for 31-May-07:** | $477.61 | |
| | | | **Total for May 2007:** | $10,127.46 | |
| | | | **Percent of Grand Total:** | 7.50% | |



Figure 16-28 Here is the result of setting conditional formatting for the two Sum text boxes.

**To see a more complex example of conditional formatting in action, open rptEmployeeRes in the sample database. That report uses conditional formatting to check for overlapping reservation requests, highlight them, and reveal a warning label in the section header.**

# Creating and Embedding a Subreport

In many of your reports, you will probably design the Detail section to display a single line of information from the underlying record source. As you learned earlier in this chapter, it's fairly easy to link several tables to get lots of detail across several *one-to-many* relationships in your database. You also saw how to use the Hide Duplicates property to display a hierarchy across several rows of detail.

However, as with forms and subforms, which you learned about in Chapter 13, you can embed subreports (or subforms) in the Detail section of your report to display multiple detail lines from a table or query that has a *many* relationship to the *one* current line printed in the Detail section. You must use this technique when you want to display information from more than one *many* relationship on a single page. In the Conrad Systems Contacts database, for example, if you want to provide details about contact events and products owned by a contact, you must use subreports. You could create a very complex query that joins all the information, but you'd get one row for each unique combination of contact event and product. If a contact has 100 events and owns six products, each of the six product rows is matched with each of the 100 contact event rows. You'll get 600 rows for that contact in a query that joins the tblContacts, tblContactEvents, and tblContactProducts tables—each product record appears 100 times, and each contact event record appears six times.

## Understanding Subreport Challenges

Subreports present a unique challenge. Unlike a subform where you can scroll through all available related rows in one window, a subreport has no scroll bar. The subreport expands to list all the related rows. If the rows won't fit on one page, it can be difficult to repeat the header information at the top of the subsequent pages. Although you can define a report header in a report that you use as a subreport, that header prints only once at the top of the subreport space on the page where the subreport starts.

To understand how this works, let's examine two approaches to listing department information in a report with related employee information in a subreport. In the HousingDataCopy2.accdb sample database, open rptDepartmentsWSubBad in Design view, as shown in Figure 16-29. When you drop a report onto the design of another report to create a subreport, Access sizes the subreport control to the height of one line from the report inside the control. The figure shows the subreport control expanded so that you can see the subreport inside it. We selected the control and dragged down the bottom edge, but you might find it easier to change the Height property in the property sheet because the bottom sizing box is difficult to grab with your mouse pointer.

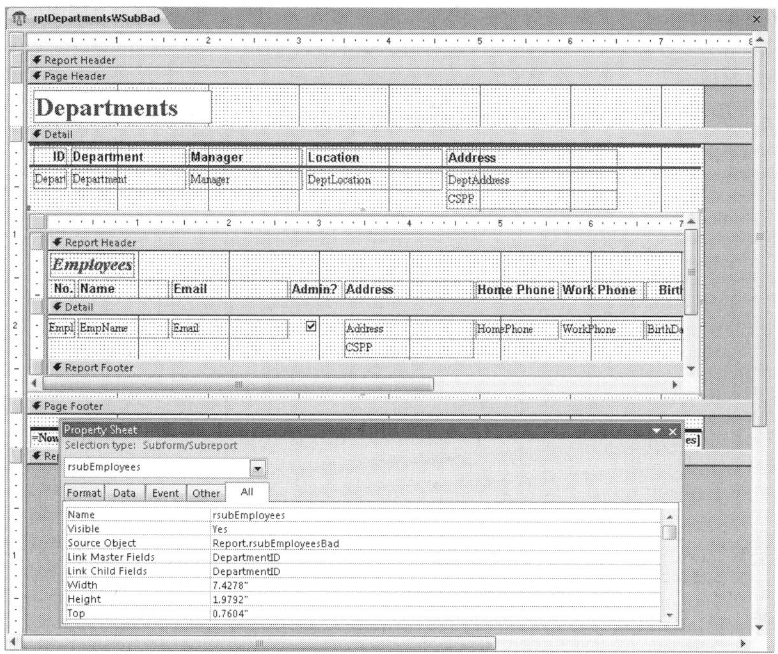


**Figure 16-29** This report displays departments with related employees in a subreport.

The outer report, Departments, uses a query based on the tblDepartments and tblEmployees tables to provide information about each department and the department's manager. The report inside the subreport control, Employees, has another query on the tblEmployees table. The report looks simple enough—a heading for each department row and a heading inside the subreport to provide column headings for the employee information. You can also see that a subreport works just like a subform—you define the Link Master Fields and Link Child Fields properties of the subreport control to link the information from the two reports.

Now switch to Print Preview, and go to the fourth and fifth pages of the report, as shown in Figures 16-30 and 16-31, to see what really happens when a department has more employees than will fit on one page.

Departments

# Departments

| ID | Department | Manager | Location | Address |
|---|---|---|---|---|
| 4 | Product Development | Kramer, James D. | Headquarters, MD 501 | 1234 Main Street<br>Chicago, IL 60601 |

***Employees***

| No. | Name | Email | Admin? | Address | Home Phone | Work Phone | Birth Date |
|---|---|---|---|---|---|---|---|
| 37 | Caron, Nicole | NCaron@ProseWare.co | ☐ | 5678 3rd Boulevard<br>Mingo Junction, OH 4393 | (740) 555-0129 | (740) 555-0172 | 11/11/1978 |
| 28 | Dumitrascu, Adria | ADumitrascu@ProseWa | ☐ | 2345 Willow Street<br>Winnsboro, LA 71295 | (318) 555-0138 | (318) 555-0173 | 1/14/1963 |
| 11 | Fort, Garth | GFort@ProseWare.com | ☐ | 2345 Main Drive<br>Walker, LA 70785 | (225) 555-0145 | (225) 555-0169 | 9/3/1942 |
| 9 | [illegible] | [illegible] | ☐ | 7090 Willow Boulevard<br>Youngstown, OH 44505 | (330) 555-0131 | (330) 555-0152 | [illegible] |
| 22 | Hines, Mike | MHines@ProseWare.co | ☐ | 6789 1st Avenue<br>Russells Point, OH 43348 | (937) 555-0143 | (937) 555-0175 | 12/25/1976 |
| 3 | Kramer, James D. | JKramer@ProseWare.c | ☐ | 7890 Main Street<br>Westlake, TX 76262 | (254) 555-0145 | (254) 555-0174 | 4/7/1949 |
| 4 | Kuppa, Vamsi | VKuppa@ProseWare.co | ☐ | 4567 Central Parkway<br>Wolcott, IN 47995 | (219) 555-0107 | (219) 555-0160 | 1/11/1948 |
| 35 | Martin, Benjamin | BMartin@ProseWare.co | ☐ | 5678 Church Avenue | (541) 555-0139 | (541) 555-0189 | 9/14/1942 |

Page: 4 No Filter

**Figure 16-30** The top of the fourth page of the departments and employees report displays the header information.

Departments

# Departments

| No. | Name | Email | Admin? | Address | Home Phone | Work Phone | Birth Date |
|---|---|---|---|---|---|---|---|
| 26 | Steiner, Alan | ASteiner@ProseWare.c | ☐ | 3456 2nd Boulevard<br>Callao, VA 22435 | (804) 555-0140 | (804) 555-0153 | 10/26/1947 |

**Figure 16-31** The top of the fifth page of the departments and employees report has missing headers.

As you can see, the fifth page has nothing more than the page header to help identify the information being printed. The detail department information printed once on the fourth page, as did the report header from the subreport. When the subreport overflowed onto a second page, the column heading information from the report header defined for the subreport didn't print again.

To see how to solve this problem, open rptDepartmentsWSub in Design view, as shown in Figure 16-32. Again, the figure shows the subreport control expanded so that you can see the subreport inside it.

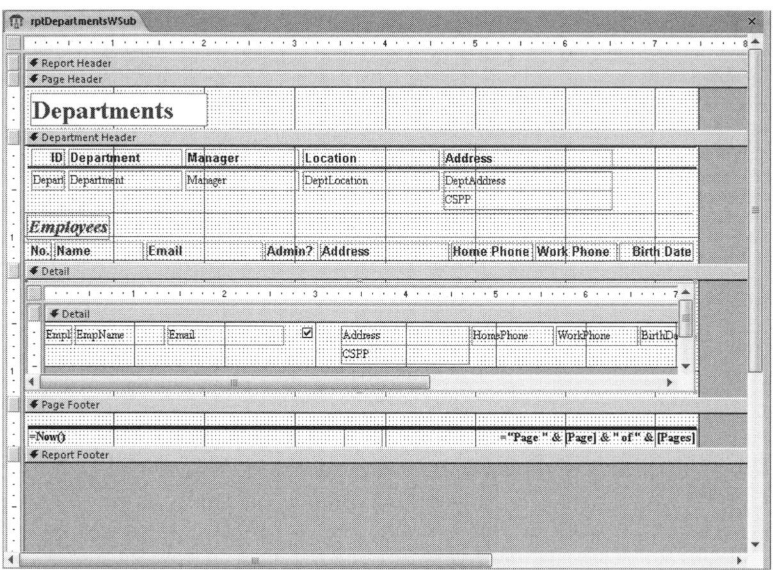


**Figure 16-32** This design of a report and subreport handles the page overflow problem.

Can you figure out the difference? The secret is the outer report has a group defined on department, even though there is only one detail row per department. All the department information and the headers for the columns in the subreport appear in this group header. Remember that you set the Repeat Section property of a group header to Yes to force it to appear again at the top of a page if the information in the Detail section overflows the page. The Detail section contains only the subreport, and the subreport has no headers. If you switch to Print Preview and go to the fifth page in this report, as shown in Figure 16-33, you can see that the appropriate headers appear again when the Product Development department overflows onto another page.

**Departments**

| ID | Department | Manager | Location | Address |
|---|---|---|---|---|
| 4 | Product Development | Kramer, James D. | Headquarters, MD 501 | 1234 Main Street<br>Chicago, IL 60601 |

***Employees***

| No. | Name | Email | Admin? | Address | Home Phone | Work Phone | Birth Date |
|---|---|---|---|---|---|---|---|
| 21 | Seamans, Mike | MSeamans@ProseWare | ☐ | 5678 4th Boulevard<br>Scotland, SD 57059 | (605) 555-0129 | (605) 555-0170 | 6/18/1940 |
| 26 | Steiner, Alan | ASteiner@ProseWare.c | ☐ | 3456 2nd Boulevard<br>Callao, VA 22435 | (804) 555-0140 | (804) 555-0153 | 10/26/1947 |

**Figure 16-33** The top of the fifth page of the departments and employees report in this sample has headers correctly repeated.

## Building a Report with a Subreport

The manager of Housing Administration has just asked you to produce a report that summarizes for each facility the revenue by month. You know the manager is someone who likes to see a visual representation as well as the data, so you need to design a report that will ultimately display a revenue chart as well. You'll learn how to add the PivotChart in the last section of this chapter.

### Building the Subreport Query

If all you needed to do was display total revenue by facility and by month, you could build one totals query that joins the tblFacilities table with the tblReservations table and group by facility. However, the need to add the chart means you'll need a subreport to calculate the monthly totals so that you can display the chart that graphically shows all the month values immediately below the numerical data. If you try to add a chart to the Detail area of a report that displays totals by month, the chart will show one graph point for the current month, not all months.

In the previous examples, you have been using a complex query to calculate revenue by day—an accounts receivable perspective. But guests in a hotel usually don't pay for their stay until the day they check out. So, to calculate actual revenue received for a month, you should use the check-out date and the total amount owed.

Start a new query on the tblReservations table. In the query design grid, include the FacilityID (you'll need this field to provide the link between the subreport and the main report), CheckOutDate, and TotalCharge fields. You could turn this into a totals query to sum the total charge by month, but it's just as easy to do that in the report. Your query should look like Figure 16-34. You can find this query saved in the sample database as qryXmplFacilityRevenue.

### Designing the Subreport

The report you need for the subreport is very simple. Click the Report Design button in the Reports group on the Create tab to start designing your report. If you want your report to look like the Facility Occupancy report earlier in this chapter, click the AutoFormat button in the AutoFormat group on the Arrange tab, and select the Access 2007 style from the gallery of options. Remember from the discussion in the previous section that you'll see what's in the report header and report footer of a report that you use as a subreport, but Access never displays the page header or page footer. Click the Page Header/Footer button in the Show/Hide group on the Arrange tab. Now click the Report Header/Footer button in the same group. You now need to bind this report to the qryXmplFacilityRevenue query (or the query you created earlier). Open the property sheet and set Record Source to qryXmplFacilityRevenue.

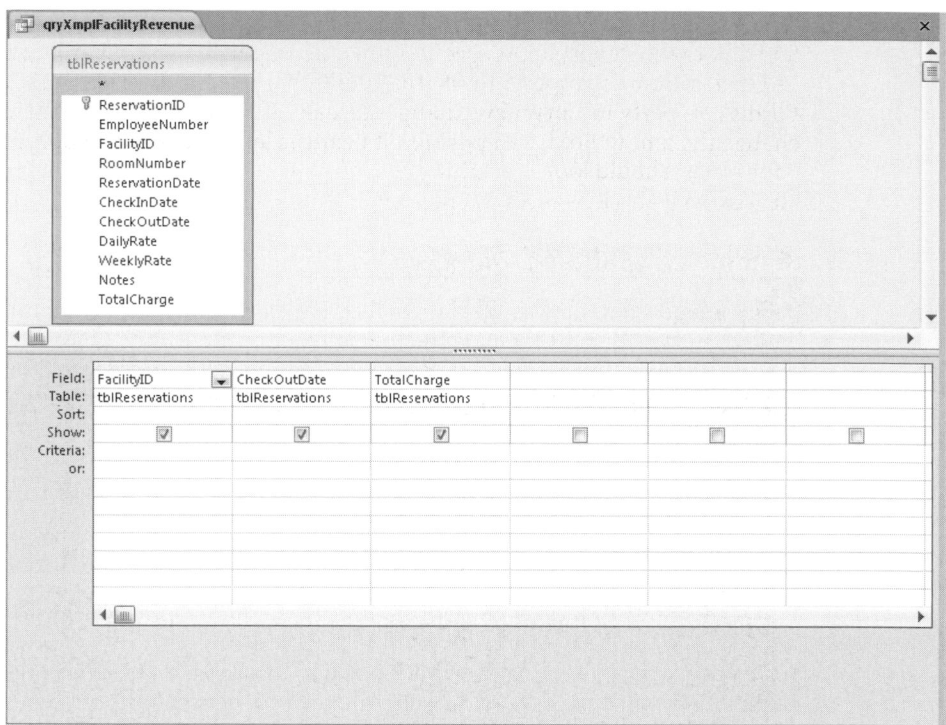


**Figure 16-34** This query for the subreport calculates revenue by facility and month.

Open the Group, Sort, And Total pane by clicking the Group & Sort button in the Grouping & Totals group on the Design tab. Click the Add A Group button to start a new grouping specification. Select the CheckOutDate field in the Select box, click the More button to expand the option list, set the group interval to By Month, and then close the pane. Because you want the report to calculate and display totals by month only, close up the Detail section to zero height. Reduce the report design area to about 5.5 inches. Close up the Report Header section to zero height because you'll add the column labels to the outer report.

Draw a line across the top of the CheckOutDate Header section starting near the left edge and extending to about 5.1 inches wide. In the Property Sheet window, set the Border Style property to Solid and the Border Width property to 1 PT. Underneath this line about 1.5 inches from the left, drag and drop the CheckOutDate field from the Field List window, and delete the attached label. In the Property Sheet window, set the Format property to **mmmm yyyy** to display the month name and four-digit year, and change the Width property to 1.5 inches. Drag and drop the TotalCharge field from the field list into the CheckOutDate Header section about 3.75 inches from the left, and delete the attached label. In the Property Sheet window, expand the width to 1.2 inches, change the Name property of the control to **TotalChargeSum**, and change the Control Source to **=Sum([TotalCharge])**. (Remember, you must change the name of the control to avoid a circular reference in the expression!) Line up the two text boxes in the CheckOutDate Header section horizontally.

Finally, click the Text Box button in the Controls group on the Design tab, and add a text box to the Report Footer section lined up under the TotalChargeSum text box. Set its Control Source property to **=Sum([TotalCharge])**, change the font to Bold, and set the Format property to Currency. Change the caption of the attached label to **Grand Total**, change the font to Bold, and position it near the left edge of the Report Footer section. Your report should look something like Figure 16-35. You can find this report saved as rsubXmplFacilityRevenueByMonth in the sample database.

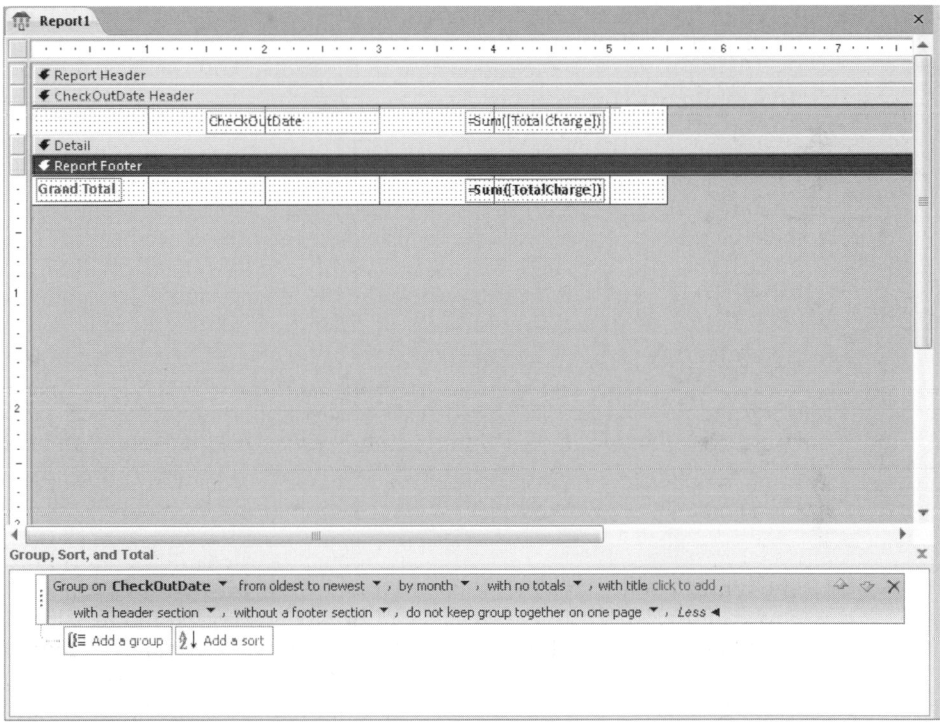


**Figure 16-35** This is your subreport to summarize revenue by month.

## Embedding a Subreport

You can find the query you need for the outer report saved as qryRptFacilities in the sample database. This query includes the FacilityID, FacilityName, and FacilityAddress fields. It also includes an expression (named FacilityCSPP) that concatenates the FacilityCity, FacilityStateOrProvince, and FaciltyPostalCode fields so that they display nicely on one line in the report.

Click the Report Design button in the Reports group on the Create tab to start your report design. Click the AutoFormat button in the AutoFormat group on the Arrange tab, and select the Access 2007 style from the gallery of options. Expand the report to 6.5 inches wide. Open the Property Sheet window, and enter **qryRptFacilities** in the Record Source property to bind the report to the saved query. Expand the Page Header section to 0.5 inch, add a label control to the Page Header section, and type **Facility Revenue** in the label. Change Font Size to 20, size the label to fit, bold the text, and position it in the upper-left corner of the Page Header section.

Open the Group, Sort, And Total pane by clicking the Group & Sort button in the Grouping & Totals group on the Design tab. Click the Add A Group button to start a new grouping specification. Select the FacilityName field in the Select box, click the More button to expand the option list, set the last column to Keep Header And First Record Together On One Page, and then close the pane. Expand the FacilityName Header section to about 1.25 inches high to give yourself some room to work. Select the FacilityName Header section, and in the Property Sheet window, set the Force New Page property to Before Section.

Drag and drop all four fields from the Field List window onto the FacilityName Header section of the report one at a time, as shown in Figure 16-36. Delete the attached label for the FacilityCSPP control, expand the width of the FacilityName text box to 1.6 inches, and expand the width of the FacilityAddress and FacilityCSPP text boxes to 3.2 inches. Bold the text of the three labels in the FacilityName Header section. Click the Label button in the Controls group on the Design tab, and place a label control under the FacilityCSPP text box control about 2.5 inches in from the left. Type **Month** in the label, and press Enter. (You can ignore the smart tag warning about an unattached label.) Add a second label control about 4.5 inches in from the left, type **Revenue** in the label, and press Enter. Line up the two labels horizontally, and bold their text. Click the Line Control button in the Controls group on the Design tab, and add a line at the top of the FacilityHeader section. In the Property Sheet window for this line, set the Border Style property to Solid, set the Border Width property to 1 PT, and set the Width property to 4.5 inches.

Expand the Navigation Pane if it is collapsed, click at the top of the Navigation Pane, click Object Type under Navigate To Category, and then click Reports under Filter By Group to display a list of reports in the sample database. Drag and drop the report you created in the previous section (or the rsubXmplFacilityRevenueByMonth report) from the Navigation Pane onto the Detail section of the report into the upper-right corner about 0.25 inch in from the left edge. In the Property Sheet window, set the Link Child Fields and Link Master Fields properties to **FacilityID**. Delete the label that Access attached to the subreport control, and then reduce the height of the Detail section to about 0.36 inch.

As a finishing touch, you can add a date text box control and a page number text box control to the Page Footer section as you learned to do earlier in this chapter. Also, you should change all the margins for the report to 1 inch using the Page Setup dialog box and enter a caption of **Facility Revenue** for the report in the Property Sheet window. Your report should look something like Figure 16-36. You can find this report saved as rptXmplFacilityRevenue in the sample database.

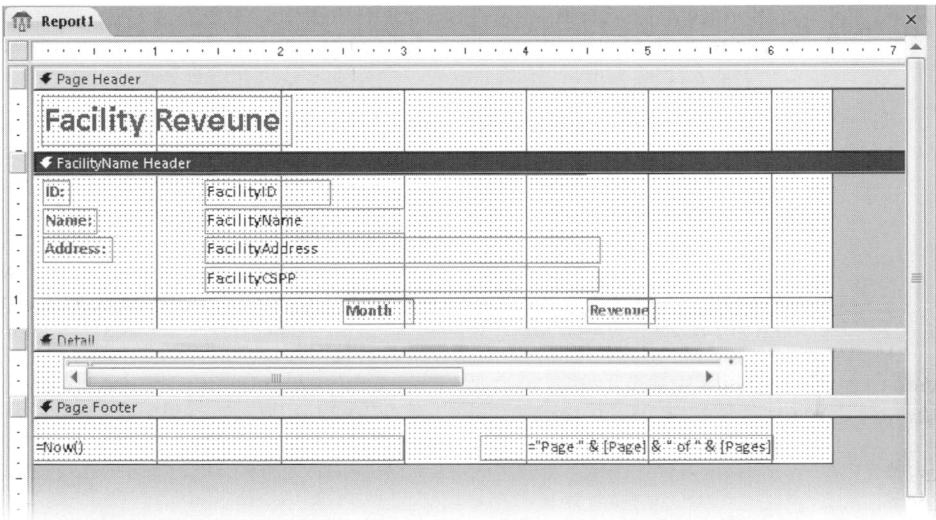


Figure 16-36 The design of your report now includes a subreport.

Switch to Print Preview to see the result as shown in Figure 16-37. If the Month and Revenue labels aren't correctly positioned over the columns in the subreport, switch to Layout view to easily make the adjustment.

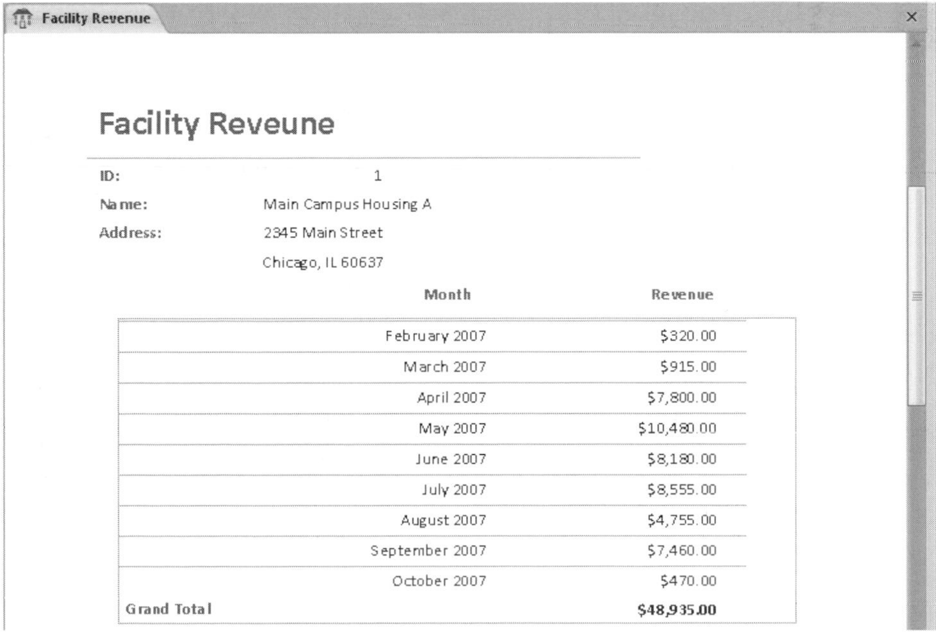


Figure 16-37 Your report now displays facility information with monthly revenue in a subreport.

# Adding a PivotChart to a Report

You can now design a form in PivotChart view to graphically display monthly revenue data. Note that a report doesn't have a PivotChart or Pivot Table view, but it is perfectly legal to embed a form into a report as a subreport. (But you cannot embed a report in a form as a subform.)

## Designing the PivotChart Form

When you built the subreport for the Facility Revenue report, you used a simple query on the tblReservations table. For the chart, you need to include the name of the facility—the ID won't make much sense in the legend for the chart. In the sample database, you can find a query named qryXmplChtFacilityRevenue that includes both the tblFacilities and tblReservations tables. The fields in the query are FacilityID and FacilityName from the tblFacilities table and CheckOutDate and TotalCharge from the tblReservations table.

To build the chart you need, select the query in the Navigation Pane, and then click the PivotChart button in the Forms group on the Create tab. This command opens a new form object in PivotChart view.

Open the chart field list, and drag and drop the FacilityName field onto the Drop Series Fields Here area of the chart. Click the plus sign next to the CheckOutDate By Month field to expand its list and drag and drop Months onto the Drop Category Fields Here area. Drag and drop the Total Charge field onto the Drop Data Fields Here area—the chart calculates a sum of this field for you. Click the Property Sheet button in the Tools group on the Design tab, and select Chart Workspace on the General tab in the Property Sheet window. Click both the Add Title and Add Legend buttons to add these elements to your chart.

Click the Chart Workspace Title element to select it. In the Property Sheet window, select the Format tab, and enter **Facility Revenue** in the Caption box. In the PivotChart, click the vertical Axis Title and in the Property Sheet window, enter **Revenue** in the Caption box. In the PivotChart, click the horizontal Axis Title, and change its Caption to **Months**. Go back to the General tab, and select the Chart Workspace. On the Show/Hide tab of the Property Sheet window, clear all the options under Show By Default and Let Users View so that users cannot modify the chart. Your chart should now look like Figure 16-38. Switch back to Design view, and set the Default View property to PivotChart. Be sure to save the form, and give it a name such as chtFacilitiesRevenue. You can find this form saved as chtXmplFacilityRevenue in the sample database.

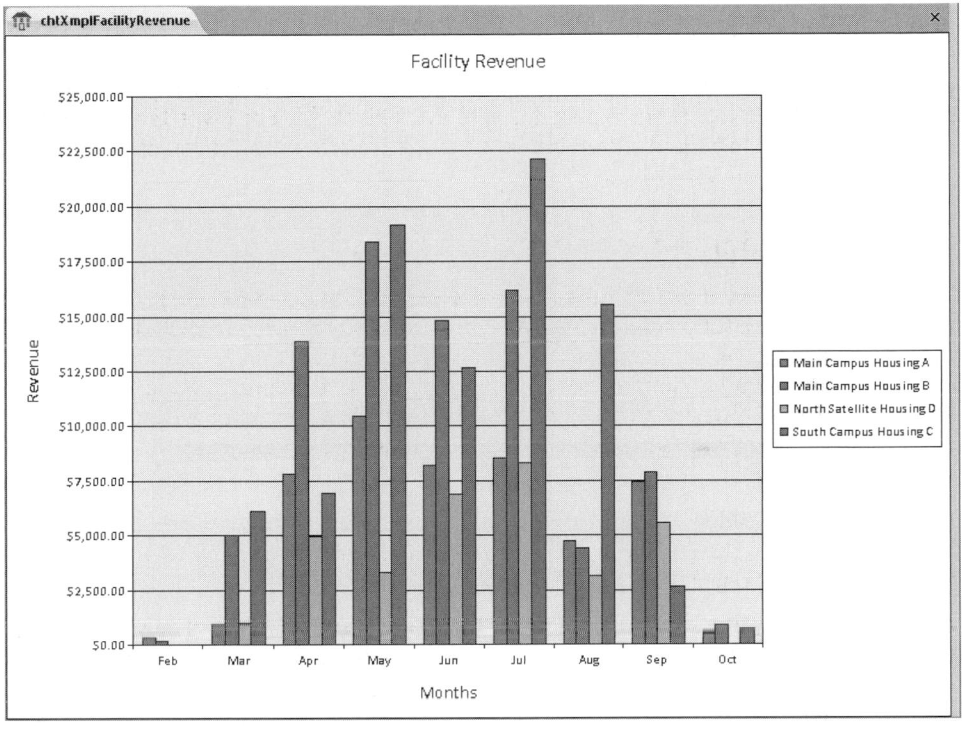


**Figure 16-38** This PivotChart form displays facility revenue by month.



## Embedding a PivotChart in a Report

The rest is easy. Go to the Navigation Pane, and select the report you created in the previous section to display facilities with revenue by month in a subreport. Open that report in Design view. (You can also open the sample rptXmplFacilityRevenue report.) Select the subreport control, and click the Size To Fit button in the Size group on the Arrange tab to make sure the subreport is exactly one line high to give yourself some room to work. Don't worry about displaying all the lines in the subreport–when you dragged and dropped it onto the report, Access set its Can Grow property to Yes. When you view the report, Access will expand the subreport control to display all the lines.

Expand the Detail section to about 5.5 inches high. Make sure the Use Control Wizards button in the Controls group is turned off, then click the Subform/Subreport button in the Controls group on the Design tab, and finally draw the control in the Detail section under the previous subreport approximately 5.5 inches wide and 4 inches high. The size of the subreport control affects the resolution of the chart you're going to put inside it, so you want it big enough to be easily readable. Delete the label from the control. Move the subreport control up under the previous subreport control.

With the new subreport control selected, open the Property Sheet window, and set the Source Object property to the PivotChart form you created earlier. (Or, you can use the example chtXmplFacilityRevenue form in the sample database.) Set both the Link Child Fields and Link Master Fields properties to FacilityID. Your report design should now look like Figure 16-39. Notice that the subreport window shows you the Form view design of the form, not the chart.

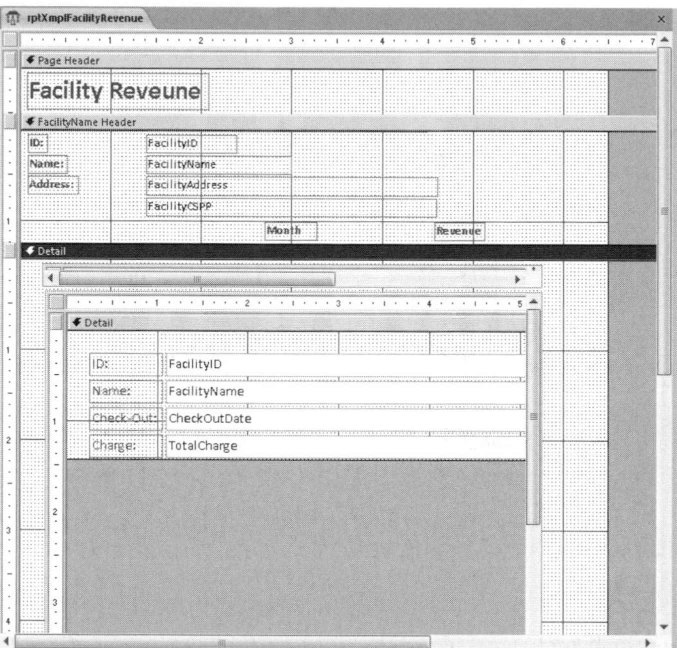


**Figure 16-39** Your report now includes an embedded PivotChart form as a subreport.

Switch to Print Preview to see the result, as shown in Figure 16-40. Now that layout should make the facilities manager happy! You can find the report saved as rptXmplFacilityRevenueChart in the sample database.

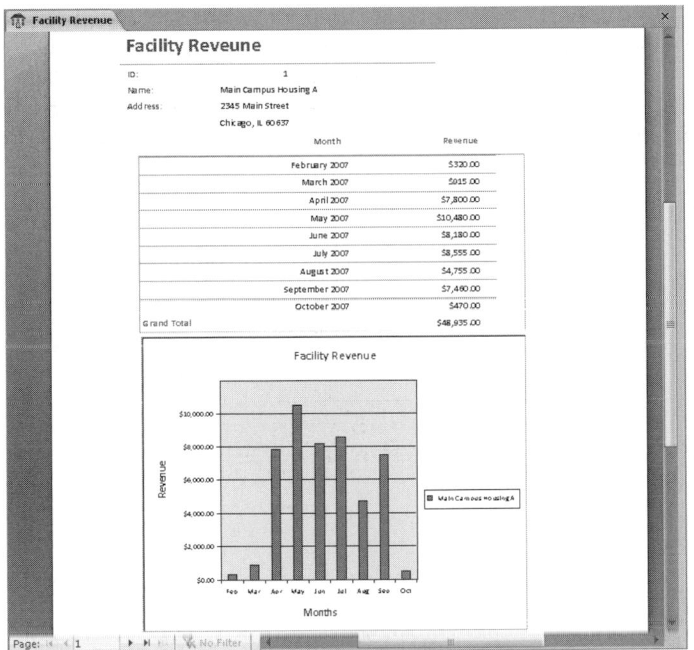


**Figure 16-40** Here is your completed report with an embedded subreport and PivotChart in Print Preview.

At this point, you should thoroughly understand the mechanics of constructing reports and working with complex formulas. The next part of the book explores how to apply all you've learned to this point to building an Access project that uses Microsoft SQL Server to store your tables and queries (views, stored procedures, and functions).

# PART 4
# Automating an Access Application

CHAPTER 17

# Understanding Event Processing



Although you can make Microsoft Office Access 2007 do a lot for you by setting properties when you design forms and reports, you really can't make your application "come alive" until you build macros or Visual Basic procedures that respond to *events*. An event can be as simple as the user clicking a button—and your code responds by opening a related form or report. An event can also trigger complex actions, such as creating a booking record when the user selects an available room.

In this chapter, you'll first learn what event processing is all about—both in Microsoft Windows and specifically within Office Access 2007. The second part of the chapter contains a comprehensive reference for all the events available within Access, a discussion of event sequence, and a list of the specific macro actions you can use to respond to events.

## Access as a Windows Event-Driven Application

If you're reading this book, you're using the 2007 Microsoft Office system and Windows. You probably use Windows every day and don't give a second thought to how it actually works. Understanding Windows is essential to programming events in Access 2007.

### Understanding Events in Windows

Windows is an event-driven and message-based operating system. When you start an application on your system, that application sends messages to Windows to tell Windows that it wants to respond to certain events. When an event occurs (such as resting your mouse pointer on the application window or clicking somewhere), Windows sends a message to the application to notify it that the event happened. The message usually includes critical information, such as the location of the mouse pointer when the event occurred. The application then responds to the event—usually by sending a message to Windows to act upon the event. Figure 17-1 shows you a conceptual view of this process.

For example, when you have Windows Explorer open and click a file name, Windows sends a message to Windows Explorer to tell it where you clicked. Windows Explorer sends a message back to Windows to tell it to highlight what you selected. Another example is the clock utility that runs on your taskbar. Windows starts this utility when

Windows initializes unless you've set a taskbar option to not display the clock. When the utility starts, it asks Windows to notify it when the system clock time changes. When the clock utility receives a message from Windows that the system clock time has changed to a different minute, it sends a message back to Windows to tell it to change the characters displayed on the taskbar.

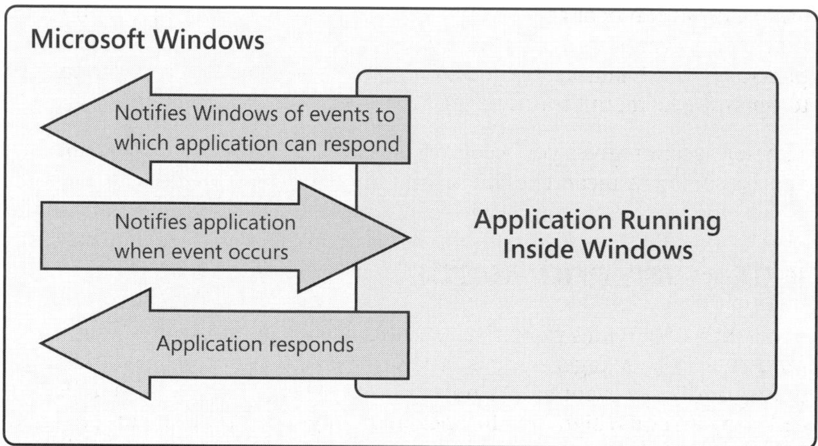


**Figure 17-1** Applications running in Windows send messages and respond to events.

The most important aspect of this entire process is that the user is in control of the applications that are running. As the user of your personal computer, you decide what you want the applications to do next. And because Windows can handle multiple messages at a time, you can start a process in an application (perhaps a search in Windows Explorer for a file) and then switch to or start another application to do something else (such as playing a game of solitaire while you wait for the search to finish).

## Leveraging Access Events to Build an Application

If you think of forms and reports in your Access application as little applications running under Access, you have the right idea. When you set an event property (one of the properties on the Event tab in the property sheet in a report, a form, or a control on a form or report that points to a macro or a Visual Basic procedure, you're notifying Access that you want to respond to that event. The code you write in your macro or Visual Basic procedure provides the response to the occurrence of the event.

Access passes on to forms, reports, and controls on forms and reports some typical Windows events such as mouse clicks (the Click and DblClick events) or characters entered from the keyboard (the Change, KeyDown, and KeyPress events). Access also defines a wide range of events that are specific to the objects it supports. For example, the BeforeUpdate event signals that the value in a control is about to change or a record being edited in the form is about to be saved. You can perform data validation in your macro or Visual Basic code that responds to BeforeUpdate and have your macro or code send a message back to Access to cancel the save if some business rule is about to be violated.

Although events in Access occur in a specific sequence, you should keep in mind that other events can occur while any code you've written to respond to an event is running. Also, some events signal that an action is about to happen but might not have completed yet. For example, the form Open event signals that a command has been issued to open the form, but the form isn't displayed on the screen yet.

The next section gives you a comprehensive overview of all events in Access 2007 and describes how you can use them.

## Summary of Form and Report Events

Access 2007 provides more than 60 different events on forms, form controls, and reports that can trigger macros or Visual Basic procedures. You indicate that you want to respond to an event by providing the name of a macro, a Visual Basic function (preceded by an equal sign), or the special settings [Event Procedure] or [Embedded Macro] as the setting of the event property in the Property Sheet window. When you specify [Event Procedure], Access looks for a Visual Basic procedure in the module stored with the form or report that has the name of the event. When the event property is set to [Embedded Macro], Access executes the related macro embedded in the form or report definition. For details about Visual Basic procedures, see Chapter 19, "Understanding Visual Basic Fundamentals." For details about creating macros, see Chapter 18, "Automating Your Application with Macros."

The tables in this section summarize those events and organize them in the following functional categories:

- Opening and closing forms and reports
- Changing data
- Detecting focus changes
- Detecting filters applied to forms and reports
- Trapping keyboard and mouse events
- Detecting changes in PivotTables and PivotCharts
- Printing
- Trapping errors
- Detecting timer expiration

> **Note**
>
> The event property names listed on the following pages are the names you will see in the property sheet in form or report Design view. To reference an event property from a macro or a Visual Basic procedure, do not include the blanks in the name. For example, the On Load event property in a form property sheet is the OnLoad property of the form. The exceptions to this rule are the 18 events associated with PivotTables and PivotCharts. For those event properties, the name of the event property is the same as the name of the event, which might not match the property name you see in the property sheet.

Table 17-1 **Opening and Closing Forms and Reports**[1]

| Event Property (Event Name) | Description |
|---|---|
| On Close (Close) | Runs the specified macro, Visual Basic function, or Visual Basic event procedure when the user or a close command in your code requests to close the form or the report but before Access clears the screen. Your code that responds to the event cannot cancel the Close event. For forms, the Close event occurs after the Unload event. |
| On Load (Load) | Runs the specified macro, Visual Basic function, or Visual Basic event procedure when Access loads a form or report and then displays the records in the recordset. Your code that responds to the event can set values in controls or set form, report, or control properties. The Load event occurs after the Open event and before the Resize event. Your code cannot cancel a Load event. |
| On Open (Open) | Runs the specified macro, Visual Basic function, or Visual Basic event procedure when the user or an open command in your code requests to open the form or the report but before Access displays the first record. To gain access to a control on the form or report, your code must specify a GoToControl action or SetFocus method to set the focus on the control. The Open event occurs before Access loads the form or report recordset, so your code that responds to the event can prompt the user for parameters and apply filters. Your code can also change the form or report record source in this event. |
| On Resize (Resize) | Runs the specified macro, Visual Basic function, or Visual Basic event procedure when a form or report changes size. This event also occurs when a form or report opens, after the Load event but before the Activate event. Your code can use this event to force immediate repainting of the resized form or report or to recalculate variables that are dependent on the size of the form. This property has no effect when you are using the single-document interface unless you have also set the Pop Up or Modal property to Yes. When you open a report in Print Preview, this event occurs only when Access opens the report; the event does not occur again if the user resizes the window in Print Preview. |

| Event Property (Event Name) | Description |
|---|---|
| On Unload (Unload) | Runs the specified macro, Visual Basic function, or Visual Basic event procedure when the user or your code requests that the form or report be closed but before Access removes the form or report from the screen. Your code can cancel an Unload event if it determines that a form should not be closed. |

[1] These events occur for all views of forms and reports except Design view.

**Table 17-2 Changing Data[2]**

| Event Property (Event Name) | Description |
|---|---|
| After Del Confirm (AfterDelConfirm) | Runs the specified macro, Visual Basic function, or Visual Basic event procedure after the user has requested that one or more rows on the form be deleted and after the user has confirmed the deletion. The AfterDelConfirm event also occurs if your code that responds to the BeforeDelConfirm event cancels the deletion. In a Visual Basic procedure, you can test a status parameter to determine whether the deletion was completed, was canceled by your code in the BeforeDelConfirm event, or was canceled by the user. If the deletion was successful, you can use the Requery action within your code that responds to the AfterDelConfirm event to refresh the contents of the form or combo boxes. Your code cannot cancel this event. In an Access project (.adp), this event occurs before the Delete event. |
| After Insert (AfterInsert) | Runs the specified macro, Visual Basic function, or Visual Basic event procedure after the user has saved a new record. Your code can use this event to requery a recordset after Access has inserted a new row. Your code cannot cancel this event. |
| After Update (AfterUpdate) | Runs the specified macro, Visual Basic function, or Visual Basic event procedure after the data in the specified form or form control has been updated. See "Understanding Event Sequence and Form Editing" on page 882 for details. Your code that responds to this event cannot cancel it. In the AfterUpdate event of a control, you can, however, use a RunCommand action to choose the Undo command from the Quick Access Toolbar or execute the Undo method of the control. This event applies to all forms and to combo boxes, list boxes, option groups, text boxes, and bound object frames as well as to check boxes, option buttons, and toggle buttons that are not part of an option group. |

| Event Property (Event Name) | Description |
|---|---|
| Before Del Confirm (BeforeDelConfirm) | Runs the specified macro, Visual Basic function, or Visual Basic event procedure after Access has deleted one or more rows on the form but before Access displays the standard confirmation dialog box. If your code cancels this event, Access replaces the deleted rows and does not display the confirmation dialog box. In a Visual Basic procedure, you can display a custom confirmation dialog box and then set a return parameter to suppress the standard confirmation dialog box. In an Access project (.adp), this event occurs before the Delete event. |
| Before Insert (BeforeInsert) | Runs the specified macro, Visual Basic function, or Visual Basic event procedure when the user types the first character in a new record. This event is useful in providing additional information to a user who is about to add records. If your code cancels this event, Access erases any new data on the form. This event occurs prior to the BeforeUpdate event. |
| Before Update (BeforeUpdate) | Runs the specified macro, Visual Basic function, or Visual Basic event procedure before Access saves changed data in a control to the form's record buffer or saves the changed record to the database. See "Understanding Event Sequence and Form Editing" on page 882 for details. Your code that responds to this event can examine both the current and previous values of a control. Your code can cancel this event to stop the update and place the focus on the changed control or record. This event is most useful for performing complex validations of data on forms or in controls. This event applies to the same controls as the AfterUpdate event. |
| On Change (Change) | Runs the specified macro, Visual Basic function, or Visual Basic event procedure whenever the user changes any portion of the contents of a combo box control or a text box control. Your code cannot cancel this event. See also the KeyDown and KeyPress keyboard events. |
| On Delete (Delete) | Runs the specified macro, Visual Basic function, or Visual Basic event procedure just before Access deletes one or more rows. This event occurs once per row being deleted, and your code that responds to the event can examine the data in each row to be deleted. Your code can provide a customized warning message. Your code can also provide automatic deletion of dependent rows in another table (for example, of all the orders for the customer about to be deleted) by executing a delete query. Your code can cancel this event to prevent individual rows from being deleted. (Cancel the BeforeDelConfirm event to cancel deletion of all rows.) |

| Event Property (Event Name) | Description |
|---|---|
| On Dirty (Dirty) | Runs the specified macro, Visual Basic function, or Visual Basic event procedure whenever the user first changes the contents of a bound control on a bound form (a form that has a record source). This event also occurs if your code changes the value of a bound control from a macro (SetValue) or a Visual Basic procedure. Your code that responds to this event can verify that the current record can be updated. Your code can cancel this event to prevent the update. After this event occurs, the Dirty property of the form is True until the record is saved. |
| On Not In List (NotInList) | Runs the specified macro, Visual Basic function, or Visual Basic event procedure when the user types an entry in a combo box that does not exist in the current recordset defined by the Row Source property for the combo box. Your code cannot cancel this event. Your code can allow the user to create a new entry for the combo box (perhaps by adding a record to the table on which the Row Source property is based). You can also use the List Items Edit Form property to tell Access to open a form to add or edit the records in the recordset of the combo box. In a Visual Basic procedure, you can examine a parameter passed to the event procedure that contains the unmatched text. Your code can also set a return value to cause Access to display the standard error message, display no error message (after your code has issued a custom message), or requery the list after your code has added data to the Row Source property. |
| On Undo (Undo) | Runs the specified macro, Visual Basic function, or Visual Basic event procedure when the user undoes a change in a form or a text box or combo box control that has been committed to the form's record buffer. See "Understanding Event Sequence and Form Editing" on page 882 for details. The Undo event does not occur when the user chooses the Undo Typing command. Your code that responds to the event can examine both the current and previous values of the control and cancel the event if the change should not be undone. |
| On Updated (Updated) | Runs the specified macro, Visual Basic function, or Visual Basic event procedure after the data in a form's object frame control changes. Your code cannot cancel this event. In a Visual Basic procedure, your code can examine a status parameter to determine how the change occurred. |

[2] These events occur for forms in Form view or Datasheet view. They do not apply to forms in Design, PivotTable, PivotChart, or Layout view.

**CAUTION!**

You can cause an endless loop if your code changes the contents of a control within the event procedure for the control's Change event.

Table 17-3 **Detecting Focus Changes**[3]

| Event Property (Event Name) | Description |
| --- | --- |
| On Activate (Activate) | Runs the specified macro, Visual Basic function, or Visual Basic event procedure in a form or a report when the Form or Report window receives the focus and becomes the active window. This event does not occur for pop-up or modal forms. This event also does not occur when a normal Form or Report window regains the focus from a pop-up or modal form unless the focus moves to another form or report. Your code cannot cancel this event. |
| On Current (Current) | Runs the specified macro, Visual Basic function, or Visual Basic event procedure in a bound form or report when the focus moves from one record to another but before Access displays the new record. Access also triggers the Current event when the focus moves to the first record as a form or report opens. This event is most useful for keeping two open and related forms synchronized. Your code cannot cancel this event. Your code can, however, use GoToRecord or similar action to move to another record if it decides that the form display should not move to the new record. This event does not occur for reports displayed in Print Preview. |
| On Deactivate (Deactivate) | Runs the specified macro, Visual Basic function, or Visual Basic event procedure when a form or a report loses the focus to a window within the Access application that is not a pop-up or modal window. Your code cannot cancel this event. |
| On Enter (Enter) | Runs the specified macro, Visual Basic function, or Visual Basic event procedure when the focus moves to a bound object frame, a combo box, a command button, a list box, an option group, or a text box, as well as when the focus moves to a check box, an option button, or a toggle button that is not part of an option group. Your code cannot cancel this event. This event occurs only when the focus moves from another control on the same form or report. If the user changes the focus to another control with the mouse, this event occurs before LostFocus in the current control and before the Enter, GotFocus, MouseDown, MouseUp, and Click events for the new control. If the user changes the focus to a control using the keyboard, this event occurs after the KeyDown, Exit, and LostFocus events in the control that previously had the focus but before the GotFocus, KeyPress, and KeyUp events in the control that is receiving the focus. This event does not occur for reports displayed in Print Preview or forms displayed in PivotTable or PivotChart view. |

| Event Property (Event Name) | Description |
|---|---|
| On Exit (Exit) | Runs the specified macro, Visual Basic function, or Visual Basic event procedure when the focus moves from a bound object frame, a combo box, a command button, a list box, an option group, or a text box, as well as when the focus moves from a check box, an option button, or a toggle button that is not part of an option group to another control on the same form or report. Your code cannot cancel this event. This event does not occur when the focus moves to another window. If the user leaves a control using the mouse, this event occurs before the Enter, GotFocus, MouseDown, MouseUp, and Click events in the new control. If the user leaves a control using the keyboard, the KeyDown and Exit events in this control occur, and then the Enter, KeyPress, and KeyUp events occur in the new control. This event does not occur for reports displayed in Print Preview or forms displayed in PivotTable or PivotChart view. |
| On Got Focus (GotFocus) | Runs the specified macro, Visual Basic function, or Visual Basic event procedure when an enabled form or report control receives the focus. If a form or report receives the focus but has no enabled controls, the GotFocus event occurs for the form or report. Your code cannot cancel this event. The GotFocus event occurs after the Enter event. Unlike the Enter event, which occurs only when the focus moves from another control on the same form or report, the GotFocus event occurs every time a control receives the focus, including from other windows. This event does not occur for reports displayed in Print Preview or forms displayed in PivotTable or PivotChart view. |
| On Lost Focus (LostFocus) | Runs the specified macro, Visual Basic function, or Visual Basic event procedure when an enabled form or report control loses the focus. The LostFocus event for the form or report occurs whenever a form or report that has no enabled controls loses the focus. Your code cannot cancel this event. This event occurs after the Exit event. Unlike the Exit event, which occurs only when the focus moves to another control on the same form or report, the LostFocus event occurs every time a control loses the focus, including to other windows. This event does not occur for reports displayed in Print Preview or forms displayed in PivotTable or PivotChart view. |

[3] These events do not apply to forms or reports in Design view.

Table 17-4 **Detecting Filters Applied to Forms and Reports**[4]

| Event Property (Event Name) | Description |
|---|---|
| On Apply Filter (ApplyFilter) | Runs the specified macro, Visual Basic function, or Visual Basic event procedure when a user applies a filter on a form or report from the user interface or via the ApplyFilter command. Setting the form or report's Filter, OrderBy, ServerFilter, FilterOn, or OrderByOn properties from code does not trigger this event. Your code can examine and modify the form or report's Filter and Order By properties or cancel the event. Within a Visual Basic procedure, you can examine a parameter that indicates how the filter is being applied. |
| On Filter (Filter) | Runs the specified macro, Visual Basic function, or Visual Basic event procedure when the user opens the Filter By Form or the Advanced Filter/Sort window. Your code can use this event to clear any previous Filter or Order By setting, set a default Filter or Order By criterion, or cancel the event to prevent the window from opening and provide your own custom filter form. Within a Visual Basic procedure, you can examine a parameter that indicates whether a user has asked to open the Filter By Form or the Advanced Filter/Sort window. |

[4] These events apply to forms in Form or Datasheet view and reports in Report view.

Table 17-5 **Trapping Keyboard and Mouse Events**[5]

| Event Property (Event Name) | Description |
|---|---|
| On Click (Click) | Runs the specified macro, Visual Basic function, or Visual Basic event procedure when the user clicks a command button or clicks an enabled form, report, or control. Your code cannot cancel this event. The Click event occurs for a form or report only if no control on the form or report can receive the focus. |
| On Dbl Click (DblClick) | Runs the specified macro, Visual Basic function, or Visual Basic event procedure when the user double-clicks a bound object frame, a combo box, a command button, a list box, an option group, or a text box, as well as when the user double-clicks a check box, an option button, or a toggle button that is not part of an option group. The Click event always occurs before DblClick. That is, when the user clicks the mouse button twice rapidly, the Click event occurs for the first click followed by DblClick for the second click. Access runs the macro or Visual Basic procedure before showing the user the normal result of the double-click. Your code can cancel the event to prevent the normal response to a double-click of a control, such as activating the application for an ActiveX object in a bound control or highlighting a word in a text box. The DblClick event occurs for a form or report only if no control on that form or report can receive the focus. |

| Event Property (Event Name) | Description |
| --- | --- |
| On Key Down (KeyDown) | Runs the specified macro, Visual Basic function, or Visual Basic event procedure when the user presses a key or a combination of keys. Your code cannot cancel this event. In a Visual Basic procedure, you can examine parameters to determine the key code (the numeric code that represents the key pressed) and whether the Shift, Ctrl, or Alt key was also pressed. You can also set the key code to 0 in Visual Basic to prevent the control from receiving keystrokes. If the form or report has a command button whose Default property is set to Yes (this indicates that the command button responds to Enter as though the button had been clicked), KeyDown events do not occur when the Enter key is pressed. If the form or report has a command button whose Cancel property is set to Yes (this indicates that the command button responds to the Esc key as though the button had been clicked), KeyDown events do not occur when the Esc key is pressed. See also the Change event. The KeyDown event occurs before KeyPress and KeyUp. If the key the user presses (such as the Tab key) causes the focus to move to another control, the control that has the focus when the user presses the key signals a KeyDown event, but the control that receives the focus signals the KeyPress and KeyUp events. If you set the form's KeyPreview property to Yes, this event also occurs for the form or report. |
| On Key Press (KeyPress) | Runs the specified macro, Visual Basic function, or Visual Basic event procedure when the user presses a key or a combination of keys that would result in a character being delivered to the control that has the focus. (For example, KeyPress does not occur for the arrow keys.) Your code cannot cancel this event. In a Visual Basic procedure, you can examine the ANSI key value and set the value to 0 to cancel the keystroke. The KeyPress event occurs after KeyDown and before KeyUp. If the form or report has a command button whose Default property is set to Yes, the KeyPress event occurs for the form or report and the command button when the Enter key is pressed. If the form or report has a command button whose Cancel property is set to Yes, the KeyPress event occurs for the form or report and the command button when the Esc key is pressed. See also the Change event. If you set the form or report's KeyPreview property to Yes, this event also occurs for the form or report. |
| On Key Up (KeyUp) | Runs the specified macro, Visual Basic function, or Visual Basic event procedure when the user releases a key or a combination of keys. Your code cannot cancel this event. In a Visual Basic procedure, you can examine parameters to determine the key code and whether the Shift, Ctrl, or Alt key was also pressed. If you set the form or report's KeyPreview property to Yes, this event also occurs for the form or report. If the form or report has a command button whose Default property is set to Yes, the KeyUp event occurs for the form or report and the command button when the Enter key is released. If the form or report has a command button whose Cancel property is set to Yes, the KeyUp event occurs for the form or report and the command button when the Esc key is released. |

| Event Property (Event Name) | Description |
|---|---|
| On Mouse Down (MouseDown) | Runs the specified macro, Visual Basic function, or Visual Basic event procedure when the user presses any mouse button. Your code cannot cancel this event. In a Visual Basic procedure, you can determine which mouse button was pressed (left, right, or middle); whether the Shift, Ctrl, or Alt key was also pressed; and the X and Y coordinates of the mouse pointer (in twips) when the button was pressed. (Note: There are 1440 *twips* in an inch.) |
| On Mouse Move (MouseMove) | Runs the specified macro, Visual Basic function, or Visual Basic event procedure when the user moves the mouse over a form, a report, or a control. Your code cannot cancel this event. In a Visual Basic procedure, you can determine which mouse button was pressed (left, right, or middle) and whether the Shift, Ctrl, or Alt key was also pressed. You can also determine the X and Y coordinates of the mouse pointer (in twips). |
| On Mouse Up (MouseUp) | Runs the specified macro, Visual Basic function, or Visual Basic event procedure when the user releases any mouse button. Your code cannot cancel this event. In a Visual Basic procedure, you can determine which mouse button was released (left, right, or middle); whether the Shift, Ctrl, or Alt key was also pressed; and the X and Y coordinates of the mouse pointer (in twips) when the button was released. |
| On Mouse Wheel (MouseWheel) | Runs the specified macro, Visual Basic function, or Visual Basic event procedure when the user rolls the mouse wheel while the focus is on a form or report. In a Visual Basic procedure, you can determine whether rolling the wheel caused the form to display a new page and the count of rows that the view was scrolled. (When the user rolls the mouse wheel, the form scrolls up or down through the records in the form.) |

[5] These events apply to forms in Form or Datasheet view and to reports in Report view.



Table 17-6 **Detecting Changes in PivotTables and PivotCharts**

| Event Property (Event Name) | Description |
|---|---|
| After Final Render (AfterFinalRender) | In PivotChart view, runs the specified macro, Visual Basic function, or Visual Basic event procedure after all elements in the chart have been rendered (drawn on the screen). Your code cannot cancel this event. |
| After Layout (AfterLayout) | In PivotChart view, runs the specified macro, Visual Basic function, or Visual Basic event procedure after all charts have been laid out but before they have been rendered. In a Visual Basic procedure, you can reposition the title, legend, chart, and axis objects during this event. Your code can also reposition and resize the chart plot area. Your code cannot cancel this event. |

| Event Property (Event Name) | Description |
|---|---|
| After Render (AfterRender) | In PivotChart view, runs the specified macro, Visual Basic function, or Visual Basic event procedure when a particular chart object has been rendered. In a Visual Basic procedure, you can examine the drawing object and the chart objects and use methods of the drawing object to draw additional objects. Your code cannot cancel this event. This event occurs before the AfterFinalRender event. |
| Before Query (BeforeQuery) | In PivotTable view, runs the specified macro, Visual Basic function, or Visual Basic event procedure when the PivotTable queries its data source. Your code cannot cancel this event. |
| Before Render (BeforeRender) | In PivotChart view, runs the specified macro, Visual Basic function, or Visual Basic event procedure before an object is rendered. In a Visual Basic procedure, you can determine the type of rendering and the type of object that is about to be rendered. Your code can cancel this event if it determines that the object should not be rendered. This event occurs before the AfterRender and AfterFinalRender events. |
| Before Screen Tip (BeforeScreenTip) | In PivotTable or PivotChart view, runs the specified macro, Visual Basic function, or Visual Basic event procedure before a ScreenTip is displayed. In a Visual Basic procedure, you can examine and change the text of the tip or hide the tip by setting the text to an empty string. Your code cannot cancel this event. |
| On Cmd Before Execute (CommandBeforeExecute) | In PivotTable or PivotChart view, runs the specified macro, Visual Basic function, or Visual Basic event procedure before a command is executed. In a Visual Basic procedure, you can determine the command to be executed and cancel the event if you want to disallow the command. This event occurs before the CommandExecute event. |
| On Cmd Checked (CommandChecked) | In PivotTable and PivotChart view, runs the specified macro, Visual Basic function, or Visual Basic event procedure when the user has selected (checked) a command. In a Visual Basic procedure, you can determine the command selected and disallow the command by setting the value of the Checked parameter to False. Your code cannot cancel this event. |
| On Cmd Enabled (CommandEnabled) | In PivotTable and PivotChart view, runs the specified macro, Visual Basic function, or Visual Basic event procedure when a command has been enabled. In a Visual Basic procedure, you can determine the type of command and disable it. Your code cannot cancel this event. |

| Event Property (Event Name) | Description |
| --- | --- |
| On Cmd Execute (CommandExecute) | In PivotTable and PivotChart view, runs the specified macro, Visual Basic function, or Visual Basic event procedure after a command has executed. In a Visual Basic procedure, you can determine the type of command and issue additional commands if desired. Your code cannot cancel this event. |
| On Data Change (DataChange) | In PivotTable view, runs the specified macro, Visual Basic function, or Visual Basic event procedure when the data fetched or calculated by the PivotTable has changed. In a Visual Basic procedure, you can examine the reason for the change, which could include changing the sort, adding a total, or defining a filter. Your code cannot cancel this event. This event often precedes the DataSetChange event. |
| On Data Set Change (DataSetChange) | In PivotTable view, runs the specified macro, Visual Basic function, or Visual Basic event procedure when the data source has changed. Your code cannot cancel this event. |
| On Connect (OnConnect) | In PivotTable view, runs the specified macro, Visual Basic function, or Visual Basic event procedure when the PivotTable connects to its data source. Your code cannot cancel this event. |
| On Disconnect (OnDisconnect) | In PivotTable view, runs the specified macro, Visual Basic function, or Visual Basic event procedure when the PivotTable disconnects from its data source. Your code cannot cancel this event. |
| On PivotTable Change (PivotTableChange) | In PivotTable view, runs the specified macro, Visual Basic function, or Visual Basic event procedure when a field, field set, or total is added or deleted. In a Visual Basic procedure, you can examine the reason for the change. Your code cannot cancel this event. |
| On Query (Query) | In PivotTable view, runs the specified macro, Visual Basic function, or Visual Basic event procedure when the PivotTable must requery its data source. Your code cannot cancel this event. |
| On Selection Change (SelectionChange) | In PivotTable or PivotChart view, runs the specified macro, Visual Basic function, or Visual Basic event procedure when the user makes a new selection. Your code cannot cancel this event. |
| On View Change (ViewChange) | In PivotTable or PivotChart view, runs the specified macro, Visual Basic function, or Visual Basic event procedure when the table or chart is redrawn. In a Visual Basic procedure, you can determine the reason for a PivotTable view change. When the form is in PivotChart view, the reason code is always –1. Your code cannot cancel this event. |

Table 17-7 **Printing**

| Event Property (Event Name) | Description |
|---|---|
| On Format (Format) | Runs the specified macro, Visual Basic function, or Visual Basic event procedure just before Access formats a report section to print. This event is useful for hiding or displaying controls in the report section based on data values. If Access is formatting a group header, your code has access to the data in the first row of the Detail section. Similarly, if Access is formatting a group footer, your code has access to the data in the last row of the Detail section. Your code can test the value of the Format Count property to determine whether the Format event has occurred more than once for a section (due to page overflow). Your code can cancel this event to keep a section from appearing on the report. |
| On No Data (NoData) | Runs the specified macro, Visual Basic function, or Visual Basic event procedure after Access formats a report that has no data for printing and just before the reports prints. Your code can cancel this event to keep a blank report from printing. |
| On Page (Page) | Runs the specified macro, Visual Basic function, or Visual Basic event procedure after Access formats a page for printing and just before the page prints. In Visual Basic, you can use this event to draw custom borders around a page or add other graphics to enhance the look of the report. |
| On Paint (Paint) | Runs the specified macro, Visual Basic function, or Visual basic event procedure just before Access paints a formatted section of a form or report. If you open your report in Layout view or Report view, this event occurs instead of the Format or Print events. If you are using the Format event during printing or displaying your report in Print Preview, you might also need to use the Paint event to see the same result in Layout view or Report view. Your code cannot cancel this event. |
| On Print (Print) | Runs the specified macro, Visual Basic function, or Visual Basic event procedure just before Access prints a formatted section of a report. If your code cancels this event, Access leaves a blank space on the report where the section would have printed. |
| On Retreat (Retreat) | Runs the specified macro, Visual Basic function, or Visual Basic event procedure when Access has to retreat past already formatted sections when it discovers that it cannot fit a "keep together" section on a page. Your code cannot cancel this event. |

Table 17-8 **Trapping Errors**

| Event Property (Event Name) | Description |
|---|---|
| On Error (Error) | Runs the specified macro, Visual Basic function, or Visual Basic event procedure whenever a run-time error occurs while the form or report is active. This event does not trap errors in Visual Basic code; use the On Error statement in the Visual Basic procedure instead. Your code cannot cancel this event. If you use a Visual Basic procedure to trap this event, you can examine the error code to determine an appropriate action. |

Table 17-9 **Detecting Timer Expiration**

| Event Property (Event Name) | Description |
|---|---|
| On Timer (Timer) | Runs the specified macro, Visual Basic function, or Visual Basic event procedure when the timer interval defined for the form or report elapses. The Timer Interval property defines how frequently this event occurs in milliseconds. If the Timer Interval property is set to 0, no Timer events occur. Your code cannot cancel this event. However, your code can set the Timer Interval property for the form to 0 to stop further Timer events from occurring. |

You should now have a basic understanding of events and how you might use them. In the next section, you'll see some of these events in action.

## Understanding Event Sequence and Form Editing

One of the best ways to learn event sequence is to see events in action. In the WeddingMC.accdb sample database on the companion CD, you can find a special form that you can use to study events. Open the sample database, and then open the WeddingEvents form, as shown in Figure 17-2. (The form's Caption property is set to Wedding List.)



When you open the form, it also opens an event display pop-up form that shows the events that have occurred. All the events (except the Mouse and Paint events that fire so frequently that they would make it hard to study other events) are set to write the event name to the pop-up window. The pop-up window shows the most recent events at the top. (The event names displayed in the window show an underscore rather than a blank between words in the name.) When you open the form, the initial events are as follows:

1. **Form Open** This signals that the form is about to open.
2. **Form Load** This signals that the form is now open and the record source for the form is about to be loaded.
3. **Form Resize** The form's Auto Resize property is set to Yes, so this indicates that Access is resizing the window to show an exact multiple of rows. (The form's Default View property is set to Continuous Forms.)

4. **Form Activate** The form has now received the focus.
5. **Form Current** The form has now moved to the first row in the record source.
6. **Title Enter** The first control in the tab order has been entered.
7. **Title GotFocus** The first control in the tab order now has the focus.

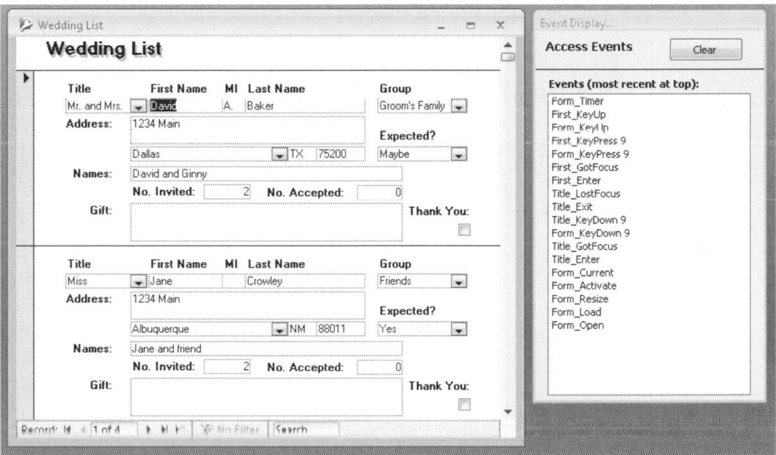


**Figure 17-2** Use the WeddingEvents form to study event sequence.

After the form opened, we pressed the Tab key to move from the Title field to the First Name field. (The name of the control is First.) The form has its Key Preview property set to Yes, so you can see the keyboard events for both the form and the controls. The events occurred in the following sequence:

1. **Form KeyDown** The form detected that the Tab key (key code 9) was pressed.
2. **Title KeyDown** The Title combo box control detected that the Tab key was pressed.
3. **Title Exit** Pressing the Tab key caused an exit from the Title combo box control.
4. **Title LostFocus** The Title combo box control lost the focus as a result of pressing Tab.
5. **First Enter** The First text box control (First Name) was entered.
6. **First GotFocus** The First text box control received the focus.
7. **Form KeyPress** The form received the Tab key.
8. **First KeyPress** The First text box control received the Tab key.
9. **Form KeyUp** The form detected that the Tab key was released.
10. **First KeyUp** The First text box detected that the Tab key was released.

In Figure 17-2, you can also see a Form Timer event listed. The Timer Interval property for this form is set to 20,000 (the value is milliseconds), so you should see the timer event occur every 20 seconds as long as you have the form open.

You can have fun with this form moving around and typing new data. You'll be able to see each character that you enter. You'll also see the control and form BeforeUpdate and AfterUpdate events when you commit changed values. You can also switch to PivotChart or PivotTable view to watch events related to those views.

Figure 17-3 shows you a conceptual diagram of how editing data in a form works and when the critical Current, BeforeUpdate, and AfterUpdate events occur.

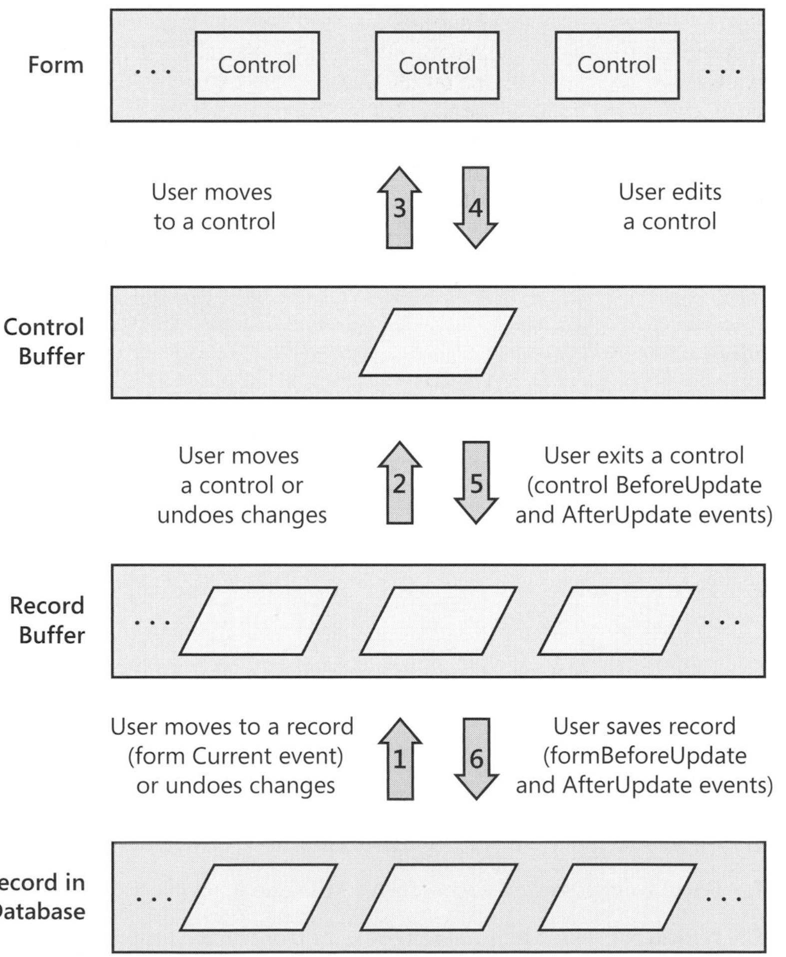


**Figure 17-3** Many events occur behind the scenes when you edit data on a bound form.

Of course, the ultimate goal is to update data in your database table. When Access opens a form, it builds a special buffer to contain the contents of the current record displayed on the form. As you move from control to control on the form, Access fetches the field bound to each control from this record buffer and puts it into a special control buffer. As you type in the control, you're changing the control buffer and not the record buffer or the actual record in the table.

If you have changed the data in a control and then you move to another control, Access signals the BeforeUpdate event for the control. If you do not cancel the event, Access then copies the updated contents of the control buffer into the record buffer and signals the control's AfterUpdate event. Access then fetches into the control buffer the contents of the field bound to the control to which you moved from the record buffer and displays it in the control.

If you undo any edit, Access signals the appropriate Undo event and refreshes either the control buffer from the record buffer (if you undo a control) or the original record from the table into the record buffer (if you undo all edits). When you save a changed record—either by clicking the Save button in the Records group on the Home tab, by moving to another record, or by closing the form—Access first signals the BeforeUpdate event of the form. If you do not cancel this event, Access writes the changed record to your table and signals the AfterUpdate event of the form.

Now that you understand events and event sequence, the next chapter discusses macros and how you can design macro actions to respond to form and report events.

CHAPTER 18

# Automating Your Application with Macros



In Microsoft Office Access 2007, you can define a macro to execute just about any task you would otherwise initiate with the keyboard or the mouse. The unique power of macros in Office Access 2007 is their ability to automate responses to many types of events without forcing you to learn a programming language. The event might be a change in the data, the opening or closing of a form or a report, or even a change of focus from one control to another. Within a macro, you can include multiple actions and define condition checking so that different actions are performed depending on the values in your forms or reports.

Macros are particularly useful for building small, personal applications or for prototyping larger ones. As you'll learn in Chapter 19, "Understanding Visual Basic Fundamentals," you probably should use Microsoft Visual Basic for complex applications or for applications that will be shared by several users over a network. However, even if you think you're ready to jump right into Visual Basic, you should study all the macro actions first. You'll find that you'll use nearly all of the available macro actions in Visual Basic, so learning macros is an excellent introduction to programming in Access in general.

**Note**

The examples in this chapter are based on the Wedding List Macro (WeddingMC.accdb) sample database on the companion CD included with this book. The results you see from the samples in this chapter might not exactly match what you see in this book if you have changed the sample data in the files. Also, all the screen images in this chapter were taken on a Microsoft Windows Vista system with the display theme set to Blue. Your results might look different if you are using a different operating system or a different theme.

In this chapter, you will

- Learn about the various types of actions you can define in macros
- Tour the macro design facility and learn how to build both a simple macro and a macro with multiple defined actions
- Learn how to manage the many macros you need for a form or a report by creating a macro group
- See how to add conditional statements to a macro to control the actions Access performs
- Learn about the new macro features in Access 2007 including embedded macros, error trapping in macros, temporary variables, and macro actions that are not trusted.
- Learn how to reference other form and report objects in macros
- Understand some of the actions automated with macros in the Wedding List Macro sample database

**Note**

In Article 6, "Macro Actions," on the companion CD, you'll find summaries of the macro actions and of the events that can trigger a macro. You might find that article useful as a quick reference when you're designing macros for your applications.

# Uses of Macros

Access 2007 provides various types of macro actions that you can use to automate your application. With macros, you can

- Open any table, query, form, or report in any available view or close any open table, query, form, or report.
- Open a report in Print Preview or Report view or send a report directly to the printer.
- Send the output data from a report to a Rich Text Format (.rtf) file, a Windows Notepad (.txt) file, or a Snapshot (.snp) format file. You can then open the file in Microsoft Word or Notepad.
- Execute a select query or an action query. You can base the parameters of a query on the values of controls in any open form.

- Include conditions that test values in a database, a form, or a report and use the results of a test to determine what action runs next.
- Execute other macros or execute Visual Basic functions. You can halt the current macro or all macros, cancel the event that triggered the macro, or quit the application.
- Trap errors caused during execution of macro actions, evaluate the error, and execute alternate actions.
- Set the value of any form or report control or set selected properties of forms and form controls.
- Emulate keyboard actions and supply input to system dialog boxes.
- Refresh the values in forms, list box controls, and combo box controls.
- Apply a filter to, go to any record in, or search for data in a form's underlying table or query.
- Execute any of the commands on any of the Access Ribbons.
- Move and size, minimize, maximize, or restore any window within the Access workspace when you work in multiple-document interface mode.
- Change the focus to a window or to any control within a window or select a page of a report to display in Print Preview.
- Display informative messages and sound a beep to draw attention to your messages. You can also disable certain warning messages when executing action queries.
- Rename any object in your database, make another copy of a selected object in your database, or copy an object to another Access database.
- Delete objects in your database or save an open object.
- Import, export, or attach other database tables or import or export spreadsheet or text files.
- Start an application and exchange data with the application using Dynamic Data Exchange (DDE) or the Clipboard. You can send data from a table, query, form, or report to an output file and then open that file in the appropriate application. You can also send keystrokes to the target application.

Consider some of the other possibilities for macros. For example, you can make moving from one task to another easier by using command buttons that open and position forms and set values. You can create very complex editing routines that validate data entered in forms, including checking data in other tables. You can even check something like the customer name entered in an order form and open another form so that the user can enter detailed data if no record exists for that customer.

INSIDE OUT **Do We Recommend Using Macros?**

In versions prior to Access 2007, we would have strongly recommended against using macros. Now that macros offer error trapping and the ability to create and manipulate simple variables, we can recommend using them for all simple applications and perhaps even moderately complex ones. Macros still won't work well for a complex production application. The debugging facilities are very limited. If you run into any problem in your macro code, it can be very difficult to figure out the solution. Most complex applications also require manipulating recordsets behind the scenes, and you can't do that at all with macros.

Even if you plan to use Visual Basic from the very beginning, it's still worth your while to learn the basics of programming with macro actions. In truth, the best (and perhaps only) way to perform certain actions in Visual Basic is to execute the equivalent macro action. For example, the only way to open a form that does not have any Visual Basic code is to execute the OpenForm action from within your Visual Basic procedure. (When a form has a module, an advanced way to open one or more copies of a form is to set a module object to the form's module.) As you'll learn in the next chapter, you execute macro actions in Visual Basic as methods of a special object called DoCmd. (In Article 6, on the companion CD, we note the macro actions that have better native equivalents in Visual Basic.)

# The Macro Design Facility—An Overview

The following sections explain how to work with the macro design facility in Access 2007.

## Working with the Macro Design Window

Open the Wedding List Macro sample database (WeddingMC.accdb) from the folder where you installed the sample files. (The default location is \Microsoft Press\Access 2007 Inside Out on your C drive.) As you'll discover later in this chapter, a special macro called *Autoexec* runs each time you open the database. This macro determines whether the database is trusted, opens an informational form for a few seconds, and then tells you which macro to run to start the application. We'll look at that macro in some detail later.

On the Create tab, in the Other group, click the arrow on the New Object button, and click Macro from the list of three options. (The top half of the New Object button displays the last type of new object created–Macro, Module, or Class Module. If you see the Macro icon in the top half of the New Object button, you can also click that button to begin creating a new macro.) Access opens a new Macro window similar to the one shown in Figure 18-1. In the upper part of the Macro window, you define your new macro; and in the lower part, you enter settings, called *arguments*, for the actions you've selected for your macro. The upper part shows at least two columns, Action and Comment. You can view all five columns shown in Figure 18-1 by clicking the Macro Names, Conditions, and Arguments buttons in the Show/Hide group on the Design tab.

> **Note**
>
> You can cause the Macro Name and Condition columns to appear automatically for any new macro by selecting the Names Column and Conditions Column check boxes under Show In Macro Design in the Display section of the Advanced category in the Access Options dialog box.

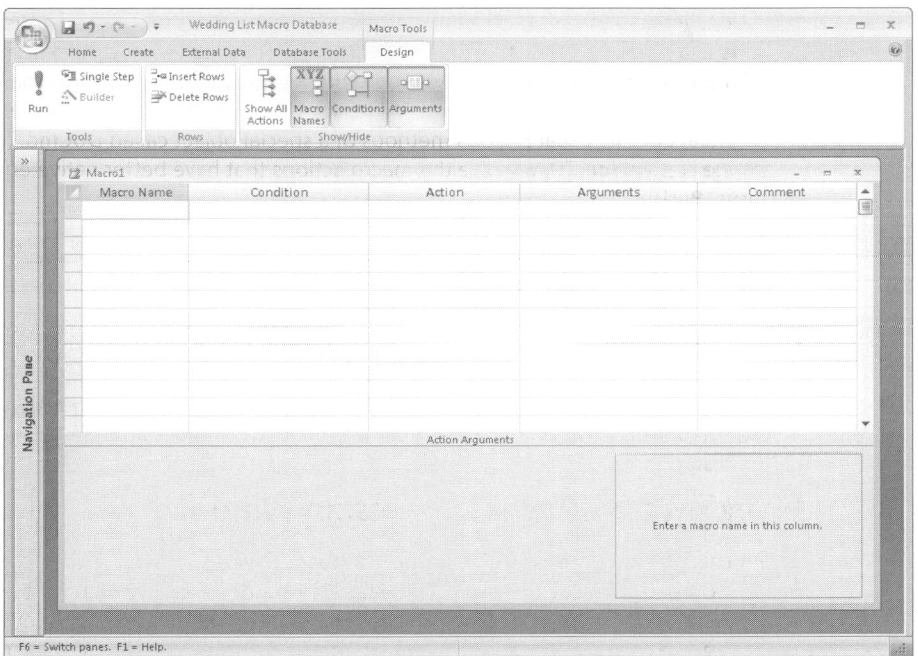


**Figure 18-1** A new Macro window displays columns where you can define your macro.

Notice that the area at the lower right displays a brief help message. The message changes depending on where the insertion point is located in the upper part of the window. (Remember: You can always press F1 to open a context-sensitive Help topic.)

In the Action column, you can specify any one of the 70 macro actions provided by Access 2007. If you click any box in the Action column, an arrow appears at the right side of the box. Click this arrow to open a list of the macro actions, as shown in Figure 18-2.

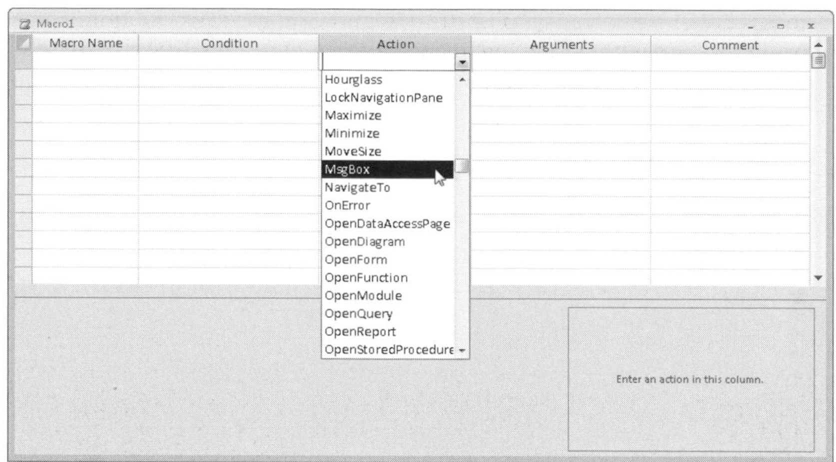


**Figure 18-2** The list of macro actions displays 70 actions you can use in Access 2007.

## TROUBLESHOOTING

### Why doesn't the list include all the macro actions available?

Access 2007 includes 70 macro actions, but not all these actions can run in a database that is not trusted. By default, Access displays only the macro actions that can run in a trusted database in the Action column. To see the complete list of macro actions, click the Show All Actions button in the Show/Hide group on the Design tab. When you select an action that can run only in a trusted database, Access displays an exclamation point on the selection button to the left. If a macro in your application includes actions that can run only in a trusted database, your user must trust your database to be able to run the macro.

To see how the Macro window works, select the MsgBox action now. (Scroll down the list to find MsgBox.) You can use the MsgBox action to open a pop-up modal dialog box with a message in it. This is a great way to display a warning or an informative message in your database without defining a separate form.

Assume that this message will be a greeting, and type **Greeting message** in the corresponding box in the Comment column. You'll find the Comment column especially useful for documenting large macros that contain many actions. You can enter additional comments in any blank box in the Comment column (that is, any box without an action next to it).

After you select an action such as MsgBox, Access displays argument boxes in the lower part of the window, as shown in Figure 18-3, in which you enter the arguments for the action. If you display the Arguments column, Access shows you a summary of the arguments that you have entered for each action. The Arguments column is a new feature in

Access 2007. When you display this column, you can see a summary of the arguments for each action without having to click each action row to see the arguments in the lower part of the design window.

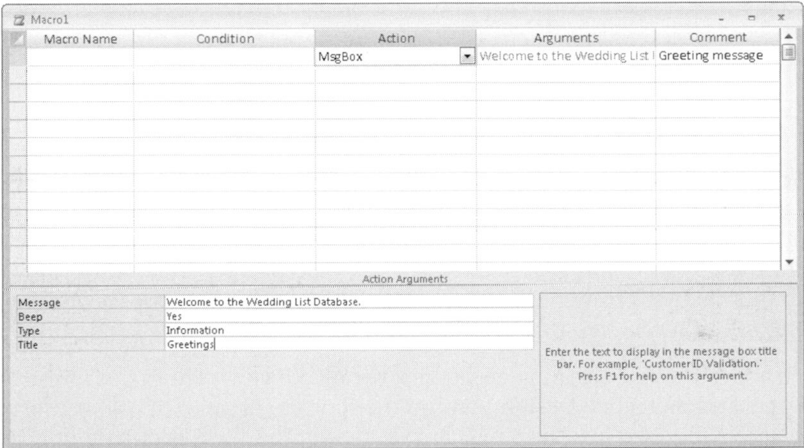


**Figure 18-3** Enter arguments for the MsgBox action to display a greeting message.

**Note**

As you can in the Table and Query windows in Design view, you can use the F6 key to move between the upper and lower parts of the Macro window.

You use the Message argument box in the lower part of the design window to set the message that you want Access to display in the dialog box you're creating. The setting in the Beep argument box tells Access whether to sound a beep when it displays the message. In the Type argument box, you can choose a graphic indicator, such as a red critical icon, that will appear with your message in the dialog box. In the Title argument box, you can type the contents of your dialog box's title bar. Use the settings shown in Figure 18-3 in your macro.

## Saving Your Macro

You must save a macro before you can run it. Click the Save button on the Quick Access Toolbar, or click the Microsoft Office Button and then click Save. When you do so, Access opens the dialog box shown in Figure 18-4. Enter the name **TestGreeting**, and click OK to save your macro.

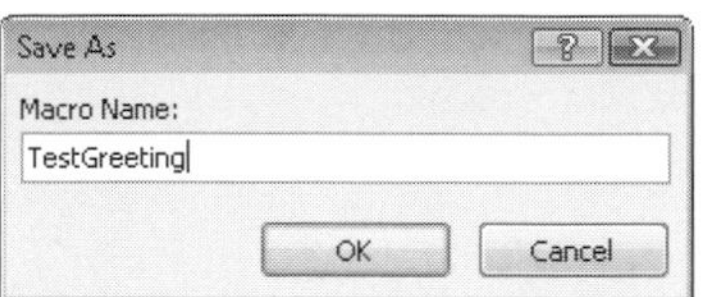


**Figure 18-4** Enter a name for this test macro in the Save As dialog box.

## Testing Your Macro

You can run some macros (such as the simple one you just created) directly from the Navigation Pane or from the Macro window because they don't depend on controls on an open form or report. If your macro does depend on a form or a report, you must link the macro to the appropriate event and run it that way. (You'll learn how to do this later in this chapter.) However you run your macro, Access provides a way to test it by allowing you to single step through the macro actions.

To activate single stepping, right-click the macro you want to test in the Navigation Pane, and then click Design View on the shortcut menu. This opens the macro in the Macro window. Click the Single Step button in the Tools group on the Design tab. Now when you run your macro, Access opens the Macro Single Step dialog box before executing each action in your macro. In this dialog box, you'll see the macro name, the action, and the action arguments.

Try this procedure with the TestGreeting macro you just created. Open the Macro window, click the Single Step button, and then click the Run button in the Tools group on the Design tab. The Macro Single Step dialog box opens, as shown in Figure 18-5. Later in this section, you'll learn how to code a condition in a macro. The Macro Single Step dialog box also shows you the result of testing your condition.

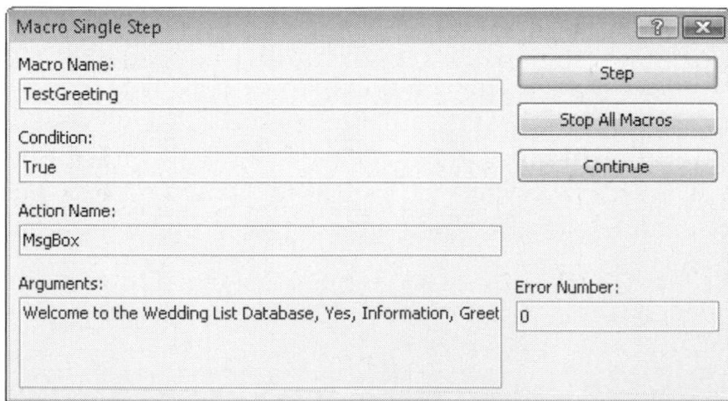


**Figure 18-5** The Macro Single Step dialog box allows you to test each action in your macro.

If you click the Step button in the dialog box, the action you see in the dialog box will run, and you'll see the dialog box opened by your MsgBox action with the message you created, as shown in Figure 18-6. Click the OK button in the message box to dismiss it. If your macro had more than one action defined, you would have returned to the Macro Single Step dialog box, which would have shown you the next action. In this case, your macro has only one action, so Access returns you to the Macro window.

**Figure 18-6** Access displays the dialog box you created by using the MsgBox action in the TestGreeting macro.

If Access encounters an error in any macro during the normal execution of your application, Access first displays a dialog box explaining the error it found. You then see an Action Failed dialog box, which is similar to the Macro Single Step dialog box, containing information about the action that caused the problem. At this point, you can click only the Stop All Macros button. You can then edit your macro to fix the problem. We'll discuss handling errors in "Trapping Errors in Macros" on page 910.

Before you read on in this chapter, you might want to return to the Macro window and click the Single Step button again so that it's no longer selected. Otherwise you'll continue to single step through every macro you run until you exit and restart Access or click Continue in one of the Single Step dialog boxes.

# Defining Multiple Actions

In Access 2007, you can define more than one action within a macro, and you can specify the sequence in which you want the actions performed. The Wedding List Macro database contains several examples of macros that have more than one action. Open the database if it is not open already. Click the Navigation menu at the top of the Navigation Pane, click Object Type under Navigate To Category, and then click Macros under Filter By Group to display a list of macros available in the Wedding List Macro database. Right-click the macro named AutoexecXmpl, and then click Design View on the shortcut menu to open the Macro window. Figure 18-7 shows the macro.

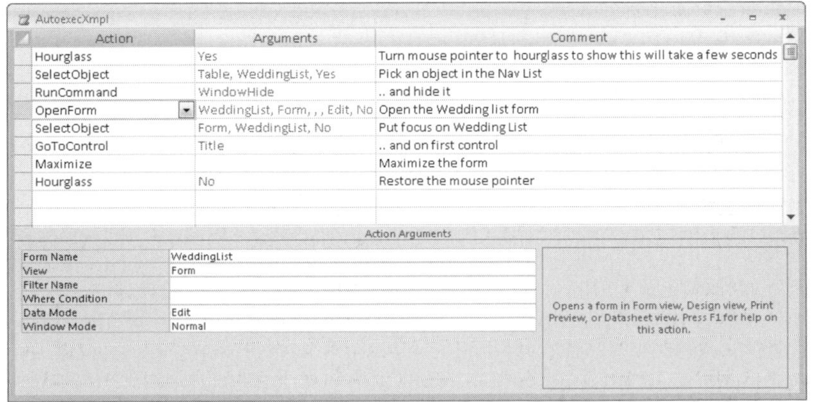


**Figure 18-7** The AutoexecXmpl macro defines multiple actions that Access executes when you run the macro.

INSIDE OUT

### Autoexec Macros—A Special Type of Macro

If you create a macro and name it Autoexec, Access runs the macro each time you open the database in which it is stored. The preferred method to run startup code is to define a startup form in the Application Options section of the Current Database category in the Access Options dialog box. For details, see Chapter 24, "The Finishing Touches."

In the Wedding List Macro sample database, the Autoexec macro examines the IsTrusted property of the CurrentProject object (CurrentProject defines all the executable code) to see whether the database is trusted. (You can trust the database by placing it in a trusted location.) If the database is not trusted, the macro opens a dialog form with instructions on how to create a trusted folder. If you open this database in a trusted location, the macro displays a copyright form followed by a message box telling you to run the AutoexecXmpl macro to start the application.

If this macro were named Autoexec, Access would execute each action automatically whenever you open the database. This sample macro is an example of a macro you might design to start the application when the user opens your database.

We defined eight actions in this macro. First, the Hourglass action displays an hourglass mouse pointer to give the user a visual clue that the next several steps might take a second or two. It's always a good idea to turn on this visual cue, even if you think the next several actions won't take very long. Next, the SelectObject action puts the focus on a known object in the Navigation Pane, and the RunCommand-WindowHide action hides the selected window (the Navigation Pane).

The next action, OpenForm, opens the WeddingList form. As you can see in Figure 18-7, the OpenForm action has six arguments that you can use to define how it should work. The Form Name argument indicates the form you want to open. The View argument tells Access what view you want. (The seven choices for the View argument are Form, Design, Print Preview, Datasheet, PivotTable, PivotChart, and Layout.) You can ask Access to apply a filter to the form when it opens either by specifying the name of a query that defines the filter in the Filter Name argument or by entering filter criteria in the Where Condition argument. You can click in the argument box and then click the Build button that Access reveals to open the Expression Builder, which can help you create the filter.

Edit is the default for the Data Mode argument, which allows the user to add, edit, or delete records while using this form. The other choices for this argument are Add, which opens the form in Data Entry mode, and Read Only, which opens the form but does not allow any changes to the data. The default setting for the Window Mode argument is Normal, which opens the form in the mode set by its design properties. You can override the design property settings to open the form in Hidden mode, as an icon in Icon mode, or in the special Dialog mode. When you open a form hidden, the user can reveal it only by adding the Unhide Window command to the Quick Access Toolbar and then clicking the command. When you open a form in Dialog mode, Access does not run further actions or Visual Basic statements until you close that form.

Access doesn't always wait for one action to complete before going on to the next one. For example, an OpenForm action merely starts a task to begin opening the form. Particularly if the form displays a lot of data, Access might take several seconds to load all the data and finish displaying the form. Because you're running Windows, your computer can handle many tasks at once. Access takes advantage of this by going to the next task without waiting for the form to completely open. However, because this macro is designed to maximize the WeddingList form, the form must be completely open in order for this to work.

You can force a form to finish opening by telling Access to put the focus on the form. This macro does so by using the SelectObject action to identify the object to receive the focus (in this case, the WeddingList form), followed by the GoToControl action to put the focus on a specific control on the form. After the GoToControl action puts the focus on the control, the Maximize action sizes the active window (the window containing the object that currently has the focus) to fit the entire screen. The final action in the macro (the Hourglass again) restores the mouse pointer to let the user know that the macro is finished.

**Note**

Because macros might be used by inexperienced programmers, Access automatically restores Hourglass when it finishes running a macro. If it didn't do this, the mouse pointer would continue to show an hourglass. The user would think that Access is broken. However, it's good practice to always restore what you turn off, which is why the sample AutoexecXmpl macro includes Hourglass-No at the end even though it isn't required. As you'll learn in the next chapter, Visual Basic isn't quite so forgiving. If you turn the mouse pointer to an hourglass in a Visual Basic procedure and forget to turn it back on before your code exits, your mouse pointer will forever display an hourglass!

Learning to define multiple actions within a macro is very useful when you want to automate the tasks you perform on a day-to-day basis. Now that you've learned how to do this, the next step is to learn how to group actions by tasks.

## Grouping Macros

You'll find that most of the forms you design for an application require multiple macros to respond to events—some to edit fields, some to open reports, and still others to respond to command buttons. You could design a separate macro saved with its own unique name in the Database window to respond to each event, but you'll soon have hundreds of macros in your application.

You can create a simpler set of more manageable objects by defining *macro objects* that contain several named macros within each object. (This sort of macro object is called a *macro group* within Access 2007 Help.) One approach is to create one saved macro object per form or report. Another technique is to categorize macros by type of action—for example, one macro containing all the OpenForm actions and another containing all the OpenReport actions.

Let's take a look at a form that depends on a macro group. Figure 18-8 shows the PrintOptions form from the Wedding List Macro database in Form view. This form contains two command buttons, Print and Cancel, each of which triggers a different macro. The two macros are contained within a macro object called DoReport.

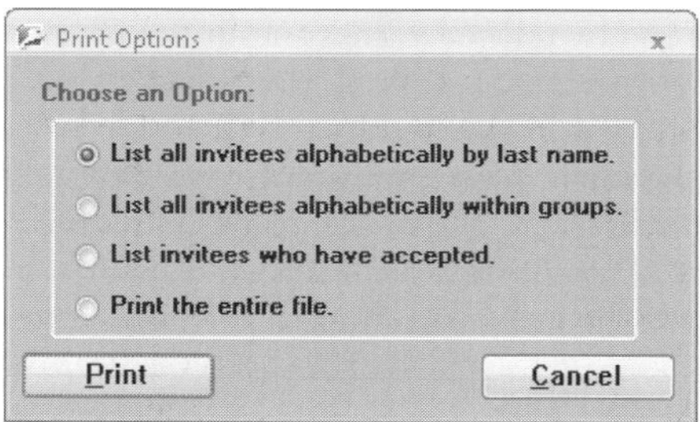


**Figure 18-8** The two command buttons on the PrintOptions form run macros.

To look at the macro object, right-click the DoReport macro in the list of macro objects in the Navigation Pane, and then click Design view on the shortcut menu to open this macro object in the Macro window. Figure 18-9 shows the macro.

DoReport

| Macro Name | Condition | Action | Arguments | Comment |
|---|---|---|---|---|
| | | | | Click event of the Print Report button on Wedding |
| Options | | OpenForm | PrintOptions, Form, , , Edit, No | Open the print options |
| | | | | |
| | | | | Click event of the Print button on PrintOptions for |
| PrintIt | 1=[Forms]![PrintOptions]![opt | RunMacro | DoReport.Alpha, , | Check the option group value - 1 = Alpha by last na |
| | ... | StopMacro | | ... exit once we've decided |
| | | | | |
| | 2=[Forms]![PrintOptions]![opt | RunMacro | DoReport.Groups, , | 2 = Alpha within Group |
| | ... | StopMacro | | ... exit once we've decided |
| | | | | |
| | 3=[Forms]![PrintOptions]![opt | RunMacro | DoReport.Accepted, , | 3 = List Accepted |
| | ... | StopMacro | | ... exit once we've decided |
| | | | | |
| | 4=[Forms]![PrintOptions]![opt | RunMacro | DoReport.PrintF, , | 4 = List All |

Action Arguments

| | |
|---|---|
| Form Name | PrintOptions |
| View | Form |
| Filter Name | |
| Where Condition | |
| Data Mode | Edit |
| Window Mode | Normal |

Opens a form in Form view, Design view, Print Preview, or Datasheet view. Press F1 for help on this action.

**Figure 18-9** The DoReport macro group includes nine individual macros.

To create a group of named macro procedures within a macro object, you must open the Macro Name column in the macro design window. (If you don't see the Macro Name column, click the Macro Names button in the Show/Hide group on the Design tab.) You can create a series of actions at the beginning of the macro definition, without a name, that you can reference from an event property or a RunMacro action by using only the name of the macro object. As you saw earlier in the AutoexecXmpl macro, naming a macro object in a RunMacro action (without any qualifier) asks Access to run the unnamed actions it finds in that macro object.

To create a set of named actions within a macro object, place a name on the first action within the set in the Macro Name column. To execute a named set of actions within a macro object from an event property or a RunMacro action, enter the name of the macro object, a period, and then the name from the Macro Name column. For example, to execute the PrintIt set of actions in the DoReport macro, enter DoReport.PrintIt in the event property or the Macro Name parameter.

In the sample DoReport macro, each of the nine names in this column represents an individual macro within the object. (You must scroll down to see the other names.) The first macro, Options (triggered by the Print Report button on the WeddingList form), opens the PrintOptions form, and the second macro, PrintIt, determines which report was selected. The next four macros, Groups, Alpha, Accepted, and PrintF, display the appropriate report in Print Preview mode, based on the result of the second macro. The Cancel macro merely closes the PrintOptions form if the user clicks the Cancel button. The NoRecords macro cancels opening a report when the report's record source has no data, and the ErrReport macro handles errors. As you might have guessed, Access runs a macro starting with the first action of the macro name specified and executes each action in sequence until it encounters a StopMacro action, another macro name, or no further actions. As you'll see later, you can control whether some actions execute by adding tests in the Condition column of the macro.

If you open the PrintOptions form in Design view (see Figure 18-10) and look at the properties for each of the command buttons, you'll see that the On Click property contains the name of the macro that executes when the user clicks the command button. If you open the list for any event property, you can see that Access lists all macro objects and the named macros within them to make it easy to select the one you want.

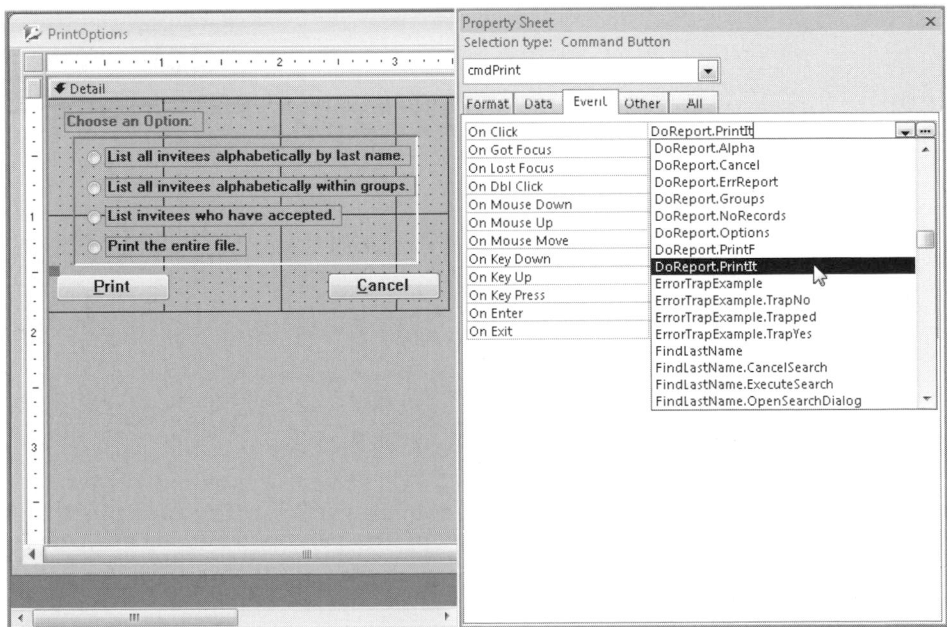


**Figure 18-10** You can see that Access lists all macro objects and named macros in the various event properties.

Remember, the macro name is divided into two parts. The part before the period is the name of the macro object, and the part after the period is the name of a specific macro within the object. So, for the first command button control, the On Click property is set to DoReport.PrintIt. When the user clicks this button, Access runs the PrintIt macro in the DoReport macro object. After you specify a macro name in an event property, you can click the Build button next to the property, and Access opens that macro in a Macro window.

# Understanding Conditional Expressions

In some macros, you might want to execute some actions only under certain conditions. For example, you might want to update a record, but only if new values in the controls on a form pass validation tests. Or you might want to display or hide certain controls based on the value of other controls.

The PrintIt macro in the DoReport macro group is a good example of a macro that uses conditions to determine which action should proceed. Right-click the DoReport macro in the Navigation Pane, and then click Design View on the shortcut menu to see the Macro window. Click in the Condition column of the first line of the PrintIt macro, and press Shift+F2 to open the Zoom window, shown in Figure 18-11. (If you can't see the Condition column, click the Conditions button in the Show/Hide group on the Design tab.)

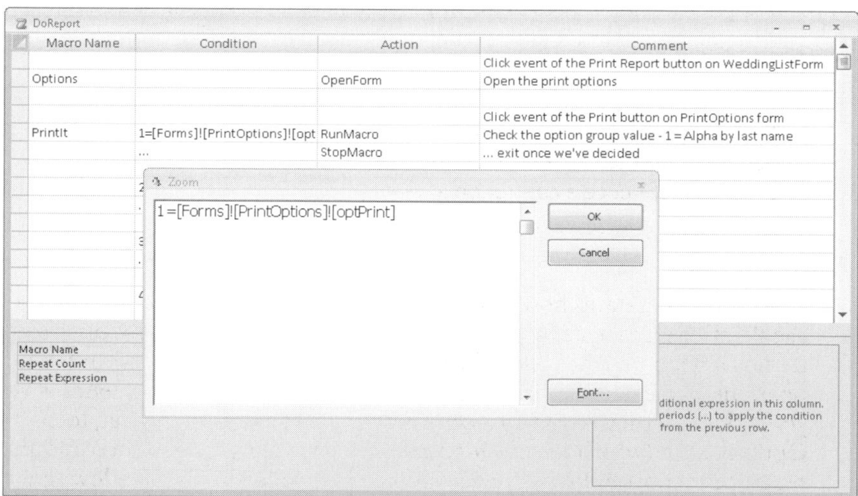


**Figure 18-11** In the Zoom window, you can see we added a condition in the DoReport macro group.

As you saw earlier, this macro is triggered by the On Click property of the Print button on the PrintOptions form. This form allows the user to print a specific report by selecting the appropriate option button and then clicking the Print button. If you look at the form in Design view (see Figure 18-10), you'll see that the option buttons are located within an option group control on the form. Each option button sets a specific numeric value (in this case 1 for the first button, 2 for the second button, 3 for the third button, and 4 for the fourth button) in the option group, which you can test in the Condition column of a macro.

When you include a condition in a macro, Access won't run the action on that line unless the condition evaluates to True. If you want to run a series of actions on the basis of the outcome of a test, you can enter the test in the Condition column on the first action line and enter an ellipsis (...) in the Condition column for the other actions in the series. This causes Access to evaluate the condition only once and execute additional actions (those with an ellipsis in the Condition column) if the original test evaluated to True.

In this particular example, the condition tests the value of the option group control on the form. You can reference any control on an open form by using the syntax

```
FORMS!formname!controlname
```

where *formname* is the name of an open form and *controlname* is the name of a control on that form. In this case, the direct reference is *[FORMS]![PrintOptions]![optPrint]*. (*optPrint* is the name of the option group control. You can see this in the Name property on the Other tab of the property sheet for this control.) See "Referencing Form and Report Objects" on page 919 for more details about the rules for referencing objects in Access.

INSIDE OUT **When to Use Brackets**

If your object names do not contain any embedded blanks or other special characters, you don't need to surround *formname* or *controlname* with brackets when you use this syntax to reference a control on a form; Access inserts the brackets as needed.

After you understand how to refer to the value of a control on a form, you can see that the PrintIt macro tests for each of the possible values of the option group control. When it finds a match, PrintIt runs the appropriate named macro within the macro object to open the requested report and then stops. If you look at the individual report macros, you'll see that they each run a common macro, DoReport.Cancel, to close the PrintOptions form (which isn't needed after the user chooses a report) and then open the requested report in Print Preview and put the focus on the window that displays the report.

## Using Embedded Macros

Access 2007 includes a new feature to create *embedded macros* in the event procedures for forms, reports, and controls. The macros you have been creating and opening thus far in this chapter are macro objects that you can access from the Navigation Pane. You save embedded macros, however, within the event procedures for forms and reports. You cannot see or run these macros directly from the Navigation Pane.

## Editing an Embedded Macro

To edit an embedded macro, you must first open a form or report in Design view. The fdlgNotTrusted form in the Wedding List Macro database contains two embedded macros, each of which is attached to the Click event of one of the two command buttons. Select this form in the Navigation Pane, and open it in Design view. Click the Property Sheet button in the Tools group on the Design tab to open the form's property sheet. Next, click the command button labeled Print These Instructions, or select cmdPrint from the selection list on the property sheet to view the properties for this command button, as shown in Figure 18-12.

**Figure 18-12** The property sheet lists any embedded macros attached to events.

Notice that [Embedded Macro] appears in the On Click property—this indicates that a macro is stored with the form design that responds to this event. To view and edit the macro attached to this event property, click the Build button on the right side of this property line. Access opens a macro design window, as shown in Figure 18-13. Notice that in the macro title bar Access displays the name of the form, the object name the embedded macro is attached to (in this case, the cmdPrint command button), and the specific event of the object that runs the embedded macro.

With the macro design window open, you can now view and edit the macro conditions (not used in this sample macro), actions, arguments, and comments. For the cmdPrint command button, you can see we attached a simple macro that executes the RunCommand action. In the Command argument, we selected the Print command, which tells Access to print the object that has the focus—in this case, the fdlgNotTrusted form. The application displays this form only if the database is trusted. We provide this print button so that you can print the instructions for creating a trusted location displayed on the form.

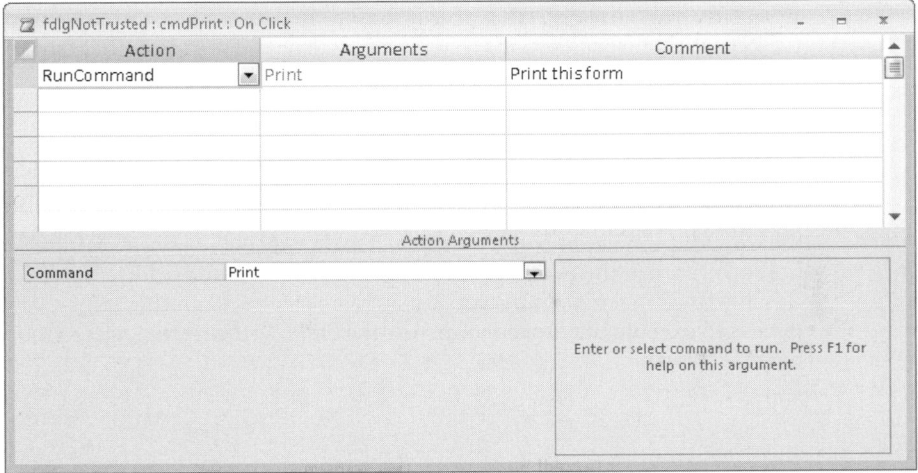


**Figure 18-13** The macro design window shows the embedded macro we created to respond to the Click event of the cmdPrint button on the fdlgNotTrusted form.

Close the macro design window for this embedded macro, and then click the Close button on the form (or select cmdCancel from the selection list). You'll see [Embedded Macro] displayed in the On Click property for this command button. Click the Build button for this property to open the macro design window shown in Figure 18-14. This embedded macro uses the Close action to tell Access to close the fdlgNotTrusted form when the user clicks this command button.

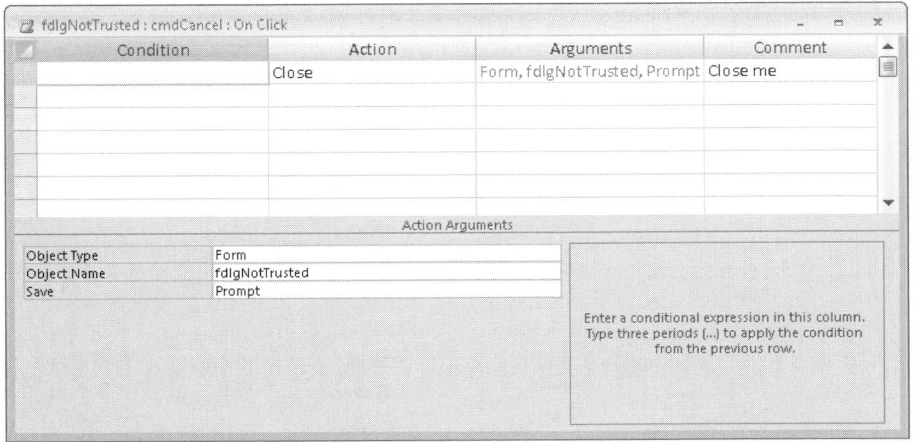


**Figure 18-14** The Close button on the fdlgNotTrusted form executes an embedded macro to close the form.

We set the Save argument of the Close action to Prompt, which instructs Access to ask the user whether any changes to the form design should be saved on closing. (The form opens in Form view, so the user shouldn't be able to make any changes.) We selected this setting because choosing any other option causes the Close action to be not trusted. We'll discuss actions that are not trusted later in this chapter.

The two embedded macros you've seen on this form are simple macros with only one action each. You're not limited to using only one action in an embedded macro. You can create a very complex macro, such as the DoReport macro you saw previously in this chapter, with several macro actions using several conditions. However, there is one important difference when designing a complex embedded macro. If you create named macro groups in an embedded macro, Access executes only the actions defined in the first group when the event to which this macro responds occurs. To execute the additional named macro groups, you must create a call within the first set of actions to tell Access to execute the other groups—as the DoReport macro object demonstrated earlier in this chapter.

INSIDE OUT **Embedded Macros Stay with Their Controls**

If you attach embedded macros to a specific control on a form or report, Access saves the macro with the control. If you cut or copy this control to the Clipboard and then paste it back on the form or report, Access keeps the embedded macro attached to the control.

## Creating an Embedded Macro

Close the macro design window if you still have it open, and let's create a new embedded macro to display a message box when this form opens. From the list under Selection Type near the top of the property sheet, select Form to display all the properties of the form. Click the Event tab, and click the On Open property. To create a new embedded macro, click the Build button at the right end of the property. Access opens the Choose Builder dialog box, as shown in Figure 18-15.

If you select the Macro Builder option, Access opens a new macro design window where you can create your embedded macro. If you select Expression Builder, Access opens the Expression Builder dialog box where you can build an expression to enter in the property. If you select Code Builder, Access opens the Visual Basic Editor where you can write a Visual Basic code procedure for this event property. (We'll discuss Visual Basic in the next two chapters—Chapter 19 and Chapter 20, "Automating Your Application with Visual Basic.") Select the Macro Builder option, and then click OK to begin creating a new embedded macro.

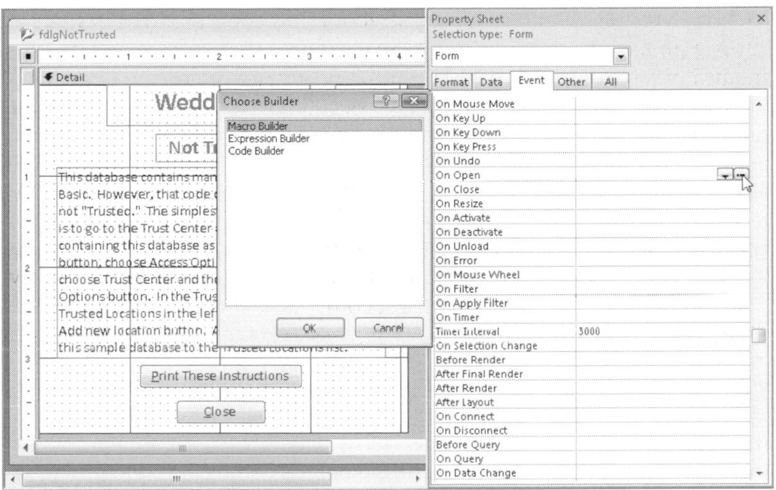


**Figure 18-15** Select Macro Builder in the Choose Builder dialog box to create an embedded macro.

To display a message box, select MsgBox in the Action column. In the Message argument, enter the following text:

**This database is not trusted, so it cannot execute all the code needed to automate this application. Please read and follow the instructions displayed in the form that opens after you close this message in order to have the application function properly.**

In the Beep argument, leave the default setting Yes, and change the Type argument to Warning! to provide a visual cue that something is wrong and call attention to the message. In the Title argument, enter **Embedded Macro Test**. Your finished macro should look something like Figure 18-16.

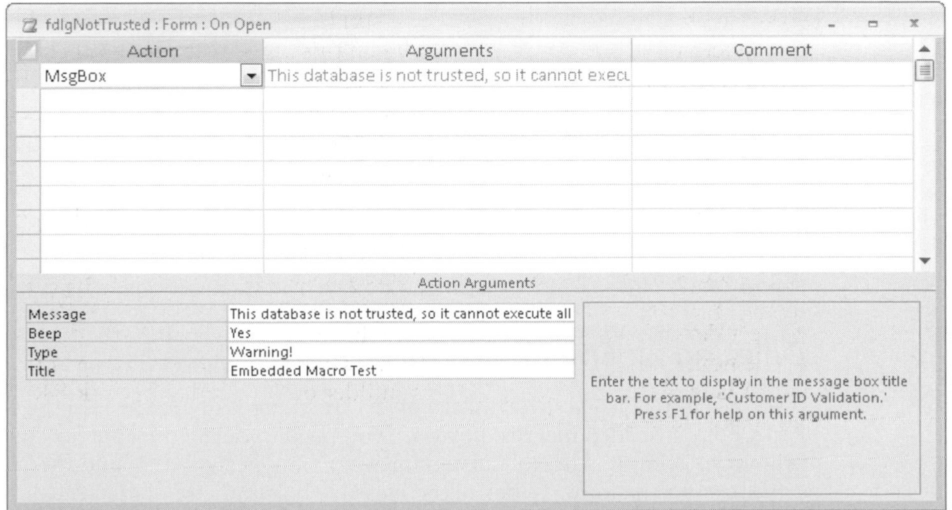


**Figure 18-16** The MsgBox action displays a message box in Access.

### INSIDE OUT Enabling the Choose Builder Dialog Box

In Chapter 19, you'll learn that you can select [Event Procedure] from the list in an event property and then click the Build button to open the Visual Basic Editor to create the appropriate procedure. In the initial release of Access 2007, Microsoft failed to also provide an [Embedded Macro] option that you could use in the same way to create a macro to respond to the event. You also cannot type [Embedded Macro] in the property and click the Build button. You must leave the property blank, click the Build button, and choose Macro Builder in the Choose Builder dialog box.

But there's a catch. To see the Choose Builder dialog box, you must not select the Always Use Event Procedures check box in the Forms/Reports section in the Object Designers category of the Access Options dialog box. (The option is cleared by default.) If you select that check box, Access always opens the Visual Basic Editor window when you click the Build button in any event property. The only way to create a new embedded macro is to select Macro Builder in the Choose Builder dialog box. If you intend to use embedded macros, you must leave the Always Use Event Procedures check box cleared.

Click Save on the Quick Access Toolbar to save this new embedded macro, and then close the macro design window. You'll notice that Access now displays [Embedded Macro] on the On Open property line. Note that if you don't click Save before closing the macro design window, Access prompts you to save the changes and update the property. If you click No, Access does not save the embedded macro. Click the Save button again on the Quick Access Toolbar to save the changes to the form itself. Switch to Form view (or close the form and then open it in Form view from the Navigation Pane), and notice that Access now displays a message box, as shown in Figure 18-17. Click OK in the message box, and Access then displays the not trusted form. Click the Close button to close the form.

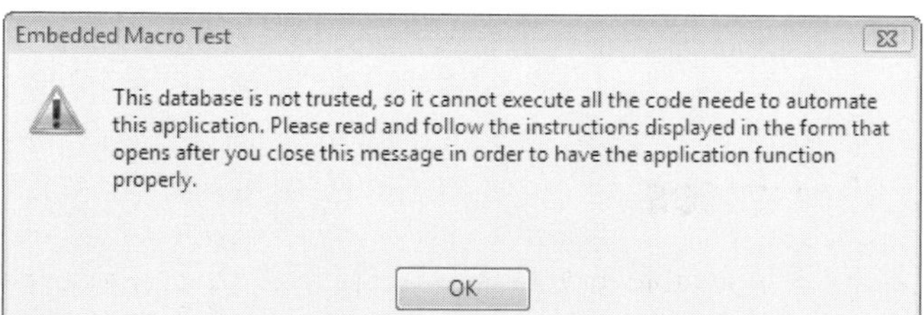


**Figure 18-17** Your embedded macro now displays a message box before the form opens.

## Deleting an Embedded Macro

If you need to delete a saved macro object, you can easily delete it in the Navigation Pane. For embedded macros, however, you need to delete the contents in the specific property. Open the fdlgNotTrusted form again in Design view, and then open the property sheet for the form. To delete the message box embedded macro you just created, find the On Open property on the Event tab, highlight [Embedded Macro], and then press Delete to delete the embedded macro. Click Save on the Quick Access Toolbar to save your changes, and then close the form.

**CAUTION!**

Access does not warn you that it deletes the macro associated with an event property when you clear the property setting. You also cannot undo clearing the property to get the macro back. If you delete a complex macro that was previously saved in the form design, click the Microsoft Office Button, and click Save As to save the form with a new name. (Or close the form without saving if you're willing to discard other changes.) You can then open the original form in Design view to recover the macro. Remember that when you copy and paste a control from one form to another, Access also pastes any attached embedded macros, so you can copy the control and its macro from the old form to the new one to get the macro back in the new form.

**INSIDE OUT** **Embedded Macros Won't Work with Earlier Access Versions**

If you create a database in the .mdb file format, Access 2007 allows you to create embedded macros for forms, reports, and controls just like you can in an .accdb file format database. But if you open the .mdb database with an earlier version of Access—2000, 2002, or 2003—the embedded macros do not function. In fact, you cannot see any [Embedded Macro] entries for event properties when you open an .mdb database with an earlier Access version. If you create an .mdb format database using Access 2007 that will be opened and run with a previous version of Access, do not create embedded macros for your application.

## Using Temporary Variables

You can use a temporary variable in Access to store a value that can be used in other macros, event procedures, expressions, and queries. As you'll learn in Chapter 24, we use a variable to store the user name when you log in to the Conrad Systems Contacts and Housing Reservations sample databases. Variables are very useful when you need Access to remember something for later use. You can think of a temporary variable in a macro as writing yourself a note to remember a number, a name, or an address so that you can recall it at a later time. All variables have a unique name. To fetch, set, or examine a variable, you reference it by its name. Temporary variables stay in memory until you close the database, assign a new value, or clear the value.

To see an example of using a temporary variable in the Wedding List Macro sample database, open the ValidateCitySetStateAndZip macro in Design view. We'll study this macro in more detail in "Validating Data and Presetting Values" on page 928, but for now we'll focus on creating a temporary variable. Creating a temporary variable in a macro is easy—Access creates the variable for you when you reference it for the first time in a SetTempVar action. In Figure 18-18, you can see that in the AskEdit macro in the ValidateCitySetStateAndZip macro group, we created a new temporary variable called AddFlag and set its value to True in the Expression argument.

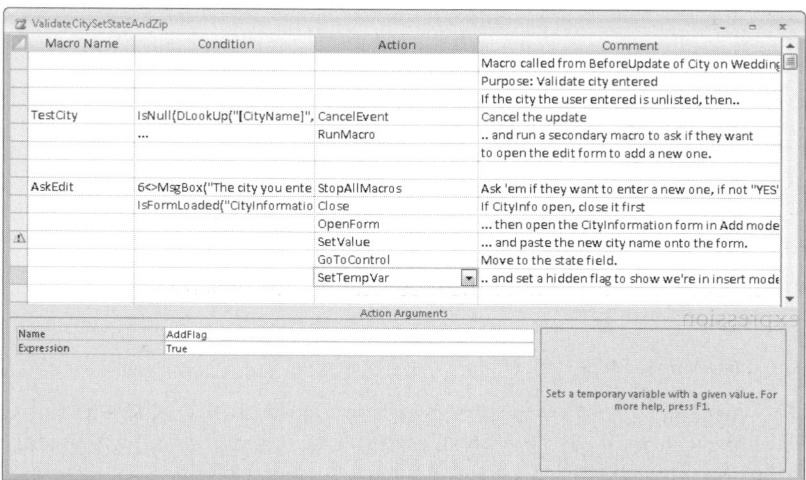


**Figure 18-18** The AskEdit macro in the ValidateCitySetStateAndZip macro uses a temporary variable to indicate that the CityInformation form has been opened in Data Entry mode.

The AskEdit macro runs from the BeforeUpdate event of the City combo box on the WeddingList form when the user enters a new city name that isn't in the row source. The macro first executes a MsgBox function in the condition of the first action to ask the user whether the new city should be added. If the user clicks the Yes button in the dialog box displayed by the MsgBox function, the function returns the value 6. (We'll explain more about the MsgBox function later.) If the user clicks No, the macro halts. When the user clicks Yes, the macro calls the IsFormLoaded custom Visual Basic function (in the modUtility module object) to determine whether the CityInformation form is open. If it is, the macro closes it. The macro then opens the CityInformation form in Data Entry mode and copies the new city name from the WeddingList form to the CityInformation form.

The application uses the AddFlag variable to let code in another macro know that this macro has closed and reopened the CityInformation form in Data Entry mode. The RefreshCityList macro that executes in response to the AfterInsert event in the CityInformation form is also stored in the ValidateCitySetStateAndZip macro. The macro tests the AddFlag variable set in the AskEdit macro. Scroll down the macro rows in the macro design window until you come to the RefreshCityList macro, as shown in Figure 18-19.

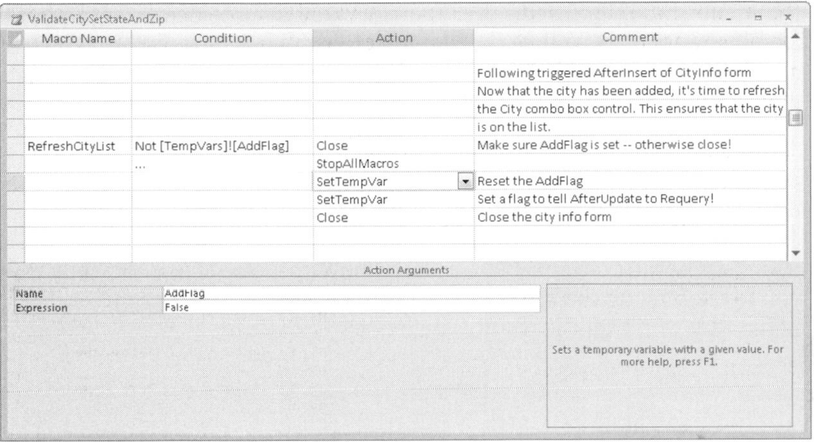


**Figure 18-19** The RefreshCityList macro in the ValidateCitySetStateAndZip macro tests and sets temporary variables.

In the Condition column for the first action in this macro, you can see the following expression:

```
Not [TempVars]![AddFlag]
```

This test checks to see whether the AddFlag temporary variable has been set. If not, then the user must be using the CityInformation form to add a new record independent of the WeddingList form, so the macro closes the form and stops (the StopAllMacros action). If the AddFlag temporary variable is True, the macro resets the AddFlag temporary variable to False, sets another temporary variable (RequeryFlag, not shown in the figure) to let the macro that responds to the AfterUpdate event of the City combo box do a requery, and closes the CityInformation form.

Note the special syntax you need to use to reference a temporary variable anywhere other than in an action specifically related to temporary variables. When you create a temporary variable in a macro, Access adds the variable to the special collection of the database called TempVars. When an object is a member of a collection (Access treats temporary variables as objects), you can reference the object by naming the collection, using an exclamation point separator, and then naming the object. So, to reference a temporary variable in macros, queries, event procedures, and even Visual Basic code, use the following syntax:

```
[TempVars]![<name of temporary variable>]
```

You can have as many as 255 temporary variables defined at any time in your Access 2007 database. By using temporary variables in the various macros in the ValidateCitySetStateAndZip macro object, you can change the way Access executes the various macro actions based on actions taken in other macros.

If you need to clear the value stored in a temporary variable and delete the variable, you can use the RemoveTempVar macro action. The RemoveTempVar action requires only one argument—Name—and it clears any value stored in the temporary variable of that name and then deletes the variable. If you need to delete all temporary variables from memory, you can use the RemoveAllTempVars action. This action requires no arguments because it clears all temporary variables, similar to what would occur if you closed the database.

Although removing a temporary variable technically deletes it from the TempVars collection, you won't get an error if you attempt to reference a temporary variable that doesn't exist. If you attempt to fetch the value of a nonexistent temporary variable, Access returns the value Null. For this reason, you should be careful when naming and using temporary variables. If you set a temporary variable in one macro and then think you're referencing the same variable in another macro but slightly misspell the variable name, you won't get the results you expect.

### Note

Access 2007 allows you to create temporary variables in macros if you save your database in the .mdb file format. If, however, you open the .mdb database with an earlier version of Access—2000, 2002, or 2003—the temporary variables do not function, and you will receive error messages when your macros run. If you have users still using previous Access versions, do not use temporary variables created in macros for your application.

## Trapping Errors in Macros

Access 2007 is the first Access version to support trapping and handling errors within macros. During the normal process of running your application, Access can (and most likely will) encounter errors. Access might encounter errors in your code that it cannot resolve–such as a syntax error in a predicate used to filter a form. In those cases, Access cannot proceed further. Other errors might occur that are not quite so catastrophic but happen in the normal processing of your application. For example, you might use the OnNoData event of a report to display a message box saying no records were found. If your code then cancels the report from opening, Access returns an error if a subsequent action attempts to reference the report that didn't open. If there's no error trap in the macro, Access displays an ugly and confusing dialog box to the user.

To see how error trapping works in Access 2007, open the ErrorTrapExample macro in Design view. We created this simple macro specifically to show you two things–how Access handles an unexpected error with no error trapping and how you can trap and respond to an error. In Figure 18-20, you can see the macro names, conditions, actions, and arguments for this example macro.

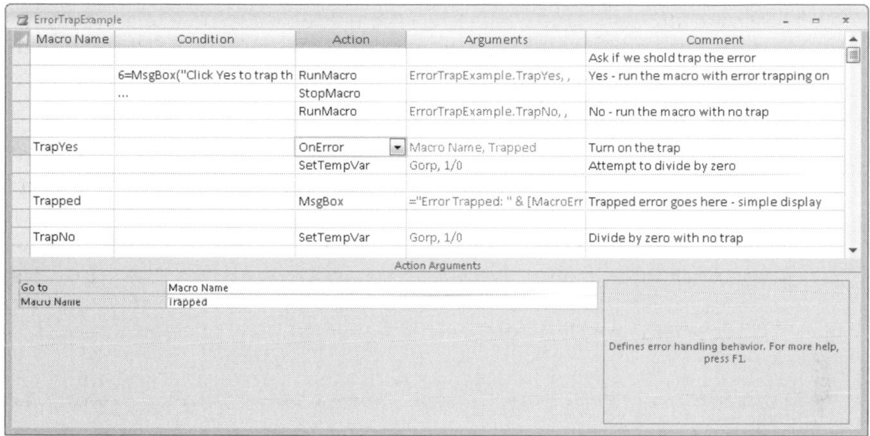

**Figure 18-20** The ErrorTrapExample macro demonstrates error handling in Access 2007.

In the first line of the macro, we call the MsgBox function in the Condition column to ask whether you want to use error trapping. (You can learn more about the settings in the MsgBox function in Table 18-4 on page 932.) If you click the Yes button in the dialog box displayed by MsgBox, the function returns the value 6. So when you click Yes, the condition is True, and the RunMacro action calls the TrapYes macro. If you click No, the condition is False, so the macro executes the second RunMacro that calls the TrapNo macro.

The first action in the TrapYes macro uses the new OnError macro action to tell Access how it should proceed if any error occurs. The OnError action has two arguments—Go To and Macro Name. The options in the Go To argument are Next, Macro Name, and Fail. If you select Next in the Go To argument, Access does not halt the macro when an error occurs—it simply goes on to the next action. If you select Macro Name in the Go To argument, Access runs the macro you specify in the Macro Name argument. If you select Fail, you're basically turning error trapping off.

In all cases, Access records the error number and error description information in the MacroError object. If you have trapped the error by specifying Macro Name or Next, you can examine the error in a Condition statement to determine what action, if any, to take. For simple errors (such as an OpenReport that might be canceled), you can choose Next and check to see whether an error has occurred in the Condition line on the next action. For more complex errors, you should go to another macro that can test for several potential errors that you plan to handle. In this example, we tell Access to run the Trapped macro if any errors occur.

> **Note**
>
> If you specify a macro name in the Go To argument of the OnError action, the macro must exist in the same macro object. You cannot reference a macro in a different macro object when using the OnError action.

The next line in the TrapYes macro uses the SetTempVar action to create a temporary variable named Gorp and set it to an invalid mathematical expression of 1/0—dividing by zero will cause an error. Because we asked Access to trap any error, Access runs the Trapped macro when the error occurs. Although we could have examined the error and perhaps taken some other action, for this simple example we used another MsgBox action to tell Access to display a message containing the error number and description of the error. Click this MsgBox action, and notice the following text in the Message argument:

```
="Error Trapped: " & [MacroError].[Number] & ", " & [MacroError].[Description]
```

All errors in Access have both a unique error number and a description. When an error occurs in a macro, the Number property of the MacroError object contains the error number, and the Description property of the MacroError object contains text describing the error associated with the number. The Message argument of the MsgBox action asks Access to fetch the Number and Description properties and display them in the message.

Finally, the TrapNo macro executes the assignment of an invalid value to a temporary variable without first setting an error trap. To see how this process works, click the Run button in the Tools group on the Design tab. Because the first action contains a call to the MsgBox function in the Condition column, Access displays the message box shown in Figure 18-21 asking whether you want to trap the error as part of evaluating the condition.

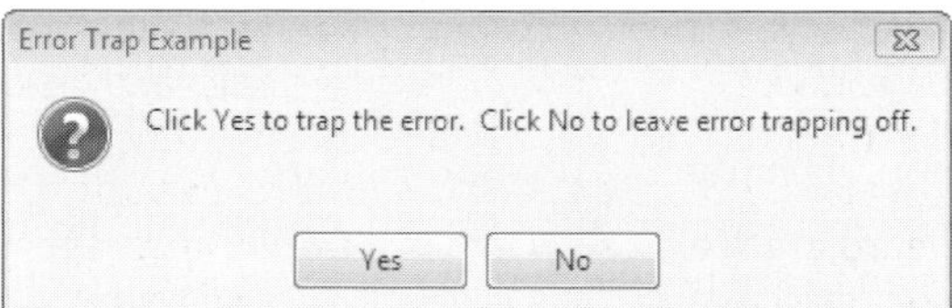


**Figure 18-21** When you run the ErrorTrapExample macro, it first asks you whether you want to trap the error.

Click No to see what happens when the error isn't trapped. First, Access displays a message box telling you the nature of the error, as shown in Figure 18-22.

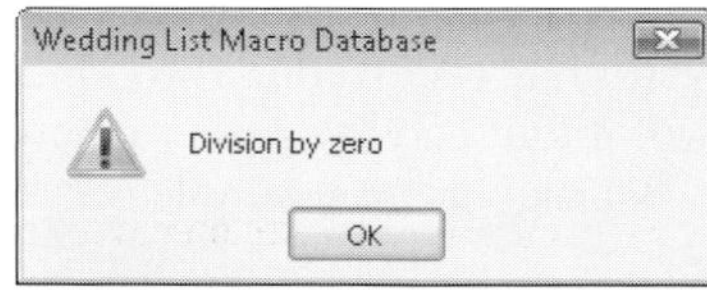


**Figure 18-22** Access cannot divide a number by zero, so it displays an application error message.

Click OK in this message box, and then Access displays the Action Failed dialog box, as shown in Figure 18-23. Not very user friendly, is it? Access displays the Action Failed dialog box whenever it encounters an unhandled error while running a macro. Access displays the specifics of where the error occurred in the Macro Name, Condition, Action Name, and Arguments boxes. Access displays the error number currently stored in the MacroError object in the Error Number box. The 2950 error number indicates that Access encountered an application error and had to display an application error message. As you'll see when we trap the error, this isn't the error number associated with the Divide By Zero error!

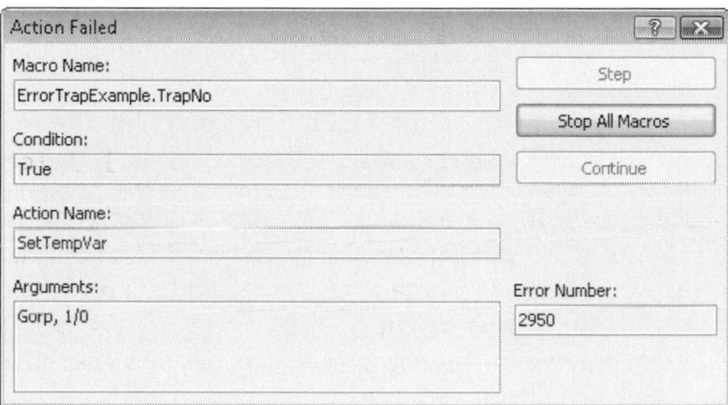


**Figure 18-23** Access displays an Action Failed dialog box if it encounters an unhandled error.

The only button you can click in this dialog box is the Stop All Macros button. When you click this button, Access stops running the macro so that you can continue working in your application. You can imagine the support calls you're going to get from your users if this dialog box appears often in your applications. Click the Stop All Macros button to close the Action Failed dialog box.

Now let's see what happens when the macro traps the error. Run the macro again, and click Yes when the code asks you whether you want to trap the error. This runs the TrapYes macro (shown earlier in Figure 18-20), which executes OnError followed by the SetTempVar that generates an error. Access traps the error and executes the Trapped macro as requested. That macro asks Access to display another message box with the error number and description, as shown in Figure 18-24. Notice that Access displays the correct error number (11) and error description (Division By Zero) in the message text.

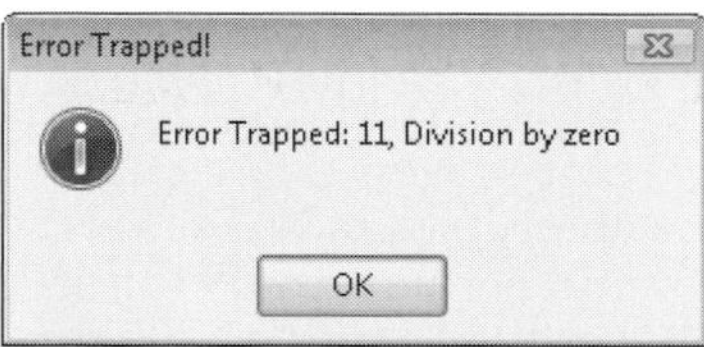


**Figure 18-24** By trapping an error in a macro, you can display a helpful message to the user.

In a completed application, you probably would not need to display the error details to the user, but for debugging your application, the information in the MacroError object can be very useful. For an end user, it could be more informative to display a message such as "While attempting to calculate a value, the application divided a number by zero. Please recheck the numbers you entered before proceeding."

Click OK in the message box, and notice what happens when you do trap the error—nothing! Because we trapped the error, Access does not display the confusing Action Failed dialog box.

Earlier in this chapter you saw the DoReport macro that is used with the PrintOptions form. This macro also uses error trapping to handle the possibility that a report might not contain any records. Close the ErrorTrapExample macro, and then open the DoReport macro in Design view. In the Groups, Alpha, Accepted, and PrintF macros, you can see that we used the OnError action just before each OpenReport action. Scroll down until you can see the PrintF macro, as shown in Figure 18-25.

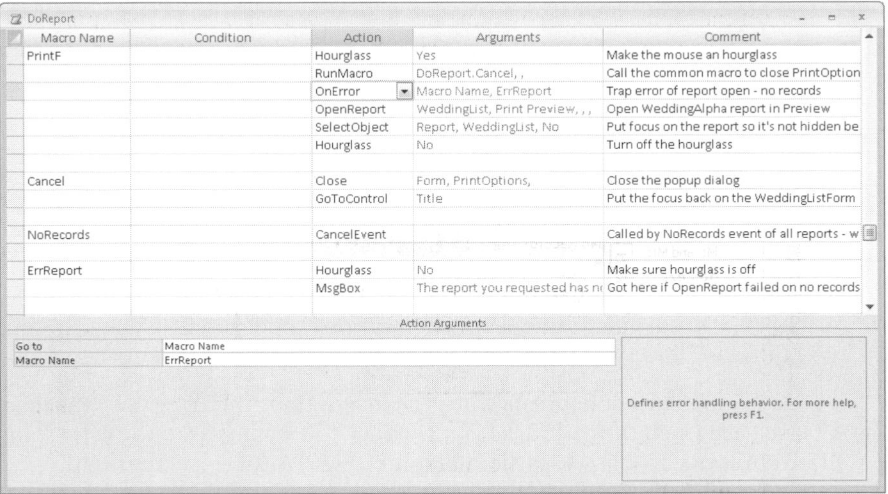


| Macro Name | Condition | Action | Arguments | Comment |
|---|---|---|---|---|
| PrintF | | Hourglass | Yes | Make the mouse an hourglass |
| | | RunMacro | DoReport.Cancel, , | Call the common macro to close PrintOption |
| | | OnError | Macro Name, ErrReport | Trap error of report open - no records |
| | | OpenReport | WeddingList, Print Preview, , , | Open WeddingAlpha report in Preview |
| | | SelectObject | Report, WeddingList, No | Put focus on the report so it's not hidden be |
| | | Hourglass | No | Turn off the hourglass |
| | | | | |
| Cancel | | Close | Form, PrintOptions, | Close the popup dialog |
| | | GoToControl | Title | Put the focus back on the WeddingListForm |
| | | | | |
| NoRecords | | CancelEvent | | Called by NoRecords event of all reports - w |
| | | | | |
| ErrReport | | Hourglass | No | Make sure hourglass is off |
| | | MsgBox | The report you requested has n | Got here if OpenReport failed on no records |

**Figure 18-25** The DoReport macro uses the OnError action to handle the possibility that no records are returned in the report.

The first line of the macro turns the mouse pointer into an hourglass. The second line calls the Cancel macro that closes the PrintOptions form and puts the focus back on the WeddingList form. The third line sets the error trap. We selected Macro Name in the Go To argument and ErrReport in the Macro Name argument to tell Access to go to the ErrReport macro if any errors occur. The fourth line attempts to open the report.

In each of the four reports in this sample database, the On No Data event property specifies the NoRecords macro. When the report has no records, this macro executes the CancelEvent action to prevent the report from opening. If the report opening is canceled, Access encounters an error on the next line of our macro—SelectObject. Access cannot put the focus on a report that isn't opened, so we need to plan for this possibility. Because we're trapping all errors, the user won't see the ugly Action Failed dialog box. Instead, the ErrReport macro runs, and this macro restores the mouse pointer and displays an informative message telling the user that the report requested has no records.

To test how this works, close the DoReport macro, and then open the WeddingList form in Form view. Click the Print button on this form to open the PrintOptions form.

On the PrintOptions form, select List Invitees Who Have Accepted. Unless you have changed the sample data, this report should return no records. Click the Print button to run the PrintIt macro in the DoReport macro group. This macro looks at the option you chose on the PrintOptions form and runs the Accepted macro. That macro attempts to open the WeddingAccepted report with a filter to return only the records where the value in the Accepted field is greater than zero.

Because no records qualify, the NoData event in the WeddingAccepted report runs the NoRecords macro and cancels the opening of the report. Next, the macro attempts to set the focus on the WeddingAccepted report. Because the report is now closed, this causes an error—2489, if you're curious—that Access returns to the macro that attempted to set the focus. Because we turned on error trapping, the ErrReport macro displays a message to inform you that no records were found in the report, as shown in Figure 18-26.

**Figure 18-26** The error handling in the DoReport macro presents an informative message if the report contains no records.

If you want to see what happens when the error isn't trapped, open the DoReport macro object, scroll down to the Accepted macro, type **False** in the Condition column next to the OnError action so that the error trap isn't set, and save the macro. Try to run the report again from the WeddingList form, and you'll see the ugly error messages that result when you don't trap the error. Be sure to remove the False condition from the Accepted macro and save it again so that the application works properly.

If you want to use macros in your application, you should add appropriate error handling using the OnError action. A well-designed Access application should always display helpful messages to users when errors occur.

INSIDE OUT **Clearing the MacroError Object**

The MacroError object contains only the information from the last reported error. Access retains this information in the MacroError object until either the macro stops running, another error occurs, or you run the ClearMacroError action. If you need to continue running your macro after an error is handled and expect to possibly test the MacroError object again (perhaps after setting OnError to Next), you can use the ClearMacroError action to clear the contents of the MacroError object. The ClearMacroError action requires no arguments.

## Understanding Macro Actions That Are Not Trusted

Earlier in this chapter we mentioned that Access 2007 has trusted and not trusted macro actions. As you might recall from Chapter 2, "Exploring the New Look of Access 2007," the Trust Center settings in the Access Options dialog box control whether Access disables certain content in your database. If your database is not trusted, Access might silently disable any potentially malicious macros or VBA code depending upon the Trust Center settings you enabled or disabled. So what exactly is a malicious macro? In Microsoft's terms, a *malicious* macro runs an action that could potentially do harm to your computer or files, such as deleting a file.

Access 2007 separates macro actions into two categories—those that will run in any database, even in a database that is not trusted (*trusted* macros), and those that can run only in a database that is trusted (*not trusted* macros). Note that if you select Enable All Macros in the Trust Center Macro Settings section (not recommend by Microsoft), Access treats all macro actions as trusted even when the database is not trusted.

**Note**

If you are in a corporate network environment, you should check with your Information Technology department to determine whether your company has established guidelines concerning enabling content in Access databases.

Access 2007 recognizes 32 macro actions as potentially unsafe to run in a database that is not trusted. Seven of the actions are not trusted only when you select certain arguments. Table 18-1 lists the macro actions that Access will run only when the database is trusted. The Comments column lists special cases dependent on the arguments you choose or an alternative trusted method you can use.

Table 18-1 **Macro Actions That Are Not Trusted**

| Action | Comments |
|---|---|
| Close | Setting the Save argument to Prompt is trusted. |
| CopyDatabaseFile | |
| CopyObject | |
| DeleteObject | |
| Echo | |
| OpenDataAccessPage | |
| OpenDiagram | |
| OpenForm | Setting the View argument to Design or Layout is not trusted. |
| OpenFunction | |
| OpenModule | |
| OpenQuery | Setting the View argument to Design is not trusted. |
| OpenReport | Setting the View argument to Design or Layout is not trusted. |
| OpenStoredProcedure | |
| OpenTable | Setting the View argument to Design is not trusted. |
| OpenView | |
| Printout | |
| Quit | Setting the Options argument to Prompt is trusted. |
| Rename | |
| RunApp | |
| RunCommand | Commands that affect objects in Design or Layout view are not trusted. |
| RunSavedImportExport | |
| RunSQL | |
| Save | |
| SendKeys | |
| SetValue | Use the trusted SetProperty action instead of SetValue to change the Enabled, Visible, Locked, Left, Top, Width, Height, Fore Color, Back Color, or Caption properties of forms, reports, or controls. |
| SetWarnings | |
| ShowToolbar | |
| TransferDatabase | |

| Action | Comments |
|---|---|
| TransferSharePointList | |
| TransferSpreadsheet | |
| TranferSQLDatabase | |
| TransferText | |

In the Wedding List Macro sample database, you can find a macro that shows you all the macro actions that are not trusted. Open the mcrXmplNotTrustedActions macro in Design view to see all 32 macro actions that are not trusted, as shown in Figure 18-27.

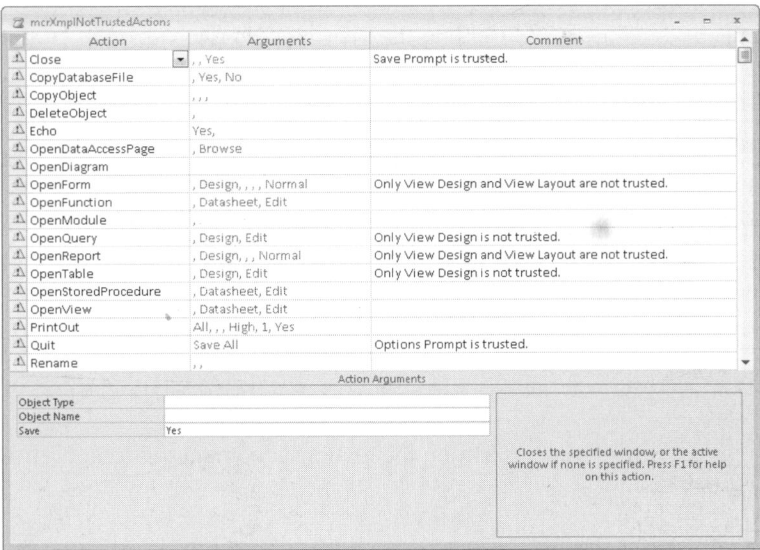


**Figure 18-27** Macro actions that are not trusted display an exclamation mark in the left column of the macro design window.

Note that when you select a macro action or argument that is not trusted, Access displays an exclamation mark on the selector button of the macro line. When you're designing your macros, you can use this visual aid to easily see whether any of your macro actions will not run in a database that is not trusted.

# Making Your Application Come Alive with Macros

Throughout this book, you've learned how to perform common tasks by using Ribbon commands or by finding the object you want in the Navigation Pane and opening it. In working with your database, you've probably also noticed that you perform certain tasks repeatedly or on a regular basis. You can automate these tasks by creating macros to execute the actions you perform and then associating the macros with various form or control events, such as the Current event of a form, the Click event of a command button, or the DblClick event of a text box. In the following sections, you'll use examples from the Wedding List Macro sample database (WeddingMC.accdb) to understand how macros can help automate your application.

## Referencing Form and Report Objects

As you create macros to automate tasks that you repeat frequently, you'll often need to refer to a report, a form, or a control on a form to set its properties or values. Before we dig into some of the macros in the Wedding List Macro, you need to know how to code these references. You can find the syntax for referencing reports, forms, report and form properties, controls, and control properties in the following sections.

### Rules for Referencing Forms and Reports

You can refer to a form or a report by name, but you must first tell Access which *collection* contains the named object. Open forms are in the Forms collection, and open reports are in the Reports collection. To reference a form or a report, you follow the collection name with an exclamation point to separate it from the name of the object to which you are referring. You must enclose an object name that contains blank spaces or special characters in brackets ([ ]). If the object name contains no blanks or special characters, you can simply enter the name. However, it's a good idea to always enclose an object name in brackets so that your name reference syntax is consistent.

For example, you refer to a form named WeddingList as follows:

```
Forms![WeddingList]
```

You refer to a report named WeddingList as follows:

```
Reports![WeddingList]
```

### Rules for Referencing Form and Report Properties

To reference a property of a form or a report, follow the form or report name with a period and the property name. You can see a list of most property names for a form or a report by opening the form or the report in Design view and displaying the property sheet while you have the form or the report selected. With macros, you can change most form or report properties while the form is in Form view or from the Print, Format, and Paint events of a report as Access prints or displays it.

You refer to the Scroll Bars property of a form named CityInformation as follows:

```
Forms![CityInformation].ScrollBars
```

You refer to the Caption property of a report named CityInformation as follows:

```
Reports![CityInformation].Caption
```

**Note**

The names of properties do not contain embedded blank spaces, even though the property sheet shows blanks within names. For example, BackColor is the name of the property listed as Back Color in the property sheet.

## Rules for Referencing Form and Report Controls and Their Properties

To reference a control on a form or a report, follow the form or report name with an exclamation point and then the control name enclosed in brackets. To reference a property of a control, follow the control name with a period and the name of the property. You can see a list of most property names for controls by opening a form or a report in Design view, selecting a control (note that different control types have different properties), and opening its property sheet. You can change most control properties while the form is in Design view.

You refer to a control named State on the WeddingList form as follows:

```
Forms![WeddingList]![State]
```

You refer to the Visible property of a control named Accepted on a report named WeddingList as follows:

```
Reports![WeddingList]![Accepted].Visible
```

## Rules for Referencing Subforms and Subreports

When you embed a subform in a form or a report, the subform is contained in a *subform control*. A subreport embedded in a report is contained in a *subreport control*. You can reference a subform control or a subreport control exactly as you would any other control on a form or a report. For example, suppose you have a subform called RelativesSub embedded in the WeddingList form. You refer to the subform control on the WeddingList form as follows:

```
Forms![WeddingList]![RelativesSub]
```

Likewise, you can reference properties of a subform or a subreport by following the control name with a period and the name of the property. You refer to the Visible property of the RelativesSub subform control as follows:

```
Forms![WeddingList]![RelativesSub].Visible
```

Subform controls have a special Form property that lets you reference the form that's contained in the subform control. Likewise, subreport controls have a special Report property that lets you reference the report contained in the subreport control. You can follow this special property name with the name of a control on the subform or the subreport to access the control's contents or properties. For example, you refer to the LastName control on the RelativesSub subform as follows:

```
Forms![WeddingList]![RelativesSub].Form![LastName]
```

You refer to the FontWeight property of the LastName control as follows:

```
Forms![WeddingList]![RelativesSub].Form![LastName].FontWeight
```

## Opening a Secondary Form

As you learned in Chapter 10, "Using Forms," it's easier to work with data by using a form. You also learned in Chapter 13, "Advanced Form Design," that you can create multiple-table forms by embedding subforms in a main form, thus allowing you to see related data in the same form. However, it's impractical to use subforms in situations such as the following:

- You need three or more subforms to see related data.
- The main form is too small to display the entire subform.
- You need to see the related information only some of the time.

The solution is to use a separate form to see the related data. You can open this form by creating a macro that responds to one of several events. For example, you can use a command button or the DblClick event of a control on the main form to give your users access to the related data in the secondary form. This technique helps reduce screen clutter, makes the main form easier to use, and helps to speed up the main form when you're moving from record to record.

You could use this technique in the WeddingList form. It would be simple to create a macro that would respond to clicking the City Info button by opening the CityInformation form and displaying all records from the CityNames table, including the best airline to take and the approximate flying time from each city to Seattle, Washington. However, if you're talking to your friend Jane in Albuquerque, New Mexico, it would be even more convenient for the CityInformation form to display only Albuquerque-related data, rather than the data for all cities. In the following section, you'll create a macro that opens the CityInformation form based on the city that's displayed for the current record in the WeddingList form.

### Creating the SeeCityInformation Macro

Open the Wedding List Macro sample database (WeddingMC.accdb). Click OK on the opening message so that no objects are opened. Click the arrow on the New Object button in the Other group on the Create tab, and select Macro from the list of three options. (The top half of the New Object button displays the last type of new object created—Macro, Module, or Class Module. If you see the Macro icon in the top half of the New Object button, you can click that button to begin creating a new macro.) When the Macro window opens, collapse the Navigation Pane. Next, click the Macro Names button and the Conditions button in the Show/Hide group on the Design tab to display the Macro Name and Condition columns in the Design window. Although you won't use these columns for this macro, it's a good idea to get in the habit of displaying them because you will use them often when creating new macros.

## INSIDE OUT Always Show Macro Names and Conditions

You can display the Macro Name and Condition columns by default by clicking the Microsoft Office Button, clicking Access Options, clicking the Advanced category, and selecting both the Names Column and Conditions Column check boxes under Show In Macro Design in the Display section. The next time you create a macro, the columns will be displayed automatically.

Figure 18-28 shows the macro you are going to create. (If you simply want to view the macro, it is saved as XmplSeeCityInformation in the sample database.)

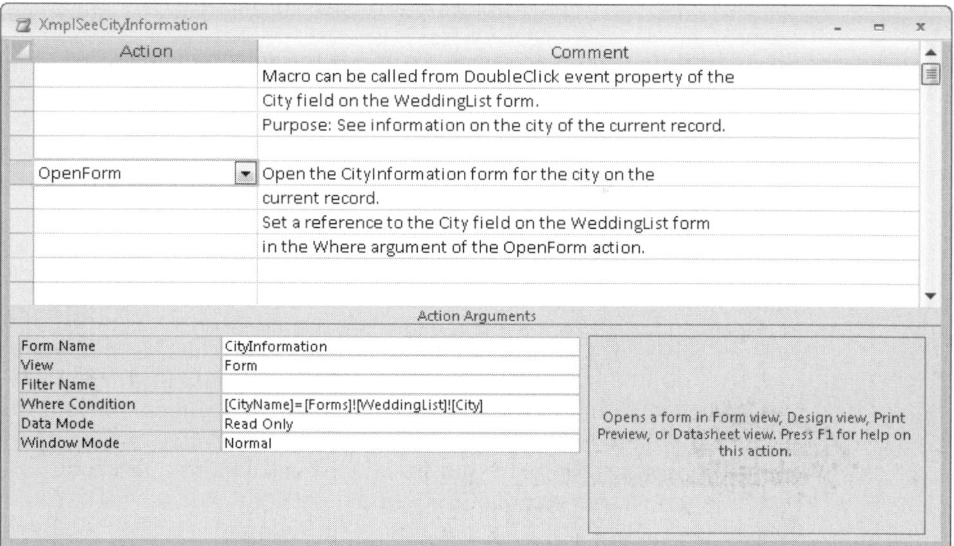


**Figure 18-28** When triggered from an event on the WeddingList form, this macro opens the City-Information form filtered on the city name.

The macro contains only one action, OpenForm. The OpenForm action not only opens the CityInformation form but also applies a filter so that the city that will be displayed matches the city currently displayed in the WeddingList form. Click in the Action column, and then choose OpenForm from the list of actions. In the Action Arguments section of the Macro window, enter the following Where Condition argument:

```
[CityName]=Forms![WeddingList]![City]
```

The Where Condition argument causes the OpenForm action to open the City-Information form showing only the rows in the form's record source whose CityName field equals the value currently shown in the City combo box on the open the Wedding-List form. (Later, you'll learn how to create a macro to synchronize these two forms as you move to different rows in the WeddingList form.)

Set the rest of the action arguments for the OpenForm action, as shown in Figure 18-28. After you finish creating the action for the macro, it's a good idea to use the Comment column to document your macro. Documenting your macro makes it easier to debug, modify, or enhance the macro in the future. It's also easier to read in English what each macro action does rather than have to view the arguments for each action line by line. Refer to Figure 18-28, and enter the information displayed in the Comment column. You can see that we've added comments about the macro in general and about the specific action the macro is designed to perform. Click the Save button on the Quick Access Toolbar, and save the macro as SeeCityInformation.

Next, you can associate the macro with the City combo box control on the WeddingList form. Click the WeddingList form in the Navigation Pane, right-click the name, and click Design View to open the form in Design view. Click the City combo box control, and then click the Property Sheet button in the Tools group on the Design tab. When the property sheet opens, click the Event tab. You'll want to trigger the SeeCityInforma-tion macro from the DblClick event, so click the On Dbl Click property box, and select the macro from the On Dbl Click event property's drop-down list. You'll find a macro called SeeCityInfo already entered here, as shown in Figure 18-29. We created a slightly different version of the macro and saved it in the form so that the application is fully functional when you first open it. You can change the event property to your macro (SeeCityInformation) to test what you've built.

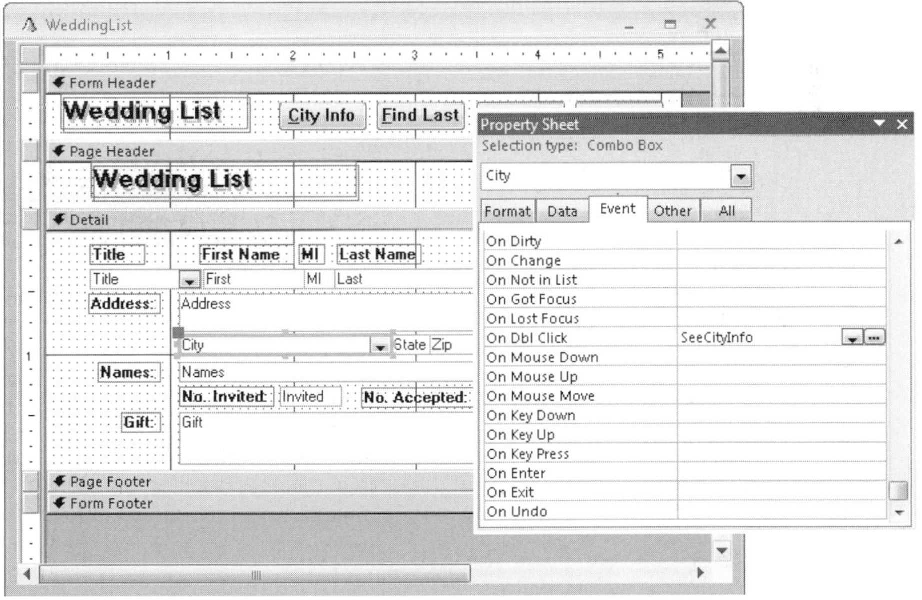


**Figure 18-29** Select the macro you created for the DblClick event of the City combo box control.

You can also associate the macro with the City Info button by changing the button's On Click event property to point to the macro. Click Save on the Quick Access Tool-bar to save your changes, switch to Form view, and then maximize the form. Scroll down one or two records, and double-click the City combo box. The CityInformation form opens, and the data displayed should be for the city in the current record in the WeddingList form. Your screen should look like the one shown in Figure 18-30.

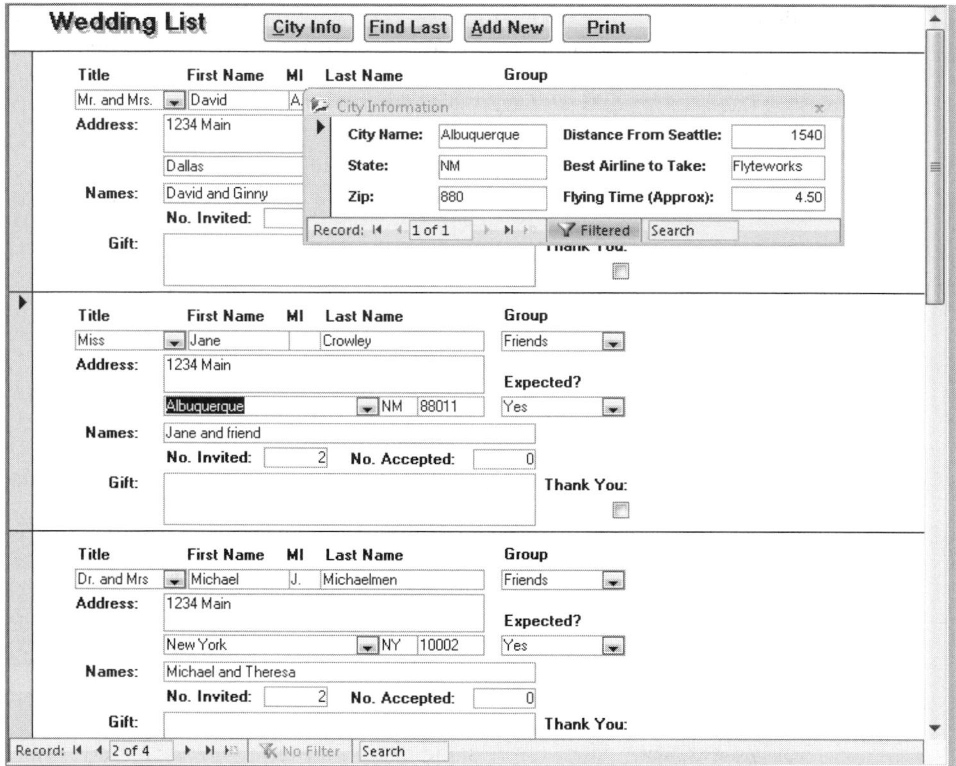


**Figure 18-30** The CityInformation form displays a matching city in the WeddingList form.

Linking two related forms in this manner is very useful, but what happens to the data displayed in the CityInformation form when you move to a new record in the WeddingList form? Try scrolling through the records using the record selector. You'll find that the data in the CityInformation form changes as you move through records in the WeddingList form. The data changes because we've set one of the events on the WeddingList form to execute a macro that keeps the data displayed on the two forms synchronized. In the next section, you'll walk through the steps to re-create this macro yourself.

## Synchronizing Two Related Forms

In the previous section, you learned how to open a secondary form from a main form based on matching values of two related fields in the two forms. In the following sections, you'll create a macro that synchronizes the data in a companion form when the selected record changes in a main form.

## Creating the SyncWeddingAndCity Macro

Click the arrow on the New Object button in the Other group on the Create tab, and click Macro from the list of three options to create a new query. When the macro design window opens, maximize it so that it fills the entire screen. Figure 18-31 shows the actions and comments you'll create for this macro. (You can find this sample macro saved as XmplSyncWeddingAndCity.)

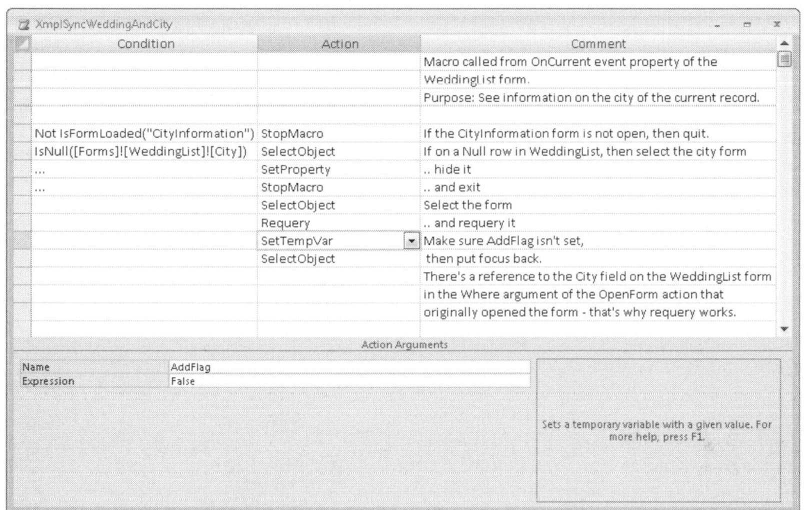
XmplSyncWeddingAndCity
Condition
Action
Comment
Macro called from OnCurrent event property of the
WeddingList form.
Purpose: See information on the city of the current record.
Not IsFormLoaded("CityInformation")
StopMacro
If the CityInformation form is not open, then quit.
IsNull([Forms]![WeddingList]![City])
SelectObject
If on a Null row in WeddingList, then select the city form
...
SetProperty
.. hide it
...
StopMacro
.. and exit
SelectObject
Select the form
Requery
.. and requery it
SetTempVar
Make sure AddFlag isn't set,
SelectObject
then put focus back.
There's a reference to the City field on the WeddingList form
in the Where argument of the OpenForm action that
originally opened the form - that's why requery works.
Action Arguments
Name
AddFlag
Expression
False
Sets a temporary variable with a given value. For more help, press F1.

**Figure 18-31** You'll create these conditions, actions, and comments for the SyncWeddingAndCity macro.

You'll create this macro in the same basic manner that you created the SeeCity-Information macro. Enter the needed conditions in the Condition column, select the actions from the Action column, and type the associated comments in the Comment column. Table 18-2 lists the settings for the actions.

> **Note**
>
> Some code and expression examples in this chapter are too long to fit on a single printed line. A line that ends with the ➘ symbol means that the code shown on the following line should be entered on the same line.

Table 18-2 **Actions, Arguments, and Settings in SyncWeddingAndCity**

| Condition | Action | Argument | Setting |
|---|---|---|---|
| Not IsFormLoaded➘ ("CityInformation") | StopMacro | | |
| IsNull([Forms]!➘ [WeddingList]!➘ [City]) | SelectObject | Object Type | Form |
| | | Object Name | CityInformation |
| ... | | In Database Window | No |
| ... | SetProperty | Control Name | |
| | | Property | Visible |
| | | Value | 0 |
| | StopMacro | | |
| | SelectObject | Object Type | Form |
| | | Object Name | CityInformation |
| | | In Database Window | No |
| | Requery | | |
| | SetTempVar | Name | AddFlag |
| | | Expression | False |
| | SelectObject | Object Type | Form |
| | | Object Name | WeddingList |
| | | In Database Window | No |

This macro has a couple of conditions that determine which parts of the macro execute. The first condition uses the IsFormLoaded function, which is included in the modUtility module of the Wedding List Macro database. This function checks to see whether a form (whose name you've provided to the function) is currently open. (The form can be hidden.) The syntax for the function is IsFormLoaded("*formname*"), where *formname* is the name of the form in question. You must enclose the name of the form in double quotation marks in order for the function to work. The *Not* before the function expression tells Access to evaluate the converse of the True/False value returned from the function. So, this condition will be true only if the form is *not* loaded. If the companion CityInformation form isn't open, there's nothing to synchronize, so the macro action on this line—StopMacro—executes and the macro ends.

Now that we know the companion CityInformation is open, we need to decide whether the value on which that form is filtered is valid. Remember, when you created the SeeCityInformation macro that opens the CityInformation form, you included a Where Condition to filter what's displayed in the CityInformation form to match the city in the current record in the WeddingList form. However, it's a bad idea to reference an empty value in a Where Condition argument. In fact, in some cases you'll get an error message. When you move beyond the last row in the WeddingList form or click New Record under the Go To button in the Find group on the Home tab, you'll be in a new blank row in which the City field has no value. In this case if you force the CityInformation form to refresh, it will go blank because it's a read-only form and there will be no rows returned if the filter compares to an empty value.

It probably makes more sense to test for an empty, or Null, value and hide the companion form if you're in a new row in the WeddingList form. The second line in this macro uses the IsNull built-in function to check for this condition. If City is Null, the macro hides the CityInformation form by setting the value of the Visible property to 0 (or false), and then the macro ends. On the third line, the ellipsis (...) in the Condition column tells Access to run this action only if the previous condition is true. This lets you enter the condition only once—and Access tests the condition only once. In this case, if the City is Null, Access runs not only the SetProperty action on line 3 but also the StopMacro action on line 4—which ends macro execution at this point. Note that the form is *still* open even though you can't see it. If you move back to a row in the WeddingList form that contains data, this macro executes again, but the actions to hide the CityInformation form and to stop will be skipped because the City field won't be Null anymore.

The CityInformation form displays the city details for the current record in the WeddingList form because your macro opened the CityInformation form with a filter pointing to the City control on the WeddingList form. However, the CityInformation form doesn't "know" when you move to a different record in the WeddingList form, so Access never reapplies the filter. Access does save the Where Condition argument you specified in the Filter property of the CityInformation form. To display the appropriate city information when the user moves to a new record in the WeddingList form, all you need to do is requery the CityInformation form to make Access reevaluate the filter. The macro selects the CityInformation form to make sure it has the focus (this also reveals the form if it was hidden) and then executes a Requery action with no value specified in the Control Name argument. With no control name specified, Access knows to requery whatever form or report has the focus.

Finally, the SetTempVar action sets a value that's tested by other macros, and the SelectObject command ensures that the form has the focus after setting the value of the AddFlag temporary variable. We'll explain more about using SetTempVar in "Passing Status Information Between Linked Forms" on page 934.

After you have the synchronization macro you need, save it as SyncWeddingAndCity. The last step is to associate the macro with the Current event of the WeddingList form. To do that, right-click the WeddingList form in the Navigation Pane, and click Design View to open the form in Design view. Click the Property Sheet button in the Tools group on the Design tab to open the property sheet for the form, and then click the On Current property box. Use the list to select your SyncWeddingAndCity macro. (You'll find the example XmplSyncWeddingAndCity macro set in this property in the form.) Your screen should look like the one shown in Figure 18-32.

When you finish, save and close the form. Open the form in Form view, double-click the City combo box control, and move to the second record. Your screen should look like the one shown in Figure 18-30, assuming that Jane Crowley's record is the current one.

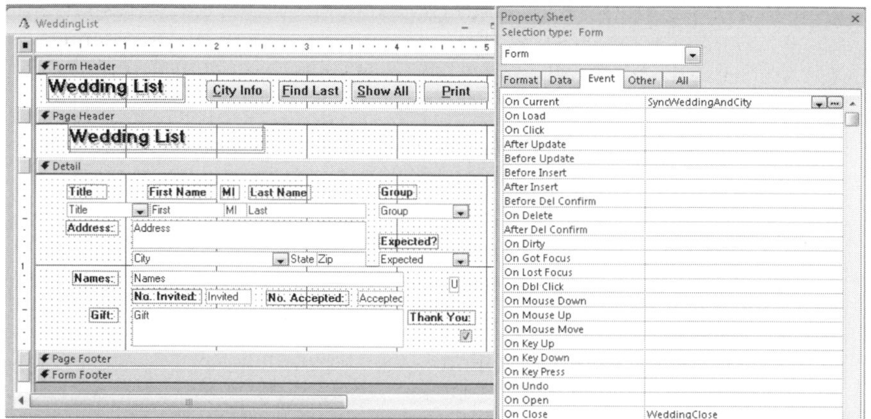


**Figure 18-32** Associate the SyncWeddingAndCity macro with the On Current event property of the WeddingList form.

Test the macro by moving through the records in the WeddingList form. As you move from record to record, the data in the CityInformation form should change to reflect the city displayed in the current record of the WeddingList form. If you move to the blank record at the end of the recordset, the CityInformation form disappears. Move back to a row containing data, and it reappears!

Using a macro to synchronize two forms containing related data is a technique that works well with almost any set of forms, and you can use it in a number of situations. In the next section, you'll learn how to create a more complex macro set of named macros within a macro object, also sometimes referred to as a *macro group*. When you group macros by task, you'll see that this is a good way to organize your work and to keep from cluttering your database with dozens of macro objects.

## Validating Data and Presetting Values

Two tasks you'll commonly automate in your applications are validating data that a user enters in a field and automatically setting values for specific fields. You'll now explore several macro objects saved in the sample database and learn how they perform these tasks on both the WeddingList form and the CityInformation form.

### Validating Data

A problem you'll often encounter when you create database applications is ensuring that the data the users enter is valid. Three types of invalid data are unknown entries, misspelled entries, and multiple versions of the same entry:

- **Unknown entries** A good example of this error is an entry such as *AX* in a state field. No state name is abbreviated as *AX*, but a user who tries to enter *AZ* might accidentally hit the X key instead of the Z key.
- **Misspelled entries** This sort of error is quite common among users with poor typing or spelling skills and among very fast typists. In this case, you might see entries such as *Settle*, *Seatle*, or *Saettle* for *Seattle*.

- **Multiple versions** These errors are common in poorly designed databases and in databases that are shared by a number of users. You might see entries such as *ABC Company, Inc.*; *ABC Company, Incorporated*; *ABC Co., Inc.*; or *A B C Company Inc.*

You can use macros to validate data and help reduce errors. In the next section, you'll create a macro for the WeddingList form that validates the city that the user enters in the City field. If the city doesn't exist in the CityNames table, the macro then executes the following steps:

1. It displays a message indicating that the city is currently unlisted and asks whether the user wants to enter a new city name.
2. If the user wants to create a new city record, another macro runs that opens the CityInformation form in Data Entry mode and copies the city name the user just typed.
3. If the user successfully saves a new row, a macro associated with the AfterInsert event of the CityInformation form sets a temporary variable.
4. Back in the WeddingList form, the city name gets revalidated, and if the city entry is a new one, a macro triggered by the AfterUpdate property of the City field sets the combo box to the new name. When the city name is validated, this macro also automatically enters the state name and the first three digits of the ZIP Code.

## Understanding the ValidateCitySetStateAndZip Macro Group

In the Navigation Pane, find the ValidateCitySetStateAndZip macro, and open it in Design view. Be sure the Macro Name and Condition columns are displayed. Figure 18-33 shows the first macro and its associated actions.

ValidateCitySetStateAndZip

| Macro Name | Condition | Action | Arguments | Comment |
|---|---|---|---|---|
| | | | | Macro called from BeforeUpdate of City on WeddingListForm |
| | | | | Purpose: Validate city entered |
| | | | | If the city the user entered is unlisted, then.. |
| TestCity | IsNull(DLookUp("[CityName]", | CancelEvent | | Cancel the update |
| | ... | RunMacro | ValidateCitySetState | .. and run a secondary macro to ask if they want |
| | | | | to open the edit form to add a new one. |
| | | | | |
| AskEdit | 6<>MsgBox("The city you ente | StopAllMacros | | Ask 'em if they want to enter a new one, if not "YES", then exit |
| | IsFormLoaded("CityInformatio | Close | Form, CityInformati | If CityInfo open, close it first |
| | | OpenForm | CityInformation, For | ... then open the CityInformation form in Add mode. |
| | | SetValue | [Forms]![CityInform | ... and paste the new city name onto the form. |
| | | GoToControl | State | Move to the state field. |
| | | SetTempVar | AddFlag, True | .. and set a hidden flag to show we're in insert mode! |

Action Arguments

| | |
|---|---|
| Macro Name | ValidateCitySetStateAndZip.AskEdit |
| Repeat Count | |
| Repeat Expression | |

Runs a macro. You can use this action to run a macro from within another macro, repeat a macro, run a macro based on a certain condition, or attach a macro to a custom menu command. Press F1 for help on this action.

**Figure 18-33** This figure shows the Macro window for the first two macros in the ValidateCitySetStateAndZip macro group.

The first three lines of the macro are comments, and TestCity is the name of the first macro in the object. You can see the actions for this macro listed in Table 18-3.

**Table 18-3 Actions, Arguments, and Settings in the TestCity Macro**

| Action | Argument | Setting |
|---|---|---|
| CancelEvent | | |
| RunMacro | Macro Name | ValidateCitySetStateAndZip.AskEdit |

To understand how this macro works, let's take a look at the condition that validates the city name. What we want to do is look up the name just entered in the CityName field to find out whether it exists in the CityNames table. If it doesn't exist, the first line of the macro executes a CancelEvent action. The second line then calls another macro that we'll examine later.

To see this condition easily, click the first line of the macro in the Condition column. Press Shift+F2 to open the expression in the Zoom box, as shown in Figure 18-34.

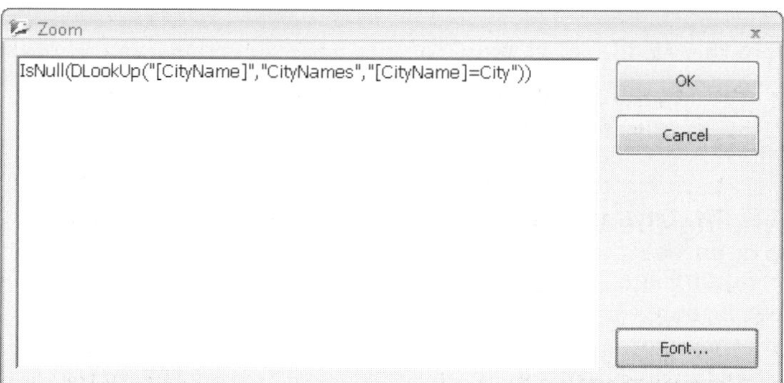


**Figure 18-34** The conditional expression in the TestCity macro uses the DLookup function to try to find the city in the CityNames table.

This condition uses two built-in functions: DLookup and IsNull. The DLookup function looks up the city name in the CityNames table. The IsNull function checks the return value of the DLookup function. If the DLookup function doesn't find the city name, it returns a Null value. This causes the IsNull function to return a True value because the return value of the DLookup function is indeed Null. If no row in the CityNames table matches the current city name in the WeddingList form, Access then executes the action associated with this condition because the condition evaluated to True. In this case, the CancelEvent macro action tells Access not to store the new value in the CityName field. By including an ellipsis (...) in the Condition column of the second action, you tell Access to run the second action only if the previous condition is true. (When you use an ellipsis, you enter the condition only once, and Access performs the evaluation only once.) So if the city doesn't exist in the CityNames table, the RunMacro action on the second line calls the AskEdit macro, which we'll look at in a moment.

On the other hand, if the DLookup function does find the city name, it returns the city name to the IsNull function. The IsNull function then returns a value of False because the return value of the DLookup function is not Null. Access disregards the action associated with this condition. Because you included an ellipsis on the second condition line, the False evaluation applies there also, so the macro ends without taking any further action.

What's the point of all of this? If you open the WeddingList form in Design view, click the City combo box, and look at its event properties, you'll find this macro "wired" into the Before Update property. If you remember from the previous chapter, you can use the BeforeUpdate event of a form or control to verify what's about to be saved. If the data is not valid, you can cancel the event to tell Access not to save the change. This is exactly what the first line of this macro is doing.

When you don't cancel a BeforeUpdate event on a control, Access accepts the changes and gives you a chance to look at the result in the AfterUpdate event. The AfterUpdate event isn't what you want to use to validate data because the data has already been saved, but it's perfect for filling in other fields on the form based on what the user just entered. As you'll see later, this application uses AfterUpdate on this control to fill in the correct state and part of the ZIP Code.

INSIDE OUT

### Why Aren't We Using the NotInList Event to Test for a New City Name?

The NotInList event occurs when the user types a name that's not in the row source of a combo box. The CityNames table is the row source of the City combo box, so NotInList seems to be an ideal choice to detect a name that's not in the CityNames table. But for NotInList to work properly, you need to be able to return a response code to the event to let Access know whether you've handled the problem and inserted a new city name. You can do that only in Visual Basic code, not in a macro. We set the Limit To List property of the combo box to No so that the NotInList event never happens. By trapping the problem in the BeforeUpdate event of the combo box, we can test the value and take appropriate action without having to return a response code to Access. As you'll learn later in the Visual Basic chapters, the NotInList event is a much better choice as long as you can return a response code.

So what happens if the user enters a city name that's not yet in the database? The AskEdit macro runs, and the first step it takes is to evaluate another condition. As you'll learn in later chapters, this sort of IF...THEN...IF logic testing is much easier to do with procedures written in Visual Basic. With macros, you have to do the first test in one macro, and if that returns a True value, you have to call another nested macro to perform a further test.

The condition on the first line of the AskEdit macro is as follows:

```
6<>MsgBox("The city you entered is not in the ➥
   database. Do you want to enter a new one?",36)
```

You've seen the MsgBox action before. This condition uses a built-in function called MsgBox that's a lot more powerful. The MsgBox function lets you not only display a message but also specify what icon you want displayed, and it provides several options for buttons to display in the message box. You set these options by adding number selections and providing the result as the second argument to MsgBox. In this case, 36 is the sum of 32, which asks for a question icon, and 4, which requests Yes and No buttons. (Intuitive, isn't it?) You can find all the option settings by searching for MsgBox Function in Access Help. For your convenience, we've listed all the option settings for the MsgBox function in Table 18-4. In addition, the function returns an integer value depending on the button the user clicks in the message box. If you look at the MsgBox Function help topic, you'll find out that when the user clicks Yes, MsgBox returns the value 6. Table 18-5 shows you the MsgBox return value settings. So if the user doesn't click Yes, the first line of this macro—a StopAllMacros action—executes, and the macro ends. If the user does click Yes, the rest of the macro executes. Table 18-6 lists all the actions and arguments for this macro.

**Table 18-4 Option Settings for the MsgBox Function**

| Value | Meaning |
|---|---|
| **Button Settings (Choose One)** | |
| 0 | OK button only |
| 1 | OK and Cancel buttons |
| 2 | Abort, Retry, and Ignore buttons |
| 3 | Yes, No, and Cancel buttons |
| 4 | Yes and No buttons |
| 5 | Retry and Cancel buttons |
| **Icon Settings (Choose One)** | |
| 0 | No icon |
| 16 | Critical (red X) icon |
| 32 | Warning query (question mark) icon |
| 48 | Warning message (exclamation point) icon |
| 64 | Information message (letter *i*) icon |
| **Default Button Settings (Choose One)** | |
| 0 | First button is the default |
| 256 | Second button is the default |
| 512 | Third button is the default |

**Table 18-5 Return Values for the MsgBox Function**

| Value | Meaning |
|---|---|
| 1 | OK button clicked |
| 2 | Cancel button clicked |
| 3 | Abort button clicked |
| 4 | Retry button clicked |
| 5 | Ignore button clicked |
| 6 | Yes button clicked |
| 7 | No button clicked |

**Table 18-6 Actions, Arguments, and Settings in the AskEdit Macro**

| Action | Argument | Setting |
|---|---|---|
| StopAllMacros | | |
| Close | Object Type | Form |
| | Object Name | CityInformation |
| | Save | Prompt |
| OpenForm | Form Name | CityInformation |
| | View | Form |
| | Data Mode | Add |
| | Window Mode | Normal |
| SetValue | Item | [Forms]![CityInformation]![CityName] |
| | Value | [Forms]![WeddingList]![City] |
| GoToControl | Control Name | State |
| SetTempVar | Name | AddFlag |
| | Expression | True |

The AskEdit macro contains several actions that Access executes if the user enters the data for a new city name and responds by clicking Yes in the MsgBox that asks whether the user wants to add the new city. The macro uses the IsFormLoaded function you saw earlier to determine whether the CityInformation form is open. If it is, the macro instructs Access to close the form. Next, Access opens the CityInformation form in Add mode and copies the city name from the WeddingList form to the CityName field of the CityInformation form by using the SetValue action. (Note that SetValue has an exclamation mark icon on the selection button to the left of the action line indicating Access will not run this action in a database that is not trusted.) SetValue inserts the city name the user typed for user convenience and to ensure that the user starts with the city name just entered. After the macro copies the city name to the CityName field, it tells Access to move the focus to the State field using the GoToControl action. Finally, the macro creates a temporary variable called AddFlag and sets the value to True to indicate that the CityInformation form is now opened in Data Entry mode. The macro attached to the AfterInsert event checks this temporary variable to determine whether it should notify the AfterUpdate event of the City control on the WeddingList form to refresh its list.

## Passing Status Information Between Linked Forms

As you just saw, the AskEdit macro creates a temporary variable called AddFlag to tell the CityInformation form's AfterInsert event macro that the WeddingList form needs to know whether a new row has been added successfully. Likewise, when the user adds a new row using the CityInformation form, the macro that runs in response to an AfterInsert event (the event that Access uses to let you know when a new row has been added via a form) needs to check the flag and pass an indicator back to the macro that responds to the AfterUpdate event of the City combo box on the WeddingList form. You'll learn in later chapters that you can also do this sort of "status indicator" passing by using variables in Visual Basic procedures.

Figure 18-35 shows the macro you need in order to respond to the AfterInsert event of the CityInformation form. You might recall from the previous chapter that Access triggers this event right after it has saved a new row. You could save the row by clicking Save in the Records group on the Home tab, moving to a new row, or closing the form. The first line has a condition that tests to be sure that the user asked to add a new row. The condition is as follows:

```
Not [TempVars]![AddFlag]
```

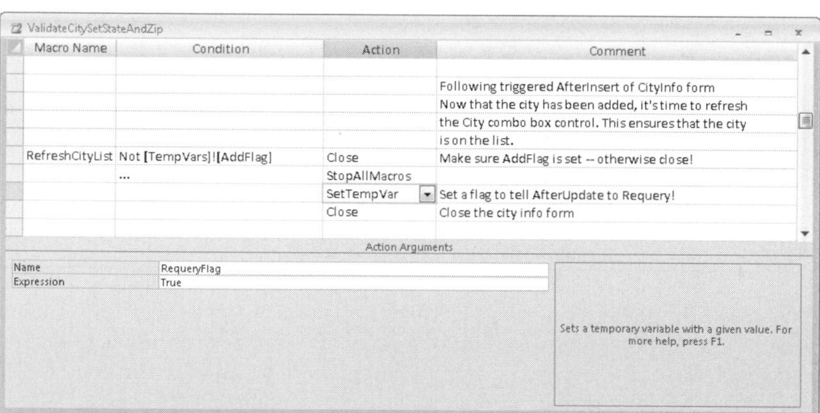


**Figure 18-35** The RefreshCityList macro sets a temporary variable to indicate a requery is needed.

If the AddFlag temporary variable is not true, the first action closes the form, and the StopAllMacros action causes the macro to end. If the variable is true, the SetTempVar action creates another temporary variable called RequeryFlag and sets the flag to let the macro that responds to the AfterUpdate event of the City combo box know that it must refresh the list in the combo box at its earliest opportunity. Finally, the macro closes the CityInformation form. Remember that the AfterInsert event could be triggered as a result of clicking the form's Close button after entering new data. Normally, you would expect an error if you try to execute a Close command while the form is already in the process of closing (you will get an error in Visual Basic). Because Access assumes that macros are most often used by beginning programmers, it is kind enough not to generate any error from either of the Close actions in this macro if this is the case.

If the user triggers the AfterInsert event by moving to another row, closing the form makes sense after adding the one row you need. If the user closes the form without entering any new data, the AfterInsert event won't happen. The user will be back in the WeddingList form with the unmatched city data still typed in the City combo box. If the user attempts to save the unmatched name again, the BeforeUpdate event runs the TestCity macro that cancels the update when the city isn't in the CityNames table. The user must either add the new value or enter a value in the list.

As a final touch, the SetTempVar action in the SyncWeddingAndCity macro that you created in Figure 18-31 sets the AddFlag temporary variable to False when you move to a new row on the WeddingList form. When you have just moved to a new row, you clearly aren't worried about adding a new row to the CityNames table. Also, there's a SelectObject action in the macro to make sure the focus is back on the WeddingList form after the macro updates the temporary variable.

## Presetting Values

Validating data is just one of the many ways you can ensure data integrity in a database. Presetting values for certain fields is another way. Although you can set the Default property of a field, sometimes you'll need to set the value of a field based on the value of another field in a form. For example, you'll want to set the values of the State field and the Zip field in the WeddingList form based on the value of the City field. You can accomplish this with a macro.

In this section, you'll examine actions in the ValidateCitySetStateAndZip macro group that set the values of the State and Zip fields in the WeddingList form based on the city entered. If you scroll down the macro design window, you can see the additional actions, as shown in Figure 18-36.

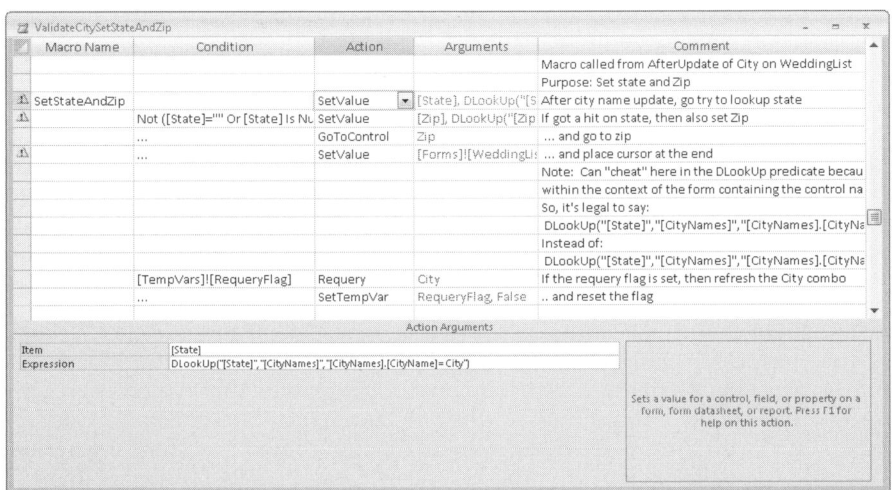


**Figure 18-36** The SetStateAndZip macro uses SetValue actions to automatically fill in the State and Zip controls.

Table 18-7 lists the actions and arguments in this macro.

**Table 18-7 Actions, Arguments, and Settings in the SetStateAndZip Macro**

| Action | Argument | Setting |
|---|---|---|
| SetValue | Item | [State] |
| | Expression | DLookup("[State]","[CityNames]", ➥ "[CityNames].[CityName]=City") |
| SetValue | Item | [Zip] |
| | Expression | DLookup("[Zip]","[CityNames]", ➥ "[CityNames].[CityName]=City") |
| GoToControl | Control Name | Zip |
| SetValue | Item | [Forms]![WeddingList]! ➥ [Zip].[SelStart] |
| | Expression | 255 |
| Requery | Control Name | City |
| SetTempVar | Name | RequeryFlag |
| | Expression | False |

When the user enters a valid city name, the first SetValue action uses the DLookup function to retrieve the matching State value from the CityNames table. If the value for State isn't blank or Null, the second SetValue action retrieves the first three digits of the ZIP Code from the table, moves the focus to the Zip control with a GoToControl action, and sets the SelStart property of the Zip control to a high value (255) to place the insertion point at the end of the data displayed in the control. Pressing the F2 key after you move to a control also places the insertion point at the end of the data in the control, so you could use a SendKeys action here instead. However, setting the SelStart property is faster and more reliable. (See Access Help for more information about the SelStart property.) The user can now enter the last two digits of the ZIP Code on the main form before moving on to the Expected field. The Condition column for the second action is as follows:

```
Not ([State]="" Or [State] Is Null)
```

The set of macros in this macro object is now complete. You can see how these macros help implement data integrity by validating data and presetting specific values. This decreases the likelihood that users will make errors. Now you'll see how to associate these macros with the appropriate events on the WeddingList form and the CityInformation form.

Right-click the WeddingList form in the Navigation Pane, and click Design View to open the form in Design view. Click the City combo box control, and then click the Property Sheet button in the Tools group on the Design tab. After the property sheet opens, click the Event tab. You should see the ValidateCitySetStateAndZip.TestCity macro associated with the BeforeUpdate event of the City combo box. Remember, this is the macro you should run to verify whether the user has entered a valid city name. The AfterUpdate event property should be set to ValidateCitySetStateAndZip.SetStateAndZip.

This macro automatically sets the matching State and Zip values whenever the user specifies a new City value. Figure 18-37 shows the result.

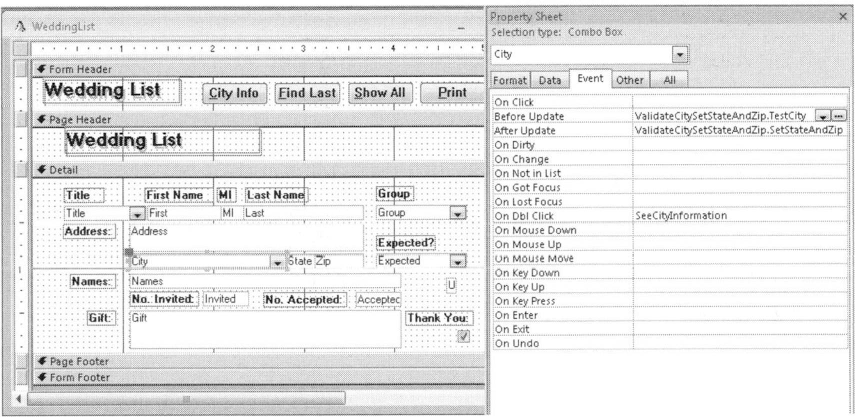


**Figure 18-37** The Before Update and After Update event properties for the City control on the WeddingList form are set to run macros in the ValidateCitySetStateAndZip macro.

Close the WeddingList form. Open the CityInformation form in Design view, and click the Property Sheet button in the Tools group on the Design tab to open the property sheet. The ValidateCitySetStateAndZip.RefreshCityList macro is set in the form's After Insert event property, as shown in Figure 18-38. Recall from the previous chapter that you could also use the form's AfterUpdate event to see changed data. However, in this case you don't care about existing rows that change. The AfterInsert event is more appropriate because Access fires this event only when a *new* row is saved, but not when an existing row is saved.

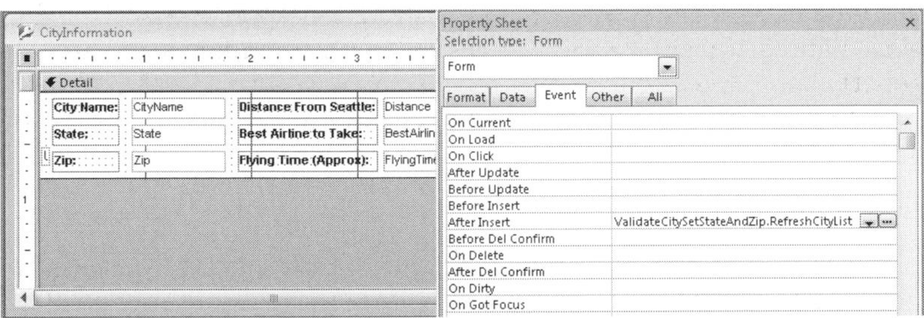


**Figure 18-38** The ValidateCitySetStateAndZip.RefreshCityList macro executes when the AfterInsert event of the CityInformation form occurs.

Close the CityInformation form. Now that you've verified that the macros are associated with the appropriate objects and events, you're ready to test how this works. Begin by closing all open objects, and then double-click the AutoexecXmpl macro in the Navigation Pane to run the macro and open the WeddingList form. Move to a new record in the WeddingList form, and enter a title, a name, an address, and a group. When the insertion point moves to the City combo box, enter **Miami**. After you press Enter or Tab, Access runs the ValidateCitySetStateAndZip.TestCity macro. Because this city doesn't currently exist in the CityNames table, the AskEdit macro runs, and Access displays the message box shown in Figure 18-39.

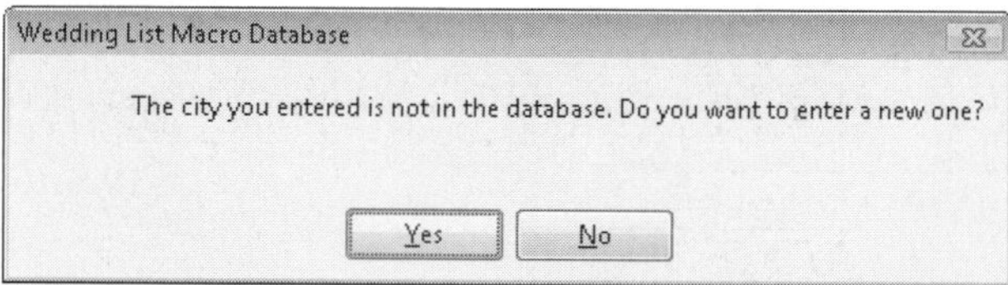


**Figure 18-39** The AskEdit macro displays a message box if you enter a new city.

After you click the Yes button, Access executes the remaining actions in the macro. Access opens the CityInformation form in Data Entry mode, copies the city name to the CityName text box control on the form, and moves the insertion point to the State field. Figure 18-40 shows the result of these actions.

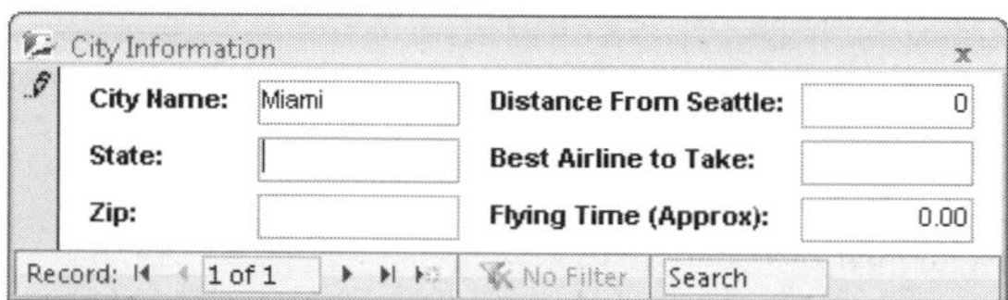


**Figure 18-40** The AskEdit macro then opens the CityInformation form where you can enter the details of the new city.

After you enter information in the remaining fields and close the CityInformation form, the AfterInsert event of the form triggers the ValidateCitySetStateAndZip.RefreshCity-List macro. After the form closes, Access moves the focus back to the WeddingList form. When you finally leave the now valid City control, the macro triggered by After-Update requeries the City combo box control and automatically updates the State and Zip fields.

## Converting Your Macros to Visual Basic

As you'll learn in the rest of this book, Visual Basic, rather than macros, is what you should use to automate any serious applications. If you've spent some time getting familiar with programming in Access in macros but would now like to move to Visual Basic, you're in luck! Access provides a handy tool to convert the actions in macros called from events on your forms and reports to the equivalent Visual Basic statements.

To see how this works, open the WeddingList form in Design view. On the Database Tools tab, in the Macro group, click the Convert Form's Macros To Visual Basic button, as shown in Figure 18-41.

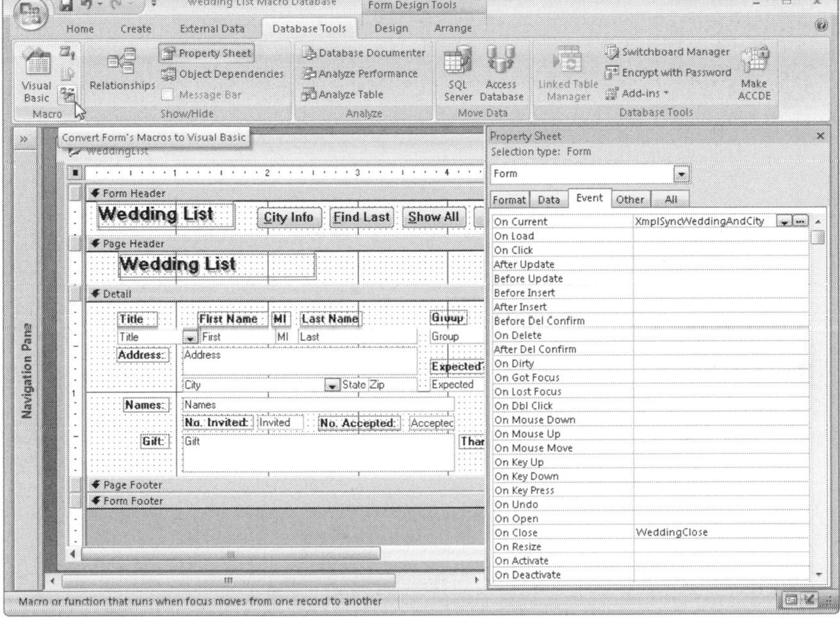


**Figure 18-41** Access includes a command to convert a form's macros to Visual Basic.

In the next dialog box, the Convert tool offers you the option to insert error-handling code and to copy the comments from your macros into the new code. You should leave both check boxes selected and then click Convert to change your macros to Visual Basic. After the tool is finished, you should see all macro references in event properties changed to [Event Procedure]. Click the On Current event property for the WeddingList form, and then click the Build button (...) to the right of the property. You'll see the converted code displayed, as shown in Figure 18-42.

> **Note**
>
> Converting your macros to Visual Basic does not delete any of your original macros. However, Access removes any embedded macros assigned to form and control properties and converts them to Visual Basic. Also, the tool doesn't convert any macros referenced by a RunMacro command—you'll have to do that yourself.

**In Chapter 20, we'll introduce you to some enhancements we made to the Wedding List sample database after we converted all the macros to Visual Basic using this wizard. You can find this version of the database saved as WeddingList.accdb on the companion CD.**

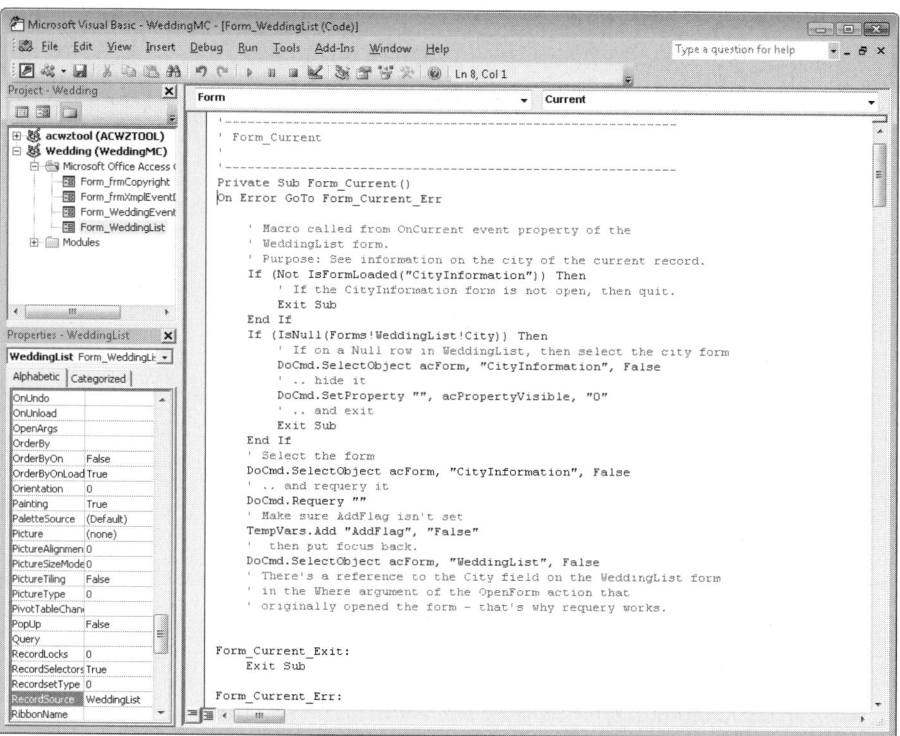

Figure 18-42 Access converted the macro from the Current event of the WeddingList form to Visual Basic.

Article 6, on the companion CD, summarizes all the actions you can include in macros. You'll find it useful to browse through that article to become familiar with the available actions and events before going on to the next two chapters, where you'll learn about Visual Basic and where you'll see how the other sample applications are automated using Visual Basic.

CHAPTER 19

# Understanding Visual Basic Fundamentals



In this chapter, you'll learn how to create, edit, and test Microsoft Visual Basic code in your Microsoft Office Access 2007 applications. The chapter covers the following major topics:

- The Visual Basic Editor (VBE) and its debugging tools
- Variables and constants and how to declare them
- The primary object models defined in access—the Access model, the Data Access Objects (DAO) model, and the ActiveX Data Objects (ADO) model.

  You'll need to understand these models to be able to manipulate objects such as forms, form controls, and recordsets in your code.
- Visual Basic procedural statements
  - Function and Sub statements
  - Property Get, Property Let, and Property Set (for use in class modules) statements
  - Flow-control statements, including Call, Do, For, If, and Select Case
  - DoCmd and RunCommand statements
  - On Error statements
- A walk-through of some example code you'll find in the sample databases

If you're new to Visual Basic, you might want to read through the chapter from beginning to end, but keep in mind that the large section in the middle of the chapter on procedural statements is designed to be used primarily as a reference. If you're already familiar with Visual Basic, you might want to review the sections on the Visual Basic Editor and the object models, and then use the rest of the chapter as reference material.

**Note**

You can find many of the code examples from this chapter in the modExamples module in the Contacts.accdb and Housing.accdb sample databases on the companion CD.

# The Visual Basic Development Environment

In Access for Windows 95 (version 7.0), Visual Basic replaced the Access Basic programming language included with versions 1 and 2 of Access. The two languages are very similar because both Visual Basic and Access Basic evolved from a common design created before either product existed. (It's called *Visual* Basic because it was the first version of Basic designed specifically for the Windows graphical environment.) In recent years, Visual Basic has become the common programming language for Microsoft Office applications, including Access, Excel, Word, and PowerPoint. Some of the 2007 Office system products (including Word and Excel) can work with an even newer variant of Visual Basic—Visual Basic .NET—but Access does not.

Having a common programming language across applications provides several advantages. You have to learn only one programming language, and you can easily share objects across applications by using Visual Basic with object automation. Office Access 2007 uses the Visual Basic Editor common to all Microsoft Office applications and to the Visual Basic programming product. The Visual Basic Editor provides color-coded syntax, an Object Browser, and other features. It also provides excellent tools for testing and confirming the proper execution of the code you write.

## Modules

You save all Visual Basic code in your database in modules. Access 2007 provides two ways to create a module: as a module object or as part of a form or report object.

### Module Objects

You can view the module objects in your database by clicking the top of the Navigation Pane and then clicking Object Type under Navigate To Category. Click the Navigation Pane menu again, and click Modules under Filter By Group. Figure 19-1 shows the standard and class modules in the Conrad Systems Contacts sample database. (We also right-clicked the top of the Navigation Pane, clicked View By on the shortcut menu, and then Details on the submenu so you can see the descriptions we've attached to all the modules.) You should use module objects to define procedures that you need to call from queries or from several forms or reports in your application. You can call a public procedure defined in a module from anywhere in your application.

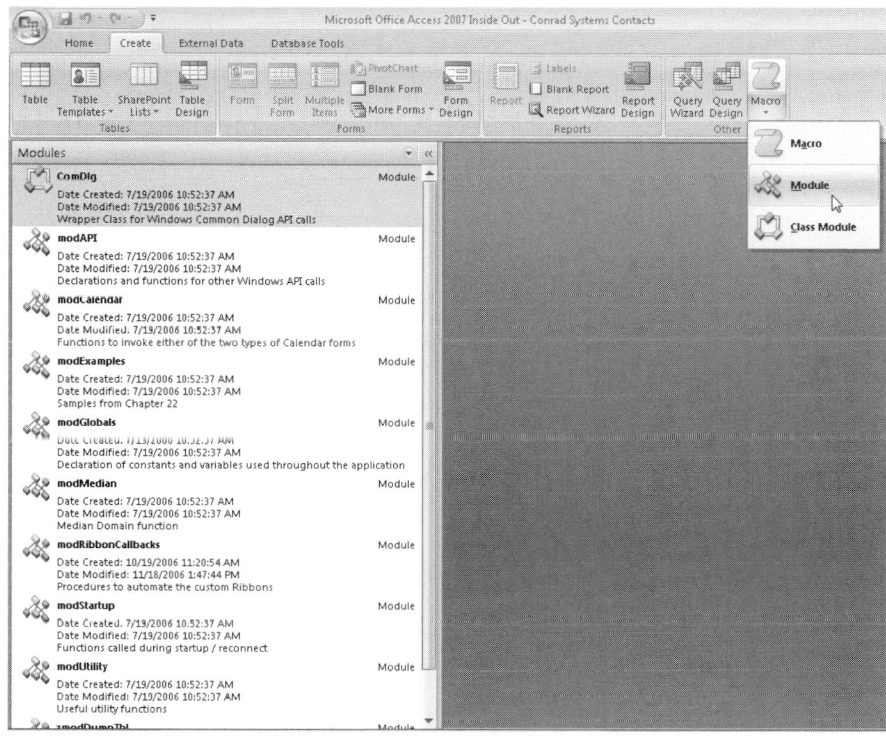


**Figure 19-1** To see all the modules in your database, click Modules under Filter By Group on the Navigation Pane menu when you have Navigate To Category set to Object Type. On the Create tab, in the Other group, click the arrow under the Macro command and then click Module to create a new standard module.

To create a new module, on the Create tab, in the Other group, click the arrow under the Macro command, and click either Module or Class Module, also shown in Figure 19-1. (This button remembers the last object type you created in your current Access session, so it might say Module or Class Module.) When you click Module, Access creates a new *standard module*. You use a standard module to define procedures that you can call from anywhere in your application. It's a good idea to name modules based on their purpose. For example, you might name a module that contains procedures to perform custom calculations for queries modQueryFunctions, and you might name a module containing procedures to work directly with Windows functions modWindowsAPIFunctions.

Advanced developers might want to create a special type of module object called a *class module*. A class module is a specification for a user-defined object in your application, and the Visual Basic procedures you create in a class module define the properties and methods that your object supports. You create a new class module by clicking the arrow under the Macro command and then clicking Class Module. You'll learn more about objects, methods, properties, and class modules later in this chapter.

## Form and Report Modules

To make it easy to create Visual Basic procedures that respond to events on forms or reports, Access 2007 supports a class module associated with each form or report. (You can design forms and reports that do not have a related class module.) A module associated with a form or report is also a class module that allows you to respond to events defined for the form or report as well as define extended properties and methods of the form or report. Within a form or report class module, you can create specially named event procedures to respond to Access-defined events, private procedures that you can call only from within the scope of the class module, and public procedures that you can call as methods of the class. See "Collections, Objects, Properties, and Methods" on page 978 for more information about objects and methods. You can edit the module for a form or a report by opening the form or report in Design view and then clicking the View Code button in the Tools group on the Design contextual tab (located under Form Design Tools). As you'll learn later, you can also open a form or a report by setting an object equal to a new instance of the form or report's class module.

Using form and report modules offers three main advantages over module objects.

- All the code you need to automate a form or a report resides with that form or report. You don't have to remember the name of a separate form-related or report-related module object.
- Access loads module objects into memory when you first reference any procedure or variable in the module and leaves them loaded as long as the database is open. Access loads the code for a form or a report only when the form or the report is opened. Access unloads a form or a report class module when the object is closed; therefore, form and report modules consume memory only when you're using the form or the report to which they are attached.
- If you export a form or report, all the code in the form or report module is exported with it.

However, form and report modules have one disadvantage: Because the code must be loaded each time you open the form or report, a form or report with a large supporting module opens noticeably more slowly than one that has little or no code. In addition, saving a form or report design can take longer if you have also opened the associated module and changed any of the code.

One enhancement that first appeared in Microsoft Access 97 (version 8.0)—the addition of the HasModule property—helps Access load forms and reports that have no code more rapidly. Access automatically sets this property to Yes if you try to view the code for a form or report, even if you don't define any event procedures. If HasModule is No, Access doesn't bother to look for an associated Visual Basic module, so the form or report loads more quickly.

**CAUTION!**

If you set the HasModule property to No in the Properties window, Access deletes the code module associated with the form or report. However, Access warns you and gives you a chance to change your mind if you set the HasModule property to No in error.

## The Visual Basic Editor Window

When you open a module in Design view, Access 2007 opens the Visual Basic Editor and asks the editor to display your code. Open the Conrad Systems Contacts sample database (Contacts.accdb), view the Modules list in the Navigation Pane, and then either right-click the modExamples object and click Design View on the shortcut menu or double-click the modExamples object to see the code for this module opened in the Visual Basic Editor, as shown in Figure 19-2. Notice that the Visual Basic Editor in Access 2007 uses the older menu and toolbar technology from previous releases, not the Ribbon used in the main Access window.

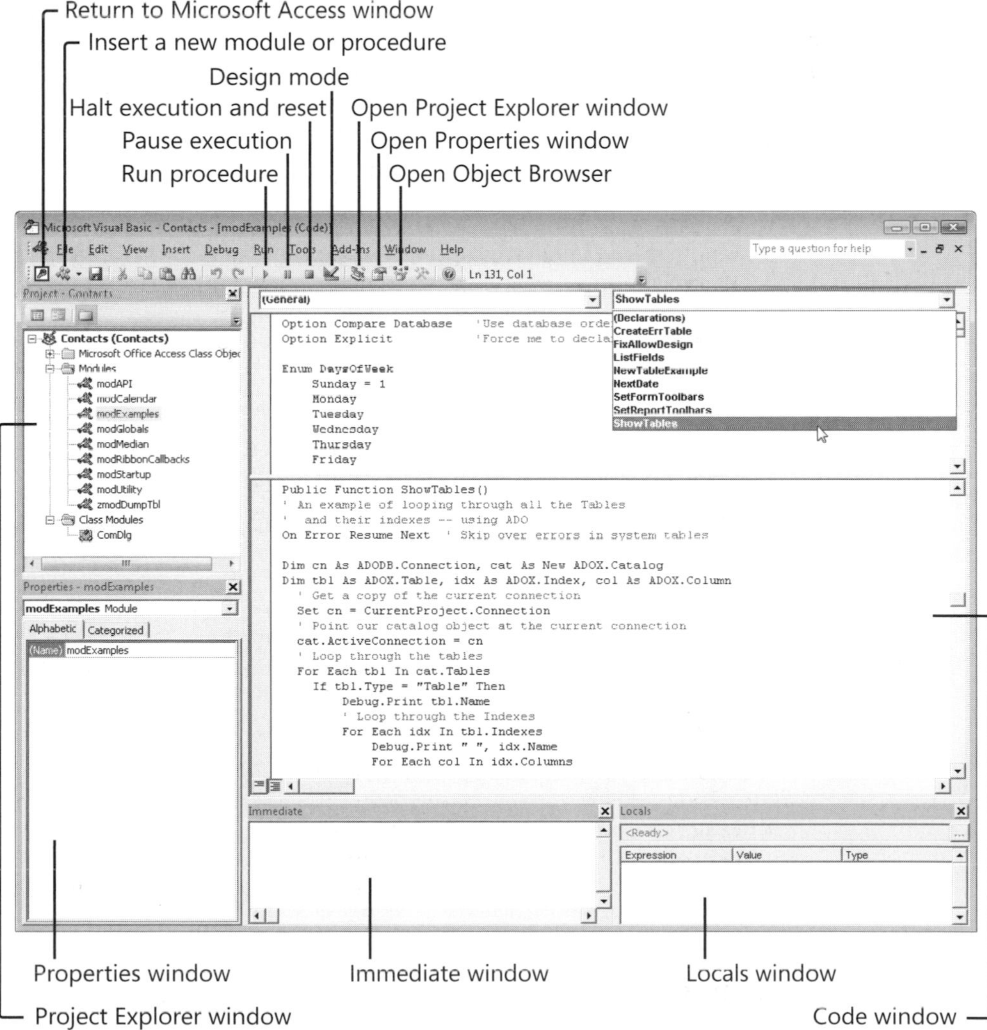


**Figure 19-2** Use the Visual Basic Editor to view and edit all Visual Basic code in your database.

What you see on your screen might differ from Figure 19-2, particularly if you have opened the Visual Basic Editor previously and moved some windows around. In the upper-left corner of the figure, you can see the Visual Basic Project Explorer window docked in the workspace. (Click Project Explorer on the View menu or press Ctrl+R to see this window if it's not visible.) In this window, you can discover all module objects and form and report class modules saved in the database. You can double-click any module to open it in the Code window, which you can see maximized in the upper-right corner.

Docked in the lower-left corner is the Properties window. (Click Properties Window on the View menu or press F4 to see this window if it's not visible.) When you have a form or report that has a Visual Basic module open in Design view in Access, you can click that object in the Project Explorer to see all its properties. If you modify a property in the Properties window, you're changing it in Access. To open a form or report that is not open, you can select it in the Project Explorer and then click Object on the View menu.

In the lower-right corner you can see the Locals window docked. (Click Locals Window on the View menu to see this window if it's not visible.) As you will see later, this window allows you to instantly see the values of any active variables or objects when you pause execution in a procedure. In the lower center you can see the Immediate window docked. (Click Immediate window on the View menu or press Ctrl+G to see this window if it's not visible.) It's called the Immediate Window because you can type any valid Visual Basic statement and press Enter to execute the statement immediately. You can also use a special "what is" command character (?) to find out the value of an expression or variable. For example, you can type **?5*20** and press Enter, and Visual Basic responds with the answer on the following line: *100*.

You can undock any window by grabbing its title bar and dragging it away from its docked position on the edge toward the center of the screen. You can also undock a window by right-clicking anywhere in the window and clearing the Dockable property. As you will see later, you can set the Dockable property of any window by clicking Options on the Tools menu. When a window is set as Dockable but not docked along an edge, it becomes a pop-up window that floats on top of other windows—similar to the way an Access form works when its Pop Up property is set to Yes, as you learned in Chapter 12, "Customizing a Form." When you make any window not Dockable, it shares the space occupied by the Code window.

You cannot set the Code window as Dockable. The Code window always appears in the part of the workspace that is not occupied by docked windows. You can maximize the Code window to fill this remaining space, as shown in Figure 19-2. You can also click the Restore button for this window and open multiple overlaid Code windows for different modules within the Code window space.

At the top of the Code window, just below the toolbar, you can see two drop-down lists.

- **Object list** When you're editing a form or report class module, open this list on the left to select the form or the report, a section on the form or the report, or any control on the form or the report that can generate an event. The Procedure list then shows the available event procedures for the selected object. Select General to view the Declarations section of the module, where you can set options or declare variables shared by multiple procedures. In a form or a report class module, General is also where you'll see any procedures you have coded that do not respond to events. When you're editing a standard module object, this list displays only the General option. In a class module object, you can choose General or Class.

- **Procedure list** Open this list on the right to select a procedure in the module and display that procedure in the Code window. When you're editing a form or report module, this list shows the available event procedures for the selected object and displays in bold type the event procedures that you have coded and attached to the form or the report. When you're editing a module object, the list displays in alphabetic order all the procedures you coded in the module. In a class module when you have selected Class in the Object list, you can choose the special Initialize or Terminate procedures for the class.

In Figure 19-2, we dragged the divider bar at the top of the scroll bar on the right of the Code window downward to open two edit windows. We clicked in the lower window and then clicked ShowTables in the Procedure list box. You might find a split window very handy when you're tracing calls from one procedure to another. The Procedure list box always shows you the name of the procedure that currently has the focus. In the Code window, you can use the arrow keys to move horizontally and vertically. When you enter a new line of code and press Enter, Visual Basic optionally verifies the syntax of the line and warns you of any problems it finds.

If you want to create a new procedure in a module, you can type either a *Function* statement, a *Sub* statement, or a *Property* statement on any blank line above or below an existing procedure and then press Enter, or click anywhere in the module and click the arrow to the right of the Insert button on the toolbar and then click Procedure, or click Procedure on the Insert menu. (For details about the Function and Sub statements, see "Functions and Subroutines" on page 1005. For details about the Property statement, see "Understanding Class Modules," page 1009.) Visual Basic creates a new procedure for you (it does not embed the new procedure in the procedure you were editing) and inserts an *End Function*, *End Sub*, or *End Property* statement. When you create a new procedure using the Insert button or the Insert menu, Visual Basic opens a dialog box where you can enter the name of the new procedure, select the type of the procedure (Sub, Function, or Property), and select the scope of the procedure (Public or Private). To help you organize your procedures, Visual Basic inserts the new procedure in alphabetical sequence within the existing procedures.

**CAUTION!**

If you type a Function, Sub, or Property statement in the middle of an existing procedure, Visual Basic accepts the statement if it's syntactically correct, but your project won't compile because you cannot place a Function, Sub, or Property procedure inside another Function, Sub, or Property procedure.

If you're working in a form or report module, you can select an object in the Object list and then open the Procedure list to see all the available events for that object. An event name displayed in bold type means you have created a procedure to handle that event. Select an event whose name isn't displayed in bold type to create a procedure to handle that event.

Visual Basic provides many options that you can set to customize how you work with modules. Click Options on the Tools menu, and then click the Editor tab to see the settings for these options, as shown in Figure 19-3.

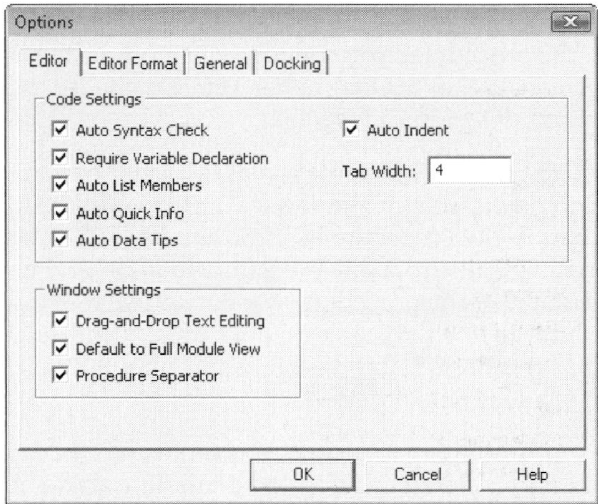


**Figure 19-3** You can customize the Visual Basic Editor by using the settings on the Editor tab in the Options dialog box.

On the Editor tab, some important options to consider are Auto Syntax Check, to check the syntax of lines of code as you enter them; and Require Variable Declaration, which forces you to declare all your variables. (Require Variable Declaration is not selected by default—you'll see later why it's important to select it.) If you want to see required and optional parameters as you type complex function calls, select the Auto List Members check box. Auto Quick Info provides drop-down lists where appropriate built-in constants are available to complete parameters in function or subroutine calls. When you're debugging code, Auto Data Tips lets you discover the current value of a variable by pausing your mouse pointer on any usage of the variable in your code.

Drag-And-Drop Text Editing allows you to highlight code and drag it to a new location. Default To Full Module View shows all your code for multiple procedures in a module in a single scrollable view. If you clear that check box, you will see only one procedure at a time and must page up or down or select a different procedure in the Procedure list box to move to a different part of the module. When you're in full module view, selecting the Procedure Separator check box asks Visual Basic to draw a line between procedures to make it easy to see where one procedure ends and another begins.

Selecting the Auto Indent check box asks Visual Basic to leave you at the same indent as the previous line of code when you press the Enter key to insert a new line. We wrote all of the sample code you'll see in this book and in the sample databases with indents to make it easy to see related lines of code within a loop or an If...Then...Else construct. You can set the Tab Width to any value from 1 through 32. This setting tells Visual Basic how many spaces you want to indent when you press the Tab key while writing code.

On the Editor Format tab of the Options dialog box, you can set custom colors for various types of code elements and also choose a display font. We recommend using a monospaced font such as Courier New for all code editing.

On the General tab, shown in Figure 19-4, you can set some important options that dictate how Visual Basic acts as you enter new code and as you debug your code. You can ignore all the settings under Form Grid Settings because they apply to forms designed in Visual Basic, not Access.

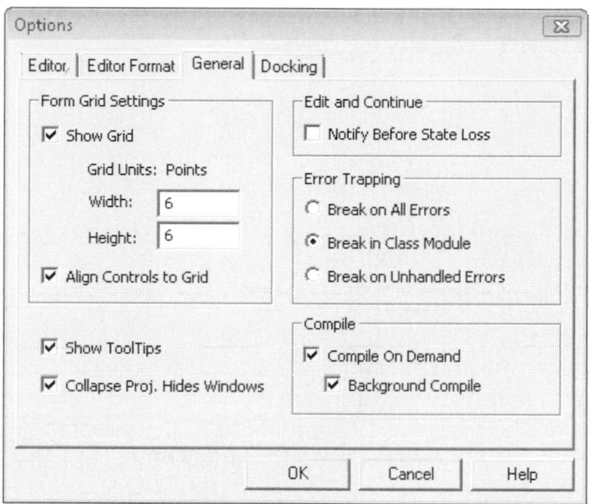


**Figure 19-4** You can modify settings to help you debug your code on the General tab in the Options dialog box.

If your code has halted, in many cases you can enter new code or correct problems in code before continuing to test. Some changes you make, however, will force Visual Basic to reset rather than let you continue to run from the halted point. If you select the Notify Before State Loss check box, Visual Basic will warn you before allowing you to make code changes that would cause it to reset.

In the Error Trapping section, you can select one of three ways to tell Visual Basic how to deal with errors. As you'll discover later in this chapter, you can write statements in your code to attempt to catch errors. If you think you have a problem in your error-trapping code, you can select Break On All Errors. With this setting, Visual Basic ignores all error trapping and halts execution on any error. If you have written class modules that can be called from other modules, to catch an untrapped error that occurs within a class module, choose Break In Class Module to halt on the statement within the class module that failed. (We recommend this setting for most testing.) If you choose Break On Unhandled Errors, and an untrapped error occurs within a class module, Visual Basic halts on the statement that invoked the class module.

The last two important options on this tab are Compile On Demand and Background Compile. With the Compile On Demand check box selected, Visual Basic compiles any previously uncompiled new code whenever you run that code directly or run a procedure that calls that code. Background Compile lets Visual Basic use spare CPU cycles to compile new code as you are working in other areas.

Finally, on the Docking tab you can specify whether the Immediate window, Locals window, Watch window, Project Explorer, Properties window, or Object Browser can be docked. We will take a look at the Immediate window and Watch window in the next section. You can use the Object Browser to discover all the supported properties and methods of any object or function defined in Access, Visual Basic, or your database application.

INSIDE OUT

**Understanding the Relationship Between Access and Visual Basic**

Access 2007 and Visual Basic work as two separate but interlinked products in your Access application. Access handles the storage of the Visual Basic project (both the source code and the compiled code) in your desktop database (.accdb) or project (.adp) file, and it calls Visual Basic to manage the editing and execution of your code.

Because Access tightly links your forms and reports with class modules stored in the Visual Basic project, some complex synchronization must happen between the two products. For example, when you open a form module and enter a new event procedure in the Visual Basic Code window, Access must set the appropriate event property to [Event Procedure] so that both the form and the code are correctly linked. Likewise, when you delete all the code in an event procedure, Access must clear the related form or control property. So, when you open a form or report module from the Visual Basic Editor window, you'll notice that Access also opens the related form or report object in the Access window.

When Access first began using Visual Basic (instead of Access Basic) in version 7.0 (Microsoft Access for Windows 95), it was possible to end up with a corrupted Visual Basic project or corrupted form or report object if you weren't careful to always compile and save both the code and the form or report definition at the same time when you made changes to either. It was particularly easy to encounter corruption if multiple developers had the database open at the same time. This corruption most often occurred when Access failed to merge a changed module back into the Visual Basic project when the developer saved changes.

Microsoft greatly improved the reliability of this process when it switched in version 9.0 (Microsoft Access 2000) to saving the entire Visual Basic project whenever you save a change. However, this change means that two developers can no longer have the same database open and be working in the code at the same time. This also means that your Access file can grow rapidly if you're making frequent changes to the code and saving your changes.

When you're making multiple changes in an Access application, we recommend that you always compile your project when you have finished changing a section of code. (Click Compile on the Debug menu in the Visual Basic Editor.) You should also save all at once multiple objects that you have changed by clicking the Save button in the Visual Basic Editor window and always responding Yes to the Save dialog box that Access shows you when you have multiple changed objects open.

## Working with Visual Basic Debugging Tools

You might have noticed that the debugging tools for macros are very primitive. You can't do much more than run macros in single-step mode to try to find the source of an error. The debugging tools for Visual Basic are significantly more extensive. The following sections describe many of the tools available in Visual Basic. You might want to scan these sections first and then return after you have learned more about the Visual Basic language and have begun writing procedures that you need to debug.

### Setting Breakpoints

If you still have the modExamples module open, scroll down until you can see all of the ShowTables function, as shown in Figure 19-5. This sample function examines all the table definitions in the current database and displays the table name, the names of any indexes defined for the table, and the names of columns in each index by printing to a special object called *Debug* (another name for the Immediate window).

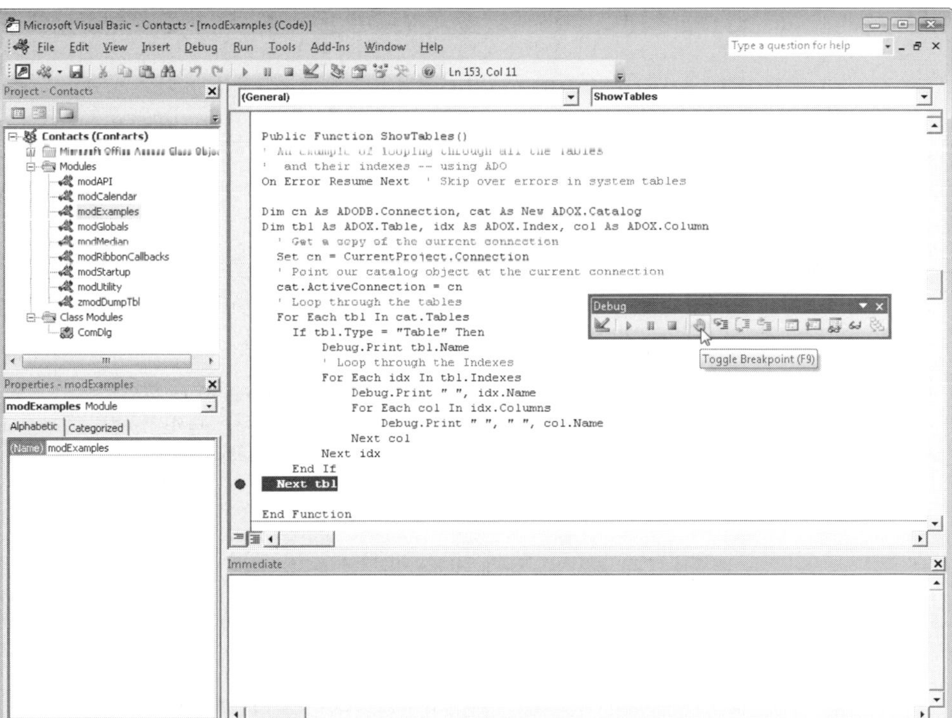


**Figure 19-5** You can set a breakpoint in a Visual Basic module to help you debug your code.

One of the most common ways to test particularly complex code is to open the module you want to examine, set a stopping point in the code (called a breakpoint), and then run the code. Visual Basic halts before executing the statement on the line where you set the breakpoint. As you'll soon see, when Visual Basic stops at a breakpoint, you can examine all sorts of information to help you clean up potential problems. While a procedure is stopped, you can look at the values in variables—including all object variables you might have defined. In addition, you can also change the value of variables, single-step through the code, reset the code, or restart at a different statement.

To set a breakpoint, click anywhere on the line of code where you want Visual Basic execution to halt and either click the Toggle Breakpoint button on the Debug toolbar (open this toolbar by right-clicking any toolbar and clicking Debug on the shortcut menu), click Toggle Breakpoint on the Debug menu, or press F9 to set or clear a breakpoint. When a breakpoint is active, Access highlights the line of code (in red by default) where the breakpoint is established and displays a dot on the selection bar to the left of the line of code. Note that you can set as many breakpoints as you like, anywhere in any module. After you set a breakpoint, the breakpoint stays active until you close the current database, specifically clear the breakpoint, or click Clear All Breakpoints on the Debug menu (or press Ctrl+Shift+F9). In the example shown in Figure 19-5, we set a breakpoint to halt the procedure at the bottom of the loop that examines each table. When you run the procedure later, you'll see that Visual Basic will halt on this statement just before it executes the statement.

## Using the Immediate Window

"Action central" for all troubleshooting in Visual Basic is a special edit window called the Immediate window. You can open the Immediate window while editing a module by clicking the Immediate Window button on the Debug toolbar or clicking Immediate Window on the View menu. Even when you do not have a Visual Basic module open, you can open the Immediate window from anywhere in Access by pressing Ctrl+G.

**Executing Visual Basic Commands in the Immediate Window** In the Immediate window (shown earlier in Figure 19-2), you can type any valid Visual Basic command and press Enter to have it executed immediately. You can also execute a procedure by typing the procedure name followed by any parameter values required by the procedure. You can ask Visual Basic to evaluate any expression by typing a question mark character (sometimes called the "what is" character) followed by the expression. Access displays the result of the evaluation on the line below. You might want to experiment by typing **?(5 * 4) / 10**. You will see the answer 2 on the line below.

Because you can type any valid Visual Basic statement, you can enter an *assignment statement* (the name of a variable, an equals sign, and the value you want to assign to the variable) to set a variable that you might have forgotten to set correctly in your code. For example, there's a public variable (you'll learn more about variables later in this chapter) called gintDontShowCompanyList that the Conrad Systems Contacts sample application uses to save whether the current user wants to see the Select Companies pop-up window when clicking Companies on the main switchboard. Some users may prefer to go directly to the Companies/Organizations form that edits all companies rather than select or filter the list. If you have been running the Conrad Systems Contacts application, you can find out the current value of the string by typing

```
?gintDontShowCompanyList
```

Visual Basic displays the value of this variable, which should be either 0 or –1. You can set the value of this string to False (0) by typing

```
gintDontShowCompanyList = 0
```

You can verify the value of the variable you just set by typing

```
?gintDontShowCompanyList
```

If you assigned 0 to the variable, you should see that value echoed in the Immediate window.

To have a sense of the power of what you're doing, go to the Database window in Access by clicking the View Microsoft Access button on the left end of the toolbar in the Visual Basic Editor window. Open the frmMain form in Form view. Click the Companies button to find out whether the Select Companies form or the Companies/Organizations form opens. If you go directly to the Select Companies form, then gintDontShowCompanyList must be False (0). Close the form that opens.

Now, go back to the Visual Basic Editor window. (An easy way to do this is to use the Windows Alt+Tab feature.) In the Visual Basic Immediate window, set the value to True by entering in the Immediate window

```
gintDontShowCompanyList = True
```

Go back to the main switchboard and try the Companies button again. Because you set the public variable to True, you should go directly to the Companies/Organizations form. Now that you have the form open to edit companies, you can set a filter directly from the Immediate window. Go back to that window and enter the expression

```
Forms!frmCompanies.Filter = "[StateOrProvince] = 'PA'"
```

If you want, you can ask what the filter property is to see if it is set correctly. Note that nothing has happened yet to the form. Next, turn on the form's FilterOn property by entering

```
Forms!frmCompanies.FilterOn = True
```

Return to the form, and you should now see the form filtered down to two rows—all the companies in the state of Pennsylvania. If you want to try another example, return to the Immediate window and enter

```
Forms!frmCompanies.Section(0).Backcolor = 255
```

The background of Section(0), the detail area of the form, should now appear red! Note that none of these changes affect the design of the form. You can close the form, and the next time you open it, the form will have a normal background color, and the records won't be filtered.

**Using Breakpoints** You saw earlier how to set a breakpoint within a module procedure. To see how a breakpoint works, open the modExamples module in the Visual Basic Editor window, find the ShowTables function, and be sure you have set a breakpoint on the `Next tbl` statement as shown in Figure 19-6.

Because the ShowTables procedure is a function that might return a value, you have to ask Visual Basic to evaluate the function in order to run it. The function doesn't require any parameters, so you don't need to supply any. To run the function, type **?ShowTables()** in the Immediate window, as shown in Figure 19-6, and press Enter.

> **Note**
>
> You can also ask Visual Basic to run any public procedure by clicking in the procedure and clicking the Run button on either the Standard or Debug toolbar.

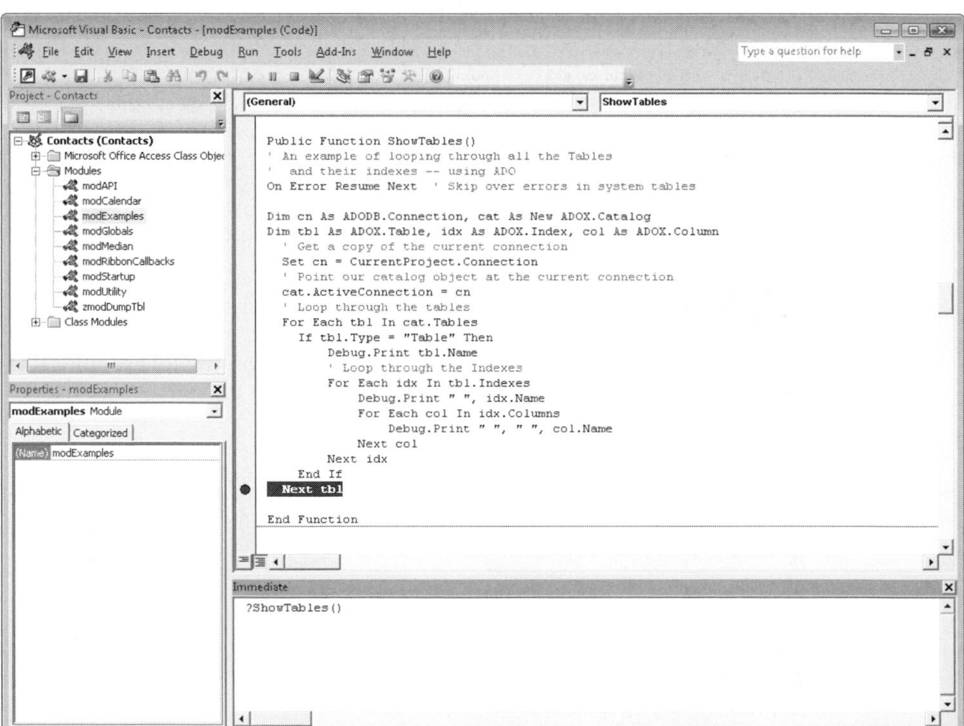


**Figure 19-6** You can execute a module function from the Immediate window.

Visual Basic runs the function you requested. Because you set a breakpoint, the code stops on the statement with the breakpoint, as shown in Figure 19-7. The first table in the database is actually a linked table (an Excel spreadsheet), so you won't see any output. Click the Continue button on the toolbar to run through the loop a second time to display the first table.

Note that we clicked Locals Window on the View menu to reveal the Locals window you can see across the bottom of Figure 19-7. (We undocked the Immediate window so you can see more of the Locals window.) In the Locals window, Visual Basic shows you all the active variables. You can, for example, click the plus sign next to the word *cat* (a variable set to the currently opened database catalog) to browse through all the property settings for the database and all the objects within the database. You can click on the *tbl* variable to explore the columns and properties in the table. See "Collections, Objects, Properties, and Methods" on page 978 for details about all the objects you see in the "tree" under the database catalog.

The Immediate window displays the output of three Debug.Print statements within the function you're running, as also shown in Figure 19-7.

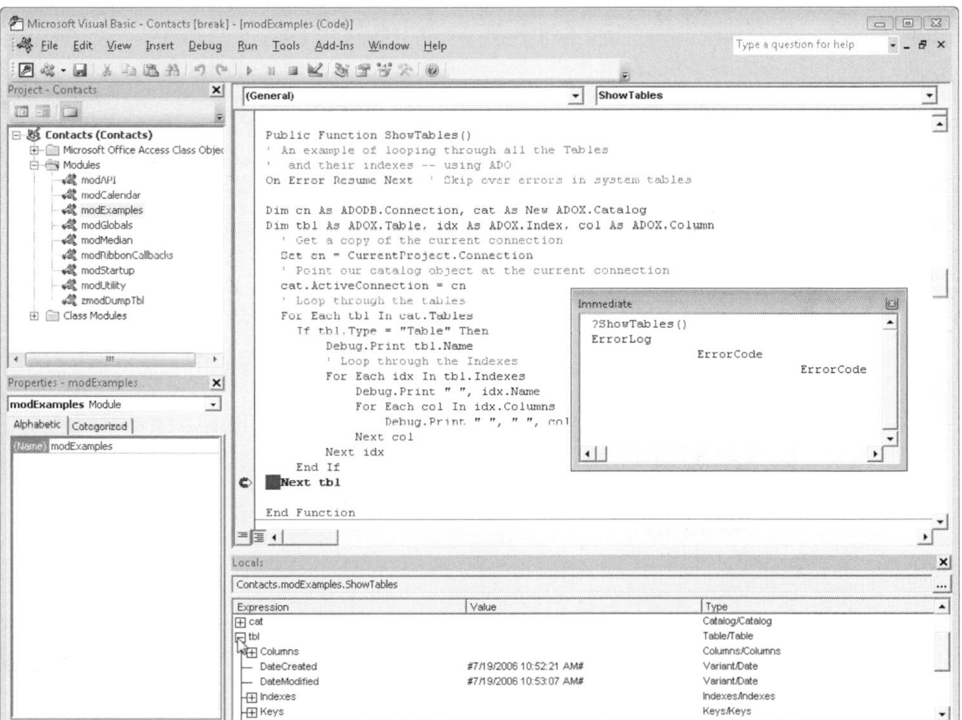


**Figure 19-7** When your Visual Basic code stops at a breakpoint, you can use the Locals window to examine variable and object values.

The first line shows the name of the first table (Errorlog) that the function found in the database. The second (indented) line shows the name of the index for that table. The third line shows the name of the one column in the index.

If you want to see the results of executing the next loop in the code (examining the next table object in the catalog), click the Continue button on the toolbar. If you want to run the code a single statement at a time, click Step Into or Step Over on the Debug menu or open the Debug toolbar and click the Step Into or Step Over button. Step Into and Step Over work the same unless you're about to execute a statement that calls another procedure. If the next statement calls another procedure, Step Into literally steps into the called procedure so that you can step through the code in the called procedure one line at a time. Step Over calls the procedure without halting and stops on the next statement in the current procedure.

When you are finished studying the loop in the ShowTables function, be sure to click the Reset button on the toolbar to halt code execution.

> **Note**
>
> The Tables collection in the catalog includes tables, linked tables, system tables, and queries. Because the ShowTables procedure only looks for tables, you will need to loop through the code several times until the procedure finds the next object that defines a table. You should quickly find the ErrorLog, ErrTable, and ErrTableSample tables, but the code must then loop through all the queries and linked tables (more than 40 of them) before finding the SwitchboardDriver table.

## Working with the Watch Window

Sometimes setting a breakpoint isn't enough to catch an error. You might have a variable that you know is being changed somewhere by your code (perhaps incorrectly). By using the Watch window, you can examine a variable as your code runs, ask Visual Basic to halt when an expression that uses the variable becomes true, or ask Visual Basic to halt when the variable changes.

An interesting set of variables in the Conrad Systems Contacts sample database are gintDontShowCompanyList, gintDontShowContactList, and gintDontShowInvoiceList (all defined in the modGlobals module). When any of these variables are set to True, the main switchboard bypasses the intermediate list/search form for companies, contacts, and invoices, respectively. You played with one of these variables earlier, but it would be interesting to trap when these are set or reset.

**CAUTION!**

There are a couple of known issues with setting breakpoints in Access 2007. First, code will not halt if you have cleared the Use Access Special Keys check box in the Application Options section of the Current Database category of the Access Options dialog box (click the Microsoft Office Button and then click Access Options). Second, the Break When Value Is True and Break When Value Changes options in the Add Watch dialog box will not work if the value or expression you're watching is changed in a form or report module that is not already open in the Visual Basic Editor. For this example to work, the form modules for frmMain, frmSignon, and frmUsers must be open. You can verify that these modules are open by opening the Windows menu in the Visual Basic Editor window. The Contacts.accdb sample file should have modules open, but these modules might not be open in your copy if you have closed them and compiled and saved the project. You can find these modules in the Project Explorer window. Open the list of objects in the Microsoft Class Objects category and then double-click the form modules that you need to open them.

To set a watch for when the value changes, open the Watch window by clicking it on the View menu, right-click in the Watch window, and click Add Watch on the shortcut menu. You can also click Add Watch on the Debug menu. You should see the Add Watch dialog box, as shown in Figure 19-8.

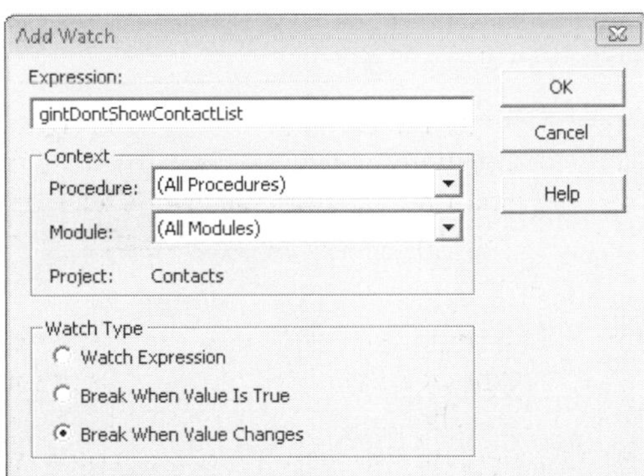


**Figure 19-8** You can set a watch for when a variable's value changes.

In the Expression box, enter the name of the variable you want the code to watch. In this case, you want to watch when the gintDontShowContactList variable changes. You don't know where the variable is set, so set the Procedure and Module selections to (All Procedures) and (All Modules), respectively. Under Watch Type, select the Break When Value Changes option, and click OK to set the watch. Go to the Immediate window and set gintDontShowContactList to True by entering **gintDontShowContactList = True** and pressing Enter. Now return to the Navigation Pane and start the application by opening the frmSplash form. (Code in the Load event of this form hides the Navigation Pane and then opens the Conrad Systems Contacts Sign On form.) Because you set a watch to halt when gintDontShowContactList changes, the code execution should halt in the module for the frmSignOn form as shown in Figure 19-9.

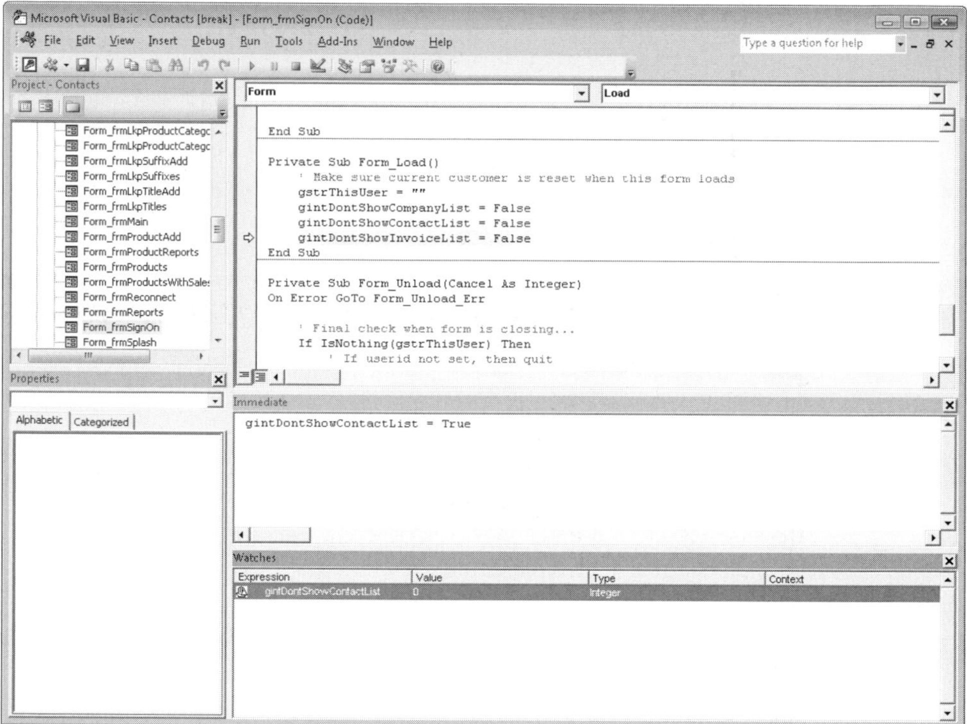


**Figure 19-9** Visual Basic code halts immediately after a watch variable has changed.

Note that the code halts on the statement immediately after the one that reset the watched variable. If you didn't set the variable to True before you started the application, Visual Basic won't halt because the value won't be changing.

Click the Continue button (or press F5) to let the code continue executing. Return to the Access window, and in the Conrad Systems Contacts Sign On dialog box, select my name (John Viescas) and press Enter or click the Sign On button. The sign on dialog box will close, and the main switchboard form opens. In the main switchboard, click the Users button to open the user edit form. The second record should be my record unless you've created other users. Select the Don't Show Contact List check box in my record and click the Save button. The procedure halts again, as shown in Figure 19-10.

It appears that this code is setting the gintDontShowContactList variable to some value on the user edit form. (As you'll learn later, Me is a shorthand way to reference the form object where your code is running, so Me.DontShowContactList references a control on the form.) Click the Continue button again to let the code finish execution. Return to the Access window and click the Close button on the Users form to return to the main switchboard.

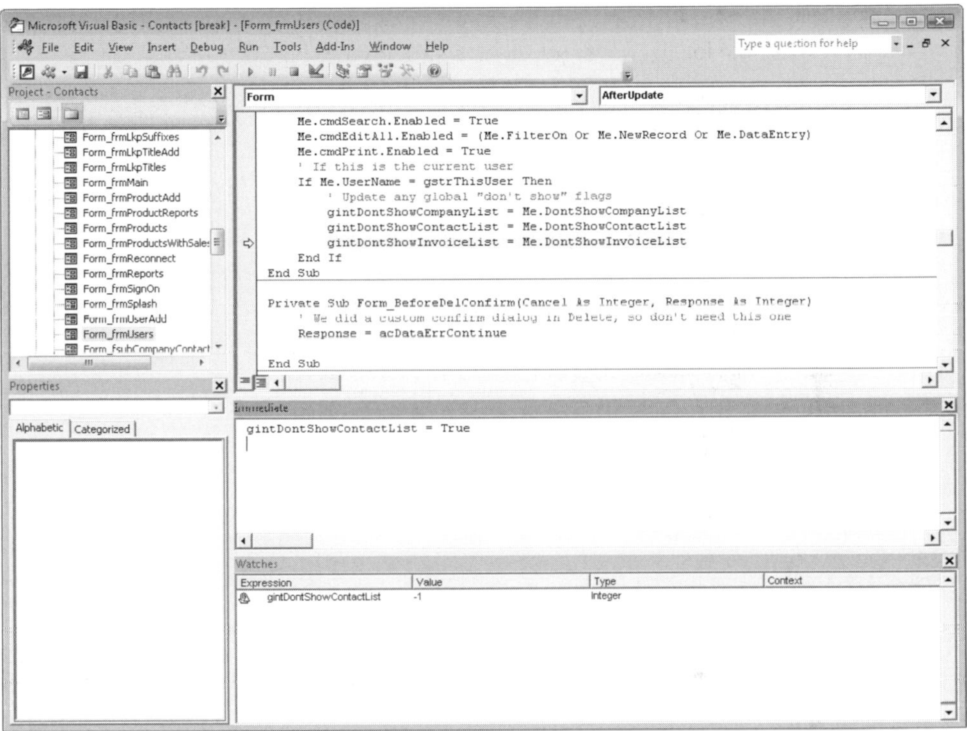


**Figure 19-10** The gintDontShowContactList variable is set to the value of a form control.

If you open frmUsers in Design view (you can't do this while the procedure is still halted) and examine the names of the check box controls on the form, you'll find that the check box you selected is named DontShowContactList. When the code behind frmUsers detects a change to the options for the currently signed-on user, it makes sure the option variables in modGlobals get changed as well. Be sure to close the frmUsers form when you're finished looking at it.

## Examining the Procedure Call Sequence (Call Stack)

After stopping code that you're trying to debug, it's useful sometimes to find out what started the current sequence of code execution and what procedures have been called by Visual Basic. For this example, you can continue with the watch on the gintDontShowContactList variable.

You should now be at the main switchboard form (frmMain) in the application. Click the Exit button to close the application and return to the Navigation Pane. (You'll see a prompt asking you if you're sure you want to exit—click Yes. You might also see a prompt offering to back up the data file—click No.) The code should halt again in the Close event of the frmMain form. Click the Call Stack button on the toolbar or click Call Stack on the View menu to see the call sequence shown in Figure 19-11.

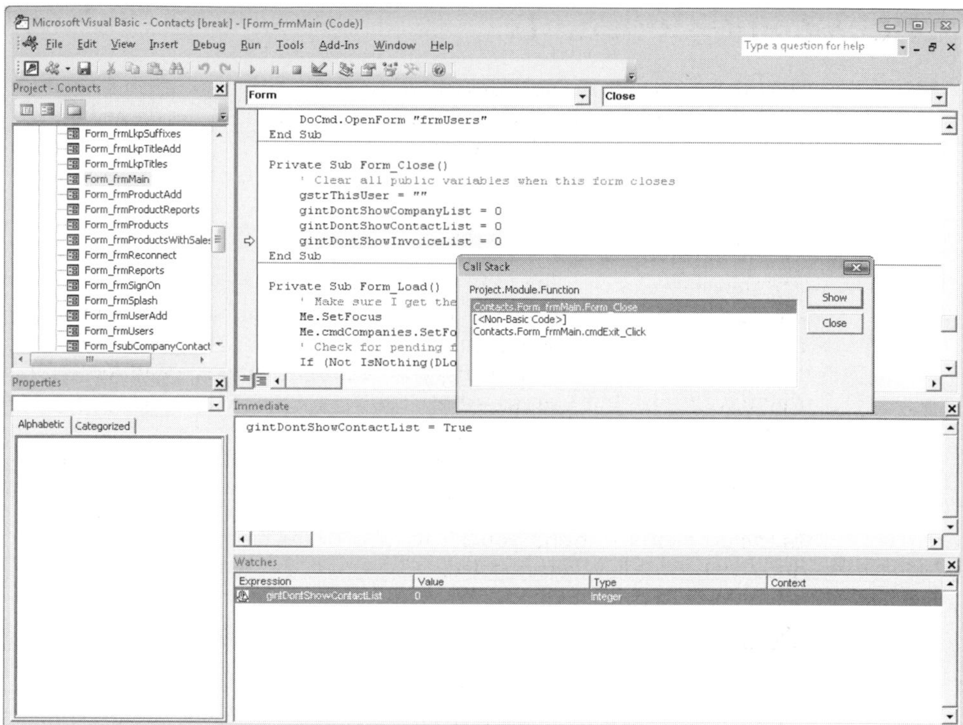

**Figure 19-11** When your code is halted, you can see the chain of code executed to the point of the halt in the Call Stack dialog box.

The Call Stack dialog box shows the procedures that have executed, with the most recent procedure at the top of the list, and the first procedure at the bottom. You can see that the code started executing in the cmdExit_Click procedure of the frmMain form. This happens to be the Visual Basic event procedure that runs when you click the Exit button. If you click that line and then click the Show button, you should see the cmdExit_Click procedure in the module for the frmMain form (the switchboard) with the cursor on the line that executes the DoCmd.Close command to close the form. This line calls the Access built-in Close command (the <Non-Basic Code> you see in the call stack list), which in turn triggered the Close event procedure for the form. It's the Close event procedure code that sets the gintDontShowContactList variable back to False (0). Be sure that the Call Stack dialog box is closed and click Continue on the toolbar to let the code finish running.

### Note

Be sure to delete the watch after you are finished seeing how it works by right-clicking it in the Watch window and clicking Delete on the shortcut menu.

# Variables and Constants

In addition to using Visual Basic code to work with the controls on any open forms or reports (as you can with macros), you can declare and use named variables in Visual Basic code for storing values temporarily, calculating a result, or manipulating any of the objects in your database. To create a value available anywhere in your code, you can define a global variable, as you can find in the modGlobals module in the Conrad Systems Contacts sample database.

Another way to store data in Visual Basic is with a constant. A *constant* is a data object with a fixed value that you cannot change while your application is running. You've already encountered some of the built-in constants in Access 2007–Null, True, and False. Visual Basic also has a large number of intrinsic constants–built-in constants that have meaningful names–that you can use to test for data types and other attributes or that you can use as fixed arguments in functions and expressions. You can view the list of intrinsic constants by searching for the Visual Basic Constants topic in Help. You can also declare your own constant values to use in code that you write.

In the following sections, you'll learn about using variables to store and calculate data and to work with database objects.

## Data Types

Visual Basic supports data types for variables and constants that are similar to the data types you use to define fields in tables. It also allows you to define a variable that is a pointer to an object (such as a form or a recordset). The data types are described in Table 19-1.

**Table 19-1 Visual Basic Data Types**

| Data Type | Size | Data-Typing Character | Can Contain |
|---|---|---|---|
| Boolean | 2 bytes | (none) | True (–1) or False (0) |
| Byte | 1 byte | (none) | Binary data ranging in value from 0 through 255 |
| Integer | 2 bytes | % | Integers from –32,768 through 32,767 |
| Long | 4 bytes | & | Integers from –2,147,483,648 through 2,147,483,647 |
| Single | 4 bytes | ! | Floating-point (imprecise) numbers from approximately $-3.4 \times 10^{38}$ through $3.4 \times 10^{38}$ |
| Double | 8 bytes | # | Floating-point (imprecise) numbers from approximately $-1.79 \times 10^{308}$ through $1.79 \times 10^{308}$ |

| Data Type | Size | Data-Typing Character | Can Contain |
|---|---|---|---|
| Currency | 8 bytes | @ | A scaled integer with four decimal places from –922,337,203,685,477.5808 through 922,337,203,685,477.5807 |
| Decimal | 14 bytes | (none) | A precise number with up to 29 digits and up to 28 decimal places from $-79.228 \times 10^{27}$ to $79.228 \times 10^{27}$ (Visual Basic in Access supports the Decimal data type only as a type within the Variant data type.) |
| String | 10 bytes plus 2 bytes per character | $ | Any text or binary string up to approximately 2 billion bytes in length, including text, hyperlinks, memo data, and "chunks" from an ActiveX object; a fixed-length string can be up to 65,400 characters long |
| Date | 8 bytes | (none) | Date/time values ranging from January 1, 100, to December 31, 9999 |
| Object | 4 bytes | (none) | A pointer to an object—you can also define a variable that contains a specific type of object, such as the Database object |
| Variant | 16 bytes through approximately 2 billion bytes | (none) | Any data, including Empty, Null, and date/time data (Use the VarType function to determine the current data type of the data in the variable. A Variant can also contain an array of Variants. Use the IsArray function to determine whether a Variant is an array.) |
| User-defined | Depends on elements defined | (none) | Any number of variables of any of the above data types |

You can implicitly define the data type of a variable by appending a data-typing character, as noted in the table above, the first time you use the variable. For example, a variable named *MyInt%* is an integer variable. If you do not explicitly declare a data variable that you reference in your code and do not supply a data-typing character, Visual Basic assigns the Variant data type to the variable. (See "Declaring Constants and Variables" on page 965 to learn how to explicitly declare data variables.) Note that although the Variant data type is the most flexible (and, in fact, is the data type for all controls on forms and reports), it is also the least efficient because Visual Basic must do extra work to determine the current data type of the data in the variable before working with it in your code. Variant is also the only data type that can contain the Null value.

The Object data type lets you define variables that can contain a pointer to an object. See "Collections, Objects, Properties, and Methods" on page 978 for details about objects that you can work with in Visual Basic. You can declare a variable as the generic Object data type, or you can specify that a variable contains a specific type of object. The major object types are AccessObject, Application, Catalog, Column, Command, Connection, Container, Control, Database, Document, Error, Field, Form, Group, Index, Key, Parameter, Procedure, Property, QueryDef, Recordset, Relation, Report, Table, TableDef, User, View, and Workspace.

INSIDE OUT **Using Option Explicit Is a Good Idea**

You can request that Visual Basic generate all new modules with an Option Explicit statement by selecting the Require Variable Declaration check box on the Editor tab of the Options dialog box, as shown in Figure 19-3. If you set this option, Visual Basic includes an Option Explicit statement in the Declarations section of every new module. This helps you avoid errors that can occur when you use a variable in your code that you haven't properly declared in a Dim, Public, Static, or Type statement or as part of the parameter list in a Function statement or a Sub statement. (See "Functions and Subroutines" on page 1005.) When you specify this option in a module, Visual Basic flags any undeclared variables it finds when you ask it to compile your code. Using an Option Explicit statement helps you find variables that you might have misspelled when you entered your code.

## Variable and Constant Scope

The scope of a variable or a constant determines whether the variable or the constant is known to only one procedure, all procedures in a module, or all procedures in your database. You can create variables or constants that can be used by any procedure in your database (public scope). You can also create variables or constants that apply only to the procedures in a module or only to a single procedure (private scope). A variable declared inside a procedure is always private to that procedure (available only within the procedure). A variable declared in the Declarations section of a module can be private (available only to the procedures in the module) or public. You can pass values from one procedure to another using a parameter list, but the values might be held in variables having different names in the two procedures. See the sections on the Function, Sub, and Call statements later in this chapter.

To declare a public *variable*, use the *Public* statement in the Declarations section of a standard module or a class module. All modules attached to forms or reports are class modules. To declare a public *constant*, use the Public keyword with a *Const* statement in the Declarations section of a standard module. You cannot declare a public constant in a class module. To declare a variable or a constant that all procedures in a module can reference, define that variable or constant in the Declarations section of the module. (A variable defined in a Declarations section is private to the module unless you use the

Public statement.) To declare a variable or a constant used only in a particular procedure, define that variable or constant as part of the procedure.

Visual Basic in Access 2007 allows you to use the same name for variables or constants in different module objects or at different levels of scope. In addition, you can declare public variables and constants in form and report modules as well as public variables and constants in standard modules.

To use the same name for public variables and constants in different module objects or form or report modules, specify the name of the module to which it belongs when you refer to it. For example, you can declare a public variable named intX in a module object with the name modMyModule and then declare another public variable named intX in a second module object, named modMyOtherModule. If you want to reference the intX variable in modMyModule from a procedure in modMyOtherModule (or any module other than modMyModule), you must use

```
modMyModule.intX
```

You can also declare variables or constants with the same name at different levels of scope within a module object or a form or report module. For example, you can declare a public variable named intX and then declare a local variable named intX within a procedure. (You can't declare a public variable within a procedure.) References to intX within the procedure refer to the local variable, while references to intX outside the procedure refer to the public variable. To refer to the public variable from within the procedure, qualify it with the name of the module, just as you would refer to a public variable from within a different module.

Declaring a public variable in a form or report module can be useful for variables that are logically associated with a particular form or report but that you might also want to use elsewhere. Like the looser naming restrictions, however, this feature can sometimes create confusion. In general, it's still a good idea to keep common public variables and constants in standard modules and to give public variables and constants names that are unique across all variable names in your application.

### Note

For information on the syntax conventions used in the remainder of this chapter, refer to "Syntax Conventions" in the "Conventions Used In This Book" section at the beginning of this book.

# Declaring Constants and Variables

The following sections show the syntax of the statements you can use to define constants and variables in your modules and procedures.

## Const Statement

Use a Const statement to define a constant.

### Syntax

```
[Public | Private] Const {constantname [As datatype]
  = <const expression>},...
```

### Notes

Include the Public keyword in the Declarations section of a standard module to define a constant that is available to all procedures in all modules in your database. Include the Private keyword to declare constants that are available only within the module where the declaration is made. Constants are private by default, and a constant defined within a procedure is always private. You cannot define a Public constant in a class module. (All constants in a class module are private.)

The *datatype* can be Byte, Boolean, Integer, Long, Currency, Single, Double, Date, String, or Variant. You cannot declare a constant as an object. Use a separate As *datatype* clause for each constant being declared. If you don't declare a type, Visual Basic assigns the data type that is most appropriate for the expression provided. (You should always explicitly declare the data type of your constants.)

The *<const expression>* cannot include variables, user-defined functions, or Visual Basic built-in functions (such as Chr). You can include simple literals and other previously defined constants.

### Example

To define the constant PI to be available to all procedures in all modules, enter the following in the Declarations section of any standard module.

```
Public Const PI As Double = 3.14159
```

INSIDE OUT

### Use Variable Naming Conventions

It's a good idea to prefix all variable names you create with a notation that indicates the data type of the variable, particularly if you create complex procedures. This helps ensure that you aren't attempting to assign or calculate incompatible data types. (For example, the names will make it obvious that you're creating a potential error if you try to assign the contents of a long integer variable to an integer variable.) It also helps ensure that you pass variables of the correct data type to procedures. Finally, including a prefix helps ensure that you do not create a variable name that is the same as an Access or Visual Basic reserved word. The following table suggests data type prefixes that you can use for many of the most common data types.

| Data Type | Prefix |
|---|---|
| Boolean | bol |
| Byte | byt |
| Currency | cur |
| Double | dbl |
| Integer | int |
| Long | lng |
| Single | sgl |
| String | str |
| User-defined (using the Type statement) | usr |
| Variant | var |
| Catalog | cat |
| Column | col |
| Command | cmd |
| Connection | cn |
| Control | ctl |
| Database | db |

| Data Type | Prefix |
|---|---|
| Document | doc |
| Field | fld |
| Form | frm |
| Index | idx |
| Key | key |
| Parameter | prm |
| Procedure | prc |
| Property | prp |
| QueryDef | qdf |
| Recordset | rst |
| Report | rpt |
| Table | tbl |
| TableDef | tbl |
| View | vew |
| Workspace | wks |

## Dim Statement

Use a Dim statement in the Declarations section of a module to declare a variable or a variable array that can be used in all procedures in the module. Use a Dim statement within a procedure to declare a variable used only in that procedure.

## Syntax

```
Dim {[WithEvents] variablename
  [([<array dimension>],... )] [As [New]
  datatype]},...
```

where <*array dimension*> is

```
[lowerbound To ] upperbound
```

## Notes

If you do not include an <*array dimension*> specification but you do include the parentheses, you must include a ReDim statement in each procedure that uses the array to dynamically allocate the array at run time. You can define an array with as many as 60 dimensions. If you do not include a *lowerbound* value in an <*array dimension*> specification, the default lower bound is 0. You can reset the default lower bound to 1 by including an *Option Base 1* statement in the module Declarations section. The *lowerbound* and *upperbound* values must be integers, and *upperbound* must be greater than or equal to *lowerbound*. The number of members of an array is limited only by the amount of memory on your computer.

Valid *datatype* entries are Byte, Boolean, Integer, Long, Currency, Single, Double, Date, String (for variable-length strings), String * *length* (for fixed-length strings), Object, Variant, or one of the object types described earlier in this chapter. You can also declare a user-defined variable structure using the Type statement and then use the user type name as a data type. You should always explicitly declare the data type of your variables. If you do not include the As *datatype* clause, Visual Basic assigns the Variant data type.

Use the New keyword to indicate that a declared object variable is a new instance of an object that doesn't have to be set before you use it. You can use the New keyword only with object variables to create a new instance of that class of object without requiring a Set statement. You can't use New to declare dependent objects. If you do not use the New keyword, you cannot reference the object or any of its properties or methods until you set the variable to an object using a Set statement.

Use the WithEvents keyword to indicate an object variable within a class module that responds to events triggered by an ActiveX object. Form and report modules that respond to events on the related form and report objects are class modules. You can also define custom class modules to create custom objects. If you use the WithEvents keyword, you cannot use the New keyword.

Visual Basic initializes declared variables at compile time. Numeric variables are initialized to zero (0), variant variables are initialized to empty, variable-length string variables are initialized as zero-length strings, and fixed-length string variables are filled with ANSI zeros (Chr(0)). If you use a Dim statement within a procedure to declare variables, Visual Basic reinitializes the variables each time you run the procedure.

## Examples

To declare a variable named intMyInteger as an integer, enter the following:

```
Dim intMyInteger As Integer
```

To declare a variable named dbMyDatabase as a database object, enter the following:

```
Dim dbMyDatabase As Database
```

To declare an array named strMyString that contains fixed-length strings that are 20 characters long and contains 50 entries from 51 through 100, enter the following:

```
Dim strMyString(51 To 100) As String * 20
```

To declare a database variable, a new table variable, and two new field variables for the table; set up the objects; and append the new table to the Tabledefs collection, enter the following:

```
Public Sub NewTableExample()
    Dim db As DAO.Database
    Dim tdf As New DAO.TableDef, _
        fld1 As New DAO.Field, _
        fld2 As New DAO.Field
    ' Initialize the table name
    tdf.Name = "MyTable"
    ' Set the name of the first field
    fld1.Name = "MyField1"
    ' Set its data type
    fld1.Type = dbLong
    ' Append the first field to the Fields
    ' collection of the table
    tdf.Fields.Append fld1
    ' Set up the second field
    fld2.Name = "MyField2"
    fld2.Type = dbText
    fld2.Size = 20
    ' Append the second field to the table
    tdf.Fields.Append fld2
    ' Establish an object on the current database
    Set db = CurrentDb
    ' Create a new table by appending tdf to
    ' the Tabledefs collection of the database
    db.TableDefs.Append tdf
End Sub
```

**See "Collections, Objects, Properties, and Methods" on page 978 for details about working with DAO objects. See "Functions and Subroutines" on page 1005 for details about the Sub statement.**

To declare an object variable to respond to events in another class module, enter the following:

```
Option Explicit
Dim WithEvents objOtherClass As MyClass

Sub LoadClass ()
    Set objOtherClass = New MyClass
End Sub

Sub objOtherClass_Signal(ByVal strMsg As string)
    MsgBox "MyClass Signal event sent this " & _
      "message: " & strMsg
End Sub
```

In class module MyClass, code the following:

```
Option Explicit
Public Event Signal(ByVal strMsg As String)

Public Sub RaiseSignal(ByVal strText As String)
    RaiseEvent Signal(strText)
End Sub
```

In any other module, execute the following statement:

```
MyClass.RaiseSignal "Hello"
```

## Enum Statement

Use an Enum statement in a module Declarations section to assign long integer values to named members of an enumeration. You can use an enumeration name as a restricted Long data type.

### Syntax

```
[Public | Private] Enum enumerationname
    <member> [= <long integer expression>]
    ...
End Enum
```

### Notes

Enumerations are constant values that you cannot change when your code is running. Include the Public keyword to define an enumeration that is available to all procedures in all modules in your database. Include the Private keyword to declare an enumeration that is available only within the module where the declaration is made. Enumerations are public by default.

You must declare at least one *member* within an enumeration. If you do not provide a *<long integer expression>* assignment, Visual Basic adds 1 to the previous value or assigns 0 if the *member* is the first member of the enumeration. The *<long integer expression>* cannot include variables, user-defined functions, or Visual Basic built-in functions (such as CLng). You can include simple literals and other previously defined constants or enumerations.

Enumerations are most useful as a replacement for the Long data type in a Function or Sub statement. When you call the function or sub procedure in code, you can use one of the enumeration names in place of a variable, constant, or literal. If you select the Auto List Members option (see Figure 19-3), Visual Basic displays the available names in a drop-down list as you type the sub or function call in your code.

## Example

To declare a public enumeration for days of the week and use the enumeration in a procedure, enter the following:

```
Option Explicit
Public Enum DaysOfWeek
    Sunday = 1
    Monday
    Tuesday
    Wednesday
    Thursday
    Friday
    Saturday
End Enum

Public Function NextDate(lngDay As DaysOfWeek) As Date
' This function returns the next date
' that matches the day of week requested
Dim intThisDay As Integer, datDate As Date
    ' Get today
    datDate = Date
    ' Figure out today's day of week
    intThisDay = WeekDay(datDate)
    ' Calculate next day depending on
    ' whether date requested is higher or lower
    If intThisDay < lngDay Then
        NextDate = datDate + (lngDay - intThisDay)
    Else
        NextDate = datDate + (lngDay + 7) - intThisDay
    End If
End Function
```

You can test the function from the Immediate window by entering the following:

```
?NextDate(Monday)
```

## Event Statement

Use the Event statement in the Declarations section of a class module to declare an event that can be raised within the module. In another module, you can define an object variable using the WithEvents keyword, set the variable to an instance of this class module, and then code procedures that respond to the events declared and triggered within this class module.

### Syntax

```
[Public] Event eventname ([<arguments>])
```

where *<arguments>* is

```
{[ByVal | ByRef] argumentname [As datatype]},...
```

### Notes

An Event must be public, which makes the event available to all other procedures in all modules. You can optionally include the Public keyword when coding this statement.

You should declare the data type of any arguments in the event's argument list. Note that the names of the variables passed by the triggering procedure can be different from the names of the variables known by this event. If you use the ByVal keyword to declare an argument, Visual Basic passes a copy of the argument to your event. Any change you make to a ByVal argument does not change the original variable in the triggering procedure. If you use the ByRef keyword, Visual Basic passes the actual memory address of the variable, allowing the event to change the variable's value in the triggering procedure. (If the argument passed by the triggering procedure is an expression, Visual Basic treats it as if you had declared it by using ByVal.) Visual Basic always passes arrays by reference (ByRef).

### Example

To declare an event that can be triggered from other modules, enter the following in the class module MyClass:

```
Option Explicit
Public Event Signal(ByVal strMsg As String)

Public Sub RaiseSignal(ByVal strText As String)
    RaiseEvent Signal(strText)
End Sub
```

To respond to the event from another module, enter the following:

```
Option Explicit
Dim WithEvents objOtherClass As MyClass

Sub LoadClass ()
    Set objOtherClass = New MyClass
End Sub
```

```
Sub objOtherClass_Signal(ByVal strMsg As string)
    MsgBox "MyClass Signal event sent this " & _
      "message: " & strMsg
End Sub
```

To trigger the event in any other module, execute the following:

```
MyClass.RaiseSignal "Hello"
```

## Private Statement

Use a Private statement in the Declarations section of a standard module or a class module to declare variables that you can use in any procedure within the module. Procedures in other modules cannot reference these variables.

### Syntax

```
Private {[WithEvents] variablename
  [([<array dimension>],... )]
  [As [New] datatype]},...
```

where *<array dimension>* is

```
[lowerbound To ] upperbound
```

### Notes

If you do not include an *<array dimension>* specification but you do include the parentheses, you must include a ReDim statement in each procedure that uses the array to dynamically allocate the array at run time. You can define an array with up to 60 dimensions. If you do not include a *lowerbound* value in an *<array dimension>* specification, the default lower bound is 0. You can reset the default lower bound to 1 by including an *Option Base 1* statement in the module Declarations section. The *lowerbound* and *upperbound* values must be integers, and *upperbound* must be greater than or equal to *lowerbound*. The number of members of an array is limited only by the amount of memory on your computer.

Valid *datatype* entries are Byte, Boolean, Integer, Long, Currency, Single, Double, Date, String (for variable-length strings), String * *length* (for fixed-length strings), Object, Variant, or one of the object types described earlier in this chapter. You can also declare a user-defined variable structure using the Type statement and then use the user type name as a data type. You should always explicitly declare the data type of your variables. If you do not include the As *datatype* clause, Visual Basic assigns the Variant data type.

Use the New keyword to indicate that a declared object variable is a new instance of an object that doesn't have to be set before you use it. You can use the New keyword only with object variables to create a new instance of that class of object without requiring a Set statement. You can't use New to declare dependent objects. If you do not use the New keyword, you cannot reference the object or any of its properties or methods until you set the variable to an object using a Set statement.

Use the WithEvents keyword to indicate an object variable within a class module that responds to events triggered by an ActiveX object. Form and report modules that respond to events on the related form and report objects are class modules. You can also define custom class modules to create custom objects. If you use the WithEvents keyword, you cannot use the New keyword.

Visual Basic initializes declared variables at compile time. Numeric variables are initialized to zero (0), variant variables are initialized to empty, variable-length string variables are initialized as zero-length strings, and fixed-length string variables are filled with ANSI zeros (Chr(0)).

### Example

To declare a long variable named lngMyNumber that can be used in any procedure within this module, enter the following:

```
Private lngMyNumber As Long
```

## Public Statement

Use a Public statement in the Declarations section of a standard module or a class module to declare variables that you can use in any procedure anywhere in your database.

### Syntax

```
Public {[WithEvents] variablename
  [([<array dimension>],... )]
  [As [New] datatype]},...
```

where *<array dimension>* is

```
[lowerbound To ] upperbound
```

### Notes

If you do not include an *<array dimension>* specification but you do include the parentheses, you must include a ReDim statement in each procedure that uses the array to dynamically allocate the array at run time. You can define an array with up to 60 dimensions. If you do not include a *lowerbound* value in an *<array dimension>* specification, the default lower bound is 0. You can reset the default lower bound to 1 by including an *Option Base 1* statement in the module Declarations section. The *lowerbound* and *upperbound* values must be integers, and *upperbound* must be greater than or equal to *lowerbound*. The number of members of an array is limited only by the amount of memory on your computer.

Valid *datatype* entries are Byte, Boolean, Integer, Long, Currency, Single, Double, Date, String (for variable-length strings), String * *length* (for fixed-length strings), Object, Variant, or one of the object types described earlier in this chapter. Note, however, that you cannot declare a Public fixed-length string within a class module. You can also declare a user-defined variable structure using the Type statement and then use the user type name as a data type. You should always explicitly declare the data type of your variables. If you do not include the As *datatype* clause, Visual Basic assigns the Variant data type.

Use the New keyword to indicate that a declared object variable is a new instance of an object that doesn't have to be set before you use it. You can use the New keyword only with object variables to create a new instance of that class of object without requiring a Set statement. You can't use New to declare dependent objects. If you do not use the New keyword, you cannot reference the object or any of its properties or methods until you set the variable to an object using a Set statement.

Use the WithEvents keyword to indicate an object variable within a class module that responds to events triggered by an ActiveX object. Form and report modules that respond to events on the related form and report objects are class modules. You can also define custom class modules to create custom objects. If you use the WithEvents keyword, you cannot use the New keyword.

Visual Basic initializes declared variables at compile time. Numeric variables are initialized to zero (0), variant variables are initialized to empty, variable-length string variables are initialized as zero-length strings, and fixed-length string variables are filled with ANSI zeros (Chr(0)).

### Example

To declare a long variable named lngMyNumber that can be used in any procedure in the database, enter the following:

```
Public lngMyNumber As Long
```

## ReDim Statement

Use a ReDim statement to dynamically declare an array within a procedure or to redimension a declared array within a procedure at run time.

### Syntax

```
ReDim [Preserve] {variablename
  (<array dimension>,...) [As datatype]},...
```

where *<array dimension>* is

```
[lowerbound To ] upperbound
```

### Notes

If you're dynamically allocating an array that you previously defined with no *<array dimension>* specification in a Dim, Public, or Private statement, your array can have up to 60 dimensions. You cannot dynamically reallocate an array that you previously defined with an *<array dimension>* specification in a Dim, Public, or Private statement. If you declare the array only within a procedure, your array can have up to 60 dimensions. If you do not include a *lowerbound* value in an <*array dimension*> specification, the default lower bound is 0. You can reset the default lower bound to 1 by including an *Option Base 1* statement in the module Declarations section. The *lowerbound* and *upperbound* values must be integers, and *upperbound* must be greater than or equal to *lowerbound*. The number of members of an array is limited only by the amount of memory on your computer. If you previously specified dimensions in a Public, Private, or Dim statement or in another ReDim statement within the same procedure, you cannot change the number of dimensions.

Include the Preserve keyword to ask Visual Basic not to reinitialize existing values in the array. When you use Preserve, you can change the bounds of only the last dimension in the array.

Valid *datatype* entries are Byte, Boolean, Integer, Long, Currency, Single, Double, Date, String (for variable-length strings), String * *length* (for fixed-length strings), Object, Variant, or one of the object types described earlier in this chapter. You can also declare a user-defined variable structure using the Type statement and then use the user type name as a data type. You should always explicitly declare the data type of your variables. If you do not include the As *datatype* clause, Visual Basic assigns the Variant data type. You cannot change the data type of an array that you previously declared with a Dim, Public, or Private statement. After you establish the number of dimensions for an array that has module or global scope, you cannot change the number of its dimensions using a ReDim statemetnt.

Visual Basic initializes declared variables at compile time. Numeric variables are initialized to zero (0), variant variables are initialized to empty, variable-length string variables are initialized as zero-length strings, and fixed-length string variables are filled with ANSI zeros (Chr(0)). When you use the Preserve keyword, Visual Basic initializes only additional variables in the array. If you use a ReDim statement within a procedure to both declare and allocate an array (and you have not previously defined the array with a Dim, Public, or Private statement), Visual Basic reinitializes the array each time you run the procedure.

### Example

To dynamically allocate an array named strProductNames that contains 20 strings, each with a fixed length of 25, enter the following:

```
ReDim strProductNames(20) As String * 25
```

## Static Statement

Use a Static statement within a procedure to declare a variable used only in that procedure and that Visual Basic does not reinitialize while the module containing the procedure is open. Visual Basic opens all standard and class modules (objects you can see in the Modules list in the Navigation Pane) when you open the database containing those objects. Visual Basic keeps form or report class modules open only while the form or the report is open.

## Syntax

```
Static {variablename [({<array dimension>},...)]
  [As [New] datatype]},...
```

where <*array dimension*> is

```
[lowerbound To ] upperbound
```

## Notes

If you do not include an <*array dimension*> specification but you do include the parentheses, you must include a ReDim statement in each procedure that uses the array to dynamically allocate the array at run time. You can define an array with up to 60 dimensions. If you do not include a *lowerbound* value in an <*array dimension*> specification, the default lower bound is 0. You can reset the default lower bound to 1 by including an *Option Base 1* statement in the module Declarations section. The *lowerbound* and *upperbound* values must be integers, and *upperbound* must be greater than or equal to *lowerbound*. The number of members of an array is limited only by the amount of memory on your computer.

Valid *datatype* entries are Byte, Boolean, Integer, Long, Currency, Single, Double, Date, String (for variable-length strings), String * *length* (for fixed-length strings), Object, Variant, or one of the object types described in this chapter. You can also declare a user-defined variable structure using the Type statement and then use the user type name as a data type. You should always explicitly declare the data type of your variables. If you do not include the As *datatype* clause, Visual Basic assigns the Variant data type.

Use the New keyword to indicate that a declared object variable is a new instance of an object that doesn't have to be set before you use it. You can use the New keyword only with object variables to create a new instance of that class of object without requiring a Set statement. You can't use New to declare dependent objects. If you do not use the New keyword, you cannot reference the object or any of its properties or methods until you set the variable to an object using a Set statement.

Visual Basic initializes declared variables at compile time. Numeric variables are initialized to zero (0), variant variables are initialized to empty, variable-length string variables are initialized as zero-length strings, and fixed-length string variables are filled with ANSI zeros (Chr(0)).

## Examples

To declare a static variable named intMyInteger as an integer, enter the following:

```
Static intMyInteger As Integer
```

To declare a static array named strMyString that contains fixed-length strings that are 20 characters long and contains 50 entries from 51 through 100, enter the following:

```
Static strMyString(51 To 100) As String * 20
```

## Type Statement

Use a Type statement in a Declarations section to create a user-defined data structure containing one or more variables.

### Syntax

```
[Public | Private] Type typename
    {variablename [({<array dimension>},...)]
      As datatype}
    ...
End Type
```

where *<array dimension>* is

```
[lowerbound To ] upperbound
```

### Notes

A Type statement is most useful for declaring sets of variables that can be passed to procedures (including Windows API functions) as a single variable. You can also use the Type statement to declare a record structure. After you declare a user-defined data structure, you can use *typename* in any subsequent Dim, Public, Private, or Static statement to create a variable of that type. You can reference variables in a user-defined data structure variable by entering the variable name, a period, and the name of the variable within the structure. (See the second part of the example that follows.)

Include the Public keyword to declare a user-defined type that is available to all procedures in all modules in your database. Include the Private keyword to declare a user-defined type that is available only within the module in which the declaration is made. You must enter each *variablename* entry on a new line. You must indicate the end of your user-defined data structure using an End Type statement.

Valid *datatype* entries are Byte, Boolean, Integer, Long, Currency, Single, Double, Date, String (for variable-length strings), String * *length* (for fixed-length strings), Object, Variant, or one of the object types described earlier in this chapter. You can also declare a user-defined variable structure using the Type statement and then use the user type name as a data type. You should always explicitly declare the data type of your variables. If you do not include the As *datatype* clause, Visual Basic assigns the Variant data type.

If you do not include an *<array dimension>* specification but you do include the parentheses, you must include a ReDim statement in each procedure that uses the array to dynamically allocate the array at run time in any variable that you declare as this Type. You can define an array with as many as 60 dimensions. If you do not include a *lowerbound* value in an *<array dimension>* specification, the default lower bound is 0. You can reset the default lower bound to 1 by including an *Option Base 1* statement in the module Declarations section. The *lowerbound* and *upperbound* values must be integers, and *upperbound* must be greater than or equal to *lowerbound*. The number of members of an array is limited only by the amount of memory on your computer.

Note that a Type declaration does not reserve any memory. Visual Basic allocates the memory required by the Type statement when you use *typename* as a data type in a Dim, Public, Private, or Static statement.

### Example

To define a user type structure named MyRecord containing a long integer and three string fields, declare a variable named usrContacts using that user type, and then set the first string to "Jones", first enter the following:

```
Type MyRecord
    lngID As Long
    strLast As String
    strFirst As String
    strMid As String
End Type
```

Within a procedure, enter the following:

```
Dim usrContacts As MyRecord
usrContacts.strLast = "Jones"
```

# Collections, Objects, Properties, and Methods

You've already dealt with two of the main collections supported by Access 2007–Forms and Reports. The Forms collection contains all the form objects that are open in your application, and the Reports collection contains all the open report objects.

As you'll learn in more detail later in this section, collections, objects, properties, and methods are organized in several object model hierarchies. An object has *properties* that describe the object and *methods* that are actions you can ask the object to execute. For example, a Form object has a Name property (the name of the form) and a Requery method (to ask the form to requery its record source). Many objects also have *collections* that define sets of other objects within the object. For example, a Form object has a Controls collection that is the set of all control objects (text boxes, labels, and so on) defined on the form.

You don't need a thorough understanding of collections, objects, properties, and methods to perform most application tasks. It's useful, however, for you to know how Access and Visual Basic organize these items so that you can better understand how Access works. If you want to study advanced code examples available in the many sample databases that you can download from public forums, you'll need to understand collections, objects, properties, and methods and how to correctly reference them.

## The Access Application Architecture

An Access 2007 desktop application (.accdb) has two major components–the application engine, which controls the programming and the user interface, and the Microsoft Access Database Engine (DBEngine), which controls the storage of data and the definition of all the objects in your database. An Access project (.adp) also uses the application engine, but it depends on its Connection object to define a link to the Microsoft SQL Server database that contains the tables, views, functions, and stored procedures used by the application.

As you'll see later, Visual Basic supports two distinct object models (Data Access Objects–DAO, and ActiveX Data Objects–ADO) for manipulating objects stored by the database engine. Figure 19-12 shows the application architecture of Access.

When you open a database, the application engine loads the appropriate object collections from the database and application files to enable it to list the names of all the tables, queries, views, database diagrams, stored procedures, forms, reports, macros, and modules to appear in the Navigation Pane. The application engine establishes the top-level Application object, which contains several useful collections, including a Forms collection (all the open forms), a Reports collection (all the open reports), a Modules collection (all the open modules, including form and report modules), a References collection (all Visual Basic library references), and a TempVars collection (all temporary variables created by macros). Each form and report, in turn, contains a Controls collection (all of the controls on the form or report). Among some of the more interesting properties of the Application object is the ADOConnectString property that contains the information you can use to connect to this database from another database.

#### Note

For backward compatibility with earlier versions and database files in the .mdb format, the Access object architecture continues to support obsolete collections, objects, and properties. For example, the Application object continues to support a CommandBars collection to allow you to manipulate any custom menus or toolbars that might have been defined using Microsoft Office Access 2003 or earlier. The CurrentProject object continues to support the AllDataAccessPages collection to allow you to find any data access pages defined in an older .mdb format file; however, the AllDataAccessPages collection is hidden and appears only when you request it or instruct the Visual Basic Editor to show hidden members. Finally, the Screen object continues to support the ActiveDataAccessPage property, but only as a hidden property.

The Application object also contains two special objects, the Screen object and the DoCmd object. The Screen object has six very useful properties: ActiveForm, ActiveReport, ActiveDatasheet, ActiveControl, PreviousControl, and MousePointer. Without knowing the actual names, you can reference the control (if any) that currently has the focus, the datasheet (if any) that has the focus, the form (if any) that has the focus, the report (if any) that has the focus, or the name of the control that previously had the focus. You can use the MousePointer property to examine the current status of the mouse pointer (arrow, I-beam, hourglass, and so on) and set the pointer. (Additional details about referencing properties of objects appear later in this chapter.) The DoCmd object lets you execute most macro actions within Visual Basic. See "Running Macro Actions and Menu Commands" on page 1026. If your application is an Access desktop database (.accdb), the DBEngine object under the Application object connects you to the

Microsoft Access Database Engine (ACE) to manipulate its objects using the Data Access Objects (DAO) model.

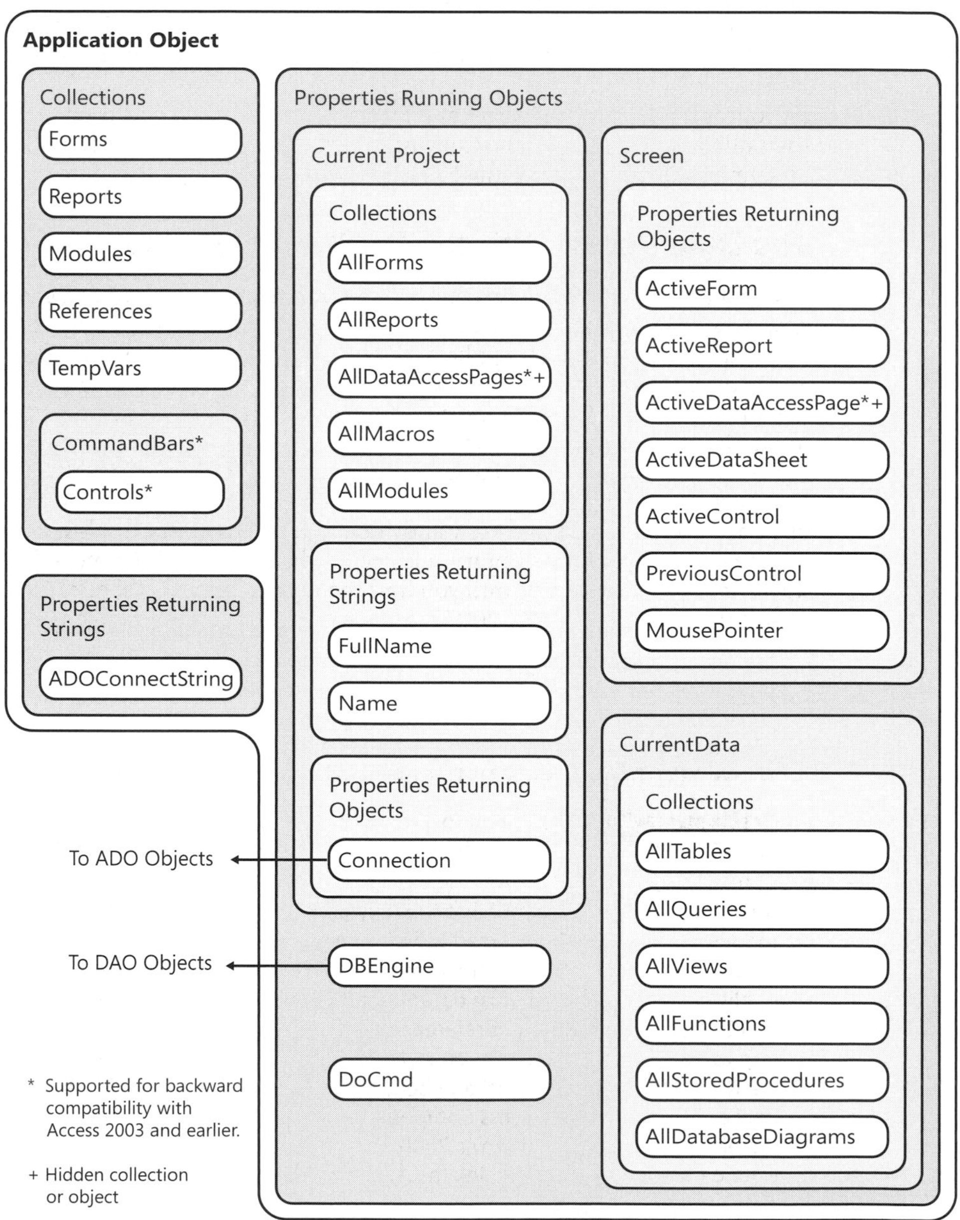


**Figure 19-12** You can explore objects in the Access application architecture from the Application object.

Two properties allow you to directly find out the names of all objects stored in your database without having to call the database engine. In an Access desktop database (.accdb), you can find out the names of all your tables and queries via the CurrentData property. In an Access project file (.adp) that is connected to SQL Server, you can additionally find out the names of database diagrams, stored procedures, functions, and views via this same property. In either type of Access file, you can discover the names of all your forms, reports, macros, and modules via the CurrentProject property. Finally, the FullName property of the CurrentProject object tells you the full path and file name of your application file, and the Name property tells you the file name only.

## The Data Access Objects (DAO) Architecture

The first (and older) of the two models you can use to fetch data and examine or create new data objects is the Data Access Objects (DAO) model. This model is best suited for use within Access desktop applications (.accdb) because it provides objects, methods, and properties specifically tailored to the way Access and the Access Database Engine work together. The latest version included with Access 2007 includes enhancements to manipulate the complex Attachment data type and multi-value fields. To use this model, you must ask Visual Basic to load a reference to the Microsoft Office 12.0 Access Database Engine Object Library. To verify that your project includes this reference, open any module in Design view and click References on the Tools menu. If you don't see the check box for this library selected at the top of the References dialog box, scroll down the alphabetical list until you find the library, select its check box, and click OK to add the reference. Access 2007 creates this reference for you in any new database that you create.

INSIDE OUT **Is the Rumor That "DAO Is Dead" Really True?**

Absolutely not! First, you need to know a bit of history. Beginning with version 9.0 (Access 2000), the Access development team introduced ActiveX Data Objects (ADO) to make it easier to work with SQL Server or other server databases as the data store for Access applications. ADO was touted as the "new direction" for data engine object models because it was designed to be more generic to work with different databases. Access 2000 also introduced the project file format (.adp) that lets you create an Access application linked directly to a database on SQL Server. Both Access 2000 and Access XP (2002) provided a default reference to the ADO library in a new database, and you had to add the DAO library if you wanted to use it. Microsoft also declared DAO "stable" (read: no new enhancements) and began distributing the Access JET database engine as part of Microsoft Data Access Components (MDAC) that you install with your operating system—Windows 98, Windows 2000, Windows XP, or Windows Vista. And so, the developer community began to think that DAO was "dead."

But DAO in many cases really works better if you're building a desktop application. DAO gives you direct access not only to all your table and query definitions but also forms, reports, macros, and modules. Also, the record source for all forms and reports creates a DAO recordset, so it doesn't make sense to try to use the entirely different ADO recordset object in your code. As of Access 2002, you can assign a recordset object you open in code directly to the Recordset property of a form. But if you're using an ADO recordset, features that you expect to work—such as updating across a join or autolookup when you set a foreign key—don't work correctly. In short, DAO was designed to work best with Access desktop applications.

When Microsoft stopped providing DAO as a default reference in new databases, many in the developer community pointed out to Microsoft that this really isn't a good idea for desktop applications. Microsoft listened to its users and changed the default library back to DAO in Office Access 2003. However, the Access development team couldn't plan any major enhancements because the JET engine had become part of Windows.

For Access 2007, the development team began creating its own new version of the JET engine—now called the Access Database Engine or ACE for short. ACE includes the new features to support the Attachment data type as well as multi-value fields, and it also supports all the features of the old JET engine, but uses an enhanced version of DAO. So no, DAO is not dead—it in a sense has been reborn in the new database engine for Access 2007.

The Application object's DBEngine property serves as a bridge between the application engine and the Access Database Engine. The DBEngine property represents the DBEngine object, which is the top-level object in the DAO hierarchy. Figure 19-13 shows you a diagram of the hierarchy of collections defined in the DAO model.

The DBEngine object controls all the database objects in your database through a hierarchy of collections, objects, and properties. When you open an Access database, the DBEngine object first establishes a Workspaces collection and a default Workspace object (the first object in the Workspaces collection). If you are opening a secured database created in the prior version format (.mdb, .mde) and your workgroup is secured, Access prompts you for a password and a user ID so that the DBEngine can create a User object in the Users collection and a Group object in the Groups collection within the default workspace. If your workgroup is not secured, the DBEngine signs you on as a default user called Admin.

Finally, the DBEngine creates a Database object within the Databases collection of the default Workspace object. If your prior version format file is secured, the DBEngine uses the current User and/or Group object information to determine whether you're authorized to access any of the objects within the database.

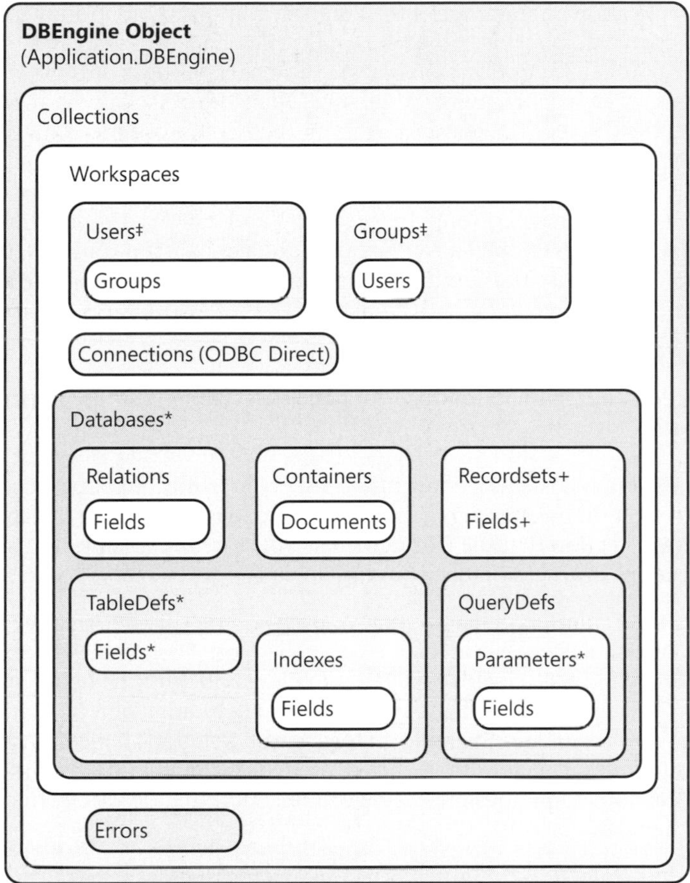


* Default collection of any object contained in the parent collection.
\+ The Access Database Engine (ACE) for Access 2007 also supports Recordset2 and Field2 objects to manipulate complex fields (attachment and multi-value).
‡ Supported for backward compatibility of user-level security in .mdb and .mde files.

**Figure 19-13** The Data Access Objects (DAO) model is specifically designed to manipulate data objects in an Access desktop database.

After the DBEngine creates a Database object, the application engine determines whether the database contains any potentially untrustworthy objects. Any database containing tables, queries, macros or Visual Basic code is deemed potentially untrustworthy. If the database is signed with a certificate that you have accepted as trustworthy or the database resides in a trusted location, the application engine enables all code. If the database is not trusted, the application engine displays a security warning message and provides the option to temporarily enable the database.

Next, the application engine checks the database's application options to find out whether to open a display form, load an application icon, and display a title or to use one or more of the other application options. You can set these options when you have your database open by clicking the Microsoft Office Button, clicking Access Options, and clicking the Current Database category in the Access Options dialog box. After checking the application options, the application engine checks to see whether a macro group named Autoexec exists in the database. If it finds Autoexec, the application engine runs this macro group. In versions 1 and 2 of Access, you'd often use the Autoexec macro group to open a startup form and run startup routines. In Access 2007, however, you should use the application options to specify a display form, and then use the event procedures or embedded macros of the startup form to run your startup routines.

**See Chapter 24, "The Finishing Touches," for details on creating startup properties and custom Ribbons.**

You can code Visual Basic procedures that can create additional Database objects in the Databases collection by opening additional .accdb files. Each open Database object has a Containers collection that the DBEngine uses to store the definition (using the Documents collection) of all your tables, queries, forms, reports, macros, and modules.

You can use the TableDefs collection to examine and modify existing tables. You can also create new TableDef objects within this collection. Each TableDef object within the TableDefs collection has a Fields collection that describes all the fields in the table, and an Indexes collection (with a Fields collection for each Index object) that describes any indexes that you created on the table. Likewise, the Relations collection contains Relation objects that describe how tables are related and what integrity rules apply between tables, and each Relation object has a Fields collection that describes the fields that participate in the relation.

The QueryDefs collection contains QueryDef objects that describe all the queries in your database. You can modify existing queries or create new ones. Each QueryDef object has a Parameters collection for any parameters required to run the query and a Fields collection that describes the fields returned by the query. Finally, the Recordsets collection contains a Recordset object for each open recordset in your database, and the Fields collection of each Recordset object tells you the fields in the recordset.

To reference any object within the DAO model, you can always start with the DBEngine object. If you want to work in the current database, that Database object is always the first database in the Databases collection of the first Workspace object. For example:

```
Dim dbMyDB As DAO.Database
Set dbMyDB = DBEngine.Workspaces(0).Databases(0)
```

Access also provides a handy shortcut object to the current database called CurrentDb. So, you can also establish a pointer to the current database as follows:

```
Set dbMyDB = CurrentDb
```

> **Note**
>
> In one of the examples at the end of this chapter, you'll learn how to create a new TableDef object and then open a Recordset object on the new table to insert rows. You can find code examples in the Conrad Systems Contacts application that manipulate objects using both DAO and ADO.

## The ActiveX Data Objects (ADO) Architecture

With Access 2000, Microsoft introduced a more generic set of data engine object models to provide references not only to objects stored by the Access Database Engine but also to data objects stored in other database products such as SQL Server. These models are called the ActiveX Data Objects (ADO) architecture. With Access 97 (version 8.0), you could download the Microsoft Data Access Components from the Microsoft Web site to be able to use the ADO model. Access 2000 and Access XP (2002) provided direct support for ADO with built-in libraries and direct references to key objects in the model from the Access Application object. As noted earlier, Access 2003 and Access 2007 provide a default reference to the Data Access Objects library (DAO), not ADO.

Because these models are designed to provide a common set of objects across any data engine that supports the ActiveX Data Objects, they do not necessarily support all the features you can find in the DAO architecture that was specifically designed for the Access Database Engine. For this reason, if you are designing an application that will always run with the Access Database Engine, you are better off using the DAO model. If, however, you expect that your application might one day "upsize" to an ActiveX data engine such as SQL Server, you should consider using the ADO architecture as much as possible. If you create your Access application as an Access project (.adp) linked to SQL Server, you should use only the ADO models.

Figure 19-14 shows you the two major models available under the ADO architecture. The basic ADODB model lets you open and manipulate recordsets via the Recordset object and execute action or parameter queries via the Command object. The ADO Extensions for DDL and Security model (ADOX) allows you to create, open, and manipulate tables, views (non-parameter unordered queries), and procedures (action queries, parameter queries, ordered queries, functions, triggers, or procedures) within the data engine Catalog object (the object that describes the definition of objects in your database). You can also examine and define Users and Groups collections defined in the Catalog object with ADOX.

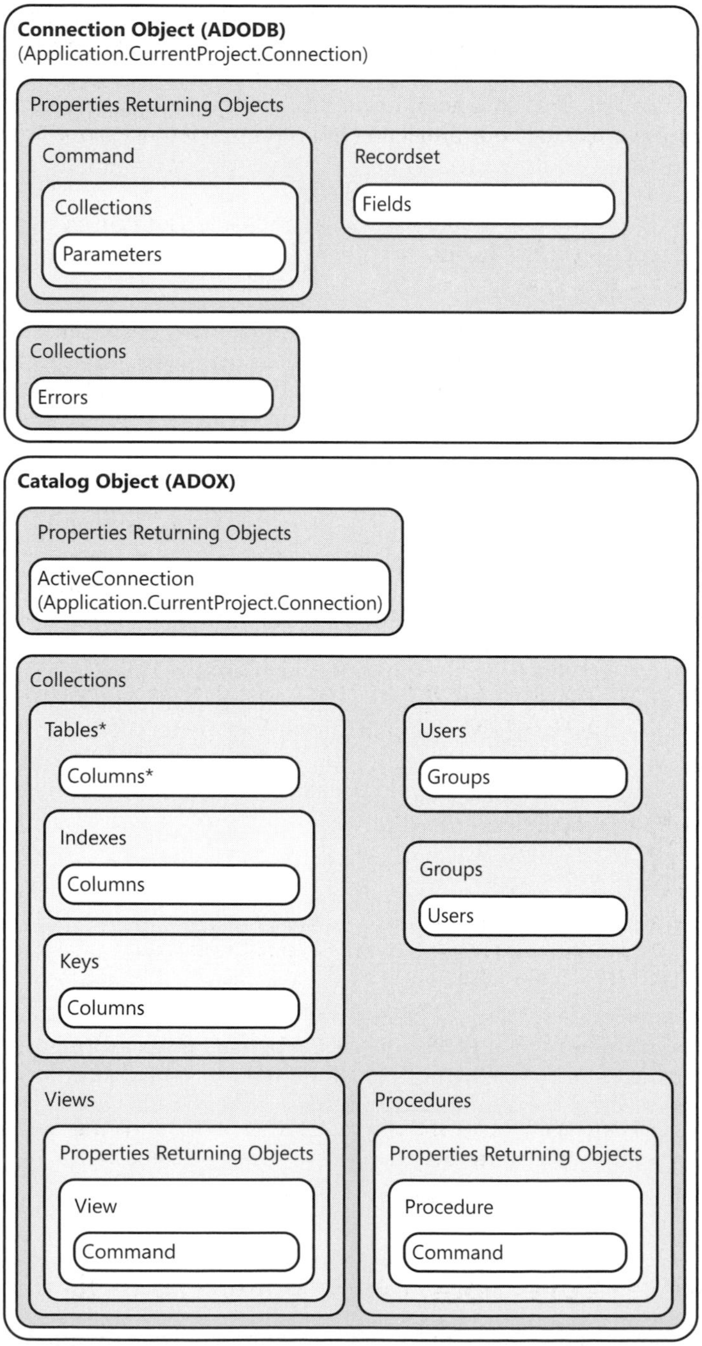


*Default collection of any object contained in the parent collection

**Figure 19-14** The ActiveX Data Objects (ADODB) and ActiveX Data Objects Extensions for DDL and Security (ADOX) models provide another way to work with the data and objects in your database.

To use the ADODB model, you must instruct Visual Basic to load a reference to the Microsoft ActiveX Data Objects Library. For objects in the ADOX model, you need the Microsoft ADO Extensions for DDL and Security Library. (You should normally find only one version on your computer. If you find multiple versions in the list, select the latest one.) To verify that your project includes these references, open any module in Design view and click References on the Tools menu. If you don't see the check boxes for these libraries selected at the top of the References dialog box, scroll down the alphabetical list until you find the library you need, select its check box, and click OK to add the reference. Access 2007 does not automatically create a reference to the ADODB library for you in any new database that you create.

Note that there are some objects in common between DAO, ADODB, and ADOX. If you use multiple models in an application, you must be careful to qualify object declarations. For example, a Recordset object type in the DAO model is DAO.Recordset, whereas a Recordset in the ADODB model is ADODB.Recordset. You cannot freely interchange a DAO recordset with an ADODB recordset—they are completely different objects.

The link to ADODB and ADOX is via the CurrentProject.Connection property. After you open an ADODB.Connection object, you can work with other collections, objects, and properties within the ADODB model. Likewise, by establishing an ADOX.Catalog object and setting its Connection property, you can work with any collection, object, or property within the ADOX model.

For all objects within either ADODB or ADOX, you must first establish a base object (connection or catalog, respectively). For example:

```
Dim cn As ADODB.Connection, rst As New ADODB.Recordset
Set cn = CurrentProject.Connection
rst.Open = "tblContacts", cn
```

Or

```
Dim catThisDB As New ADOX.Catalog, tbl As ADOX.Table
Set catThisDB.ActiveConnection = CurrentProject.Connection
Set tbl = catThisDB.Tables("tblContacts")
```

> **Note**
>
> One of the extensive examples at the end of this chapter uses ADO exclusively to manipulate recordsets in the Conrad Systems Contacts sample database.

## Referencing Collections, Objects, and Properties

In the previous chapter, you were introduced to the most common way to reference objects in the Forms and Reports collections, controls on open forms and reports, and properties of controls. There are two alternative ways to reference an object within a collection. The three ways to reference an object within a collection are as follows:

- **CollectionName![Object Name]** This is the method you used in the previous chapter. For example: *Forms![frmContacts]*.
- **CollectionName("Object Name")** This method is similar to the first method but uses a string constant (or a string variable) to supply the object name, as in *Forms("frmContacts")* or *Forms(strFormName)*.
- **CollectionName(RelativeObjectNumber)** Visual Basic numbers objects within most collections from zero (0) to CollectionName.*Count minus 1*. You can determine the number of open forms by referring to the Count property of the Forms collection: *Forms.Count*. You can refer to the second open form in the Forms collection as *Forms(1)*.

Forms and Reports are relatively simple because they are top-level collections within the application engine. As you can see in Figure 19-13, when you reference a collection or an object maintained by the DBEngine, the hierarchy of collections and objects is quite complex. If you want to find out the number of Workspace objects that exist in the Workspaces collection, for example, you need to reference the Count property of the Workspaces collection like this:

```
DBEngine.Workspaces.Count
```

(You can create additional workspaces from Visual Basic code.)

Using the third technique described above to reference an object, you can reference the default (first) Workspace object by entering the following:

```
DBEngine.Workspaces(0)
```

Likewise, you can refer to the currently open database in a desktop application (.accdb) by entering the following:

```
DBEngine.Workspaces(0).Databases(0)
```

When you want to refer to an object that exists in an object's default (or only) collection (see Figures 22-13 and 22-14), you do not need to include the collection name. Therefore, because the Databases collection is the default collection for the Workspaces collection, you can also refer to the currently open database by entering the following:

```
DBEngine.Workspaces(0)(0)
```

As you can see, even with this shorthand syntax, object names can become quite cumbersome if you want to refer, for example, to a particular field within an index definition for a table within the current database in the default Workspace object—or a column within an index definition for a table within the current catalog. For example, using this full syntax, you can reference the name of the first field in the tblContacts table in Contacts.accdb like this:

```
DBEngine(0)(0).TableDefs("tblContacts").Fields(0).Name
```

(Whew!) If for no other reason, object variables are quite handy to help minimize name complexity.

In particular, you can reduce name complexity by using an object variable to represent the current database. When you set the variable to the current database, you can call the CurrentDb function rather than use the database's full qualifier. For example, you can declare a Database object variable, set it to the current database by using the CurrentDb function, and then use the Database object variable name as a starting point to reference the TableDefs, QueryDefs, and Recordsets collections that it contains. (See "Assigning an Object Variable—Set Statement" on page 991 for the syntax of the Set statement.) Likewise, if you are going to work extensively with fields in a TableDef object or columns in a Table object, you are better off establishing an object variable that points directly to the TableDef or Table object. For example, you can simplify the complex expression to reference the name of the first field in the tblContacts table in Contacts.accdb like this:

```
Dim db As DAO.Database, tdf As DAO.TableDef
Set db = CurrentDb
Set tdf = db.Tabledefs![tblContacts]
Debug.Print tdf.Fields(0).Name
```

INSIDE OUT

**Should I Use CurrentDb or DBEngine.Workspaces(0).Databases(0)?**

When you use DBEngine.Workspaces(0).Databases(0) (or DBEngine(0)(0)) to set a database object, Visual Basic establishes a pointer to the current database. You can have only one object variable set to the actual copy of the current database, and you must never close this copy. A safer technique is to set your database variable using the CurrentDb function. Using this technique opens a new database object that is based on the same database as the current one. You can have as many copies of the current database as you like, and you can close them when you finish using them. When you use CurrentDb to establish a pointer to your database, Visual Basic refreshes all the collections and keeps them current. If you want to ensure that the collections are current (for example, to be aware of any added or deleted tables or queries), you must refresh the collections yourself when you use DBEngine(0)(0). The one small advantage to DBEngine(0)(0) is that it is more efficient because it does not refresh all collections when you establish a pointer to it.

## When to Use "!" and "."

You've probably noticed that a complex, fully qualified name of an object or a property in Access 2007 or Visual Basic contains exclamation points (!) and periods (.) that separate the parts of the name.

Use an exclamation point preceding a name when the name refers to an object that is *in* the preceding object or collection of objects. A name following an exclamation point is generally the name of an object you created (such as a form or a table). Names following an exclamation point must be enclosed in brackets ([ ]) if they contain embedded blank spaces or a special character, such as an underscore (_). You must also enclose the name of an object you created in brackets if the name is also an Access or SQL reserved word. For example, most objects have a Name property—if you name a control or field "Name," you must use brackets when you reference your object.

To make this distinction clear, you might want to get into the habit of always enclosing in brackets names that follow an exclamation point, even though brackets are not required for names that don't use blank spaces or special characters. Access automatically inserts brackets around names in property sheets, design grids, and action arguments.

Use a period preceding a name that refers to a collection name, a property name, or the name of a method that you can perform against the preceding object. (Names following a period should never contain blank spaces.) In other words, use a period when the following name is *of* the preceding name (as in the TableDefs collection *of* the Databases(0) object, the Count property *of* the TableDefs collection, or the MoveLast method *of* the DAO Recordset object). This distinction is particularly important when referencing something that has the same name as the name of a property. For example, the reference

```
DBEngine.Workspaces(0).Databases(0).TableDefs(18).Name
```

refers to the name of the nineteenth TableDef object in the current database. In the Contacts.accdb database, if you use Debug.Print or the Immediate window to display this reference, Visual Basic returns the value *tblCompanyContacts*. However, the reference

```
DBEngine.Workspaces(0).Databases(0).TableDefs(18)![Name]
```

refers to the contents of a field called Name (if one exists) in the nineteenth TableDef object in the current database. In the Conrad Systems Contacts database, this reference returns an error because there is no Name field in the tblCompanyContacts table.

## INSIDE OUT What About Me?

If you spend some time looking at any of the code behind forms and reports in the sample databases, you'll notice many references such as Me.Name or Me.ProductName. Whenever you write code in a form or report module, you'll likely need to reference some of the controls on the form or report or some of the properties of the form or report. You already know that you can reference an open form by using, for example

```
Forms![frmProducts]
```

And to reference a control on the open frmProducts form, you could use

```
Forms![frmProducts]![ProductName]
```

Rather than type the collection name (Forms) and the form name (frmProducts) each time, you can use a shortcut—*Me*. This special keyword is a reference to the object where your code is running. Also, when Access opens a form, it loads the names of all controls you defined on the form as properties of the form—which are also properties of the Me object. (It also does the same for controls on open reports.) So, you can reference the ProductName control in code behind the frmProducts form by entering:

```
Me.ProductName
```

This can certainly make entering code faster. Also, because Me is an object, your code executes more quickly.

INSIDE OUT **Is It Possible to Reference in Visual Basic Variables Created by Macros?**

You bet! As you learned in Chapter 18, "Automating Your Application with Macros," you can use the new SetTempVar, RemoveTempVar, and RemoveAllTempVars actions to create, modify, and inspect values that you can pass from one macro to another. If you create an application that uses both macros and Visual Basic, you can also create, modify, and inspect these variables by using the TempVars collection. Unlike most collections in Access where you must first create an object before you can reference it, you can both create and set a macro temporary variable by simply assigning a value to a name in the TempVars collection. For example, to create and set a temporary variable called MyTempVar, use the following:

```
TempVars!MyTempVar = "Value to pass to a macro"
```

Temporary variables are the Variant data type, so you can assign a string, a number, or a date/time value to a member of the TempVars collection. To delete a temporary variable, use the Remove method as follows:

```
TempVars.Remove MyTempVar
```

To remove all temporary variables, use the RemoveAll method as follows:

```
TempVars.RemoveAll
```

But be careful. If you reference a temporary variable that does not exist yet, you won't get any error. If you misspell a temporary variable name, Access temporarily creates the variable and returns the value Null.

## Assigning an Object Variable—Set Statement

Use the Set statement to assign an object or object reference to an object variable.

### Syntax

```
Set objectvariablename = [New] objectreference
```

### Notes

As noted earlier, you can use object variables to simplify name references. Also, using an object variable is less time-consuming than using a fully qualified name. At run time, Visual Basic must always parse a qualified name to first determine the type of object and then determine which object or property you want. If you use an object variable, you have already defined the type of object and established a direct pointer to it, so Visual Basic can quickly go to that object. This is especially important if you plan to reference, for example, many controls on a form. If you create a form variable first and then assign the variable to point to the form, referencing controls on the form via the form variable is much simpler and faster than using a fully qualified name for each control.

You must first declare *objectvariablename* using a Dim, Private, Public, or Static statement. The object types you can declare include AccessObject, Application, ADOX.Catalog, ADOX.Column, ADODB.Command, ADOX.Command, ADODB.Connection, DAO.Container, Control, DAO.Database, DAO.Document, ADODB.Error, DAO.Error, ADODB.Field, DAO.Field, DAO.Field2, Form, ADOX.Group, DAO.Group, ADOX.Index, DAO.Index, ADOX.Key, ADODB.Parameter, DAO.Parameter, ADOX.Procedure, ADODB.Property, ADOX.Property, DAO.Property, DAO.QueryDef, ADODB.Recordset, DAO.Recordset, DAO.Recordset2, DAO.Relation, Report, ADOX.Table, DAO.TableDef, ADOX.User, DAO.User, ADOX.View, and DAO.Workspace object. You can also declare a variable as the generic Object data type and set it to any object (similar to the Variant data type). In addition, you can declare a variable as an instance of the class defined by a class module. The object type must be compatible with the object type of *objectreference*. You can use another object variable in an *objectreference* statement to qualify an object at a lower level. (See the examples that follow.) You can also use an object *method* to create a new object in a collection and assign that object to an object variable. For example, it's common to use the OpenRecordset method of a QueryDef or TableDef object to create a new Recordset object. See the example in the next section, "Object Methods."

An object variable is a reference to an object, not a copy of the object. You can assign more than one object variable to point to the same object and change a property of the object. When you do that, all variables referencing the object will reflect the change as well. The one exception is that several Recordset variables can refer to the same recordset, but each can have its own Bookmark property pointing to different rows in the recordset. If you want to create a new instance of an object, include the New keyword.

## Examples

To create a variable reference to the current database, enter the following:

```
Dim dbMyDB As DAO.Database
Set dbMyDB = CurrentDb
```

To create a variable reference to the tblContacts table in the current database using the dbMyDB variable defined above, enter the following:

```
Dim tblMyTable As DAO.TableDef
Set tblMyTable = dbMyDB![tblContacts]
```

Notice that you do not need to explicitly reference the TableDefs collection of the database, as in dbMyDB.TableDefs![tblContacts] or dbMyDB.TableDefs("tblContacts"), because TableDefs is the default collection of the database. Visual Basic assumes that [tblContacts] refers to the name of an object in the default collection of the database.

To create a variable reference to the Notes field in the tblContacts table using the tblMyTable variable defined above, enter the following:

```
Dim fldMyField As DAO.Field
Set fldMyField = tblMyTable![Notes]
```

Again, you do not need to include a specific reference to the Fields collection of the TableDef object, as in tblMyTable.Fields![Notes], because Fields is the default collection.

To create a variable reference to the catalog for the current database, enter the following:

```
Dim catThisDB As New ADOX.Catalog
catThisDB.ActiveConnection = CurrentProject.Connection
```

Note that you must use the New keyword because there's no way to open an existing catalog without first establishing a connection to it. You open a catalog by declaring it as a new object and assigning a Connection object to its ActiveConnection property. The preceding example takes advantage of the existence of the Application.CurrentProject.Connection property rather than first setting a Connection object. If you already have another Catalog object open, you can create a copy of it by using

```
Dim catCopy As ADOX.Catalog
Set catCopy = catThisDB
```

To create a variable reference to the tblContacts table in the current database using the catThisDB variable defined above, enter the following:

```
Dim tblMyTable As ADOX.Table
Set tblMyTable = catThisDB![tblContacts]
```

Notice that you do not need to explicitly reference the Tables collection of the database, as in catThisDB.Tables![ tblContacts] or catThisDB.Tables("tblContacts"), because Tables is the default collection of the catalog. Visual Basic assumes that [tblContacts] refers to the name of an object in the default collection of the catalog.

To create a variable reference to the Notes column in the tblContacts table using the tblMyTable variable defined above, enter the following.

```
Dim colMyColumn As ADOX.Column
Set colMyColumn = tblMyTable![Notes]
```

Again, you do not need to explicitly reference the Columns collection of the Table object, as in tblMyTable.Columns![Notes] because the Columns collection is the default collection of a Table object.

## Object Methods

When you want to apply an action to an object in your database (such as open a query as a recordset or go to the next row in a recordset), you apply a *method* of either the object or an object variable that you have assigned to point to the object. In some cases, you'll use a method to create a new object. Many methods accept parameters that you can use to further refine how the method acts on the object. For example, you can tell the DAO OpenRecordset method whether you're opening a recordset on a local table, a dynaset (a query-based recordset), or a read-only snapshot.

Visual Basic supports many different object methods—far more than there's room to properly document in this book. Perhaps one of the most useful groups of methods is the group you can use to create a recordset and then read, update, insert, and delete rows in the recordset.

## Working with DAO Recordsets

To create a recordset, you must first declare a Recordset object variable. Then open the recordset using the DAO OpenRecordset method of the current database (specifying a table name, a query name, or an SQL statement to create the recordset) or the OpenRecordset method of a DAO.QueryDef, DAO.TableDef, or other DAO.Recordset object. (As you'll learn in "Working with ADO Recordsets," if you're working in ADO, you use the Open method of a New ADODB.Recordset object.)

In DAO, you can specify options to indicate whether you're opening the recordset as a local table (which means you can use the Seek method to quickly locate rows based on a match with an available index), as a dynaset, or as a read-only snapshot. For updatable recordsets, you can also specify that you want to deny other updates, deny other reads, open a read-only recordset, open the recordset for append only, or open a read-only forward scroll recordset (which allows you to move only forward through the records and only once).

The syntax to use the OpenRecordset method of a Database object is as follows:

```
Set RecordSetObject =  DatabaseObject.OpenRecordset(source,
    [type], [options], [lockoptions])
```

*RecordSetObject* is a variable you have declared as DAO.Recordset, and *DatabaseObject* is a variable you have declared as DAO.Database. *Source* is a string variable or literal containing the name of a table, the name of a query, or a valid SQL statement. Table 19-2 describes the settings you can supply for *type*, *options*, and *lockoptions*.

**Table 19-2 OpenRecordset Parameter Settings**

| Setting | Description |
|---|---|
| **Type (Select one)** | |
| dbOpenTable | Returns a table recordset. You can use this option only when *source* is a table local to the database described by the Database object. *Source* cannot be a linked table. You can establish a current index in a table recordset and use the Seek method to find rows using the index. If you do not specify a *type*, OpenRecordset returns a table if *source* is a local table name. |
| dbOpenDynaset | Returns a dynaset recordset. *Source* can be a local table, a linked table, a query, or an SQL statement. You can use the Find methods to search for rows in a dynaset recordset. If you do not specify a *type*, OpenRecordset returns a dynaset if *source* is a linked table, a query, or an SQL statement. |
| dbOpenSnapshot | Returns a read-only snapshot recordset. You won't see any changes made by other users after you open the recordset. You can use the Find methods to search for rows in a snapshot recordset. |
| dbOpen-ForwardOnly | Returns a read-only snapshot recordset that you can move forward through only once. You can use the MoveNext method to access successive rows. |

| Setting | Description |
|---|---|
| **Options (You can select multiple options, placing a plus sign between option names to add them together)** | |
| dbAppendOnly | Returns a table or dynaset recordset that allows inserting new rows only. You can use this option only with the dbOpenTable and dbOpenDynaset types. |
| dbSeeChanges | Asks Access to generate a run-time error in your code if another user changes data while you are editing it in the recordset. |
| dbDenyWrite | Prevents other users from modifying or inserting records while your recordset is open. |
| dbDenyRead | Prevents other users from reading records in your open recordset. |
| dbInconsistent | Allows you to make changes to all fields in a multiple table recordset (based on a query or an SQL statement), including changes that would be inconsistent with any join defined in the query. For example, you could change the customer identifier field (foreign key) of an orders table so that it no longer matches the primary key in an included customers table–unless referential integrity constraints otherwise prevent you from doing so. You cannot include both dbInconsistent and dbConsistent. |
| dbConsistent | Allows you to only make changes in a multiple table recordset (based on a query or an SQL statement) that are consistent with the join definitions in the query. For example, you cannot change the customer identifier field (foreign key) of an orders table so that its value does not match the value of any customer row in the query. You cannot include both dbInconsistent and dbConsistent. |
| **Lockoptions (Select one)** | |
| dbPessimistic | Asks Access to lock a row as soon as you place the row in an editable state by executing an Edit method. This is the default if you do not specify a lock option. |
| dbOptimistic | Asks Access to not attempt to lock a row until you try to write it to the database with an Update method. This generates a run-time error if another user has changed the row after you executed the Edit method. |

For example, to declare a recordset for the tblFacilities table in the Housing Reservations (Housing.accdb) database and open the recordset as a table so that you can use its indexes, enter the following:

```
Dim dbHousing As DAO.Database
Dim rcdFacilities As DAO.RecordSet
Set dbHousing = CurrentDb
Set rcdFacilities = dbHousing.OpenRecordSet("tblFacilities", _
  dbOpenTable)
```

To open the qryContactProducts query in the Conrad Systems Contacts database (Contacts.accdb) as a dynaset, enter the following:

```
Dim dbContacts As DAO.Database
Dim rcdContactProducts As DAO.RecordSet
Set dbContacts = CurrentDb
Set rcdContactProducts = _
  dbContacts.OpenRecordSet("qryContactProducts")
```

(Note that opening a recordset as a dynaset is the default when the source is a query.)

> **Note**
>
> Any table recordset or dynaset recordset based on a table is updatable. When you ask Access to open a dynaset on a table, Access internally builds a query that selects all columns from the table. A dynaset recordset based on a query will be updatable if the query is updatable. See "Limitations on Using Select Queries to Update Data" on page 468 for details.

After you open a recordset, you can use one of the Move methods to move to a specific record. Use *recordset*.MoveFirst to move to the first row in the recordset. Other Move methods include MoveLast, MoveNext, and MovePrevious. If you want to move to a specific row in a dynaset recordset, use one of the Find methods. You must supply a string variable containing the criteria for finding the records you want. The criteria string looks exactly like an SQL WHERE clause but without the WHERE keyword. (See Article 2, "Understanding SQL," on the companion CD.) For example, to find the first row in the qryContactProducts query's recordset whose SoldPrice field is greater than $200, enter the following:

```
rcdContactProducts.FindFirst "SoldPrice > 200"
```

To delete a row in an updatable recordset, move to the row you want to delete and then use the Delete method. For example, to delete the first row in the qryContactProducts query's recordset that hasn't been invoiced yet (the Invoiced field is false), enter the following:

```
Dim dbContacts As DAO.Database
Dim rcdContactProducts As DAO.RecordSet
Set dbContacts = CurrentDb
Set rcdContactProducts = _
  dbContacts.OpenRecordSet("qryContactProducts")
rcdContactProducts.FindFirst "Invoiced = 0"
' Test the recordset NoMatch property for "not found"
If Not rcdContactProducts.NoMatch Then
    rcdContactProducts.Delete
End If
```

If you want to update rows in a recordset, move to the first row you want to update and then use the Edit method to lock the row and make it updatable. You can then refer to any of the fields in the row by name to change their values. Use the Update method on the recordset to save your changes before moving to another row. If you do not use the Update method before you move to a new row or close the recordset, the database discards your changes.

For example, to increase by 10 percent the SoldPrice entry of the first row in the rcdContactProducts query's recordset whose SoldPrice value is greater than $200, enter the following:

```
Dim dbContacts As DAO.Database
Dim rcdContactProducts As DAO.RecordSet
Set dbContacts = CurrentDb
Set rcdContactProducts = _
  dbContacts.OpenRecordSet("qryContactProducts")
rcdContactProducts.FindFirst "SoldPrice > 200"
 ' Test the recordset NoMatch property for "not found"
If Not rcdContactProducts.NoMatch Then
  rcdContactProducts.Edit
  rcdContactProducts![SoldPrice] = _
    rcdContactProducts![SoldPrice] * 1.1
  rcdContactProducts.Update
End If
```

To insert a new row in a recordset, use the AddNew method to start a new row. Set the values of all required fields in the row, and then use the Update method to save the new row. For example, to insert a new company in the Conrad Systems Contacts tblCompanies table, enter the following:

```
Dim dbContacts As DAO.Database
Dim rcdCompanies As DAO.RecordSet
Set dbContacts = CurrentDb
Set rcdCompanies = _
  dbContacts.OpenRecordSet("tblCompanies")
rcdCompanies.AddNew
rcdCompanies![CompanyName] = "Winthrop Brewing Co."
rcdCompanies![Address] = "155 Riverside Ave."
rcdCompanies![City] = "Winthrop"
rcdCompanies![StateOrProvince] = "WA"
rcdCompanies![PostalCode] = "98862"
rcdCompanies![PhoneNumber] = "(509) 555-8100"
rcdCompanies.Update
```

Note that because all the main data tables in Contacts.accdb are linked tables, rcdCompanies is a dynaset recordset, not a table recordset.

## Manipulating Complex Data Types Using DAO

New in Access 2007 are complex data types—the Attachment data type or any field defined as multi-value. A complex data type lets you store multiple values or objects in a field within a single record. Access 2007 accomplishes this by building hidden tables that contain one row per multiple value stored. You can manipulate these rows in a recordset in code, but only using DAO.

To work with data in a complex data type field, you must first open a recordset on the table containing the field. You can either open the table directly or open a query that includes the table and its complex field(s). The secret to dealing with complex fields is the Value property of the field in the recordset returns a DAO.Recordset2 object. So, you can set a declared DAO.Recordset2 variable to the Value property to open a recordset on the hidden table. You can manipulate this recordset exactly as you can any other DAO recordset, including using the Find and Move methods, and the Edit, AddNew, Update, and Delete methods.

When the complex field is a multi-value field, the recordset returned from the Value property of the parent field contains a single field called Value. You'll find one row per multiple value stored in the complex field. When the complex field is an Attachment data type, the recordset returned from the Value property of the parent field contains three fields—FileData, FileName, and FileType. The FileData field in an attachment complex recordset supports one method, LoadFromFile, that lets you insert the complex OLE data into the record by supplying a file location and name.

The tblContacts table in the Contacts sample database contains both a multi-value field (ContactType) and an attachment field (Photo). In the modExamples module in the Contacts.accdb database, you can find the following code that displays in the Immediate window the values from both fields for all contact records.

```
Public Sub ListContactComplex()
' An example of listing all the complex values in the Contacts table
Dim db As DAO.Database, rst As DAO.Recordset, rstComplex As DAO.Recordset2
Dim fld As DAO.Field2
  ' Point to this database
  Set db = CurrentDb
  ' Open a recordset on tblContacts
  Set rst = db.OpenRecordset("SELECT * FROM tblContacts")
  ' Loop through all the records
  Do Until rst.EOF
    ' Dump out the ID and name
    Debug.Print rst!ContactID, rst!LastName, rst!FirstName
    ' Get the contact type complex field
    Set rstComplex = rst!ContactType.Value
    ' Loop through them all
    Do Until rstComplex.EOF
      ' Dump out each value
      Debug.Print " ", "Contact Type: ", rstComplex!Value
      ' Get the next
      rstComplex.MoveNext
    Loop
    ' Get the Photo Attachment recordset
    Set rstComplex = rst!Photo.Value
    ' Loop though them all
    Do Until rstComplex.EOF
```

```
      ' Dump out the data
      Debug.Print " ", "Photo FileName: ", rstComplex!FileName, _
        "  File Type: ", rstComplex!FileType
      ' Get the next
      rstComplex.MoveNext
    Loop
    ' Get the next contact
    rst.MoveNext
  Loop
  ' Close out
  rst.Close
  Set rst = Nothing
  Set rstComplex = Nothing
  Set db = Nothing
End Sub
```

If you want to find the record for John Viescas and add the value Trainer to the Contact-Type field, do the following:

```
Dim db As DAO.Recordset, rst As DAO.Recordset, rstComplex As DAO.Recordset2
  ' Set a pointer to the current database
  Set db = CurrentDb
  ' Open the contacts table
  Set rst = db.OpenRecordset("tblContacts", dbOpenDynaset)
  ' Find the record for Viescas
  rst.FindFirst "LastName = 'Viescas'"
  ' Make sure we found it
  If Not rst.NoMatch Then
    ' Get the ContactType recordset
    Set rstComplex = rst!ContactType.Value
    ' Add a new row
    rstComplex.AddNew
    ' Insert the new value
    rstComplex.Value = "Trainer"
    ' Save the new value
    rstComplex.Update
  End If
  ' Close out
  rst.Close
  Set rst = Nothing
  Set rstComplex = Nothing
  Set db = Nothing
```

To find the contact record for John Viescas, check for the value Trainer in the Contact-Type field, and delete it if it exists, do the following:

```
Dim db As DAO.Recordset, rst As DAO.Recordset, rstComplex As DAO.Recordset2
  ' Set a pointer to the current database
  Set db = CurrentDb
  ' Open the contacts table
  Set rst = db.OpenRecordset("tblContacts", dbOpenDynaset)
  ' Find the record for Viescas
  rst.FindFirst "LastName = 'Viescas'"
```

```
  ' Make sure we found it
  If Not rst.NoMatch Then
    ' Get the ContactType recordset
    Set rstComplex = rst!ContactType.Value
    ' See if Trainer exists
    rstComplex.FindFirst "Value = 'Trainer '"
    ' If it exists,
    If Not rstComplex.NoMatch Then
      ' Delete it
      rstComplex.Delete
    End If
  End If
  ' Close out
  rst.Close
  Set rst = Nothing
  Set rstComplex = Nothing
  Set db = Nothing
```

To check to see if the Photo field for contact Jeff Conrad contains a file named JeffConrad.docx and add it if it does not, the code is as follows:

```
Dim db As DAO.Recordset, rst As DAO.Recordset, rstComplex As DAO.Recordset2
  ' Set a pointer to the current database
  Set db = CurrentDb
  ' Open the contacts table
  Set rst = db.OpenRecordset("tblContacts", dbOpenDynaset)
  ' Find the record for Conrad
  rst.FindFirst "LastName = 'Conrad'"
  ' Make sure we found it
  If Not rst.NoMatch Then
    ' Get the Photo recordset
    Set rstComplex = rst!Photo.Value
    ' See if the JeffConrad.docx file exists
    rstComplex.FindFirst "FileName = 'JeffConrad.docx'"
    ' If it does not exist,
    If rstComplex.NoMatch Then
      ' Start a new attachment record
      rstComplex.Addnew
      ' Load the file
      rstComplex!FileData.LoadFromFile _
        "C:\Microsoft Press\Access 2007 Inside Out\Documents\JeffConrad.docx"
      ' Save the new row
      rstComplex.Update
    End If
  End If
  ' Close out
  rst.Close
  Set rst = Nothing
  Set rstComplex = Nothing
  Set db = Nothing
```

## Working with ADO Recordsets

Recordsets in ADO offer many of the same capabilities and options as recordsets in DAO, but the terminology is somewhat different. Because you will most often use ADO with data stored in a server database such as SQL Server, the options for an ADO recordset are geared toward server-based data. For example, ADO uses the term *cursor* to refer to the set of rows returned by the server. Fundamentally, a cursor is a pointer to each row you need to work with in code. Depending on the options you choose (and the options supported by the particular database server), a cursor might also be read-only, updatable, or forward-only. A cursor might also be able to reflect changes made by other users of the database (a keyset or dynamic cursor), or it might present only a snapshot of the data (a static cursor).

To open an ADO recordset, you must use the Open method of a new ADO Recordset object. The syntax to use the Open method of a Recordset object is as follows:

```
RecordSetObject.Open [source], [connection],
  [cursortype], [locktype], [options]
```

*RecordSetObject* is a variable you have declared as a New ADO.Recordset. *Source* is a Command object, a string variable, or string literal containing the name of a table, the name of a view (the SQL Server term for a query), the name of a stored procedure, the name of a function that returns a table, or a valid SQL statement. A stored procedure might be a parameter query or a query that specifies sorting of rows from a table or view. A function might also accept parameters. If you supply a Command object as the source, you do not need to supply a *connection* (you define the connection in the Command object). Otherwise, *connection* must be the name of a Connection object that points to the target database.

Table 19-3 describes the settings you can supply for *cursortype*, *lockoptions*, and *options*.

For example, to declare a recordset for the tblFacilities table in the Housing Reservations database (Housing.accdb) and open the recordset as a table so you can use its indexes, enter the following:

```
Dim cnThisConnect As ADODB.Connection
Dim rcdFacilities As New ADODB.RecordSet
Set cnThisConnect = CurrentProject.Connection
rcdFacilities.Index = "PrimaryKey"
rcdBooks.Open "tblFacilities", cnThisConnect, adOpenKeyset, _
    adLockOptimistic, adCmdTableDirect
```

Note that you must establish the index you want to use before you open the recordset.

Table 19-3 **RecordSetObject.Open Parameter Settings**

| Setting | Description |
|---|---|
| **CursorType (Select one)** | |
| adOpenForwardOnly | Returns a read-only snapshot cursor (recordset) that you can move forward through only once. You can use the MoveNext method to access successive rows. If you do not supply a CursorType setting, adOpenForwardOnly is the default. |
| adOpenKeyset | Returns a Keyset cursor. This is roughly analogous to a DAO dynaset. If you are using ADO to open a recordset against a source in an Access .accdb file, you should use this option to obtain a recordset that behaves most like a DAO recordset. In this type of cursor, you will see changes to rows made by other users, but you will not see new rows added by other users after you have opened the cursor. |
| adOpenDynamic | Returns a dynamic cursor. This type of cursor lets you see not only changes made by other users but also added rows. Note, however, that certain key properties you might depend on in a DAO recordset such as RecordCount might not exist or might always be zero. |
| adOpenStatic | Returns a read-only snapshot cursor. You won't be able to see changes made by other users after you've opened the cursor. |
| **LockType (Select one)** | |
| adLockReadOnly | Provides no locks. The cursor is read-only. If you do not provide a lock setting, this is the default. |
| adLockPessimistic | Asks the target database to lock a row as soon as you place the row in an editable state by executing an Edit method. |
| adLockOptimistic | Asks the target database to not attempt to lock a row until you try to write it to the database with an Update method. This generates a run-time error in your code if another user has changed the row after you executed the Edit method. You should use this option when accessing rows in an Access .accdb file. |
| **Options (You can combine one Cmd setting with one Async setting with a plus sign)** | |
| adCmdText | Indicates that *source* is an SQL statement. |
| adCmdTable | Indicates that *source* is a table name (or a query name in a desktop database). In DAO, this is analogous to opening a dynaset recordset on a table. |
| adCmdTableDirect | Indicates that *source* is a table name. This is analogous to a DAO dbOpenTable. |

| Setting | Description |
|---|---|
| adCmdStoredProc | Indicates that *source* is a stored procedure. In DAO, this is analogous to opening a dynaset on a sorted query. |
| adAsyncFetch | After fetching the initial rows to populate the cursor, additional fetching occurs in the background. If you try to access a row that has not been fetched yet, your code will wait until the row is fetched. |
| adAsyncFetchNonBlocking | After fetching the initial rows to populate the cursor, additional fetching occurs in the background. If you try to access a row that has not been fetched yet, your code will receive an end of file indication. |



To open the qryContactProducts query in the Conrad Systems Contacts database as a keyset, enter the following:

```
Dim cnThisConnect As ADODB.Connection
Dim rcdContactProducts As New ADODB.RecordSet
Set cnThisConnect = CurrentProject.Connection
rcdContactProducts.Open "qryContactProducts", _
  cnThisConnect, adOpenKeyset, adLockOptimistic, _
  adCmdTable
```

After you open a recordset, you can use one of the Move methods to move to a specific record. Use *recordset*.MoveFirst to move to the first row in the recordset. Other Move methods include MoveLast, MoveNext, and MovePrevious. If you want to search for a specific row in the recordset, use the Find method or set the recordset's Filter property. Unlike the Find methods in DAO, the Find method in ADO is limited to a single simple test on a column in the form "<*column-name*> <*comparison*> <*comparison-value*>". Note that to search for a Null value, you must say: "[SomeColumn] = Null", not "[SomeColumn] Is Null" as you would in DAO. Also, <*comparison*> can be only <, >, <=, >=, <>, =, or LIKE. Note that if you want to use the LIKE keyword, you can use either the ANSI wildcards "%" and "_" or the Access ACE/JET wildcards "*" and "?", but the wildcard can appear only at the end of the <*comparison-value*> string.

If you want to search for rows using a more complex filter, you must assign a string variable or an expression containing the criteria for finding the records you want to the Filter property of the recordset. This limits the rows in the recordset to only those that meet the filter criteria. The criteria string must be made up of the simple comparisons that you can use with Find, but you can include multiple comparisons with the AND or OR Boolean operators.

For example, to find the first row in the qryContactProducts query's recordset whose SoldPrice field is greater than $200, enter the following:

```
rcdContactProducts.MoveFirst
rcdContactProducts.Find "SoldPrice > 200"
' EOF property will be true if nothing found
If Not rcdContactProducts.EOF Then
' Found a record!
```

To find all rows in qryContactProducts where the product was sold after February 1, 2007, and SoldPrice is greater than $200, enter the following:

```
rcdContactProducts.Filter = &
  "DateSold > #2/1/2007# AND SoldPrice > 200"
' EOF property will be true if filter produces no rows
If Not rcdODetails.EOF Then
' Found some rows!
```

To delete a row in a keyset, simply move to the row you want to delete and then use the Delete method. For example, to delete the first row in the qryContactProducts query's recordset that hasn't been invoiced yet (the Invoiced field is false), enter the following:

```
Dim cnThisConnect As ADODB.Connection
Dim rcdContactProducts As New ADODB.RecordSet
Set cnThisConnect = CurrentProject.Connection
rcdContactProducts.Open "qryContactProducts", _
  cnThisConnect, adOpenKeyset, adLockOptimistic, _
  adCmdTable
rcdContactProducts.MoveFirst
rcdContactProducts.Find "Invoiced = 0"
' Test the recordset EOF property for "not found"
If Not rcdContactProducts.EOF Then
    rcdContactProducts.Delete
End If
```

If you want to update rows in a recordset, move to the first row you want to update. Although ADO does not require you to use the Edit method to lock the row and make it updatable, you can optionally use the Edit method to signal your intention to the database engine. You can refer to any of the updatable fields in the row by name to change their values. You can use the Update method on the recordset to explicitly save your changes before moving to another row. ADO automatically saves your changed row when you move to a new row. If you need to discard an update, you must use the CancelUpdate method of the recordset object.

For example, to increase by 10 percent the SoldPrice entry of the first row in the rcdContactProducts query's recordset whose SoldPrice value is greater than $200, enter the following:

```
Dim cnThisConnect As ADODB.Connection
Dim rcdContactProducts As New ADODB.RecordSet
Set cnThisConnect = CurrentProject.Connection
rcdContactProducts.Open "qryContactProducts", _
  cnThisConnect, adOpenKeyset, adLockOptimistic, _
  adCmdTable
rcdContactProducts.Filter "SoldPrice > 200"
' Test the recordset EOF property for "not found"
If Not rcdContactProducts.EOF Then
  rcdContactProducts![SoldPrice] = _
    rcdContactProducts![SoldPrice] * 1.1
  rcdContactProducts.MoveNext
End If
```

To insert a new row in a recordset, use the AddNew method to start a new row. Set the values of all required fields in the row, and then use the Update method to save the new row. For example, to insert a new company in the Conrad Systems Contacts tblCompanies table, enter the following:

```
Dim cnThisConnect As ADODB.Connection
Dim rcdCompanies As New ADODB.RecordSet
Set cnThisConnect = CurrentProject.Connection
rcdCompanies.Open "tblCompanies", cnThisConnect, _
  adOpenKeyset, adLockOptimistic, adCmdTable
rcdCompanies.AddNew
rcdCompanies![CompanyName] = "Winthrop Brewing Co."
rcdCompanies![Address] = "155 Riverside Ave."
rcdCompanies![City] = "Winthrop"
rcdCompanies![StateOrProvince] = "WA"
rcdCompanies![PostalCode] = "98862"
rcdCompanies![PhoneNumber] = "(509) 555-8100"
rcdCompanies.Update
```

### Other Uses for Object Methods

As you'll learn later in this chapter in more detail, you must use a method of the DoCmd object to execute the equivalent of most macro actions within Visual Basic. You must use the RunCommand method of either the Application or DoCmd object to execute commands you can find on any of the Access menus.

You can also define a public function or subroutine (see the next section) within the module associated with a Form or Report object and execute that procedure as a method of the form or report. If your public procedure is a function, you must assign the result of the execution of the method to a variable of the appropriate type. If the public procedure is a subroutine, you can execute the form or report object method as a Visual Basic statement. For more information about object methods, find the topic about the object of interest in Help, and then click the Methods hyperlink.

## Functions and Subroutines

You can create two types of procedures in Visual Basic—*functions* and *subroutines*—also known as Function procedures and Sub procedures. (As you'll learn later in "Understanding Class Modules" on page 1009, class modules also support a special type of function, Property Get, and special subroutines, Property Let and Property Set, that let you manage properties of the class.) Each type of procedure can accept *parameters*—data variables that you pass to the procedure that can determine how the procedure operates. Functions can return a single data value, but subroutines cannot. In addition, you can execute a public function from anywhere in Access, including from expressions in queries and from macros. You can execute a subroutine only from a function, from another subroutine, or as an event procedure in a form or a report.

## Function Statement

Use a Function statement to declare a new function, the parameters it accepts, the variable type it returns, and the code that performs the function procedure.

### Syntax

```
[Public | Private | Friend] [Static] Function functionname
  ([<arguments>]) [As datatype]
    [<function statements>]
    [functionname = <expression>]
    [Exit Function]
    [<function statements>]
    [functionname = <expression>]
End Function
```

where *<arguments>* is

```
{[Optional][ByVal | ByRef][ParamArray] argumentname[()]
  [As datatype][= default]},...
```

### Notes

Use the Public keyword to make this function available to all other procedures in all modules. Use the Private keyword to make this function available only to other procedures in the same module. When you declare a function as private in a module, you cannot call that function from a query or a macro or from a function in another module. Use the Friend keyword in a class module to declare a function that is public to all other code in your application but is not visible to outside code that activates your project via automation.

Include the Static keyword to preserve the value of all variables declared within the procedure, whether explicitly or implicitly, as long as the module containing the procedure is open. This is the same as using the Static statement (discussed earlier in this chapter) to explicitly declare all variables created in this function.

You can use a type declaration character at the end of the *functionname* entry or use the As *datatype* clause to declare the data type returned by this function. Valid *datatype* entries are Byte, Boolean, Integer, Long, Currency, Single, Double, Date, String (for variable-length strings), String * *length* (for fixed-length strings), Object, Variant, or one of the object types described earlier in this chapter. If you do not declare a data type, Visual Basic assumes that the function returns a variant result. You can set the return value in code by assigning an expression of a compatible data type to the function name.

You should declare the data type of any arguments in the function's parameter list. Note that the names of the variables passed by the calling procedure can be different from the names of the variables known by this procedure. If you use the ByVal keyword to declare an argument, Visual Basic passes a copy of the argument to your function. Any change you make to a ByVal argument does not change the original variable in the calling procedure. If you use the ByRef keyword, Visual Basic passes the actual memory address of the variable, allowing the procedure to change the variable's value in the calling procedure. (If the argument passed by the calling procedure is an expression, Visual Basic treats it as if you had declared it by using ByVal.) Visual Basic always passes arrays by reference (ByRef).

Use the Optional keyword to declare an argument that isn't required. All optional arguments must be the Variant data type. If you declare an optional argument, all arguments that follow in the argument list must also be declared as optional. You can specify a *default* value only for optional parameters. Use the IsMissing built-in function to test for the absence of optional parameters. You can also use the ParamArray argument to declare an array of optional elements of the Variant data type. When you call the function, you can then pass it an arbitrary number of arguments. The ParamArray argument must be the last argument in the argument list.

Use the Exit Function statement anywhere in your function to clear any error conditions and exit your function normally, returning to the calling procedure. If Visual Basic runs your code until it encounters the End Function statement, control is passed to the calling procedure but any errors are not cleared. If this function causes an error and terminates with the End Function statement, Visual Basic passes the error to the calling procedure. See "Trapping Errors" on page 1028 for details.

### Example

To create a function named MyFunction that accepts an integer argument and a string argument and returns a double value, enter the following:

```
Function MyFunction (intArg1 As Integer, strArg2 As _
  String) As Double
    If strArg2 = "Square" Then
      MyFunction = intArg1 * intArg1
    Else
      MyFunction = Sqr(intArg1)
    End If
End Function
```

## Sub Statement

Use a Sub statement to declare a new subroutine, the parameters it accepts, and the code in the subroutine.

### Syntax

```
[Public | Private | Friend] [Static] Sub subroutinename
  ([<arguments>])
    [ <subroutine statements> ]
    [Exit Sub]
    [ <subroutine statements> ]
End Sub
```

where <*arguments*> is

```
{[Optional][ByVal | ByRef][ParamArray]
   argumentname[()] [As datatype][ = default]},...
```

## Notes

Use the Public keyword to make this subroutine available to all other procedures in all modules. Use the Private keyword to make this procedure available only to other procedures in the same module. When you declare a sub as private in a module, you cannot call that sub from a function or sub in another module. Use the Friend keyword in a class module to declare a sub that is public to all other code in your application but is not visible to outside code that activates your project via automation.

Include the Static keyword to preserve the value of all variables declared within the procedure, whether explicitly or implicitly, as long as the module containing the procedure is open. This is the same as using the Static statement (discussed earlier in this chapter) to explicitly declare all variables created in this subroutine.

You should declare the data type of all arguments that the subroutine accepts in its argument list. Valid *datatype* entries are Byte, Boolean, Integer, Long, Currency, Single, Double, Date, String (for variable-length strings), String * *length* (for fixed-length strings), Object, Variant, or one of the object types described earlier in this chapter. Note that the names of the variables passed by the calling procedure can be different from the names of the variables as known by this procedure. If you use the ByVal keyword to declare an argument, Visual Basic passes a copy of the argument to your subroutine. Any change you make to a ByVal argument does not change the original variable in the calling procedure. If you use the ByRef keyword, Visual Basic passes the actual memory address of the variable, allowing the procedure to change the variable's value in the calling procedure. (If the argument passed by the calling procedure is an expression, Visual Basic treats it as if you had declared it by using ByVal.) Visual Basic always passes arrays by reference (ByRef).

Use the Optional keyword to declare an argument that isn't required. All optional arguments must be the Variant data type. If you declare an optional argument, all arguments that follow in the argument list must also be declared as optional. You can specify a *default* value only for optional parameters. Use the IsMissing built-in function to test for the absence of optional parameters. You can also use the ParamArray argument to declare an array of optional elements of the Variant data type. When you call the subroutine, you can then pass it an arbitrary number of arguments. The ParamArray argument must be the last argument in the argument list.

Use the Exit Sub statement anywhere in your subroutine to clear any error conditions and exit your subroutine normally, returning to the calling procedure. If Visual Basic runs your code until it encounters the End Sub statement, control is passed to the calling procedure but any errors are not cleared. If this subroutine causes an error and terminates with the End Sub statement, Visual Basic passes the error to the calling procedure. See "Trapping Errors" on page 1028 for details.

### Example

To create a subroutine named MySub that accepts two string arguments but can modify only the second argument, enter the following:

```
Sub MySub (ByVal strArg1 As String, ByRef strArg2 _
  As String)
    <subroutine statements>
End Sub
```

## Understanding Class Modules

Whenever you create event procedures behind a form or report, you're creating a *class module*. A class module is the specification for a user-defined object in your database, and the code you write in the module defines the methods and properties of the object. Of course, forms and reports already have dozens of methods and properties already defined by Access, but you can create extended properties and methods when you write code in the class module attached to a form or report.

You can also create a class module as an independent object by clicking the arrow on the New Object button in the Other group on the Create tab and then clicking Class Module or by clicking Class Module on the Insert menu in the Visual Basic Editor. In the Conrad Systems Contacts sample database (Contacts.accdb), you can find a class module called ComDlg that provides a simple way to call the Windows open file dialog box from your Visual Basic code.

As previously discussed, you define a method in a class module by declaring a procedure (either a function or a sub) public. When you create an active instance of the object defined by the class module, either by opening it or by setting it to an object variable, you can execute the public functions or subs you have defined by referencing the function or sub name as a method of the object. For example, when the frmCustomers form is open, you can execute the cmdCancel_Click sub by referencing it as a method of the form's class. (The cmdCancel_Click sub is public in all forms in the sample database so that the Exit button on the main switchboard can use it to command the form to clear edits and close itself.) The name of any form's class is in the form *Form_formname*, so you execute this method in your code like this:

```
Form_frmCustomers.cmdCancel_Click
```

When you create a class module that you see in the Modules list in the Navigation Pane, you can create a special sub that Visual Basic runs whenever code in your application creates a new instance of the object defined by your class. For example, you can create a private Class_Initialize sub to run code that sets up your object whenever other code in your application creates a new instance of your class object. You might use this event to open recordsets or initialize variables required by the object. You can also create a private Class_Terminate sub to run code that cleans up any variables or objects (perhaps closing open recordsets) when your object goes out of scope or the code that created an instance of your object sets it to Nothing. (Your object goes out of scope if a procedure activates your class by setting it to a non-static local object variable and then the procedure exits.)

Although you can define properties of a class by declaring public variables in the Declarations section of the class module, you can also define specific procedures to handle fetching and setting properties. When you do this, you can write special processing code that runs whenever a caller fetches or sets one of the properties defined by these procedures. To create special property processing procedures in a class module, you need to write Property Get, Property Let, and Property Set procedures as described in the following sections.

## Property Get

Use a Property Get procedure to return a property value for the object defined by your class module. When other code in your application attempts to fetch the value of this property of your object, Visual Basic executes your Property Get procedure to return the value. Your code can return a data value or an object.

### Syntax

```
[Public | Private | Friend] [Static] Property Get propertyname
  ([<arguments>]) [As datatype]
    [<property statements>]
    [propertyname = <expression>]
    [Exit Property]
    [<property statements>]
    [propertyname = <expression>]
End Property
```

where *<arguments>* is

```
{[Optional][ByVal | ByRef][ParamArray] argumentname[()]
  [As datatype][= default]},...
```

### Notes

Use the Public keyword to make this property available to all other procedures in all modules. Use the Private keyword to make this property available only to other procedures in the same module. When you declare a property as private in a class module, you cannot reference that property from another module. Use the Friend keyword to declare a property that is public to all other code in your application but is not visible to outside code that activates your project via automation.

Include the Static keyword to preserve the value of all variables declared within the property procedure, whether explicitly or implicitly, as long as the module containing the procedure is open. This is the same as using the Static statement (discussed earlier in this chapter) to explicitly declare all variables created in this property procedure.

You can use a type declaration character at the end of the *propertyname* entry or use the As *datatype* clause to declare the data type returned by this property. Valid *datatype* entries are Byte, Boolean, Integer, Long, Currency, Single, Double, Date, String (for variable-length strings), String * *length* (for fixed-length strings), Object, Variant, or one of the object types described earlier in this chapter. If you do not declare a data type, Visual Basic assumes that the property returns a variant result. The data type of the returned value must match the data type of the *propvalue* variable you declare in any companion Property Let or Property Set procedure. You can set the return value in code by assigning an expression of a compatible data type to the property name.

You should declare the data type of all arguments in the property procedure's parameter list. Note that the names of the variables passed by the calling procedure can be different from the names of the variables known by this procedure. If you use the ByVal keyword to declare an argument, Visual Basic passes a copy of the argument to your procedure. Any change you make to a ByVal argument does not change the original variable in the calling procedure. If you use the ByRef keyword, Visual Basic passes the actual memory address of the variable, allowing the procedure to change the variable's value in the calling procedure. (If the argument passed by the calling procedure is an expression, Visual Basic treats it as if you had declared it by using ByVal.) Visual Basic always passes arrays by reference (ByRef).

Use the Optional keyword to declare an argument that isn't required. All optional arguments must be the Variant data type. If you declare an optional argument, all arguments that follow in the argument list must also be declared as optional. You can specify a *default* value only for optional parameters. Use the IsMissing built-in function to test for the absence of optional parameters. You can also use the ParamArray argument to declare an array of optional elements of the Variant data type. When you attempt to access this property in an object set to the class, you can then pass it an arbitrary number of arguments. The ParamArray argument must be the last argument in the argument list.

Use the Exit Property statement anywhere in your property procedure to clear any error conditions and exit your procedure normally, returning to the calling procedure. If Visual Basic runs your code until it encounters the End Property statement, control is passed to the calling procedure but any errors are not cleared. If this procedure causes an error and terminates with the End Property statement, Visual Basic passes the error to the calling procedure. See "Trapping Errors" on page 1028 for details.

## Examples

To declare a Filename property as a string and return it from a variable defined in the Declarations section of your class module, enter the following:

```
Option Explicit
Dim strFileName As String
Property Get Filename() As String
    ' Return the saved file name as a property
    Filename = strFilename
End Property
```

To establish a new instance of the object defined by the ComDlg class module and then fetch its Filename property, enter the following in a function or sub:

```
Dim clsDialog As New ComDlg, strFile As String
  With clsDialog
    ' Set the title of the dialog box
    .DialogTitle = "Locate Conrad Systems Contacts Data File"
    ' Set the default file name
    .FileName = "ContactsData.accdb"
    ' .. and start directory
    .Directory = CurrentProject.Path
    ' .. and file extension
    .Extension = "accdb"
    ' .. but show all accdb files just in case
    .Filter = "Conrad Systems File (*.accdb)|*.accdb"
    ' Default directory is where this file is located
    .Directory = CurrentProject.Path
    ' Tell the common dialog that the file and path must exist
    .ExistFlags = FileMustExist + PathMustExist
    ' If the ShowOpen method returns True
    If .ShowOpen Then
      ' Then fetch the Filename property
      strFile = .FileName
    Else
      Err.Raise 3999
    End If
  End With
```

## Property Let

Use a Property Let procedure to define code that executes when the calling code attempts to assign a value to a data property of the object defined by your class module. You cannot define both a Property Let and a Property Set procedure for the same property.

### Syntax

```
[Public | Private | Friend] [Static] Property Let propertyname
  ([<arguments>,] propvalue [As datatype])
    [ <property statements> ]
    [Exit Property]
    [ <property statements> ]
End Property
```

where *<arguments>* is

```
{[Optional][ByVal | ByRef][ParamArray]
   argumentname[()] [As datatype][ = default]},...
```

## Notes

Use the Public keyword to make this property available to all other procedures in all modules. Use the Private keyword to make this property available only to other procedures in the same module. When you declare a property as private in a class module, you cannot reference the property from another module. Use the Friend keyword to declare a property that is public to all other code in your application but is not visible to outside code that activates your project via automation.

Include the Static keyword to preserve the value of all variables declared within the property procedure, whether explicitly or implicitly, as long as the module containing the procedure is open. This is the same as using the Static statement (discussed earlier in this chapter) to explicitly declare all variables created in this property procedure.

You should declare the data type of all arguments in the property procedure's parameter list. Valid *datatype* entries are Byte, Boolean, Integer, Long, Currency, Single, Double, Date, String (for variable-length strings), String * *length* (for fixed-length strings), Object, Variant, or one of the object types described earlier in this chapter. Note that the names of the variables passed by the calling procedure can be different from the names of the variables as known by this procedure. Also, the names and data types of the arguments must exactly match the arguments declared for the companion Property Get procedure. If you use the ByVal keyword to declare an argument, Visual Basic passes a copy of the argument to your property procedure. Any change you make to a ByVal argument does not change the original variable in the calling procedure. If you use the ByRef keyword, Visual Basic passes the actual memory address of the variable, allowing the procedure to change the variable's value in the calling procedure. (If the argument passed by the calling procedure is an expression, Visual Basic treats it as if you had declared it by using ByVal.) Visual Basic always passes arrays by reference (ByRef).

Use the Optional keyword to declare an argument that isn't required. All optional arguments must be the Variant data type. If you declare an optional argument, all arguments that follow in the argument list must also be declared as optional. You can specify a *default* value only for optional parameters. Use the IsMissing built-in function to test for the absence of optional parameters. You can also use the ParamArray argument to declare an array of optional elements of the Variant data type. When you attempt to assign a value to this property in an object set to the class, you can then pass it an arbitrary number of arguments. The ParamArray argument must be the last argument in the argument list.

You must always declare at least one parameter, *propvalue*, that is the variable to contain the value that the calling code wants to assign to your property. This is the value or expression that appears on the right side of the assignment statement executed in the calling code. If you declare a data type, it must match the data type declared by the companion Property Get procedure. Also, when you declare a data type, the caller receives a data type mismatch error if the assignment statement attempts to pass an incorrect data type. You cannot modify this value, but you can evaluate it and save it as a value to be returned later by your Property Get procedure.

Use the Exit Property statement anywhere in your property procedure to clear any error conditions and exit your procedure normally, returning to the calling procedure. If Visual Basic runs your code until it encounters the End Property statement, control is passed to the calling procedure but any errors are not cleared. If this procedure causes an error and terminates with the End Property statement, Visual Basic passes the error to the calling procedure. See "Trapping Errors" on page 1028 for details.

### Examples

To declare a Filename property, accept a value from a caller, and save the value in a variable defined in the Declarations section of your class module, enter the following:

```
Option Explicit
Dim strFileName As String
Property Let FileName(strFile)
  If Len(strFile) <= 64 Then _
    strFileName = strFile
End Property
```

To establish a new instance of the object defined by the ComDlg class module and then set its Filename property, enter the following:

```
Dim clsDialog As New ComDlg, strFile As String
  With clsDialog
    ' Set the title of the dialog
    .DialogTitle = "Locate Conrad Systems Contacts Data File"
    ' Set the default file name
    .FileName = "ContactsData.accdb"
  End With
```

## Property Set

Use a Property Set procedure to define code that executes when the calling code attempts to assign an object to an object property of the object defined by your class module. You cannot define both a Property Let and a Property Set procedure for the same property.

### Syntax

```
[Public | Private | Friend] [Static] Property Set propertyname
  ([<arguments>,] object [As objecttype])
    [ <property statements> ]
    [Exit Property]
    [ <property statements> ]
End Property
```

where *<arguments>* is

```
{[Optional][ByVal | ByRef][ParamArray]
   argumentname[()] [As datatype][ = default]},...
```

## Notes

Use the Public keyword to make this property available to all other procedures in all modules. Use the Private keyword to make this property available only to other procedures in the same module. When you declare a property as private in a class module, you cannot reference the property from another module. Use the Friend keyword to declare a property that is public to all other code in your application but is not visible to outside code that activates your project via automation.

Include the Static keyword to preserve the value of all variables declared within the property procedure, whether explicitly or implicitly, as long as the module containing the procedure is open. This is the same as using the Static statement (discussed earlier in this chapter) to explicitly declare all variables created in this property procedure.

You should declare the data type of all arguments in the property procedure's parameter list. Valid *datatype* entries are Byte, Boolean, Integer, Long, Currency, Single, Double, Date, String (for variable-length strings), String * *length* (for fixed-length strings), Object, Variant, or one of the object types described earlier in this chapter. Note that the names of the variables passed by the calling procedure can be different from the names of the variables as known by this procedure. Also, the names and data types of the arguments must exactly match the arguments declared for the companion Property Get procedure. If you use the ByVal keyword to declare an argument, Visual Basic passes a copy of the argument to your property procedure. Any change you make to a ByVal argument does not change the original variable in the calling procedure. If you use the ByRef keyword, Visual Basic passes the actual memory address of the variable, allowing the procedure to change the variable's value in the calling procedure. (If the argument passed by the calling procedure is an expression, Visual Basic treats it as if you had declared it by using ByVal.) Visual Basic always passes arrays by reference (ByRef).

Use the Optional keyword to declare an argument that isn't required. All optional arguments must be the Variant data type. If you declare an optional argument, all arguments that follow in the argument list must also be declared as optional. You can specify a *default* value only for optional parameters. Use the IsMissing built-in function to test for the absence of optional parameters. You can also use the ParamArray argument to declare an array of optional elements of the Variant data type. When you attempt to assign a value to this property in an object set to the class, you can then pass it an arbitrary number of arguments. The ParamArray argument must be the last argument in the argument list.

You must always declare at least one parameter, *object*, that is the variable to contain the object that the calling code wants to assign to your property. This is the object reference that appears on the right side of the assignment statement executed in the calling code. If you include an *objecttype* entry, it must match the object type declared by the companion Property Get procedure. Also, when you declare an object type, the caller receives a data type mismatch error if the assignment statement attempts to pass an incorrect object type. You can evaluate the properties of this object, set its properties, execute its methods, and save the object pointer in another variable that your Property Get procedure can later return.

Use the Exit Property statement anywhere in your property procedure to clear any error conditions and exit your procedure normally, returning to the calling procedure. If Visual Basic runs your code until it encounters the End Property statement, control is passed to the calling procedure but any errors are not cleared. If this procedure causes an error and terminates with the End Property statement, Visual Basic passes the error to the calling procedure. See "Trapping Errors" on page 1028 for details.

### Examples

To declare a ControlToUpdate property, accept a value from a caller, and save the value in an object variable defined in the Declarations section of your class module, enter the following:

```
Option Explicit
Dim ctlToUpdate As Control
Property Set ControlToUpdate(ctl As Control)
  ' Verify we have the right type of control
  Select Case ctl.ControlType
    ' Text box, combo box, and list box are OK
    Case acTextBox, acListBox, acComboBox
      ' Save the control object
      Set ctlToUpdate = ctl
    Case Else
      Err.Raise 3999
  End Select
End Property
```

To establish a new instance of the object defined by the ComDlg class module and then set its Filename property, enter the following in a function or sub:

```
Dim clsDialog As New ComDlg, strFile As String
  With clsDialog
    ' Set the title of the dialog
    .DialogTitle = "Locate Conrad Systems Contacts Data File"
    ' Set the default file name
    .FileName = "ContactsData.accdb"
  End With
```

## Controlling the Flow of Statements

Visual Basic provides many ways for you to control the flow of statements in procedures. You can call other procedures, loop through a set of statements either a calculated number of times or based on a condition, or test values and conditionally execute sets of statements based on the result of the condition test. You can also go directly to a set of statements or exit a procedure at any time. The following sections demonstrate some (but not all) of the ways you can control flow in your procedures.

# Call Statement

Use a Call statement to transfer control to a subroutine.

## Syntax

```
Call subroutinename [(<arguments>)]
```

or

```
subroutinename [<arguments>]
```

where <*arguments*> is

```
{[ByVal | ByRef] <expression> },...
```

## Notes

The Call keyword is optional, but if you omit it, you must also omit the parentheses surrounding the parameter list. If the subroutine accepts arguments, the names of the variables passed by the calling procedure can be different from the names of the variables as known by the subroutine. You can use the ByVal and ByRef keywords in a Call statement only when you're making a call to a dynamic link library (DLL) procedure. Use ByVal for string arguments to indicate that you need to pass a pointer to the string rather than pass the string directly. Use ByRef for nonstring arguments to pass the value directly. If you use the ByVal keyword to declare an argument, Visual Basic passes a copy of the argument to the subroutine. The subroutine cannot change the original variable in the calling procedure. If you use the ByRef keyword, Visual Basic passes the actual memory address of the variable, allowing the procedure to change the variable's value in the calling procedure. (If the argument passed by the calling procedure is an expression, Visual Basic treats it as if you had declared it by using ByVal.)

## Examples

To call a subroutine named MySub and pass it an integer variable and an expression, enter the following:

```
Call MySub (intMyInteger, curPrice * intQty)
```

An alternative syntax is

```
MySub intMyInteger, curPrice * intQty
```

# Do...Loop Statement

Use a Do...Loop statement to define a block of statements that you want executed multiple times. You can also define a condition that terminates the loop when the condition is false.

### Syntax

```
Do [{While | Until} <condition>]
    [<procedure statements>]
    [Exit Do]
    [<procedure statements>]
Loop
```

or

```
Do
    [<procedure statements>]
    [Exit Do]
    [<procedure statements>]
Loop [{While | Until} <condition>]
```

### Notes

The *<condition>* is a comparison predicate or expression that Visual Basic can evaluate to True (nonzero) or False (zero or Null). The While clause is the opposite of the Until clause. If you specify a While clause, execution continues as long as the *<condition>* is true. If you specify an Until clause, execution of the loop stops when *<condition>* becomes true. If you place a While or an Until clause in the Do clause, the condition must be met for the statements in the loop to execute at all. If you place a While or an Until clause in the Loop clause, Visual Basic executes the statements within the loop before testing the condition.

You can place one or more Exit Do statements anywhere within the loop to exit the loop before reaching the Loop statement. Generally you'll use the Exit Do statement as part of some other evaluation statement structure, such as an If...Then...Else statement.

### Example

To read all the rows in the tblCompanies table until you reach the end of the recordset (the EOF property is true), enter the following:

```
Dim dbContacts As DAO.Database
Dim rcdCompanies As DAO.RecordSet
Set dbContacts = CurrentDb
Set rcdCompanies = dbContacts.OpenRecordSet("tblCompanies")
Do Until rcdCompanies.EOF
    <procedure statements>
    rcdClubs.MoveNext
Loop
```

## For...Next Statement

Use a For...Next statement to execute a series of statements a specific number of times.

### Syntax

```
For counter = first To last [Step stepamount]
    [<procedure statements>]
    [Exit For]
    [<procedure statements>]
Next [counter]
```

### Notes

The *counter* must be a numeric variable that is not an array or a record element. Visual Basic initially sets the value of *counter* to *first*. If you do not specify a *stepamount*, the default *stepamount* value is +1. If the *stepamount* value is positive or 0, Visual Basic executes the loop as long as *counter* is less than or equal to *last*. If the *stepamount* value is negative, Visual Basic executes the loop as long as *counter* is greater than or equal to *last*. Visual Basic adds *stepamount* to *counter* when it encounters the corresponding Next statement. You can change the value of *counter* within the For loop, but this might make your procedure more difficult to test and debug. Changing the value of *last* within the loop does not affect execution of the loop. You can place one or more Exit For statements anywhere within the loop to exit the loop before reaching the Next statement. Generally you'll use the Exit For statement as part of some other evaluation statement structure, such as an If...Then...Else statement.

You can nest one For loop inside another. When you do, you must choose a different *counter* name for each loop.

### Example

To list in the Immediate window the names of the first five queries in the Conrad Systems Contacts database, enter the following in a function or sub:

```
Dim dbContacts As DAO.Database
Dim intI As Integer
Set dbContacts = CurrentDb
For intI = 0 To 4
    Debug.Print dbContacts.QueryDefs(intI).Name
Next intI
```

## For Each...Next Statement

Use a For Each...Next statement to execute a series of statements for each item in a collection or an array.

### Syntax

```
For Each item In group
    [<procedure statements>]
    [Exit For]
    [<procedure statements>]
Next [item]
```

### Notes

The *item* must be a variable that represents an object in a collection or an element of an array. The *group* must be the name of a collection or an array. Visual Basic executes the loop as long as at least one item remains in the collection or the array. All the statements in the loop are executed for each item in the collection or the array. You can place one or more Exit For statements anywhere within the loop to exit the loop before reaching the Next statement. Generally you'll use the Exit For statement as part of some other evaluation statement structure, such as an If...Then...Else statement.

You can nest one For Each loop inside another. When you do, you must choose a different *item* name for each loop.

### Example

To list in the Immediate window the names of all the queries in the Conrad Systems Contacts database, enter the following in a function or sub:

```
Dim dbContacts As DAO.Database
Dim qdf As DAO.QueryDef
Set dbContacts = CurrentDb
For Each qdf In dbContacts.QueryDefs
    Debug.Print qdf.Name
Next qdf
```

**CAUTION!**

If you execute code within the For Each loop that modifies the members of the group, then you might not process all the members. For example, if you attempt to close all open forms using the following code, you will skip some open forms because you are eliminating members from the group (the Forms collection) inside the loop.

```
Dim frm As Form
For Each frm In Forms
  DoCmd.Close acForm, frm.Name
Next frm
```

The correct way to close all open forms is as follows:

```
Dim intI As Integer
For intI = Forms.Count - 1 To 0 Step - 1
  DoCmd.Close acForm, Forms(intI).Name
Next intI
```

## GoTo Statement

Use a GoTo statement to jump unconditionally to another statement in your procedure.

### Syntax

```
GoTo {label | linenumber}
```

### Notes

You can label a statement line by starting the line with a string of no more than 40 characters that starts with an alphabetic character and ends with a colon (:). A line label cannot be a Visual Basic or Access reserved word. You can also optionally number the statement lines in your procedure. Each line number must contain only numbers, must be different from all other line numbers in the procedure, must be the first nonblank characters in a line, and must contain 40 characters or less. To jump to a line number or a labeled line, use the GoTo statement and the appropriate *label* or *linenumber*.

### Example

To jump to the statement line labeled SkipOver, enter the following:

```
GoTo SkipOver
```

## If...Then...Else Statement

Use an If...Then...Else statement to conditionally execute statements based on the evaluation of a condition.

### Syntax

```
If <condition1> Then
    [<procedure statements 1>]
[ElseIf <condition2> Then
    [<procedure statements 2>]]...
[Else
    [<procedure statements n>]]
End If
```

or

```
If <condition> Then <thenstmt> [Else <elsestmt>]
```

### Notes

Each condition is a numeric or string expression that Visual Basic can evaluate to True (nonzero) or False (0 or Null). A condition can also consisit of multiple comparison expressions and Boolean operators. In addition, a condition can also be the special TypeOf...Is test to evaluate a control variable. The syntax for this test is

```
TypeOf <Object> Is <ObjectType>
```

where <*Object*> is the name of an object variable and <*ObjectType*> is the name of any valid object type recognized in Access. A common use of this syntax is to loop through all the controls in a form or report Controls collection and take some action if the control is of a specific type (for example, change the FontWeight property of all labels to bold). Valid control types are Attachment, BoundObjectFrame, CheckBox, ComboBox, CommandButton, CustomControl, Image, Label, Line, ListBox, ObjectFrame, OptionButton, OptionGroup, PageBreak, Rectangle, Subform, TabControl, TextBox, or ToggleButton.

If the condition is true, Visual Basic executes the statement or statements immediately following the Then keyword. If the condition is false, Visual Basic evaluates the next ElseIf condition or executes the statements following the Else keyword, whichever occurs next.

The alternative syntax does not need an End If statement, but you must enter the entire If...Then statement on a single line. Both <*thenstmt*> and <*elsestmt*> can be either a single Visual Basic statement or multiple statements separated by colons (:).

### Example

To set an integer value depending on whether a string begins with a letter from *A* through *F*, from *G* through *N*, or from *O* through *Z*, enter the following:

```
Dim strMyString As String, strFirst As String, _
  intVal As Integer
' Grab the first letter and make it upper case
strFirst = UCase(Left(strMyString, 1))
If strFirst >= "A" And strFirst <= "F" Then
    intVal = 1
ElseIf strFirst >= "G" And strFirst <= "N" Then
    intVal = 2
ElseIf strFirst >= "O" And strFirst <= "Z" Then
    intVal = 3
Else
    intVal = 0
End If
```

## RaiseEvent Statement

Use the RaiseEvent statement to signal a declared event in a class module.

### Syntax

```
RaiseEvent eventname [(<arguments>)]
```

where <*arguments*> is

```
{ <expression> },...
```

## Notes

You must always declare an event in the class module that raises the event. You cannot use RaiseEvent to signal a built-in event (such as Current) of a form or report class module. If an event passes no arguments, you must not include an empty pair of parentheses when you code the RaiseEvent statement. An event can only be received by another module that has declared an object variable using WithEvents that has been set to the class module or object containing this class.

**See the WeddingList.accdb sample database—described in Chapter 20, "Automating Your Application with Visual Basic"—for an example using RaiseEvent to synchronize two forms.**

## Example

To define an event named Signal that returns a text string and then to signal that event in a class module, enter the following:

```
Option Explicit
Public Event Signal(ByVal strMsg As String)

Public Sub RaiseSignal(ByVal strText As String)
    RaiseEvent Signal(strText)
End Sub
```

# Select Case Statement

Use a Select Case statement to execute statements conditionally based on the evaluation of an expression that is compared to a list or range of values.

## Syntax

```
Select Case <test expression>
    [Case <comparison list 1>
        [<procedure statements 1>]]
    ...
    [Case Else
        [<procedure statements n>]]
End Select
```

where *<test expression>* is any numeric or string expression; where *<comparison list>* is

```
{<comparison element>,...}
```

where *<comparison element>* is

```
{expression | expression To expression |
  Is <comparison operator> expression}
```

and where *<comparison operator>* is

```
{= | <> | < | > | <= | >=}
```

### Notes

If the <*test expression*> matches a <*comparison element*> in a Case clause, Visual Basic executes the statements that follow that clause. If the <*comparison element*> is a single expression, the <*test expression*> must equal the <*comparison element*> for the statements following that clause to execute. If the <*comparison element*> contains a To keyword, the first expression must be less than the second expression (either in numeric value if the expressions are numbers or in collating sequence if the expressions are strings) and the <*test expression*> must be between the first expression and the second expression. If the <*comparison element*> contains the Is keyword, the evaluation of <*comparison operator*> *expression* must be true.

If more than one Case clause matches the <*test expression*>, Visual Basic executes only the set of statements following the first Case clause that matches. You can include a block of statements following a Case Else clause that Visual Basic executes if none of the previous Case clauses matches the <*test expression*>. You can nest another Select Case statement within the statements following a Case clause.

### Example

To assign an integer value to a variable, depending on whether a string begins with a letter from *A* through *F*, from *G* through *N*, or from *O* through *Z*, enter the following:

```
Dim strMyString As String, intVal As Integer
Select Case UCase$(Mid$(strMyString, 1, 1))
    Case "A" To "F"
        intVal = 1
    Case "G" To "N"
        intVal = 2
    Case "O" To "Z"
        intVal = 3
    Case Else
        intVal = 0
End Select
```

## Stop Statement

Use a Stop statement to suspend execution of your procedure.

### Syntax

```
Stop
```

### Notes

A Stop statement has the same effect as setting a breakpoint on a statement. You can use the Visual Basic debugging tools, such as the Step Into and the Step Over buttons and the Debug window, to evaluate the status of your procedure after Visual Basic halts on a Stop statement. You should not use the Stop statement in a production application.

## While...Wend Statement

Use a While...Wend statement to continuously execute a block of statements as long as a condition is true.

### Syntax

```
While <condition>
    [<procedure statements>]
Wend
```

### Notes

A While...Wend statement is similar to a Do...Loop statement with a While clause, except that you can use an Exit Do statement to exit from a Do loop. Visual Basic provides no similar Exit clause for a While loop. The *<condition>* is an expression that Visual Basic can evaluate to True (nonzero) or False (0 or Null). Execution continues as long as the *<condition>* is true.

### Example

To read all the rows in the tblCompanies table until you reach the end of the recordset, enter the following in a function or sub:

```
Dim dbContacts As DAO.Database
Dim rcdCompanies As DAO.RecordSet
Set dbContacts = CurrentDb
Set rcdCompanies = dbContacts.OpenRecordSet("tblCompanies")
While Not rcdCompanies.EOF
    <procedure statements>
    rcdCompanies.MoveNext
Wend
```

## With...End Statement

Use a With statement to simplify references to complex objects in code. You can establish a base object using a With statement and then use a shorthand notation to refer to objects, collections, properties, or methods on that object until you terminate the With statement. When you plan to reference an object many times within a block of code, using With also improves execution speed.

### Syntax

```
With <object reference>
    [<procedure statements>]
End With
```

### Example

To use shorthand notation on a recordset object to add a new row to a table, enter the following:

```
Dim rcd As DAO.Recordset, db As DAO.Database
Set db = CurrentDb
Set rcd = db.OpenRecordset("MyTable", _
  dbOpenDynaset, dbAppendOnly)
With rcd
    ' Start a new record
    .Addnew
    ' Set the field values
    ![FieldOne] = "1"
    ![FieldTwo] = "John"
    ![FieldThree] = "Viescas"
    .Update
    .Close
End With
```

To write the same code without the With, you would have to say:

```
Dim rcd As DAO.Recordset, db As DAO.Database
Set db = CurrentDb
Set rcd = db.OpenRecordset("MyTable", _
  dbOpenDynaset, dbAppendOnly)
    ' Start a new record
    rcd.Addnew
    ' Set the field values
    rcd![FieldOne] = "1"
    rcd![FieldTwo] = "John"
    rcd![FieldThree] = "Viescas"
    rcd.Update
    rcd.Close
```

# Running Macro Actions and Menu Commands

From within Visual Basic, you can execute most of the macro actions that Access provides and any of the built-in menu commands. Only a few of the macro actions have direct Visual Basic equivalents. To execute a macro action or menu command, use the methods of the DoCmd object, described below.

## DoCmd Object

Use the methods of the DoCmd object to execute a macro action or menu command from within a Visual Basic procedure.

### Syntax

**DoCmd**.*actionmethod* [*actionargument*],...

### Notes

Some of the macro actions you'll commonly execute from Visual Basic include ApplyFilter, Close, FindNext and FindRecord (for searching the recordset of the current form and immediately displaying the result), Hourglass, Maximize, Minimize, MoveSize, OpenForm, OpenQuery (to run a query that you don't need to modify), OpenReport, and RunCommand. Although you can run the Echo, GoToControl, GoToPage, RepaintObject, and Requery actions from Visual Basic using a method of the DoCmd object, it's more efficient to use the Echo, SetFocus, GoToPage, Repaint, and Requery methods of the object to which the method applies.

### Examples

To open a form named frmCompanies in Form view for data entry, enter the following:

```
DoCmd.OpenForm "frmCompanies", acNormal, , , acAdd
```

To close a form named frmContacts, enter the following:

```
DoCmd.Close acForm, "frmContacts"
```

## Executing an Access Command

To execute an Access command (one of the commands you can find on the Ribbon), use the RunCommand method of either the DoCmd or Application object and supply a single action argument that is the numeric code for the command.

### Syntax

```
[DoCmd.]RunCommand [actionargument],...
```

### Notes

You can also use one of many built-in constants for *actionargument* to reference the command you want. When you use RunCommand, you can optionally leave out the DoCmd or Application object.

### Examples

To execute the Save command in the Records group on the Home tab, enter the following:

```
RunCommand acCmdSaveRecord
```

To switch an open form to PivotChart view (execute the PivotChart View command in the Views group on the Home tab), enter the following:

```
RunCommand acCmdPivotChartView
```

To open the Find window while the focus is on a form (execute the Find command in the Find group on the Home tab), enter the following:

```
RunCommand acCmdFind
```

**Note**

Visual Basic provides built-in constants for many of the macro action and RunCommand parameters. For more information, search on "Microsoft Access Constants" and "Run-Command Method" in Help.

## Actions with Visual Basic Equivalents

A few macro actions cannot be executed from a Visual Basic procedure. All but one of these actions, however, have equivalent statements in Visual Basic, as shown in Table 19-4.

**Table 19-4 Visual Basic Equivalents for Macro Actions**

| Macro Action | Visual Basic Equivalent |
|---|---|
| AddMenu | No equivalent |
| MsgBox | MsgBox statement or function |
| RemoveAllTempVars | TempVars.RemoveAll |
| RemoveTempVar | TempVars.Remove *variablename* |
| RunApp[1] | Shell function |
| RunCode | Call subroutine |
| SendKeys | SendKeys statement |
| SetTempVar | TempVars!*variablename* = *value* |
| SetValue | Variable assignment (=) |
| StopAllMacros | Stop or End statement |
| StopMacro | Exit Sub or Exit Function statement |

[1] Database must be trusted to execute this action.

# Trapping Errors

One of the most powerful features of Visual Basic is its ability to trap all errors, analyze them, and take corrective action. In a well-designed production application, the user should never see any of the default error messages or encounter a code halt when an error occurs. Also, setting an error trap is often the best way to test certain conditions. For example, to find out if a query exists, your code can set an error trap and then attempt to reference the query object. In an application with hundreds of queries, using an error trap can also be faster than looping through all QueryDef objects. To enable error trapping, you use an On Error statement.

## On Error Statement

Use an On Error statement to enable error trapping, establish the procedure to handle error trapping (the error handler), skip past any errors, or turn off error trapping.

### Syntax

```
On Error {GoTo lineID | Resume Next | GoTo 0}
```

### Notes

Use a GoTo *lineID* clause to establish a code block in your procedure that handles any error. The *lineID* can be a line number or a label.

Use a Resume Next clause to trap errors but skip over any statement that causes an error. You can call the Err function in a statement immediately following the statement that you suspect might have caused an error to see whether an error occurred. Err returns 0 if no error has occurred.

Use a GoTo 0 statement to turn off error trapping for the current procedure. If an error occurs, Visual Basic passes the error to the error routine in the calling procedure or opens an error dialog box if there is no previous error routine.

In your error handling statements, you can examine the built-in Err variable (the error number associated with the error) to determine the exact nature of the error. You can use the Error function to examine the text of the error message associated with the error. If you use line numbers with your statements, you can use the built-in Erl function to determine the line number of the statement that caused the error. After taking corrective action, use a Resume statement to retry execution of the statement that caused the error. Use a Resume Next statement to continue execution at the statement immediately following the statement that caused the error. Use a Resume statement with a statement label to restart execution at the indicated label name or number. You can also use an Exit Function or Exit Sub statement to reset the error condition and return to the calling procedure.

### Examples

To trap errors but continue execution with the next statement, enter the following:

```
On Error Resume Next
```

To trap errors and execute the statements that follow the MyError: label when an error occurs, enter the following:

```
On Error GoTo MyError
```

To turn off error trapping in the current procedure, enter the following:

```
On Error GoTo 0
```

If you create and run the following function with zero as the second argument, such as MyErrExample(3,0), the function will trigger an error by attempting to divide by zero, trap the error, display the error in an error handling section, and then exit gracefully.

```
Public Function MyErrExample(intA As Integer, intB As Integer) As Integer
' Set an error trap
On Error GoTo Trap_Error
  ' The following causes an error if intB is zero
  MyErrExample = intA / intB
ExitNice:
  Exit Function
Trap_Error:
  MsgBox "Something bad happened: " & Err & ", " & Error
  Resume ExitNice
End Function
```

# Some Complex Visual Basic Examples

A good way to learn Visual Basic techniques is to study complex code that has been developed and tested by someone else. In the Conrad Systems Contacts and Housing Reservations sample databases, you can find dozens of examples of complex Visual Basic code that perform various tasks. The following sections describe two of the more interesting ones in detail.

## A Procedure to Randomly Load Data

You've probably noticed a lot of sample data in both the Conrad Systems Contacts and the Housing Reservations databases. No, we didn't sit at our keyboards for hours entering sample data! Instead, we built a Visual Basic procedure that accepts some parameters entered on a form. In both databases, the form to load sample data is saved as zfrmLoadData. If you open this form in Contacts.accdb from the Navigation Pane, you'll see that you use it to enter a beginning date, a number of days (max 365), a number of companies to load (max 25), a maximum number of contacts per company (max 10), and a maximum number of events per contact (max 25). You can also select the check box to delete all existing data before randomly loading new data. (The zfrmLoadData form in the Housing Reservations database offers some slightly different options.) Figure 19-15 shows this form with the values we used to load the Conrad Systems Contacts database.

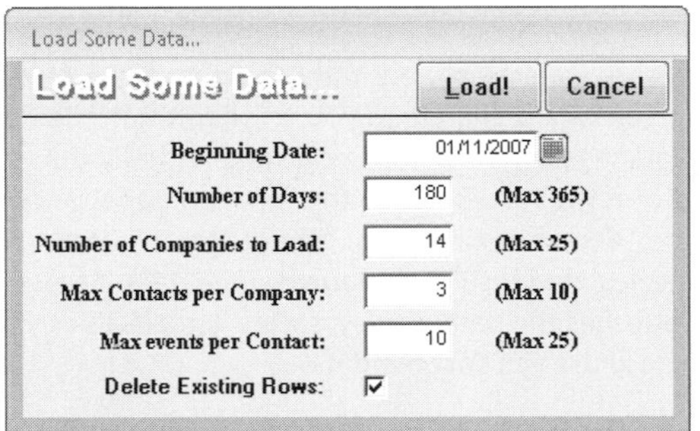


**Figure 19-15** The zfrmLoadData form in the Conrad Systems Contacts sample database makes it easy to load sample data.

As you might expect, when you click the Load button, our procedure examines the values entered and loads some sample data into tblCompanies, tblContacts, tblCompanyContacts, tblContactEvents and tblContactProducts. The code picks random company names from ztblCompanies (a table containing a list of fictitious company names) and random person names from ztblPeople (a table containing names of Microsoft employees who have agreed to allow their names to be used in sample data). It also chooses random ZIP Codes (and cities, counties, and states) from tlkpZips (a table containing U.S. postal ZIP Code, city name, state name, county name, and telephone area codes as of December 2002 that we licensed from CD Light, LLC—*www.zipinfo.com*). Figure 19-16 shows you the design of the query used in the code to pick random person names.

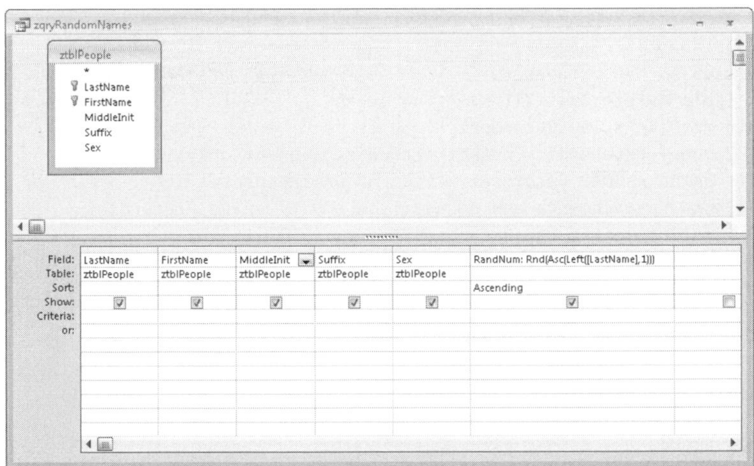


**Figure 19-16** This query returns person names in a random sequence.

The query creates a numeric value to pass to the Rnd (random) function by grabbing the first character of the LastName field and then calculating the ASCII code value. The Rnd function returns some floating-point random value less than 1 but greater than or equal to zero. Asking the query to sort on this random number results in a random list of values each time you run the query.

> **Note**
>
> If you open zqryRandomNames in Datasheet view, the RandNum column won't appear to be sorted correctly. In fact, the values change as you scroll through the data or resize the datasheet window. The database engine actually calls the Rnd function on a first pass through the data to perform the sort. Because the function depends on a value of one of the columns (LastName), Access assumes that other users might be changing this column— and therefore, the calculated result—as you view the data. Access calls the Rnd function again each time it refreshes the data display, so the actual values you see aren't the ones that the query originally used to sort the data.

If you want to run this code, you should either pick a date starting after July 9, 2007, or select the option to delete all existing records first.

You can find the code in the cmdLoad_Click event procedure that runs when you click the Load button on the zfrmLoadData form. We've added line numbers to some of the lines in this code listing in the book so that you can follow along with the line-by-line explanations in Table 19-5, which follows the listing. Because the code loads data into both a multi-value field and an attachment field in the tblContacts table, it uses the DAO object model exclusively. (You cannot manipulate multi-value or attachment fields using the ADO object model.)

```
1 Private Sub cmdLoad_Click()
2 ' Code to load a random set of companies,
  '  contacts, events, and products
  ' Database variable
3 Dim db As DAO.Database
  ' Table delete list (if starting over)
  Dim rstDel As DAO.Recordset
  ' Company recordset; Contact recordset (insert only)
  Dim rstCo As DAO.Recordset, rstCn As DAO.Recordset
  ' Photo (attachment) and ContactType (multi-value) recordset
  Dim rstComplex As DAO.Recordset2
  ' CompanyContact recordset, ContactEvent recordset (insert only)
  Dim rstCoCn As DAO.Recordset, rstCnEv As DAO.Recordset
  ' A random selection of zips
  Dim rstZipRandom As DAO.Recordset
  ' ..and company names
  Dim rstCoRandom As DAO.Recordset
  ' .. and people names
  Dim rstPRandom As DAO.Recordset
  ' A recordset to pick "close" zip codes for contacts
  Dim rstZipClose As DAO.Recordset
  ' A recordset to pick contact events
  Dim rstEvents As DAO.Recordset
  ' Place to generate Picture Path
4 Dim strPicPath As String
  ' Places for path to backend database and folder
  Dim strBackEndPath As String, strBackEndFolder As String
```

```
 ' Place to generate a safe "compact to" name
 Dim strNewDb As String
 ' Places to save values from the form controls
 Dim datBeginDate As Date, intNumDays As Integer
 Dim intNumCompanies As Integer, intNumContacts As Integer
 Dim intNumEvents As Integer
 ' Lists of street names and types
5 Dim strStreetNames(1 To 9) As String, strStreetTypes(1 To 5) As String
 ' As string of digits for street addresses and area codes
 Const strDigits As String = "1234567890"
 ' List of Person Titles by gender
 Dim strMTitles(1 To 6) As String, strFTitles(1 To 7) As String
 ' Place to put male and female picture file names
 Dim strMPicture() As String, intMPicCount As Integer
 Dim strFPicture() As String, intFPicCount As Integer
 ' Some working variables
 Dim intI As Integer, intJ As Integer, intK As Integer
 Dim intL As Integer, intM As Integer, intR As Integer
 Dim varRtn As Variant, intDefault As Integer
 Dim datCurrentDate As Date, datCurrentTime As Date
 ' Variables to assemble Company and Contact records
 Dim strCompanyName As String, strCoAddress As String
 Dim strAreaCode As String, strPAddress As String
 Dim strThisPhone As String, strThisFax As String
 Dim strWebsite As String
 Dim lngThisCompany As Long
 Dim lngThisContact As Long, strProducts As String
 ' Set up to bail if something funny happens (it shouldn't)
6   On Error GoTo BailOut
    ' Initialize Streets
7   strStreetNames(1) = "Main"
    strStreetNames(2) = "Central"
    strStreetNames(3) = "Willow"
    strStreetNames(4) = "Church"
    strStreetNames(5) = "Lincoln"
    strStreetNames(6) = "1st"
    strStreetNames(7) = "2nd"
    strStreetNames(8) = "3rd"
    strStreetNames(9) = "4th"
    strStreetTypes(1) = "Street"
    strStreetTypes(2) = "Avenue"
    strStreetTypes(3) = "Drive"
    strStreetTypes(4) = "Parkway"
    strStreetTypes(5) = "Boulevard"
    ' Initialize person titles
    strMTitles(1) = "Mr."
    strMTitles(2) = "Dr."
    strMTitles(3) = "Mr."
    strMTitles(4) = "Mr."
    strMTitles(5) = "Mr."
    strMTitles(6) = "Mr."
```

```
    strFTitles(1) = "Mrs."
    strFTitles(2) = "Dr."
    strFTitles(3) = "Ms."
    strFTitles(4) = "Mrs."
    strFTitles(5) = "Ms."
    strFTitles(6) = "Mrs."
    strFTitles(7) = "Ms."
    ' Search for male picture names (should be in Current Path\Pictures)
8   strPicPath = Dir(CurrentProject.Path & "\Pictures\PersonM*.bmp")
    ' Loop until Dir returns nothing (end of list or not found)
9   Do Until (strPicPath = "")
      ' Add 1 to the count
      intMPicCount = intMPicCount + 1
      ' Extend the file name array
10    ReDim Preserve strMPicture(1 To intMPicCount)
      ' Add the file name to the array
      strMPicture(intMPicCount) = strPicPath
      ' Get next one
      strPicPath = Dir
11  Loop
    ' Search for female picture names (should be in Current Path\Pictures)
    strPicPath = Dir(CurrentProject.Path & "\Pictures\PersonF*.bmp")
    ' Loop until Dir returns nothing (end of list or not found)
12  Do Until (strPicPath = "")
      ' Add 1 to the count
      intFPicCount = intFPicCount + 1
      ' Extend the file name array
      ReDim Preserve strFPicture(1 To intFPicCount)
      ' Add the file name to the array
      strFPicture(intFPicCount) = strPicPath
      ' Get next one
      strPicPath = Dir
13  Loop
    ' Capture values from the form
14  datBeginDate = CDate(Me.BeginDate)
    intNumDays = Me.NumDays
    intNumCompanies = Me.NumCompanies
    intNumContacts = Me.NumContacts
    intNumEvents = Me.NumEvents
    ' Open the current database
15  Set db = CurrentDb
    ' Do they want to delete old rows?
16  If (Me.chkDelete = -1) Then
      ' Verify it
17    If vbYes = MsgBox("Are you SURE you want to delete " & _
        "all existing rows? " & vbCrLf & vbCrLf & _
        "(This will also compact the data file.)", _
        vbQuestion + vbYesNo + vbDefaultButton2, gstrAppTitle) Then
        ' Open the table that tells us the safe delete sequence
18      Set rstDel = db.OpenRecordset("SELECT * FROM " & _
          "ztblDeleteSeq ORDER BY Sequence", _
          dbOpenSnapshot, dbForwardOnly)
        ' Loop through them all
```

```
19        Do Until rstDel.EOF
            ' Execute a delete
20          db.Execute "DELETE * FROM " & rstDel!TableName, _
              dbFailOnError
            ' Go to the next row
            rstDel.MoveNext
          Loop
          ' Figure out the path to the backend data
21        strBackEndPath = Mid(db.TableDefs("tblContacts").Connect, 11)
          ' Figure out the backend folder
22        strBackEndFolder = Left(strBackEndPath, _
            InStrRev(strBackEndPath, "\"))
          ' Calculate a "compact to" database name
          strNewDb = "TempContact" & Format(Now, "hhnnss") & ".accdb"
          ' Compact the database into a new name
23        DBEngine.CompactDatabase strBackEndPath, _
            strBackEndFolder & strNewDb
          ' Delete the old one
24        Kill strBackEndPath
          ' Rename the new
          Name strBackEndFolder & strNewDb As strBackEndPath
        Else
          ' Turn off the delete flag - changed mind
          Me.chkDelete = 0
25      End If
26    End If
      ' Initialize the randomizer on system clock
27    Randomize
      ' Open all output recordsets
28    Set rstCo = db.OpenRecordset("tblCompanies", dbOpenDynaset)
      Set rstCn = db.OpenRecordset("tblContacts", dbOpenDynaset)
      Set rstCoCn = db.OpenRecordset("tblCompanyContacts", dbOpenDynaset)
      Set rstCnEv = db.OpenRecordset("tblContactEvents", dbOpenDynaset)
      ' Open the random recordsets
      Set rstZipRandom = db.OpenRecordset("zqryRandomZips", dbOpenDynaset)
      Set rstCoRandom = db.OpenRecordset("zqryRandomCompanies", dbOpenDynaset)
      Set rstPRandom = db.OpenRecordset("zqryRandomNames", dbOpenDynaset)
      ' Open the Events/products list
      Set rstEvents = db.OpenRecordset("zqryEventsProducts", dbOpenDynaset)
      ' Move to the end to get full recordcount
      rstEvents.MoveLast
      ' Turn on the hourglass
29    DoCmd.Hourglass True
      ' Initialize the status bar
30    varRtn = SysCmd(acSysCmdInitMeter, "Creating Companies...", _
        intNumCompanies)
      ' Outer loop to add Companies
31    For intI = 1 To intNumCompanies
        ' Start a new company record
        rstCo.AddNew
        ' Clear the saved website
        strWebsite = ""
```

```
      ' Grab the next random "company" name
32    strCompanyName = rstCoRandom!CompanyName
      ' .. and the website
33    rstCo!Website = rstCoRandom!CompanyName & "#" & _
        rstCoRandom!Web & "##" & rstCoRandom!CompanyName & " Website"
      strWebsite = rstCo!Website
34    rstCo!CompanyName = strCompanyName
      ' Generate a random street number
35    intR = Int((7 * Rnd) + 1)
      strCoAddress = Mid(strDigits, intR, 4)
      ' Now pick a random street name
      intR = Int((9 * Rnd) + 1)
      strCoAddress = strCoAddress & " " & strStreetNames(intR)
      ' and street type
      intR = Int((5 * Rnd) + 1)
      strCoAddress = strCoAddress & " " & strStreetTypes(intR)
      rstCo!Address = strCoAddress
      ' Fill in random values from the zip code table
36    rstCo!City = rstZipRandom!City
      rstCo!County = rstZipRandom!County
      rstCo!StateOrProvince = rstZipRandom!State
      rstCo!PostalCode = rstZipRandom!ZipCode
      ' Generate a random Area Code
37    intR = Int((8 * Rnd) + 1)
      strAreaCode = Mid(strDigits, intR, 3)
      ' Generate a random phone number (0100 - 0148)
      intR = Int((48 * Rnd) + 1) + 100
      strThisPhone = strAreaCode & "555" & Format(intR, "0000")
      rstCo!PhoneNumber = strThisPhone
      ' Add 1 for the fax number
      strThisFax = strAreaCode & "555" & Format(intR + 1, "0000")
      rstCo!FaxNumber = strThisFax
      ' Save the new Company ID
38    lngThisCompany = rstCo!CompanyID
      ' .. and save the new Company
      rstCo.Update
      ' Now, do some contacts for this company
      '  - calc a random number of contacts
39    intJ = Int((intNumContacts * Rnd) + 1)
      ' Set up the recordset of Zips "close" to the Work Zip
40    Set rstZipClose = db.OpenRecordset("SELECT * FROM tlkpZips " & _
        "WHERE ZipCode BETWEEN '" & _
        Format(CLng(rstZipRandom!ZipCode) - 5, "00000") & _
        "' AND '" & Format(CLng(rstZipRandom!ZipCode) + 5, "00000") & _
        "'", dbOpenDyanaset)
      ' Move to last row to get accurate count
      rstZipClose.MoveLast
      ' Make the first contact the company default
      intDefault = True
      ' Loop to add contacts
41    For intK = 1 To intJ
        ' Start a new record
```

```
      rstCn.AddNew
      ' Put in the name info from the random people record
42    rstCn!LastName = rstPRandom!LastName
      rstCn!FirstName = rstPRandom!FirstName
      rstCn!MiddleInit = rstPRandom!MiddleInit
      rstCn!Suffix = rstPRandom!Suffix
      ' Select title  and picture based on gender of person
43    If rstPRandom!Sex = "f" Then
        ' Pick a random female title and picture
        intR = Int((7 * Rnd) + 1)
        rstCn!Title = strFTitles(intR)
        ' Make sure we have some picture file names
        If intFPicCount <> 0 Then
          ' Pick a random file name
          intR = Int((intFPicCount * Rnd) + 1)
          strPicPath = strFPicture(intR)
        Else
          ' Set empty picture name
          strPicPath = ""
        End If
44    Else
        ' Pick a random male title and picture
        intR = Int((6 * Rnd) + 1)
        rstCn!Title = strMTitles(intR)
        ' Make sure we have some picture file names
        If intMPicCount <> 0 Then
          ' Pick a random file name
          intR = Int((intMPicCount * Rnd) + 1)
          strPicPath = strMPicture(intR)
        Else
          ' Set empty picture name
          strPicPath = ""
        End If
45    End If
      ' Set contact type to "Customer" - complex data type
46    Set rstComplex = rstCn!ContactType.Value
      rstComplex.AddNew
      rstComplex!Value = "Customer"
      rstComplex.Update
47    ' Copy the company website
      rstCn!Website = strWebsite
      ' Set up a dummy email
      rstCn!EmailName = rstPRandom!FirstName & " " & _
        rstPRandom!LastName & mailto: & Left(rstPRandom!FirstName, 1) & _
        rstPRandom!LastName & "@" _
        Mid(rstCoRandom!Web, Instr(rstCoRandom!Web, http://www.) + 11)
      ' Strip off the trailing "/"
      rstCn!EmailName = Left(rstCn!EmailName, Len(rstCn!EmailName) - 1)
      ' Pick a random birth date between Jan 1, 1940 and Dec 31, 1979
      ' There are 14,610 days between these dates
      intR = Int((14610 * Rnd) + 1)
      rstCn!BirthDate = #12/31/1939# + Int((14610 * Rnd) + 1)
```

```
    ' Set Default Address to 'work'
    rstCn!DefaultAddress = 1
    ' Copy work address from Company
    rstCn!WorkAddress = strCoAddress
    rstCn!WorkCity = rstZipRandom!City
    rstCn!WorkStateOrProvince = rstZipRandom!State
    rstCn!WorkPostalCode = rstZipRandom!ZipCode
    rstCn!WorkPhone = strThisPhone
    rstCn!WorkFaxNumber = strThisFax
    ' Generate a random street number for home address
    intR = Int((7 * Rnd) + 1)
    strPAddress = Mid(strDigits, intR, 4)
    ' Now pick a random street name
    intR = Int((9 * Rnd) + 1)
    strPAddress = strPAddress & " " & strStreetNames(intR)
    ' and street type
    intR = Int((5 * Rnd) + 1)
    strPAddress = strPAddress & " " & strStreetTypes(intR)
    rstCn!HomeAddress = strPAddress
    ' Position to a "close" random zip
48  intR = rstZipClose.RecordCount
    intR = Int(intR * Rnd)
    rstZipClose.MoveFirst
    If intR > 0 Then rstZipClose.Move intR
    rstCn!HomeCity = rstZipClose!City
    rstCn!HomeStateOrProvince = rstZipClose!State
    rstCn!HomePostalCode = rstZipClose!ZipCode
    ' Generate a random phone number (0150 - 0198)
    intR = Int((48 * Rnd) + 1) + 149
    rstCn!HomePhone = strAreaCode & "555" & Format(intR, "0000")
    ' Add 1 for the fax number
    rstCn!MobilePhone = strAreaCode & "555" & Format(intR + 1, "0000")
    ' Save the new contact ID
49  lngThisContact = rstCn!ContactID
    ' If got a random photo name, load it
50  If strPicPath <> "" Then
      ' Open the special photo editing recordset
51    Set rstComplex = rstCn!Photo.Value
      rstComplex.Addnew
      rstComplex!FileData.LoadFromFile _
        (CurrentProject.Path & "\Pictures\" & strPicPath)
      rstComplex.Update
    End If
    ' Finally, save the row
    rstCn.Update
    ' Insert linking CompanyContact record
52  rstCoCn.AddNew
    ' Set the Company ID
    rstCoCn!CompanyID = lngThisCompany
    ' Set the Contact ID
    rstCoCn!ContactID = lngThisContact
    ' Make this the default company for the contact
```

```
          rstCoCn!DefaultForContact = True
          ' Set default for company - 1st contact will be the default
          rstCoCn!DefaultForCompany = intDefault
          ' Reset intDefault after first time through
          intDefault = False
          ' Save the linking row
          rstCoCn.Update
          ' Now, do some contacts events for this contact
          '  - calc a random number of events
53        intM = Int((intNumEvents * Rnd) + 1)
          ' Clear the Products sold string
          strProducts = ""
          ' Loop to add some events
54        For intL = 1 To intM
            ' Start a new row
            rstCnEv.AddNew
            ' Set the Contact ID
            rstCnEv!ContactID = lngThisContact
            ' Calculate a random number of days
            intR = Int(intNumDays * Rnd)
            datCurrentDate = datBeginDate + intR
            ' Calculate a random time between 8am and 8pm (no seconds)
            datCurrentTime = CDate(Format(((0.5 * Rnd) + 0.3333), "hh:nn"))
            ' Set the contact date/time
            rstCnEv!ContactDateTime = datCurrentDate + datCurrentTime
55 TryAgain:
            ' Position to a random event
56          intR = rstEvents.RecordCount
            intR = Int(intR * Rnd)
            rstEvents.MoveFirst
            If intR > 0 Then rstEvents.Move intR
            ' If a product sale event,
57          If (rstEvents!ContactEventProductSold = True) Then
              ' Can't sell the same product twice to the same contact
              If InStr(strProducts, _
                Format(rstEvents!ContactEventProductID, "00")) <> 0 Then
                ' ooops.  Loop back to pick a different event
58              GoTo TryAgain
              End If
            End If
            ' Set the Event Type
59          rstCnEv!ContactEventTypeID = rstEvents!ContactEventTypeID
            ' Set the follow-up
            rstCnEv!ContactFollowUp = rstEvents!ContactEventRequiresFollowUp
            ' Set the follow-up date
            If (rstEvents!ContactEventRequiresFollowUp = True) Then
              rstCnEv!ContactFollowUpDate = datCurrentDate + _
                rstEvents!ContactEventFollowUpDays
            End If
            ' Save the record
60          rstCnEv.Update
            ' If this event is a product sale,
```

```
    If (rstEvents!ContactEventProductSold = True) Then
     ' Call the routine to also add a product record!
     varRtn = Add_Product(lngThisCompany, lngThisContact, _
      rstEvents!ContactEventProductID, datCurrentDate)
     ' Add the product to the products sold string
     strProducts = strProducts & " " & _
      Format(rstEvents!ContactEventProductID, "00")
    End If
   ' Loop to do more events
   Next intL
  ' Move to the next random person record
  rstPRandom.MoveNext
  ' and loop to do more contacts
  Next intK
  rstZipClose.Close
  Set rstZipClose = Nothing
  ' Move to the next random zip record
  rstZipRandom.MoveNext
  ' Update the status bar
  varRtn = SysCmd(acSysCmdUpdateMeter, intI)
 ' Loop until done
 Next intI
 ' Clear the status bar
 varRtn = SysCmd(acSysCmdClearStatus)
 ' Done with error trapping, too
 On Error GoTo 0
 ' Be nice and close everything up
 rstCo.Close
 Set rstCo = Nothing
 rstCn.Close
 Set rstCn = Nothing
 rstCoCn.Close
 Set rstCoCn = Nothing
 rstCnEv.Close
 Set rstCnEv = Nothing
 rstZipRandom.Close
 Set rstZipRandom = Nothing
 rstCoRandom.Close
 Set rstCoRandom = Nothing
 ' Turn off the hourglass
 DoCmd.Hourglass False
 MsgBox "Done!", vbExclamation, gstrAppTitle
 DoCmd.Close acForm, Me.Name
 Exit Sub
BailOut:
 MsgBox "Unexpected error: " & Err & ", " & Error
 ' Turn off the hourglass
 DoCmd.Hourglass False
 varRtn = SysCmd(acSysCmdClearStatus)
 Resume Done
End Sub
```

Table 19-5 lists the statement line numbers and explains the code on key lines in the preceding Visual Basic code example.

**Table 19-5 Explanation of Code in Example to Load Random Data**

| Line | Explanation |
|---|---|
| 1 | Declare the beginning of the subroutine. The subroutine has no arguments. |
| 2 | You can begin a comment anywhere on a statement line by preceding the comment with a single quotation mark. You can also create a comment statement using the Rem statement. |
| 3 | Declare local variables for a DAO Database object and all the DAO Recordset objects used in this code. |
| 4 | Beginning of the declarations of all local variables. You should always explicitly define variables in your code. |
| 5 | This procedure uses several arrays in which it stores street names, street types, male person titles, female person titles, and the paths to male and female pictures. Code later in the procedure randomly chooses values from these arrays. |
| 6 | Set an error trap; the BailOut label is at line 71. |
| 7 | Code to initialize the arrays begins here. Note that separate arrays handle male and female titles. |
| 8 | Use the Dir function to find available male picture names in the Pictures subfolder under the location of the current database. Note that if you move the sample database, this code won't find any pictures to load. When Dir finds a matching file, it returns the file name as a string. The code subsequently calls Dir with no arguments inside the following loop to ask for the next picture. |
| 9 | Begin a loop to load male pictures, and keep looping until the picture file name is an empty string (Dir found no more files). |
| 10 | Note the use of ReDim Preserve to dynamically expand the existing file name array for male pictures without losing any entries already stored. |
| 11 | End of the loop started at statement number 9. |
| 12 | This loop finds all the female pictures available and loads them into the array that holds picture file names for females. |
| 13 | End of the loop started at statement number 12. |
| 14 | The next several lines of code capture the values from the form. Validation rules in the form controls make sure that the data is valid. |
| 15 | Initialize the Database object. |
| 16 | Check to see if you selected the option to delete all existing rows. |
| 17 | Use the MsgBox function to verify that you really want to delete existing data. |
| 18 | The ztblDeleteSeq table contains the table names in a correct sequence for deletes from the bottom up so that this code doesn't violate any referential integrity rules. Note that the recordset is opened as a forward-only snapshot for efficiency. |

| Line | Explanation |
|---|---|
| 19 | Start a loop to process all the table names in ztblDeleteSeq. |
| 20 | Use the Execute method of the Database object to run the DELETE SQL commands. |
| 21 | Figure out the path to the linked data file by examining the Connect property of one of the linked tables. |
| 22 | Extract the folder name of the data file using the Left and InStrRev functions. |
| 23 | Use the CompactDatabase method of the DBEngine object to compact the data file into a new one—TempContact*hhmmss*.accdb—where *hhmmss* is the current time to avoid conflicts. |
| 24 | Use the Kill command to delete the old file and the Name command to rename the compacted temp copy. |
| 25 | Terminate the If statement on line 17. |
| 26 | Terminate the If statement on line 16. |
| 27 | Initialize the randomizer so that all random recordsets are always different. |
| 28 | Open all the recordsets needed in this code. |
| 29 | Turn the mouse pointer into an hourglass to let you know the transaction is under way and might take a while. You could also set the Screen.MousePointer property to 11 (busy). |
| 30 | The SysCmd utility function provides various useful options such as finding out the current directory for msaccess.exe (the Access main program), and the current version of Access. It also has options to display messages and a progress meter on the status bar. This code calls SysCmd to initialize the progress meter you see as the code loads the data. |
| 31 | Start the main loop to load company data. |
| 32 | Save the company name from the random recordset in a local variable. |
| 33 | Generate the Web site hyperlink from the company name and the Web field. |
| 34 | Set the company name in the new company record. |
| 35 | The next several lines of code use the Rnd function to randomly generate a four-digit street address and randomly choose a street name and street type from the arrays loaded earlier. |
| 36 | Grab the city, county, state, and ZIP Code from the current row in the random ZIP Code query. |
| 37 | Use Rnd again to generate a fake phone area code and phone and fax numbers. |
| 38 | The primary key of tblCompanies is an AutoNumber field. Access automatically generates the next number as soon as you update any field in a new record. This code saves the new company ID to use in related records and writes the company record with the Update method. |
| 39 | Calculate a random number of contacts to load for the new company based on the maximum you specified in the form. |

| Line | Explanation |
|---|---|
| 40 | Open a recordset that chooses the ZIP Codes that are 5 higher or lower than the random ZIP Code for the company. (It makes sense that the employees of the company live nearby.) |
| 41 | Start the loop to add contacts for this company. |
| 42 | Update the new contacts record with a random name plucked from the random person names query. |
| 43 | The records in the ztblPeople table have a gender field to help choose an appropriate title and picture for the contact. The statements following this If statement load female data, and the statements following the Else statement on line 44 load male data. |
| 44 | This Else statement matches the If on line 43. Statements following this choose male data. |
| 45 | This End If closes the If on line 43. |
| 46 | The ContactType field is a multi-value field, so must open a recordset on the field's Value property even though we're specifying only one value. |
| 47 | Finish generating fields for the contacts record, including the Web site copied from the company, a fake e-mail name, and a random birth date and addresses. |
| 48 | Choose a random ZIP Code for the contact near the company ZIP Code from the recordset opened on line 40. Also generate phone and fax numbers. |
| 49 | The primary key for tblContacts is also an AutoNumber field, so save the new value to use to generate related records and save the new contact. |
| 50 | If the code found a good picture file name earlier (male or female), then the following code adds that picture to the record. |
| 51 | Photo is an attachment field that works similarly to multi-value fields in code. The code opens a recordset and uses the LoadFromFile method to insert the picture using its file path. |
| 52 | Create the linking record in tblCompanyContacts from the saved CompanyID and ContactID. The first contact created is always the default contact for the company. |
| 53 | Calculate a random number of events to load for this contact. |
| 54 | Start the loop to add contact events. The following several lines calculate a random contact date and time within the range you specified on the form. |
| 55 | Code at line 58 goes here if the random product picked was already sold to this contact. |
| 56 | Choose a random event. |
| 57 | If the random event is a product sale, verify that this product isn't already sold to this contact. A product can be sold to a contact only once. |
| 58 | The code loops back up to line 55 to choose another event if this is a duplicate product. |
| 59 | Finish updating the fields in the new contact event record. |

| Line | Explanation |
|---|---|
| 60 | Save the new contact event. |
| 61 | If the event was a product sale, call the Add_Product function that's also in this form module to add a row to tblContactProducts. This code passes the company ID, contact ID, product ID, and the date of the event to the function. It also saves the product ID to be sure it isn't sold again to this contact. |
| 62 | This Next statement closes the loop started on line 54. |
| 63 | Move to the next random person record. |
| 64 | Loop back up to line 41. |
| 65 | Close the recordset of ZIP Codes close to the company ZIP Code. |
| 66 | Get the next random ZIP Code for the next company. |
| 67 | Update the status bar to indicate your're done with another company. |
| 68 | Loop back up to line 31. |
| 69 | Clear the status bar and close up shop. |
| 70 | Clear the hourglass set on line 29. Also issue the final MsgBox confirming that all data is now loaded. Finally, close this form and exit. |
| 71 | Any trapped error comes here. This code simply displays the error, clears the mouse pointer and the status bar, and exits. If you don't reset the mouse pointer and clear the status bar, Access won't do it for you! |
| 72 | End of the subroutine. |

## A Procedure to Examine All Error Codes

In the Housing Reservations database (Housing.accdb), we created a function that dynamically creates a new table and then inserts into the table (using DAO) a complete list of all the error codes used by Access and the text of the error message associated with each error code. You can find a partial list of the error codes in Help, but the table in the Housing Reservations sample database provides the best way to see a list of all the error codes. You might find this table useful as you begin to create your own Visual Basic procedures and set error trapping in them.

> **Note**
>
> You can find the ADO equivalent of this example in the modExamples module in the Conrad Systems Contacts sample database.

The name of the function is CreateErrTable, and you can find it in the modExamples module. The function statements are listed next. You can execute this function by entering the following in the Immediate window:

```
?CreateErrTable
```

The sample database contains the ErrTable table, so the code will ask you if you want to delete and rebuild the table. You should click Yes to run the code. Again, we've added line numbers to some of the lines in this code listing so that you can follow along with the line-by-line explanations in Table 19-6, which follows the listing.

```
 1 Function CreateErrTable ()
   ' This function creates a table containing a list of
   '  all the valid Access application error codes
   '  You can find the ADO version of this procedure in Contacts.accdb
 2   ' Declare variables used in this function
 3   Dim dbMyDatabase As DAO.Database, tblErrTable As DAO.TableDef, _
       fldMyField As DAO.Field, idxPKey As DAO.Index
 4   Dim rcdErrRecSet As DAO.Recordset, lngErrCode As Long, _
       intMsgRtn As Integer
 5   Dim varReturnVal As Variant, varErrString As Variant, _
       ws As DAO.Workspace
     ' Create Errors table with Error Code and Error String fields
     ' Initialize the MyDatabase database variable
     ' to the current database
 6   Set dbMyDatabase = CurrentDb
 7   Set ws = DBEngine.Workspaces(0)
     ' Trap error if table doesn't exist
     ' Skip to next statement if an error occurs
 8   On Error Resume Next
 9   Set rcdErrRecSet = dbMyDatabase.OpenRecordset("ErrTable")
10   Select Case Err   ' See whether error was raised
11     Case 0   ' No error-table must exist
12       On Error GoTo 0   ' Turn off error trapping
13       intMsgRtn = MsgBox("ErrTable already " & _
           "exists. Do you want to delete and " & _
           "rebuild all rows?", vbQuestion + vbYesNo)
14       If intMsgRtn = vbYes Then
           ' Reply was YES-delete rows and rebuild
           ' Run quick SQL to delete rows
15         dbMyDatabase.Execute_
             "DELETE * FROM ErrTable;", dbFailOnError
16       Else                     ' Reply was NO-done
17         rcdErrRecSet.Close     ' Close the table
18         Exit Function          ' And exit
19       End If
20     Case 3011, 3078            ' Couldn't find table,
                                  ' so build it
21       On Error GoTo 0    ' Turn off error trapping
         ' Create a new table to contain error rows
22       Set tblErrTable = _
           dbMyDatabase.CreateTableDef("ErrTable")
         ' Create a field in ErrTable to contain the
         ' error code
23       Set fldMyField = tblErrTable.CreateField( _
           "ErrorCode", DB_LONG)
         ' Append "ErrorCode" field to the fields
         ' collection in the new table definition
```

```
    tblErrTable.Fields.Append fldMyField
    ' Create a field in ErrTable for the error
    ' description
    Set fldMyField = _
      tblErrTable.CreateField("ErrorString", _
      DB_MEMO)
    ' Append "ErrorString" field to the fields
    ' collection in the new table definition
    tblErrTable.Fields.Append fldMyField
    ' Append the new table to the TableDefs
    ' collection in the current database
    dbMyDatabase.TableDefs.Append tblErrTable
    ' Set text field width to 5" (7200 twips)
    ' (calls sub procedure)
    SetFieldProperty _
      tblErrTable![ErrorString], _
      "ColumnWidth", DB_INTEGER, 7200
    ' Create a Primary Key
    Set idxPKey = tblErrTable.CreateIndex("PrimaryKey")
    ' Create and append the field to the index fields collection
    idxPKey.Fields.Append idxPKey.CreateField("ErrorCode")
    ' Make it the Primary Key
    idxPKey.Primary = True
    ' Create the index
    tblErrTable.Indexes.Append idxPKey
    ' Set recordset to Errors Table recordset
    Set rcdErrRecSet = _
      dbMyDatabase.OpenRecordset("ErrTable")
  Case Else
    ' Can't identify the error-write message
    ' and bail out
    MsgBox "Unknown error in CreateErrTable " & _
      Err & ", " & Error$(Err), 16
    Exit Function
End Select
' Initialize progress meter on the status bar
varReturnVal = SysCmd(acSysCmdInitMeter, _
  "Building Error Table", 32767)
' Turn on hourglass to show this might take
' a while
DoCmd.Hourglass True
' Start a transaction to make it go fast
ws.BeginTrans
' Loop through Microsoft Access error codes,
' skipping codes that generate
' "Application-defined or object-define error"
' message
For lngErrCode = 1 To 32767
  varErrString = AccessError(lngErrCode)
  If IsNothing(varErrString) Or _
    ' If AccessError returned nothing, then try Error
    varErrString = "Application-defined or object-defined error" Then
    varErrString = Error(lngErrCode)
  End If
```

```
42      If Not IsNothing(varErrString) Then
43        If varErrString <> "Application-" & _
            "defined or object-defined error" Then
            ' Add each error code and string to
            ' Errors table
44          rcdErrRecSet.AddNew
45          rcdErrRecSet("ErrorCode") = lngErrCode
46          rcdErrRecSet("ErrorString") = varErrString
47          rcdErrRecSet.Update
48        End If
49      End If
        ' Update the status meter
50      varReturnVal = SysCmd(acSysCmdUpdateMeter, _
          lngErrCode)
        ' Process next error code
51    Next lngErrCode
52    ws.CommitTrans
      ' Close recordset
53    rcdErrRecSet.Close
      ' Turn off the hourglass-you're done
54    DoCmd.Hourglass False
      ' And reset the status bar
55    varReturnVal = SysCmd(acSysCmdClearStatus)
      ' Select new table in the Navigation Pane
      ' to refresh the list
56    DoCmd.SelectObject acTable, "ErrTable", True
      ' Open a confirmation dialog box
57    MsgBox "Errors table created."
58 End Function
```

Table 19-6 lists the statement line numbers and explains the code on each line in the preceding Visual Basic code example.

**Table 19-6 Explanation of Code in Example to Examine Error Codes**

| Line | Explanation |
|---|---|
| 1 | Declare the beginning of the function. The function has no arguments. |
| 2 | You can begin a comment anywhere on a statement line by preceding the comment with a single quotation mark. You can also create a comment statement using the Rem statement. |
| 3 | Declare local variables for a Database object, a TableDef object, a Field object, and an Index object. |
| 4 | Declare local variables for a Recordset object, a Long Integer, and an Integer. |
| 5 | Declare local variables for a Variant that is used to accept the return value from the SysCmd function, a Variant that is used to accept the error string returned by the AccessError function, and a Workspace object. |
| 6 | Initialize the Database object variable by setting it to the current database. |
| 7 | Initialize the Workspace object by setting it to the current workspace. |
| 8 | Enable error trapping but execute the next statement if an error occurs. |

| Line | Explanation |
|---|---|
| 9 | Initialize the Recordset object variable by attempting to open the ErrTable table. If the table does not exist, this generates an error. |
| 10 | Call the Err function to see whether an error occurred. The following Case statements check the particular error values that interest you. |
| 11 | The first Case statement tests for an Err value of 0, indicating no error occurred. If no error occurred, the table already existed and opened successfully. |
| 12 | Turn off error trapping because you don't expect any more errors. |
| 13 | Use the MsgBox function to ask whether you want to clear and rebuild all rows in the existing table. The vbQuestion intrinsic constant asks MsgBox to display the question icon, and the vbYesNo intrinsic constant requests Yes and No buttons (instead of the default OK button). The statement assigns the value returned by MsgBox so that you can test it on the next line. |
| 14 | If you click Yes, MsgBox returns the value of the intrinsic constant vbYes. (vbYes happens to be the integer value 6, but the constant name is easier to remember than the number.) |
| 15 | Run a simple SQL statement to delete all the rows in the error table. |
| 16 | Else clause that goes with the If statement on line 14. |
| 17 | Close the table if the table exists and you clicked the No button on line 13. |
| 18 | Exit the function. |
| 19 | End If statement that goes with the If statement on line 14. |
| 20 | Second Case statement. Error codes 3011 and 3078 are both "object not found." |
| 21 | Turn off error trapping because you don't expect any more errors. |
| 22 | Use the CreateTableDef method on the database to start a new table definition. This is the same as clicking the Table Design button in the Tables group on the Create tab of the Ribbon. |
| 23 | Use the CreateField method on the new table to create the first field object—a long integer (the intrinsic constant DB_LONG) named ErrorCode. |
| 24 | Append the first new field to the Fields collection of the new Table object. |
| 25 | Use the CreateField method to create the second field—a memo field named ErrorString. |
| 26 | Append the second new field to the Fields collection of the new Table object. |
| 27 | Save the new table definition by appending it to the TableDefs collection of the Database object. If you were to halt the code at this point and repaint the Navigation Pane, you would find the new ErrTable listed. |
| 28 | Call the SetFieldProperty subroutine in this module to set the column width of the ErrorString field to 7200 twips (5 inches). This ensures that you can see more of the error text when you open the table in Datasheet view. |
| 29 | Use the CreateIndex method of the TableDef to begin building an index. |

| Line | Explanation |
|---|---|
| 30 | Create a single field and append it to the Fields collection of the index. The following statement sets the Primary property of the index to True to indicate that this will be the primary key. |
| 31 | Save the new primary key index by appending it to the Indexes collection of the TableDef. |
| 32 | Open a recordset by using the OpenRecordset method on the table. |
| 33 | This Case statement traps all other errors. |
| 34 | Show a message box with the error number and the error message. |
| 35 | Exit the function after an unknown error. |
| 36 | End Select statement that completes the Select Case statement on line 10. |
| 37 | Call the SysCmd function to place a "building table" message on the status bar, and initialize a progress meter. The CreateErrTable function will look at 32,767 different error codes. |
| 38 | Turn the mouse pointer into an hourglass to indicate that this procedure will take a few seconds. |
| 39 | Use the BeginTrans method of the Workspace object to start a transaction. Statements within a transaction are treated as a single unit. Changes to data are saved only if the transaction completes successfully with a CommitTrans method. Using transactions when you're updating records can speed performance by reducing disk access. |
| 40 | Start a For loop to check each error code from 1 through 32,767. |
| 41 | Assign the error text returned by the AccessError function to the variable varErrString. If the string is empty or returned "Application-defined or object-defined error," try calling the Error function to get the text of the message. |
| 42 | Call the IsNothing function in the modUtility module of the sample database to test whether the text returned is blank. You don't want blank rows, so don't add a row if the AccessError function for the current error code returns a blank string. |
| 43 | Lots of error codes are defined as "Application-defined or object-defined error." You don't want any of these, so this statement adds a row only if the AccessError function for the current error code doesn't return this string. |
| 44 | Use the AddNew method to start a new row in the table. |
| 45 | Set the ErrorCode field equal to the current error code. |
| 46 | Save the text of the message in the ErrorString field. Because we defined the field as a memo, we don't need to worry about the length of the text. |
| 47 | Use the Update method to save the new row. |
| 48 | End If statement that completes the If statement on line 43. |
| 49 | End If statement that completes the If statement on line 42. |
| 50 | After handling each error code, update the progress meter on the status bar to show how far you've gotten. |

| Line | Explanation |
|---|---|
| 51 | Next statement that completes the For loop begun on line 40. Visual Basic increments lngErrCode by 1 and executes the For loop again until lngErrCode is greater than 32,767. |
| 52 | CommitTrans method that completes the transaction begun on line 39. |
| 53 | After looping through all possible error codes, close the recordset. |
| 54 | Change the mouse pointer back to normal. |
| 55 | Clear the status bar. |
| 56 | Put the focus on the ErrTable table in the Navigation Pane. |
| 57 | Display a message box confirming that the function has completed. |
| 58 | End of the function. |

You should now have a basic understanding of how to create functions and subroutines using Visual Basic. In the next chapter, you'll enhance what you've learned as you study major parts of the Conrad Systems Contacts, Housing Reservations, and Wedding List applications.

CHAPTER 20

# Automating Your Application with Visual Basic



Now that you've learned the fundamentals of using Microsoft Visual Basic, it's time to put this knowledge into practice. In this chapter, you'll learn how to create the Visual Basic code you need to automate many common tasks.

You can find dozens of examples of automation in the Conrad Systems Contacts, Housing Reservations, and Wedding List sample databases. As you explore the databases, whenever you see something interesting, open the form or report in Design view and take a look at the Visual Basic code behind the form or report. This chapter walks you through a few of the more interesting examples in these databases.

**Note**

You can find the code explained in this chapter in the Conrad Systems Contacts (Contacts.accdb), Housing Reservations (Housing.accdb), and Wedding List (WeddingList.accdb) sample applications on the companion CD.

## Why Aren't We Using Macros?

Although you can certainly use macros to automate simple applications, macros have certain limitations. For example, as you might have noticed when examining the list of available events in Chapter 17, "Understanding Event Processing," many events require or return parameters that can be passed to or read from a Visual Basic procedure but not a macro. Also, even though you can write a macro to handle general errors in forms and reports, you can't really analyze errors effectively within a macro nor do much to recover from an error. And as you saw in Chapter 18, "Automating Your Application with Macros," the debugging facilities for macros are very simplistic.

## When to Use Macros

Use macros in your application in any of the following circumstances:

- Your application consists of only a few forms and reports.
- You need to build a simple application that is automated using only trusted macro actions so that the application can run even when the database is not trusted.
- Your application might be used by users unfamiliar with Visual Basic who will want to understand how your application is constructed and possibly modify or enhance it.
- You're developing an application prototype, and you want to rapidly automate a few features to demonstrate your design. However, once you understand Visual Basic, automating a demonstration application is just as easy using event procedures.
- You don't need complex error evaluation and handling.
- You don't need to evaluate or set parameters passed by certain events, such as AfterDelConfirm, ApplyFilter, BeforeDelConfirm, Error, Filter, KeyDown, KeyPress, KeyUp, MouseDown, MouseMove, MouseUp, NotInList, and Updated.
- You don't need to open and work with recordsets or other objects.

In fact, we can think of only two reasons you'll ever need to use a macro:

- You must write an AutoKeys macro to define any keystrokes that you want to intercept globally in your application. However, you can also easily define custom handling of keystrokes using the KeyPress events in forms and reports. The one advantage of an AutoKeys macro is it allows you to trap keystrokes in one place. The disadvantage is it is more difficult to customize keystroke handling for individual forms and reports. You'll learn how to create an AutoKeys macro in Chapter 24, "The Finishing Touches."
- Because Microsoft Access won't run any Visual Basic code in a database that is not trusted, in an application that runs using Visual Basic you need to either write a safe AutoExec macro or embed a safe macro in your startup form's Load event. In that macro, test the IsTrusted property of the CurrentProject object and exit gracefully if the user has not trusted your application.

## When to Use Visual Basic

Although macros can be useful, a number of tasks cannot be carried out with macros, and there are others that are better implemented using a Visual Basic procedure. Use a Visual Basic procedure instead of a macro in any of the following circumstances:

- You need complex error handling in your application.
- You want to define a new function.

- You need to handle events that pass parameters or accept return values (other than Cancel).
- You need to create new objects (tables, queries, forms, or reports) in your database from application code.
- Your application needs to interact with another Windows-based program via ActiveX automation.
- You want to be able to directly call Windows API functions.
- You want to define application code that is common across several applications in a library.
- You want to be able to open and work with data in a recordset on a record-by-record basis.
- You need to use some of the native facilities of the relational database management system that handles your attached tables (such as Microsoft SQL Server procedures or data definition facilities).
- You want maximum performance in your application. Because modules are compiled, they execute slightly faster than macros. You'll probably notice a difference only on slower processors.
- You are writing a complicated application that will be difficult to debug.

Although you can now trap errors in macros in an application written using Office Access 2007, you don't have complex evaluation structures such as Select Case to help you decipher and handle the error. Quite frankly, the only reason we might recommend using macros instead of Visual Basic is when you need to write an application that can run in a database that is not trusted. But the instant that you need to use a macro action that is not trusted (our favorites are SetValue and Quit), then you might as well automate your application with Visual Basic.



# Assisting Data Entry

You can do a lot to help make sure the user of your application enters correct data by defining default values, input masks, and validation rules. But what can you do if the default values come from a related table? How can you assist a user who needs to enter a value that's not in the row source of a combo box? How do you make the display text in a hyperlink more readable? Is there a way you can make it easier for your user to pick dates and times? And how do you help the user edit linked picture files? You can find the answers to these questions in the following sections.

## Filling In Related Data

The tblContactProducts table in the Conrad Systems Contacts database has a SoldPrice field that reflects the actual sales price at the time of a sale. The tblProducts table has a UnitPrice field that contains the normal selling price of the product. When the user is working in the Contacts form (frmContacts) and wants to sell a new product, you don't want the user to have to go look up the current product price before entering it into the record.

You learned in Chapter 13, "Advanced Form Design," how to build a form with subforms nested two levels to edit contacts, the default company for each contact, and the products sold to that company and registered to the current contact. However, if you open frmContacts and click the Products tab, as shown in Figure 20-1, you'll notice that there doesn't appear to be any linking company data between contacts and the products sold. (The subform to display contact products isn't nested inside another subform to show the companies for the current contact.) Again, the user shouldn't have to look up the default company ID for the current contact before selling a product.

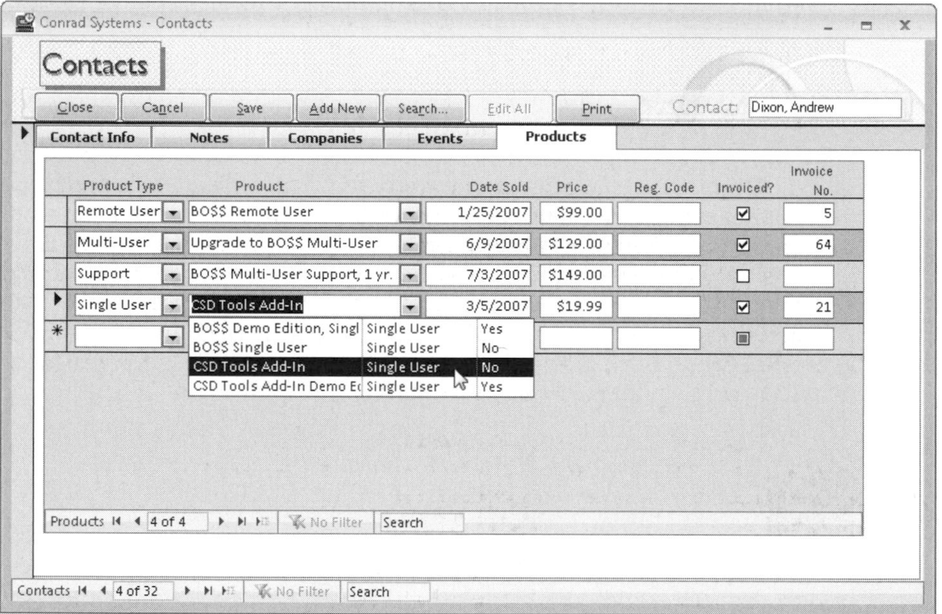


**Figure 20-1** Selling a product to a contact involves filling in the price and the default company.

As you can see, a combo box on the subform (fsubContactProducts) helps the user choose the product to sell. Part of the secret to setting the price (the SoldPrice field in tblContactProducts) automatically is in the row source query for the combo box, qlkpProductsForContacts, as shown in Figure 20-2.

You certainly need the ProductID field for the new record in tblContactProducts. Displaying the ProductName field in the combo box is more meaningful than showing the ProductID number, and, as you can see in Figure 20-1, the list in the combo box also shows you the CategoryDescription and whether the product is a trial version. But why did we include the UnitPrice, TrialExpire, and PreRequisite columns in the query's design grid?

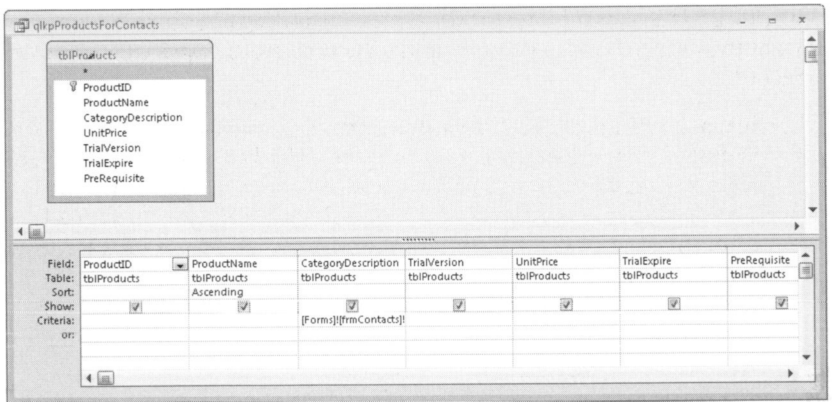


**Figure 20-2** The qlkpProductsForContacts query is the row source for the Product combo box on fsubContactProducts.



As it turns out, you can retrieve any of these fields from the current row in the combo box by referencing the combo box Column property. (You'll see later in this chapter, in "Validating Complex Data" on page 1071, how other code behind the form uses the additional fields to make sure the contact already owns any prerequisite product.) You can see the simple line of code that copies the UnitPrice field by opening the Visual Basic module behind the fsubContactProducts form. Go to the Navigation Pane, select the fsubContactProducts form, right-click the form and click Design View on the menu, and then click the View Code button in the Tools group on the Design tab. In the Visual Basic Editor (VBE) Code window, scroll down until you find the cmbProductID_After-Update procedure. The code is as follows:

```
Private Sub cmbProductID_AfterUpdate()
  ' Grab the default price from the hidden 5th column
  Me.SoldPrice = Me.cmbProductID.Column(4)
End Sub
```

Notice that you use an index number to fetch the column you want and that the index starts at zero. You can reference the fifth column in the query (UnitPrice) by asking for the Column(4) property of the combo box. Notice also that the code uses the Me shortcut object to reference the form object where this code is running. So, every time you pick a different product, the AfterUpdate event occurs for the ProductID combo box, and this code fills in the related price automatically.

If you open the frmContacts form in Design view, select the fsubContactProducts form on the Products tab, and examine the Link Child Fields and Link Master Fields properties, you'll find that the two forms are linked on ContactID. However, the tblContact-Products table also needs a CompanyID field in its primary key. Code in the module for the fsubContactProducts form handles fetching the default CompanyID for the current contact, so you don't need an intermediary subform that would clutter the form design.

If you still have the module for the fsubContactProducts form open in the VBE window, you can find the code in the Form_BeforeInsert procedure. The code is as follows:

```
Private Sub Form_BeforeInsert(Cancel As Integer)
Dim varCompanyID As Variant
  ' First, disallow insert if nothing in outer form
  If IsNothing(Me.Parent.ContactID) Then
    MsgBox "You must define the contact information on a new row before " & _
      "attempting to sell a product", vbCritical, gstrAppTitle
    Cancel = True
    Exit Sub
  End If
  ' Try to lookup this contact's Company ID
  varCompanyID = DLookup("CompanyID", "qryContactDefaultCompany", _
    "(ContactID = " & Me.Parent.ContactID.Value & ")")
    If IsNothing(varCompanyID) Then
    ' If not found, then disallow product sale
    MsgBox "You cannot sell a product to a Contact that does not have a " & _
      "related Company that is marked as the default for this Contact." & _
      "  Press Esc to clear your edits and click on the Companies tab " & _
      "to define the default Company for this Contact.", vbCritical, _
      gstrAppTitle
        Cancel = True
    Else
        ' Assign the company ID behind the scenes
        Me.CompanyID = varCompanyID
    End If
End Sub
```

This procedure executes whenever the user sets any value on a new row in the subform. First, it makes sure that the outer form has a valid ContactID. Next, the code uses the DLookup domain function to attempt to fetch the default company ID for the current contact. The query includes a filter to return only the rows from tblCompanyContacts where the DefaultForContact field is True. If the function returns a valid value, the code sets the required CompanyID field automatically. If it can't find a CompanyID, the code uses the MsgBox statement to tell the user about the error.

> **Note**
>
> The IsNothing function that you see used in code throughout all the sample applications is not a built-in Visual Basic function. This function tests the value you pass to it for "nothing"—Null, zero, or a zero length string. You can find this function in the modUtility standard module in all the sample databases.

## INSIDE OUT Understanding the Useful Domain Functions

Quite frequently in code, in a query, or in the control source of a control on a form or report, you might need to look up a single value from one of the tables or queries in your database. Although you can certainly go to the trouble of defining and opening a recordset in code, Access provides a set of functions, called domain functions, that can provide the value you need with a single function call. The available functions are as follows:

| Function Name | Description |
|---|---|
| DFirst, DLast | Return a random value from the specified domain (the table or query that's the record source) |
| DLookup | Looks up a value in the specified domain |
| DMax | Returns the highest (Max) value in the specified domain |
| DMin | Returns the lowest (Min) value in the specified domain |
| DStDev, DStDevP | Return the standard deviation of a population sample or a population of the specified domain |
| DSum | Returns the sum of an expression from a domain |
| DVar, DVarP | Return the variance of a population sample or a population of the specified domain |

The syntax to call a domain function is as follows:

```
<function name>(<field expression>, <domain name> [, <criteria> ])
```

where

<*function name*> is the name of one of the functions in the preceding list

<*field expression*> is a string literal or name of a string variable containing the name of a field or an expression using fields from the specified domain

<*domain name*> is a string literal or name of a string variable containing the name of a table or query in your database

<*criteria*> is a string literal or name of a string variable containing a Boolean comparison expression to filter the records in the domain

Note that when a domain function finds no records, the returned value is a Null, so you should always assign the result to a Variant data type variable. When you construct a criteria expression, you must enclose string literals in quotes and date/time literals in the # character. (If you use double quotes to delimit the criteria string literal, then use single quotes around literals inside the string, and vice versa.) For example, to find the lowest work postal code value for all contacts where the contact type is customer and the birth date is before January 1, 1970, enter:

```
DMin("WorkPostalCode", "tblContacts", "[ContactType] = 'customer'
And [BirthDate] < #01/01/1970#")
```

## Handling the NotInList Event

In almost every data entry form you'll ever build, you'll need to provide a way for the user to set the foreign key of the edited record on the *many* side of a relationship to point back to the correct *one* side record—for example, to set the ProductID field in the tblContactProducts table when selling a product on the Products tab of the frmContacts form. But what if the user needs to create a new product? Should the user have to open the form to edit products first to create the new product before selling it? The answer is a resounding no, but you must write code in the NotInList event of the combo box to handle new values and provide a way to create new rows in the tblProducts table.

Figure 20-3 shows you what happens when the user tries to type a product name that's not already in the tblProducts table. In this case, the customer wants to purchase a two-year support contract instead of the already available one-year product. You can see that something has intercepted the new product name to confirm that the user wants to add the new product.

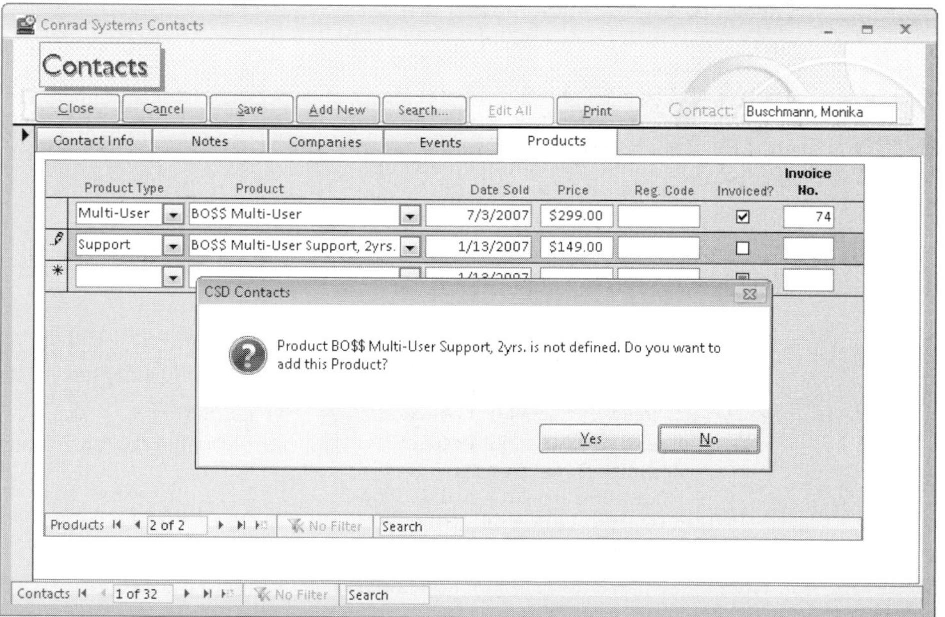


**Figure 20-3** When you enter a product that isn't defined in the database, the application asks if you want to add the new product.

First, the combo box has been defined with its Limit To List property set to Yes. Second, there's an event procedure defined to handle the NotInList event of the combo box, and it is this code that's asking whether the user wants to add a product. If the user clicks Yes to confirm adding this product, the event procedure opens the frmProductAdd form in Dialog mode to let the user enter the new data, as shown in Figure 20-4. Opening a form in Dialog mode forces the user to respond before the application resumes execution. The code that opens this form passes the product name entered and the product type that the user selected before entering a new product name. The user can fill in the price and other details. The user can also click Cancel to avoid saving the record and close the form. If the user clicks Save, the form saves the new product record and closes to allow the code in the NotInList event procedure to continue.

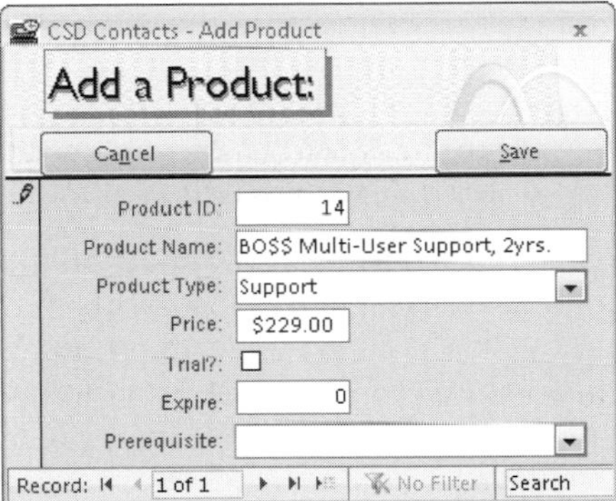


**Figure 20-4** The frmProductAdd form lets you define the details for the new product.

To see how this works, open the fsubContactProducts form in Design view, click the cmbProductID combo box, find the On Not In List event property in the Properties window, and click the Build button to open the code. The code for the procedure is shown here:

```
Private Sub cmbProductID_NotInList(NewData As String, Response As Integer)
Dim strType As String, strWhere As String
  ' User has typed in a product name that doesn't exist
  strType = NewData
  ' Set up the test predicate
  strWhere = "[ProductName] = """ & strType & """"
  ' Ask if they want to add this product
  If vbYes = MsgBox("Product " & NewData & " is not defined. " & _
    "Do you want to add this Product?", vbYesNo + vbQuestion + _
    vbDefaultButton2, gstrAppTitle) Then
    ' Yup.  Open the product add form and pass it the new name
    ' - and the pre-selected Category
    DoCmd.OpenForm "frmProductAdd", DataMode:=acFormAdd, _
      WindowMode:=acDialog, _
      OpenArgs:=strType & ";" & Me.cmbCategoryDescription
    ' Verify that the product really got added
    If IsNull(DLookup("ProductID", "tblProducts", strWhere)) Then
      ' Nope.
      MsgBox "You failed to add a Product that matched what you entered." & _
        "  Please try again.", vbInformation, gstrAppTitle
      ' Tell Access to continue - we trapped the error
      Response = acDataErrContinue
    Else
      ' Product added OK - tell Access so that combo gets requeried
      Response = acDataErrAdded
    End If
```

```
  Else
    ' Don't want to add - let Access display normal error
    Response = acDataErrDisplay
  End If
End Sub
```

As you can see, Access passes two parameters to the NotInList event. The first parameter (NewData) contains the string you typed in the combo box. You can set the value of the second parameter (Response) before you exit the sub procedure to tell Access what you want to do. You wouldn't have access to these parameters in a macro, so you can see that this event requires a Visual Basic procedure to handle it properly.

The procedure first creates the criteria string that it uses later to verify that the user saved the product. Next the procedure uses the MsgBox function to ask whether the user wants to add this product to the database (the result shown in Figure 20-3). If you've ever looked at the MsgBox function Help topic, you know that the second parameter is a number that's the sum of all the options you want. Fortunately, Visual Basic provides named constants for these options, so you don't have to remember the number codes. In this case, the procedure asks for a question mark icon (vbQuestion) and for the Yes and No buttons (vbYesNo) to be displayed. It also specifies that the default button is the second button (vbDefaultButton2)—the No button—just in case the user quickly presses Enter upon seeing the message.

If the user clicks Yes in the message box, the procedure uses DoCmd.OpenForm to open the frmProductAdd form in Dialog mode and passes it the product name entered and the product type selected by setting the form's OpenArgs property. Note the use of the named parameter syntax in the call to DoCmd.OpenForm to make it easy to set the parameters you want. You *must* open the form in Dialog mode. If you don't, your code continues to run while the form opens. Whenever a dialog box form is open, Visual Basic code execution stops until the dialog box closes, which is critical in this case because you need the record to be saved or canceled before you can continue with other tests.

After the frmProductAdd form closes, the next statement calls the DLookup function to verify that the product really was added to the database. If the code can't find a new matching product name (the user either changed the product name in the add form or clicked Cancel), it uses the MsgBox statement to inform the user of the problem and sets a return value in the Response parameter to tell Access that the value hasn't been added but that Access can continue without issuing its own error message (acDataErrContinue).

If the matching product name now exists (indicating the user clicked Save on the frmProductAdd form), the code tells Access that the new product now exists by setting Response to acDataErrAdded. Access requeries the combo box and attempts a new match. Finally, if the user clicks No in the message box shown in Figure 20-3, the procedure sets Response to acDataErrDisplay to tell Access to display its normal error message.

The other critical piece of code is in the Load event for the frmProductAdd form. The code is as follows:

```
Private Sub Form_Load()
Dim intI As Integer
  If Not IsNothing(Me.OpenArgs) Then
    ' If called from "not in list", Openargs should have
    '   Product Name; Category Description
    ' Look for the semi-colon separating the two
    intI = InStr(Me.OpenArgs, ";")
    ' If not found, then all we have is a product name
    If intI = 0 Then
      Me.ProductName = Me.OpenArgs
    Else
      Me.ProductName = Left(Me.OpenArgs, intI - 1)
      Me.CategoryDescription = Mid(Me.OpenArgs, intI + 1)
      ' lock the category
      Me.CategoryDescription.Locked = True
      Me.CategoryDescription.Enabled = False
      ' .. and clear the tool tip
      Me.CategoryDescription.ControlTipText = ""
    End If
  End If
End Sub
```

If you remember, the cmbProductID NotInList event procedure passes the original string the user entered and selected the product type (the CategoryDescription field) as the OpenArgs parameter to the OpenForm method. This sets the OpenArgs property of the form being opened. The OpenArgs property should contain the new product name, a semicolon, and the selected product type, so the Form_Load procedure parses the product name and product type by using the InStr function to look for the semicolon. (The InStr function returns the offset into the string in the first parameter where it finds the string specified in the second parameter, and it returns 0 if it doesn't find the search string.) The code then uses the two values it finds to set the ProductName and Category-Description fields. Also, when the code finds a category description, it locks that combo box so that the user can't change it to something other than what was selected on the new product row in the original form.

## Fixing an E-Mail Hyperlink

As you learned in Chapter 7, "Creating and Working with Simple Queries," one of the easiest ways to enter a hyperlink is to use the Insert Hyperlink feature. However, you can also type the hyperlink address directly into the field in a datasheet or form. Remember that a hyperlink field can contain up to four parts: display text, hyperlink address, bookmark, and ScreenTip text. If a user simply enters an e-mail address into a hyperlink field, Access 2007 recognizes the format, adds the *mailto:* protocol, and uses what the user typed as the display text. For example, if the user enters

```
jconrad@mvps.org
```

Access stores in the hyperlink field

```
jconrad@mvps.org#mailto:jconrad@mvps.org#
```

Rather than repeat the e-mail address as the display text, the end result might look better if the display text is the person's name rather than a repeat of the e-mail address. One of the forms that has an e-mail address is the frmContacts form in the Conrad Systems Contacts application. You can find the code that examines and attempts to fix the address in the AfterUpdate event procedure for the EmailName text box. (If the user enters some valid protocol other than *http://* or *mailto:*, this code won't fix it.) The code is as follows:

```
Private Sub EmailName_AfterUpdate()
' If you just type in an email name: Somebody@hotmail.com
' Access changes it to: Somebody@hotmail.com#mailto:somebody@hotmail.com#
' This code replaces the display field with the user name
Dim intI As Integer
    ' Don't do anything if email is empty
    If IsNothing(Me.EmailName) Then Exit Sub
    ' Fix up http:// if it's there
    ' This was an old bug in 2003 and earlier, but fixed in 2007
    Me.EmailName = Replace(Me.EmailName, "http://", "mailto:")
    ' Now look for the first "#" that delimits the hyperlink display name
    intI = InStr(Me.EmailName, "#")
    ' And put the person name there instead if found
    If intI > 0 Then
      Me.EmailName = (Me.FirstName + " ") & Me.LastName & _
        Mid(Me.EmailName, intI)
    End If
End Sub
```

If the user clears the EmailName text box, the code doesn't do anything. If there's something in the text box, the code uses the Replace function to search for an incorrect *http://* and replace it with the correct *mailto:* protocol identifier. As you know, a hyperlink field can optionally contain text that is displayed instead of the hyperlink, a # character delimiter, and the actual hyperlink address. The code uses the InStr function to check for the presence of the delimiter. (The InStr function returns the offset into the string in the first parameter where it finds the string specified in the second parameter.) If the code finds the delimiter, it replaces the contents of the field with the person's first and last name as display text followed by the text starting with the # delimiter. (The Mid function called with no length specification—the optional third parameter—returns all characters starting at the specified offset.)

> **Note**
>
> In Access 2003 and earlier, when you typed an e-mail address without the *mailto:* protocol prefix into a hyperlink field, Access would store the hyperlink with the *http://* protocol prefix in error. This bug has been fixed in Access 2007, but the preceding code will fix that problem if you use it in the earlier versions.

## Providing a Graphical Calendar

You can always provide an input mask to help a user enter a date and time value correctly, but an input mask can be awkward—always requiring, for example, that the user type a two-digit month. An input mask also can conflict with any default value that you might want to assign. It's much more helpful if the user can choose the date using a graphical calendar.

Access 2007 provides a new Show Date Picker property for text boxes. You can set this property to For Dates to instruct Access to display a calendar icon next to the control when it contains a date/time value and has the focus. The user can click the button to pop open a graphical calendar to select a date value. But Show Date Picker isn't available for controls other than the text box control, and the date picker lets the user enter only a date, not a date and time.

Both the Conrad Systems Contacts and the Housing Reservations sample applications provide sample calendar forms and code you can use to set a date/time value in any control. The two applications actually have two different versions of a calendar form—one that employs the Calendar ActiveX control (frmCalendarOCX), and a second (frmCalendar) that uses Visual Basic code to "draw" the calendar on a form using an option group and toggle button controls. Both forms provide an option to enter a time as well as select a date.



**TROUBLESHOOTING**

### Why isn't Access setting my defined default value for a date/time field?

Did you also define an Input Mask property? If so, then that's your problem. A date/time field is actually a floating-point number, but Access always converts and displays the character value in table and query datasheets and forms and reports. When you define an Input Mask property, any Default Value setting must match the restrictions imposed by the input mask. If the value violates the restrictions, Access won't use the default value. When you assign a default value to a date/time field, you typically use the Date or Now built-in functions. These functions return a valid date/time floating-point value—which probably won't match your input mask restrictions. To have Access use the default value, you must format it to match your input mask. For example, if your input mask is **90/00/0000\ 00:00**, then you should set the Default Value property of the field or control to **=Format(Now(), "mm/dd/yyyy hh:nn"**. This forces Access to return a string value as the default that matches your input mask.

This graphical facility is available in the sample applications wherever you see a small command button next to a control containing a date or date/time field on a form. Click the button to open the calendar and set the value. One control that uses the ActiveX version of the calendar is the ContactDateTime control on the Events tab of the frmContacts form. You can see the calendar open in Figure 20-5.

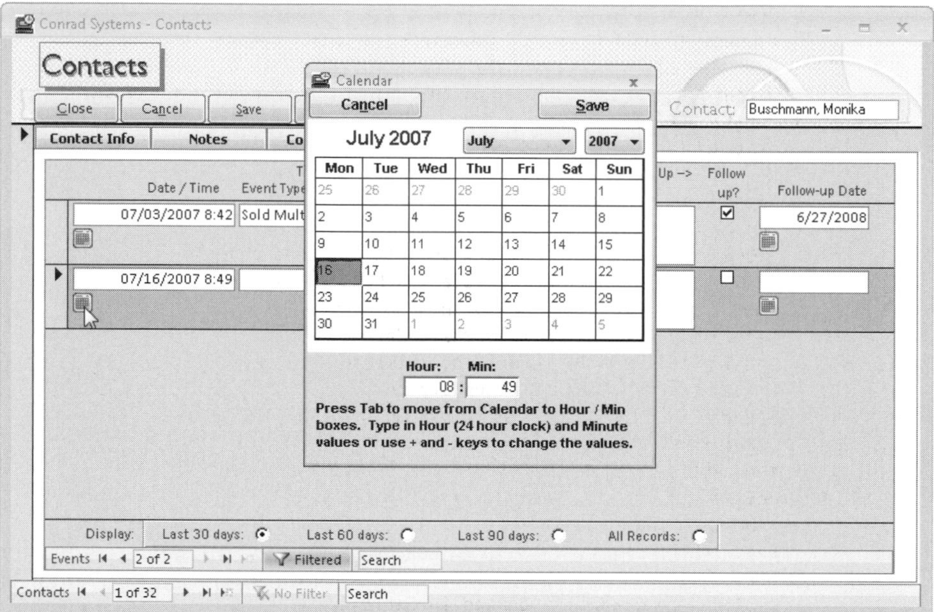


**Figure 20-5** Click the calendar command button next to the ContactDateTime control on the Events tab of the frmContacts form to open a graphical form to select the date and enter the time.

The code in the Click event of this command button calls a public function to open the form and pass it the related control that should receive the resulting date value. You can find this code, shown here, in the module for the fsubContactEvents form.

```
Private Sub cmdContactTimeCal_Click()
Dim varReturn As Variant
  ' Clicked the calendar icon asking for graphical help
  ' Put the focus on the control to be updated
  Me.ContactDateTime.SetFocus
  ' Call the get a date function
  varReturn = GetDate(Me.ContactDateTime, False)
End Sub
```

When the user clicks the command button, Access moves the focus to it. The code moves the focus back to the date field to be edited and calls the public function where the real action happens. You can find the code for the GetDateOCX function in the modCalendar module; the code is also listed here:

```
Option Compare Database
Option Explicit
' Place holder for the form class
Dim frmCalOCX As Form_frmCalendarOCX
' End Declarations Section
Function GetDateOCX(ctlToUpdate As Control, _
  Optional intDateOnly As Integer = 0)
```

```
'-----------------------------------------------------------
' Inputs: A Control object containing a date/time value
'         Optional "date only" (no time value) flag
' Outputs: Sets the Control to the value returned by frmCalendar
' Created By: JLV 11/15/02
' Last Revised: JLV 11/15/02
'-----------------------------------------------------------
' Set an error trap
On Error GoTo ProcErr
  ' Open the OCX calendar form by setting a new object
  ' NOTE: Uses a module variable in the Declarations section
  '       so that the form doesn't go away when this code exits
  Set frmCalOCX = New Form_frmCalendarOCX
  ' Call the calendar form's public method to
  '  pass it the control to update and the "date only" flag
  Set frmCalOCX.ctlToUpdate(intDateOnly) = ctlToUpdate
  ' Put the focus on the OCX calendar form
  frmCalOCX.SetFocus
ProcExit:
  ' Done
  Exit Function
ProcErr:
  MsgBox "An error has occured in GetDateOCX.  " _
    & "Error number " & Err.Number & ": " & Err.Description _
    & vbCrLf & vbCrLf & _
    "If this problem persists, note the error message and " _
    & "call your programmer.", , "Ooops . . .       (unexpected error)"
  Resume ProcExit
End Function
```

The function begins by setting an error trap that executes the code at the ProcErr label if anything goes wrong. You might remember from the previous chapter that you can open a form that has code behind it by setting an object to a new instance of the form's class module. This is exactly what this function does to get the form open. In addition, it calls the Property Set procedure for the form's ctlToUpdate property to pass it the control object that should be updated after the user picks a date value. The function also passes along an optional variable to indicate whether the control needs a date and time or a date only (intDateOnly). After the calendar form is open and has the control it needs to update, this function is finished. Notice that the object variable used to open the form is declared in this module's Declarations section. It cannot be declared inside the function because the variable would go out of scope (and the form would close) when the GetDateOCX function exits.

The final pieces of code that make all of this work are in the module behind the frmCalendarOCX form. The portion of the code that initializes the form is listed here:

```
Option Compare Database
Option Explicit
' This form demonstrates both using a custom control (MSCal.OCX)
' and manipulating a Class via Property Set
' See also the GetDateOCX function that activates this form/module.
' Place to save the "date only" indicator
```

Chapter 20

```
Dim intDateOnly As Integer
' Variable for the Property Set
Dim ctlThisControl As Control
' Optional variable for the Property Set
Dim intSet As Integer
' Place to save the date value
Dim varDate As Variant
' End Declarations Section

Private Sub Form_Load()
  ' Hide myself until properties are set
  Me.Visible = False
End Sub

Public Property Set ctlToUpdate(Optional intD As Integer = 0, ctl As Control)
' This procedure is called as a property of the Class Module
' GetDateOCX opens this form by creating a new instance of the class
'  and then sets the required properties via a SET statement.
' First, validate the kind of control passed
  Select Case ctl.ControlType
    ' Text box, combo box, and list box are OK
    Case acTextBox, acListBox, acComboBox
    Case Else
      MsgBox "Invalid control passed to the Calendar."
      DoCmd.Close acForm, Me.Name
  End Select
  ' Save the pointer to the control to update
  Set ctlThisControl = ctl
  ' Save the date only value
  intDateOnly = intD
  ' If "date only"
  If (intDateOnly = -1) Then
    ' Resize my window
    DoCmd.MoveSize , , , 3935
    ' Hide some stuff just to be sure
    Me.txtHour.Visible = False
    Me.txtMinute.Visible = False
    Me.lblColon.Visible = False
    Me.lblTimeInstruct.Visible = False
    Me.SetFocus
  End If
  ' Set the flag to indicate we got the pointer
  intSet = True
  ' Save the "current" value of the control
  varDate = ctlThisControl.Value
  ' Make sure we got a valid date value
  If Not IsDate(varDate) Then
    ' If not, set the default to today
    varDate = Now
    Me.Calendar1.Value = Date
    Me.txtHour = Format(Hour(varDate), "00")
    Me.txtMinute = Format(Minute(varDate), "00")
```

```
  Else
    ' Otherwise, set the date/time to the one in the control
    ' Make sure we have a Date data type, not just text
    varDate = CDate(varDate)
    Me.Calendar1.Value = varDate
    Me.txtHour = Format(Hour(varDate), "00")
    Me.txtMinute = Format(Minute(varDate), "00")
  End If
End Property
```

We know it looks complicated, but it really isn't. The first event that happens is the Load event for the form, and code in that event procedure hides the form until the GetDateOCX function uses the Property Set statement to pass the control to update to the form. The ctlToUpdate Property Set procedure saves the Control object (the control next to the button the user clicked on the form) in a variable in the Declarations section. If the optional intDateOnly variable is True (the control needs only a date value, not a date and time value), the form shrinks to hide those text boxes. Because the event date/time field needs a time value, this parameter is False, so you should be able to see the hour and minute text boxes. Next, the code checks to see if the control already has a value, and initializes the calendar value and two text boxes to display an optional hour and minute using either the value already in the control or the system date and time.

After the initialization code finishes, the form waits until the user enters a value and clicks Save or decides to not change the value by clicking Cancel. The code for the two procedures that respond to the command buttons is as follows:

```
Public Sub cmdCancel_Click()
  ' Close without saving
  DoCmd.Close acForm, Me.Name
End Sub

Private Sub cmdSave_Click()
' Saves the changed value back in the calling control
' Do some error trapping here in case the calling control can't
' accept a date/time value.
  On Error GoTo Save_Error
  ' Make sure we got a valid control to point to
  If intSet Then
    ' OK - save the value
    If (intDateOnly = -1) Then
      ' Passing back date only
      ctlThisControl.Value = Me.Calendar1.Value
    Else
      ' Do date and time
      ctlThisControl.Value = Me.Calendar1.Value + _
        TimeValue(Me.txtHour & ":" & Me.txtMinute)
    End If
  End If
Save_Exit:
  DoCmd.Close acForm, Me.Name
  Exit Sub
```

```
Save_Error:
  MsgBox "An error occurred attempting to save the date value.", _
    vbCritical, gstrAppTitle
  ErrorLog "frmCalendarOCX_Save", Err, Error
  Resume Save_Exit
End Sub
```

Clicking the Cancel button (cmdCancel_Click) simply closes the form without changing any value in the control passed to the form. The code that saves the value the user selects on the graphical calendar is in the Click event for the cmdSave command button. This code verifies that the Property Set procedure executed correctly and then saves the selected value back into the control object—which happens to point to the control on the form that should be updated.



INSIDE OUT

### ActiveX or Not ActiveX, That Is the Question!

If you look behind all the little calendar buttons that activate a graphical way to set a date or date/time value, you'll find that only the button next to the Birth Date field on the frmContacts form and the button next to the Date/Time field on the fsubContactEvents form use the ActiveX version of the calendar discussed in this chapter. All the others use the custom form we designed with some complex code to actually build and manipulate a calendar created with an option group control. So why did we do that?

As you learned in Chapter 13, you can probably find dozens of ActiveX controls registered on your computer, but only some of them work in Access. To complicate matters, Microsoft has issued different versions of some of these controls with each new version of Access. You can use these controls with confidence if you're installing your application on a computer that has the exact same version and service pack level of Access that you used to create the application. However, if you install your application in Runtime mode on a computer that has a different version of Access installed, your ActiveX control might not work at all. (See Chapter 25, "Distributing Your Application," for details about creating a distributable installation of your application.) The user sees a "Can't create object" error message when opening a form that uses the ActiveX control.

We discovered that even the simple Calendar ActiveX control was giving us problems when we tried to distribute applications that used it in prior versions of Access. So, we came up with a way to provide a very similar interface using standard Access controls and Visual Basic. This is why several of the calendar buttons use our custom form (frmCalendar) instead of the form that depends on the ActiveX control. We recommend that you try the ActiveX control first. If you find that your application has problems on some computers on which you attempt to install your application, you might need to get creative and build your own solution using native Access tools.

## Working with Linked Photos

Although you can certainly store and display photos in an Access application using the OLE Object data type, if your application might need to interact with a Web application, you cannot use this feature. Web applications cannot handle the internal format of a stored OLE object. Also, if your application needs to handle hundreds or thousands of photos, you could easily exceed the 2 gigabyte file size limit for an .accdb file. If you're working with your data on the Web using Microsoft Windows SharePoint Services (version 3), you can use the new Attachment data type for your photos that can store attachments more efficiently, but you still might run into file size limitations if you need to store many photos. The alternative method is to store the pictures as files and save the picture path as a text field in your tables.

The good news is the image control in Access 2007 now lets you specify a Control Source property. When this property points to a field containing a folder and file location as a text string, the image control will load the photo for you from that location. However, you should still provide features in your forms to help users to easily edit the file location information.

The Housing Reservations database (Housing.accdb) is designed to work on the Web. Open the Housing.accdb sample database and then open the frmEmployeesPlain form, as shown in Figure 20-6. The employee picture you see on the frmEmployees and frmEmployeesPlain forms is fetched by the image control from the path stored in the Photo field of the table.

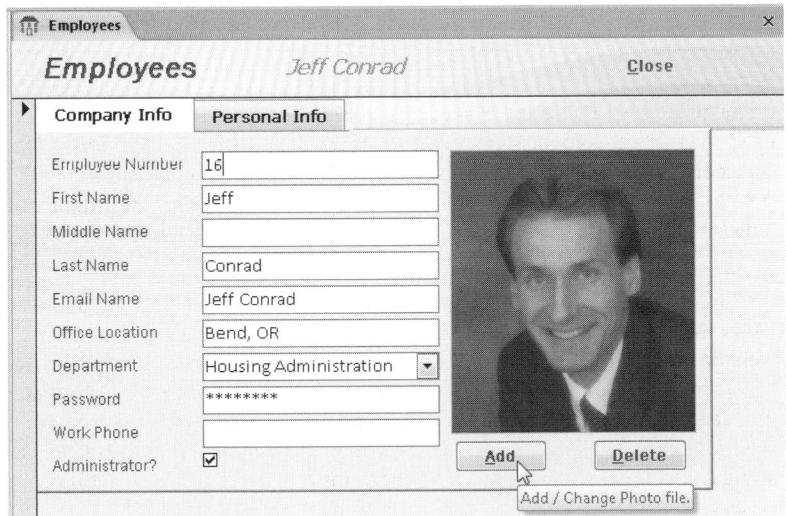


**Figure 20-6** The image control loads the photo on the Employees form from a picture path.

Notice that the user cannot see the contents of the Photo field that contains the picture path information. However, we've provided two command buttons to make it easy for the user to edit or delete the photo path information.

## Deleting and Updating an Image Path

Clearing the file name saved in the record is the easy part, so let's take a look at that first. Behind the Delete button that you can see on the frmEmployeesPlain form, you can find the following code:

```
Private Sub cmdDelete_Click()
' User asked to remove the picture
  ' Clear photo
  Me.txtPhoto = Null
  ' Set the message
  Me.lblMsg.Caption = "Click Add to create a photo for this employee."
  ' Make it visible
  ' Put focus in a safe place
  Me.FirstName.SetFocus
End Sub
```

When the user clicks the command button asking to delete the photo, the code sets the photo path to Null and displays the informative label. Setting the Photo field to Null causes the image control to remove the image. Because the background of the image control is transparent, the label control hidden behind it shows through, displaying an informative message.

The tricky part is to provide the user with a way to enter the picture path to add or update a picture in a record. Although you could certainly use the InputBox function to ask the user for the path, it's much more professional to call the Windows Open File dialog box so that the user can navigate to the desired picture using familiar tools. The bad news is calling any procedure in Windows is complex and usually involves setting up parameter structures and a special declaration of the external function. The good news is the 2007 Microsoft Office system includes a special FileDialog object that greatly simplifies this process. You need to add a reference to the Microsoft Office library to make it easy to use this object—from the VBE window, choose References from the Tools menu and be sure the Microsoft Office 12.0 Object Library is selected. After you do this, you can include code using the FileDialog object to load a picture path. You can find the following code behind the Click event of the Add button (cmdAdd) in the frmEmployeesPlain form:

```
Private Sub cmdAdd_Click()
' User asked to add a new photo
Dim strPath As String
  ' Grab a copy of the Office file dialog
  With Application.FileDialog(msoFileDialogFilePicker)
    ' Select only one file
    .AllowMultiSelect = False
    ' Set the dialog title
    .Title = "Locate the Employee picture file"
    ' Set the button caption
    .ButtonName = "Choose"
    ' Make sure the filter list is clear
    .Filters.Clear
```

```
        ' Add two filters
        .Filters.Add "JPEGs", "*.jpg"
        .Filters.Add "Bitmaps", "*.bmp"
        ' Set the filter index to 2
        .FilterIndex = 2
        ' Set the initial path name
        .InitialFileName = CurrentProject.Path & "\Pictures"
        ' Show files as thumbnails
        .InitialView = msoFileDialogViewThumbnail
        ' Show the dialog and test the return
        If .Show = 0 Then
          ' Didn't pick a file - bail
          Exit Sub
        End If
        ' Should be only one filename - grab it
        strPath = Trim(.SelectedItems(1))
        ' Set an error trap
        On Error Resume Next
        ' Set the image
        Me.txtPhoto = strPath
        ' Set the message in case Image control couldn't find it
        Me.lblMsg.Caption = "Failed to load the picture you selected." & _
          "  Click Add to try again."
      End With
      ' Put focus in a safe place
      Me.FirstName.SetFocus
    End Sub
```

The code establishes a pointer to the FileDialog object using a With statement, sets the various properties of the object including the allowed file extensions and the initial path, and then uses the Show method to display the Windows Open File dialog box. Setting the Photo field causes the image control to load the new picture, but the code also sets the message hidden behind the image control just in case the image control had a problem loading the file.

# Validating Complex Data

Although you can certainly take advantage of the Input Mask property and the field and table Validation Rule properties, your application often has additional business rules that you can enforce only by adding code behind the forms you provide to edit the data. The following examples show you how several of the business rules in the Conrad Systems Contacts and Housing Reservations applications are enforced with Visual Basic code.

## Checking for Possible Duplicate Names

When you design a table, you should attempt to identify some combination of fields that will be unique across all records to use as your primary key. However, when you create a table to store information about people, you usually create an artificial number as the primary key of the table because you would need to combine many fields to ensure a unique value. Even when you attempt to construct a primary key from first name, last name, address, postal code, and phone number, you still can't guarantee a unique value across all rows.

Using an artificial primary key doesn't mean you should abandon all efforts to identify potentially duplicate rows. Code in the frmContacts form in the Conrad Systems Contacts application checks the last name the user enters for a new record and issues a warning message if it finds any close names. For example, if the user creates a new record and enters a last name like "Viscas" (assuming John's record is still in the table), code behind the form detects the similar name and issues the warning shown in Figure 20-7.



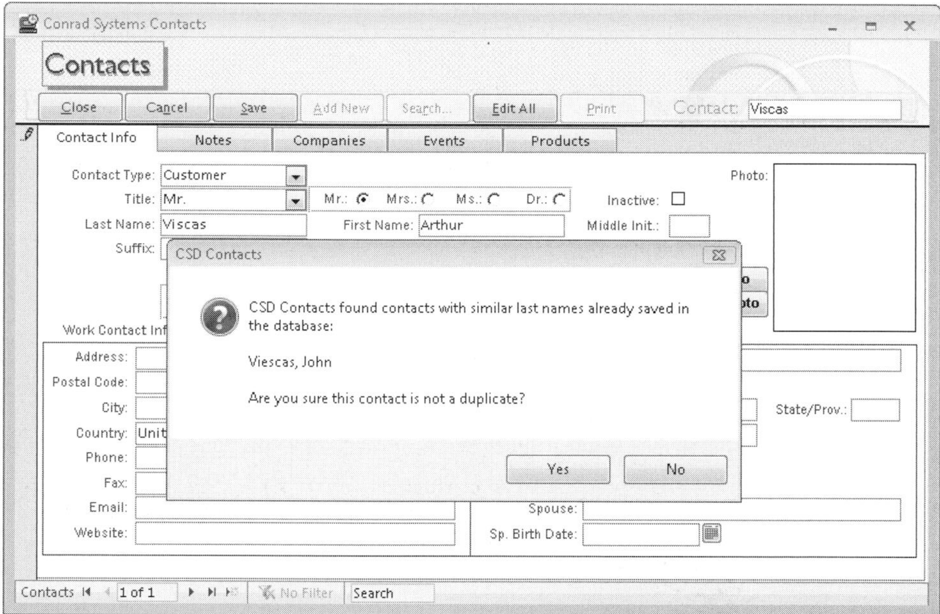


**Figure 20-7** The application warns you about a potentially duplicate name in the contacts table.

The code searches for potential duplicates by comparing the Soundex codes of the last names. The formula for generating a Soundex code for a name was created by the U.S. National Archives and Records Administration (NARA). Soundex examines the letters by sound and produces a four-character code. When the codes for two names match, it's likely that the names are very similar and sound alike. So, by using Soundex, the error-checking code not only finds existing contacts with exactly the same last name but also other contacts whose name might be the same but one or both might be slightly misspelled.

Access 2007 doesn't provide a built-in Soundex function (SQL Server does), but it's easy to create a simple Visual Basic procedure to generate the code for a name. You can find a Soundex function in the modUtility module in both the Conrad Systems Contacts and Housing Reservations sample databases. You can find the code that checks for a potentially duplicate name in the BeforeUpdate event procedure of the frmContacts form. The code is as follows:

```
Private Sub Form_BeforeUpdate(Cancel As Integer)
Dim rst As DAO.Recordset, strNames As String
  ' If on a new row,
  If (Me.NewRecord = True) Then
    ' ... check for similar name
    If Not IsNothing(Me.LastName) Then
      ' Open a recordset to look for similar names
      Set rst = CurrentDb.OpenRecordset("SELECT LastName, FirstName FROM " & _
        "tblContacts WHERE Soundex([LastName]) = '" & _
        Soundex(Me.LastName) & "'")
      ' If got some similar names, collect them for the message
      Do Until rst.EOF
        strNames = strNames & rst!LastName & ", " & rst!FirstName & vbCrLf
        rst.MoveNext
      Loop
      ' Done with the recordset
      rst.Close
      Set rst = Nothing
      ' See if we got some similar names
      If Len(strNames) > 0 Then
        ' Yup, issue warning
        If vbNo = MsgBox("CSD Contacts found contacts with similar " & _
         "last names already saved in the database: " & vbCrLf & vbCrLf & _
          strNames & vbCrLf & _
          "Are you sure this contact is not a duplicate?", _
          vbQuestion + vbYesNo + vbDefaultButton2, gstrAppTitle) Then
            ' Cancel the save
            Cancel = True
        End If
      End If
    End If
  End If
End Sub
```

The code checks only when the user is about to save a new row. It opens a recordset to fetch any other contact records where the Soundex code of the last name matches the last name about to be saved. It includes all names it finds in the warning message so that the user can verify that the new contact is not a duplicate. If the user decides not to save the record, the code sets the Cancel parameter to True to tell Access not to save the new contact.

## Testing for Related Records When Deleting a Record

You certainly can and should define relationships between your tables and ask Access to enforce referential integrity to prevent saving unrelated records or deleting a record that still has related records in other tables. In most cases, you do not want to activate the cascade delete feature to automatically delete related records. However, Access displays a message "the record cannot be deleted or changed because 'tblXYZ' contains related records" whenever the user tries to delete a record that has dependent records in other tables.

You can do your own testing in code behind your forms in the Delete event and give the user a message that more clearly identifies the problem. For example, here's the code in the Delete event procedure of the frmContacts form in the Conrad Systems Contacts application:

```
Private Sub Form_Delete(Cancel As Integer)
Dim db As DAO.Database, qd As DAO.QueryDef, rst As DAO.Recordset
Dim varRelate As Variant
  ' Check for related child rows
  ' Get a pointer to this database
  Set db = CurrentDb
  ' Open the test query
  Set qd = db.QueryDefs("qryCheckRelateContact")
  ' Set the contact parameter
  qd!ContactNo = Me.ContactID
  ' Open a recordset on the related rows
  Set rst = qd.OpenRecordset()
  ' If we got rows, then can't delete
  If Not rst.EOF Then
    varRelate = Null
    ' Loop to build the informative error message
    rst.MoveFirst
    Do Until rst.EOF
      ' Grab all the table names
      varRelate = (varRelate + ", ") & rst!TableName
      rst.MoveNext
    Loop
    MsgBox "You cannot delete this Contact because you have " & _
      "related rows in " & _
      varRelate & _
      ".  Delete these records first, and then delete the Contact.", _
      vbOKOnly + vbCritical, gstrAppTitle
    ' close all objects
    rst.Close
    qd.Close
    Set rst = Nothing
    Set qd = Nothing
    Set db = Nothing
    ' Cancel the delete
    Cancel = True
    Exit Sub
  End If
```

```
    ' No related rows - clean up objects
    rst.Close
    qd.Close
    Set rst = Nothing
    Set qd = Nothing
    Set db = Nothing
    ' No related rows, so OK to ask if they want to delete!
    If vbNo = MsgBox("Are you sure you want to delete Contact " & _
      Me.txtFullName & "?", _
      vbQuestion + vbYesNo + vbDefaultButton2, gstrAppTitle) Then
      Cancel = True
    End If
End Sub
```

The code uses a special UNION parameter query, qryCheckRelateContact, that attempts to fetch related rows from tblCompanyContacts, tblCompanies (the ReferredBy field), tblContactEvents, and tblContactProducts, and returns the name(s) of the table(s) that have any related rows. When the code finds rows returned by the query, it formats a message containing names more meaningful to the user, and it includes all the tables that the user must clear to be able to delete the contact. The standard Access error message lists only the first related table that Access finds. Even when the check for related records finds no problems, the code also gives the user a chance to decide not to delete the contact after all.

## Verifying a Prerequisite

In some applications, it makes sense to save a certain type of record only if prerequisite records exist. For example, in a school or seminar registration application, the user might need to verify that the person enrolling has successfully completed prerequisite courses. In the Conrad Systems Contacts application, it doesn't make sense to sell support for a product that the contact doesn't own. It's not possible to ask Access to perform this sort of test in a validation rule, so you must write code to enforce this business rule.

Figure 20-8 shows you the message the user sees when trying to sell support for a product that the contact doesn't own. This message also appears if the user attempts to sell the special upgrade to multi-user product, and the contact doesn't already own the prerequisite single user product.

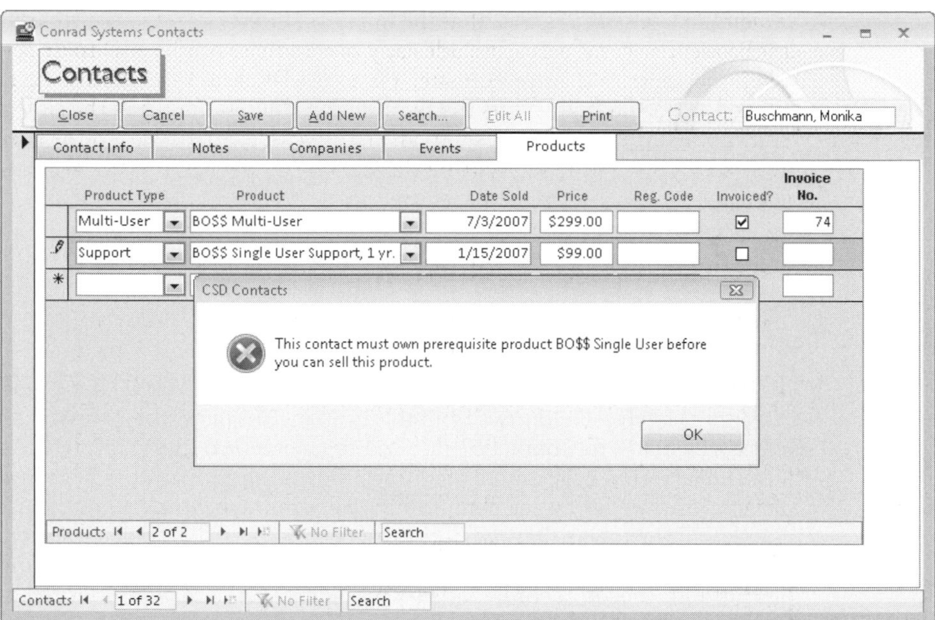


**Figure 20-8** Special business rule code won't let you sell a product with a missing prerequisite.

The code that enforces this business rule is in the BeforeUpdate event procedure of the fsubContactProducts form. The code is as follows:

```
Private Sub Form_BeforeUpdate(Cancel As Integer)
Dim lngPreReq As Long, strPreReqName As String
  ' Check for prerequisite
  If Not IsNothing(Me.cmbProductID.Column(6)) Then
    ' Try to lookup the prerequisite for the contact
    lngPreReq = CLng(Me.cmbProductID.Column(6))
    If IsNull(DLookup("ProductID", "tblContactProducts", _
      "ProductID = " & lngPreReq & " And ContactID = " & _
      Me.Parent.ContactID)) Then
      ' Get the name of the prerequisite
      strPreReqName = DLookup("ProductName", "tblProducts", _
        "ProductID = " & lngPreReq)
      ' Display error
      MsgBox "This contact must own prerequisite product " & strPreReqName & _
        " before you can sell this product.", vbCritical, gstrAppTitle
      ' Cancel the edit
      Cancel = True
    End If
  End If
End Sub
```

Remember from Figure 20-2 that the query providing the row source for the cmbProductID combo box includes any prerequisite product ID in its seventh column. When the code finds a prerequisite, it uses the DLookup function to verify that the current contact already owns the required product. If not, then the code looks up the name of the product, includes it in an error message displayed to the user, and disallows saving the product by setting the Cancel parameter to True. This enforces the business rule and makes it crystal clear to the user what corrective action is necessary.



## Maintaining a Special Unique Value

When two subjects have a many-to-many relationship in your database, you must define a linking table to create the relationship. (See Article 1, "Designing Your Database Application," on the companion CD for details about designing tables to support a many-to-many relationship.) You will often add fields in the linking table to further clarify the relationship between a row in one of the related tables and the matching row in another. Figure 20-9 shows you the table in the Conrad Systems Contacts application that defines the link between companies and contacts.

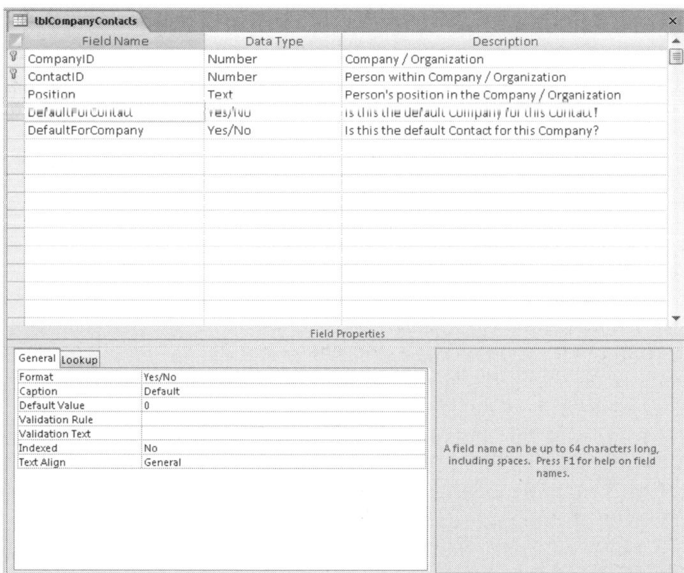


**Figure 20-9** The tblCompanyContacts table defines the many-to-many relationship between companies and contacts.

Two special yes/no fields in this table identify which company is the default for a contact and which contact is the default for a company. However, a contact can't have two or more default companies. Likewise, it doesn't make sense for a company to have more than one default contact. To verify this type of special unique value constraint you must add business rules in code behind the forms you provide the user to edit this data.

You can find the code that ensures that there is only one default company for each contact in code behind the fsubContactCompanies form in the Conrad Systems Contacts sample application (Contacts.accdb). The code is in the BeforeUpdate event procedure for the DefaultForContact control on the form. The code is as follows:

```
Private Sub DefaultForContact_BeforeUpdate(Cancel As Integer)
  ' Disallow update if there's no Company ID yet
  If IsNothing(Me.CompanyID) Then
    MsgBox "You must select a Company / Organization before" & _
      " you can set Default.", _
      vbCritical, gstrAppTitle
    Cancel = True
    Exit Sub
  End If
  ' Make sure there's only one default
  ' Check only if setting Default = True
  If (Me.DefaultForContact = True) Then
    ' Try to lookup another contact set Default
    If Not IsNothing(DLookup("ContactID", "tblCompanyContacts", _
      "ContactID = " & Me.Parent.ContactID & _
      " AND CompanyID <> " & Me.CompanyID & _
      " AND DefaultForContact = True")) Then
      ' ooops...
      MsgBox "You have designated another Company as the" & _
        " Default for this Contact." & _
        "  You must remove that designation before you" & _
        " can mark this Company as the Default.", _
        vbCritical, gstrAppTitle
      Cancel = True
    End If
  End If
End Sub
```

First, the code verifies that the user has chosen a company for this record. (The Link Child Fields and Link Master Fields properties of the subform control provide the ContactID.) Next, if the user is attempting to mark this company as the default for the contact, the code uses the DLookup function to see if any other record exists (in the tblCompanyContacts table for the current contact) that is also marked as the default. If it finds such a duplicate record, it warns the user and sets the Cancel parameter to True to prevent saving the change to the control. You'll find similar code in the fsubCompanyContacts form that makes sure only one contact is the primary for any company.

## Checking for Overlapping Data

When you build an application that tracks the scheduling of events or reservations that can span a period of time, you most likely need to make sure that a new event or reservation doesn't overlap with an existing one. This can be a bit tricky, especially when the records you're checking have start and end dates or times.

Of course, the Housing Reservations application (Housing.accdb) must make sure that an employee doesn't enter an overlapping reservation request. To see how this works, open the sample database and then open the frmSplash form to start the application. Choose any employee name you like from the combo box in the sign-on dialog box (Jack Richins is a good choice), type **password** as the password, and click the Sign On button. On the main switchboard, click the Reservation Requests button. If you see the Edit Reservation Requests dialog box (because you happened to sign on as a manager), click the Edit All button.



The Reservation Requests form won't let you enter a reservation start date in the past. Click in the blank new row in the list of reservation requests, enter a reservation request for next week for a span of several days, and save the row. (Remember, you can click the Calendar buttons that appear next to the date fields when the focus is on the field to help you choose dates.) Enter another request that overlaps the reservation you just created either at the beginning, the end, or across the middle of the reservation you just entered. Try to save the row, and you should see a warning message similar to the one in Figure 20-10.

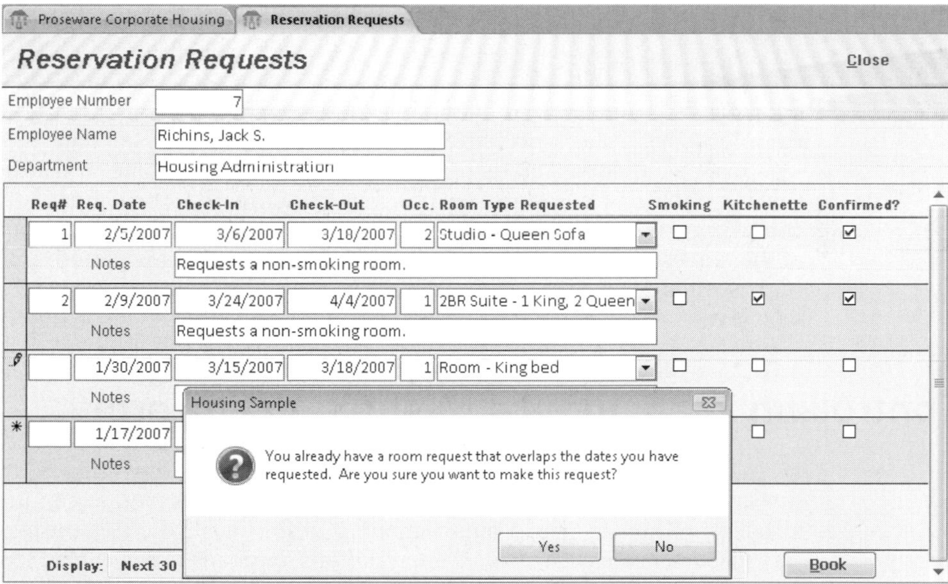


**Figure 20-10** The Housing Reservations application displays a warning when you attempt to save an overlapping reservation request.

If you click No, the code cancels your save and returns you to the record to fix it. Notice that you can click Yes to save the duplicate—the application allows this because an employee might want to intentionally reserve two or more rooms on the same or overlapping dates. The code that performs this check in the BeforeUpdate event of the fsubReservationRequests form is as follows:

```
Dim varNum As Variant
  ' Check for overlap with existing request
  ' Try to grab RequestID - will be Null on unsaved row
  varNum = Me.RequestID
  If IsNull(varNum) Then varNum = 0 ' Set dummy value
  If Not IsNull(DLookup("RequestID", "tblReservationRequests", _
    "(EmployeeNumber = " & _
    Me.Parent.EmployeeNumber & ") AND (CheckInDate < #" & Me.CheckOutDate & _
    "#) AND (CheckOutDate > #" & Me.CheckInDate & "#) AND (RequestID <> " & _
    varNum & ")")) Then
    If vbNo = MsgBox("You already have a room request " & _
      "that overlaps the dates you have " & _
      "requested.  Are you sure you want to make this request?", _
      vbQuestion + vbYesNo + vbDefaultButton2, gstrAppTitle) Then
      Cancel = True
      Exit Sub
    End If
  End If
```

The code uses the DLookup function to see if another reservation exists (but a different request ID) for the same employee with dates that overlap. The criteria asks for any record that has a check-in date less than the requested checkout date (an employee can legitimately check out and then check back in on the same date) and a checkout date that is greater than the requested check-in date. You might be tempted to build more complex criteria that checks all combinations of reservations that overlap into the start of the requested period, overlap into the end of the requested period, span the entire requested period, or are contained wholly within the requested period, but the two simple tests are all you need. (Draw it out on a sheet of paper if you don't believe us!)

## Controlling Tabbing on a Multiple-Page Form

In Chapter 13, you learned how to create a multiple-page form as one way to handle displaying more data than will fit on one page of a form on your computer screen. You also learned how to control simple tabbing on the form by setting the form's Cycle property to Current Page. One disadvantage of this approach is you can no longer use Tab or Shift+Tab to move to other pages or other records. You must use the Page Up and Page Down keys or the record selector buttons to do that. You can set Cycle to All Records to restore this capability, but some strange things happen if you don't add code to handle page alignment.

To see what happens, open the frmXmplContactsPages form in the Conrad Systems Contacts sample database (Contacts.accdb) from the Navigation Pane. Press Page Down to move to the Home Address field for the first contact. Next press Shift+Tab once (back tab). Your screen should look something like Figure 20-11.

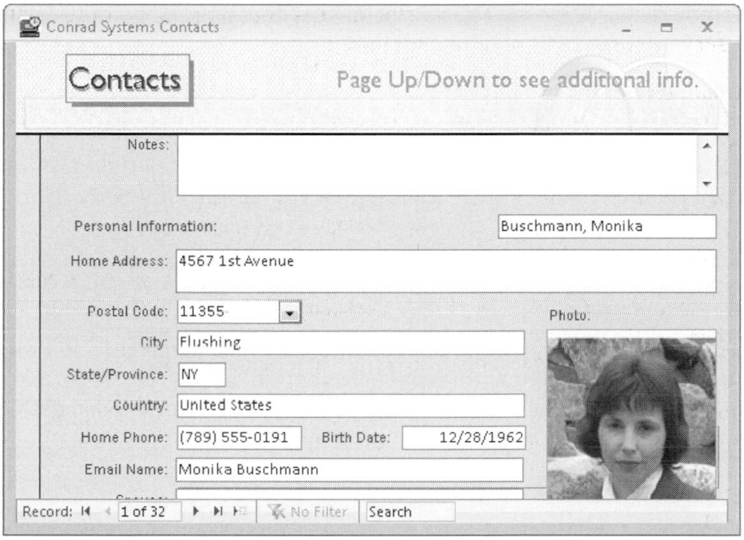

Figure 20-11 The form page doesn't align correctly when you back-tab from the Home Address field in frmXmplContactsPages.

If you leave the Cycle property set to All Records or Current Record, tabbing across page boundaries causes misalignment unless you add some code to fix it. What happens is that Access moves the form display only far enough to show the control you just tabbed to. (In this example, you're tabbing to the Notes text box control.) Open the sample frmContactsPages form that has the code to fix this problem and try the same exercise. You should discover that Shift+Tab places you in the Notes field, but the form scrolls up to show you the entire first page.

To allow tabbing across a page boundary while providing correct page alignment, you need event procedures in the Enter event for the first and last controls that can receive the focus on each page. If you examine the code behind the frmContactsPages form, you'll find these four procedures:

```
Private Sub ContactID_Enter()
    ' If tabbing forward into this field from previous record
    '  align page 1
    Me.GoToPage 1
End Sub

Private Sub HomeAddress_Enter()
    ' If tabbing forward into this field, align page 2
    Me.GoToPage 2
End Sub

Private Sub Notes_Enter()
    On Error Resume Next
    ' If tabbing backward into the last control on page 1, align it
    Me.GoToPage 1
End Sub
```

```
Private Sub Photo_Enter()
    On Error Resume Next
    ' If tabbing backward into the last control on page 2, align it
    Me.GoToPage 2
End Sub
```

This is arguably some of the simplest example code in any of the sample databases, but this attention to detail will make the users of your application very happy.



> **Note**
>
> The code also executes when you tab backward into the ContactID and HomeAddress controls or forward into the Notes or Photo controls, or you can click in any of the controls. Access realizes that the form is already on the page requested in each case, so it does nothing.

# Automating Data Selection

One of the most common tasks to automate in a database application is filtering data. Particularly when a database contains thousands of records, users will rarely need to work with more than a few records at a time. If your edit forms always display all the records, performance can suffer greatly. So it's a good idea to enable the user to easily specify a subset of records. This section examines four ways to do this.

## Working with a Multiple-Selection List Box

You work with list boxes all the time in Windows and in Access. For example, the file list in Windows Explorer is a list box, the Access 2007 Navigation Pane is a list box, and the list of properties on any tab in the property sheet is a list box. In the property, you can select only one property from the list at a time. If you click a different property, the previous object is no longer selected—this is a simple list box. In Windows Explorer, you can select one file, select multiple noncontiguous files by holding down the Ctrl key and clicking, or select a range of files by holding down the Shift key and clicking—this is a multiple-selection list box.

Suppose you're using the Conrad Systems Contacts application (Contacts.accdb) and you're interested in looking at the details for several contacts at one time but will rarely want to look at the entire list. Start the application by opening the frmSplash form, select John Viescas as the User Name, and click Sign On (no password required). Click the Contacts button on the main switchboard form, and the application opens the

Select Contacts form (frmContactList). As shown in Figure 20-12, the frmContactList form contains a multiple-selection list box.

> **Note**
>
> You won't see the Select Contacts dialog box if the Don't Show Contact List option is selected in John's user profile. If the Contacts form opens when you click the Contacts button on the main switchboard, close the form and click the Users button. Clear the Don't Show Contact List option in John's profile, save the record, and close the form. You should now see the Select Contacts dialog box when you click the Contacts button on the main switchboard.



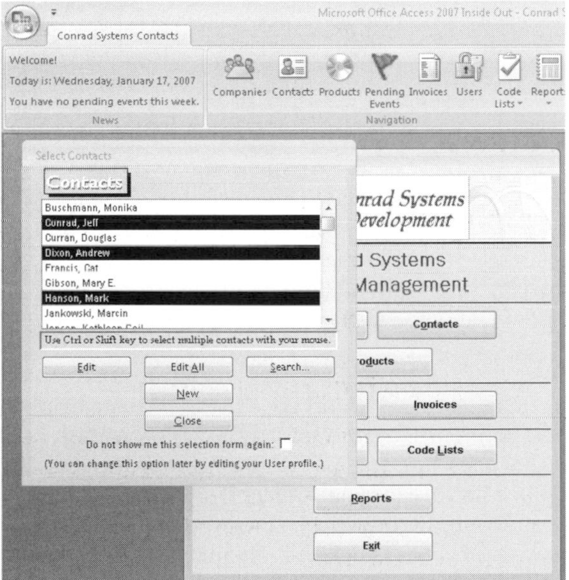


**Figure 20-12** You can select multiple contact records to edit in the frmContactList form.

In this list box, the contacts are shown in alphabetic order by last name, and the list is bound to the ContactID field in the underlying table. You can edit any single contact by simply double-clicking the person's name. You can move the highlight up or down by using the arrow keys. You can also type the first letter of a contact last name to jump to the next contact whose last name begins with that letter. You can hold down the Shift key and use the arrow keys to extend the selection to multiple names. Finally, you can hold down either the Shift key or the Ctrl key and use the mouse to select multiple names.

Figure 20-12 shows three contacts selected using the Ctrl key and the mouse. When you click the Edit button, the application opens the frmContacts form with only the records you selected. As shown in Figure 20-13, the caption to the right of the Record Number box indicates three available records and that the recordset is filtered.

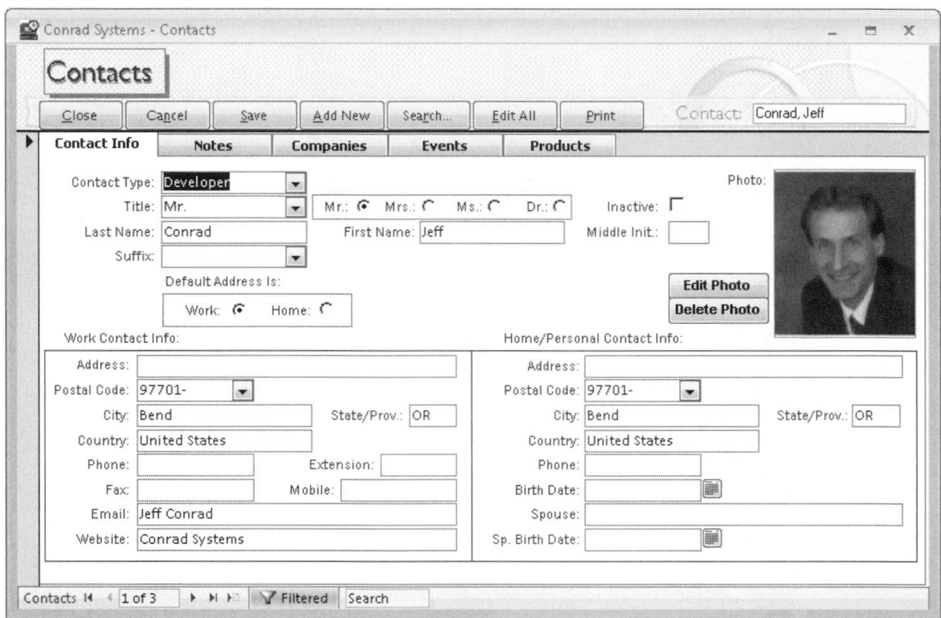


**Figure 20-13** After you select the records you want to edit in the frmContactList form, the application opens the frmContacts form displaying only those records.

To see how this works, you need to go behind the scenes of the frmContactList form. Click Exit on the main switchboard form to return to the Navigation Pane. (Click Yes in the message box that asks "Are you sure you want to exit?," and click No if the application offers to create a backup for you.) Select frmContactList, and open the form in Design view, as shown in Figure 20-14. Click the list box control, and open its property sheet to see how the list box is defined. The list box uses two columns from the qlkpContacts query, hiding the ContactID (the primary key that will provide a fast lookup) in the first column and displaying the contact name in the second column. The key to this list box is that its Multi Select property is set to Extended. Using the Extended setting gives you the full Ctrl+click or Shift+click features that you see in most list boxes in Windows. The default for this property is None, which lets you select only one value at a time. You can set it to Simple if you want to select or clear multiple values using the mouse or the Spacebar.

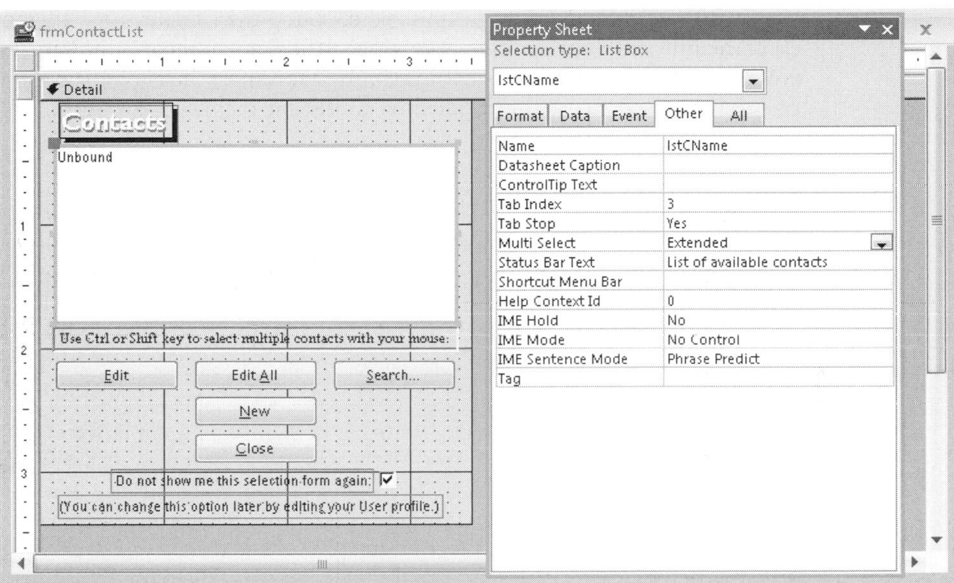


**Figure 20-14** The multiple-selection list box on the frmContactList form has its Multi Select property set to Extended.

If you scroll down to the Event properties, you'll find an event procedure defined for On Dbl Click. The code for this event procedure (which is called when you double-click an item in the list box) runs only the cmdSome_Click procedure. Right-click the cmdSome command button (the one whose caption says *Edit*), and choose Build Event from the shortcut menu to jump to the cmdSome_Click procedure that does all the work, as shown here:

```
Private Sub cmdSome_Click()
Dim strWhere As String, varItem As Variant
  ' Request to edit items selected in the list box
  ' If no items selected, then nothing to do
  If Me!lstCName.ItemsSelected.Count = 0 Then Exit Sub
  ' Loop through the items selected collection
  For Each varItem In Me!lstCName.ItemsSelected
    ' Grab the ContactID column for each selected item
    strWhere = strWhere & Me!lstCName.Column(0, varItem) & ","
  Next varItem
  ' Throw away the extra comma on the "IN" string
  strWhere = Left$(strWhere, Len(strWhere) - 1)
  ' Open the contacts form filtered on the selected contacts
  strWhere = "[ContactID] IN (" & strWhere & ") And (Inactive = False)"
  DoCmd.OpenForm FormName:="frmContacts", WhereCondition:=strWhere
  DoCmd.Close acForm, Me.Name
End Sub
```

When you set the Multi Select property of a list box to something other than None, you can examine the control's ItemsSelected collection to determine what (if anything) is selected. In the cmdSome_Click procedure, the Visual Basic code first checks the Count property of the control's ItemsSelected collection to determine whether anything is selected. If the Count is 0, there's nothing to do, so the procedure exits.

The ItemsSelected collection is composed of variant values, each of which provides an index to a highlighted item in the list box. The For Each loop asks Visual Basic to loop through all the available variant values in the collection, one at a time. Within the loop, the code uses the value of the variant to retrieve the Contact ID from the list. List boxes also have a Column property, and you can reference all the values in the list by using a statement such as

```
Me.ListBoxName.Column(ColumnNum, RowNum)
```

where *ListBoxName* is the name of your list box control, *ColumnNum* is the relative column number (the first column is 0, the second is 1, and so on), and *RowNum* is the relative row number (also starting at 0). The variant values in the ItemsSelected collection return the relative row number. This Visual Basic code uses column 0 and the values in the ItemsSelected collection to append each selected ContactID to a string variable, separated by commas. You'll recall from studying the IN predicate in Chapter 7 that a list of values separated by commas is ideal for an IN clause.

After retrieving all the ContactID numbers, the next statement removes the trailing comma from the string. The final Where clause includes an additional criterion to display only active contacts. The DoCmd.OpenForm command uses the resulting string to create a filter clause as it opens the form. Finally, the code closes the frmContactList form. (Me.Name is the name of the current form.)

## Providing a Custom Query By Form

Suppose you want to do a more complex search on the frmContacts form—using criteria such as contact type, company, or products owned rather than simply using contact name. You could teach your users how to use the Filter By Form features to build the search, or you could use Filter By Form to easily construct multiple OR criteria on simple tests. But if you want to find, for example, all contacts who own the Single User edition or whom you contacted between certain dates, there's no way to construct this request using standard filtering features. The reason for this is that when you define a filter for a subform (such as the Events subform in frmContacts) using Filter By Form, you're filtering only the subform rows. You're not finding contacts who have only a matching subform row.

The only solution, then, is to provide a custom Query By Form that provides options to search on all the important fields and then build the Where clause to solve the search problem using Visual Basic code. To start, open the Conrad Systems Contacts application. (If you have exited to the Navigation Pane, you can start the application by opening frmSplash.) Sign on, click the Contacts button on the main switchboard form, and then click the Search button in the Select Contacts dialog box. You should see the fdlgContactSearch form, as shown in Figure 20-15.

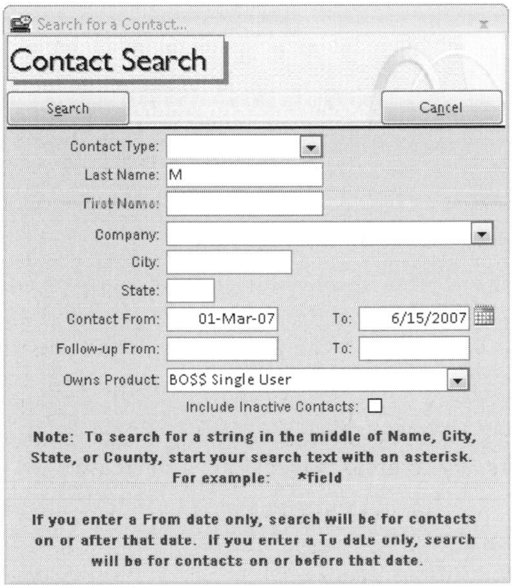

**Figure 20-15** You can design a custom Query By Form to perform a complex search.

Try selecting contacts whose last name begins with the letter *M*, whom you contacted between March 1, 2007, and June 15, 2007, and who own the BO$$ Single User product (from the Owns Product drop-down list). When you click the Search button, you should see the frmContacts form open and display two contacts.

To see how this works, you need to explore the design of the fdlgContactSearch form. Switch to the Navigation Pane (press F11), and open the form in Design view. You should see a window like that shown in Figure 20-16. Notice that the form is not bound to any record source. The controls must be unbound so they can accept any criteria values that a user might enter.

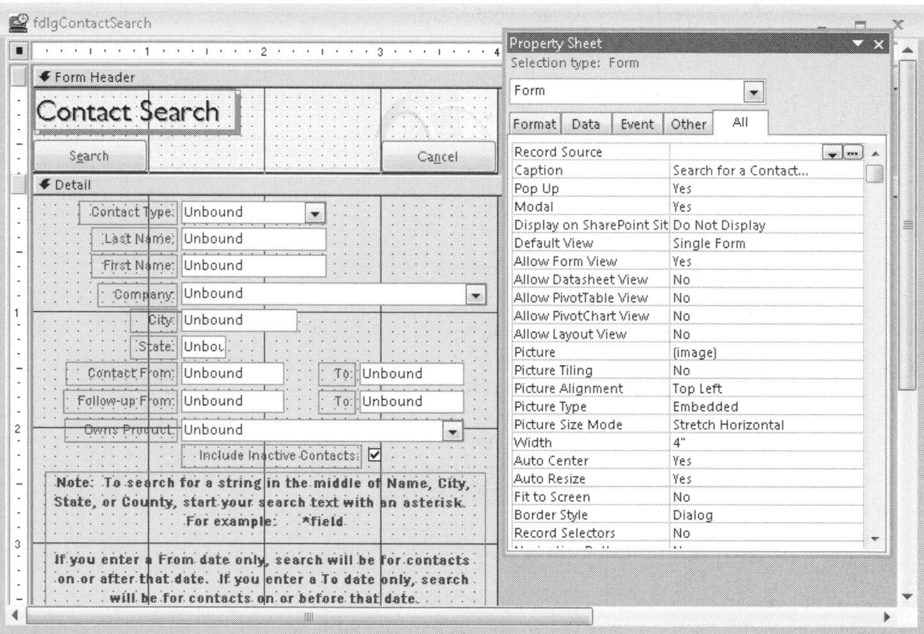


**Figure 20-16** When you look at the fdlgContactSearch form in Design view, you can see that it has no record source.

The bulk of the work happens when you click the Search button. The code for the event procedure for the Click event of the Search button is shown here:

```
Private Sub cmdSearch_Click()
Dim varWhere As Variant, varDateSearch As Variant
Dim rst As DAO.Recordset
  ' Initialize to Null
  varWhere = Null
  varDateSearch = Null
  ' First, validate the dates
  ' If there's something in Contact Date From
  If Not IsNothing(Me.txtContactFrom) Then
    ' First, make sure it's a valid date
    If Not IsDate(Me.txtContactFrom) Then
      ' Nope, warn them and bail
      MsgBox "The value in Contact From is not a valid date.", _
        vbCritical, gstrAppTitle
      Exit Sub
    End If
    ' Now see if they specified a "to" date
    If Not IsNothing(Me.txtContactTo) Then
      ' First, make sure it's a valid date
      If Not IsDate(Me.txtContactTo) Then
        ' Nope, warn them and bail
        MsgBox "The value in Contact To is not a valid date.", _
```

```
      vbCritical, gstrAppTitle
    Exit Sub
  End If
  ' Got two dates, now make sure "to" is >= "from"
  If Me.txtContactTo < Me.txtContactFrom Then
    MsgBox "Contact To date must be greater than " & _
      "or equal to Contact From date.", _
      vbCritical, gstrAppTitle
    Exit Sub
  End If
End If
Else
  ' No "from" but did they specify a "to"?
  If Not IsNothing(Me.txtContactTo) Then
    ' Make sure it's a valid date
    If Not IsDate(Me.txtContactTo) Then
      ' Nope, warn them and bail
      MsgBox "The value in Contact To is not a valid date.", _
        vbCritical, gstrAppTitle
      Exit Sub
    End If
  End If
End If
' If there's something in Follow-up Date From
If Not IsNothing(Me.txtFollowUpFrom) Then
  ' First, make sure it's a valid date
  If Not IsDate(Me.txtFollowUpFrom) Then
    ' Nope, warn them and bail
    MsgBox "The value in Follow-up From is not a valid date.", _
      vbCritical, gstrAppTitle
    Exit Sub
  End If
  ' Now see if they specified a "to" date
  If Not IsNothing(Me.txtFollowUpTo) Then
    ' First, make sure it's a valid date
    If Not IsDate(Me.txtFollowUpTo) Then
      ' Nope, warn them and bail
      MsgBox "The value in Follow-up To is not a valid date.", _
        vbCritical, gstrAppTitle
      Exit Sub
    End If
    ' Got two dates, now make sure "to" is >= "from"
    If Me.txtFollowUpTo < Me.txtFollowUpFrom Then
      MsgBox "Follow-up To date must be greater than " & _
        "or equal to Follow-up From date.", _
        vbCritical, gstrAppTitle
      Exit Sub
    End If
  End If
Else
  ' No "from" but did they specify a "to"?
  If Not IsNothing(Me.txtFollowUpTo) Then
    ' Make sure it's a valid date
```

Chapter 20

```
    If Not IsDate(Me.txtFollowUpTo) Then
      ' Nope, warn them and bail
      MsgBox "The value in Follow-up To is not a valid date.", _
        vbCritical, gstrAppTitle
      Exit Sub
    End If
  End If
End If
' OK, start building the filter
' If specified a contact type value
If Not IsNothing(Me.cmbContactType) Then
  ' .. build the predicate
  varWhere = "(ContactType.Value = '" & Me.cmbContactType & "')"
End If
' Do Last Name next
If Not IsNothing(Me.txtLastName) Then
  ' .. build the predicate
  ' Note: taking advantage of Null propagation
  '  so we don't have to test for any previous predicate
  varWhere = (varWhere + " AND ") & "([LastName] LIKE '" & _
    Me.txtLastName & "*')"
End If
' Do First Name next
If Not IsNothing(Me.txtFirstName) Then
  ' .. build the predicate
  varWhere = (varWhere + " AND ") & "([FirstName] LIKE '" & _
    Me.txtFirstName & "*')"
End If
' Do Company next
If Not IsNothing(Me.cmbCompanyID) Then
  ' .. build the predicate
  ' Must use a subquery here because the value is in a linking table...
  varWhere = (varWhere + " AND ") & _
    "([ContactID] IN (SELECT ContactID FROM tblCompanyContacts " & _
    "WHERE tblCompanyContacts.CompanyID = " & Me.cmbCompanyID & "))"
End If
' Do City next
If Not IsNothing(Me.txtCity) Then
  ' .. build the predicate
  ' Test for both Work and Home city
  varWhere = (varWhere + " AND ") & "(([WorkCity] LIKE '" & _
    Me.txtCity & "*')" & _
    " OR ([HomeCity] LIKE '" & Me.txtCity & "*'))"
End If
' Do State next
If Not IsNothing(Me.txtState) Then
  ' .. build the predicate
  ' Test for both Work and Home state
  varWhere = (varWhere + " AND ") & "(([WorkStateOrProvince] LIKE '" & _
    Me.txtState & "*')" & _
    " OR ([HomeStateOrProvince] LIKE '" & Me.txtState & "*'))"
End If
```

```
' Do Contact date(s) next -- this is a toughie
'   because we want to end up with one filter on the subquery table
'   for both Contact Date range and FollowUp Date range
' Check Contact From first
If Not IsNothing(Me.txtContactFrom) Then
  ' .. build the predicate
  varDateSearch = "tblContactEvents.ContactDateTime >= #" & _
    Me.txtContactFrom & "#"
End If
' Now do Contact To
If Not IsNothing(Me.txtContactTo) Then
  ' .. add to the predicate, but add one because ContactDateTime includes
  '  a date AND a time
  varDateSearch = (varDateSearch + " AND ") & _
    "tblContactEvents.ContactDateTime < #" & _
    CDate(Me.txtContactTo) + 1 & "#"
End If
' Now do Follow-up From
If Not IsNothing(Me.txtFollowUpFrom) Then
  ' .. add to the predicate
  varDateSearch = (varDateSearch + " AND ") & _
    "tblContactEvents.ContactFollowUpDate >= #" & Me.txtFollowUpFrom & "#"
End If
' Finally, do Follow-up To
If Not IsNothing(Me.txtFollowUpTo) Then
  ' .. add to the predicate
  varDateSearch = (varDateSearch + " AND ") & _
    "tblContactEvents.ContactFollowUpDate <= #" & Me.txtFollowUpTo & "#"
End If
' Did we build any date filter?
If Not IsNothing(varDateSearch) Then
  ' OK, add to the overall filter
  ' Must use a subquery here because the value is in a linking table...
  varWhere = (varWhere + " AND ") & _
    "([ContactID] IN (SELECT ContactID FROM tblContactEvents " & _
    "WHERE " & varDateSearch & "))"
End If
' Do Product
If Not IsNothing(Me.cmbProductID) Then
  ' .. build the predicate
  ' Must use a subquery here because the value is in a linking table...
  varWhere = (varWhere + " AND ") & _
    "([ContactID] IN (SELECT ContactID FROM tblContactProducts " & _
    "WHERE tblContactProducts.ProductID = " & Me.cmbProductID & "))"
End If
' Finally, do the Inactive check box
If (Me.chkInactive = False) Then
  ' Build a filter to exclude inactive contacts
  varWhere = (varWhere + " AND ") & "(Inactive = False)"
End If
' Check to see that we built a filter
```

Chapter 20

```
    If IsNothing(varWhere) Then
      MsgBox "You must enter at least one search criteria.", _
        vbInformation, gstrAppTitle
      Exit Sub
    End If
    ' Open a recordset to see if any rows returned with this filter
    Set rst = CurrentDb.OpenRecordset("SELECT * FROM tblContacts " & _
      "WHERE " & varWhere)
    ' See if found none
    If rst.RecordCount = 0 Then
      MsgBox "No Contacts meet your criteria.", vbInformation, gstrAppTitle
      ' Clean up recordset
      rst.Close
      Set rst = Nothing
      Exit Sub
    End If
    ' Hide me to fix later focus problems
    Me.Visible = False
    ' Move to last to find out how many
    rst.MoveLast
    ' If 5 or less or frmContacts already open,
    If (rst.RecordCount < 6) Or IsFormLoaded("frmContacts") Then
      ' Open Contacts filtered
      ' Note: if form already open, this just applies the filter
      DoCmd.OpenForm "frmContacts", WhereCondition:=varWhere
      ' Make sure focus is on contacts
      Forms!frmContacts.SetFocus
    Else
      ' Ask if they want to see a summary list first
      If vbYes = MsgBox("Your search found " & rst.RecordCount & _
        " contacts.  " & _
        "Do you want to see a summary list first?", _
        vbQuestion + vbYesNo, gstrAppTitle) Then
        ' Show the summary
        DoCmd.OpenForm "frmContactSummary", WhereCondition:=varWhere
        ' Make sure focus is on contact summary
        Forms!frmContactSummary.SetFocus
      Else
        ' Show the full contacts info filtered
        DoCmd.OpenForm "frmContacts", WhereCondition:=varWhere
        ' Make sure focus is on contacts
        Forms!frmContacts.SetFocus
      End If
    End If
    ' Done
    DoCmd.Close acForm, Me.Name
    ' Clean up recordset
    rst.Close
    Set rst = Nothing
  End Sub
```

The first part of the procedure validates the contact date from and to values and the follow-up date from and to values. If any are not valid dates or the from date is later than the to date, the code issues an appropriate warning message and exits.

The next several segments of code build up a WHERE string by looking at the unbound controls one at a time. If the corresponding field is a string, the code builds a test using the LIKE predicate so that whatever the user enters can match any part of the field in the underlying table, but not all the fields are strings. When the function adds a clause as it builds the WHERE string, it inserts the AND keyword between clauses if other clauses already exist. Because the variable containing the WHERE clause is a Variant data type initialized to Null, the code can use a + concatenation to optionally add the AND keyword. Note that because the ContactType field is a multi-value field, the code specifically searches the Value property of the field.

The underlying record source for the frmContacts form does not include either contact event or product information directly, so the procedure has to build a predicate using a subquery if you ask for a search by contact date, follow-up date, or product. In the case of contact date or follow-up date, the code builds a separate filter string (varDate-Search) because both fields are in the same table (tblContactEvents). If you ask for any date range check, the code builds criteria using a subquery that finds the ContactID from records in the tblContactEvents table that fall within the date range. For a search by product, the code builds criteria using a subquery that finds the ContactID from records in the tblContactProducts table that match the product you selected. Finally, if you leave the Include Inactive Contacts check box cleared, the code adds a test to include only records that are active.

After examining all the possible filter values the user could have entered, the code checks to see if there's anything in the filter string (varWhere). There's no point in opening the form without a filter, so the code displays a message and exits, leaving the form open to allow the user to try again.

The final part of the procedure builds a simple recordset on the tblContacts table used in both the frmContacts and frmContactSummary forms, applying the WHERE clause built by the code in the first part of the procedure. If it finds no records, it uses the MsgBox function to inform the user and then gives the user a chance to try again.

When you first open a Recordset object in code, its RecordCount property is 0 if the recordset is empty and is some value greater than 0 if the recordset contains some records. The RecordCount property of a Recordset object contains only a count of the number of rows visited and not the number of rows in the recordset. So if it finds some rows, the procedure moves to the last row in the temporary recordset to get an accurate count. When the record count is greater than 5 and the frmContacts form is not already open, the procedure uses the MsgBox function to give the user the option to view a summary of the records found in the frmContactSummary form or to display the records found directly in the frmContacts form. (As noted earlier, both forms use the same record source, so the code can apply the filter it built as it opens either form.) We'll examine how the frmContactSummary form works in the next section.

## Selecting from a Summary List

As you saw in the cmdSearch_Click procedure in the previous section, the user gets to make a choice if more than 5 rows meet the entered criteria. To examine this feature in more detail, make sure the frmContacts form is not open, and ask for a search of contacts with a Contact Type of Customer in the fdlgContactSearch form. The result should look like that shown in Figure 20-17, in which 30 contacts are categorized as customers.

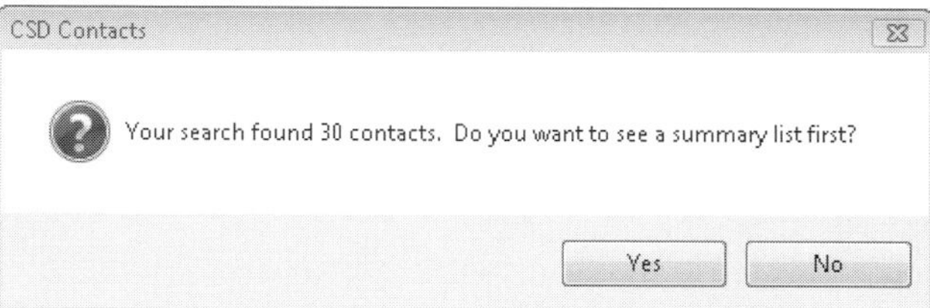


**Figure 20-17** This message box appears when the cmdSearch_Click procedure returns more than five rows.

When you click Yes, the cmdSearch_Click procedure opens the Contact Search Summary form (frmContactSummary), as shown in Figure 20-18. You can scroll down to any row, put the focus on that row (be sure the row selector indicator is pointing to that row), and then click the View Details button to open the frmContacts form and view the details for the one contact you selected. You can see that this is a very efficient way to help the user narrow a search down to one particular contact.

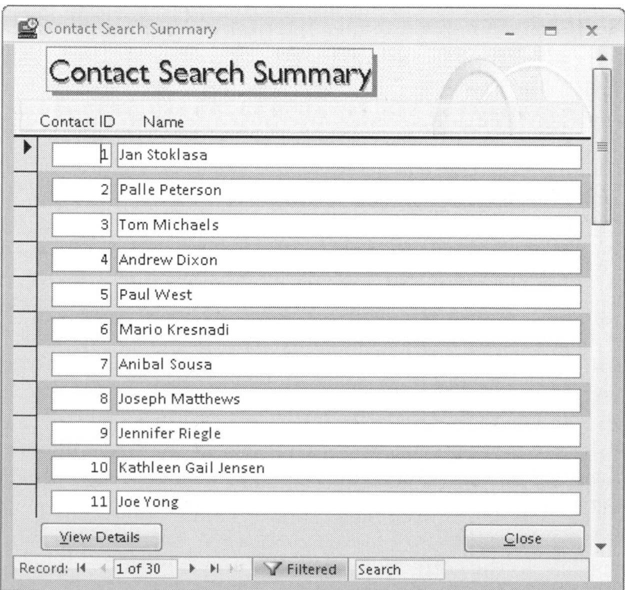


**Figure 20-18** You can select a specific contact from the search summary form.

You can also double-click either the Contact ID or the Name field to see the details for that contact. Because this list is already filtered using the criteria you specified in the fdlgContactSearch form, the code that responds to your request builds a simple filter on the one Contact ID to make opening the frmContacts form most efficient. The code behind this form that responds to your request is as follows:

```
' Set up the filter
strFilter = "(ContactID = " & Me.ContactID & ")"
' Open contacts filtered on the current row
DoCmd.OpenForm FormName:="frmContacts", WhereCondition:=strFilter
' Close me
DoCmd.Close acForm, Me.Name
' Put focus on contacts
Forms!frmContacts.SetFocus
```



## Filtering One List with Another

You might have noticed when editing products on the Products tab in the frmContacts form (see Figure 20-1) that you can first choose a product type to narrow down the list of products and then choose the product you want. There are only 11 products in the sample application, so being able to narrow down the product selection first isn't all that useful, but you can imagine how a feature like this would be absolutely necessary in an application that had thousands of products available for sale.

The secret is that the row source for the Product combo box is a parameter query that filters the products based on the product type you chose. When you use this technique in a form in Single Form view, all you need to do is requery the filtered combo box (in this case, the Product combo box) when the user moves to a new record (in the Current event of the form) and requery when the user chooses a different value in the combo box that provides the filter value (in the AfterUpdate event of the combo box providing the filter value).

However, using this technique on a form in Continuous Forms view is considerably more complex. Even though you can see multiple rows in Continuous Forms view, there is actually only one copy of each control on the form. If you always requery the Product combo box each time you move to a new row, the product name displayed in other rows that have a different product type will appear blank! When the value in a row doesn't match a value in the list, you get a blank result, not the actual value of the field.

The way to solve this is to include the display name in the recordset for the form and carefully overlay each combo box with a text box that always displays the correct value regardless of the filter. You can open the fsubContactProducts form in Design view to see how we did this. Figure 20-19 shows you the form with the two overlay text boxes (CategoryDescription and ProductName) pulled down from the underlying combo boxes (Unbound and ProductID).

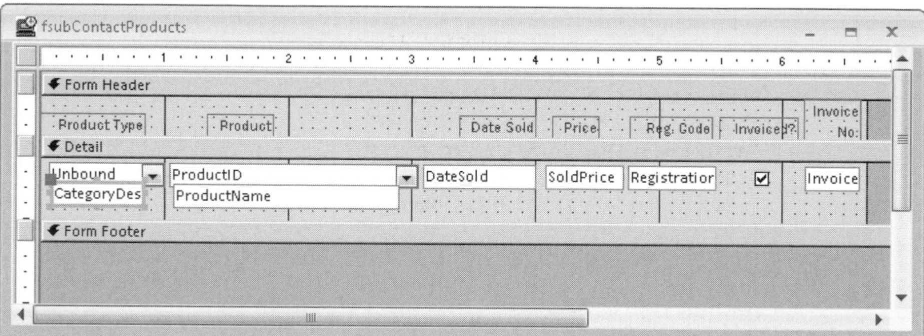


**Figure 20-19** You can solve a filtered combo box display problem by overlaying text boxes.

Notice that the control source of the Product combo box is actually the ProductID field, but the combo box displays the ProductName field. Also, the Product Type combo box isn't bound to any field at all—there is no CategoryDescription field in tblContact-Products—but it does display the CategoryDescription field from the lookup table. To make this work, you need to include the ProductName and CategoryDescription fields in the record source for this form. You don't want the user to update these values, but you need them to provide the overlay display. These two text boxes have their Locked property set to Yes to prevent updating and their Tab Stop property set to No so that the user will tab into the underlying combo boxes and not these text boxes. Figure 20-20 shows you the qryContactProducts query that's the row source for this form.

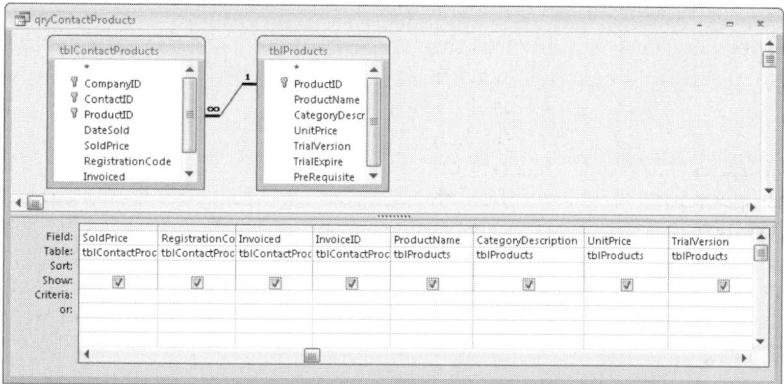


**Figure 20-20** The qryContactProducts query provides the necessary ProductName and CategoryDescription fields from a related table so that you can display the values.

To make it all work correctly, several event procedures make sure the focus goes where necessary and that the filtered Product combo box gets requeried correctly. The code behind the fsubContactProducts form that does this is as follows:

```
Private Sub CategoryDescription_GotFocus()
  ' We have some tricky "overlay" text boxes here that
  ' shouldn't get the focus.  Move focus to the underlying
  ' combo box if that happens.
  Me.cmbCategoryDescription.SetFocus
End Sub
```

```
Private Sub cmbCategoryDescription_AfterUpdate()
  ' If they pick a new Category, then requery the
  '  product list that's filtered on category
  Me.cmbProductID.Requery
  ' Set the Product to the first row in the new list
  Me.cmbProductID = Me.cmbProductID.ItemData(0)
  ' .. and signal Product after update.
  cmbProductID_AfterUpdate
End Sub

Private Sub Form_Current()
  ' If we have a valid Category Description on this row...
  If Not IsNothing(Me.CategoryDescription) Then
    ' Then make sure the unbound combo is in sync.
    Me.cmbCategoryDescription = Me.CategoryDescription
  End If
  ' Requery the product list to match the current category
  Me.cmbProductID.Requery
End Sub

Private Sub ProductName_GotFocus()
    ' We have some tricky "overlay" text boxes here that
    ' shouldn't get the focus.  Move focus to the underlying
    ' combo box if that happens.
    Me.cmbProductID.SetFocus
End Sub
```

As expected, the code requeries the Product combo box whenever you pick a new category (cmbCategoryDescription_AfterUpdate) or when you move to a new row (Form_Current). It also keeps the unbound combo box in sync as you move from row to row as long as the underlying record has a valid category. (A new record won't have a related CategoryDescription until you choose a Product ID, so the code doesn't update the unbound combo box on a new record.) Finally, if you try to click in CategoryDescription or ProductName, the GotFocus code moves you to the underlying combo box where you belong. Why didn't we simply set the Enabled property for CategoryDescription and ProductName to No? If you do that, then you can't ever click into the category or product combo boxes because the disabled text box overlaid on top would block you.

> **Note**
>
> If you want to see what the filtered combo box looks like without the overlay, make a backup copy of Contacts.accdb, open the fsubContactProducts form in Design view, move the Category Description and Product Name text boxes down similar to Figure 20-19, and save the form. Now open the frmContacts form and click on the Products tab.

# Linking to Related Data in Another Form or Report

Now that you know how to build a filter to limit what the user sees, you can probably surmise that using a filter is a good way to open another form or report that displays information related to the current record or set of filtered records in the current form. This section shows you how to do this for both forms and reports. Later in this section, you will learn how to use events in class modules to build sophisticated links.



## Linking Forms Using a Filter

You've already seen the frmContactSummary form (Figure 20-18) that uses a simple filter to link from the record selected in that form to full details in the frmContacts form. You can find similar code behind the fsubCompanyContacts form used as a subform in the frmCompanies form. Figure 20-21 shows you the frmCompanies form and the Edit This buttons we provided on the subform.

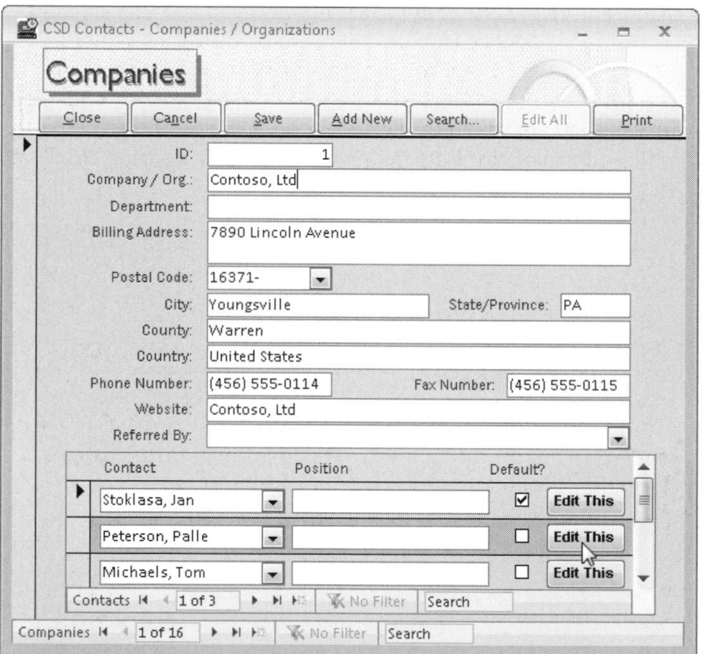


**Figure 20-21** You can provide a link from the Companies / Organizations form to details about a particular contact.

To see the details for a particular contact, the user clicks the Edit This button on the chosen contact record, and code opens the frmContacts form with that contact displayed. The code behind the button is as follows:

```
Private Sub cmdEdit_Click()
    ' Open Contacts on the related record
    DoCmd.OpenForm "frmContacts", WhereCondition:="ContactID = " & Me.ContactID
End Sub
```

And code in the form's Current event prevents the user from clicking on the button when on a new record that doesn't have a contact ID, as shown here:

```
Private Sub Form_Current()
    ' Disable "edit this" if on a new row
    Me.cmdEdit.Enabled = Not (Me.NewRecord)
End Sub
```

Setting the button's Enabled property to False causes it to appear dimmed, and the user cannot click the button.



## Linking to a Report Using a Filter

Now let's take a look at using the Filter technique to link to related information in a report. Open the frmInvoices form in the Conrad Systems Contacts application (Contacts.accdb) and move to an invoice that looks interesting. Click the Print button to open the Print Invoices form (fdlgInvoicePrintOptions) that gives you the option to see the current invoice formatted in a report, display all unprinted invoices in a report, display only unprinted invoices for the current customer, or print all invoices currently shown in the frmInvoices form. (You can use Search to filter the displayed invoices to the ones you want.) Select the Current Invoice Only option and click Print again to see the invoice in a report, as shown in Figure 20-22. (The figure shows you the sequence you see after clicking the Print button on the frmInvoices form. The Print Invoices dialog box closes after opening the report.)

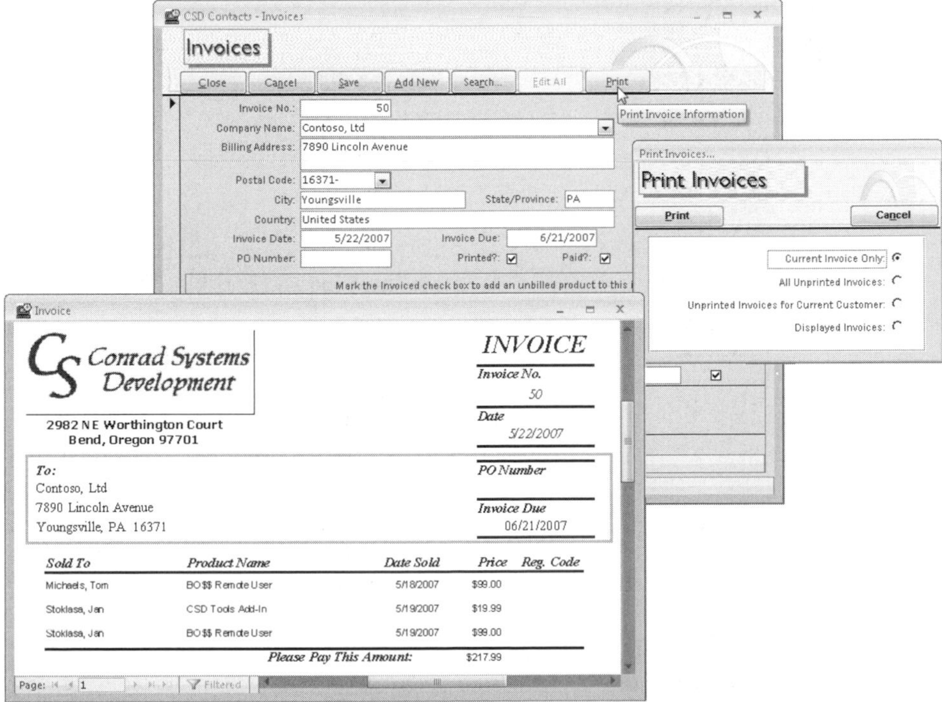


**Figure 20-22** You can ask to print only the current invoice in the Conrad Systems Contacts database.

The code from the Click event of the Print button in the fdlgInvoicePrintOptions form is as follows:

```
Private Sub cmdPrint_Click()
Dim strFilter As String, frm As Form
  ' Set an error trap
  On Error GoTo cmdPrint_Error
  ' Get a pointer to the Invoices form
  Set frm = Forms!frmInvoices
  Select Case Me.optFilterType.Value
    ' Current Invoice
    Case 1
      ' Set filter to open Invoice report for current invoice only
      strFilter = "[InvoiceID] = " & frm!InvoiceID
    ' All unprinted invoices
    Case 2
      ' Set filter to open all unprinted invoices
      strFilter = "[InvoicePrinted] = 0"
    ' Unprinted invoices for current company
    Case 3
      ' Set filter to open unprinted invoices for current company
      strFilter = "[CompanyID] = " & frm!cmbCompanyID & _
        " AND [InvoicePrinted] = 0"
    ' Displayed invoices (if filter set on form)
    Case 4
      ' Check for a filter on the form
      If IsNothing(frm.Filter) Then
        ' Make sure they want to print all!
        If vbNo = MsgBox("Your selection will print all " & _
          "Invoices currently in the " & _
          "database.  Are you sure you want to do this?", _
          vbQuestion + vbYesNo + vbDefaultButton2, _
          gstrAppTitle) Then
          Exit Sub
        End If
        ' Set "do them all" filter
        strFilter = "1 = 1"
      Else
        strFilter = frm.Filter
      End If
  End Select
  ' Hide me
  Me.Visible = False
  ' Have a filter now.  Open the report on that filter
  DoCmd.OpenReport "rptInvoices", acViewPreview, , strFilter
  ' Update the Print flag for selected invoices
  CurrentDb.Execute "UPDATE tblInvoices SET InvoicePrinted = -1 WHERE " & _
    strFilter
  ' Refresh the form to show updated Printed status
  frm.Refresh
  ' Execute the Current event on the form to make sure it is locked correctly
  frm.Form_Current
```

```
cmdPrint_Exit:
  ' Clear the form object
  Set frm = Nothing
  ' Done
  DoCmd.Close acForm, Me.Name
  Exit Sub
cmdPrint_Error:
  ' Got an error
  ' If Cancel, that means the filter produced no Invoices
  If Err = errCancel Then
    ' Exit - report will display "no records" message
    Resume cmdPrint_Exit
  End If
  ' Got unknown error - display and log
  MsgBox "Unexpected error while printing and updating print flags: " & _
    Err & ", " & _
    Error, vbCritical, gstrAppTitle
  ErrorLog Me.Name & "_Print", Err, Error
  Resume cmdPrint_Exit
End Sub
```

This first part of this procedure sets an object reference to the frmInvoices form to make it easy to grab either the InvoiceID or the CompanyID and to reference properties and methods of the form's object. The Select Case statement examines which option button the user selected on fdlgInvoicePrintOptions and builds the appropriate filter for the report. Notice that if the user asks to print all the invoices currently displayed on the form, the code first looks for a user-applied filter on the frmInvoices form. If the code finds no filter, it asks if the user wants to print all invoices. The code uses the filter it built (or the current filter on the frmInvoices form) to open the rptInvoices report in Print Preview. It also executes an SQL UPDATE statement to flag all the invoices the user printed. If you look at code in the Current event of the frmInvoices form, you'll find that it locks all controls so that the user can't update an invoice that has been printed.

## Synchronizing Two Forms Using a Class Event

Sometimes it's useful to give the user an option to open a pop-up form that displays additional details about some information displayed on another form. As you move from one row to another in the main form, it would be nice if the form that displayed the additional information stayed in sync.

Of course, the Current event of a form lets you know when you move to a new row. In the Wedding List sample database built with macros (WeddingListMC.accdb), the macros do some elaborate filtering to keep a pop-up form with additional city information in sync with the main form. However, doing it with macros is the hard way!

The primary Wedding List sample application is in WeddingList.accdb, and it uses Visual Basic to provide all the automation. With Visual Basic, we were able to declare and use a custom event in the WeddingList form to signal the CityInformation form if it's open and responding to the events. In the Current event of the WeddingList form, we don't have to worry about whether the companion form is open. The code simply signals the event and lets the City Information form worry about keeping in sync with the main form. (The user can open the City Information form at any time by clicking the City Info button on the Wedding List form.) You can see these two forms in action in Figure 20-23.

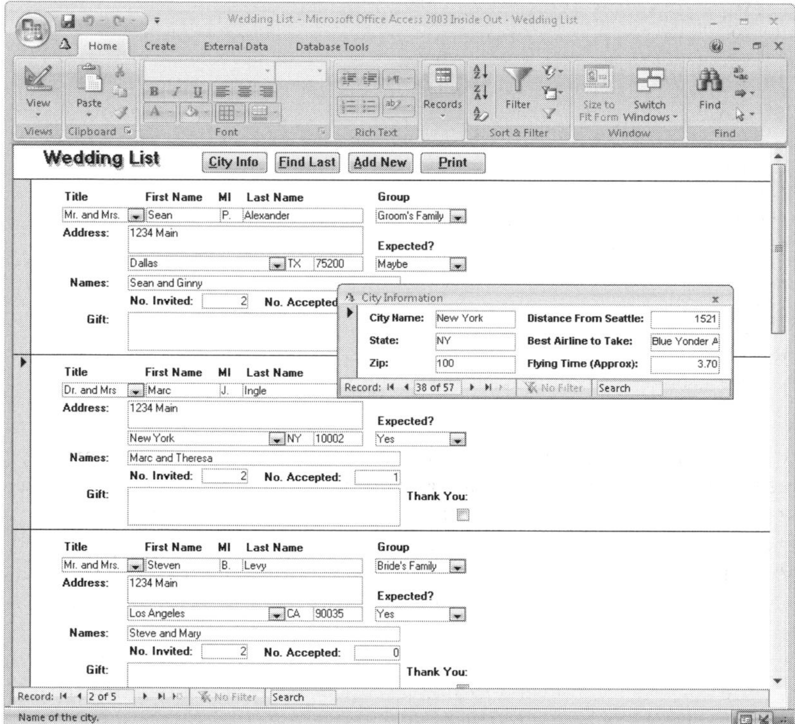


**Figure 20-23** The CityInformation form pops open over the main WeddingList form to display additional information about the invitee's home city.

Here's the code from the WeddingList class module that makes an event available to signal the CityInformation form:

```
Option Compare Database
Option Explicit
' Event to signal we've moved to a new city
Public Event NewCity(varCityName As Variant)
' End of Declarations Section

Private Sub Form_Current()
On Error GoTo Form_Current_Err
  ' Signal the city form to move to this city
  ' and pass the city name to the event
  RaiseEvent NewCity(Me!City)
Form_Current_Exit:
  Exit Sub
```

```
Form_Current_Err:
  MsgBox Error$
  Resume Form_Current_Exit
End Sub

Private Sub cmdCity_Click()
On Error GoTo cmdCity_Click_Err
  ' If the city form not open, do it
  If Not IsFormLoaded("CityInformation") Then
    DoCmd.OpenForm "CityInformation", acNormal, , , acFormReadOnly, acHidden
    ' Give the other form a chance to "hook" our event
    DoEvents
  End If
  ' Signal the form we just opened
  RaiseEvent NewCity(Me!City)
cmdCity_Click_Exit:
  Exit Sub
cmdCity_Click_Err:
  MsgBox Error$
  Resume cmdCity_Click_Exit
End Sub
```



In the Declarations section of the module, we declared an event variable and indicated that we're going to pass a parameter (the city name) in the event. In the Form_Current event procedure, the code uses RaiseEvent to pass the current city name to any other module that's listening. The code doesn't have to worry about whether any other module is interested in this event–it just signals the event when appropriate and then ends. (This is not unlike how Access works. When a form moves to a new record, Access signals the Form_Current event, but nothing happens unless you have written code to respond to the event.) Note that the variable passed is declared as a Variant to handle the case when the user moves to the new row at the end–the City control will be Null in that case. A command button (cmdCity) on the WeddingList form allows the user to open the CityInformation form. The Click event of that button opens the form hidden and uses the DoEvents function to give the CityInformation form a chance to open and indicate that it wants to listen to the NewCity event on the WeddingList form. After waiting for the CityInformation form to finish processing, the code raises the event to notify that form about the city in the current row.

The CityInformation form does all the work (when it's open) to respond to the event signaled by the WeddingList form and move to the correct row. The code is shown here:

```
Option Compare Database
Option Explicit
Dim WithEvents frmWedding As Form_WeddingList
' End of the Declarations Section

Private Sub Form_Load()
On Error GoTo Form_Load_Err
  ' If the wedding list form is open
  If IsLoaded("WeddingList") Then
    ' Then set to respond to the NewCity event
    Set frmWedding = Forms!WeddingList
  End If
```

```
Form_Load_Exit:
  Exit Sub
Form_Load_Err:
  MsgBox Error$
  Resume Form_Load_Exit
End Sub

Private Sub frmWedding_NewCity(varCityName As Variant)
  ' The Wedding List form has asked us to move to a
  ' new city via the NewCity event
  On Error Resume Next
  If IsNothing(varCityName) Then
    ' Hide me if city name is empty
    Me.Visible = False
  Else
    ' Reveal me if there's a city name, and go
    ' find it
    Me.Visible = True
    Me.Recordset.FindFirst "[CityName] = """ & _
      varCityName & """"
  End If
End Sub
```

In the Declarations section, you can find an object variable called frmWedding that has a data type equal to the class module name of the WeddingList form. The WithEvents keyword indicates that code in this class module will respond to events signaled by any object assigned to this variable. When the form opens, the Form_Load procedure checks to see that the WeddingList form is open (just in case you opened this form by itself from the Navigation Pane). If the WeddingList form is open, it "hooks" the New-City event in that form by assigning it to the frmWedding variable.

The frmWedding_NewCity procedure responds to the NewCity event of the frmWedding object. Once the Load event code establishes frmWedding as a pointer to the WeddingList form, this procedure runs whenever code in the class module for that form signals the NewCity event with RaiseEvent.

The code in the event procedure is pretty simple. If the CityName parameter passed by the event is "nothing" (Null or a zero length string), the procedure hides the form because there's nothing to display. If the event passes a valid city name, the procedure uses the FindFirst method of the Recordset object of this form to move to the correct city.

> **Note**
>
> The Recordset property of a form in an Access database (.accdb file) returns a DAO recordset in Access 2007. For this reason, you should use a DAO FindFirst method, not an ADO Find method, to locate rows in a form recordset.

# Automating Complex Tasks

The most complex Visual Basic code we've examined thus far in this chapter is the procedure to build a search clause from the data you enter in the fdlgContactSearch form. Trust us, we've only started to scratch the surface!

## Triggering a Data Task from a Related Form

One of the more complex pieces of code in the Conrad Systems Contacts sample database is triggered from the fsubContactEvents form that's part of the frmContacts form. After signing on correctly to the application, the user can open the frmContacts form, click on the Events tab, and add an event indicating the sale of a product. As soon as the user saves the record, code behind the subform automatically adds the product to the contact, as shown in Figure 20-24.



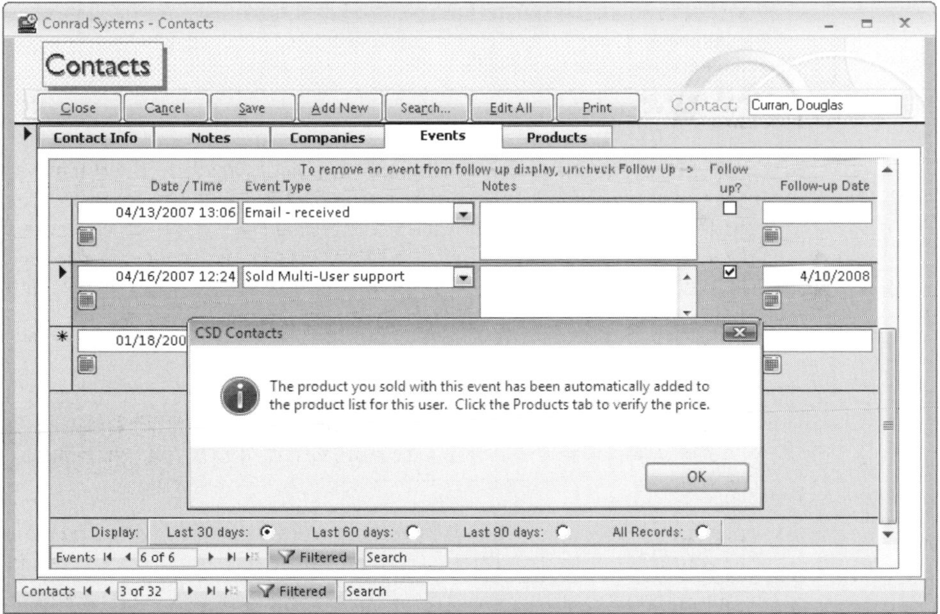


**Figure 20-24** Logging a product sale event on the Events tab automatically sells the product to the contact.

If you look behind the fsubContactEvents form, you'll find event procedures that detect when the user has created a sale event and execute an SQL INSERT command to create the related product row. The code is as follows:

```
Option Compare Database
Option Explicit
' Flag to indicate auto-add of a product if new event requires it
Dim intProductAdd As Integer
' Place to store Company Name on a product add
```

```
Dim varCoName As Variant
' End of the Declarations Section

Private Sub ContactEventTypeID_BeforeUpdate(Cancel As Integer)
  ' Did they pick an event that involves a software sale?
  ' NOTE: All columns in a combo box are TEXT
  If Me.ContactEventTypeID.Column(4) = "-1" Then
    ' Try to lookup this contact's Company Name
    varCoName = DLookup("CompanyName", "qryContactDefaultCompany", _
      "ContactID = " & Me.Parent.ContactID.Value)
    ' If not found, then disallow product sale
    If IsNothing(varCoName) Then
      MsgBox "You cannot sell a product to a Contact " & _
        "that does not have a " & _
        "related Company that is marked as the default for this Contact." & _
        "  Press Esc to clear your edits and click on the Companies tab " & _
        "to define the default Company for this Contact.", _
        vbCritical, gstrAppTitle
      Cancel = True
    End If
  End If
End Sub

Private Sub Form_BeforeUpdate(Cancel As Integer)
  ' Did they pick an event that involves a software sale?
  ' NOTE: All columns in a combo box are TEXT
  If Me.ContactEventTypeID.Column(4) = "-1" Then
    ' Do this only if on a new record or they changed the EventID value
    If (Me.NewRecord) Or (Me.ContactEventTypeID <> _
      Me.ContactEventTypeID.OldValue) Then
      ' Set the add product flag
      '- product added by AfterUpdate code for safety
      intProductAdd = True
    End If
  End If
End Sub

Private Sub Form_AfterUpdate()
Dim strSQL As String, curPrice As Currency,
Dim lngProduct As Long, varCoID As Variant
Dim rst As DAO.Recordset, strPreReqName As String
  ' See if we need to auto-add a product
  If (intProductAdd = True) Then
    ' Reset so we only do this once
    intProductAdd = False
    ' Set an error trap
    On Error GoTo Insert_Err
    ' Save the Product ID
    lngProduct = Me.ContactEventTypeID.Column(5)
    ' Fetch the product record
    Set rst = CurrentDb.OpenRecordset("SELECT * FROM tblProducts " & _
      "WHERE ProductID = " & lngProduct)
```

```
' Make sure we got a record
If rst.EOF Then
  MsgBox "Could not find the product record for this sales event." & _
    "  Auto-create of " & _
    "product record for this contact has failed.", _
    vbCritical, gstrAppTitle
  rst.Close
  Set rst = Nothing
  GoTo Insert_Exit
End If
' Check for prerequisite product
If Not IsNull(rst!PreRequisite) Then
  ' Make sure contact owns the prerequisite product
  If IsNull(DLookup("ProductID", "tblContactProducts", _
    "ProductID = " & rst!PreRequisite & " And ContactID = " & _
    Me.Parent.ContactID)) Then
    ' Get the name of the prerequisite
    strPreReqName = DLookup("ProductName", "tblProducts", _
      "ProductID = " & rst!PreRequisite)
    ' Display error
    MsgBox "This contact must own prerequisite product " & _
      strPreReqName & " before you can sell this product." & _
      vbCrLf & vbCrLf & _
      "Auto-create of product record for this contact has failed", _
      vbCritical, gstrAppTitle
    ' Bail
    rst.Close
    Set rst = Nothing
    GoTo Insert_Exit
  End If
End If
' Save the price
curPrice = rst!UnitPrice
' Done with the record - close it
rst.Close
Set rst = Nothing
' Now, find the default company for this contact
varCoID = DLookup("CompanyID", "qryContactDefaultCompany", _
  "ContactID = " & Me.Parent.ContactID.Value)
' If not found, then disallow product sale
If IsNothing(varCoID) Then
  MsgBox "You cannot sell a product to a Contact who does not have a " & _
    "related Company that is marked as the default for this Contact.", _
    vbCritical, gstrAppTitle
  GoTo Insert_Exit
End If
' Set up the INSERT command
strSQL = "INSERT INTO tblContactProducts " & _
  "(CompanyID, ContactID, ProductID, DateSold, SoldPrice) " & _
  "VALUES(" & varCoID & ", " & Me.Parent.ContactID & ", " & _
  lngProduct & ", #" & _
  DateValue(Me.ContactDateTime) & "#, " & _
  curPrice & ")"
```

```
    ' Attempt to insert the Product row
    CurrentDb.Execute strSQL, dbFailOnError
    ' Got a good add - inform the user
    MsgBox "The product you sold with this event " & _
      "has been automatically added " & _
      "to the product list for this user.  " & _
      "Click the Products tab to verify the price.", _
      vbInformation, gstrAppTitle
    ' Requery the other subform to get the new row there
    Me.Parent.fsubContactProducts.Requery
  End If
Insert_Exit:
  Exit Sub
Insert_Err:
  ' Was error a duplicate row?
  If Err = errDuplicate Then
    MsgBox "CSD Contacts attempted to auto-add " & _
      "the product that you just indicated " & _
      "that you sold, but the Contact appears " & _
      "to already own this product.  Be sure " & _
      "to verify that you haven't tried to sell the same product twice.", _
      vbCritical, gstrAppTitle
  Else
    MsgBox "There was an error attempting to auto-add " & _
      "the product you just sold: " & _
      Err & ", " & Error, vbCritical, gstrAppTitle
    ' Log the error
    ErrorLog Me.Name & "_FormAfterUpdate", Err, Error
  End If
  Resume Insert_Exit
End Sub
```

In the Declarations section of the module, you can find two variables that the event procedures use to pass information between events. (If you declare the variables inside one of the procedures, only that procedure can use the variables.) The BeforeUpdate event procedure for the contact event type checks to see if the event is a product sale (by examining one of the hidden columns in the combo box row source). If the user is trying to log a product sale and this particular contact doesn't have a default company defined, the code displays an error message and won't let the user save that event type. Remember, a record in the tblContactProducts table must have a CompanyID as well as a ContactID.

When the user attempts to save a new or changed event record, Access runs the form's BeforeUpdate event procedure. This code again checks to see if the record about to be saved is for a product sale. However, if this isn't a new record or the user is saving an old event record but didn't change the event type, the code exits because it doesn't want to add a product record twice. (If this is an existing record and the event type didn't change, this code probably created the companion contact product record the first time the user saved the record.) The code could insert the record into tblContactProducts at this point, but, as you learned in Chapter 17, the record isn't really saved until after the BeforeUpdate event finishes. So, this code sets the module variable to tell the form's AfterUpdate event procedure to perform that task after Access has saved the changed record.

After Access saves the new or changed event record, it runs the form's AfterUpdate event procedure. If the code in BeforeUpdate indicated that a product insert is required by setting the module intProductAdd variable to True, this code sets up to add the new record. It opens a recordset on the tblProducts table for the product that was just sold so that it can get the product price and check for any prerequisite product. If the product has a prerequisite but this contact doesn't own the prerequisite, the code displays an error message and exits.

Although previous code checked to see that this contact has a default CompanyID, this code checks again and exits if it can't find one. After the code has completed all checks and has the price and company ID information it needs, it inserts the new record into the tblContactProducts table using SQL. Notice that at the bottom of the procedure you can find error-trapping code that tests to see if the insert caused a duplicate record error.



## Linking to a Related Task

Let's switch to the Housing Reservations application (Housing.accdb) and take a look at the process for confirming a room for a reservation request. To see this in action, you must start the application by opening the frmSplash form, and then sign on as an administrator (Conrad, Jeff, Richins, Jack S., Schare, Gary, or Viescas, John L.) using **password** as the password. On the main switchboard, click Reservation Requests, and then click View Unbooked in the Edit Reservation Requests dialog box. You'll see the Unbooked Requests form (frmUnbookedRequests) as shown in Figure 20-25.

> **Note**
>
> The query that provides the records displayed in the frmUnbookedRequests form includes criteria to exclude any requests that have a check-in date earlier than today's date. (It doesn't make sense to confirm a reservation request for a date in the past.) The latest requested check-in date in the original database is September 15, 2007, so you will probably see an error message when you attempt to look at unbooked requests. You can use the zfrmLoadData form to load new reservations and requests that are more current into the qryUnbookedRequests query to not eliminate old requests to be able to see how the frmUnbookedRequests form works.

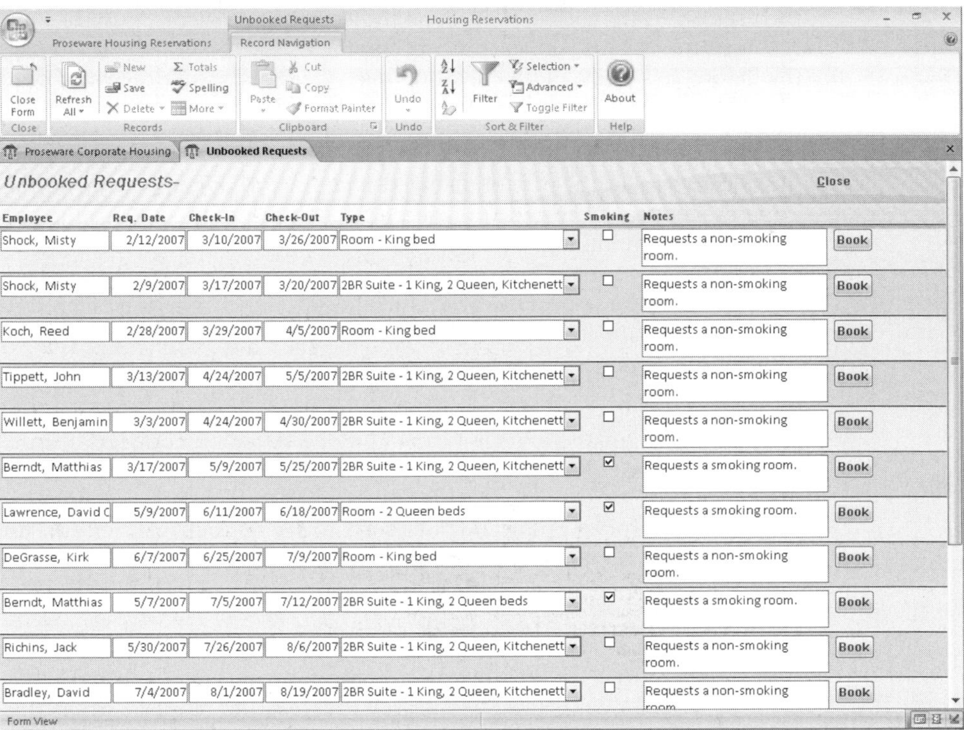


**Figure 20-25** The Unbooked Requests form lets administrators view pending requests and start the booking process.

Earlier in this chapter, in "Linking to Related Data in Another Form or Report" on page 1098, you learned one technique for using a command button to link to a related task. The key task in the Housing Reservations application for the housing manager (or any administrator) is to assign a room and book a reservation for pending requests. When you click one of the Book buttons on the Unbooked Requests form, code behind the form opens a form to show the manager the rooms that match the request and aren't booked for the time span requested. If you click the request from Kirk DeGrasse for a room with a king bed from June 7, 2007, to June 25, 2007, you'll see the list of available rooms in the fdlgAvailableRooms form as shown in Figure 20-26.

Available Rooms

| Facility | Room | Type | Smoking | Daily | Weekly | |
|---|---|---|---|---|---|---|
| Main Campus Housing B | 115 | Room - King bed | ☐ | $55.00 | $350.00 | Pick This |
| Main Campus Housing A | 107 | Room - King bed | ☐ | $55.00 | $350.00 | Pick This |
| Main Campus Housing A | 205 | Room - King bed | ☐ | $55.00 | $350.00 | Pick This |
| Main Campus Housing A | 207 | Room - King bed | ☐ | $55.00 | $350.00 | Pick This |
| Main Campus Housing A | 405 | Room - King bed | ☐ | $55.00 | $350.00 | Pick This |
| Main Campus Housing A | 407 | Room - King bed | ☐ | $55.00 | $350.00 | Pick This |
| Main Campus Housing A | 505 | Room - King bed | ☐ | $55.00 | $350.00 | Pick This |
| Main Campus Housing A | 705 | Room - King bed | ☐ | $55.00 | $350.00 | Pick This |
| Main Campus Housing A | 707 | Room - King bed | ☐ | $55.00 | $350.00 | Pick This |
| Main Campus Housing A | 805 | Room - King bed | ☐ | $55.00 | $350.00 | Pick This |
| Main Campus Housing A | 105 | Room - King bed | ☐ | $55.00 | $350.00 | Pick This |
| Main Campus Housing B | 107 | Room - King bed | ☐ | $55.00 | $350.00 | Pick This |
| South Campus Housing ( | 707 | Room - King bed | ☐ | $55.00 | $350.00 | Pick This |
| Main Campus Housing B | 207 | Room - King bed | ☐ | $55.00 | $350.00 | Pick This |
| Main Campus Housing B | 215 | Room - King bed | ☐ | $55.00 | $350.00 | Pick This |
| Main Campus Housing B | 407 | Room - King bed | ☐ | $55.00 | $350.00 | Pick This |
| Main Campus Housing B | 415 | Room - King bed | ☐ | $55.00 | $350.00 | Pick This |
| Main Campus Housing B | 507 | Room - King bed | ☐ | $55.00 | $350.00 | Pick This |

**Figure 20-26** The fdlgAvailableRooms form shows a list of available rooms matching the selected reservation request.

The code behind the Book button on the frmUnbookedRequests form is as follows:

```
Private Sub cmdBook_Click()
  ' Make sure no changes are pending
  If Me.Dirty Then Me.Dirty = False
  ' Open the available rooms form - hidden, dialog
  '  and check if any available
  DoCmd.OpenForm "fdlgAvailableRooms", _
    WhereCondition:="Smoking = " & Me.Smoking, _
    WindowMode:=acHidden
  If Forms!fdlgAvailableRooms.RecordsetClone.RecordCount = 0 Then
    MsgBox "There are no available rooms of this " & _
      "type for the dates requested." & _
      vbCrLf & vbCrLf & _
      "You can change the Room Type or dates and try again.", _
      vbInformation, gstrAppTitle
    DoCmd.Close acForm, "fdlgAvailableRooms"
    Exit Sub
  End If
```

```
  ' Show the available rooms
  ' - form will call our public sub to create the res.
  Forms!fdlgAvailableRooms.Visible = True
End Sub
```

The record source of the fdlgAvailableRooms form is a parameter query that filters out rooms already booked for the specified dates and includes the remaining rooms that match the requested room type. The code behind the Book button adds a filter for the smoking or nonsmoking request because the room type doesn't include this information but each specific available room does. Behind the Pick This button on the fdlgAvailableRooms form, you can find the following code:

```
Private Sub cmdPick_Click()
Dim intReturn As Integer
  ' Call the build a reservation proc in the calling form
  intReturn = Form_frmUnbookedRequests.Bookit(Me.FacilityID, Me.RoomNumber, _
    Me.DailyRate, Me.WeeklyRate)
  If (intReturn = True) Then
    MsgBox "Booked!", vbExclamation, gstrAppTitle
  Else
    MsgBox "Room booking failed.  Please try again.", _
      vbCritical, gstrAppTitle
  End If
  DoCmd.Close acForm, Me.Name
End Sub
```

Can you figure out what's happening? Back in frmUnbookedRequests, there's a public function called Bookit that this code calls as a method of that form. It passes the critical FacilityID, RoomNumber, DailyRate, and WeeklyRate fields to complete the booking. Back in frmUnbookedRequests, the code in the public function is as follows:

```
Public Function Bookit(lngFacility As Long, lngRoom As Long, _
  curDaily As Currency, curWeekly As Currency) As Integer
' Sub called as a method by fdlgAvailableRooms to book the selected room
' Caller passes in selected Facility, Room number, and rates
Dim db As DAO.Database, rstRes As DAO.Recordset
Dim varResNum As Variant, strSQL As String, intTrans As Integer
  ' Set error trap
  On Error GoTo BookIt_Err
  ' Get a pointer to this database
  Set db = CurrentDb
  ' Open the reservations table for insert
  Set rstRes = db.OpenRecordset("tblReservations", _
    dbOpenDynaset, dbAppendOnly)
  ' Start a transaction
  BeginTrans
  intTrans = True
  ' Get the next available reservation number
  varResNum = DMax("ReservationID", "tblReservations")
  If IsNull(varResNum) Then varResNum = 0
  varResNum = varResNum + 1
  ' Update the current row
```

```
  strSQL = "UPDATE tblReservationRequests SET ReservationID = " & _
    varResNum & " WHERE RequestID = " & Me.RequestID
  db.Execute strSQL, dbFailOnError
  ' Book it!
  rstRes.AddNew
  ' Copy reservation ID
  rstRes!ReservationID = varResNum
  ' Copy employee number
  rstRes!EmployeeNumber = Me.EmployeeNumber
  ' Copy facility ID from the room we picked
  rstRes!FacilityID = lngFacility
  ' .. and room number
  rstRes!RoomNumber = lngRoom
  ' Set reservation date = today
  rstRes!ReservationDate = Date
  ' Copy check-in, check-out, and notes
  rstRes!CheckInDate = Me.CheckInDate
  rstRes!CheckOutDate = Me.CheckOutDate
  rstRes!Notes = Me.Notes
  ' Copy daily and weekly rates
  rstRes!DailyRate = curDaily
  rstRes!WeeklyRate = curWeekly
  ' Calculate the total charge
  rstRes!TotalCharge = ((Int(Me.CheckOutDate - Me.CheckInDate) \ 7) * _
    curWeekly) + _
    ((Int(Me.CheckOutDate - Me.CheckInDate) Mod 7) * _
    curDaily)
  ' Save the Reservation Row
  rstRes.Update
  ' Commit the transaction
  CommitTrans
  intTrans = False
  ' Clean up
  rstRes.Close
  Set rstRes = Nothing
  Set db = Nothing
  ' Requery this form to remove the booked row
  Me.Requery
  ' Return success
  Bookit = True
BookIt_Exit:
  Exit Function
BookIt_Err:
  MsgBox "Unexpected Error: " & Err & ", " & Error, vbCritical, gstrAppTitle
  ErrorLog Me.Name & "_Bookit", Err, Error
  Bookit = False
  If (intTrans = True) Then Rollback
  Resume BookIt_Exit
End Function
```

It makes sense to have the actual booking code back in the frmUnbookedRequests form because the row the code needs to insert into tblReservations needs several fields from the current request record (EmployeeNumber, CheckInDate, CheckOutDate, and Notes). The code starts a transaction because it must simultaneously enter a ReservationID in both the tblReservationRequests table and the tblReservations table. If either fails, the error-trapping code rolls back both updates. Notice that the code opens the tblReservations table for append only to make the insert of the new reservation more efficient.



### Calculating a Stored Value

If you follow the rules of good table design (see Article 1, "Designing Your Database Application"), you know that storing a calculated value in a table isn't usually a good idea because you must write code to maintain the value. But sometimes, in a very large database, you need to calculate and save a value to improve performance for searching and reporting. The Housing Reservations application isn't all that large—but it could be in real life. We chose to store the calculated total charge for each reservation to show you some of the steps you must take to maintain a value like this.

Users can create and edit reservation requests, but the creation of the reservation records that contain the calculated value is controlled entirely by code, so maintaining the calculated TotalCharge value in this application is simple. You've already seen the one place where a new reservation record is created—in the public Bookit function in the frmUnbookedRequests form. The little piece of code that calculates the value is as follows:

```
' Calculate the total charge
rstRes!TotalCharge = ((Int(Me.CheckOutDate - Me.CheckInDate) \ 7) * _
  curWeekly) + _
  ((Int(Me.CheckOutDate - Me.CheckInDate) Mod 7) * _
  curDaily)
```

However, in many applications, you may not be able to control the editing of a calculated value this closely. You need to carefully consider the ramifications of saving a calculated value in your table and perhaps write code that an administrator can run to periodically verify that any saved calculated value hasn't become out of sync with the other fields used to perform the calculation.

## Automating Reports

In a typical application, you'll probably spend 80 to 90 percent of your coding effort in event procedures for your *forms*. That doesn't mean that there aren't many tasks that you can automate on *reports*. This last section shows you just a few of the possibilities.

## Allowing for Used Mailing Labels

Have you ever wanted to create a mailing label report and come up with a way to use up the remaining labels on a partially used page? You can find the answer in the Conrad Systems Contacts sample application (Contacts.accdb). Let's say you want to send a promotional mailing to all contacts who own the Single User product offering them an upgrade to Multi-User. Open the main switchboard form (frmMain), click Contacts, and then click Search in the Select Contacts pop-up window. Perform a search for all contacts who own the Single User product—you should find eight records in the original sample data. (Click No when the application asks you if you want to see a summary list first.) Click the Print button on the frmContacts form, select Avery 5163 Labels (2" × 4"), ask for the report to include the Displayed Contacts, and specify that your first page of labels is missing three used ones. Your screen should look like Figure 20-27 at this point.

**Figure 20-27** You can request mailing labels and specify that some labels have already been used on the first page.

Click the Print button in the dialog box, and you should see the labels print—but with three blank spaces first to avoid the used ones—as shown in Figure 20-28.

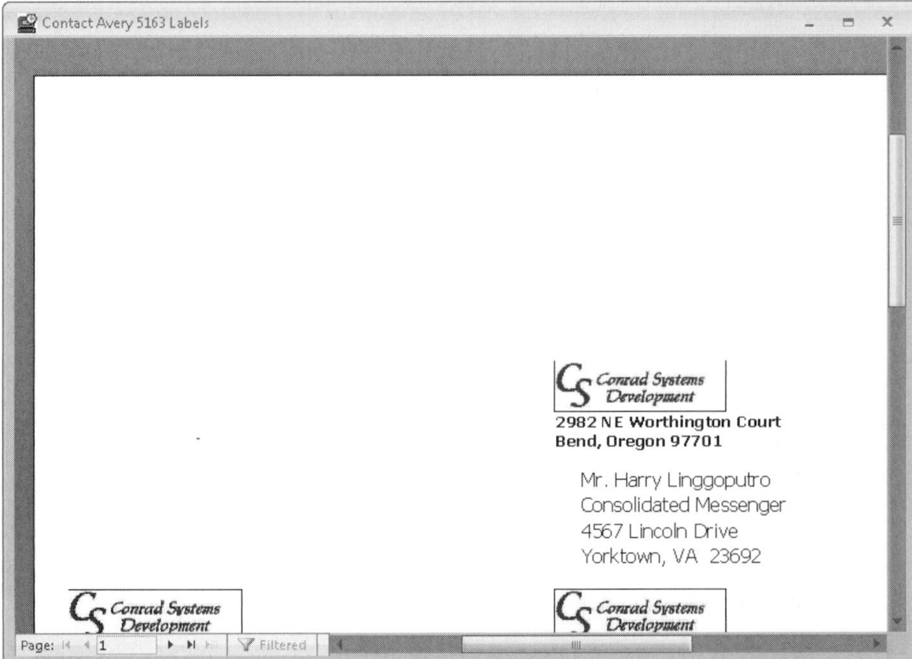


**Figure 20-28** The labels print and avoid the used ones.

You can find some interesting code in the AfterUpdate event of the option group to choose the report type in the fdlgContactPrintOptions form. The code is as follows:

```
Private Sub optReportType_AfterUpdate()
  ' Figure out whether to show the "used labels" combo
  Select Case Me.optReportType
    Case 1
      ' Show the used labels combo
      Me.cmbUsedLabels.Visible = True
      ' Hide the number of days option group
      Me.optDisplay.Visible = False
      ' up to 29 used labels on 5160
      Me.cmbUsedLabels.RowSource = "0;1;2;3;4;5;6;7;8;9;10;11;12;13;" & _
        "14;15;16;17;18;19;20;21;22;23;24;25;26;27;28;29"
    Case 2
      ' Show the used labels combo
      Me.cmbUsedLabels.Visible = True
      ' Hide the number of days option group
      Me.optDisplay.Visible = False
      ' up to 9 used labels on 5163
      Me.cmbUsedLabels.RowSource = "0;1;2;3;4;5;6;7;8;9"
```

```
    Case 3, 4
      ' Don't need the combo for Envelopes and contact list
      Me.cmbUsedLabels.Visible = False
      ' .. or the number of days filter
      Me.optDisplay.Visible = False
    Case 5, 6
      ' Don't need the used labels combo for contact events or products
      Me.cmbUsedLabels.Visible = False
      ' Do need the day filter
      Me.optDisplay.Visible = True
  End Select
End Sub
```



You can have up to 29 used labels when printing on Avery 5160 (1" × 2.625") label paper. You can have up to 9 used labels when printing on Avery 5163 (2" × 4") label paper. The combo box that you can use to indicate the number of used labels has a Value List as its row source type, so the code sets up the appropriate list based on the label type you choose.

However, the real trick to leaving blank spaces on the report is in the query that is the record source for the rptContactLabels5163 report. In the sample database, you can find a table, ztblLabelSpace, that has 30 records, and each record has one field containing the values 1 through 30. The SQL for the query is as follows:

```
PARAMETERS [Forms]![fdlgContactPrintOptions]![cmbUsedLabels] Long;
SELECT "" As Contact, "" As CompanyName, "" As Address, "" As CSZ,
Null As ContactID, "" As Zip, "" As LastName, "" As FirstName,
"" As ContactType, "" As WorkCity, "" As WorkStateOrProvince,
"" As HomeCity, "" As HomeStateOrProvince, 0 As Inactive
FROM ztblLabelSpace
WHERE ID <= [Forms]![fdlgContactPrintOptions]![cmbUsedLabels]
UNION ALL
SELECT ([tblContacts].[Title]+" ") & [tblContacts].[FirstName] & " " &
([tblContacts].[MiddleInit]+". ") & [tblContacts].[LastName] &
(", "+[tblContacts].[Suffix]) AS Contact,
Choose([tblContacts].[DefaultAddress], qryContactDefaultCompany.CompanyName,
Null) As CompanyName,
Choose([tblContacts].[DefaultAddress],[tblContacts].[WorkAddress],
[tblContacts].[HomeAddress]) AS Address,
Choose([tblContacts].[DefaultAddress],[tblContacts].[WorkCity] & ", " &
[tblContacts].[WorkStateOrProvince] & "  " & [tblContacts].[WorkPostalCode],
[tblContacts].[HomeCity] & ", " & [tblContacts].[HomeStateOrProvince]
& "  " & [tblContacts].[HomePostalCode]) AS CSZ,
tblContacts.ContactID,
Choose([tblContacts].[DefaultAddress],[tblContacts].[WorkPostalCode],
[tblContacts].[HomePostalCode]) AS Zip,
tblContacts.LastName, tblContacts.FirstName, tblContacts.ContactType,
tblContacts.WorkCity, tblContacts.WorkStateOrProvince, tblContacts.HomeCity,
tblContacts.HomeStateOrProvince, tblContacts.Inactive
FROM tblContacts
LEFT JOIN qryContactDefaultCompany
ON tblContacts.ContactID = qryContactDefaultCompany.ContactID;
```

The first SELECT statement (up to the UNION ALL) creates dummy blank columns for each field used by the report and uses the ztblLabelSpace table and a filter on the combo box in the fdlgContactPrintOptions form (Figure 20-27) to return the correct number of blank rows. The query uses a UNION with the actual query that returns contact data to display information on the report.

Because this label report prints a logo and a label control containing the return address, there's one final bit of code that keeps these from appearing on the blank labels in the rptContactLabels5163 report. The code is as follows:



```
Private Sub Detail_Format(Cancel As Integer, FormatCount As Integer)
  ' Don't print the return logo and address if this is a "spacer" record
  If IsNull(Me.ContactID) Then
    Me.imgConrad Systems.Visible = False
    Me.lblRtnAddr.Visible = False
  Else
    Me.imgConrad Systems.Visible = True
    Me.lblRtnAddr.Visible = True
  End If
End Sub
```

The Format event of the Detail section depends on the fact that the ContactID in the "spacer" rows is Null. When printing a blank row for spacing, the code hides the logo and the return address label.

## Drawing on a Report

When you want to draw a border around a report print area, sometimes you'll need to write some code to ask Access to draw lines or a border after placing the data on the page. This is especially true if one or more controls on the report can grow to accommodate a large amount of data.

We used the Report Wizard to create the basic rptContacts report using the Justified format. (We customized the report after the wizard finished.) The wizard created a fairly decent layout with a border around all the fields, but it didn't make the text box to display notes large enough to display the text for all contacts. Figure 20-29 shows you the report displaying John's contact record from the database. You can see that the notes about John are cut off at the bottom.

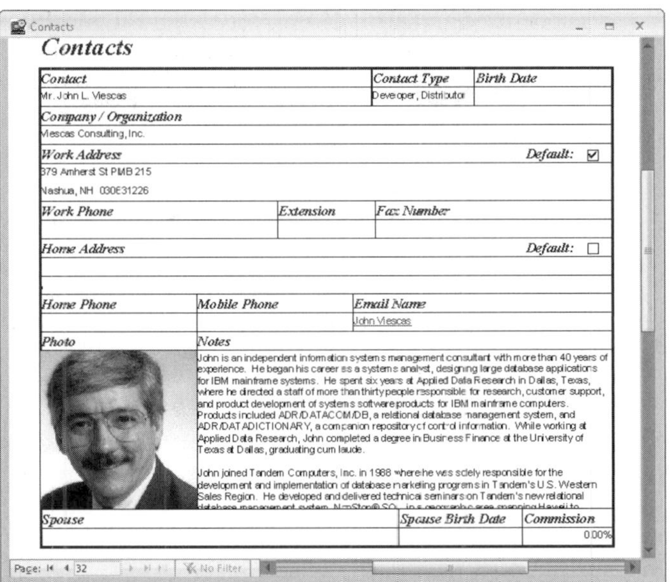


**Figure 20-29** This report uses a border around the data, but one of the text boxes isn't large enough to display all the text.

It's simple enough to change the Can Grow property of the text box to Yes to allow it to expand, but the rectangle control used to draw the border around all the text doesn't also have a Can Grow property. The solution is to remove the rectangle and use the Line method of the Report object in the report's Format event of the Detail section to get the job done. Below is the code you can find in this event procedure in the rptContacts-ExpandNotes report.

```
Private Sub Detail_Print(Cancel As Integer, PrintCount As Integer)
Dim sngX1 As Single, sngY1 As Single
Dim sngX2 As Single, sngY2 As Single, lngColor As Long
  ' Set coordinates
  sngX1 = 120
  sngY1 = 120
  sngX2 = 9120
  ' Adjust the height if Notes has expanded
  sngY2 = 7680 + (Me.Notes.Height - 2565)
  ' Draw the big box around the data
  ' Set width of the line
  Me.DrawWidth = 8
  ' Draw the rectangle around the expanded fields
  Me.Line Step(sngX1, sngY1)-Step(sngX2, sngY2), RGB(0, 0, 197), B
End Sub
```

The Line method accepts three parameters:

1. The upper-left and lower-right corners of the line or box you want to draw, expressed in *twips*. (There are 1440 twips per inch.) Include the Step keyword to indicate that the coordinates are relative to the current graphics position, which always starts at 0, 0. When you use Step for the second coordinate, you provide values relative to those you specified in the first set of coordinates.

2. The color you want to draw the line or box, expressed as a red-green-blue (RGB) value. (The RGB function is handy for this.)

3. An indicator to ask for a line, a rectangle, or a filled rectangle. No indicator draws a line. Include the letter B to ask for a rectangle. Add the letter F to ask for a filled rectangle.



Before you call the Line method, you can set the DrawWidth property of the report to set the width of the line. (The default width is in pixels.)

The only tricky part is figuring out the coordinates. On the original report, the rectangle starts at 0.0833 inch in from the left and down from the top, so multiplying that value by 1440 twips per inch gave us the starting values of 120 down from the top and 120 in from the left edge. The width of the rectangle needs to be about 6.3333 inches, so the relative coordinate for the upper-right corner is 6.3333 × 1440, or about 9,120 twips. The height of the rectangle needs to be at least 5.3333 inches, or about 7,680 twips, and the height needs to be adjusted for the amount that the Notes text box expands. The Notes text box is designed to be a minimum of 1.7813 inches high, or 2,565 twips, so subtracting 2,565 from the actual height of the Notes text box when it's formatted (the Height property is also in twips) gives you the amount you need to add to the original height of the rectangle. Trust us, we didn't get it right on the first try!

If you open the rptContactsExpandNotes report and move to John's record on page 18, you'll see that the rectangle now expands nicely to fit around the Notes text box that grew to display all the text in John's record. Figure 20-30 shows you the report with the rectangle drawn by the code behind the report.

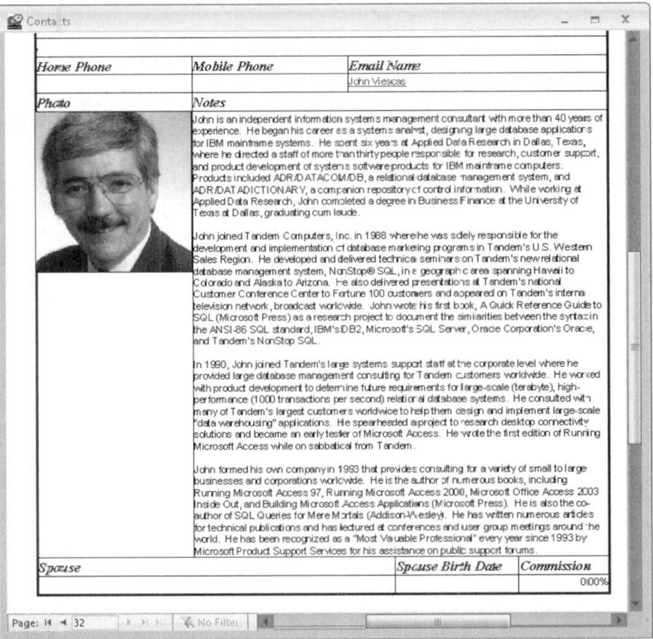


**Figure 20-30** Code in the rptContactsExpandNotes report draws a custom rectangle around expanded text.

## Dynamically Filtering a Report When It Opens

The two most common ways to open a report filtered to print specific records are

- Use the WhereCondition parameter with the DoCmd.OpenReport method (usually in code in an event procedure behind a form) to specify a filter.
- Base the report on a parameter query that prompts the user for the filter values or references control values on an open form.

In some cases, you might design a report that you intend to open from several locations in your application, and you can't guarantee that the form to provide filter values will always be open. Or, you might have multiple reports that need the same filter criteria, and you don't want to have to design a separate filter form for each report. To solve these problems, you can add code to the report to have it open its own filter dialog box from the report's Open event procedure. Let's go back to the Housing Reservations application (Housing.accdb) to take a look at a report that uses this technique.

In the Housing Reservations application, both the rptFacilityOccupancy report and the rptFacilityRevenueChart report depend on a single form, fdlgReportDateRange, to provide a starting and ending date for the report. To see the rptFacilityOccupancy report, you can start the application by opening the frmSplash form, sign on as an administrator (Conrad, Jeff, Richins, Jack S., Schare, Gary, or Viescas, John L.), click the Reports button on the main switchboard, and then click the Reservations button in the

Facilities category on the Reports switchboard. (You can also simply open the report directly from the Navigation Pane.) When you open the report, you'll see a dialog box prompting you for the dates you want as shown in Figure 20-31.

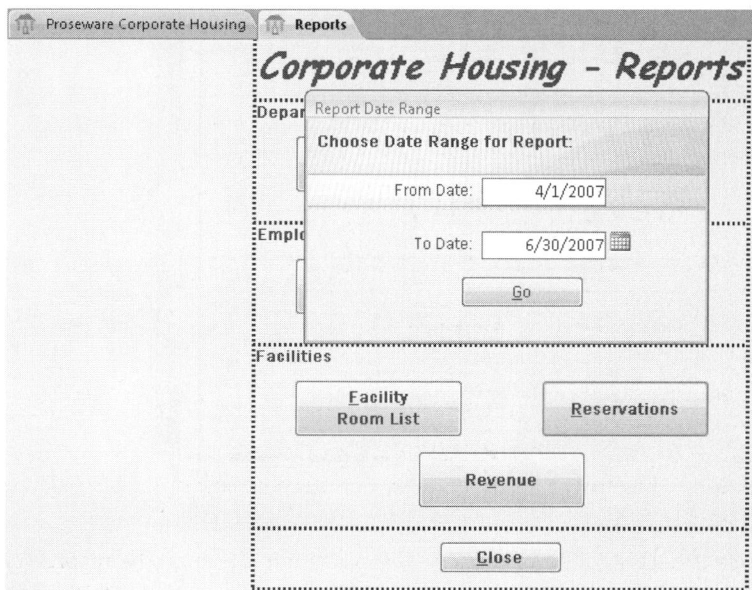


**Figure 20-31** A parameter dialog box opens from the report that you asked to view.

Unless you've reloaded the sample data, the database contains reservations from February 28, 2007 through September 26, 2007, so asking for a report for April, May, and June should work nicely. Enter the dates you want and click Go to see the report, as shown in Figure 20-32.

The report has a parameter query in its record source, and the parameters point to the from and to dates on the fdlgReportDateRange form that you see in Figure 20-31. However, the code behind the Reservations button on the Reports switchboard opens the report unfiltered. It's the code in the report's Open event procedure that opens the dialog box so that the query in the record source can find the parameters it needs. The code is as follows:

```
Private Sub Report_Open(Cancel As Integer)
  ' Open the date range dialog
  ' .. report record source is filtered on this!
  DoCmd.OpenForm "fdlgReportDateRange", WindowMode:=acDialog
End Sub
```

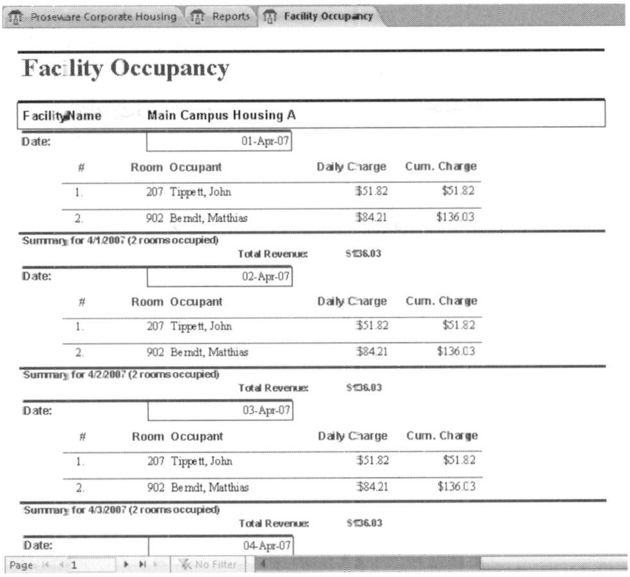

Proseware Corporate Housing | Reports | Facility Occupancy

**Facility Occupancy**

FacilityName Main Campus Housing A

Date: 01-Apr-07

| # | Room | Occupant | Daily Charge | Cum. Charge |
|---|---|---|---|---|
| 1. | 207 | Tippett, John | $51.82 | $51.82 |
| 2. | 902 | Berndt, Matthias | $84.21 | $136.03 |

Summary for 4/1/2007 (2 rooms occupied)

Total Revenue: $136.03

Date: 02-Apr-07

| # | Room | Occupant | Daily Charge | Cum. Charge |
|---|---|---|---|---|
| 1. | 207 | Tippett, John | $51.82 | $51.82 |
| 2. | 902 | Berndt, Matthias | $84.21 | $136.03 |

Summary for 4/2/2007 (2 rooms occupied)

Total Revenue: $136.03

Date: 03-Apr-07

| # | Room | Occupant | Daily Charge | Cum. Charge |
|---|---|---|---|---|
| 1. | 207 | Tippett, John | $51.82 | $51.82 |
| 2. | 902 | Berndt, Matthias | $84.21 | $136.03 |

Summary for 4/3/2007 (2 rooms occupied)

Total Revenue: $136.03

Date: 04-Apr-07

Page 1 No Filter

**Figure 20-32** The Facility Occupancy report uses a shared filter dialog box to let you specify a date range.

This works because a Report object doesn't attempt to open the record source for the report until after the code in the Open event finishes. So, you can place code in the Open event to dynamically change the record source of the report or, as in this example, open a form in Dialog mode to wait until that form closes or hides itself. The code behind the dialog form, fdlgReportDateRange, is as follows:

```
Private Sub Form_Load()
  ' If passed a parameter, reset defaults to last quarter
  If Not IsNothing(Me.OpenArgs) Then
    ' Set the start default to first day of previous quarter
    Me.txtFromDate.DefaultValue = "#" & _
      DateSerial(Year(Date), ((Month(Date) - 1) \ 3) * 3 - 2, 1) & "#"
    ' Set the end default to last day of previous quarter
    Me.txtToDate.DefaultValue = "#" & _
      DateSerial(Year(Date), ((Month(Date) - 1) \ 3) * 3 + 1, 1) & "#"
  End If
End Sub

Private Sub cmdGo_Click()
  ' Hide me so report can continue
  Me.Visible = False
End Sub
```

The code in the form's Load event checks to see if the report that is opening the form has passed a parameter in the OpenArgs property. If so, the code resets the default values for the two date text boxes to the start and end date of the previous quarter. If you look at the code behind the rptFacilityRevenueChart report, you'll find that this report

Chapter 20

asks for the different default values. But it's the code in the Click event of the Go command button that gets things rolling. The code behind the form responds to your clicking the Go button to hide itself so that the report can continue. It can't close because the record source of the report depends on the two date parameters. As noted earlier, hiding this form opened in Dialog mode allows the code in the Open event of the report to finish, which lets the report finally load its record source. As you might suspect, there's code in the Close event of the report to close the parameter form when you close the report or the report finishes printing.

As you've seen in this chapter, Visual Basic is an incredibly powerful language, and the tasks you can accomplish with it are limited only by your imagination. In the next chapter of this book, you'll learn how to set startup properties, create custom menus, and build a main switchboard form for your application.

# PART 5
# Linking Access and the Web

CHAPTER 21

# Publishing Data on the Web



The World Wide Web, built from simple low-cost servers and universal clients, has revolutionized computing. Not so long ago, the very concept of a common global information network was unthinkable. In fact, even Microsoft was unconvinced that Web technology would ever mature successfully. Originally, The Microsoft Network (MSN) was constructed with proprietary technology, modeled after similar networks such as CompuServe and Prodigy. To connect to these networks, you had to install proprietary software on your computer.

Today, the concept of living *without* the Web is just as unthinkable, and all the formerly proprietary networks (including MSN) have spent millions of dollars to convert their networks to the universal access offered by the Web. Although MSN, CompuServe (now owned by AOL), and Prodigy (owned by SBC) all still offer specialized programs that you can install to enhance your experience as a member of any of the networks, all these programs are merely customized versions of your Web browser. You can also log on to these networks with a standard Web browser.

Database applications were among the last to appear on the Web, but today they are arguably the fastest growing type of Web application. The prospect of distributing data to or collecting it from literally a world of clients, working on disparate computers and operating systems, and not requiring software distribution other than the ubiquitous browser, is simply too compelling to resist for long.

Microsoft Office Access 2007 doesn't provide a complete Web development environment. However, it does provide useful tools for developing a variety of Web database applications. This chapter explores the Web, explains how the Web capabilities of Office Access 2007 work, and provides pointers to other tools in case Access doesn't satisfy all your needs. This chapter serves as an introduction to topics that will be covered in detail in the next two chapters.

## Working with the Web

Designing and developing Web applications requires a different set of tools, a different approach, and a different mindset than performing the same tasks solely in Access. A properly designed Web application can offer significant improvements over typical desktop applications—in timeliness (frequency of update and reporting), interactivity (degree of user control), and partitioning (distributed location of application components).

With each new version of development environments, software companies provide improved tools that allow developers to more easily deliver desktop and Web solutions. Some of these tools allow developers to create desktop and Web applications that work with each other. However, there is quite a leap between desktop application development, such as Access 2007, and Web application development. Before you begin to explore ways to create Web applications, you first need to become familiar with a couple of key underlying technologies—HTML (Hypertext Markup Language) and XML (Extensible Markup Language).

## Understanding HTML

Web pages are simple text files containing a mix of textual content and codes that your browser interprets when it loads the Web page. The codes (called *tags*) that your browser understands are part of an international language specification called Hypertext Markup Language (HTML). The basic specification is documented by ISO (International Organization for Standardization) standard ISO/IEC 15445:2000. However, the standard that most software vendors implement is an enhanced version created and published by the World Wide Web Consortium (W3C), which is made up of representatives from major software vendors around the world. (You can visit the W3C Web site at *www.w3.org*.)



Actually, HTML isn't a programming language—it's a descriptive language that defines objects on your Web page. These objects can have properties, methods, and events similar to many of the objects you find in Access. You can include procedural code (known as a *script*) in your Web page definition that responds to events. The two most common scripting languages are VBScript, a second cousin to the Visual Basic you use in Access, and JavaScript, a language invented by Sun Microsystems.

Most Web page developers use an HTML editor (such as Microsoft Expression Web) to create Web pages. A good editor hides the actual coding and allows the developer to create pages—in much the same way that you create Access forms or reports—by providing a what-you-see-is-what-you-get (WYSIWYG) interface. However, most developers at one time or another must dig into the HTML to do some custom work.

INSIDE OUT **Viewing the HTML Code of a Web Page**

Most browsers can display the HTML that the browser used to create a Web page that you're viewing. In Windows Internet Explorer version 7, click Page, and then click View Source to see the code behind any Web page. When you understand the basics of HTML, this can be a fun way to discover advanced techniques.

## Introducing HTML Coding

As noted earlier, the codes in HTML that tell your browser how to format your Web page are in the form of tags. A tag begins with the < character and ends with the > character. The characters immediately following the < character identify the type of tag, and you can usually follow this tag identifier with attributes that further qualify how the tag behaves. For example, a particular type of tag might accept attributes that tell your browser what font to use or how to align the text that follows the tag.

All tags define objects on your Web page, and all Web pages begin with the <html> tag that defines the page object. Most Web page objects can contain other object definitions (for example, a table is an object, and the rows within the table are objects), and such objects require an end tag to define the end of the object. An end tag is in the form </*tagname*>, so, for example, every page ends with an </html> tag. Tags that define objects that cannot contain other objects include <br> (line break) and <img> (image), and you cannot define an end tag for these objects. Table 21-1 shows you a small subset of the HTML tags that you can use.

**Table 21-1 Common HTML Tags**

| HTML Tags | Description |
|---|---|
| <html> </html> | Designates the beginning and ending of your Web page. |
| <head> </head> | Specifies an optional heading section at the beginning of your Web page. Any text that you include in this section (with the exception of the text in a <title> tag that appears in the browser title bar—see below) does not appear on the page. In the heading section, you can define keywords for search engines and default fonts and styles to be used in the body of the page. |
| <title> </title> | Defines text that the browser displays in its title bar. You place this in the heading section. |
| <body> </body> | Designates the body section of the page. You code the majority of other tags inside the body section. |
| <script> </script> | Surrounds script language that responds to events on your page. Script languages include VBScript and JavaScript. |
| <div> </div> | Splits the page into divisions (similar to a section break in a Microsoft Office Word 2007 document) that can have different style attributes. You can optionally provide text between the begin and end tags to create a heading for the division. |
| <h1> </h1> | Surrounds a first-level heading. You can define the default attributes of headings in your heading section, or you can specify attributes for this heading following the tag name in the begin tag. |
| <h2> </h2> | Surrounds a second-level heading. |
| <p> </p> | Defines a paragraph. |
| <br> | Adds a line break. This tag does not have an end tag because you cannot define other objects inside a line break object. |

| HTML Tags | Description |
| --- | --- |
| <STRONG> </STRONG> | Formats the text between the tags with a larger font. |
| <ul> </ul> | Creates a bulleted list. Code the lines of text between these two tags. |
| <li> </li> | Defines a list item within a bulleted list. Insert the text for the line between these tags. |
| <a> </a> | Designates a hyperlink. You code the hyperlink address following the tag name inside the begin tag. Your browser displays any text or any image object you include between the begin and end tags as a hyperlink, and your browser follows the defined hyperlink when you click the text or image. You can use these tags between other tags, such as between <p> </p>, to have only a portion of the paragraph text display as a hyperlink. |
| <img> | Specifies an image object that your browser displays. You define the location of the image following the tag name inside the tag. You can surround this tag with <a> </a> to create a graphic hyperlink. Note that this tag does not have an end tag because you cannot define other objects inside an image object. |
| <table> </table> | Defines a table. Between these begin and end tags you use other tags such as <tr> </tr> (table row) to define the format of a row and <td> </td> (table data) to define the data displayed in a row. Following the tag name inside the begin tag, you can define attributes such as the width of the table, the border style, and the spacing between cells in the table. |

This is an HTML example for a very simple Web page:

```
<html>
  <head>
    <title>My Simple HTML</title>
  </head>
  <body>
    <STRONG>This is my simple page showing some simple HTML commands</STRONG>
  </body>
</html>
```

The previous HTML creates the Web page displayed in Figure 21-1.

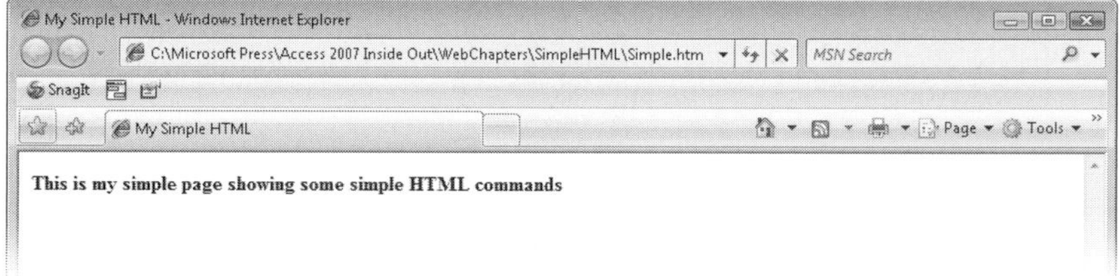


**Figure 21-1** A simple Web page is displayed in Internet Explorer.

You can find this file, called Simple.htm, on the companion CD in the WebChapters\SimpleHTML folder. You can also type the HTML commands in Notepad and save the text with the extension of .htm or .html. When you double-click the file you saved, it opens in your default browser.

INSIDE OUT **Not All Browsers Support All Tags**

The rendering of tags, members, and other features you code into your Web pages depends on which browser, such as Internet Explorer, Firefox, Opera, or Netscape, you are using to display the pages. In addition, different versions of the same browser might support different features. These limitations are known as *cross-browser issues* and can be difficult to deal with when writing advanced HTML. Writing HTML code that can be displayed on multiple browsers and platforms can be very important if you want your pages to be accessed by users all over the world. When you are creating a Web site for an intranet inside a corporation, you can usually identify which browser is the company's standard.

If you are working with an HTML editor such as Visual Studio .NET, you can look up the various tags, and in the description you can find something like the following: "This object is defined in HTML 3.2 and is defined in World Wide Web Consortium (W3C) Document Object Model (DOM) Level 1." This tells you that as long as your browser supports this version of HTML, using this tag should work. In some editors, such as Expression Web, you can specify the browser, browser version, and server type for which the editor should generate the HTML. However, when working with the simple tags mentioned here, you shouldn't have any problems with any of the browsers.



## Tag Members

As noted earlier, tags define objects on your Web page. As part of the begin tag, you can create *members*—also called *elements* (properties, methods, or events)—that let you control or further refine the object defined by the tag. Script that you write to respond to events for an object can reference members that you have defined. Table 21-2 shows you some of the member types you can define for your Web page objects.

**Table 21-2 Common HTML Object Members**

| Member | Description |
|---|---|
| Attribute/property | Like Access properties, these members describe something about the object defined by the tag. For example, a table object has *width* and *height* properties. This is the member type you are likely to use most often. |
| Behavior | Lets you specify various behaviors for the tag object. For example, in a table object, *rowover* enables alternate shading and row highlighting for table elements. |
| Collection | Every tag has at least one collection, called the *attributes* collection, which is a collection of all the members for the object defined by the tag. Additional collections depend on the object type. For example, the table object has a collection called *rows*, which is made up of the *tr* objects included in the table. |
| Event | You can include events that you want the browser to recognize, and you can write script to handle various tasks for you in response to these events. For example, the table object supports more than 50 events, including *onmouseover* and *ondblclick*. |
| Filters | Filters affect visual aspects of the object. For example, you can define a *glow* filter for the table object that sets a glow around the table. |
| Method | A *method* is an action that an object can perform, and you can write script to execute the method of the object. An example for the table object is the *focus* method, which just like an Access control's SetFocus method, causes the focus to move to the object. |
| Object | Objects can contain other objects. When an object can contain multiple instances of another object (for example, rows in a table object), those subordinate objects are in a *collection*. When an object can have only one instance of a subordinate object, that subordinate object is an *object* member. For example, most objects, including the table object, have a single *Styles* object. |
| Styles | The Styles object in HTML contains a collection of attributes that are similar to the properties you can find on the Format tab of an Access object's property sheet. For example, the table object has a Styles object that has a collection of attributes that includes *bordercolor* and *borderstyle*. You can set the style attributes either by defining them directly as attributes of the object or by setting them in the attributes collection of the Styles object. If you use the Styles object, you put a dash between the words that make up the attribute. For example, use *border-color* and *border-style* inside a Styles object. |

Now that you have a basic understanding of tags and members, let's look at some specific members of commonly used tags and then study a more complex Web page design. Table 21-3 shows you some of the members of the <a> (hyperlink), <table> (table), and <img> (image) tags.

**Table 21-3 Some Members of Commonly Used Tags**

| Tag | Member | Member Type | Description |
|---|---|---|---|
| <a> | href | Property | The URL to which you want to link. |
| | title | Property | The title of the hyperlink. Some browsers display the title as a ScreenTip for the link. |
| <table> | frame | Object | The frame around the table. |
| | border | Property | The width of the border in pixels. |
| | width | Property | The width of the table in pixels or as a percentage of the available browser window. |
| | Rows | Collection | The rows that make up the table. |
| | cellspacing | Property | The spacing between the cells in pixels. |
| | cellpadding | Property | The spacing within the cells in pixels. |
| <img> | alt | Property | A short description of the image. Most browsers display this property as a ScreenTip. |
| | src | Property | The URL of the image to display. |
| | height | Property | Overrides the defined height of the image file. |
| | width | Property | Overrides the defined width of the image file. |

You can now apply what you've learned to understanding a more complex page. The following HTML is for a page that contains a page title, two sections (<div>) with individual titles, a table in the first section that includes an image and a hyperlink, and a bulleted list in the second section:

```
<html>
  <head>
    <title>My More Complex Page</title>
  </head>
  <body>
    <div>My Favorite Types of Hotels</div>
    <table cellSpacing="1" cellPadding="1" width="300" border="1">
      <tr>
        <td width="127">Bed and Breakfasts</td>
        <td></td>
      </tr>
      <tr>
        <td width="127">Ski Lodges</td>
        <td><a href="http://www.whistlerblackcomb.com/">
        <img alt="Whistler, Canada" src=".\Images\Ski.jpg">
          </a>
        </td>
      </tr>
```

```
      <tr>
        <td width="127">Fishing Cabins</td>
        <td></td>
      </tr>
    </table>
    <br>
    <div>Features I Look For:</div>
    <ul>
      <li>
        Quiet</li>
      <li>
        Good Food</li>
      <li>
        Good Jazz Music Nearby</li>
    </ul>
  </body>
</html>
```



The previous HTML gives you the Web page displayed in Figure 21-2. Note that to display the image correctly, the Ski.jpg file must be in the Images subfolder of the location where you put your HTML.

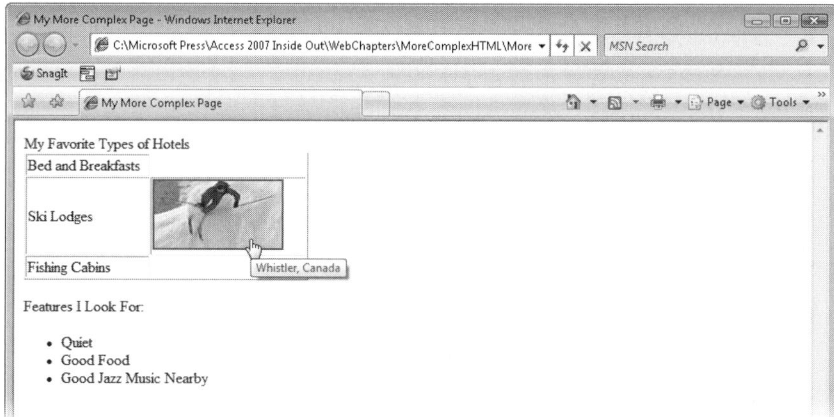


**Figure 21-2** A more complex Web page is shown with a hyperlink behind the graphic image.

You can find this file, called MoreComplexPage.htm, on the companion CD in the WebChapters\MoreComplexHTML folder.

## Editing HTML

For the two simple examples shown thus far, we typed the HTML directly into Notepad to create the page. As you can imagine, this can be a slow and tedious process for a complex Web page, especially if you are not an HTML guru. The good news: Many editors are available that create the HTML code for you. The not-so-good news: If much of your work involves creating more advanced Web pages, you are going to have to learn HTML coding.

When you first start creating Web pages, you may dread having to work in HTML. But as you become more proficient at it, you'll enjoy seeing your browser convert your code into a Web page. However, if you can use an editor such as Expression Web to create the HTML for you, all the better. You can see an example of working with HTML using Expression Web in Figure 21-3. Expression Web lets you see both the HTML and the graphical Design view of the page at the same time. Notice that Expression Web highlights the HTML code that generates the object selected in Design view.

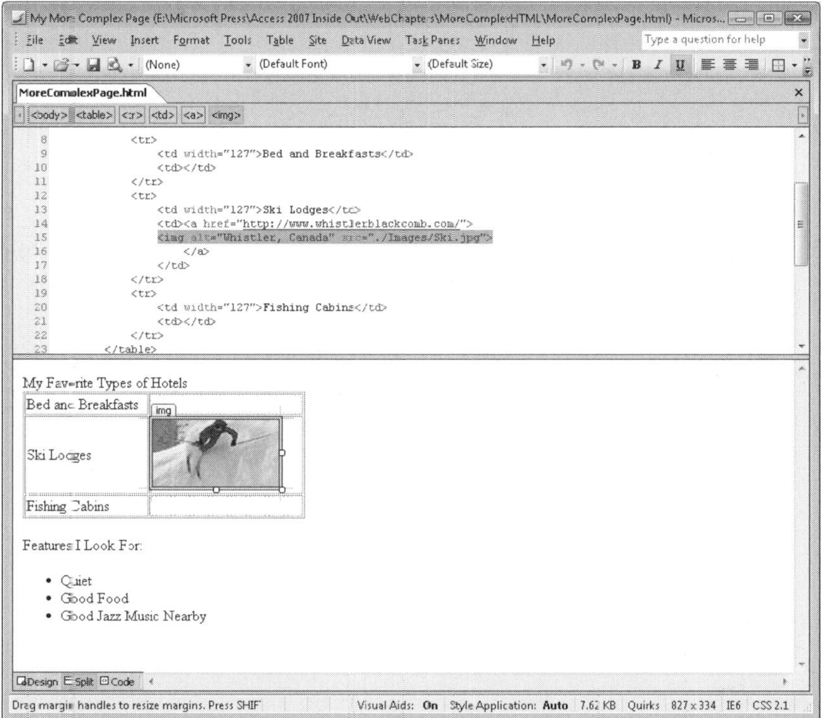


**Figure 21-3** The HTML view in Expression Web allows you to see the results of your code while editing the HTML.

For details about creating a simple HTML page from Access 2007, see "Creating a Static HTML Document" on page 1140.

# Introducing XML

With all the businesses that are accessing the Web and using software to connect to each other and exchange data, a standard way of describing the data and its structure is necessary to allow these systems to understand the data. That standard is XML (Extensible Markup Language). As with HTML, the current XML standard is based on an ISO standard, but the most commonly used version is the one maintained and published by W3C. Where HTML deals with presentation, XML deals with data. Because a file in XML format contains not only the data but also a description of the structure of the data, receiving systems know exactly how to process the data from the information included in the file.

For example, an insurance company might receive data from an outside company that manages some of its insurance claims. The insurance company needs to know which fields the file includes, the data type of the fields, and the order in which the fields occur in the data file. If the file is coded in XML, the company can easily import this file into Access or any other program that understands XML, even if the sending company changes the format or content of the file. With other file types, such as fixed-width text files, you must know the file format so that you can define the import/export specification for Access before you attempt to import the file.

One of the major features in Access 2007 is the ability to work with data published using the latest XML standards. Access 2007 can easily import and export XML files and related style sheets. You can see an example of a file imported as XML and displayed in a datasheet subform in Figure 21-4.



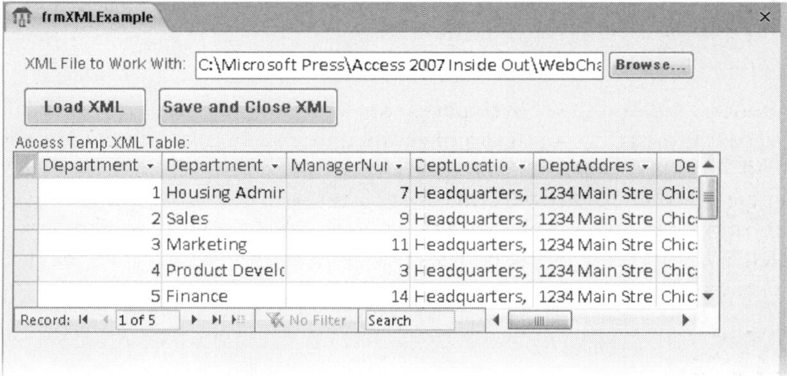


**Figure 21-4** You can load, edit, and save XML files using Access 2007.

You can find this form saved as frmXMLExample in the Housing.accdb sample database. When you first open the form, the subform window is blank. You can enter the location of any XML file in the XML File To Work With box or click the Browse button to locate an XML file on your computer. You can also use the XMLDepartments.xml file that you'll find in the WebChapters\XML folder on the companion CD. Click the Load XML button to import the file into a local table and display it in the subform window. You can actually change any of the data that you see in the subform window and then click the Save And Close XML button to write the changes back to the XML file that you imported.

When Access imports the XML file, it builds the definition of the table fields from the information in the file and then loads the data. Code behind the form then loads the table into the subform control so that you can edit it. No fancy code is required to decipher what's in the file.

Microsoft has enhanced the XML capabilities in all components of the 2007 Microsoft Office system. When you create custom Ribbons in Access 2007, you use XML to build the various tabs, groups, and other Ribbon elements. The Microsoft Internet development architecture, .NET (pronounced *dot net*), depends heavily on XML. The Internet development platform, Visual Studio .NET, makes extensive use of XML in its ADO.NET data model and manages some of its system features using XML.

With XML growing in use, does this mean you have to become an XML guru? The answer is no, but it's a good idea to know how and where you can use it. You'll learn additional details about working with XML in Chapter 23, "Using XML," and in Chapter 24, "The Finishing Touches."

# Understanding Static Web Pages

The Web pages you've seen thus far in this chapter are *static*—after you publish a page like these to a Web server, the information doesn't change until you replace or edit the text. Actually, static Web pages are the most common type of page you'll find on any noncommercial site on the Web. All the pages at the W3C Web site (*www.w3.org*) and all the pages on John's Web site (*www.viescas.com*) are static. So, you won't see any new information on John's Web site unless he edits and updates the pages.

To understand how static Web pages work (and the way the Web works in general), you need to know a bit about the architecture of the Web. Like all network applications, the World Wide Web defines two roles computers can play: client or server. (Sometimes, a single computer can serve both roles.) The client software, called a *browser*, requests files from the server and displays them on the client computer. The server software, called a *Web server*, accepts requests from browsers and transmits the requested files to the browser. Figure 21-5 provides a highly simplified diagram of these components.

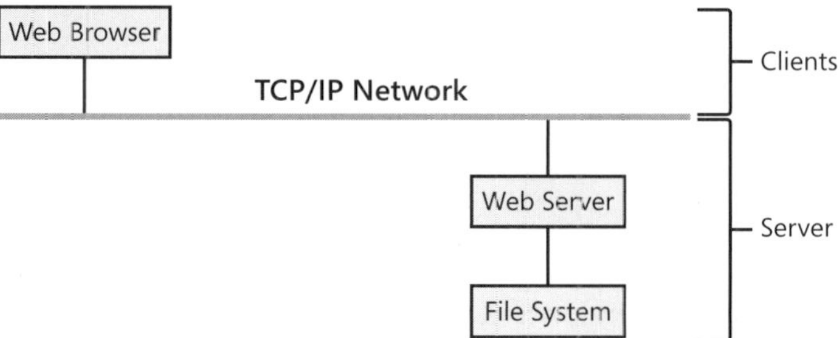


**Figure 21-5** On the World Wide Web, Web browsers connect to Web servers using TCP/IP.

> **Note**
>
> TCP/IP stands for Transmission Control Protocol/Internet Protocol. TCP describes the way computers on Internet-style networks can exchange data without loss. IP describes the identification scheme for computers on Internet-style networks.

INSIDE OUT **What Is a Protocol?**

When you connect your computer to a network, the communications software on each computer must send and receive information in a format that all the computers understand. Think of a computer network as a railway system. If one station can handle boxcars but not hopper cars, any other station that sends cargo to that station must send boxcars only. Similarly, a network protocol defines a specific type of data packaging that can be sent over your network "rails."

In early Microsoft Windows–based systems, Microsoft packaged the data using a protocol called NetBEUI. Systems networked using Novell Netware used a protocol called IPX/SPX. The World Wide Web standardized on the TCP/IP protocol. Today, most computers include software to support multiple protocols so that you can be connected to a local network using IPX/SPX, NetBEUI, or TCP/IP and also to the World Wide Web using TCP/IP.

TCP/IP is a transport protocol that defines the general packaging of the messages sent over the network. What your computer sends within the packaging parameters of a protocol depends on the applications sending and receiving the information—the application protocol. (To continue our train analogy, what kind of boxes inside the boxcar is the stationmaster on the other end prepared to unlock?) When you copy a file to a local server using Windows Explorer, Windows Explorer packages your file information in a format the receiving file system understands. Windows then wraps these packages in an available transport protocol for sending over the network.

When you work on a Web-based network (such as the World Wide Web), your browser uses standardized application protocols to send and receive information. Two of the most common Web protocols are Hypertext Transport Protocol (HTTP) for transmitting information such as Web pages and pictures and File Transfer Protocol (FTP) for uploading and downloading files.

The key to the explosive success of the World Wide Web is the broad acceptance and adoption of the transport protocol, application protocols, and page definition standard (HTML) by virtually every computer and software manufacturer. These common standards let you point your Web browser at a Web server halfway around the world to send and receive information. You don't have to worry or care about what kind of computer or operating system is installed for the Web server. For the most part, the folks who program the Web server don't have to worry about what kind of computer you're using or what Web browser you have installed.

When you publish a static page on a Web server, that server stores your text in its file system. When a browser on a client sends a request for the page to the server, the server reads the file from its file system and sends it unmodified to the client browser. To change what the server sends, you must change the text file stored in the server's file system. If the static page contains hyperlinks or script that responds to events defined on the page, it's the browser on the requesting client computer that interprets what should happen next, and it executes any script on the client computer.

What can you do if your static Web page contains a table with data generated from a database? If the data in the database is reasonably static (for example, a membership name and address list that you update once a month), it doesn't really matter that your Web page displays a static copy of data from the table. Access can make the periodic update of your Web page easy because it provides an export facility that allows you to save the data from a table, query, form, or report as an HTML table.

Of course, if you need your Web pages to display up-to-the-minute information from active database tables, static Web pages won't do at all. To solve this problem, you need to define a Web page that can dynamically fetch the latest information, format it as HTML, and send it to the requesting browser. See "Creating Dynamic Web Pages" on page 1158 to find additional information for creating dynamic Web pages from data in an Access database.

# Viewing Static HTML Pages



Figure 21-6 shows a simple HTML Web page created as a menu to allow you to link to other pages on the Web site to view reservations and requests. We used Expression Web to create the page and then added two buttons to go to the related pages. We also applied one of the simple Expression Web themes to the page. We asked Expression Web to create the hyperlinks behind the two buttons as relative links to files in the same folder, so the three pages should work together no matter where you publish them as long as all three are in the same folder. (You can find this example page saved as menu.htm in the WebChapters\StaticHTML folder on the companion CD.)

**Note**

The examples in the remainder of this chapter are based on the tables and data in the Housing Reservations database (Housing.accdb). You can find the sample Web pages in the \WebChapters\StaticHTML folder on your companion CD.

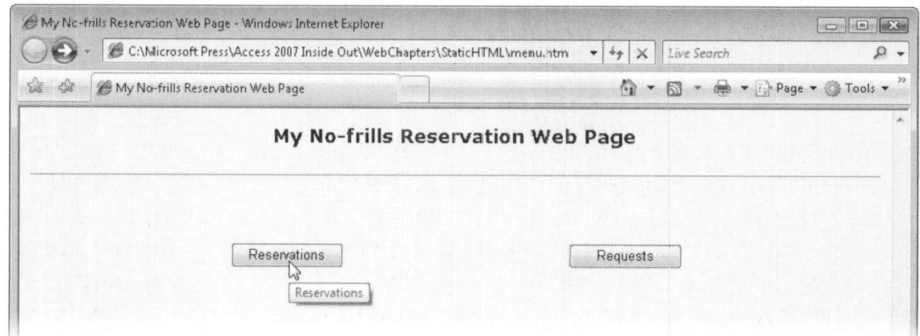


**Figure 21-6** You can create a simple HTML menu page easily using Expression Web.

If you open the simple menu page in your browser and click the Reservations button, you'll see the data from the tblReservations table in the Housing Reservations database, as shown in Figure 21-7. We created this page by exporting the tblReservations table from Access as an HTML file. To move back to the menu Web page, click the Back button of your browser.

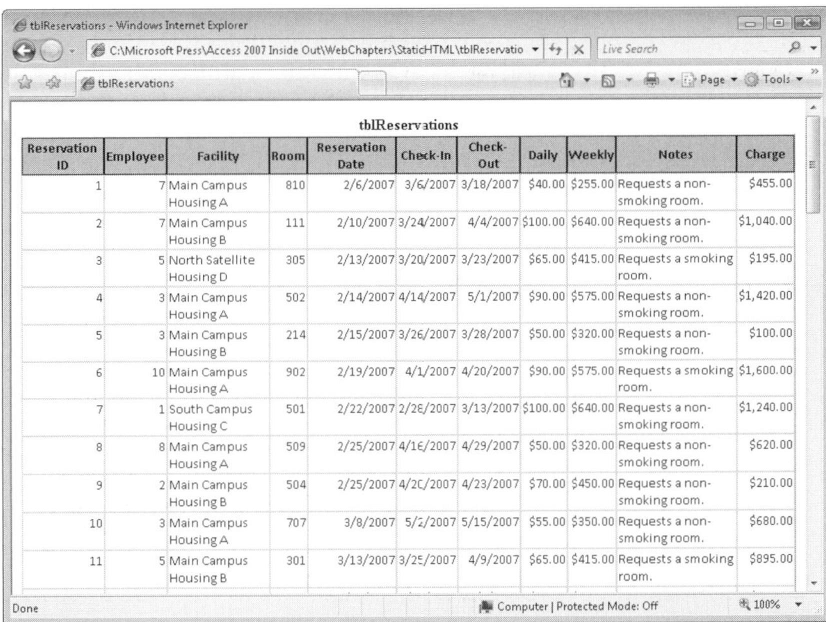


tblReservations

| Reservation ID | Employee | Facility | Room | Reservation Date | Check-In | Check-Out | Daily | Weekly | Notes | Charge |
|---|---|---|---|---|---|---|---|---|---|---|
| 1 | 7 | Main Campus Housing A | 810 | 2/6/2007 | 3/6/2007 | 3/18/2007 | $40.00 | $255.00 | Requests a non-smoking room. | $455.00 |
| 2 | 7 | Main Campus Housing B | 111 | 2/10/2007 | 3/24/2007 | 4/4/2007 | $100.00 | $640.00 | Requests a non-smoking room. | $1,040.00 |
| 3 | 5 | North Satellite Housing D | 305 | 2/13/2007 | 3/20/2007 | 3/23/2007 | $65.00 | $415.00 | Requests a smoking room. | $195.00 |
| 4 | 3 | Main Campus Housing A | 502 | 2/14/2007 | 4/14/2007 | 5/1/2007 | $90.00 | $575.00 | Requests a non-smoking room. | $1,420.00 |
| 5 | 3 | Main Campus Housing B | 214 | 2/15/2007 | 3/26/2007 | 3/28/2007 | $50.00 | $320.00 | Requests a non-smoking room. | $100.00 |
| 6 | 10 | Main Campus Housing A | 902 | 2/19/2007 | 4/1/2007 | 4/20/2007 | $90.00 | $575.00 | Requests a smoking room. | $1,600.00 |
| 7 | 1 | South Campus Housing C | 501 | 2/22/2007 | 2/28/2007 | 3/13/2007 | $100.00 | $640.00 | Requests a non-smoking room. | $1,240.00 |
| 8 | 8 | Main Campus Housing A | 509 | 2/25/2007 | 4/16/2007 | 4/29/2007 | $50.00 | $320.00 | Requests a non-smoking room. | $620.00 |
| 9 | 2 | Main Campus Housing B | 504 | 2/25/2007 | 4/20/2007 | 4/23/2007 | $70.00 | $450.00 | Requests a non-smoking room. | $210.00 |
| 10 | 3 | Main Campus Housing A | 707 | 3/8/2007 | 5/2/2007 | 5/15/2007 | $55.00 | $350.00 | Requests a non-smoking room. | $680.00 |
| 11 | 5 | Main Campus Housing B | 301 | 3/13/2007 | 3/25/2007 | 4/9/2007 | $65.00 | $415.00 | Requests a smoking room. | $895.00 |

**Figure 21-7** This simple Web site displays data exported from an Access table.

# Creating a Static HTML Document

When you want to make relatively static data available in a Web page, you can export your data in HTML format. The Web page that you create in this way won't allow users to update the data, and your users will have limited search capabilities. However, you can create automated procedures in your application that make it easy to periodically update the Web page to ensure that it is current.

The simplest way to publish data from your database to a Web page is to export the data as a simple, *static* HTML file. This type of file presents a snapshot of your data at the time you create the HTML file. To refresh the data on your Web page, you'll have to repeat the export process each time you want to present fresh data. You can use the export tools in Access to export data from a table, query, form, or report, but this has some limitations. Table 21-4 lists these objects and the options you have when you export them to HTML.

Table 21-4 **Options for Exporting Access Objects to HTML**

| Object | Data Exported | Comments |
|---|---|---|
| Table | Table datasheet | Access attempts to duplicate any formatting that you have applied to the datasheet (font, gridlines). You can also specify a template file to enhance the final output. The table name appears as a caption in the exported HTML table. |
| Query | Query datasheet | Same as a table. When you export a parameter query, Access prompts you for the parameters and exports the result of fetching the data after resolving the parameter values. |
| Form | The recordset for the outer form | Same as a table except you control formatting by setting the format of the form's Datasheet view. Access will not export data in any subform. |
| Report | The data displayed in the report | Access attempts to duplicate the format of the report but does not output any line or rectangle controls. Access also exports any data in any subreport. Access exports the report one page at a time. It assigns the file name you specify for the first page and appends *PageN* (where *N* is the subsequent page number) for the second through last pages. You can specify a template file to enhance the overall appearance of the exported pages. You can include information in the template to ask Access to generate links to the various pages of the report. |



The procedure to export to HTML is very similar for all object types. In the Navigation Pane, select the object you want to export, click the More button in the Export group on the External Data tab, and then click HTML Document. You can also right-click the object, click Export on the shortcut menu, and then click HTML Document on the submenu. For this example, open the Housing Reservations database (Housing.accdb), select tblDepartments in the Navigation Pane, click the More button in the Export group on the External Data tab, and then click HTML Document. Access displays the Export–HTML Document dialog box, as shown in Figure 21-8.

In the File Name box you can enter the location of where you want to save the exported HTML document. Click Browse to open the Windows File Save dialog box, browse to a specific folder to which you want to save the HTML document, and then click Save. (You can find the sample static HTML files installed from the companion CD in the \WebChapters\StaticHTML subfolder, as shown in Figure 21-8.) If you select the Export Data With Formatting And Layout check box, Access attempts to preserve any formatting you might have applied to the data. Be sure to leave this check box cleared for this example. The object here is to discover the simple format that Access uses to export to HTML.

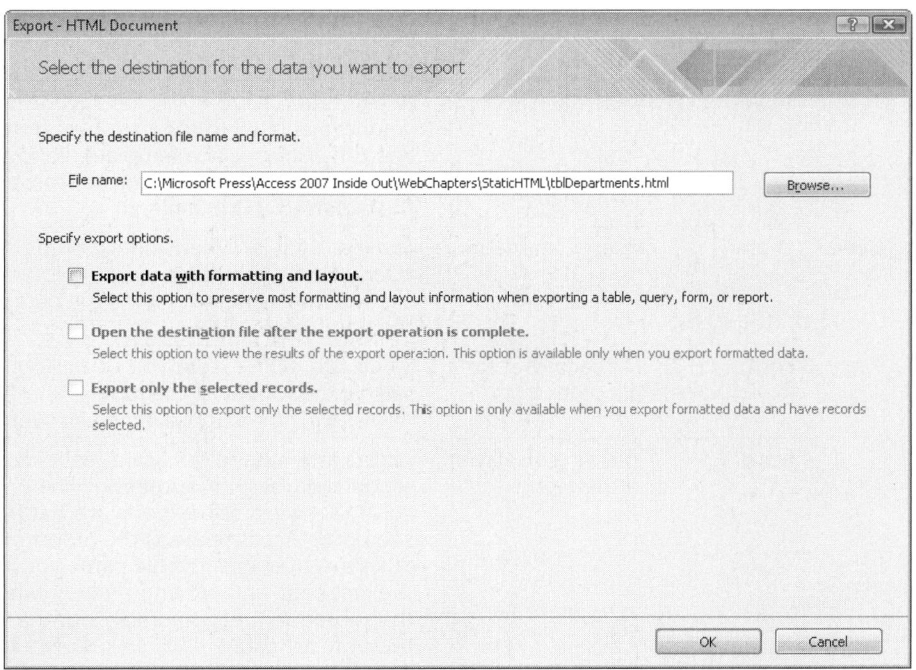


**Figure 21-8** You can export the data in an Access table as simple HTML using the Export–HTML Document dialog box.

The Export – HTML Document dialog box has two additional check boxes: Open The Destination File After The Export Operation Is Complete and Export Only The Selected Records. If you select the Export Data With Formatting And Layout check box (which we'll explore later in this chapter), Access lets you select the Open The Destination File After The Export Operation Is Complete check box. This option tells Access to open the HTML document in your default Web browser as soon as the export procedure is completed. The Export Only The Selected Records check box is available only when you have a table, query, or form open; have selected a subset of the records; and have also selected the Export Data With Formatting And Layout check box. When you select only a few of the records in a table or query and then select this check box, Access exports only the selected records. If you leave this check box cleared, Access exports all the records in the table or query, even if you selected only a few of the records.

Click OK to complete the creation of your Web page. Access displays a confirmation message in the Export – HTML Document dialog box if the export is successful. If the export fails for any reason, Access displays an error message describing the problem. Access also offers you the opportunity to save these export steps if you plan to execute them frequently. Click Close to close the dialog box, open Windows Explorer, find the page you just created, and double-click the file to open it in your Web browser. Your result should look like Figure 21-9.

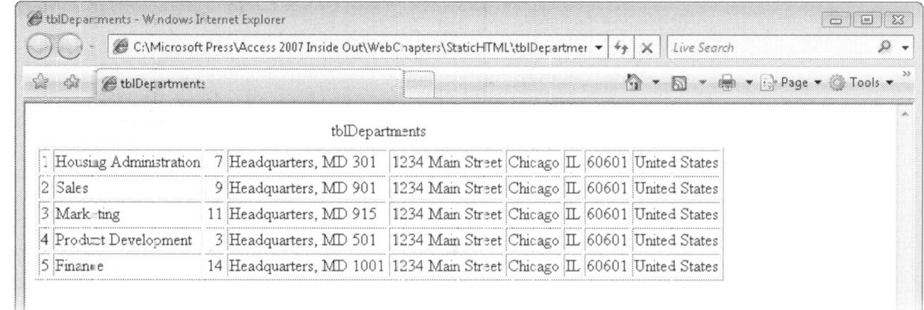


| | | | | | | | | |
|---|---|---|---|---|---|---|---|---|
| 1 | Housing Administration | 7 | Headquarters, MD 301 | 1234 Main Street | Chicago | IL | 60601 | United States |
| 2 | Sales | 9 | Headquarters, MD 901 | 1234 Main Street | Chicago | IL | 60601 | United States |
| 3 | Marketing | 11 | Headquarters, MD 915 | 1234 Main Street | Chicago | IL | 60601 | United States |
| 4 | Product Development | 3 | Headquarters, MD 501 | 1234 Main Street | Chicago | IL | 60601 | United States |
| 5 | Finance | 14 | Headquarters, MD 1001 | 1234 Main Street | Chicago | IL | 60601 | United States |

**Figure 21-9** This is data from the tblDepartments table exported to HTML using a simple format.

Not very attractive, is it? Access doesn't even provide column headings. You could certainly open this page in an HTML editor and improve it, but you have additional options in Access to minimize the work needed to make this Web page more attractive. (You can find this page saved as tblDepartmentsPlain.html in the \WebChapters\StaticHTML folder on your companion CD.)

## Improving the Look of Exported Data in HTML

Creating more attractive HTML output from Access isn't difficult. You can customize the Datasheet view of your output source to specify a font and the appearance of the gridlines in the resulting HTML table. You can also create a template file that Access can use to make the resulting HTML more appealing.

### Customizing Datasheet View

You can change the default settings for all datasheets in the Access Options dialog box. You can also customize the Datasheet view of any individual table, query, or form. To change settings for all datasheets, start by opening the Housing Reservations sample database, click the Microsoft Office Button, click Access Options, and then click the Datasheet category. You can see that you have several formatting options for datasheets, as shown in Figure 21-10.

**CAUTION!**

Keep in mind that any setting that you change in the Access Options dialog box affects the look of all datasheets in any database on your computer. However, temporarily choosing custom settings in this dialog box might be a good option when you want to export several datasheets and do not want to change the settings for the individual objects.

Chapter 21

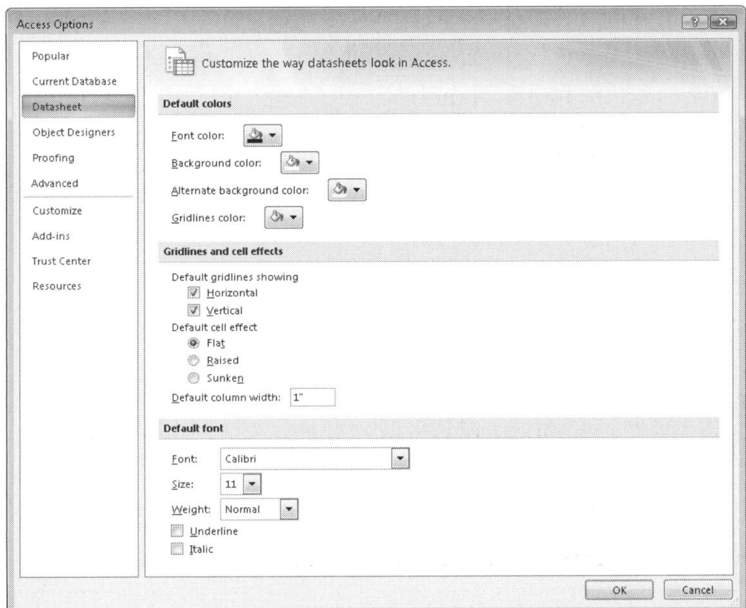


**Figure 21-10** You can change settings that affect all datasheets using the options in the Access Options dialog box.

Under Default Colors, you can choose from a palette of Access theme colors and standard colors, or you can customize your own colors for Font, Background, Alternate Background, and Gridlines. Be careful to not choose the same color for the font as for the background—the data won't be visible in the output table.

In the Default Gridlines Showing section under Gridlines And Cell Effects, you can specify whether you want Horizontal or Vertical or both gridlines displayed. Setting the Default Cell Effect changes the look of the cells in the HTML table. When you choose Raised or Sunken, Access ignores the settings for Background and Gridlines under Default Colors and ignores the Horizontal and Vertical settings under Default Gridlines Showing. When you choose Raised, Access uses Silver as the background color and Gray as the gridline color. For Sunken, Access also uses Silver as the background color and uses White for the gridlines. When you choose Raised or Sunken, be careful not to choose Silver as the color for the font because Silver is the background color. Although you can specify a default column width under Gridlines And Cell Effects, changing this setting does not affect the column widths in the HTML output. (Changing this setting does affect all datasheets that you open within Access.) Access creates the HTML table so that the column widths and heights adjust to display all the data within the width of the browser window.

Finally, under Default Font, you can choose the font name; the size; the weight (Thin, Extra Light, Light, Normal, Medium, Semi-Bold, Bold, Extra Bold, and Heavy); and whether you want the font underlined, italic, or both. The choices for Weight vary depending on the particular font you select. Keep in mind that the font you choose must also be available on the user's computer. Typical fonts on most Windows systems include Arial, Comic Sans, Courier New, Georgia, Modern, MS Sans Serif, MS Serif, Tahoma, Times New Roman, and Verdana.

If you want to set the format of the datasheet for an individual table, query, or form, you must first open the object in Datasheet view. Open the qryFacilities query in the Housing Reservations database in Datasheet view, as shown in Figure 21-11. (The query sorts by facility name.) We changed the font, font color, alternating row color, and gridlines.

**Figure 21-11** You can customize the format of an individual query in Datasheet view.



To change the font settings for this query's datasheet, use the options available in the Font group on the Home tab. You can enter the name of the font and select the style that you want—bold, italics, or underline. (Clicking the Underline button draws a line under all characters in both the column headings and the data.) You can also enter a font size or choose a size from the drop-down list. Choose a color for the font from the drop-down color palette, but be sure that you do not select a color that is the same as the background of the grid.

To see the other settings that affect the format of the datasheet, click the Datasheet Formatting Dialog Box Launcher button in the lower-right corner of the Font group on the Home tab, as shown in Figure 21-12.

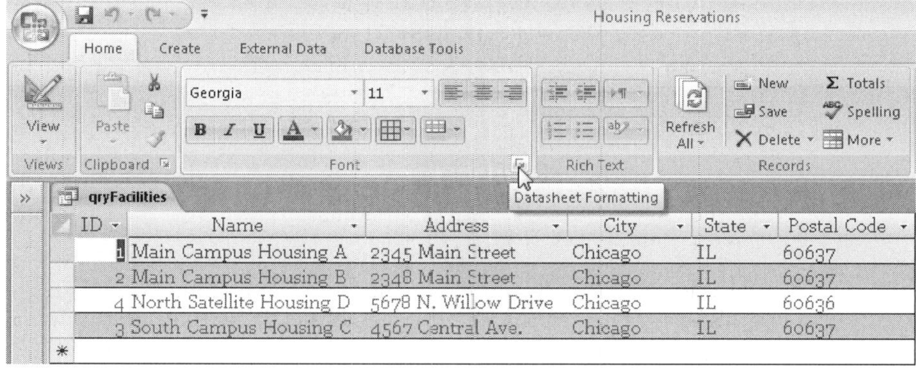


**Figure 21-12** To see additional formatting options, click the Datasheet Formatting Dialog Box Launcher button.

Access displays the Datasheet Formatting dialog box, as shown in Figure 21-13.

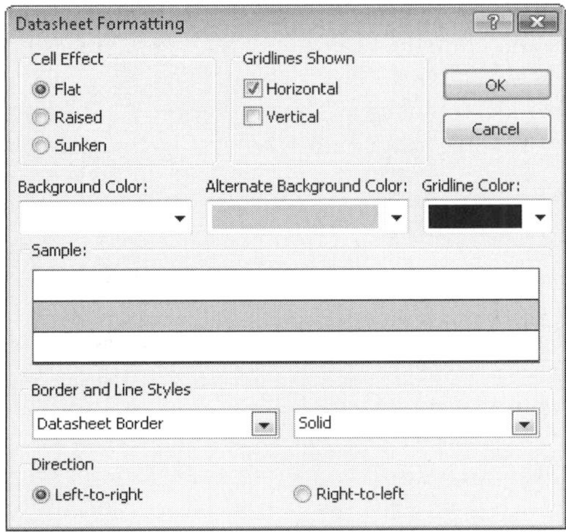


**Figure 21-13** Use the Datasheet Formatting dialog box to specify settings for a specific datasheet.

You can choose a cell effect exactly as you can in the Access Options dialog box. However, in this dialog box when you choose Raised or Sunken, Access disables the choices for Gridlines Shown. Access does change the background color, alternate background color, and gridline color to reflect the colors that it uses when you choose one of the two special effects. Although you can change settings under Border And Line Styles to affect the look of the datasheet in Access, you'll see only solid lines in the resulting HTML. If you want to see how these settings affect the datasheet in Access, select Flat under Cell Effect, select either the Horizontal or Vertical check box (or both) under Gridlines Shown, select Datasheet Border or Column Header Underline in the left combo box under Border And Line Styles, and then choose a setting in the right combo box. Choices in the right combo box include Transparent Border, Solid, Dashes, Short Dashes, Dots, Sparse Dots, Dash-Dot, Dash-Dot-Dot, and Double Solid.

When you have finished changing formatting settings, click OK, click the Save button on the Quick Access Toolbar, and then close the query. If you don't want to save your changes, close the Datasheet view, and reply No when Access asks you whether you want to save the layout changes.

After you set the options you want (either in the Access Options dialog box for all datasheets or in the Font group and Datasheet Formatting dialog box for an individual datasheet), you're ready to export the results with formatting applied. For this example, select the qryFacilities query in the Navigation Pane, click the More button in the Export group on the External Data tab, and then click HTML Document. Access opens the Export – HTML Document dialog box, as shown in Figure 21-14.

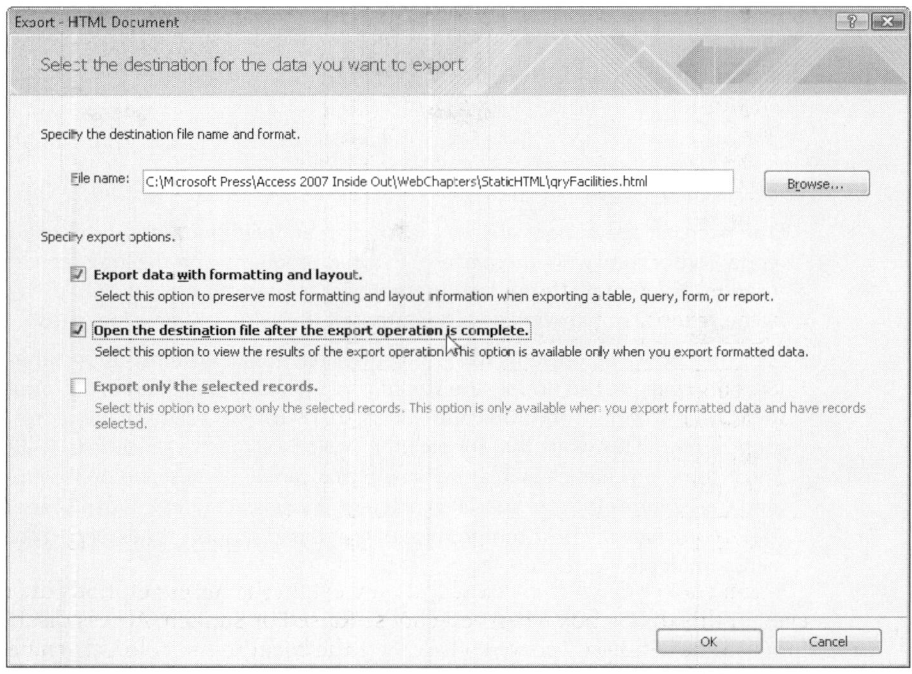


**Figure 21-14** You can export a query to HTML and preserve its formatting.

Be sure to select the Export Data With Formatting And Layout check box so that Access knows to honor the formatting of the query's datasheet. Also select the Open The Destination File After The Export Operation Is Complete check box–Access will open the HTML file in your browser as soon as it completes the export. Click OK, and Access displays the HTML Output Options dialog box, as shown in Figure 21-15.

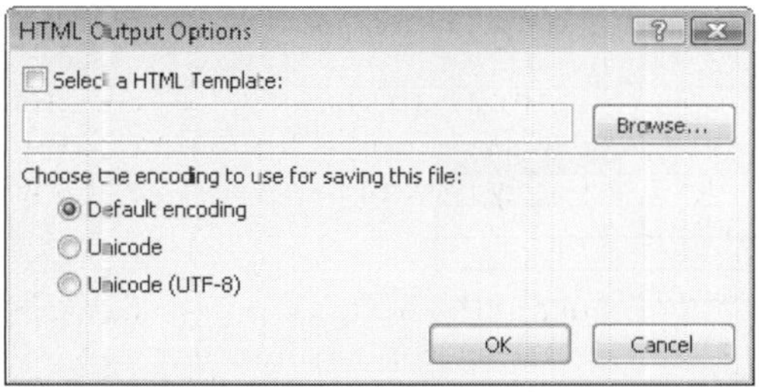

**Figure 21-15** You can choose to use an existing HTML template in the HTML Output Options dialog box.

In this dialog box, you can also select an HTML template file to further customize the output. You'll learn how to create and use a template file that includes special embedded codes that Access understands in the next section. For now, leave the Select A HTML Template check box clear. You can also select the character encoding that you want Access to use for the file. In most cases, the Default Encoding option (Windows) works just fine. If your data contains unusual characters (for example, the Swedish character å) and your Web page might be viewed on non-Windows computers, you should choose Unicode or Unicode (UTF-8).

> **What Is Unicode?**
>
> The two Unicode options are a result of international standards established by the Unicode Consortium (*www.unicode.org*) to avoid problems with the internal numeric code used by different platforms to represent special characters. For example, the character å is the value 229 on a Windows computer but the value 140 on a Macintosh.
>
> Unicode, however, presents two problems. First, not all systems support the standard. Second, Unicode can double the size of your HTML file, resulting in performance problems over slow networks. Unicode (which is UTF-16) is a 2-byte character set that is recognized by all browsers that support the Unicode standard. Unicode (UTF-8) supports most common characters in a single byte that can be understood by most platforms and uses 2 bytes to store special characters. If your data does contain special characters, UTF-8 provides the best compromise of speed and support for extended character sets across multiple platforms.



Click OK to complete the export of the query. When the export is finished, Access starts your browser and shows you the result that you can see in Figure 21-16. You can see that because you asked Access to export the data with formatting, the table now has column headings and is using the font and gridlines specified for the query datasheet. You can find this sample page saved as qryFacilitiesCustomDS.html. (After you return to the Access window, close the Export – HTML Document dialog box.)

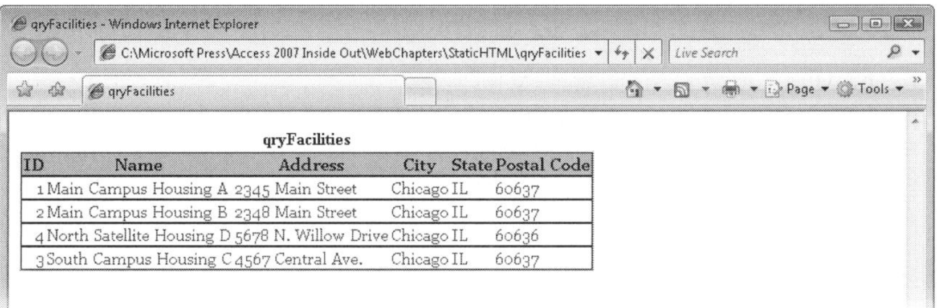


**Figure 21-16** The HTML page shows the formatted query you exported.

## Designing and Using HTML Output Templates

When you take the time to format a table, query, or form datasheet before you export it to HTML, you can see that the result is superior to the default export format. You can take this one step further by defining a template HTML file and asking Access to apply the template when it exports your data. In fact, creating a template is a good way to establish a common design for all your Web pages. Not only can you use a template to improve the appearance of data you export from Access, you can also use the same template to apply a common design to Web pages that you create from many HTML editors.

You can embed special comments in your template file (called *tokens*) that Access uses to place certain key elements in the final page. Table 21-5 lists the tokens and how Access uses them.

**Table 21-5 HTML Template Tokens Recognized by Access**

| Token | Meaning |
|---|---|
| <!--AccessTemplate_Title--> | Inserts the name of the table, query, or form, or the contents of the Caption property of the report in place of this token. |
| <!--AccessTemplate_Body--> | Inserts the exported data as an HTML table at this location. |
| <!--AccessTemplate_FirstPage--> | When you are exporting a report, places a hyperlink to the first page of the report at this location. |
| <!--AccessTemplate_PreviousPage--> | When you are exporting a report, places a hyperlink to the previous page of the report at this location. |
| <!--AccessTemplate_NextPage--> | When you are exporting a report, places a hyperlink to the next page of the report at this location. |
| <!--AccessTemplate_LastPage--> | When you are exporting a report, places a hyperlink to the last page of the report at this location. |
| <!--AccessTemplate_PageNumber--> | When you are exporting a report, places the page number at this location. |

In the \WebChapters\StaticHTML folder on your companion CD, you can find two template files. The first one, StaticTemplate.htm, does not include any of the special report tokens, so it is more suitable for exporting the datasheet of a table, query, or form. The contents of the template are as follows:

```
<html>
<head>
<title><!--ACCESSTEMPLATE_TITLE--></title>
</head>
<body leftmargin="50" background="sumiback.jpg">
<font face="Verdana" size="4" color="#333399"> <STRONG>Housing Reservation System
</STRONG></font><p>
<img src="housing.jpg" width="241" height="124">
<!--ACCESSTEMPLATE_BODY--><br>
</p>
</body>
</html>
```

The template isn't very complex, but it does specify a background graphic for the page, a heading, and an embedded JPEG file. You can see that the template places the name of the output object in the browser title bar and asks Access to insert the table results following the graphic image.

To see how this works, you can export the qryFacilityRooms query from the Housing Reservations database. We saved the query datasheet using a purple Verdana font and vertical gridlines only. Select this query in the Navigation Pane, click the More button in the Export group on the External Data tab, and then click HTML Document to open the Export – HTML Document dialog box. Click the Browse button, and navigate to the WebChapters\StaticHTML folder in the File Save dialog box. Enter **qryFacilityRooms.html** in the File Name box (Access should fill this in for you), and then click Save to return to the Export – HTML Document dialog box. Select the Export Data With Formatting And Layout check box, select the Open The Destination File After The Export Operation Is Complete check box, and then click OK. In the HTML Output Options dialog box, select the Select A HTML Template check box. Click the Browse button, find the StaticTemplate.htm file in the \WebChapters\StaticHTML folder, and then click OK. The HTML Output Options dialog box should look like Figure 21-17. Notice that the dialog box disables the encoding options when you choose the option to use a template—the encoding for your final page will be inherited from the template.



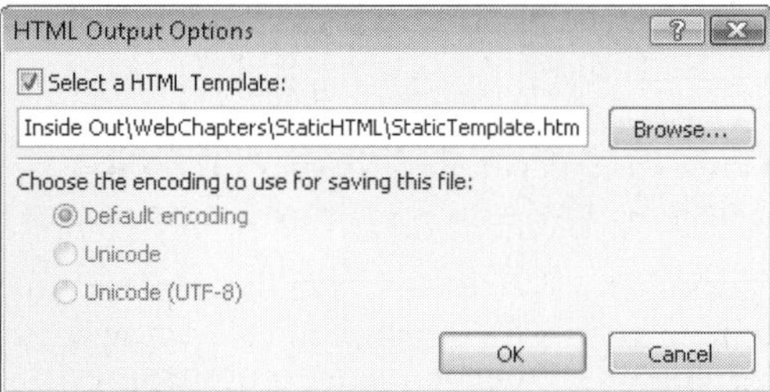


**Figure 21-17** You can specify to use a custom template when you export data to HTML.

Click OK to finish the export. Access displays the result in your browser window, as shown in Figure 21-18. You can find this Web page saved as qryFacilityRoomsCustomDSTemplate.html on the companion CD.

## TROUBLESHOOTING

### I don't see the graphic or the background on my sample page. What am I doing wrong?

Take another look at the HTML for the template file. The file specifies a background using the sumiback.jpg file. It also references the housing.jpg file to be displayed as an image. When you include file references like these in your HTML and you do not include a relative path from the current location of the Web page, your browser expects to find the files in the same folder as the Web page. If you saved your sample file to a folder other than the \WebPages\StaticHTML folder, you won't see the graphics unless you copy the two files to the folder where you saved the sample file. Copy the two files, and try opening the Web page again.

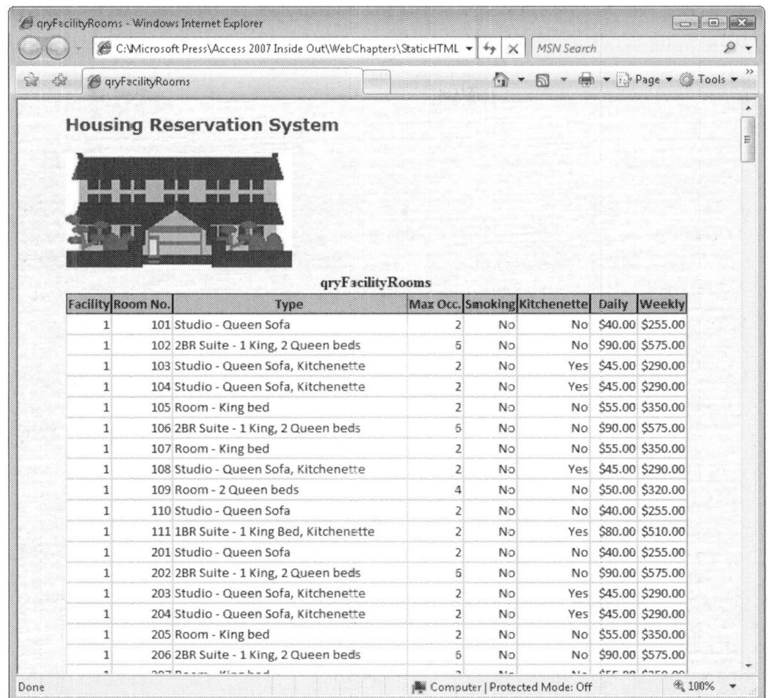


| Facility | Room No. | Type | Max Occ. | Smoking | Kitchenette | Daily | Weekly |
|---|---|---|---|---|---|---|---|
| 1 | 101 | Studio - Queen Sofa | 2 | No | No | $40.00 | $255.00 |
| 1 | 102 | 2BR Suite - 1 King, 2 Queen beds | 6 | No | No | $90.00 | $575.00 |
| 1 | 103 | Studio - Queen Sofa, Kitchenette | 2 | No | Yes | $45.00 | $290.00 |
| 1 | 104 | Studio - Queen Sofa, Kitchenette | 2 | No | Yes | $45.00 | $290.00 |
| 1 | 105 | Room - King bed | 2 | No | No | $55.00 | $350.00 |
| 1 | 106 | 2BR Suite - 1 King, 2 Queen beds | 6 | No | No | $90.00 | $575.00 |
| 1 | 107 | Room - King bed | 2 | No | No | $55.00 | $350.00 |
| 1 | 108 | Studio - Queen Sofa, Kitchenette | 2 | No | Yes | $45.00 | $290.00 |
| 1 | 109 | Room - 2 Queen beds | 4 | No | No | $50.00 | $320.00 |
| 1 | 110 | Studio - Queen Sofa | 2 | No | No | $40.00 | $255.00 |
| 1 | 111 | 1BR Suite - 1 King Bed, Kitchenette | 2 | No | Yes | $80.00 | $510.00 |
| 1 | 201 | Studio - Queen Sofa | 2 | No | No | $40.00 | $255.00 |
| 1 | 202 | 2BR Suite - 1 King, 2 Queen beds | 6 | No | No | $90.00 | $575.00 |
| 1 | 203 | Studio - Queen Sofa, Kitchenette | 2 | No | Yes | $45.00 | $290.00 |
| 1 | 204 | Studio - Queen Sofa, Kitchenette | 2 | No | Yes | $45.00 | $290.00 |
| 1 | 205 | Room - King bed | 2 | No | No | $55.00 | $350.00 |
| 1 | 206 | 2BR Suite - 1 King, 2 Queen beds | 6 | No | No | $90.00 | $575.00 |

**Figure 21-18** The HTML page displays the formatted query using the template specifications.

As you can see, the HTML page is vastly improved over the simple results that you get when you export data without formatting and a template. It's a simple matter to edit the final HTML to replace the query name in the title bar and the table caption with something more meaningful.

## Generating an HTML Page from an Access Report

Access does a much better job of exporting reports to HTML. It attempts to mimic the layout and fonts that you designed into your original report. It also places the Caption property defined for the report in the title bar of your Web browser. The two limitations are that Access cannot export bound OLE or other graphic objects (such as check boxes) and it cannot duplicate lines and rectangles that you include in the report design. When your report contains more than one page, Access creates one HTML file per page and includes hyperlinks in the pages to make it easy to navigate from one page to another.

### Creating a Template for a Report

Although Access does format reports nicely when you output them to HTML, you can further enhance the result by designing a template file. On the companion CD, you can find a template that you can use with reports, StaticTemplateReport.htm. The code in the template file is as follows:

```
<html>
<head>
<title><!--ACCESSTEMPLATE_TITLE--></title>
</head>
<body leftmargin="50" background="sumiback.jpg">
<font face="Verdana" size="4" color="#333399">
<STRONG>Housing Reservation System</STRONG></font><p>
<img src="housing.jpg" width="241" height="124">
<!--ACCESSTEMPLATE_BODY--><br>
<a href="<!--AccessTemplate_FirstPage-->">
<img border="0" id="img1" src="buttonA.jpg" height="30" width="100" alt="First">
</a>
<a href="<!--AccessTemplate_PreviousPage-->">
<img border="0" id="img1" src="buttonB.jpg" height="30" width="100"
alt="Previous"></a>
<a href="<!--AccessTemplate_NextPage-->">
<img border="0" id="img1" src="buttonC.jpg" height="30" width="100"
alt="Next"></a>
<a href="<!--AccessTemplate_LastPage-->">
<img border="0" id="img1" src="buttonD.jpg" height="30" width="100"
alt="Last"></a><b><font face="Verdana"><br>
Page <!--AccessTemplate_PageNumber-->.</font></b>
</p>
</body>
</html>
```



As noted earlier, when your report contains multiple pages, Access exports each page as a separate file and inserts hyperlinks to navigate through the pages. However, the default hyperlinks are simple text links that aren't very attractive. The sample template replaces the four links (First, Previous, Next, Last) with graphic button images. The template also inserts a page number at the bottom of each page. You can see that this template also specifies a background image and an embedded graphic and heading.

## Exporting a Report with a Template

You can use the sample template to export any of the reports in the sample Housing Reservations database. To try it out, select the rptDepartments report in the Navigation Pane, click More in the Export group on the External Data tab, and then click HTML Document to open the Export – HTML Document dialog box. Click the Browse button, navigate to the WebChapters\StaticHTML folder in the File Save dialog box, and then click Save to return to the Export – HTML Document dialog box. Select the Open The Destination File After The Export Operation Is Complete check box, as shown in Figure 21-19. Notice that Access automatically selected and dimmed the Export Data With Formatting And Layout check box—Access always exports reports to HTML formatted.

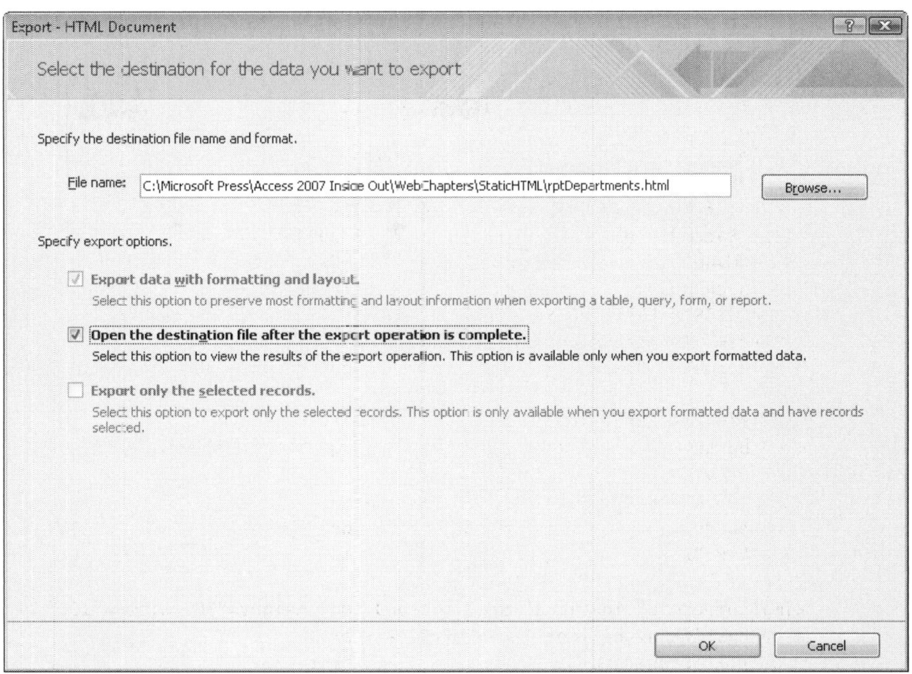


**Figure 21-19** When you export a report to HTML, Access automatically keeps any formatting.

Click OK, and Access displays the HTML Output Options dialog box that you saw earlier in Figure 21-17. Be sure to select the Select A HTML Template check box, then choose the StaticTemplateReport.htm file from the \WebChapters\StaticHTML folder as the template file, and finally click OK. Click OK again to export the report, and you should see a result in your browser as shown in Figure 21-20. (You can find an example saved as rptDepartmentsTemplate.html in the sample files.)

Notice that the check box control used to display the Admin? column on the report is missing. (You would need to change the check box on the report to a text box before exporting to fix this.) Also, the report already includes page numbers, so the page number added by the template is redundant. (We included the page number token in the template so that you can see how it works.) However, the Web page does include nice graphic hyperlinks to make it easy to move from page to page in the report. When you return to the Access window, close the Export – HTML Document dialog box.

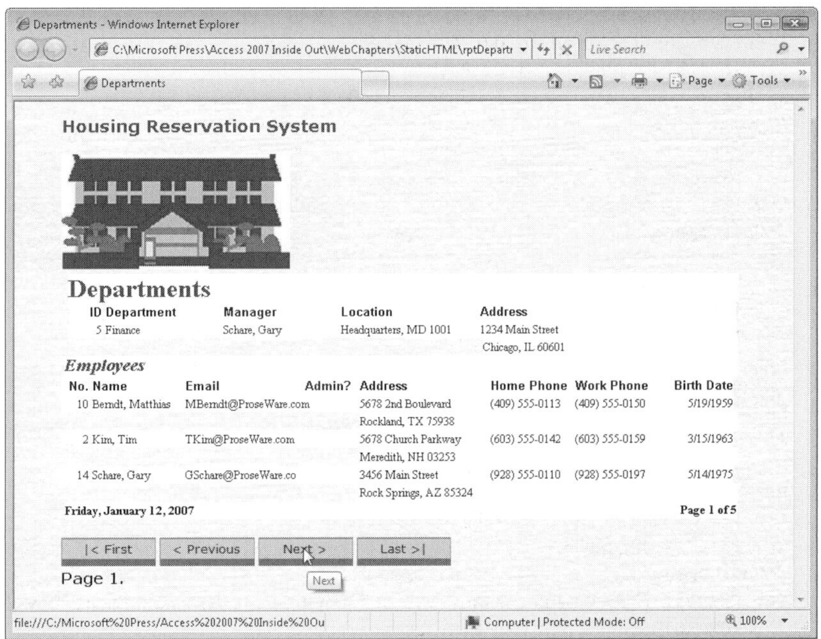


**Figure 21-20** When you export the report to HTML with a template applied, you can see the template elements with the report formatting.

## Writing HTML from Visual Basic

Remember that HTML files are actually text files containing tags and perhaps script that your browser can interpret. After you become familiar with HTML coding, you might find it easiest to create a Visual Basic procedure to rewrite static Web pages that need to be updated periodically.

Unless you have a lot of turnover in your organization, the work phone numbers for employees probably don't change very often. So, to make this information available in a Web page, a static HTML page probably works just fine. However, you need an easy way to update the information in the Web page periodically—perhaps once a month—to make sure the information is current.

In the Housing Reservations sample database (Housing.accdb), you can find a procedure in the modHTML module that does just that. The following is the Visual Basic code for the WriteHTML function that you can find in the module:

```
Public Function WriteHTML() As Integer
' Function demonstrates how to format and write a
' static Web page with embedded data
' Declare some variables
Dim db As DAO.Database, rstDept As DAO.Recordset, rstEmp As DAO.Recordset
Dim strWebPath As String, strPagePath As String
  ' Trap all errors
```

```
On Error GoTo Err_HTML
' Set up the location to put the page
strWebPath = CurrentProject.Path & "\WebChapters\StaticHTML\"
strPagePath = strWebPath & "EmployeePhone.htm"
' Delete the old page, if it's there
If Len(Dir(strPagePath)) > 0 Then
  Kill strPagePath
End If
' Open a new output file
Open strPagePath For Output As #1
' Write the HTML headings
' Using Print to avoid quotes in the output
Print #1, "<HTML>"
Print #1, "<head><title>Employee Phone List</title></head>"
Print #1, ""
Print #1, "<body leftmargin=""50"" background=""sumiback.jpg"">"
Print #1, "<p align=""left""><font size=""6"" face=""Times New Roman""" & _
  " color=darkblue>Employee Phone List</font></p>"
Print #1, ""
' Point to the current database
Set db = CurrentDb
' Open departments sorted by name
Set rstDept = db.OpenRecordset("SELECT DepartmentID, Department " & _
  "FROM tblDepartments ORDER BY Department")
' Loop through all departments
Do Until rstDept.EOF
  ' Write the table description, caption, and headings
  Print #1, "<table border=""3"" style=""border-collapse: collapse""" & _
    " bordercolor=steelblue width=""400"" cellpadding=""5"">"
  Print #1, "<caption><p align=""left"">" & _
    "<b><font face=""Verdana""" & _
    " color=""darkblue"">Department: " & rstDept!Department & _
    "</font></b></p></caption>"
  Print #1, ""
  Print #1, "<THEAD>"
  Print #1, "<TR>"
  Print #1, "<TH BGCOLOR=whitesmoke BORDERCOLOR=#000000 " & _
    "style=""border-style: double; border-width: 3"" >"
  Print #1, "<FONT style=FONT-SIZE:10pt FACE=""Verdana"" " & _
    "COLOR=darkblue>Employee Name</FONT></TH>"
  Print #1, "<TH BGCOLOR=whitesmoke BORDERCOLOR=#000000 " & _
    "style=""border-style: double; border-width: 3"" >"
  Print #1, "<FONT style=FONT-SIZE:10pt FACE=""Verdana"" " & _
    "COLOR=darkblue>Phone Number</FONT></TH>"
  Print #1, "</TR></THEAD>"
  Print #1, ""
  Print #1, "<TBODY>"
  ' Now open a recordset on the employees in this department
  ' sorted by last name, first name
  Set rstEmp = db.OpenRecordset("SELECT FirstName, MiddleName, " & _
    LastName, WorkPhone FROM tblEmployees " & _
    "WHERE DepartmentID = " & rstDept!DepartmentID & _
```

```
          " ORDER BY LastName, FirstName")
        ' Loop through all employees in this department
        Do Until rstEmp.EOF
          ' Write a table row for each employee
          Print #1, "  <tr>"
          Print #1, "    <td width=""65%"" style=""border-style: double; " & _
            "border-width: 3"">"
          Print #1, "    <font color=""darkblue"">" & _
            rstEmp!LastName & ", " & rstEmp!FirstName & _
            (" " + rstEmp!MiddleName) & _
            "</font></td>"
          Print #1, "    <td width=""35%"" style=""border-style: double; " & _
            "border-width: 3"">"
          Print #1, "    <font color=""darkblue"">" & _
            Format(rstEmp!WorkPhone, "(@@@) @@@-@@@@") & "</font></td>"
          Print #1, "  </tr>"
          ' Get next employee
          rstEmp.MoveNext
        Loop
        ' Close off the table
        Print #1, "</table>"
        Print #1, ""
        ' Create a space between tables
        Print #1, "</table>"
        Print #1, "<p> </p>"
        Print #1, ""
        ' Get the next department
        rstDept.MoveNext
      Loop
      ' Close off the Web page
      Print #1, "</Body>"
      Print #1, "</HTML>"
      ' Done - close up shop
      Close #1
      rstDept.Close
      Set rstDept = Nothing
      rstEmp.Close
      Set rstEmp = Nothing
      Set db = Nothing
      WriteHTML = True
    Exit_HTML:
      Exit Function
    Err_HTML:
      ' Display the error
      MsgBox "Error writing HTML: " & Err & ", " & Error
      ' Log the error
      ErrorLog "WriteHTML", Err, Error
      ' Bail
      Resume Exit_HTML
    End Function
```

The procedure begins by using the Dir function to check to see whether the old Web page file exists. If it finds the file, it deletes it using the Visual Basic Kill statement. Next, the procedure takes advantage of the ability to read and write files that's built into Visual Basic. The code uses the Open statement to create a new .htm file, followed by a series of Print statements to write the heading tags to the file. You can also use a Write statement to write to a file opened this way, but Write includes double quotes around string variables or literals that you write to the file. Print writes only the text you specify.

The code opens a recordset on the tblDepartments table, sorted by department name. It creates an HTML table with a caption and a heading for each department. It opens a second recordset for all the employees in the department and loads the HTML table rows using information from the employee recordset. After writing out all the employees for the current department, the code writes tags to close off the table and create a space between tables. The code moves to the next department and loops back to start a new HTML table for the next department. When it has finished with the last department, it closes off the Web page with </Body> and </HTML> tags.

You can open the modHTML module, click anywhere in the function, and click the Run button on the toolbar to run the code. After the code finishes, you can open the EmployeePhone.htm file that you can find in the \WebChapters\StaticHTML folder. Figure 21-21 shows you the result. (If you don't want to run the code, you can find the result saved as EmployeePhoneXmpl.htm in the sample files.)

**Figure 21-21** The completed Web page created by a Visual Basic procedure shows the current phone numbers of all employees.

When you combine your Visual Basic skills with your knowledge about writing HTML, the options are limitless.

# Creating Dynamic Web Pages

To create Web pages that display (and perhaps allow the user to update) data from a database, you must create a special type of Web page containing script that can fetch and update the data. The most common way to do this is to create an Active Server Page (ASP) that runs on the Web server to fetch requested information from a database, format it as HTML, and send it to the client browser. An alternate method is to use HTML forms that contain an ActiveX control and script to perform the same tasks. When you create an HTML form, you can design it to run the database code on the server or on the client.

With Microsoft's introduction of the .NET architecture and ASP.NET, creating dynamic Web pages is almost as easy as creating desktop database applications. These tools help you create ASPs or HTML forms to handle the database processing. You can also use Expression Web to build HTML forms that deliver dynamic information from your database. Let's take a brief look at these technologies.



## Delivering Dynamic Query Results

If, whenever a Web visitor requests a page, you want your Web page to query the database and return the result to the visitor, you must create a dynamic Web page. Figure 21-22 shows the most common network architecture you can build using Access as the database file server to report up-to-the-minute, live database contents. The browser requests a special kind of Web page—an ASP—that contains a mixture of HTML and script code. The script code, running on the server and working through several layers of software, opens the database, runs the query, and formats the results. The Web server then transmits the results to the Web visitor's browser as pure HTML.

> **Note**
>
> The script code generated by Microsoft products in ASPs is Microsoft Visual Basic Scripting Edition (VBScript).

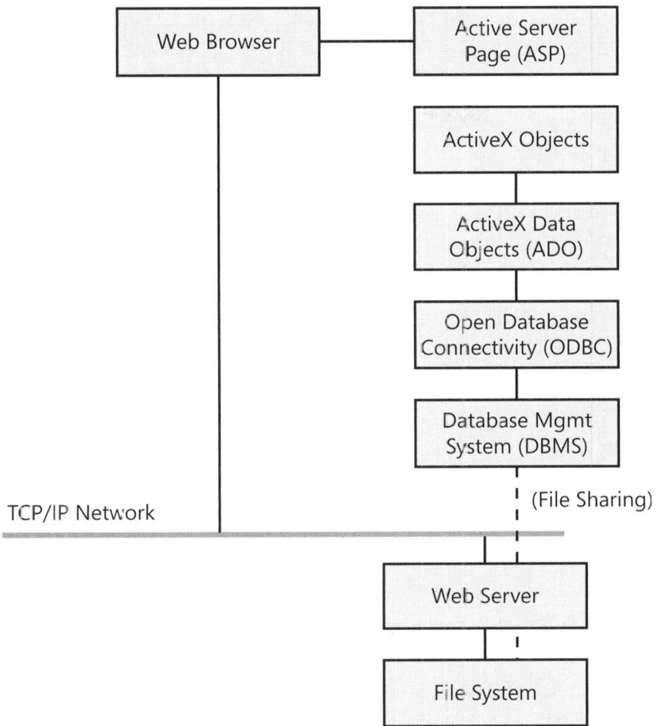


**Figure 21-22** A high-level schematic shows the delivery of database queries dynamically.



INSIDE OUT

### Installing Microsoft Internet Information Services and Expression Web

Any ASP that you create with Microsoft products is designed to work on Microsoft Internet Information Services (IIS). You can install IIS on Windows 2000 Server, Windows XP Professional, Windows Vista, or Windows Server 2003. If you have Windows Vista on your desktop computer, you can install a local IIS server to test your work. If you didn't choose to install IIS when you installed Windows Vista, you can add it later by starting the Programs And Features application in Windows Control Panel and then clicking the Turn Windows Features On Or Off link.

If you plan to use Expression Web, you must also install the Microsoft .NET Framework 2.0.

Figure 21-22 shows the following additional components. Even if you never work with these directly, it's good to know what they are so that you can decipher documentation and error messages.

- ActiveX objects are prewritten software modules that provide commonly used functions. Most VBScript code in ASPs works by loading and controlling ActiveX objects that run on the Web server. The ActiveX objects you need to build most ASPs are included with the Microsoft Office system and in the Expression Design add-on for the Expression Web product.
- ActiveX Data Objects (ADO) are collections of ActiveX objects specifically designed to process databases. As you learned in Chapter 19, "Understanding Visual Basic Fundamentals," the ADO libraries are a standard part of Access.
- Open Database Connectivity (ODBC) provides a standard interface to many different types of database systems. You configure ODBC through Windows Control Panel. See Chapter 6, "Importing and Linking Data," for details about managing ODBC connections.
- The database management system (DBMS) organizes data into databases, tables, and fields. It also accepts commands (usually coded in SQL) that update or query the database. Access 2007 and Microsoft SQL Server are typical DBMSs you can use to support ASPs.



## Processing Live Data with HTML Forms

Among the many objects Web pages can contain are various form elements: text boxes, drop-down lists (similar to combo boxes in Access forms), check boxes, option buttons, push buttons (similar to command buttons in Access forms), and ActiveX controls. Web visitors can use these to enter data and submit it to an ASP or other server-based program for processing. Typical database processing includes running customized queries and adding, changing, or deleting records in tables. Processing follows the schematic previously shown in Figure 21-22, except that the server receives form field data from the Web page and the ASP programming is more complex.

HTML forms can't provide nearly as rich or as helpful an interface as Access forms, but using HTML forms means authorized users anywhere can run your Web application without loading any additional software and regardless of the type of computer the user has. These are important considerations when you need to support many users, many environments, or both.

## Using Visual Studio .NET and ASP.NET

Microsoft's latest answer to software development, Visual Studio .NET, is an editor and project manager that lets you create both Windows desktop applications using one of several languages and Web applications using ASP.NET. .NET allows you to create applications using the programming language of your choice, including Visual Basic

.NET, Visual C++ .NET, Visual C# .NET, or Visual J# .NET. No matter which programming language you choose, the compiled version of your program shares the same run-time library with all other languages. When you build a Web application, ASP.NET lets you use any of the available programming languages to generate HTML forms and ASP pages to implement your application.

Visual Studio uses essentially the same user interface as the Visual Basic editor supplied with Access 2007. In addition, Visual Studio provides a WYSIWYG HTML editor, ActiveX controls that generate HTML whenever you save a page that contains them, an assortment of database wizards and design tools, and an interactive debugger for both ASP.NET and scripts that run on the browser. ASP.NET also lets you choose the language that you want to use behind your Web forms, including Visual Basic. Yet, despite all these aids, Visual Studio remains at heart a programmer's environment. If you're not comfortable working directly with HTML code, Visual Basic programming, and ActiveX interfaces, this probably isn't the program for you. Otherwise, rest assured that anything you can do in code, you can do in Visual Studio .NET.

**For more information about Expression Web, consult *Microsoft Expression Web Designer Inside Out* from Microsoft Press.**



# Sharing Your Data with SharePoint

It seems that every couple of years something new occurs in technology that causes a stir. For Microsoft, the latest hot buttons are .NET, XML, and now Windows SharePoint Services. In all three cases, the technologies (.NET and XML) and product (Windows SharePoint Services) have increased productivity and made life simpler for developers and users alike.

## Introducing Windows SharePoint Services

Windows SharePoint Services consists of two components: Microsoft Windows SharePoint Services (version 3) and Microsoft Office 2007 SharePoint Server. Windows SharePoint Services allows teams of people to collaborate and share documents, tasks, and schedules. Office SharePoint Server is a Web portal that lets you set up your server to handle the searching and storing of documents. You can think of Windows SharePoint Services as a front end to Office SharePoint Server, where multiple but separate team services might use the same portal service. You can see an example of a Windows SharePoint Services site in Figure 21-23. (This is a Microsoft Office Live Web site that John created.)

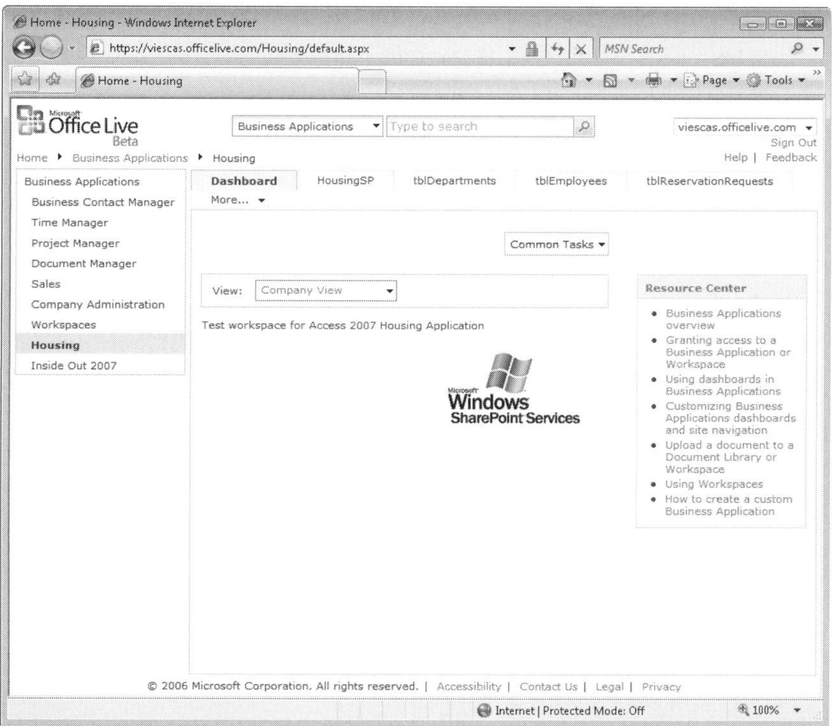


**Figure 21-23** An Office Live Web site uses Windows SharePoint Services.

Windows SharePoint Services uses ASP.NET to create Web sites that take advantage of a technology called *Web Parts*. Web Parts are custom forms that you can ask Windows SharePoint Services to dynamically include on your team site pages. These Web Parts allow you to customize your Windows SharePoint Services site with items such as announcements, contact lists, task lists, interactive discussion areas, and links to other pages relevant to the team tasks. You will learn more about Windows SharePoint Services and Web Parts and how they work in Chapter 22, "Working with Windows SharePoint Services," and in Chapter 23.

## Office and Windows SharePoint Services

The development team for the Microsoft Office system has gone to great efforts to integrate all its products with Windows SharePoint Services so that you can share on your site documents of various types, including data from Access. In addition to being able to import data from and export data to a Windows SharePoint Services site, you can create Access reports from the various lists within your site. Some of the other tasks you can perform with the Microsoft Office system and Windows SharePoint Services are

- Import data to and export data from Access
- Link to Windows SharePoint Services documents from Access to allow you to work with the data stored in Windows SharePoint Services from your Access application

- Attach local working documents to events on a Windows SharePoint Services site
- Import events into Microsoft Office Outlook 2007 to allow users to have a local copy of an event or reminder
- Store on the Windows SharePoint Services site Microsoft Office Excel 2007 worksheets and Office Word 2007 documents for sharing
- Use Office Web Components such as the PivotTable and PivotChart as Web Parts to enhance your Windows SharePoint Services site

We'll discuss additional Microsoft Office system and Windows SharePoint Services features in the next chapter. You are now ready to dig in and see how to use Access for some of your Web needs. In the next two chapters, we will delve deeper into the Windows SharePoint Services and XML topics that we discussed in this chapter.

# CHAPTER 22
# Working with Windows SharePoint Services



Microsoft Windows SharePoint Services (version 3) is a Web-based product from Microsoft that enables companies to create a central repository of many types of information that can be viewed and updated by authorized users. Windows SharePoint Services runs as a service on Microsoft Windows Server 2003 or later and uses Microsoft SQL Server to store and manage the shared data.

Any company that needs a way to improve team collaboration should find Windows SharePoint Services very useful. With a Windows SharePoint Services Web site, you can

- Provide a central location for collaborating on documents created using Microsoft Office applications.
- Create separate workspaces for different teams.
- Assign users to different groups, allowing some to view only shared data, permitting others to modify and contribute shared data, and allowing a few to customize the design of their own or shared sites.
- Create forums such as blogs and wikis using built-in templates.
- Customize a shared site using off-the-shelf Web Parts included as part of the Windows SharePoint Services product. These Web Parts include
    - Announcements that can be posted by the team leaders
    - Contact lists
    - Content from another Web page or file embedded within the main page
    - Event and issue tracking and task assignment
    - Online discussion board
    - Links to other pages or Web sites
    - Team membership lists
    - Shared document sublibrary
    - Online survey

Web Parts are a particularly powerful feature in Windows SharePoint Services. If you are a member of a group that has design permission on the team site, you can customize the Web pages presented by Windows SharePoint Services by choosing the components you want, indicating where you want the component to appear on the page, and customizing the components by setting their properties. You can also apply one of dozens of themes to the team site to give it a customized look. These features are not unlike designing a form within Microsoft Access, but you perform your design work directly within your browser.

Microsoft Office Access 2007 extends the collaboration power of Windows SharePoint Services by adding features that allow the two programs to work in tandem. In this chapter you'll learn how to

- Work within the Windows SharePoint Services user interface
- Export a table stored in Office Access 2007 to a Windows SharePoint Services list
- Import a list from Windows SharePoint Services into Access 2007 as a local table
- Link to existing SharePoint lists
- Create new lists in Windows SharePoint Services from within Access 2007
- Work with Windows SharePoint Services lists offline and later synchronize any changes
- Upload your Access 2007 database to a SharePoint site
- Publish your Access 2007 database in a document library on a SharePoint site
- Open SharePoint lists in Access 2007
- Open Access 2007 forms and reports inside a SharePoint site

### Note

The samples in this chapter are based on the Housing Reservations Windows SharePoint Services application, HousingSP.accdb, and the IssuesSample.accdb database that you can find on the companion CD. This particular Housing Reservations database is a scaled-down version of the full Housing.accdb sample you have been working with throughout this book. It is designed to be uploaded to a Windows SharePoint Services Version 3 Web site. In order to take full advantage of this database, you will need to have access to a Windows SharePoint Services Version 3 Web site to which you can connect. Also, all screen shots were taken using a Microsoft Office Live Web site, so the figures you see in this chapter might differ from what you see on your screen based on your Windows SharePoint Services Version 3 site. Many of the features of Windows SharePoint Services discussed in this chapter require version 3. Earlier versions might not offer all the features we discuss in this chapter. If you do not have access to a Windows SharePoint Services Version 3 site, you can sign up for one (with a free trial) at *http://office.microsoft.com/en-us/officelive/default.aspx*.

# Working Within the Windows SharePoint Services User Interface

In the process of writing this book, we used an Office Live Web site running Windows SharePoint Services Version 3 to test and demonstrate how Access 2007 and Windows SharePoint Services can work together. A full discussion of Windows SharePoint Services Version 3 and all its features is beyond the scope of this book, so our goal in this section is only to familiarize you with some of the user interface elements relevant to Access 2007. Figure 22-1 shows the main page we created to demonstrate the Housing SharePoint sample you'll see later in this chapter.

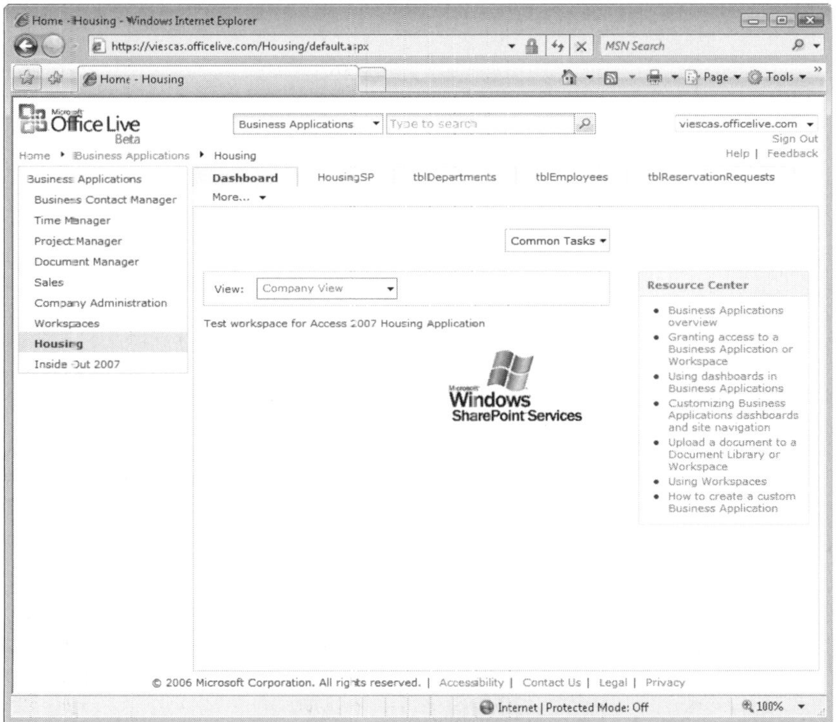


**Figure 22-1** A Windows SharePoint Services Web site allows you to collaborate and share information through a Web browser.

The left side of the page is a navigation bar similar to the Navigation Pane in Access 2007. Clicking one of these links takes you to another part of this Web site. In our example, we clicked the Housing link to access the HousingSP database. Horizontally near the top of the page is a *dashboard* that displays the internal contents of the Housing folder using tabs. You can see the name of the Housing SharePoint database (HousingSP) and some of the lists within that database–tblDepartments, tblEmployees, and tblReservationRequests.

Click the Common Tasks button to see a list of customization options, as shown in Figure 22-2. You can customize the dashboard, assign permissions to various parts of your Web site, view settings for your other applications and workspaces, create new elements on your Web site, and modify the current workspace settings.

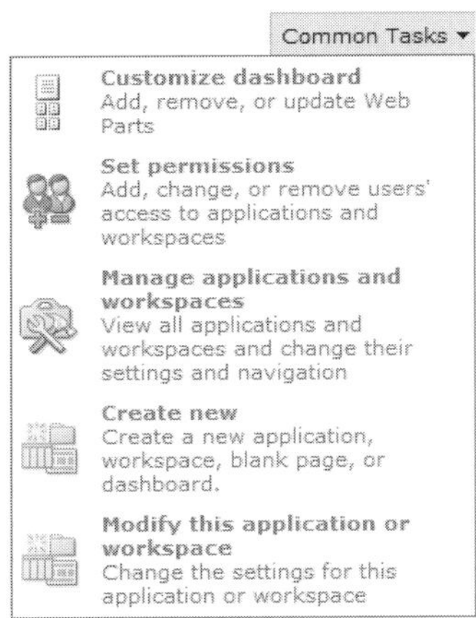


**Figure 22-2** Click Common Tasks to create, edit, and customize the various elements of your Windows SharePoint Services Web site.

## Editing Data in Lists

In Windows SharePoint Services terminology, a table is referred to as a *list* that stores information about a single subject. In a list you have *columns* (fields) that contain the different kinds of information about the subject. Similar to how you work in Access 2007, you can work with lists in different views for adding and editing records. Figure 22-3 shows the default view of an Employees list on our test site that looks like Datasheet view in Access. (This list was created as part of one of the sample business applications that Office Live loaded when we set up the Web site.) You can see the column headers—such as Last Name, First Name, and Job Title—and one employee row below the column headers. This view is also set to display all the employees.

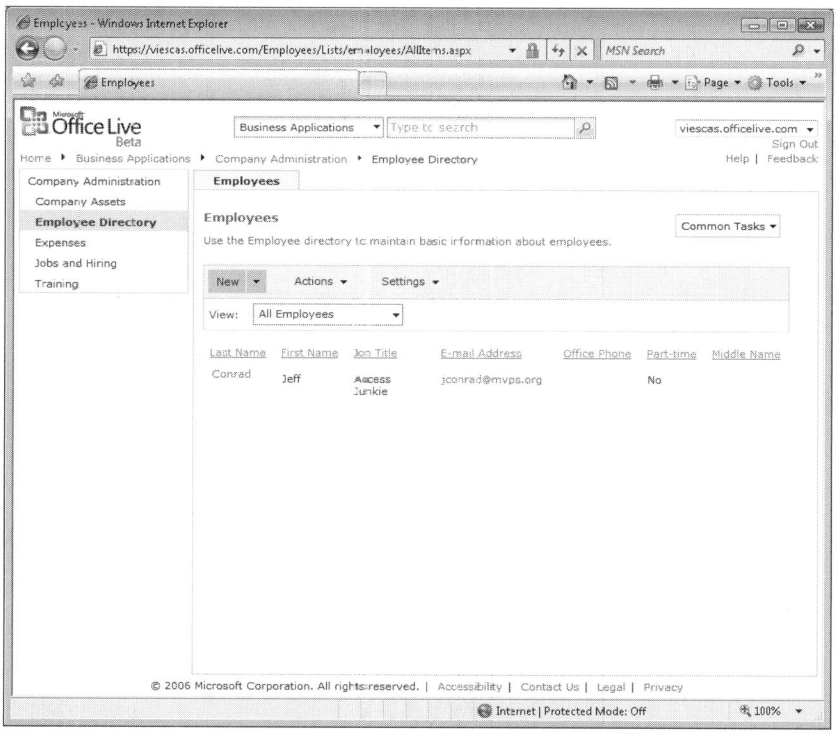


**Figure 22-3** A list displayed on a SharePoint site resembles Datasheet view of a table in Access.

Although this view resembles a datasheet, you cannot edit any of the columns or records from this specific page because this is a read-only view. In the Windows SharePoint Services user interface, you'll notice that there are no record indicators or blank rows for new records. To add a record to the Employees list, click the arrow to the right of the New button and then click the New Item command, as shown in Figure 22-4.

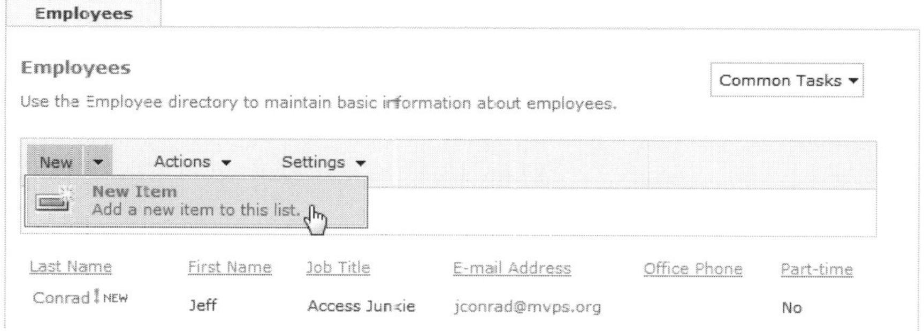


**Figure 22-4** Click the New Item command to add a new record.

Windows SharePoint Services opens a new page that resembles a blank data entry form in Access, as shown in Figure 22-5. All the column headers for this list are displayed on the left side, and text boxes for the columns are on the right side. (You can't see all the columns for the Employees list in Figure 22-5.) This single-item edit form displays a red asterisk next to any required columns—for this list, you must enter a value in Last Name.

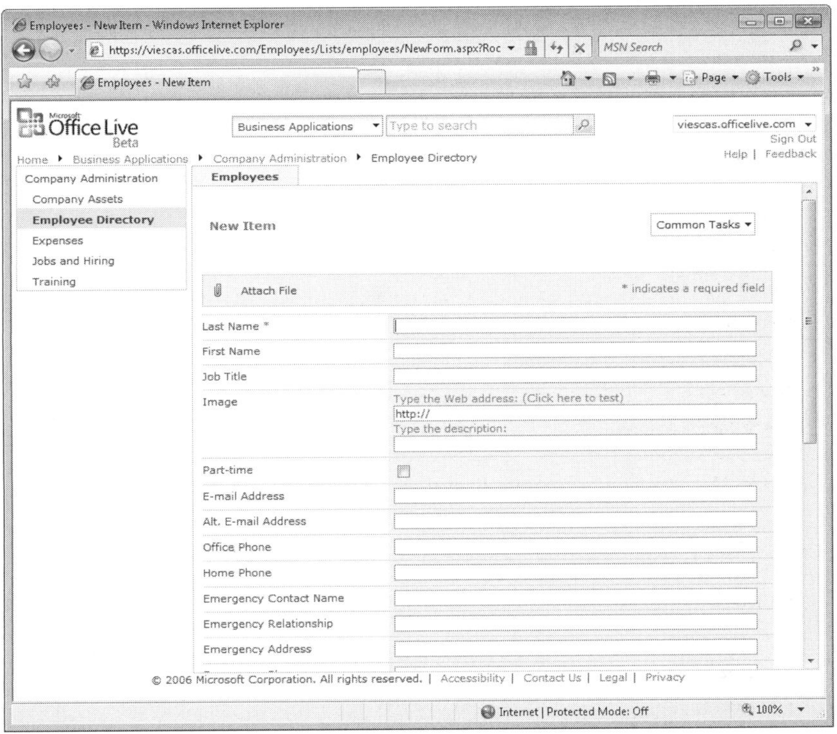


**Figure 22-5** You can add new records via a view of the list that looks like a form.

As with a data entry form in Access, you enter the information for this record into the various text boxes. In Figure 22-6 you can see we are entering John's employee information. Just like Access 2007, Windows SharePoint Services supports adding attachments to individual records. In this particular view, we can click the Attach File link, shown in Figure 22-6, to browse to a location and upload an attachment for this employee's record.

Windows SharePoint Services also supports Rich Text Format for text and memo fields. The last column in the Employees list, Notes, includes formatting buttons you can use to apply different fonts, font sizes, bolding, alignments, and colors for your text, as shown in Figure 22-7. After we click OK to save this new record, we return to the default view of the Employees list, which now displays John's record, as shown in Figure 22-8.

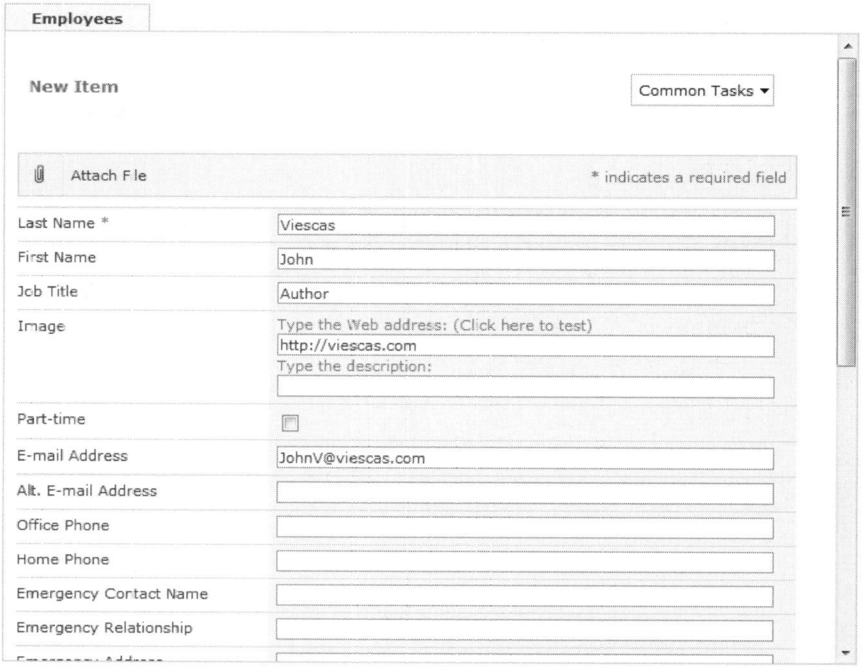

Figure 22-6 You can see John's record details being added to the form.

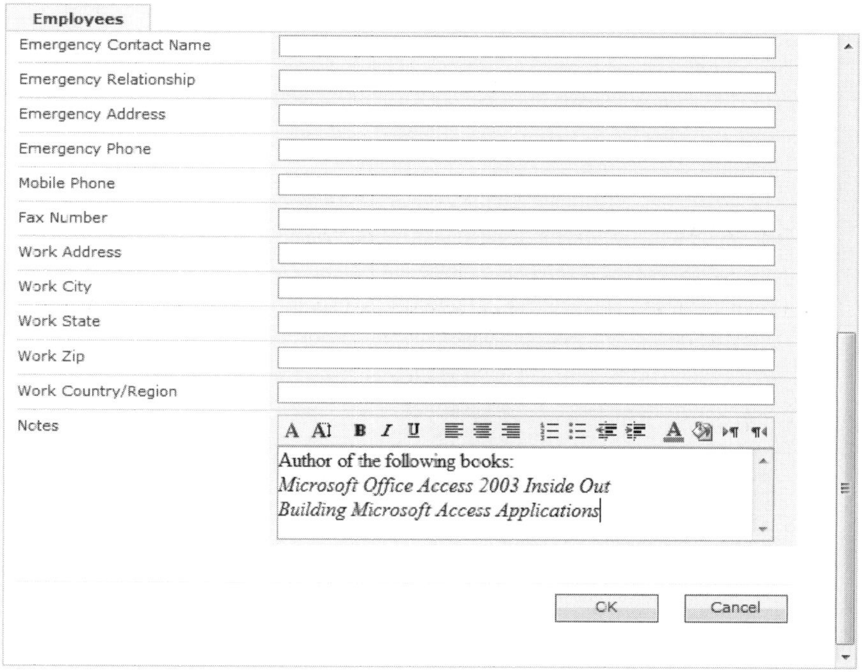

Figure 22-7 Windows SharePoint Services supports Rich Text Format for text fields.

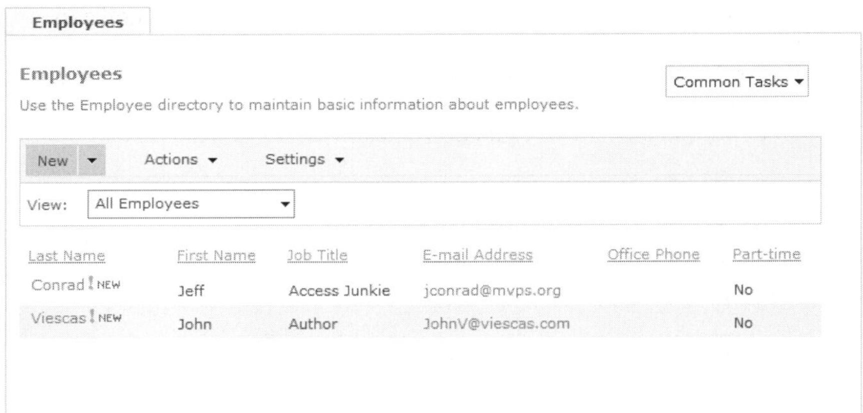


**Figure 22-8** John's record has been added to the Employees list.

## Creating New Views

Within the Windows SharePoint Services user interface, you can create new views of your lists. If a particular view shows too many columns or too few columns, you can create a custom view to display only the columns you need. You might find this feature handy for hiding certain columns from specific users or groups. You might also want to set up a Datasheet view of your list for quick data entry and editing many records. On our test site we created a Datasheet view of the Employees list. As shown in Figure 22-9, we clicked the arrow to the right of View and then clicked the Create View command to begin creating a new Datasheet view.

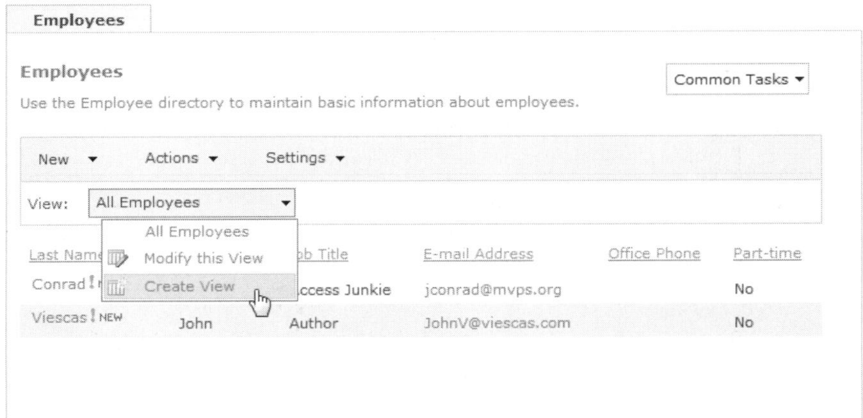


**Figure 22-9** You can create new views of your lists within Windows SharePoint Services.

The Create View page opens, where you can choose from several existing view formats, as shown in Figure 22-10. This page includes built-in views such as Standard, Calendar, Access, Datasheet, and Gantt. You can even use an existing view as a basis for creating a new view. Not all views would be appropriate for certain types of lists. For instance, a list of products would not function at all if displayed in Calendar view.

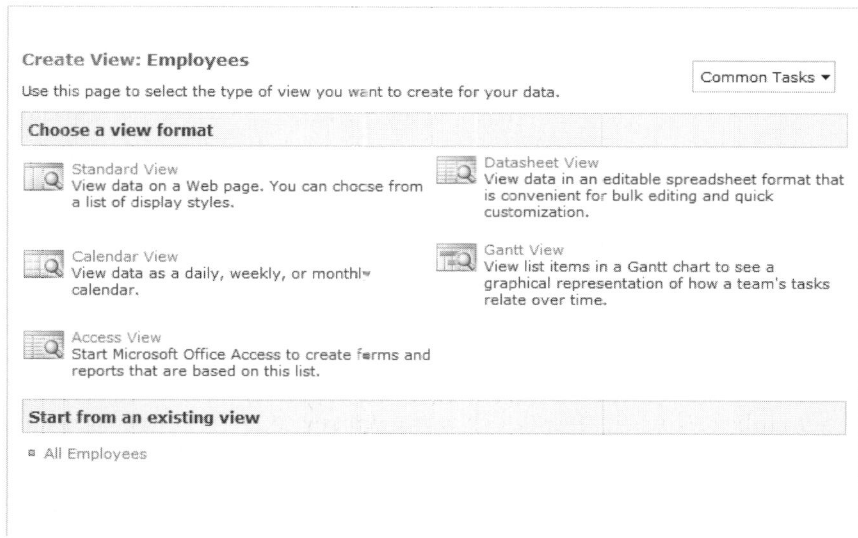


**Figure 22-10** Windows SharePoint Services offers several built-in views for your lists.

We want to create a Datasheet view of the Employees list, so we clicked the Datasheet View button to open a new page to customize our new view, as shown in Figure 22-11. On this page we can choose from any of the following options for this new list view:

- **Name** Assign a name for this new list view.
- **Audience** Designate whether this view can be seen by others or only by yourself. Public is the default.
- **Columns** Select which columns will appear in the list view and in what order. All data columns appear in the sequence defined by default. You can also choose to display other columns maintained by Windows SharePoint Services such as attachments, date created, date modified, and version.
- **Sort** Assign sorting options for one or two columns. By default, no columns are sorted—the data appears in the order entered.
- **Filter** Apply one or more filters to the list view. By default, no filters are defined.

- **Totals** Calculate totals for any of the columns. No totals are defined by default.
- **Folders** Choose to show items inside folders or in a flat view without folders. The default is to display items inside folders.
- **Item Limit** Assign a maximum number of records to display in the view. The default is to display all records.

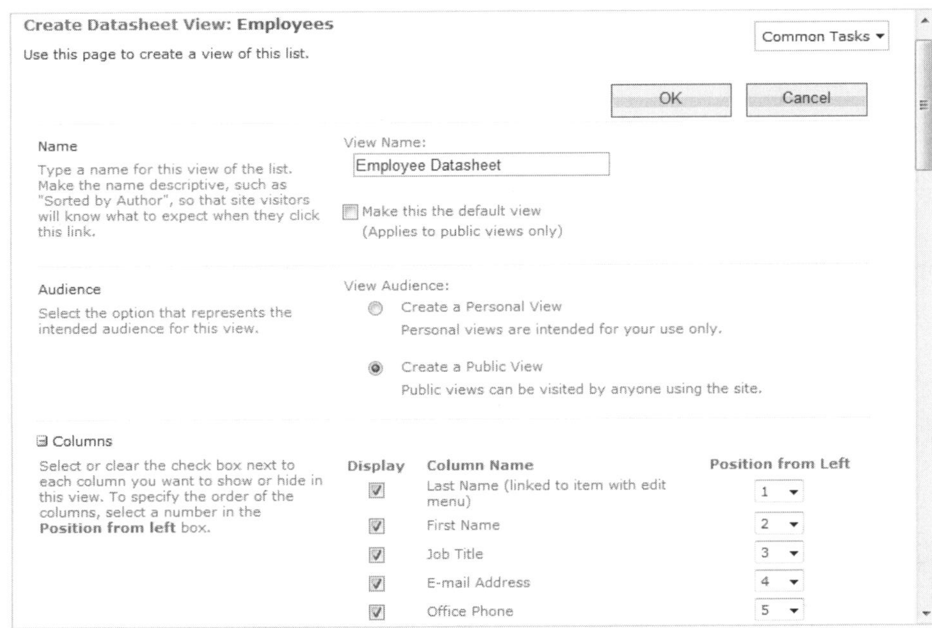


**Figure 22-11** On this page, you can choose options to customize your new Datasheet view.

In our example, we named this new view Employee Datasheet and kept all of the other options set to their defaults. In the Access world, what we are building is conceptually a query and a data entry form for the Employees list. For the query, we are deciding which fields to display and in which order to sort the fields. For the form, we are choosing the form layout (Datasheet, in this case), and specifying any totals to display for the columns. After clicking OK to save our new view, Windows SharePoint Services displays our Employee Datasheet list view, as shown in Figure 22-12.

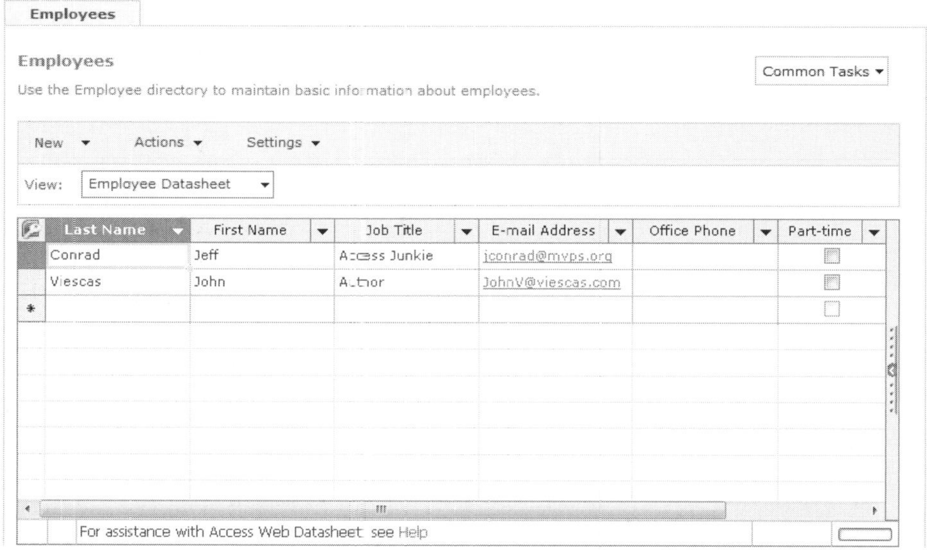


**Figure 22-12** You can now see your new Datasheet view of the Employees list.

This view now looks very similar to Datasheet view of a form you might create in Access. You can easily move through the columns and records using the Tab and arrows keys. You can click the arrows on the column headers to apply additional filters to the records. You can see a blank row at the bottom of this view for entering a new record. Windows SharePoint Services even displays an Access icon in the upper-left corner of the view!

## Adding Columns to Lists

In the Windows SharePoint Services user interface you can also add new columns to your lists. For our example, we might want to add a Middle Name column between the Last Name and First Name columns and reorder the columns to First Name, Middle Name, and Last Name. This is a three-step process—add the column to the list, add the column to the Employee Datasheet view, and then reorder the columns. To add the new column to the Employees list, we clicked the arrow to the right of Settings and then clicked the Create Column command, as shown in Figure 22-13.

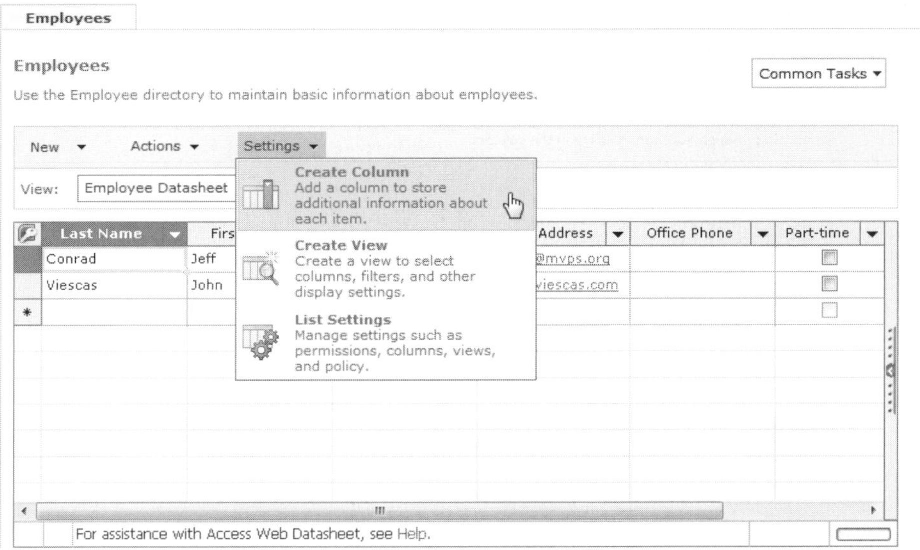


**Figure 22-13** The Create Column command adds a new column to the list.

The Create Column page opens, on which you can assign properties for the new column, as shown in Figure 22-14. In Windows SharePoint Services, you assign the following properties for the new column:

- Name and Type
- Description
- Required
- Field Size
- Default Value
- Add To Default View

Depending on the data type you choose, this page displays additional options, such as the list of values for a Choice data type or the minimum and maximum values for a Number or Currency data type. After you assign your column properties, click OK and Windows SharePoint Services adds the new column to the list.

Now that we have added the column to the list, we must add the column to our Employee Datasheet view. (However, if the Datasheet view is the default view—which it isn't in this case—and we selected the Add To Default View check box to add the column to the default view when we created it, we can skip these steps.) We have already indicated which columns to display in the Employee Datasheet view so, by default, Windows SharePoint Services does not add this column to our custom view. To add the column to the custom view, we clicked the arrow to the right of View and then clicked the Modify This View command, as shown in Figure 22-15.

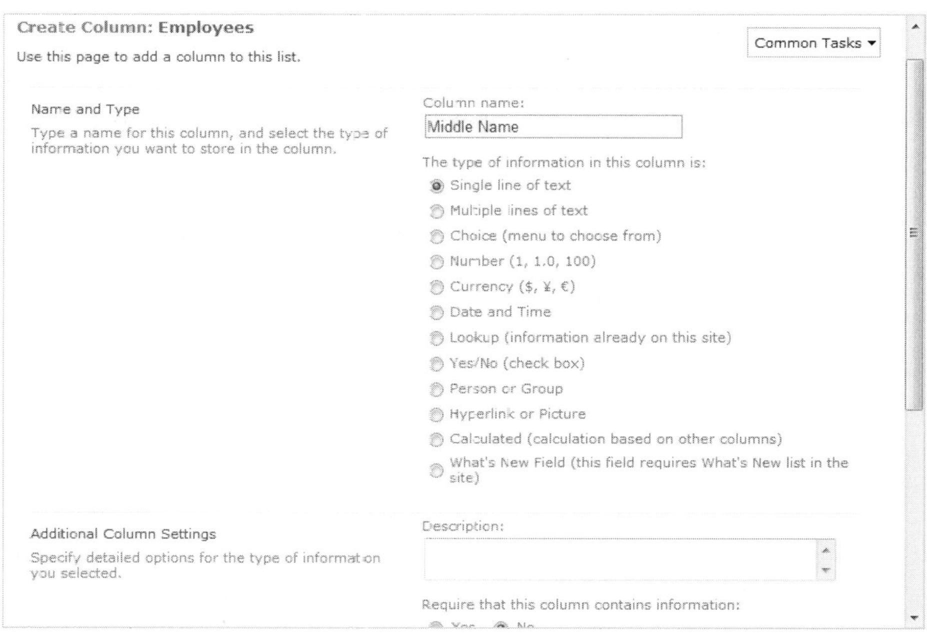


**Figure 22-14** On this page you can set properties for the new column.

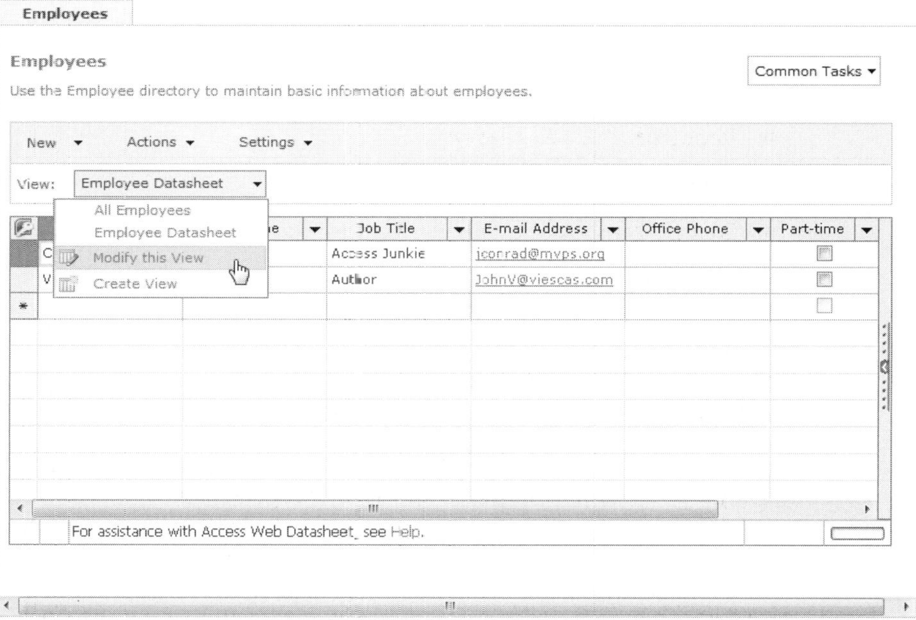


**Figure 22-15** To display the new Middle Name column, you have to add it to the Employee Datasheet view.

On the Edit Datasheet View page, you can modify the layout of the Employee Datasheet view, as shown in Figure 22-16. This page displays the name of each column with a check box to its left. Select the check box next to Middle Name to add this column to your custom view. A Position From Left box to the right of the column name lets you position each column in the view. In Figure 22-16, you can see we assigned the First Name column to the 1 position to have it appear first in the column order. When we changed the Position From Left value for the First Name column, the sequence of the other columns changed automatically. We then changed the position of the Middle Name column to 2. Windows SharePoint Services changed the sequence the other columns and assigned the Last Name column to the 3 position.

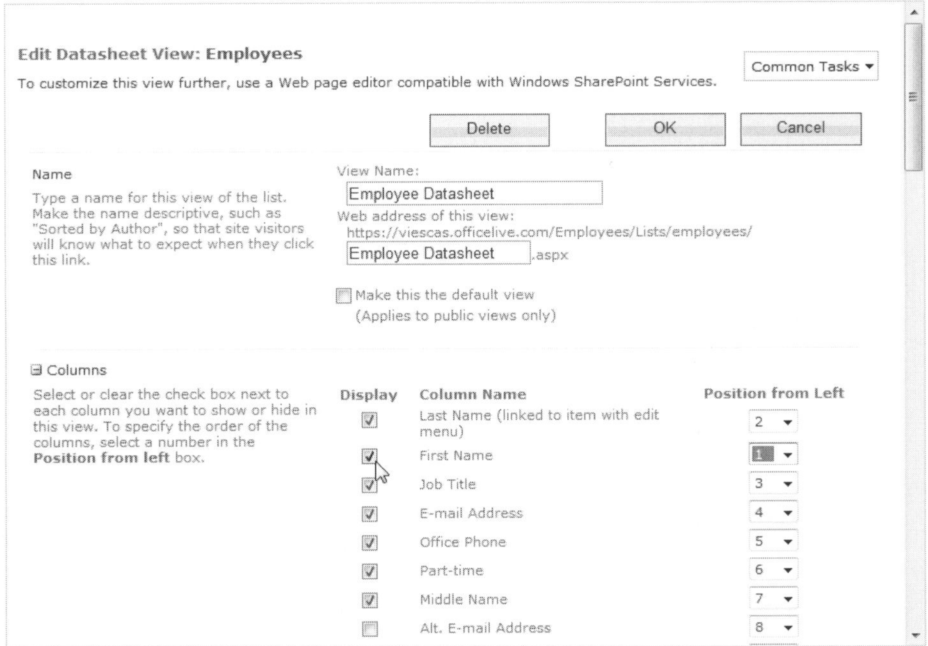


**Figure 22-16** You can adjust the display positions for the columns on the Edit Datasheet View page.

Note that you can change the name of the view on this page. You can also specify the Web page address, which by default will be the same as the name of the view. Finally, you can select the Make This The Default View check box to make this the view users see whenever they open the list. After you click OK to save the changes, you can see your revised Employee Datasheet view with the new Middle Name column, as shown in Figure 22-17. Windows SharePoint Services correctly positions the new column between the First Name and Last Name columns and places the First Name column first in the column order.

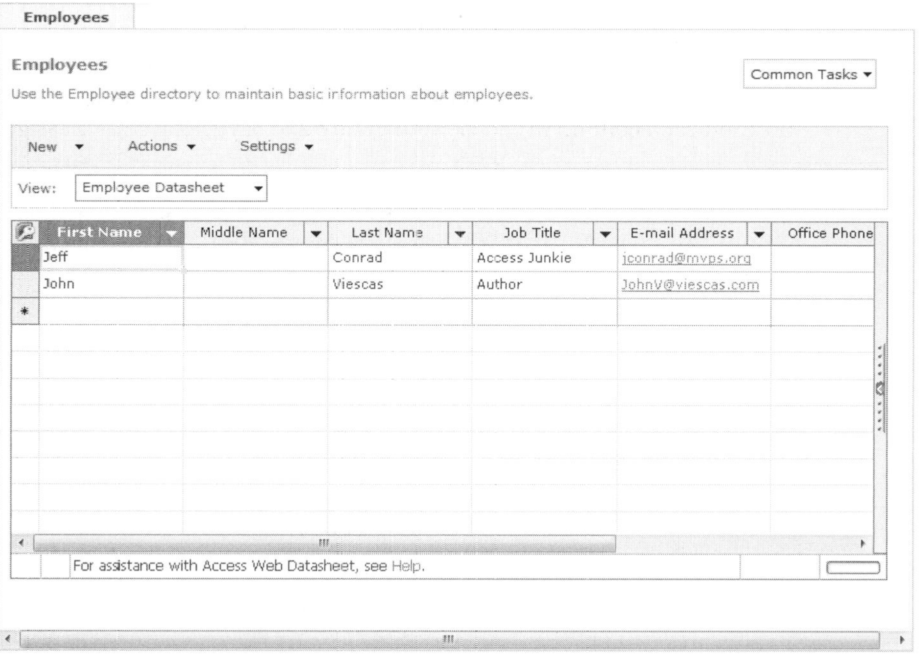


**Figure 22-17** The new Middle Name column now appears in the Employee Datasheet view.

> **Note**
>
> You might be wondering why we used a space in the name of the Middle Name column, especially considering that we recommended that you not use spaces for field names in your tables at the beginning of this book. In Windows SharePoint Services you cannot assign captions to the columns, so the column names displayed in the various views are always the actual names of the columns. For this reason, you'll probably want to include spaces in column names in lists defined in Windows SharePoint Services to make them more readable.



## Recycle Bin

One of the great advantages to having lists stored on a Windows SharePoint Services site is the Recycle Bin. In most cases, if you delete something in Access, it is gone for good. If you delete one record (or a thousand) by mistake and then close the database, those records are lost. In some situations it is possible to retrieve deleted database elements using professional recovery services, but retrieval is not always guaranteed and these services can be costly. If you're lucky, you might have a backup of your database that you can use to restore deleted records, but you still might lose some very important data depending on when you made the last backup.

Windows SharePoint Services has a built-in Recycle Bin where you can easily recover deleted records and other Windows SharePoint Services Web site elements. Suppose, for example, we accidentally deleted John's record in our Employees list that we have been working on. We can go to the Recycle Bin on a SharePoint site by navigating to the site settings (click Common Tasks and then Modify This Application Or Workspace) and clicking Deleted Items under Recycle And Restore, as shown in Figure 22-18.

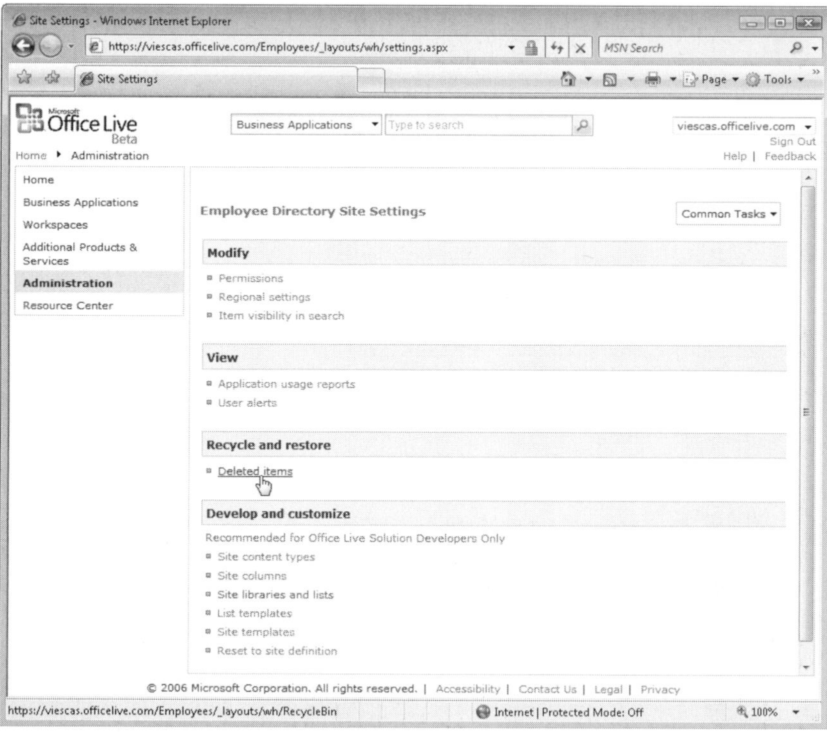


**Figure 22-18** Windows SharePoint Services includes a Recycle Bin so you can recover deleted items.

After you click Deleted Items, Windows SharePoint Services displays the Recycle Bin for the Employee Directory, as shown in Figure 22-19. The Recycle Bin shows the type of object deleted (in this case a record), the name of the deleted record, the original location of the list from which the record was deleted, who created the record, when the record was deleted, and the size of the record.

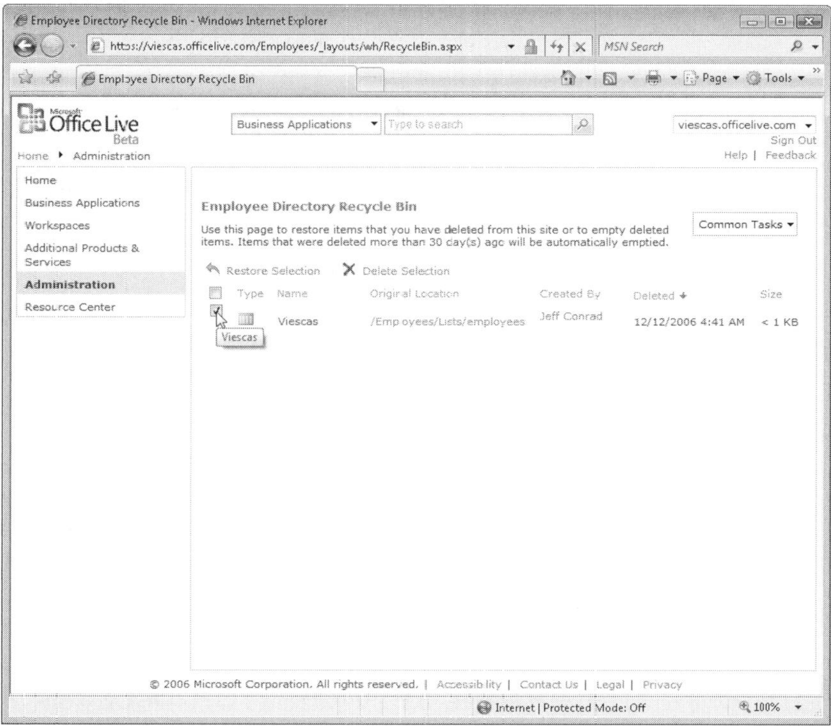


**Figure 22-19** John's record can be restored from the Recycle Bin.

The Windows SharePoint Services Recycle Bin works in much the same way as the Windows Recycle Bin. The one difference is that Windows SharePoint Services automatically empties deleted items that were deleted longer ago than 30 days. To restore John's record, we selected the check box next to his record and then clicked the Restore Selection button. Windows SharePoint Services restored John's record to the correct list, as shown in Figure 22-20.

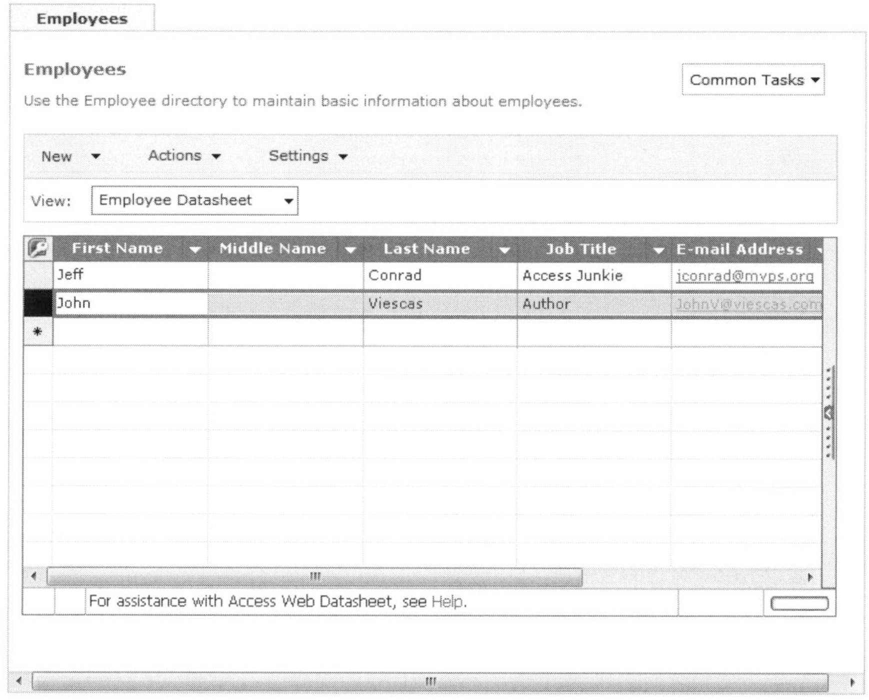


**Figure 22-20** John's record has now been completely restored.



# Using Windows SharePoint Services from Access

So far in this chapter you have read about how to work with lists within Windows SharePoint Services. You've learned how to edit data through different views, add new columns to your lists, and use the Recycle Bin to recover deleted records. Now that you are more familiar with how to work within the Windows SharePoint Services user interface, it's time to discover how you can leverage the power of Windows SharePoint Services within Access 2007.

## Exporting Data to Windows SharePoint Services

In some situations you might find that data stored in Access 2007 for your own personal use needs to be shared by several users in different locations. You might find, for example, that a list of contacts you maintain locally in an Access data table in Oregon needs to be accessed by your sales force in Paris. By exporting this table to a SharePoint site, both you and your sales force can view, add, and edit the contact information from anywhere in the world.

Access 2007 makes the process of exporting data from a table very easy. Let's start by using the Contacts database template that comes with Access for an example. Open Access and click the Contacts database template icon in the middle of the screen. Browse to a location to save this file and name it Contacts. Click the Download button to download the database to your local computer. After Access opens the database, close the opening Contacts form so that only the Navigation Pane is visible. Click the Navigation Pane menu, click Object Type under Navigate To Category, and then click All Access Objects to display a list of all objects.

This Contacts database includes only one table—Contacts—with no records. To see how records are exported to a SharePoint site, you should add some records to this table. Open the Contacts table in Datasheet view and add a couple of records of contact information, as shown in Figure 22-21.

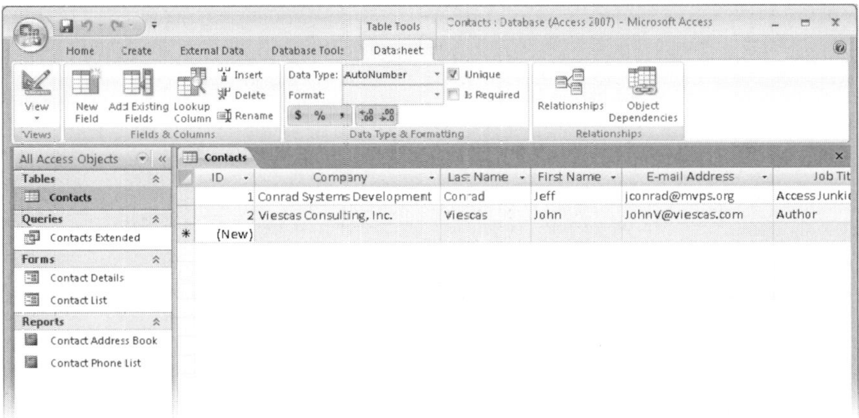


**Figure 22-21** Enter some contact records before exporting the Contacts table to a SharePoint list.

Now that you have created some records, close the Contacts table. As you learned in Chapter 6, "Importing and Linking Data," all import and export commands are located on the External Data tab of the Ribbon. Select the Contacts table in the Navigation Pane, and then on the External Data tab, in the Export group, click the SharePoint List button, as shown in Figure 22-22. Alternatively, you can right-click the table in the Navigation Pane, click the Export command on the shortcut menu that appears, and then click SharePoint List on the submenu.

Access opens the Export - SharePoint Site wizard, as shown in Figure 22-23. Under Specify A SharePoint Site, enter a valid address to a SharePoint site or subdirectory. Any SharePoint sites that you have previously imported from, linked to, or exported to are displayed in a list box. If one of these sites is the location to which you want to export the table, you can click that address and Access fills in the address text box below the list with that link. Enter a valid Windows SharePoint Services address in the text box below the list, or select a previously visited Windows SharePoint Services address from the list box.

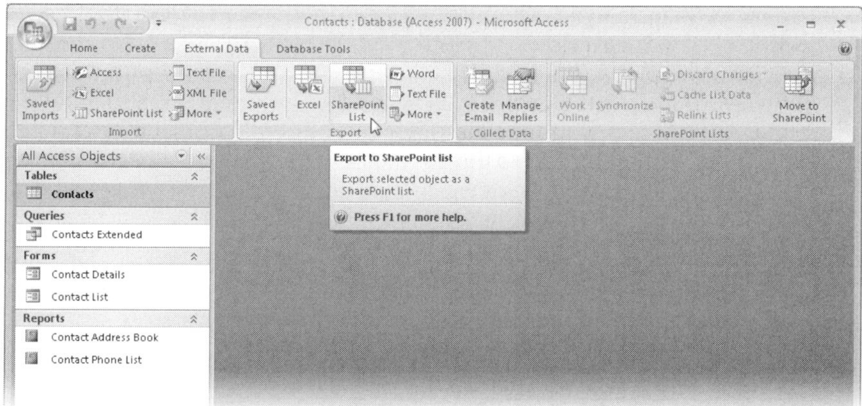


**Figure 22-22** Click the SharePoint List button to start the Export – SharePoint Site wizard.

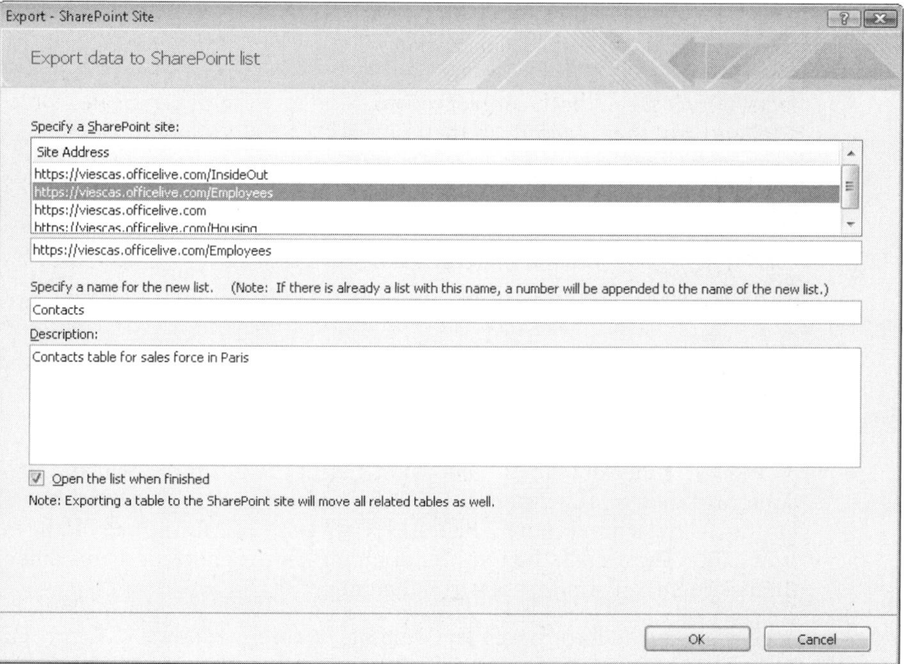


**Figure 22-23** The Export – SharePoint Site wizard helps you export a table to a SharePoint list.

Under Specify A Name For The New List, give this new list a name. Keep in mind that the name you use is exactly how it appears to users on the SharePoint site. If you name it tblContacts, for instance, that is exactly how the name is displayed to users. For our example, we kept the default name of Contacts that Access used. Also, if you use the same name as an existing list, Windows SharePoint Services appends a number to the end of the name to avoid duplication. For example, if a Contacts list is already present on our site, the new list is named Contacts1.

Under Description you can optionally enter some information to describe the use of this list. This description is shown on the SharePoint site next to the name of the list. For our example, we entered a description of "Contacts table for sales force in Paris," which you can see in Figure 22-23. Select the Open The List When Finished check box if you want Access to immediately display the new list in your browser after the export is complete. The wizard also displays a message noting that any tables related to this one are also going to be exported to the SharePoint site. We'll discuss this concept later in the chapter. Click OK to start the export process. If you are not logged on to your SharePoint site, you might be prompted to enter your logon information before continuing. During the export process, Access displays a message screen with progress indicators.

The duration of the export process depends on how many tables you are exporting, your connection speed, and the amount of data being transferred. In our simple test of this Contacts table using a high-speed connection, Access completed the task in only a few seconds. If you selected the Open The List When Finished check box in the Export – SharePoint Site wizard, your browser should open, displaying the Contacts list on the SharePoint site, as shown in Figure 22-24. You can see the name of the list, Contacts, as well as the optional description we entered in the wizard. By default, Windows SharePoint Services shows an All Items view for all lists; in this case it is called All Contacts, which shows both contact records. In our example, our sales force can now view, add, and edit these records in their Paris office using their browser.

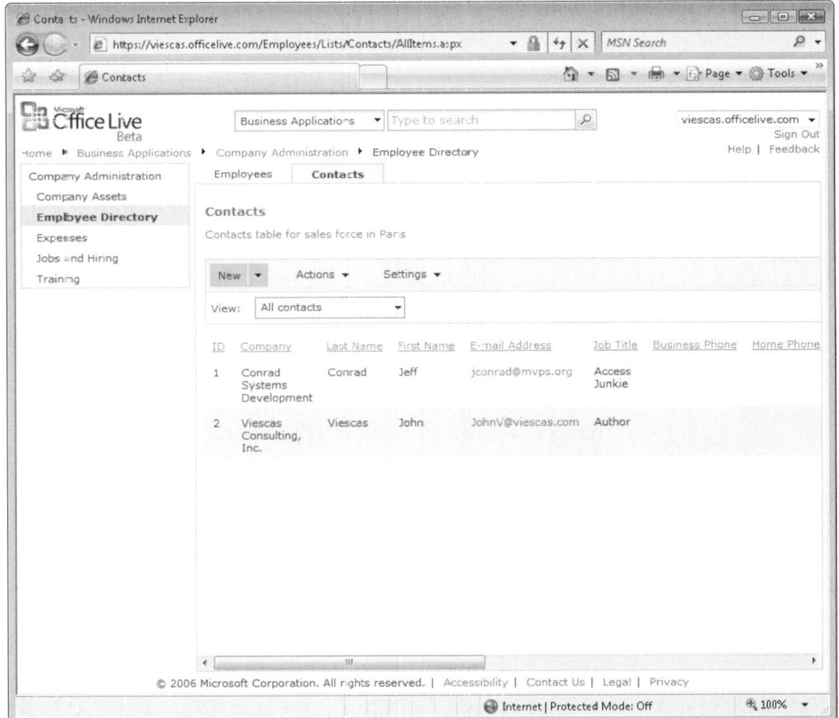


**Figure 22-24** Your new Contacts table is now displayed as a list on the SharePoint site.

When the export is complete, Access displays a confirmation message on the last page of the wizard, as shown in Figure 22-25. This page also offers you the option to save the export steps you just performed if you plan to repeat these steps on a regular basis. You can execute saved exports by clicking the Saved Exports button in the Export group on the External Data tab of the Ribbon. If the export process encounters any problems, Access displays a message on this page informing you of the errors and creates a local table of those it encounters. We'll discuss this error table later in the chapter. Click Close to close the wizard.

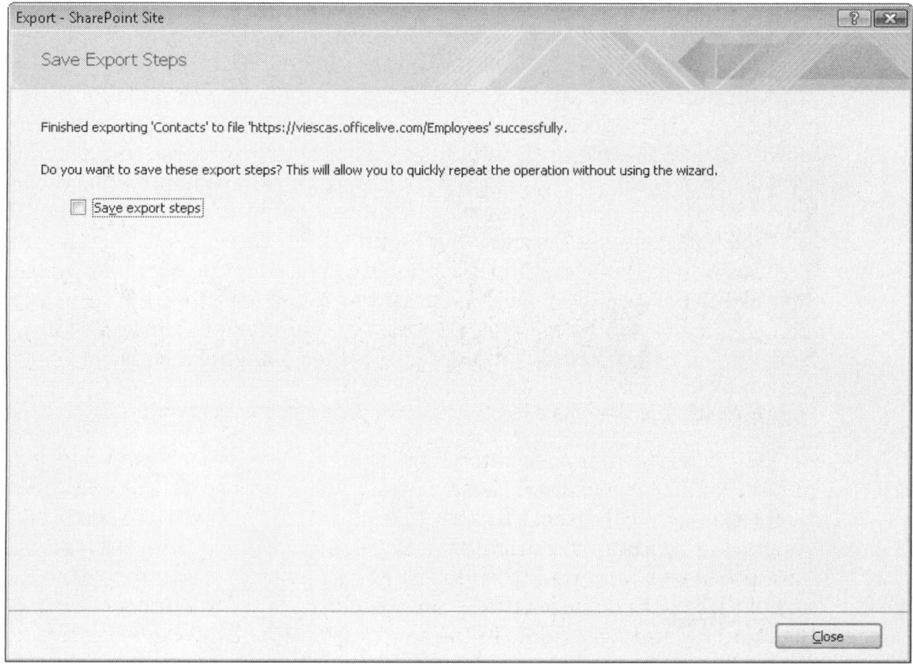


**Figure 22-25** Access confirms whether the table export was successful on the last page of the wizard.

## Importing a List from Windows SharePoint Services

Importing a list into Access 2007 from a SharePoint site works in much the same way as exporting a table. In this case, you are downloading data from a SharePoint site and saving a local copy of the data in an Access table. After Access creates the table and imports the records, you can use all the powerful tools at your disposal in Access—queries, forms, and reports—to analyze the data.

Continuing with our Contacts table example, let's import the Contacts list from the SharePoint site to the Contacts database we created earlier. You already have a

Contacts table in this database, so if you import the list, Access appends a number (in this case, 1) to the name of the imported table—Contacts1. You can either temporarily rename the existing Contacts table in your database to a new name, perhaps OldContacts, or just delete the table. We deleted the existing Contacts table by right-clicking the table in the Navigation Pane and clicking Delete on the shortcut menu.

Begin the import process by opening the Contacts database in Access and on the External Data tab, in the Import group, clicking the SharePoint List button, as shown in Figure 22-26.

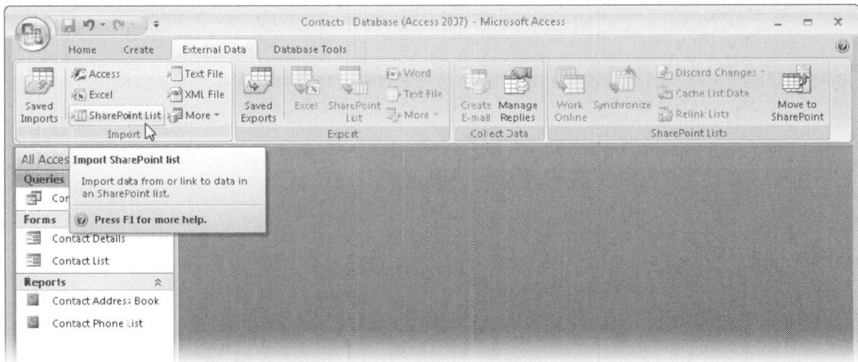


**Figure 22-26** Click the SharePoint List button to start the import process.

Access opens the first page of the Get External Data – SharePoint Site wizard, as shown in Figure 22-27. You can use this wizard to either import or link to Windows SharePoint Services lists. We'll discuss linking in the next section. Under Specify A SharePoint Site, enter a valid address to a SharePoint site or subdirectory. Any SharePoint sites that you have previously imported from, linked to, or exported to are displayed in a list box. If one of these sites is the location from which you want to import the table, you can click that address and Access fills in the address text box below the list with that link. Enter a valid Windows SharePoint Services address in the text box, or select a previously visited Windows SharePoint Services address from the list box. Select the first option, Import The Source Data Into A New Table In The Current Database, to import the list and records to a local table and then click Next.

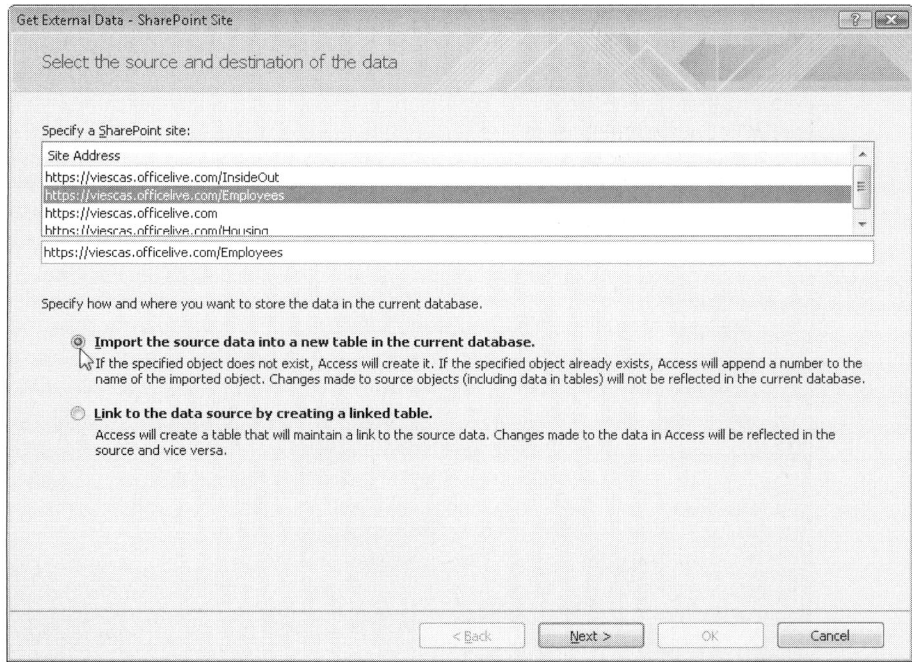


**Figure 22-27** You can import or link to Windows SharePoint Services lists using this wizard.

The second page of the wizard displays all the lists found in the SharePoint site directory that you specified on the previous page, as shown in Figure 22-28. Select a check box in the Import column to specify which list to import to Access. The Type column displays icons representing the different types of lists. User-defined lists, for example, are shown in orange, and built-in Windows SharePoint Services lists are shown in gray. The Name column displays the names of the lists on the SharePoint site. The fourth column, Items To Import, shows a list of views. If the list has more than one view defined in Windows SharePoint Services, you can select which specific view you want to import. The default view, All Contacts, is the only view defined in our example. The last column, Last Modified Date, displays the date the list was last modified.

Near the bottom of this page is an option to import the display values from any lookup fields instead of the actual lookup field ID. If you think a list has one or more related lookup lists, and you want to fetch the linking ID instead of the lookup value, clear this check box so that you fetch the actual ID value. For example, if an Orders list is related to a Customers list, clearing this check box fetches the Customer ID instead of the customer name that might be defined in a lookup. If you leave this item selected, you'll see the customer name imported in the Customer ID field. In this case there are no related or lookup tables for Contacts, so this option does not apply.

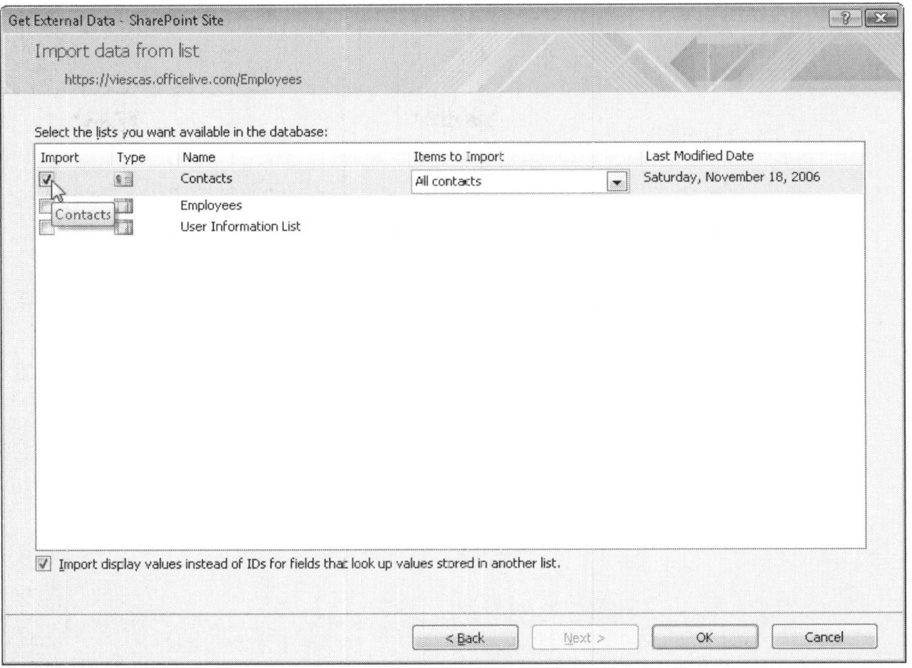


**Figure 22-28** Select which lists to import to Access on the second page of the wizard.

Select the check box for the Contacts list, leave the other options set to their defaults, and then click OK to begin the import process. Access creates a new local table in your database and then imports the records. After the import process is complete, Access displays the last page of the wizard, as shown in Figure 22-29. A message at the top of this page indicates whether the import process was a success or if any problems were encountered. The wizard also displays an option to save your import steps in case you want to perform the exact import procedure again in the future. You can execute saved imports by clicking the Saved Imports button in the Import group of the External Data tab on the Ribbon. Click Close to dismiss the wizard.

Access now displays the new Contacts table in the Navigation Pane. Open the table in Datasheet view to confirm that the table includes the two contacts records, as shown in Figure 22-30. You can now analyze the data using queries and reports or build data entry forms for adding records to the table or editing them. Note, however, that you've made a *copy* of the data stored on the SharePoint site. Any changes you make to the local copy won't be reflected in the Web site list. If you want to be able update the data in the list directly from Access, read on to the next section.

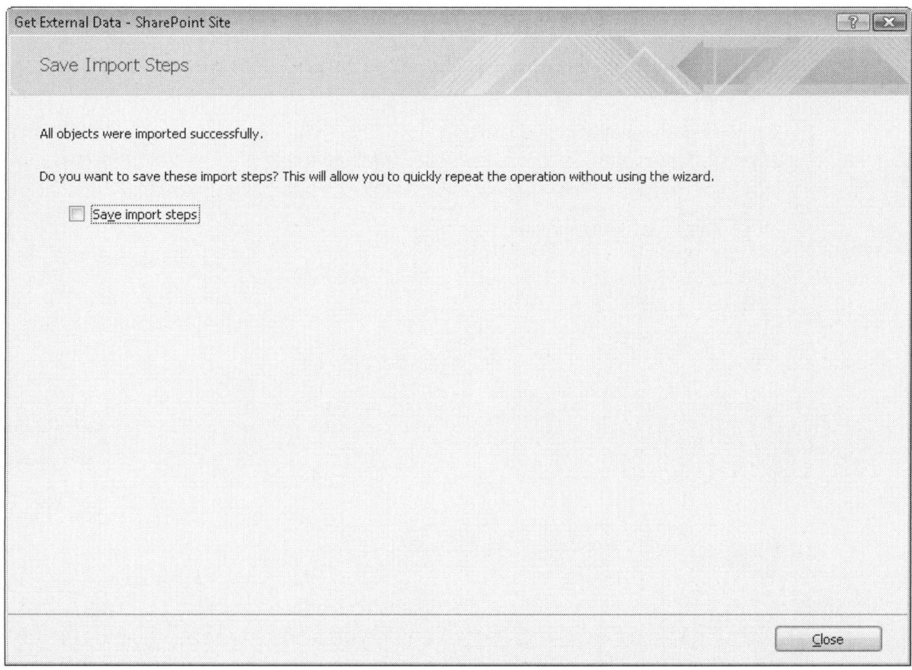


**Figure 22-29** The last page of the wizard asks if you want to save the import steps.



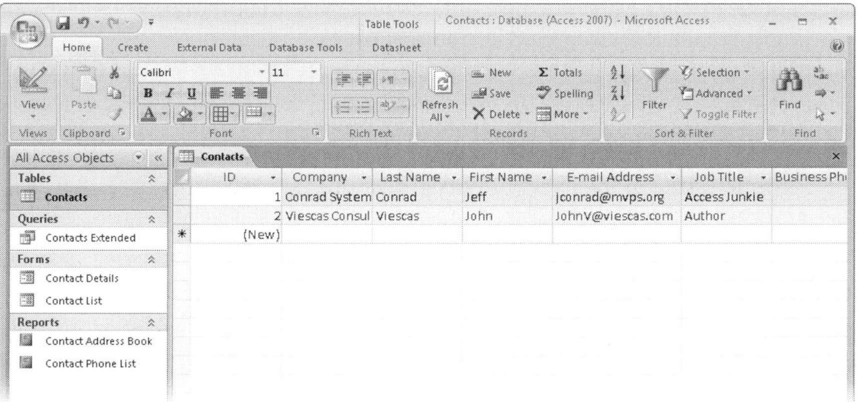


**Figure 22-30** The Contacts list from the SharePoint site has now been imported as a local table into Access.

**TROUBLESHOOTING**

**Why doesn't my imported Windows SharePoint Services list include all the records?**

Earlier in this chapter, you learned how to create different views of a list in Windows SharePoint Services. You can define filters, include only certain columns, and assign sort orders to a custom view. If your custom view restricts the number of records returned, Access follows those rules and imports only those specific records. So, for example, if you define a custom view that shows only contacts whose last name equals Viescas and then import that view into Access, the only records imported are ones where the last name equals Viescas. If you need to import all the records into Access, make sure you import a view that returns all the records in the list.

## Linking a Windows SharePoint Services List into Access

As you might recall from Chapter 6, we discussed the differences between deciding to import from or link to another data source. If you need to share your data with other users or if the data changes frequently, you should consider linking to instead of importing from another data source. You just imported a Contacts list from a SharePoint site to an Access database. If you add new records, edit existing records, or delete records in this table, these changes are not reflected in the list on the SharePoint site. This can be problematic if all users need to have the most up-to-date data available to them. You could make changes to your local table and then export the table to the SharePoint list, but what if another user had also made changes to the records in the list? You can see the dilemma this causes when trying to keep accurate data.

Fortunately, with Access you can link to a SharePoint site just as you can to other data sources. If you export an Access table to Windows SharePoint Services and then link it back, this allows both your desktop application users and authorized members of your Windows SharePoint Services team to work with and update the same data. To link to a SharePoint list from Access, click the SharePoint List button in the Import group on the External Data tab, as shown in Figure 22-31.

Access opens the first page of the Get External Data – SharePoint Site wizard, shown in Figure 22-32. This particular wizard is the same one you used for importing lists from a SharePoint site in the previous section. Enter a valid Windows SharePoint Services address in the address text box below the list of previously visited sites or select a previously visited Windows SharePoint Services address from the list box. Select the second option, Link To The Data Source By Creating A Linked Table, to link to an existing list on a SharePoint site and then click Next.

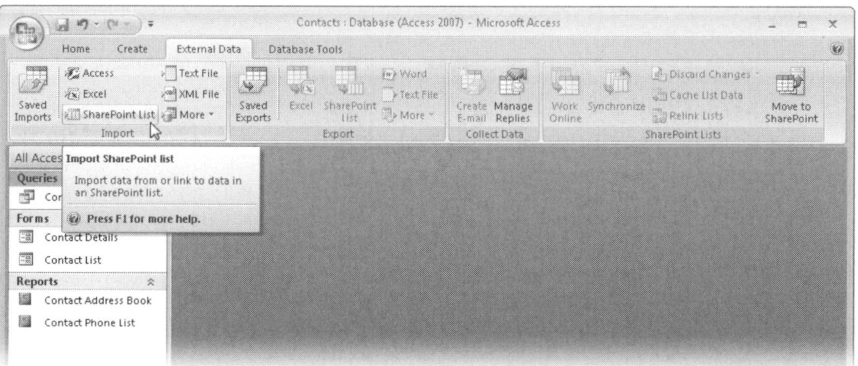

**Figure 22-31** Click the SharePoint List button to start the Get External Data – SharePoint Site wizard.

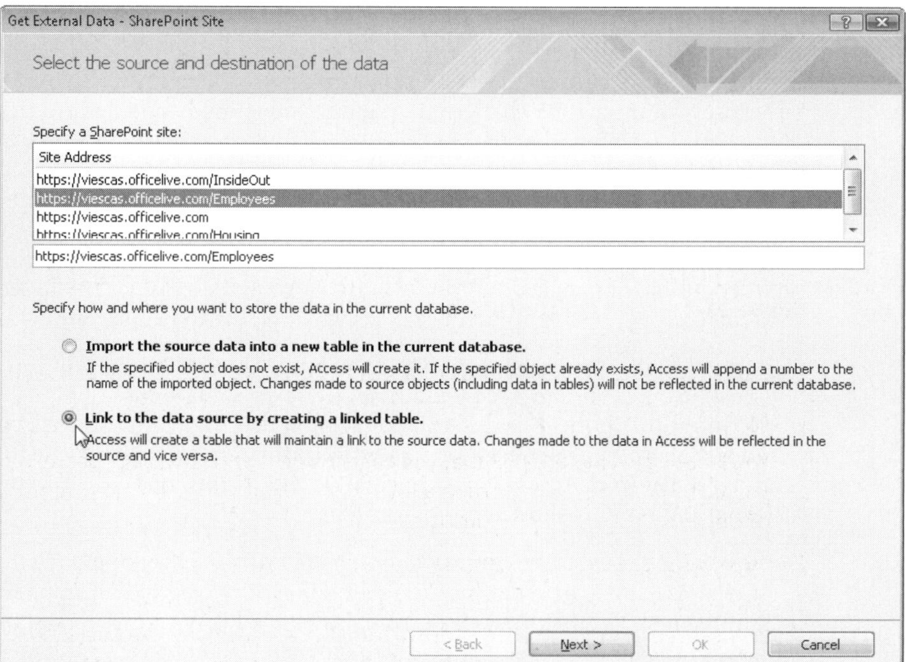

**Figure 22-32** Select the link option on the first page of the wizard to link to a list.

The second page of the wizard displays all the lists found in the SharePoint site directory that you specified on the previous page, as shown in Figure 22-33. Select a check box in the Link column to specify which list you want to link to Access. The Type column displays icons representing the type of list. User-defined lists, for example, are shown in orange when clicked, and built-in Windows SharePoint Services lists are shown in gray when clicked or not clicked. The Name column displays the names of the lists on the SharePoint site. The last column, Last Modified Date, displays the date the list was last modified. Select the Link check box next to Contacts and then click OK to start the link process.

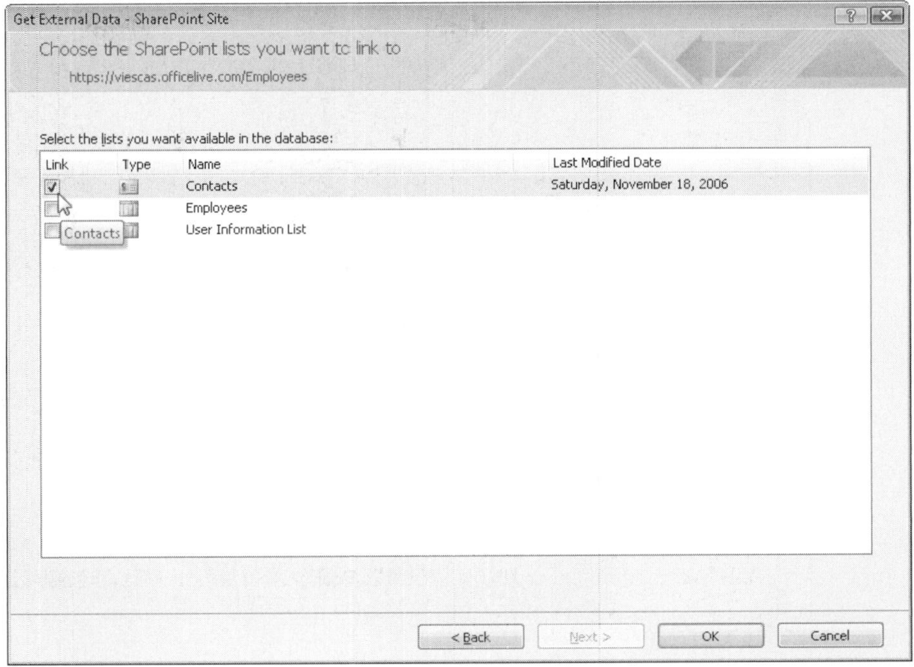


**Figure 22-33** Select the list you want to link to on this wizard page.

> **Note**
>
> You'll notice in Figure 22-33 that you cannot select any views on a SharePoint site as you can when you are importing a list. Access allows you to link only to the full list as opposed to views created from lists.

Access creates a link to the Windows SharePoint Services Contacts list and marks the icon for linked Windows SharePoint Services tables in the Navigation Pane with a blue arrow, as shown in Figure 22-34. If Access finds a duplicate name, it generates a new name by adding a unique integer to the end of the name as described earlier. Because objects such as forms, reports, macros, and modules might refer to the linked table by its original name, you should carefully check name references if Access has to rename a linked table.

On the status bar at the bottom of the Access window shown in Figure 22-34, you'll notice that Access displays Online With SharePoint. This message appears on the status bar whenever you have any active links to a SharePoint site.

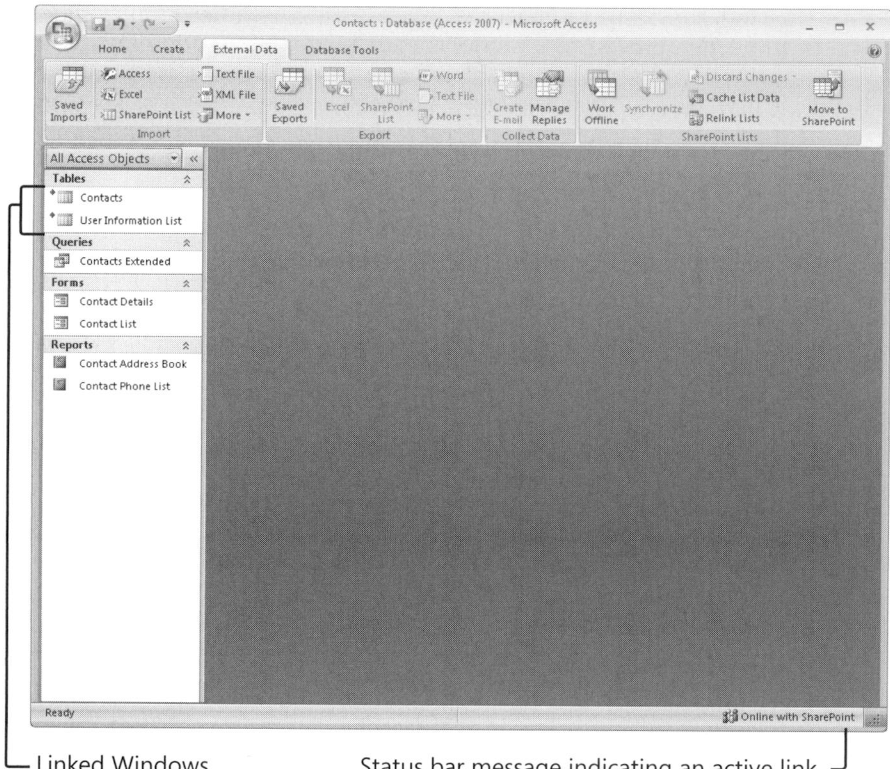


**Figure 22-34** Access now has a link to the Contacts list on the SharePoint site.



INSIDE OUT

### Do Not Delete the User Information List Link!

You might have noticed that Access created a link to the User Information List in addition to the Contacts list, even though you did not explicitly link to that list. Access adds links to other related lists such as those used for lookup values. Every list in Windows SharePoint Services includes hidden columns for Created By and Modified By dates, and this data is stored in the User Information List in Windows SharePoint Services. If you delete this link, Access displays error messages, like this one, whenever you attempt to update records in the list.

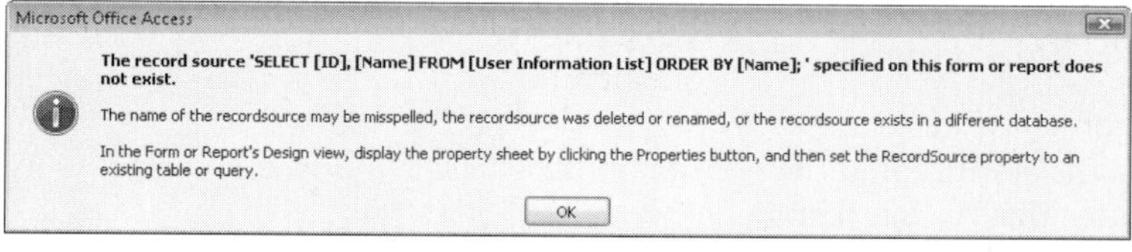

You can now use this Contacts list just like the original table in this application. In Figure 22-35, you can see that we opened the Contact List form in Access bound to the linked table, and both contact records are there. If you add a new record to the Contacts table using this form, the Contacts list on the SharePoint site is also updated. Note that using data from a SharePoint list as a linked table in Access requires a high-speed Internet connection or local area connection to your intranet server. Performance will be poor over a dial-up connection.

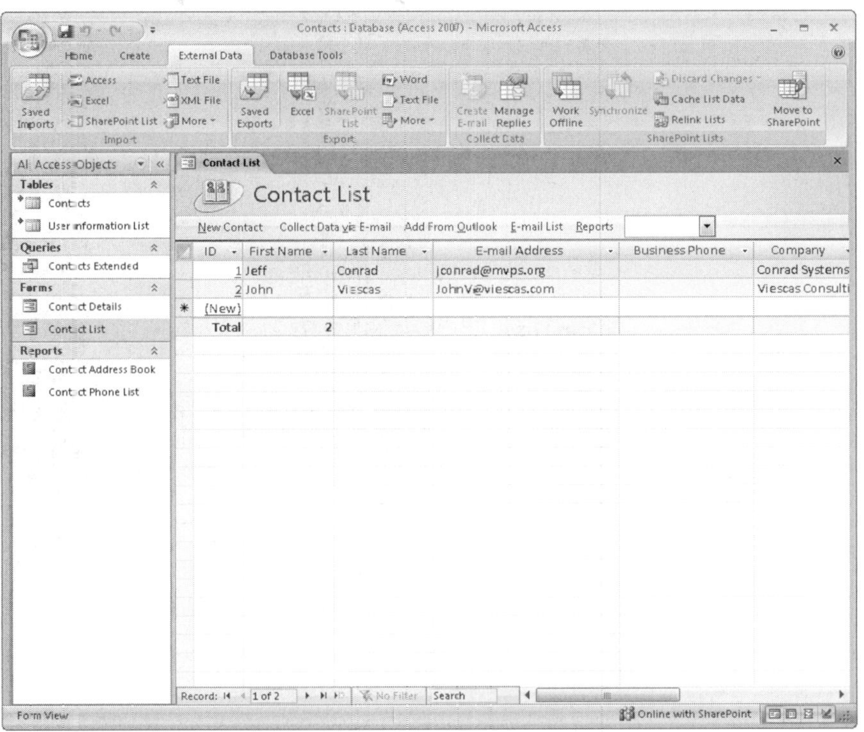

**Figure 22-35** You can update a linked SharePoint list just like local tables or tables linked to other data sources.

Also note that Windows SharePoint Services doesn't enforce referential integrity. If you use Windows SharePoint Services lists as the tables in your application, your application must perform additional checks to ensure that data integrity is maintained. For example, you might have a Contact Events list that includes the Contact ID field from the Contacts list. Before allowing a user to delete a Contacts record, you should check to see that no related records exist in the Contact Events list. If records exist, you can either delete them or disallow deleting the Contacts records. You'll learn more about working with recordsets in code behind forms in Chapter 20, "Automating Your Application with Visual Basic."

## Using SharePoint List Options with Linked Lists

When you have a linked list, Access 2007 offers several options for interacting directly with the SharePoint site interface through a shortcut menu. If you've been following along to this point, you should still have an active link to the Windows SharePoint Services Contacts list. Close the Contact List form if it's still open, and then right-click the Contacts table link in the Navigation Pane, as shown in Figure 22-36.

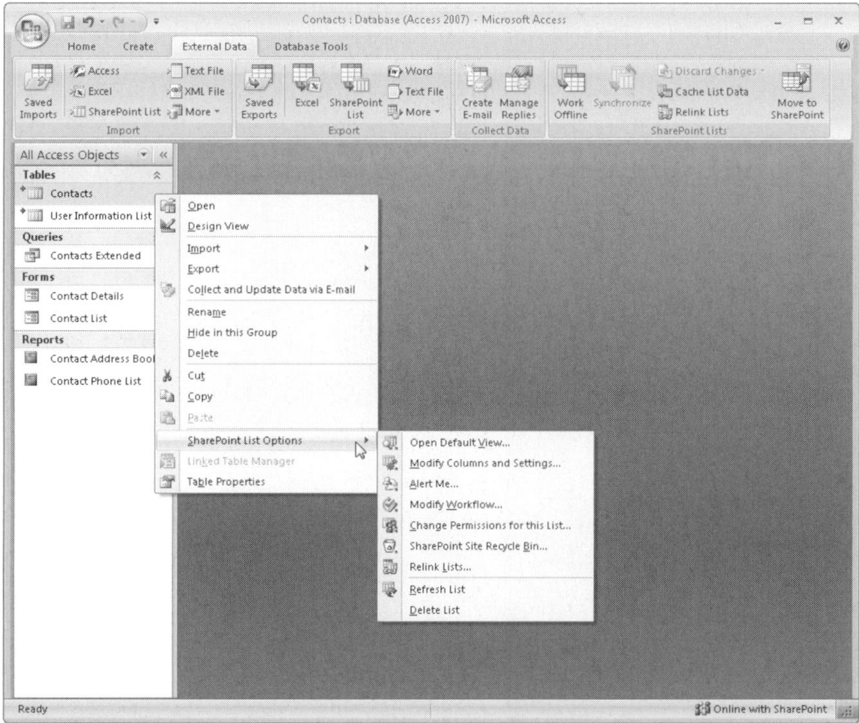


**Figure 22-36** You can interact directly with the Windows SharePoint Services interface from within Access by using commands on the shortcut menu of a linked list.

You can do any of the following from the SharePoint List Options submenu:

- **Open Default View** This option sends a command to the SharePoint site and opens the default view for the list. In our example, Windows SharePoint Services displays the All Contacts view.
- **Modify Columns And Settings** This option opens a page where you can modify the design of the list. Similarly to modifying a table in an Access database, you can rename columns, change data types, change the sequence of columns, delete columns, or add new columns.
- **Alert Me** This option opens a page on the SharePoint site where you can set options to be notified via e-mail if any data is added to this list, if data is modified, or even if data is deleted.

- **Modify Workflow** This option takes you to the Workflow page for this list where you can modify existing workflow rules or add new workflow rules. You can use workflow rules to attach business logic to items in a SharePoint, similarly to setting validation rules in an Access table.
- **Change Permissions For This List** This option opens a page on the SharePoint site where you can view and change the users and their permissions levels.
- **SharePoint Site Recycle Bin** This option opens the Recycle Bin page on the SharePoint site where you can restore items (lists, views, rows, and so on) to your site or permanently delete them. Windows SharePoint Services stores elements in the Recycle Bin for 30 days and automatically purges anything left in the Recycle Bin longer than that.
- **Relink Lists** This option opens the Relink Lists To New Site dialog box so that you can relink your lists to a new SharePoint site location. This dialog box, shown here, works in much the same way as the Linked Table Manager for relinking tables when the data source location has changed. You might need to use this facility if you have moved your lists to a new Web site.

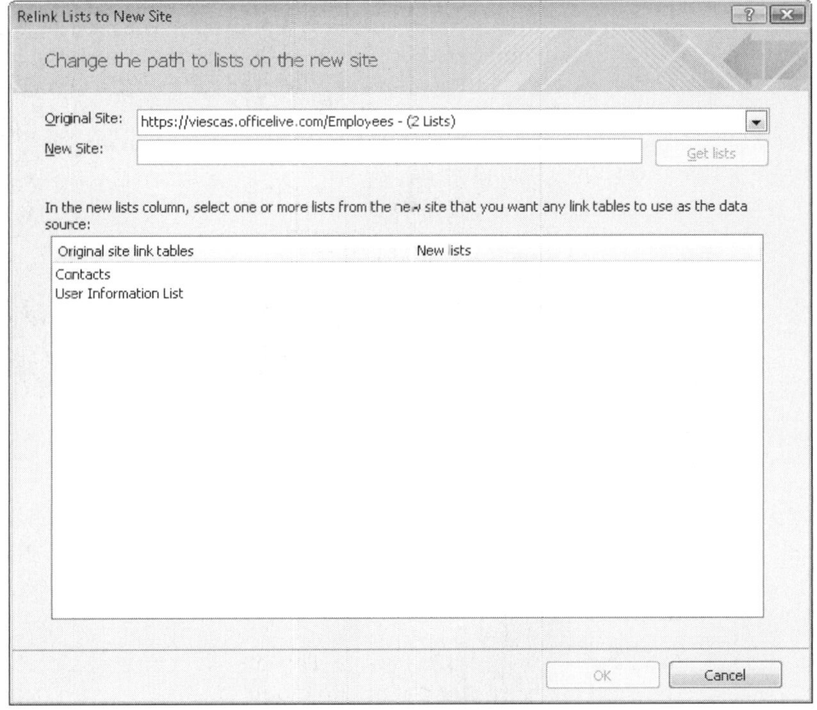


- **Refresh List** This option causes Access to refresh the list from the SharePoint site.

- **Delete List** This option deletes the selected list from the SharePoint site. Access displays a message asking you to confirm the deletion. If you accidentally delete a list by mistake, you can recover it in the Recycle Bin.

> **Note**
>
> When you open a database that has tables linked to Windows SharePoint Services lists and if you're not currently logged on to your SharePoint site, you'll see a standard Web site logon dialog box where you must enter your user name and password and click OK.

## Creating a New Windows SharePoint Services List from Within Access

Access 2007 also includes a powerful new feature that lets you dynamically create new lists on a Windows SharePoint Services site. With only one click on a Ribbon button and a few wizard options to set, you're essentially creating a new table as a list directly in Windows SharePoint Services. We'll continue using our Contacts database and our existing SharePoint site to demonstrate this functionality. If you have any objects open in this database, close them so that you see only the Navigation Pane. On the Create tab, in the Tables group, click the SharePoint Lists button. Access displays a menu of six options, as shown in Figure 22-37.

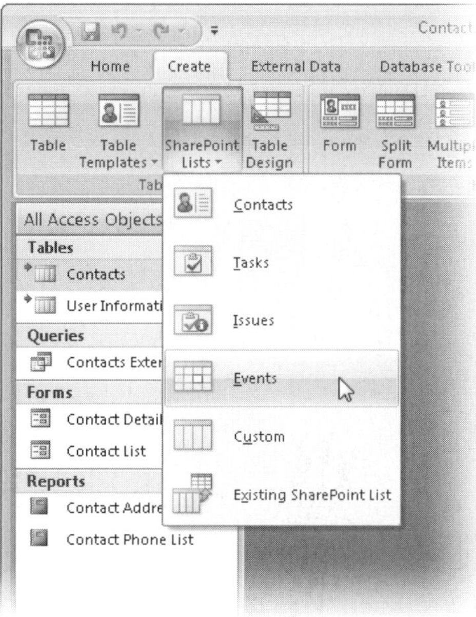


Figure 22-37 You can create new lists on a SharePoint site from within Access.

## Using an Existing List Template

The first four options—Contacts, Tasks, Issues, and Events—create a new list on the SharePoint site and a table in Access that links to that list using a built-in template. These first four options are commonly used list styles on a SharePoint site. The Custom option, discussed in the next section, creates a new list on the SharePoint site with only three visible columns—ID, Title, and Attachments. The Existing SharePoint List option opens the Get External Data - SharePoint Site wizard to import or link to a Windows SharePoint Services list.

Let's step through creating a new Events list on the SharePoint site so that we can coordinate vacation scheduling with our sales force in Paris. Click the Events option on the SharePoint Lists menu, as shown in Figure 22-37. Access opens the Create New List wizard, shown in Figure 22-38. Under Specify A SharePoint Site, enter a valid address to a SharePoint site or subdirectory on that site. Enter a valid Windows SharePoint Services address in the text box or select a previously visited Windows SharePoint Services address from the list box.

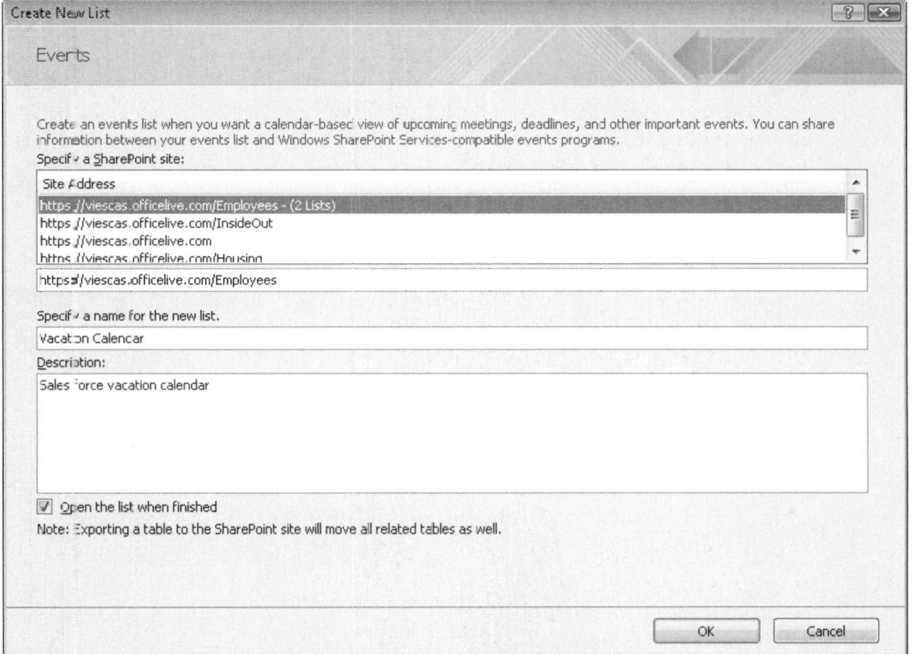


**Figure 22-38** To create a new list, specify a name for the list and the location of the SharePoint site.

Under Specify A Name For This List, give this new list a name. Keep in mind that the name you use is exactly how it appears to users on the SharePoint site. We decided to name our new list Vacation Calendar. Under Description you can optionally enter some information to describe the use of this list. We entered a description of "Sales force vacation calendar," which you can see in Figure 22-38. This description appears on the SharePoint site next to the name of the list. Leave the Open The List When Finished check box selected so that Access immediately displays the new table in Datasheet view after you create the list. Click OK to create the new list.

Access sends commands to the SharePoint site to create the new list and then creates a new table linked to the Vacation Calendar list. Access also opens the new table in Datasheet view, as shown in Figure 22-39. This new table has 21 fields, such as Location, Start Time, End Time, and Description, which you can use to describe an event.

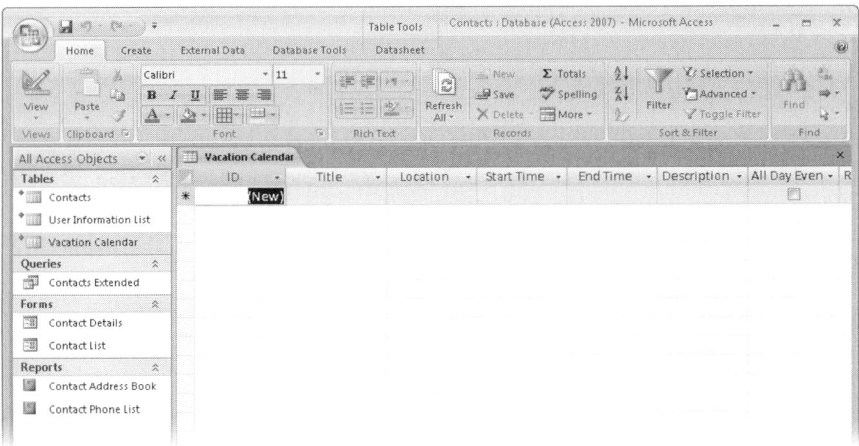


**Figure 22-39** Access created a new list on a SharePoint site and a table linked to the list.

If you use Internet Explorer to navigate to the address you specified for the list, you should now see the new Vacation Calendar list on the SharePoint site. This type of list is perfectly suited for display in a Calendar view. As you can see in Figure 22-40, the default view for the Vacation Calendar list is Calendar. The Vacation Calendar list also has two other views—All Events and Current Events—that display the records in a more traditional Datasheet view. At the moment, the Calendar view is empty because no records have been created in the list.

Switch back to Access, and let's add a new record to the table to see how easily we can interact with the Calendar view on the SharePoint site. Our sales manager, John, is going to be on vacation from October 30 through November 3. You can enter this data directly into the table's Datasheet view in Access, or you could build a data entry form. As you learned in Part 3 of this book, you have a lot more control over how data is entered if you use a form instead of entering data directly into a table datasheet, but for this simple exercise we entered John's vacation schedule into the table's Datasheet view, as shown in Figure 22-41. (If you're following along with this example, select a start and end time within the current month.)

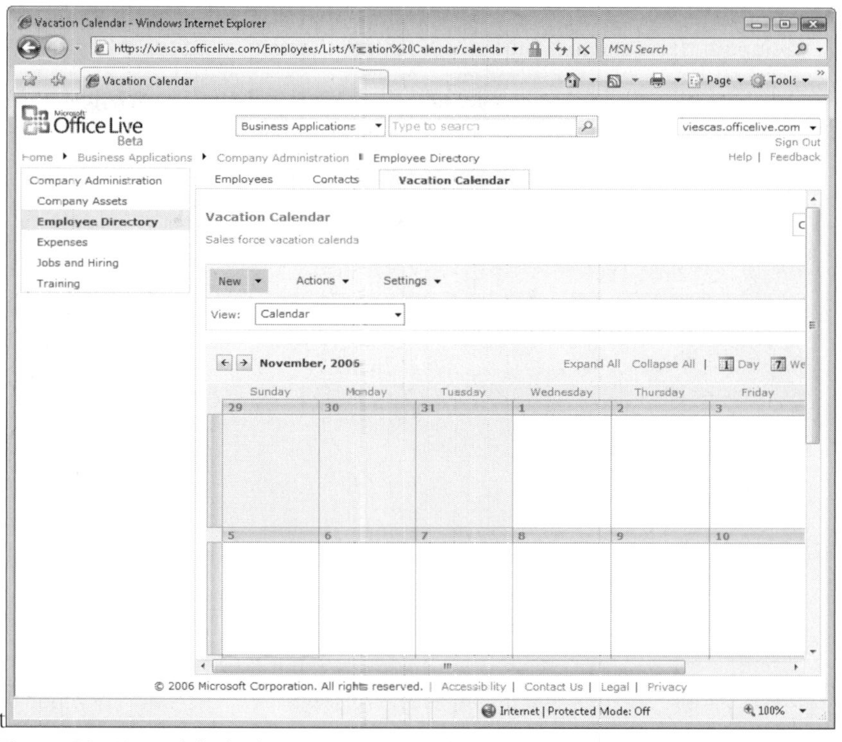

Figure 22-40 By default, the new Vacation Calendar list is displayed in Calendar view.

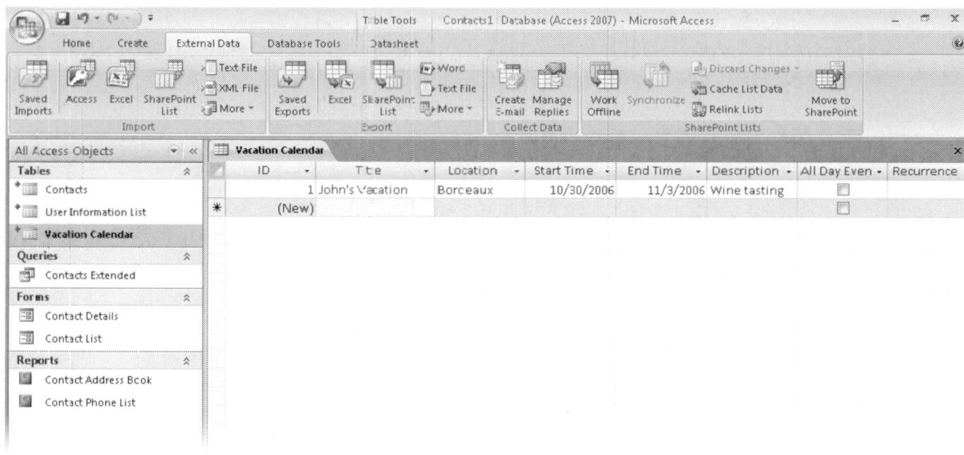

Figure 22-41 Enter a vacation record into the table to see it displayed on the SharePoint site.

After you move from the record or save it by clicking the Save button in the Records group on the Home tab, Access saves the information on the Windows SharePoint Services site. Go to the Windows SharePoint Services site using your browser, click the Refresh button, and navigate to the appropriate month and year to see the changes reflected in the Calendar view, as shown in Figure 22-42. John's vacation schedule can now be seen by any users of our Windows SharePoint Services site.

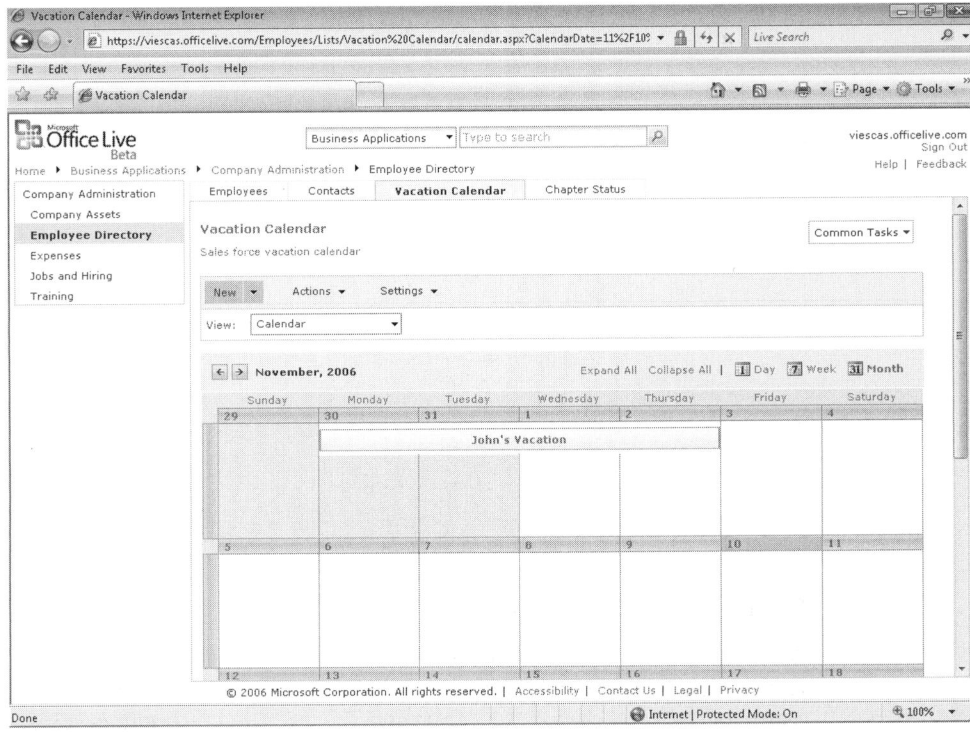


**Figure 22-42** John's vacation schedule now appears as a block of time in the Calendar view.

If you click on the block of time in the Calendar view, Windows SharePoint Services displays a single-list view showing the details of John's record that we entered in Access, as shown in Figure 22-43.

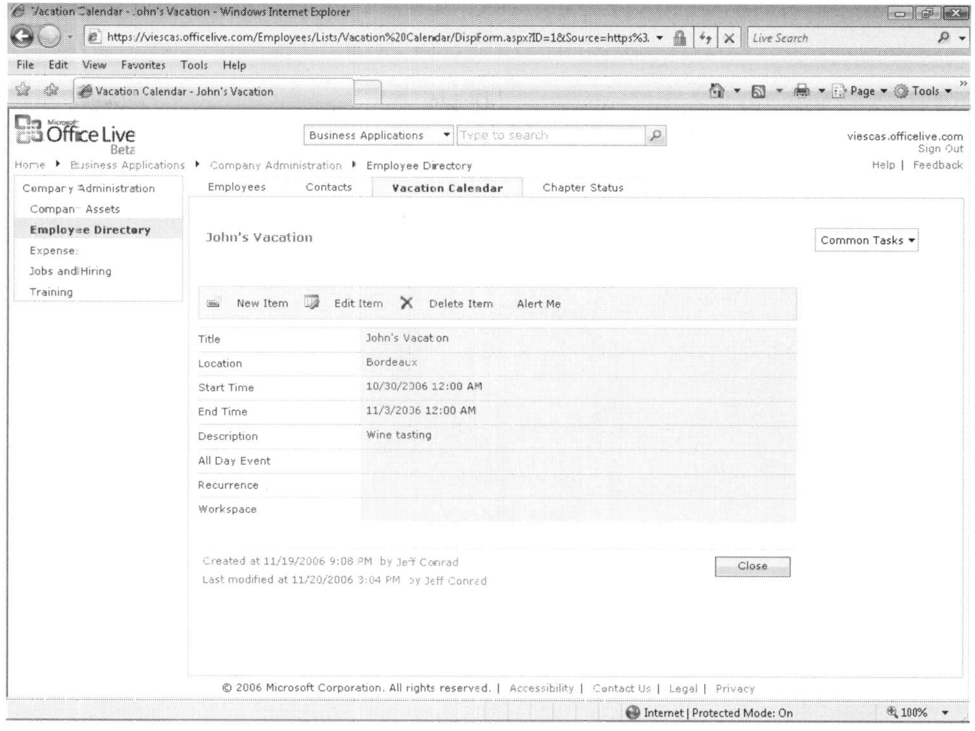


**Figure 22-43** The single-list view shows the details of John's schedule.

## Creating a Custom List

You can also create a new custom list on a SharePoint site through Access 2007. When you choose this option, Windows SharePoint Services does not use one of its built-in templates for the list structure. In Access, if you have any database objects open, close them now so that only the Navigation Pane is visible. On the Create tab, click the SharePoint Lists button in the Tables group, as shown in Figure 22-44.

Next, click the Custom option. Access opens the Create New List wizard, as shown in Figure 22-45. Enter a valid Windows SharePoint Services address in the text box or select a previously visited Windows SharePoint Services address from the list box. Under Specify A Name For This List, we entered Chapter Status. In the Description box we entered "Status of chapters for Microsoft Press," as you can see in Figure 22-45. Leave the Open The List When Finished check box selected and then click OK to create the new list.

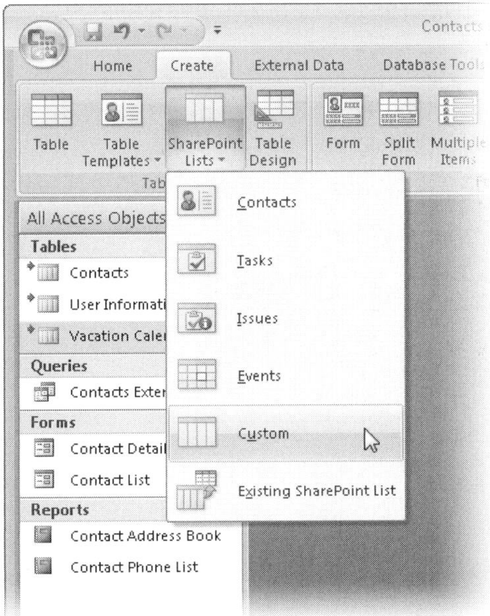


**Figure 22-44** Click the Custom option to create a custom list on the SharePoint site.

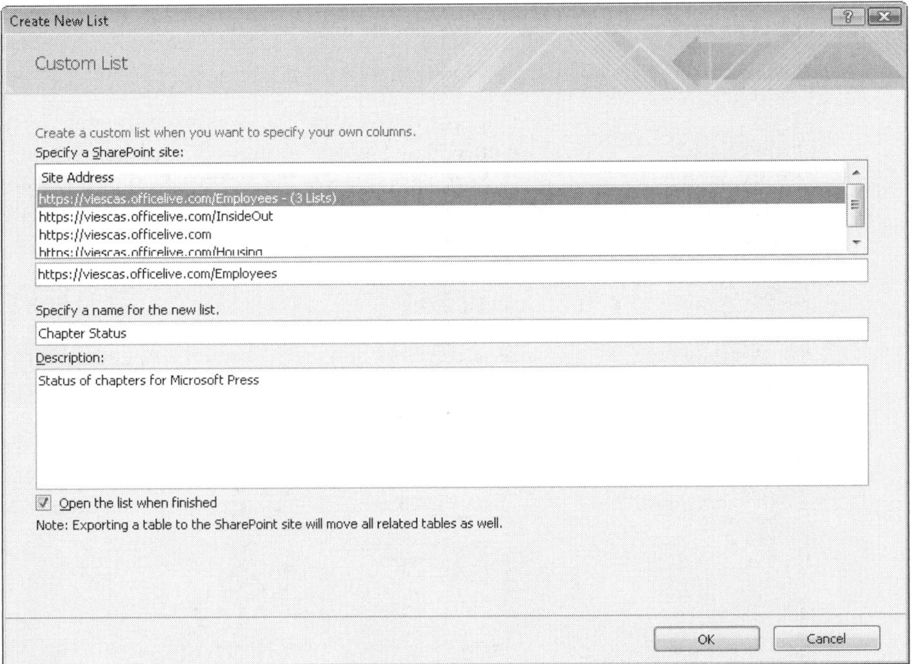


**Figure 22-45** Enter a name for the custom list and the location of the SharePoint site.

Access instructs Windows SharePoint Services to create a new default list, creates a table linked to the list, and opens the new list in Datasheet view, as shown in

Figure 22-46. A Windows SharePoint Services custom list by default contains only ID, Title, and Attachments columns.

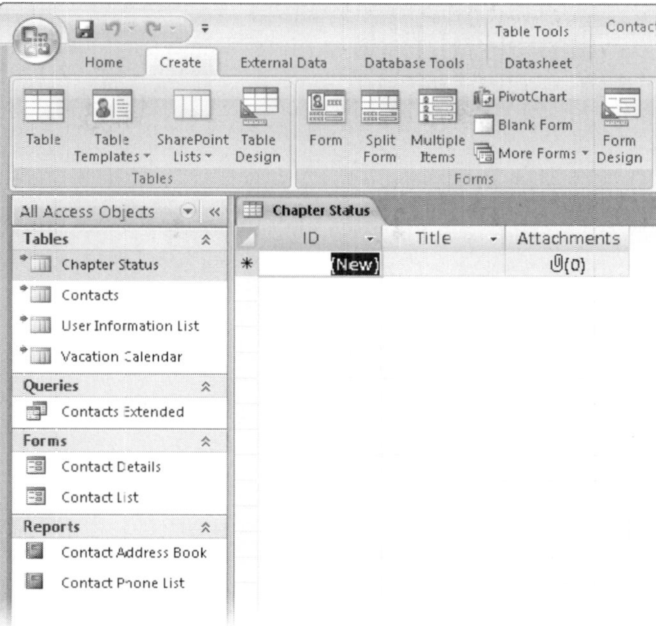


**Figure 22-46** By default, the new list includes three columns.

If you go to the SharePoint site in your browser, you can see the new custom list, as shown in Figure 22-47. The only view created so far is the All Items view, and the list is empty. Windows SharePoint Services displays the description of the list that we entered in the wizard beneath the list name. In this view, the Attachment column is to the left of the Title column, and the ID column is hidden.

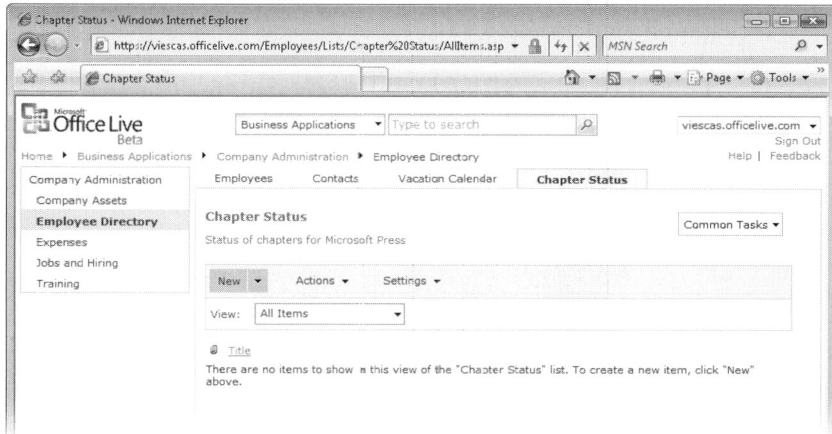


**Figure 22-47** The new custom list shows up in the browser window.

Go back to Access, and let's take a closer look at the table that Windows SharePoint Services created. Right-click the Chapter Status linked table in the Navigation Pane and click Design View on the shortcut menu. Access displays a warning message that Chapter Status is a linked table and that you cannot change any of its properties. Click Yes in the message box to open the table in Design view, as shown in Figure 22-48.

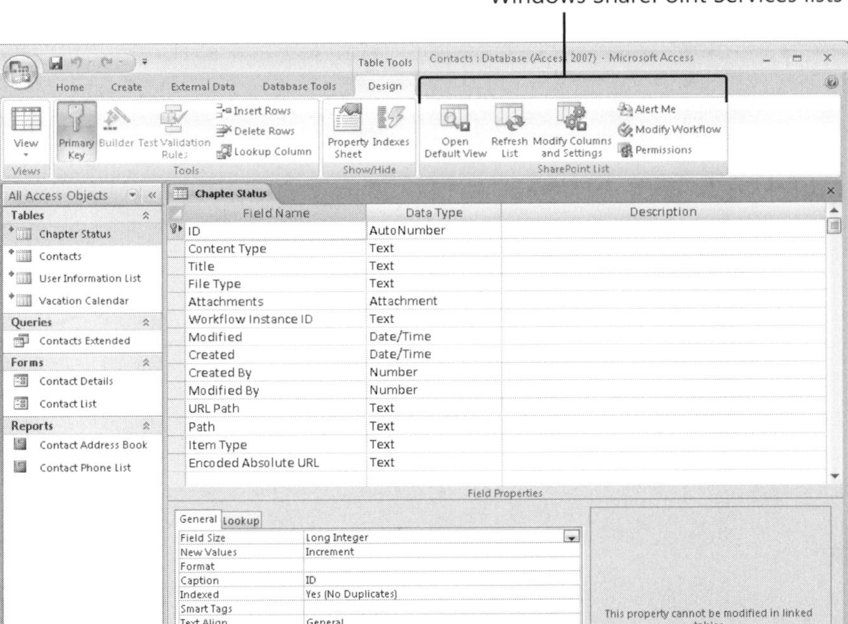


**Figure 22-48** Access displays all the hidden columns of the list in the table's Design view.

You'll immediately notice that instead of seeing only three fields as you did in Datasheet view, Access displays 14 fields in Design view. These extra fields are hidden columns that Windows SharePoint Services uses to maintain the list. You can also see in Figure 22-48 a new group on the Design contextual tab under Table Tools called SharePoint List. Access displays this group only when you are working with tables that are linked to Windows SharePoint Services lists. In the SharePoint List group, you can do the following:

- **Open Default View** This option sends a command to the Windows SharePoint Services browser and opens the default view for that list.
- **Refresh List** This option causes Access to refresh the list from the SharePoint site. If any column properties have changed, Access closes the table.

- **Modify Columns And Settings** This option opens the SharePoint site to a page where you can modify the design of the list. Similar to modifying a table in an Access database, you can rename columns, change data types, change the sequence of columns, delete columns, or add new columns. Just as with other linked tables, to make changes to the source table, you must make them in the source data store, in this case on the SharePoint site.
- **Alert Me** This option opens a page on the SharePoint site where you can set options to be notified via e-mail if any data is added to this list, if data is modified, or even if data is deleted.
- **Modify Workflow** This option takes you to the Workflow page for this list where you can modify existing workflow rules or add new workflow rules.
- **Permissions** This option opens a page on the SharePoint site where you can view and change the users and their permission levels.

After you create a custom list, you can use these commands to modify your list according to your specific needs. Close the Design view for this table now.

## Migrating an Access Database to a Windows SharePoint Services Site

You'll learn in Part 7 of this book that you can use an SQL server as a data source for an Access project file. You can also use a Windows SharePoint Services site as a data source for your Access 2007 database. You can either *publish* or *move* your Access 2007 database when migrating to a SharePoint site. When you publish your database, you are simply copying your database to the Windows SharePoint server so that others can open and use it. Any changes you make to the data in the local copy are not reflected in the copy on the SharePoint site. If you change queries, forms, reports, macros, or modules, you must republish your database to make the copy on the server current.

When you move your database, Access makes a backup copy of your database, uploads all the tables into Windows SharePoint Services lists, and replaces all the tables with a link to the appropriate list so that any data editing you perform in the local copy is reflected in the copy on the SharePoint site. You can set form and report properties so that Access creates a view of the SharePoint list that points to the form or report in the moved database. If you change queries, forms, reports, macros, or modules in your local copy, you must republish your database to make the copy on the server current.

Similar to the process of upsizing an Access database to SQL Server, Access 2007 includes a Move To SharePoint Site Wizard that walks you through the process of moving your tables and data to Windows SharePoint Services lists. By moving your database, you can share the data with many users and take advantage of the Windows SharePoint Services security, version control, and Recycle Bin. Users can update and view the data either through links to the lists in an Access 2007 database or by using their browser.

When you move an Access 2007 database to a SharePoint site, Access places an entire copy of the database in a document library on the site. Users can open the database from the SharePoint site and download a copy to their local computer to work with the data. By having a copy of your database objects on a SharePoint site, users can always have the latest copy of the queries, forms, reports, macros, and modules.

> **Note**
> Before we began the next steps in this chapter, we deleted all the existing lists we previously created on our SharePoint site.

## Publishing Your Database to a Windows SharePoint Services Site

Publishing a database to a SharePoint site is somewhat similar to copying a database to a file server where users can obtain a copy of the data, work with it, and send changes back to the server. When you open a published database on the SharePoint site, Access downloads a cached copy of the file for you to use. Any changes you make to the data or objects are not reflected in the database on the SharePoint site unless you republish the changes.

Close the current Contacts database if you haven't already done so; we'll use another new Contacts database template that comes with Access for an example of publishing a database. Open Access if you closed it, and click the Contacts database template icon in the middle of the Getting Started screen. Browse to a location in the right task pane to save this file and name it Contacts. Beneath the file path, you can see an option to create and link your database to a SharePoint site, as shown in Figure 22-49. If you select this check box and then click Download, Access downloads the database template to your computer and then prompts you for the address of your SharePoint site. After you provide the appropriate address, Access creates a new list for each table in the sample database on the SharePoint site and then creates a link to each list in the database. You also have the option to move a copy of the entire database up to the SharePoint site. (We discuss moving a database in the following sections.)



To continue our publishing example, clear the Create And Link Your Database To A SharePoint site check box, and then click the Download button to download the database to your local computer. After Access opens the database, close the open Contact List form so that only the Navigation Pane is visible. Click the Navigation Pane menu, click Object Type under Navigate To Category, and then click All Access Objects to display a list of all objects.

This Contacts database includes only one table—Contacts—with no records. To publish the database, click the Microsoft Office Button, point to the Publish option, and then click Document Management Server, as shown in Figure 22-50.

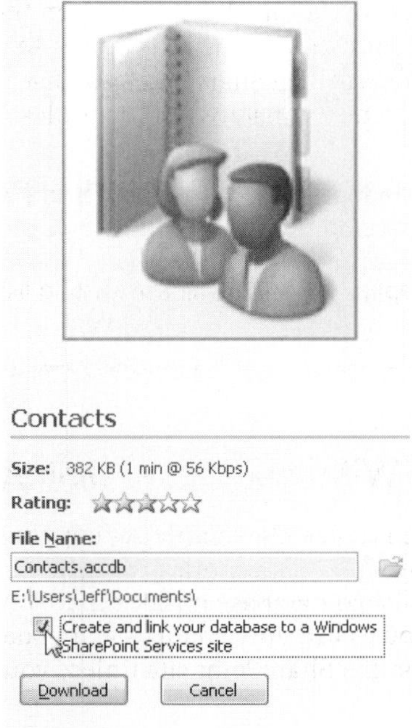


**Figure 22-49** The right task pane on the Getting Started screen includes an option to create links to a SharePoint site when you create the database.

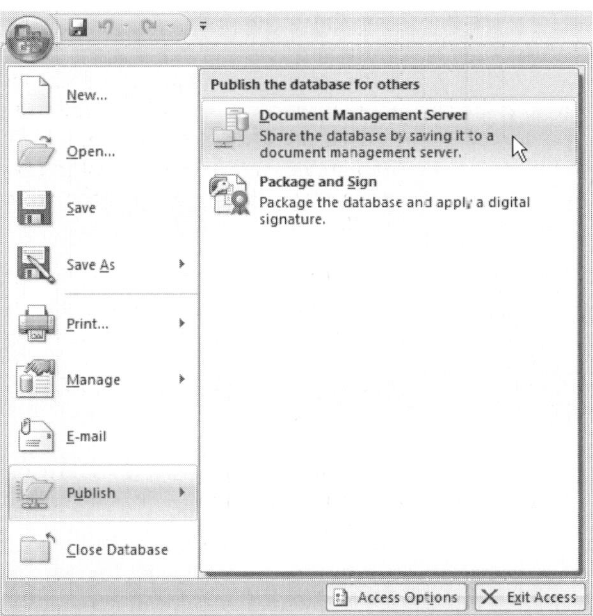


**Figure 22-50** Click Document Management Server to begin publishing your database.

**Note**

You can publish an Access database to a SharePoint site only if the database is in the Access 2007 .accdb file format.

Access opens the Publish To Web Server dialog box, as shown in Figure 22-51. You need to specify the address to the workspace on the SharePoint site in the File Name box. (If you're working in a corporate environment, you might need to ask your network administrator for this information.) We entered the address to the InsideOut workspace on our SharePoint site. Click Publish. You should see a standard Windows logon dialog box to verify your credentials on the SharePoint site. Enter your user name and password and click OK to continue.

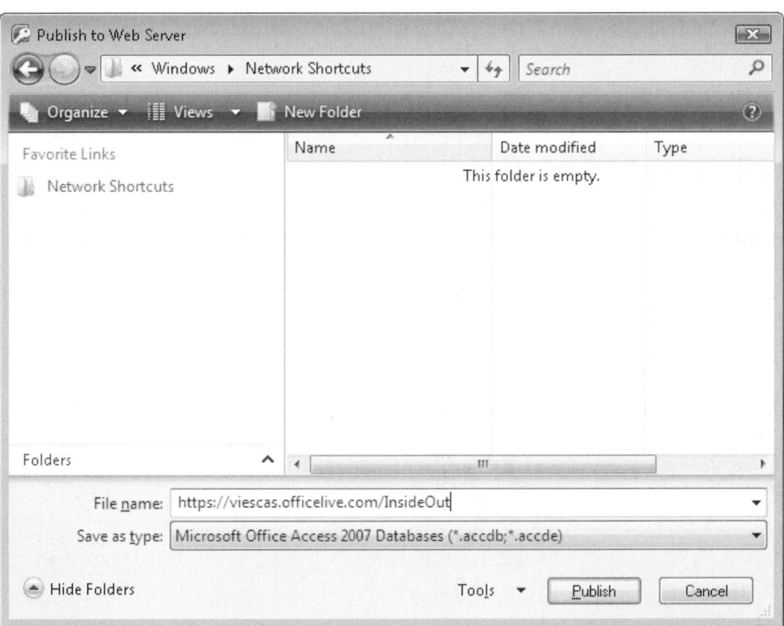


**Figure 22-51** Enter the address to your SharePoint site in the Publish To Web Server dialog box.

Access then shows the contents of the InsideOut workspace on our SharePoint site and enters the name of the file, Contacts, in the File Name text box. In our case, we selected the Shared Documents library under Document Libraries, as shown in Figure 22-52. Click the Publish button to begin publishing your database to the SharePoint site.

During the publishing process, Access sets a property in the database to note that it has been published. After the process is complete, Access opens the Contacts database again and displays the Contact List form, as shown in Figure 22-53. You'll notice that there is no link to the Contacts table in this database, and no Online With SharePoint message appears on the status bar. Note, however, that Access knows that you have published this database, and it provides you with a handy button on the Message Bar that enables you to republish any changes.

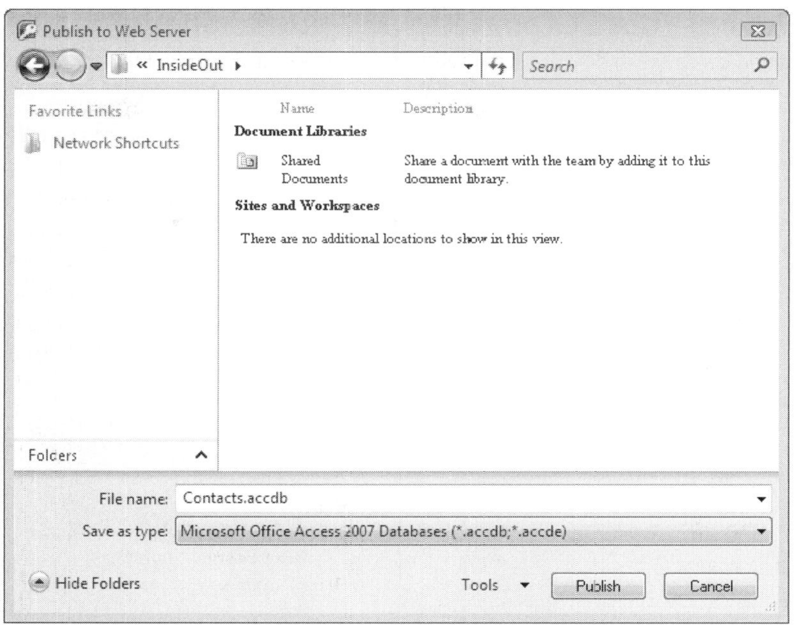


**Figure 22-52** Select the Shared Documents library to publish the Contacts database.

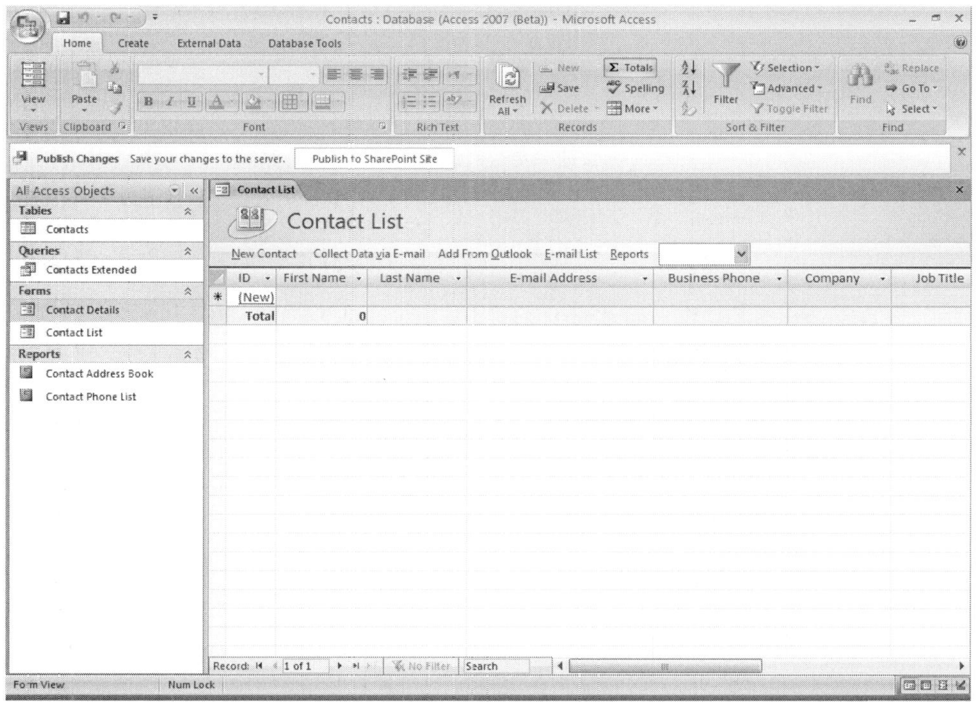


**Figure 22-53** The published database does not have active links to any list on the SharePoint site.

## Moving Your Database to a Windows SharePoint Services Site

To show you the process of moving an Access 2007 database to a Windows SharePoint Services site, we'll use the Issues Sample database on the companion CD. (You previously used this sample in Chapter 2, "Exploring the New Look of Access 2007.") This database already has data in the two tables—Contacts and Issues—so you can see how Access moves data to a SharePoint site. Begin by opening the Issues Sample database (IssuesSample.accdb), and then close the Issue List form so that only the Navigation Pane is visible. Next, on the External Data tab, click the Move To SharePoint button in the SharePoint Lists group, as shown in Figure 22-54.

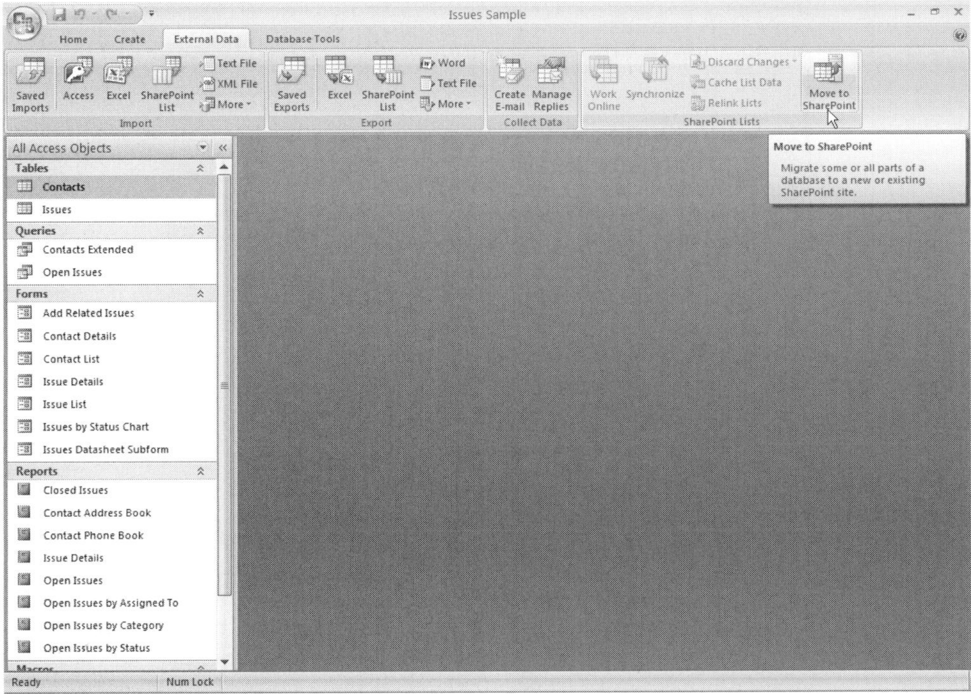


**Figure 22-54** The Move To SharePoint button facilitates the process of moving your database to a SharePoint site.

### Note

You can move an Access database to a SharePoint site only if the database is in the Access 2007 .accdb file format.

Chapter 22

Access opens the Move To SharePoint Site Wizard, as shown in Figure 22-55. Enter the address for your SharePoint site in the What SharePoint Site Do You Want To Use? text box. If you select the Save A Copy Of My Database To The SharePoint Site And Create Shortcuts To My Access Forms And Reports check box, Access uploads an entire copy of your database into a document library on that SharePoint site. If you clear this check box, Access creates only new lists for the tables, moves the data to those lists, and creates linked local tables in the Access database.

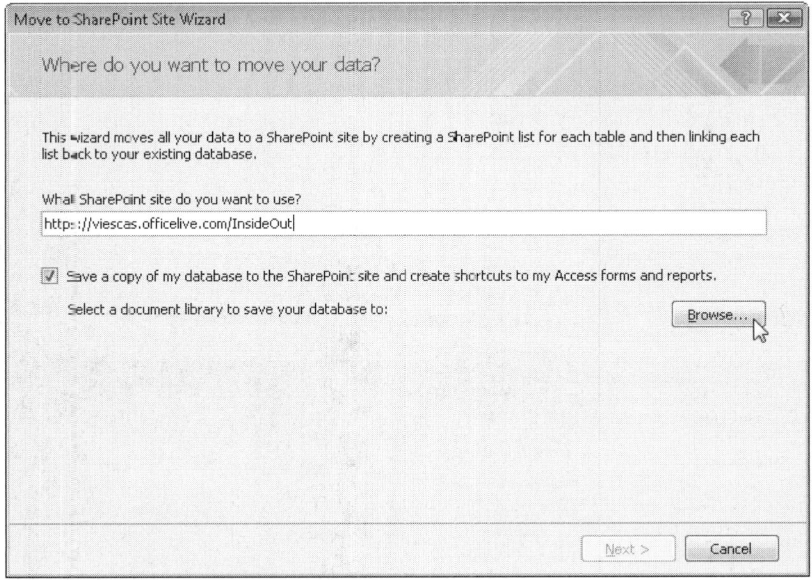


**Figure 22-55** On the first page of the wizard, enter the address of your SharePoint site and decide whether you want to upload a copy of the database.

Click the Browse button to browse for a document library location in which to save your database. If you're not currently logged on to your SharePoint site, you'll see a standard Windows logon dialog box, as shown in Figure 22-56. Enter your user name and password and then click OK to proceed.

> **Note**
>
> The Office Live Web site we used to demonstrate migrating a database authenticates users using a Windows Live ID—an e-mail address.

**Figure 22-56** You might need to log on to your SharePoint site before proceeding.

After you log on to your SharePoint site, Access displays a Location dialog box showing the various document libraries, sites, and workspaces on the site, as shown in Figure 22-57. For our example, we chose to upload a copy of the database into the Shared Documents library in the InsideOut workspace, as shown in Figure 22-58.

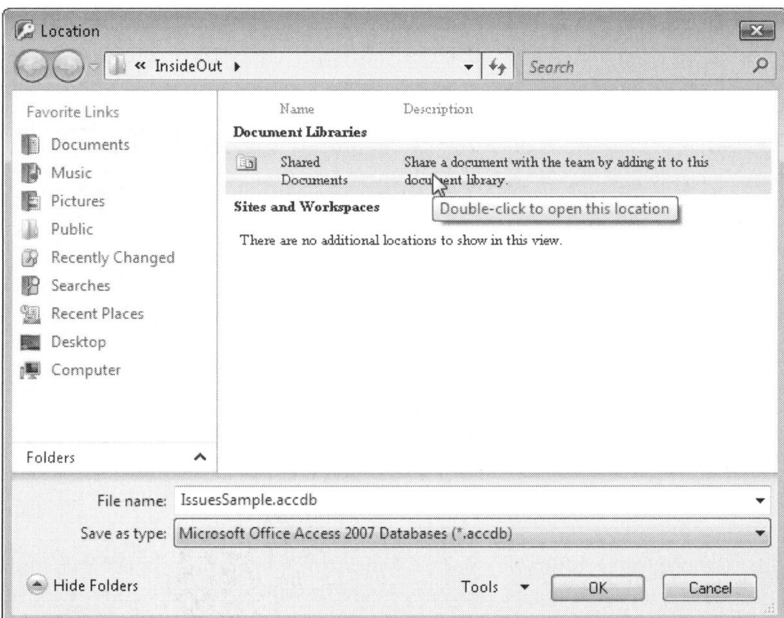


**Figure 22-57** Select the document library where you want to save the database.

After you navigate to the correct folder in which to upload your database, click OK to continue. The Move To SharePoint Site Wizard now displays the folder where Access will save the database, as shown in Figure 22-59. Verify that the information is correct, and click Next to begin the process of moving your database.

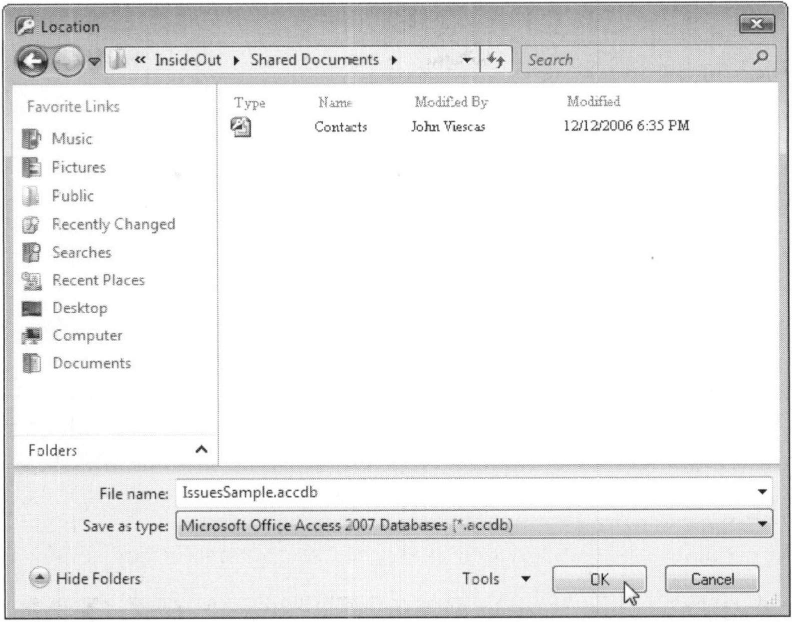

**Figure 22-58** After selecting the document library in the workspace, click OK to save the database in that location.

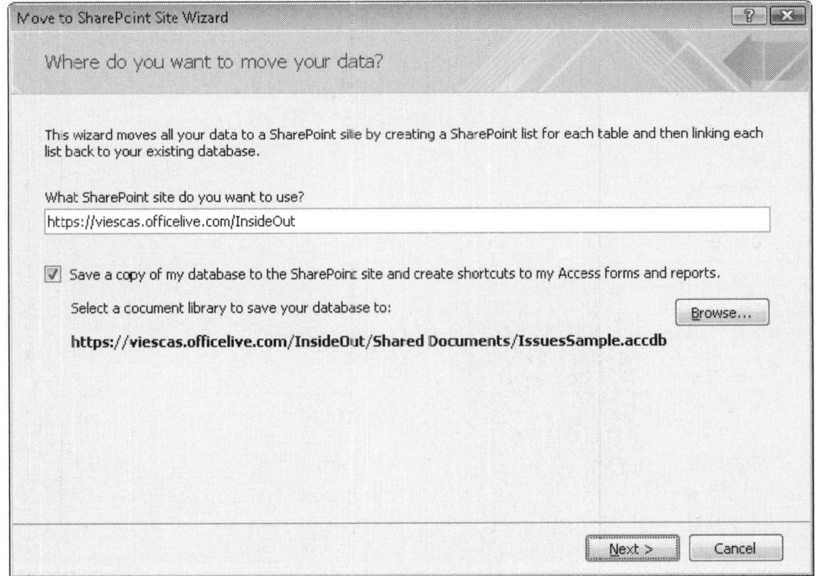


**Figure 22-59** The wizard displays the location on the SharePoint site where the migrated database will be saved.

Access displays several progress screens as it creates new lists for the two tables, copies the data to the new lists, and moves a copy of the entire database to the InsideOut folder on our SharePoint site.

> **Note**
>
> If the data in a table that you're moving to Windows SharePoint Services closely matches one of the built-in Windows SharePoint Services templates, Access uses that. Otherwise, Access instructs Windows SharePoint Services to build a custom list.

After Access completes the migration process, the final page of the wizard confirms that the move was successful. You can select the Show Details check box to find out the actions taken and any error that occurred during the migration process. As you can see in Figure 22-60, Access successfully created two new lists on the SharePoint site—Contacts and Issues. Access always creates a backup of your database before beginning the migration process, and you can see the name and location of the database on this page of the wizard. You can also see the full address path to the location of your database on the SharePoint site. Finally, Access informs you that it created a log table of issues it encountered when moving the tables to the SharePoint site. Click Finish to close the wizard.

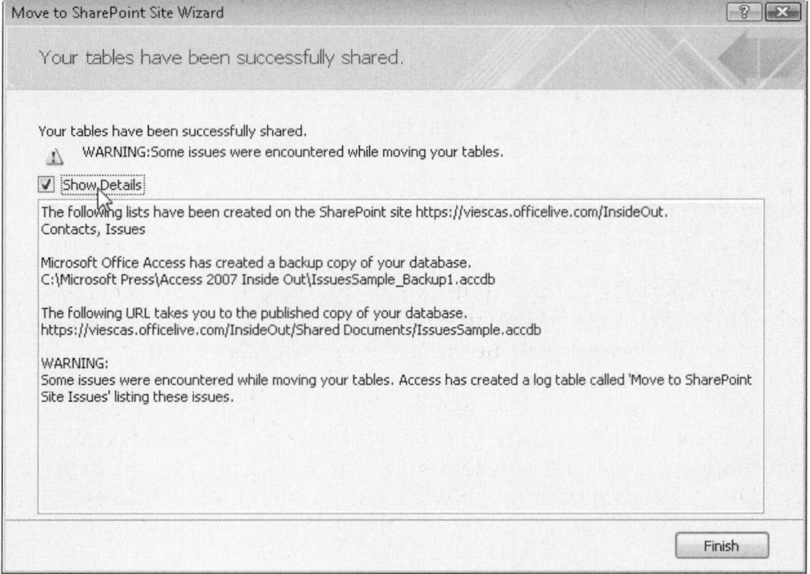


**Figure 22-60** Select the Show Details check box to see any issues Access encountered during the migration process.

After you close the wizard, Access opens your new database and displays the startup form, Issue List, as shown in Figure 22-61. You can see in the Navigation Pane that Access created links to the new Contacts and Issues lists on the SharePoint site as well as the User Information List. The status bar notifies you that you are currently online with the SharePoint site. You'll also notice that the Message Bar displays a Publish Changes message, and Access created a new local table called Move To SharePoint Site Issues.

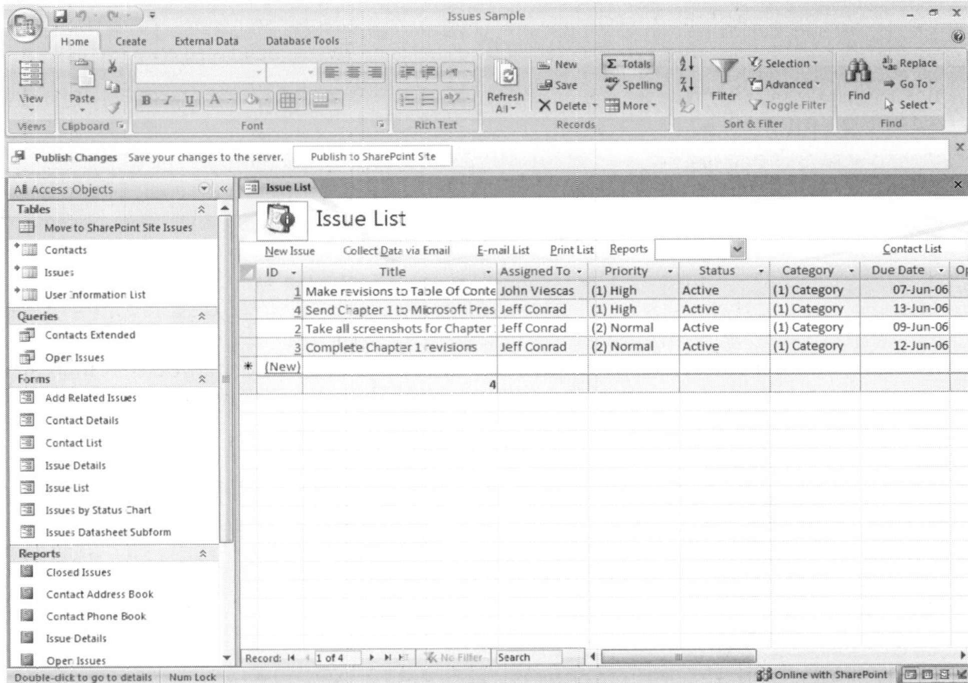


**Figure 22-61** The database on your computer is now linked to the SharePoint site.

Close the Issue List form and then open the Move To SharePoint Site Issues table to see what problems Access encountered when moving your database. In Figure 22-62, we collapsed the Navigation Pane and expanded the column widths of the first two fields so that you can read them. Windows SharePoint Services Version 3 does not support referential integrity so Access created a log entry in this table for the three relationships that had referential integrity defined. Windows SharePoint Services Version 3 also does not support validation rules, so the Opened Date and Due Date fields will not have their validation rules enforced in the Windows SharePoint Services lists.

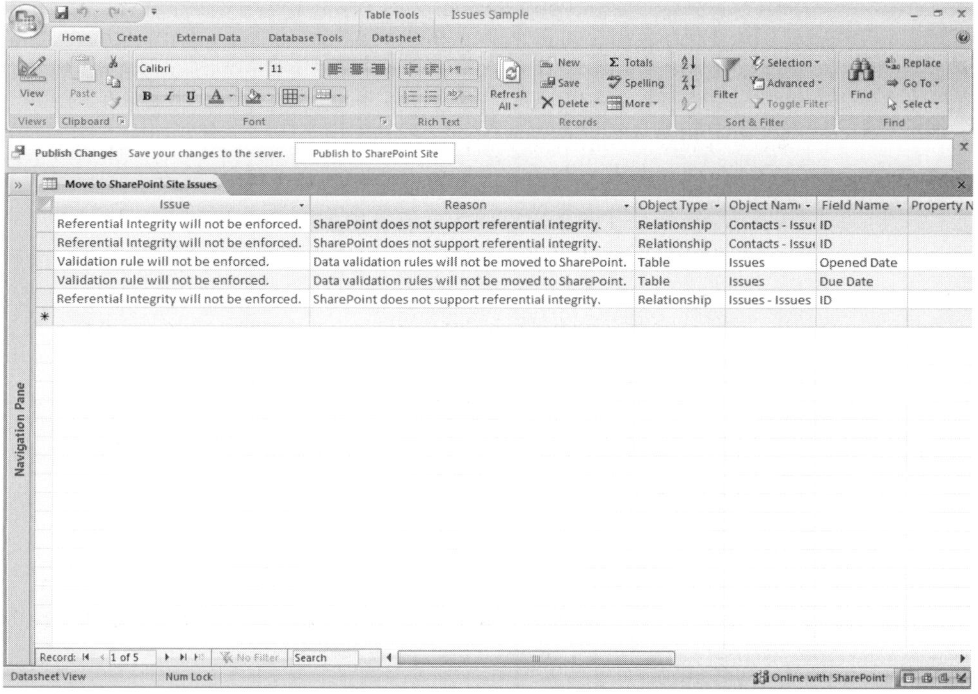


| Issue | Reason | Object Type | Object Nam | Field Name | Property N |
|---|---|---|---|---|---|
| Referential Integrity will not be enforced. | SharePoint does not support referential integrity. | Relationship | Contacts - Issu | ID | |
| Referential Integrity will not be enforced. | SharePoint does not support referential integrity. | Relationship | Contacts - Issu | ID | |
| Validation rule will not be enforced. | Data validation rules will not be moved to SharePoint. | Table | Issues | Opened Date | |
| Validation rule will not be enforced. | Data validation rules will not be moved to SharePoint. | Table | Issues | Due Date | |
| Referential Integrity will not be enforced. | SharePoint does not support referential integrity. | Relationship | Issues - Issues | ID | |

**Figure 22-62** Access creates a log table for any problems it encounters when moving your tables to Windows SharePoint Services lists.

When you migrate an Access 2007 database to a SharePoint site, you need to be aware that Windows SharePoint Services does not support certain data types. You also need to be aware of the following issues when migrating an Access 2007 database to Windows SharePoint Services:

- Windows SharePoint Services does not support dates prior to 1900. You will not be able to move any data that contains dates prior to 1900. If you have a date/time field with some dates earlier than 1900, Access exports the column but Windows SharePoint Services leaves blanks in those records for that column.
- Windows SharePoint Services converts any new line characters in text fields to either a memo field or a Multiple Lines of Text field.
- Windows SharePoint Services does not support referential integrity, so any relationships that have this enforced are ignored when you move the table to a list.
- Windows SharePoint Services does not support cascading updates and cascading deletes, so these will not be applied to the Windows SharePoint Services lists. You will need to write VBA code to delete and update related records. You'll learn how to do this in Chapter 20.
- Windows SharePoint Services ignores any relationship where the primary key is not an integer or the relationship does not relate to the ID column.

- Windows SharePoint Services does not support default values for fields that are dynamic—such as Date(), which changes each day—and ignores these when moving your tables to lists. Windows SharePoint Services accepts only static default values such as numbers, text, and standard dates, which do not change.
- Windows SharePoint Services supports automatic numbering of fields only in a list for the ID column.
- Windows SharePoint Services does support any multi-field indexes in lists, and ignores these indexes when you move your data to a list.
- Windows SharePoint Services supports unique indexes only for the ID column, and ignores any other indexes when you move your data to a list.
- Windows SharePoint Services does not support data validation rules, and ignores these when you move your data to a list.
- Windows SharePoint Services converts any ReplicationID fields to Single Line of Text data types.
- Windows SharePoint Services converts any decimal fields to Number data types.

INSIDE OUT

### Finding the Primary Key Data in a Windows SharePoint Services List

When you export a table to a new SharePoint list, you might not see the primary key data in the default view. If your primary key is an AutoNumber or Number data type, Windows SharePoint Services moves this data into a hidden _ID column in the new list. Windows SharePoint Services defaults to not displaying any hidden _ID columns in the default view. You'll need to modify the view in order to display this hidden column.



In Figure 22-63, you can see the Issues Sample database uploaded to the Shared Documents library in the InsideOut folder. You can also see that Access created new Contacts and Issues lists on the SharePoint site. Now that you have migrated the data to lists, other users who have the appropriate permissions can view, edit, and delete records through either the views on the SharePoint site or by opening the Access database in the Shared Documents library. If some of your users do not have Access 2007 installed, they can still view, edit, and delete records by using their browser.

## Republish a Database to a Windows SharePoint Services Site

Regardless of whether you publish or move a database to a Windows SharePoint Services site, you might occasionally need to republish your database. In Figure 22-53 on page 1211, you might have noticed a Publish To SharePoint Site button on the Message Bar after publishing a copy of the database to Windows SharePoint Services. Any changes you make to the data or database objects in the local copy of the Contacts database will not appear on the SharePoint site unless you republish these changes.

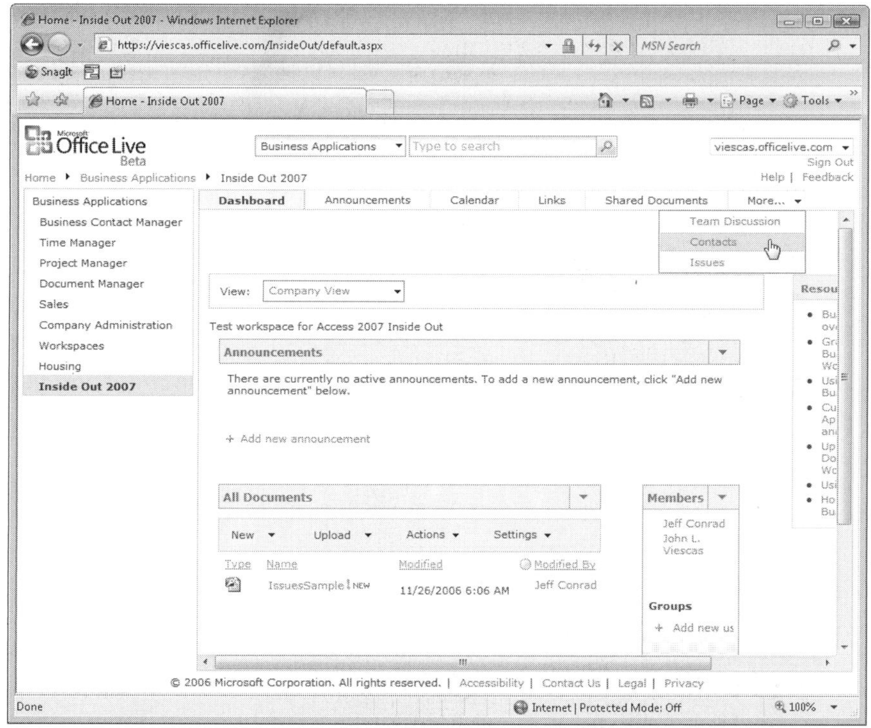

**Figure 22-63** The Issues Sample database has now been migrated to the SharePoint site.

In Figure 22-61 in the previous section, you can see the same Publish To SharePoint Site button, but in a database that you moved to Windows SharePoint Services. When you move a database, Access 2007 modifies the local copy, replacing the tables with links to the SharePoint lists. Any changes you make to data using the local copy will appear in the shared lists on the SharePoint site. However, any changes you make to queries, forms, reports, macros, or modules must be republished to appear in the shared copy on the server.

In this case, we'll work with the worst-case example, the published Contacts database. We'll add some records and make a change to one of the database objects to show you how this process works. If you followed along and created a Contacts database and published it, reopen the database now. Add a couple of records to the Contacts table using the Contact List form, as shown in Figure 22-64.

After you enter the records, switch to Design view on the Contact List form by right-clicking the form's tab and clicking Design View on the shortcut menu. Change the caption of the label in the Form Header section to **Conrad Systems Development Contact List**, as shown in Figure 22-65. Close the form and save the changes you made.

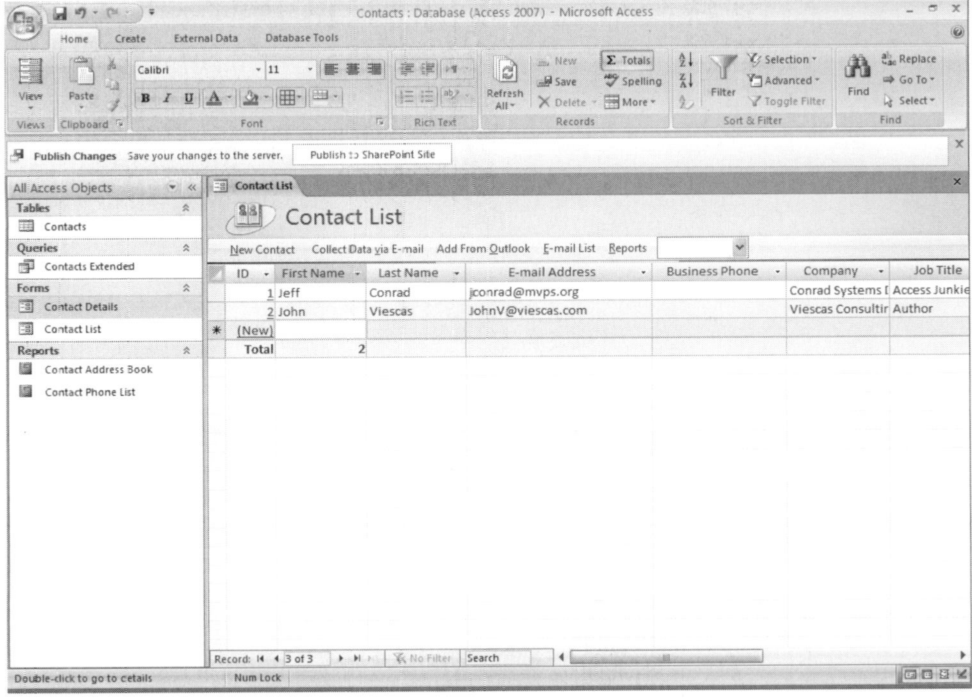


**Figure 22-64** Add some records to the Contacts table for this example.

To republish these changes to the SharePoint site, click the Publish To SharePoint Site button on the Message Bar. (If you accidentally closed the Message Bar, you can reopen it by clicking the Database Tools tab, and then selecting the Message Bar check box in the Show/Hide group.) If you are prompted for your logon information by the SharePoint site, enter your user name and password and click OK to continue. Access remembers the specific folder in which you saved the database, as shown in Figure 22-66. If the correct folder is not showing, locate the proper document library and then click Publish.

Access prompts you that a Contacts database file already exists in the same location and asks if you want to overwrite the existing file. Click Yes to confirm the overwrite and Access republishes the revised database to the SharePoint site. After the republishing procedure is complete, Access reopens the database and shows the Contact List form.

> **Note**
>
> Use this same procedure for a database that you have moved to a SharePoint site, but you need to republish your database only when you have made a change to a query, form, report, macro, or module in your local copy of the database.

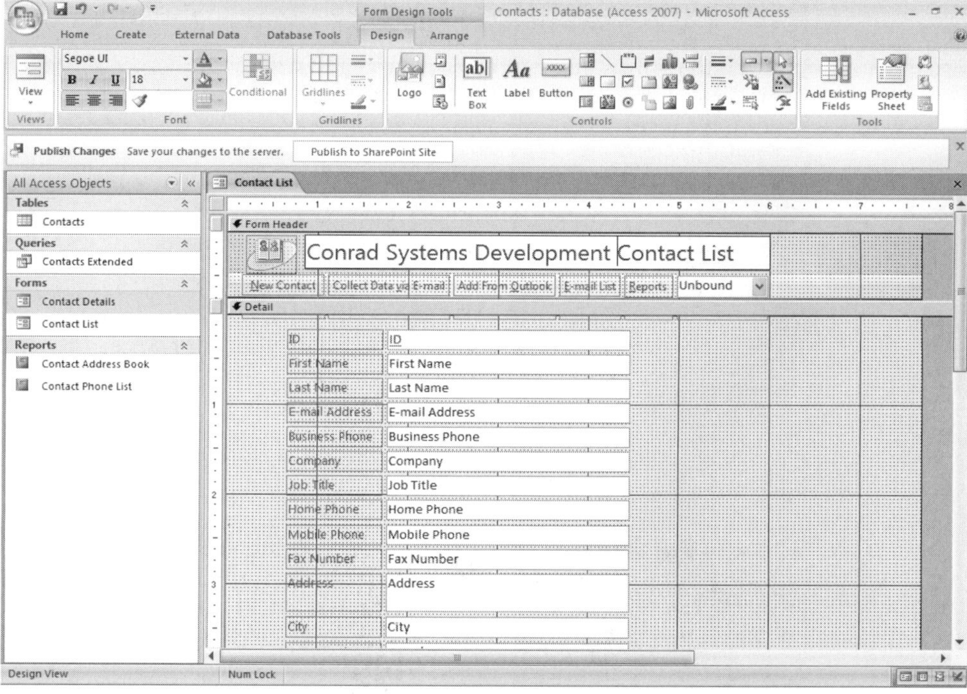

Figure 22-65 Change the label caption in the Form Header section.

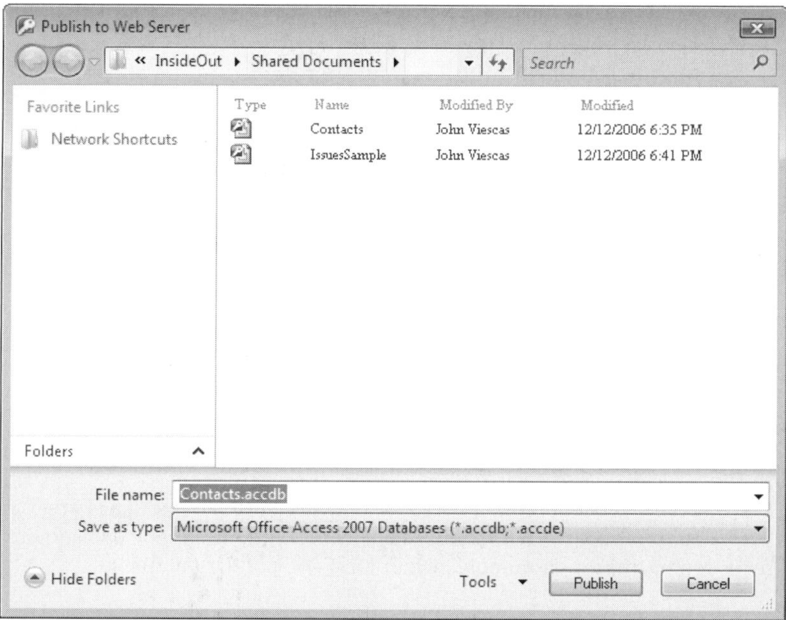

Figure 22-66 Navigate to the folder on the SharePoint site to republish the database changes.

## Opening the Database from Windows SharePoint Services

Users with appropriate permissions can open a database directly from a Windows SharePoint Services document library using their browser. In this example, we'll open the Contacts database we republished in the previous section. If your local copy of the Contacts database is still open, close it now.

In Figure 22-67 you can see that we navigated to the Shared Documents library in the InsideOut folder on our test SharePoint site. You can double-click directly on the name of the Contacts database to open it in Access 2007. Alternatively, if you click the arrow next to the name of the Contacts database (you must point to this database to see the arrow), Windows SharePoint Services displays a list of options; click the Edit In Microsoft Office Access option to view this database using Access 2007. However, if you choose this option, Access downloads a copy to a temporary folder on your computer and opens it as read-only. This option works when all you want to do is edit data in a database that has been moved to a SharePoint site. But if the database has simply been published, you won't be able to do anything except browse the data. (We'll show you how to modify the data in a read-only database in just a moment.)

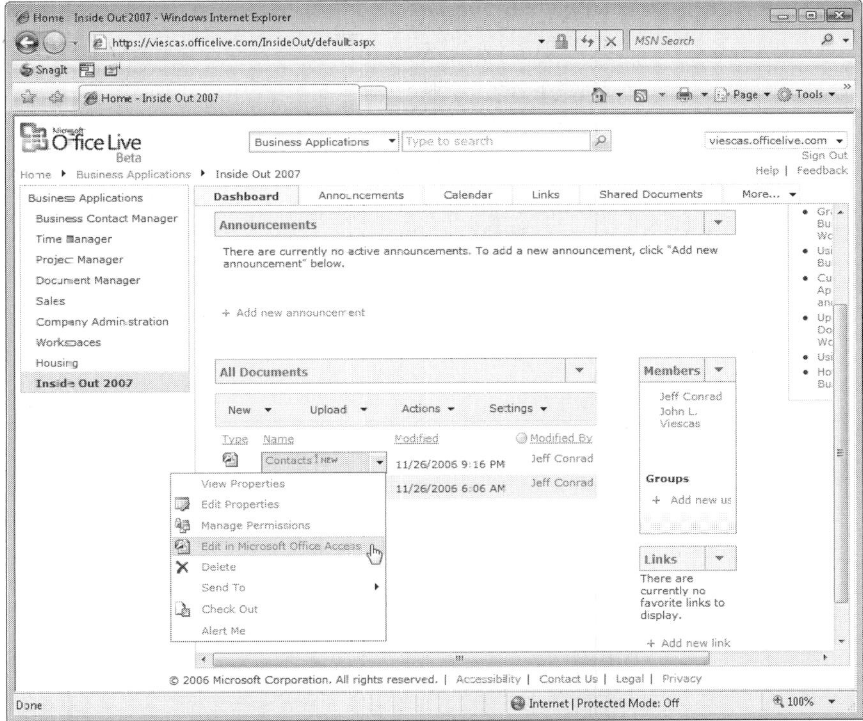


**Figure 22-67** When you open a published Access 2007 database using Edit In Microsoft Office Access, your browser downloads and opens a read-only copy of the database.

In this case, you're opening a published database, so double-click the database name to open it. Windows Internet Explorer displays a File Download dialog box with a warning message that some files can be harmful to your computer, as shown in Figure 22-68.

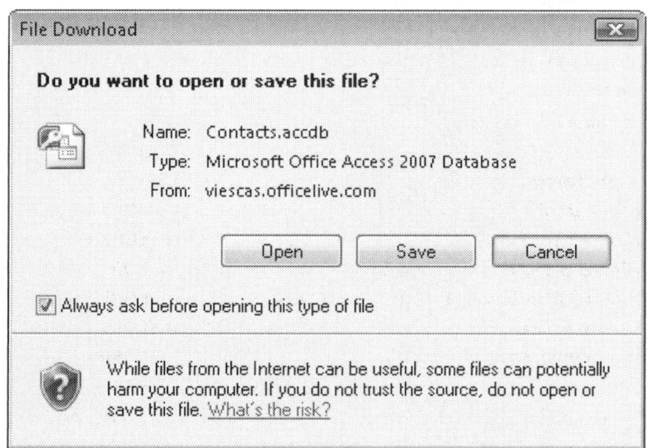


**Figure 22-68** Internet Explorer asks if you want to open the database or save a copy for editing.

If you click Open, Internet Explorer downloads a copy of the database to a temporary folder on your local hard drive and then calls Access to open the file. If you choose this option, Access opens the database in read-only mode. (You cannot make any design changes to the objects or change any of the data in the tables if the database is read-only.) If the database had links to Windows SharePoint Services lists, you could change the data in any linked tables. If you only want to view data in the database, the Open option should work just fine for you. If you click Save, the Windows Save As dialog box opens, as shown in Figure 22-69. You can select a folder on your hard drive and save a copy of the database. In this case, Access does not open the database in read-only mode, so you can make changes to the data and objects. If you click Cancel, Windows SharePoint Services stops the download process.



## TROUBLESHOOTING

### Why can't I make any changes to my published database?

If you select the Edit In Microsoft Office Access option for a published Access 2007 database, your database opens in read-only mode. You can only view data in this situation. If you moved the database instead of publishing it, you'll be able to edit the data and database objects.

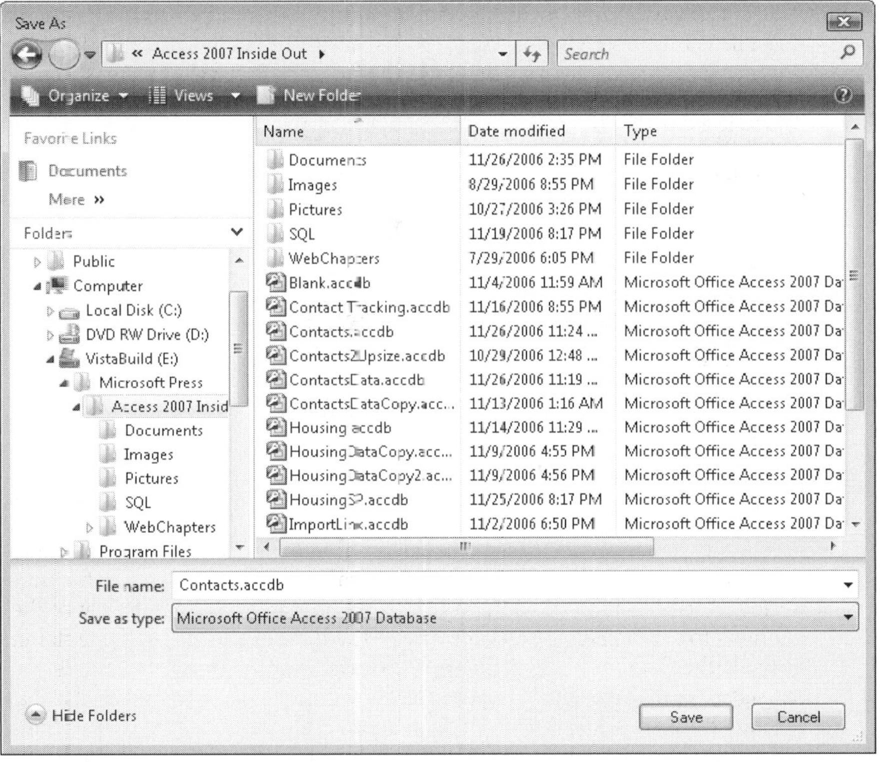

**Figure 22-69** Select a folder to save a local copy of the database.

Either change the name of the database or save it in a different location than the Access 2007 Inside Out folder so as not to overwrite the existing Conrad Systems Contacts database–Contacts.accdb. Click the Save button in the File Download dialog box, navigate to a folder in which to save the database, and then click the Save button in the Save As dialog box to download a copy of the database from the SharePoint site. If necessary, click Close to close the Download Complete dialog box. Access opens the database and displays the Contact List form with our two records in the Contacts table, as shown in Figure 22-70. You can now view, edit, and delete records and make design-level changes to the database objects. Remember that in order to have the information reflected in the database on the SharePoint site, you will need to republish the database by clicking the Publish To SharePoint Site button on the Message Bar. Close this database after you are finished.

### Note

If you save a copy of the database to an untrusted location, Access 2007 disables any harmful content in the database including all Visual Basic code and certain macro actions. To avoid this, you should download the database to a trusted location.

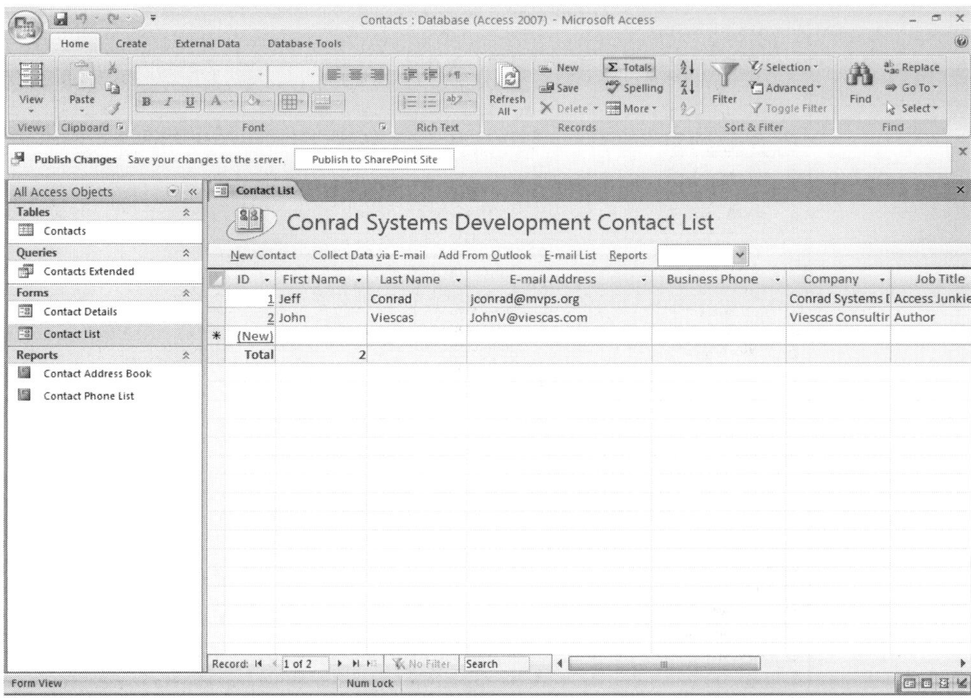


**Figure 22-70** Use the Save option to download a local copy of the database for editing.



## Working Offline

Occasionally, you might need to work with data stored in lists on a SharePoint site when you are disconnected. If your Windows SharePoint Services lists are stored on an internal server not accessible from the Internet, this could pose a problem if you need to view, edit, or delete records while away from your local intranet. Access 2007 and Windows SharePoint Services Version 3 allow you to work offline with data from the lists and then later synchronize your offline changes with the server after you reconnect.

Earlier in this chapter, you saw us move the Issues Sample database, which linked to lists on our test SharePoint site. You'll now see how we can take the data offline, make some changes, and later resolve any conflicts that might occur with data still on the server. In Access, open the Issues Sample database you migrated earlier in this chapter. (You might need to log on to the SharePoint site when reopening this database.) In Figure 22-71, you can see the links to the Contacts and Issues lists as well as to the User Information List table. The status bar indicates that we are online with our SharePoint site, and the Message Bar displays the Publish Changes message. Remember from earlier in this chapter that we can make changes to the data in the tables because we have links to the list in this database.

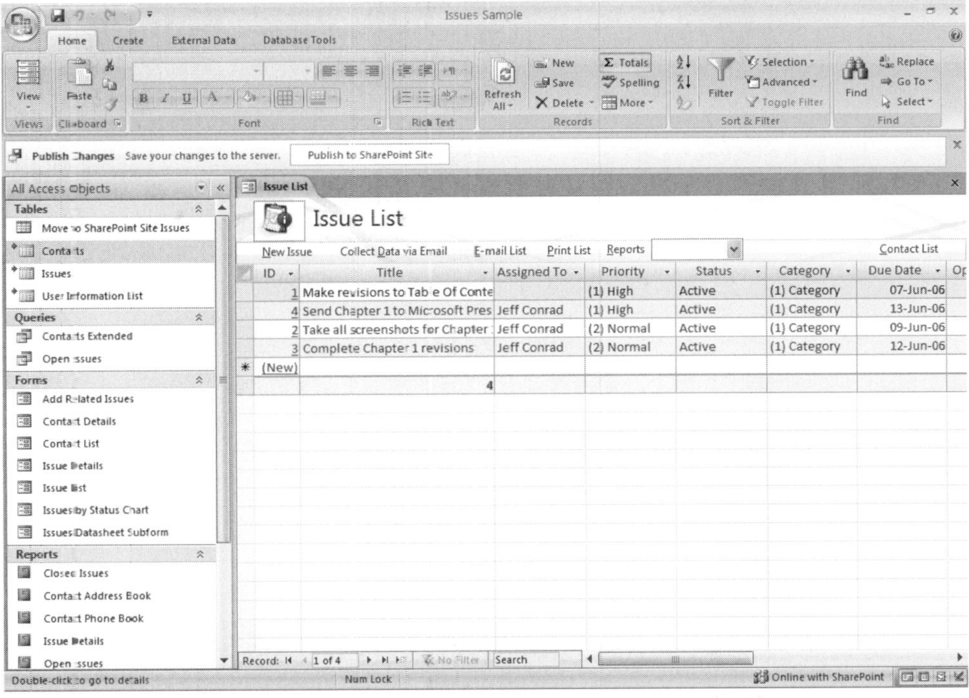

**Figure 22-71** Reopen the Issues Sample database and verify that you are working online with the SharePoint site.

Disconnect from the SharePoint site by closing the Issue List form and then on the External Data tab of the Ribbon, in the SharePoint Lists group, clicking the Work Offline button, as shown in Figure 22-72. Access downloads a copy of all the data currently on the server and temporarily disconnects the active links to the Windows SharePoint Services lists. You might see Access display some progress screens for each list depending on how much data it needs to download.

Access changes the icon for the linked lists to give you a visual cue that your links are now disconnected from the SharePoint site. Access also changes the status bar message to Offline With SharePoint to indicate that you are now working offline, as shown in Figure 22-73. Now that you have a local copy of all the data, you can analyze the data with queries, view and edit data through forms, and run reports while disconnected from the server. You'll also probably see a performance increase because you are now working only with data stored locally in the database.

Open the Issue List form, and let's make some changes to a couple of the records. Change the status of the issue records with IDs of 1 and 4 from Active to Resolved, as shown in Figure 22-74. Also, add a new record to the Issues table using the Issue List form. In Figure 22-74, you can see that we added a record concerning Chapter 22. You might notice that Access has used a negative number for the ID value instead of a positive value. Access uses negative numbers for ID values when you are working offline.

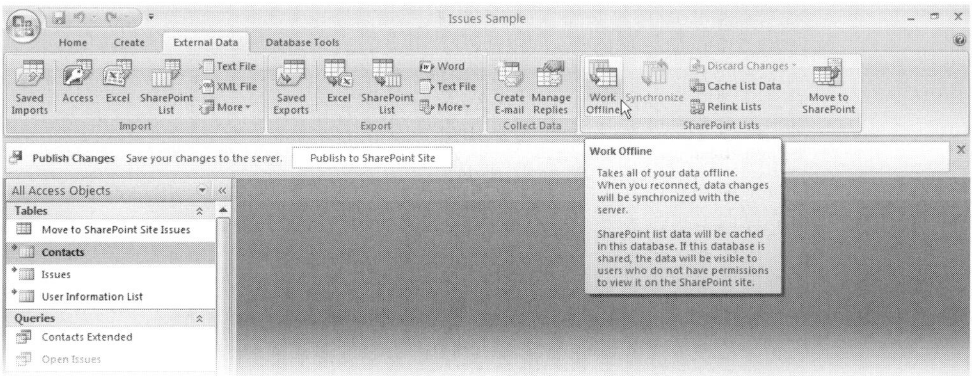


**Figure 22-72** Click the Work Offline button to disconnect from the SharePoint site.

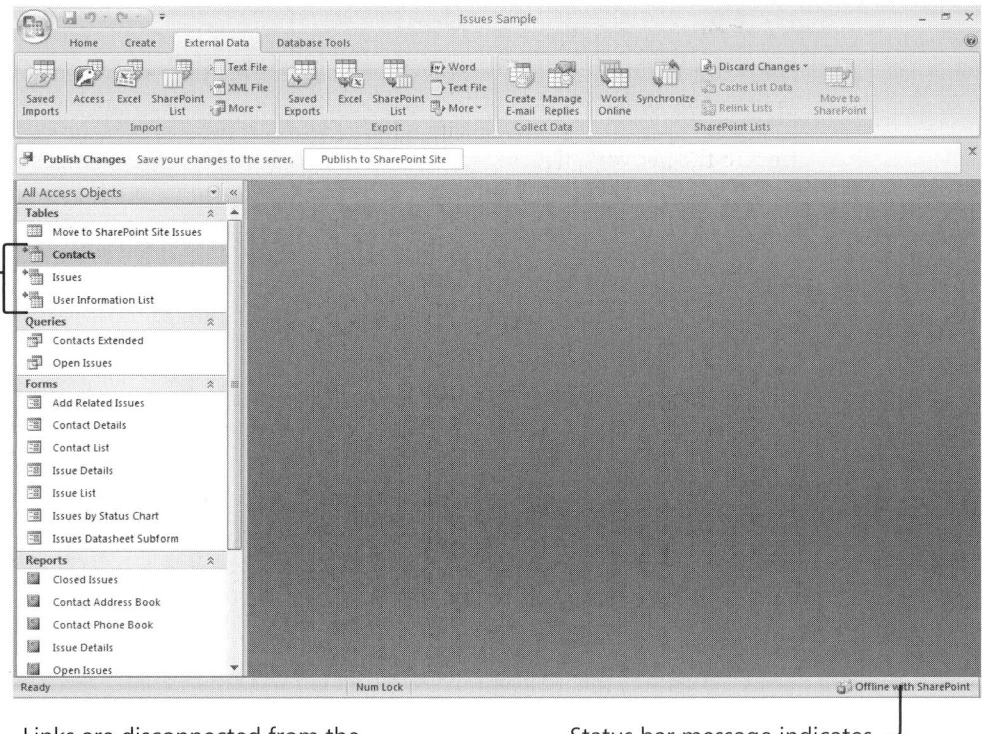


**Figure 22-73** Your database is now disconnected from the Windows SharePoint Services lists, but you can still edit the data.

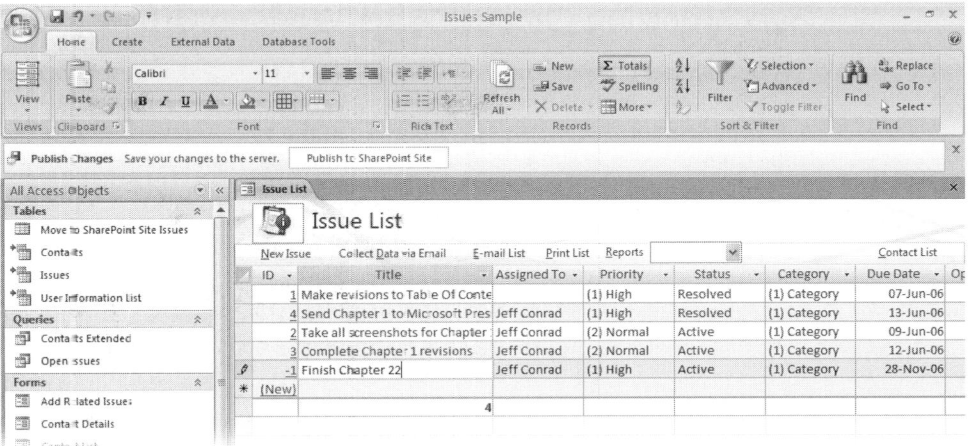


**Figure 22-74** You can edit and add records while working offline.

After you make the changes to the records, close the Issue List form and then open the Issues table in Datasheet view. In Figure 22-75, you can see that Access flags all records edited or added while offline with a pencil icon in the record selector. When you reconnect to the network, Access looks for this flag to synchronize changes with the server. If you want to discard all changes you made to the records while offline, you can click the arrow to the right of the Discard Changes button in the SharePoint Lists group on the External Data tab and then click either Discard All Changes or Discard All Changes And Refresh. The latter option not only ignores all changes you made while you had the database offline but also refreshes the data from the SharePoint site.

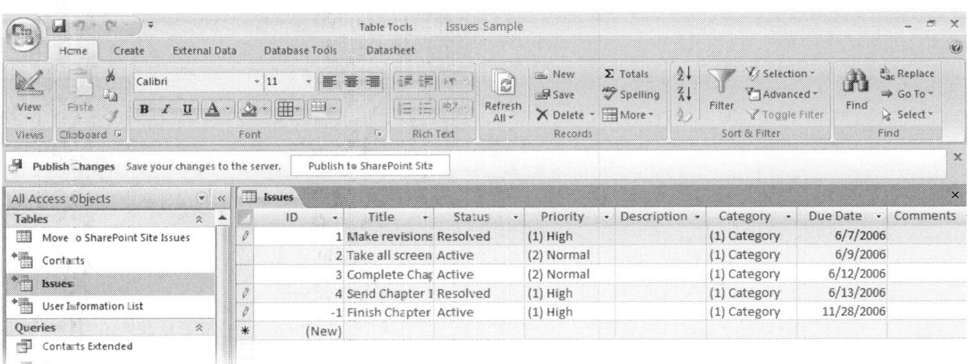


**Figure 22-75** Access displays a pencil icon next to records that you changed while offline.

## Synchronizing Changes After Working Offline

While you are disconnected from the server, it is possible that someone else might edit the same records you changed. As a result, you now have a conflict between your local copy of the data and the server data. Let's assume that while you were away from the office, someone else changed the status of the same two records from Active to Closed, but you changed them from Active to Resolved. In Figure 22-76, you can see within the browser window on the SharePoint site that the records with IDs of 1 and 4 were edited. (Someone else could also make changes through links from another database as well.)

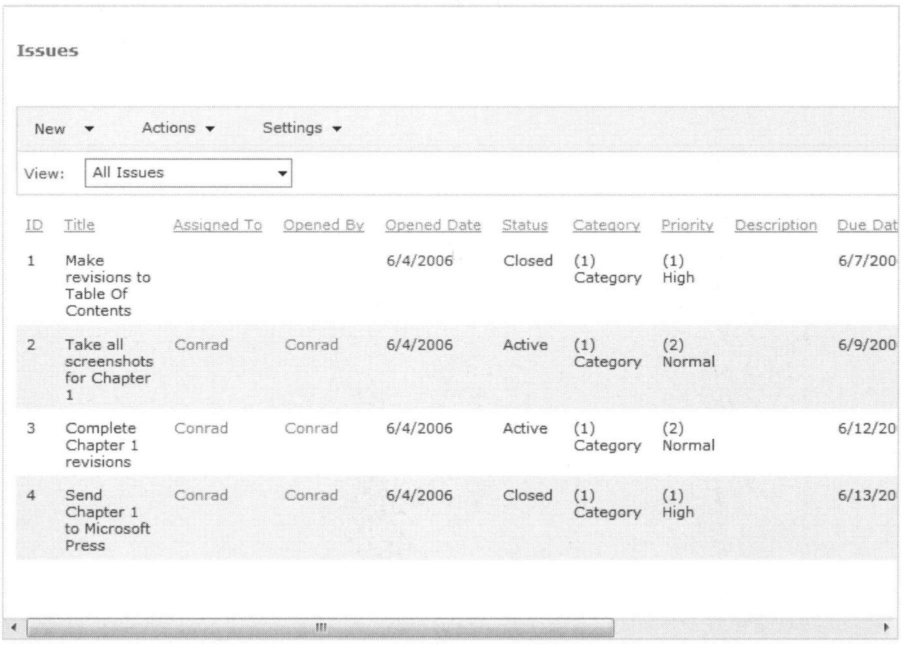


| ID | Title | Assigned To | Opened By | Opened Date | Status | Category | Priority | Description | Due Dat |
|---|---|---|---|---|---|---|---|---|---|
| 1 | Make revisions to Table Of Contents | | | 6/4/2006 | Closed | (1) Category | (1) High | | 6/7/200 |
| 2 | Take all screenshots for Chapter 1 | Conrad | Conrad | 6/4/2006 | Active | (1) Category | (2) Normal | | 6/9/200 |
| 3 | Complete Chapter 1 revisions | Conrad | Conrad | 6/4/2006 | Active | (1) Category | (2) Normal | | 6/12/20 |
| 4 | Send Chapter 1 to Microsoft Press | Conrad | Conrad | 6/4/2006 | Closed | (1) Category | (1) High | | 6/13/20 |

**Figure 22-76** The data on the SharePoint site changed while you were offline.

To reconnect to the SharePoint site and synchronize the data, click the Work Online button in the SharePoint Lists group on the External Data tab, as shown in Figure 22-77. If you click the Synchronize button, Access attempts to resolve any data conflicts, updates any data that has been changed between the local copy and the server copy, but keeps the links disconnected from the server.

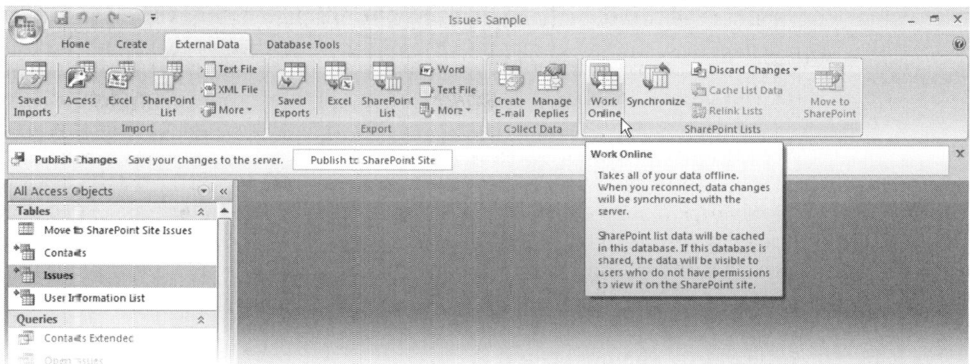


**Figure 22-77** Click the Work Online button to reestablish links to the Windows SharePoint Services lists.

Access now attempts to reconnect the links to the lists on the SharePoint site, but it finds some data conflicts in the Issues table. If any conflicts exist between data in the local copy of the database and the data in the Windows SharePoint Services lists, Access displays the Resolve Conflicts dialog box, as shown in Figure 22-78. In this case, Access correctly spots that two records have data conflicts. The Resolve Conflicts dialog box has Previous and Next buttons in the upper-right corner. You can use these buttons to move back and forth between the records that have data conflicts. (These buttons appear dimmed if only one conflict is found in a table.) Access displays the number of conflicts it finds near the top of the dialog box. In our case Access shows a message of "Details – 1 of 2," meaning two records have data conflicts.



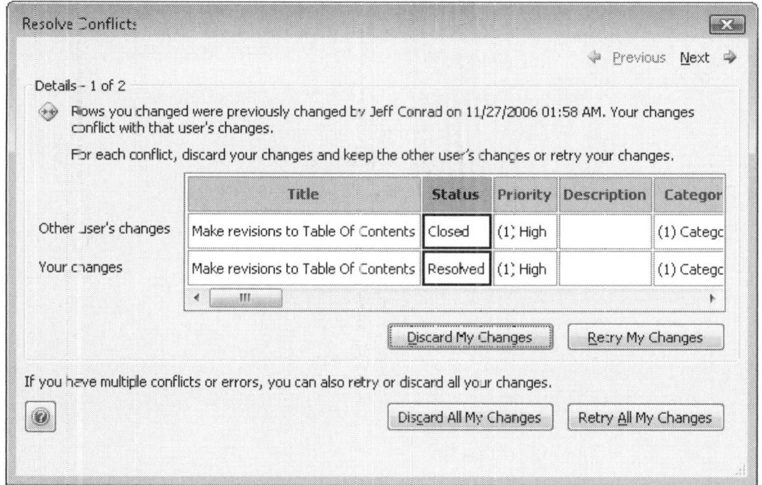


**Figure 22-78** Access displays the Resolve Conflicts dialog box whenever data conflicts occur.

The Resolve Conflicts dialog box shows who changed the data on the server and the date and time it was changed. In the middle of the dialog box Access displays all the fields in the list, and highlights what the other user changed in the record on the SharePoint site as well as the changes you made to the same record. In our example, you can see that the Status field was changed to Closed on the server and we changed it to Resolved in our local copy of the data.

If you want to keep the changes that the other user made, click the Discard My Changes button. If you want to keep the changes you made to the record, click the Retry My Changes button. For each record conflict, you need to decide whether you want to keep your changes or discard them. If you want to discard all your data changes, click the Discard All My Changes button at the bottom of the dialog box. If you want to keep all your record changes, click the Retry All My Changes button. If you have additional data conflicts in other tables, you'll need to resolve those conflicts as well. (If two people from two locations try to resolve conflicts at the same time, the last user's changes are saved.) As you might recall, we added one new record to the Issues table. Access had no problems adding this record to the Windows SharePoint Services Issues list because there were no data conflicts. We want to keep the changes we made, so click the Retry All My Changes button. After the data conflicts are resolved, Access relinks your tables to the Windows SharePoint Services lists and changes the status bar message to indicate that you are back online. In Figure 22-79 you can see Access has completed the relinking process and opened the Issue List form.

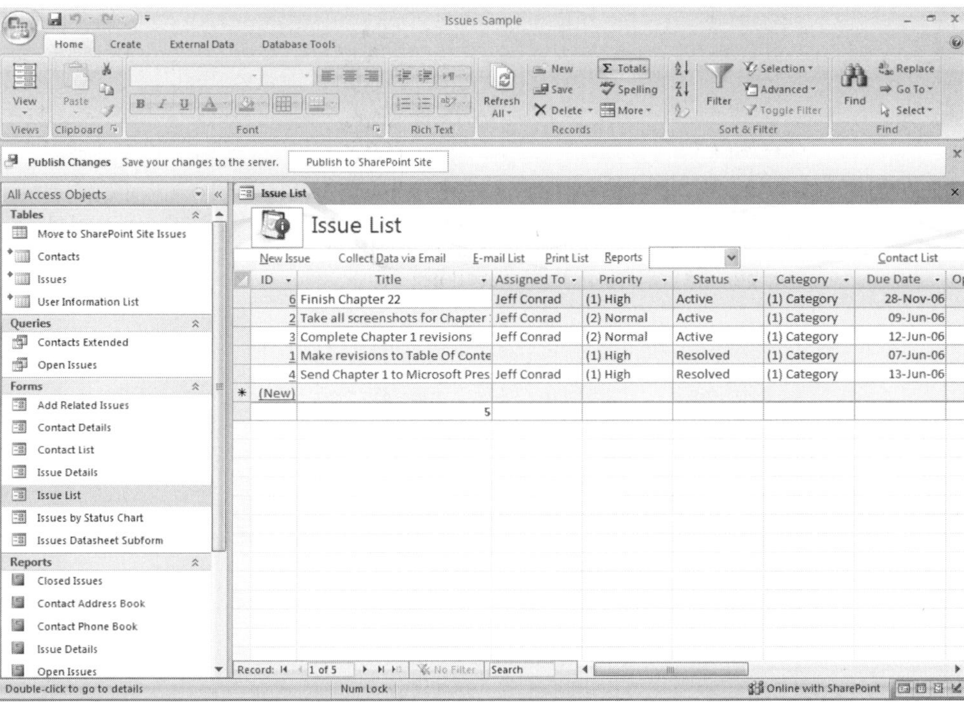


**Figure 22-79** Access relinks the tables when you go back online.

Our record changes were accepted and uploaded to the SharePoint site and now show up in both our local copy of the database, in any database linked to the lists on the server, and in the lists on the server. In Figure 22-80 you can see all the updated data in the Issues list on the SharePoint site.

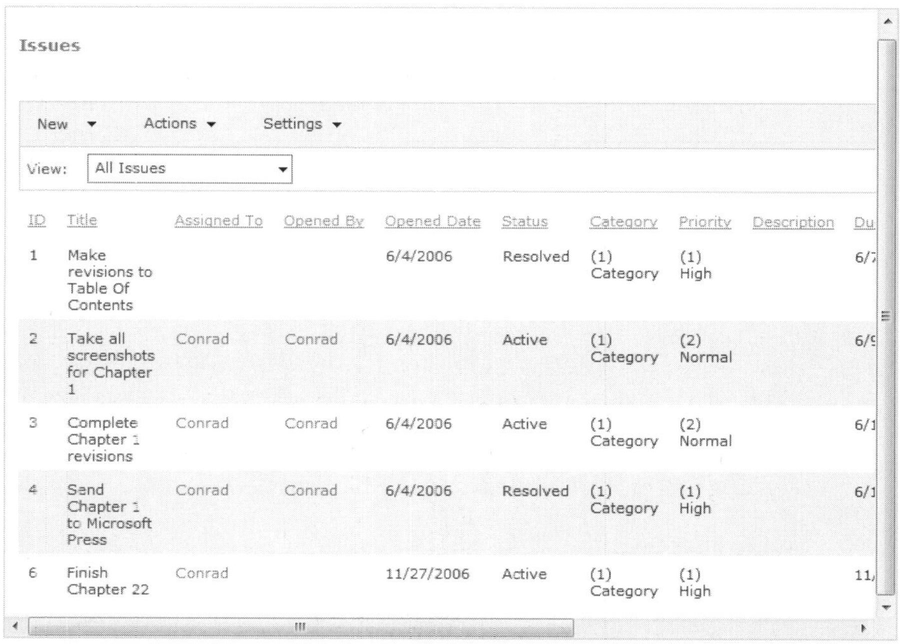


**Figure 22-80** The Issues list on the SharePoint site now includes all the changes we made while working offline.

You should now have a good grasp of working within the user interface of a Windows SharePoint Services Version 3 site. You have also learned how to leverage the collaborative benefits of Windows SharePoint Services with Access 2007.

CHAPTER 23

# Using XML



Today's modern companies are increasing productivity and cutting costs by finding ways to share more and more information online. When data can be shared in a universal format, it doesn't matter whether an employee is down the hall, across the street, or thousands of miles away. The online sharing of information also makes it easier for companies to expand into global markets. Customers half a world away can explore a company's products and services and place orders online. Companies can tap into vendors worldwide to find the best products at the best price.

The World Wide Web has certainly been an enabling technology for increasing productivity and expanding markets. As explained in Chapter 21, "Publishing Data on the Web," the Web works because of the universal acceptance of protocol and language standards. Hypertext Markup Language (HTML) enables a Web page to be displayed on any computer and in any browser anywhere in the world. As an adjunct to HTML, Extensible Markup Language (XML) defines a standard and universal way to share data files or documents. Microsoft Windows SharePoint Services leverage both these technologies to provide an enhanced Web-based data and information sharing mechanism to help companies increase productivity.

This chapter explores XML in more detail and shows you how you can take advantage of these technologies to share information more readily from your Microsoft Office Access 2007 applications.

**Note**

The XML examples in this chapter are based on the tables and data in the Housing Reservations application (Housing.accdb) and on various XML documents (files) located in the WebChapters\XML folder on the companion CD. The Ribbon examples are based on the tables and forms in the Conrad Systems Contacts application (Contacts.accdb).

# Exploring XML

The current XML standard is based on an ISO standard, but the most commonly used version is the one maintained and published by W3C (World Wide Web Consortium). Because a file in XML format contains not only the data but also a description of the structure of the data, XML-enabled receiving systems know exactly how to process the data from the information included in the file.

An XML document can contain data from a single table or from an entire database. An XML document can also have supporting files that describe details about the table schema (for example, field properties and indexes) or that describe how the recipient should lay out (format) the data for display (for example, fonts and column sizes).

Like HTML, XML uses tags to identify descriptive elements. Examples include the name of a table or the name of a field in an XML data file, the names of table properties or index properties in an XML schema file, and the size and color of a border or the name of a style sheet template in an XML layout file. However, where most browsers are forgiving of errors in HTML, such as a missing end tag in a table row, most software that can process XML insists that the tags in an XML file be very precise and follow strict rules. An XML document or set of documents that contain precise XML are said to be *well formed*.

## Well-Formed XML

Although you will create most XML documents using a program such as Office Access 2007 that always creates well-formed XML, you might occasionally need to view and edit XML files that you receive from outside sources. You should understand the following rules that apply to well-formed XML:

- Each XML document must have a unique root element that surrounds the entire document.
- Any start tag must have an end tag. Unlike HTML that supports stand-alone tags (such as <br>), XML requires all tags to have explicit ends. However, some tags within XML are self-contained. For example, you code an object definition tag within a schema file like this (the /> characters at the end of the string define the end of the tag):

  ```
  <od:object-type attributes />
  ```
- Tags cannot overlap. For example, you cannot start the definition of one table field and then start the definition of a second table field without ending the first one.
- When you need to include certain characters that are reserved for XML syntax (such as <, &, >, ", ') within the data portion of an element, you must use a substitute character sequence. For example, you indicate a single quote within data using the special sequence *&apos*.
- All tags in XML are case-sensitive. For example, </tblfacilities> is an invalid end tag for the begin tag <TBLFacilities>.

As you examine the XML examples in this chapter, you should not encounter any XML that is not well formed.

## Understanding XML File Types

XML documents can be made up of a single file if necessary. However, when you want to send more than the table name, field names, and data content, you can generate additional files that help the recipient understand data properties and format the data as you intended. The five types of files that can make up a set of XML documents about one table or group of tables are as follows:

- Data document (.xml) contains the names of tables and fields and the data in the fields.
- Schema document (.xsd) contains additional information about the properties of the tables (such as indexes defined on the table) and properties of the fields (such as data type or length).
- Presentation (layout) document (.xsl) specifies the layout of the data, including fonts and column and row spacing.
- Presentation layout extension (.xsx) document specifies additional properties used by the designer.
- Web package (.htm) is a version of the information contained in the data, schema, and presentation documents compiled into HTML format ready for display in a browser.

When you create XML documents to display on your own Web site, you most likely will use all five file types to completely describe the data and format it for presentation. When you are sending a data file to another organization or business application, you usually send only the data and schema documents—the essential information that the recipient needs to understand your data.

### Note

Although you can embed schema and presentation information inside a data document, you should normally send the information as separate files. Not all applications that can process XML can handle a combined file that contains the data and the schema or the data and the schema and the presentation specification. In general, it's a good idea to keep the data values, the data definition, and the layout specifications separate.

One of the best ways to understand XML files is to study some examples. So, let's look at the files Access 2007 creates when you ask it to export a small table such as the tblFacilities table in the Housing Reservations application as XML. You can learn how to create these documents from Access in "Exporting Access Tables and Queries" on page 1246.

## The XML Data Document (.xml)

The data document contains very basic information about your table and the fields within the table as well as the data from the table. The data document for the tblFacilities table (tblFacilities.xml) is as follows:

```
<?xml version="1.0" encoding="UTF-8"?>
<dataroot xmlns:od="urn:schemas-microsoft-com:officedata"
xmlns:xsi="http://www.w3.org/2001/XMLSchema-instance"
xsi:noNamespaceSchemaLocation="tblFacilities.xsd"
    generated="2007-01-21T12:56:27">
<tblFacilities>
<FacilityID>1</FacilityID>
<FacilityName>Main Campus Housing A</FacilityName>
<FacilityAddress>2345 Main Street</FacilityAddress>
<FacilityCity>Chicago</FacilityCity>
<FacilityStateOrProvince>IL</FacilityStateOrProvince>
<FacilityPostalCode>60637</FacilityPostalCode>
</tblFacilities>
<tblFacilities>
<FacilityID>2</FacilityID>
<FacilityName>Main Campus Housing B</FacilityName>
<FacilityAddress>2348 Main Street</FacilityAddress>
<FacilityCity>Chicago</FacilityCity>
<FacilityStateOrProvince>IL</FacilityStateOrProvince>
<FacilityPostalCode>60637</FacilityPostalCode>
</tblFacilities>
<tblFacilities>
<FacilityID>3</FacilityID>
<FacilityName>South Campus Housing C</FacilityName>
<FacilityAddress>4567 Central Ave.</FacilityAddress>
<FacilityCity>Chicago</FacilityCity>
<FacilityStateOrProvince>IL</FacilityStateOrProvince>
<FacilityPostalCode>60637</FacilityPostalCode>
</tblFacilities>
<tblFacilities>
<FacilityID>4</FacilityID>
<FacilityName>North Satellite Housing D</FacilityName>
<FacilityAddress>5678 N. Willow Drive</FacilityAddress>
<FacilityCity>Chicago</FacilityCity>
<FacilityStateOrProvince>IL</FacilityStateOrProvince>
<FacilityPostalCode>60636</FacilityPostalCode>
</tblFacilities>
</dataroot>
```

The first line is a comment tag that notes the version of the XML standard that Access used to generate this file and states that the characters in the file comply with an 8-bit character-set standard. The next line starts the required root element of the document and identifies that the schema definition can be found in the file tblFacilities.xsd. The remaining lines, up to the </dataroot> end tag, identify the four rows in the table and the six fields within each row, including the data content of each field. Note that each row starts with a <tblFacilities> tag and ends with a </tblFacilities> tag. Likewise, each field begins and ends with a tag that names the field, and the data contents of each field appears between the begin and end field tags.

You can see that this file primarily contains information about the data contents. Except for the implied sequence of fields in each row and the sequence of rows within the table, no information about the definition of the table or the fields is in this file. Although this example file contains the data from only one table, it is possible to include the data from multiple tables in one XML file.

### The Schema File (.xsd)

To find the structural definition of the table and fields, you must look in the companion schema file. Understanding how to read a schema file can be useful if you attempt to import an XML file sent to you but you don't seem to be getting the results you expect. The beginning of the schema file for the tblFacilities table (tblFacilites.xsd) is as follows:

```
<?xml version="1.0" encoding="UTF-8"?>
<xsd:schema xmlns:xsd="http://www.w3.org/2001/XMLSchema" xmlns:od="urn:schemas-micro-
soft-com:officedata">
<xsd:element name="dataroot">
<xsd:complexType>
<xsd:sequence>
<xsd:element ref="tblFacilities" minOccurs="0" maxOccurs="unbounded"/>
</xsd:sequence>
<xsd:attribute name="generated" type="xsd:dateTime"/>
</xsd:complexType>
</xsd:element>

<xsd:element name="tblFacilities">
  <xsd:annotation>
  <xsd:appinfo>
  <od:index index-name="FacilityPostalCode" index-key="FacilityPostalCode "
    primary="no" unique="no" clustered="no" order="asc"/>
  <od:index index-name="PrimaryKey" index-key="FacilityID " primary="yes"
    unique="yes" clustered="no" order="asc"/>
  <od:tableProperty name="Orientation" type="2" value="0"/>
  <od:tableProperty name="OrderByOn" type="1" value="0"/>
  <od:tableProperty name="NameMap" type="11" value="
CswOVQAAAAByioucQ0Z3T40beJpq7gFyAAAAAPb4bxHZceJAAAAAAAAAAAB0AGIA
bABGAGEAYwBpAGwAaQB0AGkAZQBzAAAAAAAAAAJ8VD08qACpMs5fBc7lh6boHAAAA
coqLnENGd0+NG3iaau4BckYAYQBjAGkAbABpAHQAeQBJAEQAAAAAAAAAAXutJYWBV
kEKh+5avJU3lowcAAAByioucQ0Z3T40beJpq7gFyRgBhAGMAaQBsAGkAdAB5AE4A
YQBtAGUAAAAAAAAAAmf/iHgqvp0KuAX5jWsirtgcAAAByioucQ0Z3T40beJpq7gFy
RgBhAGMAaQBsAGkAdAB5AEEAZABkAHIAZQBzAHMAAAAAAAAAAbWoQcZl0wEa/hQ5v
XmRRvQcAAAByioucQ0Z3T40beJpq7gFyRgBhAGMAaQBsAGkAdAB5AEMAaQB0AHkA
AAAAAAAA+ri0bFFbYUKAk99BNF1kGAcAAAByioucQ0Z3T40beJpq7gFyRgBhAGMA
aQBsAGkAdAB5AFMAdABhAHQAZQBPAHIAUAByAG8AdgBpAG4AYwBlAAAAAAAAAA0ik
G2+R0v9Ij2tojSM0wTUAAAAAEeO/9Ndx4kAAAAAAAAAAAHQAbABrAHAAWgBpAHAA
cwAAAAAAAACkC3HuUea3S7cpPZBX0k4VBwAAAHKKi5xDRndPjRt4mmruAXJGAGEA
YwBpAGwAaQB0AHkAUABvAHMAdABhAGwAQwBvAGQAZQAAAA==
"/>
  <od:tableProperty name="DefaultView" type="2" value="2"/>
  <od:tableProperty name="Description" type="10"
    value="Table for Housing Facility records"/>
  <od:tableProperty name="SubdatasheetName" type="10" value="[None]"/>
  <od:tableProperty name="GUID" type="9" value="coqLnENGd0+NG3iaau4Bcg=="/>
```

Chapter 23

```
  <od:tableProperty name="Filter" type="12"
    value="((tblFacilities.FacilityID=1))"/>
</xsd:appinfo>
</xsd:annotation>
<xsd:complexType>
<xsd:sequence>
```

The first line is a comment like the one found in the companion XML data file. The second line defines the beginning of the root element—the schema. The next eight lines, beginning with <xsd:element name="dataroot"> and ending with </xsd:element>, link this schema to the dataroot object defined in the tblFacilities XML file.

The tag <xsd:element name="tblFacilities"> begins the definition of the table. The information following the <xsd:appinfo> tag defines application-specific information about the structure of the table—in this case, the two indexes defined on the table. Notice that even though a desktop database (.accdb) doesn't use a clustered property, the schema definition includes this property for compatibility with SQL Server.

Following the heading information, you can find segments that define each of the six fields in the tblFacilities table. The definition of the first field, FacilityID, is as follows:

```
<xsd:element name="FacilityID" minOccurs="0" od:jetType="longinteger"
    od:sqlSType="int" type="xsd:int">
  <xsd:annotation>
  <xsd:appinfo>
  <od:fieldProperty name="Required" type="1" value="0"/>
  <od:fieldProperty name="ColumnWidth" type="3" value="-1"/>
  <od:fieldProperty name="ColumnOrder" type="3" value="1"/>
  <od:fieldProperty name="ColumnHidden" type="1" value="0"/>
  <od:fieldProperty name="Description" type="10" value="Unique Facility ID"/>
  <od:fieldProperty name="DecimalPlaces" type="2" value="255"/>
<od:fieldProperty name="DisplayControl" type="3" value="109"/>
<od:fieldProperty name="Caption" type="12" value="ID"/>
  <od:fieldProperty name="GUID" type="9" value="nxUPTyoAKkyzl8FzuWHpug==
"/>
</xsd:appinfo>
</xsd:annotation>
</xsd:element>
```

The tag beginning with <xsd:element name="FacilityID" starts the definition of the FacilityID field. The tag specifies a data type for both the Access desktop database engine (notice the reference is to the Microsoft JET database engine) as well as for SQL Server.

The remaining five fields are all text fields. The start tag for each field defines the JET data type (text) and the SQL Server data type (nvarchar) inside the tag. Each field start tag is then followed by tags that define the simple data type as a string as well as restrictions on the maximum length of each field. The last several lines in the schema definition are end tags that close up the last field, the sequence of fields started just before the first field definition, the complex type tag just before that, the element tag that started the table definition, and finally the end tag for the entire schema.

You can see that it's not too difficult to figure out what the schema is describing as long as you can sort out the pairs of begin and end tags. However, you probably wouldn't want to attempt to build such a schema file from scratch.

## The Presentation (Layout) Document (.xsl)

As noted earlier, you can optionally include a presentation document (also called a *style sheet*) to describe how the table defined by the .xsd file and the data within the file included in the .xml file should be displayed. If you ask Access to also create a presentation document (tblFacilities.xsl) for the tblFacilities table, its contents will be as follows:

```
<?xml version="1.0"?>
<xsl:stylesheet version="1.0"
  xmlns:xsl="http://www.w3.org/1999/XSL/Transform"
  xmlns:msxsl="urn:schemas-microsoft-com:xslt"
  xmlns:fx="#fx-functions" exclude-result-prefixes="msxsl fx">
<xsl:output method="html" version="4.0" indent="yes"
  xmlns:xsl="http://www.w3.org/1999/XSL/Transform"/>
<xsl:template match="//dataroot"
  xmlns:xsl="http://www.w3.org/1999/XSL/Transform">
    <html>
      <head>
        <META HTTP-EQUIV="Content-Type"
          CONTENT="text/html;charset=UTF-8"/>
        <title>tblFacilities</title>
        <style type="text/css">
        </style>
      </head>
      <body link="#0c0000" vlink="#050000">
        <table border="1" bgcolor="#ffffff" cellspacing="0"
          cellpadding="0" id="CTRL1">
          <colgroup>
            <col style="TEXT-ALIGN: right; WIDTH: 0.9375in"/>
            <col style="WIDTH: 0.9375in"/>
            <col style="WIDTH: 0.9375in"/>
            <col style="WIDTH: 0.9375in"/>
            <col style="WIDTH: 0.6979in"/>
            <col style="WIDTH: 0.9375in"/>
          </colgroup>
          <tbody>
            <tr>
              <td>
                <div align="center">
                  <strong>ID</strong>
                </div>
              </td>
              <td>
                <div align="center">
                  <strong>Name</strong>
                </div>
              </td>
```

Chapter 23

```
                <td>
                  <div align="center">
                    <strong>Address</strong>
                  </div>
                </td>
                <td>
                  <div align="center">
                    <strong>City</strong>
                  </div>
                </td>
                <td>
                  <div align="center">
                    <strong>State</strong>
                  </div>
                </td>
                <td>
                  <div align="center">
                    <strong>Postal Code</strong>
                  </div>
                </td>
              </tr>
            </tbody>
            <tbody id="CTRL2">
              <xsl:for-each select="tblFacilities">
              <!-- Cache the current node incase the a field is formatted -->
              <xsl:value-of select="fx:CacheCurrentNode(.)"/>
                <tr>
                  <td>
                    <xsl:value-of select="FacilityID"/>
                  </td>
                  <td>
                    <xsl:value-of select="FacilityName"/>
                  </td>
                  <td>
                    <xsl:value-of select="FacilityAddress"/>
                  </td>
                  <td>
                    <xsl:value-of select="FacilityCity"/>
                  </td>
                  <td>
                    <xsl:value-of select="FacilityStateOrProvince"/>
                  </td>
                  <td>
                    <xsl:value-of select="FacilityPostalCode"/>
                  </td>
                </tr>
              </xsl:for-each>
            </tbody>
          </table>
        </body>
      </html>
    </xsl:template>
```

```
  <msxsl:script language="VBScript" implements-prefix="fx"
  xmlns:msxsl="urn:schemas-microsoft-com:xslt">
<![CDATA[
...
Standard data conversion VBScript functions included by Access
removed for brevity.
...
]]></msxsl:script>
</xsl:stylesheet>
```

Notice that the file begins with a comment and the required root element tag. The tag following the root tag specifies that the output format is HTML—ideal for a Web page. The next tag (<xsl:template ...>) identifies the start of the template.

What follows is pure HTML—the tags you would expect to see in an HTML page to define a table layout and its headings. About two-thirds of the way into the listing, following the tags that define the column headings (ID, Name, Address, City, State, and Postal Code), you can find an <xsl:for-each ...> tag that identifies the XML table that provides the data. This directive is followed by six blocks of <xsl:value-of ...> directives, one for each field in the table.

Following the end of the template (</xsl:template> tag), Access includes a large amount of code written in VBScript that defines a series of data transformation functions and the VBScript equivalent of many Access built-in functions. The style sheet doesn't need most of these functions for a simple table like tblFacilities, but it might need them if you have exported the result of a query to XML and that query uses functions in expressions. As Access developers, we become spoiled by the broad range of Visual Basic functions that we can use in queries, but many simply don't exist in VBScript. So, Access must include script that emulates these functions.

The script ends, as you would expect, with an </xsl:stylesheet> end tag to terminate the stylesheet object.

## The Presentation Layout Extension Package (.xsx)

Access 2007 also creates a presentation layout extension file that includes a few simple directives that are used by any designer package (such as Microsoft Expression Web). Your designer might modify this file if you choose to edit the XML file. Because we created the sample files on a Western language system, the sample file contains a single directive to the designer to lay out text from left to right.



## The Web Package (.htm)

The final file that you can optionally create when you export to XML is an HTML (.htm) file containing the commands necessary to bring together the other four files and output standard HTML that your browser can display. This file contains VBScript that executes in the ONLOAD event of the Web page, and the script uses the Document

Object Model (DOM) to convert the XML information to HTML descriptive tags. The Web package file (tblFacilities.htm) for the tblFacilities table is as follows:

```
<HTML xmlns:signature="urn:schemas-microsoft-com:office:access">
<HEAD>
<META HTTP-EQUIV="Content-Type" CONTENT="text/html;charset=UTF-8"/>
</HEAD>
<BODY ONLOAD="ApplyTransform()">
</BODY>
<SCRIPT LANGUAGE="VBScript">
  Option Explicit
  Function ApplyTransform()
    Dim objData, objStyle
    Set objData = CreateDOM
    LoadDOM objData, "tblFacilities.xml"
    Set objStyle = CreateDOM
    LoadDOM objStyle, "tblFacilities.xsl"
    Document.Open "text/html","replace"
    Document.Write objData.TransformNode(objStyle)
  End Function
  Function CreateDOM()
    On Error Resume Next
    Dim tmpDOM
    Set tmpDOM = Nothing
    Set tmpDOM = CreateObject("MSXML2.DOMDocument.5.0")
    If tmpDOM Is Nothing Then
      Set tmpDOM = CreateObject("MSXML2.DOMDocument.4.0")
    End If
    If tmpDOM Is Nothing Then
      Set tmpDOM = CreateObject("MSXML.DOMDocument")
    End If
    Set CreateDOM = tmpDOM
  End Function
  Function LoadDOM(objDOM, strXMLFile)
    objDOM.Async = False
    objDOM.Load strXMLFile
    If (objDOM.ParseError.ErrorCode <> 0) Then
      MsgBox objDOM.ParseError.Reason
    End If
  End Function
</SCRIPT>
</HTML>
```

Notice that the script code doesn't use the XSD file at all! It doesn't need this file because the data file (.xml) and the presentation file (.xsl) contain all the information necessary to create the Web page. The Document.Write statement is the command that actually writes the final HTML to your browser to display the table. If you open the tblFacilities.htm file in your browser, you'll see the result shown in Figure 23-1.

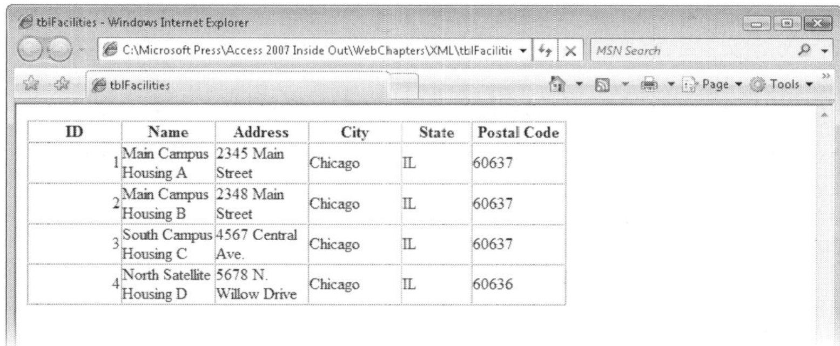


| ID | Name | Address | City | State | Postal Code |
|---|---|---|---|---|---|
| 1 | Main Campus Housing A | 2345 Main Street | Chicago | IL | 60637 |
| 2 | Main Campus Housing B | 2348 Main Street | Chicago | IL | 60637 |
| 3 | South Campus Housing C | 4567 Central Ave. | Chicago | IL | 60637 |
| 4 | North Satellite Housing D | 5678 N. Willow Drive | Chicago | IL | 60636 |

**Figure 23-1** The tblFacilities.htm file displayed in Windows Internet Explorer shows the data and the fields in the tblFacilities table.

> **Note**
>
> Depending upon your browser settings, you might not be able to see the page because you have your browser security options set to disable running scripts. If you're using Internet Explorer version 6 or 7, click the top of the browser window (where the warning message is displayed), click Allow Blocked Content, and then click Yes in the Security Warning dialog box to view the page.

If you're using Internet Explorer 7, you can click the Page button and then click View Source to open in Notepad the final HTML generated by the script. The final HTML the browser uses looks like the HTML you found in the presentation file (.xsl) with the data merged from the data file (.xml).

**For more information on the HTML and XML standards, you can visit the Web site of the World Wide Web Consortium (W3C) at *www.w3.org/*.**

# Using XML in Microsoft Access

Access 2007 not only allows you to import and export data from multiple, related tables, it also supports the exporting of forms and reports that look similar to the original object in your Access application. The new table templates feature that you saw in Chapter 4, "Creating Your Database and Tables," and all the Ribbons you have been working with in Access 2007 also depend on XML technology.

## Exporting and Importing XML from the User Interface

From the Navigation Pane of any Access desktop database (.accdb) or project file (.adp), you can export any table, query (view, function, or stored procedure in a project file), form, or report by selecting the object in the Navigation Pane, clicking the More button in the Export group on the External Data tab, and then clicking XML File. (You can also right-click the object in the Navigation Pane, click Export on the shortcut menu, and then click XML File.) You can also import any XML file as a table by clicking the XML File button in the Import group on the External Data tab. The following sections show you how to perform these actions.

## Exporting Access Tables and Queries

You can export an entire table and any related tables as well as the data extracted by a query and any related data; or you can open a table or query datasheet, select several rows, and export only the selected data. If you have previously applied a filter to your table or query datasheet, you can also ask the XML export facility to apply that filter to select the data to be exported.

Let's take a look at exporting the tblFacilities table and one of its related tables in the Housing Reservations database (Housing.accdb). Open the database and select the tblFacilities table in the Navigation Pane. Click the More button in the Export group on the External Data tab and then click XML File. Access shows you the Export – XML File wizard, as shown in Figure 23-2. In the File Name box, enter the location where you want to save the exported files and the name of the file. You can click the Browse button to open the File Save dialog box and browse to the folder in which you want to save the files. (In our example, we are saving to the \WebChapters\XML folder.)

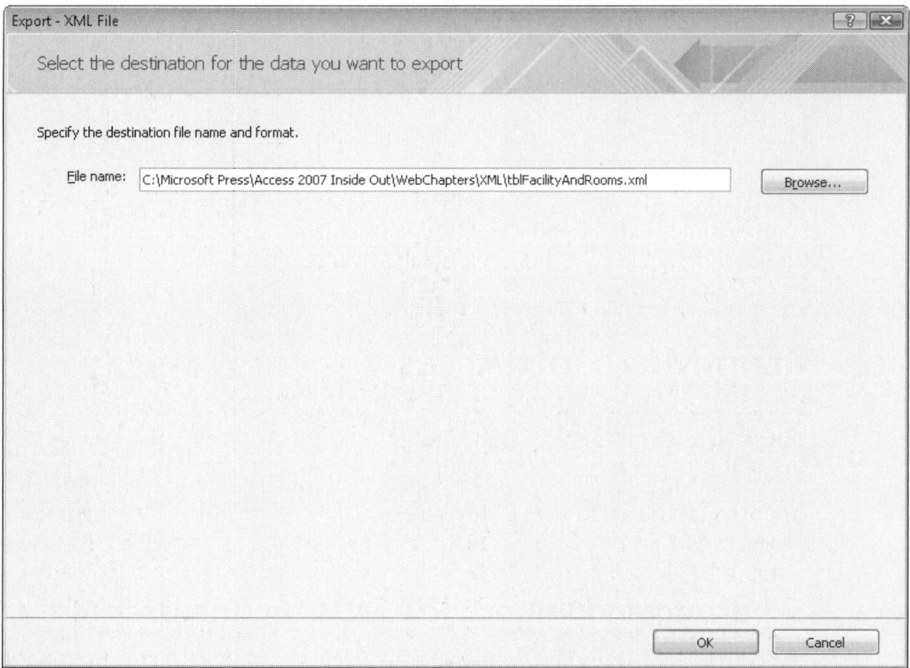


**Figure 23-2** Specify a destination folder and name for your exported XML document on the first page of the Export – XML File wizard.

In this exercise, you'll export both the four records from the tblFacilities table as well as the related records from the tblFacilityRooms table, so change the file name to **tblFacilityAndRooms**, as shown in Figure 23-2. Click OK, and Access shows you the Export XML dialog box, as shown in Figure 23-3.

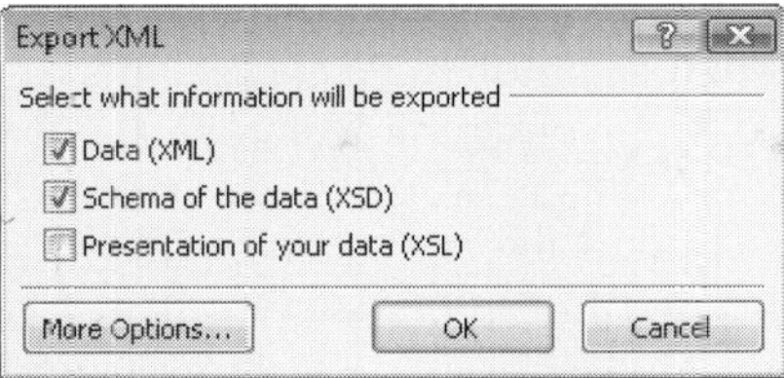


**Figure 23-3** Access displays the Export XML dialog box when you export a table to an XML file.

Notice that the Export XML dialog box assumes that you want to export both the data file (.xml) and the schema file (.xsd). If you also want to export the presentation file (.xsl) and create an HTML file that loads the data using the style sheet, select the Presentation Of Your Data (XSL) check box. If you want to quickly export your data with the default options, you can click OK to complete the export process. However, let's first take a look at some of the options you can choose. Click the More Options button, and Access shows you the expanded Export XML dialog box shown in Figure 23-4.

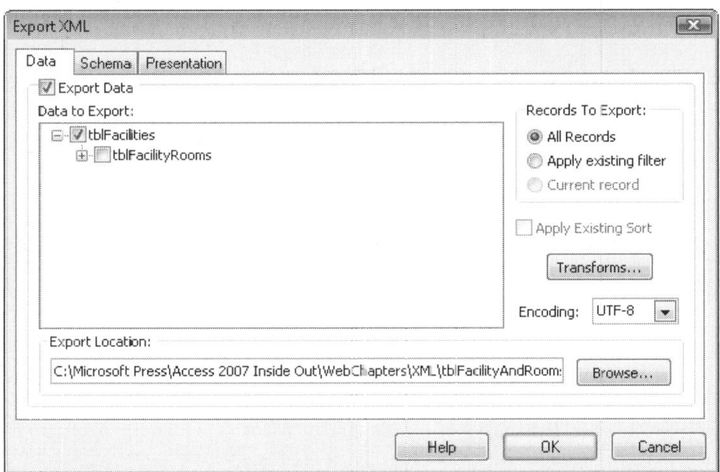


**Figure 23-4** Click the More Options button shown in Figure 23-3 to display additional XML export customizing options.

In the expanded dialog box, you can see three tabs corresponding to the three major types of files you can choose to export. (The Presentation tab includes both the presentation file and the companion HTML file.) If you left the Data (XML) check box selected in the original dialog box, you'll see the Export Data check box selected on the Data tab. Notice that Access shows you the first table that it finds related to the tblFacilities table–tblFacilityRooms. Go ahead and select the check box next to that table to include the related information in your XML files. You can also click the plus sign next to the table name to see other related tables that you might want to include—in this case you could expand the tree of relationships and choose tblReservations, tblReservation-Requests, and even tblEmployees and tblDepartments.

In the upper right of the dialog box, you can select which records to export under Records To Export. The default is to export all records in all tables that you select. Because we previously applied a filter to tblFacilities in Datasheet view and then saved the filter, you can also see an Apply Existing Filter option offered. Unfortunately, Access doesn't give you any clues about the saved filter, so you would need to remember the last filter that you applied and saved with the table to take advantage of this option. There's also a dimmed option to export the current record, but you'll see that option available only when you have opened the table in Datasheet view, selected a record, and then started an export to an XML file. (You can try this on your own by opening tblFacilities in Datasheet view, selecting one record, clicking the More button in the Export group on the External Data tab, and then clicking XML File.)

Directly under the Records To Export section, you can see a dimmed check box labeled Apply Existing Sort. As you might surmise, Access would show you this option if you had previously sorted the data in the table in Datasheet view and saved the sort. Directly under the sort option is a Transforms button. If you previously saved a presentation file (.xsl) or created a presentation transform file (.xslt), you can click this button to specify the file. (Creating XSLT transformation files is beyond the scope of this book.) The export facility applies the transformation to your XML file after it completes the export.

In the Encoding box, you can choose options to export the text in UTF-8 (single-byte character set) or UTF-16 (extended character set). You should choose UTF-16 only if your data contains non-Latin characters. (English and most European languages use a Latin character set.) Finally, you can change your mind about where you want to store the resulting file and what name you want to give to the file by typing in the Export Location box or by clicking the Browse button to navigate to a new location. Click the Schema tab to see the options that you can specify for the schema file, as shown in Figure 23-5.

If you selected the Schema Of The Data (XSD) check box in the initial Export XML dialog box (Figure 23-3), you'll see the Export Schema check box selected here. As you can see, you have the options to include the primary key and index definitions in your schema file and to export all the table and field properties. You can also choose to embed the schema inside the XML data document file, but choosing Create Separate Schema Document (the default) gives you more flexibility. Finally, you can specify an alternate location for the schema file, but you should normally store it in the same location as the data document. On the last tab, Presentation, you can specify options for your presentation file (.xsl), as shown in Figure 23-6. (We have selected the Export Presentation check box on this tab.)

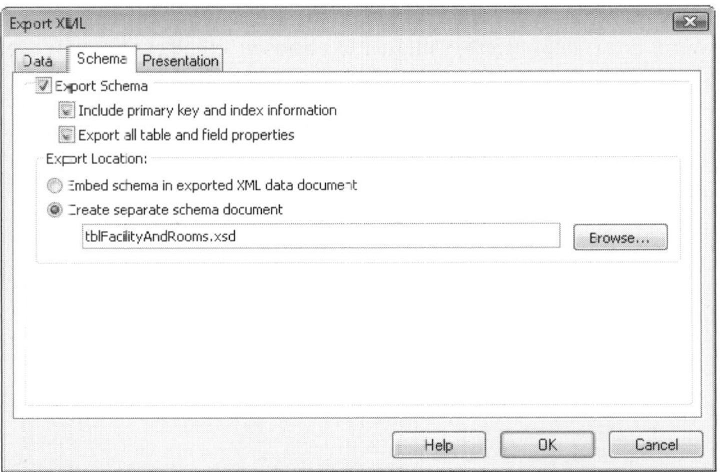


**Figure 23-5** You can select options to export the table definition on the Schema tab of the Export XML dialog box.

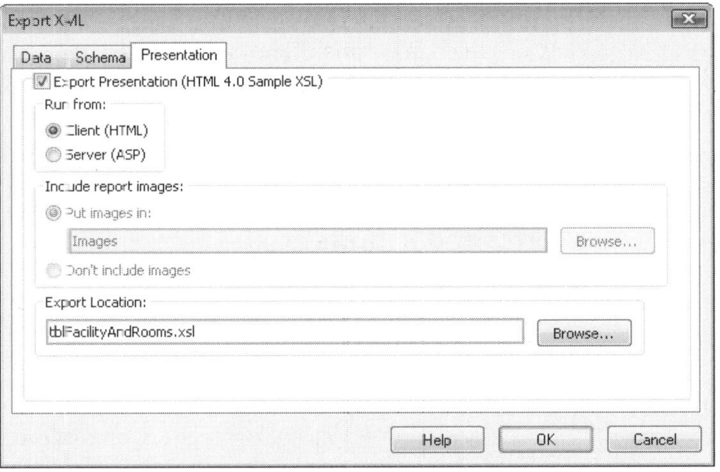


**Figure 23-6** Select the Export Presentation check box on the Presentation tab in the Export XML dialog box to create an HTML file.

Notice that you have the option to create a standard HTML file (.htm) by selecting Client (HTML) or an Active Server Page file (.asp) by selecting Server (ASP). You can open an HTML file directly in your browser, but you must publish an Active Server Page to a Web server that supports dynamic pages and then request it from the server to be able to open it. Remember, however, that you're publishing your data as static XML, so neither the HTML nor the Active Server Page will fetch current data from your database or allow you to update the data in the XML file. Also, even though you have selected multiple tables on the Data tab, the Web pages will display data only from the first table. (This is a limitation of the export XML facility in Access 2007.)

As you'll see later when you ask to export a form or report to XML, Access makes the Include Report Images options available to allow you to include any graphics that you have used in the design of your form or report in the resulting Web page. (Yes, this option applies to forms, too!)

Click OK to complete the export. The last page of the Export – XML File wizard asks you whether you want to save the export steps for future use. You don't need to save these steps, so click Close to close the wizard. When you open the resulting tblFacility-AndRooms.htm file in your browser, it should look exactly like Figure 23-1, but if you open the XML file, you'll see that Access included the data for both tables. You can find the sample files saved on the companion CD as tblFacilityAndRoomsXmpl.htm, .xml, .xsd, and .xsl.

INSIDE OUT **Exporting to ASP**

If you're running Microsoft Windows XP Professional or Windows Vista and have installed and started Internet Information Services, you can export your data as an Active Server Page to your server folders (usually C:\Inetpub\wwwroot) by selecting the Server (ASP) option under Run From on the Presentation tab. Be sure to export the XML, XSD, and XSL files to the same Web folder as the Active Server Page. You can then view the resulting Active Server Page by opening your browser and asking it to display this address: *http://localhost/tblFacilityAndRooms.asp*

## Exporting Access Forms and Reports

A useful feature in Access is the ability to create Web pages from your Access forms and reports. Unlike when you export the data from a table or query to create a simple formatted Web page, you can export the data behind a form or report and create a special presentation file that emulates the look of the original object in Access. To do this, Access creates a special version of the XSL file using an extension to the language called ReportML. This language extension includes special tags to support form and report formatting, and you can open these files only in a browser that supports the version of VBScript and the Document Object Model (DOM) that understands them (such as Internet Explorer version 6 and later).

You might find this feature useful to produce Web reports that look similar to the design of the original object. To update the data periodically, all you need do is replace the XML file containing the data used by the Web page. The one drawback to this process is you can export only forms and reports that do not include subforms or subreports. Although Access will let you export a form that has one or more subforms, it will export and format only the data shown in the outer form.

Let's take a look at a simple form in the Housing Reservations application (Housing.accdb) that exports nicely as XML. Open the database, and select the frmDepartments form in the Navigation Pane. Click the More button in the Export group on the External Data tab, and then click XML File to start the process.

On the first page of the Export - XML File wizard (shown previously in Figure 23-2), you can type a location and name for the export file. You can also click the Browse button to browse for a new location. For this example, select the \WebChapters\XML folder as you did in the previous example. You can keep the default name Access provided—frmDepartments.xml—for the file name and then click OK to continue. In the initial Export XML dialog box (shown in Figure 23-3), you'll see the option to export the data selected. Because you want to see the data formatted similar to the form, also make sure that the Schema Of The Data (XSD) and Presentation Of Your Data (XSL) check boxes are selected, and then click the More Options button to look at the options you can customize. Figure 23-7 shows you the options on the Data tab.

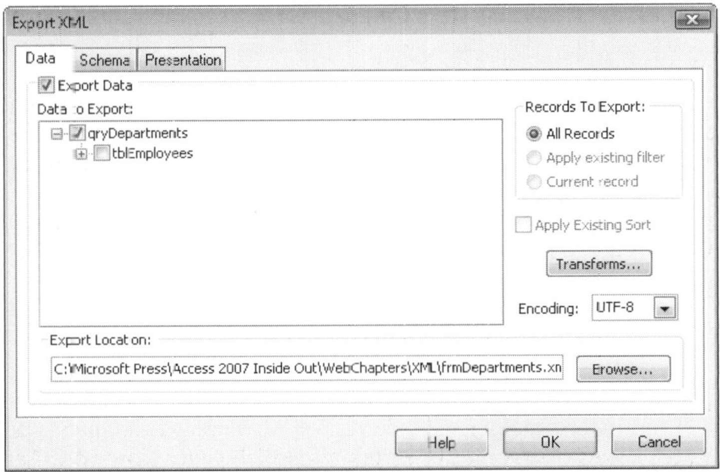


**Figure 23-7** The Data tab options when exporting a form as XML are the same as when exporting a table

Notice that Access gives you the option to include additional related tables, but keep in mind that you'll see only the first table in the resulting Web page. If you opened the form in Form view first, Access would also offer you the option to export the current record only.

The options on the Schema tab are exactly as you saw earlier when exporting a table (Figure 23-5). Click the Presentation tab to see additional options related to exporting a form, as shown in Figure 23-8.

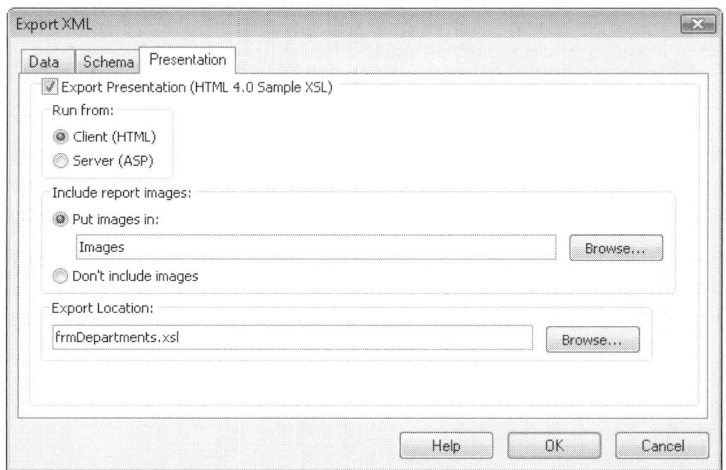


**Figure 23-8** The Presentation tab of the Export – XML dialog box lets you set options to include images when you export a form as XML.

Notice that Access now gives you the option to export any images. We created the original form using the Form Wizard and chose the Trek format, which applies a light orange pattern bitmap to the form background. If you want the resulting Web page to include the background, you should leave the Put Images In option selected. Click OK to export the form and its data. Click Close on the last page of the Export – XML File wizard, and don't save the export steps. When you open the HTM file, it should look like Figure 23-9.

Notice that the ReportML style specification does a fairly good job of copying the fonts and styles from the original form. However, it also displays all labels, text boxes, combo boxes, and list boxes that you designed on the form, including a hidden label. When you open the form in the application, that label is revealed only when you're creating a new department. Also, the form background is the background of the Web page, but it doesn't display behind the actual form area. (The screen illustration printed in this book might not make that obvious—open the sample file to see the difference.) Finally, the page includes all the records strung back-to-back. You can find this set of files saved in the WebChapters\XML subfolder on the companion CD as frmDepartmentsXmpl.htm, .xml, .xsd, and .xsl.



We think Access does a better job of exporting reports than forms (as long as they don't have subreports) into an HTML/XML result that looks very much like the original. You can try this yourself by selecting the rptDepartments report in the Navigation Pane and following the same export steps that you did for the frmDepartments form. Your end result displayed in a Web page should look like Figure 23-10. You can find this set of files saved in the WebChapters\XML subfolder on the companion CD as rptDepartmentsXmpl.htm, .xml, .xsd, and .xsl.

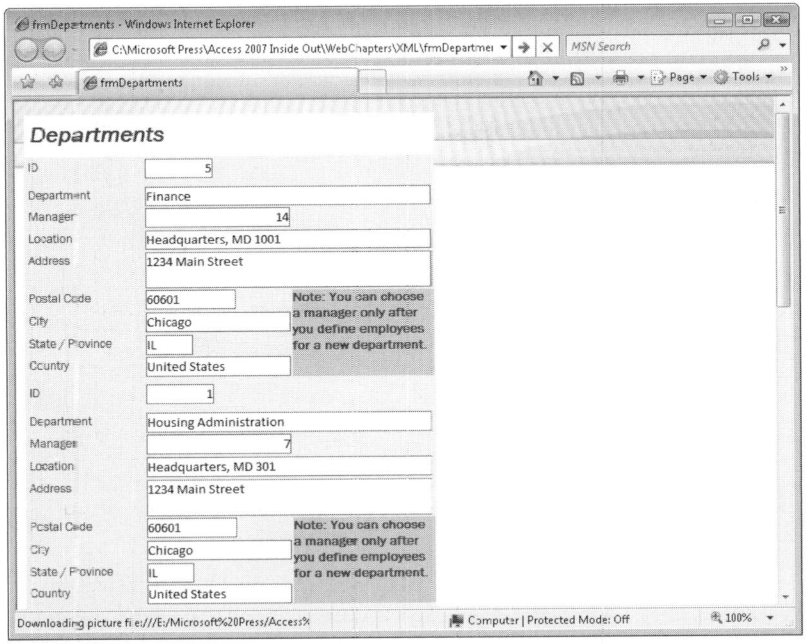


Figure 23-9 The frmDepartments form exported as XML is shown here displayed in a Web page.

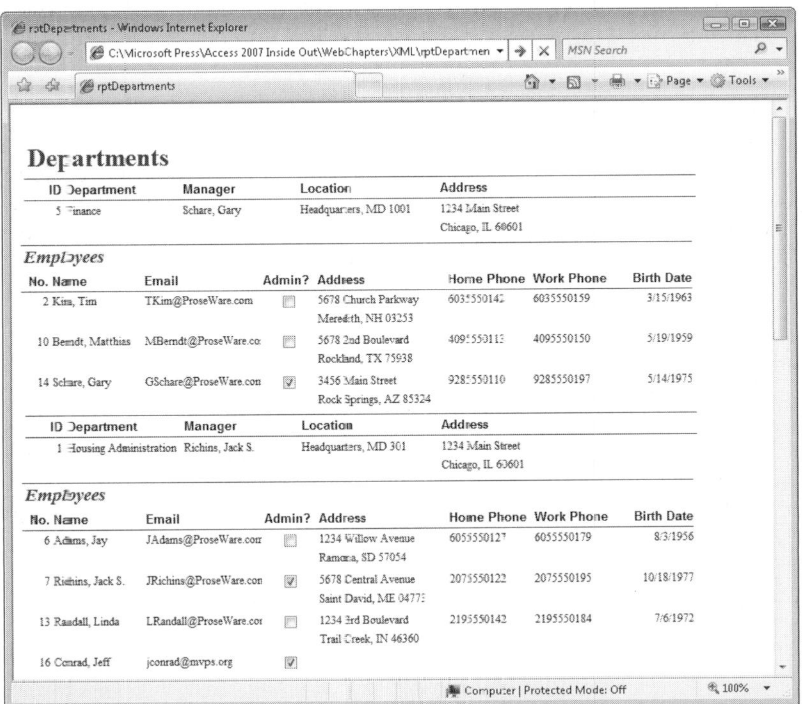


Figure 23-10 The rptDepartments report in the Housing Reservations database is exported as XML and displayed in a Web page.

Chapter 23

The result looks remarkably like the original. To make it look perfectly the same, you would need to dig into the presentation file and fix the display specifications for the phone numbers and the birth date.

## Importing XML Files

As you learned in Chapter 6, "Importing and Linking Data," you can import or link many types of database files and text and spreadsheet files into your Access database. In Access 2007, you can also import XML files, but you cannot link to them. Access 2007 also supports XML files that contain multiple tables. When you import XML that includes multiple tables, Access creates one table in your database for each table it finds in the file.

To begin importing an XML file, click the XML File button in the Import group on the External Data tab. Access opens the Get External Data – XML File wizard, as shown in Figure 23-11.

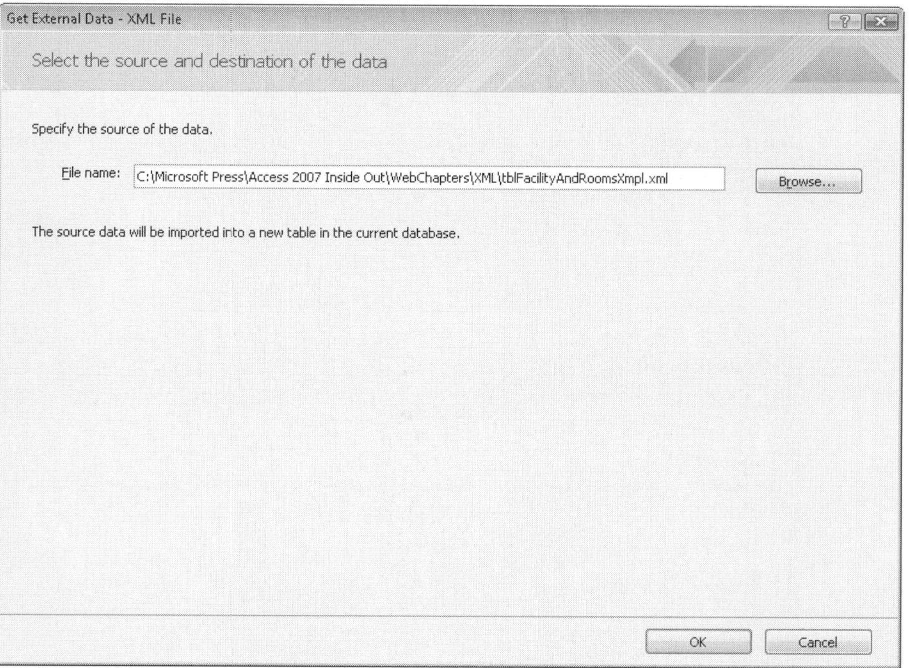


**Figure 23-11** Select the location and name of the XML file to import on the first page of the Get External Data – XML File wizard.

On the first page of the wizard you need to type the location and name of the XML file you want to import. You can click the Browse button to choose a different location than the default folder that Access chooses. In this case, let's choose the sample XML file you previously created that includes data from both the tblFacilities table and the tblRooms table (tblFacilityAndRoomsXmpl.xml). Click OK to start the process, and Access displays the Import XML dialog box, as shown in Figure 23-12.

> **Note**
>
> If you ask Access to import an XSD file, Access creates a table with the specified data structure but does not import the data. Remember, the data is in the XML file; the XSD file contains only the schema definition.

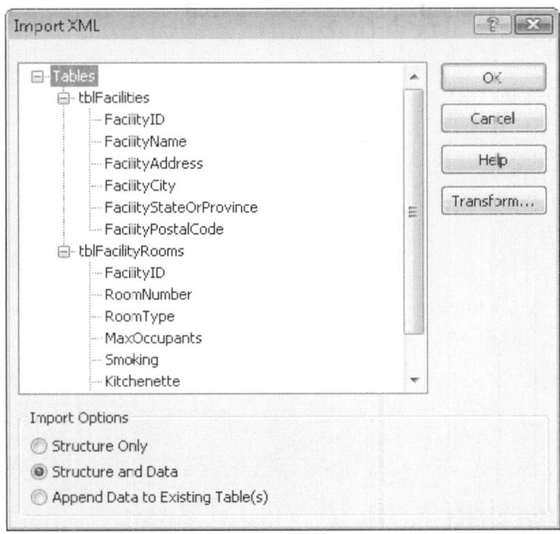


**Figure 23-12** The Import XML dialog box displays options for importing XML files.

When you first see this dialog box, Access shows you the tables it found in the XML file. You can click the plus sign next to any table name to verify the field names. You can click the Transform button to specify any XSLT file that you need in order to convert the data into a format that Access can use. This file originally came from Access, so you don't need to apply any transformation.

In the Import Options section, you can select options to import only the structure (from the XSD file or embedded schema in the XML file) or the structure and the data (the default) or to append the data to existing tables of the same name. In this case, you know that the Housing Reservations database already contains these tables, so attempting to append the data will result in duplicate primary key value errors. So, leave the default Structure And Data option selected, and click OK. On the last page of the Get External Data – XML File wizard, you can choose to save the export steps you just performed for future use. You don't need to save these steps, so click Close to close the wizard.

Because the two tables already exist in the database, Access appends a number to the names of the tables it is importing from the XML file to avoid duplicate names. You can see the two new tables (tblFacilities1 and tblFacilityRooms1) in the Navigation Pane and one of them (tblFacilities1) opened in Design view in Figure 23-13. Notice that the new table correctly includes the primary key definition as well as all the other field properties. Remember that when you created this XML file earlier, we had you select the Export All Table And Field Properties option on the Schema tab in the Export XML dialog box. If you had not selected that option, Access would not be able to create any of these field properties.

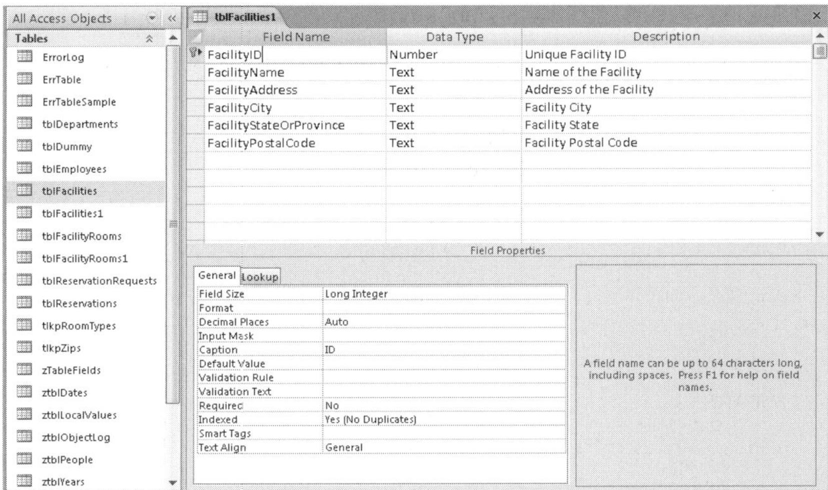


**Figure 23-13** The two tables imported into Access from an XML file contain all the correct data and field properties.

## Importing and Exporting XML in Visual Basic

Importing and exporting XML from the user interface works well for simple one-time tasks, but what if you need to automate the process to make it easy for users of your application to work with XML data? You took a brief look at the example frmXML-Example form in Chapter 21. Now let's look behind the form to understand the code that automates importing and exporting XML data.

Access 2007 provides two methods of the Application object—ImportXML and ExportXML—that enable you to deal with XML files in Visual Basic code. The syntax for the ImportXML command is as follows:

```
[Application.]ImportXML <data source file> [, <import option> ]
```

where <*data source file*> is the path and file name of the file you want to import and <*import option*> is acAppendData, acStructureAndData (the default), or acStructure-Only. Notice that the three options match the options you saw in the Import XML dialog box in Figure 23-12. If the table(s) in the file you want to import already exist, Access appends a numeric digit to the table name(s).

The syntax for the ExportXML command is as follows:

```
[Application.]ExportXML <object type>, <object name>, [ <data file> ],
  [ <schema file> ], [ <presentation file> ], [ <image path> ], [ <encoding> ],
  [ <options> ], [ <filter> ], [ <additional data object> ]
```

*<object type>* is acExportForm, acExportFunction, acExportQuery, acExportReport, acExportServerView, acExportStoredProcedure, or acExportTable.

*<object name>* is the name of the object that you want to export.

*<data file>* is the path and file name of the XML file you want to create. If the file already exists, ExportXML overwrites it.

*<schema file>* is the path and file name of the XSD file you want to create. If the file already exists, ExportXML overwrites it.

*<presentation file>* is the path and file name of the XSL file you want to create. If the file already exists, ExportXML overwrites it.

Note that although all the export file names (data, schema, and presentation) are optional, you must specify at least one of them.

*<image path>* is the folder path where you want to store any images when exporting a form or report.

*<encoding>* is acUTF16 or acUTF8 (the default).

*<options>* are one or more options that you can add together using a plus sign operator (+). The options are as follows:

| Option Intrinsic Constant | Description |
|---|---|
| acEmbedSchema | Embeds the schema within the XML data file. When you include the option, ExportXML ignores any <schema file> specification. |
| acExcludePrimaryKeyAndIndexes | Does not include the primary key or index definitions in the schema data. |
| acExportAllTableAndFieldProperties | Includes the primary key and all field property definitions in the schema data. |
| acLiveReportSource | When <object type> is acExportFunction, acExportServerView, or acExportStoredProcedure, creates a link to your SQL Server database. |
| acPersistReportML | When the <object type> is acExportForm or acExportReport, includes ReportML code in the presentation file. |
| acRunFromServer | Creates an Active Server Page file instead of an HTML file when you ask for a <data file> and <presentation file>. |

*<filter>* is a criteria string to filter the records to be exported.

*<additional data object>* is an object of the AdditionalData data type that you can create by executing the CreateAdditionalData method of the Application object. You specify an additional table name by executing the Add method of the object and supplying the table name as a string.

In the Housing Reservations database (Housing.accdb), the frmXMLExample form demonstrates how you might import an XML file and load it into a form for editing and then export the file when you have finished making changes. Figure 23-14 shows you the form opened in Form view.

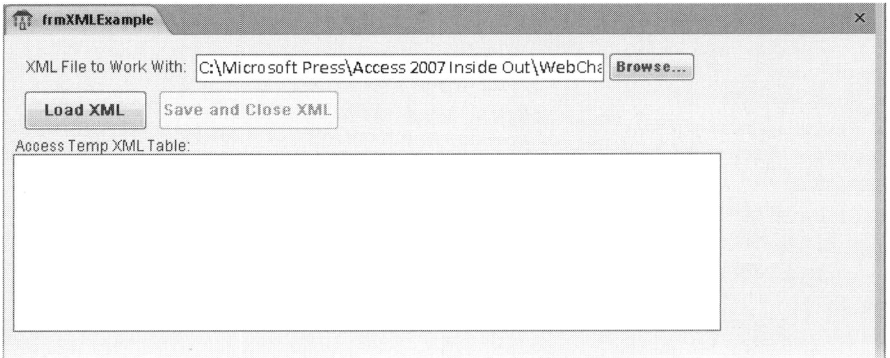


**Figure 23-14** The frmXMLExample sample form allows you to import XML data, edit the data, and then export the data when you have finished making your changes.

The form is designed to initially point to a sample XML file that you can find on the companion CD in the WebChapters\XML subfolder–xmlDepartments.xml. You can click the Browse button to point to any XML file, but you should not use any of the other sample XML files that you find in the subfolder because these are all named the same as objects that already exist in the database. Also, the code depends on the name of the file matching the name of the table defined inside the file. Click the Load XML button to import the file and display the data in the Access Temp XML Table window, as shown in Figure 23-15.

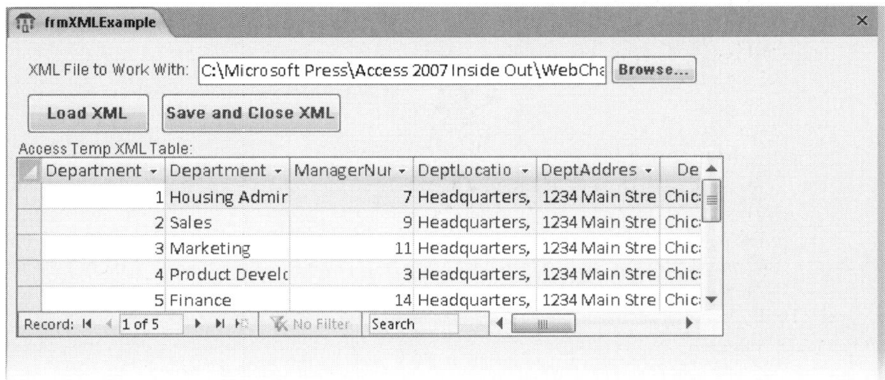


**Figure 23-15** After you click the Load XML button, an XML file is loaded into a window in the form so that you can edit the data.

The data is actually a copy of the data you can find in the tblDepartments table. You can type in any field to change the values, just as you can in a subform datasheet that's bound to a live table in your database. To save your changes, click the Save And Close XML button to export the changed data back to the original XML file. When you load the XML file again, you should see your changes.

To understand how this works, you need to examine the code behind the Load and Save command buttons. Here's the code from the Load procedure:

```
Private Sub cmdLoadXML_Click()
' New table name created from imported XML document
Dim strTableName As String
  ' Turn off screen updates
  Application.Echo False, "Importing XML..."
  ' Turn on error handling
  On Error GoTo cmdLoadXML_Err
  ' Get the table name to be from the XML document name
  ' Note, this will work only if you name the file
  ' the same name as the table inside the XML file.
  strTableName = Mid(Me.txtXMLDocument, InStrRev(Me.txtXMLDocument, "\") + 1)
  strTableName = Left(strTableName, Len(strTableName) - 4)
  ' Change error handling to skip if the next gets an error
  On Error Resume Next
  ' Delete the old XML table, if it exists
  DoCmd.DeleteObject acTable, strTableName
  ' Turn error handling back on
  On Error GoTo cmdLoadXML_Err
  ' Import the XML document
  Application.ImportXML Me.txtXMLDocument, acStructureAndData
  ' Set the subform Source Object property to the table just imported.
  Me.subXML.SourceObject = "Table." & strTableName
  ' Enable the SaveXML button to let them save the XML
  Me.cmdSaveXML.Enabled = True
  ' Indicate XML is loaded
  intXMLLoaded = True
  ' Turn screen updating back on.
  Application.Echo True
  ' Exit the routine
  Exit Sub
' Error-handling routine
cmdLoadXML_Err:
  ' Turn screen updating back on.
  Application.Echo True
  ' Tell the user the problem
  MsgBox "An error has occurred importing the XML: " & Err.Description
  ' Exit the routine
  Exit Sub
End Sub
```

As noted earlier, this code depends on the table name inside the XML file to match the name of the file. (You could also open the XML file or the XSD file as text and scan for the table name tag.) The ImportXML command is very straightforward. The code takes advantage of the fact that you can specify a table in the SourceObject property of a subform control to display the imported table.

The code behind the Save button is as follows:

```
Private Sub cmdSaveXML_Click()
Dim strTableName As String
  ' Get the table name to be from the XML document name
  ' Note, this will work only if you name the file
  ' the same name as the table inside
  strTableName = Mid(Me.txtXMLDocument, InStrRev(Me.txtXMLDocument, "\") + 1)
  strTableName = Left(strTableName, Len(strTableName) - 4)
  ' Export the table back out to the XML document
  Application.ExportXML acExportTable, strTableName, _
    Me.txtXMLDocument, _
    Left(Me.txtXMLDocument, Len(Me.txtXMLDocument) - 4) & ".xsd"
  ' Clean up by resetting the Source Object of the subform to "".
  Me.subXML.SourceObject = ""
  ' Delete the XML table
  DoCmd.DeleteObject acTable, strTableName
  ' Point the focus off the cmdSaveXML button
  Me.cmdLoadXML.SetFocus
  ' Disable the cmdSaveXML button
  Me.cmdSaveXML.Enabled = False
  ' Turn off XML Loaded flag
  intXMLLoaded = False
End Sub
```

Notice that the ExportXML command also rewrites the schema file, but that's probably not necessary. The code also clears the subform by setting its SourceObject property to an empty string. It must do this so that it can delete the temporary table object—if the object were still open in the subform control, Access wouldn't allow the DeleteObject command.

As you can see, Access 2007 provides extensive features to work with XML files in your database applications. You not only can import and export XML files and export some forms and reports from the user interface but also can import and export XML from Visual Basic procedures.



# Modifying Table Templates

In Chapter 4, you learned how to get a jump-start on creating a new table by using one of the five table templates available in Access 2007—Contacts, Tasks, Issues, Events, and Assets. You started creating your contacts table in that chapter by using the Contacts table template as a base, and then you modified the resulting table to meet your specific needs. To define these table templates, Access uses special documents coded in XML that describe the table and field properties. Access reads this schema information when you click one of the five template gallery buttons on the Ribbon and builds your table based on these properties. In the following sections, we'll show you how to modify the templates so that they generate tables that more closely match what you want.

## Adding a New Field to a Table Template

The five template files have .accfl extensions and are located in the Program Files\ Microsoft Office\Templates\1033\Access folder on your C drive in a default 2007 Microsoft Office system installation. You can open the .accfl files using Notepad or an XML reader. For our tests, we used Notepad to edit the XML.

> **Note**
>
> You can download Microsoft Visual Basic 2005 Express Edition from Microsoft to help you create and edit XML files: *http://msdn.microsoft.com/vstudio/express/vb/*.

> **CAUTION!**
>
> If you want to follow along in this section to modify these template files, be sure to make a backup copy and place it in a different folder. If you leave the backup copy in the same folder as the template, Access creates duplicates of every field for that template.

When you used the built-in template to build your contacts table in Chapter 4, you might remember that Access did not automatically create a middle initial field–you had to manually add this field to the table design. Wouldn't it be nice if Access added this field every time you used the Contacts table template? By changing the XML schema information in the Contacts.accfl file, you can have Access create a middle initial field for you. Before you begin, let's take a look at the original fields that Access creates with this template. Create a blank new database, called ModifyTableTemplate, and save it in a trusted location. Next, close the default new Table1 that Access creates for new databases. Now click the Table Templates button in the Tables group on the Create tab, and then click Contacts. Access creates a new table called Table1 with 18 fields to describe a contact. Switch to Design view, and save the table as OriginalContacts when Access prompts you for a name. As you can see in Figure 23-16, Access did not create a middle initial field for you.

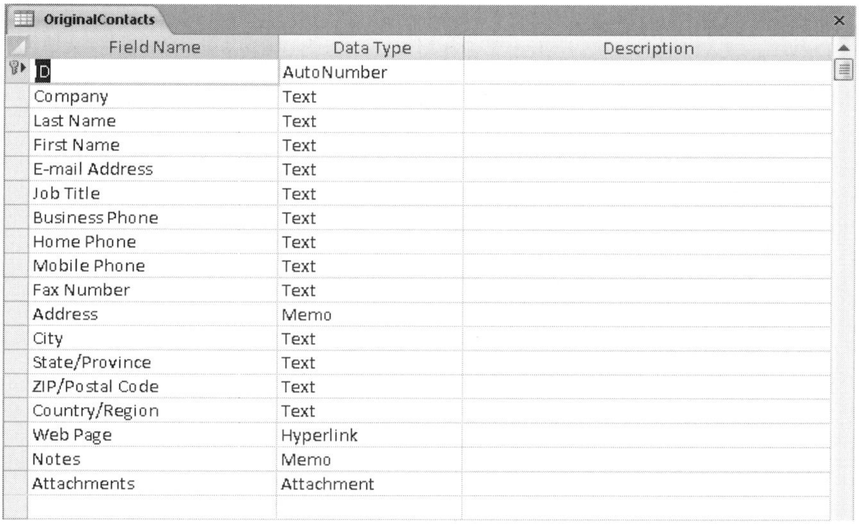

OriginalContacts

| Field Name | Data Type | Description |
|---|---|---|
| ID | AutoNumber | |
| Company | Text | |
| Last Name | Text | |
| First Name | Text | |
| E-mail Address | Text | |
| Job Title | Text | |
| Business Phone | Text | |
| Home Phone | Text | |
| Mobile Phone | Text | |
| Fax Number | Text | |
| Address | Memo | |
| City | Text | |
| State/Province | Text | |
| ZIP/Postal Code | Text | |
| Country/Region | Text | |
| Web Page | Hyperlink | |
| Notes | Memo | |
| Attachments | Attachment | |

**Figure 23-16** The original Contacts.accfl file includes schema information for 18 fields.

Close the database, and now let's change the schema information to create a new middle initial field. Open the Contacts.accfl file with Notepad or an XML editor, and scroll down until you come to the following area that describes the First Name field:

```
</xsd:element>
  <xsd:element name="First_x0020_Name" minOccurs="0" od:jetType="text"
      od:sqlSType="nvarchar">
    <xsd:annotation>
      <xsd:appinfo>
        <od:fieldProperty name="ColumnWidth" type="3" value="-1"/>
        <od:fieldProperty name="ColumnOrder" type="3" value="0"/>
        <od:fieldProperty name="ColumnHidden" type="1" value="0"/>
        <od:fieldProperty name="Required" type="1" value="0"/>
        <od:fieldProperty name="AllowZeroLength" type="1" value="0"/>
        <od:fieldProperty name="DisplayControl" type="3" value="109"/>
        <od:fieldProperty name="IMEMode" type="2" value="0"/>
        <od:fieldProperty name="IMESentenceMode" type="2" value="0"/>
        <od:fieldProperty name="UnicodeCompression" type="1" value="1"/>
        <od:fieldProperty name="TextAlign" type="2" value="0"/>
        <od:fieldProperty name="AggregateType" type="4" value="-1"/>
        <od:fieldProperty name="WSSFieldID" type="10" value="FirstName"/>
        <od:fieldProperty name="GUID" type="9" value="8LewvB2Zg02/47ANPW8KHA=="/>
      </xsd:appinfo>
    </xsd:annotation>
    <xsd:simpleType>
      <xsd:restriction base="xsd:string">
        <xsd:maxLength value="50"/>
      </xsd:restriction>
    </xsd:simpleType>
```

INSIDE OUT **Forming Field Names with Spaces in XML**

You might have noticed that the name assigned to the First Name field includes a strange x0020 specification in the middle. Names coded in HTML or XML cannot embed spaces or special characters, so you must enter special codes if you want to include a space in the generated name. The hexadecimal code for a space in the ASCII character set is 20 (decimal 32), so the _x0020_ embedded within the name instructs XML to use an actual space in the name. If you scan down further in the .accfl file, you'll find that the character / is embedded in State/Province using the code _x002F_ (decimal 47). You can find the ASCII decimal codes for special characters in Access Help by searching for *ASCII character chart*.

You could type similar XML to create another field, but the First Name field has most of the same properties that we want to set for the middle initial field. To make the task easier, let's make a copy of this code and change what we need. Highlight and copy all the previous code to the Clipboard, place your insertion point just after the </xsd:simpleType> line, press Enter, and then paste the code back into the file. You now have a duplicate entry of the First Name field.

In this second copy of the XML code, you need to change the field name and the maximum length. Look for the following line of code that has the field name:

```
<xsd:element name="First_x0020_Name" minOccurs="0" od:jetType="text"
od:sqlSType="nvarchar">
```

Change the *element name* to **="MiddleInitial"** (without any spaces) in order to have Access name the new field MiddleInitial. You'll also need to make the same change in this line of code:

```
<od:fieldProperty name="WSSFieldID" type="10" value="FirstName"/>
```

Change the *value* to **="MiddleInitial"** to complete changing the field name. To change the length of the field (a middle initial should be restricted to one character), find the following lines of code:

```
<xsd:restriction base="xsd:string">
    <xsd:maxLength value="50"/>
</xsd:restriction>
```

Change the value 50 to 1, and then save and close the Contacts.accfl file.

Note

Although the table templates clearly specify the MaxLength property for text fields, the initial release of Access 2007 fails to apply this property. As a result, all text fields in templates are created with the maximum length of 255. You should change this property of any text field that you add to a template in anticipation of fixing this problem in future updates to the product.

Open the ModifyTableTemplate.accdb database you created earlier, click the Table Templates button in the Tables group on the Create tab, and then click Contacts. Access creates another table called Table1 and opens it in Datasheet view. Switch to Design view, and name the table ContactsInitial. In Figure 23-17, you can see Access creates the MiddleInitial field and places it after the First Name field. Each time you use the Contacts table template from this point, Access creates this additional field.

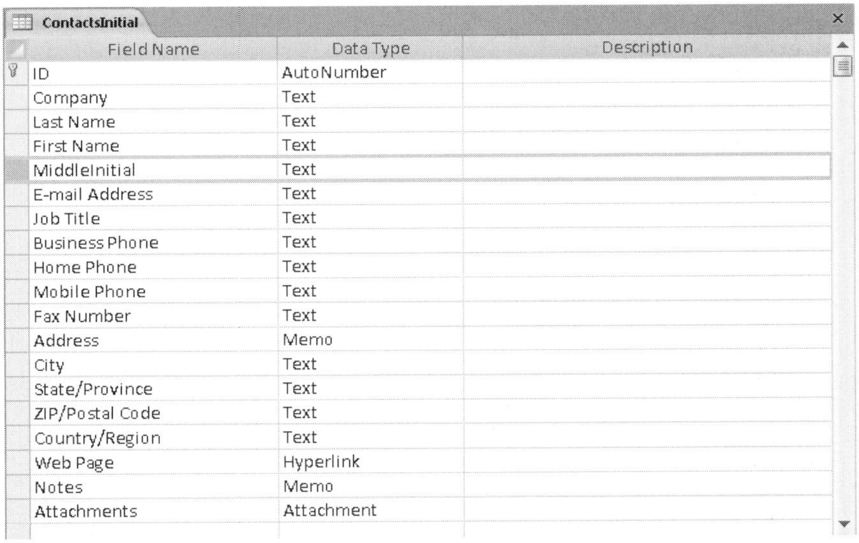

ContactsInitial

| Field Name | Data Type | Description |
|---|---|---|
| ID | AutoNumber | |
| Company | Text | |
| Last Name | Text | |
| First Name | Text | |
| MiddleInitial | Text | |
| E-mail Address | Text | |
| Job Title | Text | |
| Business Phone | Text | |
| Home Phone | Text | |
| Mobile Phone | Text | |
| Fax Number | Text | |
| Address | Memo | |
| City | Text | |
| State/Province | Text | |
| ZIP/Postal Code | Text | |
| Country/Region | Text | |
| Web Page | Hyperlink | |
| Notes | Memo | |
| Attachments | Attachment | |

**Figure 23-17** Access creates the MiddleInitial field because you added XML schema information.

## Modifying a Field in a Table Template

You can also modify the existing field properties by changing the XML in the .accfl files. You've noticed by now that all the field names for the five table templates include spaces—Last Name, First Name, and so on. We recommend you do not include spaces in your field names unless you plan to migrate the database to Windows SharePoint Services (version 3). You could take the time to change all the field names whenever you need to use the table template commands, but if you change the XML schema information, Access can do the work for you each time.

Close the ModifyTableTemplate.accdb database you've been working on if you still have it open. Open the Contacts.accfl file in Notepad or an XML editor. For this example, let's change the properties only for the First Name field so that Access does not create a space when it builds this field.

If you look through the XML code near the beginning of the file, you'll notice there is property information for all the indexes in the table. Look for the index called First Name shown next.

```
<od:index index-name="First Name" index-key="First_x0020_Name " primary="no"
unique="no" clustered="no" order="asc"/>
```

In the XML schema, the First Name field is always referenced as "First_x0020_Name." If you eliminate the extra characters between the two words in each instance, Access creates the field with the name FirstName. It could be tedious to manually search through all the XML for each instance of First_x0020_Name. To make your job easier, you can use the Replace command in Notepad, and enter **First_x0020_Name** in the Find What box and **FirstName** in the Replace With box. Click Find Next, and then click Replace for each instance of First_x0020_Name that Notepad highlights. (Note you could also change the index name from First Name to FirstName if you prefer.) You should find two instances you'll need to change. Save and close the template file when you're finished.

Open your ModifyTableTemplate accdb database again, and let's see the results. Click the Table Templates button in the Tables group on the Create tab, and then click Contacts. Access creates another table called Table1 and opens it in Datasheet view. Switch to Design view, and name the table ContactsRevised. In Figure 23-18, you can see Access created the FirstName field with no spaces in the field name. Each time you use the Contacts table template from this point, Access creates the FirstName field with no spaces. If you like, you can open the template file again and remove all the spaces and special characters in the other field names. By examining the XML in the five .accfl files, you can create additional fields and modify existing field properties in any of the table templates to tailor them more to your needs.

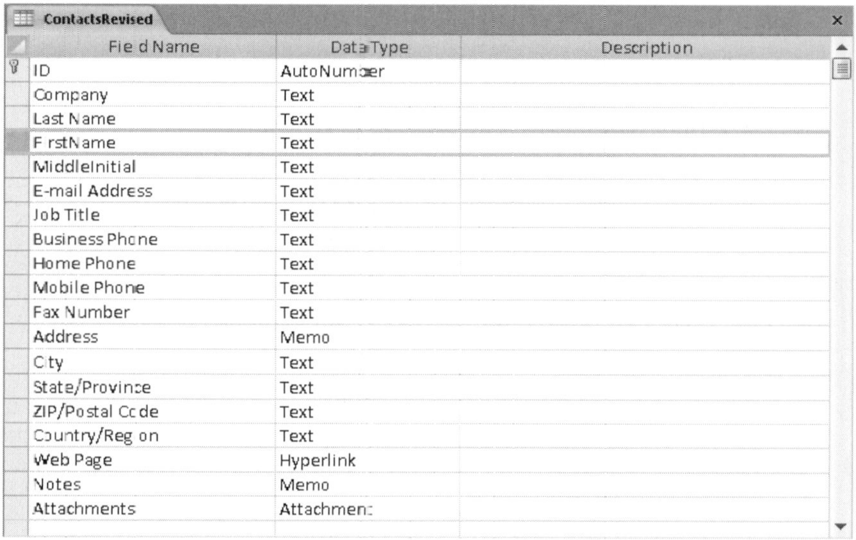

ContactsRevised

| Field Name | Data Type | Description |
|---|---|---|
| ID | AutoNumber | |
| Company | Text | |
| Last Name | Text | |
| FirstName | Text | |
| MiddleInitial | Text | |
| E-mail Address | Text | |
| Job Title | Text | |
| Business Phone | Text | |
| Home Phone | Text | |
| Mobile Phone | Text | |
| Fax Number | Text | |
| Address | Memo | |
| City | Text | |
| State/Province | Text | |
| ZIP/Postal Code | Text | |
| Country/Region | Text | |
| Web Page | Hyperlink | |
| Notes | Memo | |
| Attachments | Attachment | |

**Figure 23-18** The FirstName field now has no spaces when you use the revised table template.

# Customizing the Ribbon with XML

So far in this chapter you've learned about XML file types, how to import and export Access objects and data using XML, and how to modify table templates by changing the schema in the template files. Access 2007 and most applications in the 2007 Office release use XML in another important user interface element—Ribbons. Throughout this book you've seen how to use the Ribbon commands on the four main tabs—Home, Create, External Data, and Database Tools—as well as on the many contextual tabs. You even might have noticed the custom Ribbons we created in the Conrad Systems Contacts (Contacts.accdb) and Housing Reservations (Housing.accdb) sample databases when you opened any of the forms and reports used by the application. In the following sections, you'll learn what steps are necessary to create a simple custom Ribbon for a form. You'll see how to create XML for this Ribbon that displays existing groups from the four main Ribbon tabs. You'll also create a new data entry form and assign your new Ribbon to this form to test the new commands.

## Creating a USysRibbons Table

When you open an Access 2007 database, Access looks for a local table called USysRibbons during the startup process to see whether it needs to load any custom Ribbons. If Access does not find this table, it proceeds with loading all built-in Ribbons. You can also load custom Ribbons into your application by writing Visual Basic code to load the XML stored in a different table or defined within your code. We'll discuss how to do this in Chapter 24, "The Finishing Touches."

Access does not create a local table called USysRibbons when you create a new blank database or use one of the database templates—you need to create this table yourself. For Access to use the USysRibbons table, the table must contain the two fields listed in Table 23-1. The RibbonName field is a unique name used to identify the name of the Ribbon. The RibbonXml field contains the XML used to define the custom Ribbon. The XML must be well-formed XML in order for Access to interpret the code and apply it to the Ribbon. Note that you can have additional fields in this table if you want (such as a field that documents what's on your custom Ribbon), but Access looks for only the two fields listed in Table 23-1 when loading your Ribbons.

**Table 23-1 USysRibbons Table Fields**

| Field Name | Data Type |
|---|---|
| RibbonName | Text |
| RibbonXml | Memo |

By default, Access does not display in the Navigation Pane any local tables that start with the prefix USys because it considers these to be system tables. Depending upon what settings you have configured in the Navigation Options dialog box, you might not be able to see any system tables. For example, if you create and save a new table with the name USysRibbons, you might not see this new table in the Navigation Pane.

In the Conrad Systems Contacts database, we have included this table to load the custom Ribbons we use in the application. Open the Contacts.accdb database, and click OK in the opening message box. Click the menu at the top of the Navigation Pane, click Object Type under Navigate To Category, and then click Tables under Filter By Group to display a list of tables available in this database. If you scroll through the list of tables, you'll notice you do not see a table called USysRibbons. To see this table in the Navigation Pane, right-click the menu at the top of the Navigation Pane, and click Navigation Options. In the Display Options section in the Navigation Options dialog box, select the Show System Objects check box to display all system objects in the database, as shown in Figure 23-19.

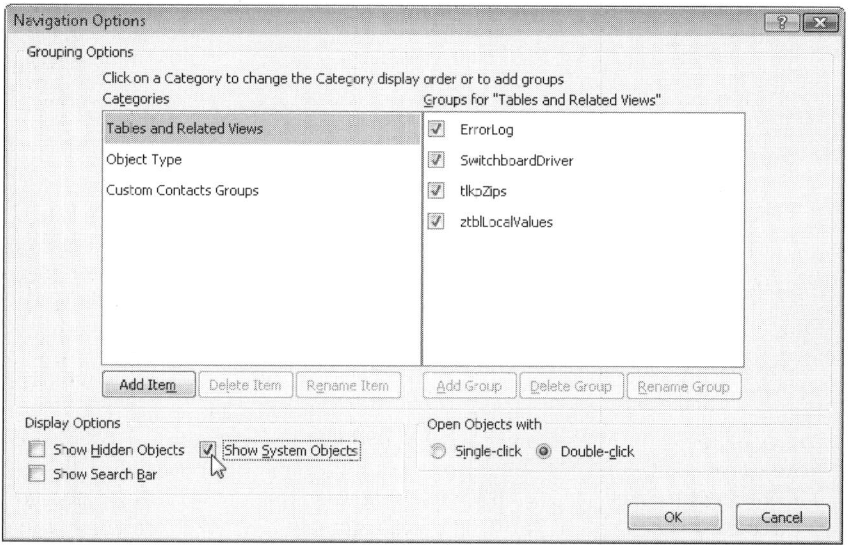


**Figure 23-19** Select the Show System Objects check box to display the USysRibbons table.

Click OK to close the Navigation Options dialog box, and then review the list of tables in the Navigation Pane. You'll notice you can now see six tables that start with the prefix MSys and the USysRibbons table. Right-click the USysRibbons table in the Navigation Pane and click Design View on the shortcut menu to see this table in Design view. In Figure 23-20, you can see the table has one additional field—ID—with a data type of AutoNumber. Remember that Access needs to have only the RibbonName and RibbonXml fields and will ignore any other fields. We added the ID field and used it as the primary key for the table to make sure our entries are unique.

**CAUTION!**

Do not attempt to modify or delete the system tables with the MSys prefix. Access uses these tables internally to manage the various objects and other elements of your database.

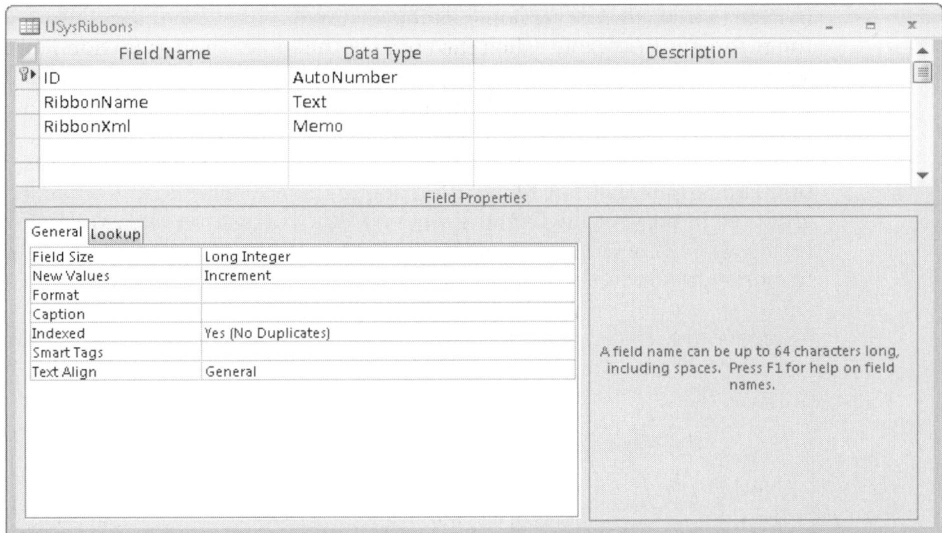


**Figure 23-20** Access looks for a table called USysRibbons during startup to load custom Ribbons.

Switch to Datasheet view by clicking the arrow in the Views group on the Design tab and clicking Datasheet View from the list of available views. You'll notice that there are three records in the USysRibbons table, as shown in Figure 23-21. Each of the records in this table denotes a specific custom Ribbon. You can see the names of each of the Ribbons in the RibbonName field–rbnForms, rbnPrintPreview, and rbnCSD. The rbnForms Ribbon is used by most of the data entry forms in the Conrad Systems Contacts database, the rbnPrintPreview Ribbon is used by the reports, and the rbnCSD Ribbon is displayed for the frmMain, frmCodeLists, and frmReports forms.

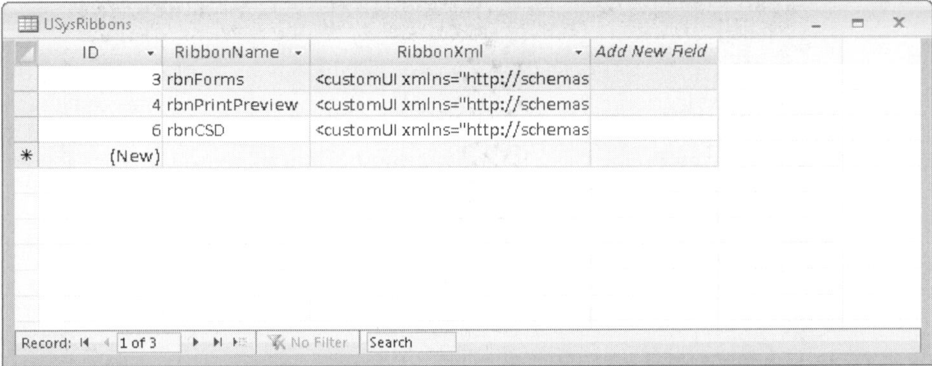


**Figure 23-21** The Conrad Systems Contacts database includes three custom Ribbons.

In the RibbonXml field, you can see the XML for each of these three custom Ribbons. The well-formed XML in these fields, however, is not particularly easy to read in table Datasheet view. You can place your insertion point in the field and use the arrow keys to read the XML, you can press Shift+F2 to open the Zoom box, or you can expand the height of the individual rows. However, a much easier way to view and modify the XML is to create a form bound to this table. In the Conrad Systems Contacts database (and the Housing Reservations database as well), we created a form to add and edit the records in this table. Click the menu at the top of the Navigation Pane, click Object Type under Navigate To Category, and then click Forms under Filter By Group to display a list of forms available in the this database. Find the form called zfrmChange-RibbonXML, and open it in Form view, as shown in Figure 23-22. If you use the record navigation buttons, you can see the XML for each of the three custom Ribbons. (You'll study the three existing Ribbons in more detail in Chapter 24, so don't be concerned about understanding the XML at this point.) We used the Form Wizard to create this form, but you could just as easily create one from scratch if you'd like. Creating a form to work with your USysRibbons table is not a requirement, but you'll have an easier time viewing and modifying your XML by using a large text box on a form for the RibbonXml field.

> **Note**
>
> Now that you understand how to change your settings in the Navigation Options dialog box to view system objects like the USysRibbons table in the Navigation Pane, we recommend you change your settings back to *not* display system objects. Right-click the menu at the top of the Navigation Pane, and click Navigation Options. In the Display Options section in the Navigation Options dialog box, clear the Show System Objects check box, and click OK. You'll be using our zfrmChangeRibbonXML form in the remaining sections to work with the data in the USysRibbons table, so you don't need to see this table in the Navigation Pane.

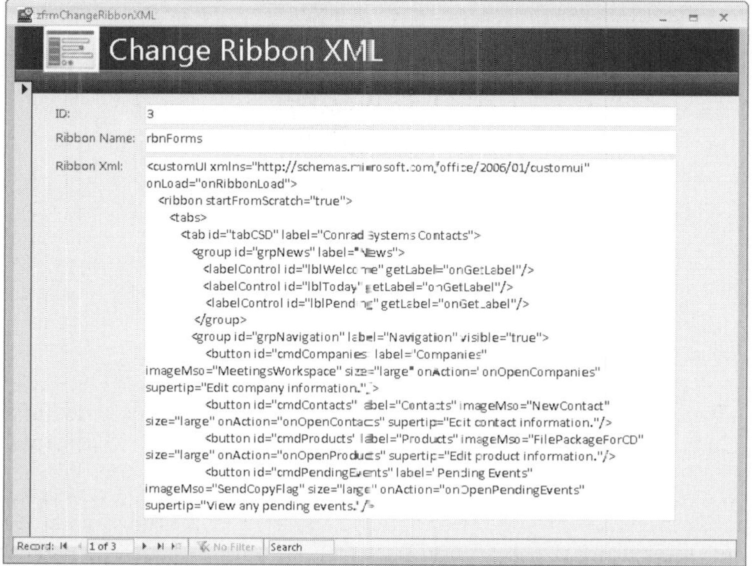


**Figure 23-22** You'll have an easier time editing your XML for the USysRibbons table if you use a form.

## Creating a Test Form

Most of the forms and reports in the Conrad Systems Contacts database each already have a custom Ribbon applied. In the next section, we'll walk you through creating XML for a new form Ribbon. Before we build the XML, let's first create a new data entry form based on the tblContacts table. We'll use this new form to test the XML without disturbing any of the existing database objects. First, close the zfrmChangeRibbonXML form if you still have it open. Next, click the menu at the top of the Navigation Pane, click Object Type under Navigate To Category, and then click Tables under Filter By Group. Finally, select the tblContacts table in the Navigation Pane, and click the Form button in the Forms group on the Create tab. Access creates a new columnar form based on the table and opens it in Form view, as shown in Figure 23-23. Click the Save button on the Quick Access Toolbar, name the form frmRibbonTest, and then close the form.

**Figure 23-23** Create a test form on the tblContacts table to use for your Ribbon testing.

## Building the Ribbon XML

To create a custom Ribbon for a form or report, you must first create the XML in a text editor such as Notepad or Notepad 2007 or in Visual Basic 2005 Express Edition. We used the Notepad text editor to create our XML. To create well-formed XML for Ribbons, you need to use the Microsoft Office system XML Schema Reference, which contains the schema information that Access 2007 needs to validate the Ribbon customizations. You might also want to download the Microsoft Office system Document

Lists of Control IDs, which contains a complete list of the control IDs of the built-in tabs, groups, buttons, and other commands. Each button, group, and tab is assigned a unique control ID in the Ribbon schema file. You can use these controls IDs to place existing built-in Ribbon elements onto your custom Ribbons.

> **Note**
>
> If you use an editor such as Notepad 2007 or a tool such as Visual Basic 2005 Express Edition, you can use Microsoft IntelliSense to assist with constructing your XML. You can download the free XML Notepad 2007 editor from Microsoft at *www.microsoft.com/downloads/details.aspx?familyid=72D6AA49-787D-4118-BA5F-4F30FE913628&displaylang=en.*
>
> You can download Visual Basic 2005 Express Edition from Microsoft at *http://msdn.microsoft.com/vstudio/express/vb/.*
>
> You can download the Microsoft Office system XML Schema Reference for Ribbons from Microsoft at *www.microsoft.com/downloads/details.aspx?familyid=15805380-f2c0-4b80-9ad1-2cb0c300aef9&displaylang=en.*
>
> You can download the Microsoft Office system Document Lists of Control IDs from Microsoft at *www.microsoft.com/downloads/details.aspx?familyid=4329d9e9-4d11-46a5-898d-23e4f331e9ae&displaylang=en.*

## Hiding Existing Ribbon Elements

Open Notepad (or an XML editor) to begin building your XML. We'll create a custom Ribbon for our test form that includes two groups from the Home tab and hides all the built-in main tabs. As we proceed, you'll test each step to see the Ribbon take shape. The XML for Ribbons needs to start with the following line:

```
<customUI xmlns="http://schemas.microsoft.com/office/2006/01/customui">
```

The first line tells Access which schema file to use when building this specific Ribbon. The next line should be as follows:

```
<ribbon startFromScratch="true">
```

If you specify true, Access hides the four main tabs on the Ribbon when your custom Ribbon is loaded. In addition, when you click the Microsoft Office Button, Access shows only the New, Open, Save As, Close Database, Access Options, and Exit Access options. Also, the Quick Access Toolbar shows no options except the arrow—and you can select only the options to place the Quick Access Toolbar above or below the Ribbon or minimize the Ribbon. If you want to have a more controlled interface and show only your custom Ribbons to users, you should set this XML attribute to True. If you set startFromScratch to False, Access does not hide any of the main Ribbon tabs, and it doesn't hide any options when you click the Microsoft Office Button. Any new tabs that you create appear to the right of the Database Tools tab.

After these first two lines, you can begin to build any tabs, groups, buttons, and other Ribbon elements. For now, let's complete this simple XML example with some ending tags for ribbon and customUI. Your XML up to this point should look like the following:

```
<customUI xmlns="http://schemas.microsoft.com/office/2006/01/customui">
   <ribbon startFromScratch="true">
   </ribbon>
</customUI>
```

## Testing Your XML

As you build your XML, it's a good idea to test it along the way to ensure that everything is working properly. You'll have an easier time debugging any issues in your XML if you systematically test it after each major step. Highlight all the XML you've created so far, and copy it to the Clipboard. Next, open the zfrmChangeRibbonXML form in the Conrad Systems Contacts database in Form view, and navigate to a new record. In the Ribbon Name text box, enter **rbnTest** for the name of this Ribbon. Finally, press the Tab key to move to the Ribbon Xml text box, and paste in the XML content from the Clipboard. Your record in the form should look like Figure 23-24.

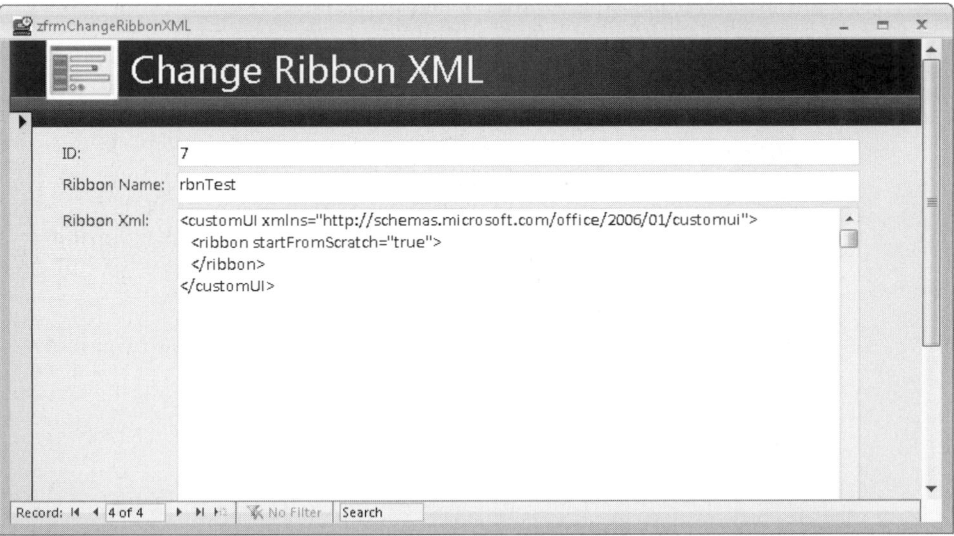


**Figure 23-24** Create a new record in the USysRibbons table for your test Ribbon by using the zfrmChangeRibbonXML form.

Close the zfrmChangeRibbonXML form to save your changes to the USysRibbons table. To display this Ribbon for your test form to see how it looks, you need to assign the rbnTest Ribbon to the Ribbon Name property of the form. Before you do this, however, you need to first close the database and then reopen it. You'll remember we mentioned earlier that Access loads all the Ribbons found in the USysRibbons table during the application startup process. Because you just added this new record to the table, Access has not loaded this Ribbon into memory. If you opened the Property Sheet window for your test form at this point, you will not see rbnTest as an available option on the Ribbon Name property. (Note that you can type rbnTest in the property line, but you still won't see this Ribbon displayed until you close and reopen the database.)

Close the database now and then reopen it to have Access load your new test Ribbon into memory. After you reopen the database, open your test form–frmRibbonTest–in Design view. Click the Property Sheet button in the Tools group on the Design tab to open the property sheet for the form. On the Other or All tab of the property sheet, click the arrow on the Ribbon Name property line, and then select rbnTest from the list of four Ribbons. Click the Save button on the Quick Access Toolbar to save your changes and then switch to Form view to see the result.

When you switch views, you'll notice the entire Ribbon disappears, as shown in Figure 23-25. Access also hides all the options on the Quick Access Toolbar except for the arrow to open the Customize Quick Access Toolbar menu. Click the Microsoft Office Button, and you'll see that Access reduces the number of options, as we discussed previously. Because you specified startFromScratch=True in your XML and did not specify any other custom tabs, Access presents a very limited user interface. Unless you want to provide any features such as filtering and sorting directly on your forms, you clearly need to improve this custom Ribbon beyond the bare essentials.

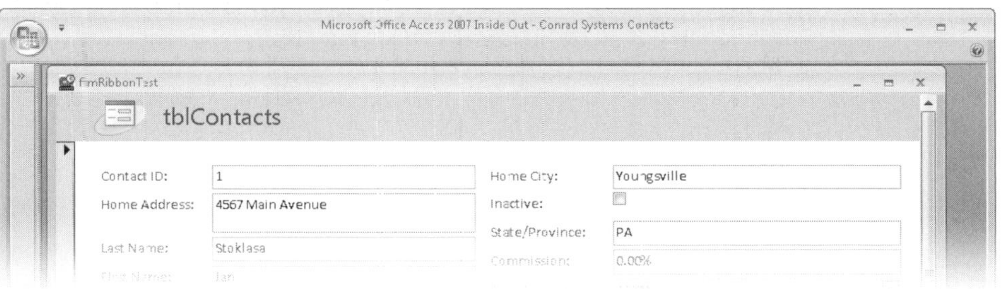


**Figure 23-25** The simple XML you created earlier completely hides the Ribbon.

Chapter 23

### INSIDE OUT Displaying Ribbon Errors

If you create XML for a Ribbon that is not well formed, Access will not display your custom Ribbon. In this situation, Access displays the built-in four main Ribbon tabs because it cannot interpret and display the appropriate customization elements. Access is not forgiving in this case, because even a single line of XML that is not well formed causes Access to revert to showing all the main tabs of the Ribbon. You will have a difficult time debugging the XML and finding the cause of the problem because Access does not automatically display errors when it encounters errors in your XML.

Fortunately, Access includes an option that you can enable to display errors in these cases. Click the Microsoft Office Button, click Access Options, click the Advanced category, and then scroll down to the General area. If you select the Show Add-In User Interface Errors check box (cleared by default) and then click OK, Access displays a dialog box if it finds any problems in your XML. For example, if you select the Show Add-In User Interface Errors check box and add an extra < at the beginning of the third line of the XML you've been working with up to this point, Access displays the following error message when you open your test form (after you close and reopen the database):

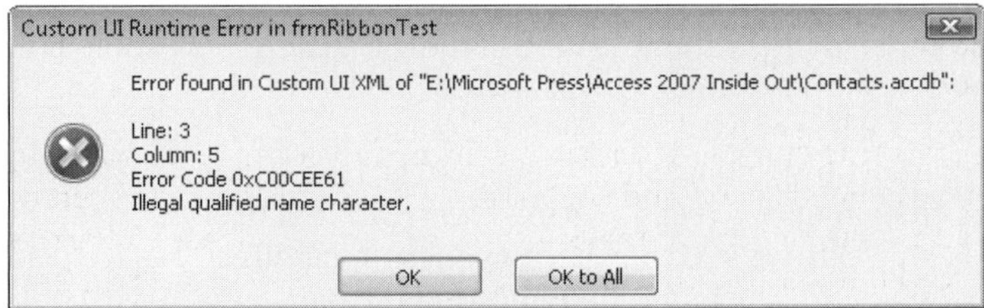


You can see in the error message text that Access found a problem on line 3 of your XML. Selecting this option can help you debug your XML for Ribbons.

## Creating Tabs

Creating an interface with no Ribbon showing, such as the one you just tested in the previous section, might work for some applications, but what if you want to provide your users with the same navigation and filter options for your forms that normally appear on the Home tab? To add buttons and controls to your custom Ribbon, you first need to create a tab to hold these controls. The Access Ribbon schema uses a *tabs* tag to denote a new tab to appear on the Ribbon.

Open Notepad (or an XML editor), and return to the XML file you were creating earlier. To create a new tab, you first need to use a tabs tag (<tabs>) followed by a line with the following syntax:

```
<tab id=UniqueTabName label=LabelCaption
```

The UniqueTabName must be a unique name for the current Ribbon XML. The Label-Caption attribute is optional, but if you don't provide a caption for the tab, Access displays a small, empty tab header. At the end of any XML for the tab, you also need to provide an ending tab tag (</tab>) for each tab and an ending tabs tag (</tabs>) following all the individual tab tags. For this example, we'll create a new tab called tabTest with a caption called Navigation. Add the following XML between the two ribbon tags (<ribbon> and </ribbon>) to create this new tab:

```
    <tabs>
      <tab id="tabTest" label="Navigation">
      </tab>
    </tabs>
```

Your completed XML should now look like the following:

```
<customUI xmlns="http://schemas.microsoft.com/office/2006/01/customui">
  <ribbon startFromScratch="true">
    <tabs>
      <tab id="tabTest" label="Navigation">
      </tab>
    </tabs>
  </ribbon>
</customUI>
```

Now let's test this markup with our test form and see how it looks. Highlight all the XML you've created so far, and copy it to the Clipboard. Next, open the zfrmChange-RibbonXML form in the Conrad Systems Contacts database in Form view, and navigate to the record that has rbnTest in the Ribbon Name text box. Press Tab to move to the Ribbon XML text box, and paste the XML content from the Clipboard, overwriting the previous XML. Next, close the zfrmChangeRibbonXML form to save your changes to the USysRibbons table. Finally, close the database, reopen it, and then open the frmRibbonTest form in Form view. Access now displays the Ribbon at full height with a new tab and caption of Navigation, as shown in Figure 23-26.

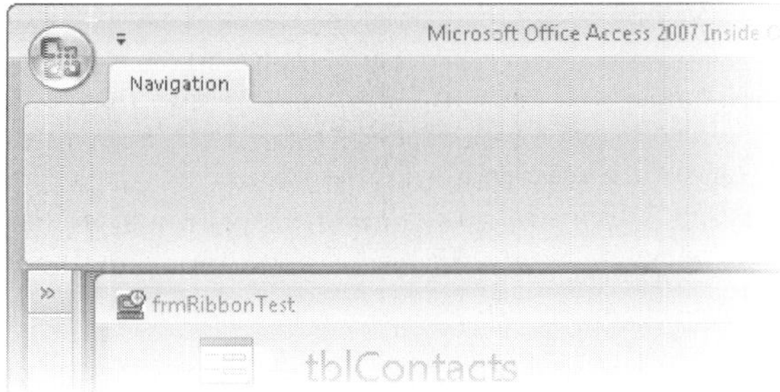


**Figure 23-26** You can create custom tabs for your Ribbons.

## Adding Built-In Groups to Tabs

Now that you have a new tab created in your markup, you can begin the process of adding different controls to this tab. For this test form, it would help your users to navigate through the contact records if they could use some of the built-in buttons and commands found on the Home tab—specifically the Records, Sort & Filter, and Find groups. You could write your own XML to create custom buttons that mimic the actions of each of the individual buttons in those three groups; but to make things easier, you can use the RibbonX architecture to copy buttons, commands, and options found in a built-in group onto one of your custom tabs. (We'll show you how to create individual custom buttons on tabs in Chapter 24).

Open Notepad (or an XML editor), and return to the XML file you were creating earlier. To use an existing built-in group on a custom tab, use the following syntax:

```
<group idMso=ControlID>
```

You can add this tag anywhere within a tab definition (delimited with <tab> </tab> tags). You can use the idMso attribute to denote a built-in control ID—a built-in control defined in the RibbonX architecture. Every button, group, and tab on the built-in Ribbon has an internal control ID that you can reference. In this case, you're going to show how to use the idMso attribute to refer to a specific group that you want to use on your tab. To help identify the names of these groups, you can use the Microsoft Office system Document Lists of Control IDs Excel spreadsheet that contains a complete list of these internal control IDs. For this example, you want to add the Records group on the Home tab to your custom Navigation tab to help your users add, save, and delete records. The control ID for the Records group is GroupRecords. At the end of any XML for a new group, you also need to provide an ending group tag. Add the following XML between the tab tags to create this new group:

```
        <group idMso="GroupRecords">
        </group>
```

Your completed XML up to this point should now look like the following:

```
<customUI xmlns="http://schemas.microsoft.com/office/2006/01/customui">
  <ribbon startFromScratch="true">
    <tabs>
      <tab id="tabTest" label="Navigation">
        <group idMso="GroupRecords">
        </group>
      </tab>
    </tabs>
  </ribbon>
</customUI>
```

Now let's test this XML with our test form to see how it looks. As you did previously, highlight all the XML you've created so far, and copy it to the Clipboard. Next, open the zfrmChangeRibbonXML form in the Conrad Systems Contacts database in Form view, and navigate to the record that has rbnTest in the Ribbon Name text box. Press Tab to move to the Ribbon XML text box, and paste the XML content from the Clipboard, overwriting the existing XML. Next, close the zfrmChangeRibbonXML form to save your changes to the USysRibbons table. Finally, close the database, reopen it, and then open the frmRibbonTest form in Form view. Access now displays all the buttons and commands from the Records group on your custom Navigation tab, as shown in Figure 23-27. If you test some of the buttons, you'll see that they all work just as they do on the Home tab.

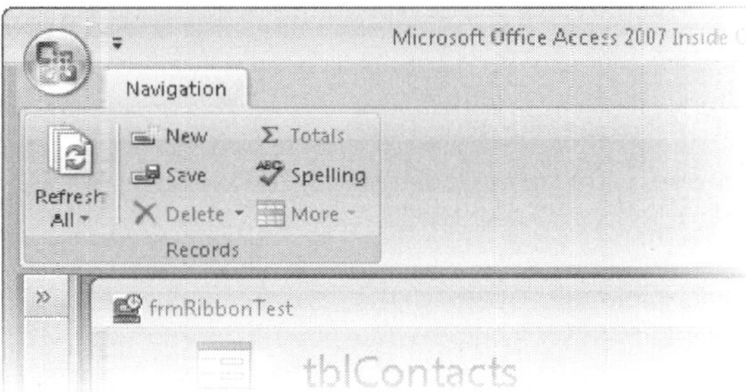


**Figure 23-27** The built-in Records group now appears on your custom Ribbon.

INSIDE OUT

### Finding Control IDs for Built-In Controls

You can also find the control IDs for built-in controls listed in the Customize category in the Access Options dialog box. Click the Microsoft Office Button, click Access Options, and then select the Customize category. In the list on the left, you can see the built-in Access commands. If you rest your mouse pointer on one of these commands, Access displays a ScreenTip that lists the internal control ID. To help you identify control groups, Access displays an icon with a down arrow next to any group names. The internal control ID for the Records group on the Home tab—GroupRecords—is within the parentheses on the ScreenTip, as shown here.

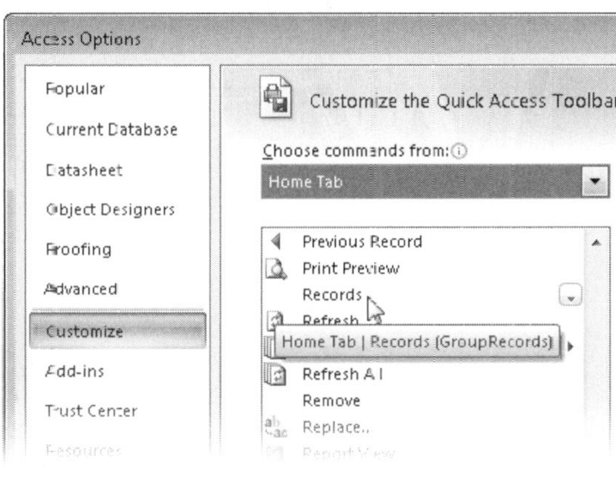


Chapter 23

Now that you've added the Records group to your tab, let's finish the XML by adding the Sort & Filter and Find groups to your custom Ribbon. Open Notepad (or an XML editor), and return to the XML file you were creating earlier. The control ID for the Sort & Filter group is GroupSortAndFilter, and the control ID for the Find group is GroupFindAccess. Add the following XML after the group end tag and before the tab end tag:

```
<group idMso="GroupSortAndFilter">
</group>
<group idMso="GroupFindAccess">
</group>
```

Your final XML should now look like the following:

```
<customUI xmlns="http://schemas.microsoft.com/office/2006/01/customui">
  <ribbon startFromScratch="true">
    <tabs>
      <tab id="tabTest" label="Navigation">
        <group idMso="GroupRecords">
        </group>
        <group idMso="GroupSortAndFilter">
        </group>
        <group idMso="GroupFindAccess">
        </group>
      </tab>
    </tabs>
  </ribbon>
</customUI>
```

Now test your completed XML on your test form. As you did previously, highlight all the XML you've created so far, and copy it to the Clipboard. Next, open the zfrmChangeRibbonXML form in the Conrad Systems Contacts database in Form view, and paste the XML content from the Clipboard into the Ribbon XML text box on the rbnTest record, overwriting the existing XML. Close the zfrmChangeRibbonXML form to save your changes to the USysRibbons table. Close the database, and reopen it to have Access load the new Ribbon changes. Finally, open the frmRibbonTest form in Form view to see the results. Access now displays all the buttons and commands from the Records, Sort & Filter, and Find groups on your custom Navigation tab, as shown in Figure 23-28. With only a few lines of XML, you've created a custom Ribbon that you can use in your application. You could assign this Ribbon to any of the forms in your application. Also, because the XML is stored in a local table, you could easily import this table into another database and reuse the Ribbon for those forms.

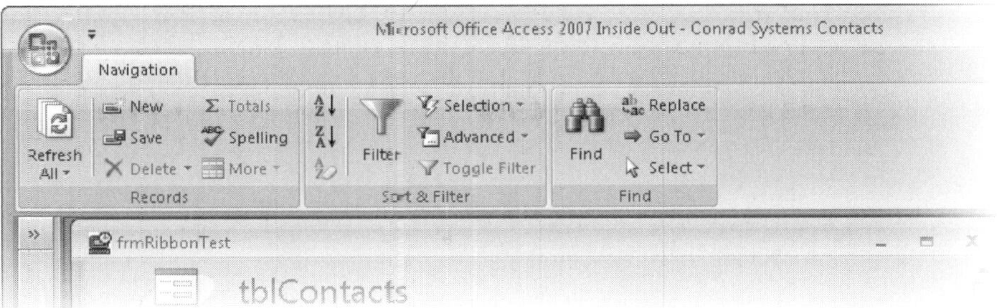


**Figure 23-28** The custom Ribbon you created now includes buttons and commands from three built-in groups.

You should now have a good grasp of the technologies included in Access 2007 to integrate with the Web. In Part 6 of this book, we'll expand our discussion of RibbonX architecture and show you the more advanced concepts of using Visual Basic with Ribbons. We'll show you how to create your own custom buttons and load custom Ribbon schemes. You'll also learn about additional features you can use after you've finished designing your database application.

PART 6

# After Completing Your Application

CHAPTER 24

# The Finishing Touches



You're in the home stretch. You have almost all the forms and reports required for the tasks you want to implement in your application, but you need some additional forms to make it easier to navigate to different tasks. To add a professional touch, you should design a custom Ribbon for your main navigation forms, another custom Ribbon for most data entry forms, and perhaps one for reports. You should take advantage of built-in tools to check the efficiency of your design, and you should make sure that none of your forms and reports allow Layout view. Finally, you need to set the startup properties of your database to let Microsoft Office Access 2007 know how to get your application rolling, and you need to perform a final compile of your Visual Basic code to achieve maximum performance.

**Note**

The Ribbon examples in this chapter are based on the custom Ribbons in Contacts.accdb, Contacts.adp, and Housing.accdb on the companion CD included with this book. All screen images in this chapter were taken on a Microsoft Windows Vista system with the display theme set to Blue. Your results might look different if you are using a different operating system or a different theme.

## Creating Custom Ribbons

When your application is running, the user probably won't want or need some of the Office Access 2007 design features. However, you might want to provide some additional buttons on your form Ribbon so that the user has direct access to commands such as Save Record and Refresh All. For example, open the Conrad Systems Contacts sample database (Contacts.accdb), open the frmContactsPlain form (which uses the built-in Ribbon), and then open the frmContacts form. As you click each form window, Access changes the Ribbon. You can see some useful differences between the two Ribbons, as shown in Figure 24-1.

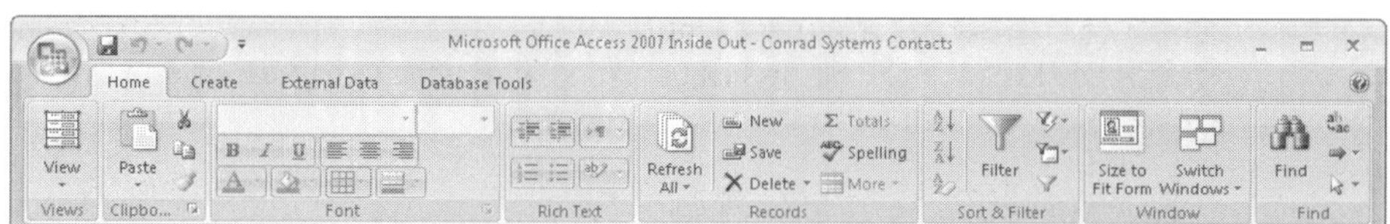

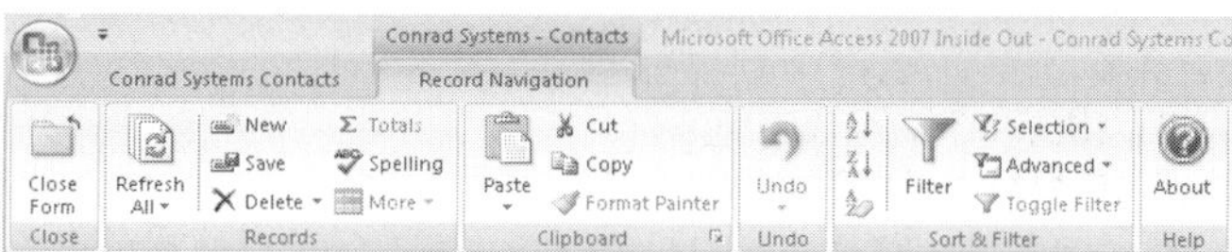

**Figure 24-1** The standard Ribbon (top) displays many commands and tabs your end users won't need, compared to the custom form Ribbon (bottom) from the Conrad Systems Contacts sample database.

Buttons, groups, and tabs the user won't need (such as the buttons in the Views and Windows groups) aren't available on the custom Ribbon. Also, Access disables all the buttons on the Quick Access Toolbar for the frmContacts form, such as Undo, Save, and Quick Print. (None of the forms in the Conrad Systems Contacts database are designed to be printed.) However, the custom Ribbon does have a Close Form button added at the left end of the Record Navigation tab, and we provided a custom Undo command because Undo is no longer available on the Quick Access Toolbar. In the Conrad Systems Contacts application, all forms (except frmContactsPlain and a few other example forms) have their Ribbon Name properties set to use the custom Ribbon.

The same is true of the built-in tabs. For example, you don't want your users to be able to create new database objects using the buttons on the Create tab or to be able to use the tools available on the Database Tools tab. For most forms, you also don't want the user to be able to switch to PivotTable or PivotChart view using the View button. The following sections show you how to build a custom main Ribbon and custom Ribbons for forms and reports.

## Loading Ribbon XML

In Chapter 23, "Using XML," you learned the basic structure of Ribbon XML and how to create a USysRibbons table to store the XML for each of your custom Ribbons. You learned that Access searches for this table during startup and that if it finds this table (and correct fields within the table), Access loads these custom Ribbons into memory. In the Conrad Systems Contacts (Contacts.accdb) sample database, we created three custom Ribbons for the application in the USysRibbons table–rbnCSD, rbnForms, and rbnPrintPreview.

After you define custom Ribbons in the USysRibbons table, you can specify that Access load a specific custom Ribbon each time you open the database. To accomplish this, click the Microsoft Office Button, click Access Options, and then click the Current Database category. In the Ribbon And Toolbar Options section, click the arrow on the Ribbon Name option, and then select your custom Ribbon from the list of loaded Ribbons, as shown in Figure 24-2. (Note that you might need to close and reopen the database to see any new Ribbon you just created appear in the list.) Click OK to save your changes, and close the Access Options dialog box. The next time you open your database, Access applies that custom Ribbon.

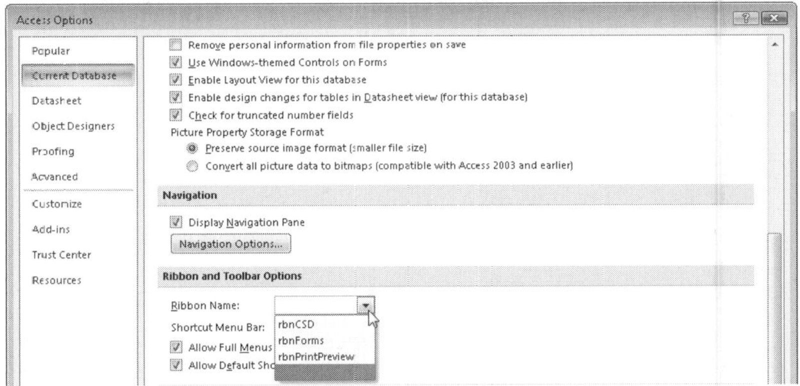


**Figure 24-2** In the Current Database category in the Access Options dialog box, you can select a specific custom Ribbon to load each time you open the database.

> **Note**
>
> To prevent Access from automatically loading any custom Ribbons during the startup procedure, press and hold the Shift key when you open the database.

When you create a USysRibbons table, Access takes care of the work of loading your custom Ribbons. You can also load custom Ribbons into your application by using the LoadCustomUI method. When you dynamically load your Ribbon customization using the LoadCustomUI method, you can store your XML in a table with a different name, in a different database, or in a Visual Basic module.

## Syntax

**Application.LoadCustomUI(***CustomUIName, CustomUIXML***)**

## Notes

*CustomUIName* is a string variable or literal containing the unique name of the custom Ribbon to be associated with this XML, and *CustomUIXML* is a string variable or literal that contains the well-formed XML that defines your custom Ribbon.

If you want to dynamically load custom Ribbons, you need to call the LoadCustomUI method each time you open the database. In the Conrad Systems Contacts project file (Contacts.adp), we use this method to load the same Ribbons you see in the Conrad Systems Contacts database (Contacts.accdb). Close Contacts.accdb if you still have it open, and then open the Contacts.adp file. After you establish a connection to your SQL server, click OK in the opening message box. Next, click the menu at the top of the Navigation Pane, click Object Type under Navigate To Category, and then click Tables under Filter By Group to display a list of tables available in this project file. If you open the ztblRibbons table in Datasheet view, you'll notice we have the same custom Ribbons in this table—rbnForms, rbnPrintPreview, and rbnCSD—as we have in the USysRibbons table in the Contacts.accdb sample database.

INSIDE OUT

### Loading Ribbons into Access Data Projects

Because all tables for an Access project file are stored in SQL Server, you cannot define a local USysRibbons table to have Access automatically load your custom Ribbons. Defining a USysRibbons table on the SQL server doesn't work because those tables don't become available until after Access has completed the initialization of the project file. For more information about working with project files, see Part 7, "Designing an Access Project," on the companion CD.

Close the ztblRibbons table, and let's examine the Visual Basic code we use to load these custom Ribbons. Click the menu at the top of the Navigation Pane, click Object Type under Navigate To Category, and then click Modules under Filter By Group to display a list of Visual Basic modules available in this project file. Right-click modRibbonCallbacks in the Navigation Pane, and click Design View on the shortcut menu to open the Visual Basic Editor. The first function in this module—LoadRibbons—and the declarations above it use the LoadCustomUI method as follows:

```
' This serves as a cached copy of the RibbonUI.
' We can use this to then invalidate the Ribbon and refresh the controls
Public gobjRibbon1 As IRibbonUI
Public gobjRibbon2 As IRibbonUI

Public Function LoadRibbons() As Integer
' Code called by frmCopyright and frmSplash to verify custom Ribbon load
Dim rst As New ADODB.Recordset
    ' Set an error trap
    On Error GoTo LoadRibbon_Err
    ' Do nothing if gobjRibbon is set
    If Not (gobjRibbon1 Is Nothing) Then
        ' Set OK return
        LoadRibbons = True
    Else
        ' Try to load - open recordset on Ribbons
        rst.Open "SELECT * FROM ztblRibbons", CurrentProject.Connection, _
            adOpenKeyset, adLockOptimistic
        Do Until rst.EOF
            Application.LoadCustomUI rst!RibbonName, rst!RibbonXML
            rst.MoveNext
```

```
        Loop
        ' Close out
        rst.Close
        Set rst = Nothing
        LoadRibbons = True
    End If
LoadRibbon_Exit:
    Exit Function
LoadRibbon_Err:
    ' Silently log error
    ErrorLog "LoadRibbons", Err, Error
    LoadRibbons = False
    Resume LoadRibbon_Exit
End Function
```

The first line of code in the LoadRibbons function creates a new ADO recordset that the code uses to fetch the records from the custom Ribbon definition table. Next, the code instructs Access to go to the LoadRibbon_Err line if any errors occur. The If statement checks to see whether Access has already loaded customization by verifying whether a cached copy of the RibbonUI has been set. If the main custom Ribbon has been loaded, Is Nothing returns a value of False to indicate Access already has loaded the Ribbon. If the custom Ribbon isn't loaded, the code following the Else line executes. To load the custom Ribbons, the code opens an ADO recordset on the ztblRibbons table, loops through each record in the recordset, and calls the LoadCustomUI method once for each record. The code uses the RibbonName field from the recordset to pass the name to the LoadCustomUI method, and the RibbonXML field contains the well-formed XML that defines each of our custom Ribbons. After Access loads each Ribbon, the code closes the recordset and sets it to Nothing. The last line before the End If statement returns a value of True for the LoadRibbons function, indicating success. The last part of the code has an exit procedure and our error handling code to handle the case if Access encounters an error.

As you can see, you can use the LoadCustomUI method to load a custom Ribbon from a different table, but you're not limited to storing the XML in a table. You could also store the XML directly within a code module and set it to a string variable.

## Using Ribbon Attributes

The RibbonX architecture contains many controls and attributes you can use in your applications. To help you understand some of the elements you can create with RibbonX, we'll look at the custom Ribbons we created in the Conrad Systems Contacts sample database. Open the Contacts.accdb sample database, and click OK in the opening message box. Next, open the frmSplash form in Form view either by double-clicking the form in the Navigation Pane or by right-clicking it and clicking Open on the shortcut menu. The frmSplash form is displayed for a few seconds and then opens the frmSignOn form where you can sign in to the database. Select Jeff's name from the User Name combo box, and click the Sign On button to sign in to the database. (Neither of the users has a password assigned.) Access opens the frmMain form and displays the custom main Ribbon for this database, as shown in Figure 24-3. The main Ribbon in this database, rbnCSD, has a tab called Conrad Systems Contacts and four groups—News, Navigation, Exit, and About. The News group displays three labels, one of which displays the name of the current user signed in to the database. (You'll learn how to dynamically change the Ribbon later in this chapter.) The remaining three groups display custom buttons that allow you to navigate to the various parts of the application.

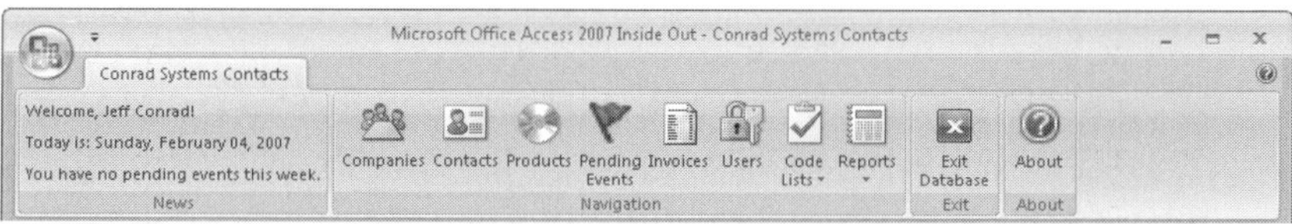


**Figure 24-3** The main Ribbon in the Conrad Systems Contacts database displays custom controls.

You can see in Figure 24-3 that all built-in Ribbon elements are hidden. As you recall from Chapter 23, if you set the startFromScratch attribute to True, Access hides all four built-in Ribbon tabs, displays limited options when you click the Microsoft Office Button, and displays a limited Quick Access Toolbar.

When you build a custom Ribbon definition, you can either define an entire custom Ribbon or define XML that modifies one of the built-in Ribbons. In your XML, you define custom controls. You assign *attributes* to your controls to define how they look and where they are positioned, and you define *callbacks* for your controls to define how they act. In Visual Basic terms, you can think of an attribute as a property of a control object and a callback as a method or event of a control object. When an attribute of a control is a callback, it is essentially the same as an event property of an Access control—you assign to a callback attribute the name of a procedure that will handle the event. You can also copy attributes of built-in controls by using an attribute name that is a Control ID, and you can reference a control in another custom Ribbon using a Qualified ID.

Let's take a look at attributes you can assign to controls first. Table 24-1 lists the RibbonX attributes you can use in your XML customization.

**Table 24-1 RibbonX Attributes**

| Attribute | Value or Type | Description |
|---|---|---|
| description | String | Defines the text shown in menu controls when itemSize="large". |
| enabled | True or False | Returns the control's enabled state. Disabled controls (enabled = False) appear dimmed in the Ribbon. |
| getDescription | Callback | Names the macro or procedure that can set the description attribute of a control. |
| getEnabled | Callback | Defines the macro or procedure that can set the enabled state of a control. |
| getImage | Callback | Names the macro or procedure that can set the image attribute of a control. |
| getLabel | Callback | Defines the macro or procedure that can set the label attribute of a control. |

| Attribute | Value or Type | Description |
|---|---|---|
| getPressed | Callback | Names the procedure that can respond to the current state of a toggle button or check box. |
| getSupertip | Callback | Names the procedure that can set the Enhanced ScreenTip of a control. |
| getTooltip | Callback | Names the procedure that can set the ToolTip of a control. |
| getVisible | Callback | Names the procedure that can set the visibility state of a control |
| id | String | Provides the Unique ID for a user-defined control. |
| idMso | Control ID | Provides the Control ID for a built-in Ribbon element. |
| idQ | Qualified ID | Provides the qualified name of a control on another Ribbon. |
| image | String | Defines the image displayed on the control. |
| imageMso | Control ID | Provides the icon of a built-in control. |
| insertAfterMso | Control ID | Positions a custom control after a built-in control. |
| insertAfterQ | Qualified ID | Positions a custom control after a control defined by another Ribbon using a qualified name. |
| insertBeforeMso | Control ID | Positions a custom control before a built-in control. |
| insertBeforeQ | Qualified ID | Positions a custom control before a control defined by another Ribbon using a qualified name. |
| label | String | Returns a control's label text. |
| onAction | Callback | Defines the macro or procedure called when a user clicks this control. |
| pressed | True or False | Returns the state of a toggle button or check box control. |
| showLabel | True or False | Determines whether a control label is visible. |
| size | Normal or Large | Sets the image size of a custom control. |
| supertip | String | Defines the text to display an enhanced ScreenTip when the user rests their mouse pointer on the control. |
| tooltip | String | Defines the text to display as a ToolTip. |
| visible | True or False | Returns the visible status of a control. |

In addition to attributes you can use in your XML customization, you can create many types of controls using RibbonX. Table 24-2 lists the types of controls you can use in a custom Ribbon definition and their associated attributes (properties) and callbacks (event properties).

**Table 24-2 RibbonX Controls**

| Control Name | Attributes | Callbacks |
|---|---|---|
| button | description, enabled, id, idMso, idQ, image, imageMso, insertAfterMso, insertAfterQ, insertBeforeMso, insertBeforeQ, keytip, label, screentip, showImage, showLabel, size, supertip, tag, and visible | getDescription, getEnabled, getImage, getKeytip, getLabel, getScreentip, getShowImage, getShowLabel, getSize, getSupertip, getVisible, and onAction |
| buttonGroup | id, idQ, insertAfterMso, insertAfterQ, insertBeforeMso, insertBeforeQ, and visible | getVisible |
| checkBox | description, enabled, id, idMso, idQ, insertAfterMso, insertAfterQ, insertBeforeMso, insertBeforeQ, keytip, label, screentip, supertip, tag, and visible | getDescription, getEnabled, getKeytip, getLabel, getPressed, getScreentip, getSupertip, getVisible, and onAction |
| comboBox | enabled, id, idMso, idQ, image, imageMso, insertAfterMso, insertAfterQ, insertBeforeMso, insertBeforeQ, label, maxLength, screentip, showItemImage, showImage, showLabel, sizeString, supertip, tag, and visible | getEnabled, getImage, getItemCount, getItemID, getItemImage, getItemLabel, getItemScreentip, getItemSupertip, getKeytip, getLabel, getScreentip, getShowImage, getShowLabel, getSize, getSupertip, getText, getVisible, and onChange |
| dialogBox-Launcher | None<br>Note that you must create a button inside a dialogBoxLauncher tag and then use the attributes of that button to specify attributes for the dialogBoxLauncher. | None<br>Note that you must create a button inside a dailogBoxLauncher tag and then use the callbacks of that button to specify events for the dialogBoxLauncher. |
| dropDown | enabled, id, idMso, idQ, image, imageMso, insertAfterMso, insertAfterQ, insertBeforeMso, insertBeforeQ, keytip, label, screentip, showImage, showItemLabel, showLabel, supertip, tag, and visible | getEnabled, getImage, getItemCount, getItemID, getItemImage, getItemLabel, getItemScreentip, getItemSupertip, getKeytip, getLabel, getScreentip, getSelectedItemID, getSelectedItemIndex, getShowImage, getShowLabel, getSize, getSupertip, getText, getVisible, and onChange |

| Control Name | Attributes | Callbacks |
|---|---|---|
| dynamicMenu | description, enabled, id, idMso, idQ, image, imageMso, insertAfterMso, insertAfterQ, insertBeforeMso, insertBeforeQ, keytip, label, screentip, showImage, showLabel, size, supertip, tag, and visible | getDescription, getEnabled, getContent, getImage, getKeytip, getLabel, getScreentip, getShowImage, getShowLabel, getSize, getSupertip, and getVisible |
| editBox | enabled, id, idMso, idQ, image, imageMso, insertAfterMso, insertAfterQ, insertBeforeMso, insertBeforeQ, keytip, label, maxLength screentip, showImage, showLabel, sizeString, supertip, tag, and visible | getEnabled, getImage, getKeytip, getLabel, getScreentip, getShowImage, getShowLabel, getSupertip, getText, getVisible, and onChange |
| gallery | columns, description, enabled, id, idMso, idQ, image, imageMso, insertAfterMso, insertAfterQ, insertBeforeMso, insertBeforeQ, itemHeight, itemWidth, keytip, label, rows, screentip, showImage, showItemImage, showItemLabel, showLabel, size, sizeString, supertip, tag, and visible | getDescription, getEnabled, getImage getItemCount, getItemHeight, getItemID, getItemImage, getItemLabel, getItemScreentip, getItemSupertip, getItemWidth, getKeytip, getLabel, getScreentip, getSelectedItemID, getSelectedItemIndex, getShowImage, getShowLabel, getSize, getSupertip, getText, getVisible, and onAction |
| group | id, idMso, idQ, image, imageMso, insertAfterMso, insertAfterQ, insertBeforeMso, insertBeforeQ, keytip, label, screentip, supertip, and visible | getImage, getKeytip, getLabel, getScreentip, getSupertip, and getVisible |
| labelControl | enabled, id, idMso, idQ, insertAfterMso, insertAfterQ, insertBeforeMso, insertBeforeQ, label, screentip, showLabel, supertip, tag, and visible | getEnabled, getLabel, getScreentip, getShowLabel, getSupertip, and getVisible |
| menu | description, enabled, id, idMso, idQ, image, imageMso, insertAfterMso, insertAfterQ, insertBeforeMso, insertBeforeQ, itemSize, keytip, label, screentip, showImage, showLabel, size, supertip, tag, and visible | getDescription, getEnabled, getImage, getKeytip, getLabel, getScreentip, getShowImage, getShowLabel, getSize, getSupertip, and getVisible |
| menuSeparator | id, idQ, insertAfterMso, insertAfterQ, and insertBeforeQ | getTitle |

| Control Name | Attributes | Callbacks |
|---|---|---|
| separator | id, idQ, insertAfterMso, insertAfterQ, insertBeforeMso, insertBeforeQ, and visible | getVisible |
| splitButton | enabled, id, idMso, idQ, insertAfterMso, insertAfterQ, insertBeforeMso, insertBeforeQ, keytip, label, screentip, showLabel, size, supertip, tag, and visible | getEnabled, getKeytip, getShowLabel, getSize, getSupertip, and getVisible |
| tab | id, idMso, idQ, insertAfterMso, insertAfterQ, insertBeforeMso, insertBeforeQ, keytip, label, tag, and visible | getKeytip, getLabel, and getVisible |
| toggleButton | description, enabled, id, idMso, idQ, image, imageMso, insertAfterMso, insertAfterQ, insertBeforeMso, insertBeforeQ, keytip, label, screentip, showImage, showLabel, size, supertip, tag, and visible | getDescription, getEnabled, getImage, getKeytip, getLabel, getPressed, getScreentip, getShowImage, getShowLabel, getSize, getSupertip, getVisible, and onAction |

Now that you know the attributes and callbacks available in the RibbonX architecture, you can begin to study how we created the main Ribbon in the Conrad Systems Contacts database. If you still have the frmMain form open, click the Exit button to close it, and then click Yes to confirm that you want to exit. Next, find the zfrmChangeRibbonXML form in the Navigation Pane, and open it in Form view. Finally, move to the third record in the table where the Ribbon Name text box displays rbnCSD. Listed next is the XML customization for this Ribbon in the Ribbon XML text box. We've added line numbers to this code listing so that you can follow along with the line-by-line explanations in Table 24-3, which follows the listing.

```
1 <customUI xmlns="http://schemas.microsoft.com/office/2006/01/customui"
2  onLoad="onRibbonLoad1">
3  <ribbon startFromScratch="true">
4    <tabs>
5       <tab id="tabCSD" label="Conrad Systems Contacts">
6          <group id="grpNews" label="News">
7             <labelControl id="lblWelcome" getLabel="onGetLabel"/>
8             <labelControl id="lblToday" getLabel="onGetLabel"/>
9             <labelControl id="lblPending" getLabel="onGetLabel"/>
10           </group>
11          <group id="grpNavigation" label="Navigation" visible="true">
12              <button id="cmdCompanies" label="Companies"
13                imageMso="MeetingsWorkspace" size="large"
14                onAction="onOpenCompanies"
15                supertip="Edit company information."/>
16              <button id="cmdContacts" label="Contacts" imageMso="NewContact"
17                size="large" onAction="onOpenContacts"
```

```
      supertip="Edit contact information."/>
    <button id="cmdProducts" label="Products"
      imageMso="FilePackageForCD" size="large"
      onAction="onOpenProducts"
      supertip="Edit product information."/>
    <button id="cmdPendingEvents" label="Pending Events"
      imageMso="SendCopyFlag" size="large"
      onAction="onOpenPendingEvents"
      supertip="View any pending events."/>
     <button id="cmdInvoices" label="Invoices"
       imageMso="CustomTableOfContentsGallery" size="large"
       onAction="onOpenInvoices"
       supertip="Edit invoice information."/>
     <button id="cmdUsers" label="Users"
       imageMso="FileDocumentEncrypt"
       size="large" onAction="onOpenUsers"
       supertip="Edit user information."/>
 <splitButton id="sbCodeList" size="large">
   <button id="cmdCodeLists" imageMso="NewTask"
     onAction="onOpenCodeLists" label="Code Lists"/>
   <menu id="sbMnuCodeLists">
      <button id="cmdContactTypes" label="Contact Types"
         imageMso="NewTask" onAction="onOpenContactTypes"/>
      <button id="cmdEventTypes" label="Event Types"
         imageMso="NewTask" onAction="onOpenEventTypes"/>
      <button id="cmdProductCategories" label="Product Categories"
         imageMso="NewTask" onAction="onOpenProductCategories"/>
      <button id="cmdPersonTitles" label="Person Titles"
         imageMso="NewTask" onAction="onOpenPersonTitles"/>
      <button id="cmdPersonSuffixes" label="Person Suffixes"
         imageMso="NewTask" onAction="onOpenPersonSuffixes"/>
    </menu>
  </splitButton>
  <splitButton id="sbReports" size="large">
    <button id="cmdReports" imageMso="CreateReport
      onAction="onOpenReports" label="Reports"/>
    <menu id="sbMnuReports" supertip="View reports ">
      <button id="cmdCompanyReports" label="Company Reports"
        imageMso="CreateReport" onAction="onOpenCompanyReports"/>
      <button id="cmdContactReports" label="Contact Reports"
        imageMso="CreateReport" onAction="onOpenContactReports"/>
      <button id="cmdProductReports" label="Product Reports"
        imageMso="CreateReport" onAction="onOpenProductReports"/>
    </menu>
  </splitButton>
</group>
<group id="grpExit" label="Exit">
  <button id="cmdExitDatabase" label="Exit Database"
    imageMso="PrintPreviewClose" size="large"
    onAction="onCloseDatabase" supertip="Exit the database."/>
</group>
<group id="grpAbout" label="About">
```

Chapter 24

```
70            <button id="cmdHelpAbout" label="About" size="large"
71              imageMso="Help" onAction="onOpenFormEdit" tag="frmAbout"
72              supertip="View the About form."/>
73          </group>
74        </tab>
75      </tabs>
76    </ribbon>
77  </customUI>
```

Table 24-3 **Explanation of XML in the rbnCSD Ribbon**

| Line(s) | Explanation |
|---|---|
| 1 | Tells Access which schema file to use when building this specific Ribbon. |
| 2 | Specifies a procedure that processes the RibbonLoad event when Access first displays the Ribbon. In this event, you can save a pointer to the Ribbon to enable your code to dynamically update it. (We'll explain how to update the Ribbon later in this chapter.) |
| 3 | Hides all built-in Ribbon elements. |
| 4 | Specifies the beginning tag to create a new set of tabs. |
| 5 | Creates a new tab with a Control ID called tabCSD and displays Conrad Systems Contacts in the tab caption. |
| 6 | Creates a new group with a Control ID called grpNews and displays News as the group label. |
| 7 | Creates a new label control, lblWelcome, and specifies the onGetLabel procedure to respond to the getLabel event to dynamically update the text displayed in the label. |
| 8 | Creates a new label control, lblToday, that also calls onGetLabel. |
| 9 | Creates a new label control, lblPending, that also calls onGetLabel. |
| 10 | Ends group tag for the grpNews group. |
| 11 | Creates a new group with a Control ID called grpNavigation and displays Navigation as the group label. |
| 12-15 | Creates a new button, cmdCompanies, with a label of Companies. Instead of specifying an image attribute, we used imageMSO to copy the image from the built-in control named FilePackageForCD. The button size is set to large, and the onAction attribute issues a callback to the onOpenCompanies procedure. Finally, we designate text to display as a supertip. |
| 16–18 | Creates a new button, cmdContacts, with a label of Contacts, an image copied from a built-in control, and a callback defined. |
| 19–22 | Creates a new button, cmdProducts, with a label of Products, an image copied from a built-in control, and a callback defined. |
| 23–26 | Creates a new button, cmdPendingEvents, with a label of Pending Events, an image copied from a built-in control, and a callback defined. |
| 27–30 | Creates a new button, cmdInvoices, with a label of Invoices, an image copied from a built-in control, and a callback defined. |

| Line(s) | Explanation |
|---|---|
| 31–34 | Creates a new button, cmdUsers, with a label of Users, an image copied from a built-in control, and a callback defined. |
| 35 | Creates a new split button, sbCodeList, with a large size. |
| 36–37 | Creates a new button, cmdCodeLists, with a label of Code Lists, an image copied from a built-in control, and a callback defined. This button becomes the top half of the split button. If you click the top half of the button, Access calls the onAction procedure for this button. |
| 38 | Creates a new menu control, sbMnuCodeLists, for the bottom half of the split button. |
| 39–40 | Creates a new button, cmdContactTypes, with a label of Contact Types, an image copied from a built-in control, and a callback defined. |
| 41–42 | Creates a new button, cmdEventTypes, with a label of Event Types, an image copied from a built-in control, and a callback defined. |
| 43–44 | Creates a new button, cmdProductCategories, with a label of Product Categories, an image copied from a built-in control, and a callback defined. |
| 45–46 | Creates a new button, cmdPersonTitles, with a label of Person Titles, an image copied from a built-in control, and a callback defined. |
| 47–48 | Creates a new button, cmdPersonSuffixes, with a label of Person Suffixes, an image copied from a built-in control, and a callback defined. |
| 49 | Ends the menu tag for menu sbMnuCodeLists. |
| 50 | Ends the split button tag for sbCodeList. |
| 51 | Creates a new split button, sbReports, with a large size. |
| 52–53 | Creates a new button, cmdReports, with a label of Reports, an image copied from a built-in control, and a callback defined. This button becomes the top half of the split button. If you click the top half of the button, Access calls the onAction procedure for this button. |
| 54 | Creates a new menu control, sbMnuReports, for the bottom half of the split button with a supertip. |
| 55–56 | Creates a new button, cmdCompanyReports, with a label of Company Reports, an image copied from a built-in control, and a callback defined. |
| 57–58 | Creates a new button, cmdContactReports, with a label of Contact Reports, an image copied from a built-in control, and a callback defined. |
| 59–60 | Creates a new button, cmdProductReports, with a label of Product Reports, an image copied from a built-in control, and a callback defined. |
| 61 | Defines the ending menu tag for menu sbMnuReports. |
| 62 | Defines the ending split button tag for sbReports. |
| 63 | Defines the ending group tag for the grpNavigation group. |
| 64 | Creates a new group with a Control ID called grpExit and displays Exit for the group label. |

| Line(s) | Explanation |
|---|---|
| 65–67 | Creates a new button, cmdExitDatabase, with a label of Exit Database, an image copied from a built-in control, and a callback defined. |
| 68 | Ends the group tag for the grpExit group. |
| 69 | Creates a new group with a Control ID called grpAbout and displays About for the group label. |
| 70–72 | Creates a new button, cmdHelpAbout, with a label of About, an image copied from a built-in control, and a callback defined. A custom tag value is assigned to this control using the tag attribute. |
| 73 | Defines the ending group tag for the grpAbout group. |
| 74 | Defines the ending tag for the tabCSD tab. |
| 75 | Defines the ending tabs tag. |
| 76 | Defines the ending ribbon tag. |
| 77 | Defines the ending customUI tag. |

## Creating VBA Callbacks

As you reviewed the XML customization for the rbnCSD Ribbon, you no doubt noticed that most of the buttons used the onAction callback. When you use onAction, you specify a saved macro object (you cannot use an embedded macro on a form or report in this case) or a Visual Basic for Applications (VBA) procedure to respond to the event—the user clicking the button. (You can think of onAction for a button in a Ribbon as the same as On Click for a command button on an Access form.) In the Conrad Systems Contacts sample database (Contacts.accdb), we defined all the procedures to respond to callback events for our custom Ribbons in the module modRibbonCallbacks. Let's take a look at some of these VBA procedures so that you can see how everything ties together. Close any objects you have open at the moment, right-click modRibbonCallbacks in the Navigation Pane (you might need to adjust your Navigation Pane display to see the modules), and click Design View on the shortcut menu to open this module in Design view.

Scroll down the procedures and functions in this module until you come to the onOpenCompanies procedure. This procedure responds to the On Click event of the very first button defined in our custom Ribbon—the cmdCompanies button. The procedure is as follows:

```
Public Sub onOpenCompanies(control As IRibbonControl)
' User wants to open Companies
    ' Make sure frmMain is there
    If IsFormLoaded("frmMain") Then
        ' Yes - execute the Companies procedure
        Form_frmMain.cmdCompanies_Click
    End If
End Sub
```

The idea is to duplicate what happens when the user clicks the Companies button in the main switchboard form. That form (frmMain) already has code to process the request, so why duplicate it? If you remember from Chapter 19, "Understanding Visual Basic Fundamentals," you can make any procedure in a form's class module a method of the form by declaring it Public. We did exactly that with the cmdCompanies_Click procedure in the frmMain form so that this onAction procedure can call it and not duplicate the code to open Companies. The procedure first verifies that the frmMain form is open because a call to the public method will fail if the form is closed. If the frmMain form is open, the procedure calls the cmdExit_Click procedure as a method of the form. If you scroll through the other procedures in the modRibbonCallbacks modules, you'll find that most of them follow this same pattern—they run an existing command button Click event procedure on the frmMain form.

## Dynamically Updating Ribbon Elements

When Access first opens a custom Ribbon, it issues callbacks for all the controls in order to set their attributes. Note that, other than for the custom Ribbon defined in the Ribbon Name property in the Current Database category of Access Options, Access opens a custom Ribbon when it is first referenced in the Ribbon Name property of a form or report that you open or that your application code opens. Executing the LoadCustomUI method of the Application object loads the Ribbon definition into memory, but it does not actually open the Ribbon.

After a Ribbon is loaded, the Ribbon is static, and Access does not update any elements. If you want to update the Ribbon, such as change the text in a label control to display the current user's name, you must explicitly tell Access to reinitialize the entire Ribbon or a control on the Ribbon. Fortunately, the RibbonX architecture allows you to save a copy of a pointer to the Ribbon in a public variable so you that can update it at a later time. In RibbonX terms, you *invalidate* a control (or the entire Ribbon) to force Access to reload the object and issue any attribute setting callbacks. At the beginning of the XML customization for rbnCSD, you'll recall seeing this line of code:

```
<customUI xmlns="http://schemas.microsoft.com/office/2006/01/customui"
  onLoad="onRibbonLoad1">
```

The first procedure in the modRibbonCallbacks module is onRibbonLoad. In the procedure called by onRibbonLoad, you can save a pointer to the Ribbon that is being opened. If you do not plan to ever update any of your Ribbon elements, you do not need to add the onRibbonLoad attribute to the <customUI> element. Access calls the onLoad callback only once during the process of opening the custom Ribbon for the first time. The following is the onRibbonLoad1 procedure that executes in the onLoad callback of the rbnCSD custom Ribbon:

```
' This is the customUI onLoad event handler for main ribbon
Public Sub onRibbonLoad1(ribbon As IRibbonUI)
    ' Cache a copy of the Ribbon so we can refresh later at any time
    Set gobjRibbon1 = ribbon
End Sub
```

The IRibbonUI object is a parameter that you can use to save a pointer to the opened custom Ribbon. The IRibbonUI class provides methods that you can use to invalidate a single control in your customization or the entire Ribbon. Table 24-4 lists these methods.

**Table 24-4 IRibbonUI Methods**

| Method | Description |
|---|---|
| Invalidate() | Access reinitializes all custom controls. |
| InvalidateControl(string controlID) | Access reinitializes one specific control. |

After you signed in to the Conrad Systems Contacts database, you'll recall seeing the user name displayed in the News group. To update the display of the three labels in the News group, we use the following onGetLabel procedure:

```
' This serves as a getLabel callback for the labels.
' We determine which Control ID was passed from the Ribbon
' and set the label appropriately.
Public Sub onGetLabel(control As IRibbonControl, ByRef label)
    Select Case control.Id
        Case "lblWelcome"
            ' Update welcome information
            label = GetWelcomeMessage()
        Case "lblToday"
            ' Update Time
            label = "Today is: " & FormatDateTime(Date, vbLongDate)
        Case "lblPending"
            ' Update Pending Events message
            label = GetPendingEventsNumber
    End Select
End Sub
```

We use a Select Case procedure to test the value of the label Control ID passed into the onGetLabel procedure. For the lblWelcome label, we update the display by calling the GetWelcomeMessage function to retrieve the name of the user currently signed in to the database. For the lblToday label, we retrieve the current date from the Windows system date and format it to display as Long Date. For the lblPending label, we retrieve the number of pending events for the current user by calling the GetPendingEventsNumber function.

You might be wondering, when does Access know to update these labels? On the frmSignOn form, you have to select a user name and provide a password. In the Click event of the cmdSignOn command button, we have this code just before the form close code:

```
    ' Refresh the data in the Ribbon
    gobjRibbon1.InvalidateControl "lblWelcome"
    gobjRibbon1.InvalidateControl "lblPending"
```

A few lines above this code, Access saves the user name to a public string variable, gstrThisUser, which is referenced in the GetWelcomeMessage function and the

GetPendingEventsNumber function. We invalidate the lblWelcome control in the cmdSignOn procedure, which causes Access to refresh this specific control and change the label's text. We also invalidate the lblPending control so that the correct number of pending events is displayed for the current user. After you've saved a pointer to the Ribbon, you can invalidate the controls or the entire Ribbon as often as you need.

## Loading Images into Custom Controls

The easiest way to display images on a custom button in your Ribbon customization is to use the imageMso attribute. As you'll recall from Chapter 23, you can use the imageMso attribute to apply an existing icon from Access 2007 or from any 2007 Microsoft Office system applications that support Ribbons. All the custom command buttons on the Ribbons in the Conrad Systems Contacts and Housing Reservations sample databases reuse icons and images from other built-in controls.

You can also load images from an attachment field stored in a table or use the LoadPicture method to load image files stored in a folder. In the Housing Reservations sample database (Housing.accdb), we store all the pictures for the employees in a table called USysRibbonImages. (Note that you can name your table whatever you like, but we chose to name our table with the USys prefix so that it appears in the Navigation Pane only if you have enabled your Navigation Options to display system objects.) Open the Housing.accdb database now (close Contacts.accdb if you have it open), and click OK in the opening message box. Next, open the frmSplash form in Form view. After a few seconds, the frmSplash form closes, and then frmSignOn opens. Select Jeff's name from the User Name combo box, and enter **password** in the Password text box. (All the passwords in this sample database are **password**.) Finally, click the Sign On button to sign in to the database under Jeff's name. Access opens the frmMain form and displays a custom Ribbon with Jeff's picture in the News group, as shown in Figure 24-4.

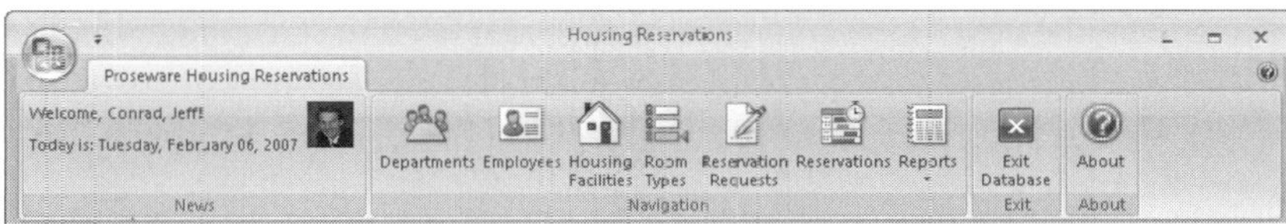


**Figure 24-4** You can load images from attachment fields onto custom controls in your Ribbons.

Access is placing the image on a button in the News group, cmdPicture, that has no onAction attribute assigned to it. (We don't want anything to happen if you click the button, but we're using the button to display our custom image.) If you were to sign on as a different user, Access would update the picture because we invalidated the control in the Click event of the cmdSignOn button on the frmSignOn form. To set the picture, we use the getImage callback attribute of the custom cmdPicture control in our main Ribbon. The getImage callback runs the GetButtonImage function in the modRibbonCallbacks module listed here:

```
Public Function GetButtonImage(control As IRibbonControl, ByRef image)
    ' This function displays a picture of the logged on user
    ' The command button in the Welcome group will update from
```

```
    ' a picture stored in an Attachment field in the table USysRibbonImages.
    ' We have to load a hidden form in order to grab the picture
    Dim frmRibbonImages As Form
    Static rsForm As DAO.Recordset2
    Dim rsAttachments As DAO.Recordset2
    If frmRibbonImages Is Nothing Then
        ' Form is not opened, so open it
        DoCmd.OpenForm "zfrmUSysRibbonImages", WindowMode:=acHidden
        Set frmRibbonImages = Forms("zfrmUSysRibbonImages")
        Set rsForm = frmRibbonImages.Recordset
    End If
    ' Find the picture for the logged on user
    rsForm.FindFirst "UserID='" & gstrThisEmployee & "'"
    If rsForm.NoMatch Then
        ' User not found so set the image to nothing
        Set image = Nothing
    Else
        ' Found a match, so update the display on the Ribbon
        Set image = frmRibbonImages.RibbonImages.PictureDisp
    End If
End Function
```

To load an image from an attachment field onto a custom Ribbon, you have to assign an object that is in the correct format. The PictureDisp property of an Attachment control bound to a picture in an attachment field returns the correct object type. Using an open form bound to the table that contains the attachment field is a simple way to get what we need. (You could also write a COM object in C#, but that's far beyond the scope of this book!) We created a special form, zfrmUSysRibbonImages, especially for this purpose. The code opens this form in hidden mode so it never becomes visible on screen. Next, the code searches the records in the table for a match to the public variable that contains the name of the user signed in to the database–gstrThisEmployee. If no match is found, Access sets the image to nothing. If a match is found, Access updates the image on the custom button with the picture stored in the attachment field.

## Hiding Options on the Microsoft Office Button

You've previously learned that if you set the startFromScratch attribute of your customization to True, Access hides some of the options available when your Ribbon is open and you click the Microsoft Office Button. You can selectively hide buttons and commands by using the <officemenu> tags and setting the visible attribute for the built-in controls to false. For example, if you want to hide the New, Open Database, and Save As options, use the following XML example in a custom Ribbon that you load:

```
<customUI xmlns="http://schemas.microsoft.com/office/2006/01/customui">
    <ribbon startFromScratch="true">
      <officeMenu>
          <button idMso="FileNewDatabase" visible="false"/>
          <button idMso="FileOpenDatabase" visible="false"/>
          <splitButton idMso="FileSaveAsMenuAccess" visible="false" />
      </officeMenu>
    </ribbon>
 </customUI>
```

Chapter 24

If you click the Microsoft Office Button using this customization, you'll see a very limited set of options available for your users, as shown in Figure 24-5.

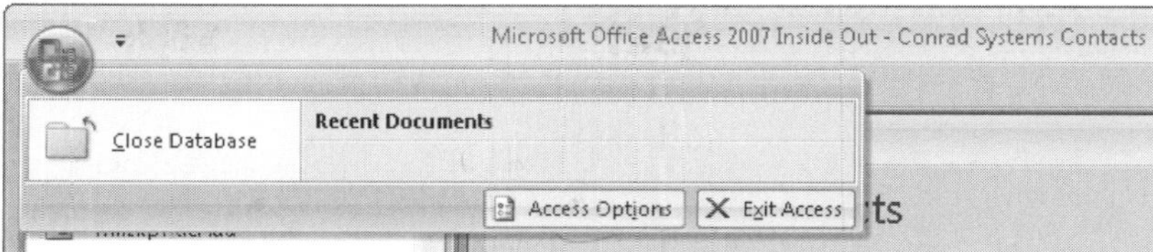


**Figure 24-5** You now have limited options available when you click the Microsoft Office Button.

## Setting Focus to a Tab

The RibbonX architecture does not provide a method to place the focus on a specific tab, which is unfortunate. In the Conrad Systems Contacts and Housing Reservations sample databases, we wanted to display our main Ribbon at all times. For the data entry forms, we wanted to still see the main tab when the custom Ribbon for forms is open but put the focus on the Navigation tab as a visual cue for the users of the application. Instead, the Navigation tab opens to the right of the main tab but does not receive focus. Fortunately, RibbonX does provide a TabSetFormReportExtensibility element that you can use for these cases.

When you use the TabSetFormReportExtensibility element, Access places the content into the current tabSet, moves the focus to this tab, and places a caption above the tab. The tab caption matches the Caption property of the current form or report if this property is set. If no caption is set, Access uses the current name of the object. In the rbnForms custom Ribbon in both Conrad Systems Contacts and Housing Reservations, we duplicated all the controls in the main Ribbon–rbnCSD or rbnProseware–and then added the XML necessary to display the tab we wanted with groups and controls for form navigation. The specific customization for these follows this format:

```
  <contextualTabs>
    <tabSet idMso="TabSetFormReportExtensibility">
        <tab id="tabRecNav" label="Record Navigation">
....(remaining XML customization here)....
        </tab>
    </tabSet>
</contextualTabs>
```

In essence we created our own contextual tab that appears next to the main Ribbon tab but receives the focus when the data entry forms open, as shown in Figure 24-6.

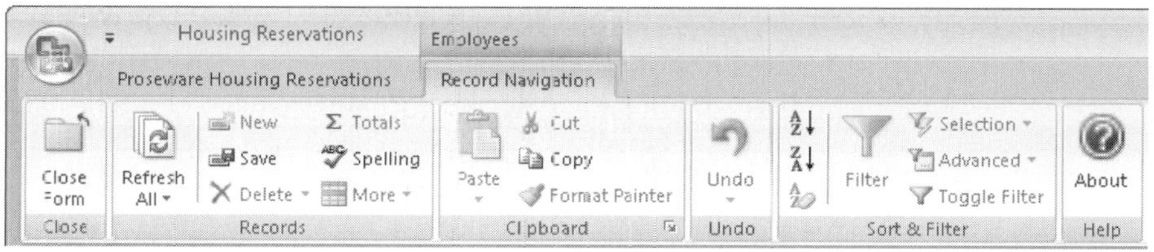


**Figure 24-6** Use the TabSetFormReportExtensibility element to set focus to a specific tab.

Quite frankly, we could write an entire book about Ribbon customization, but you should have enough information at this point to get started building your own custom Ribbons. For more information, visit the Microsoft Developer Network Web site at *http://msdn.microsoft.com/*. In the remainder of this chapter, you'll learn additional techniques that you can use to customize your applications for your users.

# Fine-Tuning with Performance Analyzer

Even the most experienced database designers (including us) don't always take advantage of all the techniques available to improve performance in an Access application. Fortunately, Access provides Performance Analyzer to help you do a final analysis after you build most of your application. In this section, we'll let Performance Analyzer analyze the Housing Reservations sample database (Housing.accdb). To start Performance Analyzer, click the Analyze Performance button in the Analyze group on the Database Tools tab. Access opens the dialog box shown in Figure 24-7.

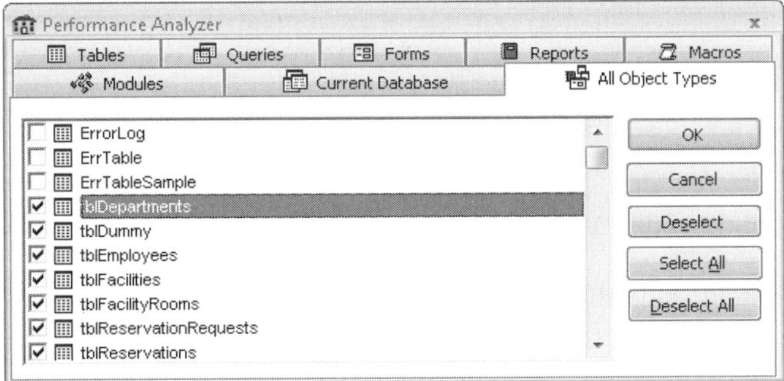


**Figure 24-7** You can select which objects to analyze from the eight tabs of Performance Analyzer.

You can select a specific category of objects to analyze—Current Database (which lets you analyze table relationships), Tables, Queries, Forms, Reports, Macros, Modules, or All Object Types. Within a category, you can select the check box next to an object name to select it for analysis. You can click the Select All button to ask Performance Analyzer to examine all objects or click Deselect All if you made a mistake and want to start again. In this example, we chose the All Object Types tab, clicked Select All, and then clicked sample tables, queries, forms, and reports that aren't part of the actual application (all the extra examples we built for the book) to deselect them. (In the Housing Reservations database, select all tables that have names beginning with "tbl" or "tlkp," and select all queries, forms, and reports except those that have names beginning with the letter *z* or that have "Example," "Xmpl," or "USys" as part of the object name.)

Click OK to run Performance Analyzer. Performance Analyzer opens a dialog box that shows you its progress as it analyzes the objects you selected. When it is finished, Performance Analyzer displays the results of its analysis, similar to those shown in Figure 24-8.

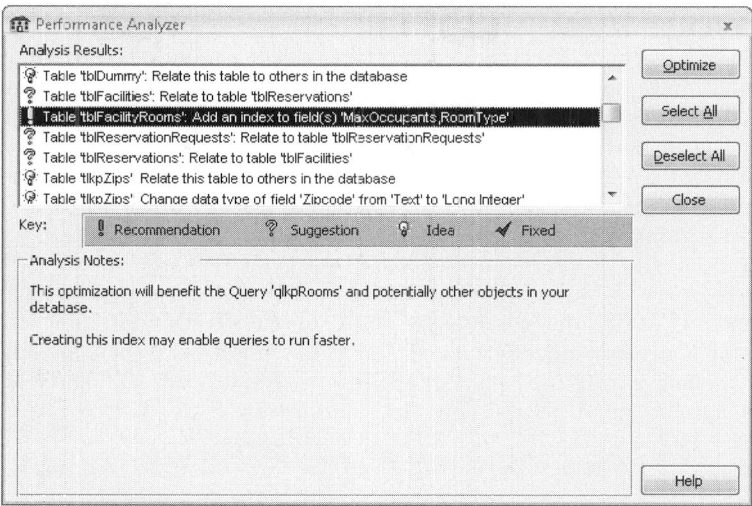


**Figure 24-8** Performance Analyzer displays recommendations to improve your application.

You can scan the list of recommendations, suggestions, and ideas displayed by Performance Analyzer. (Notice the key below the Analysis Results list.) Click any *recommendation* or *suggestion* that you like, and then click the Optimize button to have Performance Analyzer implement the change on the spot. After Performance Analyzer implements a change, you'll see a check mark next to the item. If you like, you can click the Select All button to highlight all the recommendations and suggestions and then click Optimize to implement the fixes.

Personally, we'd rather choose the ones we want one at a time. For example, the idea to change the PostalCode field from text to long integer won't work if you're storing Canadian or European postal codes in your database. Also, we know that tblReservations is already related to tblFacilities through the tblFacilityRooms table, so adding a direct relationship between tblFacilties and tblReservations would be redundant.

Although you can implement recommendations and suggestions directly from Performance Analyzer, you can't do so with *ideas*. Most ideas are changes that could potentially cause a lot of additional work. For example, changing a data type of a field in a table might improve performance slightly, but it might also cause problems in dozens of queries, forms, and reports that you've already built using that table field. Other ideas are fixes that Performance Analyzer isn't certain will help; they depend on how you designed your application. We recommend that you look at the recommendations and suggestions and implement the ones that make the most sense for your application.

# Disabling Layout View

You might have noticed as you built new forms and reports in your Access 2007 databases that Access sets the new Allow Layout View property to Yes by default. This is a handy feature while you're building forms and reports because it allows you to align, position, and resize controls while you view live data. When you're ready to put your application in production, however, you need to reset this new property to No for all your forms and reports so that the users see your forms and reports as you intended. You could open every form and report in Design view, change the property, and save the form or report. But why do it the hard way? In the Access Options dialog box, you can select an option that disables the ability to open forms and reports in Layout view. Click the Microsoft Office Button, click Access Options, and then click the Current Database category. In the Application Options section, clear the Enable Layout View For This Database check box, as shown in Figure 24-9.

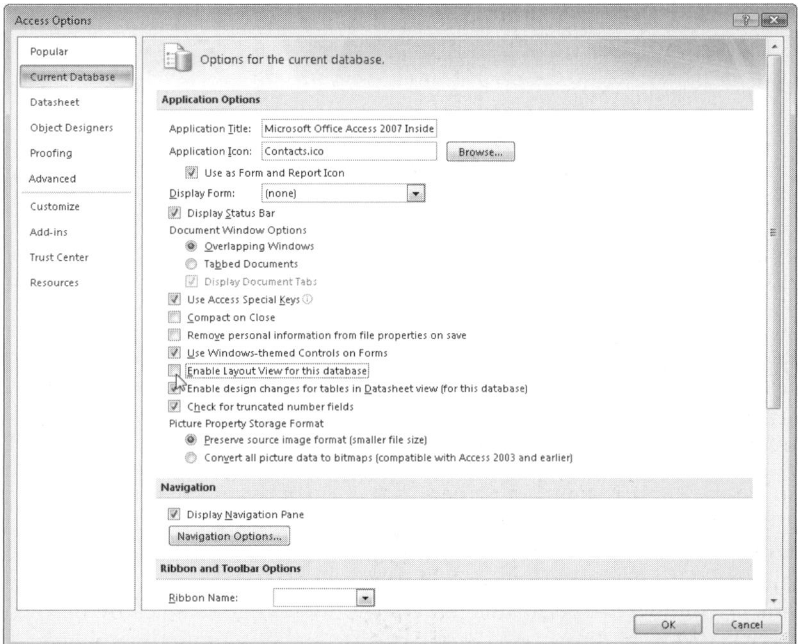


**Figure 24-9** You can disable the ability to view objects in Layout view in the Access Options dialog box.

When you clear this option, Access does not show Layout View as an option in the Views group on the Ribbon or on any shortcut menus.

# Defining Switchboard Forms

Usually the last forms that you build are the switchboard forms that give the user direct access to the major tasks in your application.

## Designing a Switchboard Form from Scratch

Your main switchboard form should be a simple form with a logo, a title, and perhaps as many as eight command buttons. The command buttons can be used to open the forms that you defined in the application. Figure 24-10 shows the main switchboard form for the Conrad Systems Contacts database in Design view.

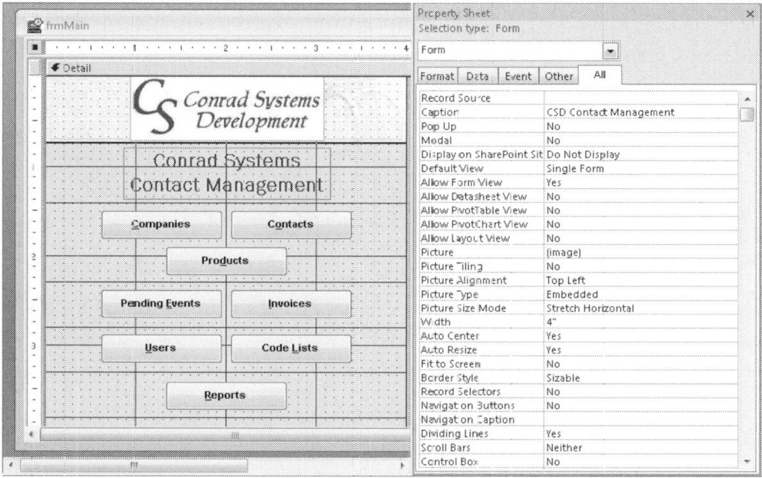


**Figure 24-10** The main switchboard form for the Conrad Systems Contacts database has command buttons to guide users through the application.

One feature worth mentioning here is the use of the ampersand (&) character when setting each control's Caption property. You can use the ampersand character to define a shortcut key for the control. In the Caption property for the Companies command button, for example, the ampersand precedes the letter *C*. The letter *C* becomes the shortcut key, which means that you can choose the Companies button by pressing Alt+C as well as by more traditional methods such as clicking the button with the mouse or tabbing to the button and pressing the Spacebar or the Enter key. You must be careful, however, not to duplicate another shortcut key letter. For example, the shortcut key for the Contacts command button in this example is *O*, to avoid conflict with the C access key for the Companies command button.

INSIDE OUT **Let Access Show You Any Keyboard Shortcut Duplicates**

If you select the Check For Keyboard Shortcut Errors check box in the Error Checking section in the Object Designers category in the Access Options dialog box, Access displays a smart tag next to any command button or label that has a duplicate shortcut key defined.

You can use a shortcut key to make it easier to select any control that has a caption. For command buttons, the caption is part of the control itself. For most other controls, the caption is in the attached label. For example, you can define shortcut keys to select option buttons or toggle buttons in an option group by including an ampersand in the caption for each button in the group.

For each command button, you need a simple event procedure to handle the Click event and to open the appropriate form. Here is the procedure for the Products button:

```
Private Sub cmdProducts_Click()
  ' Open the Product edit/create form
  DoCmd.OpenForm "frmProducts"
End Sub
```

If you have a custom Ribbon, you should set the Ribbon Name property of your switchboard form to point to the name of the custom Ribbon. If you also have a custom Ribbon used for data entry forms, you should set the form's Ribbon Name property to it. In the Conrad Systems Contacts and Housing Reservations applications, a single custom Ribbon is used for all data entry forms, and a different Ribbon is used for navigation forms—such as frmCodeLists, frmProductReports, and frmSignOn.

## Using the Switchboard Manager to Design Switchboard Forms

If your application is reasonably complex, building all the individual switchboard forms you need to provide the user with navigation through your application could take a while. Access has a Switchboard Manager utility that helps you get a jump on building your switchboard forms. This utility uses a creative technique to handle all switchboard forms by dynamically modifying a single form. It uses a driver table named Switchboard Items to allow you to define any number of switchboard forms with up to eight command buttons each. Information in the table tells the code behind the switchboard form how to modify the buttons displayed and what to do when the user clicks each of the buttons.

**Note**

The Conrad Systems Contacts application (Contacts.accdb) has a SwitchboardSample form that we created with the Switchboard Manager. Because we renamed the objects and fixed the embedded macros behind the SwitchboardSample form to use the SwitchboardDriver table, you can't use the Switchboard Manager to modify this form. You can open the SwitchboardSample form to see how a form built by the Switchboard Manager works, and you can follow along with the steps in this chapter to build your own switchboard.

To start the Switchboard Manager, click the Switchboard Manager button in the Database Tools group on the Database Tools tab. The utility checks to see whether you already have a switchboard form and a Switchboard Items table in your database. If you don't have these, the Switchboard Manager displays the message box shown in Figure 24-11, which asks you whether you want to build them.

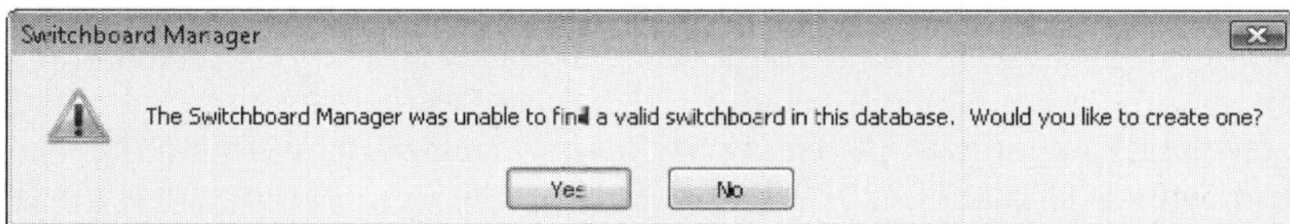


**Figure 24-11** This message box appears if the Switchboard Manager does not find a valid switchboard form and Switchboard Items table in your database.

Click Yes to allow the Switchboard Manager to continue. After it builds a skeleton switchboard form and a Switchboard Items table (or after it establishes that you already have these objects in your database), it displays the main Switchboard Manager window. Unless your application is very simple, you won't be able to provide all the navigation your users need on one switchboard with eight options—especially considering that you should use one of the options to provide a way for the user to exit the application. So, you should plan additional switchboards that the user can navigate to from the main switchboard. One way to lay out the additional switchboards is to plan one switchboard for each major subject or group of similar features in your database.

You should first define all the switchboards that you need (called *pages* in the Switchboard Manager) because a page must be defined before you can create a button to navigate to or from the page. To build an additional switchboard page, click the New button, and enter a name for the new switchboard in the Create New dialog box, as shown in Figure 24-12. Click OK to create the page.

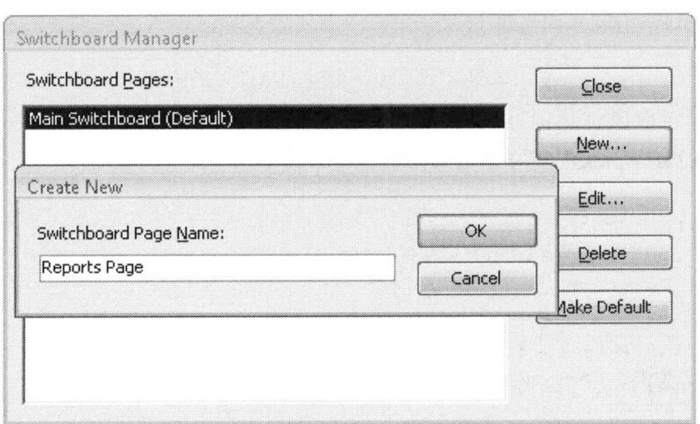


**Figure 24-12** To add a switchboard page to the main switchboard form, click the New button, and give your page a name.

After you create the additional switchboard pages that you need, you can select one in the main Switchboard Manager window and click the Edit button to begin defining actions on the page. You'll see a window similar to the one shown in the background in Figure 24-13. Use this window to create a new action, edit an existing action, or change the order of actions. Figure 24-13 shows a new action being created. When you create a new action, the Switchboard Manager places a button on the switchboard page to execute that action. In the Text box, enter the caption that you want displayed next to the button. (Note that if you enter an ampersand (&) before one of the letters in the caption to make that letter the access key for the button, the switchboard form does not recognize it as a keyboard shortcut.) Choose the action you want from the Command drop-down list. The Switchboard Manager can create actions such as moving to another switchboard page, opening a form in add or edit mode, opening a report, switching to Design view, exiting the application, or running a macro or a Visual Basic procedure. If you choose an action such as opening a form or report, the Edit Switchboard Item dialog box shows you a list of appropriate objects in the second drop-down list.

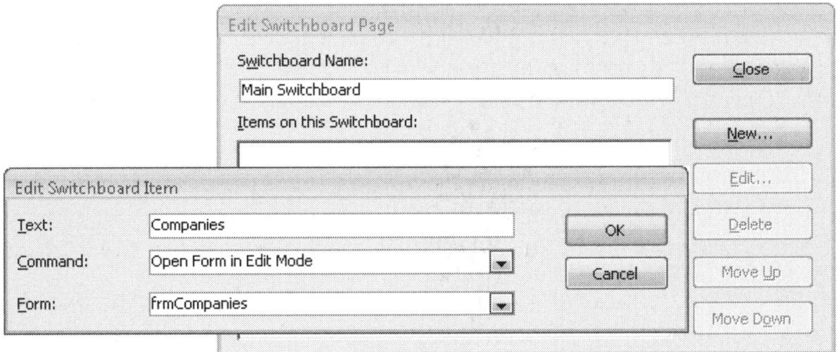


**Figure 24-13** Click the New button to create a new action on a switchboard page.

On the main switchboard page, you should create actions to open other pages and an action to exit the application. On each subsequent page, you should always provide at least one action to move back through the switchboard-page tree or to go back to the main switchboard page, as shown in Figure 24-14.

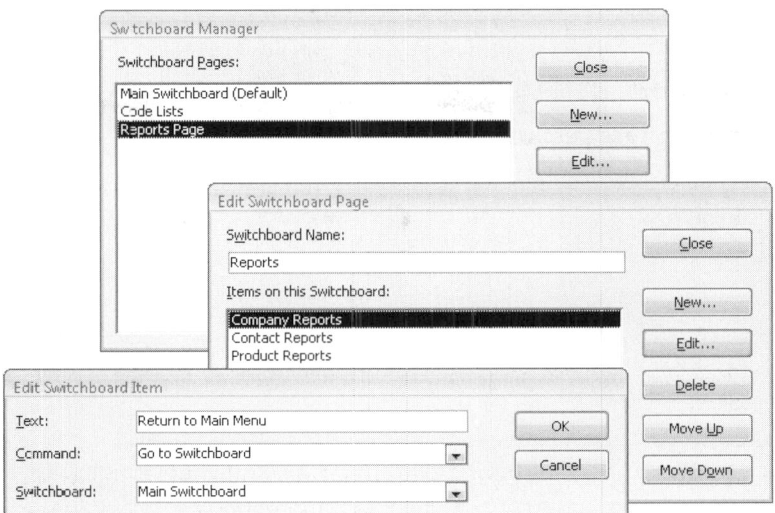


**Figure 24-14** Make sure you create an action to return to the main switchboard form from another switchboard page.

On the SwitchboardSample form, we created buttons to open Companies, Contacts, Products, Pending Events, and Invoices. We also created buttons to open pages to show code lists that can be edited and the available reports. On the Code Lists page, we added entries to open Contact Types, Event Types, Product Categories, Person Titles, Person Suffixes, and Users. We also added a button to return to the main menu. On the Reports page, we added entries to open Company Reports, Contact Reports, and Product Reports as well as a button to return to the main menu.

After you finish, the Switchboard Manager saves the main switchboard form with the name *Switchboard*. You can rename this form if you want. If you want to rename the Switchboard Items table, be sure to edit the embedded macro in the On Open property of the Switchboard form so that it refers to the new name. You'll also need to change the record source of the form and edit the embedded macro in the On Click property of both the Option1 command button and the OptionLabel1 text box control.

Figure 24-15 shows an example Switchboard form for the Conrad Systems Contacts database (the SwitchboardSample form). We edited the form design to add the Conrad Systems logo. You can further customize the look of this form as long as you don't remove an option button or attached label or change the names of these controls.

We personally prefer to design our own switchboard forms so that we can add specialized code behind some of the command buttons. But you can see that the Switchboard Manager is a handy way to quickly design a complex set of switchboard pages without a lot of work.

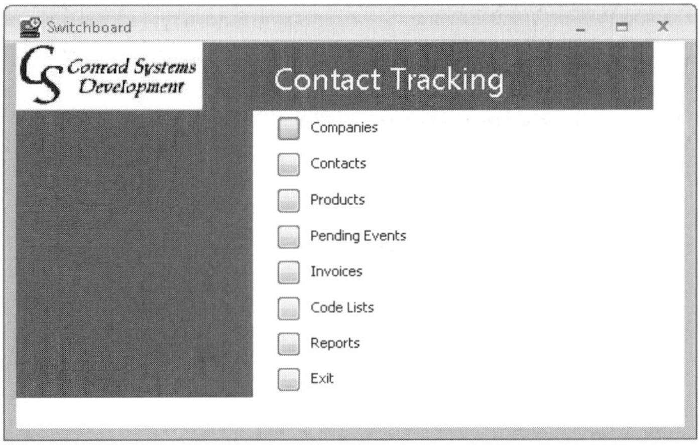

**Figure 24-15** The main switchboard form of our example shows options to other areas of the application.

# Controlling How Your Application Starts and Runs

Especially if you're distributing your application for others to use, you probably want your application to automatically start when the user opens your database. As noted in the previous section, you should design switchboard forms to help the user navigate to the various parts of your application. You should also set properties and write code to ensure that your user can cleanly exit your application.

## Setting Startup Properties for Your Database

At this point, you know how to build all the pieces you need to fully implement your database application. But what if you want your application to start automatically when you open your database? One way is to create a macro named *AutoExec*–Access always runs this macro if it exists when you open the database (unless you hold down the Shift key when you open the database). In the Conrad Systems Contacts database, we use an AutoExec macro to first determine whether the database is being run in a trusted environment. You can also specify an opening form in the startup properties for the database. You can set these properties by clicking the Microsoft Office Button, clicking Access Options, and then clicking the Current Database category, as shown in Figure 24-16.

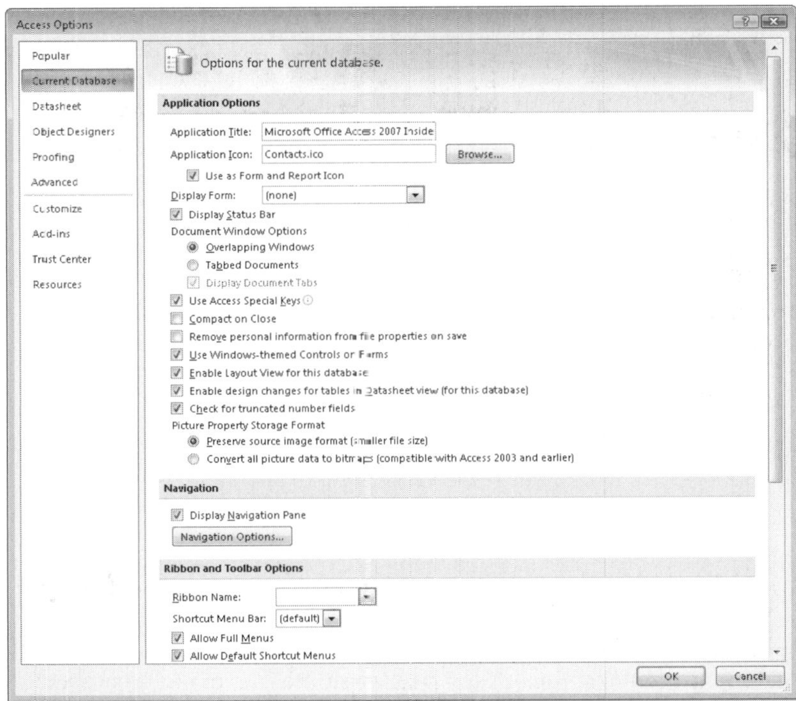


**Figure 24-16** You can set startup properties for your database in the Current Database category of the Access Options dialog box.

You can specify which form opens your database by selecting a form from the Display Form list. You can also specify a custom title for the application, an icon for the application, and a custom Ribbon to override the built-in Ribbon. If you always open the database with its folder set to the current directory, you can simply enter the icon file name, as shown in Figure 24-16. If you're not sure which folder will be current when the application opens, you should enter a fully qualified file name location. Note that you can also ask Access to display the icon you specify as the form and report icon instead of the standard Access icons.

If you clear the Display Navigation Pane check box, Access hides the Navigation Pane when your application starts. (As you'll learn later, you can also write code that executes in your startup form to ensure that the Navigation Pane is hidden.) You can also hide the status bar if you want by clearing the Display Status Bar check box. We like to use the SysCmd function to display information on the status bar, so we usually leave the Display Status Bar check box selected. We recommend you always clear the Enable Design Changes For Tables In Datasheet View (For This Database) check box. If you leave this check box selected, your users can make design changes to your tables displayed in Datasheet view, as well as any forms that open in Datasheet view.

Finally, you can disable special keys—such as F11 to reveal the Navigation Pane, Ctrl+G to open the Debug window, or Ctrl+Break to halt code execution—by clearing the Use Access Special Keys check box. As you can see, you have many powerful options for customizing how your application starts and how it operates.

## Starting and Stopping Your Application

Although you can set startup properties asking Access to hide the Navigation Pane, you might want to include code in the Load event of your startup form to make sure it is hidden. All the sample databases provided with this book open the frmCopyright form as the startup form. Note that the AutoExec macro in these sample databases first checks to see whether the database is running in a trusted location. If the database is in a trusted location, the macro opens frmCopyright; otherwise, the macro opens the fdlgNotTrusted form followed by the frmCopyrightNotTrusted form. The copyright forms display information about the database. In the trusted version, code behind the form checks connections to linked tables. In both the Conrad Systems Contacts and Housing Reservations sample applications, the code behind the frmCopyright form tells you to open the frmSplash form to actually start the application.

When the frmSplash form opens, code in the Load event uses the following procedure to make sure the Navigation Pane is hidden:

```
' Select the Navigation Pane
DoCmd.SelectObject acForm, "frmSplash", True
' .. and hide it
RunCommand acCmdWindowHide
```

The procedure hides the Navigation Pane by selecting a known object in the Navigation Pane to give the Navigation Pane the focus and then executing the WindowHide command. The splash form waits for a timer to expire (the Timer event procedure) and then opens a form to sign on to the application. When you sign on successfully, the frmMain form finally opens.

The frmMain form in the Conrad Systems Contacts application has no Close button and no Control menu button. The database also has an AutoKeys macro defined that intercepts any attempt to close a window using the Ctrl+F4 keys. (You'll learn about creating an AutoKeys macro in the next section.) So, you must click the Exit button on the frmMain form to close the application. On the other hand, the frmMain form in the Housing Reservations application does allow you to press Ctrl+F4 or click the Close button to close the form and exit the application.

You should always write code to clean up any open forms, reset variables, and close any open recordsets when the user asks to exit your application. Because the user can't close the frmMain form in Conrad Systems Contacts application except by clicking the Exit button, you'll find such clean-up code in the command button's Click event. In the frmMain form in the Housing Reservations database, the clean-up code is in the form's Close event procedure. The code in both forms is similar, so here's the exit code in the Conrad Systems Contacts sample application.

```
Private Sub cmdExit_Click()
Dim intErr As Integer, frm As Form, intI As Integer
Dim strData As String, strDir As String
Dim lngOpen As Long, datBackup As Date
Dim strLowBkp As String, strBkp As String, intBkp As Integer
Dim db As DAO.Database, rst As DAO.Recordset
  If vbNo = MsgBox("Are you sure you want to exit?", _
    vbYesNo + vbQuestion + vbDefaultButton2, _
      gstrAppTitle) Then
      Exit Sub
  End If
  ' Trap any errors
  On Error Resume Next
  ' Make sure all forms are closed
  For intI = (Forms.Count - 1) To 0 Step -1
    Set frm = Forms(intI)
    ' Don't close myself!
    If frm.Name <> "frmMain" Then
      ' Use the form's "Cancel" routine
      frm.cmdCancel_Click
      DoEvents
    End If
    ' Note any error that occurred
    If Err <> 0 Then intErr = -1
  Next intI
  ' Log any error beyond here
  On Error GoTo frmMain_Error
  ' Skip backup check if there were errors
  If intErr = 0 Then
    Set db = CurrentDb
    ' Open ztblVersion to see if we need to do a backup
    Set rst = db.OpenRecordset("ztblVersion", dbOpenDynaset)
    rst.MoveFirst
    lngOpen = rst!OpenCount
    datBackup = rst!LastBackup
    rst.Close
    Set rst = Nothing
    ' If the user has opened 10 times
    ' or last backup was more than 2 weeks ago...
    If (lngOpen Mod 10 = 0) Or ((Date - datBackup) > 14) Then
      ' Ask if they want to backup...
      If vbYes = MsgBox("CSD highly recommends backing up " & _
        "your data to avoid " & _
        "any accidental data loss.  Would you like to backup now?", _
        vbYesNo + vbQuestion, gstrAppTitle) Then
        ' Get the name of the data file
        strData = Mid(db.TableDefs("ztblVersion").Connect, 11)
        ' Get the name of its folder
        strDir = Left(strData, InStrRev(strData, "\"))
        ' See if the "BackupData" folder exists
        If Len(Dir(strDir & "BackupData", vbDirectory)) = 0 Then
          ' Nope, build it!
```

Chapter 24

```
          MkDir strDir & "BackupData"
        End If
        ' Now find any existing backups - keep only three
        strBkp = Dir(strDir & "BackupData\CSDBkp*.accdb")
        Do While Len(strBkp) > 0
          intBkp = intBkp + 1
          If (strBkp < strLowBkp) Or (Len(strLowBkp) = 0) Then
            ' Save the name of the oldest backup found
            strLowBkp = strBkp
          End If
          ' Get the next file
          strBkp = Dir
        Loop
        ' If more than two backup files
        If intBkp > 2 Then
          ' Delete the oldest one
          Kill strDir & "BackupData\" & strLowBkp
        End If
        ' Now, setup new backup name based on today's date
        strBkp = strDir & "BackupData\CSDBkp" & _
          Format(Date, "yymmdd") & ".accdb"
        ' Make sure the target file doesn't exist
        If Len(Dir(strBkp)) > 0 Then Kill strBkp
        ' Create the backup file using Compact
        DBEngine.CompactDatabase strData, strBkp
        ' Now update the backup date
        db.Execute "UPDATE ztblVersion SET LastBackup = #" & _
          Date & "#", dbFailOnError
        MsgBox "Backup created successfully!", vbInformation, gstrAppTitle
      End If
      ' See if error log has 20 or more entries
      If db.TableDefs("ErrorLog").RecordCount > 20 Then
        ' Don't ask if they've said not to...
        If Not (DLookup("DontSendError", "tblUsers", _
          "UserName = '" & gstrThisUser & "'")) Then
          DoCmd.OpenForm "fdlgErrorSend", WindowMode:=acDialog
        Else
          db.Execute "DELETE * FROM ErrorLog", dbFailOnError
        End If
      End If
    End If
    Set db = Nothing
  End If
  ' Restore original keyboard behavior
  ' Disabled in this sample
'  Application.SetOption "Behavior Entering Field", gintEnterField
'  Application.SetOption "Move After Enter", gintMoveEnter
'    Application.SetOption "Arrow Key Behavior", gintArrowKey
  ' We're outta here!
frmMain_Exit:
  On Error GoTo 0
  DoCmd.Close acForm, Me.Name
```

```
    ' In a production application, would quit here
    DoCmd.SelectObject acForm, "frmMain", True
    Exit Sub
frmMain_Error:
    ErrorLog "frmMain", Err, Error
    Resume frmMain_Exit
End Sub
```

After confirming that the user really wants to exit, the code looks at every open form. All forms have a public cmdCancel_Click event procedure that this code can call to ask the form to clear any pending edits and close itself. The DoEvents statement gives that code a chance to complete before going on to the next form. Notice that the code skips the form named frmMain (the form where this code is running).

If there were no errors closing all the forms, then the code opens a table that contains a count of how many times this application has run and the date of the last backup. Every tenth time the application has run or every two weeks since the last backup, the code offers to create a backup of the application data. If the user confirms creating a backup, the code creates a Backup subfolder if it does not exist, deletes the oldest backup if there are three or more in the folder, and then backs up the data using the Compact-Database method of the DBEngine.

Next, the code checks to see whether more than 20 errors have been logged by code running in the application. If so, it opens a dialog box that gives the user the option to e-mail the error log, print out the error log, skip printing the error log this time, or turn off the option to print the log. Because the error log option form opens in Dialog mode, this code waits until that form closes. Finally, the code closes this form and selects an object in the Navigation Pane to reveal that pane. If this weren't a demonstration application, the code would use the Quit method of the Application object to close and exit Access.

This might seem like a lot of extra work, but taking care of details like this really gives your application a professional polish.

## Creating an AutoKeys Macro

As noted earlier, the Conrad Systems Contacts sample application (Contacts.accdb) has an AutoKeys macro defined to intercept pressing Ctrl+F4. You can normally press this key combination to close any window that has the focus, but the application is designed so that you must close the frmMain form using the Exit button, not Ctrl+F4. You can create an AutoKeys macro to define most keystrokes that you want to intercept and handle in some other way. You can define something as simple as a StopMacro action to effectively disable the keystrokes, create a series of macro actions that respond to the keystrokes, or use the RunCode action to call complex Visual Basic code. Figure 24-17 shows you the AutoKeys macro in the Conrad Systems Contacts database open in Design view.

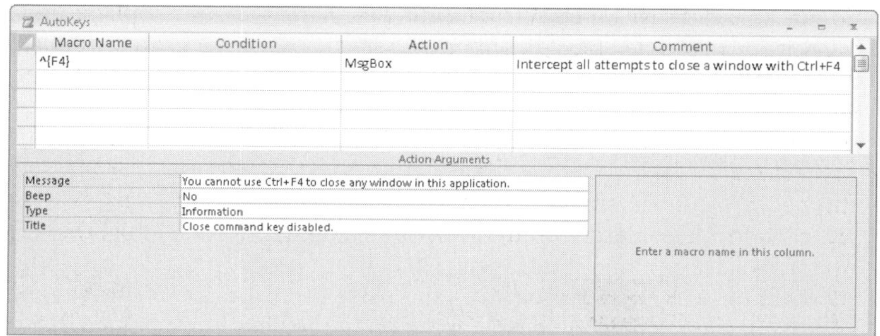


**Figure 24-17** The design of this AutoKeys macro intercepts the Ctrl+F4 key combination.

The critical part of a macro defined in an AutoKeys macro group is the macro name. When the name is a special combination of characters that match a key name, the macro executes whenever you press those keys. Table 24-5 shows you how to construct macro names in an AutoKeys macro group to respond to specific keys.

**Table 24-5 AutoKeys Macro Key Codes**

| AutoKeys Macro Name | Key Intercepted |
|---|---|
| ^letter or ^number | Ctrl+[the named letter or number key] |
| {Fn} | The named function key (F1–F12) |
| ^{Fn} | Ctrl+[the named function key] |
| +{Fn} | Shift+[the named function key] |
| {Insert} | Insert |
| ^{Insert} | Ctrl+Insert |
| +{Insert} | Shift+Insert |
| {Delete} or {Del} | Delete |
| ^{Delete} or ^{Del} | Ctrl+Delete |
| +{Delete} or +{Del} | Shift+Delete |

Keep in mind that you can also intercept any keystroke on a form in the KeyDown and KeyPress events when you want to trap a particular key on only one form or control.

# Performing a Final Visual Basic Compile

The very last task you should perform before placing your application in production is to compile and save all your Visual Basic procedures. When you do this, Access stores a compiled version of the code in your database. Access uses the compiled code when it needs to execute a procedure you have written. If you don't do this, Access has to load and interpret your procedures the first time you reference them—each and every time you start your application. For example, if you have several procedures in a form module, the form will open more slowly the first time because Access has to also load and compile the code.

To compile and save all the Visual Basic procedures in your application, open any module—either a module object or a module associated with a form or report. Choose Compile *project-name* from the Debug menu, as shown in Figure 24-18. If your code compiles successfully, be sure to save the result by choosing File, Save or by clicking the Save button on the toolbar. (If you have errors in any of your code, the compiler halts on the first error it finds, displays the line of code, and displays an error message dialog box.) After successfully compiling and saving your Visual Basic project, close your database and compact it, as described in Chapter 5, "Modifying Your Table Design."

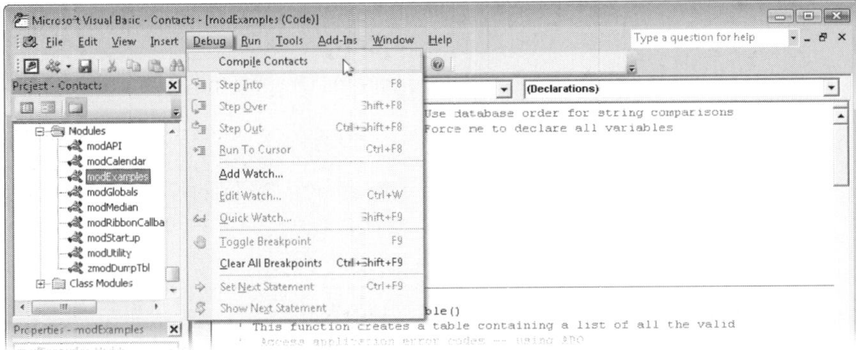


**Figure 24-18** Choose the Debug, Compile *project-name* command to compile all the Visual Basic procedures in your database.

As you've seen in this book, you can quickly learn to build complex applications. You can use the relational database management system in Access 2007 to store and manage your data locally or on a network, and you can access information in other popular database formats or in any server-hosted or mainframe-hosted database that supports the Open Database Connectivity (ODBC) standard. You can get started with macros to become familiar with event-oriented programming and to prototype your application. With a little practice, you'll soon find yourself writing Visual Basic event procedures like a pro. In the final chapter, you'll learn how to set up your application so that you can distribute it to others.

CHAPTER 25

# Distributing Your Application



Although you can certainly use Microsoft Office Access 2007 to create database applications only for your personal use, most serious users of Office Access 2007 eventually end up building applications to be used by others. If you have created a stand-alone desktop database application and your users all have the same version of Access installed on their computers, you can simply give them a copy of your database file to run. However, most database applications become really useful when multiple users share the data.

In Chapter 6, "Importing and Linking Data," you learned about linking tables from another database and using the Linked Table Manager. In Part 7, "Designing an Access Project," on the companion CD, you'll learn about some of the advantages of using a client/server architecture to allow multiple users running the same application to share data. Both these topics help you understand how to design and secure a multi-user application. However, they don't provide you with the techniques you can employ in your application design to ensure that your application installs and runs smoothly and to ensure that your users can't tamper with your code. In this chapter, you'll learn

- How to split a desktop database to use shared data on a server and linked tables on each client computer and how to create code that verifies and corrects linked table connection properties when your application starts
- The advantages of runtime mode and design considerations for using it
- How to create an execute-only version of your application so that users can't tamper with your code
- Techniques for creating application shortcuts to simplify starting your application
- How to apply an encrypted database password to your database
- How to package your database and digitally sign it
- Tools you can use in Access 2007 Developer Extensions and Runtime to distribute your application to users who don't have Access

# Using Linked Tables in a Desktop Database

Your first foray into the world of shared applications will most likely involve copying your completed database to a file server and instructing users to open the database from the server. That's basically not a good idea because Access doesn't run on the server—it runs on each user's desktop. If you have several users sharing a database file, the copy of Access running on each user computer has to load all your "code" definitions—the queries, forms, reports, macros, and modules—over the network. If one user applies a sort or filter to a form and then closes it, Access will try to save the changed definition in the copy on the server, and it might run into locking or corruption problems if another user has the form open at the same time. Also, if your application needs to keep information about how each user works with the application, it would be more complicated to store this information in the database because all users share the same file.

The solution is to create a data-only .accdb file on a server and use linked tables in a desktop application that you install on multiple desktop computers and link to the data server. When you separate the data tables into a shared file on a server, you're actually building a simple client/server application. The main advantage to splitting your database over simply sharing a single desktop database is that your application needs to retrieve only the data from the tables over the network. Because each user will have a local copy of the queries, forms, reports, macros, and modules, Access running on each user workstation will be able to load these parts of your application quickly from the local hard drive. Using a local copy of the desktop application on each client computer also makes it easy to create local tables that save settings for each user. For example, the Conrad Systems Contacts application allows each user to set a preference to open a search dialog box for companies, contacts, and invoices or to display all records directly.

## Taking Advantage of the Database Splitter Wizard

You could split out the tables in your application into a separate file and link them into the database that contains all your queries, forms, reports, and modules "by hand" by first creating a new empty database (see Chapter 4, "Creating Your Database and Tables") and then importing all your tables into that database using the techniques described in Chapter 6. You could then return to your original database and delete all the tables. Finally, you could move the data database (the one containing the tables) to a file server and then link these tables into your original code database (the one containing all your queries, forms, reports, and modules), again using the techniques in Chapter 6.

INSIDE OUT

### Is Your Desktop Application Designed for Client/Server?

When you build a desktop database application, it's all too easy to design forms and reports that always display all records from your tables when the user opens them. It's also tempting to create combo boxes or list boxes that display all available values from a lookup table. These issues have little to no impact when you're the only user of the application or you share your application with only a few other users. However, fetching all rows by default can have serious performance implications when you have multiple users who need to share a large amount of data over a network.

A successful client/server application fetches only the records required for the task at hand. You can design an application so that it never (or almost never) opens a form to edit data or a report to display data without first asking the user to specify the records needed for the task at hand. For example, the Conrad Systems Contacts application opens a list of available companies, contacts, or invoices from which the user can choose only the desired records. This application also offers a custom query by form search to filter specific records based on the criteria the user enters.

You can also design the application so that it uses information about the current user to filter records. For example, the Housing Reservations database always filters employee and reservations data to display information only for the currently signed on employee. When a department manager is signed on, the application shows data only for the current manager's department.

Even so, the two main sample applications aren't perfect examples. Both applications use a ZIP Code table that contains more than 50,000 records to help users enter valid address data, and this huge table is the row source for several combo boxes. In the desktop database version, each user has a local copy of the ZIP Code table, so the performance impact is minimal. If you decide to split your database application into a client/server architecture, you need to think about keeping any tables similar to this in the local database on each user's computer. You could certainly do this with a ZIP Code table because the data is relatively static.

The bottom line is you should take a look at the way your desktop application fetches data for the user. If it always fetches all records all the time, it's probably not a good candidate for upsizing to a client/server application.

Fortunately, there's an easier way to do this in one step using the Database Splitter wizard. Open your original database, and on the Database Tools tab, in the Move Data group, click Access Database. (You can try this with one of your own databases or a backup copy of the Housing.accdb sample database.) The wizard displays the page shown in Figure 25-1.

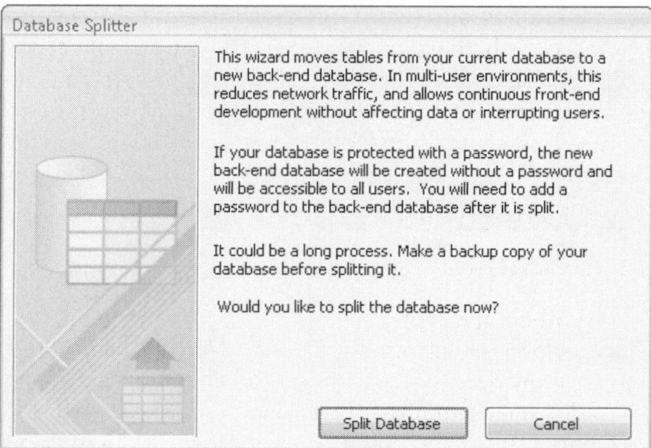


**Figure 25-1** The Database Splitter wizard helps you move the tables into a separate database.

When you click the Split Database button, the wizard opens a second page where you can define the name and location of the back-end, or data-only, database. Be sure to choose a location for this database on a network share that is available to all potential users of your application. Click the Split button on that page, and the wizard exports all your tables to the new data-only database, deletes the tables in your original database, and creates links to the moved tables in your original database. You can now give each user a copy of the code database—containing your queries, forms, reports, modules, and linked table objects pointing to the new data-only database—to enable them to run the application using a shared set of tables.

One disadvantage to using the Database Splitter wizard is that it splits out all tables that it finds in your original desktop database. If you take a look at the desktop database version of the Conrad Systems Contacts application (Contacts.accdb), you can see that the application also uses some local tables (tables that remain in the code database). For example, the ErrorLog table contains records about errors encountered when the user runs the application. If the error was caused by a failure in the link to the server, the code that writes the error record wouldn't be able to write to this table if the table was in the server database. The database also contains local copies of lookup tables that aren't likely to change frequently, such as the tlkpStates table that contains U.S. state codes and names and the ztblYears table that provides a list of years for the frmCalendar form. Access can fetch data from local tables faster than it can from ones linked to a database on a server, so providing local copies of these tables improves performance.

Although splitting a database application makes it easier for multiple users to share your application, this technique works well only for applications containing a moderate amount of data (less than 200 MB is a good guideline) with no more than 20 simultaneous users. Remember that Access is fundamentally a desktop database system. All the work—including solving complex queries—occurs on the client computer, even when you have placed all the data on a network share. Each copy of Access on each client computer uses the file sharing and locking mechanisms of the server operating system.

Access sends many low-level file read, write, and lock commands (perhaps thousands to solve a single query) from each client computer to the file server rather than sending a single SQL request that the server solves. When too many users share the same application accessing large volumes of data, many simple tasks can start, taking minutes instead of seconds to complete.

## Creating Startup Code to Verify and Correct Linked Table Connections

If you were careful when you created your linked tables, you used a Universal Naming Convention (UNC) path name instead of a physical or logical drive letter. Unless the network share name is different on various client computers, this should work well to establish the links to the data file when the user opens your application. However, even "the best-laid schemes o' mice an' men gang aft aglee."[1] (Or, if you prefer, Murphy's law is always in force.)

In Chapter 6, you learned how to use the Linked Table Manager to repair any broken connections. However, you can't expect your users to run this wizard if the linked table connections are broken. You should include code that runs when your startup form opens that verifies and corrects the links if necessary. Also, you might over time make changes to the structure of the data tables and issue an updated version of the client desktop database that works with the newer version of the tables. Your startup code can open and check a version table in the shared data database and warn the user if the versions don't match.

You can find sample code that accomplishes all these tasks in the desktop database version of the Conrad Systems Contacts database (Contacts.accdb). Open the database, and then open the modStartup module. Select the ReConnect function, where you'll find the following code:

```
Public Function ReConnect()
Dim db As DAO.Database, tdf As DAO.TableDef
Dim rst As DAO.Recordset, rstV As DAO.Recordset
Dim strFile As String, varRet As Variant, frm As Form
Dim strPath As String, intI As Integer
' This is a slightly different version of reconnect code
' Called by frmSplash - the normal startup form for this application
    On Error Resume Next
    ' Point to the current database
    Set db = CurrentDb
    ' Turn on the hourglass - this may take a few secs.
    DoCmd.Hourglass True
    ' First, check linked table version
    Set rstV = db.OpenRecordset("ztblVersion")
    ' Got a failure - so try to reattach the tables
    If Err <> 0 Then GoTo Reattach
    ' Make sure we're on the first row
    rstV.MoveFirst
```

[1] Burns, Robert. "To a Mouse, On Turning Her Up in Her Nest With the Plough." 1785.

```
' Call the version checker
If Not CheckVersion(rstV!Version) Then
    ' Tell caller that "reconnect" failed
    ReConnect = False
    ' Close the version recordset
    rstV.Close
    ' Clear the objects
    Set rstV = Nothing
    Set db = Nothing
    ' Done
    DoCmd.Hourglass False
    Exit Function
End If
' Versions match - now verify all the other tables
' NOTE: We're leaving rstV open at this point for better efficiency
'   in a shared database environment.
'  JET will share the already established thread.
' Turn on the progress meter on the status bar
varRet = SysCmd(acSysCmdInitMeter, "Verifying data tables...", _
    db.TableDefs.Count)
' Loop through all TableDefs
For Each tdf In db.TableDefs
    ' Looking for attached tables
    If (tdf.Attributes And dbAttachedTable) Then
        ' Try to open the table
        Set rst = tdf.OpenRecordset()
        ' If got an error - then try to relink
        If Err <> 0 Then GoTo Reattach
        ' This one is OK - close it
        rst.Close
        ' And clear the object
        Set rst = Nothing
    End If
    ' Update the progress counter
    intI = intI + 1
    varRet = SysCmd(acSysCmdUpdateMeter, intI)
Next tdf
' Got through them all - clear the progress meter
varRet = SysCmd(acSysCmdClearStatus)
' Turn off the hourglass
DoCmd.Hourglass False
' Set a good return
ReConnect = True
' Edit the Version table
rstV.Edit
' Update the open count - we check this on exit to recommend a backup
rstV!OpenCount = rstV!OpenCount + 1
' Update the row
rstV.Update
' Close and clear the objects
rstV.Close
Set rstV = Nothing
```

```
    Set db = Nothing
    ' DONE!
    Exit Function

Reattach:
    ' Clear the current error
    Err.Clear
    ' Set a new error trap
    On Error GoTo BadReconnect
    ' Turn off the hourglass for now
    DoCmd.Hourglass False
    ' ... and clear the status bar
    varRet = SysCmd(acSysCmdClearStatus)
    ' Tell the user about the problem - about to show an open file dialog
    MsgBox "There's a temporary problem connecting to the CSD data." & _
      "  Please locate the CSD data file in the following dialog.", _
      vbInformation, "CSD Contacts Manager"
    ' Establish a new ComDlg object
    With New ComDlg
        ' Set the title of the dialog
        .DialogTitle = "Locate CSD Contacts Data File"
        ' Set the default file name
        .FileName = "ContactsData.accdb"
        ' ... and start directory
        .Directory = CurrentProject.Path
        ' ... and file extension
        .Extension = "accdb"
        ' ... but show all accdb files just in case
        .Filter = "CSD File (*.accdb)|*.accdb"
        ' Default directory is where this file is located
        .Directory = CurrentProject.Path
        ' Tell the common dialog that the file and path must exist
        .ExistFlags = FileMustExist + PathMustExist
        If .ShowOpen Then
            strFile = .FileName
        Else
            Err.Raise 3999
        End If
    End With
    ' Open the "info" form telling what we're doing
    DoCmd.OpenForm "frmReconnect"
    ' ... and be sure it has the focus
    Forms!frmReconnect.SetFocus
    ' Attempt to re-attach the Version table first and check it
    Set tdf = db.TableDefs("ztblVersion")
    tdf.Connect = ";DATABASE=" & strFile
    tdf.RefreshLink
    ' OK, now check linked table version
    Set rst = db.OpenRecordset("ztblVersion")
    rst.MoveFirst
    ' Call the version checker
    If Not CheckVersion(rst!Version) Then
```

```
        ' Tell the caller that we failed
        ReConnect = False
        ' Close the version recordset
        rst.Close
        ' ... and clear the object
        Set rst = Nothing
        ' Bail
        Exit Function
    End If
    ' Passed version check - edit the version record
    rst.Edit
    ' Update the open count - we check this on exit to recommend a backup
    rst!OpenCount = rst!OpenCount + 1
    ' Write it back
    rst.Update
    ' Close the recordset
    rst.Close
    ' ... and clear the object
    Set rst = Nothing
    ' Now, reattach the other tables
    ' Strip out just the path name
    strPath = Left(strFile, InStrRev(strFile, "\") - 1)
    ' Call the generic re-attach function
    If AttachAgain(strPath) = 0 Then
        ' Oops - failed.  Raise an error
        Err.Raise 3999
    End If
    ' Close the information form
    DoCmd.Close acForm, "frmReconnect"
    ' Clear the db object
    Set db = Nothing
    ' Return a positive result
    ReConnect = True
    ' ... and exit
Connect_Exit:
    Exit Function
BadReconnect:
    ' Oops
    MsgBox "Reconnect to data failed.", vbCritical, _
      "CSD Contacts Manager"
    ' Indicate failure
    ReConnect = False
    ' Close the info form if it is open
    If IsFormLoaded("frmReconnect") Then DoCmd.Close acForm, "frmReconnect"
    ' Clear the progress meter
    varRet = SysCmd(acSysCmdClearStatus)
    ' ... and bail
    Resume Connect_Exit
End Function
```

The code begins by attempting to open the linked ztblVersion table. If the open generates an error, the code immediately jumps to the Reattach label about halfway down the listing. If the version-checking table opens successfully, the code next calls the

CheckVersion function (not shown here) that compares the version value in the table with a public constant saved in the modGlobals module. If the versions don't match, that function displays an appropriate error message and returns a False value to this procedure. If the version check fails, this procedure returns a False value to the original calling procedure (in the frmSplash form's module) and exits.

If the versions do match, the code next loops through all the table definitions in the database and attempts to open a recordset on each one to verify the link. Note that the code leaves the recordset on the version-checking table open. If it didn't do this, each subsequent open and close would need to establish a new network connection to the file server, and the checking of all tables would take minutes instead of seconds. Note also that the code uses the SysCmd system function to display a progress meter on the Access status bar.

If all linked tables open successfully, the procedure returns True to the calling procedure and exits. If opening any of the tables fails, the code immediately jumps to the Reattach label to attempt to fix all the links.

The code beginning at the Reattach label clears all errors, sets an error trap, and then displays a message informing the user that there's a problem. After the user clicks OK in the dialog box, the code creates a new instance of the ComDlg class module, sets its properties to establish an initial directory and ask for the correct file type, and uses the ShowOpen method of the class to display a Windows Open File dialog box. The class module returns a True value if the user successfully locates the file, and the code retrieves the class module's FileName property to find out the path and name of the file chosen by the user. If the ShowOpen failed, the code raises an error to be logged by the error-handling code at the end of the procedure.

Next, the code opens a form that is a dialog box informing the user that a reconnect is in progress. The code attempts to fix the link to the version-checking table using the path and file the user selected. Notice that the code sets the Connect property of the TableDef object and then uses the RefreshLink method to reestablish the connection. If the table isn't in the file the user selected, the RefreshLink method returns an error, and the code after the BadReconnect label near the end of the procedure executes because of the error trap.

After checking that the version of the code matches the version of the database, the code calls the AttachAgain function (not shown here) and passes it the path and file name. You can also find this function in the modStartup module. The function loops through all the TableDef objects, resets the Connect property for linked tables, and uses RefreshLink to fix the connection. Because this sample database also has some linked Microsoft Excel worksheets, you'll find that code in the AttachAgain function checks the type of linked table and sets up the Connect property appropriately.

If you'd like to see how this code works, you can open the Contacts.accdb file and then use Windows Explorer to temporarily move the ContactsData.accdb, Fictitious Companies.xlsx, and Fictitious Names.xlsx files to another folder. Open the frmSplash form, and you should see the code prompt you to identify where you moved the ContactsData.accdb file. The code in the AttachAgain procedure assumes that the two Excel files are in the same folder as the ContactsData.accdb file.

You can study the other functions called by the Reconnect function in the modStartup module on your own. We provided comments for every line of code to help you understand how the code works.

# Understanding Runtime Mode

When Access starts in runtime mode, it does not allow the user to access the Navigation Pane or to use any of the built-in Ribbons. So, the user can only run your application, not edit any of the objects. As you might expect, many keystrokes are also unavailable, such as pressing F11 to show the Navigation Pane or pressing Ctrl+Break to halt Visual Basic code execution. If you also download the Access 2007 Developer Extensions and Runtime tools, you can distribute your database with the modules to execute in runtime mode to users who do not have Access installed on their systems. For more information about the new Access 2007 Developer Extensions and Runtime tools, see *http://msdn2.microsoft.com/en-us/office/bb229700.aspx*.

However, to execute successfully in runtime mode, your application must have the following:

- All features of the application must be implemented with forms and reports. The user will not have access to the Navigation Pane to execute queries or to open tables.
- The application must have a startup form or an AutoExec macro that opens a startup form.
- All forms and reports must have custom Ribbons because runtime mode does not provide the built-in Ribbon.
- You must implement error trapping in all your macros and Visual Basic procedures. Any untrapped errors cause the application to exit.
- If you automate your application with Visual Basic or use macro actions that are not trusted, you must ensure either that the user places your database in a trusted location or that you digitally sign the database and instruct the user how to trust the signature. For more about digitally signing a database, see "Packaging and Signing Your Database" on page 1336.
- The application should execute the Quit method of the Application object to terminate. If you simply close the final form, the user will be left staring at an empty Access workspace.

The primary sample databases, Conrad Systems Contacts (Contacts.accdb) and Housing Reservations (Housing.accdb), meet the preceding requirements except the startup form is set to frmCopyright to display important information each time you open one of the databases, and the Exit button on the main switchboard form merely closes the form and attempts to return to the Navigation Pane.

If you would like to see what runtime mode looks like, you can test it using existing databases. Open the Housing.accdb desktop database, click the Microsoft Office Button, click Access Options, and then click the Current Database category. In the Application Options section, select frmSplash in the Display Form list, and then click OK. Close the Housing.accdb database. The sample files include a shortcut, Housing Runtime, that opens this database in runtime mode. This shortcut should work as long as you installed the 2007 Microsoft Office system in the default folder (C:\Program Files\Microsoft Office\Office 12) and the sample files in the default folder (C:\Microsoft Press\Access 2007 Inside Out). If necessary, you can change the shortcut by right-clicking the shortcut and selecting Properties on the shortcut menu. The target setting in this shortcut is as follows:

```
"C:\Program Files\Microsoft Office\Office12\MSACCESS.EXE"
   "C:\Microsoft Press\Access 2007 Inside Out\Housing.accdb" /runtime
```

After you change the Display Form setting in the Access Options dialog box and correct any settings in the shortcut target, you can double-click the shortcut to start the application in runtime mode. Click OK in the opening message box, and then sign on as any employee of your choosing to see the main switchboard form. Try pressing F11 to see whether anything happens—the Navigation Pane should not appear. You can move around in the application using the command buttons on the various switchboard forms and the buttons on the custom Ribbons. When you click Exit on the main switchboard, code in the form closes all open forms and then closes the switchboard. You'll be left looking at a blank Access workspace and a very limited set of options when you click the Microsoft Office Button. You can click Close Database from here to close this limited copy of Access or click the Exit button. Be sure to open the Housing.accdb file again, click Exit on the sign-on form, and then change Display Form in the Access Options dialog box back to (none).

INSIDE OUT **Change the File Extension to Test the Runtime Mode**

You can also test your application in runtime mode by changing the file extension on your database. In Windows Explorer, right-click the Housing.accdb sample database file, click Rename, and change the file name to Housing.accdr. Windows prompts you that changing the file extension might make the file unusable. Click Yes in this message box and then open the Housing.accdr database. You'll see the limited Ribbon, Quick Access Toolbar, and Microsoft Office Button options as you did when using the runtime shortcut.

## Creating an Execute-Only Database

Even if you have secured your database, you might still want to be sure that no one can examine or change the Visual Basic procedures you created. After you have fully compiled your Visual Basic project, Access no longer needs the original text of your Visual Basic statements. You can create a special execute-only copy of your database by using one of the utilities supplied with Access. An additional advantage of an execute-only database is that it might be significantly smaller than a copy that contains all the code—particularly if you have written many Visual Basic procedures.

To create an execute-only copy of any completed database application, open the database, and close any open objects. Click the Make ACCDE button in the Database Tools group on the Database Tools tab. (Note that if you're using an Access .adp project file, this button says Make ADE.) The Save As dialog box asks you for a location and name for your new database or project. It then makes sure the current database is fully compiled and saved, copies the database to a new file with the appropriate .accde or .ade extension, removes the Visual Basic source code, and compacts the new file.

If you open an .accde file (you can find a file called Contacts.accde on the companion CD), you'll find that you can't open any Visual Basic module—neither the module of any form or report module nor any module object. You also won't be able to open a form or a report in Design view or Layout view. (This is an additional benefit of an .accde file.) Figure 25-2 shows the Modules list in the Contacts.accde database file. Notice that the Design View button is disabled on the shortcut menu, indicating that you cannot view the source code of an existing module and that the only way to run code is through the database application's interface. The Module and Class Module buttons in the Other group on the Create tab are also disabled so that you cannot create new modules. You'll find that the Design View option is also disabled for all forms and reports, and all the commands in the Forms and Reports groups on the Create tab are unavailable.

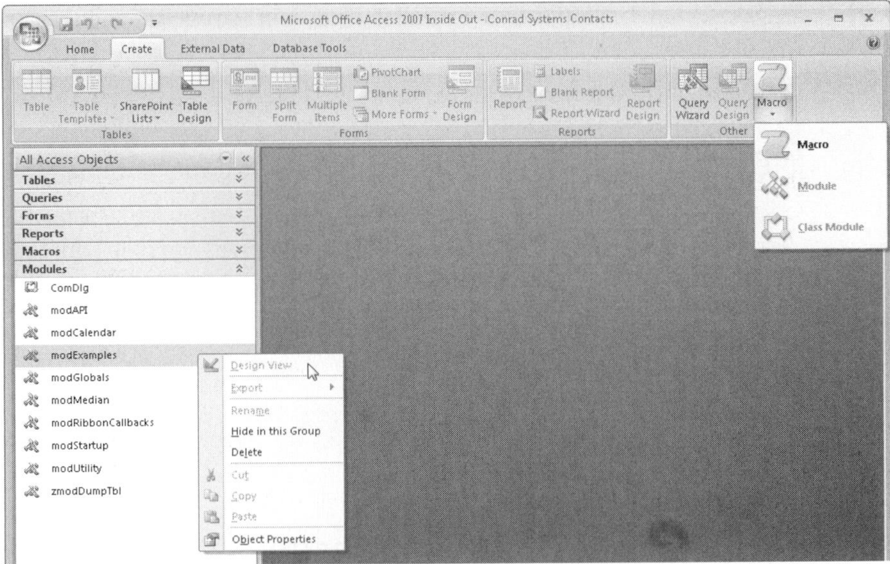


**Figure 25-2** You can't edit any modules in the Contacts.accde database file.

## Creating an Application Shortcut



When you're all done, you might need to create a way for users to easily start your application. If your users all have a copy of Access, you could give them your database application files and simply instruct them to open the appropriate file. But what if the user doesn't have Access, so you have to set them up to execute your application with the runtime version of Access? What if you want to also define certain utility functions that the user might need to execute from time to time? The answer is to create a shortcut.

You use shortcuts all the time in Windows to start programs on your computer. When you install an application on your computer, the setup program usually creates a shortcut that it adds to your Start menu. Some setup programs also add a shortcut on your desktop. The icon for a shortcut on your desktop has a small white box in the lower-left corner with an arrow in it. You can right-click a shortcut and choose Properties from the shortcut menu to see the definition of the shortcut.

To create a shortcut on your Windows desktop for your Access application, right-click the desktop, click New, and then click Shortcut. You can also create a shortcut in a folder by opening Windows Explorer, navigating to the folder you want, pressing the Alt key to view the menu bar, clicking New on the File menu, and then clicking Shortcut. In either case, Windows opens the Create Shortcut wizard to help you find the program you want the shortcut to open. Click the Browse button, and find C:\Program Files\Microsoft Office\Office12\MSACCESS.EXE. Click OK to select the file, and then click the Next button. Give your shortcut a name, such as the name of the database you plan to open with the shortcut, and then click Finish.

Right-click your new shortcut, and click Properties. You'll see a dialog box similar to the one shown in Figure 25-3.

At the top of the Shortcut tab is the icon the shortcut displays and the name of the shortcut. You can click the General tab and enter a new name to rename your shortcut. Target Type tells you that this shortcut starts an application. Target Location displays the original location of the program that this shortcut starts. The Target box allows you to specify the program or file that you want to run. Note that at this point your new shortcut starts only the Access program—it doesn't specify a file to open or any parameters. You can specify the database file name and enter any parameters used by the program in the Target box.

Immediately following the name of the Access program in the Target box, enter a space followed by the database you want to open (with its full path). If the path or file name contains any blanks or special characters, you must enclose the file path in double quotes. Follow the name of the database with the options you need to perform the task you want. For example, to open the Housing.accdb sample database from the default installation, the target setting in this shortcut is as follows:

```
"C:\Program Files\Microsoft Office\Office12\MSACCESS.EXE"
   "C:\Microsoft Press\Access 2007 Inside Out\Housing.accdb"
```

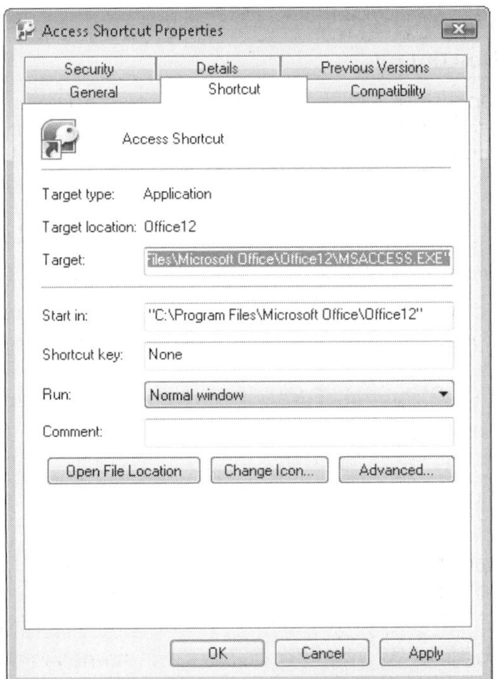


**Figure 25-3** You can modify the Target setting for a Windows shortcut in the shortcut's Properties dialog box.

> **Note**
>
> You can also specify only the name of a database file in the Target box in a shortcut, and Windows opens the program that can process this file (in this case, Access) when you double-click the shortcut. However, Access won't recognize any parameters that you include after the file name. You must specifically ask to open the Access program (MSACCESS.EXE) and add the file name and parameters.

Table 25-1 summarizes the shortcut command-line options you can use. When you include multiple command-line options, separate each with a space.

Table 25-1 **Access Shortcut Command-Line Options**

| Option | Description |
|---|---|
| *<database>* | Opens the specified database. If the path or file name contains blanks, you must enclose the string in double quotes. Must be the first option after the folder and file location for MSACCESS.EXE. |
| /cmd *<command string>* | Specifies a program parameter that can be retrieved by a Visual Basic procedure using the built-in Command function. Must be the last option on the command line. |
| /compact [*<target>*] | Compacts and repairs the specified database but does not open the database. If you omit the target file name, Access compacts the database into the original file name and location. |
| /convert *<target>* | Converts the specified version 11 or earlier database to Access 2007 file format and stores it in the target file. |
| /excl | Opens the specified database with exclusive access. Only one user at a time can use a database that is opened exclusively. |
| /profile *<userprofile>* | Specifies the name of a user profile in the Windows registry. You can use a profile to override database engine settings and specify a custom application title, icon, or splash screen. |
| /pwd *<password>* | Specifies the password for the user named in the /user parameter. If the password contains the / or ; character, enter the character twice. For example, if the password is #ab/cd;de, enter **#ab//cd;;de**. This option applies to Access 2003 and earlier (.mdb) format databases that have user-level security implemented. |
| /repair | Repairs the specified database but does not open the database. |
| /ro | Opens the specified database in read-only mode. |
| /runtime | Specifies that Access will execute with runtime version options. |
| /user *<userid>* | Specifies the logon user ID. This option applies to Access 2003 and earlier (.mdb) format databases that have user-level security implemented. |
| /wrkgrp *<workgroupfile>* | Uses the specified workgroup file. This option applies to Access 2003 and earlier (.mdb) format databases that have user-level security implemented. |
| /x macroname | Runs the specified macro after opening the specified database. |

Using a command-line option, you can also create a shortcut to perform the maintenance task of compacting your database. For example, to compact the Contacts.accdb database and save the compacted version to a file named ContactsCompact.accdb in the same folder, enter the following in the Target box:

```
"C:\Program Files\Microsoft Office\OFFICE12\MSACCESS.EXE"
    "C:\Microsoft Press\Access 2007 Inside Out\Contacts.accdb" /compact
    "C:\Microsoft Press\Access 2007 Inside Out\ContactsCompact.accdb"
```

This previous text assumes you've installed the sample files in the default folders. In the Start In box, specify the starting folder for the application. In the Shortcut Key box, you can enter a single letter or number that the user can press with Ctrl+Alt+ to run the shortcut. The shortcut key must be unique for all shortcuts on your system. In the Run list, you can choose to start the application in a normal-size window (the default), minimized as an icon on your taskbar, or maximized to fill your screen. In the Comment box, you can enter text that appears when the user rests the mouse pointer on the shortcut.

Click the Open File Location button to verify that the target you entered is valid. Click the Change Icon button to select a different icon stored within the target program (MSACCESS.EXE has 68 available icons) or to locate an icon file on your hard disk. Click the Advanced button if you need to set up this shortcut to run under a specific Windows user ID.

On the Compatibility tab of the Properties dialog box, you can find an option to run the program in compatibility mode as though it's running on an older operating system such as Windows 2000 or Windows XP. You can also force your display to 256 colors, use 640×480 screen resolution, or disable Windows themes when this program runs. On the Security tab, you can allow or deny permissions to use this shortcut for specific Windows users or groups.

After you have completed the settings you want, click OK to save your changes to the shortcut. You can now double-click the shortcut to run the program with the options you specified.

# Encrypting Your Database

Access 2007 includes a new feature to encrypt your database with a password. You can use this feature to prompt users for a password before opening the database. When you encrypt the database, Access makes the data unreadable to tools that can read binary data stored in the physical file.

To encrypt your database with a password, you must first open your database in exclusive mode. Click the Microsoft Office Button, and then click Open. Select your database, and then in the Open dialog box, click the arrow on the Open button, and then click Open Exclusive, as shown in Figure 25-4.

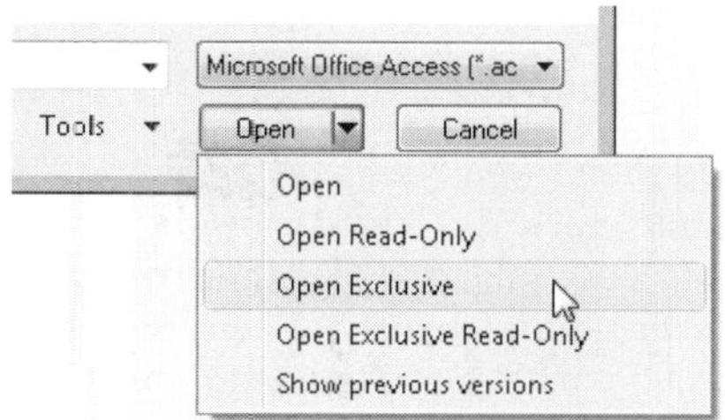


**Figure 25-4** You must open your database in exclusive mode to encrypt the database with a password.

After your database opens, click the Encrypt With Password button in the Database Tools group on the Database Tools tab. Access opens the Set Database Password dialog box, as shown in Figure 25-5. Enter your password in the Password text box, and then reenter it in the Verify text box. Click OK, and Access checks to see whether the two passwords match. If the passwords match, the next time you open the database, Access prompts you for the database password.

If you want to remove the password later, you'll need to open the database in exclusive mode and then click the Decrypt Database button in the Database Tools group on the Database Tools tab. In the Unset Database Password dialog box, type your password in the Password text box, and then click OK. The next time you open the database, Access does not prompt you for a password.

**Figure 25-5** Enter your password in the Set Database Password dialog box.

INSIDE OUT **How Useful Is Encryption?**

Encrypting your database does provide a thin layer of security, but it's not foolproof. If you distribute this database to many users, each user has to know the password in order to open and use the database. Because all users need to share one common password, we don't recommend encryption for multiple-user scenarios. If you're creating this database for your own personal use, encrypting might be an option to keep other people out of your database. Just remember, however, a determined hacker could still gain access to your database given enough time and determination.

## Packaging and Signing Your Database

If you want to send a database to other users, you can certainly put it in a zip file and e-mail it. However, unless the recipient really trusts that the e-mail came from you (it's easy to spoof a sending e-mail address), the recipient might not be willing to open your file. Access 2007 provides a new tool that lets you compress your database file and include it inside a file that is digitally signed.

So, what is "digitally signed?" If you've surfed the Web at all, you've probably encountered several digitally signed files. For example, when a Web site wants to download and install an ActiveX control and you have security enabled in your browser, your browser prompts you to decide whether to download and run the file. If the file is digitally signed, you'll see verified information about the publisher that has been authenticated over the Web by a commercial certificate authority such as VeriSign, GeoTrust, or GoDaddy. In many cases, you can select an option to accept all signed files from a specific trusted source (such as Microsoft) so that you won't be prompted again if you encounter another signed file from the same source.

The new tool in Access 2007 lets you package your database into a compressed Deployment file (.accdc) and then sign it with a digital certificate ready to send to your users. When a user attempts to open your file, Access 2007 uses the digital certificate to verify the source of the file and that all objects in the database have not been changed since the database was signed. If the user trusts the digital certificate, Access 2007 opens and extracts your database file ready for the user to run.

But there's one catch. If you need to distribute this database to other users, you must purchase a digital certificate from a commercial certificate authority, and they're not inexpensive. When you own a commercial certificate, you can use it to "sign" any file that you publish (perhaps on your Web site) or send to others. The program that the recipient uses to open the file can send the certificate information over the Web to the validating authority. The validating authority verifies the certificate and sends back information about the publisher of the file. The recipient can decide to trust the information to avoid being prompted in the future, decide to open the file anyway, or cancel the open.

## INSIDE OUT Using a Self-Signing Certificate

If you want to test how packaging and signing works, you can create and use a self-signing certificate. The 2007 Microsoft Office system includes a tool to create self-signing digital certificates—SelfCert—that you can use for packaging databases. These certificates, however, are valid only for the computer on which you create them. To create a digital certificate for yourself, click the Windows Start button, click All Programs, click your Microsoft Office folder, click Microsoft Office Tools, and then click Digital Certificate For VBA Projects. In the Create Digital Certificate dialog box, enter the name of the certificate you want to create, and then click OK. Because a self-signing digital certificate is valid only on the computer on which you create it, if you package and sign a database with a self-signing certificate and then send it to someone else, the certificate is no longer valid.

To package and digitally sign your database, open the database, click the Microsoft Office Button, click Publish, and then click Package And Sign. Access opens the Select Certificate dialog box, as shown in Figure 25-6. Click the View Certificate button to review all the details of the selected certificate. Select the certificate you want to use from the list, and then click OK. (In this example, we used a self-signing certificate for demonstration purposes.)

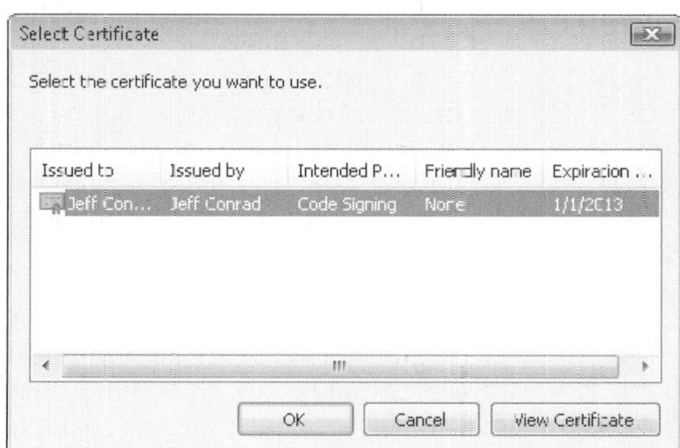


**Figure 25-6** Select the digital certificate you want to use to sign the package.

Access opens the Create Microsoft Office Access Signed Package dialog box, as shown in Figure 25-7. Enter or browse to the location in which you want to save your signed database package. In the File Name box, enter a name for this new packaged file, and then click Create. Access compresses your database, "signs" the file using the digital certificate you selected, and places the database and signature into an .accdc file in the location you specified.

> **Note**
>
> You can package and sign only those databases saved in the .accdb file format. In addition, you can include only one database in a package. If you want to digitally sign the Visual Basic code in an .mdb or .adp file, open the Visual Basic Editor, and click Digital Signature on the Tools menu. Your VBA project must be compiled. If you make any further changes to your database after signing it, the digital signature becomes invalid.

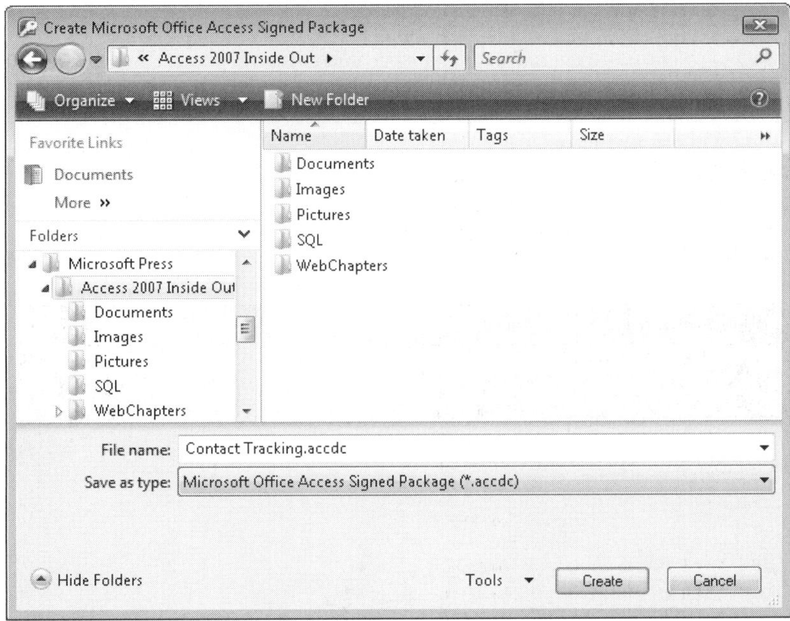


**Figure 25-7** Enter a file name and location for your packaged database.

When you (or your user) open a signed database, Access displays the Microsoft Office Access Security Notice dialog box, shown in Figure 25-8, if you have not previously trusted this publisher. If you're unsure of the source of this certificate, you can click the Show Signature Details link to examine all the details about the publisher. If you click Trust All From Publisher, Access always trusts any files from this source. You can see a list of trusted publishers in the Trusted Publishers list in the Trust Center that you can access from the Access Options dialog box.

**Figure 25-8** Click Open if you trust the publisher and want to open the database.

Click Open if you trust the publisher, and Access opens the Extract Database To dialog box, as shown in Figure 25-9. Enter a name in the File Name text box, select a location to save the extracted database, and then click OK. Access extracts the database from the .accdc file, saves it to the location you specified, and then opens the extracted file. Note that Access might still disable content in this database depending upon your settings in the Trust Center.

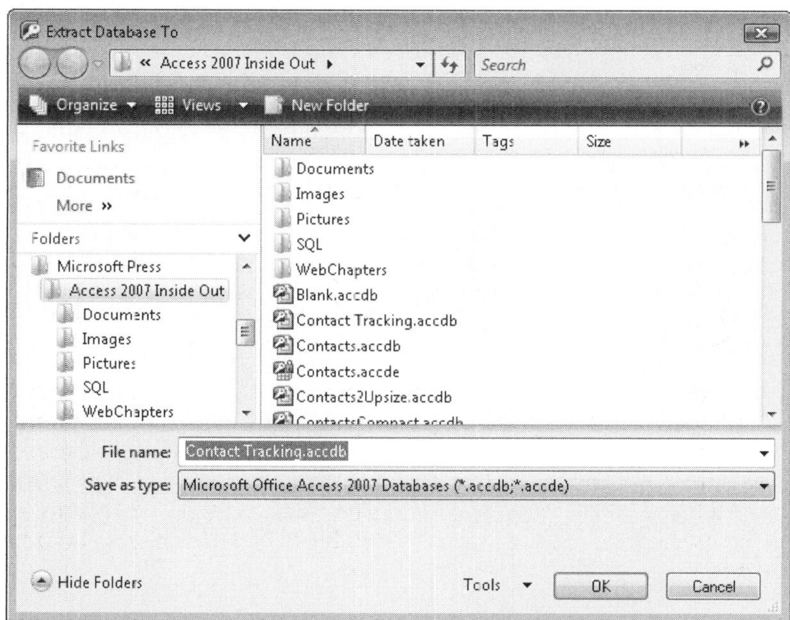


**Figure 25-9** Select a location to extract the packaged database.

# Understanding the Access 2007 Developer Extensions and Runtime

You can obtain additional tools and a license to freely distribute runtime versions of your applications by downloading the Access 2007 Developer Extensions and Runtime from this location: *http://msdn2.microsoft.com/en-us/office/bb229700.aspx*. In previous versions, you had to purchase the developer tools and runtime extensions separately. The big news is that, for Access 2007, Microsoft is offering these tools at no additional charge. This set of software includes the following:

- A royalty-free license to distribute the runtime modules for Access 2007. This allows you to provide your application to users who do not have Access.
- A Package Solution wizard that helps you create installation files that include your database application, the runtime modules necessary to run your application, and any supporting files (such as ActiveX controls or icons). The wizard creates a standard Microsoft Windows Installer setup file (.msi).
- A source code database to help you discover how the wizards included with this package work.
- A Save As template that you can use to create the database templates to appear on the Getting Started screen. The template files have .accdt extensions.
- White papers on conditional formatting, normalization, and managing SQL Server security.

This concludes the printed portion of *Microsoft Office Access 2007 Inside Out*. If you're interested in building project files that link directly to tables and queries stored in Microsoft SQL Server, be sure to read the chapters in Part 7 that you can find on the companion CD. The companion CD also includes a host of reference articles that you'll find essential for increasing your knowledge about building applications using Access.

APPENDIX

# Installing Your Software



This book assumes you have installed Microsoft Office Access 2007 as part of Microsoft Office Professional 2007 or Microsoft Office Ultimate 2007. To install Microsoft Office and related software for a single user, you need a Microsoft Windows–compatible computer configured as follows

- A Pentium 500 megahertz (MHz) or faster processor (Pentium III is recommended as a minimum).
- Microsoft Windows Vista, Microsoft Windows XP with Service Pack 2 (or later), or Windows Server 2003 with Service Pack 1 (or later) operating system.
- At least 256 megabytes (MB) of random access memory (RAM); 512 MB is recommended.
- A hard drive with at least 527 MB of free space for a minimum installation when your network administrator has set up an install package for you on a server. When you perform a local installation, you need up to 3 gigabytes (GB) on your primary hard drive for the installation files and programs. At the end of the Microsoft Office system install, you have the option to leave some of the installation files on your hard drive, which requires up to an additional 240 MB of free space. You need an additional 40 MB to 240 MB of space to install Microsoft SQL Server 2005 Express Edition (depending upon the components you want to install).
- A CD-ROM or DVD-ROM drive. (A DVD-ROM is recommended.) If you are installing over a network, no disc drive is required.
- A mouse or other pointing device.
- A 1024×768 or greater monitor display.

Other options required to use all features include the following:

- A multimedia computer for sound and other multimedia effects.
- Dial-up or broadband Internet access
- Microsoft Mail, Microsoft Exchange, Internet SMTP/POP3 service, or other MAPI-compliant messaging software for e-mail.

- Microsoft Exchange Server 2000 or later for advanced collaboration functions.
- Microsoft Internet Explorer 6.0 or later to run Microsoft InfoPath.
- Connection to an Internet service provider or a local copy of Microsoft Internet Information Services (IIS) installed.

# Installing the Microsoft Office System

Before you run the Microsoft Office system setup program, be sure that no other applications are running on your computer.

If you're installing from the Office Professional 2007 or Office Ultimate 2007 CD-ROM or DVD-ROM, insert the first disc. On most systems, the Microsoft Office system setup program starts automatically. If the setup program does not start automatically, click the Run command on the Windows Start menu. In the Run dialog box, type **x:\setup.exe** (where *x* is the drive letter of your CD-ROM drive), and click OK. If you see the User Account Control dialog box and you're logged on as a nonadministrative user, specify the user name and password for an administrative account, and click Continue. If you're logged on as an administrator, click Continue.

To install from a network drive, use Windows Explorer to connect to the folder in which your system manager has placed the Microsoft Office system setup files. Run Setup.exe in that folder by double-clicking it. If you're installing the Microsoft Office system from a Master License Pack, click Run on the Start menu, and include a PIDKEY= parameter and the 25-character volume-license key in the open box, as in:

```
x:\setup.exe PIDKEY=1234567890123456789012345
```

Note that the setup program might take several minutes after it displays its opening screen to examine your computer and determine what programs you currently have installed—be patient! If you didn't supply a license key on the command line, the setup program first asks for a valid product key. If you're installing from a CD or DVD, you can find the product key in the materials included with the 2007 Office release installation package. Enter a valid key, and click Continue to go to the next page. The setup program asks you to confirm that you accept the license agreement. Select the I Accept The Terms Of This Agreement check box, and then click Continue. The setup program asks whether you want to install now or to customize your installation.

## Choosing Options When You Have No Previous Version of Microsoft Office

When you install the 2007 Office release on your computer, you can choose between two options—Install Now or Customize, as shown in Figure A-1. If you click Install Now, the setup program installs all the programs and components that Microsoft considers most useful to the majority of users. The fastest way to complete an install is to click Install Now. If you don't want to tailor the installation to your specific needs by clicking

Customize, click Install Now in order to include Access 2007 so that you can work through the examples in this book.

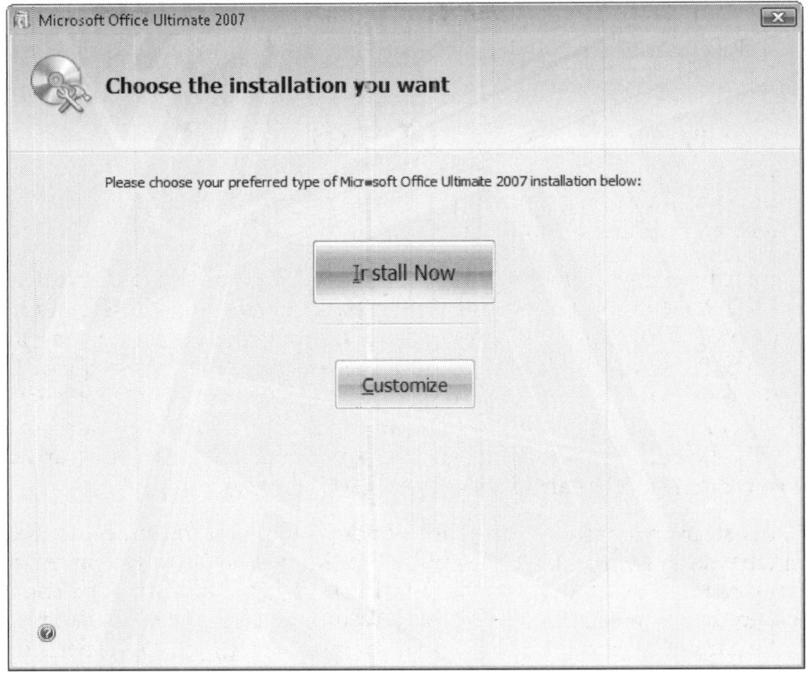


**Figure A-1** Click Install Now to install the default Office Ultimate 2007 programs.

We like to click Customize to pick the options we need. The Customize install option allows you to choose only some of the applications or include additional features that Microsoft considers optional. When you click Customize, the setup program displays a window with three tabs—Installation Options, File Location, and User Information, as shown in Figure A-2.

The setup program shows you the available options for the Microsoft Office system and each program in a hierarchical view. By default, the setup program selects all programs, but it selects only some of the features for several of the programs. Click the plus sign next to any category to expand it and see the options in subcategories. When you see a category that interests you, click the arrow next to the disk drive icon to choose options for all items in that category and its subcategories. To work through all the examples in this book, you should select the Run All From My Computer option for Microsoft Office Access, as shown in Figure A-3. Choosing this option selects the Run From My Computer option for all subcategories. When you select Installed On First Use, the installation program creates a shortcut for the program on your Start menu, but you'll be prompted to install the application when you select the shortcut the first time. Choosing Not Available causes the installation program to neither install the program nor provide a shortcut.

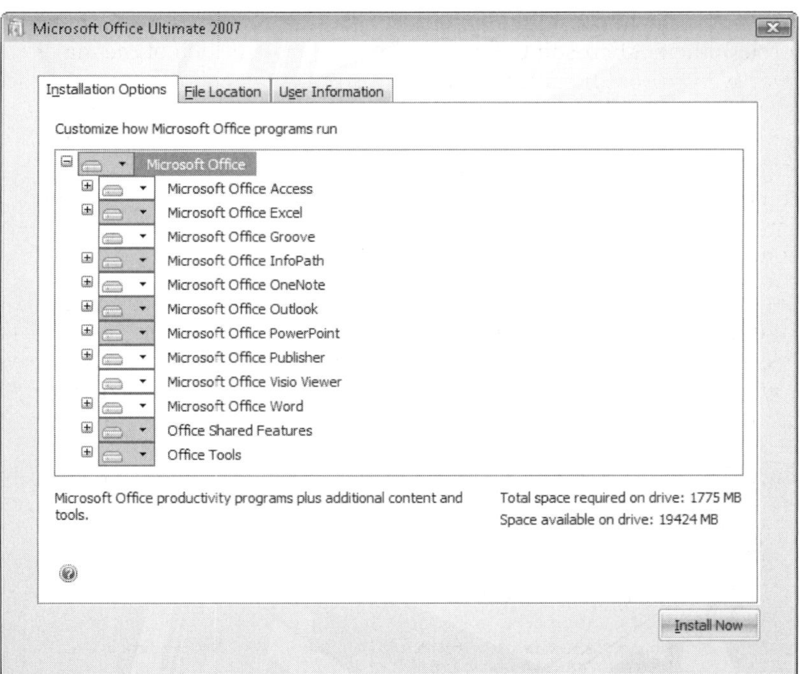


**Figure A-2** The Installation Options tab allows you to choose which programs and options to install.

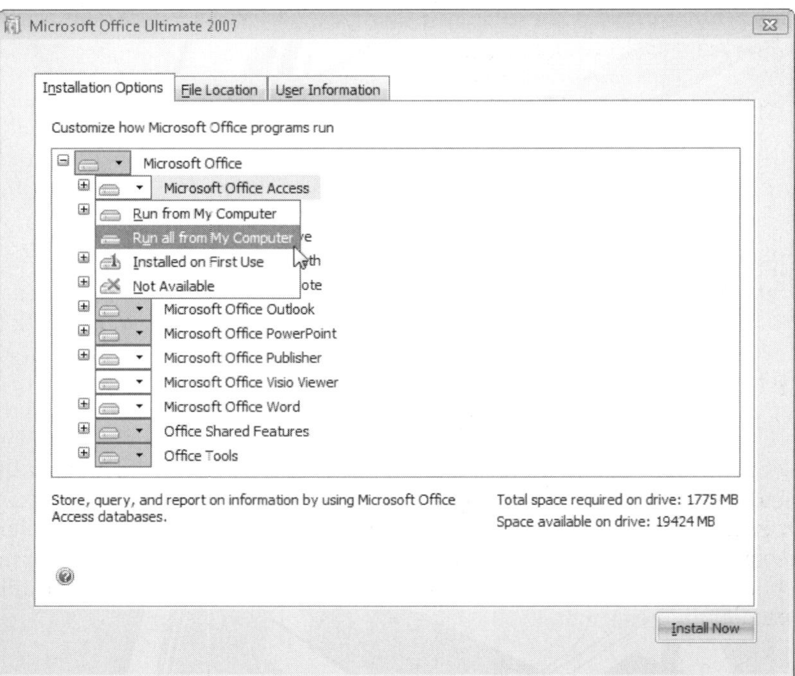


**Figure A-3** Choose Run All From My Computer to install Access 2007 components.

We personally like to begin by selecting the Run All From My Computer option for the top-level item, Microsoft Office. We then go through each of the major categories and selectively choose Installed On First Use or Not Available for options that we do not want. For example, you might want to go to the Office Shared Features category and remove some of the extra fonts under International Support. Under Office Tools, you might want to remove the Microsoft Script Editor (HTML Source Editing) options if you plan to also install Microsoft Expression Web. If you're unsure about any option, you can click the title of the option to see a brief description in the lower part of the window.

On the File Location tab, you see a box with a default location chosen, as shown in Figure A-4. You can enter a different program file location or click the Browse button to select a location on your hard drive. We recommend that you keep the default location. You'll see summary information on how much space is required and available on your hard drive in the middle of the window.

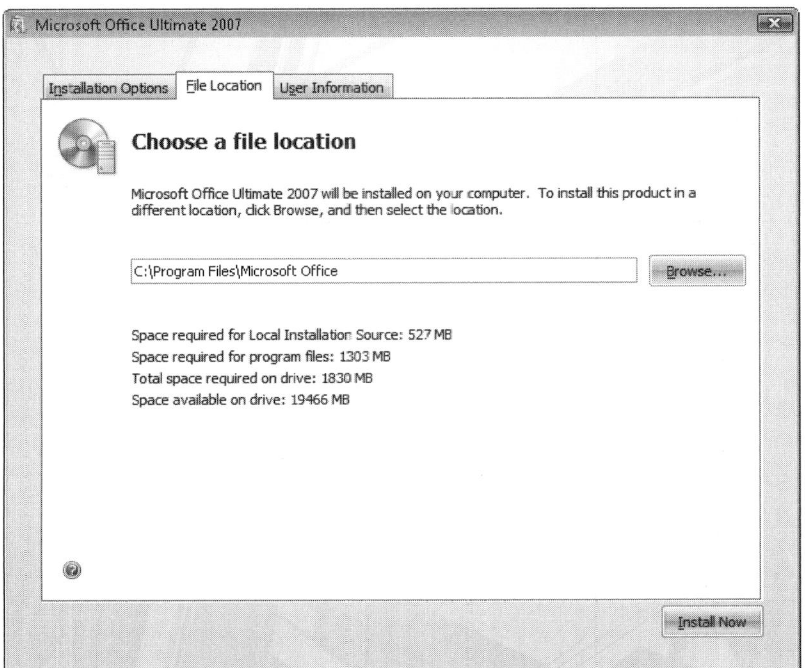


**Figure A-4** Select an installation folder on the File Location tab.

On the User Information tab, you can enter personal information about yourself and your company, as shown in Figure A-5. Type your name in the Full Name text box, your initials in the Initials text box, and your organization or company name in the Organization text box. (Note, if you do not fill in these boxes here, the first Microsoft Office system program you open after installation prompts you for your full name and initials.)

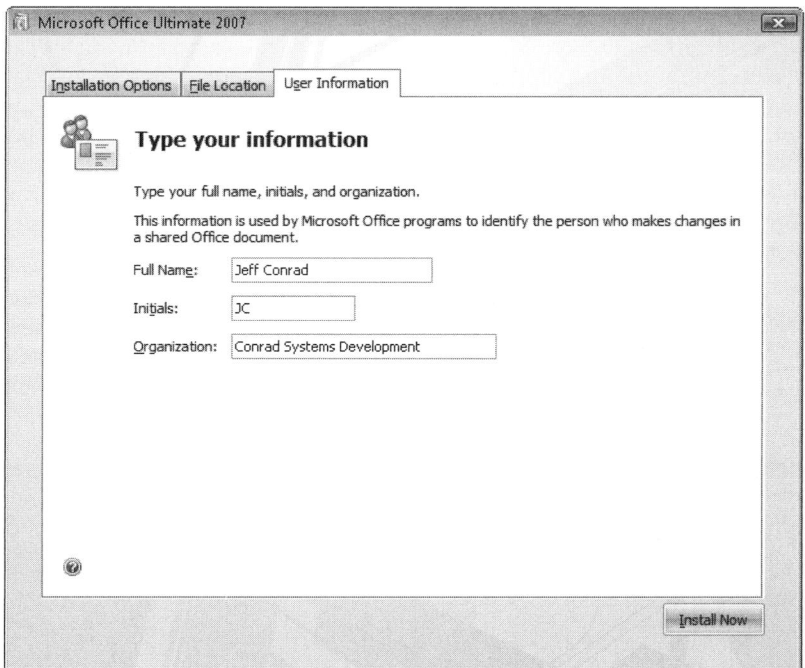


**Figure A-5** Enter your personal information on the User Information tab.

After you have finished making your selections, click Install Now to proceed. If you're not sure, you can click any of the three tabs to verify the options you selected. When the setup program finishes, it shows you a setup completed window, as shown in Figure A-6. In this final window, you can select options to open your Web browser to check for additional updates. You can click the Help icon in the lower-left corner of the window to display information about registering your copy of the 2007 Office release. Click Close to close the setup program window.

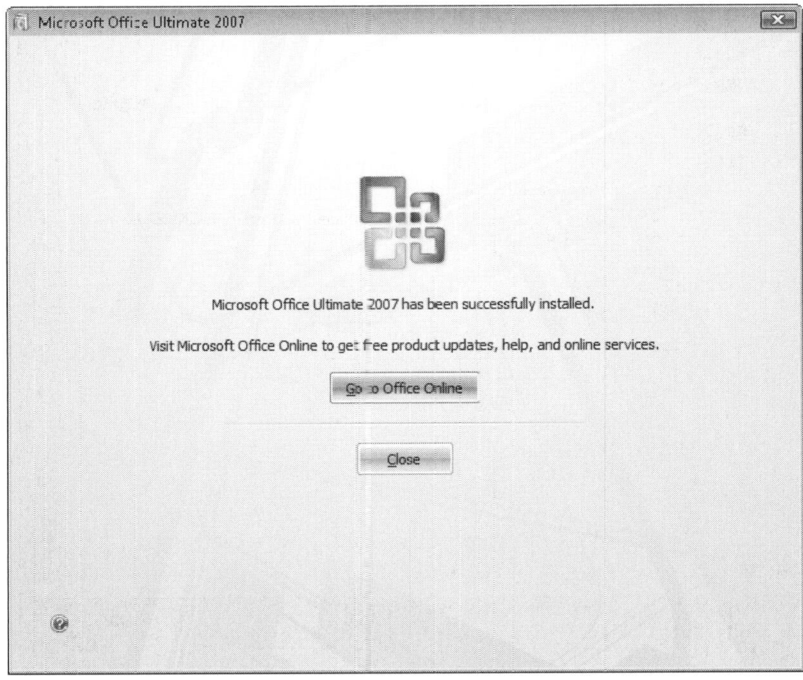


**Figure A-6** The setup program displays this message when the installation process completes.

## Choosing Options to Upgrade a Previous Version of Microsoft Office

When you have a previous version of any of the Microsoft Office programs installed on your computer, the setup program shows you different options after you accept the license agreement, as shown in Figure A-7. If you click Upgrade, the setup program installs all the programs and components that Microsoft considers most useful to the majority of users and removes any previous versions of Microsoft Office programs. The fastest way to complete an install is to click Upgrade.

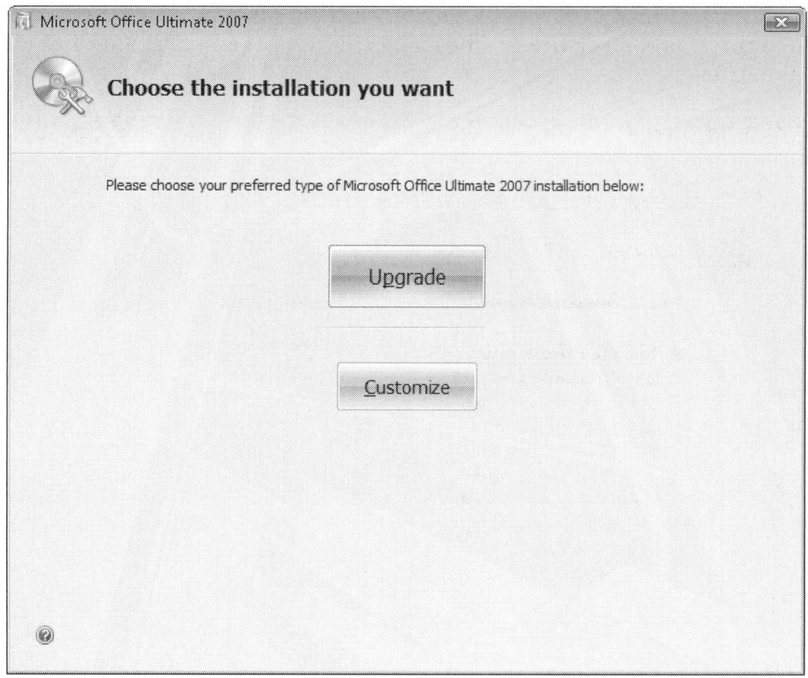


**Figure A-7** When you have previous versions of Microsoft Office programs installed, you can choose either Upgrade or Customize.

We like to click Customize to pick the options we need. The Customize install option allows you to choose only some of the applications to install and to not remove previous versions. When you click Customize, the setup program displays a window with four tabs—Upgrade, Installation Options, File Location, and User Information, as shown in Figure A-8.

The Installation Options, File Location, and User Information tabs display the same options you learned about in the previous section. The setup program displays the Upgrade tab only when you have previous versions of Microsoft Office programs installed on your computer. If you select Remove All Previous Versions, the setup program removes any existing Microsoft Office programs before installing the 2007 Office release programs. If you select the Keep All Previous Versions option, the setup program does not remove any existing Microsoft Office programs before installing the 2007 Office release programs. Notice that you cannot choose to keep a previous version of Microsoft Office Outlook if you have chosen to install Office Outlook 2007. If you select Remove Only The Following Applications, you can choose which existing Microsoft Office programs to keep.

As professional Microsoft Access developers, we keep several versions of Access installed on our primary development computers so that we can continue to support older applications that we wrote. (We actually have Access 97, 2000, 2002, 2003, and 2007 installed!) You might also want to keep an older version of Excel, Microsoft

Office PowerPoint, or Microsoft Office Word. To keep an older version, you must clear the appropriate check box for the application under Remove Only The Following Applications.

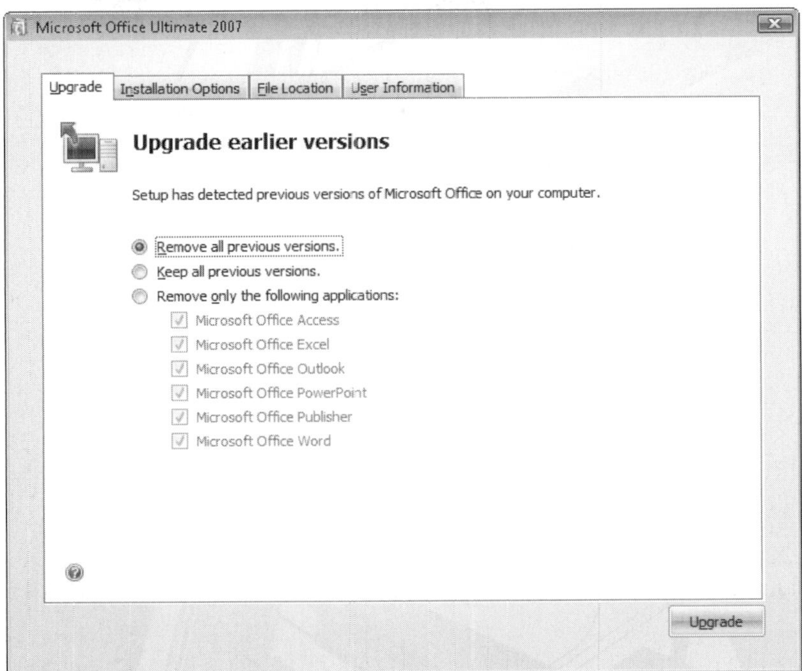


**Figure A-8** You can choose to keep or remove existing Microsoft Office programs on the Upgrade tab.

As you learned in the previous section, you can change which of the 2007 Office release components are installed on the Installation Options tab, change the installation folder on the File Location tab, and specify your user name information on the User Information tab. After clicking Upgrade, the setup program proceeds and displays the setup completed window in Figure A-6 when it is finished. You can click the Help icon in the lower-left corner of the window to display information about registering your copy of the 2007 Office release. Click Close to close the setup program window.

# Installing SQL Server 2005 Express Edition

If you intend to build Access project files (.adp file name extension) that link directly to a database defined in SQL Server, you should install SQL Server 2005 Express Edition on your desktop computer to facilitate building and testing your application. SQL Server 2005 Express Edition is a special version of SQL Server 2005 configured to run on any operating system supported by the 2007 Office release–Windows Vista, Windows XP with Service Pack 2, or Windows Server 2003 with Service Pack 1. With SQL Server 2005 Express Edition installed, you can use an Access project file to create

Appendix

databases and define tables, views, diagrams, and stored procedures that you can later move to SQL Server on a network. You normally install SQL Server 2005 Express Edition on your desktop computer. However, you can also install SQL Server 2005 Express Edition on a server. If you need to install SQL Server 2005 Express Edition on a server, you must install from that server's console.

SQL Server 2005 Express Edition has its own setup program—you can't install SQL Server 2005 Express Edition using the setup program in the 2007 Office release. You can download SQL Server 2005 Express Edition from Microsoft's Web site at this location: *http://msdn.microsoft.com/vstudio/express/default.aspx*. Be sure to download the .NET Framework 2.0 if you haven't installed it yet. Also download both SQL Server 2005 Express Edition and SQL Server Management Studio Express.

After you download the SQL Server 2005 Express Edition setup file to your computer and run the program, it shows you the license agreement that you must accept in order to unpack the installation files to your hard drive. (Note, if you see the User Account Control dialog box and you're logged on as a nonadministrative user, specify the user name and password for an administrative account, and click Continue. If you're logged on as an administrator, click Continue to see the license agreement.) After you accept the license agreement by selecting the I Accept The Licensing Terms And Conditions check box and clicking Next, the program displays a dialog box listing the prerequisite components that will be installed, as shown in Figure A-9. Click Install to begin the installation process.

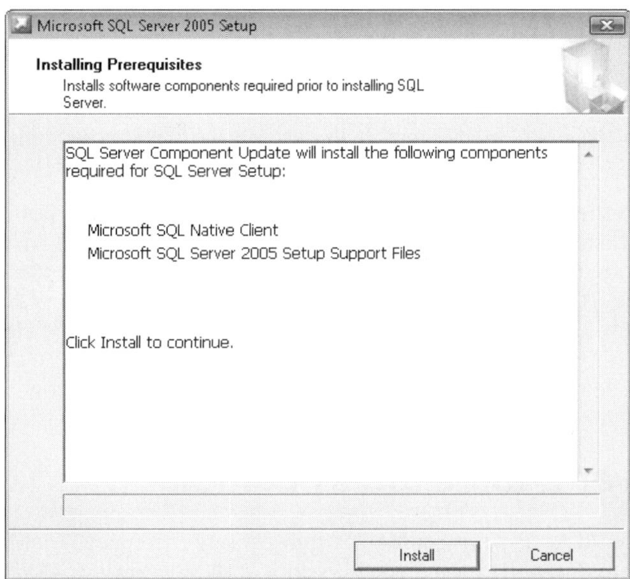


**Figure A-9** Click Install to install the prerequisite components needed for SQL Server 2005 Express Edition.

After the prerequisite components are installed, click Next to continue. The setup program then performs a scan of your current computer configuration. After the scan is complete, the setup program displays the Microsoft SQL Server 2005 Setup Wizard, as shown in Figure A-10. Click Next to continue.

**Figure A-10** Click Next to begin the installation process for SQL Server 2005 Express Edition.

The wizard displays the System Configuration Check page, as shown in Figure A-11. The wizard checks to see that all necessary components and system requirements are met before proceeding. If any problems exist, such as not having the .NET Framework 2.0 installed, the wizard displays an error message in the Status column. You'll need to review what components or system requirements need to be met in order to install SQL Server 2005 Express Edition. If your computer passes all the requirement tests, click Next to proceed.

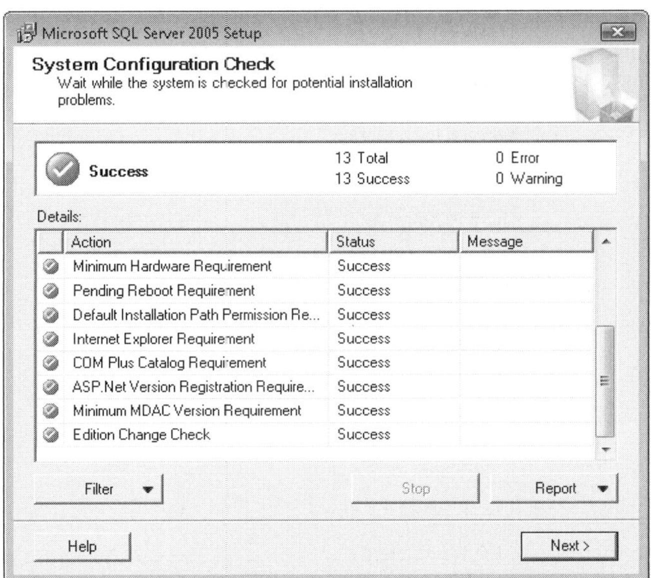


**Figure A-11** If your computer meets all the prerequisites for installation, you can click Next to proceed.

The wizard next displays the Registration Information page, as shown in Figure A-12. Enter your name in the Name text box (this is a required field) and your company or organization name in the Company text box. If you clear the Hide Advanced Configuration Options check box (selected by default), you see a number of additional pages along with the Authentication Mode and Error And Usage Report Settings pages shown later in this section. Click the Help button in the lower-left corner of the wizard for more information on each page. Click Next to proceed.

The next page of the setup wizard, Feature Selection, displays the components you can install with SQL Server 2005 Express Edition, as shown in Figure A-13. The wizard shows you all the available options for SQL Server 2005 Express Edition in a hierarchical view. By default, the wizard does not select Client Components, but you should install those options. Click the plus sign next to any category to expand it and see the options in subcategories. When you see a category that interests you, click the arrow next to the disk drive icon to choose options for all items in that category and its subcategories. We selected the Will Be Installed On Local Hard Drive option for all components. The installation path for the program is listed near the bottom of this page. If you want to change this location, click the Browse button, and browse to a different location to install SQL Server 2005 Express Edition. Click the Disk Cost button to display each volume drive on your computer, the amount of total disk space for each drive, the amount of free disk space available on each drive, the amount of required space needed to install the components, and the difference in size remaining. Click Next to proceed.

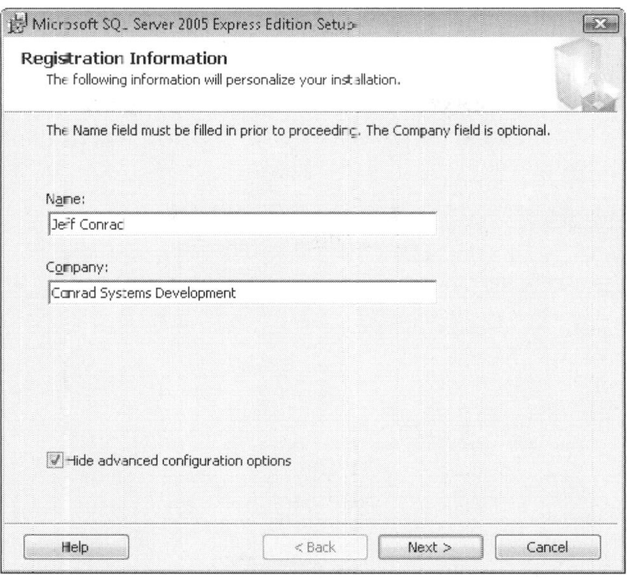


**Figure A-12** Enter your name and company on this page of the setup wizard.

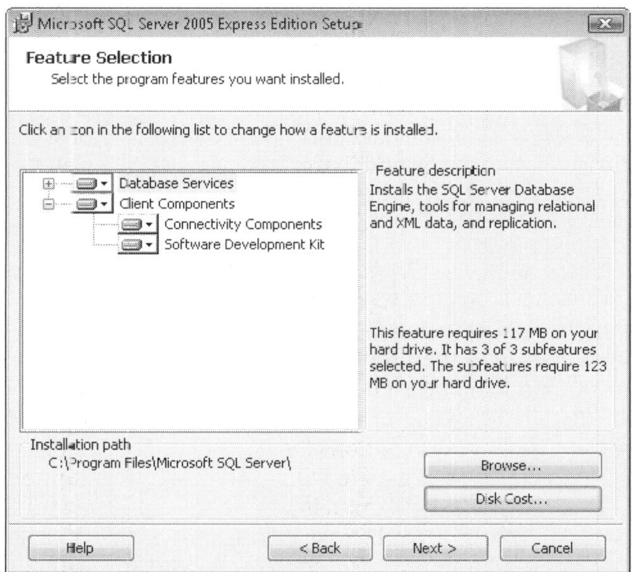


**Figure A-13** Select the components you want to install on the Feature Selection page.

The wizard next displays the Authentication Mode page, as shown in Figure A-14. We strongly recommend that you use Windows Authentication Mode. When you do this, only Windows-authenticated users who have been granted permission on your server can gain access to it. (The members of the Administrators group on your computer automatically have permission.) If you use SQL Server security, anyone who discovers the password to the sa user ID can gain access to your server. If you choose to use Mixed Mode (Windows Authentication And SQL Server Authentication), the password for the sa user account should be at least six characters and can be as long as 128 characters. A password should also contain some combination of letters, numbers, and symbols such as # or ) to make it more difficult to discover. Click Next to continue.

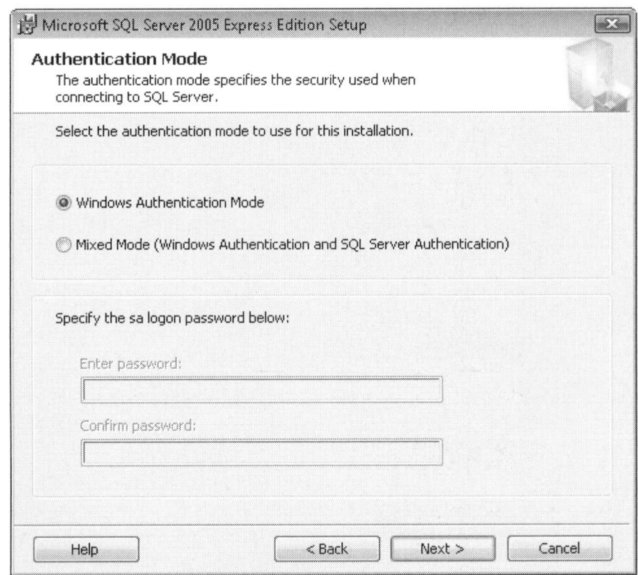


**Figure A-14** Select an authentication mode to use with SQL Server 2005 Express Edition.

The wizard next displays the Configuration Options page, as shown in Figure A-15. On this page, you can create separate instances for users who do not have administrator permissions. Select Enable User Instances (selected by default) to allow separate instances or clear this check box to disable the functionality. Select Add User To The SQL Server Administrator Role (cleared by default) to add the user installing SQL Server 2005 Express Edition to the administrator role. If you're installing SQL Server 2005 Express Edition on a Windows Vista computer, we recommend selecting this option because the installation wizard does not add the user running the installation to the administrator role. Click Next to proceed.

The wizard next displays the Error And Usage Report Settings page, as shown in Figure A-16. If you select the first check box (cleared by default), SQL Server 2005 Express Edition automatically sends error reports to either Microsoft or an internal corporate IT department. If you select the second check box (also cleared by default), SQL Server 2005 Express Edition automatically sends usage reports to Microsoft on what features you are using in the program. Microsoft uses this data to make improvements in future releases. Click Next to proceed.

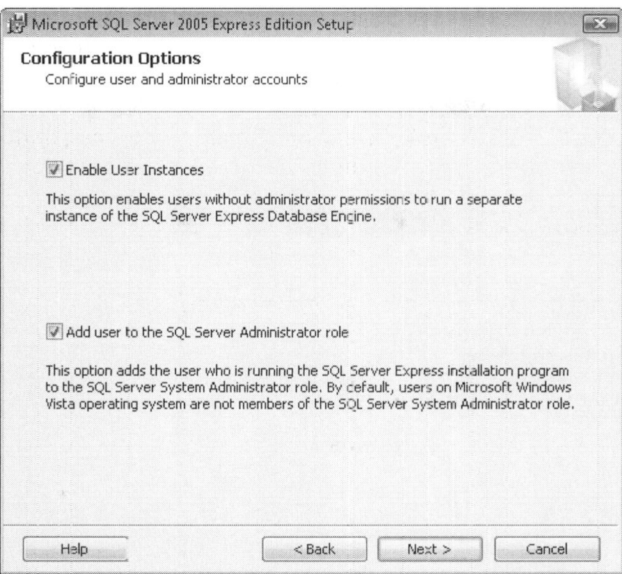


**Figure A-15** Select user and administrator options on the Configuration Options page.

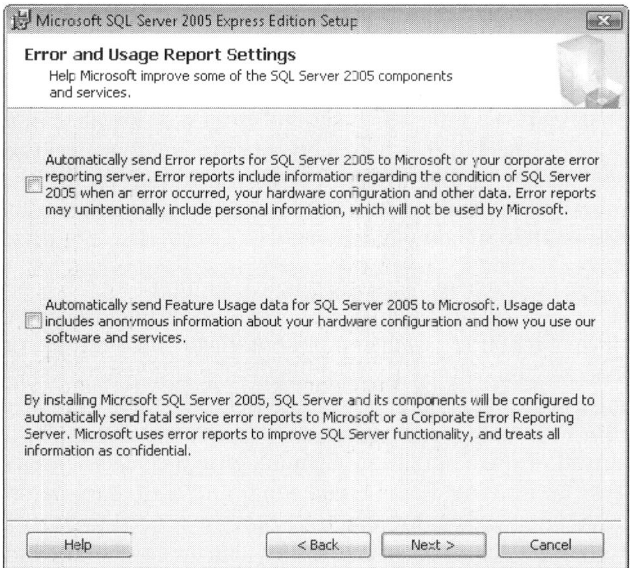


**Figure A-16** These two options allow you to report errors and usage data to either Microsoft or your company's IT department.

The last page of the setup wizard, Ready To Install, displays the components that will be installed on your computer, as shown in Figure A-17. If you want to change any of your installation options, click the Back button to return to previous setup wizard pages. If you want to cancel the installation process, click the Cancel button. Click the Install button to proceed with the installation.

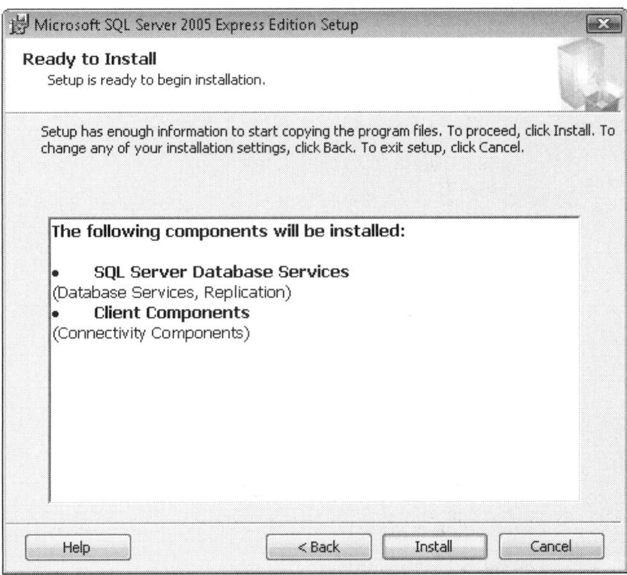


**Figure A-17** Click Install to complete the installation process.

The wizard displays a dialog box that shows you the progress and time remaining for the installation. On a fast computer, the installation should complete in two to three minutes. You can click Cancel in this dialog box at any time to cancel the installation. On the Setup Progress page, shown in Figure A-18, the Status column should display Setup Finished next to each component that the setup wizard installed. Click Next to continue when the installation completes.

Figure A-19 shows the last page of the setup wizard, Completing Microsoft SQL Server 2005 Setup. Click the Summary Log link to open a Summary file in Notepad detailing the success or failure of installing each component. If you encountered errors during the installation process, you can use this log file to diagnose where the error occurred. Click the Surface Area Configuration Tool link to install a utility that helps configure the surface area of your SQL Server installation. You can use this utility to start or stop unused components after the installation. By managing the surface area of your SQL Server 2005 Express Edition installation, you can improve the security on your system by reducing potential entry points for attacks. Note, you'll need to download and install SQL Server 2005 Service Pack 2 to use this utility. The text box at the bottom of this page displays additional information and links concerning SQL Server 2005. Click Finish to close the setup wizard.

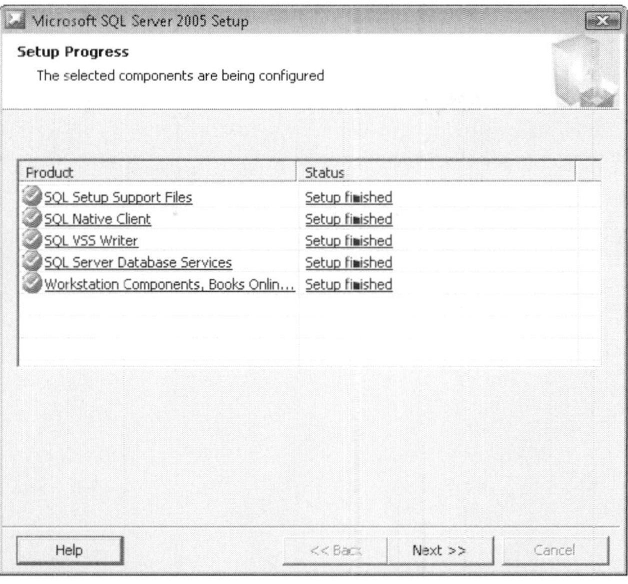


**Figure A-18** The setup wizard displays a status message next to each installed component.

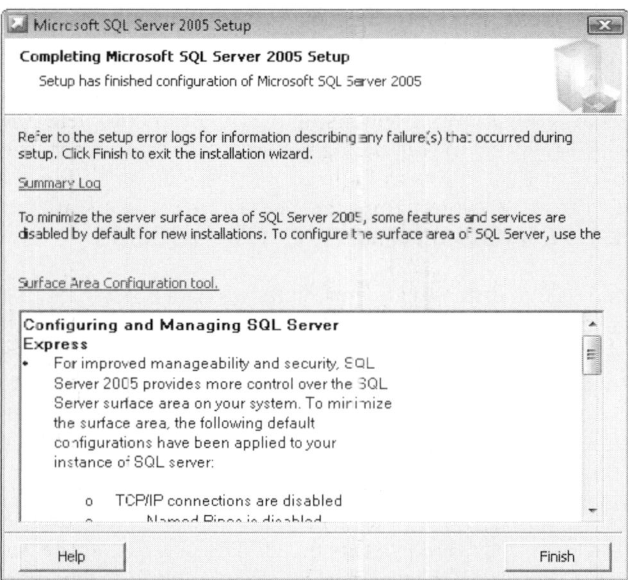


**Figure A-19** You can review any errors that might have occurred during the installation on the last page of the setup wizard.

After the installation completes, you can start the SQL Server Configuration Manager by clicking the SQL Server Configuration Manager option on the Configuration Tools submenu of the Microsoft SQL Server 2005 program group. (If you don't find the program on your Microsoft SQL Server 2005 menu, you can also start it from C:\Windows\System32\SQLServerManager.msc.) In the Configuration Manager, select SQL Server 2005 Services, and be sure the SQL Server (SQLEXPRESS) service is marked as Running. If it is not running, right-click the service name, and click Start on the shortcut menu. The Configuration Manager presents options, as shown in Figure A-20. You can close the SQL Server Configuration Manager program window, but the service continues to run.

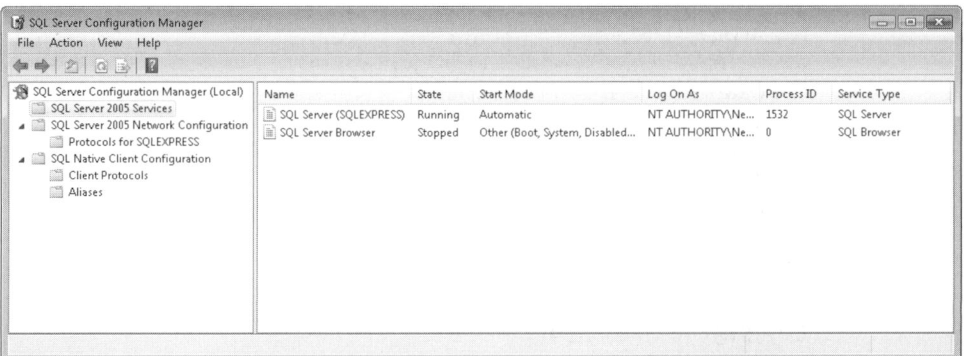


**Figure A-20** The SQL Server Configuration Manager displays the status of your SQL Server services.

To be able to manage your databases, we recommend that you also install the SQL Server Management Studio Express program. This program provides a graphical interface to create, modify, and delete databases, tables, views, stored procedures, functions, security settings, and more.

# Converting from a Previous Release of Access

Access 2007 (version 12 of Access) can work with the data and tables in a database file created by Access version 2, version 7 (Access for Windows 95), version 8 (Access 97), version 9 (Access 2000), version 10 (Access 2002), and version 11 (Access 2003). For version 2, you can only import the tables and queries in the old database into a new database that you create using Access 2007. Depending on the complexity of the application, you might be able to open and run a version 7 or version 8 database application with version 12, but you won't be able to modify any of the objects in the database. You can open a version 9, version 10, or version 11 database with version 12 and modify any of the objects in the database.

You can convert a version 7 or version 8 database file to either the Access 2000 format (version 9), the Access 2002-2003 format (versions 10 and 11), or the Access 2007 .accdb format (version 12). Before you begin the conversion process, make sure all Access Basic or Visual Basic for Applications (VBA) modules are compiled in your earlier version database. If you want to convert your database to the .accdb file format, start Access 2007, click the Microsoft Office Button, and then click Convert. Access opens the Save As dialog box. You must specify a different file name or location for your converted database because Access won't let you replace your previous version file directly. Click Save to convert the database. If you want to convert your database to the Access 2000 or Access 2002-2003 format, start Access 2007, click the Microsoft Office Button, click the arrow next to Save As, and then click either Access 2000 Database or Access 2002-2003 Database. Access opens the Save As dialog box. You must specify a different file name or location for your converted database because Access won't let you replace your previous version file directly. Click Save to convert the database.

If you open a version 2, version 7, or version 8 database in Access 2007, you will see a dialog box offering to convert the database to the current version or attempt to modify the database for shared use between versions. For these versions, we recommend that you attempt to convert them rather than modify them for shared use. You won't be able to convert a database that contains anything other than tables and queries. You must create a new Access 2007 format database and import tables and queries from a version 2 database that has forms, reports, macros, or modules. You can also convert an earlier version database by creating a new Access 2007 format database and then importing all the objects from the older version database.

## Conversion Issues

Access 2007 reports any objects or properties that it is unable to convert by creating a table called Convert Errors in your converted database. The most common problems you're likely to encounter are Visual Basic libraries that were available in a previous version but not in Access 2007 and obsolete code that you created in a user-defined function.

Other changes that might affect the conversion of your application code or how your converted application runs include the following:

- In versions 7 and earlier, you had to use macros to construct custom menus. Access 2007 continues to support macros for custom menus, but you might want to rebuild custom Ribbons using XML.
- As of version 8, DoMenuItem is no longer supported. The conversion utility replaces this command in all macros with the equivalent RunCommand action or method. The DoMenuItem method in Visual Basic code is still supported for backward compatibility, but you should locate and change these statements after converting your database.
- In version 8, you could create a formatted Windows dialog box with the MsgBox action or function, separating the sections of the message with the @ character. Version 9 and later no longer support this feature. You should remove the @ character used in this way in code you wrote for version 8.
- Versions 7 and 8 supported the Microsoft DAO 2.5/3.*x* compatibility library for databases converted from previous versions. Version 9 and later no longer support this library. You will need to replace the reference to this library to the Microsoft Office 12.0 Access Database Engine Object Library after you convert

the database, and you might need to change old Visual Basic statements that depended on the older version of Data Access Objects (DAO).

- If you convert a database by importing its objects, your new database might not compile or execute properly. The problem is most likely a reference to an obsolete Visual Basic code library. You can correct this by opening any module in the Visual Basic Editor and then clicking Tools, References. Remove any libraries marked MISSING, and attempt to compile the project.
- Unless you also have Microsoft Office 2003 installed on your computer, you won't be able to edit any data access pages that you created in Access 2003.

# Index to Troubleshooting Topics

# Index

## Symbols and Numbers

## B

## D

## E

## G

## H

## I

## J

## N

## P

## Q

## T

## U

## V

## W

## Y



## Z